September 21–24, 2012
San Francisco, CA, USA

Association for
Computing Machinery

Advancing Computing as a Science & Profession

MobileHCI'12

Proceedings of the 14th International Conference on

Human Computer Interaction with Mobile Devices and Services

Sponsored by:

SIGCHI

Supported by:

Nokia, Grand, Google, FX Pal, Telefonica, Yahoo! Labs

Association for
Computing Machinery

Advancing Computing as a Science & Profession

The Association for Computing Machinery
2 Penn Plaza, Suite 701
New York, New York 10121-0701

Notice to Past Authors of ACM-Published Articles
ACM intends to create a complete electronic archive of all articles and/or other material previously published by ACM. If you have written a work that has been previously published by ACM in any journal or conference proceedings prior to 1978, or any SIG Newsletter at any time, and you do NOT want this work to appear in the ACM Digital Library, please inform permissions@acm.org, stating the title of the work, the author(s), and where and when published.

ISBN: 978-1-4503-1281-3 (Digital)

ISBN: 978-1-4503-1885-3 (Print)

Additional copies may be ordered prepaid from:

ACM Order Department
PO Box 30777
New York, NY 10087-0777, USA

Phone: 1-800-342-6626 (USA and Canada)
+1-212-626-0500 (Global)
Fax: +1-212-944-1318
E-mail: acmhelp@acm.org
Hours of Operation: 8:30 am – 4:30 pm ET

Printed in the USA

MobileHCI 2012 Chairs' Welcome

It is our great pleasure to welcome you to the *2012 ACM International Conference on Human-Computer Interaction with Mobile Devices and Services – MobileHCI 2012.*

MobileHCI is the world's leading conference in the field of Human Computer Interaction concerned with portable and personal devices and with the services to which they enable access. Mobile HCI provides a multidisciplinary forum for academics, hardware and software developers, designers and practitioners to discuss the challenges and potential solutions for effective interaction with and through mobile devices, applications, and services.

The conference continues to attract a significant number of submissions; this year we received 212 valid paper submissions. We have continued our commitment to improve the quality of the review process. A senior program committee of 38 internationally renowned scientists from academia and industry was assembled. Each paper received 3 or more high-quality peer reviews, as well as an additional meta review by the assigned PC member. Following last year's successful cross-Atlantic, split committee meeting, the 38 committee members assembled in two locations (Palo Alto and Berlin) that were linked by audio and video connections. This provided an opportunity for the papers and reviews to be discussed in detail and all final decisions to be agreed upon by the Program Committee as a whole.

The outcome of this process was that 54 of the 212 submissions were accepted (25%) for inclusion in the final Program, to be presented in San Francisco in September 2012. Of these, 39 were full papers and 15 were notes. A shepherding process was also used in which 6 of the 54 accepted papers were revised and improved under the expert guidance of a dedicated committee member. In our commitment to continually improving the quality of the Program, 8 papers/notes were given special recognition of excellence by being nominated for consideration as a Best Paper. A jury, consisting of 5 members of the Program Committee, was established to judge which of these papers represented the highest caliber of research in the field to be deserving of the Best Paper award. The final decision is to be revealed at the conference itself.

Putting together *MobileHCI 2012* was a team effort. Therefore, before closing, we would like to thank all the contributors and volunteers who have made this conference possible. We first thank the authors for providing the content of the program. We are also very grateful to the program committee and the senior program committee, who worked very hard in reviewing papers and providing feedback for authors. This conference could not have happened without our committee: thanks to all of them for their time and effort, and to their various institutions for sparing their time to help us move this important research field forward.

Special thanks also go to: Philippe Palanque, the SigCHI Adjunct Chair for Specialized Conferences, for shepherding us in the process of bringing this conference under the umbrella of the ACM; to Ashley Cozzi from ACM for helping us navigate contracts and budgets; to the MobileHCI steering Committee for their support and guidance; and to Lisa Tolles from Sheridan Proceedings Service for helping us pull the content together. Finally, we extend our deepest gratitude to our sponsor, ACM SIGCHI, for taking the risk to support this conference, and to our generous corporate supporters whose endorsement and support were essential in pulling this conference together.

We hope that you will find this program interesting and thought-provoking, that the conference will provide you with a valuable opportunity to share ideas with other researchers and practitioners from institutions around the world, that you will consider sharing with others who could not be here the ideas, inspirations and provocations you experience and that you will consider supporting this conference series with your contributions in the future.

Elizabeth Churchill
and Sriram Subramanian
MobileHCI 2012 General Chairs

Patrick Baudisch
and Kenton O'Hara
MobileHCI 2012 Program Chairs

Table of Contents

Session 8: Mobile Augmented Reality

Session Chair: Michael Rohs *(University of Hanover)*

Session 9: Understanding Touch

Session Chair: Enrico Rukzio *(Ulm University & Lancaster University)*

Session 10: Multiplexing

Session Chair: Elizabeth Bales *(University of California, San Diego)*

Session 11: Non-visual Interaction

Session Chair: Eve Hoggan *(University of Helsinki)*

MobileHCI 2012 Conference Organization

General Chairs: Elizabeth Churchill *(Designing Associates, USA)*
Sriram Subramanian *(University of Bristol, UK)*

Program Chairs: Patrick Baudisch *(Hasso Plattner Institute, Germany)*
Kenton O'Hara *(Microsoft Research, Cambridge, UK)*

Posters Chairs: Pourang Irani *(University of Manitoba, Canada)*
Jason Alexander *(University of Lancaster, UK)*

Interactive Installation Chairs: David A. Shamma *(Yahoo Research, USA)*
Les Nelson *(PARC, USA)*
Alex Olwal *(MIT Media Lab, USA)*

Workshop Chairs: Parisa Eslambolchila *(Swansea University, UK)*
Daniel Ashbrook *(Nokia Research Center, USA)*

Tutorials Chairs: Aaron Quigley *(University of St. Andrews, UK)*
Jeff Pierce *(Samsung Electronics, USA)*

Doctoral Consortium Chair: Ravin Balakrishnan *(University of Toronto, Canada)*

Panels Chairs: Frank Bentley *(Motorola Solutions, USA)*
Henriette Cramer *(Mobile Life, Sweden)*

E-Publication Chairs: Rodrigo de Oliveira *(Telefonica Research, Spain)*
Mauro Cherubini *(Google, Switzerland)*

Local Arrangements Chairs: Thea Turner *(FXPAL, USA)*
Kris Mihalic *(Zynga, USA)*

Sponsorship Chairs: Marco de SÃ *(Yahoo Research, USA)*
Ed Cutrell *(Microsoft Research, India)*
Björn Hartmann *(University of California, Berkeley, USA)*

Social Buzz Chairs: Steve Viller *(University of Queensland, Australia)*
Alexandra Wellenmann *(University of Gothenburg, Sweden)*
Mattias Rost *(Mobile Life, Sweden)*

Student Volunteer Chairs: Jessica Cauchard *(University of Bristol, UK)*
Brent Hecht *(Northwestern University, USA)*

Design Chair: Andrés Lucero *(Nokia Research Center, Finland)*

Web Chair: Mark Marshall *(University of Bristol, UK)*

Program Committee (continued):

Mark Perry *(Brunel University, UK)*
Mauro Cherubini *(Telefonica, Spain)*
Michael Rohs *(University of Munich, Germany)*
Mike Fraser *(University of Bristol, UK)*
Nuria Oliver *(Telefonica, Spain)*
Paul Marshall *(University College London, UK)*
Per Ola Kristensson *(University of St Andrews, UK)*
Pourang Irani *(University of Manitoba, Canada)*
Roderick Murray-Smith *(Glasgow University, UK)*
Russell Beale *(University of Birmingham, UK)*
Sebastian Boring *(University of Calgary, Canada)*
Sian Lindley *(Microsoft Research Cambridge, UK)*
Steve Brewster *(Glasgow University, UK)*
Yang Li *(Google, USA)*

MobileHCI'12 Additional Reviewers

Robert Adelmann
Ana Afonso
Andrew Aftelak
Jason Alexander
Dzmitry Aliakseyeu
Hana Al-nuaim
Florian Alt
Tomohiro Amemiya
Saleema Amershi
Morgan Ames
Margarita Anastassova
Adrienne Andrew
Anupriya Ankolekar
Edward Anstead
Lisa Anthony
Caroline Appert
Ahmed Arif
Ilhan Aslan
Mobolaji Ayoade
Chris Baber
Naveen Bagalkot
Madeline Balaam
Matthias Baldauf
Tyler Baldwin
Dirk Balfanz
Rafael Ballagas
Linas Baltrunas
Louise Barkhuus
Tom Bartindale
Eric Baumer
Dominikus Baur
Benjamin Bederson
Ben Bedwell
Ashweeni Beeharee
Frauke Behrendt
Pascal Belin
Marek Bell
Peter Bennett
Frank Bentley
Xiaojun Bi
Andrea Bianchi
Gerald Bieber
Pascal Bihler
Jon Bird
Renaud Blanch
Matthias Böhmer
Susanne Boll
Matthew Bonner
Chris Bowers
Andrew Bragdon
Gregor Broll
A.J. Brush
Stefano Burigat
Jenna Burrell
Daragh Byrne
Xiang Cao
Stefan Carmien
Luis Carriço
Scott Carter
Steven Castellucci
Jessica Cauchard
Olivier Chapuis
Chi-Hua Chen
Thomas Chesney
Alvin Chin
Karen Church
James Clawson
Andy Cockburn
Sunny Consolvo
Gregorio Convertino
Céline Coutrix
Lisa Cowan
Anna Cox
David Coyle
Henriette Cramer
Yanqing Cui
Edward Cutrell
Chandrika Cycil
Mary Czerwinski
Laura Dabbish
Raimund Dachselt
Peter Dalsgaard
Alexander De Luca
Marco de Sá
Sebastian Denef
Laurent Denoue
Debayan Dhar
David Doermann
Tanja Döring
Luís Duarte
Lucy Dunne
Paul Dunphy
Andreas Dünser
Abigail Durrant
Martin Ebner
Florian Echtler
Niklas Elmqvist
Philip Ely
Andreas Emrich
Arvid Engström
Parisa Eslambolchilar
Georg Essl
Daniel Fallman
Ava Fatah gen Schieck
Steven Feiner
Mikael Fernstrom
Denzil Ferreira
Joel Fischer
Daniel Fitton
Rowanne Fleck
Richard Fletcher
Clifton Forlines
Adrian Friday
Jonas Fritsch
Richard Fung
Steffen Gauglitz
Sven Gehring
Aaron Genest
Gloria Gomez
Jorge Gonçalves
Daniel Gonçalves
Sandy Gould
Connor Graham
Raphael Grasset
Thomas Grill
Andrea Grimes Parker
Jim Grimmett
Tovi Grossman
Yves Guiard
François Guimbretière
Sidhant Gupta
Sean Gustafson
Carl Gutwin
Mieke Haesen
Jonna Häkkilä

Malcolm Hall
Tim Halverson
Martin Halvey
Teng Han
Vicki Hanson
Chris Harrison
Amir Alexander Hasson
Kirstie Hawkey
Brent Hecht
Jeffrey Heer
Niels Henze
Steffen Hess
Wilko Heuten
Clint Heyer
Otmar Hilliges
Thomas Hillman
Jon Hindmarsh
Uta Hinrichs
Toda Hiroyuki
Christina Hochleitner
Simon Holland
Christian Holz
Elaine Huang
Scott Hudson
Stephane Huot
Amy Hurst
Wolfgang Hürst
Zahid Hussain
Takeo Igarashi
Jussi Impio
Shamsi Iqbal
Ali Israr
Shahram Izadi
Robert Jacob
Giulio Jacucci
Mohit Jain
Myoung Hoon Jeon
Rose Johnson
Matt Jones
Anirudha Joshi
Marko Jurmu
Topi Kaaresoja
Vaiva Kalnikaite
Santosh Kalwar
Maryam Kamvar
Shaun Kane
Marije Kanis
Panagiotis Karampelas
Amy Karlson
Konstantinos Kazakos
Vassilis-Javed Khan
Varun Khanduja
Julie Kientz
Yoshifumi Kitamura
Jayne Klenner-Moore
Hendrik Knoche
Sebastian Knödel
Andreas Komninos
Vassilis Kostakos
Sven Kratz
Christian Kray
Stefan Kreitmayer
John Krumm
Hannu Kukka
Andrew Kun
June-Jei Kuo
Hideaki Kuzuoka
Ki-Uk Kyung
Jarmo Laaksolahti
Denis Lalanne
Shyong Lam
Eric Laurier
Effie Law
Christopher Le Dantec
Eric Lecolinet
Seungyon Claire Lee
Luis Leiva
Tuck Leong
Gilly Leshed
Vincent Levesque
Kevin Li
Frank Chun Yat Li
Hai-Ning Liang
Chunyuan Liao
Ann Light
Brian Lim
Siân Lindley
Conor Linehan
Agnes Lisowska Masson
Qiong Liu
Sara Ljungblad
Markus Löchtefeld
Peter Lonsdale
Pedro Lopes
Andrés Lucero
Rosemary Luckin
Joanna Lumsden
Kris Luyten
Scott MacKenzie
Allan MacLean
Rui Madeira
Charlotte Magnusson
Nasim Mahmud
Sylvain Malacria
Tanya Markow
Chris Marmo
Nicolai Marquardt
Gary Marsden
Mark Marshall
Catherine Marshall
Stefan Marti
Benoît Martin
Christopher Mcadam
Joe McCarthy
Marilyn McGee-Lennon
David McGookin
Indrani Medhi
Tao Mei
Johanna Mercurio
Alexander Meschtscherjakov
Nicholas Micallef
Takashi Miyaki
Ann Morrison
Lee Morton
Christiane Moser
Ingrid Mulder
Jörg Müller
Catherine Mulligan
Miguel Nacenta
Frank Nack
Hiromi Nakamura
Elena Nazzi
David Nguyen
Maria Normark
Lauren Norrie
James Norris
Petteri Nurmi
Stina Nylander
Ian Oakley
Marianna Obrist
William Odom

Rodrigo de Oliveira
Thomas Olsson
Eamonn O'Neill
Jacki O'Neill
Elisa Oreglia
Sebastian Osswald
Jeni Paay
Brian Pagán
Joshua Palay
Nirmal Patel
Fabio Paternò
Eric Paulos
Andriy Pavlovych
Dianne Pawluk
Sonja Pedell
Martin Pielot
Jeffrey Pierce
James Pierce
Thomas Pietrzak
Laura Pina
Benjamin Poppinga
Ivan Poupyrev
Costin Pribeanu
Ahmad Rahmati
Kari-Jouko Räihä
Nitendra Rajput
Gonzalo Ramos
Jussi Rantala
Dimitrios Raptis
Umar Rashid
Matthias Rath
Pei-Luen Patrick Rau
Dana Raveh
Janet C Read
Stuart Reeves
Thomas Reitmaier
Gerhard Reitmayr
Stefan Rennick-Egglestone
Francesco Ricci
Yann Riche
Hendrik Richter
Jochen Rick
Julie Rico
Jens Riegelsberger
Simon Robinson
Tom Rodden
Mario Romero
John Rooksby
José Rouillard
George Roussos
Jaime Ruiz
Sonja Rümelin
Norman Sadeh
Dario Salvucci
Pedro Santana-Mancilla
Gerhard Schall
Raimund Schatz
Michael Schellenbach
Dominik Schmidt
Johannes Schöning
Katie Seaborn
Abigail Sellen
Vidya Setlur
Mike Sharples
John Shearer
Gilles Simon
Mikael B. Skov
Diana Smetters
Timothy Sohn
Hyunyoung Song
Henrik Sørensen
Daniel Spelmezan
Jan Stage
Christoph Stahl
Danae Stanton Fraser
Craig Stewart
Steven Strachan
Sara Streng
Hank Strub
Wolfgang Stuerzlinger
Simone Stumpf
Sriram Subramanian
Mengu Sukan
Petra Sundström
Rahul Swaminathan
Laurel Swan
Gerd Szwillus
Atau Tanaka
Karen Tang
Anthony Tang
Markus Tatzgern
Nick Taylor
Simon Taylor
Loren Terveen
Jakob Tholander
Emma Thom
Bruce Thomas
Sabine Timpf
Khai Truong
Leon Urbas
Stephen Uzor
Kaisa Väänänen-Vainio-Mattila
Asimina Vasalou
Radu-Daniel Vatavu
Akos Vetek
Frank Vetere
Jesse Vig
Yon Visell
Juergen Vogel
Daniel Vogel
Bruno von Niman
Bruce Walker
Lorna Wall
James Wallace
Jingtao Wang
Rainer Wasinger
Janet Wesson
Tara Whalen
Stevejohn Whittaker
Daniel Wigdor
David Wilfinger
John Williamson
Katharine Willis
Graham Wilson
Andrew Wilson
Max Wilson
Sarah Wiseman
Jacob Wobbrock
Katrin Wolf
Maria Wolters
Min Wu
Volker Wulf
Qian Xu
Xing-Dong Yang
Koji Yatani
Chuang-wen You
Massimo Zancanaro
Clint Zeagler
Shengdong Zhao
Yu Zheng

Mobile HCI 2012 Sponsor & Supporters

Sponsor: SIGCHI

Champion Supporter: NOKIA

Donors:

Graphisme, animation et nouveaux médias
grand
Graphics, Animation and New Media

Google™

FX PAL

Telefónica
Telefónica
Investigación y Desarrollo

YAHOO!® LABS

Understanding Tablet Use: A Multi-Method Exploration

Hendrik Müller
Google, Inc.
76 9th Ave
New York, NY 10011
United States
hendrikm@google.com

Jennifer L. Gove
Google, Inc.
1600 Amphitheatre Parkway
Mountain View, CA 94043
United States
jgove@google.com

John S. Webb
Google, Inc.
76 9th Ave
New York, NY 10011
United States
jwebb@google.com

ABSTRACT

Tablet ownership has grown rapidly over the last year. While market research surveys have helped us understand the demographics of tablet ownership and provided early insights into usage, there is little comprehensive research available. This paper describes a multi-method research effort that employed written and video diaries, in-home interviews, and contextual inquiry observations to learn about tablet use across three locations in the US. Our research provides an in-depth picture of frequent tablet activities (e.g., checking emails, playing games, social networking), locations of use (e.g., couch, bed, table), and contextual factors (e.g., watching TV, eating, cooking). It also contributes an understanding of why and how people choose to use tablets. Popular activities for tablet use, such as media consumption, shopping, cooking, and productivity are also explored. The findings from our research provide design implications and opportunities for enriching the tablet experience, and agendas for future research.

Author Keywords

Tablet; mobile devices; diary study; video diary; contextual inquiry; field interviews; user requirements

ACM Classification Keywords

H.5.m. Information interfaces and presentation (e.g., HCI): Miscellaneous

INTRODUCTION

The emergence of tablet computers (tablets) have provided a new device format for users to enjoy access to a wide variety of digital experiences and information. People search the internet, they communicate with friends, they download mobile applications (apps) so that they can access everyday information, they watch videos, and they play games on their tablets. Existing insights into tablet ownership and use are available primarily through market research studies. Pew Internet has been measuring tablet ownership since May of 2010, when it recorded US ownership at 3% [26]. By August 2010, their survey showed that ownership had grown to 10% [28]. More recently tablet ownership has risen sharply, to 19% of the US population [31]. The prominence of tablet devices is also reflected in the level of app usage, with 75% of those (8% of all US adults) having downloaded an app to their device, and 38% reporting using six or more apps per week [28]. Aside from this body of market research, there is little other published research available on tablet use at this time.

Given this lack of information about tablet use, our goals were to provide a detailed picture of how people are using tablets today. We investigated when, where, why, and how people interact with content on their tablets. We explored activities including, but not limited to, media consumption, shopping, cooking, and productivity. Our research that employed a combination of diary study, interview, and observational methods took place in September and October of 2011, with 33 participants across three locations in the US.

MobileHCI'12, September 21–24, 2012, San Francisco, CA, USA.

RELATED WORK

While little has been published around how consumers use tablets, it is important to note that over the past few years there has been substantial research conducted around how consumers use smartphones. There have also been investigations into some specialized applications of tablet use. We will review these topics as a basis for approaching our research into understanding everyday tablet use.

Smartphones have been quickly adopted by consumers in the US. A 2011 Pew Internet study reports that one third of adults in the US own a smartphone [30]. Additionally, studies by Nielsen have shown that ownership is increasing across all age groups [24]. Studies on smartphone use have focused on search and mobility, location, and app use; and a variety of methodologies have been applied including exploratory methodologies [1, 7, 6], survey research [30, 33], and log analysis [8, 14, 3].

Amin et al. (2009) used a web-based diary tool to understand searches done on the go; they found that mobile searches are primarily conducted when people are with others [1]. More recently, online diaries and interviews have been used to explore the trend towards more people using their phones from stationary environments, primarily home and work. Church and Oliver (2011) found that mobile phones are primarily used for communication and that search behavior is shaped by location, social factors, and other aspects of context [7]. Similarly, Chau et al. (2011) found that location, context, and the social environment trigger information needs [6].

Logging and tracking methodologies have also been applied to gain more insight into how people use their mobile phones. Early studies focused primarily on search behavior and more recently studies have started to track the use of apps. Church et al. (2008) examined six million search requests and characterized the differences between search behavior on desktop computers and mobile phones, finding mobile search queries to have shorter query length, be more focused, and centered around transactional content, navigational queries, and adult content. The authors anticipated mobile specific opportunities such as taking advantage of touch-based displays and localization, and making the mobile search experience more personalized [8]. A study by Kamvar et al. (2009) similarly found mobile searches to be more targeted than those on desktop [14]. Verkasalo et al. (2010), conducted both a tracking study and a survey that confirmed that perceived behavioral control is directly linked to perceived enjoyment and the usefulness of apps that people choose to use [33].

With the proliferation of apps, logging and tracking has been applied to uncover patterns of app usage. The types of apps used have been found to differ throughout the day, e.g., news apps are accessed in the morning, games apps at night, and communication apps are used throughout the day [3]. A Nielsen tracking study revealed that certain types of apps such as those related to shopping, games, and video viewing, are differentially accessed by age [21]. And while smartphones themselves provide a diversity of functionality, to which apps contribute, a recent study has illustrated that users can aptly, and happily, navigate the "seams" that are a current characteristic of smartphones [2]. The authors suggest that design and development priority be given to building systems that allow for "assemblability" so that users can build their own personal experiences with their phones, adapting the features and functionality to their own lifestyle needs.

Turning to examine tablet use, there has been little use of exploratory and in-depth research methods to uncover details and patterns of activities that characterize consumer-focused tablet use. There are however, different strands and bodies of research that detail tablet use in specific applied contexts. Use of tablet computers has been found to afford greater collaboration, creativity, and expressiveness in children with learning disabilities, including those with autism spectrum disorders [13]. Many of the opportunities envisioned for tablet use in general education and learning have focused on social, collaborative use as well as expressiveness, and indeed, have resulted in gains in these specific areas [32, 5, 34]. The use of tablets for increasing the efficiency and effectiveness in education environments has been examined widely [15, 4, 9], and the use of tablets in health and medical settings has been investigated [12, 11]. However, since we have seen such a rapid shift in tablet design and adoption over the last couple of years, tablet use in these contexts is likely going through some substantial change. We have reached the point now in the developed world, at which tablet computers are being designed for consumers en masse, and, in contrast to the niche areas of their application, we see tablets very rapidly gaining in adoption and use in several everyday contexts. Now is the time therefore, that we need to understand what the landscape looks like for tablet users that have adopted this new form-factor product so readily.

One major methodological approach has already been applied to understanding consumer tablet usage, and this is the survey method. Findings, such as those from Pew Internet, provide us with demographic information about tablet use [27]. Methodologically similar studies by Nielsen tell us that tablet ownership is changing, that it is becoming a popular device with older users now, as well as younger [22], and that for a significant proportion of people, tablet ownership reduces the amount that they use other devices [23] while aggregate device usage is generally increasing [22].

The goal of our work was to investigate how people are using their tablet devices, and apply exploratory methodologies to do so. We wanted to understand the activities people choose to do on their tablets and the places that they do them. We were interested in whether the activities done on tablet devices are self-contained, or required other devices, and we were interested in finding out about the extent to which the activities that people are conducting on tablets also bridge into the "real world", such as shops or restaurants. An additional goal was to collect rich examples of tablet use.

STUDY METHODOLOGY

To gather comprehensive insights about how tablets are used we employed a variety of research methods: 1) written diaries, 2) video diaries, 3) follow-up in-home interviews, and 4) contextual inquiry observations. We selected this set of methods to understand different aspects of tablet usage and triangulate varying insights. While the diary study portion allowed us to collect a large amount of self-reported data over a longer period of time, the follow-up interviews and contextual inquiries enabled us to gather rich data about specific use cases.

Participants

A total of 33 participants were recruited from three locations across the US: San Francisco (12), New York (11), and Milwaukee areas (10). This allowed us to draw participants from urban, suburban, and rural areas. Participants were recruited against several criteria, including gender, age, education, occupation, family situation, commuting habits, length of tablet ownership, and characteristics of their tablet. These criteria were guided by previous research by both Nielsen [17, 19, 18, 25] and Pew Internet [29], to target a sample of participants that was representative of the current US population of tablet users as possible. Participants were incentivised for their time investment with a gift cheque and could keep the small video cameras that were provided to complete the video diaries.

Of all 33 participants who took part in the diary study, 39% (13) were men and 61% (20) were women. They ranged in age from 18 to 70, with the following distribution across the different age ranges: 18-23 (18%), 24-30 (30%), 31-40 (39%), 41-70 (12%). All participants owned a tablet: 73% (24) owned an Apple iPad and 27% (9) owned an Android-based tablet. For 82% (27) of those participants, the tablet they used during the time of the study was the first tablet they had ever owned. While 39% (13) of all participants were still new to using their tablets (they had owned it for less than three months), 61% (20) had owned their tablet for more than three months at the time of the study.

After the diary study had commenced, we selected a subset of 18 participants to participate in follow-up field visits, six from each location. They were again chosen to reflect the same participant requirements outlined above. Finally, we conducted contextual inquiries sessions with four of those participants, to gain further insights.

Procedure

In this section, details are provided about the four different research methods that were used.

Written Diaries

To uncover all of the activities that are carried out on tablets, participants were asked to complete a written diary entry whenever they used their tablet over the two-week study period. We used Google Forms to collect written diary entries, accessible to the participants through the browser of their desktop computer. The diary questions were designed to capture details about each activity, including an explanation of the activity itself, the time and length of the activity, the context in which that activity was conducted (e.g., location, secondary activity, other people), as well as information about transitions to and from other connected devices or the real world. The diary questions included a set of open-ended as well as several closed-ended questions. Each participant was called periodically to check on their involvement, and, as a reminder to them, to complete the question set every time they used their tablet. Participants were not able to review their previous diary submissions.

It is important to point out the limitations of this diary study research method, which are mainly a result of the self-reported nature of this data gathering technique. Participants may forget to record some activities, resulting in under-reported activity frequencies. Overall, the diary study methodology allowed us to collect rich information about each instance of tablet use, when it occurred naturally, without having to be present with the participant to observe them.

Video Diaries

In addition to the written diary entries, participants completed five video diary submissions, based on specific assignments that were requested on five different days, spread over the two-week period. We used a vendor that provided an online portal specifically created for collecting video diary data. Each video diary question was designed to capture information about the participant and their tablet use with greater richness beyond the textual diary entries. Participants were asked to record either their face or the tablet screen, depending on the question asked. Each participant was provided with a small video camera with a stand for simple recording, to enable them to easily complete the required video diaries.

Through five specific tasks, participants were asked to introduce themselves and describe their day, to provide background information about their tablet, to walk through their tablet apps, and to detail recent shopping and search related activities. They received an alternative assignment if they had not used their tablets for such activities recently.

Follow-up Interviews

Throughout the two-week diary study, we reviewed participants' responses. This helped us to select a subset of 18 participants to visit for follow-up interviews in their homes, six per location (New York, San Francisco, Milwaukee areas). The goal of the interviews was to broaden our understanding of the function of the tablet in the participants' lives, understand how it is used alongside other devices they own, learn about and observe the context they are using their tablet in, and follow up with questions about specific use cases described in their diary entries. Each interview lasted 90 minutes, for which we used a semi-structured interview guide.

Contextual Inquiry

Both when reviewing the diary submissions and when conducting the follow-up interviews, the researchers identified areas for which we would be able to collect richer data and gain unique insights through conducting contextual inquiries. We followed up with four participants we had previously interviewed and the contextual inquiries lasted two hours each. During each contextual inquiry, we observed the participants' activities, recorded their interactions with the tablet and other devices, and periodically asked follow-up questions for clarification. The activities that we observed included looking up recipes and cooking, family use before, during and after dinner, and productivity tasks in a workplace environment.

RESULTS

Once the research was completed, we had collected 774 written diary entries, 157 video diary answers, 18 detailed participant profile write-ups from the field visits, and observations from four contextual inquiries, together with the raw video recordings, transcriptions, and photos. We conducted the analysis in three stages: 1) quantitative analysis of the written diaries, 2) qualitative analysis of the field research and video diaries, and 3) triangulation of insights to develop a set of conclusions.

Over the course of the two-week period, our participants had reported 774 incidences of tablet use with an average of 23.5 per participants (min=1, max=72, standard deviation=17.2). As these numbers indicate, there was a range in the number of tablet use incidences reported by each participant, with 80% of all diary entries submitted by 17 out of the 33 participants. Note that due to limitations of the diary study approach, it is unlikely that these numbers reflect the exact volume of actual tablet use, but rather a lower bound on their true usage. All open-ended responses to diary questions were coded using a bottom-up approach; with similar activities being grouped to then turn those into frequency distributions. The data from the video diaries, field visits, and contextual inquiries were analyzed in a two-day workshop during which we followed a bottom-up affinity diagramming approach. Finally, we reviewed the diary study analysis to triangulate its findings with those from the insights from the generated affinity diagram. This analysis process resulted in a set of insights about the overall distribution of tablet activities, correlations of tablet activities to contextual factors, and learnings about specific

Activity	Incidences		Participants	
Email checking	146	18.9%	28	84.8%
Playing games	84	10.9%	17	51.5%
Social networking	51	6.6%	19	57.6%
Looking up information	45	5.8%	19	57.6%
Listening to music	39	5.0%	12	36.4%
Watching TV/videos	34	4.4%	16	48.5%
Shopping: Browsing	31	4.0%	19	57.6%
Reading a book	27	3.5%	10	30.3%
Lightweight creation	27	3.5%	7	21.2%
Checking the weather	25	3.2%	11	33.3%
Reading news	25	3.2%	15	45.5%
Surfing the Web	22	2.8%	15	45.5%
Shopping: Purchasing	22	2.8%	15	45.5%
Local search	22	2.8%	11	33.3%
Recipe search, cooking	21	2.7%	12	36.4%
Reading a blog	19	2.5%	6	18.2%
Finding, installing apps	17	2.2%	9	27.3%
Checking calendar	15	1.9%	6	18.2%
Managing finances	13	1.7%	8	24.2%
Viewing documents	10	1.3%	6	18.2%

Table 1. Top tablet activities (90% of all reported incidences listed).

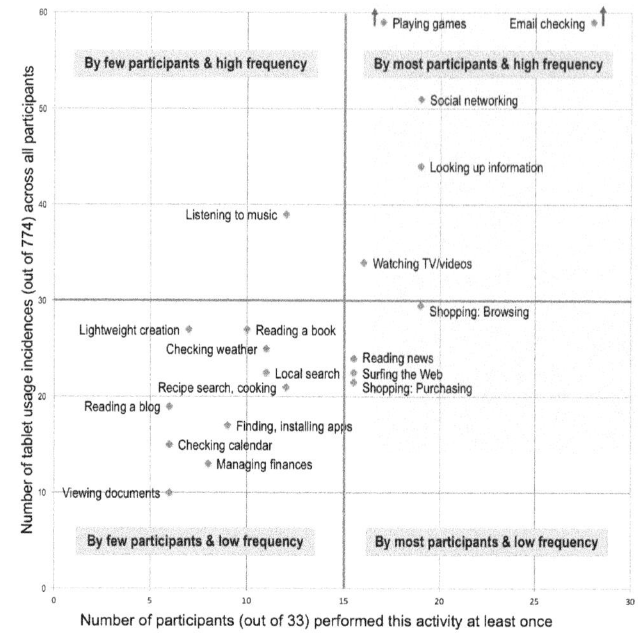

Figure 1. Top activities: Number of incidences vs. participants.

areas, including media consumption, shopping, cooking, and productivity. The remainder of this paper describes the details of our findings.

Overview of Tablet Activities

Across all reports of tablet use, the most frequent activities were found to be: Checking emails (with light responding), playing games, social networking, looking up and searching information, listening to music, shopping (browsing and purchasing), lightweight content creation (e.g., notes, lists, forms), reading a book, checking the weather, reading news, watching TV/movies/videos, and conducting a local search (refer to Table 1 for details). These results are similar to a Nielsen report which found that email, social networking, and watching videos were the top three activities [23], though we found that playing games, information seeking, and listening to music were more common than watching videos.

It is important to explore whether the reported tablet activities are common across participants or if they can be accounted for by just a few participants who do them frequently. We divided the activities into four distinct groups (see the quadrants in Figure 1): Activities reported 1) by few participants with low frequency, 2) by few participants with high frequency, 3) by a high number of participants with low frequency, and 4) by a high number of participants with high frequency. Hence, email checking, playing games, social networking, looking up information, watching TV or videos, shopping, reading news, and surfing the Web are distinct among activities, in being both common across participants and activities that are done frequently.

The structure of the diary questions allowed us to further dissect these activities. We first broke them down by personal vs. work. About 91% of reported tablet use was for personal purposes, while only 9% were related to work. Tablets were predominantly used for fun and relaxation. This was confirmed during the follow-up interviews in which many participants who described activities such as cooking, watching videos, and playing games were found to be particularly passionate about doing these on their tablet. Other personal tablet activities included those that were previously done on other devices, like checking email, social networking sites, their calendar, or the weather. Participants also enjoyed collaborating on activities with their kids and reading the news. For some families, tablets have become a central shared device that can be used by several family members, e.g., for playing games, reading a story book together, or for educational purposes. In such cases the tablet is not exclusively used in a collaborative setting, and members of the family may use it as a personal device as well. Only a small portion of participants used their tablets primarily for work-related tasks, which we will address in detail later.

Previous research has shown that use of computers and mobile phones differs depending on the day of the week [10], and so we evaluated if this also applies to tablet computers. Tablets were used for more activities (i.e., more unique instances of tablet use) during a typical weekday as compared to a typical weekend day: 61% of usage (1.86 incidences) occurred on a typical weekday and 39% (1.21 incidences) occurred during a typical weekend day. Besides the difference in the number of activities, tablets were also used overall for longer total duration during a typical weekday (an average participant spent about 48 minutes using their tablet) as compared to a typical weekend day (36 minutes). Weekdays showed more frequent email checking, managing of calendars, and checking the weather, but also included longer activities such as listening to music or social networking; however, activities such as watching videos, playing games, reading, and shopping were more frequently done on weekends.

Our findings show that tablets are being used repeatedly for the same activities, as has also been found to be the case for mobile phones [7].

We further asked participants to describe those activities that either involved another connected device or an action in the real world (i.e., without using the tablet). About 18% (138 incidences) of all reported tablet use involved another device besides the tablet, either before, during, or after using the tablet. The most frequent activities that included the use of another device were: checking emails (e.g., writing longer replies from their laptop/computer), looking up and searching information (e.g., conducting intensive research), and shopping (e.g., making the purchase after having browsed through options). Furthermore, about 12% (90 incidences) of all reported tablet use was started or continued in the real world. The most frequent of these activities included: checking emails (e.g., discussing or answering the email in person), looking up and searching information (e.g., providing the answer to a question they encountered in the real world), reading a book (e.g., a discussion of the book content), local search (e.g., going to the found store or restaurant), and shopping (e.g., making a purchase in a store).

Context of Tablet Use

To guide future product development, it is important to fully understand the contexts of tablet use. In the diary study, we asked participants to explain the place and situation they were in each time they used their tablet. We then coded their responses by the location and the secondary activity mentioned. In this section, we will discuss tablet activities regarding the participants' locations and other activities participants were engaged in while using their tablet. Examples of how participants described their contexts of use included:

> I was sitting on my couch having a cup of coffee.
>
> I was sitting on my bed and I had just woken up.
>
> I was sitting in my car waiting for the street to be cleaned and save myself a parking spot.
>
> I was at my home office desk while doing work emails with my laptop.
>
> Outside in my backyard, sitting on my patio relaxing.
>
> I was on the train going back home from work.
>
> I was home in my apartment and I just carried the iPad around with me when I changed rooms.

Common Locations

The most common locations for using tablets included those within their home (living room, couch, table, kitchen), at work (office, desk, meeting), while on the go (car, train, subway), and in other places (restaurant, gym, classroom). See Table 2 for details. Note that we developed the location codes based on the greatest specificity provided by the participants' diary submissions, e.g., while some participants may have only referenced their bedroom, others were more specific and called out that the specific location was their bed. As a result of this, the categories are of varying levels of granularity.

Location	Incidences		Participants	
Couch	182	23.51%	23	69.7%
Bed	128	16.54%	22	66.7%
Home	97	12.53%	18	54.6%
Table	70	9.04%	13	39.4%
Kitchen	67	8.66%	15	45.5%
Office	46	5.94%	11	33.3%
Desk	28	3.62%	9	27.3%
Bedroom	26	3.36%	7	21.2%
Car	25	3.23%	6	18.2%
Restaurant/café	21	2.71%	6	18.2%
Gym	12	1.55%	6	18.2%
Classroom	10	1.29%	4	12.1%
Commuting	10	1.29%	5	15.2%

Table 2. Top tablet use locations (90% of all incidences listed).

The data also provides a picture of the most common locations for the different activities (see Figure 2 for details):

- Email checking: Mostly on the couch and in bed.
- Playing games: Mostly on the couch, at home, in the car.
- Looking up info: Mostly in the kitchen, on couch, in bed.
- Listening to music: Mostly in the kitchen and in the office.
- Shopping: Mostly in bed, on the couch, in the kitchen.
- Light-weight content creation: Mostly while at a table.
- Reading: Happens quite evenly in any location.
- Checking weather: Mostly in the bedroom or in bed.
- Watching TV/videos: Mostly in bed, on couch, at the gym.
- Recipe search, cooking: Mostly in the kitchen.

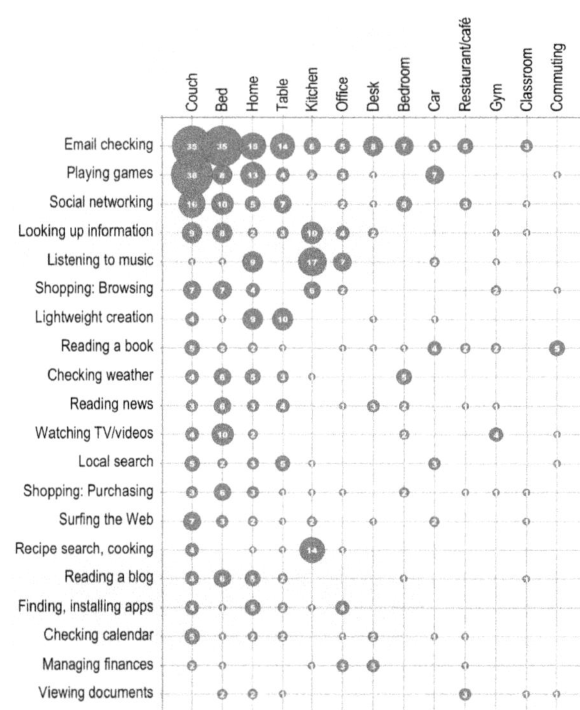

Figure 2. Frequency of top tablet activities by top locations.

Secondary activity	Incidences		Participants	
Watching TV	99	31.33%	20	60.6%
Eating/drinking	80	25.32%	13	39.4%
Cooking	32	10.13%	9	27.3%
Waiting somewhere	20	6.33%	9	27.3%
Getting dressed	15	4.75%	2	6.1%
Talking with others	14	4.43%	8	24.2%
Watching child/dog	10	3.16%	5	15.2%
Reading	10	3.16%	2	6.1%
Working	7	2.22%	5	15.2%
Exercising	6	1.9%	6	18.2%

Table 3. Top secondary activities (90% of all reported sec. activities).

During our follow-up interviews, we gathered more insights about the locations where tablets are used today. Seven interview participants said they used the tablet while in bed because the form factor fits the relaxed setting of being in bed. As the tablet was often placed close to their bed, they were likely to use it last thing before they went to sleep as well as the first thing after waking up.

This data also showed that tablets are more likely to stay at home as compared to being fully mobile devices; 82% of all incidences of tablet use occurred at home. Given the findings of a study by Church and Oliver (2011) [7] on the location of smartphones, we had already anticipated that a significant proportion of tablet activities would occur at a stationary location; however, tablets turned out to be even less mobile than smartphones. For most participants, their tablet stayed at home and was used in many rooms within the house from living room, to kitchen, to bedroom, to bathroom. The only exception to tablets remaining in the home was when people travelled, in which case the tablet tended to become a laptop replacement and was, hence, taken with them outside of their home. Fewer participants took their tablets everywhere (such as to work, school, the gym, cafes, or the park) as compared those who used it mainly at home.

Secondary Activities

We further classified tablet use by the participant's level of engagement, differentiating between partially and fully engaged use. We categorized an activity as fully engaged when the participant did not describe any other activity besides using the tablet; hence, partial engagement was defined as using the tablet while doing something else. Of all reported tablet incidence, 41% (316 out of 774) showed partial engagement. Note that this number is to be considered as a lower bound as it is possible that participants under-reported or forgot to explain those activities they were engaged in outside their tablet use.

The most frequently reported non-tablet activities that participants were doing at the same time they were using their tablet were: Watching TV, eating or drinking, cooking, waiting somewhere, getting dressed, talking with others, and exercising, among others (see Table 3 for more details for each). Those tablet activities that included secondary activities were: Listening to music, checking the weather, checking and light responding to emails, recipe search and cooking, social net-

Figure 3. Frequency of top tablet activities by top secondary activities.

working, and looking up information. Further relating tablet activities to secondary activities away from the tablet highlighted, for example, that playing games occurs frequently while waiting, that checking of emails and social networks is done often while eating, and that recipe searches happen mostly while cooking (refer to Figure 3 for more details).

The most frequent secondary activity performed while using the tablet was watching TV (by 61% of all participants, 31% of all secondary activities), as our diary study analysis as well as other research that has since been conducted [16, 25, 20] showed. Participants explained that their tablets can enhance the TV experience by extending that activity, through for example, looking up related information about the program that they were watching. An example of this would be searching a movie database for the names of movie actors. However, the diary study data also showed that people sometimes do unrelated activities on their tablet at the same time as watching TV. Some were constantly switching their focus between the TV program and their tablet activity, while others were simply accompanying their partner engaged in watching TV by being in the same location. The tablet form factor affords lightweight interaction that compliments TV watching better than a laptop, and having a bigger screen than a smartphone makes it easier to divide attention between the TV and the tablet screen.

Insights about Specific Areas

Our research revealed that certain activities on the tablet warrant a fuller exploration and description. They are compelling either because people are particularly passionate about them, because they are very engaged in the activity while carrying it out, or because it requires sustained effort and interaction. We will look at these areas of shopping, media consumption, cooking, and productivity, in this section.

Shopping

We found that many participants like to do shopping research through browsing (window shopping) on the tablet but then often made the actual purchases either on their computer or in person at a physical store. During the two-week diary study, 58% of all participants (19) did some form of product browsing activities on their tablet (31 out of 774 incidences), while 42% of all made an actual purchase on their tablet during the time of the diary study (22 out of total 774 incidences). This differentiation between browsing and purchasing is also highlighted by shopping-related activities having a higher percentage of transitions from or to other devices (30%) or the real world (17%), than many other activities.

> It's always just a bit more effortless on the laptop [shopping] but every now and then when I'm sitting in front of a movie I'll purchase items through my iPad. – iPad user

There were several reasons why purchases tended not to be made on tablets. During our follow-up interviews, most participants said they were often not signed into their accounts on shopping sites. These participants explained that they did not have their account information stored in the tablets' browser and they couldn't always remember their username and/or password. It was therefore more convenient to switch to the desktop or laptop computer, where this information was already stored. Participants also described how it is often difficult to enter payment information and "checkout" on the tablet with the attempt sometimes failing because the site is not optimized for tablet interaction. We also heard from many iPad users that the lack of Flash support was a reason they would move from window shopping on their tablet to the computer. Other reasons included that the tablet form factor (especially the keyboard) can make purchasing more difficult in comparison to a computer with a full, tactile keyboard.

> It's too much pain to sign in on the tablet. By the time I do that, I have ordered it already on my computer. – iPad user

Through our in-depth interviews, we learned that many participants went directly to trusted shopping sites such as Amazon, Target, eBay, or Craigslist. We observed several participants as they went back and forth across such sites mentally comparing the products and prices that they saw. We observed that when shopping, most participants appeared not to be interested in finding additional stores to buy the item from if their favorite, known sources will do.

> Usually when I do any kind of shopping, my main app is Safari so I can jump through the sites that way. – iPad user

Lastly, most participants who shopped on their tablets explained they preferred to do so on full sites in the browser over apps or mobile sites. Reasons for this included having a larger number of products listed on full sites, product details can be expanded to a greater degree, and there is often additional filtering functionality available. We also observed that participants preferred the richer browsing experience afforded by the full sites (over apps) because it is familiar and consistent with their experience on a computer.

As more people continue to pursue shopping activities on tablets, it is important to find ways for creating a more seamless experience both on the tablet itself and across devices.

Media Consumption

Media consumption activities explored in our study included watching television, movies and videos, listening to music, and reading news, blogs, magazines and books. These media consumption activities were carried out by the majority of participants. 78% of all participants (26 out of 33) used media on their tablet at least once during the study. Media consumption was also among the most frequent activities accounting for 19% of all 774 incidences.

Watching television, movies, and videos was reported by 16 out of 33 participants (34 out of a total 774 incidences) in the diary study. During the subsequent interviews, participants told us how they liked that the tablet provided a bigger form factor compared to their phone for consuming media. They also said that since their tablets were more portable, cool (temperature) and lighter than a laptop it made it easier to watch television, movies, and videos in bed. They also used the tablet for media consumption in other locations including the living room, at the kitchen table, or at the gym. Participants reported that they had migrated some activities they previously performed on laptops and smartphones to the tablet. The types of activities that they had transitioned tended to be leisurely activities such as media consumption that better fit the fun and leisurely experience that participants associate with their tablets. We also found that participants were surprised at how much they were using their tablets to watch television, movies and video. They reported accessing this media primarily through specific apps, e.g., Netflix, iTunes, YouTube, Facebook, PBS, ABC, and HBO.

> I didn't think I was going to use this [iPad] to be a TV to watch HBO. The resolution on it is really, really good so I feel like I have a little personal TV to myself. – iPad user

One of the key areas of media consumption reported by participants was reading content, with 61% of participants (20 out of 33) reporting reading either a book, news, blog, or a magazine on their tablet. Of the 33 participants in the diary study, 15 reported reading news (24 out of 774 incidences), 10 reading a book (27), 6 reading a blog (18), and 4 reading a magazine (7).

> After work today, I decided to do some reading on my tablet to relax. Reading on my tablet is so easy and it actually can be more fun. I also think that it is easier on my eyes as well. – Android tablet user

Reading a book occurred primarily at home (on the couch or in bed) and when commuting. Participants reported finding it easy and convenient to download and read books on their tablet. They were reading in the evening in bed before going to sleep and also when they had some free time during the day, typically in sessions lasting less than one hour. Participants primarily used native apps (e.g., Slate, Wall Street Journal, Fox News) and aggregators (e.g., Flipboard, Pulse) to access news content, though several reported using the browser to surf across favorite news sites (e.g., CNN, NYTimes, and local news providers). While the majority of participants did their reading of magazine, blog, and news content at home, a few reported doing so at work, while commuting and at other locations such as a gym or cafe.

Participants also reported that *listening to music* was a key activity they did with their tablet. During the diary study, 36% of participants (12 out of 33) used their tablet for listening to music. Interestingly, the top location for listening to music via the tablet was in the kitchen while cooking a meal. Tablets were also used for listening to music while at work. Participants reported accessing the music with apps, or streaming via the browser, via services such as Pandora and Spotify.

> I accessed Pandora on my iPad to play some low key music while cooking breakfast for my child. I like having music on while I am cooking or baking especially with my child around. We sing and dance to the music together and it makes for a nice, mellow bonding time while eating. – iPad user

Our research showed that many activities are migrating from participants TVs, computers, and phones to the tablet and of particular interest are some of the activities around media consumption that have high levels of engagement. We expect to see more of these activities happening on tablets as more content and delivery channels become available.

Cooking

The extent to which participants used their tablets for recipes and cooking was surprising. During the diary portion of the study, 36% of all participants (12 out of 33) described using their tablets for finding recipes and for following instructions while cooking. When we only look at female participants, 45% of all (9 out of 20) used their tablet for such activities. Many did this fairly regularly, often a couple of times a week. In comparison to other activities (such as accessing the news, emailing, or social networking) it is a less frequent activity, but has a higher average sustained length. Also of particular note, some participants were very passionate about using their tablet for recipes and cooking, particularly enjoying the experience, and citing it as a good benefit to owning a tablet computer. The form factor of the tablet resonated in terms of being an ideal cooking companion for some people.

The benefits that participants saw to using the tablet as a cookery resource included not having to print recipes to take them to the kitchen, not having to plug the tablet in, and being able to put the tablet close to the cooking area. The issues included knowing to change the settings to disable the dimming function of the tablet. If the user did not do this, they regularly needed to touch the tablet to reactivate the light. Also, a number of recipe websites were not mobile optimized for tablet devices, resulting in a less satisfying experience. Some users also spoke about being concerned about getting food on to their tablet during the cooking process, and keeping it at a suitable distance within the cooking vicinity can be somewhat frustrating.

We found that the recipes that participants accessed came from four sources: 1) directly accessing favorite recipe websites (e.g., `allrecipies.com`, `foodnetwork.com`, `cooks.com`, `bettycrocker.com`), 2) searching and finding recipes via search results, 3) directly accessing favorite apps (e.g., Epicurious, Jamie Oliver's 20-minute meals), and 4) directly accessing favorite cooking video shows (e.g., Netflix, YouTube). It seemed to be that participants typically stuck to their preferred source for their recipes, whether a particular show, a favorite app or website, or whether they always searched in a browser, since they talked to us about the primary way they access recipes. However, not all sources were created equal, and using recipes accessible through videos proved quite problematic. While we were observing one participant, it was clear that the pace of the video was too fast to easily follow. She had to rewind it a lot, and found that difficult to control. She had to watch the whole episode from the beginning a few times, because the instructions went by so quickly.

We also discovered that online solutions that create a shopping list are beneficial. For example, the Epicurious app has a shopping list function, and three participants described taking their phone to the store with a shopping list, and switching to their tablet at home to follow the recipe.

> I used Epicurious to build my shopping list, snapshot the list and emailed it to my iPhone. – iPad user.

As we have seen, there are a variety of ways to find recipes using a tablet; and our study has also revealed a diversity of ways that users are saving recipes. These include: 1) bookmarking recipes in the browser, 2) using a tagging service, 3) storing the recipe using Evernote, 4) copying and pasting recipes into the Notes app on the tablet, and 5) "favoriting," "liking," or using similar marking mechanisms in cookery apps. Through our contextual inquiries, we found that the time while the recipe is cooking is "down-time" during which the tablet was used for media consumption (as described previously), and we also observed participants using their tablet as an entertainment device while cooking.

While finding recipes and cooking with tablets is understandably not a frequent activity, in comparison to checking email or playing games, this study revealed that using tablets for recipes and cookery is an important activity for many tablet owners, and should be considered as a key use case for their development and design.

Productivity

The diary study revealed that 39% of all participants (13 out of 33) performed at least one productivity-focused task with their tablet. Such activities included document creation, document editing, file management, and file transfer. When including "email checking with light responding", 88% of all participants (29 out of 33) did a productivity-related activity with their tablet.

Participants used a wide variety of tools on the tablet for productivity tasks including 1) Evernote for syncing notes across multiple devices and for collecting recipes, 2) QuickOffice to view documents, 3) Google Docs to view and edit documents, 4) Notes for shopping and task lists, 5) Cosi for syncing lists, 6) AutoCad for reviewing drawings, and 7) email apps for reminders and file management. One participant who was a student used her iPad for reading PDFs, note-taking during class, and sending files through email for subsequent use on her laptop. Another participant, also a student, used her tablet as a laptop replacement for activities such as reviewing and taking notes in class, editing documents and sending emails to herself for future reference.

> I was studying in my office today and used QuickOffice on my iPad to take notes as I read. Not having a keyboard always makes this process a little less fluid and easy than using my laptop, but it's worth it to have the smaller device to carry around. It also takes up less space on my desk or table when I work, which is nice too. – iPad user

Document and content creation related activities included: email checking with light responding (146 incidences), lightweight content creation (27), creating and editing of documents (4), and creating notes and shopping lists (3). Participants reported that typing on the tablet was a major pain point which they found frustrating and it often limited the amount of data entry they were willing to do before moving to another device such as a laptop or desktop computer. Other productivity related activities included: checking the calendar with light managing (15), viewing documents (10), and transferring data (2).

Managing files and transferring data from the computer to the tablet (and visa versa) proved difficult for participants (e.g., difficulty opening zip files and working with large spreadsheets). Several participants complained about the lack of printing capability with their tablet. These participants had workarounds such as emailing items to themselves and switching devices (for example, one participant switched to a laptop to print coupons). Another participant described how she successfully emailed attached files from her laptop and opened them on the tablet with QuickOffice.

> I was trying to access a document through my email in order to view it on the iPad. I was able to access the email and download the document in order to study it later on in the day. – iPad user

Other productivity related insights included participants creating shopping lists and reminders on their tablets using the Notes app, email and other apps.

While in many cases productivity tasks were not easy to perform on the tablet, a number of participants were willing to put up with many of these issues for the convenience afforded by the form factor of the device (e.g., lightweight, small).

CONCLUSION

In this paper, we have presented results from a multi-method study conducted during September and October 2011, which explored in detail how tablets are being used today. Thirty-three participants from across three locations in the U.S. took part in a diary study, 18 were visited for follow-up interviews, and with 4 we conducted contextual inquiries. Our results include a detailed breakdown of tablet activities, with the most frequent activities being checking emails, playing games, social networking, and looking up information. We found that tablets are primarily used for personal purposes, and that users are very passionate about certain activities, particularly those for which the tablet form factor provides unique interactions or usability affordances. Our data also showed that tablets are used more during weekdays and that a portion of tablet activities include a transition from or to other devices or actions in the real world. We also found that tablet use mostly occurs in the home (e.g., couch, bed, table, kitchen) and often while doing other activities away from the tablet (e.g., watching TV, eating, cooking, waiting). Finally, we discussed qualitative insights about some of the most engaging activities, including media consumption, shopping, cooking, and productivity.

By better understanding current tablet activities and their context, these findings may serve as a basis for anyone designing and developing applications and sites for tablets. Especially for highly engaging tablet activities, we need to consider the constraints and opportunities of the context of use; for example, using tablets while lying in bed may require a tailored user experience and a particular interaction technique. It is also important to take better advantage of the disposition of tablet users by providing more opportunities for playful interactions and explorations in terms of how content is presented and revealed. Furthermore, website designers need to ensure their sites offer the full feature set while being tailored towards tablets. They should make a concerted effort to optimize their existing sites to "just work" on tablets, using responsive design. This will result in reduced effort of developing separate sites for each device, but it also encourages cross-device consistency and a unified user experience. At the same time, sites need to take advantage of the unique affordances of tablet devices to support gestures like touch and swipe.

As people continue to migrate many of their media consumption activities to tablet devices, website designers should optimize their entertainment content to make it more accessible on these devices (of varying screen sizes), as well as offer easy transitions between the actual media content and related material. In particular for shopping and productivity-related activities, it is important to provide a seamless experience across all of the user's devices, so that activities started on one of their devices can easily be continued on another. It is worth exploring how tablets can be integrated into the real-world shopping experience as well as making online shopping easier, so that tablets can provide great user experiences for purchasing in-store as well as on the tablet itself. The tablet also has the potential to become a state-of-the-art device to support the end-to-end cooking experience, including support for recipe selection, ingredients shopping, step-by-step cooking help, healthy eating, gathering friends, and so forth.

Finally, our findings also point to several unexplored areas of research. It is important to understand more about how tablet use differs from that of other computing devices (especially laptops, netbooks, and smartphones), including understanding how and why people transition between those devices. We would also like to explore how tablets are used with other people or in the proximity of other people, to better understand the impact of different social situations. We intend to repeat this combination of quantitative and qualitative research on tablet usage periodically to uncover how motivations and behavior changes in relation to tablets over time.

ACKNOWLEDGMENTS

We would like to thank all the participants who took part in this study, as well as those that helped us make this research be a success (recruiting vendor, online portal providers, interview transcribers, interview observers, and analysis workshop participants), and in particular our research partner Marianne Berkovich.

REFERENCES

1. Amin, A., Townsend, S., Ossenbruggen, J., and Hardman, L. Fancy a drink in canary wharf?: A user study on location-based mobile search. In *Proc. INTERACT '09*, Springer-Verlag (2009), 736–749.
2. Barkhuus, L., and Polichar, V. E. Empowerment through seamfulness: Smart phones in everyday life. *Personal Ubiquitous Comput. 15* (2011), 629–639.
3. Böhmer, M., Hecht, B., Schöning, J., Krüger, A., and Bauer, G. Falling asleep with Angry Birds, Facebook and Kindle: A large scale study on mobile application usage. In *Proc. MobileHCI '11*, ACM (2011), 47–56.
4. Chandrasekar, S., Tront, J. G., and Prey, J. C. WriteOn1.0: A tablet PC-based tool for effective classroom instruction. In *Proc. ITiCSE '09*, ACM (2009), 323–327.
5. Chipman, G., Fails, J. A., Druin, A., and Guha, M. L. Paper vs. tablet computers: A comparative study using Tangible Flags. In *Proc. IDC '11*, ACM (2011), 29–36.
6. Chua, A. Y. K., Balkunje, R. S., and Goh, D. H.-L. Fulfilling mobile information needs: A study on the use of mobile phones. In *Proc. ICUIMC '11*, ACM (2011).
7. Church, K., and Oliver, N. Understanding mobile web and mobile search use in today's dynamic mobile landscape. In *Proc. MobileHCI '11*, ACM (2011).
8. Church, K., Smyth, B., Bradley, K., and Cotter, P. A large scale study of European mobile search behaviour. In *Proc. MobileHCI '08*, ACM (2008), 13–22.
9. Guelman, C., De Leone, C., and Price, E. The influence of tablet PCs on students use of multiple representations in lab reports. In *Proc. PER '09*, vol. 1179 of *PER Conference* (2009), 153–156.
10. Halvey, M., Keane, M. T., and Smyth, B. Predicting navigation patterns on the mobile-internet using time of the week. In *Special interest tracks and posters WWW '05*, ACM (2005), 958–959.
11. Heslop, L., Weeding, S., Dawson, L., Fisher, J., and Howard, A. Implementation issues for mobile-wireless infrastructure and mobile health care computing devices for a hospital ward setting. *Journal of Medical Systems 34*, 4 (2010), 509–518.
12. Holzner, B., Schauer-Maurer, G., Stockhammer, G., Muigg, A., Hutterer, M., and Giesinger, J. Patient reported outcome monitoring using a tablet PC is suitable for measuring quality of life in patients with gliomas. *Wiener medizinische Wochenschrift 1946 161*, 1-2 (2011), 6–12.
13. Hourcade, J. P., Bullock-Rest, N. E., and Hansen, T. E. Multitouch tablet applications and activities to enhance the social skills of children with autism spectrum disorders. *Personal Ubiquitous Comput. 16*, 2 (2012).
14. Kamvar, M., Kellar, M., Patel, R., and Xu, Y. Computers and iphones and mobile phones, oh my!: A logs-based comparison of search users on different devices. In *Proc. WWW '09*, ACM (2009), 801–810.
15. Kurtz, B. L., Fenwick, Jr., J. B., and Ellsworth, C. C. Using podcasts and tablet PCs in computer science. In *Proc. ACM-SE 45*, ACM (2007), 484–489.
16. Nielsen. Multitasking at home: Simultaneous use of media grows, Sept. 2009. `http://goo.gl/FI2ba`.
17. Nielsen. The connected devices age: ipads, kindles, smartphones and the connected consumer, Sept. 2010. `http://goo.gl/9QeFA`.
18. Nielsen. Connected devices: Does the ipad change everything?, Oct. 2010. `http://goo.gl/MPpQf`.
19. Nielsen. Who is buying the ipad, and will they also buy an iphone?, Aug. 2010. `http://goo.gl/OoHui`.
20. Nielsen. 40% of tablet and smartphone owners use them while watching tv, Oct. 2011. `http://goo.gl/HolIh`.
21. Nielsen. App-happy with android: The most popular android apps by age, Dec. 2011. `http://goo.gl/8sDfC`.
22. Nielsen. Changing demographics of tablet and ereader owners in the us, Aug. 2011. `http://goo.gl/oubJr`.
23. Nielsen. Connected devices: How we use tablets in the u.s., May 2011. `http://goo.gl/yDO06`.
24. Nielsen. Generation app: 62% of mobile users 25-34 own smartphones, Nov. 2011. `http://goo.gl/KO6sh`.
25. Nielsen. In the u.s., tablets are tv buddies while ereaders make great bedfellows, May 2011. `http://goo.gl/ylQO2`.
26. Pew Research Center. Mobile access 2010, July 2010. `http://goo.gl/1DMWp`.
27. Pew Research Center. A snapshot of e-reader and tablet owners, July 2010. `http://goo.gl/uqgTZ`.
28. Pew Research Center. Half of adult cell phone owners have apps on their phones, Nov. 2011. `http://goo.gl/wdJEe`.
29. Pew Research Center. How mobile devices are changing community information environments, Mar. 2011. `http://goo.gl/76BA5`.
30. Pew Research Center. Smartphone adoption and usage, July 2011. `http://goo.gl/hzcjd`.
31. Pew Research Center. Tablet and e-book reader ownership nearly double over the holiday gift-giving period, Jan. 2012. `http://goo.gl/1kIjr`.
32. Steinweg, S. B., Williams, S. C., and Stapleton, J. N. Faculty use of tablet PCs in teacher education and K-12 settings. *TechTrends 54* (2010), 54–61.
33. Verkasalo, H., Lpez-Nicols, C., Molina-Castillo, F. J., and Bouwman, H. Analysis of users and non-users of smartphone applications. *Telematics and Informatics 27*, 3 (2010), 242 – 255.
34. Wyeth, P., McEwan, M., Roe, P., and MacColl, I. Expressive interactions: Tablet usability for young mobile learners. In *Proc. OzCHI '11*, ACM (2011).

Exploring iPhone Usage: The Influence of Socioeconomic Differences on Smartphone Adoption, Usage and Usability

Ahmad Rahmati[1], Chad Tossell[2], Clayton Shepard[1], Philip Kortum[2], and Lin Zhong[1]
[1] Dept. of Electrical and Computer Engineering, [2] Dept. of Psychology, Rice University, Houston, TX
{rahmati, chad.tossell, cws, pkortum, lzhong}@rice.edu

ABSTRACT
Previous studies have found that smartphone users differ by orders of magnitude. We explore this variability to understand how users install and use native applications in ecologically-valid environments. A quasi-experimental approach is applied to compare how users in different socioeconomic status (SES) groups adopt new smartphone technology along with how applications are installed and used. We present a longitudinal study of 34 iPhone 3GS users. 24 of these participants were chosen from two carefully selected SES groups who were otherwise similar and balanced. Usage data collected through an in-device programmable logger, as well as several structured interviews, identify similarities, differences, and trends, and highlight systematic differences in smartphone usage. A group of 10 lower SES participants were later recruited and confirm the influence of SES diversity on device usage. Among our findings are that a large number of applications were uninstalled, lower SES groups spent more money on applications and installed more applications overall, and the lowest SES group perceived the usability of their iPhones poorly in comparison to the other groups. We further discuss the primary reasons behind this low score, and suggest design implications to better support users across SES brackets.

Author Keywords
Smartphones; Socioeconomic Status; SES; Applications; Diversity; User Study; iPhone; Mobile.

ACM Classification Keywords
H.1.2 [Models and Principals]: User/Machine Systems

INTRODUCTION
Understanding user diversity is a central tenet of human-computer interaction (HCI) research [1]. With an understanding of how users vary, designers can better support a broad range of individuals with different backgrounds, capabilities, skills and interests. Smartphone users have been described as extremely diverse [2]. Yet, little research has moved towards understanding these differences in more precise ways. To this end, we contribute a naturalistic and longitudinal study of how different SES groups use their iPhones. The study leverages an in-device, programmable, continuously running logger that collects device usage, complemented by regular interviews with the participants.

Our study has two unique features. First, unlike prior work that has very limited information about the participants [3-5], it achieves more statistical control over potentially confounding variables. Our users are extremely similar in age, attend college at the same university, live in similar dorms, and have the exact same experience levels with their device. However, they differ in their SES backgrounds, which we show is important for explaining user variance.

Second, our study logs smartphone usage for a longer period of time. Data is collected from most of our iPhone users for twelve months. In contrast, prior work is based on studies lasting at most a few months on Android and Windows Mobile based smartphones. This yearlong study allows us to study the adoption and long-term evolution of user behavior, which has been previously impossible. We chose the iPhone as, at the time of the study, it represented the cutting edge of smartphone design for usability, accounting for over a third of the US mobile Internet traffic as of April 2010 [6]. Additionally, iPhone users have access to the largest number of third-party applications, with over 300,000 officially released apps as of October, 2010. This enables our study to paint a comprehensive picture of how iPhone users employ their devices in real environments and capture longitudinal trends that were previously missed.

Taken together, the two unique features highlighted above enable us to contribute unique findings in this paper instead of presenting mere usage statistics. After we describe the research that informs the current study in the Related Work section, we describe the logging methodology used to collect real-world usage data from 34 participants. Because our users are all new smartphone users, we present results longitudinally to show device adoption and trends. While smartphone users are known to be diverse [2], we look not only at what the users do with the iPhones, but the influence of SES on how users differ.

In the Diversity and Dynamics of Usage section, we describe aggregate usage patterns. This includes the first empirical look at how users install and uninstall applications from the Apple App Store. We demonstrate the importance of a try-before-you-buy App Store, and show that web based versions of applications often entice users to install the full application.

In the Effect of Socioeconomic Status section, we carefully examine the affects of SES by utilizing our two carefully selected participant subsets. They both attend the same

MobileHCI'12, September 21–24, 2012, San Francisco, CA, USA.

small private college, have similar experience with their iPhones, are equal in gender distribution, and are similar in other regards as well; except they differ in SES. We find that SES has a significant impact on usage, suggesting different needs and preferences for these groups of users in their specific contexts. In particular, we find that the web usage of low SES users is more of an extension to their PC-based web access, and that users' disappointment with the browsing experience on smartphones decreases their usage. Our findings indicating that lower SES users spend more time on the phone and more money on applications, suggest that the positioning and marketing of manufacturers who position their devices in a low end (cheap) – high end (expensive) manner, where the lower end phones are unable to run the latest high-resource-usage applications and games, and/or have a lower quality camera / display, is unfruitful.

Since the above SES differences manifested across a number of interactive behaviors, in the Lower Income Smartphone Users section, we recruit ten more users from one of the most underprivileged regions in a major metropolitan city. Usage patterns logged from these individuals confirm the influence of SES is important to understand the variance in how smartphone technology is adopted and used in real environments. Furthermore, the lowest SES group perceived their iPhone usability as poor in comparison to the other groups. Limited battery lifetime was their primary reason behind this low score.

Our findings have strong implications not only for understanding smartphone users, but for device and application design, optimization, and evaluation. In the Implications section, we highlight the value of long-term user studies with carefully selected participants. While we show the feasibility and limitations of smartphones as a primary device for IT access, especially for cost effective IT access in underserved communities, our results strongly suggest smartphone users could benefit from a better web browsing experience. Last but not least, we assess the one-size-fits-all phone paradigm, and show that even among our limited set of participants, there are distinctively different usage patterns that would benefit from phones with different hardware and software configurations.

RELATED WORK

Although there has been little work understanding the influence of SES on device usage, human factors of mobile devices have been an active research area for more than a decade. Most HCI studies in mobile space employ either lab-based evaluation or a short period of field trials [7]. In the last few years, as smartphones began to be widely adopted, there have been several relatively long-term field studies that we build upon in the present report.

The MIT Reality Mining project [8] studied 100 users of Nokia Symbian 60 series phones for one year. In [9], we studied 12 high-school users of Windows Mobile smartphones for four month. Both of these studies used previous generation phones, and their usage does not generalize to current smartphones. More importantly, they were severely limited in their data collection capabilities. The first recorded running application, currently associated cell tower, and visible Bluetooth devices. The second recorded the screen status and detailed network conditions.

In [2], the authors studied 33 users of Android smartphones for 7 – 21 weeks. The authors did not have access to the participants for interviews or have demographic information about them beyond several predetermined user types. The data was analyzed mostly for usage statistics in the form of distributions, and the authors concluded that smartphone users are very different, without providing insights into why. In contrast, our study employed participants selected in a controlled manner, and a much longer period of study. This enabled us to gain insight into the long-term evolution of smartphone usage, and illuminate the differences and similarities of smartphone users. Moreover, with a superset of usage data, we are able to also analyze many new aspects of smartphone usage, including App Store utilization, application usage, and web access.

Most recently, using the methodology described in a previous report [10], we characterized user differences in mobile space by examining how the Internet was accessed on smartphones over time [11]. We found systematic differences between users, showing some were more exploratory and others concentrated their usage on favorite resources. These findings motivated design suggestions to better support users across a behavioral spectrum. However, this previous study only examined native applications that accessed the Internet. Heavily-used applications such as text messaging and voice phone were not examined.

Previous studies have shown that SES differences are important to consider for the design of other technologies. In [12], Goel et al. revisited the digital divide and found, among other differences, that SES differences drove how frequently web pages were accessed. Individuals in lower SES brackets accessed the web more than their higher SES peers. Similarly, we logged usage from iPod Touch devices and found that lower SES users without access to other technologies used their iPod Touch substantially more for activities commonly used on PCs [13].

This study analyzes all native applications used by a set of new iPhone users over a period of one year. This data reveals important influences of SES on application installation and usage through a longitudinal lens. Additionally, user differences in the types of applications installed and used over time reveal important distinctions between individuals and suggest more tailored functionality and systems to support smartphone users.

FIELD STUDY AND DATA ANALYSIS

Field Study Participants

Our main 24 users were young college students with an average age of 19.7 years (*SD* =1.1 years), and the study lasted from February 2010 to February 2011. These 24 balanced participants were recruited from two distinct SES groups from Rice University, Houston, TX. They all lived

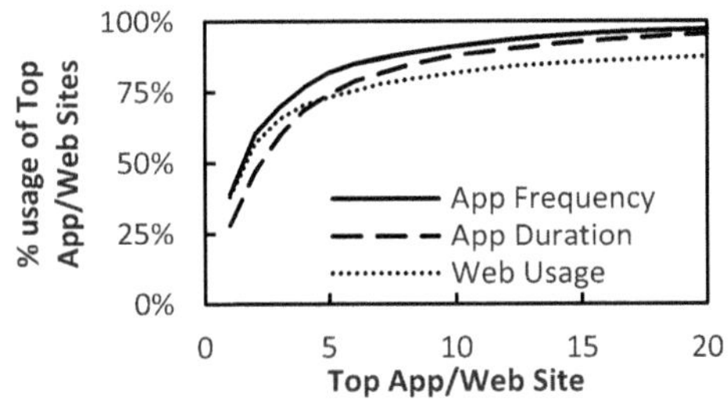

Figure 1: A small number of applications and websites dominate usage

on campus in dormitories. The low SES group was comprised of 13 students who received needs-based-scholarships and had a household income of under $60,000. The 11 users in the high SES group did not receive scholarships and their household income was over $80,000. Other factors, including their major, gender, race, PC access, and game console ownership, were balanced across groups. All had access to the university's computing labs, and a PC or laptop at their residence. All high, and 11 of the low SES participants had a personal laptop.

Every participant received a free iPhone for their participation, and was required to use the outfitted iPhone as their primary device for the entire year. Additionally, each participant received free service coverage, including 450 voice call minutes per month, unlimited data, and unlimited SMS, during the study. We helped all participants port their phone numbers to the iPhones.

Finally, approximately six months into the study, we added a third participant group of 10 students from a public community college in an underprivileged section of the same metropolitan area. We provided the same service plan and instrumented device to these participants, but for six months, from September 2010 to February 2011. The 10 users (M = 24.2 years, SD = 2.23 years) were in a lower SES bracket than the main 24 participants; they reported their annual income between $35,000 and $0. Yet, we note that there are other differences, beyond SES, between this group and the first two SES groups (e.g., occupation, age, and children). Therefore, we use this dataset carefully, and only in the Lower Income Smartphone Users section.

Data Collection

Logger Design and Implementation

The key component of the field study is an in-device, programmable logging software that collects almost all aspects of iPhone usage and context *in situ*. To run the logger in the background continuously, we had to jailbreak the iPhone 3GSs and exploit a setting provided by iOS 3.1.3, the latest at the beginning of our study. It starts the daemon process, as well as restarts it anytime it is killed. The main logger daemon is written as a shell script in bash and utilizes components written in various languages, including C, perl, awk, SQL, and objective C. Furthermore, the logger daemon is able to call built in functions, manage child processes, install and use programs from repositories, run custom programs, and add new features. We have implemented the logger in a modular and robust fashion, thus a new iOS release may break individual components, but the main functionality is unaffected. In order to monitor and update the logger, it is programmed to report the logged data and, if necessary, update itself every day through an encrypted connection, via rsync [14], to a lab server. We employed several methods to limit energy consumption, and our measurements show that the logger consumed on average 5% of the battery per day.

While the logger recorded a plethora of context information, for this work we focus on logs regarding application installation, uninstallation, price, genre, and usage, as well as web usage. We note that given the nature of the study, there were short-term lapses in the log files of five users. These lasted from a few days up to over a month, and were caused by a number of reasons. These include bugs in our code, lost, stolen or damaged phones, travel, and phones that were accidentally erased by the users. We substitute data from missing days with the all time average of that user in order to maintain each user's uniqueness and to avoid magnifying the impact of short-term fluctuation in usage. We note that since there are only short periods of missing data on few users, we regenerate missing samples, and we analyze macro-dynamics (e.g., monthly usage) the overall effect of missing data is negligible.

Complementary Interviews

Since our study design allowed us to have access to the participants, we collected self-reported data alongside automated logging. The self reports were used to assess the participants' perceptions of their usage and their access to other IT resources, as well as help interpret the logged data.

Assuring Privacy

Collecting data from smartphones in the field naturally incurs privacy issues. We employ the following methods to protect privacy while retaining relevant information for research. First, we leverage one-way hashing to preserve the uniqueness of a data entry without revealing its content. For example, we hash the recorded phone numbers, names, and email addresses. With hashing, we can still construct call statistics without knowing actual phone numbers. Second, we perform information extraction in the device. For example, we extract emoticons from emails and text messages without collecting the raw content. Finally, we structure the research team so that the data analysis and logger development team do not directly interact with the participants, in order to avoid linking data to the actual users. A separate human factors team acts as the interface with our participants, but does not deal directly with the logger or access the raw data. This enables us to contact the participants in a privacy sensitive manner when necessary, for example to schedule impromptu interviews with users who exhibit a drastic change in behavior.

DIVERSITY AND DYNAMICS OF USAGE

In this section, we analyze the diversity and dynamics of application adoption and usage, for both built-in and App

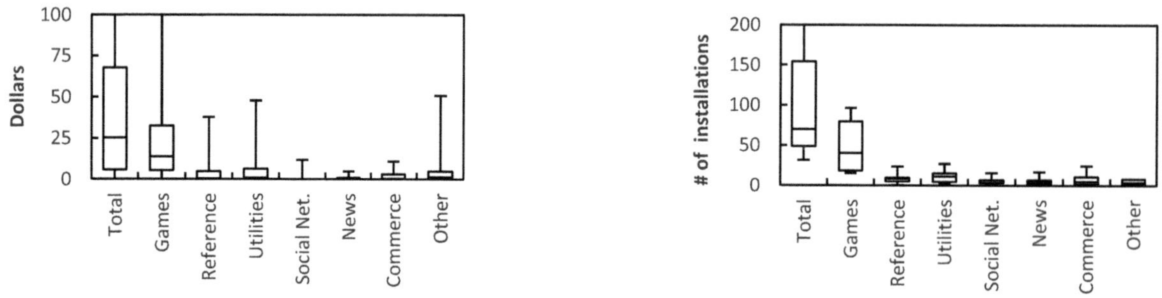

Figure 2: There is significant user diversity in paid application installations in terms of number (left) and cost (right). Broken down by category. Boxes: 2nd / 3rd quartiles. Whiskers: maximum / minimum. Horizontal lines: median

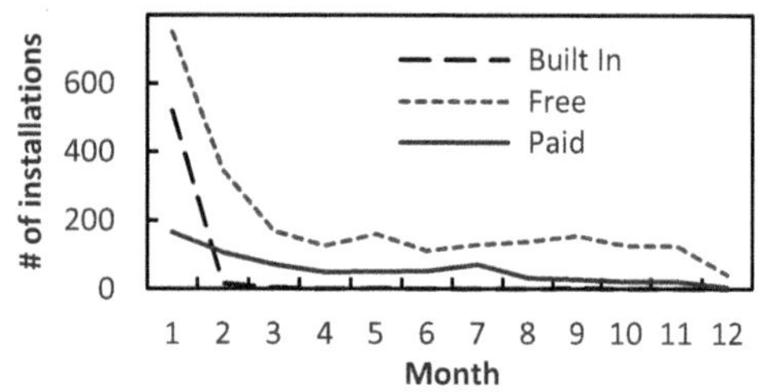

Figure 3: The ratio of paid to free application installations remained steady through the study, at ~ 20%.

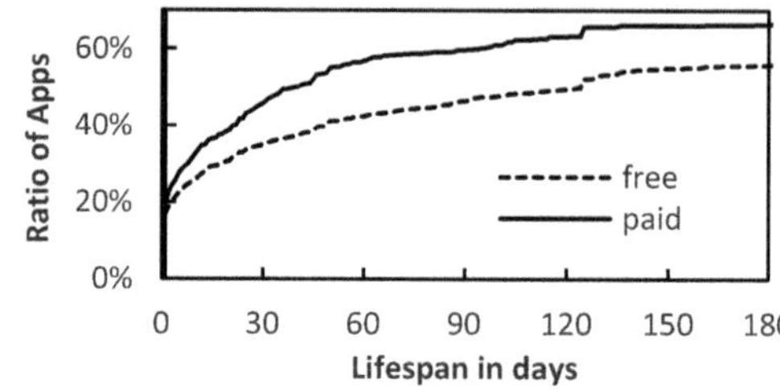

Figure 4: Paid applications have a shorter lifespan compared to free applications.

Table 1: We assigned categories to applications based on the genres reported by the App Store

Category	*Genres*	*Notes*
Games	Games, Entertainment, Media	Entertainment and media consumption
Utilities	Utilities and Productivity	Calculators, alarm clocks, todo lists
Reference	Books, Education, and Reference	Information resources
News	News, Sports, Travel, Weather	Contemporaneous information resources
Commerce	Business, Finance, Lifestyle (shopping)	Shopping or financial apps
Social Networking	Social Networking	Facebook, MySpace, Twitter
Other	Health, Navigation, Medical, Photography	Only a few (162) applications

Store applications. Our findings confirm the diversity of usage, yet, we will see in the later sections how we can extract order from this seemingly diverse usage.

Application Usage

Our 24 participants installed over 3400 applications over the course of the study, of which over 2000 were unique. Our participants also purchased almost 750 applications, of which 500 were unique, from the Apple App Store, spending over $1300. We were surprised to see 62% of the 3400 applications installed by our users were uninstalled during the study. We define the *lifespan* of an application as the time between its installation and its uninstallation. We notice that many applications have a short lifespan, (e.g., 20% were uninstalled within a day, and 31% within two weeks,) indicating that users tried but disliked them.

In order to analyze and more importantly present such a huge data set for behaviors and trends, we carefully assigned categories to applications, as shown in Table 1. The App Store already reports 20 genres for applications, but to the inconsistency of App Store genres and the fact that a certain application may be tagged by multiple genres, we had to carefully and manually categorize them. Further assisting us in analyzing the data set is the fact that each user's usage converges to a small set of applications. Figure 1 shows the median percentage of usage by each user's monthly top applications. We can see that a small number of applications constitute a large share of our participant's usage in terms of frequency and duration. Approximately 40% of application usage is from the top application, and more than 90% is attributed to the top 10 applications.

The category with the most applications installed was games, accounting for over 50% of application installs, over 50% of money spent, and approximately 5% of application usage. In contrast, social networking applications, mostly being free, only accounted for less than 2% of money spent, but accounted for 8% of application usage. As expected, there was a wide variation between users in adopting paid and free applications. Our users spent a median of $25 on 14 applications, as shown in Figure 2, and all but two users purchased at least one application. Figure 3 shows the total number of adopted applications during the study, broken in to built-in, free and paid applications. The ratio of paid to free applications stays relatively constant over time, at around 20%. Surprisingly, paid applications had a shorter lifespan overall, as shown in Figure 4. The large number of paid application with one day lifespan shows that users frequently purchase applications which they quickly determine they dislike, losing money in the process. The larger number of paid application uninstalls in the next months can be attributed to the large number of paid games.

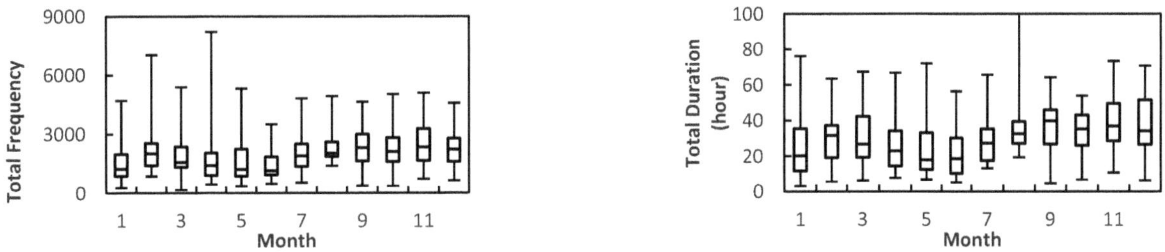

Figure 5: Application usage very diverse throughout the study, in terms of both frequency (left) and duration (right). Boxplots show 2nd / 3rd quartiles. Whiskers: maximum / minimum. Horizontal lines: median

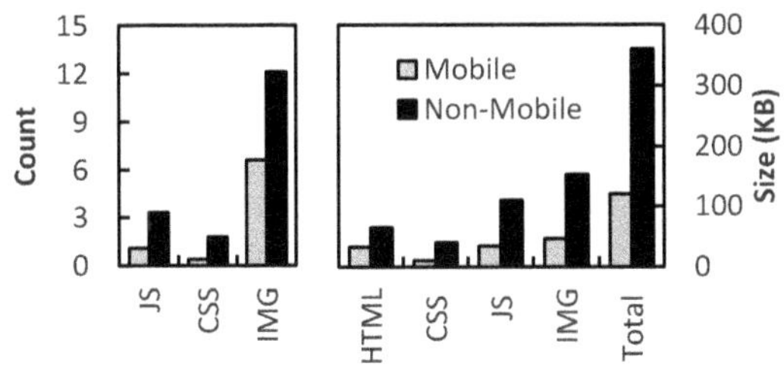

Figure 6: Mobile web pages are less content rich, in terms of the number of resources (right) and their sizes (right)

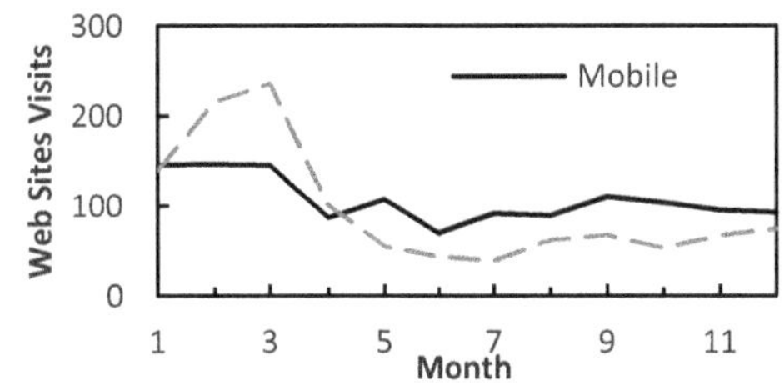

Figure 7: Median visits to mobile and non-mobile website per month

Even though categorizing applications allows us to analyze the application usage of our users, there is still a significant variation between application usage amount and frequency among different users. The differences, even among the second and third quartiles, highlight the fact that the average or median user alone is unable to serve as a benchmark for mobile usage. Instead, it is necessary to consider a wide variation of users and usage. Figure 5 shows a box plot of application usage by different users, for both frequency (left) and duration (right).

Web Usage

Similar to application usage, each participant's web usage converges to a small set of websites. As shown in Figure 1, the top website of a user accounts for 28% of web usage (median); and the user's top 10 websites accounts for 87% of usage. Compared to application usage, we found that users were more inclined to explore new web sites than applications, which is intuitive since visiting a new website requires much less commitment and time than installing an application. The key supporting evidence is the month-to-month similarity of web usage, which is significantly lower than that of application usage, at (0.73 – 0.94), compared to (0.85 - 0.97) for application frequency.

While iPhone applications are developed for a smartphone environment, and are often tailored to the specific features of the smartphone platform, we expect web browsing to be an extension and supplement to users' regular browsing.

Our findings support this hypothesis, but strongly suggest users are disappointed with their web browsing experience. The users' responses to open-ended survey questions on their web browsing experience indicated that they generally were disappointed. Further, contrary to application usage, we observed a significant decrease in participants' web usage throughout the study. We hypothesize that the disappointment was due to poor web browsing usability caused by factors such as connection latencies [15] and size of the device [11] according to the users' survey responses.

In order to further study the decrease in web usage, we analyze the web content browsed by our users. Our participants accessed both mobile and non-mobile websites. We classify web pages based on URL keyword matching; URLs that "m.", "mobile.", "iphone.", etc. are classified as mobile. Some popular websites, such as google.com, use the same URL for both mobile and non-mobile versions. In those cases, we assume the mobile version was used. Mobile web pages are less content rich than their non-mobile counterparts, in terms of styles (CSS), scripts (JS), multimedia content (IMG), and HTML size, as shown in Figure 6. Overall, the phone had to download 120KB for the typical mobile page and 3 times more, or 360KB, for the non-mobile page.

Our results in Figure 7 indicate that the drop in web usage through the study was due to a drop in non-mobile web usage, while mobile web usage, presumably better fit for mobile devices, remained relatively stable. The clear message for web designers is to develop a mobile version of their content. Indeed, this is even more important for users in lower SES brackets and new smartphone users as they transition and learn how to install native applications.

EFFECT OF SOCIOECONOMIC STATUS

Our second interest in this study is to assess the differences between SES groups in overall usage of their iPhones. We had expected differences to be minimal (e.g., how much they spent in App Store purchases) since both groups lived in the same dormitories on campus, and had no significant bias in their gender, major, PC access, or game console ownership. Surprisingly, our findings suggest stronger and broader differences in how they used their devices.

Application Usage

The low SES group consistently used more applications than their high SES counterparts, approximately 40% more,

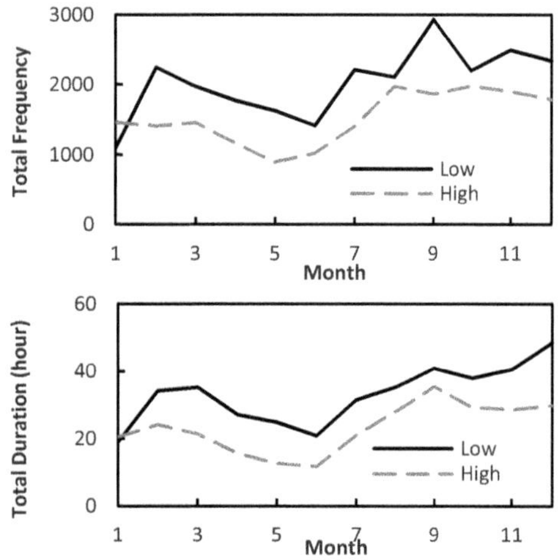

Figure 8: Median application usage was higher for low SES participants, in terms of both frequency (top) and duration (bottom)

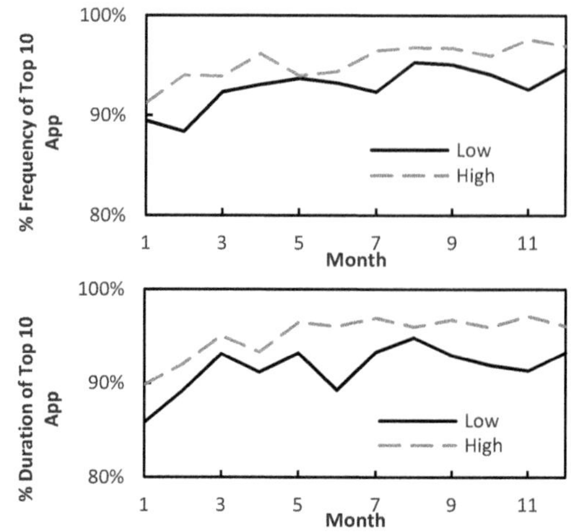

Figure 9: The top 10 applications contributed to a larger fraction of usage for high SES groups, in terms of both frequency (top) and duration (bottom)

both in terms of frequency and duration (Figure 8). For control, we assessed the differences between the low and high SES groups over the entire study period of one year. Visits to native applications and the web were combined for each user within each quarter. A 2 (SES: Low vs. High) x 4 (Time: quarters) analysis of variance (ANOVA) revealed that the low SES users more frequently launched applications compared to their higher SES peers ($F(1, 22) = 9.73$, $p = .01$). A main effect for Time or interaction was not found. A similar main effect for SES was found for duration of usage ($F(1,22) = 8.13$, $p = .02$). The low SES users also consistently used a more diverse set of applications throughout the study, as shown in Figure 9 by the top 10 applications' smaller fraction of usage. The diversity is in part due to the low SES participants' higher variety of games used. Overall, the higher device usage and application variety in the low SES users suggests that the iPhones are used for both hedonic and utilitarian reasons (as defined in [15]) by the low SES group, but primarily for the latter for the high SES group. We hypothesize that this may be due to the low SES users having fewer or less interesting *outside options*, including access to entertainment devices.

Figure 10 is a radar chart showing application usage for each SES group, for the top 10 applications or application categories, normalized to the overall average usage of each application. Four of these applications or application categories revealed how SES groups differed: Facebook, phone, games, and utilities. Logistic regression confirms this statement; we compared the standardized logistic regression coefficients of each application or application category, as suggested in [16], to find the dominant predictors of SES. The results show that the top 3 dominant applications in frequency are utilities, games and phone; and top 3 in duration are Facebook, games and utilities, which comprise the exact same four applications.

Web Usage

By comparing the SES groups, we noticed that Web usage was initially much higher in the low SES group. However, the usage of both groups dropped, and their differences disappeared through the course of the study, as shown in Figure 11. Similar to the prior subsection, we used ANOVA for URL visits. Interestingly, it revealed that there were no main effects for SES or Time. However, a significant interaction showed that the lower SES group accessed the web more at the beginning of the study; over time, however, the differences in web use between SES groups attenuated, $F(3, 66) = 4.60$, $p = .01$. Correspondingly, duration of use followed similar patterns. The low SES users spent more time on the web early on; however, differences between the SES groups diminished as a function of experience.

While iPhone applications are developed for a smartphone environment, and are often tailored to the specific features of the smartphone platform, we can expect web browsing to be an extension and supplement to users' regular browsing. Higher initial usage for the low SES participants shows that smartphone web usage is more of an extension to their PC-based web usage. Indeed, interviews with both SES groups suggest that even though they both had access to personal and university PCs, the lower SES group owned older and lower-quality computers. In contrast with application usage, both SES groups had similar diversity in web usage, as shown in Figure 12. We attribute the similarity to the participants' previously established web browsing habits.

App Store Purchases

We had expected the low SES users to spend less on paid applications, but were surprised to find the opposite. They spent a median of $31 on a median of 17 applications, compared to $15 on 6 applications for their high SES peers (i.e., twice as much money on three times as many applications). Looking deeper into the data, we found that the low SES users were more money conscious and presumably more careful in their purchases compared to their high SES peers. This is shown by their significantly different prices paid per hour usage of paid applications. By dividing the total each user spent in the App Store by the total paid application usage duration, we calculate the cost per hour for paid ap-

Figure 10: Application usage, relative to each application's average usage, for both SES groups in terms of frequency (left) and duration (right)

plications (price / duration). We found that the low SES users had significantly lower prices paid per hour (median: \$1.0 vs. \$2.6), which is substantial even considering the increased overall usage of the low SES users.

LOWER INCOME SMARTPHONE USERS

In the previous section, differences in SES influenced how users accessed their phones. The differences showed, among other things, the increased volume of usage for the lower SES group. In this section, we examine the use of iPhones in another group of community college students in one of the most underserved sections of a major metropolitan area. We limit the use of the data from this very low SES group, as there are other differences, beyond SES, between this group and the other two groups, such as occupation, age, and children.

Application Use

As expected, these ten users used their phone much more than the above users. However, the extent of the differences was surprising. Most comparisons between SES groups are presented as per use per day (PUPD) to account for the differences in study duration. Medians are used because of the large positive skew in the distributions. We found that the ten very low SES users from the community college accessed their devices 50% more frequently than our other users. As shown in Table 2, the very low SES group accessed applications at twice the rate of the high SES group. The differences in time consumed by applications were substantial as well. Interestingly, the differences between the frequency and duration of visits show that the nature of their interactions varied. The highest SES group spent less than a minute on average on each application. In contrast, though the lowest SES group yielded more app launches, the amount of time they spent within these launches was over one minute. This seemed to result from a wider diversity of resources used as shown by the amount of visits consumed by both the top 10% of applications and websites.

What applications drove these differences? The low SES students in the above section accessed the web, Facebook, iPod, and YouTube more than their high SES peers. This lower income group accessed Facebook and YouTube substantially more relative to their other applications (Figure 10). As reported more in the next section, this group did not access the web or utilities applications as much. In other words, for these users the device was much more for social networking and passive entertainment. Interestingly, we again found that the SES level impacted the amount of apps installed and how much money was spent in the App Store. Overall, the very low users installed twice as many applications as the high SES group, which is significant even though most application installs were towards the beginning of the study. The former installed roughly two applications every three days. In contrast, both higher SES groups installed only one application during this same period. The lowest SES group spent more money on applications, contrary to our expectations. Table 2 shows the money spent by the very low SES users compared to the higher SES students. The dollar amounts are similar to the highest SES group, even though they used their phones for half the time.

Table 2: Effect SES on application adoption and usage

SES:	*High*	*Low*	*Very Low*
App visits / day	57	74	96
Duration / day (min)	53	77	122
% Top 10 app visits	94	90	84
All app installs	0.30	0.37	0.64
Paid apps / month	0.5	1.4	2.3
\$ / month spent on apps	\$1.3	\$2.6	\$3.0
% Top 10 web visits	95	91	82

Web Usage

We explored what users did on their web browsers to understand the above differences. Interestingly, even though the very low SES group showed very diverse usage, their adoption of the web was substantially slower than higher SES students. The very low SES users web usage generally increased during the six months, and their sixth month of usage significantly surpassed the main participants by 260%. Instead of applying a "PC mental model", the lowest SES users seemed to use their iPhones as mobile phones first. The fact that it was not until the second full month that the web was accessed regularly across users further attests to this finding. Once adopted, the web was accessed frequently. The very low SES group followed almost the reverse trajectory of the main participants, reported above.

We also notice a difference in the websites the very low SES group visited, compared to the 24 main participants. The URLs visited by each user were manually categorized into ten categories (Table 3). To increase reliability, we recruited three students to categorize the URL visits. The results yielded substantial agreement (*Kappa* = .83) [17]. The disagree-

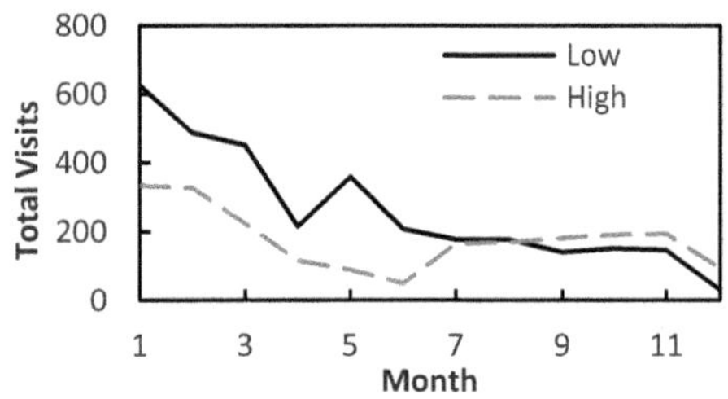

Figure 11: Median web usage was initially higher for low SES users, but became similar to high SES users

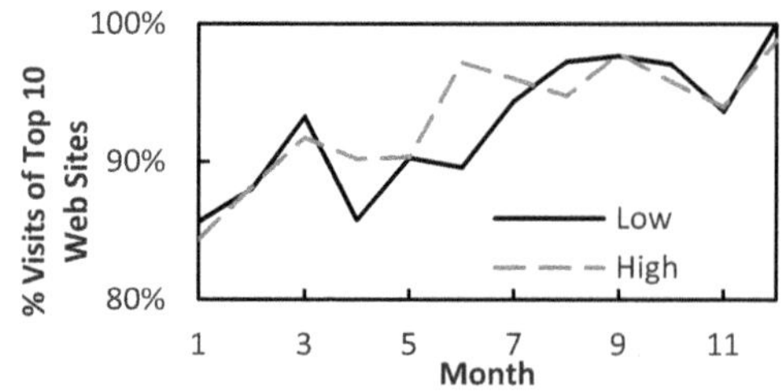

Figure 12: The top 10 websites contributed to a similar fraction of usage for both SES groups

ments were reconciled by the authors. Most importantly, the main participants accessed their institution's website much more than the community college users, 24% vs. 2% of all web visits. Two other categories with large differences were religious and adult websites.

Table 3: Per Use Per Day (PUPD) comparisons by SES

Category	*High & Low SES (%)*	*Very Low SES (%)*
Search	31	40
Institutional	24	2
Social / Blog	11	16
News / Sports	10	9
Commerce	10	8
Religion	4	9
Adult	4	10
Games/Movies	3	4
Health	2	1
Travel	1	1

Usability

One aspect not usually captured in logged data is perceived usability of the device. We surveyed our users to assess the usability of the iPhone after the study was completed, using the system usability scale (SUS) [18]. The SUS is a ten question survey with scores ranging from 0 to 100, and has been validated extensively in a number of studies on a wide range of technologies [19].

The iPhone scored well overall across all users ($M = 74.8$, $SD = 9.26$). A one-way ANOVA comparing the three different groups in our study (high SES, low SES, and very low SES users)was significant showing that one of the group means was significantly different than the grand mean ($F(2,31) = 8.51$, $p = .001$). A Bonferroni post-hoc revealed that the low ($M = 80.76$, $SD = 10.97$) and high ($M = 80.01$, $SD = 11.98$) SES users did not reliably differ. However, the very low SES group ($M = 61.4$, $SD = 14.04$) was significantly lower than both other groups ($p < .01$).

What drove these differences? Open-ended questions revealed several factors. Most notable was that 9 of the 10 users mentioned their battery was either deficient or not functioning. Because these users were new smartphone owners, their perceptions of battery life did not match the actual battery life. 50% of the users complained to the researchers of bad batteries during the study period. The only other usability problems were related to page loading delays. This was mentioned by both groups; however, it was mentioned by 84% of the main participants (high and low SES), vs. 20% of the very low SES participants.

Energy Drain

These scores prompted us to assess the energy drain recorded in both groups. Recall that the lowest SES users not only used the phones more than others, but accessed YouTube and Facebook more frequently, relative to other applications. Such data and video intensive applications have increased power consumptions. This can be quantitatively seen in Figure 13. It shows the boxplot of each users average battery consumption per day, recharges (>1% charge) per day, and low battery warnings (at 20%) per day. Note that short duration syncing can count as a (partial) recharge, and that we normalize battery consumption with the energy capacity of a full battery. We can see that the very low SES group consumes significantly more battery energy per day, and runs into more low battery situations. We note that over time, they appeared to learn the constraints of the battery and used their device more efficiently, reducing complaints.

IMPLICATIONS

We now elaborate on several implications of our finding on the design and evaluation of smartphones and smartphone applications. Clearly, SES differences influenced how iPhones were used. We controlled for experience with the device, type of device, temporal context, and other demographic factors (e.g., all students at the same university, age, gender, etc.) in the first study. Our findings suggest clear usage differences based on SES levels. In the second study, we found a very low SES group that accessed their device even more than the earlier groups and used it for more diverse functions. Of course, these users differ in other ways outside of SES (e.g., community college students, occupation, age, and children). We submit that SES, however, is at least a contributing factor in driving higher usage in the latter group and suggest several design implications to better support users at every SES level.

Application Development

First, our results provide insights into promoting third-party smartphone applications. Our findings regarding the application lifespan (Figure 4) show that users often try out applications for short periods, (e.g., a day). Unfortunately, neither the Apple App Store nor the Android Market offers try-before-you-buy as a universal feature. Instead, users are typically expected to purchase applications based on reviews and word of mouth. However, our findings clearly indicate that users would benefit from a try-before-you-buy feature, such as the one introduced by the recent Windows Phone 7 plat-

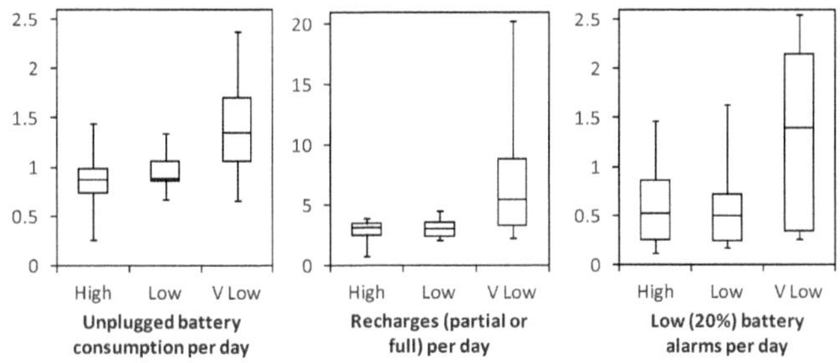

Figure 13: Very low SES users had significantly higher battery demands. Boxplot of users average battery consumption per day, recharges (>1% charge) per day, and low battery warnings (at 20%) per day.

form. This would enable them to waste less money, as well as potentially explore and purchase more applications. Additionally, real estate on iPhones is important and a try-before-you-buy store can facilitate users to quickly "clean house" if an application is not useful or engaging. Some operating systems, such as Windows Phone have already developed this feature. Our traces showing higher month-to-month diversity in web usage (Figure 12) highlight the fact that smartphone users are more comfortable exploring websites and web applications than downloading applications. Indeed, it is natural for users to be more adventurous in accessing different web sites than using applications; visiting a web site takes much less commitment than installing an application. This suggests that an application provider could reach a larger audience by providing a web service similar to its installation-based application when appropriate, so that first-time users can more easily assess them.

Designing Mobile Content

Second, many have envisioned feature-rich smartphones that provide cost-effective access to information technologies and entertainment, especially for users from underserved communities. This was one of the key motivations for our study to focus on SES. Our results support this vision: the low SES users tend to use smartphones more frequently and for more time than their high SES peers. Clearly, the web browser is more central to supporting low SES users adopt smartphone technology. When the low SES users first received their smartphones, they seem to use mental models developed through PC or laptop usage, manifesting as an increased reliance on the browser.

Over time, however, this reliance diminished in favor of native application use which was adopted earlier by their higher SES peers. In other words, low SES users, in addition to apps, require access to the mobile web to do things that could once only be done on PCs. Because many of these pages were not optimized for mobile use, it appeared they relied less on their browsers as a function of experience. Recall that the low SES users accessed more non-mobile sites which required more resources to load. The resulting page loading delays [20] have been noted as a primary cause of web usage declines on PCs [21]. Clearly, this is also a primary problem for the mobile web and this is especially problematic for low SES users. We note that since only a few top websites are most commonly used, we suspect predictive capabilities can be leveraged to preload their most common resources and improve performance.

Smartphone Design

Third, based on the results of our SES comparisons, we identify several key groups of users that phones must cater to. We acknowledge that we observe these from a very narrow demography of smartphone users (college students), and that a broader user population likely has many more and different groups. Nonetheless, the significant differences in our narrow demographic strongly suggest that the one-size-fits-all paradigm fails to serve the best interest of users. Instead, multiple mobile platforms with appropriately selected features are more likely to compliment the needs of different user groups. While some features can be achieved through software and/or OS customizations, others require hardware changes (e.g., a hardware keyboard, game controller buttons, and small form factor).

Our very low SES users had much higher overall usage, placing greater requirements on the device's battery. Their web browsing was also shown to be more of an extension to their PC experience, increasing the value of larger screen sizes for them. Since both battery capacity and screen size come as a tradeoff to compactness, we hypothesize that, different users would significantly benefit from different choices in terms of these tradeoffs (e.g., higher capacity battery and larger displays for low SES users).

DISCUSSION

Field Evaluations

Our study provides important insights into how the field evaluation of smartphone and its service should be designed and carried out. First, our results demonstrate the importance of controlling for demographic factors to understand user differences. Prior work on smartphone usage was not particularly prudent in participant selection and, not surprisingly, failed to reveal any difference [2], or failed to provide conclusive evidence for speculated differences [9].

Second, our results demonstrated that extraordinary care must be taken in drawing conclusions from data collected by giving out devices and studying them in field for a short period of time (e.g., shorter than three months). Our results show that the first months see a significantly different degree of exploration and diversity in usage than in the remaining months (e.g., Figure 3, Figure 7, and Figure 9). Moreover, because usage continues to evolve even one year into the study, conclusions drawn using data collected from a short period of time should be generalized with care. Examples include the seasonal variation in usage, and applications losing appeal, as is often the case with games.

Third, our study demonstrated the value of following the same users for a long period of time. This is shown both by the significant usage changes in the later months of the study, and the SUS findings for the lower income users. However, this method is financially and administratively expensive, and therefore, can only be applied to relatively few participants. As a result, this method is complementary to those that gather data from a large number of users but only sparsely, such as [3].

User Perception vs. Actual Usage

Application usage patterns tell only part of the story. Our interviews provided complementary insights into what applications the users consider as the most important components of their iPhones, and the context in which applications are used. The interviews also gave us insight into why users utilize particular applications. The primary mismatch we found was what users perceived to be driving usability problems. Many of the lowest SES users reported their batteries were bad and requested new ones. This led to poor usability scores. Clearly, however, they used the device very frequently for a wide range of purposes. If we only gathered usage, we might suspect that their high volume reflects high perceived usability. On the contrary, the lowest SES users accessed their devices more than others at the same experience level. However, they also reported that the iPhone was not usable. The clear takeaway is that perceived usability reports are important to supplement logged data for a more holistic understanding.

CONCLUSION

We presented our findings from studying 34 iPhone 3GS users in the field. We highlighted the influence of SES on device usage, and revealed important differences between users that should impact how mobile content and technology is designed. Returning to our statement at the beginning of this report, one primary role of HCI is to understand user differences and better design technologies and content to support a wide range of users.

This study shows the influence of SES diversity in explaining how users access their devices. Indeed, users with the same device accessed it quite differently, though we contribute that they differ systematically. SES was one factor that influenced these differences. On one hand, the iPhone offered the lowest SES users access to technology for information and entertainment that was used very frequently, much more than others at higher SES levels. This suggests the device provided useful capabilities. On the other hand, the prevalent complaints about the battery life led to poor perceived usability. Thus, system designers should not only continue to work on energy efficiency, but in the mean time provide users with more options regarding the tradeoff between battery capacity and device bulk.

In particular, we found the device was poorly suited to serve the very low SES group. This suggests that different usage groups are best served by different phone designs. Our findings obviously don't cover all SES groups or smartphone users, and only focuses on a limited snapshot. Yet, our work raises questions and hypothesis beyond the scope of this paper. We hope that our findings will motivate researchers from multiple disciplines to work together toward answering them and, as a result, to offer even more insights into better mobile content and technologies.

ACKNOWLEDGEMENTS

This work was supported in part by the NSF grants NetSE-1012831, HCC-0803556, and CRI-0751173.

REFERENCES

1. Shneiderman, B., Universal usability. *Communications of the ACM*, 2000.
2. Falaki, H., Mahajan, R., Kandula, S., Lymberopoulos, D., Govindan, R. and Estrin, D., Diversity in Smartphone Usage. in *Proc. ACM MobiSys*, 2010.
3. Huang, J., Xu, Q., Tiwana, B., Mao, Z., Zhang, M. and Bahl, P., Anatomizing Application Performance Differences on Smartphones. in *Proc. ACM MobiSys*, 2010.
4. Falaki, H., Lymberopoulos, D., Mahajan, R., Kandula, S. and Estrin, D., A First Look at Traffic on Smartphones. in *Proc. Internet Measurement Conference (IMC)*, 2010.
5. Bohmer, M., Hecht, B., Schoning, J., Kruger, A. and Bauer, G., Falling asleep with Angry Birds, Facebook and Kindle: a large scale study on mobile application usage. in *Proc. ACM MobileHCI*, 2011.
6. AdMob. AdMob April 2010 Mobile Metrics Report *http://metrics.admob.com/2010/05/april-2010-mobile-metrics-report/* April 2010.
7. Hagen, P., Robertson, T., Kan, M. and Sadler, K., Emerging research methods for understanding mobile technology use. in *Proc. ACM OZCHI*, 2005.
8. Eagle, N. and Pentland, A., Reality mining: sensing complex social systems. *Personal Ubiquitous Computing*, 2006.
9. Rahmati, A. and Zhong, L., Studying Smartphone Usage: Lessons from a Four-Month Field Study. *IEEE Transactions on Mobile Computing*, 2012.
10. Shepard, C., Rahmati, A., Tossell, C., Zhong, L. and Kortum, P., LiveLab: measuring wireless networks and smartphone users in the field. *SIGMETRICS Perform. Eval. Rev.*, 2010.
11. Tossell, C., Kortum, P., Rahmati, A., Shepard, C. and Zhong, L., Characterizing web use on smartphones. in *Proc. SIGCHI Conf. on Human Factors in Computing Systems (CHI)*, 2012.
12. Goel, S., Hofman, J.M. and Sirer, M.I., Who Does What on the Web: Studying Web Browsing Behavior at Scale. in *Proc. Int. Conf. on Weblogs and Social Media*, 2012.
13. Tossell, C., Jardina, J.R., Kortum, P.T., Peres, S.C., Shepard, C.W., Rahmati, A. and Zhong, L., Effects of Socioeconomic diversity on iPod Touch Device Use in Real-World Environments. in *Proc. Human Factors and Ergonomics Society (HFES)*, 2011.
14. rsync. an open source utility that provides fast incremental file transfer *http://samba.anu.edu.au/rsync/*.
15. Lee, I., Kim, J. and Kim, J., Use Contexts for the Mobile Internet: A Longitudinal Study Monitoring Actual Use of Mobile Internet Services. *Int. Journal of Human-Computer Interaction*, 2005.
16. Menard, S., Six approaches to calculating standardized logistic regression coefficients. *The American Statistician*, 2004.
17. Landis, J.R. and Koch, G.G., The Measurement of Observer Agreement for Categorical Data. *Biometrics*, 1977.
18. Brooke, J., SUS-A quick and dirty usability scale. *Usability evaluation in industry*, 1996.
19. Bangor, A., Kortum, P.T. and Miller, J.T., An Empirical Evaluation of the System Usability Scale. *International Journal of Human-Computer Interaction*, 2008.
20. Wang, Z., Lin, X., Zhong, L. and Chishtie, M., Why are Web Browsers Slow on Smartphones? in *Proc. ACM HotMobile*, 2011.
21. Sears, A. and Jacko, J.A. *The human-computer interaction handbook: fundamentals, evolving technologies, and emerging applications*. Lawrence Erlbaum, 2003.

A Note Paper on Note-Taking: Understanding Annotations of Mobile Phone Calls

Juan Pablo Carrascal*
Universitat Pompeu Fabra
jp.carrascal@upf.edu

Rodrigo de Oliveira
Telefonica Research
oliveira@tid.es

Mauro Cherubini*
Google
mauroc@google.com

ABSTRACT

Note-taking has been largely studied in contexts of work meetings. However, often people need to remember information exchanged in informal situations, such as during mobile phone conversations. In this paper we present a study conducted with 59 subjects who had their phone calls semi-automatically transcribed for later annotation. Analysis of the 621 calls and the subjects' annotation behavior revealed that phone recall is indeed a relevant user need. Furthermore, identifying patterns in phone calls such as numbers and names provide better indicators of annotation than variables related to the callers' profile, context of calls, or quality of service. Our findings suggest implications for the design of mobile phone annotation tools.

Author Keywords

phone call; annotation; context; mobile information

ACM Classification Keywords

H.5.2 Information Interfaces and Presentation: User Interfaces (D.2.2, H.1.2, I.3.6)

INTRODUCTION

Lots of information is exchanged every day during mobile phone calls. While a consistent part of this information could be ephemeral as supporting our social needs, another part of it might be important to remember as being functional to our lives. For example, we might receive a phone call to remember to buy some groceries on our way back home, to pick kids from school because our partner is busy, or we might agree to meet a colleague at a specific time in a restaurant.

It can be speculated that most people have a good memory for remembering important details shared during phone calls, while others require taking notes in order to avoid forgetting. To date however, there is little support of applications for this latter case and it is frequently experienced by many the cumbersome situation of having hands tight and needing to take notes while on the phone. Perhaps, this is due to the lack of studies that have tackled this issue.

*Research conducted while working for Telefonica Research.

MobileHCI'12, September 21–24, 2012, San Francisco, CA, USA.

Many studies in the past have focused on how people take notes during work-related meetings [1, 7, 3, 8]. However, how people take notes during daily mobile phone calls it is a different and less studied topic. More specifically, we have little evidence of what is important to remember during mobile conversations and which factors, whether contextual or demographic, play a role in this process.

RELATED WORK

In the recent years, scholars focused extensively on work-related meetings, during which participants also have the need to take annotations. Mobile phone calls can be considered as a two-people meetings but they are different from formal work-related gatherings. Typical mobile phone calls tend to be relatively short in time when compared to work meetings. Also, while in mobile phone calls parties tend to quickly share information with ad-hoc formalisms between greetings and salutations, work meetings tend to be rather structured following agendas and action points.

People normally take notes during meetings and in many other situations of daily life to record important issues and remember things that have been discussed [1]. Geyer and colleagues [3] note how: "personal notes primarily serve as a memory aid for individuals to remember important facts, actions, ideas, and decisions but are hardly useful for persons other than the author". In formal work settings, notes take a structured form and usually include action items. Often also formal minutes of the meetings are recorded to create a shared group memory and to make the meeting more efficient [3].

Despite the rise of Information Capture and Retrieval (ICR) technology for collaborative exchanges, the most common recording techniques used in meetings today are still pens, paper or notebooks, and sometimes laptops [7]. More sophisticated techniques comprise the recording of the audio and sometimes the audio-video trace of the meeting [3]. However, the drawback of these techniques is that they require a timestamped indexing of the content to alleviate retrieval of relevant information.

Notes that people take for themselves during meetings contain "personally important points and in particular details on action items that the note-taker needs to deal with later" [1]. Personal notes usually mention decisions, names, dates and actions [7]. Whittaker and colleagues [7] analyzed the content of people's notes and found that in 30% of the cases personal notes concerned comments that could supply context for action.

Whittaker et al. [6] have studied note taking as the primary way of recording what occurred during a meeting. Subjects in their study reviewed regularly their notes after the meeting (33%). The large majority of people in their sample (70%) reported difficulty in taking notes due to various reasons, like the failure to note facts that turned out to be important later, illegible names, lack of time, and notes that lacked the right level of summarization for *a posteriori* understanding. One of the most significant problem with personal notes is that taking notes reduces the ability of people to participate in the conversation [7].

ICT systems developed in the past aimed at addressing some of these issues. Hindus & Schmandt [4] presented a system that allowed people to mark interesting portions of an ongoing telephone conversation. Degen et al. [2] modified a handheld tape recorder so that users could mark the audio while it was being recorded. Wilcox et al. [8], designed a system called Dynamite, which allowed users to attach keywords to recorded notes so to create an index of the content. Whittaker et al. [5] looked as well at how to improve voicemail by allowing users to visually inspect its content and enabling annotations.

All these findings come from studies of work meetings while little work has focused on understanding the role of annotations as support of daily mobile phone conversations. With this work we aim at shedding some light in this area by highlighting *annotation habits*, an initial overview of *how* people make these annotations, and some evidences of *problematic aspects* related to annotations made during mobile calls.

METHODOLOGY

We designed a quantitative experiment to collect a large sample of mobile phone calls, their annotations –if any–, and contextual parameters at the time of the calls.

Participants

A total of 59 subjects (41 male) participated actively in the user study, *i.e.* answered the pre-study questionnaire and made at least one phone call during the study. Their mean age was 31.05 years ($s = 7.4$), they were all living in Spain and reported being fluent in speaking Spanish –a requirement of the study. The sample was well geographically distributed (37 unique cities) and included only subjects that had at least the basic education (primary school: 3.4%), followed by 3.4% who finished secondary school, 78% that concluded technical school or obtained a bachelor degree, and 15.2% who had either a masters or a doctorate degree. The reported annual income suggests that all social classes were represented in the sample (27%, 19%, 25%, 20%, and 9% earned up to €10K, €20K, €30K, €40K, and €40K+ a year respectively).

Procedure

The study spanned over 50 days. It was conducted amongst participants who voluntarily registered after following advertisements in popular Web portals in Spain. We had to limit participation to people who owned and used an iPhone or Android mobile, since we only had VoIP applications available for these platforms. We invited participants via email, asking them to fill a registration questionnaire which, besides general demographics, asked relevant questions such as calling habits and general note-taking habits during phone calls.

We offered participants free calls to mobile or fixed phone lines inside the Spanish territory. To be able to make free calls, they had to install a VoIP application on their mobile phones and configure it to connect through our servers. Participants were allowed to make calls either using the VoIP application–in which case they would contribute it to our study–or the native phone application so as to prevent us from having access to the conversation. We explicitly explained them how to switch between these two options. Whenever participants used our VoIP application, a short message was played to both the caller and the callee informing them that the call was going to be recorded and transcribed. Transcriptions were first generated automatically and later manually inspected and corrected by an expert before being presented to participants.

We developed a web application which allowed participants to interact with call data. It displayed a list of phone calls, and for every call, its transcription, date, duration, status and callee number, as well as a related questionnaire. Participants were asked to:

1. Enter the web application and confirm that they wanted to contribute the calls. Participants were allowed to delete a call within a 24 hour period if they considered it to have sensible content. They could review call data to assist the decision.
2. To select and highlight pieces of text that they considered important, or worth remembering, from the transcriptions. In case there was no important text, to explicitly declare so.
3. To answer a questionnaire related to each phone call.

Measures

The questionnaire associated to each phone call included several questions: 1) Relationship with callee; 2) Who was with the caller at the time of the call; 3) Location of the caller at the time of the call; 4) Objective of the call; 5) Level of importance of the call; 6) Reasons for highlighting text (if applicable); 7) Whether the caller could take written notes a the time of the call; 8) How important was to take notes during the call; and 9) General questions about sound and transcription quality. Given that participants reported objectives of calls in free text, these were manually classified by two coders as either: "discuss topic", "appointment", "give/receive information", "ask favor", or "social". Inter-rater reliability was highly acceptable ($K = .81, p < .001$).

RESULTS AND DISCUSSION

Patterns of phone calls and annotation habits in the study were consistent to self-reported data. During the 50 days of the study deployment, participants made 621 calls with a total duration time of 87,035 seconds ($\bar{x} = 140.15$; $s = 191.991$). Quality of the calls was considered acceptable ($q2 = 3$: acceptable, $q1 = 3$: acceptable, $q3 = 4$: good). Transcriptions of the calls and annotations yielded a total of 811,453 characters ($\bar{x} = 1,306.69$; $s = 1889.6$) and 44,744 characters ($\bar{x} = 72.05$; $s = 219.59$) respectively. The average number of calls per participant was 10.53 ($s = 8.69, min = 1, max = 32$), and they annotated an average of 4.61 of their calls ($s = 5.36, min = 0, max = 29$). Hence, about 44% of all phone calls were annotated, which is consistent with the participants' self-reported annotation habits captured by the pre-study questionnaire (34% and 46% indicated taking notes frequently using mobile phones and paper/pencil respectively). Likewise, participants called family members more often than friends, and called friends more often than work colleagues, which reveals the same order reported in the pre-study questionnaire. These findings support consistency between the participants' behavior in the study and how they perceive their behavior in real life.

Phone Recall Needs

Recalling information from calls is a general need and not necessarily a simple task. While 15% of the participants reported that this need rarely occurs, almost half of the sample agreed it occurs sometimes (48%), and over one third indicated it happens frequently (37%). No one reported the absence of this need. When evaluating the easiness to recall information obtained in phone calls, 37% said it is either easy or very easy, 36% reported it is neither easy nor difficult, and the remaining 27% agreed the recall task is at least difficult. These results suggest the importance of supporting recall of phone conversations.

Mobile phone is the primary tool to support recall. Several tools can be used to annotate phone calls. According to our sample, mobile phones and regular paper and pencil are the most important ones–46% and 34% respectively use them frequently for this task. Note that our sample is composed only by smartphone users, hence the popularity of mobile phones as the primary annotation source. Participants reported taking *a posteriori* notes of phone conversations using text-based notepads and audio-based memo applications (25% record audio notes for phone calls at least once a week).

Dynamics of Phone Annotation

If the call is important, expect important notes to be taken. As one might expect, the participants' evaluation of the importance of the calls strongly correlates to the importance of the corresponding annotations ($\rho = .50, p < .001$). This means that the higher one thinks is the importance of a call, the more likely important annotations will be made for it.

If the call is important, callers tend to get prepared for taking notes. While 65% of all calls happened when users had one hand holding the phone and the other hand free (usual setting when attending a phone call), this figure increased to 91% when call annotations were considered important. From this result, we raised the hypothesis that callers would make sure to have their hands free when making important calls because of the higher probability of taking notes during them. Indeed a significant association ($\phi = .11, p = .007$) was found between importance of the call (*i.e.* whether the call had at least some importance) and ability to take notes (*i.e.* whether the participant had at least one hand free to take notes). As there is no off-the-shelf solution for creating hands-free notes during a phone call, apparently people tend to change their behavior right before the call to ensure that at least one of their hands will be free for taking notes.

Transcribing the entire conversation is indeed not efficient. Only 5.5% of the characters in the transcribed calls were highlighted in the participants' annotations. This result is in agreement with previous work in the sense that providing full transcripts of conversations most likely overload users thus switching their recall problem for information retrieval [7].

Annotations have patterns and these are better indicators of note-taking than most of the variables observed in the study, i.e. *contextual, quality of service (QoS) and caller profile.* In the preliminary questionnaire, participants were asked about the kinds of information they find themselves trying to remember after a phone call. About 79% mentioned pieces of information that necessarily include numbers (*e.g.*, phone numbers, dates, prices, addresses) and 34% mentioned information related to names (*e.g.*, addresses, contacts). Therefore, we implemented three parsers to count numbers, names, and interrogative adverbs (*i.e.* why, where, how, when) in the phone call transcriptions respectively. According to Table 1, these pattern variables have significant medium correlations with the length of notes ($\rho = .33, \rho = .31, \rho = .30$ respectively), and these are higher than most correlations with other variables observed in this study–call length is the only exception ($\rho = .41$). In other words, the more numbers, names, and interrogative adverbs are mentioned in a call, the higher the probability to take notes and also the longer the annotations might be.

From the data shown in Table 1, we can highlight at least three interesting findings. First, none of the callers' demographic variables (*i.e.* gender, age, education and income) revealed significant correlations with the annotation variables.

The second interesting result is the fact that QoS variables are positively correlated to taking phone notes. Moreover, quality of call is positively correlated to both the note taking activity ($\rho = .18$) and duration of calls ($\rho = .20$). One possible explanation is that the better the quality of calls, the more time users engaged in a phone conversation, thus increasing the probability of taking notes.

And finally, contextual variables played distinct roles on the note-taking activity. Although the call place and callee information did not reveal any significant relationship with phone annotation, information about the caller's companion, the call objective, and the call length did. Phone calls next to work colleagues were positively correlated with taking notes ($\rho = .11$), probably due to the nature of the call objective (information: $\rho = .11$; appointment: $\rho = .08$). On the other hand, phone calls with no companion were inversely related to generation of notes ($\rho = -.09$). Stronger interaction effects were revealed by call length ($\rho = .35$) and social calls, i.e. calls reported by participants as *"just to chat"* or *"say hello"* ($\rho = -.26$). The former result could indicate that the lengthier the call, the higher chances of taking notes, whereas the latter result is an indication that social calls tend to have significantly fewer annotations.

In summary, the results of this study suggest that taking notes

Table 1. **Correlations/Associations between annotation-related variables (Note Taken: Yes/No; Note Length in number of characters) and other variables related to the call task.**

Variable	Source	Coefficient*	
		Note Taken	Note Length
Total numbers/call	Pattern	**.29**	**.33**
Total names/call	Pattern	**.28**	**.31**
Total adverbs/call	Pattern	**.25**	**.30**
Gender	Profile	.07	.06
Age	Profile	-.01	-.05
Education	Profile	-.02	-.01
Income	Profile	.02	.02
Recall frequency	Profile	**-.10**	-.07
Recall easiness	Profile	-.04	**-.12**
Note mobile frequency	Profile	-.02	.00
Note paper frequency	Profile	**-.11**	**-.18**
Call quality	QoS	**.18**	**.20**
Transcription quality	QoS	**.12**	**.08**
Call length (chars)	Contextual	**.35**	**.41**
Call length (seconds)	Contextual	**.29**	**.35**
Call who: mate	Contextual	.04	.04
Call who: family	Contextual	-.05	-.06
Call who: friend	Contextual	.04	.06
Call who: work	Contextual	-.03	-.04
Call with: alone	Contextual	**-.09**	**-.09**
Call with: mate	Contextual	.06	.07
Call with: family	Contextual	.05	.03
Call with: friend	Contextual	-.05	-.04
Call with: work	Contextual	**.11**	**.10**
Call from: home	Contextual	.04	.03
Call from: work	Contextual	.05	.05
Call from: commute	Contextual	-.07	-.05
Call why: discuss topic	Contextual	.04	**.08**
Call why: appointment	Contextual	**.08**	.06
Call why: info	Contextual	**.11**	.06
Call why: ask favor	Contextual	**.08**	**.10**
Call why: social	Contextual	**-.26**	**-.23**

* Correlations between ordinal and non-normal interval variables were assessed using Spearman's Rho (ρ). Associations between dichotomous variables were assessed using the χ^2 derived Phi coefficient (ϕ). Coefficients in bold are significant at $p < .05$.

during mobile phone calls is a common need, and that such need is not well satisfied by current off-the-shelf solutions. Participants of our study chose to be prepared whenever they felt that a call was important, leaving at least one hand free for taking notes. The importance of the notes taken was, unsurprisingly, correlated with the stated importance of the call. Advanced smartphones users used their devices more frequently than pen and paper for taking notes. However, the latter method was still widely used.

Another interesting finding was that participants annotated mostly information containing numbers and names, such as phone numbers, addresses, dates, or contacts. These patterns can be easily identified signaling the importance to annotate calls. Further semantical analysis might reveal more complex patterns and potentially refine our conclusions.

IMPLICATIONS FOR DESIGN

Our study provide evidence that users tend to have at least one of their hands free during calls they consider to be important. While being on the go, this probably implies limiting user's mobility. In order to overcome this problem, we emphasize the need to assist users in creating automatic annotations during mobile phone calls. We can speculate that for the callee this need might be even greater given that s/he cannot anticipate important incoming calls. Mobile phones shall be the most suitable devices to enable such solution as they were reported to be the primary phone annotation tools for the participants of our study–all smartphone users. The lack of viable solutions for automatic hands-free annotation of phone calls implies that currently the process must be accomplished offline, after the call has finished, thus increasing the possibility for important pieces of information to get lost.

An important feature for a practical solution is to avoid full call transcription and rather focus on important pieces of information towards preventing the user's information overload. According to our study, these pieces of information usually appear in patterns, such as phone numbers, dates, addresses, prices, shop/to-do lists, contact names, activities, among others. The application should be able to recognize these patterns and annotate them for later recall.

Finally, the mobile application should not only look for patterns in the call, but also leverage its embedded sensors to gather relevant contextual information for the note-taking activity, such as with whom the caller is (alone *vs.* with work colleagues) and what is the objective of the call (social *vs.* non-social). By identifying call context, call QoS–via analysis of the microphone signal, and patterns in the calls, the need to annotate a phone call might be detected and potential annotations inferred.

Acknowledgments. We thank Diego Urdiales, Isabel Ordas, Miguel Angel Santiago, Sergio Romero and all participants of the study. Telefonica Research participates in the Torres Quevedo subprogram (MICINN), cofinanced by the European Social Fund, for researchers recruitment.

REFERENCES

1. Bothin, A., and Clough, P. Participants ' personal note-taking in meetings and its value for automatic meeting summarisation. *Information Technology and Management* (2011), 1–19.
2. Degen, L., Mander, R., and Salomon, G. Working with audio: integrating personal tape recorders and desktop computers. In *Proceedings of the SIGCHI conference on Human factors in computing systems*, CHI '92, ACM (New York, NY, USA, 1992), 413–418.
3. Geyer, W., Richter, H., and Abowd, G. D. Towards a smarter meeting record–capture and access of meetings revisited. *Multimedia Tools Appl. 27* (December 2005), 393–410.
4. Hindus, D., and Schmandt, C. Ubiquitous audio: capturing spontaneous collaboration. In *Proceedings of the 1992 ACM conference on Computer-supported cooperative work*, CSCW '92, ACM (New York, NY, USA, 1992), 210–217.
5. Whittaker, S., Davis, R., Hirschberg, J., and Muller, U. Jotmail: a voicemail interface that enables you to see what was said. In *Proceedings of the SIGCHI conference on Human factors in computing systems*, CHI '00, ACM (New York, NY, USA, 2000), 89–96.
6. Whittaker, S., Hyland, P., and Wiley, M. Filochat: handwritten notes provide access to recorded conversations. In *Proceedings of the SIGCHI conference on Human factors in computing systems: celebrating interdependence*, CHI '94, ACM (New York, NY, USA, 1994), 271–277.
7. Whittaker, S., Tucker, S., Swampillai, K., and Laban, R. Design and evaluation of systems to support interaction capture and retrieval. *Personal Ubiquitous Comput. 12* (January 2008), 197–221.
8. Wilcox, L. D., Schilit, B. N., and Sawhney, N. Dynomite: a dynamically organized ink and audio notebook. In *Proceedings of the SIGCHI conference on Human factors in computing systems*, CHI '97, ACM (New York, NY, USA, 1997), 186–193.

Patterns of Usage and Context in Interaction with Communication Support Applications in Mobile Devices

Vassilios Stefanis
University of Patras / RACTI
Rion, Patras, Greece
stefanis@ceid.upatras.gr

Athanasios Plessas
University of Patras / RACTI
Rion, Patras, Greece
plessas@ceid.upatras.gr

Andreas Komninos
Glasgow Caledonian University
Glasgow UK
ako2@gcu.ac.uk

John Garofalakis
University of Patras / RACTI
Rion, Patras, Greece
garofala@ceid.upatras.gr

ABSTRACT

Contact lists are one of the most frequently used applications on mobile devices. Users are reluctant to delete or remove contacts from their repositories and as modern smartphones provide an unlimited contact list storage space, these become increasingly large, sometimes measuring several hundred entries. In this paper we present our findings from two experiments with user-subjective and quantitative data concerning the use of mobile contact lists. We examine the role that frequency and recency of usage plays in the determination of a contact's importance, with a view to aid the speed and efficacy of the information seeking and retrieval process during the use of the contact list application.

Author Keywords

Mobile PIM, Contact Lists, Context Awareness

ACM Classification Keywords

H.5.2 [Information Interfaces and Presentation]: User Interfaces

General Terms

Human Factors, Design, Theory

INTRODUCTION

Undeniably, mobile devices have become part of daily life, replacing in many ways traditional personal information management (PIM) tools such as the calendar and address book. Given that the primary raison d'être of mobile devices, in their most popular manifestation (mobile phones), is to enable communication, clearly the importance of the contact list application and its usability in such devices is paramount. A typical communication task (making a call, or sending an email) involves finding the name and number of the desired contact as a fundamental part of completing the process. One advantage of "electronic" contact lists is that they afford their users a very large storage space in which to store contact details, with most devices offering the ability to store several hundred or even thousand contacts in their internal memory. Given the ample space for contacts, users can quickly build large contact repositories, which include many contacts that are only needed temporarily or are very infrequently used, as well as other unrelated items such as PINs, passwords and other information scraps. Mobile devices pose notoriously difficult problems in information access and retrieval, due to the unique characteristics of that platform, such as small screens, awkward keyboards and input methods, simultaneous engagement in other tasks (e.g. walking), lack of a stable resting place as they are held in the hand and so forth. The existence of large contact repositories aggravates the problem of information access, in the sense that finding the desired contact to call or text usually requires fairly lengthy interaction and often results in frustration due to errors (e.g. calling the wrong person and starting all over again). Based on anecdotal stories and discussions with users, we were prompted to ask the question of whether the Pareto Principle (otherwise known as the 80/20 rule) actually applied to the use of contact list applications on mobile devices. If this was proven to be true, then this would have obvious implications for the design of mobile phone contact applications. In effect, it would mean that prioritization of contacts in the way a contact list is presented, according to the frequency of their use, would be highly desirable and in the spirit of well-accepted mobile design guidelines (e.g. Palm's Path to Enlightenment[1]). As a natural extension to this question, one has to ask whether frequency of use should be the only criterion for prioritization. In the following sections, we describe our findings from two investigations that we performed (one based on mobile users perceptions and another based on real usage data extracted from mobile phones) in examining the validity of the Pareto Principle in mobile contact list usage and furthermore our design for

[1] Zen of Palm: http://www.accessdevnet.com/docs/zenofpalm.pdf (accessed 3/3/2012)

context aware criteria for the prioritization of contacts in a list.

BACKGROUND

Although the contact list application is arguably the most frequently used function of a mobile phone, surprisingly little research has been published on evaluating its usability. In 1999, Bocker and Suwita [4] examined the usability of a C10 phone and found that although almost all users had no issues finding and calling a given contact from the phone book (94% success), this rate dropped significantly to 73% when asked to find and call the same contact from a call list. Clockar et al. also investigated the usability of several mobile phone models and found that while users typically had almost no problem calling a contact from the phonebook, there were more problems when asked to check their missed call list [6]. These findings were supported by our initial conversations with users, in which they indicated that in order to avoid searching for a contact to call or text, they would resort to looking in the call list first, particularly if it was someone they remembered having talked to recently. This is particularly true also for semi-literate users [3]. However,,this might not always be the best strategy to adopt in terms of effectiveness [4, 6].

Gaur [7] recommends two interesting options for enhancing the usability of a contact list. First, marking up a contact with a Bluetooth signature of a person (to later aid the exchange of data, or notify of their vicinity) and possibly something more interesting, the use of geo-tagging to help people remember where they met a particular contact. Rhee et al. [11] recommend an altogether different approach, where a "life diary" that monitors all of a user's activities becomes a communication gateway. The user is able to respond in any manner to any event, e.g. send an email prompted after a phone call, return a call from SMS etc. This negates the need to search for contacts in a hierarchical process to achieve a task and is much closer to our anecdotal stories that seemed to support the 80/20 rule. The authors however do not present any evaluation of their design.

Improving the contact list using context awareness was examined in a key paper by Oulasvirta et al. [10]. Perhaps the most significant finding therein was the fact that ultimately, and in line with Brown et al. [5], in situations where social factors are likely to be key to the adoption of an application, context awareness should be used to present information to the user while leaving ultimate control over the course of action to them, rather than automating it fully. Oulasvirta also makes a recommendation on the adoption of *unremarkable computing* as a design principle that makes computing transparent and supportive of the natural flow of activity, something that he attributes to Tolmie et al.[12], but possibly something that emerges from the initial theories of Weiser on the nature of ubiquitous computing. Further work by Ankolekar et al [1] discusses how a combination of contextual cues might offer usability advantages but leaves the categorisation of contacts to users and does not present any tangible research into one of the most often used applications of mobile devices

Perhaps the most relevant item of work in this topic area is that from Jung et al. [9] who investigated the improvement of a mobile contact list using as primary design drivers the efficiency of accessing contacts and the need to differentiate important contacts. They found that users responded very positively to being able to quickly access the *top 10* contacts in terms of communication frequency, those whose *birthday* was soon approaching and additionally those contacts who were *recently added* as three special category views that helped differentiate potentially important contacts from the rest of the repository. The authors did not report any experiments in mixing the two categories in a single view and while their findings seem to align with our hypothesis for the need for differentiation, top 10 seems a rather convenient and ad-hoc number to use. Their implementation does not allow ultimate control to users, with regard to who goes into a top N list, fully automating this process for the users.

Given the small body of literature on mobile contact applications, perhaps the Personal Information Management community has findings to offer, which might be applicable to the design of mobile PIM tools. From the body of literature available, the work of Whittaker et al.[13] stands out as fundamentally important for the purposes of this paper. They asked 17 users to rate the importance of their email contacts and found that 19% of these were rated as "important" (cf. the Pareto Principle). For these contacts, the hypotheses that users would interact with them more frequently and that they would send and receive communication more frequently than from non-important contacts were verified to be true in field and lab experiments. Equally important was the finding that recent communication was very much more likely to have come from Important contacts. In the field of PIM, several authors subscribe to the school of thought that believes that as personal repositories get larger, the solution to personal information retrieval is better and more powerful search engines. It is argued that a user should not have to make a decision on whether to keep or discard information, since the search engine will ensure that information will always be found when searched for. Bergman et al. [2] wondered whether there was a middle ground in asking the question of whether to keep or discard information and considered the option of a "*Gray Area*" for folders, a visual widget at the bottom of a folder where information, which was not as important, could be placed. The researchers mention that in a recent study under review, out of 70 subjects questioned, 59 preferred one of three "demoting" designs they saw over the support offered in current operating systems.

The practice of actively promoting certain elements in a PIM data set has been observed in the past. Users find clever ways to manipulate the system in order to differentiate between important and non-important items in a collection, such as placing the letter 'a' in the beginning of a file name, so it would be placed on top of a folder's contents list and thus be quickly accessible [8]. Others use numbers to impose different levels of hierarchy (e.g. 1_My Pictures, 2_My Documents) on a filesystem that has no formal support for these. This practice was also recently observed in mobile contact lists. A mobile operator in the UK (O2 – Telefonica) preloads mobile devices with useful numbers such as customer services or balance enquiries in the contact lists. The entries for these preloaded numbers are preceded by a '>' character (e.g. >O2 Customer Service), obviously in an attempt to keep them separate from regular contacts. This practice was also encountered with the contact list of one of our subjects, who preceded his most important contacts with the character '1' (e.g. "1mummy"), to keep them at the top of his list. This was also seen in [9]. The technology behind contact list UIs in today's devices is still based on just alphabetic lists. The Android OS provides a feature of presenting a contact list by use frequency, though again this is too simplistic a view of importance, considering just one type of context. In [14] we showed that a context-adaptive contact list can yield a significant usability advantage for users and presented one such design for a UI informed by context. For the purposes of that work, we emulated the awareness of context for the purposes of our evaluation, however, in [15] we proposed a context-oriented framework which could be used to drive a UI such as the one we discussed in [14]. We believe that one important factor in these schemes which must be retained, if they are to be formally facilitated in a UI, is the fact that users maintain ultimate control over what is promoted and what isn't.

HYPOTHESIZED CRITERIA FOR CONTEXT-ORIENTED MOBILE CONTACT LISTS

Based on the theoretical background reviewed in the previous sections and adhoc discussions with participants in our previous study [15], we hypothesized that *the criteria for contact importance cannot be static*; after all, users' lives and priorities change continuously during the day and a truly context-aware device should continuously adapt to these changing circumstances. This gave us further insight into the question of what are the criteria for determining the importance of a mobile contact. In discussing the importance of contacts with participants, we suggest that important contextual cues that relate to mobile contacts might be the following:

H1: Frequency and recency of use: In [13], it is shown that frequency of use and recency of communication seem to be a fairly reliable criterion to signify the importance of email contacts. In [9] this observation seems to be supported although the authors seem to base this only on subjective evaluations (the users stated they liked that feature but no formal investigation was carried out to see if the top 10 presented contacts actually were the most important ones for each user). Could it then be proven true that this criterion applies to mobile as well as email contacts?

H2: Personal preference: In the field of IR, a great amount of effort has been put into the problem of obtaining implicit relevance feedback from users. However, even designers of the best of systems admit that the ultimate form of feedback is that which comes directly and explicitly from the user themselves. Would the users feel comfortable with a fully automated system making promotion choices for them, or does some form of control (even if it doesn't result in optimal performance) afford the contact list application greater satisfaction in its use?

Though the rest of this paper focuses on the analysis of H1 and H2, it is natural to assume that additional contextual information might also play a role in determining contact importance. We believe that such criteria could be spatial context (where is the user currently in terms of actual coordinates or abstracted locations, e.g. "London" or "Work"), temporal context (the weekday, time of day and perceived meaning, e.g. "2pm on a Sunday") and task or current activity context (what is the user engaged in just now, e.g. "in a meeting with John Doe" or "commuting from work"). The "implications for design" and "future work" sections of this paper discuss how interface design could be informed by these additional criteria, though investigation of these is left in the sphere of future work.

Two final questions remain to be asked in the investigation of this topic. Firstly, what is the relationship between the aforementioned hypothesized context criteria (Q1)? Is one more important over the other, or does their weight also vary depending on a fourth (or more) types of context? The second question that remains unanswered is, assuming that determining contact importance has been made possible, how does this information get relayed to the user through the contact list UI (Q2)? We are not fully convinced that the design proposals in [9] (presenting multiple group views that the user navigates through) is optimal. Under the principle of *unremarkable computing*, we hypothesize that it is not necessary for the user to know why a particular contact has been promoted, neither that they should have to explicitly change the interface's display modes with every search for a contact. A single but intelligently adaptive user interface should suffice. The following sections discuss our findings concerning the proposed criteria H1 and H2 and present some preliminary UI mockups that could emerge.

USER-SUBJECTIVE ESTIMATION OF MOBILE CONTACTS USAGE

We began our investigation by conducting a survey of the usage of contacts in mobile contact lists. Our aim was to find out the frequency of use of contacts and whether a distinct pattern would emerge that would allow us to judge the importance of contacts. We wrote a mobile application that uses the J2ME JSR-75 PIM API to export a copy of the contact lists of 28 subjects (26 male, 2 female) aged between 18 and 31 years to a text file. We began our analysis by examining the size of the contact lists of our participants. In total, the participants' contact lists contained 3004 entries. We found that on average, each contact list contained 107 entries (mean. =107.57, stdev. =81.46, min. =16, max =372), which shows that searching and filtering contacts has to be made on a considerable corpus. This fact explains why users mentioned frequently resorting to their call lists and using special characters to "promote" contacts.

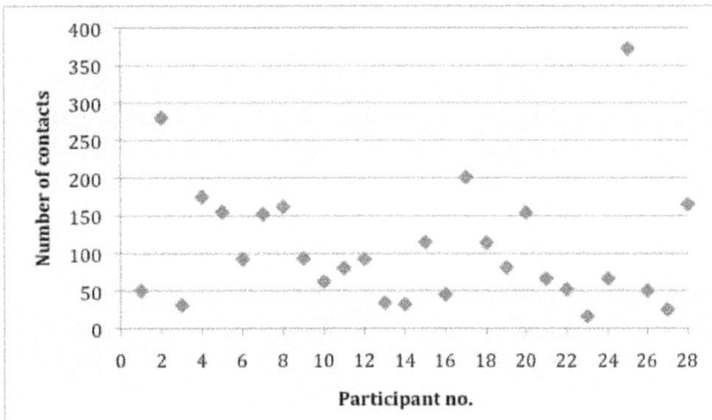

Figure 1. Distribution of contacts amongst participants

We formatted the contact lists into spreadsheets and sent these back to the participants over email, asking them to tell us for every contact therein, how long had it been since they last used that particular contact. To facilitate their input, the spreadsheet columns could only be populated with pre-determined answers. We additionally asked the participants to subjectively evaluate the importance of each of their contacts and indicate those who they perceived as very important (not only in terms of frequency of use, but also importance due to emotional, work or other reasons). Unfortunately, not all participants returned their annotated contact lists, and as such we received 14 (13 male, 1 female) responses to our request for data. Table 1 shows the answers the 14 subjects provided and a breakdown of the statistics for each answer.

Cumulative percentages from Table 1 show that 31% of the contacts were used in the last month and 40% in the last two. The cumulative percentage for the periods of 1-2, 2-3 and 3-6 months, shows that only 23% of contacts were used between the last 1-6 months. Finally, it is striking to see that 46% of the contacts haven't been used for at least 6 months or were never used. The design implications from these findings are obvious – it appears that just under half of the contacts objectively don't seem to be of much use to the subjects in our experiment. If we remove these seemingly unused contacts from consideration, we are left with the data as shown in Table 2.

Confirming our suspicion mentioned in the introduction, the *Pareto Principle* seems to arise again in the adjusted data, with ~19% of the contacts in our sample being used at least once on a weekly basis, aligning with Whittaker et al.'s observation of a relationship between frequency and importance. As mentioned previously, we asked our participants to indicate how many contacts they thought of as important, regardless of frequency of use. Of the 14 respondents, 9 (8 male, 1 female) provided this information, which resulted in the interesting findings in Table 3, which seem to confirm that frequency of use is a strong indicator of importance, although we cannot ignore the fact that entries exist across all frequency categories. This leads to the conclusion that in designing a UI that allows quick access to important contacts, we should allow users to define who these might be.

I use this contact every week	131	10.03%
I used this contact within the last month	280	21.44%
I used this contact between 1-2 months ago	118	9.04%
I used this contact between 2-3 months ago	82	6.28%
I used this contact between 3-6 months ago	90	6.89%
I haven't used this contact for 6 months or more	341	26.11%
I never used this contact	264	20.21%
Total	*1306*	*100.00%*

Table 1. Contact List Usage Pattern

I use this contact every week	131	18.69%
I used this contact within the last month	280	39.94%
I used this contact between 1-2 months ago	118	16.83%
I used this contact between 2-3 months ago	82	11.70%
I used this contact between 3-6 months ago	90	12.84%
Total	*701*	*100.00%*

Table 2. Adjusted Contact List Usage Pattern

Frequency of Use of contacts :	% of Important Contacts
Every week	42.86%
Within the last month	36.51%
Between 1-2 months ago	8.73%
Between 2-3 months ago	1.59%
Between 3-6 months ago	1.59%
Not used for 6 months or more	0.79%
Never used	2.38%

Table 3. Subjective Importance & its relation to use frequency

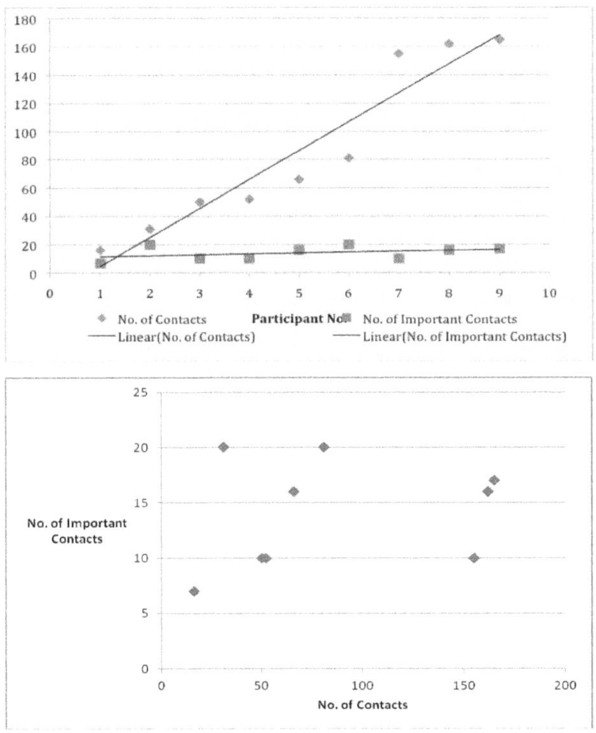

Figure 2. Size of contact list v. number of important contacts

Finally we examined the relationship between the size of a contact list and the number of important contacts contained therein. We found that the number of important contacts remained relatively steady despite the increase in size of the contact lists (Fig. 2) and that no statistically significant correlation can be found between the number of contacts and number of important contacts ($r(9)=0.21$, $p>0.58$) According to these findings, contact list UI should, as such, be able to provide quick access to approximately 20 important contacts.

MOBILE CONTACTS USAGE BASED ON REAL DATA

The second part of our research included an analysis of real data extracted from mobile phones. For this purpose we wrote an Android application that extracts the contact list (and "starred" status), the call log, the SMS log and the existing contact groups from the mobile device in a text file. The application was delivered to 42 subjects with Android smartphones, however only 34 datasets were considered as valid, since some were incomplete (e.g. extremely small number of records in call log or SMS log etc.). Concerning the 34 subjects that we take into account in our analysis, 31 of them were male and 3 female, while their age ranges were from 19 to 39 years old and they were from varied backgrounds, though most were Computer Science students. In this section we present findings from the statistical analysis of the overall dataset. Once again, we began our analysis by examining the size of the contact lists of our participants. In total, the participants' contact lists contained 5384 entries. We found that on average, each contact list contained 158 entries (mean. =158.35, stdev. =84.74, min. =33, max =344), results that are quite similar to those from our first experiment. An interesting point is that 15 of the participants had used a feature of the Android OS that allows users to indicate their personal preferences (marking a contact as starred) and promotes the preferred contacts at the top of the contact list's favorite tab.

The extracted logs covered a different time period in days for each mobile phone (mean=.48.88, stdev=41.66, min.=8, max=187). We calculated the sparsity of communication for each mobile user, by dividing the number of outgoing communications (calls and SMS) by the number of days that the call log covered, as an indicator of the daily phone usage. In Figure 3, the relationship between sparsity, outgoing communication and contact list size is shown. It is apparent that the way people use their mobile phones to communicate does not depend on the size of their contact lists. This is in line with our previous subjective findings, if one is to accept a relationship between the frequency of use and the importance of a particular contact.

Moreover, we examined the relationship between the size of a contact list and the number of starred contacts contained therein, obviously excluding any users who did not use the "starred" contact feature. Once again, we observed that the number of important contacts (since a starred contact can be perceived as declared important) remained relatively steady despite the increase in size of the contact lists (Fig. 4). We found no statistically significant correlation between the number of contacts and outgoing calls ($r(34) = 0.15$, $p>0.4$) or sparsity ($r(34) = 0.03$, $p>0.85$).

We also examined the correlation between number of starred contacts and number of total contacts, where again we could not ascertain statistical significance ($r(15)=0.21$, $p>0.46$). In this case, however, the average number of starred contacts (mean=6.2, stdev.=3,16) is lower than the number of important contacts in our subjective study. We assume that this difference is the result of a combination of reasons: a) people tend to overestimate the importance of some contacts and this is also the reason why they are reluctant to delete contacts from their contact list and b) people tend to set up their starred contacts once and they do not usually change this setting.

As a result, the number of contacts that a contact list should provide quick access to, seems to be smaller than assumed earlier from the subjective user reports. (approximately 10 important contacts).

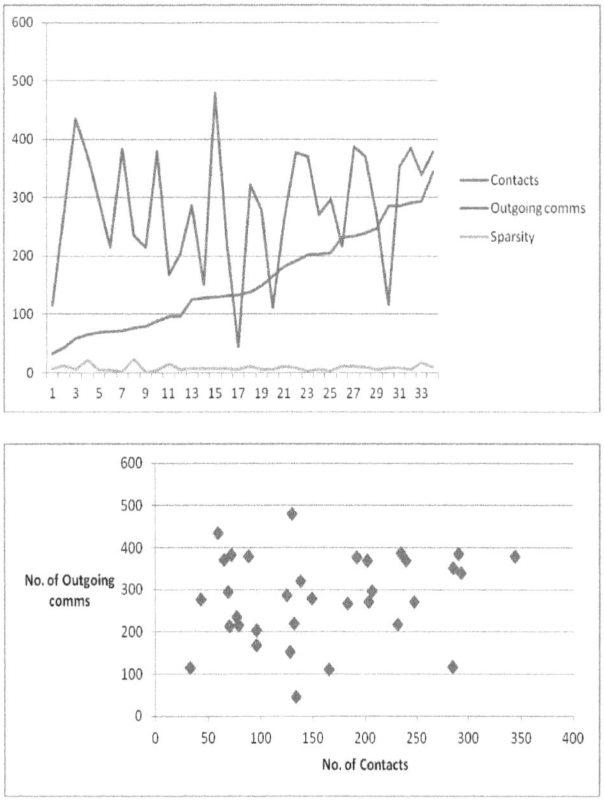

Figure 3 a (top) and b. Relationship between contact list size, outgoing communication and sparsity for each subject

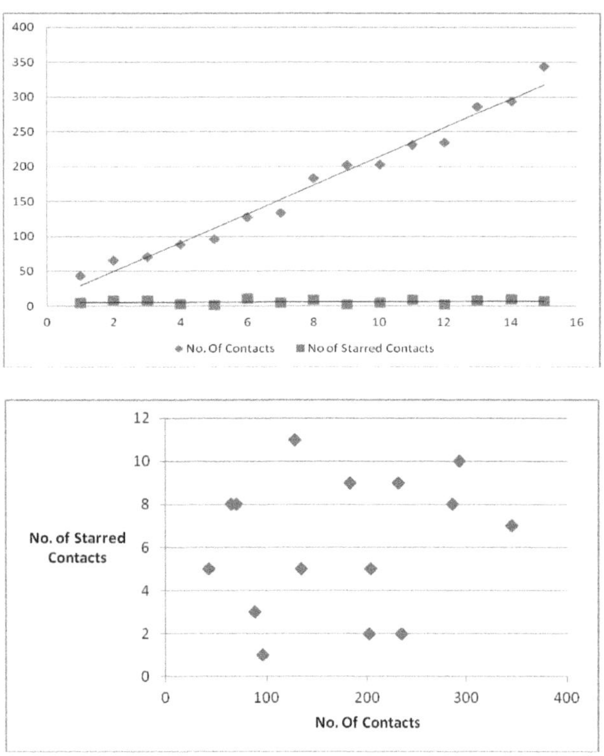

Figure 4 a(top) and b. Size of contact list vs. number of starred contacts

We also examined the percentage of outgoing calls towards starred contacts (figure 5). Some participants had the same number of starred contacts (e.g. 2, 5, 8, 9). An interesting finding is that for most users the percentage of outgoing calls towards starred contacts is significantly high. Specifically, for 60% of mobile users that use the "starred" feature of Android more than 50% of their outgoing calls were to starred contacts, a fact that reinforces our opinion about the importance of personal preference as a contextual cue related to mobile contacts. On the other hand, there are a number of participants who do not seem to communicate very much with their starred contacts. The same explanation as earlier about setting this feature only once could also apply in this case (most of these participants have the fewest starred contacts). Moreover, the fact that a participant considers a contact as being important in real life does not necessarily mean that she communicates this contact often using the mobile phone. For example, while a participant had his father as a starred contact, he claimed that he does not use his mobile phone to communicate with him since they live at the same place.

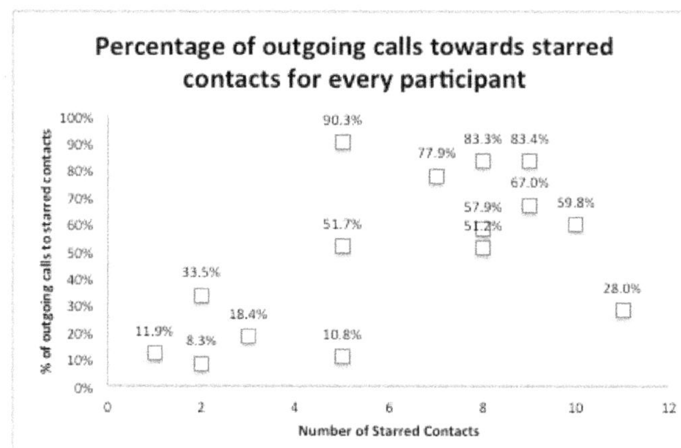

Figure 5. Number of starred contacts and percentage of outgoing calls towards starred contacts for each participant

Next, we examined if some form of the *Pareto Principle* is also valid for real usage data. For this reason, we calculated for each participant the percentage of contacts to whom 80% of outgoing calls were made and the percentage of outgoing calls that were made to the 20% of contacts with the highest call frequency. We should note here that we did not take into account contacts from the contact list that the participants had not called during the period that the call log covers. Only 15,92% (857) of the contacts in the contact lists of all participants were present in the call logs, while the rest 84,08% were not used at all. The results for each participant are presented in Figure 6. The first observable outcome is that the proportion of calls made to the 20% most frequently called contacts declines, as the proportion of contacts that makes up for 80% of the calls rises. This is expectable behavior and we observe that there is a clear negative correlation in this case ($r(34)=-0.78$, $p<0.01$)

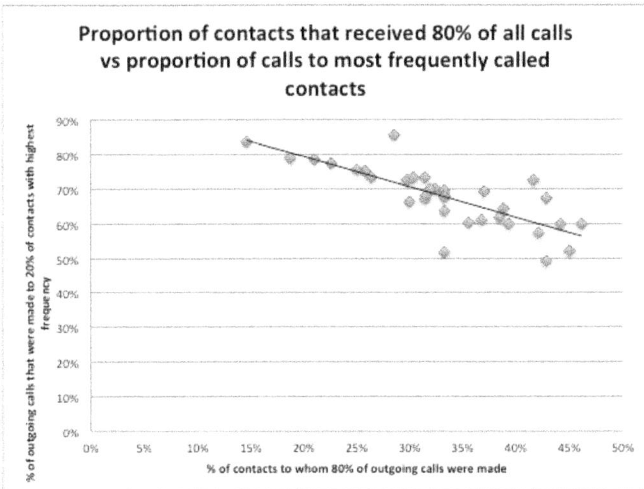

Figure 6. Percentage of contacts to whom 80% of outgoing calls were made and % of outgoing calls that were made to the 20% of contacts with highest call frequency for each participant

While the *Pareto Principle* does not seem to arise in the exact form of the 80/20 rule, for most participants there seems to be a relatively stable relation: 80% of outgoing calls are usually made to 25%-35% of contacts and usually 65%-75% of outgoing calls are made to the 20% of contacts with the highest frequency. This finding is in line with our belief that the proposed H1 criterion plays a highly important role as a contextual cue for mobile contacts. In addition, it seems that a relatively small percentage of contacts are frequently used (remember that in our analysis we excluded contacts that were not used at all), while the user has to search in a large repository (contact list) to retrieve the required record and for this reason mobile contact lists UIs should take this into account.

Finally, we proceeded to examine the relationship between calling frequencies and the number of contacts that correspond to each frequency value (i.e., the number of contacts called once for all mobile users, the number of contacts called twice and so on). In order to achieve that, as the call logs cover different time periods we performed a normalization on the data by extrapolating the usage behavior for a set period equal to the average + 1 stdev for all users (i.e. 49 days, mean=48 days, stdev=41). Then, we sorted the pairs of outgoing calls and number of contacts by the number of outgoing calls and calculated the cumulative Poisson probability for each pair. As shown in figure 7, the data can be split in three discrete areas of high, low and unpredictable (chaotic) probability behavior. From this data, we can see that all contacts in our dataset have a probability of having up to 8 calls associated with them of almost 1. The behavior then varies unpredictably until it settles in the region of 31 calls. This means that for our population dataset, if a contact has received more than 31 calls, it then belongs to a very special group of rare contacts. In fact, this group represents just 7.3% of the contact population with at least one call in the extrapolated period (832 contacts). The chaotic area represents approximately 21.5% while the high probability area represents 71.2%. We cannot of course claim that the group of rare contacts is persistently important because they have received a large number of calls, however they must have, at some point in the users' log of daily life, been important due to the large volume of calls made to them.

A very similar behavior in the distribution of the cumulative probabilities arises even if the data is not normalized as in our previous example. We wanted to see whether this pattern of behavior was repeatable for various timeframes of call log coverage and thus split our dataset in five distinct groups of log coverage periods (Table 4) and performed the same analysis for each group. We were surprised to find that the same behavioural pattern in the distribution of probabilities arises for each group, irrespectively of the size of the coverage period (Figure 8). Particularly surprising was the fact that the size of the low probability area (thus possibly contacts) in relation to the respective dataset remains the same (Figure 9) and hovers around the 11% mark (av. 10.93%, stdev=1.7%). The findings for group 5 show irregular behavior, but this is due to the fact that we only had two users that fell within this group. These results indicate a critical point where a phase shift between commonality and rarity for a contact, in terms of their usage frequency, occurs.

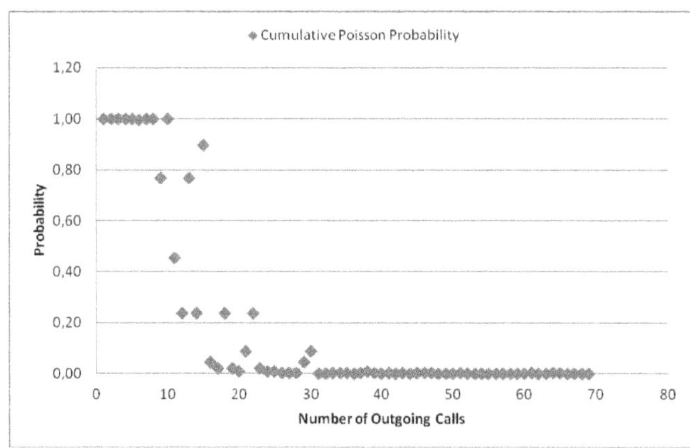

Figure 7. Overall cumulative Poisson probability distribution

Group	MinDays	MaxDays	Av Days	D-Days
1	8	14	11	7
2	17	31	24	15
3	35	64	49.5	30
4	74	115	94.5	42
5	170	187	178.5	18

Table 4. Groups of users and call log coverage periods (gaps in the groups are due to the sparsity of data)

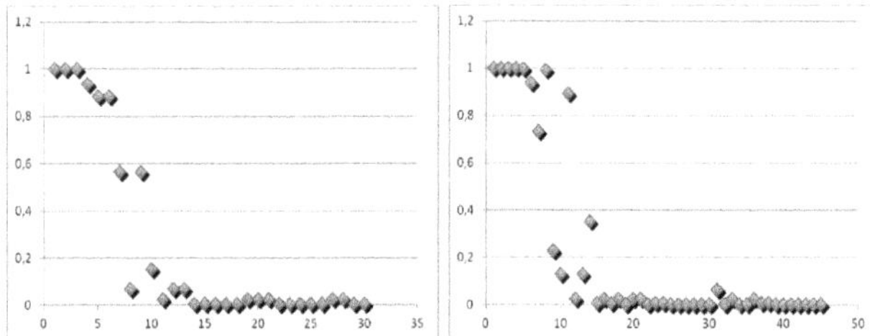

Figure 8. Cumulative Poisson probability distributions for groups 2 (left) and 3 (right)

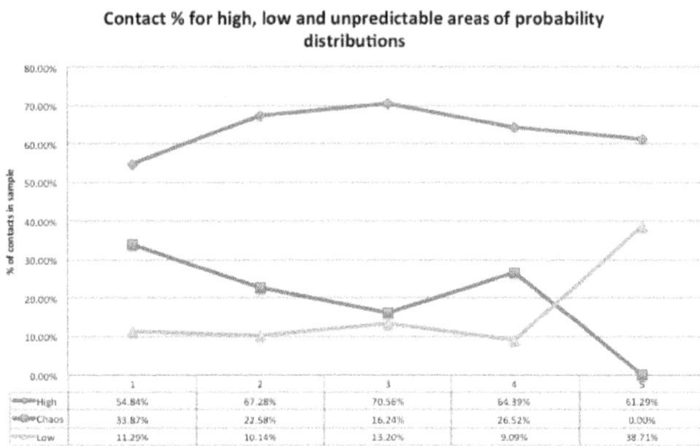

Figure 9. Relative size of the high, low and chaotic probability areas for the different groups.

This is an important finding because it shows that we can abstract the number of contacts that are potentially important under the frequency of use criterion for any user, irrespectively of the dataset covering any given time period of interest. As such, we can find the contacts that are "globally" important to the user according to the frequency criterion for his entire data log, as well as those contacts that are "locally" important in terms of a pre-determined temporal context (e.g. this week, last month). Furthermore, based on this figure, and assuming that use frequency is the primary criterion, we can further limit the application of other criteria to just the body of the contacts that are locally contextually important. The design implications of this finding for the improvement of mobile applications to support or encourage communications by minimizing searching behaviours are discussed in the next section.

IMPLICATIONS FOR DESIGN AND USABILITY

Understanding the importance of contacts given the user's current context can yield significant advantages in the usability of mobile applications that make use of a contact list, whether these are for calling, texting, communication via social or VOIP netwoks, sharing files and also discovering content pertinent to particular contacts (e.g. messages, files, pictures etc). An adaptive interface that permits quick access to important contacts offers a distinct usability advantage [14].

We hypothesized that importance can be estimated using a variety of contextual information. An interface informed by context can hide the source of its behavior or expose it and afford the user direct control over it. To highlight our vision, we discuss a few concept interface designs.

In figure 8 a one-dimensional hybrid interface is presented, where contacts are sorted alphabetically, but for each letter the important contacts are on top of the list and the remaining follow in alphabetical order. In contrast with our previous work [14], we can now safely limit the number of important contacts presented to the user using a threshold, as discussed in the previous section. This threshold can be adapted based on the time window used to sample frequency and recency data, so that it can represent a temporal locality (last 7 days) or global importance (complete log history). Such an interface abstracts and hides the mechanics of importance estimation from the user by revealing just the ordered and grouped contacts' names, without offering clues or control on how this is achieved. As such the user does not know whether the grouping is due to call frequency, recency, location or time. In our example, the user is only given information on the perceived location (work) and a button to change it, in case this is wrong. In figure 4b, the context is exposed, allowing the user to understand more fully why a contact has been selected as important (e.g. Jon Marshall has been called only 15 times but tried calling 15 minutes ago, so the user might want to get back to this person. Of course their importance shall fade very quickly if the user does not react). The downside of course is the potential information overload, which may ultimately detract from the goal of offering speedy access.

Figure 10. Hybrid one-dimensional mapping of importance (important contacts are highlighted in bold but ordered alphabetically so as to maintain user familiarity with existing UIs).

In figure 5 we show some concept renderings of 2-d and 3-d retrieval interfaces. In the case of 2 dimensions, the dimension of time can be preserved and as a result the user is able to retrieve the most important contacts during each time period. Figure 5a shows a more powerful interface, inspired by Apple's Time Machine software for restoring backed up data. In this example, the user is afforded control over the context information used by the device to calculate contact importance and can move time backwards and forwards, by using the time slider on the right, as well as manually change their location. This allows the user to gain future insight, as well as refer back to the past. Finally, in the case of 3 dimensions an example of how this technique extends beyond the domain of contact lists is presented. The respective figure (5b) shows how several personal information items or communication tasks (contacts, e-mails, SMSs etc.) could be projected in a 3-dimensional space (with possible dimensions presented on the axes of time, importance and distance from current location).

At this point in time our work focuses on a context-enabled contact list and following trials will extend to support a richer information space that will include all types of media and information pertinent to those contacts, enabling a new mode of context-based search and retrieval for mobile devices. As it can be seen, the determination of contact importance can naturally lead to the prediction of tasks or means of communication, facilitating use of the device and encouraging communication.

Figure 11a (left) and 9b (right). Retrieval UIs using 2D (left) and 3D (right) projections of item (contacts, e-mails, photos etc.) importance combined with retained, unprojected dimensions (time, distance from current location).

CONCLUSIONS AND FUTURE WORK

We presented our investigation of 2 context criteria for the design of adaptive mobile contact list applications. We performed two experiments, one based on users' perceptions and another based on the analysis of data collected from Android devices. We present findings that support the importance of proposed criterion H1 (frequency & recency of use) in the design of mobile contact list UIs. It seems that the largest part of a mobile user's outgoing communication involves a small number of contacts from her usually large contact list repository. These findings support that further research is needed in order to create new mobile UIs that will include the appropriate number of contact elements presented in an efficient manner. We also found evidence that user preference for importance (H2) should also be catered for in an adaptive UI for mobile contact lists. We strongly believe that the weights of the above mentioned criteria are not static, but dynamic, changing according to the mobile social user context. To evaluate the relationship between importance hypotheses, we are currently testing an adaptive contact list UI, informed by the design principles supported by H1 & H2. The most important contribution of this work however is evidence that user calling behavior demonstrates a repeatable pattern of use which is exploitable for the design of context-relevant contact and communication UIs regardless of the temporal scale of observed interaction.

As stated previously, frequency, recency and personal preference might not be the only contextual criteria for importance. Our research opens up questions regarding other contextual information such as *location* and *temporal context.* Our participants indicated that their calling habits depend on the location they are in. For example, when at work, they tend to use their mobile to contact work colleagues. In the evenings, when they are at home or out having fun, they would rarely do that, spending instead most of their communication time to connect with friends, relatives and some work colleagues who they are friendly with at a personal level. Could, as such, location and temporal context inform the dynamics of contact list displays?

Social, Task and activity context might also play an important role in determining contact importance. Knowing who a person is likely to need to communicate or collaborate with in the near future could also have an impact on elevating that contact's importance, even temporarily. Contacts who are regularly unimportant can suddenly become of critical importance for a short period of time, for example, when on our way to meet someone. Could the contact list interface with a user's calendar and try to guess their upcoming activities, who they're going to meet, and prepare itself accordingly to support the user in the likely event they need to call that person? If so, how long before or after the meeting does that contact remain important?

In the future we intend to complete the analysis of our collected data, performing a more detailed processing that will include recency dependencies, contact groups and incoming communication. Furthermore, we are preparing another experiment that will run simultaneously in our participants' mobile devices collecting data for the same period of time and enhancing them with spatial information as well as activity information from users' calendars, enabling us to better examine hypotheses 3 and 4.

ACKNOWLEDGEMENTS

This work has in part been supported by the National Strategic Reference Framework (NSRF) (Regional Operational Programme – Western Greece) under the title "Advanced Systems and Services over Wireless and Mobile Networks" (number 312179).

REFERENCES

1. Ankolekar, A., Szabo, G., Luon, Y., Huberman, B.A., Wilkinson, D., Wu, F. Friendlee: a mobile application for your social life. In *Proc. MobileHCI '09*, ACM Press (2009), 1-4 .
2. Bergman, O., Beyth-Marom, R., Nachmias, R., Whittaker, S. The User-Subjective Approach: A New Direction for PIM Systems Design. *Proc. CHI2008*, ACM Press (2008), 1-4.
3. Bhamidipaty, A., Deepak, P. *SymAB: Symbol-Based Address Book for the Semi-literate Mobile User.* Lecture Notes In Computer Science, Volume 4662/2007, Springer (2007), 389-392.
4. Böcker, M., Suwita, A. Evaluating the Siemens C10 mobile phone – Beyond "Quick and Dirty" Usability Testing. *Proc. HFT'99*, (1999), 1-10.
5. Brown, B., Randell, R. *Building a context sensitive telephone: some hopes and pitfalls for context sensitive computing*. CSCW Journal, special edition on context aware computing, 13(3), 329-345.mobile applications. IEEE Pervasive Computing Special Issue on The Smart Phone, 4, 2 (2005), 51-59.
6. Clockar, T., Carr, D., Hedman, A., Johansson, T., Bengtsson, F. Usability of Mobile Phones. In *Proc. of the 19th International Symposium on Human Factors in Telecommunications*, (2003), 197-204.
7. Gaur, S. *Mobile Phone Contact Book: The Social Approach*. Services and social networking on the Internet, Antti Ylä-Jääski, in Laura Takkinen (eds.) TKK Technical Reports in Computer Science and Engineering. (2008).
8. Jones, W., Phuwanartnurak, A. J., Gill, R., Bruce, H. Don't take my folders away! Organizing personal information to get things done. *In CHI '05 extended abstracts on human factors in computing systems*, ACM Press (2005), 1505-1508.
9. Jung, Y., Anttila, A., Blom, J. Designing for the Evolution of Mobile Contacts Applications. In *Proc. MobileHCI'08*, ACM Press (2008), 449-452.
10. Oulasvirta, A., Raento, M., Tiita, S. ContextContacts: Re-Designing Smartphone's Contact Book to Support Mobile Awareness and Collaboration. In *Proc. MobileHCI'05*, ACM Press (2005), 167-174.
11. Rhee, Y., Kim, J., Chung, A. *Your Phone Automatically Caches your Life*. Interaction 13(4): 42-44, (2006).
12. Tolmie, P., Pycock, J., Diggins, T., MacLean, A., Karsenty, A. Unremarkable computing. In *Proc. CHI'02*, ACM Press (2002), 399-406.
13. Whittaker, S., Jones, Q., Terveen, L. Contact Management: Identifying Contacts to Support Long-Term Communication. In *Proc. of CSCW 2002* , (2002), 216-225.
14. Bergman O., Komninos A., Liarokapis D., Clarke J. You Never Call...Demoting Unused Contacts on Mobile Phones Using DMTR, *Personal & Ubiquitous Computing, Springer, Online First (2011)*
15. Komninos, A., Liarokapis, D. The Use of Mobile Contact List applications and a Context-Oriented Framework to Support their Design, *Mobile HCI 2009, Bonn, Germany* (2009)

An Exploration of Inadvertent Variations in Mobile Pressure Input

Craig Stewart[1], Eve Hoggan[1], Laura Haverinen[1], Hugues Salamin[2], and Giulio Jacucci[1]

[1]Helsinki Institute for Information Technology
Department of Computer Science, University of Helsinki, Helsinki, Finland
{firstname.lastname}@hiit.fi

[1]Helsinki Institute for Information Technology
Department of Computer Science, University of Helsinki, Helsinki, Finland
{firstname.lastname}@hiit.fi

ABSTRACT
This paper reports the results of an exploratory study into inadvertent grip pressure changes on mobile devices with a focus on the differences between static lab-based and mobile walking environments. The aim of this research is to inform the design of more robust pressure input techniques that can accommodate dynamic mobile usage. The results of the experiment show that there are significant differences in grip pressure in static and walking conditions with high levels of pressure variation in both. By combining the pressure data with accelerometer data, we show that grip pressure is closely related to user movement.

Author Keywords
Pressure, mobile interaction, accidental triggers, implicit interaction.

ACM Classification Keywords
H.5.2 User Interfaces: Haptic I/O, Input Devices and Strategies.

NTRODUCTION
Mobile devices afford many different input techniques through their increasing power and range of sensors. Recent research has begun to focus on alternative uses for our sense of touch in mobile interaction. Tactile feedback (commonly vibrotactile stimulation of the skin) is the best understood and most used sub-modality within touch but pressure is also part of the same sensory system and can be used for mobile input [7]. The results of various different studies on explicit pressure input have shown that users can distinguish and apply up to ten pressure levels with high degrees of accuracy when navigating through a standard menu with visual and audio feedback [11].

Pressure does not have to be applied directly to the device display but can also be applied to the sides (if equipped with an appropriate sensor), which means that users can apply pressure to the device by squeezing it. We use squeezing in many everyday activities, for example squeezing a loved one's hand. Some previous research has been conducted on grip-sensing [6] [10], which has shown that grasping is an effective interaction technique.

Pressure created by squeezing the device is an ideal input mechanism for use during phone calls where the device is positioned at the user's ear making it difficult to interact via the display. Such pressure input can be used to augment phone calls with extra information. Adding an extra channel of information to speech communication has been investigated in some previous research. For example, Chang *et al.*[2] developed ComTouch a device that augments remote voice communication using pressure input. More specifically, the device converts hand pressure into vibration intensity with a single actuator. Robinson *et al.* [8] developed TapBack, which provides callers with an augmented experience with interactive voice sites by enabling touch-based gestures on the back-of-device to be used during a call.

Unfortunately, mobile environments can hinder the usability of an input technique. Although there has been a small amount of research on the effects of walking on explicit pressure input [4, 11] there has been little investigation of inadvertent changes in pressure input. As stated by Hinckley and Sinclair [5], 'because touch sensors require zero activation force, they may be prone to accidental activation due to inadvertent contact'. In order for systems to be effective in dynamic mobile environments, inadvertent forces applied to the device need to be examined and should perhaps be taken into account to minimize accidental triggering of the input mechanism. We hypothesise that there are high variations in pressure data due to the context of the user. In other words, different aspects of mobile environments may have an effect on the pressure levels applied to mobile devices; for example, a user's grip on the device may vary in force when walking as opposed to sitting or whilst walking at different speeds.

In existing systems, pressure levels from 0 to 3N have been used [9] because the sensor accommodates this range and it is an appropriate ergonomic range for humans. We argue that the pressure level ranges for robust explicit input should not only be based on the sensor's capabilities but should also consider inadvertent grip pressure changes.

Our research questions were: what pressure range should be used for explicit pressure input? What are the differences

MobileHCI'12, September 21–24, 2012, San Francisco, CA, USA.

between the average inadvertent pressure level applied to a mobile device when a user is walking and seated? What contextual factors influence inadvertent pressure levels? If we understand the inadvertent interaction better we may be able to design something more robust to mobile usage.

EXPERIMENT

To investigate inadvertent changes in grip force on mobile devices we chose to record grip pressure levels during phonecalls in static and mobile conditions.

Hardware

The prototype mobile phone used in this experiment (Figure 1) was developed by augmenting a standard Nokia N900[1] with a Force Sensing Resistor (FSR). The left-hand side of the device contains no buttons so this is a convenient location to place a large pressure sensor. The sensor itself measures approximately 100mm in length and 14mm in width, providing almost complete coverage of the side of the device. Additionally double-sided tape was used to affix the sensor to the device.

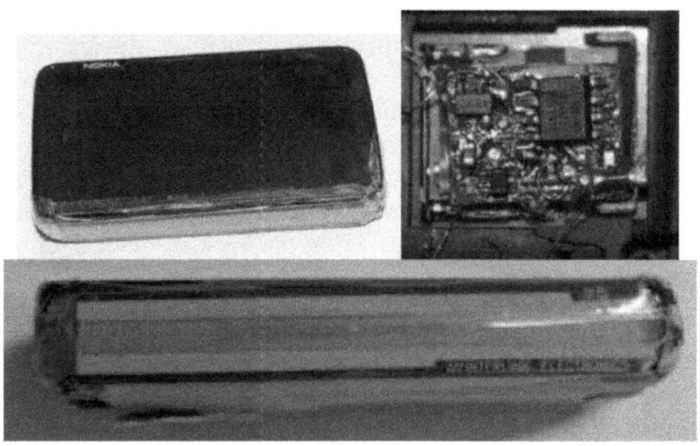

Figure 1: Prototype mobile phone with pressure sensor (top left). The sensor hardware design can fit within the microsd card slot (15mm by 11mm) of the Nokia N900 (top right). FSR attached to side of device (bottom).

The implementation of the Force Sensing Resistor-based pressure sensor is based on the design proposed by Stewart *et al.* [9] and supported by the datasheet of the FSR manufacturer[2]. The op-amp based circuit linearizes the sensor output such that changes in the amount of force applied, results in a similar change in output voltage across the range of pressure used. The output voltage from the op amp is then sampled by an 8-bit microcontroller (Atmel attiny13) at 40 Hz, and resulting data is sent to the host system by a hardware-based serial port. The digital representation of the sensor output is between 0 (no contact) and 195 (extremely firm grip). The range of the sensor was determined informally by asking various lab partners to squeeze the phone as tightly as possible and the sensitivity of the sensor adjusted to limit over saturation of the sensor output.

Logging

During the study we recorded 3D acceleration, FSR, location data and the conversation between the experimenter and subject. The resulting accelerometer and FSR data files were then synchronized and interpolated to a regular 40 Hz sampling rate.

Methodology

28 participants took part in the experiment. The participants were all right-handed, consisted of 16 females and 12 males and aged between 22 and 38 (mean 27.9, std 5.86).

We used a within-subjects design where the conditions were: walking (following a predefined route outdoors whilst talking on the phone) and static (seated at a desk in the lab whilst talking on the phone). All subjects performed both conditions and the ordering of walking and static conditions was fully counterbalanced.

During the walking condition, the participants were asked to follow a predetermined route of 1.4km with varying terrain. The average time to walk the route was 17 minutes 55 seconds. The researcher walked, at a reasonable distance, behind the participant to ensure the participants safety. Additionally, if participants became unsure of the route, the experimenter could provide directional information. The participants were asked to talk on the phone to the researcher and hold the phone in a natural manner.

RESULTS

Analyses focused on participants' inadvertent pressure applied to the device whilst seated and walking. The average pressure values for each mobility condition were calculated and a paired samples t-test showed a significant main effect of mobility condition($t=7.49$, $df=1$, $p=0.0001$) with significantly higher pressure levels occurring in the outdoor walking condition.

Pressure Variations

For pressure input to be used in an explicit manner, the system needs filter out unintentional changes in sensor values. A simple approach to achieve this would be to apply a minimum threshold value that the applied pressure should exceed to be considered intentional as opposed to unintentional. However, if we were to suggest that the mean pressure level should be used as a threshold, inadvertent triggers would still occur due to the large variations in pressure levels as demonstrated in Figure 2. In order to avoid any accidental triggering of pressure input, the minimum pressure threshold at which input can be activated must account for the increase in pressure variability in mobile scenarios.

1 www.nokia.com/gb-en/products/phone/n900/

2 http://www.sparkfun.com/datasheets/Sensors/Pressure/fsrguide.pdf

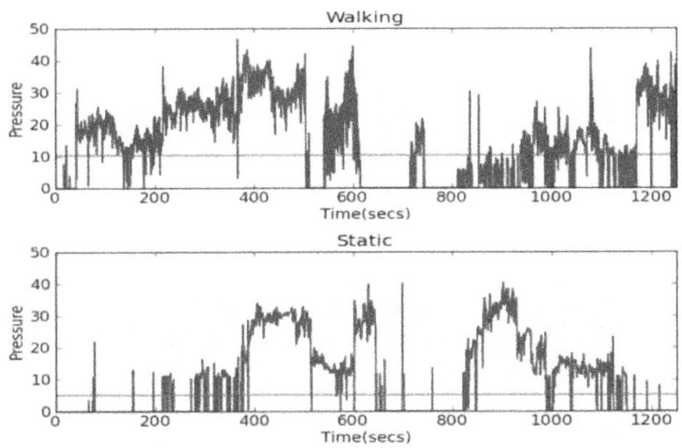

Figure 2: Example Pressure Traces for Participant 10 in the Static and Walking Conditions (with basic mean threshold level shown in red). The digitised sensor voltage 0 - 195 is mapped to voltage of 0 to 2.5v. approx. 0 – 3N.

Acceleration versus Inadvertent Pressure

To further test the effects of a dynamic mobile environment on inadvertent pressure applied to the device, we decided to examine the mobile pressure data in relation to the accelerometer data to determine whether there are any similarities between the inadvertent grip pressure and accelerometer energy in the walking condition. It has been shown in previous work that target selection time and accuracy in mobile tapping task depend on the gait of the user [1] [3]. Therefore it seemed possible that the variance in pressure is also affected by variance in accelerometer readings.

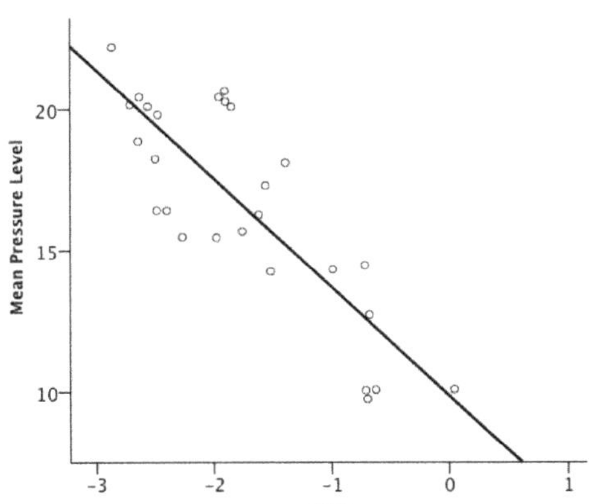

Figure 3: Predicting Mean Pressure Levels from Accelerometer Data[3].

A per sample linear regression analysis was employed to predict the pressure levels whilst walking from the accelerometer data averaged across the whole conversation (R^2 = .83) (Figure 3). Mean pitch of acceleration measurements was most strongly related to the mean pressure level. As the mean acceleration pitch moves towards zero, the pressure decreases. Additionally device roll (in radians) and acceleration magnitude mean had a non-trivial association(r>=. 1).

The inadvertent pressure levels were also analysed with respect to the participants' walking speed. Figure 4 shows the linear trend between walking speed (meters per second) and pressure levels (R^2 = 0.74).

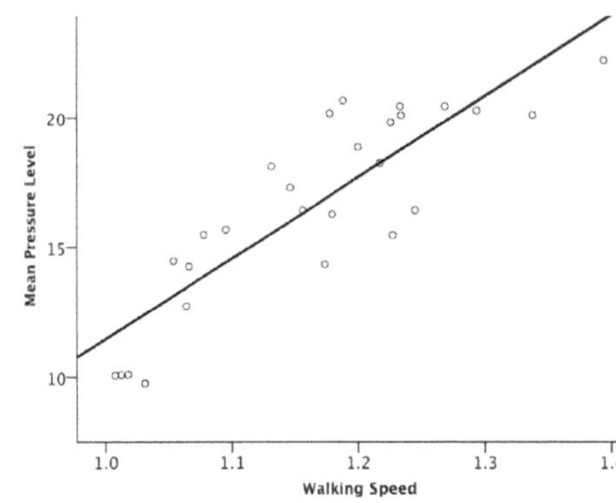

Figure 4: Predicting Mean Pressure Levels from Walking Speed (meters per second)

The significant difference in pressure variations between the stationary and walking conditions (Figure 2) showed that walking increases the amount of pressure variations applied to the device. The increasing linear trend between the walking speed and pressure levels shows that an increase of 1.1 to 1.2 meters per second results in a significant increase in pressure, t(12)=4.74, p<0.01.

Sensor Usage Analysis

By taking all of the above results into account, we wanted to explore the remaining design space for explicit pressure input. We were interested in determining the range of pressure levels available for explicit pressure input. Figure 5 shows the range of pressure values obtained (walking and static) with respect to the overall range of the FSR.

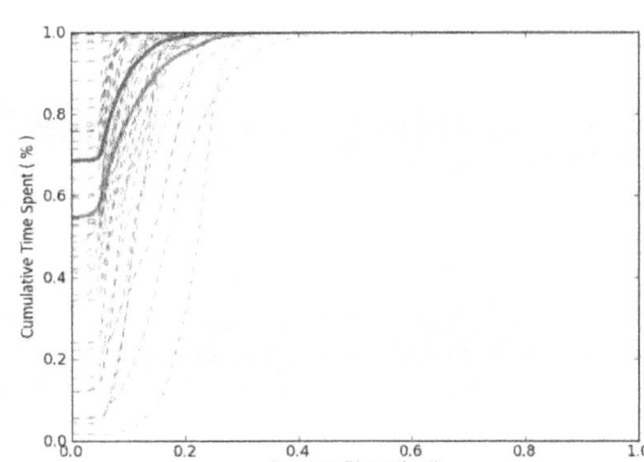

Figure 5: Cumulative Time Spent vs. Normalized Pressure Range (Indoor/Outdoor: Blue/Red, Dashed/Bold lines: Individuals / Mean).

On average, the inadvertent pressure applied to the device by participants was 20% (up to 0.6N) of the overall range of the FSR. This result suggests that the remaining 80% of the sensor range could still be used for explicit pressure input.

3 Pitch mean/std: the mean and standard deviation for the pitch (in radians) of the device as determined from accelerometer,.

DISCUSSION AND CONCLUSIONS

The exploratory experiment described here investigated the inadvertent pressure levels applied by users when holding and talking on a mobile device in a static lab-based and mobile walking environment. In response to our research questions:

What are the differences between the average inadvertent pressure level applied when a user is walking and seated?

The results show that significantly higher levels of inadvertent pressure occurred in the walking condition compared to the static condition. However, there was also more pressure variation in the walking condition than the static condition which makes it difficult to create an explicit threshold based on the average pressure levels.

What pressure range should be used for explicit pressure input?

The FSR data shows that inadvertent pressure levels commonly ranged from 0 to 0.6N. This means that thresholds above 0.6N would be more robust for explicit pressure input.

What contextual factors influence inadvertent pressure levels?

The analysis showed a relationship between the mean pressure levels and acceleration. For example, as the mean acceleration magnitude, the mean and standard deviation for the roll of the device, walking speed and the mean acceleration pitch increase, the pressure levels increase. This means that, as users' movements increase, they increase their grip on the device. These results suggest the possibility of using accelerometer data to dynamically adapt a threshold level for intentional pressure input. However the analysis with the accelerometer data did not fully explain the variations or changes in inadvertent pressure during phone calls whilst users are walking. There may be other contributing factors in mobile environments.

Future Work

Future studies will examine additional factors that may affect a user's grip on a mobile device. The dimensions of the device, weather, terrain, conversation topic or emotional state of the user may affect the user's grip. By using multiple pressure sensors we will be able to access more informative data about subtle changes in grip pressure and assess ergonomic factors. This would enable us to develop an adaptive threshold that takes these variances into account. This would lead to a more robust approach to designing explicit pressure input mechanisms that can tolerate dynamic mobile usage. Although this experiment focused on grip pressure during voice calls, it is likely that the results could be applied to other mobile use case scenarios too. Another interesting use for the data collected in this experiment and future work revolves around implicit interaction. We may be able to infer additional information about users through their inadvertent grip pressure such as conversation dynamics or as an extra measure of context to allow feedback to be adapted based on the user's situation.

ACKNOWLEDGMENTS

This work was partially funded by the Nokia Research Center (NRC) Finland and Finnish Funding Agency for Technology and Innovation (Tekes) collaboration project HEI.

REFERENCES

[1] Bergstrom-Lehtovirta, J., Oulasvirta, A. and Brewster, S. The effects of walking speed on target acquisition on a touchscreen interface. *In Proc. of MobileHCI (Stockholm, Sweden, 2011).* ACM, pp. 143-146.

[2] Chang, A., O'Modhrain, S., Jacob, R., Gunther, E. and Ishii, H. ComTouch: Design of a Vibrotactile Communication Device. *In Proc. of DIS (London, UK, 2002).* ACM Press, pp. 312 - 320.

[3] Crossan, A., Murray-Smith, R., Brewster, S., Kelly, J. and Musizza, B. Gait phase effects in mobile interaction. *In Proc. of the CHI '05 extended abstracts* (Portland, OR, USA, 2005). ACM, pp. 1312-1315.

[4] Heo, S. and Lee, G. Forcetap: extending the input vocabulary of mobile touch screens by adding tap gestures. *In Proc. of MobileHCI (Stockholm, Sweden, 2011).* ACM, pp. 113-122.

[5] Hinckley, K. and Sinclair, M. Touch-sensing input devices. *In Proc. of CHI (Pittsburgh, Pennsylvania, United States, 1999).* ACM, pp. 223-230.

[6] Kim, K.-E., Chang, W., Cho, S.-J., Shim, J., Lee, H., Park, J., Lee, Y. and Kim, S. Hand grip pattern recognition for mobile user interfaces. *In Proc. of the 18th conference on Innovative applications of artificial intelligence - Volume 2 (Boston, Massachusetts, 2006).* AAAI Press, pp. 1789-1794.

[7] McCallum, D. C., Mak, E., Irani, P. and Srinivasan, S. PressureText: pressure input for mobile phone text entry. *In Proc. of CHI extended abstracts (2009).* ACM, pp. 4519-4524.

[8] Robinson, S., Rajput, N., Jones, M., Jain, A., Sahay, S. and Nanavati, A. TapBack: towards richer mobile interfaces in impoverished contexts. *In Proc. of CHI (Vancouver, BC, Canada, 2011).* ACM, pp. 2733-2736.

[9] Stewart, C., Rohs, M., Kratz, S. and Essl, G. Characteristics of pressure-based input for mobile devices. *In Proc. of CHI (Atlanta, Georgia, USA, 2010).* ACM, pp. 801 - 810.

[10] Taylor, B. T. and V. Michael Bove, J. Graspables: grasp-recognition as a user interface. *In Proc. of CHI (Boston, MA, USA, 2009).* ACM, pp. 917-926.

[11] Wilson, G., Brewster, S. A., Halvey, M., Crossan, A. and Stewart, C. The effects of walking, feedback and control method on pressure-based interaction. *In Proc. of MobileHCI (Stockholm, Sweden, 2011).* ACM, pp. 147-156.

The Fat Thumb: Using the Thumb's Contact Size for Single-Handed Mobile Interaction

Sebastian Boring, David Ledo, Xiang 'Anthony' Chen,
Nicolai Marquardt, Anthony Tang, Saul Greenberg
Dept. of Computer Science, University of Calgary, 2500 University Dr. NW, Calgary, AB, T2N 1N4, Canada
[sebastian.boring, dledomai, anthony.xiangchen, nicolai.marquardt, tonyt, saul.greenberg]@ucalgary.ca

ABSTRACT
Modern mobile devices allow a rich set of multi-finger interactions that combine modes into a single fluid act, for example, one finger for panning blending into a two-finger pinch gesture for zooming. Such gestures require the use of both hands: one holding the device while the other is interacting. While on the go, however, only one hand may be available to both hold the device and interact with it. This mostly limits interaction to a single-touch (i.e., the thumb), forcing users to switch between input modes explicitly. In this paper, we contribute the *Fat Thumb interaction technique*, which uses the thumb's *contact size* as a form of simulated pressure. This adds a degree of freedom, which can be used, for example, to integrate panning and zooming into a single interaction. Contact size determines the mode (i.e., panning with a small size, zooming with a large one), while thumb movement performs the selected mode. We discuss nuances of the *Fat Thumb* based on the thumb's limited operational range and motor skills when that hand holds the device. We compared *Fat Thumb* to three alternative techniques, where people had to precisely pan and zoom to a predefined region on a map and found that the *Fat Thumb* technique compared well to existing techniques.

Author Keywords
Mobile device; touch-screen; single-handed interaction

ACM Classification Keywords
H.5.2 [Information interfaces and presentation]: User Interfaces: Input Devices and Strategies, Interaction Styles.

INTRODUCTION
Today, many mobile devices are equipped with multi-touch screens allowing for different content manipulations by using multiple fingers. For example, users can interact with a map by varying the number of touch points (i.e., panning the map with one finger, zooming with the two finger pinch gesture), rather than by selecting dedicated controls (e.g., menus, buttons) to switch between modes. This is especially important for mobile devices, as it reduces the number of controls cluttering the small display.

MobileHCI'12, September 21–24, 2012, San Francisco, CA, USA.

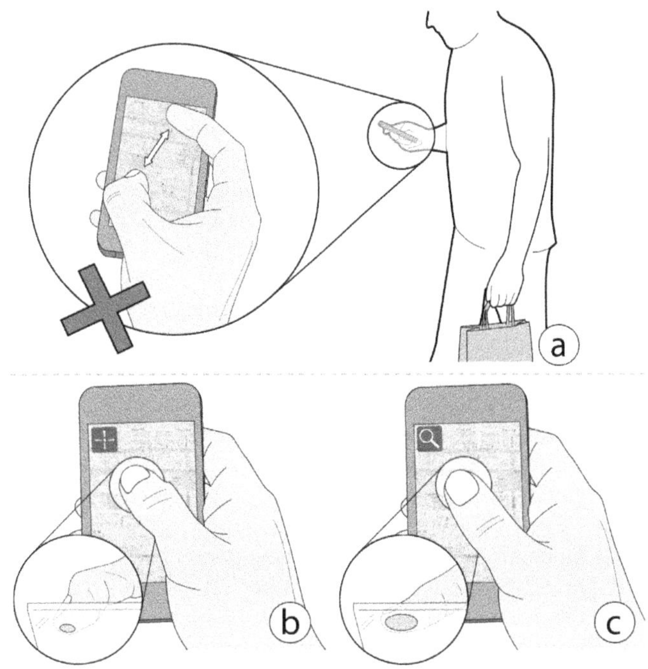

Figure 1. Performing multi-touch actions on a device with just one hand requires awkward hand postures (a); the *Fat Thumb* technique allows fluent single-handed mobile interaction through contact size; e.g., panning (b) and zooming (c) a map.

Yet multi-touch gestures on mobile devices require both hands: one to hold the device, and the other to perform the gestures. This can be problematic, as there are many situations – such as when a person is carrying a bag – when only one hand is available to both hold and interact with the device [14]. Multi-touch actions during such one-handed use become awkward. Figure 1a illustrates such a scenario, where we see how performing the thumb/index finger pinch gesture while holding the device in the same hand requires awkward hand postures. This leads to less precision, more fatigue, and insecure grip of the device (see Figure 1a, left). Alternately, users may perform a sequence of single touch operations to achieve the same result. However, this usually involves an input mode switch between actions: selecting modes via buttons and menus, single-touch gestures recognized as mode-switches [19,22], or employing different hand parts (e.g., touching and tilting the device) [12].

To mitigate this problem, we contribute *Fat Thumb*: a method for one-handed input on a mobile device that caters to the thumb's limited operational range. It uses the thumb's *contact size*, where changing the thumb's *pitch* fluidly allows for

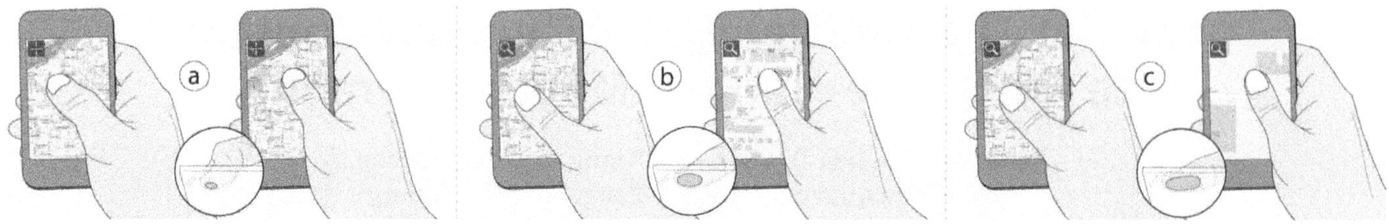

Figure 2. Walkthrough of pan and zoom example: movement with small contact size pans the map (a), increasing contact size switches to zoom (b), and further increasing the contact causes faster zoom operation (c).

transitioning between different modes of interaction (Figure 1b,c). The thumb's *movement* then performs the selected mode. We illustrate and evaluate this technique in a pan-and-zoom task in comparison to exiting single-handed techniques (i.e., a slider, *Tilt-to-Zoom* [12], and *CycloStar* [22]). Our findings demonstrate that the *Fat Thumb* technique compared well to existing one-handed pan-and-zoom techniques, with participants overwhelmingly preferring it.

THE FAT THUMB INTERACTION TECHNIQUE

To illustrate the application of the *Fat Thumb* interaction technique, we use pan and zoom in a map as the driving example throughout this paper [24]. Figure 2 shows a walkthrough of *Fat Thumb* in this scenario (also see the video figure): (a) shows how moving the thumb with a small contact size pans the content. In (b), increasing the contact size switches to the zoom, and moving the thumb in zoom mode around its joint with the palm allows zooming in (right direction) and out (left direction). Finally, in (c) further increasing the contact decreases the control-display (CD) ratio resulting in faster zoom operations.

Fat Thumb has three major differences compared to existing techniques for single-handed mobile device input:

1. It does not require the user to break out of a gesture to switch modes (as with a *Slider*). Instead, it allows for mode switching by adjusting the contact size while moving the thumb. It reduces clutching operations like *Tilt-to-Zoom* [12], thumb fatigue, and avoids moving other hand parts (e.g., the wrist in *Tilt-to-Zoom*).
2. It optimizes for the thumb's limited operational range and motor skills. Compared to other methods, it avoids precise circular strokes as required in *CycloStar* [22], or repositioning the thumb to control a slider.
3. *Fat Thumb* uses the contact size instead of an actual measure of applied pressure. Therefore, the approach causes less friction than pressure-based input systems, even when moving the thumb with a large contact size, which in turn decreases fatigue.

RELATED WORK

Fat Thumb builds on prior reports of the thumb's limitations on mobile devices, as well as prior offerings of single-handed interaction methods designed to mitigate these limitations. We also leverage related work on pressure-based systems, and on using contact shape as an input parameter for touch screen interaction.

The Thumb's Limitation on Mobile Devices

Single-handed interaction with a mobile device presents unique challenges not found in larger interactive touch screens and surfaces [7]. Often, the thumb of the hand holding the device is the only finger that is available for input [13]. Because the hand's key muscles are employed to hold the device [17], the degrees of freedom for input are limited to the thumb's joints (see Figure 3a). Both the *metacarpophalangeal* (MCP) and the *interphalangeal* (IP) joint control the movement of the thumb's tip to and away from the palm. The *carpometacarpal* (CMC) joint enables thumb rotation around the wrist [20], however, that joint is also 'connected' to the device as it secures the grip [28].

Since the thumb's CMC joint cannot be moved without changing the grip, the thumb's length limits its reachability (Figure 3b,c). Considering these kinematic properties (the thumb's movement and its reachability) has strong implications for the ergonomics of an interaction. In a 3 × 3 region matrix, Parhi et al. showed that the center target is the most preferred [27]. Karlson et al. and Henze et al. confirmed this for larger numbers of targets [9,17]. Although lower right regions (when used with the right hand) appear to be within the thumb's reach, fully bending the thumb around its MCP and IP joints requires users to use a different grip of the device [13]. As well, the lower left region is less preferred as it is at the thumb's angular limits [29].

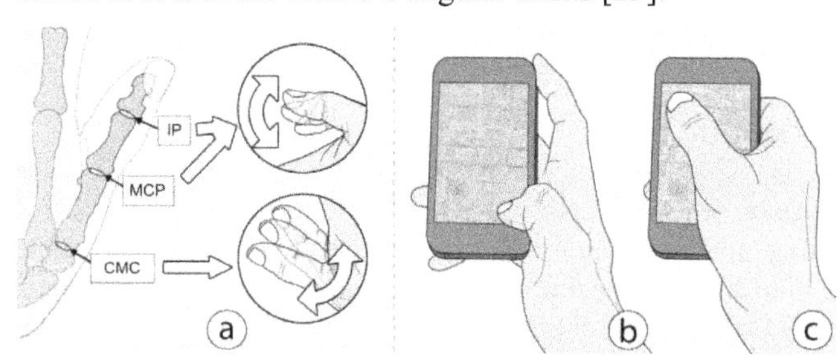

Figure 3. The joints of the thumb (a) limit its movement and reachability on the mobile touch screen. Especially lower right (b) and upper left (c) are hard to reach for right-handed users.

The thumb can perform movements in two directions: rotating around the CMC joint and rotating around both IP and MCP joints. Karlson et al. found that certain thumb motions were ergonomically difficult: moving the thumb diagonally (to and away from the palm) and horizontally requires more effort resulting in longer task times [17]. This suggests that employing the thumb's IP and MCP joints for motion is less suitable than the CMC joint.

Fat Thumb considers these limitations by: (1) not requiring placing the thumb near the device's edges; and (2) restricting its relative movement (in modes that do not require absolute and direct input) around the CMC joint.

Single-Handed Mobile Interaction using Touch

Gestures can be used to overcome limited input capabilities (e.g., only one touch point is sensed) or to increase the expressiveness of an interaction [40]. For example, Olwal et al. presented *Rubbing*, a technique for zooming in and out by performing fast strokes using a single finger [26]. Similar to the *Virtual Scroll Ring* [25], Malacria et al. show that using a circular motion around the point of interest for zooming performs better than *Rubbing* as it requires less high-speed movements [22]. Unlike *Fat Thumb*, these methods were designed for stationary screens (thereby allowing the user to freely position their hand and arm); thus it is unclear how well these work in a mobile context.

Researchers explored designs that account for the thumb's limitations. *ThumbSpace* improves accuracy for small targets that are out of the thumb's reach [19]. *AppLens* and *LaunchTile* use scalable user interfaces to access multiple applications on the same screen [18], similar to *ZoneZoom* on mobile phones featuring a keypad [31]. With *TapTap* users perform a tap to temporarily zoom into a sub-region (with a fixed zoom factor), followed by selecting the target with another tap [33]. With *MicroRolls*, Roudaut et al. demonstrate how users can perform 16 gestures by rolling the finger rather than sliding it, e.g., rolling left has a different meaning than rolling right [34]. *TapSense* allows for using different hand parts (e.g., a knuckle) to select a mode [8]. Hinckley et al.'s *Sensor Synaesthesia* uses the device's accelerometers to zoom in or out while the thumb is not moving [12]. These methods involve an action on a single location to switch the input mode. In contrast, *Fat Thumb* allows for continuous movement of the thumb on the display. Like *MicroRolls*, *Fat Thumb* allows for thumb-rolling, but unlike *MicroRolls*, it can be combined with motion.

Pressure on Mobile Devices

Pressure as input parameter is closely related to the contact size (i.e., more pressure suggests a larger contact size due to flattening of the thumb). Using a stylus for input, Ramos et al. found that a level of six different pressure values is optimal and distinguishable by users [30]. In *GraspZoom*, users can press the back of the device to temporarily switch from panning to a zooming mode [24]. Stewart et al. used pressure from the front, back or sides of a mobile device and found that applying pressure from the device's sides works best [36]. Shi et al. tested different mapping functions, such as fisheyes [35]. However, none of these systems explore the use of pressure while simultaneously moving the finger.

Pressure-sensitive input has been predominantly used for text entry [23], Clarkson et al. added pressure sensors under a regular phone's keypad, e.g., to replace multi-tapping with different pressure levels [5]. Brewster et al. extend this to keyboards on touch screens to distinguish between lower- and uppercase [3]. Wilson et al. evaluated pressure-based techniques in mobile settings (i.e., while people were walking) and found that there is hardly any difference to the performance while being seated [38]. *Fat Thumb* allows for similar input styles, except that it measures contact size instead of pressure (unlike *Glimpse* [6]), while still exploiting the user's mental model of simulated pressure.

Contact Shapes as Additional Information for Input

Capacitive and vision-based touch screens allow sensing of the contact's shape and size respectively [7,21]. Instead of only giving the contact point (calculated from the shape's center of mass), contact shapes allow for disambiguation of different hand parts touching the surface. In *Sphere*, menus can only be triggered with a finger, while placing the palm on a menu item does not affect it [2]. Moscovich uses contact size to allow for a subsequent selection of all targets that were covered by a finger [25]. *SimPress* uses small contact sizes to simulate a *hover* state and larger ones for selecting a target [2]. *ShapeTouch* discriminates coarse contact shapes of the finger *vs.* hand to change modes [4]; *Fat Thumb* also uses contact shape to change modes, but differs as it only relies on fine-grained variations in thumb's contact shape. Rogers et al.'s *AnglePose* further uses a conventional capacitive touch screen to track the finger's angle in 3D [32]. This work further focuses on using the thumb's pitch (much like *Fat Thumb*) for a variety of applications.

The contact shape and size can be used for input correction or to increase selection accuracy. In the aforementioned *MicroRolls*, the contact size gives information about the finger's angle [34]. Holz et al. present a refined model that considers the contact's change over time to differentiate moving from rolling the finger [15]. Wang et al. use the contact's shape to estimate the finger's rotation [37]. With the limitations of a capacitive touch screen on a consumer mobile device, *Fat Thumb* approximates these techniques.

DESIGNING FAT THUMB: CONTACT SIZE AS INPUT

Our overall goal is to allow for more expressiveness while only using the thumb as the input finger. As current UIs primarily track x,y positions of touch points, applications make use of buttons to switch modes which are usually located alongside the device's edges. However, this is costly: they use scarce screen space and they require more targeting and taps. Furthermore, Karlson et al. found that the device's center presents a "sweet spot", where the borders of the display are rather hard to reach and are not preferred by users [17]. Yet, permanently placing controls for mode switching at the screen's center is not an option, as they clutter the screen. For these reasons, we set out to add another input dimension – the thumb's contact size – to complement the x,y position *while* the thumb is in motion. That is, we wanted to exploit this third dimension for mode switching as one moves the thumb two-dimensionally on the display, giving different meanings to motion.

Pressure vs. thumb-tip angle. People can use two methods to alter contact size: pressure, and thumb-tip angle. First, people can adjust a finger's contact size by applying more or less pressure to the surface. The problem is that contact size only changes slightly on rigid surfaces (unlike on softer surfaces, such as used in *Liquid Displacement Sensing* [10]) leading to rather coarse and almost binary input values (see Figure 4). Vision-based systems can do better: because they operate with infrared light, they can use the contact point's brightness as an estimate of pressure: the brighter the blob, the more pressure applied. Likewise, a matrix of infrared emitters and detectors embedded directly behind the display provides similar information about the contact shape and size [14]. Yet most of today's mobile devices use a capacitive sensor matrix: this only allows sensing of the contact size (i.e., whether a pixel on the display is covered or not). This can be used to determine the outline of each contact point (e.g., [21]), but not the actual pressure of that touch.

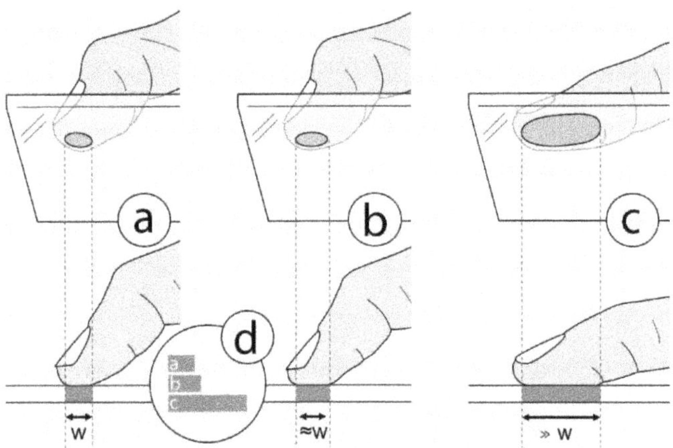

Figure 4. Compared to the original state (a), the contact size only slightly changes when using pressure (b), but changes significantly when pitching the thumb (c) on rigid surfaces. The callout shows the differences between all states (d).

Even if high accuracy pressure sensing becomes available on mobile devices, it has another fundamental drawback: applying more pressure increases the thumb tip's friction on the surface. As the thumb has to overcome resistance introduced by this friction, the force applied to move it might cause unwanted, coarse thumb movements, which affects movement accuracy. Thus, with this approach a user *either* performs regular two-dimensional input (with little or no pressure) *or* applies pressure. Although this would allow for switching modes in place, we decided against it, as it rules out mode switching while the thumb is in motion.

Instead of changing the contact size through pressure, people can also adjust it using the thumb-tip angle. Holz et al. identified the importance of all three angles (*roll*, *pitch*, and *yaw*) of the fingertip for precise touch input [16]. For our case, the thumb's orientation (*yaw*) likely does not affect the contact size itself. However, both the thumb's *pitch* and *roll* will change the contact size. Although implemented on a pixel-resistive touch screen, Roudaut et al.'s *MicroRolls* can make use of this effect. For instance, rolling the thumb to one side decreases its contact size. Likewise, the higher the finger's pitch, the lower its contact size gets (see Figure 4a, and c). For each of these strategies, friction only slightly increases and still allows for finger movement. Thus, this approach allows a combination of the two parameters (i.e., the thumb's x,y-coordinates plus the contact size).

APPLYING FAT THUMB TO PAN & ZOOM OPERATIONS

With contact size as additional dimension, we can integrate two (or more) modes into the same style of operation. As mentioned earlier, we chose zooming and panning a map – a common task on mobile devices – as our driving example. The usual method of *one finger move* (pan) and *two-finger pinch* (zoom) is awkward when the same hand also holds the device (see Figure 1). We mitigate this with the *Fat Thumb* approach, where we will show how both panning and zooming can be controlled through the thumb's motion with different contact sizes for each of the modes. The basic idea is that a person pans during a normal touch (small contact area) but rotates the thumb somewhat to zoom (large contact area).

Details and nuances of *Fat Thumb* pan and zoom are explained below. Because the range of contact sizes slightly varies among users (due to different thumb sizes), we use the following notation: *0* represents the smallest possible contact size, *1* the largest possible one, and fractions indicate sizes between these extremes. Both the smallest and largest possible contact size is obtained through a one-time calibration on a per-user basis.

Mapping Contact Sizes to Different Modes

The thumb's motion is naturally mapped to pan operations in an absolute and direct fashion. That is, whenever the thumb moves, the location it 'holds' underneath it moves with it accordingly. In contrast, when the mode is switched to *zoom*, the thumb's relative movement adjusts the level of zoom. That is, in this mode, moving the thumb in a certain direction (e.g., vertically up or down) zooms the map in or out with a zoom factor based on moved distance: the map does not move but only increases or decreases in size.

In both cases, the thumb's *contact size* determines the mode while the thumb's *movement* simultaneously performs the action associated to that mode. We assumed that it is slightly easier to move the thumb with a small contact size (i.e., only the tip touches the surface) as it (1) is the natural way we use mobile touch screens and (2) introduces slightly less thumb-tip friction. Also, we assumed that people use *panning* more frequently than *zooming*. For these reasons, we attribute smaller contact sizes (i.e., $size \leq 0.5$) to pan operations and larger ones (i.e., $size > 0.5$) to zoom interactions. Further investigation is needed to determine whether 0.5 is the best possible threshold for switching modes.

Panning. The thumb's movement while *panning* remains unchanged, which is compatible to how panning is performed in today's applications (see Figure 5a). However, we assume that because users are solely employing their thumb instead of their index finger (in two-handed scenarios), they will use multiple short strokes close to the center rather than longer ones from corner to corner. This is due to the thumb's limited operational range for movements.

Zooming. As zooming with a single touch point is not done in an absolute fashion, there needs to be a meaningful mapping between the relative thumb movements and resulting zoom factors. As discussed before, one of the best fits for thumb motion is rotating it around its CMC joint (see Figure 5b). The relative nature of *zooming* (with some constraints to the origin of interaction as discussed in the next section) allows for such movements. For the interaction, it means that the angular change around the CMC joint as rotation center between two contact locations determines the zoom factor (see Figure 5b).

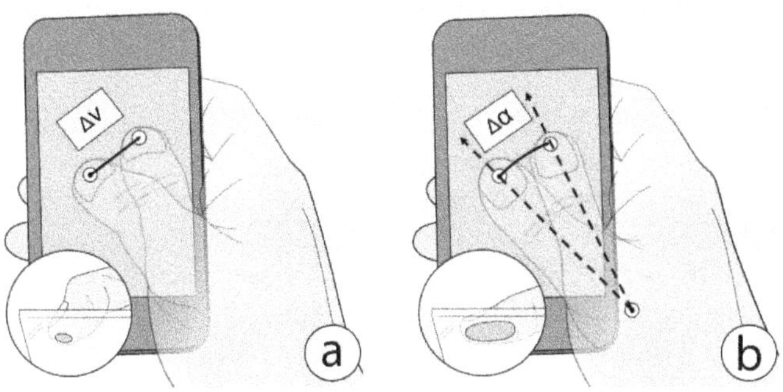

Figure 5. Mapping of thumb movements to panning (a) and zooming (b) a map.

Users can switch between these modes without lifting the finger off the display by altering the thumb tip's angle. That is, once the contact size changes from lower than 0.5 to greater then 0.5, the mode instantly changes. Thus, as described later, *Fat Thumb* allows seamlessly switching between the two modes to a certain extent.

Improvements: Zoom Center and Speed

Selecting the zoom center. The widely used, absolute two-finger *pinch* defines the zoom center (i.e., the location that remains fixed during a zoom operation) as the center point between the two touch points. With *Fat Thumb's* relative single touch point it remains unclear where the zoom origin should be located. One option is to use the center of the display as fixed point. Yet, this may be sub-optimal, as it may require subsequent panning to the actual desired region of interest. We can improve on this by taking the point where the mode changed to zoom (i.e., the first point with a contact size larger than 0.5) as the zoom origin for subsequent relative motions to zoom in or out. Although this only allows for coarsely selecting area of interest (i.e., it is still not pixel-exact), it likely reduces the amount of subsequent corrective pan (and potentially zoom) actions.

Zoom Speed. If the targeted region is much smaller (and larger respectively) than what is currently shown on the display, users may want to alter the magnification or demagnification factor of the zoom operation. With *linear* mapping, the thumb has to be moved by a large distance (potentially with several clutching operations) to accomplish this. Naturally, increasing the zoom factor (i.e., more change per angular change) allows for large changes with minor movements, but may lead to unwanted *overshooting effects*. As alternative, we decided to make use of the contact size again: until now, zoom occurs if the contact size is greater than 0.5 without considering the actual value. Instead, the actual value between 0.5 and 1 can be used to amplify the zoom speed. That is, more precise but slower zooming occurs when the contact size is close to 0.5. Faster and coarse zooming happens for contact sizes close to 1. Between these values, the amplification factor changes linearly.

IMPLEMENTATION

Fat Thumb (see Figure 6) runs on a standard Apple iPhone 4S (iOS version 5.1.1). The device's display has a resolution of 640 × 960 pixels and a diagonal of 3.5" (i.e., 329 dpi). Its 800 MHz dual-core A5 processor allows for smooth operations (60 touch points per second) even with larger, tiled map imagery. The iPhone's API only provides the major radius (and *not* the shape and orientation) in pixels of a contact point's ellipse, which is obtained as follows:

```
NSValue *val = [touch valueForKey:@"_pathMajorRadius"];
float size = [val floatValue]; // size in pixels
```

Conceptually, our application can be ported to other platforms as long as the touch screen of corresponding devices gives at least the contact size or (even better) its shape.

Adjusting the Sensed Touch Location

The iPhone's API reports touch events with their location corresponding to the contact area's center of gravity. For *Fat Thumb*, this has two major drawbacks: (1) especially when in zoom mode (i.e., covering a larger area with the thumb), the user's perceived touch location differs from the sensed location. And (2), altering the contact size by tilting the thumb leads to changes of the contact point's center. Previous vision-based systems allow for detecting the finger's contact size and orientation, allowing for a 'corrected' contact coordinate. Although the iPhone used for our prototype (unlike other devices) does not report the finger's orientation, the restricted position of the thumb allows for a reasonable approximation of the touch location as perceived by a user. Our prototype assumes that the contact point's ellipse is collinear with the thumb's orientation. Since the thumb roughly originates from the same position (unless the device is gripped differently), we can use the sensed location to estimate the thumb's orientation. To do so, we further need the (mostly fixed) location of the hand's CMC joint. With these two parameters, we can calculate the orientation vector and its angle.

With the orientation vector and sensed location, our prototype then calculates the point close to the finger's tip. In informal tests with several users, we found this rough approximation works reasonably well when the thumb is not heavily flexed (i.e., the tip is not close to the palm). Nevertheless, this correction fails (if the orientation is not natively reported by the sensing hardware) once users adjust the grip in a way that the CMC joint is repositioned significantly.

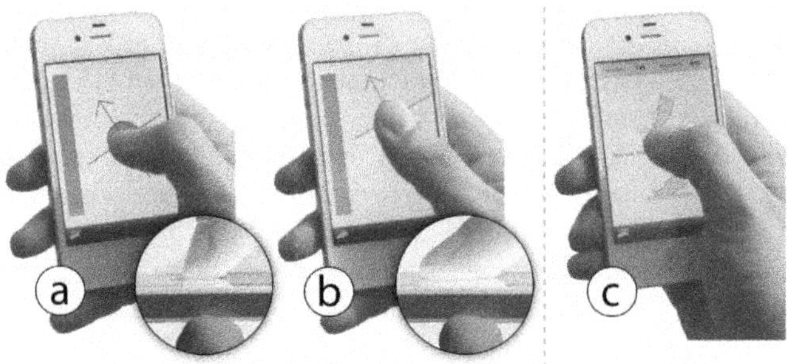

Figure 6. The *Fat Thumb* visualizer (a,b) and calibration screen (c). Callouts show the thumb's pitch angle.

One-time Setup and Calibration

At first launch, users perform a one-time calibration to measure the smallest and largest contact size (see Figure 6c). To do so, they place their thumb on the display and alter the thumb tip's angle while touching the display. This procedure requires only a few contact points, and takes less than a minute. To reduce errors, the implementation uses an interval that increases/decreases the lower/upper bound of the measured values by 2.5% (i.e., we used 95% of the interval to cut off noise). Users can verify their calibration with the Visualizer (see Figure 6a,b), and recalibrate if needed. Once satisfied, the values are stored in the device and they can start using *Fat Thumb*. The current implementation further requires users to specify in which hand they hold the device. While this should suffice in most cases, we acknowledge that detecting the hand holding the device (e.g., *HandSense* [39]) is a more elegant approach.

Limitations

Our implementation currently has two limitations: (1) the thumb's contact point (even with the aforementioned adjustment) will move a short distance during lift-off. That is, the map may (depending on the last sensed contact size) zoom or pan a bit. We currently circumvent this by ignoring the last three touch events (i.e., about 50 ms of the interaction for a touch rate of 60 Hz). And, (2) the thumb always has slightly varying contact sizes while in motion on the display (the differences increase when moved towards the screen's corners). However, *Fat Thumb* was specifically designed to work in the display's center; thus, avoiding the aforementioned case. If used in other scenarios, the *Fat Thumb* technique has to be adjusted.

EVALUATING SINGLE-HANDED PAN AND ZOOM

We conducted a user study to validate *Fat Thumb*. We were especially interested in how *Fat Thumb* compares to existing single-handed, single-touch approaches for controlling pan and zoom. The task was simple and familiar to users: given a predefined area of a map, participants had to use pan and zoom to fit and center it on the entire display.

Interface Conditions

Participants performed this task using four different interface conditions, each of which allows for panning and zooming content. In all conditions, panning was implemented as it is normally performed on touch screen devices.

- **Slider**: we added a slider on the right side of the screen (for left-handed use, the slider was displayed on the left side) that enabled for zooming in or out. The *Slider* did not offer absolute selection of zoom factors, as we were interested in thumb movements on the device. Although not commonplace on mobile multi-touch devices, it is the most known controls for zooming.
- **CycloStar**: this is a gesture-based technique [22]. Users had to perform a circular gesture to zoom in (clockwise) or out (counter-clockwise) around the center point of the drawn circle. Although not intended for thumb-use, we were interested in the limits of gesture-based interactions in single-handed scenarios. We chose *CycloStar* over Olwal et al.'s *Rubbing* [26] as pilot tests indicated that *Rubbing* less accurate and more fatiguing.
- **Tilt-to-Zoom**: this technique makes use of the built-in accelerometers [12]. To map tilting operations to changes in zoom factor, we used the same transfer function and parameters as described by Hinckley et al. [11].
- **Fat Thumb**: we implemented this condition as described before (including its improvements).

We did not include the iPhone's built-in pan/zoom methods for the following two reasons: first, its elaborate pinch gesture usually requires two hands; while possible with one hand by using the thumb and index finger, it requires an awkward hand posture. And second, the iPhone's single-handed zoom feature (i.e., double-tap to increase the zoom factor by a fixed amount) implements zooming in a discrete fashion instead of a continuous one. It further requires a tap with two fingers to zoom out, introducing problems similar to those found in the pinch gesture.

Task

Participants were presented with a series of individual area alignment tasks. We used three different area sizes (each of them mirrored the aspect ratio of the display to allow for perfect alignment) located diagonally from the center with constant distance. We avoided search times by making targets at least partially visible on screen, i.e., where they at least intersect with the display's boundaries. We also did not use different distances as panning is performed equally in all techniques, thus adding constant time to each task. We asked participants to bring the area into the display's center as quickly and accurately as possible.

Before starting a trial, participants saw the semi-transparent red target area (to minimize the time required for visual search during the task), as well as a *start button*. When participants pressed the *start button*, the button disappeared and timing began. They had to center and fit the red target area into the display's boundaries, which required a series of pan and zoom operations with the given technique. The error was given in offset, which describes the difference in both the display's total area and the target area (i.e., an offset of 0% indicates that they fit perfectly). The offset was displayed at the bottom of the screen and updated frequently so that participants were aware of the current offset at all times. When a participant was satisfied with the alignment (and the offset value shown respectively), they performed a double-tap to end the trial. Timing was stopped after a successful alignment. Subsequently, the map was reset and the start button displayed and the process would repeat for the next trial. Overall, we recorded task time, target offset, and the number of strokes used during a trial. We also recorded all finger movements (i.e., every touch point with its contact size) as well as the target offset over time.

Study Design

We used a repeated measures within-subjects factorial design. Independent variables were *Technique* (*Slider*, *CycloStar*, *Tilt-to-Zoom*, and *Fat Thumb*), target area *Direction* (*NE*, *NW*, *SW*, and *SE*), and target area *Size* (*Small*, *Medium*, and *Large*). Targets had a fixed distance from the mobile display's center in each direction.

Technique was counter-balanced across our participants. We created pairs of each the four *Directions* and the three *Sizes*. These were presented in random order within each block. For each *Technique*, we had one practice and four timed blocks in the experiment. After completing one *Technique*, participants were asked to fill out a standard device assessment questionnaire. After the study, we asked them to rank the four *Techniques*. Each participant completed the study in 120 minutes or less, a time that included training of all techniques at the beginning of the study.

Apparatus

We conducted the experiment on an Apple iPhone 4S, and its standard 1.94" × 2.91" (640 × 960 pixel) retina display with 329 dpi. All techniques functioned as previously described. The map had 24 image tiles (4 rows, 6 columns); each tile was 2048 × 2048 pixels to increase iPhone performance (larger images significantly slow down this device). Since the map did not have the same aspect ratio (to force pan operations), it was scaled down so that it had the same height as the display, but was still wider. The resulting scale factor was about 0.12. The target sizes were (fully zoomed out): *Small* (75 × 112.5 pixels; 0.23" × 0.34"), *Medium* (150 × 225 pixels; 0.46" × 0.68"), and *Large* (225 × 337.5 pixels; 0.68" × 1.03"). Their center was horizontally and vertically located 293 (0.89") and 257.8 (0.78") pixels away from the display's center, regardless of their size.

To mimic a realistic scenario of panning and zooming a map while 'on-the-go', participants were not allowed to use their second hand at any time during the experiment, nor were they allowed to rest their forearm on any surface during a trial. However, they were seated and could take breaks in between trials if fatigued.

Participants

We recruited 16 participants (10 female) ranging in age from 19 to 32 years (avg.: 23.8 years). 8 of them had corrected vision, and three were left-handed. 14 own a mobile phone, and 15 were familiar with using touch-based mobile devices (median = 4, 5-point Likert scale where 5 equals highly experienced) and had used a mapping application before. They received $15 as compensation for their time.

Hypotheses

Based on our understanding of single-handed thumb use on mobile devices we hypothesized the following: (H1) for *Small* targets, *Fat Thumb* outperforms all other techniques in terms of offset. (H2) *Fat Thumb* outperforms the other techniques in terms of task time with comparable offsets for *Small* areas. (H3) *Fat Thumb* and *Tilt-to-Zoom* require the least amount of strokes for *Small* and *Medium* targets due to their clutch-free nature. (H4) *Fat Thumb* is the most preferred technique (particularly with respect to fatigue) as it is designed for the thumb's limited operational range.

RESULTS

We compared task completion time, target area offset, and the number of strokes used per trial with a separate repeated measures within-subjects analyses of variance (ANOVA). For pair-wise post hoc tests, we used Bonferroni-corrected confidence intervals to compare against $\alpha = 0.05$. In cases where the assumption of sphericity was violated, we corrected the degrees of freedom using Greenhouse-Geisser. All unstated *p*-values are $p > 0.05$.

We first performed a 4 × 4 (*Technique* × *Block*) within-subjects ANOVA and found significant main effects for *Block* and *Technique* regarding task time (all $p < 0.003$), but not offset and number of strokes. Post hoc multiple means comparison tests showed that *Block 1* differed significantly from *Blocks 2–4* (all $p < 0.017$). Thus, we excluded *Block 1* from subsequent analyses and aggregated the remaining *Blocks*. To verify that we can also aggregate across *Location*, we performed a 4 × 4 (*Technique* × *Location*) within subject ANOVA and found no main effects or interactions.

Offsets

With the aggregated offsets we performed a 4 × 3 (*Technique* × *Size*) within subjects analysis of variance. We found significant main effects for *Technique* ($F_{1.913,28.691} = 31.723$, $p < 0.001$). There was, however, no significant main effect for *Size*, or an interaction between *Technique* and *Size*. With post hoc multiple means comparisons we found that *Fat Thumb* was more accurate than *Slider* for *Small* and *Medium Sizes* (all $p < 0.022$). Also, *Fat Thumb* was more accurate – for all *Sizes* – than *Tilt-to-Zoom* (all $p < 0.042$), and *CycloStar* (all $p < 0.001$). This supports H1.

Figure 7 shows the offsets per *Technique* and *Size*. Most interestingly, the offset for each *Technique* is higher when *Size* increases. We attribute this to users rapidly overshooting the target as most techniques are designed for rapid

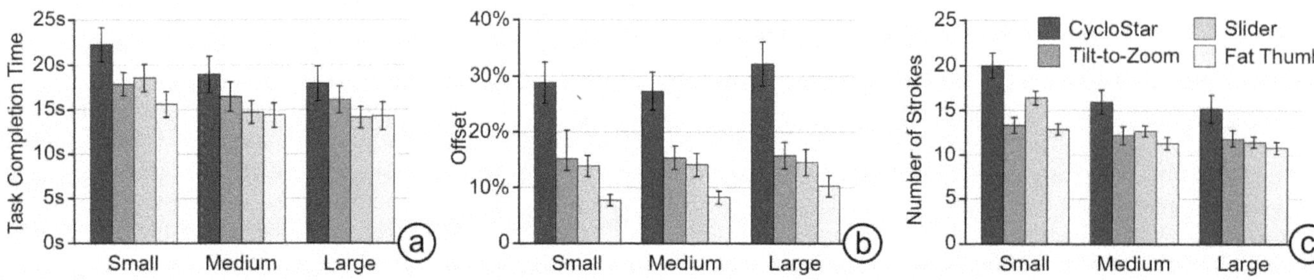

Figure 7. Task completion time (a), offset (b), and number of strokes (c) clustered by *Size* (error bars: 95% confidence interval).

zooming. The figure also reveals that *CycloStar* had the highest offset, which we believe has two reasons: (1) as expected, the technique is hard to perform using the thumb. And, (2) the technique caused user frustration, ending trials once an acceptable alignment was achieved. Overall, *Fat Thumb* had the least offset (M = 8.8%, SD = 1.5%), followed by *Slider* (M = 14.2%, SD = 2.5%), *Tilt-to-Zoom* (M = 15.4%, SD = 2.6%), and *CycloStar* (M = 29.4%, SD = 4.2%). However, one may argue that offsets of up to 15% may be acceptable depending on the task, which then only renders *CycloStar* as insufficient technique.

Task Completion Time

We measured task time from the moment the start button was pressed until participants double-tapped the target. We performed a 4 × 3 (*Technique* × *Size*) within subjects ANOVA and found significant main effects for *Technique* ($F_{3,45}$ = 4.133, $p < 0.011$), *Size* ($F_{2,30}$ = 37.744, $p < 0.001$), and a *Technique* × *Size* interaction ($F_{6,90}$ = 2.755, $p < 0.017$).

Figure 7 illustrates how task completion times increased with decreasing target area size for *CycloStar*. For the other techniques, the task time barely changes for *Large* and *Medium* sized targets, but changes for *Small* ones. This behavior may be explained with overshooting effects for targets that need high zoom factor adjustment. To discover the nature of the *Technique* × *Size* interaction, we ran separate ANOVA tests for each *Size* level. For *Large* areas, we found that there is no significant difference across techniques. For *Medium* areas, we found that *Slider* and *Fat Thumb* differ significantly from *CycloStar* (all $p < 0.04$). For *Small* areas, *Fat Thumb* differs significantly from *CycloStar* ($p < 0.02$). However, *Fat Thumb* does not show any significant difference regarding task completion time compared to *Slider* or *Tilt-to-Zoom* (thus, we reject H2). Nevertheless, there is a trend that it does not increase task time if targets get smaller while maintaining low offsets.

Overall, *Fat Thumb* was the fastest (M = 14.78s, SD = 1.94s), followed by *Slider* (M = 15.79s, SD = 1.74s), and *Tilt-to-Zoom* (M = 16.77s, SD = 1.81s). *CycloStar* was the slowest among all techniques (M = 19.68s, SD = 2.17s).

Number of Strokes

For each technique, we analyzed the number of strokes (i.e., one stroke begins with the finger being placed down and ends when it is released) that participants needed to complete a trial. We performed a 4 × 3 (*Technique* × *Size*) within subjects ANOVA and found significant main effects for *Technique* ($F_{2.015,30.228}$ = 14.002, $p < 0.001$) and *Size* ($F_{2,30}$ = 114.848, $p < 0.001$). We further found a *Technique* × *Size* interaction ($F_{6,90}$ = 14.571, $p < 0.001$).

Figure 7 suggests that the number of strokes is related to task completion time, thus leading to similar results. We separately analyzed each *Size* level and found significant main effects for each level ($p < 0.001$). For *Small* target areas, *Fat Thumb* and *Tilt-to-Zoom* significantly differ from the other techniques (all $p < 0.028$), with *Fat Thumb* presumably having fewer strokes. This supports H3. For *Medium* sized targets, *Fat Thumb* also differs significantly from *CycloStar* and *Slider* (all $p < 0.005$). *Tilt-to-Zoom*, however, only differs significantly from *CycloStar* ($p < 0.002$). Unsurprisingly, for *Large* targets, Figure 7 indicates that all but *CycloStar* have comparable number of strokes. However, only *Fat Thumb* differs significantly ($p < 0.023$).

Overall, *Fat Thumb* required the least strokes (M = 11.67, SD = 0.81), followed by *Tilt-to-Zoom* (M = 12.46, SD = 1.23), and *Slider* (M = 13.51, SD = 0.75). The most strokes were needed for *CycloStar* (M = 17.01, SD = 1.54).

Subjective Preferences

After each *Technique*, participants filled a questionnaire to assess the particular input technique. *Fat Thumb* scored consistently well across all categories on a five-point Likert scale. Most importantly, both *Fat Thumb* and *Tilt-to-Zoom* only caused little fatigue for fingers (median = 2), while *Slider* (median = 4), and *CycloStar* caused high fatigue for fingers (median = 4.5). Also, *Fat Thumb* ranked better for wrist fatigue (median = 2) than *Slider* and *Tilt-to-Zoom* (both median = 3) and *CycloStar* (median = 4). Furthermore, *Fat Thumb* was ranked the easiest to use (median = 4), followed by *Slider* (median = 3.5), *Tilt-to-Zoom* (median = 3), and *CycloStar* (median = 1). Consistently with these results, *Fat Thumb* had the highest general comfort (median = 4), followed by *Slider* and *Tilt-to-Zoom* (median = 3), and both *CycloStar* (median = 1.5).

After they completed the study, participants ranked the four *Techniques* by preference: We found a significant difference in ranks ($\chi^2(3) = 29.325$, $p < 0.001$). Post hoc analysis with Wilcoxon Signed-Rank Tests further revealed significant differences for all pairs (all $p < 0.038$) except *Slider* and *Tilt-to-Zoom*. Overall, they ranked *Fat Thumb* highest (11), followed by *Slider* (4), *Tilt-to-Zoom* (1), and *CycloStar* (0), which proves our hypothesis H4.

DISCUSSION

Our study results support all but one of our hypotheses. *Fat Thumb* proved to be more accurate for *Small* targets than the other techniques (H1). In Figure 7, one can observe that *Fat Thumb's* task time and offset also does not increase much when target areas get smaller. Our results also showed that both *Fat Thumb* and *Tilt-to-Zoom* had the least number of strokes as expected (H3). As with offset and task time, for smaller target sizes, the number of strokes only slightly increases. However, further testing with a larger range of target sizes is needed to confirm this trend.

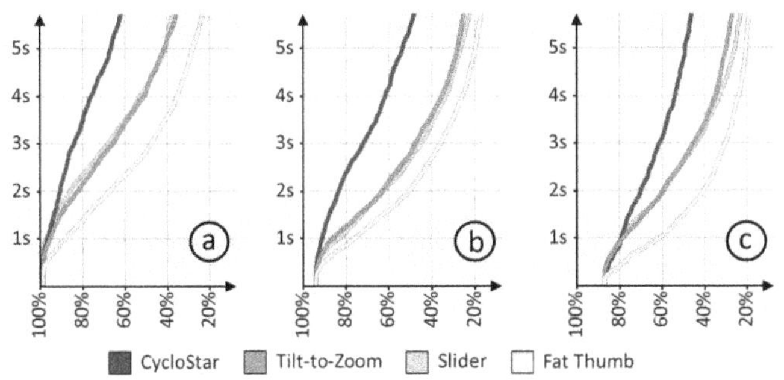

Figure 8. Progress of offset over time (first 5 seconds) for *Small* (a), *Medium* (b), and *Large* areas (c).

Surprisingly, however, the task time of *Fat thumb* did not show a significant difference to all other techniques for *Small* targets as hypothesized (H2): We assumed that one of the reasons was that participants tried to be highly precise – leading to high task times for all techniques. We plotted the progression of aggregated offsets over time to identify how much time of the overall task participants spent on fine-grained adjustments. As shown in Figure 8, *Fat Thumb* was the technique that approached the final offset faster than the other techniques. For example, *Fat Thumb* reaches 20% offset of *Medium* targets about two seconds faster than *Tilt-to-Zoom* and *Slider* We believe that this offset already is sufficient in our scenario, but acknowledge that other use-cases could potentially be harmed by this offset rate.

The gesture-based *CycloStar* approach proved poor for one-handed use. We believe that this is due to the thumb's limited operational range and not due to the original idea. *CycloStar* was designed for use with the index finger while the other hand holds the device, and in those cases it may fare well. The subjective ratings of our participants support this as *CycloStar* had the highest fatigue for wrist and finger. To understand these ratings, we analyzed the strokes performed on the device. In particular, we identified the areas participants used during the study and compared them against findings regarding 'good' and 'bad' areas on a PDA-sized touch device as identified in the literature [17]. As shown in Figure 9, *Fat Thumb* and *Tilt-to-Zoom* unsurprisingly used the center of the device. However, *CycloStar* almost used the entire touch screen. We assume that these reasons (i.e., large area of use, and fast movements) were the main sources for (1) low comfort and low ease-of-use, as well as (2) high fatigue. Thus, we suggest that *CycloStar* is not well suited for single-handed mobile touch-based interaction.

For task time and number of strokes, both *Fat Thumb* and *Tilt-to-Zoom* performed equally. However, *Tilt-to-Zoom* had lower subjective ratings regarding wrist and finger fatigue as well as the general comfort (H4). In addition, participants stated that tilting the display decreased the visibility during the task, which explains the higher offset of *Tilt-to-Zoom*. *Slider* had comparable results for *Large* targets, but permanently requires costly screen space. Also, its subjective ratings were consistently lower than *Fat Thumb*'s ratings. We assume that the necessity of reaching the side of the device introduced by the *Slider* lead to this effect.

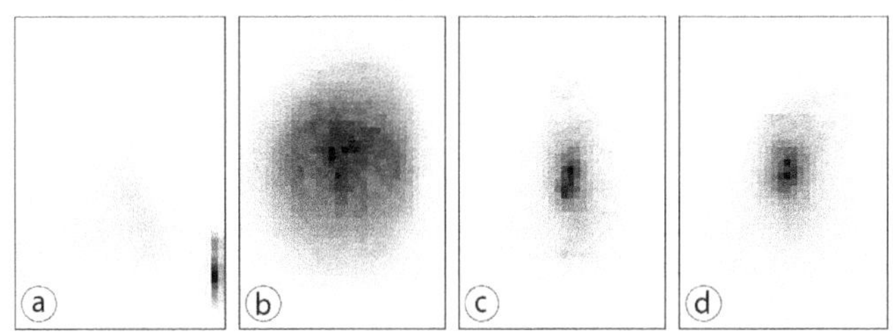

Figure 9. Heatmaps of touch points: *Slider* (a), *CycloStar* (b), *Tilt-to-Zoom* (c), and *Fat Thumb* (d).

One potential drawback of *Fat Thumb* is slightly higher occlusion introduced by larger contact sizes. While this may turn into a problem in selecting small targets, it does not interfere with our pan/zoom scenario. As well, *Fat Thumb* and its mapping could be implemented on a back-of-the-device touch pad (see [1]), eliminating occlusion.

CONCLUSIONS AND FUTURE WORK

We presented *Fat Thumb*, an alternative technique that adds a dimension to touch input on a mobile device, thus giving different meanings to touch motion. We do this by making use of the thumb's contact size to allow for seamless mode switching. We demonstrated the technique by integrating panning and zooming into a single operation where the contact size determines the mode while moving the thumb performs it. Our user study of panning/zooming revealed that *Fat Thumb* is at least as fast as other existing techniques, non-fatiguing, and the preferred technique, all while having the lowest offset rates for smaller target areas of all techniques. Together with *Tilt-to-Zoom*, *Fat Thumb* required the least number of strokes, in part because participants could switch between modes without lifting their finger.

While our study applied *Fat Thumb* to panning and zooming operations, we believe that *Fat Thumb* can be used for a variety of tasks. To explore this, we will investigate how many different contact size levels can actually be perceived and used by people, as studied with pressure levels [30]. Based on this, we will identify other single-handed mobile interactions made possible through *Fat Thumb*.

ACKNOWLEDGMENTS

This research is partially funded by the iCORE/NSERC/SMART Chair in Interactive Technologies, Alberta Innovates Technology Futures, NSERS, and SMART Technologies Inc. The authors thank Matthew Dunlap, Marian Dörk, and Uta Hinrichs for their valuable feedback.

REFERENCES

1. Baudisch, P. and Chu, G. Back-of-device interaction allows creating very small touch devices. *Proc. CHI*, ACM (2009).
2. Benko, H., Wilson, A.D., and Baudisch, P. Precise selection techniques for multi-touch screens. *Proc. CHI*, ACM (2006).
3. Brewster, S.A. and Hughes, M. Pressure-based text entry for mobile devices. *Proc. MobileHCI*, ACM (2009).
4. Cao, X., Wilson, A., Balakrishnan, R., Hinckley, K., and Hudson, S. ShapeTouch: Leveraging Contact Shape on Interactive Surfaces. *Proc. TABLETOP*, IEEE (2008).
5. Clarkson, E.C., Patel, S., Pierce, J., and Abowd, G.D. Exploring Continuous Pressure Input for Mobile Phones. *GVU Techreport; GIT-GVU-06-20*, Georgia Inst. of Tech. (2006).
6. Forlines, C., Shen, C., and Buxton, B. Glimpse: a novel input model for multi-level devices. *Proc. CHI EA*, ACM (2005).
7. Han, J.Y. Low-cost multi-touch sensing through frustrated total internal reflection. *Proc. UIST*, ACM (2005).
8. Harrison, C., Schwarz, J., and Hudson, S.E. TapSense: enhancing finger interaction on touch surfaces. *Proc. UIST*, ACM (2011), 627–636.
9. Henze, N., Rukzio, E., and Boll, S. 100,000,000 Taps: Analysis and Improvement of Touch Performance in the Large. *Proc. MobileHCI*, ACM (2011).
10. Hilliges, O., Kim, D., and Izadi, S. Creating malleable interactive surfaces using liquid displacement sensing. *Proc. TABLETOP*, IEEE (2008), 157–160.
11. Hinckley, K., Pierce, J., Sinclair, M., and Horvitz, E. Sensing techniques for mobile interaction. *Proc. UIST*, ACM (2000).
12. Hinckley, K. and Song, H. Sensor synaesthesia: touch in motion, and motion in touch. *Proc. CHI*, ACM (2011).
13. Hirotaka, N. Reassessing current cell phone designs. *Proc. CHI*, ACM (2003), 938–939.
14. Hodges, S., Izadi, S., Butler, A., Rrustemi, A., and Buxton, B. ThinSight: versatile multi-touch sensing for thin form-factor displays. *Proc. UIST*, ACM (2007), 259–268.
15. Holz, C. and Baudisch, P. The generalized perceived input point model and how to double touch accuracy by extracting fingerprints. *Proc. CHI*, ACM (2010), 581–590.
16. Holz, C. and Baudisch, P. Understanding touch. *Proc. CHI*, ACM (2011), 2501–2510.
17. Karlson, A.K., Bederson, B.B., and Contreras-Vidal, J.L. Studies in One-Handed Mobile Design: Habit, Desire and Agility. *Tech report HCIL-2006-02*, Comp. Sci. Dept, University of Maryland, MD (2006).
18. Karlson, A.K., Bederson, B.B., and SanGiovanni, J. AppLens and launchTile: two designs for one-handed thumb use on small devices. *Proc. CHI*, ACM (2005), 201–210.
19. Karlson, A.K. and Bederson, B.B. ThumbSpace: Generalized One-Handed Input for Touchscreen-Based Mobile Devices. *Proc. INTERACT*, Springer, 324–338.
20. Kuo, L.-C., Cooney, W.P., Chen, Q.-S., Kaufman, K.R., Su, F.-C., and An, K.-N. A kinematic method to calculate the workspace of the trapeziometacarpal joint. *Mechanical Engineers Journal of Engineering in Medicine 218*, 2 (2004).
21. Lee, S., Buxton, W., and Smith, K.C. A multi-touch three dimensional touch-sensitive tablet. *Proc. CHI*, ACM (1985).
22. Malacria, S., Lecolinet, E., and Guiard, Y. Clutch-free panning and integrated pan-zoom control on touch-sensitive surfaces. *Proc. CHI*, ACM (2010), 2615–2624.
23. McCallum, D.C., Mak, E., Irani, P., and Subramanian, S. PressureText: pressure input for mobile phone text entry. *Proc. CHI*, ACM (2009), 4519–4524.
24. Miyaki, T. and Rekimoto, J. GraspZoom: zooming and scrolling control model for single-handed mobile interaction. *Proc. MobileHCI*, ACM (2009).
25. Moscovich, T. and Hughes, J.F. Navigating documents with the virtual scroll ring. *Proc. UIST*, ACM (2004), 57–60.
26. Olwal, A., Feiner, S., and Heyman, S. Rubbing and tapping for precise and rapid selection on touch-screen displays. *Proc. CHI*, ACM (2008), 295–304.
27. Parhi, P., Karlson, A.K., and Bederson, B.B. Target size study for one-handed thumb use on small touchscreen devices. *Proc. MobileHCI*, ACM (2006), 203–210.
28. Pascoe, J., Ryan, N., and Morse, D. Using while moving: HCI issues in fieldwork environments. *ACM ToCHI 7*, (2000), 417–437.
29. Perry, K.B. and Hourcade, J.P. Evaluating one handed thumb tapping on mobile touchscreen devices. *Proceedings GI*, Canadian Information Processing Society (2008), 57–64.
30. Ramos, G., Boulos, M., and Balakrishnan, R. Pressure widgets. *Proc. CHI*, ACM (2004), 487–494.
31. Robbins, D.C., Cutrell, E., Sarin, R., and Horvitz, E. ZoneZoom: map navigation for smartphones with recursive view segmentation. *Proc. AVI*, ACM (2004), 231 – 234.
32. Rogers, S., Williamson, J., Stewart, C., and Murray-Smith, R. AnglePose: robust, precise capacitive touch tracking via 3d orientation estimation. *Proc. CHI*, ACM (2011), 2575–2584.
33. Roudaut, A., Huot, S., and Lecolinet, E. TapTap and MagStick: improving one-handed target acquisition on small touch-screens. *Proc. AVI*, ACM (2008), 146–153.
34. Roudaut, A., Lecolinet, E., and Guiard, Y. MicroRolls: expanding touch-screen input vocabulary by distinguishing rolls vs. slides of the thumb. *Proc. CHI*, ACM (2009).
35. Shi, K., Irani, P., Gustafson, S., and Subramanian, S. PressureFish: a method to improve control of discrete pressure-based input. *Proc. CHI*, ACM (2008), 1295–1298.
36. Stewart, C., Rohs, M., Kratz, S., and Essl, G. Characteristics of pressure-based input for mobile devices. *Proc. CHI*, ACM (2010), 801–810.
37. Wang, F., Cao, X., Ren, X., and Irani, P. Detecting and leveraging finger orientation for interaction with direct-touch surfaces. *Proc. UIST '09*, ACM (2009), 23–32.
38. Wilson, G., Stewart, C., and Brewster, S.A. Pressure-based menu selection for mobile devices. *Proc. MobileHCI*, ACM (2010), 181–190.
39. Wimmer, R. and Boring, S. HandSense: discriminating different ways of grasping and holding a tangible user interface. *Proc. TEI*, ACM (2009), 359–362.
40. Wu, M. and Balakrishnan, R. Multi-finger and whole hand gestural interaction techniques for multi-user tabletop displays. *Proc. UIST*, ACM (2003), 193–202.

The Hold-and-Move Gesture for Multi-touch Interfaces

Alexander Kulik **Jan Dittrich** **Bernd Froehlich**

Bauhaus-Universität Weimar
Bauhausstrasse 11, 99423 Weimar, Germany
<first name>.<last name>@uni-weimar.de

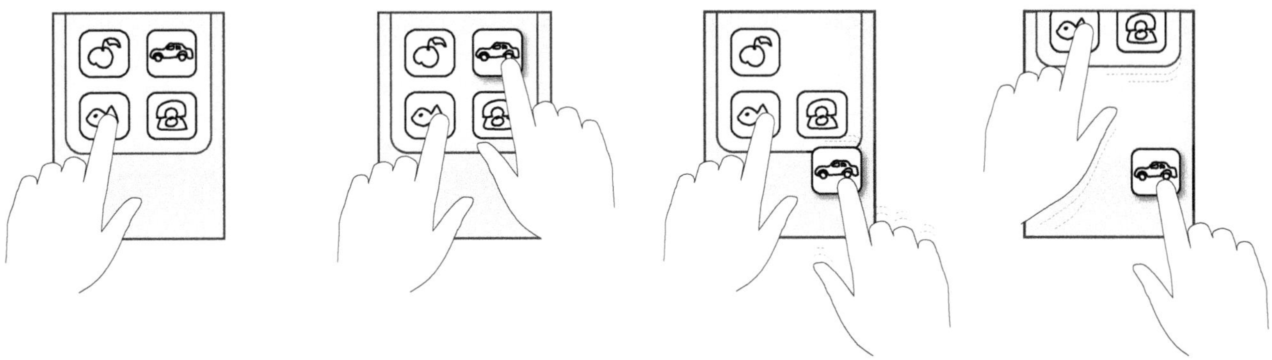

Figure 1. The *hold-and-move* gesture. (a) The first contact point (here a finger of the left hand) is always associated with the background. (b) The second contact point (here a finger of the right hand) selects an item. (c) The item can now be moved in relation to the background that is held with the left hand. (d) The left hand may perform panning of the background and even clutching while the right hand holds on to the selected item.

ABSTRACT

We present the two-finger gesture hold-and-move as an alternative to the disruptive long-tap which utilizes dwell times for switching from panning to object dragging mode in touch interfaces. We make use of a second finger for object selection and manipulation while workspace panning is operated with the first finger. Since both operations can be performed simultaneously, the cumbersome and hard-to-control autoscrolling function is no longer needed when dragging an object beyond the currently visible viewport. Single-finger panning and pinch zooming still work as expected. A user study revealed that hold-and-move enables faster object dragging than the conventional dwell-time approach and that it is preferred by most users.

Author Keywords

Multi-touch; dwell times; navigation; manipulation; hold-and-move.

ACM Classification Keywords

H.5.2. Information Interfaces and Presentation: Input devices and strategies; Interaction styles.

INTRODUCTION

Mode switching based on dwell times is widely used with mobile touch devices. It generally toggles between reference frames for motion input, e.g. panning or scrolling the entire interaction space vs. dragging individual items. Motion input from a single finger is primarily used for moving the entire screen content. Dragging individual items requires that they are first selected by a long tap based on a predefined dwell time. This can be very annoying. Dwell times often take too long if the user wants to switch to the respective mode and they may also occur accidentally.

We developed the hold-and-move interaction technique (Figure 1), which uses an implicit input differentiation based on Guiard's "left-hand precedence in action" principle [8]. Hold-and-move associates the first contact point with the background and thus motion input from a single finger always controls panning. In order to manipulate individual items, the background must be held with the first finger. A second finger may then select an individual item and move it in relation to the background. In addition, the first finger may perform panning of the background and clutching while the second finger holds on to the selected item. The manipulative gesture consistently ties the fingers to the graphics displayed under the contact point, which enforces the physicality of the interface.

The development of the hold-and-move pattern was motivated by an exploratory study on the timing of common multi-touch input actions. We observed that dwell times between a touch event and the actual motion onset are an intrinsic characteristic of touch-based input and that their duration depends heavily on the activity. On average we recorded 130 ms dwell time during object dragging tasks if the functionality is directly available (without the requirement of an initial long tap). A regular long tap with a typical duration of 500 ms is therefore an interruption of the natural interaction flow. Simply reducing this threshold, however, is rarely feasible as it would increase the chance of false positives during navigation tasks.

The analysis of the pinch-zoom gesture confirmed the symmetric nature of this input action. Both fingers are placed down almost simultaneously with only 55 ms time difference on average. Hence, we designed the hold-and-move gesture as a complementary asymmetric two-finger gesture. It can be distinguished from symmetric input based on the time difference between both touch events. We found three main advantages of this approach:

- The disruptive long tap can be avoided.
- The asymmetric gesture is compatible with established one-finger gestures and can be clearly distinguished from symmetric two-finger input like pinch zooming.
- Manipulation and navigation can be operated simultaneously.

Mode switching based on dwell times provokes interferences between the two input modalities, e.g., object dragging and panning. Hold-and-move avoids this. The asymmetric two-finger gesture may instead interfere with other two-finger input, e.g., pinch zooming. Our studies indicate that this rarely happens as the pinch-zoom gesture is generally initiated symmetrically. A comparative user study revealed that hold-and-move can be more efficient than the dwell-time approach and that it is preferred by most users. We further analyzed the timing structure of the hold-and-move pattern and derive guidelines for its implementation.

RELATED WORK

Guiard's analysis [8] on asymmetric bi-manual activity inspired the design of many highly effective human computer interfaces (e.g. [5, 3, 11, 6]). Unlike our approach, asymmetric bi-manual interaction techniques generally require the explicit identification of input from the user's dominant and non-dominant hand. Towards this end, several researchers recently proposed to operate tasks of the non-dominant hand with direct touch input while the dominant hand performs more accurate operations with a pen device [21, 4, 10].

Other approaches to increase the expressiveness of direct motion input build on explicit mode switching [13, 15], distinct hand shapes [7] or various motion gestures [20, 16, 18, 17]. Li et al. [13] compared different mode switching techniques for pen-operated interfaces: dwell times, pressing the pen's barrel button, pressure and mode switching with additional input from the non-dominant hand. Dwell times showed the worst performance whereas the best results were achieved with bi-manual input. This observation clearly supports our approach to circumvent dwell times by exploiting the additionally available information of multi-touch devices.

Lank et al. [12] also analyzed mode switching with the non-dominant hand for pen input. They were focusing their research on the initiation pattern and found that the mode switching action triggered by the non-dominant hand generally precedes the dominant hand's action. Following the principles of naïve physics, Siio et al. suggested to use the palm of the pen-operating hand to fixate a virtual background for inking as if it were paper to write on [19].

Lü et al. [14] introduced a drawing-based selection technique for small targets on mobile touch devices. They note that drawing requires a mode change in most applications and suggest to hold the background with one finger before drawing with another one. While this idea is similar to our hold-and-move technique, it is also more constrained to serve only this particular application. The implementation details and the usability aspects of such a bi-manual mode switching technique are not addressed in their publication. In that sense, our work is complementary to theirs. We contribute an analysis of the timing parameters to distinguish hold-and-move from other two-point motion input, describe its general applicability and verify its usability benefits in a formal study.

THE TIMING OF TOUCH GESTURES

We were interested in the timing of common input actions on touch-screen devices. In particular, we analyzed unconscious dwell times in common panning and object-dragging tasks and also the time difference between both touch events initiating a pinch-zoom gesture. We expected that dwell times between a touch event and the respective motion onset would occur naturally, both in panning and dragging tasks. In case of occurrence, we were also measuring its duration to derive an optimal dwell time for mode switching. For the symmetric pinch-zoom actions requiring two instead of only a single contact point, we also expected intrinsic timing characteristics that would allow a clear distinction from other two point touch gestures.

Experimental Setup

We asked ten students from our campus to perform a series of dragging, panning and zooming tasks using a mobile touch device (Apple iPod® touch 2). All participants but one stated to have only marginal previous experience with touchscreen interfaces. With detailed instructions and preparatory training we ensured that our test users were fluently operating the device during the data gathering. The purpose of the study was not explained to the participants.

Mobile devices are operated in different situations. On account of this we involved two *support* conditions in our experiments. All participants performed the tests while seated, half of the tests with the device held in their non-dominant hand (Figure 2 a, c, d) and the other half with only the dominant hand involved and the device fixed to the table surface (Figure 2 b).

For every touch input we recorded the time of the contact event and the corresponding motion onset. The latter was defined as a deviation from the contact position larger than 1.7 mm (11 px). In informal tests this position threshold was found to eliminate involuntary motion input while maintaining the responsiveness of the interface. Dwell times were measured as the time difference between these two events.

For zooming gestures we computed the time difference between the contact events of both fingers. In the following we explain the experimental tasks and the involved variables in detail.

Dragging

Dragging an on-screen object always involves selecting it at its current position and moving it to the desired target position. We expected a short dwell time between these subsequent actions as both are aimed movements that require a certain amount of planning.

The *dragging* experiment consisted of a docking task that was designed in correspondence to the main menus of many touch-based mobile devices. A grid of gray squares was displayed with white outlines on a black background. One of these items was highlighted with a green fill color designating it as the object to be dragged. Another one or two squares with white fill color marked the docking targets (Figure 2a).

We randomized the number of target options (one or two) and also varied the grid size (6x6 or 4x4 items) as such variations may affect the duration of dwell times. Each participant performed 120 docking tasks in four consecutive blocks, with short breaks of about one minute in between. If an item had been released outside the target area, it jumped back to its original position. The task had to be repeated in this case, which resulted in additional dragging actions for our records.

Panning

Depending on the users' intentions, panning a large map or scrolling a page may expose different timing structures. If a user is searching for a salient target or if the target distance is known, the motion behavior corresponds to aimed movement in pointing tasks [9]. On mobile devices this type of scrolling task is generally accomplished with a series of rapid strokes (flicks).

If users are scanning the displayed graphics or reading a text instead, panning operations are rather slow and continuous [1]. We expected that this difference between panning operations would also affect dwell times. Thus, we designed two panning tasks, both of which consisted of vertically scrolling a text on the display.

In the *Search* condition we instructed the users to scroll down until they recognized a text passage highlighted with a blue rectangle on a light gray background. The marker was set to 3 cm in width and 1.5 cm in height, thus easily recognizable even if the screen content was moving rapidly (Figure 2b).

The *Read* condition on the other hand consisted of reading a short text of about 200 words (Figure 2c). Thereafter some related questions were asked in order to motivate the users to read the article thoroughly instead of only skimming it.

Panning inertia as provided by the operating system was enabled during all tests. The line height was always set to 7 mm on the screen, such that 13 lines were be visible at once. The tasks were not repeated but they required a series of panning actions for completion. In the *search* condition, the target was 120 lines away from the initially visible workspace area, in the *read* condition the text stretched over 51 lines.

Zooming

Currently, zooming is the most relevant gesture on mobile devices that involves more than one contact point. Many other meaningful gestures can be performed with two fingers. However, the gestural vocabulary for mobile touch devices can only be extended with input patterns that can be clearly differentiated from the established ones. Toward a better understanding of the pinch-zoom gesture, we designed another experiment to capture and identify its timing characteristics.

The screen showed two rectangles, a smaller one containing a short text nested inside a larger one (Figure 2d). The users were instructed to zoom in until the small rectangle fully filled the screen without cutting away any part of the contained letters. Then they were asked to zoom out until the minimal zoom level of 50% of the initial value was obtained and finally zoom back in to the initial state. This procedure had to be sequentially repeated for at least three times. Some participants did the task more often which provided us with a larger database for the evaluation.

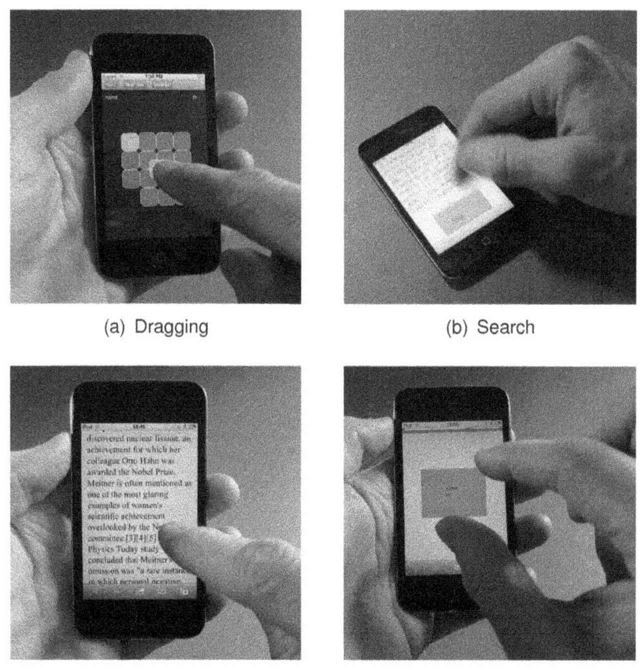

(a) Dragging (b) Search

(c) Reading (d) Zoom

Figure 2. Experimental tasks for measuring the timing of common touch gestures. The *Search* task is shown in the *support* condition with the device fixed to the table surface. All others with the device held in the non-dominant hand.

Recorded Time Intervals

We recorded 1545 dragging actions, 315 panning actions in the *read* condition and 474 panning actions in the *search* condition. From this data we extracted dwell times between the contact event of the finger touching the screen surface and the corresponding motion onset. From the 618 recorded pinch-zoom gestures we derived the average time difference between the contact events of both involved fingers.

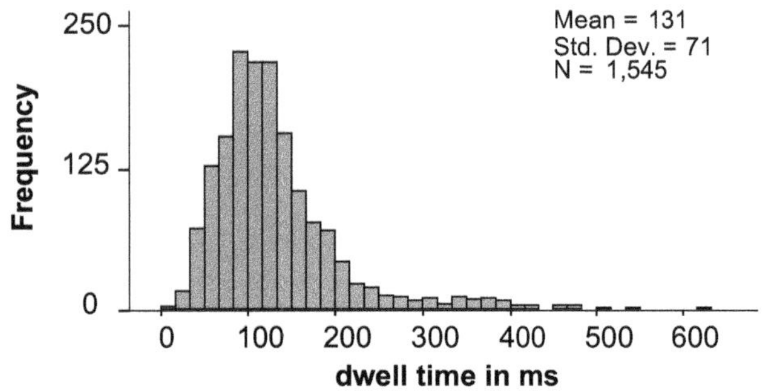

Figure 3. Histogram of dwell times during the *dragging* experiment

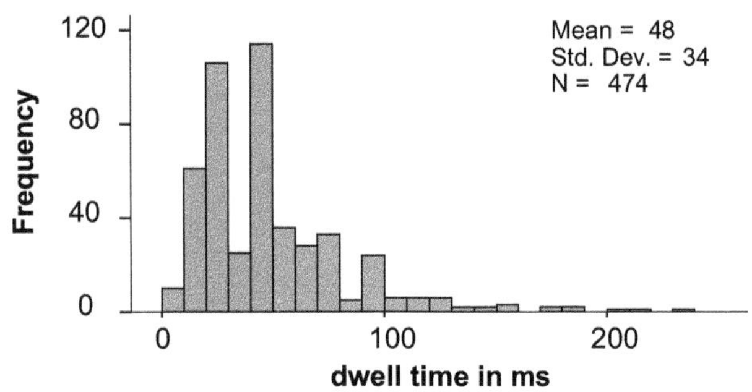

Figure 4. Histogram of dwell times during the *search* experiment

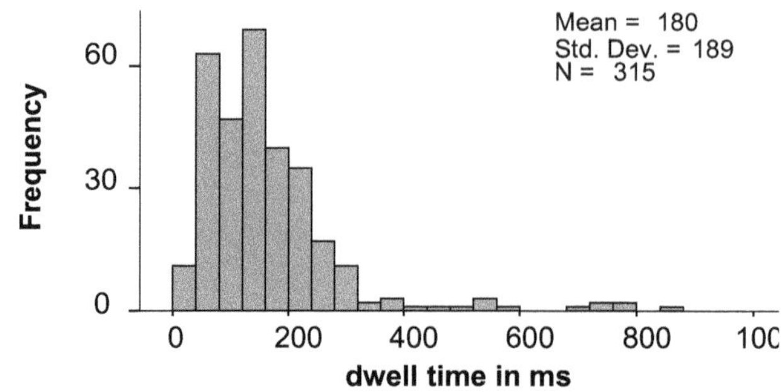

Figure 5. Histogram of dwell times during the *read* experiment

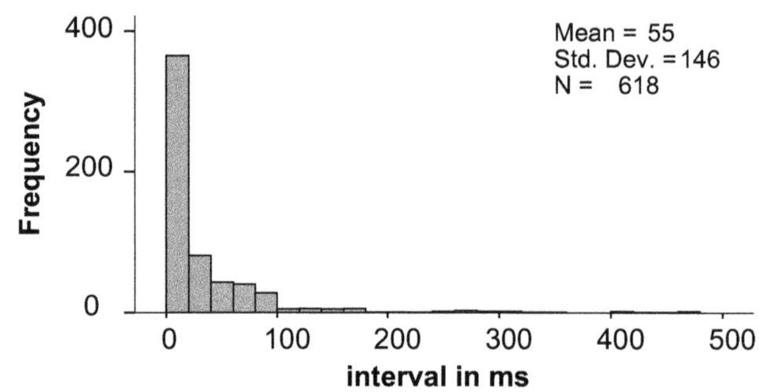

Figure 6. Histogram of time differences between the contact of both fingers with the screen surface when initiating a pinch-zoom gesture

The results from the dragging and panning tests revealed that dwell times are indeed an implicit characteristic of touch input (Table 1). We also observed that their duration is clearly different among the tested tasks. The average dwell time during dragging tasks was 131 ms (*sd*=71 ms) (Figure 3). For panning tasks we measured average dwell times of 48 ms (*sd*=34 ms) if participants were scanning for salient targets (Figure 4), but if they were asked to read a displayed text with diligence, average dwell times increased to 180 ms with a standard deviation of 189 ms (Figure 5).

Regarding the pinch-zoom gesture, we observed that both fingers generally touch the surface almost simultaneously. We excluded 19 outliers from our records with a time difference of more than 1000 ms. In the other 599 cases the time differences were under 500 ms with a mean of 55 ms and a standard deviation of 145 ms (Figure 6).

Design Considerations

It seems quite obvious to exploit dwell times for implicit mode switching since they are an implicit characteristic of dragging tasks. However, we measured much shorter time intervals than the commonly used threshold of 500 ms. Dwell times above 500 ms occurred naturally in only 3 of all recorded dragging actions. In the other 1542 cases the dwell time would have been disruptive. Thus, reducing the threshold bears the potential to increase the fluency of interaction. During more than half of all recorded dragging actions a dwell time longer than 100 ms occurred. Hence, this value could be a better suited dwell-time threshold - if interferences with panning actions can be avoided.

Our measurements indicate that this may be possible in tasks that require only rapid flicks to navigate through the displayed content. Panning actions in the *search* condition exposed with 48 ms on average the shortest dwell times in our experiments. 95% of all rapid panning gestures we recorded in this condition involved a dwell time shorter than 110 ms (see Table 1).

percentiles	**min**	**5%**	**median**	**95%**	**max**
	dwell times				
dragging	11	46	111	270	624
search	4	12	42	110	237
read	10	44	141	452	2032
	interval between two contact events				
zooming	0	0	18	143	478

Table 1. Percentiles of recorded time intervals during different input actions (all data in ms).

On the other hand, the data recorded in the *read* condition shows that dwell times during panning actions significantly increase if the task is cognitively more demanding. While reading a text our test users induced dwell times of 180 ms on average. This is longer than the dwell times recorded during dragging actions. While reading, a threshold of 110 ms would have been exceeded in 63% of all recorded panning actions. In order to avoid involuntary mode switching for at least 95% of all the panning actions in the *read* condition, the threshold would have to be set to a value above 452 ms. This corresponds to the Apple® design guidelines for long press gestures [2]. The default duration here is 500 ms. In our recorded data, this interval was exceeded in only 1% of all panning actions. We conclude that the common dwell time threshold of 500 ms is well adjusted to reduce the chance of involuntary activation. We also note, however, that it frequently interferes with the interaction flow during object manipulation.

In our study the pinch-zoom gesture exhibits a highly symmetric initiation pattern for most cases. The interval between the contact events of both fingers was less than 100 ms in 93% of the cases. The 19 excluded outliers show that pinch zoom is not necessarily initiated symmetrically, but in more than 98% of our records it was. We conclude that any input from two fingers that touch the screen with a time difference of more than 100 ms is most probably not meant to initiate a pinch-zoom gesture. It could thus be interpreted differently.

THE HOLD-AND-MOVE INPUT PATTERN

Li et al. [13] found that asymmetric bi-manual interaction can be an advantageous alternative to the disruptive long tap. Following the principles of Guiard [8], high-level motion input like navigation ought to be assigned to the non-dominant hand while the dominant hand performs object manipulation within the provided reference frame. Guiard also observed precedence of action of the non-dominant hand as a general principle of asymmetric bi-manual activities. We suggest that this principle can be directly exploited for the interpretation of multi-touch input.

We implemented the hold-and-move gesture as follows: The first finger is always assigned to *hold* the background (Figure 1a). A second touch input is used to select and *move* individual items relative to the background if the touch occurs at least 100ms after the first touch event (Figure 1b & c). In the following, we refer to this time parameter as the hold time – as opposed to the dwell time to discern a long tap. If both touch events occur within less than 100ms their input is interpreted as a pinch-zoom gesture instead. An interaction sequence of hold and move only ends when both fingers release the touch sensitive surface. The assignment of fingers to background or foreground thus remains in effect if only one finger is released, which naturally enables clutching. Long-distance panning operations can be controlled with successive input of one finger while the other one keeps holding a dragged item. (Figure 1d).

The mode switching technique clearly consists of two steps: holding the background followed by the selection of a foreground item. Hence, it should be easily distinguishable from the pinch-zoom gesture. Recall that we measured intervals shorter than 100 ms between both touch events in 93% of the 618 recorded pinch-zoom gestures. During this initial data gathering, only a single input mode had to be operated. We expected that the awareness of a second two-finger input mode would further increase the accuracy of the symmetric pinch-zoom initiation.

Target-based zooming is still available alongside with hold-and-move. Only the initiation of the input gesture matters for the differentiation between symmetric input like zooming (almost simultaneous contact of both fingers) and asymmetric input like hold-and-move (successive touch of both fingers). Thereafter, motion input may be induced symmetrically or asymmetrically.

We identify the following main advantages of using hold-and-move for mode switching:

- It eliminates involuntary object selection during panning as well as workflow interruption during intended object manipulation.
- The two-handed technique omits the need for automatic scrolling to drag an item beyond the visible screen area.
- It facilitates successive object manipulations. Once the background is attached to one finger, several objects can be sequentially dragged with another finger.

USER STUDY

We evaluated the performance and user acceptance of both the long-tap and the hold-and-move mode switching techniques in two test applications using an Apple iPod® touch 4 device. Both test applications were focusing on object dragging. Only little workspace panning and no zooming was required for task completion. Nevertheless, both types of workspace navigation were continuously available during all tests in order to observe potential issues of interference: between hold-and-move and zooming as well as between object selection with the long-tap and panning.

Hold-and-move was implemented as described above with a 100 ms hold time threshold to discern the zooming functionality. The *long-tap* implementation used the common dwell time of 500 ms and provided autoscroll functionality that was actuated if the fingertip was less than 4 mm away from the screen border.

Experimental Tasks

Our two test scenarios (*List* and *Grid*), both consisted of several object manipulation tasks that also required some navigation input. The basic activity of moving icons or pictures across the screen was implemented as a color association task. The users were asked to drag colored items (red, green, blue, gray) to corresponding text fields naming the color.

If a dragged object was released on the incorrect target position, it was automatically moved back to its origin. After having moved a matching item to each visible target field, one set of tasks was accomplished and another version was loaded, proffering a different sorting of targets and pieces to be dragged.

Note that the association from color to text added a constant cognitive load to the task. This was meant to reproduce a realistic situation in that users focus on accomplishing a certain task rather than the correct operation of the interface.

Grid

The color and text items were presented in a four by four grid structure (Figure 7 left). The first and third row each contained the four differently colored items. For each item there was a corresponding target field showing the name of the respective color in the line below. Besides this fixed vertical structure all items were placed randomly on the horizontal axis such that the users had to sort them while performing the task. Eight color items had to be dragged to the corresponding text fields on the line below. The subtask sequence was accomplished when all 8 items had been placed correctly. Then the next sequence was loaded.

List

The color items were presented in a list structure. The first three entries on top of the list always consisted of the color items red, green and blue in randomized order (Figure 7 right). Below, further entries contained gray items. All color items could be selected and moved across the screen, but only one red, green or blue item had to be dragged to the target position indicated by the word naming the respective color. We included seven different target distances (1–7 steps down in the list with Fitts' IDs ranging from 0.3–1), each appearing twice in random order. For the larger distances 5–7 the target position was sometimes too far away from the source to see both simultaneously on the screen. The users had to navigate to the target position in order to identify which item to drag there. Dragging the item to the target position correspondingly involved navigation. This second input mode was provided simultaneously in the *hold-and-move* condition or with autoscroll in the *long-tap* condition.

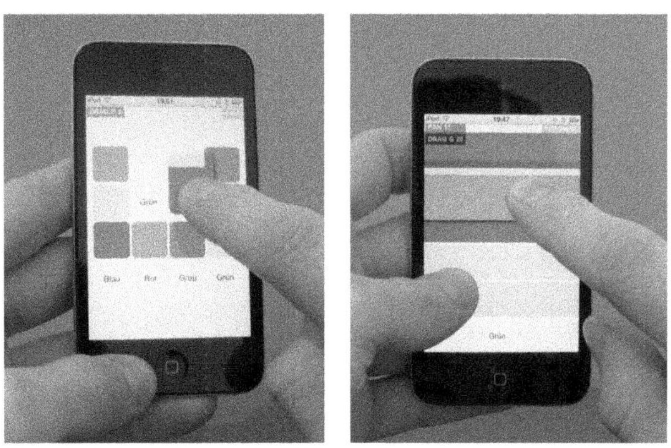

Figure 7. The test scenarios *Grid* (with *long-tap*) on the left and *List* (with *hold-and-move*) on the right.

Participants

20 people participated in the study, four of which were female, 16 male. The age ranged from 20 to 33 with a mean of 24.75. Six of the 20 participants claimed to use touch-screen devices on a daily basis, while 3 claimed to have no experiences with them. On a 5 point scale ranging from no experiences (1) to daily use (5) the mean was 3.77.

Design and Procedure

The participants were advised to hold the device in portrait orientation and in their non-dominant-hand. With each technique every participant performed six sets of eight dragging tasks in the *Grid* condition and thereafter 14 dragging tasks in the *List* condition. The order of techniques was counterbalanced. Each session started with a learning phase involving 6 dragging actions in a more holistic chess task that required also a lot of panning and zooming to manipulate the small chess pieces. No data was logged during the chess task, but it served the participants to subjectively explore the usability of the respective techniques. After all tests had been completed, we asked the participants to rate the suitability of both techniques for each scenario.

Hypotheses

We assumed that users would complete the dragging tasks faster in the *hold-and-move* condition – not because the dwell time in the *long-tap* condition is a disadvantage by itself but rather due to the users' difficulties to cope with the interruption of their workflow. In the *Grid* condition the dragging tasks were presented in sets of eight. This allowed users to take advantage of activity planning. In particular they could minimize the effort in the *hold-and-move* condition. Holding the background once enabled the object manipulation mode for all consecutive dragging actions. We thus expected a bigger advantage for *hold-and-move* in this scenario.

Results

Data was collapsed and entered into a 2 (*scenarios*)×2 (*techniques*) analysis of variance. Normality was verified using the Kolmogorov-Smyrnov test. We found significant main effects for task ($F_{(1,19)} = 56.0, p < 0.01$) and technique ($F_{(1,19)} = 62.7, p < 0.01$) as well as a significant interaction between these two independent variables ($F_{(1,19)} = 8.6, p < 0.01$). Post-hoc comparisons using Tuckey's HSD test revealed significant differences between the tested *techniques* in both *scenarios* ($p < 0.01$ for the *Grid* condition and $p < 0.05$ for the *List* condition).

As can be seen in table 2 the performance difference between both *techniques* is more pronounced in the *Grid* condition. A more detailed review of the data revealed that these additional benefits are indeed related to the improved integration of subsequent manipulation tasks. We observed that users were setting a new reference with an initiating touch event only twice within one set of the eight dragging tasks – just before starting to manipulate another group of four items in one line. Hence, the competitive edge for our novel gesture is less pronounced if we compare both techniques only in the first and the fifth dragging subtask: 2119 ms (*sd*=1267 ms) for *hold-and-move* vs. 2940 ms (*sd*=1565 ms) in the *long-tap* condition.

The impact of the target distance in the *List* condition was visible in the results, but no difference between *techniques* could be found in that regard. Overall we found considerable performance advantages of the *hold-and-move* technique as compared to the *long-tap* interface in both test scenarios (Figure 8).

	Grid	List
long-tap	2866 (1459)	3459 (2151)
hold-and-move	1366 (991)	2651 (2395)

Table 2. Mean task completion times in ms for both tested *techniques* (lines) in the two usage *scenarios* (columns). Standard deviation in parenthesis

Subjective user ratings reflect the quantitative results. The average usability rating of the two techniques on a 5-point Likert scale was similar with a mean of 4.0 for *hold-and-move* and a mean of 3.7 for the dwell times, indicating that both

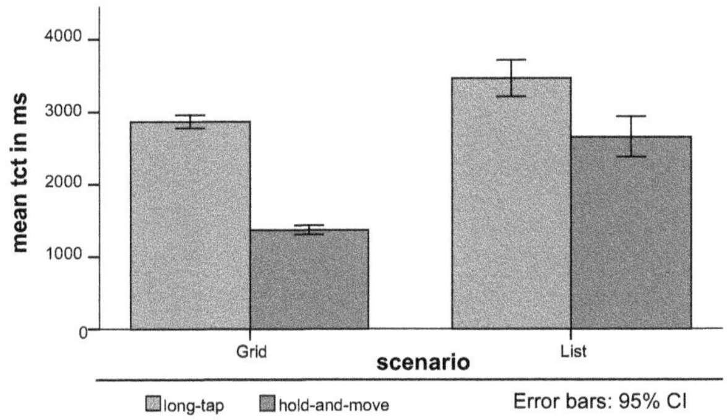

Figure 8. Mean task completion times in ms.

techniques were well suited for the given tasks. Most users had a clear preference for one of both techniques. Ten users preferred *hold-and-move* to operate the chess game while six voted for the *long-tap*. For the *List* sorting task eleven users preferred *hold-and-move* while seven users preferred the *long-tap*. Regarding the *Grid* task, many users appreciated the benefits of *hold-and-move* for successive object manipulation. Sixteen of 20 users preferred the novel technique in the *Grid* condition while three voted for the *long-tap*. Only few users were undecided in some scenarios.

Error Analysis

Different types of erroneous input may occur with the two mode-switching techniques at test. Dwell-time-based object manipulation may interfere with other motion input from one finger, e.g. panning. Hold-and-move, on the other hand, can interfere with zooming that is also operated with motion input from two fingers. In both cases, the correct interpretation of the user's input critically depends on the timing.

Quantifying such mode switching errors is not trivial. Without a predefined input sequence, we cannot easily know which mode changes were intended and which were not. Additionally, we must consider false positives (the mode changed although not intended) and false negatives (the intended mode change was not achieved).

False Positives

From our initial study on the timing of touch gestures we derived that a dwell time of 500 ms is a well suited threshold to minimize false positives during panning. Only 14 of the 789 recorded panning actions involved a dwell time longer than 500 ms.

We also estimated the rate of false positives for the hold-and-move gesture from the records of pinch-zoom gestures we gathered during this initial study. In 7% of the 618 recorded pinch zoom gestures, both fingers touched the screen surface with a time difference longer than our threshold of 100 ms. They would have had invoked the object manipulation mode although their input was meant to control the zoom level. We expected, though, that users would initiate the pinch-zoom gesture more accurately with both fingers simultaneously if they are aware of a second two-finger gesture that is initiated asymmetrically instead.

During our second study comparing hold-and-move to dwell-time based mode switching we recorded 483 hold-and-move gestures, 446 of them were completed with the successful docking of one or more dragging items. In the other 37 cases the gesture may have been initiated involuntarily. This is plausible if both touch events occurred within the range of time intervals we measured for pinch-zoom gestures. We define this range based on the average interval we measured for pinch-zoom gestures plus three times standard deviation ($55\ ms + 3 * 145\ ms = 493\ ms$). In 18 cases of our 37 error candidates both fingers touched the screen within a shorter interval, which would correspond to a rate of 3.7% false positives for a hold-time threshold of 100 ms.

False Negatives

Towards an estimate of false negatives, we can compare the frequency of "unnecessary" input actions. Most of our experimental tasks did not require panning or zooming as the source and the target position were displayed on visible screen area. Any panning or zooming would thus be inefficient and can be interpreted as an error.

In the *Grid* task users could benefit from the integration of up to eight subsequent dragging operations in one hold-and-move sequence while the long-tap involves a mode selection for each subsequent dragging operation. Thus, we only consider the first dragging action from each of these sets for the error analysis. Some of the *List* tasks involved target positions off screen and therefore required panning or zooming. This should have the same impact on the performance with both techniques, but to account for this difference we distinguish short and long target distances in the analysis. Distances of up to 4 rows were always defined to be short since the targets were always visible without navigation.

Zooming occurred rarely in all tasks and with both techniques (see Table 3). The slightly higher number of zooming actions in the *hold-and-move* condition, indicates that involuntary input may have occurred, but none of the small differences proved to be statistically significant. We conclude that hold-and-move did not had a relevant impact on the operability of pinch zoom during our experiments. Although we applied a rather low threshold of 100ms, only one of 20 users noticed the possibility of interfering with pinch-zoom input.

	Grid	**short List**	**large List**
	zooming input		
long-tap	0.13 (0.47)	0.12 (0.49)	0.26 (0.64)
hold-and-move	0.13 (0.59)	0.07 (0.28)	0.19 (0.61)
	panning input		
long-tap	1.62 (1.01)	1.66 (0.95)	2.98 (1.405)
hold-and-move	0.58 (1.59)	0.42 (0.97)	2.08 (3.028)

Table 3. Average numbers of panning and zooming actions per dragging task. Standard deviation in parentheses.

For mode selection based on dwell times false negatives are indicated by an increased amount of panning actions. We observed that the average number of panning actions per docking task is more than two times higher in the *long-tap* condition as compared to *hold-and-move* (see table 3). A MANOVA reveals that the rate of panning actions differs significantly between techniques ($F_{(1,19)} = 25.68, p < 0.01$) and also between the three groups of tasks ($F_{(2,38)} = 30.06, p < 0.01$), while the interaction between both factors is not significant. We conclude that indications of input errors related to dwell times can be found in all task conditions. User feedback supports this observation. Five participants explicitly complained about being interrupted by dwell times.

Hold-Time Analysis

With a minimal hold-time threshold of 100 ms, false negatives do not seem to occur at all. Instead, we observe a chance to invoke the object manipulation mode involuntarily. This risk can be reduced by maximizing the applied threshold. Our records from 446 successful hold-and-move gestures, indicate that this is a feasible approach. The average hold time was 658 ms (*sd*=485 ms). Interestingly, this is longer than commonly applied dwell times of about 500 ms, which confirms our assumption that the reason for the inferior performance of the *long-tap* is not the dwell time itself. User feedback indicates that the drawback rather results from the difficulties to cope with the workflow interruption.

Only 5% of the hold-and-move gestures were executed with a hold time of less than 190ms (Table 4). We reasoned that such extremely short hold times only occurred because our study was focused on consecutive dragging tasks. Consequently, we suggest a hold-time threshold above 150ms (corresponding to the 95% percentile value of pinch-zoom input) and below 190ms (corresponding to the 5 percentile value of hold-and-move gestures). Depending on the target user group and different applications, other values may offer a better suited balance (see figure 9).

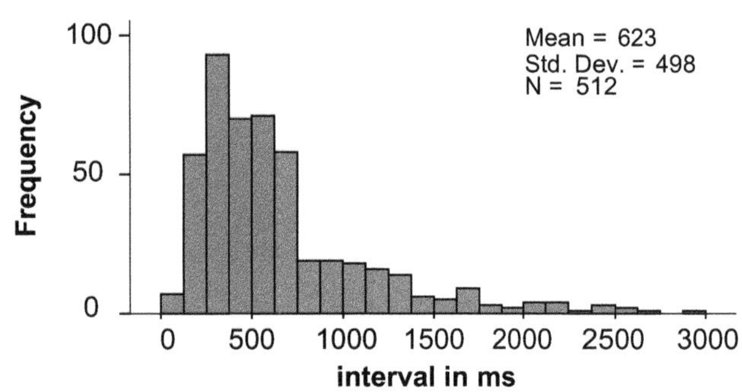

Figure 9. Histogram of recorded time differences between the contact of both fingers with the screen when initiating a hold-and-move input gesture.

percentile	**min.**	**5%**	**median**	**95%**	**max.**
hold time	103	189	514	1681	2927

Table 4. Hold time extrema (all data in ms).

Discussion

The results of our user study demonstrate that the hold-and-move gesture is an efficient alternative to the disruptive long-tap. Note that we tested with a very basic implementation of the technique. In practice, we expect that applications will take further information into account. Most obviously, context information should be included as known from using the long tap for object selection, which is only executed if the finger rests on top of a selectable item. In applications with a sparse distribution of selectable items, this simple adaptation would directly enable to operate zooming even after asymmetric initiation.

Compared to the long-tap, hold-and-move has the limitation in that it cannot be operated using only the thumb when holding the device in one hand. This will be less of a restriction for larger devices that are generally not operated single-handedly, like tablet devices. In addition, there is no technical reason that one-finger dragging based on dwell time cannot be made available in the interface in addition to the two-finger hold-and-move gesture.

It is important to consider that the normal mode of interaction for both techniques is navigation via panning and scrolling. We tested them both in manipulation-focused tasks. We expect that hold-and-move is beneficial also for navigation tasks that do not require a secondary input modality, since it prevents accidental mode switching (false-positives). Hold-and-move demands a second touching finger and cannot be triggered involuntarily in single-touch navigation (e.g. if leaving the finger on the screen while reading).

CONCLUSIONS AND FUTURE WORK

We designed the two finger object dragging pattern hold-and-move to avoid the disruptive long-tap in touch interface implementations. Our approach involves a second finger to enable the smooth execution of object selection followed by object dragging. With the novel technique regular workspace panning remains available during dragging. As a side effect, the cumbersome and hard-to-control workspace autoscrolling function is no longer needed when dragging an object beyond the currently visible viewport. Involuntary object selection during panning is also eliminated. Our user study revealed that the hold-and-move pattern allows for faster object dragging than the conventional dwell-time approach and is preferred by most users. We also showed that the novel gesture can be applied without affecting the recognition quality of the established single-finger panning and pinch-zoom gestures.

Pinch zooming mimics squeezing and stretching the screen content. Consequently, the finger motion is induced along the vector between both initial touch positions. Instead, for hold-and-move motion input is induced in the direction of a target position that is independent of the orientation of the initial touch positions. This observation could be used to further reduce involuntary mode changes. The implementation of the hold-and-move pattern could also benefit from the possibility to adapt the thresholds to the user and from context sensitivity. For example, if there are no objects near the second finger that can be dragged, the user is likely to start a pinch zoom even though the threshold for enabling this gesture has been exceeded.

While object dragging may be only rarely required in common mobile phone applications, the mode-switching technique enables many other functionalities that are similarly operated. Selecting snippets of text and images from websites and pasting them into a new document is currently a cumbersome task. Hold-and-move bears the potential to operate such tasks with comparable productivity as with the mouse in desktop environments. Furthermore, it provides a reliable basis for drawing-based interaction techniques like Gesture Avatar [14].

Our investigations into the timing structure of common multi-touch gestures and of our hold-and-move pattern provide a solid basis for designing and implementing further multi-touch gestures that do not require any additional hardware. Such gestures can be easily integrated into multi-touch enabled operating systems for mobile devices, which would extend the slowly evolving multi-touch language.

ACKNOWLEDGMENTS

This work was supported by the German Federal Ministry of Education and Research (BMBF) under grant 03IP704 (project Intelligentes Lernen).

Many thanks go to Felicitas Höbelt and Daniel Fischer who provided the software for the test applications. We also thank the participants of our studies and the reviewers of this paper for their helpful comments.

REFERENCES

1. Andersen, T. H. A simple movement time model for scrolling. In *Ext. Abstracts CHI 2005*, ACM Press (2005), 1180–1183.
2. UILongPressGestureRecognizer class reference. http://developer.apple.com/library/ios/#documentation/uikit/reference/UILongPressGestureRecognizer_Class/Reference/Reference.html.
3. Bier, E. A., Stone, M. C., Pier, K., Buxton, W., and DeRose, T. D. Toolglass and magic lenses: the see-through interface. In *Proc. Siggraph 1993*, ACM Press (1993), 73–80.
4. Brandl, P., Forlines, C., Wigdor, D., Haller, M., and Shen, C. Combining and measuring the benefits of bimanual pen and direct-touch interaction on horizontal interfaces. In *Proc. AVI 2008*, ACM Press (2008), 154–161.
5. Buxton, W., and Myers, B. A study in two-handed input. In *Proc. CHI 1986*, ACM Press (1986), 321–326.
6. Cutler, L. D., Fröhlich, B., and Hanrahan, P. Two-handed direct manipulation on the responsive workbench. In *Proc. I3D 1997*, ACM Press (1997), 107–114.
7. Epps, J., Lichman, S., and Wu, M. A study of hand shape use in tabletop gesture interaction. In *Ext. Abstracts CHI 2006*, ACM Press (2006), 748–753.
8. Guiard, Y. Asymmetric division of labor in human skilled bimanual action: The kinematic chain as a model. In *Journal of Motor Behavior*, vol. 19 (1987), 486–517.
9. Hinckley, K., Cutrell, E., Bathiche, S., and Muss, T. Quantitative analysis of scrolling techniques. In *Proc. CHI 2002*, ACM Press (2002), 65–72.
10. Hinckley, K., Yatani, K., Pahud, M., Coddington, N., Rodenhouse, J., Wilson, A., Benko, H., and Buxton, B. Manual deskterity: an exploration of simultaneous pen + touch direct input. In *Ext. Abstracts CHI 2010*, ACM Press (2010), 2793–2802.
11. Kabbash, P., Buxton, W., and Sellen, A. Two-handed input in a compound task. In *Proc. CHI 1994*, ACM Press (1994), 417–423.
12. Lank, E., Ruiz, J., and Cowan, W. Concurrent bimanual stylus interaction: a study of non-preferred hand mode manipulation. In *Proc. Graphics Interface 2006*, CIPS (2006), 17–24.
13. Li, Y., Hinckley, K., Guan, Z., and Landay, J. A. Experimental analysis of mode switching techniques in pen-based user interfaces. In *Proc. CHI 2005*, ACM Press (2005), 461–470.
14. Lu, H., and Li, Y. Gesture avatar: a technique for operating mobile user interfaces using gestures. In *Proc. CHI 2011*, ACM Press (2011), 207–216.
15. Matejka, J., Grossman, T., Lo, J., and Fitzmaurice, G. The design and evaluation of multi-finger mouse emulation techniques. In *Proc. CHI 2009*, ACM Press (2009), 1073–1082.
16. Olwal, A., Feiner, S., and Heyman, S. Rubbing and tapping for precise and rapid selection on touch-screen displays. In *Proc. CHI 2008*, ACM Press (2008), 295–304.
17. Roth, V., and Turner, T. Bezel swipe: conflict-free scrolling and multiple selection on mobile touch screen devices. In *Proc. CHI 2009*, ACM Press (2009), 1523–1526.
18. Roudaut, A., Lecolinet, E., and Guiard, Y. Microrolls: expanding touch-screen input vocabulary by distinguishing rolls vs. slides of the thumb. In *Proc. CHI 2009*, ACM Press (2009), 927–936.
19. Siio, I., and Tsujita, H. Mobile interaction using paperweight metaphor. In *Proc. UIST 2006*, ACM Press (2006), 111–114.
20. Wu, M., and Balakrishnan, R. Multi-finger and whole hand gestural interaction techniques for multi-user tabletop displays. In *Proc. UIST 2003*, ACM Press (2003), 193–202.
21. Yee, K.-P. Two-handed interaction on a tablet display. In *Ext. Abstracts CHI 2004*, ACM Press (2004), 1493–1496.

Brush-and-Drag: A Multi-touch Interface For Photo Triaging

Seon Joo Kim,[1] Hongwei Ng, Stefan Winkler
Advanced Digital Sciences Center (ADSC)
University of Illinois at Urbana-Champaign
Singapore 138632
stefan.winkler@adsc.com.sg

Peng Song, Chi-Wing Fu
School of Computer Engineering
Nanyang Technological University (NTU)
Singapore 639798
cwfu@ntu.edu.sg

ABSTRACT
Due to the convenience of taking pictures with various digital cameras and mobile devices, people often end up with multiple shots of the same scene with only slight variations. To enhance photo triaging, which is a very common photowork activity, we propose an *effective and easy-to-use brush-and-drag interface* that allows the user to interactively explore and compare photos within a broader scene context. First, we *brush* to mark an area of interest on a photo with our finger(s); our tailored segmentation engine automatically determines corresponding image elements among the photos. Then, we can *drag* the segmented elements from different photos across the screen to explore them simultaneously, and further perform simple finger gestures to interactively rank photos, select favorites for sharing, or to remove unwanted ones. This novel interaction method was implemented on a consumer-level tablet computer and demonstrated to offer effective interactions in a user study.

Author Keywords
Digital photo collections; User interaction

ACM Classification Keywords
H.5.2 Information Interfaces and Presentation: User interfaces; I.4.6 Image Processing and Computer Vision: Segmentation

INTRODUCTION
Digital cameras have become affordable and nearly ubiquitous with their integration into mobile devices, enabling people to take pictures and videos almost anywhere and anytime. Due to this convenience and the low cost of digital memory, people often take multiple shots of the same scene, and then select the best picture(s) from the set afterwards. This is especially common for photos that involve people, e.g., family photos with energetic babies and kids, or photos of certain important events such as weddings or graduation ceremonies. In these cases, we want to capture the best moment with the most natural and touching faces with the right gazes for all the subjects, and share our favorite photos with family and friends. Many modern consumer-level cameras (even basic models) now offer features that facilitate this behavior, such as powerful continuous burst-shooting modes. As a result, users often end up with a large number of photos, which later require tedious photowork (photowork refers to activities people perform with their digital photos after capture but prior to end use such as sharing [16], such as assessment, selection, edit, organization, and annotation). Among these photowork activities, one of the most common and time consuming tasks is *photo triaging* or photo sorting.

Existing photo software provides very limited computational or interface support for photo triaging. For example, when using Adobe Photoshop, Google Picasa, or Apple iPhoto, this basic task still relies on a primitive interaction method: flipping through the photos and viewing them one by one. The user has to go back and forth among the candidate photos to look for the relevant image features, to compare their differences, to select his/her favorite(s), and/or to remove the undesirable photos. Given the difficulty of recalling differences between images, this simple method becomes ineffective and progressively more time consuming when there are more photos in the set. On top of this, one typically needs to go back and forth a number of times to check or verify the differences. Using thumbnail images as an alternative does not work well either because the relevant image features to be compared are often too small in a thumbnail view, thus relevant details such as facial expressions are not easily recognizable. This is especially problematic on mobile devices such as laptops or tablets with limited screen space and resolution.

This paper introduces a novel and effective user interface to improve the process of photo triaging: browsing, sorting, and selecting photos from a candidate set that contains multiple images of the same scene with similar content. We are particularly interested in developing novel multi-touch-based interactions for photo triaging on a mobile tablet computer such as the Apple iPad 2. This family of platforms has become highly popular among the general public as evidenced by the iPad's record-setting adoption rate.[2] Hence, devising interactions for mobile devices is becoming increasingly important [6,13,17,19,22], yet photo browsing interfaces for mobile devices are still based on rather primitive interaction methods.

MobileHCI'12, September 21-24, 2012, San Francisco, CA, USA.

[1] SJ Kim is now with SUNY Korea.

[2] http://www.appleinsider.com/articles/10/10/05/apples_ipad_proclaimed_to_have_fastest_adoption_rate_ever.html

Specifically, we propose a novel *brush-and-drag* interface, which works as follows. After grouping a set of similar photos interactively in a thumbnail view, the user can *brush* to mark an area of interest on one of the photos in the set directly with his/her finger(s). Then, our tailored segmentation engine automatically determines the corresponding image elements across all the photos in the group. After that, the user can *drag* with one or two fingers to bring out the corresponding image elements and spread them out on the tablet surface, thus revealing the related area of interest on all photos simultaneously. Finally, the user can perform various simple finger gestures to interactively rank and re-order the photos, select the favorite for sharing, or remove some of them.

This is a focus+context design: our interface allows the user to selectively choose any area/object of interest by brushing (focus) while retaining the overview photo (context). Thus, the photo triaging process becomes more flexible and user-centric. We implemented our interface design on the Apple iPad 2 and evaluated it with a number of users. Results show that our interface outperforms the conventional photo triaging method (browsing photos by flipping) in both objective and subjective measurements. As demonstrated by our user study, participants were able to select favorite photographs from groups of similar images more quickly with our interface.

RELATED WORK

Photo browsing and triaging have been active research topics in human-computer interaction. Several user studies have been performed to analyze how people manage their digital photo collections. Rodden and Wood [24] suggested that digital photos are easier to manage than their non-digital counterparts. They found that simple browsing features were much more important to users than more advanced features like content-based image retrieval or voice annotation by speech recognition. Later, Kirk et al. [16] introduced the notion of "photowork" and similarly concluded that image searching features have much less relevance than new ways of browsing photos.

Apted et al. [3] introduced a multi-user, multi-touch, collaborative interface for sharing photos on a tabletop display and studied various design issues when using it with young adults and older users. Additionally, social aspects of sharing photos online have been studied by Miller and Edwards [20] and Ames et al. [2], who investigated various requirements for mobile photoware, including image capture, upload, annotation, archiving, sharing, and viewing. These user studies again suggested that basic features for photo browsing such as triaging, displaying thumbnails, and sorting are much more important to users than advanced features.

A large amount of research effort has been devoted to improving the user interaction and visualization capabilities for digital photo browsing. Kang and Shneiderman [15] introduced a scatter plot thumbnail display and a drag-and-drop interface as a tool for searching and browsing photos, while Bederson [5] proposed a zoomable image browser using quantum treemaps and bubblemaps. Platt et al. [23] developed an overview+detail design, where the overview of the photo collection is generated by an image clustering algorithm, and the details are shown as an ordered list of photos. Graham et al. [12] applied a cluster analysis of the times when photographs were taken in order to summarize the photo collection. Huynh et al. [14] proposed a zoomable layout for displaying large photo collections by trading off screen space utilization to more effectively convey the temporal order of pictures. Shneiderman et al. [27] presented an integrated interface for annotating, browsing, and sharing photo collections, supporting exploratory search needs of personal digital photo users. Other photowork activities studied in the HCI research community include photo annotation [9, 28], photo sharing [11, 20], and photo storytelling [10, 31].

While thumbnail view or grid layout approaches allow us to view and sort multiple photos simultaneously, we argue that detailed features such as faces could be too small to see clearly, especially on tablets or handheld mobile devices, whose display sizes are relatively smaller. In addition, users do not have the ability to flexibly select and examine the details. In comparison, our interaction design provides the users with an interface to mark up feature details and compare them more flexibly and effectively with the support of multi-touch gestures and an interactive image segmentation engine.

Interfaces for browsing and exploring photos have also been studied in the computer graphics community. Snavely et al. [29] introduced an interactive 3D photo browsing interface, which puts photographs in a virtual 3D space relative to their corresponding camera viewpoints. Ballan et al. [4] extended this 3D interface design for exploring videos. Agarwala et al. [1] proposed the idea of digital photomontage, where image regions from a set of photos can be interactively composited seamlessly into a desired target image. Such a technique was later integrated into various commercial products, including Adobe Photoshop's Groupshot and Microsoft's PhotoFuse. The motivation of this method is similar to ours, i.e., helping the user to come up with a good representative photo from a set. However, their work focused on merging and compositing image elements from different photos while users still need to look for good image features among a photo set before selecting the preferred image parts for photo composition. Our proposed system on the other hand provides an interactive solution for efficiently comparing user-desired image features among photos, and it can complement the photomontage framework particularly in the triaging and selection process.

DESIGN ISSUES

We propose the brush-and-drag interface as an effective means for photo triaging (Figure 1). The interface is targeted at tablet/handheld computers and general-public users. Before presenting it, we enumerate a number of design issues incurred in this setting.

- **Easy-to-use, familiar interaction gestures.** We aim to develop easy-to-use and intuitive interaction gestures that are familiar to general-public users and consistent with the way touch interfaces have been developed in common surface computing applications.

Figure 1. The brush-and-drag interface. (a) A given group of similar photos. (b) We use a natural *brush* gesture with our finger(s) to mark an area/object of interest in one of these photos. Our tailored segmentation engine quickly segments the corresponding image elements in the photo group. (c) We can then *drag* the segmented image elements to spread them out for better examination. This user-centric design allows the user to decide the size and the area of interest. It also maintains the overall photo context while enabling the user to focus on the selected area of interest for comparison and photo triaging (focus+context). Note that the normally black background of the tablet display was changed to white for printing purposes.

- **User input imprecision.** Since we rely on finger contacts on the multi-touch surface to provide input to the system, our system should not assume precise touch input due to the fat finger footprint, similar to other touch interfaces.
- **Visual feedback.** Since photo triaging requires a series of interaction stages, our interface should strive to inform the user about the changes in the interaction stages and actions they perform via appropriate visual feedback.
- **Focus+context interaction.** Due to the limited screen size and resolution available on tablet computers, we have to consider both the photo overview and the focus on details in the user interface. Hence, we take a focus+context approach to the interaction design, which allows users to stay within the overall photo context while focusing on and interacting with specific areas of interest.
- **Efficient computation.** Since the interface is intended to run interactively on a tablet computer, we should minimize the memory and computational overhead required by any supporting computation and algorithms in the system, in particular the image segmentation engine.

INTERACTION SCENARIO

The interaction scenario of our photo browsing tool consists of the following four stages:

- **Stage 0:** Before entering the main brush-and-drag interface, which starts from stage 1 below, the user first groups a set of similar looking photos in the *thumbnail view* of a photo album, see Figure 2.
- **Stage 1:** Being presented with the first photo from the selected group, the user can then *brush* to mark an area/object of interest on it directly with his/her finger(s), see Figure 1(b). This triggers our image segmentation engine to automatically select the corresponding image elements from the other photos in the set.
- **Stage 2:** The user can *drag* out the corresponding image elements with his/her finger(s) to arrange them along the dragging path for quick and intuitive comparisons in a focus+context style, see Figure 1(c).
- **Stage 3:** The user can further perform *a variety of easy-to-use photo triaging activities*, by manipulating the segmented image elements with his/her finger(s) to rank and re-order the photos, to select the favorite(s) for sharing, or to delete some of them.

We now present the details of each of these stages below.

Stage 0: Grouping Similar Photos

Like conventional digital photo browsers, our system starts with a thumbnail view of the photo collection. While comparing features and object details with thumbnail images can be difficult, the user can still identify similar photographs in this view. Thumbnails are arranged according to the time when the photos were taken by checking the photos' meta information. Hence, similar photos are automatically placed close to one another. Additionally, we introduce gaps between neighboring photos when the difference between their timestamps is relatively larger than others as a simple visual guide for the user; of course, other forms of visual indicators can also be envisaged.

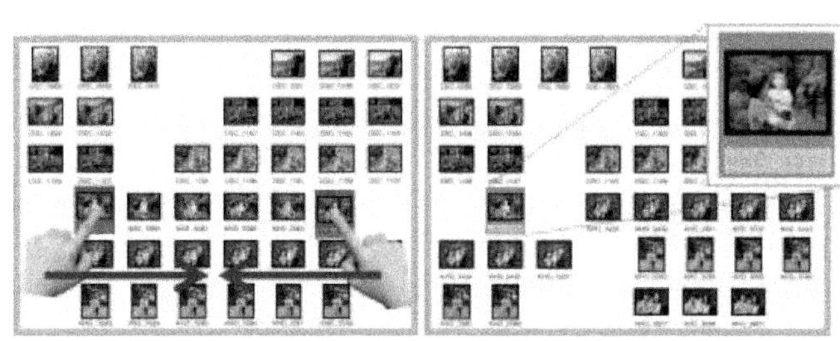

Figure 2. Stage 0: Thumbnail images are automatically arranged according to their photo-taking timestamps. (Left) The user can group photos by pressing on the first and the last photo of the set with two fingers, and then collapsing them into a batch. (Right) The thumbnail for the resulting photo batch is presented in a different style.

Our system provides an easy way of grouping photos into a batch as follows:

- First, the user places one finger on the first photo and another finger on the last photo in a group, see Figure 2 (left).

- Then, the user can do a pinching gesture to collapse all photos in-between into a batch.
- The icon for the newly-created photo batch is then presented in a different style, see also Figure 2 (right).
- Finally, a simple one-finger tap on a photo batch takes the user to the next interaction stage, *brushing*.

If the user taps on a single photo thumbnail instead of a batch icon, a full view of the photo is presented, and the user can browse the collection using the standard flipping/scrolling gesture. In this way, our interface works just like a conventional photo browser.

Stage 1: Brushing

Upon tapping on a photo batch icon in the thumbnail view, we enter the brushing interaction stage, which starts by showing a full view of the first photo in the batch. There are two modes of interaction in this stage, namely *scrolling mode* and *brushing mode*. When the interface enters this stage, it starts in scrolling mode, which allows the user to browse through different photos using the standard flipping gesture. Brushing is not allowed in this mode because it may be confused with this gesture. For disambiguation, we provide a button on the top-right corner of the interface in the form of a paint brush icon, which allows the user to switch between scrolling and brushing modes. There is also a home icon shown on the top left, which returns the user to the initial thumbnail view at any time, cf. Figure 1(b).

After the user taps the brush icon, it changes to a blue paintbrush as a visual metaphor to indicate that the brush is now ready to use. Now, the system enters the brushing mode. The working scenario is as follows:

- First, the user marks an area/object of interest by freely brushing with his/her finger(s), which is one of the core features of our brush-and-drag design. Multiple fingers can be used simultaneously for brushing by taking advantage of the increased degrees of freedom provided by the multi-touch surface. This feature allows the user to intuitively deal with varying object sizes without having to control the diameter of the brush stroke explicitly. Note that an area of interest does not have to comprise just one object, as the user may be interested in focusing on multiple objects that are located next to each other, as shown in Figure 3.
- Once the finger(s) is/are lifted from the multi-touch surface, our system initiates the segmentation engine to automatically determine the corresponding image elements across all photos in the batch. This segmentation engine is another key contribution of this work. Users only need to mark the area of interest in one of the photos. The engine can then determine the corresponding image elements across all photos in the batch. This user-driven segmentation further enhances the interaction capabilities and personalization of photo browsing. Details of our interactive segmentation engine are described in the Appendix.
- Once the segmentation is complete, the system automatically switches to the *pre-dragging mode* of stage 2 (dragging stage), and the top-right brush icon disappears, since we are no longer in the brushing mode. At the same time, the segmented element will be highlighted against a dimmed background, see Figure 3. If the user is not satisfied with the segmentation result, he/she can go back to brushing mode by double tapping the background. This removes the highlighting and makes the brush icon re-appear on the photo. The user can then start over with brushing. Alternatively, the user may tap the brush icon to revert back further to the scrolling mode of this stage.

Figure 3. Interactive segmentation by brushing: (top) brush strokes and (bottom) segmentation results highlighted by dimming the background. Brushing with multiple fingers naturally allows the user to widen the area of interest, which facilitates marking larger objects.

Stage 2: Dragging

The dragging stage has two modes: the *pre-dragging mode* followed by the *dragging mode*. We enter the pre-dragging mode after the segmentation. In this mode, the segmented image elements are highlighted against a dimmed background, as shown in Figure 3.

The user can now perform a dragging gesture with one or two fingers, which is a natural and intuitive action to spread out the segmented image elements along the dragging path. Two possible dragging gestures are supported in the pre-dragging mode, as can be seen in Figure 4:

- One-finger drag, in which the system automatically estimates the scale factor for the segmented elements, aiming at distributing them efficiently along the dragging path.
- Two-finger drag, where the size of the image elements is scaled relative to the distance between the two fingers, and image elements closer to the fingers are scaled relatively larger. This view can be helpful when sorting photos later on, because the preferred photos placed near the end of the dragging path are larger.

Using the dragging action described above, we can spread out the segmented image elements and present them all together over the given photo, following the idea of focus+context. However, the image elements presented at this point may be too cluttered, thus affecting the focus+context visualization as well as the subsequent interactions. We propose two mechanisms to resolve this issue:

- Once the finger(s) reach the tablet boundary (within a margin) as in Figure 5 (step 2), our interface automatically and progressively reduces the size of the context photo toward

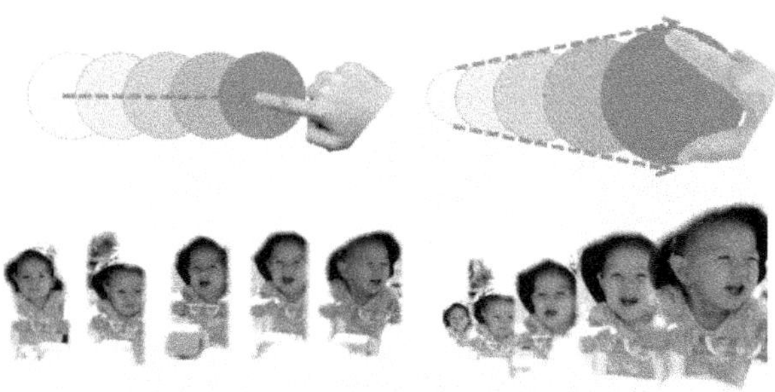

Figure 4. Dragging gestures. (Left) The one-finger drag uses the same size for all image elements. (Right) The two-finger drag scales the image elements similar to perspective viewing.

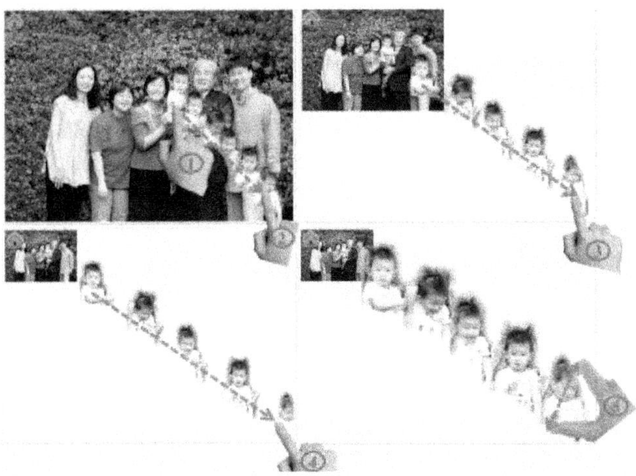

Figure 5. Automatic resizing allows us to interactively balance context and detail. After the dragging finger(s) reach the tablet boundary, the size of the context photo reduces progressively (see steps 1-4), making space for the image elements. The user can also perform a two-finger pinch to further adjust the size of the image elements (step 5).

the opposite direction (Figure 5, steps 3 and 4), making additional room for the image elements. Auto-resizing stops when the finger(s) are lifted up from the tablet surface. This mechanism allows the user to interactively balance the utilization of screen space between the main context photo and the details (segmented elements).

- Occasionally, there may be a large number of similar photos in a batch (perhaps 10 or more). In this case, the displayed elements would be either too small for effective comparison or too cluttered if the user tries to resize them (see Figure 6 (left)). To resolve this issue, we introduce the idea of a general dragging path, which allows the user to drag and spread the image elements along an arbitrary path rather than a straight line (the default) to better utilize screen space. Figure 6 illustrates this mechanism. The general path drag can be initiated after the default straight-line drag by simply pressing the context photo area with two fingers.

After the initial drag, the user may perform:

- A two-finger pinch to additionally adjust and fine-tune the size of image elements.

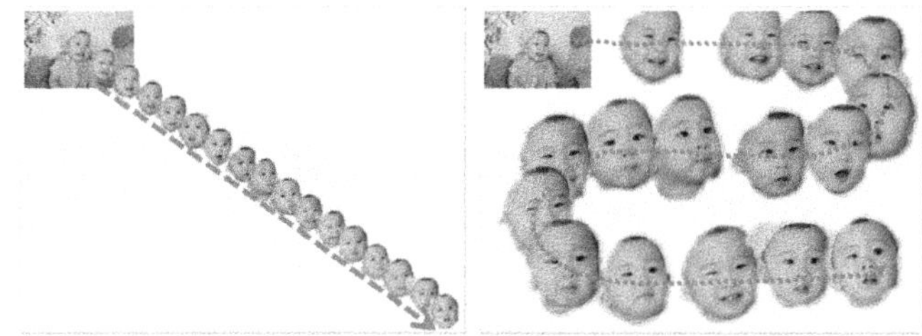

Figure 6. General path dragging. (Left) With a large number of images (16 in this example), a straight line arrangement of elements may not be effective. (Right) Users can drag the elements along a general path, which utilizes screen space more efficiently and allows more elements to be displayed at a larger size.

- A tap on an image element to switch the current main context photo to the photo associated with the tapped image element, enabling photo browsing by detail selection.
- A long press of 0.3 seconds on any image element, which takes the user to the triaging stage. This is different from a re-dragging gesture, which consists of a one-finger drag starting from the first element on the path to re-adjust and move an existing dragging path.
- A double tap on the main context photo takes the user back to pre-dragging mode, where the segmentation result is shown on the full-size view.

Stage 3: Photo Triaging Activities

In this stage, our user interface presents the overall context, which is the main context photo at the corner, as well as the focus/detail, which is an array of dragged image elements corresponding to the area/object of interest the user intended to explore earlier. This focus+context style of presenting the image segments provides not only the views on the user-marked image elements, but also interactions on these elements, making the photo triaging process more efficient by directly working with the focused elements.

Once we spread out the image segments along a dragging path, a long press on an image element enables the user to select that element and enter the *photo triaging stage*. The selected image element becomes more transparent to visually indicate the selection. The user can then perform the following photo triaging activities, as illustrated in Figure 7:

- Drag the selected image element to the star icon located near the top right corner of the interface to mark the associated photo as a favorite. A star will also appear in the top-right corner of the selected image element to indicate success.
- Drag the image element to one of the social network icons on the lower left to share the associated photo with friends.
- Delete a photo by dragging the associated image element to the recycle bin icon on the lower right. After this action, the related image element will disappear, and the associated photo will be moved into the recycle bin.
- Rank or sort photos interactively by dragging the selected image element and dropping it to a preferred location along

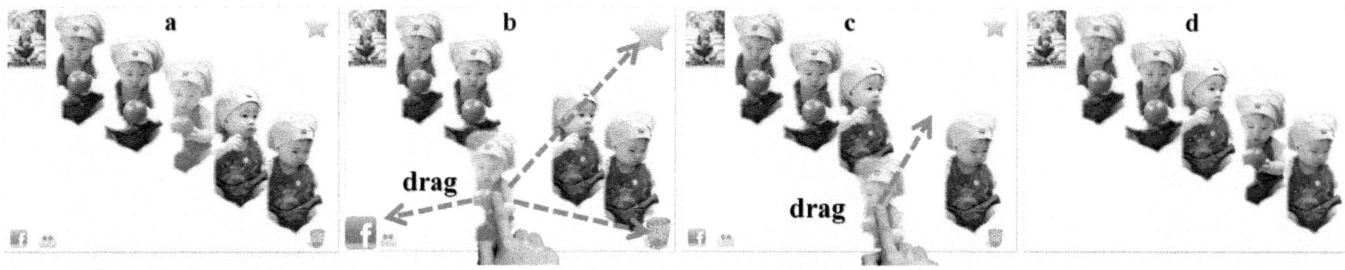

Figure 7. Photo triaging activities. (a) An image element is selected by a long press, and the selection is indicated by making it transparent. (b) The user can drag the selected element to one of the two social network icons to share and post it, to the star icon to mark it as a favorite, or to the recycle bin icon to throw it away. (c) The user can also rank or sort the images by interactively moving them before or after other image elements in the sequence. (d) The resulting photo order after sorting.

the path. The positions of other image elements will be rearranged accordingly.

- Go back to pre-dragging mode by double-tapping on the main context photo.

USER STUDY

To evaluate the effectiveness of our proposed interface, we conducted a user study, in which we compare our interface with the standard photo browser provided by Apple on the iPad 2. The reason behind this choice is that most existing photo applications on the iPad focus on enhancing and re-touching photos, whereas the basic photo browsing function remains very similar among different photo applications, without specific features for photo selection and sorting. The standard browser offers a thumbnail view as well as a simple browsing function, where the user flips from one photo to the next by a finger drag gesture. Note that our interface is also designed and developed to run on Apple's iPad 2.

Our evaluation is task-based. In each task, the participants were asked to select a favorite photo from a group of similar pictures, and the time taken by each of them to do the selection was recorded, so that we can use these measurements to evaluate the effectiveness of the two interfaces.

Test Photos

We compiled four sets of photos, which contain 4, 6, 8, and 10 similar images, respectively. We chose photo collections of a baby in various settings as the test sets, because this represents a common type of family photo, where one would usually take a large number of similar photos. Differences between photos in a set include facial expressions, the subject's poses, and modest changes in the background due to the camera motion. We have a progressively increasing number of photos in these sets, hoping to see how the number of photos may affect the task performance.

Participants

We recruited 24 participants for the user study and randomly divided them into two equally-sized groups (G1 and G2). G1 performed favorite photo selection on the four sets using Apple's standard photo browser followed by our interface, whereas G2 used the two interfaces in reverse order. There were no significant differences between the groups in terms of age and level of familiarity on using tablet computers and multi-touch interfaces. G1 comprises 8 males and 4 females, from 24 to 47 (mean 30.8) years old, and G2 comprises 7 males and 5 females, from 25 to 45 (mean 31.8) years old.

Notice that the same pre-defined sets of test photos were used for both G1 and G2 in order to minimize potential bias in the contents. When presented to the participants, the photos within each set were randomly arranged for each user and each interface.

Procedure

First, participants were asked to fill out a form with basic information including gender, age, and familiarity of using tablet computers. Then we briefly explained the procedure of the study, instructed them how to use the two interfaces, and let them practice with both (about a minute for Apple's browser and about 5 minutes for the brush-and-drag interface) so they could familiarize themselves with the two interfaces before doing the tasks.

After that, the participants started to perform the task of selecting their favorite photo from each test set. The participants in G1 were asked to select photos using the Apple's browser first. They started with the 4-photo set and ended with the 10-photo set. The participants in G2 were asked to perform the same task using our brush-and-drag interface first with the same order of sets. During the task, we measured the time taken by each participant to select a photo from each set. After the experiments, participants were asked to fill out a questionnaire and rate various aspects of the two interfaces.

Results

For the time measurements, we only use the results from the first round of selection before the participants switch to the second interface, which is our interface for G1 and Apple's standard photo browser for G2. The results from the user study confirmed that the participants indeed completed the selection task faster in the second round. Some reported to us that they could remember some of the photos they saw in the previous round, and thus could simply search for the same favorite photo they selected previously. However, we also encountered one participant who selected different favorite photos with different interfaces, reporting to us that his mood during the selection affected his choice. The reason why we require all participants to try both interfaces is that we also ask participants to rate both interfaces.

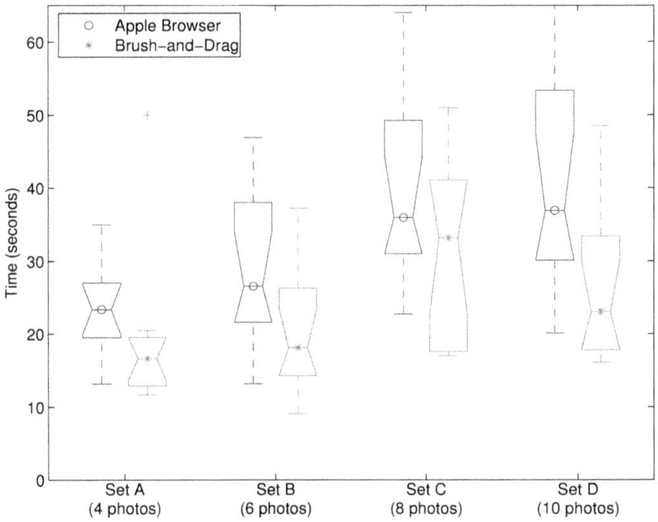

Figure 8. Box-and-whisker plots[3] of the time taken for favorite photo selection for each test set and group. Participants were able to select their favorites more quickly using our interface (red/stars) compared to Apple's (blue/circles).

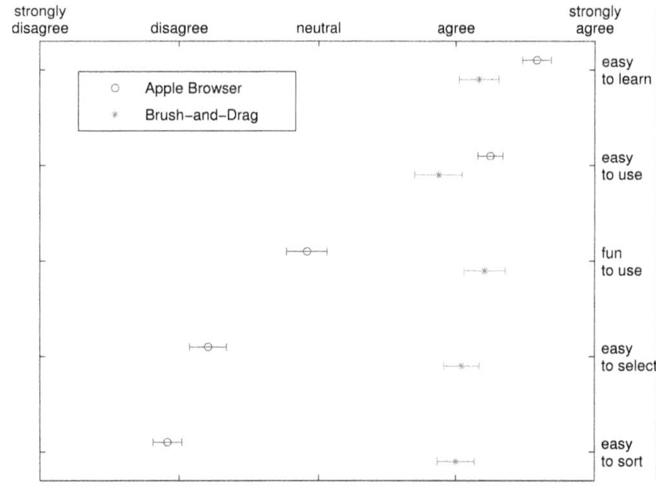

Figure 9. User ratings (means and 95% confidence intervals) of various aspects on a scale from 1 (strongly disagree) to 5 (strongly agree). Our system (red/stars) fairs well in all categories.

Figure 8 shows box-and-whisker plots of the time participants took to select their favorite photo. For all test sets, photos were selected more quickly using our interface. Our interface can save the participants about 37% of selection time for the photo set with 10 images, and about 30% on average for all sets. Unfortunately we did not have enough test sets to investigate effects of image content.

Ratings

For the subjective ratings such as usability, we use ratings of both interfaces from both G1 and G2. After finishing the given tasks, participants were asked to rate the two interfaces on various aspects on a Likert scale from 1 (strongly disagree) to 5 (strongly agree). The results are presented in Figure 9.

We expected our brush-and-drag interface to facilitate the photo comparison, which is reflected in the ratings from the users. Somewhat surprisingly perhaps, participants found the brush-and-drag interface almost as easy to learn and use as the Apple photo browser, although a few did mention that ours was harder to pick up. In addition, they viewed our interface more fun to use. They liked the interactive selection of the area of interest as well as the handling of a group of image elements via dragging. Most importantly perhaps, we outperformed the conventional browser in terms of ease of photo triaging (selection and sorting), which is the main goal of this paper. All rating differences are significant at a level of at least 0.001 according to a paired t-test, except for ease-of-use ($p = 0.0128$).

[3] The boxes indicate the 25th and 75th percentile of the data, and the vertical line inside the box represents the median. The dents on the boxes indicate the 95% significance levels. The whiskers show the data within 1.5 times the interquartile range of the lower and upper quartiles, respectively; data beyond this range is plotted individually as crosses.

DISCUSSION

The questionnaire asked participants about their approach to photo-taking and selection. The large majority said they regularly took 3 or more photos of the same scene in order to capture a good shot, with some taking up to 8 or 10 in certain situations. Multiple shots were considered most useful for people, especially children and group shots, as well as moving objects. People's expressions were almost unanimously cited as the main criterion for choosing photos, with image clarity (i.e., sharpness, color balance, lighting, etc.) second, which matches findings from previous studies on image appeal [26].

Most participants performed the given tasks as we had intended. However, a few participants also came up with interesting alternative approaches. For example, in the segmentation stage, rather than brushing directly on the area of interest as they were shown in the training, some participants attempted to circle or outline it instead. Our segmentation engine is not designed for that, and the resulting image elements were typically much larger than the participant expected. However, it can be considered as an equally intuitive way of selecting an area/object of interest, and the segmentation engine could be adapted to handle both types of input, possibly by recognizing high-level stroke semantics and image features. Other alternatives to brushing can also be envisaged, e.g., selection by rubber-banding, or simply clicking on different image features. These may be more suitable for traditional PC platforms with mouse input rather than touch screens.

Another example is the use of the segmented image elements for the favorite photo selection task. Again, most participants followed the training and relied primarily on the different elements to make their choices: they enlarged the image elements and reduced the size of the context photo. Some participants however decided to use small image elements while keeping the context photo at the original size. To them the image elements served as a form of thumbnails, with which they could quickly switch between the different full-size images. Compared to the conventional photo browser, where flipping can only be done between neighboring images, the random-access capability we provided still enabled the participants to make their selections more quickly.

The placement of the segmented elements by dragging them along a user-specified path could also be facilitated by the system automatically choosing the optimal distribution of elements on the screen (depending on their content and shape) to maximize screen space usage. The user could subsequently make adjustments to the placement if necessary.

Most people brushed either the face(s) or person(s) in the images as the area of interest. This can be expected based on the comments from participants we received as well as other photowork studies, which show that people or faces and their expressions are among the most important features and selection criteria. It also led some participants to suggest that the system could offer automatic pre-segmentation of faces or people in the photo for comparison; the user could then choose to accept or override the suggestion.

Other comments revolved around certain design choices, such as the placement of buttons on the interface, or the need to perform a long press to initiate photo triaging functionalities, which could still be optimized. For some functions, soft buttons may be more intuitive than double-clicks. Phase 0 could be automated using photo timestamps and some image similarity criteria.

Some other limitations of the system still need to be addressed as well. The segmentation algorithm did not always give participants the desired result. It also requires the object/subject of interest to be in a similar position and location across photos, even though some variations are possible. More advanced tracking or identification methods would have to be employed to detect substantial movements. Furthermore, the user can only select a single contiguous area of interest; while this may be sufficient for the majority of cases, it would be interesting to extend the interface to facilitate the comparison of multiple disjoint areas in a photo.

CONCLUSIONS

This paper introduced a new interaction design, a *brush-and-drag* interface, for supporting efficient photo triaging. Users can interactively select objects of interest to facilitate common photowork activities on a conventional tablet computer. By a natural brush gesture, users can flexibly mark any area of interest in a photo, and by further dragging out the marked object, they can browse and explore corresponding image elements across a group of similar photos at the same time.

Compared to the traditional way of flipping back and forth between photos, which is a rather tedious and time-consuming process that requires our eyes to constantly search and compare, our interface features a user-centered design, offering the flexibility to choose where to brush and what areas to mark. Furthermore, after corresponding elements are dragged out, we offer a novel user experience for photo triaging activities, allowing users to directly make use of the segmented elements for the selection of favorites as well as sharing and deleting photos. Finally, our focus+context design allows users to maintain an overview of the entire photo context while exploring the details of interest.

Future Extensions

We mostly focused on family photos such as portraits, because this is one of the most common situations where people take multiple shots (as was also confirmed by the participants in our study). It will be interesting to develop a similar triaging system for landscape photos, which bring different challenges for the interaction design. For portrait photos, interesting features are centered around the subject itself, that is, people are interested in finding photos with interesting facial expressions, gestures, or poses. For landscape photos, other features are often more important, e.g., focus, view point, zoom setting, and color, whereas the scene itself is static.

While our interface is aimed at the general public, we would like to extend our work and focus on a more specialized group in the future, namely professional photographers, who often take even more similar photos, e.g., at weddings, studio photo sessions, photo-shoots for a magazine, etc. It would be interesting to further tailor our framework to match their needs.

Finally, while interaction will remain essential to the task of photo triaging, there are a number of opportunities for additional automation and intelligence, which can further reduce the load on the user and minimize the necessary time-consuming interactions. We would like to explore the application of computer vision and computer graphics techniques to enhance photowork activities as well as to integrate photo composition capabilities.

APPENDIX: INTERACTIVE SEGMENTATION

Interactive image segmentation has been around for a while in computer vision and computer graphics [18,21,25]. Our contribution here is that corresponding image elements are segmented out from multiple images simultaneously. The user only needs to mark the element(s) of interest on one of the photos, which is a novel feature to our knowledge.

The segmentation engine in our system adopts the general framework of graphcut-based segmentation [7, 18, 25]. The goal is to label each pixel x as either foreground ($l_x = 1$) or background ($l_x = 0$). For this labeling problem, we only consider a local region in the image, specifically a bounding box that surrounds the brush strokes. This is to reduce the computation time, which is crucial for making our interactive system responsive on a tablet computer. Note that we also down-sample the images for faster computation.

Given a local region to work with, a probabilistic color model for the foreground is first computed using the color information of the brushed pixels. It is represented by a Gaussian Mixture Model (GMM) with 5 components ($p^f(\cdot)$). At the same time, we construct a GMM for the background ($p^b(\cdot)$) by randomly sampling 10% of the pixels in the region that was not brushed. Then, the optimized labels for all pixels in the image are computed by minimizing the following energy term using the graphcut solver from [8, 30]:

$$E = E_d + \omega E_s \, , \quad (1)$$

Figure 10. Interactive segmentation with brushing: note the variety of baby poses as well as the camera motion; our engine can still reasonably segment them out at interactive speed.

where E_d is the data term:

$$E_d(l_x) = \begin{cases} K & \forall x \in S \\ l_x L^f + (1 - l_x) L^b & \forall x \notin S \end{cases}, \quad (2)$$

$L^f = -\ln p^f(I_x)$, $L^b = -\ln p^b(I_x)$ with I_x being the color at pixel x, S is the set of brushed pixels, and K is a constant. The smoothness is enforced between adjacent pixels (**p**,**q**) with the weight ω and the following cost function [25]:

$$E_s(l_{\mathbf{p}}, l_{\mathbf{q}}) = \begin{cases} 0 & \text{if} \quad l_{\mathbf{p}} = l_{\mathbf{q}} \\ e^{-\beta ||\mathbf{I_p} - \mathbf{I_q}||^2} & \text{if} \quad l_{\mathbf{p}} \neq l_{\mathbf{q}}. \end{cases} \quad (3)$$

where $\beta = (2 < ||\mathbf{I_p} - \mathbf{I_q}||^2 >)^{-1}$ and $< . >$ denotes the expectation over an image sample. For details, please see [25] and references therein. Note that since the image element selected by the user as well as the image background have similar color profiles throughout the set of images, we are able to reuse the GMMs which were trained using the pixels selected by the user in the base image for segmenting all the other images instead of requiring the user to brush the image element in each of the image, hence saving the user the extra work and time needed to train the GMMs for each image.

Figure 10 shows the segmentation results for a case with a fair amount of camera motion among photos. Since the position of the subject is relatively similar, our segmentation algorithm still performs well enough for our task of comparing the brushed elements, even though the results may not be good enough for other applications.

ACKNOWLEDGMENTS

This work is supported by a research grant from the Human Sixth Sense Program at ADSC from Singapore's Agency for Science, Technology and Research (A*STAR), as well as A*STAR SERC grant no. 092 101 0063.

REFERENCES

1. Agarwala, A., Dontcheva, M., Agrawala, M., Drucker, S., Colburn, A., Curless, B., Salesin, D., and Cohen, M. Interactive digital photomontage. *ACM Transactions on Graphics (Proc. SIGGRAPH) 23*, 3 (2004), 294–302.
2. Ames, M., Eckles, D., Naaman, M., Spasojevic, M., and House, N. Requirements for mobile photoware. *Journal of Personal and Ubiquitous Computing 14* (2010), 95–109.
3. Apted, T., Kay, J., and Quigley, A. Tabletop sharing of digital photographs for the elderly. In *Proc. ACM Conference on Human Factors in Computing Systems (CHI)* (2006), 781–790.
4. Ballan, L., Brostow, G. J., Puwein, J., and Pollefeys, M. Unstructured video-based rendering: Interactive exploration of casually captured videos. *ACM Transactions on Graphics (Proc. SIGGRAPH) 29*, 4 (2010), 87:1–87:11.
5. Bederson, B. PhotoMesa: A zoomable image browser using quantum treemaps and bubblemaps. In *Proc. Annual ACM Symposium on User Interface Software and Technology* (2001), 71–80.
6. Böhmer, M., and Bauer, G. Exploiting the icon arrangement on mobile devices as information source for context-awareness. In *Proc. 12th International Conference on Human Computer Interaction with Mobile Devices and Services (MobileHCI)* (2010), 195–198.
7. Boykov, Y., and Jolly, M.-P. Interactive graph cuts for optimal boundary & region segmentation of objects in N-D images. In *Proc. International Conference on Computer Vision (ICCV)* (2001), 105–112.
8. Boykov, Y., and Kolmogorov, V. An experimental comparison of min-cut/max-flow algorithms for energy minimization in vision. *IEEE Transactions on Pattern Analysis and Machine Intelligence 26*, 9 (2004), 1124–1137.
9. Cui, J., Wen, F., Xiao, R., Tian, Y., and Tang, X. EasyAlbum: An interactive photo annotation system based on face clustering and re-ranking. In *Proc. ACM Conference on Human Factors in Computing Systems (CHI)* (2007), 367–376.
10. Durrant, A., Rowland, D., Kirk, D. S., Benford, S., Fischer, J. E., and McAuley, D. Automics: Souvenir generating photoware for theme parks. In *Proc. ACM Conference on Human Factors in Computing Systems (CHI)* (2011), 1767–1776.
11. Frohlich, D., Kuchinsky, A., Pering, C., Don, A., and Ariss, S. Requirements for photoware. In *Proc. ACM Conference on Computer Supported Cooperative Work* (2002), 166–175.
12. Graham, A., Garcia-Molina, H., Paepcke, A., and Winograd, T. Time as essence for photo browsing through personal digital libraries. In *Proc. ACM/IEEE-CS Joint Conference on Digital Libraries* (2002), 326–335.
13. Henze, N., and Boll, S. Evaluation of an off-screen visualization for magic lens and dynamic peephole interfaces. In *Proc. 12th International Conference on Human Computer Interaction with Mobile Devices and Services (MobileHCI)* (2010), 191–194.
14. Huynh, D. F., Drucker, S. M., Baudisch, P., and Wong, C. Time quilt: Scaling up zoomable photo browsers for large, unstructured photo collections. In *Proc. CHI Extended Abstracts* (2005), 1937–1940.

15. Kang, H., and Shneiderman, B. Visualization methods for personal photo collections: Browsing and searching in the PhotoFinder. In *Proc. IEEE International Conference on Multimedia and Expo (ICME)* (2000), 1539 – 1542.

16. Kirk, D., Sellen, A., Rother, C., and Wood, K. Understanding photowork. In *Proc. ACM Conference on Human Factors in Computing Systems (CHI)* (2006), 761–770.

17. Kratz, S., Brodien, I., and Rohs, M. Semi-automatic zooming for mobile map navigation. In *Proc. 12th International Conference on Human Computer Interaction with Mobile Devices and Services (MobileHCI)* (2010), 63–72.

18. Liu, J., Sun, J., and Shum, H.-Y. Paint selection. *ACM Transactions on Graphics (Proc. SIGGRAPH) 28*, 3 (2009), 69:1–69:7.

19. McAdam, C., Pinkerton, C., and Brewster, S. A. Novel interfaces for digital cameras and camera phones. In *Proc. 12th International Conference on Human Computer Interaction with Mobile Devices and Services (MobileHCI)* (2010), 143–152.

20. Miller, A. D., and Edwards, W. K. Give and take: a study of consumer photo-sharing culture and practice. In *Proc. ACM Conference on Human Factors in Computing Systems (CHI)* (2007), 347–356.

21. Mortensen, E. N., and Barrett, W. A. Intelligent scissors for image composition. In *Proc. SIGGRAPH* (1995), 191–198.

22. Mulloni, A., Dünser, A., and Schmalstieg, D. Zooming interfaces for augmented reality browsers. In *Proc. 12th International Conference on Human Computer Interaction with Mobile Devices and Services (MobileHCI)* (2010), 161–170.

23. Platt, J. C., Czerwinski, M., and Field, B. A. PhotoTOC: Automatic clustering for browsing personal photographs. Tech. Rep. MSR-TR-2002-17, Microsoft Research, 2002.

24. Rodden, K., and Wood, K. R. How do people manage their digital photographs? In *Proc. ACM Conference on Human Factors in Computing Systems (CHI)* (2003), 409–416.

25. Rother, C., Kolmogorov, V., and Blake, A. "GrabCut": Interactive foreground extraction using iterated graph cuts. *ACM Transactions on Graphics (Proc. SIGGRAPH) 23*, 3 (2004), 309–314.

26. Savakis, A. E., Etz, S. P., and Loui, A. C. Evaluation of image appeal in consumer photography. In *Proc. SPIE Human Vision and Electronic Imaging*, vol. 3959 (San Jose, CA, Jan. 23–28, 2000), 111–120.

27. Shneiderman, B., Bederson, B. B., and Drucker, S. M. Find that photo! Interface strategies to annotate, browse, and share. *Communications of the ACM 49* (April 2006), 69–71.

28. Shneiderman, B., and Kang, H. Direct annotation: A drag-and-drop strategy for labeling photos. In *Proc. International Conference on Information Visualization* (2000), 88–95.

29. Snavely, N., Seitz, S. M., and Szeliski, R. Photo tourism: Exploring photo collections in 3D. *ACM Transactions on Graphics (Proc. SIGGRAPH) 25*, 3 (2006), 835–846.

30. Szeliski, R., Zabih, R., Scharstein, D., Veksler, O., Kolmogorov, V., Agarwala, A., Tappen, M., and Rother, C. A comparative study of energy minimization methods for Markov random fields. In *Proc. European Conference on Computer Vision (ECCV)* (2006), 16–29.

31. Van House, N. A. Collocated photo sharing, story-telling, and the performance of self. *International Journal of Human-Computer Studies 67*, 12 (2009), 1073–1086.

A Longitudinal Review of Mobile HCI Research Methods

Jesper Kjeldskov and Jeni Paay
Department of Computer Science
Aalborg University, Denmark
{jesper, jeni}@cs.aau.dk

ABSTRACT

This paper revisits a research methods survey from 2003 and contrasts it with a survey from 2010. The motivation is to gain insight about how mobile HCI research has evolved over the last decade in terms of approaches and focus. The paper classifies 144 publications from 2009 published in 10 prominent outlets by their research methods and purpose. Comparing this to the survey for 2000-02 show that mobile HCI research has changed methodologically. From being almost exclusively driven by engineering and applied research, current mobile HCI is primarily empirically driven, involves a high number of field studies, and focus on evaluating and understanding, as well as engineering. It has also become increasingly multi-methodological, combining and diversifying methods from different disciplines. At the same time, new opportunities and challenges have emerged.

Author Keywords

Research methods; research purpose; literature survey

ACM Classification Keywords

A.1. [General Literature]: introductory and survey;

General Terms

Design, Human Factors

INTRODUCTION

In 2003 we did a comprehensive literature survey of Mobile Human-Computer Interaction research. The purpose of the survey was to generate an empirically grounded characterization of state-of-the-art and current practices within this growing area of mobile computing. At that time, Mobile HCI and interaction design research was still very much in its infancy as an academic research area. Widely commercially successful devices had only been around for about a decade, and leading conferences had only a few years of history behind them. As a consequence only a small body of knowledge existed about this emerging research field, and no coherent sets of methods and techniques for research had yet been established.

The literature survey [3] contributed to bringing this issue on the agenda. It reviewed 102 mobile HCI publications from 2000-02. Inspired by a similar study in Information Systems [11]. Each paper was classified in terms of its research method and purpose (see table 1), extracted from [11] with supplementary input from [1][5][6][8][12].

MobileHCI'12, September 21–24, 2012, San Francisco, CA, USA.

TRENDS AND ASSUMPTIONS

The literature survey revealed a strong bias towards applied research for engineering and laboratory experiments for evaluation, as shown in figure 13. Put simply, mobile interaction design research in the early 2000s was dominated by building new systems in a trial-and-error manner, and evaluating them in laboratory settings – if evaluating them at all. There was very little going on in terms of trying to understand the phenomenon of mobility itself in relation to interaction design and technology use, and to use such insight when designing and building actual interactive systems. Nor was much attention given to the role of real world context in relation to understanding, building or evaluating interactive mobile systems [3]. In essence this echoed a fundamental segregation between use- and technology-centeredness depending on whether the involved researchers were primarily interested in *people* or *systems*. On a more general level, it became apparent that methodology seemingly played a very small role. The approaches taken often remained unexplained, their suitability unchallenged, and their limitations and alternatives not discussed.

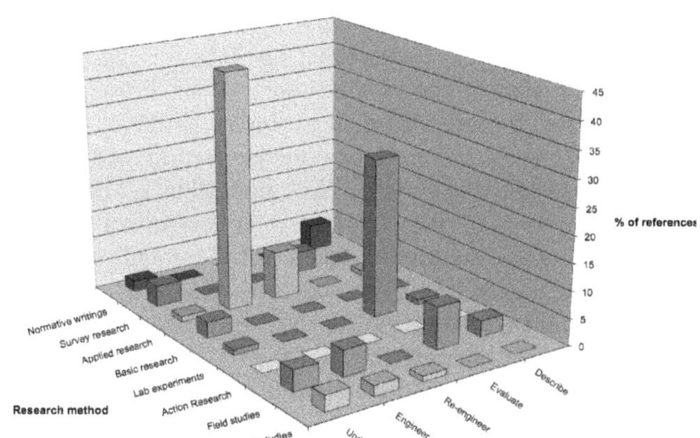

Figure 1. Distribution on methods and purpose in 2000-02 (%)

Based on our more detailed analysis of what types of research and purposes were missing, or largely underrepresented, we cautioned that the bias towards trial-and-error building of interactive systems, evaluations only in the lab, and the lack of research for understanding design and use in real world contexts, would limit the quality and

Method	**Case studies**	Intensive empirical investigations of contemporary phenomena within small size entities such as groups, organizations, individuals, systems or tools in real-life context with the researcher distinct from the phenomena being studied
	Field studies	Characterized by taking place in "the real world" covering a range of qualitative and quantitative approaches from ethnographic studies of phenomena in their social and cultural context to field experiments in which a number of independent variables are manipulated
	Action research	A method through which researchers not only add to the body of scientific knowledge but also apply that knowledge to the object of interest through intervention and participation in the activity being studied
	Lab experiments	Characterized by taking place in a controlled environment created for the purpose of research or in dedicated laboratories allowing a detailed focus on specific phenomena of interest with a large degree of experimental control
	Survey research	Informs research gathers large amounts of data through various techniques such as questionnaires and interviews from a known sample of selected respondents assumed to be independent of their environment
	Applied research	Builds on trial and error on the basis of reasoning through intuition, experience, deduction and induction. Typically the desired outcome of an applied research process is known while means of accomplishing it is not. This makes applied research very goal oriented.
	Basic research	Characterized by trial and error based development of new theories and the study of well-known problems to which neither solutions nor methods are known, relying on the competences of the researcher
	Normative writings	Cover the body of "non-research" writings about phenomena of interests such as concept development writings organizing ideas for stimulating future research, presentation of truth describing ideas that seem intuitively correct, and descriptions of applications.
Purpose	**Understanding**	The purpose of research focusing on finding the meaning of studied phenomena through, for example, frameworks or theories developed from collected data.
	Engineering	The purpose of research focused towards developing new systems or parts of systems, for example an interaction technique for a mobile device, or a mobile application or device.
	Re-engineering	The purpose of research focusing on improving existing systems by redeveloping them such as, for example, adapting a web browser to a small display.
	Evaluating	The purpose of research assessing or validating products, theories or methods, for example, the usability or user experience of a specific application, or a theory of interaction.
	Describing	The purpose of research focusing on defining desirable properties of products, for example, a mobile guide system, or mobile HCI method.

Table 1. Overview of research methods and purposes

scope of the body of knowledge about mobile human-computer interaction being accumulated, and thereby inhibit the advancement and impact of the research field in the future. In particular we found from our analysis that three underlying, and unfortunate, assumptions appeared to be characterizing mobile HCI research at the time:

- We already know what to build
- Context is not important
- Methodology matters very little

We already know what to build
The prevalent approach of applied research for engineering indicated an assumption at the time that we already knew what systems to build and what problems to solve, such as limited screen real estate, limited means for interaction, and limited network bandwidth. We just didn't know yet exactly how to build these systems and how to solve those problems, but the solutions existed out there and were just waiting to be uncovered. Only very little research addressed the more fundamental questions of what is useful and what is perceived problematic from a user-perspective, and evaluations focused on functionality rather than context-centred and user-centred issues. Given the young age of the research field we argued that this could hardly be true and that, on the contrary, young emerging research fields such as this particularly require research addressing such fundamental issues. Continuing to do research on the basis of the assumption that we already know the problem would, in it self, make it very difficult to set this assumption aside and identify the more fundamental challenges at hand.

Context is not important
The limited focus on real-world studies indicated an assumption that context was not really important for what we build, and that interactive mobile computer systems are by definition suitable solutions. Building and evaluating interactive systems on the basis of applied research and laboratory experiments also results in very concrete conclusions about very specific solutions. These conclusions can be difficult to generalize and therefore it can be difficult to elevate our learning from the systems we develop, and study in use, to an abstract level where knowledge can be transferred to other design cases, technologies, domains, users, purposes, etc. This limits our ability to move forward at a pace beyond incremental steps from one specific design to the next. Hence, in our opinion, the assumption, that building and evaluating systems by trial and error is better than grounding engineering, evaluation and theory in user-based studies, seriously weakened mobile HCI research at the time.

Methodology matters very little
The final observation, that only few studies were based on an explicit methodological foundation, indicated an assumption that methodology mattered very little in mobile HCI research. We presented this supposition as a particularly problematic one because it is a well-known fact that the choice of method clearly influence the results subsequently produced [6]. Applied research is, for example, viewed as a rather poorly performing method for problem solving because it requires researchers to investigate a very large space of possibilities.

REASONS

Having provided a snapshot of current practice within mobile HCI research and outlined a number of problematic consequences of this in [3], it was natural to continue by asking *why* research was currently being done this way?

In our opinion, a part of the answer is that bias towards applied research for engineering combined with laboratory experiments for evaluations is simply natural for a young and technologically driven area of research. Applied research and lab experiments are not as such easier than field studies, case studies, and action research, but they are a more straightforward way to start when exploring a new field of emerging technology. Before we can study and understand phenomena like use contexts, usability, and user experiences of new technology we simply need this technology to be available to us in some concrete and functioning form. However, if a field of *emerging technology* is to evolve into a field of *applied technology*, it is important not to get stuck in research methodologies where solutions are created and put to use by trial-and-error rather than grounded in real world context. Applied research methods alone do not create a field of where technology is applied well to real world problems. Another part of the answer, we believe, is that rather than mobile technologies being not ready for studies in natural settings, the body of mobile HCI research and researchers were probably not ready for natural settings research. In the early 2000s only very few studies had been published that used natural setting research methods within mobile HCI. Consequently only very few examples existed for others to be inspired by and to follow. Also, the whole debate about doing natural setting mobile research had not even really started yet. It was also still very unclear exactly how to make use of "new" methods like field studies, case studies, and action research in mobile HCI, and unclear exactly what value they could possibly bring to a specific project.

Finally, and somewhat related to the other two points, a part of the answer could also be attributed to the fact that in the early 2000s the *multi-disciplinarity* of mobile HCI was not yet strong. Like other areas of emerging technologies it was very much dominated by engineering and computer science. In terms of methodology this meant that methods and techniques from, for example, social science, the humanities, and the arts did not yet have a strong presence in the minds and traditions of the dominant mobile HCI researchers at the time, and not a lot of researchers from those disciplines were yet working with mobile HCI.

In summary, there were indeed very good reasons why the methodological landscape of mobile HCI research looked the way it did in 2003. The research up to that point had been fundamental in the creation and shaping of the field. It had created technological possibilities that allowed a paradigmatic shift away from the desktop and opened up for a wide range of new and interesting uses of computer technology within a wide range of interesting domains.

OPPORTUNITIES

Supplementing the descriptive analysis of state-of-the-art in mobile HCI research we also used the literature survey to identify opportunities for future research. The most obvious opportunities lay in responding directly to the assumptions outlined above: 1) conduct research that aimed at studying and understanding the problem space, 2) explore the importance and role of context, and 3) undertake methodological research, for example, development of new methods and techniques for studying, designing, and evaluating. Related to this, but on a more specific level, other opportunities lay in explicitly responding to the gaps in research methods and purposes identified.

In particular, the noticeable lack of *field studies* presented an enormous opportunity to use this method for exploring rich real-world use cases, contexts and user needs to gain deeper understanding of these. As a particular approach, we suggested that learning from other disciplines that have struggled with the study of similar "slippery" phenomena, such as ethnography, could provide important methodological insight. We also proposed that field studies within mobile HCI could be used to inform the engineering of new designs, and the re-engineering of existing ones, through identification of needs and opportunities for innovation. Finally, in response to the bias towards evaluating in laboratory settings, we promoted the opportunity for systematic investigation of field studies for this purpose, as mobility and context can be difficult to emulate in a laboratory. The clear lack of *survey* and *case study* research also presented interesting opportunities. In the field of Information Systems, for example these approaches are used widely. Survey research is often used to collect large amounts of data from, for example, a large segment of actual end-users of a system, enabling much wider reaching power of generalization. Case studies within mobile HCI could increase learning from existing systems within real-world contexts, for example mobile systems and infrastructure within organizations. Such case studies would enable close scrutiny of specific phenomena in specific contexts, which could then be used to enrich the collective knowledge in the discipline and to enable key issues to be described and understood. The issues generated could then be used to generate hypotheses to propagate further research. The very limited amount of *basic research* indicated an opportunity for the development of theoretical frameworks to promote description and understanding. Specifically, we promoted the opportunity for applying theories from other disciplines to the area of mobile HCI. Finally, the complete absence of *action research* pointed to both the lack of an established body of knowledge within the discipline and the unwillingness to implement mobile systems uncertain to succeed. This was perhaps not surprising, given the cost of technology and associated implementation overhead. Nonetheless, this was, again, an opportunity to develop new knowledge in the discipline through studies of practice and intervention.

7 YEARS LATER

In 2010, inspired by [4], we felt it was time to follow up on the survey, and see how the research field had developed in terms of approaches and focus. The second literature review took its offset in research papers on the topic of mobile HCI published in ten top outlets in 2009. These papers constitute all publications related to mobile human-computer interaction in 2009 in the top-level conference proceeding series and journals listed in table 2 below.

Outlet	Count
Mobile HCI Conference (MobHCI)	38
CHI Conference (CHI)	46
UIST Symposium (UIST)	6
Personal and Ubiquitous Computing (PUC)	27
Transactions on Computer-Human Interaction (TOCHI)	3
International Journal of Human-Computer Studies (IJHCS)	8
International Journal of Human-Computer Interaction (IJHCI)	7
Journal of Computer-Supported Cooperative Work (JCSCW)	2
Behaviour and Information Technology (BIT)	2
Interacting with Computers (IwC)	5
Total	**144**

Table 2. Selected outlets and paper counts

While other conferences and journals exist in which interesting research on mobile human-computer interaction is presented, we found that the listed conferences and journals provided a solid and adequately representative base for this study given the number of publications on the topic and the general level of the reviewing processes for these conferences and journals.

While other conferences and journals exist in which interesting research on mobile HCI is presented, we found that the listed conferences and journals provided a solid and adequately representative base for this study given the number of publications on the topic and the general level of the reviewing processes for these conferences and journals.

Through a thorough manual reading of titles, abstracts, and sometimes introductions, of all papers published in the selected ten outlets that year, a total of 144 papers were identified as falling within the field of mobile HCI (table 2). A paper was selected for the study if it was in any way related to mobile devices and HCI. Thus a paper would be omitted if it focused only on mobile network protocol design or did not involve any aspect of mobility of users or systems. All papers were printed, numbered, read through and classified by identifying the purpose of the presented work and the research methods applied in achieving this. The classification was done in three steps. First the two authors of this paper classified each paper independently over a period of two weeks. To ensure consistency, the initial classification was then evaluated by looking through all papers a second time on a single day. Secondly, the classification of each paper was by the two authors in collaboration. Thirdly, we invited the first authors of all 144 papers to provide a self-assessment of their method and purpose. This was received for 55 of the papers, and was used to discuss the classification further where disparities were observed, resulting in some modifications. The self-assessment was highly consistent with the initial joint classification by the two authors. But the final classification contains 12 method disparities and 14 purpose disparities from the self-assessment, where we believed that our own classification was more correct and consistent with the classification of the other papers.

FINDINGS

The classification of research methods and purpose in 2009 is shown in table 3. Since several papers (44%) involved multiple methods and purposes, these appear more than once in the table. As in 2003, an example of this is papers presenting an engineered and evaluated system. As a consequence of this, some aggregate percentages in the findings section will amount to more than 100%.

The first observation that stands out from the 2009 literature survey is the sheer number of publications on the topic. In the first literature review we found 102 papers in the same outlets over a period of 3 years. By relative comparison this number had more than quadrupled by 2009 (424% increase). On the basis of this it is fair to say that mobile HCI is a highly active area of research and has grown substantially in the last 7 years. It is also interesting to notice that while the selected articles from 2009 included the full proceedings of the specialised annual Mobile HCI conference, there were actually more papers published on the topic at the annual ACM Conference on Human Factors in Computing Systems (CHI) that year. Out of the 246 full and short papers in the Proceedings of CHI 2009 almost a fifth (19%) concerned human-computer interaction with mobile systems or devices. This shows that mobile HCI is now a substantial part of mainstream HCI research.

Table 3 shows that in 2009, 49% of mobile HCI research falls within the lab experiment category (71 of 144 papers). The secondly most used method is field studies accounting for 35% of the research (50 out of 144 papers). The third most used method is applied research with 30% (43 of 144 papers). 21% of the papers report from survey research and 6% from case studies. 4% involved basic research and 2% normative writing. Only one entry was found for action research (<1%). Looking at research purpose, 68% of mobile research is done for the purpose of evaluating, of which 63% is done through lab experiments, 29% through field studies, and 7% through surveys. 40% of the reported research involves building systems, 72% of which is done through applied research. Research for understanding mobile HCI represents 31% of the papers, of which 43% is done through field studies and 32% through surveys. 7% of the classified papers describe aspects of mobile HCI, 60% of which is informed by surveys.

Thus within mobile HCI research in 2009 there is a clear tendency towards evaluating systems, and doing so in laboratory settings. Building systems is also a central activity, closely followed by research for understanding.

Method/ purpose	Case studies	Field studies	Action research	Lab experiment	Survey research	Applied research	Basic research	Normative writings
Understand	10, 54, 107, 136	8, 14, 28, 38, 46, 56, 61,63, 76, 79, 83, 87, 88, 92, 102, 110, 126, 129, 134	3	15, 42, 52, 77, 101	20, 26, 39, 43, 57, 61, 69, 70, 89, 90, 95, 100, 114, 117, 119, 122			131
Engineer	6	5, 40, 123		31, 62, 81, 94	39, 137, 141	1, 2, 7, 11, 13, 16, 17, 19, 21, 24, 27, 28, 36, 45, 46, 47, 58, 59, 65, 66, 74, 80, 82, 85, 96, 98, 104, 108, 111, 113, 114, 115, 116, 118, 120, 125, 128, 138, 140, 143, 144	29, 51, 109, 127, 130	
Re-engineer				35		37, 44	97	
Evaluate	84	9, 22, 39, 40, 43, 45, 58, 60, 75, 81, 86, 93, 96, 98, 104, 111, 112, 115, 123, 124, 128, 132, 138, 139, 141		4, 5, 6, 7, 11, 12, 13, 16, 17, 21, 22, 24, 25, 29, 30, 31, 32, 34, 35, 36, 37, 43, 44, 47, 48, 50, 51, 53, 55, 58, 62. 64, 65, 66, 71, 73, 74, 78, 80, 82, 89, 91, 99, 103, 104, 105, 106, 108, 109, 112, 116, 118, 119, 121, 125, 127, 130, 133, 137, 140, 142, 143, 144	1, 17, 18, 55, 75, 120, 135			
Describe	33, 93				23, 49, 50, 67, 68			41, 72

Table 3. Classification of mobile HCI research in 2009. Numbers refer to the list of reviewed papers.

Looking in more detail at the current distribution of papers on their research methods and purposes, a number of interesting observations can be made. Most interestingly, the literature survey shows that by 2009 the research area of mobile HCI is characterized by:

- Focus on evaluating, engineering and understanding
- Increased empirical research
- Multi-methodological research

Evaluating, engineering and understanding

The review shows that mobile HCI has become about evaluating, engineering and understanding mobile systems and their use (figure 2). From a user-experience perspective, this development towards multiple purposes is a positive advancement as it reflects better the different and well-acknowledged phases of the traditional user-centred design cycle than a purely engineering driven approach. However, looking more detailed at the specific research projects reported in the mobile HCI literature, those different phases are in fact still poorly integrated. Research with the purpose of *understanding* and research with the purpose of *engineering* are still very separate, and rarely appears together or as outcomes from the same project. Engineering systems is still predominantly done by trial-and-error based on potentially good ideas (73,6%), and studies aiming to understand mobile HCI phenomena reportedly seldom lead to new systems or designs (0,7%).

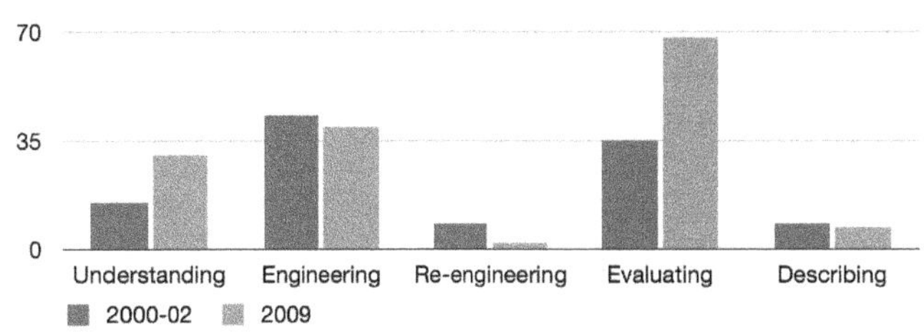

Figure 2. Research purposes in 2000-02 and 2009 (%)

Furthermore, while systems are today typically evaluated empirically (84%), these evaluations reportedly seldom lead to understanding beyond specific findings in relation to the concrete solutions being studied (1%). Hence, it seems that the broader scope of mobile HCI research in 2009 compared to 2000-02 is now reflecting the presence of *two* distinct approaches rather than one: a use- and a technology-centred one, depending on whether the involved researchers are primarily interested in *people* or *systems*. The first approach aims primarily at understanding mobile user experiences theoretically and conceptually, and the second aims primarily at building new mobile systems and evaluating them in use. Within both approaches *users* play an important role, but in first they are the *objects* of the research, while in the second they are research *subjects* in the study of technology. According to Rasmussen [9] such clear-cut distinction tends to cause the potentially fruitful dialectics between the two approaches to disappear. If one of the two approaches is considered 100% good and the other 100% bad, from either side of the divide, then one is destined to subsume the other. Dialectic thinking, on the other hand, encourages us to develop a synthesis at a higher stage of the opposing interests, as also discussed by Dahlbom and Mathiassen [2]. This is not simply a matter of finding a balance between the two but about transcending beyond opposing views and shaping a new unity at another level [7]. Hence, in order to strengthen the "interaction" part of mobile human-computer interaction a closer integration of these two approaches, the use- and the technology-centred one, is needed.

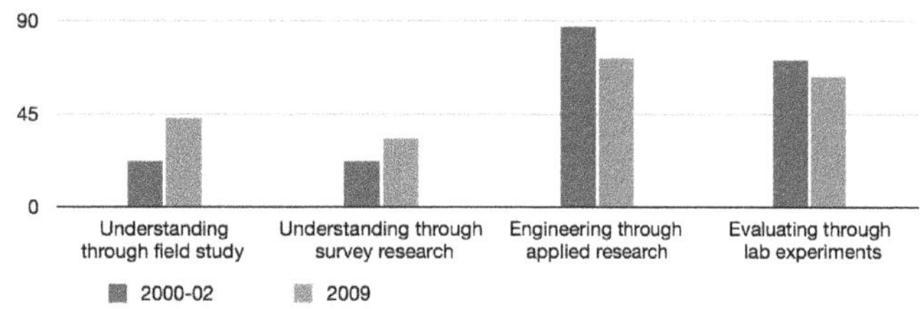

Figure 3. Research for understanding, engineering and evaluating by their dominating methods (%)

Another observation from looking at the three prevailing purposes is that they are each still dominated by the same particular methods as they were 7 years ago. This is illustrated in figure 3. Understanding is still done primarily through field and survey research (76% totally), engineering is done 3/4 through applied research (72%), and evaluations are done 2/3 through lab studies (63%). This means that while the overall focus of mobile HCI has shifted towards more research for understanding and evaluating, the research done *within* the different categories of research purposes is still to a large degree being carried out as before. Focus may have shifted, but methods used for particular purposes mostly have not.

The slight outlier here is research for the purpose of understanding. Not only is more research done overall with this purpose compared to 7 years ago, it is also done by more varying methods than research with any of the other purposes. Accordingly, figure 3 above depicts two groups of research for understanding informed by field studies and survey research, which accounts for 43% and 33% of the research for this purpose respectively. Looking more detailed at this research it is even evident that the category of *field studies* itself is beginning to diversify notably into varying *types* of field methods, such as field ethnographies and field experiments, and that there is even an evolving hybrid of field studies and survey research emerging in the form of "field surveys", such as cultural probes. This indicates that researchers concerned with *understanding* mobile HCI phenomena are successfully evolving their methodological repertoire to fit better with the contemporary research challenges facing them. This is not in the same way clearly evident for the other areas of focus.

Increased empirical research

The second general observation is that whereas applied technical research dominated the field 7 years ago, mobile HCI is today characterized by an increased amount of empirical research. As can be seen from figure 4, there has been a significant increase in the use of empirical methods. Because the total amount of research has increased this is true in both relative and absolute numbers. Most notably the relative amount of survey research has almost tripled, field studies have more than doubled, and lab experiments have almost doubled. On the contrary the relative amount of applied research has decreased by nearly 1/3.

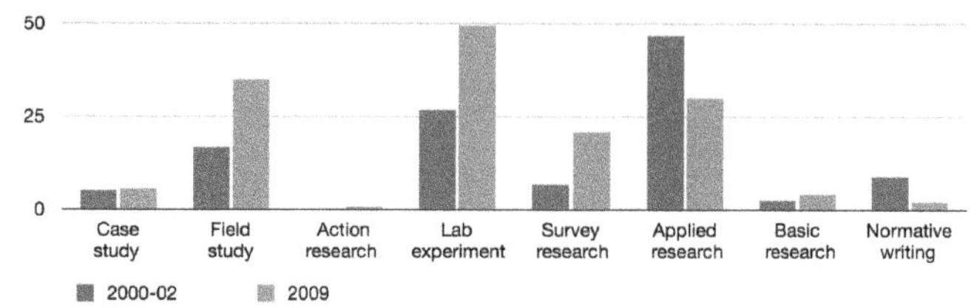

Figure 4. Mobile HCI research methods, 2000-02 & 2009 (%)

This means that mobile HCI is evolving as a research field towards a better balance between natural, artificial, and environment independent settings, and therefore also towards a better balance between the different use potentials of the specific research conducted. Research in natural, artificial, and environment independent settings have very different fundamental strengths and weaknesses, and balancing them well allows the field as a whole to draw on the relative strong points of particular types of research settings while compensating for their limitations.

Multi-methodological research

What can also be observed from the distribution of research methods in figure 4 is that no single method is now dominating mobile HCI but that it has become multi-methodological. Seven years ago mobile HCI was dominated by applied research but today there are just as many field studies, even more lab experiments, and also a substantial body of survey research. Hence the cumulative methodological repertoire of mobile HCI researchers seems to have broadened. Secondly, almost half of the reviewed papers (44%) reported on *explicit combinations* of multiple methods for multiple purposes. For example, it is now the rule rather than the exception to combine engineering with empirical evaluations (84%) where 7 years ago this was a much more rare occurrence (18%). This means that mobile HCI is evolving as a research field towards a more balanced distribution of research methods from across the broader range of disciplines involved. It does not, however, mean that these methodological foundations are *integrated* across disciplinary boundaries in an *inter*-disciplinary way [10], but the increasing explicit combination of methods is a good starting point for evolving in such direction. At the same time it is also important to notice that the amount of case studies, action research and basic research is, still, almost non existing. This shows that there is still a bias towards environment independent or artificial setting research, or in case of natural setting research, a bias towards basing it on snapshots of the real world rather than on longitudinal and in-depth studies of real world practice.

The tendency towards multi-methodological research indicates that mobile HCI researchers are discovering a need for diversifying their approaches and working more closely with other disciplines. As a part of this diversification, the specific category of *field studies* has notably changed. It now includes at least three notable sub categories of field ethnographies, field experiments, and field surveys, as described in table 3 below.

Field study	Description	%
Field ethnography	Qualitative and quantitative approaches to natural setting research where the researcher is present in the field from full-scale ethnographic studies of phenomena in their social and cultural context to smaller scale observational studies and contextual inquiry.	54%
Field experiment	Natural setting research where a number of independent variables are manipulated in the study of a particular phenomenon under controlled but realistic conditions. This includes, for example, usability tests and quasi experiments in real use contexts.	28%
Field survey	Natural setting research where survey techniques such as questionnaires, diaries, log files, interviews etc. are use for data collection rather than the researcher being present in the field. This includes, for example, cultural probe studies and the like.	18%

Table 3. Three notable emerging variations of field studies

Looking in detail at the papers in the field study column of table 2, field ethnographies and field surveys are both used roughly 50-50 for understanding and evaluating while field experiments are primarily used for evaluating (79%). Increasing methodological diversification can also be observed within studies for evaluation, although not as strongly. Whereas multiple methods appeared in only 5% of the evaluation studies 7 years ago, this is now the case of 9% of all evaluations. These multi-method evaluations typically span across different types of research settings. Unexpectedly, however, only 5% explicitly combines *field* and *lab* based methods, which is the same proportion as 7 years ago. This is surprising in the light of the long lasting debate on lab versus field evaluations within mobile HCI. It indicates that the view, which we share and promote, that lab and field evaluations both have justification, albeit for studying different things, and therefore should be combined and integrated, has not been widely established.

DISCUSSION

Based on the recent research review it appears that the three implicit assumptions dominating the area of mobile HCI a decade ago have changed, or are in the process of changing. Firstly, the multi-methodological character of recent research shows that methodology is now considered an important component of research and something that can be used actively as a means to shape research and guide its focus and contribution. Secondly, the increased amount of empirical and theoretical research into understanding phenomena surrounding and influencing mobile user experiences shows that the broader context is now indeed considered an important factor for mobile HCI. Finally, the increased amount of field studies research shows that, at least within some parts of the mobile HCI community it is clear that we do not already know what to build and what problems to solve. Unfortunately, however, as engineering is still predominantly informed by applied research, knowing what systems to build and what problems to solve still appears to be the assumption within the more technical camps of mobile HCI.

One of the things that is perhaps most disconcerting about current research practice in mobile HCI is the continuing lack of *case study* and *action research*. While there is a clear increase in natural setting research in the form of field ethnographies, field experiments and field surveys, there is still a gap in research that really embraces the full extend and complexity of the real world in which the mobile systems we design and develop are used. Field ethnographies, -experiments and -surveys are all good at grounding our knowledge in the real world, but they are often limited in terms of their scope, depth and duration, and typically don't involve an element of intervention during the progress of the study. Hence field the types of field studies currently dominating mobile HCI research often leave us with incomplete snapshots of use rather than the comprehensive accounts of it that case study and action research could facilitate providing.

Another disconcerting observation is the apparent segregation of mobile HCI research and researchers into two camps primarily interested in *people* or in *systems*. This segregation, of course, stems from the multi-disciplinarily of the research field, but maintaining such divide sadly also sustain an unfortunate implicit assumption that people and technology can, and perhaps even should, be studied separately. In turn, such assumption can be partially responsible for researchers in the people- and technology-oriented camps continuing to investigate the same types of questions and problems as before in a disconnected manner, rather than developing and investigating new shared ones in collaboration. In our view, not doing this impede the ability of mobile HCI research to continue informing the creation of better mobile devices, systems and services.

New opportunities and challenges

The distribution of research methods and purpose in the second research methods review offers a number of new opportunities and challenges within the area of mobile HCI. Most importantly, we believe that it is important that the current trajectory of doing *more* field work is extended with a move towards doing *better* field work. This does not just mean that we should improve the way we apply methods for field work, but also that we could be applying a different set of natural setting research methodologies when going into the field. Whereas field ethnographies, -experiments and -surveys offer a valuable opportunity for studying real-world phenomena and situating our design proposals in context, more *case studies* in mobile HCI could facilitate increased learning from both new and existing systems within real-world context through broader scope, increased depth and longer durations of our empirical studies, as exemplified in reviewed paper no. 6,

10, 33, 54, 84, 93, 107 and 136. As pointed out in [3] such case studies enable closer scrutiny of mobile system use and user experience, which would in turn increase the collective knowledge in the discipline and inform the generation of new hypotheses to guide further research. In extension of this, the maturity and proliferation of mobile technologies throughout society today means that some of the reasons for not doing action-research based empirical work discussed in [3] have disappeared, making this approach a currently underutilized opportunity for developing knowledge in the discipline through longitudinal deployment and evaluation in practice, as exemplified in reviewed paper no. 3.

The second opportunity and challenge facing current mobile HCI is, in our opinion, to transcend beyond the research questions and problems currently directing the focus of the people- and technology- oriented camps of mobile HCI respectively. Due to this continued divide we are at risk of missing the holistic nature of the mobile HCI challenges currently at hand, as mobile technologies have matured considerably and now pervade almost every aspect of our lives, work and leisure. What is needed then is a shift where new and shared problems are framed in a way that force new ways of thinking and operating [10]. This facilitates what Rogers et al. describe as *"reconceptualizing the domain of interest through using a modified unit of analysis"*. Hereby, the scope can be broadened while still allowing the use of existing concepts and theory. Candidates for such modified units of analysis for mobile HCI could be entities like "context" or "mobile device ecosystems".

Other opportunities include more basic research, and research that seeks to integrate, or at least combine, fieldwork better with engineering. In terms of evaluating, there are also still opportunities for exploring alternatives to field studies and lab experiments, such as case studies and action research for achieving better ecological validity. Finally, survey research could be explored even more for widening the scope and generalizability of evaluations.

CONCLUSIONS

This paper has provided a snapshot of mobile HCI research in 2009 based on a review and of 144 top-level publications classified by their methods and purpose. This is compared to a similar review from 2000-02. From this review and comparison we have identified a number of methodological trajectories within mobile HCI research showing that the research field is extending its focus and its repertoire of methods and techniques. Mobile HCI is no longer dominated by engineering systems using applied approaches, but has become a highly empirically driven area of research with a growing focus on understanding the phenomena of mobile HCI. However, there are still opportunities and challenges for mobile HCI research. Firstly, there is need and opportunity for doing better field research by applying more in-depth and longitudinal natural setting methodologies such as case studies and action research. Secondly, there is need and opportunity for distilling and defining a set of new research questions and problems, that transcends focus on either people or technology and are shared more broadly within the community. Other new opportunities lie in simply trying to populate the "less crowded" areas of table 3.

LIMITATIONS

The present study echo the limitations related to the methods and purpose categories potentially being criticised for being unclear and overlapping, and sometimes orthogonal. Hence it can sometimes be difficult to decide which category a paper belongs to, and the study relies on the researchers and authors' understanding of these.

ACKNOWLEDGEMENTS

We would like to thank everyone who provided a self-assessment of their selected research article.

REFERENCES

1. Basili, V.R., Selby, R.W. and Hutchins, D.H. Experimentation in software engineering. *IEEE Transactions on Software Engineering*, (1986), 733-743
2. Dahlbom, B. and Mathiassen L. *Computers in context.* Malden, MA, Blackwell Publishers Inc. 1993
3. Kjeldskov, J. and Graham, C. A Review of MobileHCI Research Methods. *Proc. Mobile HCI 2003,* LNCS, Springer-Verlag (2003), 317-335
4. Kjeldskov, J., Skov, M.B. and Stage, J. Does Time Heal? A Longitudinal Study of Usability. *Proc. OzCHI 2005,* Canberra, Australia. ACM Press (2005), 1-10
5. Lewis, I.M. *Social Anthropology in Perspective.* Cambridge University Press, 1985
6. Myers, M.D. Qualitative Research in Information Systems. *MIS Quarterly 21,* 2 (1997), 241-242
7. Nonaka, I., and Toyama, R. A firm as a dialectical being: towards a dynamic theory of a firm. *Industrial and Corporate Change 11,* 5 (2002), 995-1009.
8. Rapoport, R.N. Three Dilemmas in Action Research. *Human Relations 23,* 4 (1970), 499-513
9. Rasmussen L. B. From human-centred to human-context centred approach: looking back over 'the hills', what has been gained and lost? *AI & Society,* 21 (2007), 471-495.
10. Rogers Y. Scaife M. and Rizzo A. Interdisciplinarity: an Emergent or Engineered Process. In Interdisciplinary Collaboration. Mahwah, New Jersey: LEA, 2005
11. Wynekoop, J.L. and Conger, S.A. A Review of CASE Research Methods. *Proc. Working Conference on The Information Systems Research Arena* (1990)
12. Yin, R. K. *Case Study Research, Design and Methods, 2nd ed.* Newbury Park, Sage Publications, 1994

LIST OF REVIEWED PAPERS

1. Amemiya T., Maeda T., and Ando H. 2009. Location-free haptic interaction for large-area social applications. PUC, 13, 5
2. Ankolekar A., Szabo G., Luon Y., Huberman B., Wilkinson D., and Wu F. 2009. Friendlee: a mobile application for your social life. MobHCI'09.
3. Aoki P., Honicky R. J., Mainwaring A., Myers C., Paulos E., Subramanian S., Woodruff, A. 2009. A vehicle for research: using street sweepers to explore the landscape of environmental community action. CHI'09
4. Arvanitis T. N., Petrou A., Knight J. F., Savas S., Sotiriou S., Gargalakos M., Gialouri, E. 2009. Human factors and qualitative pedagogical evaluation of a mobile augmented reality system. PUC, 13, 3
5. Baber C., Smith P., Butler M., Cross J., Hunter J. 2009. Mobile technology for crime scene examination, IJHCS, 67, 5
6. Bardram J. 2009. Activity-based computing for medical work in hospitals. TOCHI. 16, 2
7. Baudisch P. and Chu G. 2009. Back-of-device interaction allows creating very small touch devices. CHI'09
8. Bedwell B., Schnädelbach H., Benford S., Rodden T., Koleva B. 2009. In support of city exploration. CHI'09
9. Bell M., Reeves S., Brown B., Sherwood S., MacMillan D., Ferguson J., Chalmers, M. 2009. EyeSpy: supporting navigation through play. CHI'09
10. Benford S., Giannachi G., Koleva B., Rodden T. 2009. From interaction to trajectories: designing coherent journeys through user experiences. CHI'09
11. Bergman J., Kauko J., Keränen J. 2009. Hands on music: physical approach to interaction with digital music. MobHCI'09
12. Brewster S., Hughes M. 2009. Pressure-based text entry for mobile devices. MobHCI'09
13. Broll G., Keck S., Holleis P., Butz A. 2009. Improving the accessibility of NFC/RFID-based mobile interaction through learnability and guidance. MobHCI'09
14. Brown L., Sellen A., Krishna R., Harper R. 2009. Exploring the potential of audio-tactile messaging for remote interpersonal communication. CHI'09
15. Brumby D., Salvucci D., Howes A. 2009. Focus on driving: how cognitive constraints shape the adaptation of strategy dialing while driving. CHI'09
16. Bruns E. Bimber O. 2009. Adaptive training of video sets for image recognition on mobile phones. PUC, 13, 2
17. Buechley L., Eisenberg M. 2009. Fabric PCBs, electronic sequins, and socket buttons: techniques for e-textile craft. PUC, 13, 2
18. Chao P., Chen G. 2009. Augmenting paper-based learning with mobile phones. IwC, 21, 3
19. Chen H., Jin, Q. 2009. Ubiquitous Personal Study: a framework for supporting information access and sharing. PUC, 13, 7
20. Chen Y., Katz, J. 2009. Extending family to school life: College students' use of the mobile phone, IJHCS. 67, 2
21. Cherniavsky N., Chon J., Wobbrock J., Ladner R., Riskin, E. 2009. Activity analysis enabling real-time video communication on mobile phones for deaf users. UIST'09
22. Cherubini M., Anguera X., Oliver N., de Oliveira R. 2009. Text versus speech: a comparison of tagging input modalities for camera phones. MobHCI'09
23. Cho G., Lee S., Cho, J. 2009. Review and Reappraisal of Smart Clothing. IJHCI, 25, 6
24. Choi M., Kim, G. 2009. TouchBall: a design and evaluation of a hand-held trackball based touch-haptic interface. CHI'09
25. Chung J., Schmandt C.2009. Going my way: a user-aware route planner. CHI'09
26. Chung N., Kwon S. 2009. Effect of trust level on mobile banking satisfaction: a multi-group analysis of information system success instruments. BIT. 28, 6
27. Coronato A., Esposito M., Pietro, G. 2009. A multimodal semantic location service for intelligent environments. PUC, 13, 7
28. Cosley D., Baxter J., Lee S., Alson B., Nomura S., Adams P., Sarabu C., Gay, G. 2009. A tag in the hand: supporting semantic, social, and spatial navigation in museums. CHI'09
29. Costanza E., Huang J. 2009. Designable visual markers. CHI'09
30. Crossan A., McGill M., Brewster S., Murray-Smith R. 2009. Head tilting for interaction in mobile contexts. MobileHCI'09
31. Dai L., Sears A., Goldman R. 2009. Shifting the focus from accuracy to recallability: A study of informal note-taking on mobile information technologies. TOCHI. 16, 1
32. De Luca A., von Zezschwitz E., Hußmann, H. 2009. Vibrapass: secure authentication based on shared lies. CHI'09
33. de Sá M., Carriço L. 2009. A mobile tool for in-situ prototyping. MobHCI'09
34. Decle F., Hachet M. 2009. A study of direct versus planned 3D camera manipulation on touch-based mobile phones. MobHCI'09
35. Dunlop M., Taylor F. 2009. Tactile feedback for predictive text entry. CHI'09
36. Echtler F., Nestler S., Dippon A., Klinker G. 2009. Supporting casual interactions between board games on public tabletop displays and mobile devices. PUC, 13, 8
37. Ecker R., Broy V., Butz A., De Luca A. 2009. pieTouch: a direct touch gesture interface for interacting with in-vehicle information systems. MobHCI'09
38. Eckles D., Wightman D., Carlson C., Thamrongrattanarit A., Bastea-Forte M., Fogg B. J. 2009. Social responses in mobile messaging: influence strategies, self-disclosure, and source orientation. CHI'09
39. Froehlich J., Dillahunt T., Klasnja P., Mankoff J., Consolvo S., Harrison B., Landay J. 2009. UbiGreen: investigating a mobile tool for tracking and supporting green transportation habits. CHI'09
40. Frohlich D., Rachovides D., Riga K., Bhat R., Frank M., Edirisinghe E., Wickramanayaka D., Jones M., Harwood W. 2009. StoryBank: mobile digital storytelling in a development context. CHI'09
41. Fröhlich P., Simon R., Baillie L. 2009. Mobile Spatial Interaction. PUC, 13, 4
42. Gao Q., Rau P., Salvendy G. 2009. Perception of Interactivity: Affects of Four Key Variables in Mobile Advertising. IJHCI. 25, 6
43. Garzonis S., Jones S., Jay T., O'Neill, E. 2009. Auditory icon and earcon mobile service notifications. CHI'09
44. Gellersen H., Fischer C., Guinard D., Gostner R., Kortuem G., Kray C., Rukzio E., Streng S. 2009. Supporting device discovery and spontaneous interaction with spatial references. PUC, 13, 4
45. Ghiani G., Paterno F., Santoro C., Spano L., 2009.UbiCicero: A location-aware, multi-device museum guide. IwC, 21, 4
46. Harper R., Taylor S. 2009. Glancephone: an exploration of human expression. MobHCI'09
47. Harrison C., Hudson S. 2009. Abracadabra: wireless, high-precision, and unpowered finger input for very small mobile devices. UIST'09
48. Harrison C., Lim B., Shick A., Hudson, S. 2009. Where to locate wearable displays?: reaction time performance of visual alerts from tip to toe. CHI'09
49. Heikkinen J., Olsson T., Väänänen-Vainio-Mattila K. 2009. Expectations for user experience in haptic communication with mobile devices. MobHCI'09
50. Heo J., Ham D., Park S., Song C., Yoon W. 2009. A framework for evaluating the usability of mobile phones based on multi-level, hierarchical model of usability factors. IwC, 21, 4
51. Hinckley K., Dixon M., Sarin R., Guimbretiere F., Balakrishnan R. 2009. Codex: a dual screen tablet computer. CHI'09
52. Hoggan E., Crossan A., Brewster S., Kaaresoja T. 2009. Audio or tactile feedback: which modality when? CHI'09
53. Inbar O., Lavie T., Meyer J. 2009. Acceptable intrusiveness of online help in mobile devices. MobHCI'09
54. Jeong H., Arriaga R. 2009. Using an ecological framework to design mobile technologies for pediatric asthma management. MobHCI'09
55. Kaasinen E., Kulju M., Kivinen T., Oksman V. 2009. User acceptance of mobile TV services. MobHCI'09
56. Karapanos E., Zimmerman J., Forlizzi J., Martens J. 2009. User experience over time: an initial framework. CHI'09
57. Karlson A., Brush A., Schechter S. 2009. Can i borrow your phone?: understanding concerns when sharing mobile phones. CHI'09
58. Kenteris M., Gavalas D., Economou D. 2009. An innovative mobile electronic tourist guide application. PUC, 13, 2
59. Keränen J., Bergman J., Kauko J. 2009. Gravity sphere: gestural audio-tactile interface for mobile music exploration. CHI'09
60. Kim, D., Steinfield C., Whitten P. (2009). The Effects of Different Presentation Modalities on a Person Identification Task. IJHCI, 25, 2
61. Klasnja P., Consolvo S., Jung J., Greenstein B., LeGrand L., Powledge P., Wetherall D. 2009. "When I am on Wi-Fi, I am fearless". CHI'09
62. Koleva B., Egglestone S., Schnädelbach H., Glover K., Greenhalgh C., Rodden T., Dade-Robertson M. 2009. Supporting the creation of hybrid museum experiences. CHI'09
63. Kostakos V., Nicolai T., Yoneki E., O'Neill E., Kenn H., Crowcroft J. 2009. Understanding and measuring the urban pervasive infrastructure. PUC, 13, 5
64. Kratz S., Ballagas R. 2009. Unravelling seams: improvoing mobile gesture recognition with visual feedback techniques. CHI'09
65. Kratz S., Rohs M. 2009. HoverFlow: expanding the design space of around-device interaction. MobHCI'09
66. Kray C., Rohs M., Hook J., Kratz S. 2009. Bridging the gap between the Kodak and the Flickr generations: A novel interaction technique for collocated photo sharing. IJHCS, 67, 12
67. Krumm J. 2009. A survey of computational location privacy. PUC, 13, 6
68. Langheinrich M. 2009. A survey of RFID privacy approaches. PUC, 13, 6
69. Lee K., Chung N., 2009. Understanding factors affecting trust in and satisfaction with mobile banking in Korea: A modified DeLone and McLean's model perspective. IwC, 21, 5-6
70. Lee S. 2009. Mob Internet Services from Consumers' Perspective. IJHCI, 25, 5
71. Lee S., Zhai, S. 2009. The performance of touch screen soft buttons. CHI'09
72. Lefrere P. 2009. Activity-based scenarios for and approaches to ubiquitous e-Learning. PUC, 13, 3
73. Leichtenstern K. André E. 2009. Studying multi-user settings for pervasive games. MobHCI'09

74. Li F., Dearman D., Truong K. 2009. Virtual shelves: interactions with orientation aware devices. UIST'09
75. Licoppe C., Morel, J. 2009. The collaborative work of producing meaningful shots in mobile video telephony. MobHCI'09
76. Lindley S., Harper R., Randall D., Glancy M., Smyth N. 2009. Fixed in time and time in motion: mobility of vision through a SenseCam lens. MobHCI'09.
77. Little, L., Briggs, P. 2009. Private whispers/public eyes: Is receiving highly personal information in a public place stressful? IwC. 21, 4
78. Liu, J., Zhong, L., Wickramasuriya, J., and Vasudevan, V. 2009. User evaluation of lightweight user authentication with a single tri-axis accelerometer. MobHCI'09
79. Ljungblad, S. 2009. Passive photography from a creative perspective: If I would just shoot the same thing for seven days, it's like, what's the point?. CHI'09.
80. Lorenz, A., De Castro, C. F., and Rukzio, E. 2009. Using handheld devices for mobile interaction with displays in home environments. MobHCI'09
81. Magielse R., Markopoulos P. 2009. HeartBeat: an outdoor pervasive game for children. CHI'09
82. McCallum D. Irani P. 2009. ARC-Pad: absolute+relative cursor positioning for large displays with a mobile touchscreen. UIST'09
83. Medhi I., Gautama S., Toyama K. 2009. A comparison of mobile money-transfer UIs for non-literate and semi-literate users. CHI'09
84. Menold N. 2009. How to Use Information Technology for Cooperative Work: Development of Shared Technological Frames. CSCW, 18
85. Miyaki T., Rekimoto J. 2009. GraspZoom: zooming and scrolling control model for single-handed mobile interaction. MobHCI'09
86. Morrison A., Oulasvirta A., Peltonen P., Lemmela S., Jacucci G., Reitmayr G., Näsänen J., Juustila A. 2009. Like bees around the hive: a comparative study of a mobile augmented reality map. CHI'09
87. Nancy A. Van House Collocated photo sharing, story-telling, and the performance of self. IJHCS. 67, 12
88. Näsänen J., Oulasvirta A., and Lehmuskallio A. 2009. Mobile media in the social fabric of a kindergarten. CHI'09
89. Ni T., Baudisch, P. 2009. Disappearing mobile devices. UIST'09.
90. Nylander S., Lundquist T., Brännström, A. 2009. At home and with computer access: why and where people use cell phones to access the internet. CHI'09
91. Oakley I., Park J., 2009. Motion marking menus: An eyes-free approach to motion input for handheld devices. IJHCS, 67, 6
92. Oulasvirta A., Estlander S., Nurminen, A. 2009. Embodied interaction with a 3D versus 2D mobile map. PUC, 13, 4
93. Paay J., Kjeldskov J., Howard S., and Dave B. 2009. Out on the town: A socio-physical approach to the design of a context-aware urban guide. TOCHI, 16, 2
94. Paek T., Lee B., Thiesson B. 2009. Designing phrase builder: a mobile real-time query expansion interface. MobHCI'09
95. Parkkola H., Saariluoma P., Berki, E. 2009. Action-oriented classification of families' information and communication actions: exploring mothers' viewpoints. BIT, 28, 6
96. Patel N. Clawson J., Voida A., Lyons K. 2009. Mobiphos: A study of user engagement with a mobile collocated-synchronous photo sharing application. IJHCS, 67, 12
97. Patel N., Clawson J., Starner T. 2009. A model of two-thumb chording on a phone keypad. MobHCI'09
98. Pielot M., Henze N., Boll S. 2009. Supporting map-based wayfinding with tactile cues. MobHCI'09
99. Price K., Lin M., Feng J., Goldman R., Sears A., Jacko J. 2009. Nomadic Speech-Based Text Entry: A Decision Model Strategy for Improved Speech to Text Processing. IJHCI, 25, 7
100. Puikkonen A., Häkkilä J., Ballagas R., Mäntyjärvi J. 2009. Practices in creating videos with mobile phones. MobHCI'09
101. Rahman M., Gustafson S., Irani P., Subramanian S. 2009. Tilt techniques: investigating the dexterity of wrist-based input. CHI'09
102. Reilly D., Mackay B., Watters C., Inkpen K. 2009. Planners, navigators, and pragmatists: collaborative wayfinding using a single mobile phone. PUC, 13, 4
103. Ren X., Zhou X. 2009. The Optimal Size of Handwriting Character Input Boxes on PDAs. IJHCI, 25, 8
104. Robinson S., Eslambolchilar P., Jones M. 2009. Sweep-Shake: finding digital resources in physical environments. MobHCI'09
105. Rohs M., Essl G., Schöning J., Naumann A., Schleicher R., Krüger A. 2009. Impact of item density on magic lens interactions. MobHCI'09
106. Rohs M., Schleicher R., Schöning J., Essl G., Naumann A., Krüger A. 2009. Impact of item density on the utility of visual context. PUC, 13, 8
107. Rooksby J., Rouncefield M., Sommerville I. 2009. Testing in the Wild: The Social and Organisational Dimensions of Real World Practice. CSCW, 18
108. Roth V., Turner T. 2009. Bezel swipe: conflict-free scrolling and multiple selection on mobile touch screen devices. CHI'09
109. Roudaut A., Lecolinet E., Guiard Y. 2009. MicroRolls: expanding touch-screen input vocabulary by distinguishing rolls vs. slides of the thumb. CHI'09
110. Rowland D., Flintham M., Oppermann L., Marshall J., Chamberlain A., Koleva B., Benford S., Perez C. 2009. Ubikequitous computing: designing interactive experiences for cyclists. MobHCI'09
111. Rukzio E., Müller M., Hardy R. 2009. Design, implementation and evaluation of a novel public display for pedestrian navigation. CHI'09
112. Sadeh N., Hong J., Cranor L., Fette I., Kelley P., Prabaker M., Rao J. 2009. Understanding and capturing people's privacy policies in a mobile social networking application. PUC, 13, 6
113. Salzmann C., Gillet D., Mullhaupt P. 2009. End-to-end adaptation scheme for ubiquitous remote experimentation. PUC, 13, 3
114. Schall G., Mendez E., Kruijff E., Veas E., Junghanns S., Reitinger B., Schmalstieg D. 2009. Handheld Augmented Reality for underground infrastructure visualization. PUC, 13, 4
115. Schöning J., Krüger A., Cheverst K., Rohs M., Löchtefeld M., Taher F. 2009. PhotoMap: using spontaneously taken images of public maps for pedestrian navigation tasks on mobile devices. MobHCI'09
116. Seewoonauth K., Rukzio E., Hardy R., Holleis P. 2009. Touch & connect and touch & select. MobHCI'09
117. Shin D. 2009. Understanding User Acceptance of DMB in South Korea Using the Modified Technology Acceptance Model. IJHCI. 25, 3
118. Shirazi., Alt F., Schmidt A., Sarjanoja A., Hynninen L., Häkkilä J., Holleis P. 2009. Emotion sharing via self-composed melodies on mobiles. MobHCI'09
119. Snowdon C., Kray, C. 2009. Exploring the use of landmarks for mobile navigation support in natural environments. MobHCI'09
120. Song H., Grossman T., Fitzmaurice G., Guimbretiere F., Khan A., Attar R., Kurtenbach G. 2009. PenLight: combining a mobile projector and a digital pen for dynamic visual overlay. CHI'09
121. Spelmezan D., Hilgers A., Borchers J. 2009. A language of tactile motion instructions. MobHCI'09
122. Spiekermann S. 2009. RFID and privacy: what consumers really want and fear. PUC, 13, 6
123. Stahl A., Höök K., Svensson,M., Taylor A., Combetto M. 2009. Experiencing the Affective Diary. PUC, 13, 5
124. Stevens C. Schubert E., Morris R., Frear M., Chen J., Healey S., Schoknecht C., Hansen S., Cognition and the temporal arts: Investigating audience response to dance using PDAs that record data during live performance. IJHCS, 67, 9
125. Strachan S. and Murray-Smith R. 2009. Bearing-based selection in mobile spatial interaction. PUC, 13, 4
126. Sun X., May, A. 2009. The role of spatial contextual factors in mobile personalization at large sports events. PUC, 13, 4
127. Takayama L., Sison J., Lathrop B., Wolfe N., Chiang A., Nielsen A., Nass C. 2009. Bringing design considerations to the mobile phone and driving debate. CHI'09
128. Takeuchi Y., Sugimoto M. 2009. A user-adaptive city guide system with an unobtrusive navigation interface. PUC 13, 2
129. Tang C., Carpendale S. 2009. A mobile voice communication system in medical setting: love it or hate it?. CHI'09
130. Taylor B., Bove V. 2009. Graspables: grasp-recognition as a UI. CHI'09
131. Terrenghi L., Quigley A., Dix A. 2009. A taxonomy for and analysis of multi-person-display ecosystems. PUC, 13, 8
132. Tsai J., Kelley P., Drielsma, P., Cranor L., Hong J., Sadeh, N. 2009. Who's viewed you?: the impact of feedback in a mobile location-sharing app. CHI'09
133. Turunen M., Melto A., Hella J., Heimonen T., Hakulinen J., Mäkinen E., Laivo T., Soronen H. 2009. User expectations and user experience with different modalities in mobile phone controlled home entertainment system. MobHCI'09
134. Verkasalo H. 2009. Contextual patterns in mobile service usage. PUC, 13, 5
135. von Watzdorf S., Michahelles F. 2009. Evaluating mobile phones as risk information providers. MobHCI'09
136. Waern A., Montola M., Stenros J. 2009. The three-sixty illusion: designing for immersion in pervasive games. CHI'09
137. Wang Q., Hsieh T., Paepcke A., 2009. Piles across space: Breaking the real-estate barrier on small-display devices. IJHCS, 67, 4
138. White S., Feiner S. 2009. SiteLens: situated visualization techniques for urban site visits. CHI'09
139. Wilfinger D., Weiss A., Tscheligi M. 2009. Exploring shopping information and navigation strategies with a mobile device. MobHCI'09
140. Wiltse H. Nichols, J. 2009. PlayByPlay: collaborative web browsing for desktop and mobile devices. CHI'09
141. Wyche S., Caine K., Davison B., Patel S., Arteaga M., Grinter R. 2009. Sacred imagery in techno-spiritual design. CHI'09
142. Yang X., Mak E., Irani P., Bischof W. 2009. Dual-Surface input: augmenting one-handed interaction with coordinated front and behind-the-screen input. MobHCI'09
143. Yatani K. Truong K. 2009. SemFeel: a user interface with semantic tactile feedback for mobile touch-screen devices. UIST'09
144. Yu K., Tian F., Wang K. 2009. Coupa: operation with pen linking on mobile devices. MobHCI'09

EdgeSplit: Facilitating the Selection of Off-Screen Objects

Zahid Hossain[1], Khalad Hasan[1], Hai-Ning Liang[2], Pourang Irani[1]

[1]Department of Computer Science, University of Manitoba, Winnipeg, Manitoba, Canada {zahid, khalad, irani}@cs.umanitoba.ca

[2]Department of Computer Science & Software Engineering Xian Jiaotong-Liverpool University Suzhou, China haining.liang@xjtlu.edu.cn

ABSTRACT

Devices with small viewports (e.g., smartphones or GPS) result in interfaces where objects of interest can easily reside outside the view, into off-screen space. Researchers have addressed this challenge and have proposed visual cues to assist users in perceptually locating off-screen objects. However, little attention has been placed on methods for directly selecting these objects. Current designs of off-screen cues can result in overlaps that can make it difficult to use the cues as handles through which users can select the off-screen objects they represent. In this paper, we present *EdgeSplit*, a technique that facilitates both the *visualization* and *selection* of off-screen objects on small devices. EdgeSplit exploits the space around the device's borders to display proxies of off-screen objects and then partitions the border regions to allow for non-overlapping areas that make selection of objects easier. We present an effective algorithm that provides such partitioning and demonstrate the effectiveness of EdgeSplit for selecting off-screen objects.

Author Keywords

Off-screen object visualization; off-screen target selection.

ACM Classification Keywords

H.5.2. [Information Interfaces and Presentation]: User Interfaces. Graphical User Interfaces Information.

INTRODUCTION

Maps and many other workspaces are often considerably larger than the available display on mobile devices. This often requires users to navigate and inspect objects located outside of the viewport. Off-screen visualization techniques can assist users in determining where objects of interest may be located (Figure 1a) [1,5,4]. The effectiveness of these techniques has primarily been based on how accurately users can locate or judge the relative positions of objects. While significant effort has been expended on visualizing [1, 5], less effort has been invested [6] in facilitating the selection of targets that are located in the off-screen space. Allowing users to inspect off-screen objects via their on-screen proxies can minimize unnecessary navigation. For example, instead of issuing multiple navigation commands, the user can enable selection by directly selecting the on-screen proxy.

We introduce *EdgeSplit* (Figure 1b), a novel technique that facilitates both, the visualization *and* selection of off-screen targets. EdgeSplit displays off-screen objects via proxies placed on the border of the device, in its 'radar' space. These proxies are pixel size representations of the relative locations of the off-screen objects. EdgeSplit then tessellates the 'radar' region into rectilinear polygons, thus ensuring the space designated for one target does not overlap with that of another (Figure 1b). This can alleviate cases of ambiguous selection that could occur with existing methods for off-screen visualization (Figure 1a).

(a) (b)

Figure 1. (a) Off-screen objects represented via Wedge [4] can make it difficult to select an item of interest; (b) EdgeSplit enables the visualization+selection of objects located outside of the main viewport. Off-screen objects are represented as proxy 'dots' around the border of the device. The borders are divided into rectilinear areas, with each area hosting one object and through which users can select objects.

We compared EdgeSplit to a state-of-the-art off-screen visualization technique, Wedge [4] (Figure 1a), in a selection task and in a task to identify the relative positions of objects. Results of our experiment suggest that EdgeSplit facilitates rapid and accurate selection of off-screen objects.

RELATED WORK

EdgeSplit is inspired by off-screen visualization cues and selection techniques.

Off-screen location cues

Several techniques provide location information about off-screen objects. Halo [1] draws circles around off-screen objects, part of which protrude into the viewport to give a sense for where an object is located. To mitigate the concern of overlapping arcs with Halo, Wedge [4], represents an off-screen object using an acute isosceles triangle, thus providing information about the direction and distance of off-screen objects. These techniques can lead to clutter and overlap, making them difficult to use for selecting objects. Overview+detail interfaces show miniature 'dot' representations of objects in the workspace. These interfaces can occlude the main workspace. To avoid such occlusion, EdgeRadar [5] shifts the overview proxy 'dots' to the four edges of the screen (Figure 2a). The proxies convey relative distance and direction of their off-screen counterpart.

Target selection

Target selection is a well-studied area but less so for off-screen objects. *Hopping* [6] is a proxy technique that bring targets closer to the user's cursor to allow for rapid selection. Other techniques, such as *Area Cursor* [7] and *Bubble Cursor* [3], work effectively on desktop interfaces. On touch devices, touch augmentations with high-precision call-outs as used in Shift [8] allow users to select small and clustered targets. Shift's call-out opens when refined selection is necessary. As an alternative to touch enhancements, researchers have suggested that the workspace on which the targets are located be modified. Starburst [2] tessellates the workspace so that each target in a cluster has its own region. Selection can be effectuated quickly and more accurately in dense clusters with such partitioning methods. We exploit this approach in the design of EdgeSplit.

EDGESPLIT

EdgeSplit has two components. The first component is inspired by EdgeRadar [5] and provides a mechanism to visually represent off-screen objects. EdgeSplit uses four docked rectangles (or 'radars') to display proxies of objects located outside the viewport. An off-screen object is represented by a 'dot' on a radar resulting in less clutter and overlap of such cues in comparison to other techniques (e.g., Wedge [4] or Halo [1]). The second component is designed for rapid selection of off-screen objects. Given the small size of these dot-type cues, EdgeSplit tessellates the radar space along the device's edges into polygons such that each subdivided area hosts only one proxy and through which the object can be selected. This technique uses the entire space of EdgeRadar and provides users with non-overlapping areas for selection, thus making it superior to other techniques.

We implemented two space partitioning algorithms in the design of EdgeSplit. The first was inspired by the Voronoi space partitioning method, used in systems such as StarBurst [2] and Bubble Cursor [3]. Partitioning with this method however provided zones with small areas in the radar zones, making them difficult to select.

One of our contributions is a novel partitioning method, as per the following description. (1) objects are sorted according to their positions along the x and y axes; (2) vertical and horizontal bisecting lines are drawn between neighboring proxy objects, thus generating a set of partitioned cells (Figure 2b-c); (3) we assign adjacent off-screen proxies a unique color (Figure 2d); (4) each partitioned cell is assigned the color of its closest proxy (Figure 2d); (5) this is repeated for all targets (Figure 2e), thus creating a pattern seen in Figure 2f (also in Figure 1b). Each colored region hosts at most one object and its selection occurs upon touching the region.

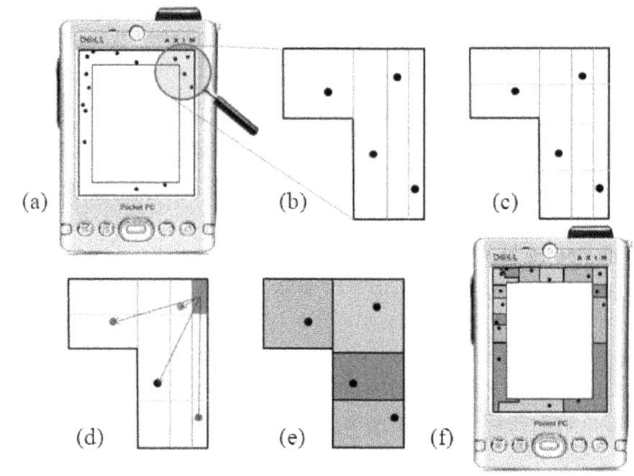

Figure 2. The partitioning algorithm used in EdgeSplit: (a) Targets are presented as 'proxy dots' along the edge of the device; (b) vertical and (c) horizontal bisecting lines are drawn between each proxy; (d) neighboring proxies are assigned a unique color; (e) all cells are filled with the color of its closest proxy; (f) the algorithm is applied to all partitioned cells.

EXPERIMENT

In this experiment we compare the performance with *EdgeSplit* to *VoronoiSplit* and *Wedge* [4] (see Figure 3). We chose Wedge because its visual cues have minimal overlap in comparison to other techniques (e.g., Halo), and provides a good size handle for selection. We did not include zooming, panning, and scrolling as these techniques often require considerable navigational effort from users. In our experiment, the intrusion depth for Wedge was equivalent to the space provided by the radar regions. We modified Wedge so that it would allow for the selection of targets, by touching directly on any region of its visible segment. We implemented all other features of Wedge (including overlap avoidance) as described in [4].

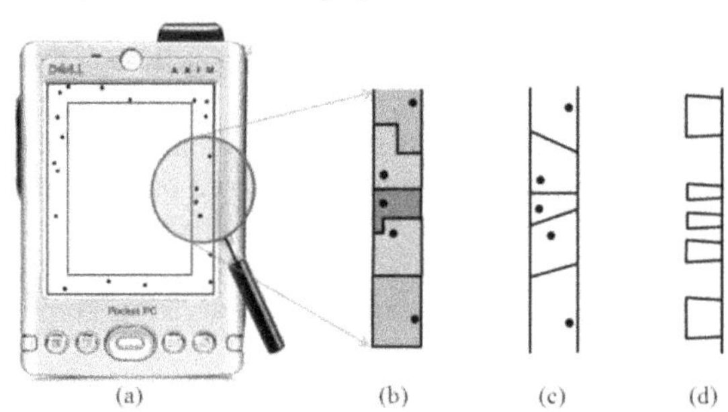

Figure 3. (a) Proxies of off-screen objects; (b-d) represented using EdgeSplit, VoronoiSplit and Wedge. Rectilinear regions in EdgeSplit facilitate selection of objects.

Methods

Apparatus

The experiment ran on Dell Axim X30 Pocket PC with a 3.5" TFT (resistive) touch screen and dimensions of 116×75×12mm. Participants could interact with regions and objects of interest through direct touch. Our techniques should provide similar performance regardless of the touch screen type. The system was developed using C# .NET.

Participants

Twelve participants (all males) between the ages of 21 and 35 were recruited from a local university to participate in this study. All participants were right-handed and had experience using mobile devices.

Design

We used a 3×2×2×2 within-subject design with four independent variables: *Technique* (*EdgeSplit; VoronoiSplit; Wedge*), *Task* (*Select*; *Closest*: finding the closest target), *Target Distance* (*Near*; *Far*), and *Target Density* (*Low*; *High*). The two distances were intended to help determine whether there would be any effect of target distance in these tasks. We also included *Target Density* to assess if the number of distractors along an edge would affect performance. Two densities were used along an edge: *Low* (1-3 distractors), and *High* (4-6 distractors). Therefore, with 3 *Techniques, 2 Tasks,* 2 *Target Distance,* 2 *Target Density,* 8 repetitions and 12 participants, we collected 2304 trials.

Tasks and procedure

The goal target (or object) was always placed at a random distance from the center of the screen (for *Near*, it was at most 60 pixels from the edge and for *Far*, from 60 pixels to a maximum of 240 pixels). In the first task participants were asked to *Select* the goal target (drawn in red). In the second task, participants were asked to select the off-screen object that was closest to a randomly place on-screen target (drawn in red). To provide assistance with ambiguous target selection, we implemented Shift [8]. In the *Select* task the goal target was displayed in red and the distractors in black. Participants had 25 seconds per trial to select the target. All participants were shown how each task and technique would work and received 16 practice trials per technique, with more practice trials if requested. Participants then performed the trials which were counterbalanced by techniques using a Latin Square design. All other variables were presented randomly. At the end of the study, participants filled an exit questionnaire. The experiment lasted 50 minutes.

Measures

We collected task completion time and number of attempts. *Task completion time* was the time from when participants click the Start button to when they successfully selected the target. The *number of attempts* was logged by the number of times participants attempted to select the target. In the Closest task, if participants failed to properly identify the closest target, they were requested to repeat the trial. Upon completion, participants ranked their preferences for the techniques using a 1-5 Likert scale.

Hypotheses

The properties of the three techniques led to the following hypotheses:

H1: The availability of larger selection regions in *EdgeSplit* and *VoronoiSplit* will lead users to achieve better time completion with these than with *Wedge*.

H2: *EdgeSplit* and *VoronoiSplit* make most effective use of the available space, thus requiring users to make fewer attempts to select a target with these than with *Wedge*.

Results

The data were analyzed using Repeated-Measures ANOVA and Bonferroni corrections for post-hoc comparisons.

Task Completion Time

Completion time measured the time from the target's appearance to the time participants successfully selected it.

The RM-ANOVA yielded a significant main effect of *Technique* ($F_{2,22}$=55.91, p<0.001) on completion time. Post-hoc comparisons showed that *EdgeSplit* (M=2808ms, s.e.=126) was significantly faster than *VoronoiSplit* (M=3042ms, s.e.=144; p<0.01). In addition, both techniques were significantly faster than *Wedge* (M=4253ms, s.e.=157; p<0.001) (Figure 4a).

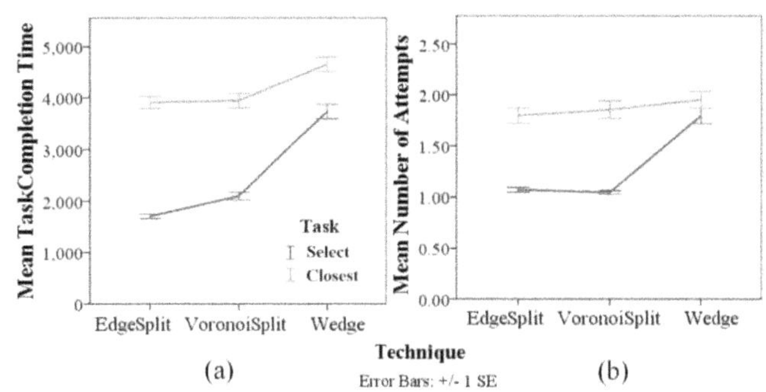

Figure 4. (a) Task completion time by technique and task; (b) Number of attempts by technique (Error bar: ± 1 SE).

There was a significant effect of *Task* on completion time ($F_{1,11}$=103.99, p<0.001), with participants performing significantly faster in the *Select* task (M=2558ms, s.e.=131) than the *Closest* task (M=4177ms, s.e.=138; p<0.001). We found a significant effect of *Target Density* on task completion time. Participants were significantly faster with *Low* density targets (M=3173ms, s.e.=121) than *High* density targets (M=3562ms, s.e.=117; p<0.001). However, we did not find any main effect of *Target Distance* ($F_{1,11}$= 0.01, p=0.93). There were significant interaction effects between *Technique* × *Task* ($F_{2,22}$=17.21, p<0.001). Participants were faster in the *Select* task for all techniques (*EdgeSplit*: M=1709ms, s.e.=101; *VoronoiSplit*: M=2099ms, s.e.=121; *Wedge*: M=3867ms, s.e.=261) than in the *Closest* Task (*EdgeSplit*: M=3907ms, s.e.=187, *VoronoiSplit*: M=3986ms, s.e.=193; *Wedge*: M=4639ms, s.e.=142).

There were also significant interaction effects between *Technique* × *Distance* ($F_{2,22}$=15.83, p<0.001) and *Task* × *Distance* ($F_{1,11}$=7.23, p<0.05). Participants performed better when targets were located at *Near* (M=2666ms) than *Far* (M=2950ms) distance with *EdgeSplit*. For *VoronoiSplit*, we found similar results with *Near* (M=2895ms) followed by *Far* (M=3189ms). However, for *Wedge*, participants were slower in selecting a target at *Near* distance (M=4523ms) than *Far* (M=3983ms). Wedge uses the size of the triangles to represent distance: the nearer the targets to the edge, the smaller the visible portion of the triangle and hence the more difficult to select (see Figure 3d above).

Number of Attempts

We counted the number of times a participant attempted to select a target and recorded these as *number of attempts* for that trial. The trial did not stop until the proper target was selected or it was timed out (after 25s).

The RM-ANOVA yielded significant main effects of *Technique* ($F_{2,22}$=15.97, p<0.001) on the number of attempts. Post-hoc analysis showed that *Wedge* (M=1.89, s.e.=0.1) had significantly higher number of attempts than *EdgeSplit* (M=1.44, s.e=0.07) and *VoronoiSplit* (M=1.45, s.e.=0.08) (p<0.01). However, there was no significant difference between the last two (Figure 3b).

There were main effects of *Task* ($F_{1,11}$=28.28, p<0.001) on number of attempts. Participants made more attempts in the *Closest* task (M=1.86, s.e.=0.11) than in the *Select* task (M=1.32, s.e.=0.05). However, we did not find any main effects of *Target Distance* ($F_{1,11}$=2.23, p=0.18) and *Target Density* ($F_{1,11}$=4.92, p=0.05). Finally, there was an interaction effect for *Technique* × *Task* ($F_{2,22}$=12.95, p<0.001). The *Select* task required fewer attempts for all techniques (*EdgeSplit:* M=1.07, s.e.=0.03; *VoronoiSplit*: M=1.04, s.e.=0.02; *Wedge:* M=1.83, s.e.=0.12) compare to the *Closest* task (*EdgeSplit*: M=1.8, s.e.=0.13; *VoronoiSplit*: M=1.85, s.e.=0.16; *Wedge*: M=1.94, s.e.= 0.1).

Subjective feedback

On a 5-point Likert scale participants preferred *EdgeSplit* (M=4.17) the most followed by *VoronoiSplit* (M=4.08) and *Wedge* (M=2). They also expressed that both *EdgeSplit* and *VoronoiSplit* (both M=3.83) were relatively easier to use than *Wedge* (M=1.83).

Discussion

Task Completion Time

Our results reveal that *EdgeSplit* and *VoronoiSplit* facilitate better off-screen target *visualization+selection* than *Wedge* (affirming **H1**). EdgeSplit afforded the best overall result (in completion times and number of attempts). This was primarily due to *EdgeSplit*'s larger selection area than *Wedge*, while its rectilinear regions provided easier access than the polygonal regions of *VoronoiSplit*.

We decomposed task completion time into: (1) *Decision time* (beginning of the trial to the time when a participant made a selection); and (2) *Selection time* (the time from the first touch to the end of the trial). We found that *Decision time* was similar across the techniques (EdgeSplit: 1766ms; VoronoiSplit: 1761ms; and Wedge: 1716ms). In contrast, there were differences in *Selection* time. Our results showed that *EdgeSplit* was the fastest in *Selection Time* for both tasks (*Locate*: 571ms; *Closest*: 1485ms), followed by *VoronoiSplit* (*Locate*: 704ms; *Closest*: 1789ms). *Wedge*, took the longest (*Locate*: 2384ms; Closest: 2566ms).

Number of attempts

Our results suggest that the total number of attempts for the *Locate* task was lower than for the *Closest* task for all techniques. For the *Locate* trials, *VoronoiSplit* exhibited the lowest number of attempts (M=1.04), closely followed by *EdgeSplit* (M=1.07). This supports **H2**. Due to the smaller selection area of the triangles, *Wedge* performed poorly (M=1.79). For the *Closest* task, the number of attempts was relatively high (from 1.80 to 1.95 attempts/trial). *EdgeSplit* had the lowest number of attempts (M=1.8), followed by *VoronoiSplit* (M=1.85) and *Wedge* (M=1.95).

CONCLUSIONS AND FUTURE WORK

In this paper, we open discussion on the selectability of off-screen cues. We propose EdgeSplit, an effective partitioning algorithm that facilitates visualization+ selection of off-screen content. EdgeSplit achieves completion times comparable to an existing state-of-the-art technique (Wedge) for identifying the relative position of objects. We also show that for off-screen object selection, EdgeSplit can facilitate improved selection over a voronoi partitioning method or against Wedge. Our results are encouraging and will allow further exploration on the effectiveness of EdgeSplit for other tasks, target layouts in corners, and real-world applications such as in GPS applications.

REFERENCES

1. Baudisch, P. and Rosenholtz, R. 2003. Halo: a technique for visualizing off-screen objects. *CHI '03*, 481-488.
2. Baudisch, P., Zotov, A., Cutrell, E., and Hinckley, K. 2008. Starburst: a target expansion algorithm for nonuniform target distributions. *AVI '08*, 129-137.
3. Grossman, T. and Balakrishnan, R. 2005. The bubble cursor: enhancing target acquisition by dynamic resizing of the cursor's activation area. *CHI '05*, 281-290.
4. Gustafson, S., Baudisch, P., Gutwin, C., and Irani, P. 2008 Wedge: clutter-free visualization of off-screen location. CHI '08, 787-796.
5. Gustafson, S. and Irani, P.P. 2007. Comparing visualizations for tracking off-screen moving targets. *CHI '07*.
6. Irani, P., Gutwin, C., and Yang, X. 2006. Improving selection of off-screen targets with hopping. CHI'06, 299-308.
7. Kabbash, P. and Buxton, W. 1995. The "Prince" technique: Fitts' law and selection using area cursors. *CHI'95*, 273-279.
8. Vogel, D. and Baudisch, P. 2007. Shift: A Technique for Operating Pen-Based Interfaces Using Touch. CHI'07, 657-666.

Around Device Interaction for Multiscale Navigation

Brett Jones, Rajinder Sodhi, David Forysth, Brian P. Bailey
University of Illinois at Urbana-Champaign
Urbana, IL
{brjones2, rsodhi2, daf, bpbailey}@illinois.edu

Giuliano Maciocci
Qualcomm Corporate R&D
Cambridge, UK
gmaciocc@qualcomm.com

ABSTRACT

In this paper we study the design space of free-space interactions for multiscale navigation afforded by mobile depth sensors. Such interactions will have a greater working volume, more fluid control and avoid screen occlusion effects intrinsic to touch screens. This work contributes the first study to show that mobile free-space interactions can be as good as touch. We also analyze sensor orientation and interaction volume usage, resulting in strong implications for how sensors should be placed on mobile devices. We describe a user study evaluating mobile free-space navigation techniques and the impacts of sensor orientation on user experience. Finally, we discuss guidelines for future mobile free-space interaction techniques and sensor design.

Author Keywords

Around Device Interaction; Pan and Zoom; Multiscale Navigation; Free-space Interaction; Depth Sensor

ACM Classification Keywords

H.5.2 **[User Interfaces]**: Input devices and strategies.

INTRODUCTION

A fundamental constraint of mobile devices is that the display and interaction real-estate is limited by the physical device size. This is particularly a problem when navigating large datasets on a mobile device. Users may navigate large datasets by exploring a map, browsing an image, arranging home-screen icons, reading a lengthy news article or playing a game. Currently, the limited screen size can result in small, repetitive navigation gestures. In a multiscale (pan-and-zoom) space, the user will have to frequently switch between panning and zooming to locate points of interest. Furthermore, with a touch screen the user's finger occludes valuable information [32].

With new depth sensing technology, we can unlock some of the fundamental constraints of mobile devices. The rise of low-cost commercial depth sensors like Microsoft's Kinect Sensor, will soon allow the integration of rich depth sensors into mobile devices [20]. These depth sensors will create new free-space interactions with mobile devices through real-time 3D tracking of multiple fingers [12]. As an added benefit, these sensors will be used for other applications as well. Depth sensors can aid in object detection and recognition [23], 3D scanning and reconstruction [17] and augmented reality applications [7].

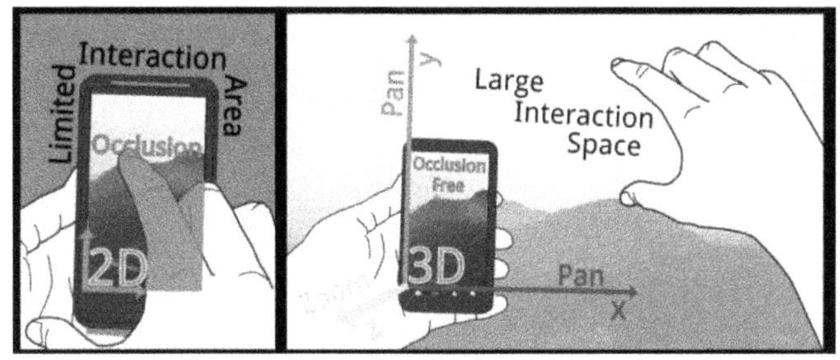

Figure 1. Touch screen interactions (left) can be complemented by mobile free-space interactions (right) which bring interaction off the surface. This enables a larger working space, provides higher degree input and eliminates screen occlusion.

By tracking fingers with a mobile depth sensor, we can shift interaction to the space around the mobile device, called Around Device Interaction (ADI) or mobile free-space interaction. ADI provides an interaction space an order of magnitude larger than the touch screen. ADI offers higher dimensional input, enabling new interaction paradigms. Also, ADI eliminates the problem of screen occlusion. We do not envision ADI replacing touch screen interactions, instead we envision ADI as a complement to touch, used for shorter, more intense interactions.

There are two main questions in Around Device Interaction: 1) *Is ADI useful?* 2) *Is ADI technically feasible*? Prior work in Around Device Interaction has focused on sensing technology and technical feasibility. Before we worry about feasibility, we must first know if Around Device Interaction is ever useful. If ADI isn't as good as the status quo (touch) then it will never be adopted. We focus on the first question and analyze the interactions under the assumption that we have feasible tracking technology. We utilize a commercial tracking system to evaluate user experience independent of tracking effects. Also before we start manufacturing mobile depth sensors we must answer, w*here should the sensor go?* To answer this question, we analyze sensor orientations through our simulated framework, to guide further research in sensing technology.

We present a user study that empirically compares free-space interaction techniques, using a multi-scale visual search task representative of navigating a large image or map. We evaluate four free-space interaction techniques that differ in clutch input, simultaneity and speed control, and compare them to touch screen interaction. We also evaluate the impact of sensor orientation on user experience with three different simulated sensor configurations. Our results show that Around Device Interaction performs similar to touch, with the majority of users preferring free-space interaction techniques to the touch screen. Furthermore, we present implications for the design of future Around Device Interaction techniques and how sensors should be placed on mobile devices.

RELATED WORK

We start with a broad overview of previous work and focus on its specific impacts to the design space in the next section (see *Design Space* section).

Device Motion

Informational spaces can be navigated by moving the mobile device through space. Since Fitzmaurice's early work with the Chameleon system introduced the concept [6], many projects have explored device motion. Device motion has been used for modal selection, text input, navigation and games [30,34]. Also, the tracking systems used for device motion have been updated from magnetic and pulley-based tracking to camera-based tracking [11,30]. Unlike device motion interfaces, ADI doesn't distract the user by requiring moving the focus as a means for navigation and ADI easily extends to allow for more complex interactions.

Distant Interactions

Previous work in virtual reality/tiled displays has mapped out parts of the design space of free-space interactions. Vogel et al. explored free-hand pointing operations and clutching gestures for tiled displays [29]. Similarly, Nancel et al. investigated free-space interactions for pan-and-zoom navigation on tiled displays [26]. In contrast to these works, Around Device Interaction represents a unique design space for free-space interactions, because the mobile device constrains the types of bi-manual interactions that are possible. Whereas Nancel et al. focused on comparing various types of constrained input, we focus on finding the best possible free-space interactions.

Around Device Interactions

Initial forays into Around Device Interaction focused on sensing technologies and introduced simple interactions like selection [4] or course gestures [19,21]. More complex 2D interactions were explored in Imaginary Interfaces [10], which examined scenarios where no mobile display device was present. The project explored 2D graffiti gestures, 2D visuospatial memory, and 2D pointing. Similarly, Ens et al. explored user performance in 2D off-screen pointing [5]. In contrast to previous work, we are the first to tackle more complex 3D Around Device Interactions.

Magnetic Sensing

Previous work in Around Device Interaction has focused on sensing modalities for tracking fingers or hands. One possible approach utilizes a magnetometer to track a magnetic ring worn by the user [1,13,19]. This approach has the benefit of providing un-constrained input around the mobile device, at the cost of requiring the user to wear an input ring, issues with interference and the approach does not scale well to tracking multiple fingers.

Depth-Based Sensing

Previous work has shown promise in using low resolution mobile depth sensors for ADI. The SideSight project explored detecting interactions to the side of a mobile device laying on a tabletop [4]. The prototype featured two arrays of 10 IR proximity sensors located on the side of the device, with a similar project exploring forward facing sensor [21]. Recently, the PalmSpace project used a depth sensor to track the orientation of the user's palm next to a mobile device, in order to rotate 3D models [22]. They experimented with a back facing and a side facing depth sensor configuration; finding in a pilot study that users preferred a side facing sensor and finding in their main study that users were faster setting rotations using a back facing sensor. In this work, we further explore the impacts of sensor configuration on user experience, focus on translational (not rotational) tasks and explore differences in clutch input, simultaneity and speed control.

DESIGN SPACE

The survey by Hinckley et al. in 1994, laid out the fundamental parameters of the design space of spatial input [14]. We build upon this survey and enumerate the design space of Around Device Interaction for pan-and-zoom navigation, explaining our design choices grounded in previous research.

We start by pointing out the unique constraints of mobile free-space interactions:

- The user holds the mobile device in their non-dominant hand limiting the input from that hand.
- The user's focus is on the device screen, discouraging movement of the non-dominant hand and discouraging interactions that lead to screen occlusion.
- The user's dominant hand must be kept free for traditional touch input, eliminating physical devices held in the dominant hand.

Reference Frame

All interactions are relative to the frame of reference of the mobile device and non-dominant hand, similar to Imaginary Interfaces [10]. Previous work has demonstrated that cognitively, the actions of the dominant hand are in the frame of reference of the non-dominant hand [16]. The touch screen uses a direct interaction metaphor, where moving a finger is equivalent to dragging around the informational space. We adopt the same metaphor where user motions are translated into world motions. If a user moves their finger right, the world moves right. Panning is accomplished in the xy-plane defined by the touchscreen (see Figure 1). In keeping with this metaphor, if a user moves a finger away from the phone in the z-direction, the world also moves away from the user (zooms out).

Clutch Input

We use physical buttons on the phone for delineating input (clutch input), which is one choice amongst a host of clutching mechanisms [14]. Recently, Vogel et al. found that users preferred tensing or relaxing the index finger over a thumb trigger gesture, when interacting with tiled displays [29]. Nancel et al. [26] used physical buttons (mice) in each hand for tiled displays and Wilson introduced pinching the index finger and thumb together as a clutch for tabletop interaction [33]. In ADI, the user is already holding a device with button affordances in their non-dominant hand and has a thumb available for input. Therefore, we use the physical buttons on the phone (volume buttons) for clutching input and explore using one or two clutch buttons in the user study.

Simultaneity

Panning and zooming represents a three dimensional input space that can be explored using differing degrees of simultaneity. We explore three kinds of simultaneity in the user study: simultaneous, system selected and separated. Pan-and-zoom can be accomplished simultaneously in three dimensions at once, as in [18]. Also, pan-and-zoom can be made independent and system selected by an intelligent system, as Nacenta et al. [25] did with spatial manipulations on tabletops. Or pan-and-zoom can be separated by individual clutches, like the clutches used in [15] for separating tools.

Speed Control

In this work we look at using spatial input for variable speed control. The optimal speed or Control/Display (C/D) gain for spatial input is dependent on a complicated mixture of user dependent variables such as learning and physical ability [36]. Furthermore, control/display gain can be variable based on other input. For instance, previous work explored controlling scrolling speed using pressure [28]. We examine controlling the speed based on spatial input. For instance, the speed of a zoom motion (along the z-axis) could be controlled by the user's position along the x-axis.

Hands vs. Fingers

Different muscle groups can have different degrees of control; for instance fingers are more precise than hands [35]. Therefore, in contrast to recent work that relied on hand input [26], we track fingers for more precise input.

Sensor Orientation

When using an oriented sensor, such as a depth sensor, the interaction is necessarily confined to a finite volume surrounding the mobile device. Should the depth sensor be oriented on the side of the phone , the front of the phone, or somewhere else? We will look at three different simulated sensor orientations and their effects on user experience.

Sensing Technology

The rise of commercial depth sensors, such as the Kinect, have enabled tracking multiple finger-tips in real-time from a rigidly mounted sensor [12,27]. Additionally, new approaches in depth sensors show promise for smaller, mobile sized sensors [20]. However, existing approaches in depth based finger tracking [12,27,31] are not yet capable of achieving the level of robust, precise, pose invariant tracking needed for an empirical user study. For example, in the user study conducted in [12], only frontal views were supported and tracking errors were still identified in 36% of tests. Also, practical considerations exclude existing depth sensors from use in the user study. An existing depth sensor attached to a mobile device would be too large, weigh too much and have too large a minimum working distance.

Furthermore, this work is interested in proving the usability of ADI without interference from the tracking system. Before the implementation details of tracking are solved, we would like to determine if the end interactions are worthwhile. Therefore, we use a commercial tracking system to simulate the mobile depth sensors and evaluate the usability of the gestures under the best possible tracking circumstances. We are confident that existing technical limitations will be quickly resolved, enabling depth-based Around Device Interaction.

USER STUDY

We conducted an experiment analyzing five interaction techniques and three simulated sensor orientations using a within-subjects counterbalanced design. We wanted to determine which interaction techniques are the most successful and why. Specifically we were interested in differences in the clutch input, the degree of simultaneity and the speed control. Additionally, we wanted to determine the impact of constraining input on user experience and whether this differs with varying sensor orientation.

Interaction Techniques

After defining the variables of the design space grounded in previous work, we created a spreadsheet of possible interactions (with some variables being mutually exclusive). We then engaged in rapid prototyping with frequent informal user evaluations, resulting in multiple interaction prototypes. We conducted informal user studies evaluating the prototypes on the visual search task. We then selected four promising representative samples from the design space that differ in clutch input, degree of simultaneity and speed control for user evaluation (see Figure 2).

2 Button

The *2 Button* (*2B*) technique uses two physical button clutches for panning and zooming, ensuring independent movement. With the pan button depressed, motions in the

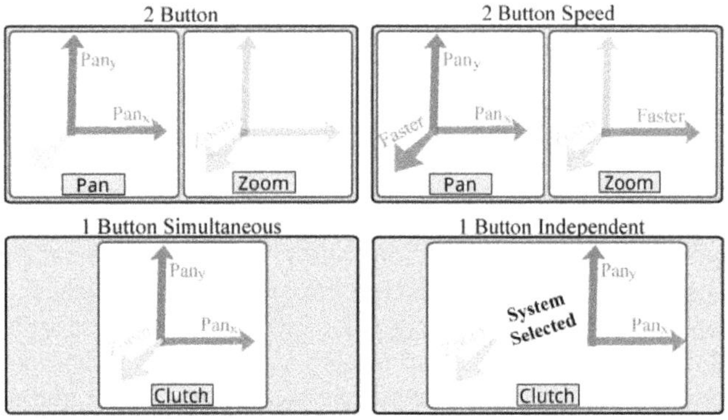

Figure 2. The selected interaction techniques differ in clutch input, speed control and degree of simultaneity.

xy-plane lead to panning, with the z-component being ignored; zooming has the reverse mapping.

2 Button Speed

The *2 Button Speed* (*2B Speed*) technique is the same as *2B*, except the user can control the speed of the navigation. The speed of the pan decreases as the user moves farther away from the device (slower along the + z-axis). Similarly, the speed of the zoom increases as the user moves farther away from the device (faster along the + x-axis).

1 Button Simultaneous

The *1 Button Simultaneous* (*1B Sim*) technique allows for panning and zooming simultaneously, with a single button to clutch input.

1 Button Independent

The *1 Button Independent* (*1B Ind*) technique automatically separates out pan and zoom actions. The system selects between panning or zooming based on the primary direction of the instantaneous velocity (projected into the xy-plane for panning and z-axis for zooming). In order to avoid unnecessary mode switching, the system uses an inverted quadratic falloff function to select between the modes.

Touch Screen

A touch screen implementation of the task was provided to serve as a frame of reference for the subjects. The implementation panned by dragging a single finger on the screen and used the standard pinch to zoom gesture, zooming about the center of the screen.

For all free-space techniques, there is a dampening function (an inverted quadratic falloff) applied to the tracking input to ensure that small jitters in the tracker do not lead to unintended movements. Also, the zoom for all techniques is accomplished about the center of the screen. In order to compare techniques, we have a fixed maximum speed/gain across all techniques that we determined through an informal pilot study (as in [36]).

Sensor Orientation

In order to understand the impacts of sensor orientation on user experience, we compared un-constrained input with three simulated sensor orientations. With each simulated depth sensor the input space was constrained to the bounds detectable by a simulated sensor. If the user moved out of the sensor area, the user was presented with a "Tracking Lost" notification and the system stopped responding until simulated tracking was regained.

The volume constraints are frustums, simulating the working volume of a depth sensor camera. The simulated sensors have an aspect ratio of 4:3, a minimum working distance of 0.1m and a maximum working distance of 0.5m.

The *Front* sensor faces the user along the + z-axis, towards the user. The *Side* sensor points along the + x-axis, to the user's right. The *FrontSide* sensor points at a 45° angle between the *Front* and *Side*. The *Front* and *Side* sensors have a 55° field of view, while the *FrontSide* sensor has a 65° field of view to capture more of the input space.

Visual Search Task

We devised a multiscale feature based visual search task that is motivated by visual search on a large dataset (see Figure 3). When viewing a large dataset, the user may zoom into a region of interest, examine the region while panning, and then zoom out to find another region.

Previous work in multiscale image navigation has used a task introduced by Guiard et al., that is the logical extension of a Fitts's target acquisition task into a multiscale environment [3,8,26]. The task consists of zooming out of a series of concentric circles, locating and panning to a target set of circles, then zooming and panning to the center of the target circles. This task represents an unlikely extrema of large dataset navigation. For a real world example of this

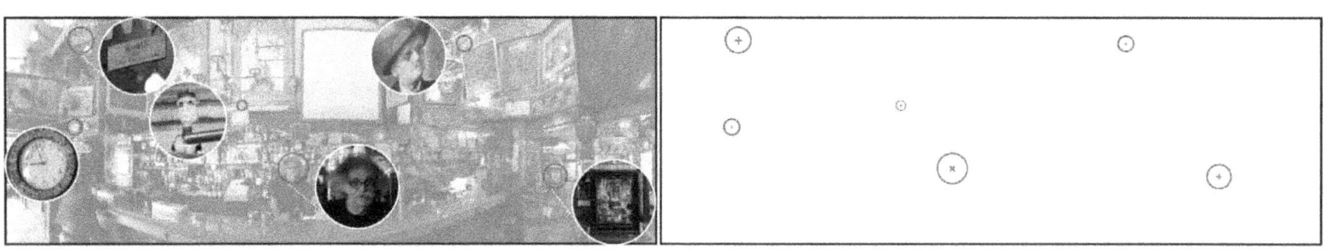

Figure 3. When viewing large datasets on a small screen, the user must engage in a significant amount of panning and zooming in order to accomplish a visual search. Here we depict an example with an image[1] that has interest points at a variety of scales. (left) A high resolution image with sample interest points (red) and close ups (white). (right) An abstracted version of the image, where the interest points are circles. This abstract version forms the basis of the task used in the user study.

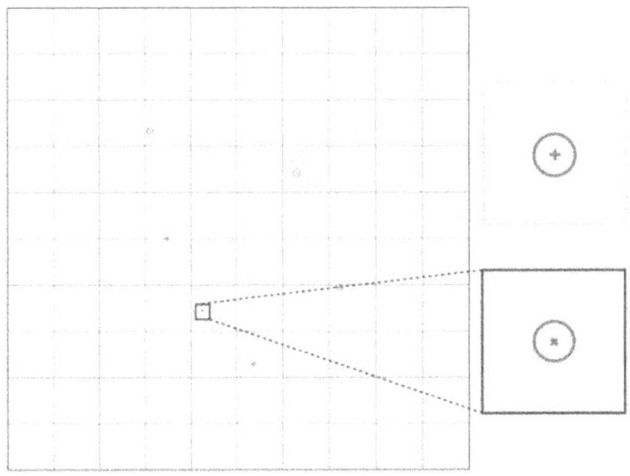

Figure 4. Feature based multiscale visual search task. (left) The user must search a series of six circles with a '+' sign in the center (right top) and find the circle with the 'x' in the center (right bottom). The circles are distributed in the space with a Gaussian distribution that is altered to enforce a dead zone in the center, with the circles scaled based on a uniform distribution.

task, imagine a user viewing a map with a detailed view of a city block. The user zooms out until they can see the entire country, then zooms and pans to another city block on the other side of the country. This task is very zoom heavy and requires a large amount of navigation. The results of this task are easily measured and the concentric circles of the task are designed to ensure that users cannot get lost. Therefore users can 'sprint' through the interface and studies can compare their fastest movement times.

We believe that a visual search task with moderate levels of pan and zoom is more representative of multiscale navigation. Also, we would like to explore the effects of screen size and finger occlusion, which will not be significant issues if the user can never get lost.

We designed a visual search task where the user must find a target (a circle with an 'x') out of a set of five distractors (circles with a '+' sign). The task is depicted in Figure 4. Once the user has found the correct target, the completion condition is the same as the Guiard task. The user must place the target circle within a certain radius, and the zoom level must be within a desired range. Visual feedback is provided when the pan or zoom end condition is met.

In order to understand the dimensions of the space, we will describe all measurements in abstract units where the zoom range is [0.01, 20.0], with a starting zoom level of 1.0 and a completion zoom level of 20.0. Each circle has a radius uniformly chosen between [5.0, 20.0], with a '+' or 'x' size of [0.5, 2.0]. The circles are distributed randomly in the space with a Gaussian distribution, $\mu = 0.0$ and $\sigma^2 = 2500.0$. The distribution of the circles is offset to enforce a dead-zone of 3000.0 units, to ensure that no circles are initially visible on the screen.

Participants

We recruited 12 participants (5 female) through fliers distributed widely in the area. The participants had no affiliation with the investigators. The participants ranged in age from 18-30 years. All participants were undergraduate or graduate students, with backgrounds distributed throughout the liberal arts, fine arts, sciences and engineering. Due to the narrow age range of the participants, we recruited one additional participant that was affiliated with the investigators, in the age range [50-60]. We excluded this participant's qualitative data from the analysis.

By chance, all participants were right handed. All participants had experience using a smartphone or other touch screen device. Participants varied in self-reported uncorrected visual acuity, with no subjects identifying as color blind.

Experimental Setup

We used a HTC Desire smartphone (released April 2010) running Android 2.3. The phone weighs 135g with dimensions [119 mm, 60 mm, 11.9 mm], has a 3.7" 480x800 display with a dual-touch screen. The experiment also uses 2 hard buttons inset in the side of the phone (volume buttons).

In order to simulate a mobile depth sensor of the future, we used a NaturalPoint OptiTrack system that tracks infrared reflective spheres at 100 Hz. The subject wears two spheres connected by a wire on their index finger, which are adjusted with Velcro. Additionally, a set of three spheres connected in a rigid body are affixed to the phone for tracking.

A desktop PC (Intel Core i7) simulated the depth sensor, translating finger positions into the phone's coordinate system. The PC processed all input from the phone (button presses) and the tracker then sent results to the phone for display. It is important to note that there was a lag in response time, due to the network communication between all components. However, the touch implementation processed the touch data directly on the phone. Therefore the touch implementation had considerably less lag than the free-space gestures.

Procedure

During the user study, participants were seated in a chair with armrests, as recommended in [14], to help combat fatigue. Normally, we envision ADI to be used for shorter interactions than the length of the user study. Each participant started by answering a brief demographic questionnaire about their visual acuity and age. Next, the subject was familiarized with the task during a pre-training phase using the *Touch* technique. Once the subject was comfortable with the task and the touch screen interface, free-space interactions were explained using the *1B Sim* technique as an exemplar.

Then, the participant used each of the five interaction techniques with the order counterbalanced across participants. For each technique, the participant trained by performing at least two trials, stopping when they felt comfortable with the technique. The participant then completed 6 measured trials. In between techniques, the subject set down the phone and answered an inter-task questionnaire. The inter-task questionnaires were based on a 5 point Likert scale. The questions asked the subject to rate: *how easy it was to accomplish the task (with this technique), how comfortable it was to accomplish the task, how comfortable you would feel using (this technique) in public places, and your overall level of satisfaction (with the technique).*

After the questionnaire the participant was asked how the interface felt and was asked to explain their questionnaire answers, with the investigators asking relevant questions. Quotations and notes were recorded by a secondary experimenter. This period served as a rest period for the subject and the subject was told that they could rest at any point during the study.

In order to elicit feedback about the impact of sensor orientation on user experience, we asked the subject to interact with three simulated sensor configurations. For each interaction volume constraint, the *1B Sim* technique was used as a representative technique for the free-space interactions. After the subject felt familiar with the volume constraints, they were asked to interact in the constrained space for at least 2 minutes. Afterwards, the subject answered a questionnaire (same questions as above) and discussed how each volume constraint felt.

Finally, the subject was asked to uniquely rank the techniques and volumes, on a variety of factors. H*ow easy it was to accomplish the task*, *your overall satisfaction* and *your overall level of comfort*. In order to rank the item, the participant placed a label {a-e} corresponding to each item next to an ordered list of the ranking criteria, without ties. Finally, the participant was asked to verbally explain their rankings with investigators asking relevant questions.

The entire session lasted between 75-90 minutes, with around 60-75 minutes of interaction with frequent breaks. The location of the index finger in relation to the phone was stored over the course of the interactions, along with the usage of the clutch button.

RESULTS

As an overview of the results, we found that *1B Sim* performed significantly better than all other free-space interaction techniques. With *1B Sim* showing equivalent movement times to *Touch*. Most participants preferred free-space techniques to *Touch* (8/12), with 6 preferring *1B Sim*.

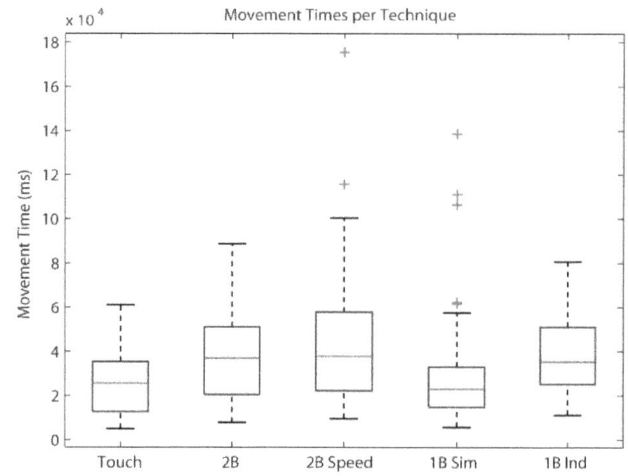

Figure 5. A boxplot of the movement times shows that the distribution is non-normal, due to noise in the visual search task. *1B Sim* outperforms the other free-space techniques and shows equivalent times to Touch. The boxplot shows medians (red), interquartile range (blue) and outliers (red+).

	Touch	2B	2B Speed	1B Sim	1B Ind
Median	**25.56**	36.98	37.82	**23.05**	35.37

Figure 6. Median movement times for each technique (seconds).

Free-space interactions were found to be more fatiguing and users would be less likely to use them in public settings. Constraining the working interaction volume greatly impacts user experience, with tradeoffs between sensor orientations.

Interaction Techniques

The visual search task has an inherent amount of uniformly distributed noise in the movement times. The user may find the target circle anywhere between their first and sixth attempt. Thus, we do not expect the data to be normally distributed. To analyze the data we will turn to non-parametric methods, which do not assume an underlying probability distribution.

We present the results in Figure 5 using a boxplot. First, we notice that *1B Sim* clearly outperformed the other free-space techniques and performed similar to touch screen. This is confirmed by the median movement times, see Figure 6. We also note that the data is non-symmetric with a heavy weight near the lower movement times, also indicating a non-normal distribution.

In our statistical analysis we would like to confirm that the data is non-Gaussian, also that *1B Sim* and *Touch* are significantly different from the other techniques and that *1B Sim* and *Touch* are equivalent. We start with a Lilliefors test, which confirms that the data is not Gaussian for all techniques, except for *2B*. The p-values for each technique are [0.047, 0.142, <0.001, < 0.001, 0.036].

Two-way Kolmogorov-Smirnov (KS) tests show that *2B*, *2B Speed*, and *1B Ind* are significantly different from *Touch* (all $p < 0.009$). Similarly, *1B Sim* is significantly different from *2B, 2B Speed* and *1B Ind* (all $p < 0.0005$). A two way KS test between *Touch* and *1B Sim* yields a strong negative result with p=0.65, indicating that the two probability distributions are indistinguishable. We confirmed these results with the more sensitive, 2-way Anderson Darling (AD) test [24]. Two-way AD results confirm that *Touch* and *1B Sim* are significantly different from the other techniques (all $p < 0.0001$). And a two-way AD test between *Touch* and *1B Sim* yields a negative result with p=0.343, showing that the results are not significantly distinguishable by a strong non-parametric test.

1B Sim clearly performs better than the other free-space interactions; however there are a considerable number of outliers present in Figure 5. These outliers come from an anomalous user who performed consistently worse than all other users on all techniques, see Figure 7. While the reason for the drastic performance differences is unknown, it is important to note that a small percentage of users may have difficulty with the coordinated spatial movement required by mobile free-space interactions.

Volume Utilization

When interacting with un-constrained free-space input, users make use of a surprisingly large volume (Figure 8a). For instance, the space used to zoom ranged over 0.8 m, [0.3, -0.5]. Observations of the users indicate that they were heavily immersed in the task. Users would frequently end up in seemingly un-natural positions in order to accomplish a particular pan or zoom operation. Especially at the end condition, users frequently ended with their arm at or above the level of their head. This may indicative that prolonged training with the bi-manual clutch is necessary for more comfortable input.

With un-constrained input, users have a strong preference for interactions directly to the right and slightly behind the mobile device. For instance *1B Sim* movements have a mean, $\mu = [0.123\,\text{m}, 0.048\,\text{m}, -0.102\,\text{m}]$, and standard deviation, $\sigma = [0.095\,\text{m}, 0.068\,\text{m}, 0.130\,\text{m}]$. Among the four free-space interaction techniques we found that *1B Sim* had the largest variance, with *2B* having the least variance.

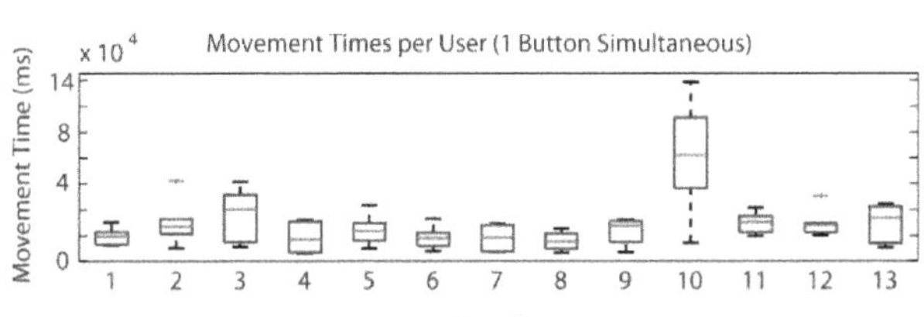

Figure 7. The outliers in the *1B Sim* movement times are due to a single user, who performed consistently worse than all other users on all techniques. It is important to note that a small percentage of users may have difficulty with the coordinated spatial movement required by mobile free-space interactions.

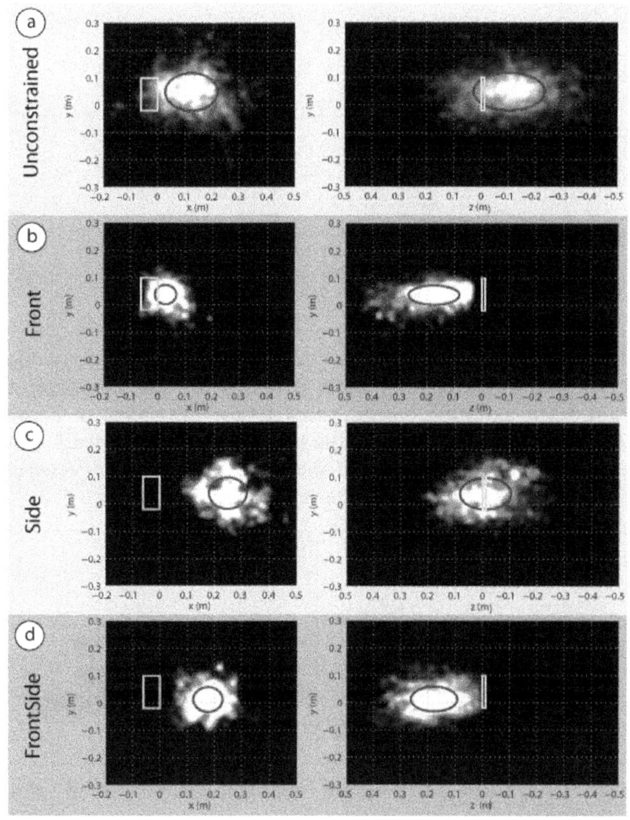

Figure 8. Heat maps showing the sample density of the finger tracker in relation to the mobile device (green). The left column shows a frontal projection of the tracking data (Z projection), the right column shows a side projection of the tracking data (x projection with left=towards user, right=away from user). The mean and std. dev. are displayed as a blue ellipse. All figures are drawn with the same axis to enable quick comparison.

Also, users' movements within the volume are not axis aligned. As Figure 9 shows, when users are attempting to zoom they drift in both the x-axis and y-axis. We see that users drift based upon cognitive and physiological constraints. In the x-axis zooming motions form the shape of a cone centered to the right of the users head. In the y-axis zooming motions follow the path of an ellipse. This non-linear warping on the input space is largely responsible for the poor performance of *1B Ind.*

Clutching

The difference in interaction volume usage between *1B Sim* and *2B* can be explained by differences in clutching frequency. With *2B*, users frequently reset their hand position when they switched from pan to zoom (see Figure 10), using less interaction volume but with slower task completion times. Whereas with *1B Sim,* users clutched less, simultaneously panned and zoomed for a longer time, used more interaction volume, and had faster task completion times. Therefore, designers should be aware of the trade-offs between clutching frequency, volume usage and movement times. The increased clutching of *1B Ind* is

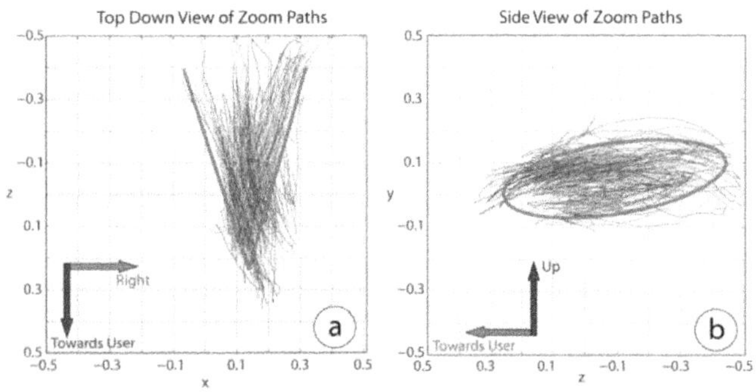

Figure 9. Users do not follow the z-axis exactly when zooming. (a) A top down view of zoom paths (using *2B*) demonstrates that while zooming, users' paths follow the shape of a cone. The apex of the cone is to the right of the user's head. (b) A side view of zoom paths demonstrates that while zooming, users' paths in the y-axis follows an elliptical motion.

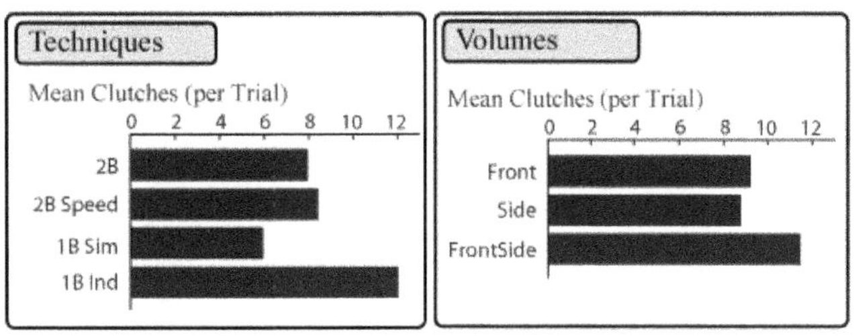

Figure 10. Mean clutching per technique and simulated sensor orientation.

largely due to user's re-clutching due to the system incorrectly classifying their non-linear movements.

Rankings

Most users preferred free-space interaction techniques over *Touch* (8/12) for ease of use. Specifically, 6 users preferred *1B Sim* and 2 users preferred *2B*. The technique ranked hardest to use was *1B Ind* (6 users) followed *2B Speed* (4 users). The mean rankings of the techniques show similar results with *1B Sim*=4.25, *Touch*=3.58 (Figure 11). Friedman tests shows that *Touch* and *1B Sim* are significantly preferred over *2B Speed* and *1B Ind* (all $p < 0.02$). *Touch* was preferred for comfort by 8 users, with 4 users preferring *1B Sim*. Friedman tests show that *Touch* is significantly more comfortable than *2B*, *2B Speed*, and *1B Ind* (all $p < 0.021$), and that *1B Sim* is significantly more comfortable than *2B Speed* and *1B Ind.*

Sensor Orientation

With the simulated sensor's volume constraints, the user's movement is shifted away from the natural un-constrained position. In the *Front* constraint (Figure 8b) users stay to the right of the screen, even though the available space is symmetric about the screen. The *Front* constraint shows a cylinder of heavy use slightly to the right of the phone and extending towards the user. As one user noted "My hand was getting in the way of the screen and it would be a problem if you had to move to the left because your hand would cross the screen." We noticed users accidentally contacting the phone or their face during zooming actions. One user said "Didn't like *Front*, it felt like I was going to hit my face." When using the *Front* condition, the phone was usually held as far away as possible to expand the limited interaction area. Users commented that this made the screen harder to see.

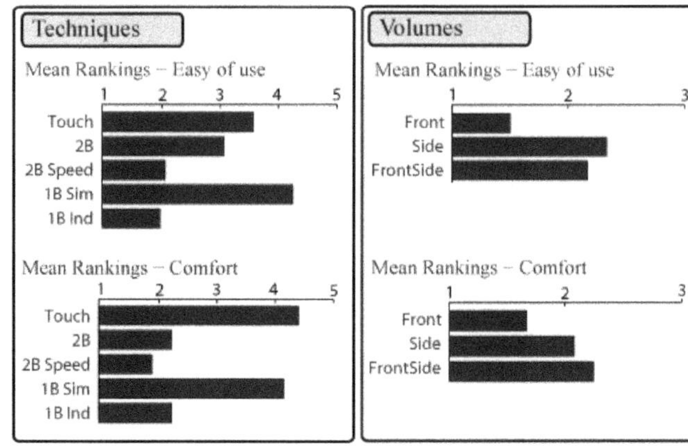

Figure 11. Mean rankings in the end questionnaire for (left) techniques and (right) interaction volumes.

The *Side* constraint volume is the closest to the un-constrained input space (Figure 8c), except movement is shifted farther to the right of the device. One user commented "I feel like it was okay but I had to hold my hand farther than I would like." With the Side constraint, users often held the phone quite close to their face as there was no danger of hitting oneself in the face.

With the *FrontSide* volume constraint (Figure 8d), the users frequently moved their dominant hand close to the right side of their face and held the phone closer to their face than *Front* but farther than *Side*. As one user put it "The [*FrontSide*] was a lot more normal. You still get some space but you aren't moving in your face."

Rankings

The mean rankings of volume constraints show that *Side* and *FrontSide* were clearly preferred over *Front* for ease-of-use and overall satisfaction, with *Side* significantly preferred over *Front* (Friedman test $p=0.021$). However the comfort/fatigue rankings are closer. Users commented that while Front felt constraining and occluded the screen, they would be more likely to use it in public places. One user sums it up nicely "In public places, [*Front*] is more comfortable. The reason being is that you are pointing at the phone."

DISCUSSION

One of the main findings of our study was that a free-space technique performed equivalent to touch screen interaction. This contrasts with previous work [26], which found that their constrained interactions (touch screen) outperformed their unconstrained interactions (free-space). Our design space is fundamentally different from [26], as we were looking at mobile devices instead of tiled displays, we pan-and-zoomed with one hand (instead of two), we evaluated more free-space interactions and we had a higher c/d gain.

Future work should evaluate if our interactions transfer to tiled displays.

Fatigue from free-space interactions could represent an obstacle to user adoption [14]. However, we expect free-space interactions to be used for short, more intense interactions as a supplement to touch screen interactions. The results from our study show that fatigue is a concern, but not an overriding one. Figure 11 shows that the comfort/fatigue ratings for *1B Sim* were only slightly worse than touch. Further empirical analysis of fatigue in free-space interactions represents necessary future work for the community.

Interaction Techniques

We found that simultaneous pan/zoom navigation is preferred by users. Our results show that for mobile free-space interaction techniques, the 3D input space is a logical mapping to pan-and-zoom operations. One user confirmed "It felt like the world was there and it was moving how the world should move." If the mapping of high degree of freedom input is too complex or doesn't fit a real-world metaphor then user experience will suffer. With *2B Speed* users commented that they mostly ignored the speed control. One user said "I thought it was difficult, it was a little more complex for me." Users also indicated that they used the zoom speed more than the pan speed. As zoom has only one dimension it may have been easier to cognitively grasp the concept of the speed control.

The largest caveat to simultaneous navigation is that the desired gain (speed) of panning and zooming will depend on the user. Not all users perform equally at mobile free-space interaction techniques. The majority of users were able to complete the training free-space task almost immediately; however, a subset of users spent a much longer time in the training phase. This may be due to differences in spatial coordination and eye-hand coordination. We informally tested our best user after the user study and found that the user was capable of handling a much more sensitive interaction. Additionally, the gain on pan and zoom should be independent of each other. One user commented that the task was more zoom than pan, and that they would prefer to have a faster zoom.

Designers should also consider the ergonomics of the clutch buttons. Most users indicated that the most uncomfortable portion of the free-space interactions was clicking the physical buttons used for clutching. As one user put it "I didn't like the button switching, I can feel it in my hand." The volume buttons on the HTC Desire are recessed, causing the users to exert force to them hold down. The ergonomics of a button clutch should be explored carefully. Alternatively, a touch strip on the side of the phone could provide a pressure-less clutch and serve as modal input or scrolling input.

All interactions should be designed to compensate for the non-linear warping of user input, as shown in Figure 9. Given the highly structured pattern across users, it seems probable that machine learning approaches could compensate for this warping.

Sensor Orientation

Constrained input had a negative impact on user perceptions of mobile spatial input. There are distinct trade-offs between all of the tested sensor orientations. A well-placed single depth sensor aimed at the 'natural' sweet-spot (un-constrained μ) on the side of the device with a wide field of view could be optimal. Alternatively, multiple depth sensors could achieve the best of both worlds: the large interaction space of *Side* and the public acceptability of *Front*. Most importantly, users' natural movements are very close to the device. All sensors should have a very small minimum working distance, which has the added benefit of allowing mixed interactions between the touch screen and free-space.

Sensors that are oriented to the side will have to balance ease-of-use with design constraints of left-handed and right-handed users. With a side facing depth sensor, the device could be intrinsically "handed" with separate phones for right-handed and left-handed users. Or preferably, devices could be orientation independent, with left-handed users simply holding the device with a 180 degree rotation.

In the recent PalmSpace project [22], they found that users performed rotation tasks faster with a back facing sensor, as opposed to a side facing sensor. These results are probably due to the difference in rotational vs. translational tasks. In PalmSpace a user only rotated their hand without moving it, whereas with our interactions a user naturally moved their fingers/hand over great distances. With a back facing sensor, translational tasks would cause the user to uncomfortably cross their arms. Future work should explore which centered interactions are better for a back facing sensor, and which translational tasks are better for a side facing sensor.

CONCLUSION AND FUTURE WORK

Mobile free-space interaction techniques unlock a larger interaction space, eliminate screen occlusion, enable higher dimensional input and provide an immersive, natural user experience.

In this work we iteratively explored the design space and created a set of mobile free-space interaction techniques for multi-scale navigation. We conducted a user study evaluating the interaction techniques and the implications of sensor orientation on user experience. Results show that for multiscale navigation, the majority of users preferred free-space interactions to touch screen, with equivalent movement times. Constraining the interaction volume has large implications for ease-of-use. And sensor placement decisions will have to balance ergonomic, social and user performance factors against hardware decisions.

As future work, we plan on expanding on the gesture set of mobile free-space interactions. For instance, mixed interactions between touch screen and free-space are rich with novel applications. Visualization of the user's movement, while taking away valuable screen real-estate, may prove effective at guiding movement and communicating tracking errors. Also, off-screen visualization techniques (i.e. Halos [2], Wedges [9]) could be combined with ADI to improve user performance in multiscale navigation. Mobile free-space gestures naturally extend to collaboration and sharing interaction volumes is an interesting line of inquiry. Furthermore, a more comprehensive understanding of fatigue is necessary for free-space interactions.

To investigate the practical challenges of creating interactions around mobile devices using depth images, we recently constructed a finger-tracking prototype using a short-range depth sensor. In future work we will explore the practical impacts of depth sensor parameters such as resolution, noise, field of view etc., on user interaction.

ACKNOWLEDGEMENTS

This work is supported by a Qualcomm Innovation Fellowship, by the National Science Foundation under Grant No. IIS-1029035, and by the Office of Naval Research under a MURI award.

REFERENCES

1. Ashbrook, D., Baudisch, P., and White, S. Nenya: subtle and eyes-free mobile input with a magnetically-tracked finger ring. *ACM CHI*, (2011), 2043–2046.
2. Baudisch, P. and Rosenholtz, R. Halo : a Technique for Visualizing Off-Screen Locations. *ACM CHI*, (2003), 481-488.
3. Bourgeois, F. and Guiard, Y. Multiscale pointing: facilitating pan-zoom coordination. *ACM CHI EA*, (2002), 758–759.
4. Butler, A. and Izadi, S. SideSight: multi-touch interaction around small devices. *ACM UIST*, (2008).
5. Ens, B. Characterizing User Performance with Assisted Direct Off-Screen Pointing. *ACM MobileHCI*, (2011), 485-494.
6. Fitzmaurice, G.W., Zhai, S., and Chignell, M.H. Virtual reality for palmtop computers. *ACM Transactions on Information Systems 11*, 3 (1993), 197-218.
7. Gordon, G., Billinghurst, M., Bell, M., et al. The use of dense stereo range data in augmented reality. *IEEE ISMAR*, (2002), 14-23.
8. Guiard, Y. and Beaudouin-Lafon, M. Target acquisition in multiscale electronic worlds. *International Journal of Human-Computer Studies 61*, 6 (2004), 875-905.
9. Gustafson, S., Baudisch, P., and Gutwin, C. Wedge : Clutter-Free Visualization of Off-Screen Locations. *ACM CHI*, (2008).
10. Gustafson, S., Bierwirth, D., and Baudisch, P. Imaginary Interfaces: Spatial Interaction with Empty Hands and Without Visual Feedback. *ACM UIST*, (2010), 3–12.
11. Hachet, M., Pouderoux, J., and Guitton, P. A Camera-Based Interface for Interaction with Mobile Handheld Computers. *ACM I3D*, (2005), 65-73.
12. Hackenberg, G., McCall, R., and Broll, W. Lightweight palm and finger tracking for real-time 3D gesture control. *IEEE VR*, (2011).
13. Harrison, C. and Hudson, S. Abracadabra: wireless, high-precision, and unpowered finger input for very small mobile devices. *ACM UIST*, (2009), 1-4.
14. Hinckley, K., Pausch, R., Goble, J.C., and Kassell, N.F. A survey of design issues in spatial input. *ACM UIST*, (1994), 213-222.
15. Hinckley, K., Pausch, R., Goblel, J.C., and Kassell, N.F. Passive Real-World Interface Props for Neurosurgical Visualization. *ACM CHI*, (1994), 452-458.
16. Hinckley, K., Pausch, R., Proffitt, D., Patten, J., and Kassell, N. Cooperative bimanual action. *ACM CHI*, (1997), 27–34.
17. Izadi, S., Newcombe, R., Kim, D., et al. KinectFusion: Real-Time Dynamic 3D Surface Reconstruction and Interaction. *SIGGRAPH (Talk)*, (2011).
18. Jacob, R.J.K. and Sibert, L.E. The perceptual structure of multidimensional input device selection. *ACM CHI*, (1992), 211-218.
19. Ketabdar, H. and Yüksel, K.A. Towards Using Embedded Magnetic Field Sensor for Around Mobile Device 3D Interaction. *ACM MobileHCI*, (2010), 153-156.
20. Kirmani, A., Colac, A., Wong, F.N.C., and Goyal, V.K. CODAC : A Compressive Depth Acquisition Camera Framework. *IEEE ICASSP*, (2012).
21. Kratz, S., Laboratories, D.T., and Rohs, M. HoverFlow : Expanding the Design Space of Around-Device Interaction. *ACM MobileHCI*, (2009).
22. Kratz, S., Rohs, M., Guse, D., Müller, J., Bailly, G., and Nischt, M. PalmSpace : Continuous Around-Device Gestures vs . Multitouch for 3D Rotation Tasks on Mobile Devices. *AVI*, (2012).
23. Lai, K., Bo, L., Ren, X., and Fox, D. Sparse Distance Learning for Object Recognition Combining RGB and Depth Information. *IEEE ICRA*, (2011).
24. Mason, D.M. A Modified Kolmogorov-Smirnov Test Sensitive to Tail Alternatives. *Statistics 11*, 3 (2011), 933-946.
25. Nacenta, M.A., Baudisch, P., Benko, H., and Wilson, A. Separability of spatial manipulations in multi-touch interfaces. *Graphics Interface*, Canadian Information Processing Society (2009), 175–182.
26. Nancel, M., Wagner, J., Pietriga, E., Chapuis, O., and Mackay, W. Mid-air pan-and-zoom on wall-sized displays. *ACM CHI*, (2011), 177–186.
27. Oikonomidis, I., Kyriazis, N., and Argyros, A. Efficient model-based 3D tracking of hand articulations using Kinect. *BMVC*, British Machine Vision Association (2011).
28. Ramos, G. and Balakrishnan, R. Zliding : Fluid Zooming and Sliding for High Precision Parameter Manipulation. *ACM UIST*, (2005), 143-152.
29. Vogel, D. and Balakrishnan, R. Distant freehand pointing and clicking on very large, high resolution displays. *ACM UIST*, (2005), 33.
30. Wang, J., Canny, J., Berkeley, U.C., Hall, S., Road, H., and Jose, S. Camera Phone Based Motion Sensing: Interaction Techniques, Applications and Performance Study. *ACM UIST*, (2008).
31. Wang, R.Y., Paris, S., and Popovi, J. 6D Hands : Markerless Hand Tracking for Computer Aided Design. *ACM CHI*, (2011).
32. Wigdor, D., Forlines, C., Baudisch, P., Barnwell, J., and Shen, C. LucidTouch : A See-Through Mobile Device. *ACM UIST*, (2007), 269-278.
33. Wilson, A. Robust computer vision-based detection of pinching for one and two-handed gesture input. *ACM UIST*, (2006), 255.
34. Yee, K.-ping. Peephole Displays : Pen Interaction on Spatially Aware Handheld Computers. *ACM CHI*, (2003).
35. Zhai, S., Milgram, P., and Buxton, W. The influence of muscle groups on performance of multiple degree-of-freedom input. *ACM CHI*, (1996), 308-315.
36. Zhai, S. Human Performance in Six Degree of Freedom Input Control. *Industrial Engineering*, 1995.

Dynamic Visualization of Large Numbers of Off-screen Objects on Mobile Devices: an Experimental Comparison of Wedge and Overview+Detail

Stefano Burigat
stefano.burigat@uniud.it

Luca Chittaro
luca.chittaro@uniud.it

Andrea Vianello
andrea.vianello@uniud.it

HCI Lab
Department of Mathematics and Computer Science
University of Udine
Via delle Scienze 206, 33100, Udine, Italy

ABSTRACT

Overview+Detail [25] and Wedge [16] have been proposed in the literature as effective approaches to resolve the off-screen objects problem on mobile devices. However, they have been studied with a small number of off-screen objects and (in most studies) with static scenarios, in which users did not have to perform any navigation activity. In this paper, we propose improvements to Wedge and Overview+Detail which are specifically aimed at simplifying their use in dynamic scenarios that involve large numbers of off-screen objects. We compare the effectiveness of the two approaches in the considered scenario with a user study, whose results show that Overview+Detail allows users to be faster in searching for off-screen objects and more accurate in estimating their location.

Author Keywords

Visualization; mobile devices; map navigation; peripheral awareness; off-screen objects; Overview+Detail; Wedge

ACM Classification Keywords

H.5.2 Information Interfaces and Presentation: User Interfaces—*Evaluation/methodology, Graphical user interfaces (GUI)*

INTRODUCTION

People increasingly use mobile devices to display large information spaces such as web pages or maps. Unfortunately, the small screen of mobile devices greatly increases the complexity of exploring these information spaces at an adequate level of detail, forcing users to carry out multiple zooming and panning actions [5]. This could be problematic, for example, when the user of a mobile map application (e.g. Google Maps) wants to know the location of objects of interest around her, such as banks, restaurants or hotels. Due to the limited size of displays, the zooming and panning actions needed to look for this information could make users lose the global context when examining the details of the visualization and vice versa [12]. As a consequence, the user may not be aware of the presence of relevant objects located off-screen (the *off-screen objects problem*) and thus may not be able to reach them.

Overview+Detail (hereinafter, O+D) and Contextual Cues Techniques are the two approaches that have been explored most in the literature to mitigate the off-screen objects problem. O+D provides both detail and context information by typically displaying two separate views simultaneously, one for the context and one for the detail [25]. With this approach, the overview can be used to highlight all objects of interest that are outside the detail view. Contextual Cues Techniques, such as Halo [3] or Wedge [16], augment the detail view with abstract shapes (or *proxies*), displayed near the border of the screen, to make users aware of relevant objects that are outside the view area. In particular, Wedge exploits isosceles triangles (called *wedges*) to point at off-screen objects: for each off-screen object, the tip of a triangle is made to coincide with the object, while the base as well as part of the two legs of the triangle are visible on the screen. By mentally extending the visible part of the legs, users should be able to estimate the position of the corresponding off-screen object (see Figure 1).

Several user studies have been carried out to evaluate the effectiveness of O+D and Contextual Cues Techniques as solutions to the off-screen objects problem. These studies revealed that both approaches are effective in helping users to carry out spatial tasks with off-screen objects. In particular, the effectiveness of Wedge stands out among Contextual Cues Techniques. However, these studies had limitations that make it difficult to generalize their results to typical real-world usage scenarios. Most studies involved spatial tasks, such as finding the closest off-screen object, that required users to only look at a static configuration of off-screen objects, thus neglecting the possible effect of panning and zooming actions on user's ability to make sense of the visualization. Moreover, all studies involved a small number of off-screen objects (typically less than 10), while real-world scenarios often involve larger numbers. Since there is evidence that even a small increase in the number of off-screen objects negatively affects user performance in spatial tasks [7], the effectiveness of the two approaches with larger numbers of objects is dubious.

The aim of our work is to propose improvements to O+D and to the most effective Contextual Cues Technique (Wedge) to simplify their use in dynamic scenarios with large numbers of off-screen objects whose relative position to the border of the screen changes as a consequence of user's navigation actions. With a user study, we investigate whether the two modified approaches are as effective in a complex and dynamic scenario as they are in the static scenarios used in past studies.

The paper is organized as follows. Section 2 surveys related work. Section 3 discusses in more detail the motivations for our work. Section 4 describes the two approaches we compared in the study. Section 5 describes the experimental evaluation and reports results, which are then discussed in Section 6.

RELATED WORK

In this section, we focus on O+D and Contextual Cues Techniques, illustrating how these approaches aim to solve the off-screen objects problem and highlighting their strengths and weaknesses.

Overview+Detail

O+D typically provides two simultaneous views of an information space: an overview of the whole space and a detail view of a specific portion of the space. In the overview, a graphical highlight (the *viewfinder*) shows which is the portion of space displayed by the detail view [25]. The two views can support zooming and panning and they can be *tightly coupled*, if the manipulation of one view is immediately reflected in the other view, or *loosely coupled* if the manipulation of one view results in an update of the other view only when users complete their panning or zooming actions. Studies in the desktop HCI literature show that the overview allows users to be faster in performing search tasks in an information space compared to a scrolling interface [2, 4, 24] and can help users to acquire information during navigation [21]. However, O+D seems to be worse than zooming and Focus+Context interfaces in terms of task completion times [1, 18, 20, 21]. Nonetheless, O+D was almost always preferred by users, probably because it helps users to build a better mental model of the explored information space [23].

On mobile devices, O+D can be problematic due to the small size of displays: information in the overview might be difficult to read and the overview may cover a sizable part of the detail view. Moreover, it could be complex for users to relate the two views [12]. The reduced size of the overview can also negatively affect interaction, making it more difficult for users to manipulate the viewfinder. Additionally, a small panning action on the overview can result in large jumps in the detail view.

Few empirical studies have been carried out on mobile O+D. In their work on web page visualization, Roto et al. [26] proposed a browser that automatically reformats page content and, during scrolling, displays a small overview containing a thumbnail of the whole page. Users found the proposed browser more usable compared to a traditional mobile browser. In [10], O+D was compared with a detail-only zooming interface, in a study where users had to perform search tasks in a scatterplot using a PDA. Users with high spatial ability were faster when using the zooming interface, suggesting that the use of a single larger detail view on mobile devices can be preferable to an O+D solution. Burigat et al. [9] compared two different implementations of O+D and a zooming interface, in a study where users had to navigate maps, diagrams and web pages. The two O+D solutions differed in terms of the information included in the overview: one showed only the outline of overview and viewfinder while the other showed a thumbnail of the considered information space. Results reveal that a small thumbnail of the information space in the overview helps users to be faster in carrying out search tasks on maps. Moreover, O+D helps users to recall the position of objects in the considered information space. In a subsequent study [6], Burigat and Chittaro compared different implementations of O+D, to better understand the effects of highlighting objects of interest in the overview and the possibility to directly manipulate the viewfinder. Results show that both factors are beneficial to users in map search tasks, with manipulability providing the highest performance improvement.

Contextual Cues Techniques

Contextual Cues Techniques augment the detail view with abstract shapes placed near the border of the screen to provide awareness of off-screen objects.

City Lights [28], one of the first Contextual Cues Techniques proposed in the literature, encodes off-screen objects with lines displayed at the border of the screen. The lines correspond to the orthogonal projection of objects on the edges of the display. Moreover, line color encodes the distance of objects. EdgeRadar [17] represents off-screen objects by using points, placed into narrow areas all along the edges of the screen. Points which are closer to the border represent farther off-screen objects. Scaled Arrows and Stretched Arrows are two other Contextual Cues Techniques proposed in [8]. In Scaled Arrows, the orientation of arrows placed along the border encodes the direction of off-screen objects while the size of arrows is inversely proportional to the distance of the objects from the edges of the screen. Stretched Arrows differ from Scaled Arrows by encoding distance with the length of arrows. In both techniques, larger arrows correspond to closer objects.

Unlike the above mentioned solutions, Halo [3] is a Contextual Cues Technique that surrounds every off-screen object with a circle large enough to enter the display area, exploiting the human ability to visually complete a circle by looking at only a portion of it, to derive position and distance of off-screen objects. Baudisch et al. [3] found that users were faster in carrying out spatial tasks on a map with Halo, compared to a technique that encodes off-screen objects with static arrows and labels for distance indication. In [8], Halo was compared with Scaled Arrows and Stretched

Arrows, in a study where users had to carry out spatial tasks on a map. Halo scored better in distance estimation, while Scaled Arrows scored better in user preference and in the task that required the relative distance order of off-screen objects. Moreover, users were faster and more accurate with the two arrow approaches when the number of off-screen objects increased. The comparison between Halo and EdgeRadar in [17] revealed that EdgeRadar is preferable to help users keep track of moving off-screen objects. In [22], the authors propose an approach based on Halo, which uses oval halos in order to reduce overlap among off-screen proxies. However, the distortion negatively affected distance estimation and user accuracy in locating off-screen objects. Another Halo variant, HaloDot [15], adds a small dot at the intersection between a circle and the intrusion border, i.e. the inner limit of the area where halos are visible, to improve direction awareness of off-screen objects. Moreover, the authors use color and transparency to encode the relevance of off-screen objects and use an aggregation approach to mitigate clutter among proxies. The results of a comparison with Halo pointed out that HaloDot allows users to search faster for relevant objects of interest and that the aggregation is useful.

As mentioned above, Wedge [16] is a Contextual Cues Technique that exploits triangles (*wedges*) to make users aware of off-screen objects. With Wedge, users were more accurate in identifying the location of off-screen objects compared to using Halo, especially when the number of objects was larger, likely because wedges take up less space on the border of the screen compared to Halo. A study described in [7] compared Wedge with Scaled Arrows and O+D. In the O+D condition, off-screen objects were represented by points in the overview. Results pointed out that O+D was more effective when users had to reason in terms of the spatial configuration of off-screen objects, such as finding the pair of objects which are closest to each other. However, Wedge was more effective when only distance information of the off-screen objects was important. When users had to identify the correct location of off-screen objects, no significant differences were found among the three approaches. Finally, results showed that with a slightly larger number of objects user performance was negatively affected with all approaches.

MOTIVATIONS OF THE STUDY

In general, the previously summarized studies pointed out that Wedge and O+D are more effective than other approaches in helping users to carry out spatial tasks in large information spaces on mobile devices. However, most of these studies had important limitations in terms of the employed scenarios. More specifically:

- Most tasks involved a relatively small number of off-screen objects. In [3], Halo was compared with the arrow-based technique employing 5 off-screen objects. In the comparison among Halo, Scaled Arrows and Stretched Arrows described in [8] the number of objects ranged from 5 to 8. The same number of objects was used in [7], where Wedge was compared with Scaled Arrows and O+D. In [16], the comparison between Wedge and Halo involved 5 objects even if the density of these objects on the screen was set to simulate more cluttered conditions.
- Almost all of the tasks involved only static scenarios, i.e., users were presented with a predefined configuration of off-screen objects and never had to perform any navigation activity in the considered information space.
- Some of the studies (e.g., [3, 16]) were carried out only on mobile device emulators running on a desktop computer with a mouse rather than on actual mobile devices.

As a consequence of these limitations, results of studies on the off-screen objects problem cannot be easily generalized to more complex and dynamic scenarios. As an example of dynamic scenario, consider a user who needs to know the position of underground stations or bus stops, located around her, in order to reach a destination. In the center of a big city, the number of these objects of interest is likely to be very high and in this case, by looking at the map at the zoom level required to see map details, a lot of these objects of interest might be outside the screen. Thus, the user has to perform panning actions to see where the desired objects of interest are located. This might have a significant impact on Contextual Cues Techniques since the relative position of all off-screen objects with respect to the border of the screen changes. Finally, with a large number of off-screen objects, which is a realistic scenario when dealing with e.g. underground stations or bus stops, the user could find it difficult to make sense of the visualization and identify the most relevant objects of interest for her purposes.

Our work was thus aimed at studying Wedge and O+D in dynamic scenarios with large numbers of off-screen objects, proposing possible improvements to the two approaches aimed at making them more effective in such scenarios and, eventually, understanding whether the effectiveness of Wedge and O+D in static scenarios with low numbers of off-screen objects would transfer to more complex scenarios.

THE CONSIDERED APPROACHES

In this section, we describe the two approaches we compared in our study, illustrating the changes we made to Wedge and O+D to improve their use in dynamic scenarios with large numbers of objects.

As discussed in previous sections, Wedge is based on local models of amodal perception which suggest that the human visual system completes the occluded part of an object by connecting the extension of visible contours [27], which, in this case, are the visible part of the legs of wedges associated to off-screen objects (Fig. 1). The base of each wedge is a key graphical element that helps users to discriminate among legs belonging to different triangles. A key feature of Wedge is that triangles have three degrees of freedom since it is possible to change rotation, aperture and intrusion of each triangle while keeping it pointed at the same location. These features are important to improve location accuracy and to display wedges at the corners of the screen. In Wedge, the degrees of freedom are also used by an iterative overlap resolution algorithm.

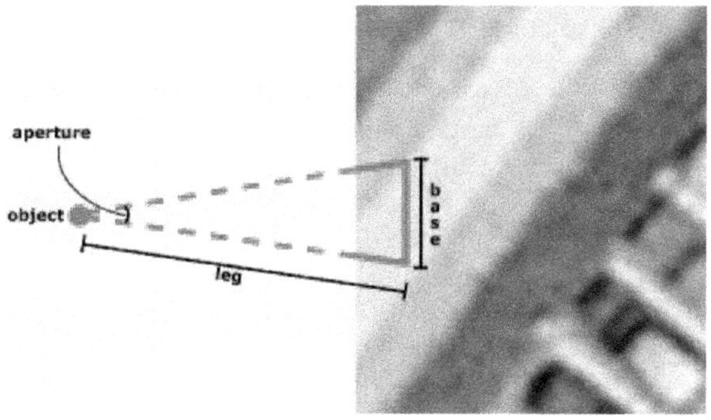

Figure 1. Each wedge consists of two legs and a base. Part of the two legs and the base are visible on the screen while the tip of the wedge coincides with the off-screen object.

After implementing Wedge on mobile devices, we examined the effect of increasing the number of off-screen objects. We started with a configuration of 20 off-screen objects randomly positioned around the visualized portion of a map. Figure 2 shows the resulting visualization with (Fig. 2a) and without (Fig. 2b) activation of the overlap resolution algorithm. Even with such a relatively low number of off-screen objects, making sense of the visualization in a dynamic scenario might be difficult, especially in the areas where the density of wedges is higher. It must also be noted that the effect of the overlap resolution algorithm, while noticeable, does not sensibly improve the visualization, mainly because several overlaps cannot be resolved. Setting the number of off-screen objects to 30, we obtained visualizations such as those in Fig. 2c (with overlap resolution) and Fig. 2d (without overlap resolution). As it can be seen, clutter greatly increases with respect to the 20 objects configuration and the overlap resolution algorithm does not improve the visualization. For this reason, we did not use the (computationally expensive) overlap resolution algorithm during the user study.

From these examples, it is clear that the largest triangles have a significant impact on the readability of the visualization since they take more screen space along the border of the screen and create several overlaps with smaller wedges. Larger wedges are associated to off-screen objects which are farther from the visualized area and in many real-world scenarios are less important for users. For this reason, we extended Wedge with two mechanisms that reduce the visibility of the largest wedges to simplify the visualization and reduce clutter.

The first mechanism acts on the transparency of wedges, changing it according to the distance of the corresponding off-screen objects. The farther the off-screen object is from the displayed area, the higher the transparency level of the corresponding wedge. The mapping between distance and transparency is based on two distance thresholds. All wedges associated to off-screen objects which are farther than a maximum threshold will use a predefined high level of transparency. Wedges associated to objects which are closer than a minimum threshold will be displayed with 100% opacity. All other wedges will be displayed with a level of transparency directly proportional to the distance of the

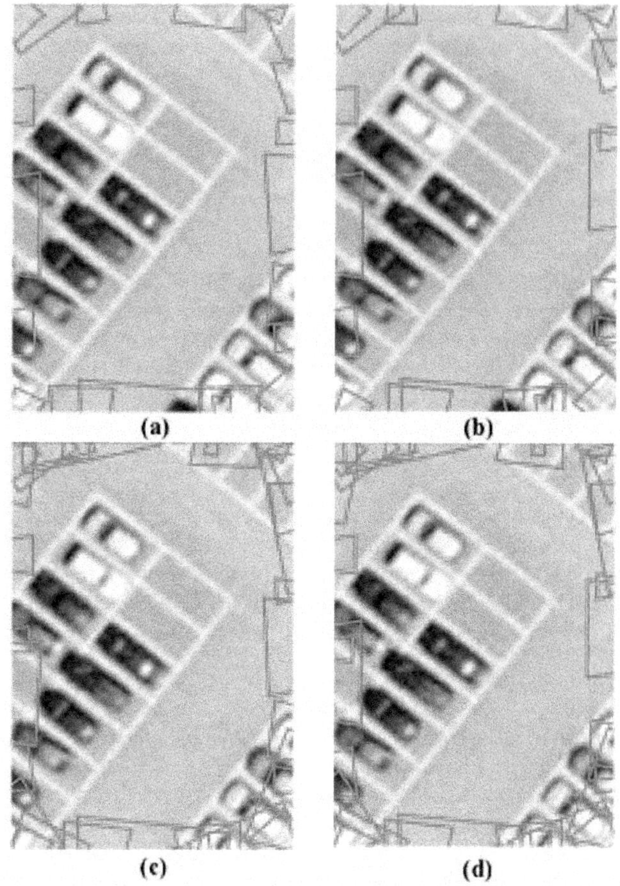

Figure 2. Examples of configurations with 20 off-screen objects (a)-(b) and 30 off-screen objects (c)-(d). In (b) and (d), the algorithm to resolve overlaps was not used.

corresponding off-screen object. This mechanism makes it easier for the user to identify the closest off-screen objects while keeping awareness of all off-screen objects. Figure 3b shows an example of the application of this mechanism to the configuration of 40 off-screen objects displayed in Fig. 3a.

The second mechanism we added to Wedge displays only those wedges corresponding to off-screen objects whose distance from the border of the screen is lower than a predefined threshold. This mechanism can reduce clutter in the case of a large number of distant objects, making wedges associated to closer objects more visible. The drawback is that it does not keep users aware of the global configuration of off-screen objects. Figure 3c shows an example of the application of this mechanism.

Activating the two mechanisms at the same time further declutters the visualization, as Fig. 3d shows.

Our study compared Wedge with a classic O+D approach that shows an overview of the information space as a small-scale thumbnail at the bottom right corner of the screen. A semi-transparent viewfinder in the overview highlights the area of the information space displayed in the detail view. Following the suggestions about overview size given in

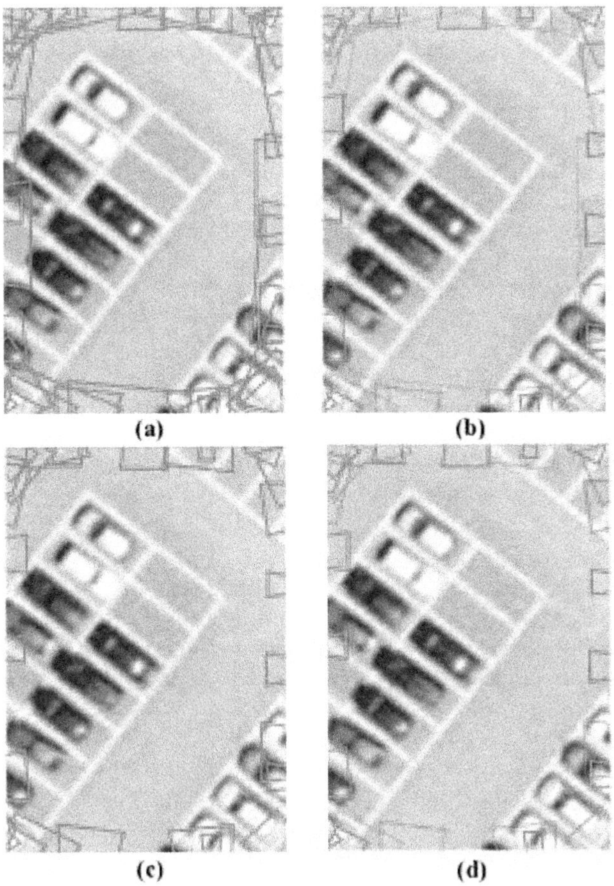

Figure 3. (a) Example of configuration with 40 off-screen objects. (b) Example of application of the transparency mechanism. (c) Example of application of the distance mechanism. (d) Example of application of both transparency and distance mechanisms.

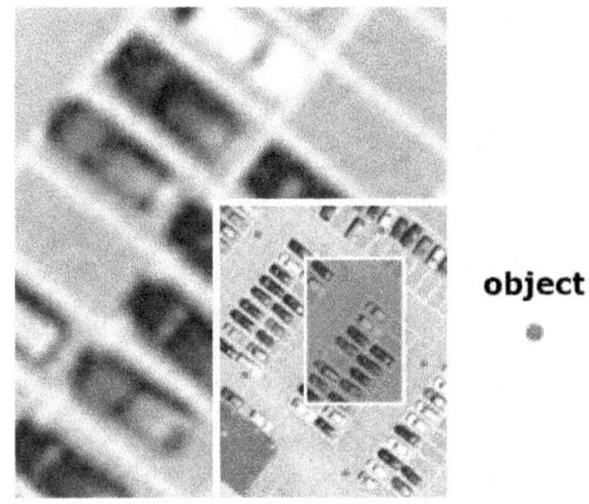

Figure 4. Close-up of the overview in the O+D visualization. The overview displays objects of interest as colored dots.

[20], our overview covers about 15% of the detail view, a compromise between legibility of its content and occlusion of the detail view. In the overview, objects of interest were displayed as colored dots (Figure 4). We extended the visualization with the same distance mechanism used in Wedge, based on displaying only those dots associated to objects which are closer than a predefined distance threshold, to reduce clutter due to a high density of dots. However, we did not add the transparency mechanism because we found that it negatively affected readability of the visualization, due to the small size of dots in the overview. Moreover, dots did not overlap, thus making transparency much less useful as a way to reduce clutter in the visualization.

USER STUDY

To evaluate the effectiveness of the two approaches based on Wedge and O+D in a dynamic situation with a large number of off-screen objects, we defined a complex scenario in which users had to navigate a map containing two categories of objects: target objects that users had to find and dangerous objects that users had to avoid. Target objects were positioned as a trail while dangerous objects framed the path, constraining user navigation. Users had to follow the sequence of target objects, tapping on each of them, while keeping dangerous objects outside of the display area during navigation. The scenario thus combines two tasks, i.e. Closest ([3, 7, 8, 16]) and Avoid ([3, 16]), that have been used in the literature to compare techniques for off-screen objects visualization. Such scenario reflects possible complex mobile phone usage scenarios, such as following a tour of points of interest while avoiding traffic jams or other obstacles.

The scenario was designed as a game to increase user involvement. In the game, users had to navigate the map (by dragging it) following a trail of coins (target objects) while avoiding monsters (dangerous objects). Users could collect coins by tapping on them on the screen. Coins where positioned in such a way that at most one could be on screen at any time while the others were all off-screen. Each collected coin gave users a 10 points bonus. Each time a monster entered the screen, the user would get a penalty of 10 points. Moreover, the user had 10 seconds to collect the next coin before expiration of a timer and an additional 10 points penalty. The timer was included to make the game more challenging but the 10 seconds time interval was large enough to let users easily complete the task. Indeed, during the study, the timer expired only 3 times. The timer had also the function of recreating the situation in which a user has a short period of time to look at her mobile phone screen, and thus to evaluate which is the closest object of interest or which are the objects to keep out of the screen. The goal of the game was to obtain the maximum possible score, collecting all coins.

Figure 5 shows the interface of the game with Wedge (Fig. 5a) and O+D (Fig. 5b), respectively. In the Wedge condition, wedges associated to coins were yellow, while wedges associated to monsters were red. In the O+D condition, the overview displayed coins as yellow points and monsters as red points. In both conditions, the distance threshold was set to 300 pixels. In the Wedge condition, the minimum and maximum transparency thresholds were set respectively to 100 and 300 pixels. We chose these values because they guarantee maximum visibility to the closest objects, reducing at the same the clutter caused by the biggest wedges. The thresholds in the two conditions assured that, if the same

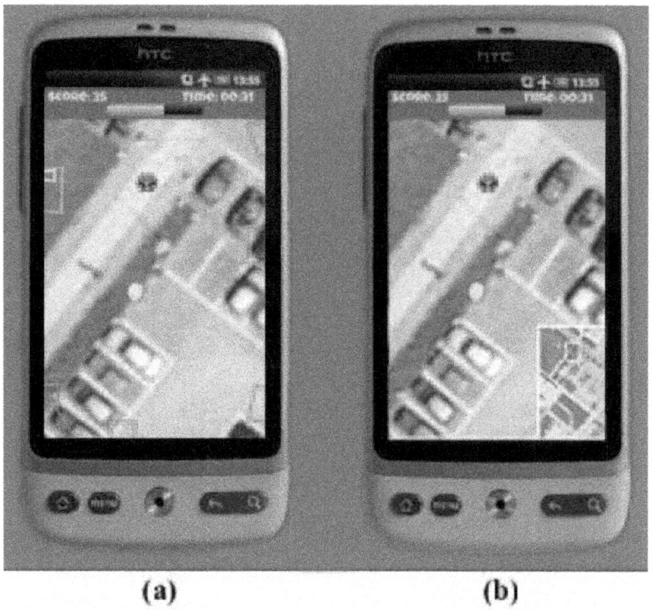

Figure 5. The game interface with Wedge (a) and O+D (b). The status bar at the top of the screen shows total score, total time and the remaining time before expiration of the timer. Both examples in the figure show a coin, a monster and a number of off-screen objects.

portion of the map were showed in the detail view, the number of points visible in the overview was the same as the number of wedges placed along the border of the screen. In both interfaces, the status bar located at the top of the screen showed global score, total time and the progress bar displaying remaining time before expiration of the timer (top of Fig. 5a and 5b).

We also took into consideration the effect of the complexity of the configuration of objects on user performance. We thus prepared 4 configurations of objects, two of which were of lower difficulty and two of higher difficulty. In high difficulty configurations, the trail of coins followed a more winding path. Each configuration contained 20 coins and 20 monsters.

Hypotheses

Considering the results of the only study that compared Wedge and O+D in a static scenario [7], one would be led to expect that Wedge could be more effective than O+D in our game scenario. Indeed, that study revealed that users were better at estimating distance of multiple off-screen objects with Wedge. This ability could be useful to monitor multiple monsters in the game, allowing users to tune their panning actions and make less errors. Wedge might also be preferred by users in a game scenario, due to its more attractive graphical aspect. However, since the static scenarios with a few off-screen objects used in the literature are very different from the dynamic scenario with larger numbers of off-screen objects in our study, there is no guarantee that past results would transfer to the new context. Moreover, considering how we prepared the configurations of objects, we would expect that users take more time and make more errors while playing with the high difficulty configurations than with the low difficulty ones, regardless of the visualization.

Participants

The study involved a sample of 16 users (8 male and 8 female) recruited among university students. Their age ranged from 21 to 28 ($M = 24.5, SD = 1.79$). Four users were left-handed, even if one of them played with the right hand, and 12 were right-handed. All users had normal or corrected-to-normal vision. On a self-reported scale ranging from 1 (low familiarity) to 7 (high familiarity), users had a high level of familiarity with mobile devices ($M = 6.13, SD = 1.02$) while they where slightly less familiar with mobile touchscreen devices ($M = 5.50, SD = 1.63$). Almost half of the users played less than once a month with video games for console or computer and with video games for mobile devices.

Materials

The study was carried out on a HTC Desire mobile phone with Android 2.2, featuring a 1GHz processor and a 3.7 inches touch screen with a resolution of 320x533 pixels. During the evaluation, a 320x463 area displayed the considered map while two menu bars were displayed at the top of the screen: a 25-pixels tall Android notification bar and the 45-pixels tall status bar containing elapsed time, total score and the progress bar, as shown at the top of Fig. 5a and 5b. In the O+D condition, the overview was located at the bottom right corner of the screen and covered a maximum area of 140x160 pixels (15% of the detail view). In both conditions, users could drag the displayed map in the desired direction using their fingers. While using O+D, users could not move the viewfinder in the overview to carry out panning actions. During the evaluation, the device was in portrait mode and placed on a table over a mat to avoid sliding. Figure 5 shows examples of the two considered approaches on the mobile phone.

The following questionnaires were administered to users in different phases of the study. A *demographic questionnaire* was used to collect data about users (age, sex, occupation, dominant hand and sight defects) and their familiarity with mobile devices and touchscreen mobile devices. Familiarity was measured on a 7-levels Likert scale where 1 corresponded to low familiarity and 7 to high familiarity. Moreover, the questionnaire contained two items asking how often users played with video games for console or computer and with video games for mobile devices. The possible answers were: never, almost once a month, several times a month, several times a week, every day less than 1 hour, every day about 1-3 hours, every day more than 3 hours.

The *NASA Task Load Index* (TLX) [19] was used to measure subjective mental workload experienced by users during game sessions. NASA-TLX is a subjective workload assessment technique that derives an overall score based on a weighted average of ratings on six sub-scales: mental demand, physical demand, temporal demand, performance, effort, and frustration level. We administered to users a computerized version of the NASA-TLX (installed on a mobile device) [11] at the end of each game session. NASA-TLX scores can range in the 1-100 interval.

A modified version of the *Player Enjoyment Scale* (PES) was used to evaluate the enjoyment perceived and the experience of flow in a gaming activity [13]. PES is based on the EGameFlow scale [14] and includes 13 bipolar statements, both positive and negative, with scores from 1 (strongly disagree) to 7 (strongly agree). We removed the 7th and 12th items ("The difficulty of challenges in the game increased as my skills improved" and "I experienced an altered sense of time while playing the game") because no increase of difficulty was planned (participants played a single level of the game) and the gaming session was short (five minutes). We had to slightly change the 8th item ("The game provided new challenges with an appropriate pacing") into "The game proceeded with an appropriate pacing", because the challenges of the game did not change during each session. A total enjoyment score is obtained by reversing the negative item scores and summing them to positive item scores. Since we removed the two above mentioned items of the PES, our modified version of the scale (for brevity, mPES) returns a score that can range from 11 to 77.

We also asked participants to rate three additional statements ("I found it difficult to understand the information about off-screen objects provided by wedges/overview", "I found the information about off-screen objects provided by wedges/overview useful", "I found the game difficult") to better evaluate user perception of the two considered approaches.

Experimental design and procedure

The study was based on a 2x2 within subjects design with Approach (Wedge and O+D) and Difficulty of objects configuration (low difficulty and high difficulty) as independent variables. We used a Latin square design to guarantee that the order of presentation of experimental conditions as well as their association with objects configurations were counterbalanced to mitigate order effects.

Participants carried out the evaluation in a seated position. They were individually briefed about the nature of the experiment and were asked to fill in the demographic questionnaire. Afterwards, the experimenter described in detail the two approaches and presented training tasks to users, to let them familiarize with the interfaces and clarify possible doubts concerning interfaces or tasks. The evaluation consisted of four game sessions. Users played two times with each approach, with two different configurations of objects (low difficulty and high difficulty). To start a task, users had to tap on a "Start" button that was initially displayed on the screen. Each task ended when users collected the last coin. After two sessions with an approach, users were asked to fill in the NASA-TLX and the mPES questionnaires. After the test, users were also asked to express their preference on the considered approaches. Tests had an average length of 30 minutes.

For each user, we automatically recorded time spent to complete each session, total score and total number of penalties, i.e. the appearance of a monster on the screen and the expiration of the timer.

Results

Task completion time

Figure 6 shows the mean completion times for all four possible combinations of Approach and Difficulty of objects configuration.

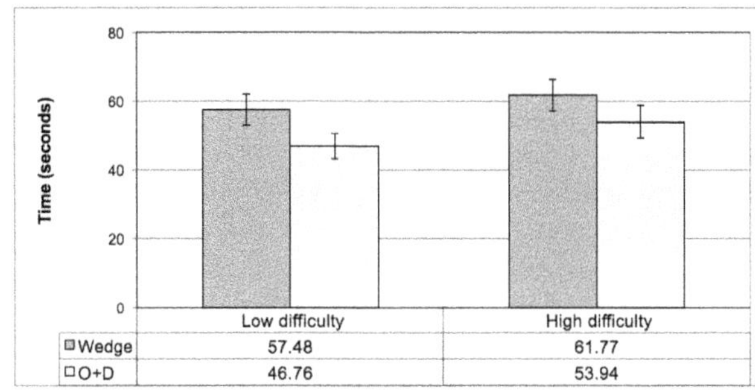

Figure 6. Mean completion times (capped bars indicate $\pm 1SE$) with the two approaches, for the two levels of difficulty.

Task completion times were subjected to the Kolmogorov-Smirnov test of normality prior to further analysis. The test revealed no significant deviation from the normal distribution. A two-way repeated measures ANOVA was then carried out, revealing no significant interaction between Approach and Difficulty ($F(1,15) = 0.30, p = 0.59$). A significant main effect of Approach was detected, ($F(1,15) = 9.18, p < 0.01, \eta^2 = 0.38$): users spent less time to carry out game sessions using O+D. A significant main effect of Difficulty was also detected, ($F(1,15) = 6.15, p < 0.05, \eta^2 = 0.29$): users took more time to complete the task when playing with a high difficulty configuration of objects.

Errors

Figure 7 shows the mean number of errors for all four possible combinations between Approach and Difficulty of objects configuration. We only analyzed errors due to monsters entering the screen because the number of timer expiration errors was negligible (only 3 over the whole experiment).

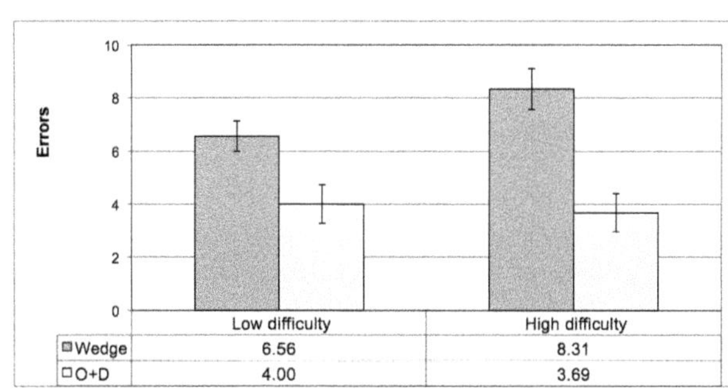

Figure 7. Mean number of errors (capped bars indicate $\pm 1SE$) with the two approaches, for the two levels of difficulty.

The Kolmogorov-Smirnov test of normality revealed no significant deviation from the normal distribution. A two-way repeated measures ANOVA was then carried out, which revealed no significant interaction between Approach and Difficulty, ($F(1, 15) = 3.63, p = 0.07$), and no significant main effect of Difficulty ($F(1, 15) = 1.11, p = 0.31$). However, a significant main effect of Approach was detected, ($F(1, 15) = 29.92, p < 0.0001, \eta^2 = 0.67$): users made less errors using O+D.

Subjective mental workload

Figure 8 shows means of the subjective mental workload we measured with the NASA-TLX. We report means for both the overall score and the six individual sub-scale ratings: mental demand (MD), physical demand (PD), temporal demand (TD), performance (PE), effort (EF), and frustration level (FL). A Wilcoxon signed-rank test on the overall scores pointed out a significant effect ($W = 15, p < 0.01, r = 0.48$) suggesting that users experienced less mental workload while using O+D. The Wilcoxon signed-rank test on sub-scale ratings revealed a significant effect for temporal demand ($W = 22, p < 0.05, r = 0.38$), performance ($W = 19.5, p < 0.05, r = 0.44$) and effort ($W = 18, p < 0.05, r = 0.39$).

Game enjoyment

Figure 9 shows the mean overall mPES scores. The data was analyzed with a Wilcoxon signed-rank test, which revealed a significant difference between the means ($W = 6.50, p < 0.01, r = 0.54$), with users perceiving O+D as more enjoyable than Wedge.

The Wilcoxon signed-rank test on each individual mPES statement revealed a significant effect for items "I perceived a sense of control on the game" ($W = 3.5, p < 0.01, r = 0.48$) (Fig. 10) and "While playing I always knew what was the next step" ($W = 3, p < 0.01, r = 0.58$) (Fig. 11) with O+D getting better scores. The Wilcoxon signed-rank test on the additional statements we asked users revealed a significant effect for item "I found the game difficult" ($W = 4, p < 0.05, r = 0.39$) (Fig. 12) with O+D getting a better score.

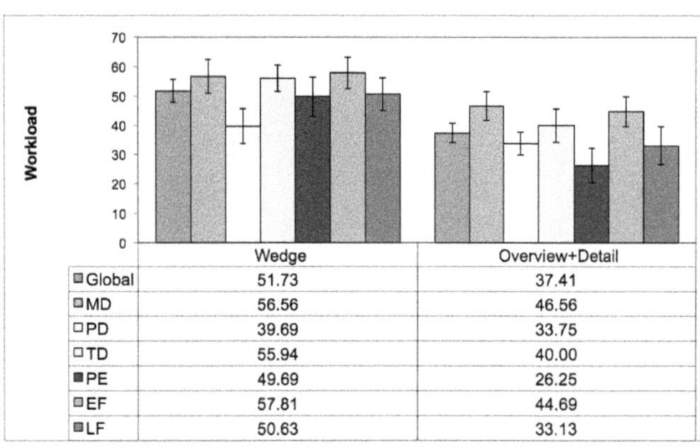

	Wedge	Overview+Detail
Global	51.73	37.41
MD	56.56	46.56
PD	39.69	33.75
TD	55.94	40.00
PE	49.69	26.25
EF	57.81	44.69
LF	50.63	33.13

Figure 8. Mean overall and sub scale workload ratings (capped bars indicate $\pm 1SE$) for the two approaches.

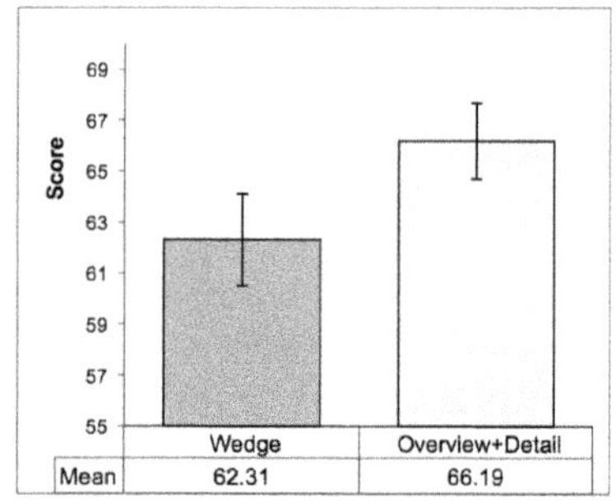

Figure 9. Mean overall scores of mPES (capped bars indicate $\pm 1SE$).

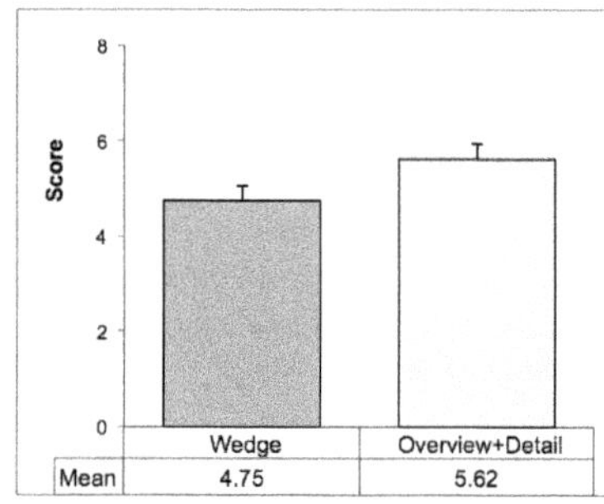

Figure 10. Mean overall scores (capped bars indicate $\pm 1SE$) for item "I perceived a sense of control on the game".

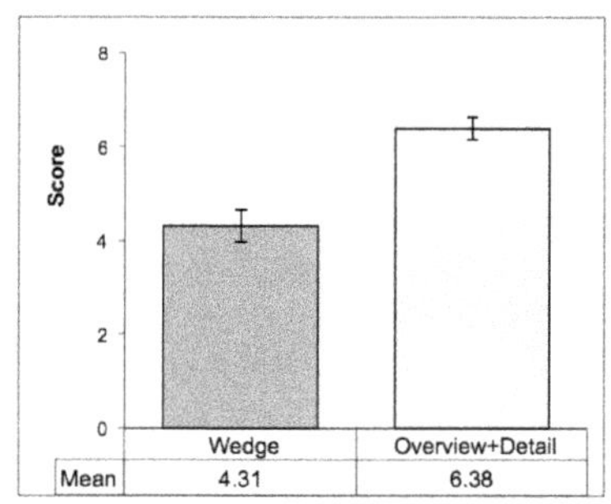

Figure 11. Mean overall scores (capped bars indicate $\pm 1SE$) for item "While playing I always knew what was the next step".

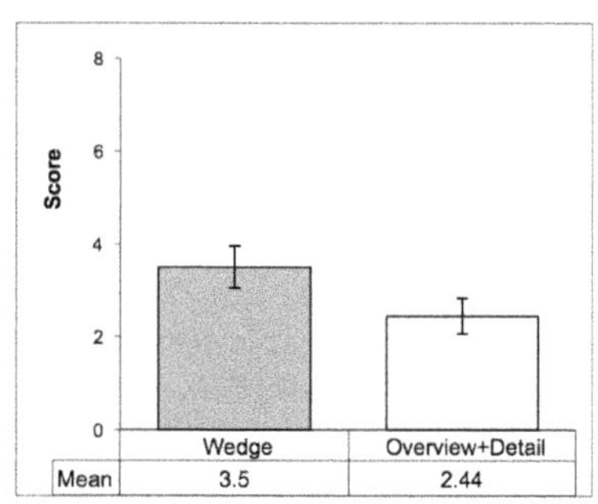

Figure 12. Mean overall scores (capped bars indicate $\pm 1SE$) for item "I found the game difficult".

Subjective preference

Four users preferred Wedge while the other 12 preferred O+D. A chi-square test revealed a significant difference between the scores ($\chi^2(1, N = 16) = 4, p < 0.05$) with O+D being the preferred approach.

DISCUSSION AND CONCLUSIONS

Overall, our evaluation found that the better results that Wedge obtains over O+D in static scenarios with a few off-screen objects do not transfer to a dynamic scenario with larger numbers of objects. In the latter context, O+D seems to be a more effective approach to off-screen objects visualization.

Users were faster while using O+D in terms of the time spent to carry out tasks. A possible explanation of this result could be that each panning action with Wedge changes the position and size of proxy shapes, while the position of off-screen objects in the overview does not change during navigation. Thus, users might spend more time with Wedge because they need to partially re-evaluate the visualization after every navigation action. Moreover, the presence of the viewfinder in the overview probably acts as a navigation aid that let users better orient and navigate in the information space. Note that this result is different from what was obtained in the study described in [7], where no difference was found between Wedge and O+D for the time needed by users to find the off-screen object nearest to the screen, probably because the scenario considered in that study was static.

Users made more errors using Wedge than using O+D. Again, the presence of static information in the overview might allow users to more easily avoid dangerous objects compared to the need to constantly re-evaluate wedges in Wedge. Users commented that the information provided by wedges changed too rapidly during navigation to allow them to easily spot monsters that could enter the screen. As for task completion times, this result differs from what was obtained in [7], where no significant differences were found between Wedge and O+D in the Closest task (in which users had to identify the off-screen object closest to the border of the screen) and in the Locate task (in which users had to estimate the exact location of every off-screen object).

Considering the configuration of objects, users took more time to complete the high difficulty configurations compared to the low difficulty ones, regardless of the type of approach used. However, contrary to our hypothesis, they did not make more errors when playing with high difficulty configurations. A possible explanation could be that users spent more time to keep dangerous objects out of the screen.

In NASA-TLX results, Wedge scored worse in all ratings. In particular, the differences were significant for the overall score and for the temporal demand, performance and effort sub-scale factors. These results suggest that the information provided by Wedge requires more mental workload in a dynamic context. As in previous results, this could be explained by the fact that the global context needs to be re-evaluated after every minimal panning action, increasing perceived effort. The increased temporal demand perceived by users could be due to the additional time needed to evaluate the situation compared to O+D. Finally, the low rating for performance could be due to the high number of errors made by users.

The mPES scores showed that users enjoyed playing with O+D more than playing with Wedge. The significant difference for the item "While playing I always knew what was the next step" could be a consequence of the fact that, when using O+D, users had a better sense of the global situation, similarly to what emerged in [7]. The significant difference we found for the item "I found the game difficult" could be due to the higher number of errors made by users using Wedge and the higher difficulty users had to understand the information provided by wedges. Globally, these factors could have negatively influenced the perceived enjoyment.

Users' subjective preference reflects performance. In general, user comments show that the information provided by O+D was more useful to understand the global position of off-screen objects and allowed users to more easily navigate the map. The few negative comments about O+D mentioned that the overview occluded part of the detail view while the use of wedges did not occlude a sizable portion of the map, even if it also did not allow users to easily determine the overall configuration of off-screen objects.

In conclusion, the results of the study point out that O+D seems to be more effective than Wedge as a solution to visualize the position of off-screen objects in the considered context, making it more appropriate for real-world usage scenarios.

ACKNOWLEDGMENTS

Andrea Vianello acknowledges the financial support of the PRIN 2008 project "Descriptive Geometry and Digital Representation: intelligent user interfaces to support modeling and navigation in 3D graphics application for architecture and design".
Stefano Burigat acknowledges partial financial support of the Italian Ministry of Education, University and Research (MIUR) under a law 17/1999 project.

REFERENCES

1. Baudisch, P., Good, N., Bellotti, V., and Schraedley, P. Keeping things in context: a comparative evaluation of focus plus context screens, overviews, and zooming. In *Proc. Conference on Human Factors in Computing Systems*, ACM Press (2002), 259–266.

2. Baudisch, P., Lee, B., and Hanna, L. Fishnet, a fisheye web browser with search term popouts: a comparative evaluation with overview and linear view. In *Proc. Conference on Advanced Visual Interfaces*, ACM Press (2004), 133–140.

3. Baudisch, P., and Rosenholtz, R. Halo: a technique for visualizing off-screen locations. In *Proc. Conference on Human Factors in Computing Systems*, ACM Press (2003), 481–488.

4. Beard, D., and Walker, J. Navigational techniques to improve the display of large two-dimensional spaces.

Behaviour and Information Technology 9, 6 (1990), 451–466.

5. Bederson, B., and Hollan, J. Pad++: a zooming graphical interface for exploring alternate interface physics. In *Proc. Conference on User Interface Software and Technology*, ACM Press (1994), 17–26.
6. Burigat, S., and Chittaro, L. On the effectiveness of overview+ detail visualization on mobile devices. *Personal and Ubiquitous Computing* (2011), doi: 10.1007/s00779-011-0500-3.
7. Burigat, S., and Chittaro, L. Visualizing references to off-screen content on mobile devices: A comparison of arrows, wedge, and overview+ detail. *Interacting with Computers 23*, 2 (2011), 156–166.
8. Burigat, S., Chittaro, L., and Gabrielli, S. Visualizing locations of off-screen objects on mobile devices: a comparative evaluation of three approaches. In *Proc. Conference on Human-Computer Interaction with Mobile Devices and Services*, ACM Press (2006), 239–246.
9. Burigat, S., Chittaro, L., and Parlato, E. Map, diagram, and web page navigation on mobile devices: the effectiveness of zoomable user interfaces with overviews. In *Proc. Conference on Human-Computer Interaction with Mobile Devices and Services*, ACM Press (2008), 147–156.
10. Büring, T., Gerken, J., and Reiterer, H. Usability of overview-supported zooming on small screens with regard to individual differences in spatial ability. In *Proc. Conference on Advanced Visual Interfaces*, ACM Press (2006), 233–240.
11. Cao, A., Chintamani, K., Pandya, A., and Ellis, R. Nasa tlx: Software for assessing subjective mental workload. *Behavior research methods 41*, 1 (2009), 113–117.
12. Chittaro, L. Visualizing information on mobile devices. *IEEE Computer 39*, 3 (2006), 40–45.
13. Chu Yew Yee, S., Duh, H., and Quek, F. Investigating narrative in mobile games for seniors. In *Proc. Conference on Human Factors in Computing Systems*, ACM Press (2010), 669–672.
14. Fu, F., Su, R., and Yu, S. Egameflow: A scale to measure learners' enjoyment of e-learning games. *Computers & Education 52*, 1 (2009), 101–112.
15. Gonçalves, T., Afonso, A., Carmo, M., and Pombinho, P. Evaluation of halodot: visualization of relevance of off-screen objects with over cluttering prevention on mobile devices. In *Proc. IFIP Conference on Human-computer interaction*, Springer-Verlag (2011), 300–308.
16. Gustafson, S., Baudisch, P., Gutwin, C., and Irani, P. Wedge: clutter-free visualization of off-screen locations. In *Proc. Conference on Human Factors in Computing Systems*, ACM Press (2008), 787–796.
17. Gustafson, S., and Irani, P. Comparing visualizations for tracking off-screen moving targets. In *Proc. Conference on Human Factors in Computing Systems*, ACM Press (2007), 2399–2404.
18. Gutwin, C., and Skopik, A. Fisheyes are good for large steering tasks. In *Proc. Conference on Human Factors in Computing Systems*, ACM Press (2003), 201–208.
19. Hart, S., and Staveland, L. Development of NASA-TLX (task load index): Results of empirical and theoretical research. *Human mental workload 1* (1988), 139–183.
20. Hornbæk, K., Bederson, B., and Plaisant, C. Navigation patterns and usability of zoomable user interfaces with and without an overview. *ACM Transactions on Computer-Human Interaction 9*, 4 (2002), 362–389.
21. Hornbæk, K., and Frøkjær, E. Reading patterns and usability in visualizations of electronic documents. *ACM Transactions on Computer-Human Interaction 10*, 2 (2003), 119–149.
22. Irani, P., Gutwin, C., and Yang, X. Improving selection of off-screen targets with hopping. In *Proc. Conference on Human Factors in Computing Systems*, ACM Press (2006), 299–308.
23. Nekrasovski, D., Bodnar, A., McGrenere, J., Guimbretière, F., and Munzner, T. An evaluation of pan & zoom and rubber sheet navigation with and without an overview. In *Proc. Conference on Human Factors in Computing Systems*, ACM Press (2006), 11–20.
24. North, C., and Shneiderman, B. Snap-together visualization: can users construct and operate coordinated visualizations? *International Journal of Human-Computer Studies 53*, 5 (2000), 715–739.
25. Plaisant, C., Carr, D., and Shneiderman, B. Image-browser taxonomy and guidelines for designers. *IEEE Software 12*, 2 (1995), 21–32.
26. Roto, V., Popescu, A., Koivisto, A., and Vartiainen, E. Minimap: a web page visualization method for mobile phones. In *Proc. Conference on Human Factors in Computing Systems*, ACM Press (2006), 35–44.
27. Sekuler, A., Palmer, S., and Flynn, C. Local and global processes in visual completion. *Psychological Science 5*, 5 (1994), 260–267.
28. Zellweger, P., Mackinlay, J., Good, L., Stefik, M., and Baudisch, P. City lights: contextual views in minimal space. In *Proc. Conference on Human Factors in Computing Systems*, ACM Press (2003), 838–839.

How to Position the Cursor? An Exploration of Absolute and Relative Cursor Positioning for Back-of-Device Input

Khalad Hasan[1], Xing-Dong Yang[2], Hai-Ning Liang[3], Pourang Irani[1]

[1]Depart. of Computer Science
University of Manitoba
Winnipeg, Manitoba, Canada
{khalad, irani}@cs.umanitoba.ca

[2]Depart. of Computer Science
University of Alberta
Edmonton, Alberta, Canada
xingdong@cs.ualberta.ca

[3]Department of Computer Science & Software Engineering
Xian Jiaotong-Liverpool University
Suzhou, China
haining.liang@xjtlu.edu.cn

ABSTRACT

Observational studies indicate that most people use one hand to interact with their mobile devices. Interaction on the back-of-devices (BoD) has been proposed to enhance one-handed input for various tasks, including selection and gesturing. However, we do not possess a good understanding of some fundamental issues related to one-handed BoD input. In this paper, we attempt to fill this gap by conducting three studies. The first study explores suitable selection techniques; the second study investigates the performance and suitability of the two main modes of cursor movement: Relative and Absolute; and the last study examines solutions to the problem of reaching the lower part of the device. Our results indicate that for BoD interaction, relative input is more efficient and accurate for cursor positioning and target selection than absolute input. Based on these findings provide guidelines for designing BoD interactions for mobile devices.

Author Keywords

Back-of-device input, touch input, selection mechanism, relative and absolute cursor positioning.

ACM Classification Keywords

H.5.2. [**Information interfaces and presentation**]: User Interfaces, Input Devices, Interaction Styles.

General Terms

Design, Experimentation, Human Factors.

INTRODUCTION

When interacting with a mobile device such as a smartphone, people often chose to use only one hand [9]. One-handed interaction is convenient and allows users to multitask by freeing their other hand for tasks such as holding a bus handle. Karlson et al. [9] have found that users prefer using one hand for two handed tasks. Despite some advantages, this form of interaction imposes several limitations, such as occlusion and reachability [8, 20, 27]. Prior studies have shown that these challenges can be overcome by allowing users to interact with the back-side of the device [1, 15, 18], or *back-of-device input*. Back-of-device (BoD) input allows users to control an on-screen cursor from behind the screen, thus reducing occlusion and improving the performance of some routine tasks, such as pointing and steering [26].

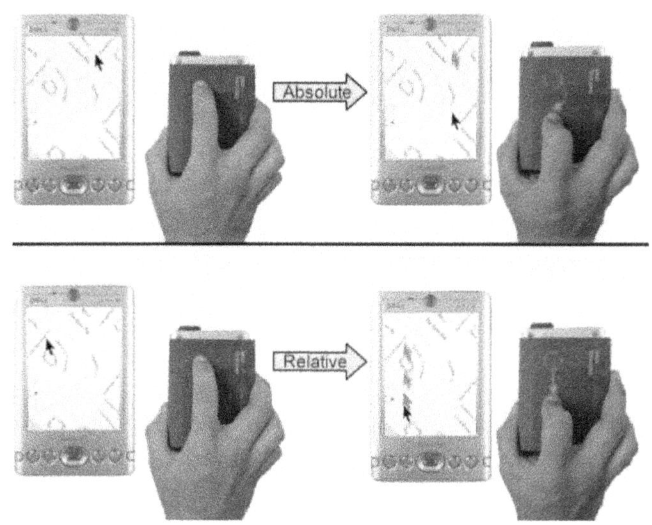

Figure 1. One-handed back-of-device input using the index finger (actual device used in our studies). In this case a touch pad senses input, allowing for both absolute (top) and relative (bottom) input, each of which present different affordances and limitations.

Cursor movement can be performed in either absolute or relative mode, and their hybrid variants [12, 19]. In absolute mode, the input device's input space has a one-to-one mapping to the screen's display space (Figure 1, top). In relative mode, the user's hand motion maps to the motion of the cursor so that the direction of the cursor's movement is consistent with the direction of the user's hand movement. (Figure 1, bottom). Despite the wide array of applications benefitting from BoD input (from pointing to text-entry) [1, 10, 16, 18, 21, 25, 26], very little research has focused on studying *selection mechanisms* and *positioning control* for *one-handed back-of-device* input. This has left some fundamental questions unanswered, such as: (1) What selection mechanism is suitable for the BoD input? (2) Which mode of cursor positioning (absolute or relative) is preferable on the back? (3) How will target size and location affect performance with these two modes?

To answer these questions, we conducted three separate studies and from the results we make the following contributions: (1) identify suitable selection mechanisms for one-handed BoD input; (2) explore the benefits of absolute and relative cursor control for BoD input; (3) examine two variations of absolute pointing mode to resolve the reachability issues discovered in our studies.

RELATED WORK

One-handed interaction

One-handed interaction is a very common method for operating mobile devices. Several in-situ observations demonstrated that at least 74% of mobile users employ only one hand when interacting with their cellular devices [8]. The thumb is thus naturally the main input method in such contexts [8, 13]. However, the thumb is often prone to inaccurate selection [20], and can be too short to reach the entire screen [8]. To alleviate concerns with thumb interaction, Applens and LaunchTile resorted to using thumb gestures as input [9]. With Applens, users could very easily navigate a grid of values using simple thumb gestures. LaunchTile allowed users to access parts of a tabular region (such as a calendar) by pressing on soft buttons associated with an area of the grid. User gestures were correct 87% of the time, implying that thumb gestures are memorable.

A study on the biomechanical limitations of thumb input revealed that users do not interact with all areas of a device with equal facility [8]. User grip, hand size, device ergonomics, and finger dexterity can strongly impact thumb reach. These results led to the development of ThumbSpace [6], which provides a miniature proxy window of the entire touch-screen. The position of the proxy window is user-defined and thus enhances thumb reach. In an extensive study, users performed better at selecting distant targets using Thumbspace than other techniques. Used in conjunction with Shift [20], ThumbSpace can be precise for target selection with the finger [7].

These findings suggest that there is sufficient evidence for the use of one-handed interaction techniques on mobile devices. However, in addition to problems of inaccurate finger pointing, which can be resolved with techniques such as Shift [20], one-handed input is also prone to limited reach. To resolve these primary concerns, researchers have proposed using the space on the back of a mobile device to interact with virtual content.

Back-of-device input

There has been significant recent activity considering the potential of BoD interaction [1, 10, 15, 16, 25]. BlindSight [10], and RearType [16] support text-entry from the back of a mobile phone by placing a key pad behind the screen. HybridTouch has a trackpad mounted on the back of a PDA to enable gesture based commands for tasks such as scrolling and panning. LucidCursor [25] has an optical sensor on the back of a PDA, allowing users to control a cursor from the back-side. NanoTouch [1] demonstrates that BoD input can lead to very small devices by avoiding on-screen finger occlusion.

However, when interacting with the back of the device, the user has limited knowledge of her finger position. LucidTouch [21] uses a rear-mounted camera to provide constant on-screen feedback of back-of-device finger movements and positions. Most other systems simply use an auxiliary sensor (such as a trackpad) on the back-side [1, 18, 22, 26], and the cursor(s) only shows up after the user's finger touches the back.

Cursor positioning through the device's back-side can be controlled with either absolute or relative movement (Figure 1). In absolute mode, a one-to-one mapping between the input and the display space positions the cursor at the touch location. In relative mode, the cursor position is updated with motions of the user's finger. In absolute mode, the cursor jumps discretely from location to location; whereas in relative mode the cursor always moves in continuous trajectories without any jumps and often requires users to perform clutching actions.

Existing systems for BoD input primarily rely on absolute input [1, 2, 21] or relative input [18, 23, 26]. Yang et al. [26] show that pointing and steering tasks on a mobile device can be carried out more precisely and efficiently with relative control than absolute control. However, in their study the two positioning modes were not used on the same side of the device. In their setup, absolute control was used on the front of the device, while relative control was used on the back. To the best of our knowledge, very little is known on which of these two control mechanisms works best for cursor control for BoD input.

Absolute positioning can be faster than relative control because it allows for rapid cursor displacement from one area to another [12]. However, absolute control for BoD can be imprecise and prone to reachability issues akin to on-screen input [8].On the other hand, relative control can be slow, particularly in cases requiring a large amount of clutching [26], but has the added benefit of precise cursor control [19]. Also, relative control does not require a one-to-one mapping between the input space and display space, allowing users to easily reach remote targets. It is unclear which of these two styles allow for more effective BoD input.

Selection mechanisms

There are several mechanisms that allow target selection while interacting from the back-side. Common techniques rely on land-on and lift-off operations. In land-on, selection occurs when the finger first touches the input component of the device, whereas in lift-off the target is selected when the finger is lifted after contact. Double tap, a combination of land-on and lift-off, is another possibility in which a selection would take place on a sequence of land-on, lift-off, and land-on actions. In addition, buttons placed on or around the device can serve to select targets.

There has been little research examining selection mechanisms and interaction from the backside. In one experiment, Baudish and Chu [1] compared target selection on lift-off and on pressing a button placed on the side of a device while users interacted through its back-side. They found that users committed more errors using lift-off across devices smaller than 2.4″. In terms of time spent per task, they found that users did better with lift-off than the side button for the 2.4″ device. In a second experiment, they found that given targets with sizes of 1.4mm, 2.8mm, 5.5mm, and 11mm participants made few errors and took less time in target selection with the side button than lift-off. Lift-off also has the unwanted effect of always having an active selection, i.e. once the user commits to touching the screen an object will get selected the moment the lift-off.

EXPERIMENT 1: SELECTION MECHANISMS

This first study investigated selection mechanisms when interaction is carried out from the back-side. We were mainly concerned with finding out which selection mechanism(s) would be suitable for absolute and relative modes.

Apparatus

The study was conducted on Dell Axim X30 with a 624 MHz processor, 53×71mm (240 × 320) TFT touch screen, and a size of 81×127×18mm. We placed a trackpad (from Ergonomic®) on the back of the device, and adjusted the size and the position of the trackpad so that they were mapped on a one-to-one basis with the touch screen in the front. We could have used other forms of sensors, but this provided the most pragmatic method for obtaining either absolute or relative input on the back of the device. The application was implemented in C#.NET.

Participants

Twelve participants (10 males) between the ages of 21 and 30 were recruited from a local university to participate in this study. Participants were all right-handed.

Task and procedure

We used a target acquisition task in which participants interacted with the device with their right hand. Each trial began when a participant clicked a "Start" button which was placed randomly but at a fixed distance of 100 pixels (1 pixel = 0.22 mm in real world units) away from the center of the screen. Tapping on the region of the trackpad directly underneath the button would start the trial. The button would then be replaced by a cursor pointer which participants would have to position in a square-shaped target to select it. The target was always placed at the center of the display. A trial ended either if a successful selection was made or if the participants failed to do so within 25 secs. Warm-up trials were given to participants prior to starting the experiment. The experiment lasted about 45 minutes.

Experimental conditions

Target selection mechanisms

We considered several existing techniques as potential candidates, e.g. lift-off, dwell, double-tap, hardware button, etc. However, some of them are not suitable for BoD input. For example, we did not include a lift-off selection as it is always active, i.e. the moment the finger rests on the back touch sensor, selection has to be invoked. We also excluded dwell because of its speed overhead. In this experiment, we tested three selection mechanisms: *side-button*, *double-tap*, and *frontside-touch*. *Side-button* allowed participants to make a selection by pressing their thumb on a button placed on the side of the device. Double-tap was implemented in a standard way as how it works on a touchpads. To make a selection using *double-tap*, participants would have to tap the touchpad twice inside the target within a short time frame (300ms). *Frontside-touch* was derived from dual-surface input [26], in which the selection was made by tapping anywhere on the front display using the thumb.

Relative cursor movement

In relative mode, participants were asked to move the cursor anywhere inside the target in the same way as with a trackpad and make a selection with one of the three techniques. A control-display ratio of 1:1 was used, and no cursor enhancements and acceleration were included to avoid confounds. Clutching was needed if a single movement did not bring the cursor inside the target.

Absolute cursor movement

Initially, we wanted participants to land a finger on the area exactly underneath the target. Informal trials indicated a high percentage of errors, often requiring a few attempts before landing on the target. This was mainly due to the discrete nature of movements or lack of continuous visual feedback. We experimented with several modifications, and found the approach used by [1] to be easy to use and provided high accuracy. In their technique, as long as the finger was left on the trackpad, users could drag the cursor and move it to the intended target. Once on the target, they could make a selection. We used this method of absolute cursor movement for all our experiments.

Experimental design

The experiment employed a 2×3×3 within-subject factorial design. The independent variables were *Cursor Movement Mode* (*Relative* and *Absolute*),*Selection Mechanism* (*side-button*, *double-tap*, and *frontside-touch*), and *Target Size* (*14*, *22*, *30* pixels or 3.1, 4.8, 6.6 mms). Each trial was repeated 6 times, with the presentation of *Cursor Movement Mode* and *Selection Mechanism* counterbalanced using a Latin Square design and *Target Size* presented randomly.

Dependent measures include selection time and error rate. Since our main focus was to investigate the performance of selection techniques, pointing time, i.e. the time the cursor traveled from the start button to the target, was excluded from the analysis. Thus selection time was measured from when the cursor entered the target to when the target was selected successfully. An error occurred if participants made the selection outside the target area. The trial did not stop until the target was successfully selected.

Hypotheses

Based on the properties of our selection techniques and cursor positioning modes, we had the following hypotheses:

H1: Side-button will have the lowest selection time as it requires the least amount of hand movement for selection;

H2: Double tap with absolute mode will result in higher errors as participants need to tap twice on the target.

Results

Selection time

For both absolute and relative modes, *side-button* and *front-side-touch* had similar performance times, with *double-tap* being the slowest mechanism (Figure 2 left).

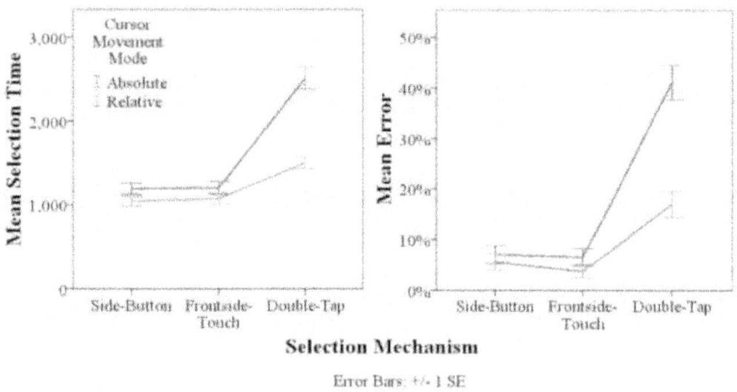

Figure 2. Left: Mean selection time across all techniques. Right: Mean error rates across all techniques.

We further analyzed the data separately for each mode using the Repeated-Measures ANOVA and Bonferroni corrections for post-hoc comparisons.

In *absolute mode*, there were significant effects for both *Selection Mechanism* ($F_{2,22}$=28.72, p<0.001)and *Target Size* ($F_{2,22}$=20.4, p<0.001), and a significant interaction effect between *Selection Mechanism×Target Size* ($F_{4,44}$=12.09, p<0.001). Post-hoc comparisons showed the *side-button* (M=1195ms, s.e.=84) and *frontside-touch*(M=1201ms, s.e.=104) were significantly faster than *double-tap* (M=2618ms, s.e.=252; p<0.001). There was no significant difference between *frontside-touch* and *side-button* (p=1). Similarly, post-hoc showed significant differences among all three target sizes (p<0.02) (Figure 3 left).

In *relative mode*, there were significant effects for both *Selection Mechanism* ($F_{2,22}$=6.87, p<0.01) and *Target Size* ($F_{2,22}$=13.16, p<0.001), but no interaction effect was found between *Selection Mechanism×Target Size* ($F_{4,44}$=1.00, p=0.41). Post-hoc pair-wise tests indicated a significant effect between *side-button* (M=1044ms, s.e.=96) and *double-tap* (M=1512ms, s.e.=100), and *frontside-touch* (M=1077ms, s.e.=109) and *double-tap* (all p<0.02), but not between *side-button* and *frontside-touch* (p=1).In addition, there was a significant effect between target sizes of 14 and 22 (p<0.02) and 14 and 30 (p<0.002), but no significant difference between 22 and 30 (p=0.45).

Error rate

Participants made fewer errors with *side-button* and *front-side-touch*. *Double-tap* led to the highest number of errors for both absolute and relative modes (Figure 2 right).

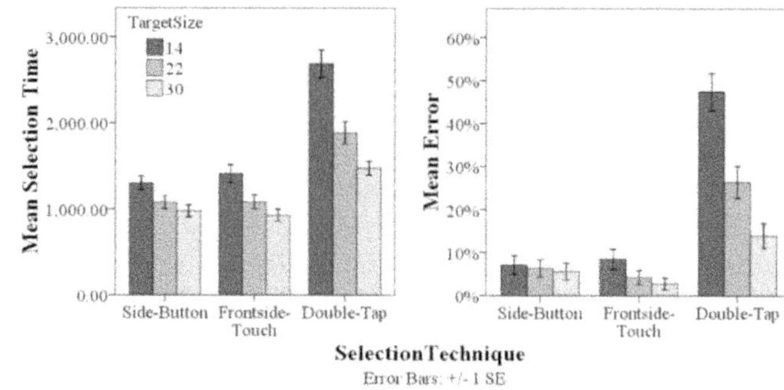

Figure 3. Left: Mean Selection time; Right: Error rate - according to target size and technique.

For *absolute mode*, we found significant effects for *Selection Mechanism* ($F_{2,22}$=67.9) and *Target Size* ($F_{2,22}$=17.72,) as well as a significant interaction effect between *Selection Mechanism× Target Size* ($F_{4,44}$=20.09; all p<0.001). Post-hoc comparisons showed that there were significant effects between double tap (43%, s.e. 3%) and the other two mechanisms (both p<0.001), but not between frontside-touch (7%, s.e. 2%) and side-button (7%, s.e. 2%; p=1). There were significant differences among the three target sizes (p<0.05) (Figure 3, right).

For *relative mode*, we found significant effects for both *Selection Mechanism* ($F_{2,22}$=12.63, p<0.001) and *Target Size* ($F_{2,22}$=3.716, p<0.05) as well as a significant interaction effects for *Selection Mechanism×Target Size* ($F_{4,44}$=4.45, p<0.005). Post-hoc pair-wise tests showed that there were significant differences between side-button (6%, s.e. 2%) and double-tap (17%, s.e. 2%; p<0.01), frontside-touch (3%, s.e. 1%) and double-tap (p<0.01); no significant differences were found between frontside-touch and side-button (p=1). In terms of target size, post-hoc tests indicated significant differences for target sizes of 14 and 22 (p<0.02), but not for target size of 14 and 30 (p=0.37) and of 22 and 30 (p=1).

User preference

Data collected from the post-experiment questionnaire indicated that participants preferred *side-button* (*M*=3.8 on a 5-point Likert scale, as compared to *frontside-touch* (*M*=2.9) and *double-tap* (*M*=2.3)) with both absolute and relative modes. They also expressed that both side-button (*M*=3.8) and frontside-touch (*M*=3.4) were relatively easier to use than double-tap (*M*=2.1).

Discussion

The results show that *double-tap* in its standard implementation is not a suitable selection mechanism for BoD input. It has a higher selection time and is more error prone, especially with absolute pointing mode, thus supporting H2. This is mainly due to the lack of feedback of the finger's contact location, which leaves space for future exploration and improvements for double-tap for BoD input. *Side-button* and *frontside-touch* have led to similar task completion times and error rates (partially rejects our H1). This seems to suggest that assigning cursor movement and target selection to a different finger may be beneficial.

Participants appear to prefer the side-button over front-side touch. One reason may be because of ergonomics: activation with the thumb was relatively comfortable. Also, unlike frontside-touch, there is no occlusion of the display. In addition, with frontside-touch, although activation was performed by touching anywhere on the display, several participants felt that this did not match their model of how it should work because they linked the area they would touch with selecting a component or target located in that area.

The results also show that target size has a significant impact on performance and number of errors for both modes, especially when dealing with small targets (e.g., 14 pixels). However, relative mode seems to be affected by big targets (e.g., 22 pixels and up).

Overall, these observations on selection mechanism suggest that side-button is the preferred technique for BoD input. Frontside-touch has several limitations (e.g., occlusions, low user rating) and double-tap has a higher selection time and error rate. Therefore, we selected *side-button* as the selection technique for the next two experiments.

EXPERIMENT 2: ABSOLUTE VS. RELATIVE CURSOR MOVEMENT

While the previous experiment focused on selection mechanisms, this study investigatesusers' ability to move the cursor with either absolute or relative control. We were particularly interested in exploring which mode is most effective for one-handed BoD input.

Apparatus

We used the same apparatus as in the previous experiment.

Participants

Twelve participants (11 males) between the ages of 21 and 35 were recruited from a local university to participate in this study. All participants were right-handed, and had at least 1 year of experience with mobile devices.

Task and procedure

We used a target acquisition task, where we placed a target in one of 9 cells in a 3×3 grid (Figure 4). Upon clicking the Start button, a square target was placed in the center of a randomly picked cell. The distance between the Start button and all the targets was fixed (80 pixels or 17.6 mm).The Start button was located at the center cell. However when a target was placed in that cell, the Start button was moved to another randomly-chosen cell with the same distance. Participants were asked to perform the task using either absolute or relative cursor control. Informed by the first study, selection was carried out with *side-button*.

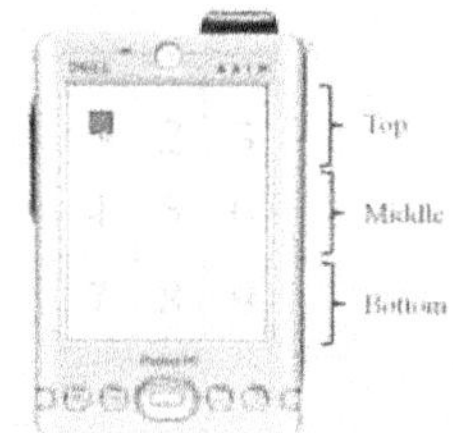

Figure 4.The 3×3 grid where targets were placed randomly at the center of cells.

A trial started after the Start button was clicked, and ended if a successful selection was made or if the participants failed to do so within 25 seconds. Participants were allowed to press the side button multiple times to make the correct selection. Warm-up trials were given to the participants prior to the experiment. The entire experiment lasted about 45 minutes. At the end of the experiment, the participants filled out a questionnaire.

Experimental design

The experiment employed a 2×3×9 within-subject factorial design. The independent variables were *Cursor Movement Mode* (*Relative* and *Absolute*), *Target Size* (*14*, *22*, *30* pixels), and *Location* (*1-9*). Each trial was repeated 3 times, with the presentation of *Cursor Movement Mode* counterbalanced using a Latin Square design, while *Target Size* and *Location* were selected randomly.

Dependent measures included task completion time and number of attempts. Completion time was measured from the time when the Start button was clicked to when the target was successfully selected. Number of attempts was measured by the number of times a participant pressed the side button to complete the task.

Hypothesis

The purpose of the experiment was to evaluate the performance (task time and number of attempts) of each mode, target size and location. We hypothesized the following:

- **H3**: Selection of targets located in the lower regions of the device will take longer than those located in the middle and top portions.

Results

We analyzed the data using the Repeated-Measures ANOVA and Bonferroni corrections for post-hoc comparisons. Trials with timeouts were removed (less than 1%) from the analysis. For simplicity of result analysis, we grouped the locations into three different *Target Positions*: Top (Locations 1-3), Middle (Locations 4-6) and Bottom (Locations 7-9). This division was also used in [8] for studying one-handed input selection.

Task completion time

Figure 5 summarizes the completion time for both cursor movement modes by target size (Left) and target position

(Right). Overall participants were significantly faster working with *Relative* mode (M=3,043ms; s.e.=155) than with *Absolute* mode (M=3,801ms; s.e.=153; $p<0.001$).

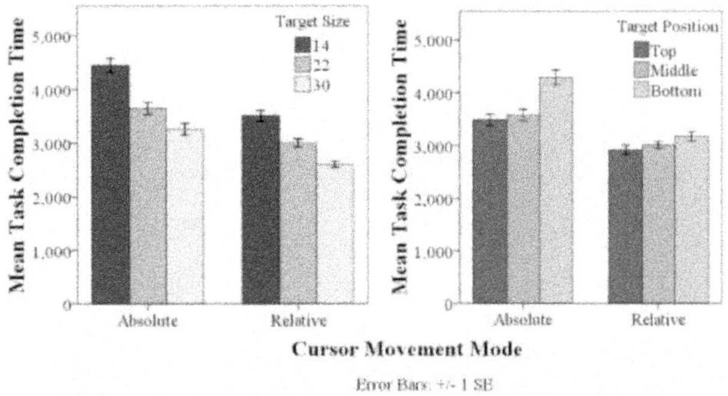

Figure 5. Left: Mean task completion time according to cursor movement mode and target size; Right: Mean task completion time according to target position.

We found significant effects for all three independent variables (*Cursor Movement Mode*: $F_{1,11}$= 32.37;*Target Size*: $F_{2,22}$=45.35; and *Target Position*:$F_{2,22}$=17.72, all $p<0.001$).There was also a significant interaction effect for *Target Size × Target Position* ($F_{4,44}$=2.72; $p<0.05$).

In both cursor modes, it took the participants longer to complete the task as the target size decreased. Similarly, the lower the location of the targets, the longer it took the participants to complete the task. Post-hoc tests revealed significant effects among all three target sizes ($p<0.01$). Also, there was a significant effect of targets located in *Bottom* (M=3,751ms; s.e.=163) with other two positions: *Top* (M=3,212ms; s.e.=147) and *Middle* (M=3,304ms; s.e.=139); $p<0.005$). However, there was no significant effect of target located in *Top* and *Middle* (p=0.90).

Number of attempts

Recall that users were allowed multiple selections before completing a trial, resulting in multiple attempts. As Figure 6 shows, in either mode the number of attempts increases when target sizes decrease (left figure). Interestingly, in relative mode, the number of attempts increases if the targets were located in the *Bottom* position.

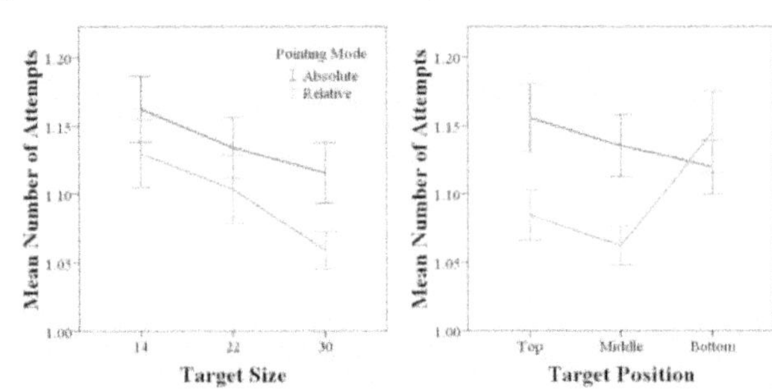

Figure 6. Left: Average number of attempts according to cursor movement mode and target size; Right: Average number of attempts according to target position.

User preference

Participants indicated a stronger preference for *Relative* mode over *Absolute* mode (M=3.92 vs. M=2.92 based on a 5-point Liker scale). They felt that *Relative* mode was relatively easier to use than *Absolute* (M=3.92 vs. M=2.83). In addition, participants noted that *Relative* allowed greater control and precision and also let them reach remote targets with ease. Figure 7 shows how participants rated the regions in terms of 'ease-of-use' (1=easy; 9=difficult). Regions on the bottom were rated as the most difficult to use, followed by the regions on the right side of the screen.

Absolute

4.00	2.75	4.67
3.42	2.33	5.67
6.50	6.83	8.83

Relative

3.67	3.00	4.92
3.00	2.25	5.83
6.75	6.67	8.92

Figure 7. The participants' ratings of ease-of-use according to each region (1=easy; 9=difficult).

Discussion

The analysis confirmed **H3**. Targets located on the bottom row were more difficult to select, particularly in *Absolute* mode. In *Relative* mode, it was not as difficult because participants were able to clutch their index finger on the upper part of the trackpad to move the cursor toward the target. In *Absolute* mode, however, clutching was not available and because of the biomechanical characteristics of the index finger, reaching targets in the bottom row was difficult. One reason for this difference might have been the fixed distance we selected for this experiment, requiring a minimal number of clutches in *Relative* mode (we observed 1.9 clutches on average).

Regardless of the mode, target size had a significant effect on selection time, reinforcing the findings from the first experiment. In addition, Relative mode led to faster selections and fewer attempts based on the target sizes we tested. These sizes were similar to those tested in [1] and it's possible that we would observe cross-over effects between Absolute and Relative modes for larger targets.

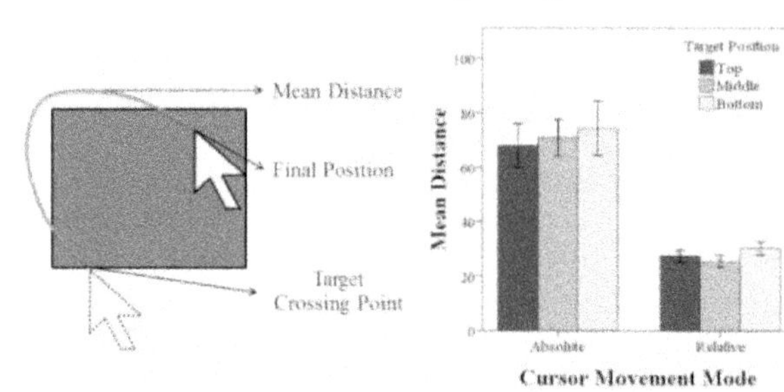

Figure 8. Left: Mean distance calculation; Right: Mean distance in Cursor movement (in pixels) and target position.

We also recorded mean distance traveled by the cursor before completing a selection. This distance was computed by looking at the distance the cursor traveled once it intersected the target to its final position at selection (Figure 8 left). Absolute cursor movement resulted in twice as much movement across all the positions (68 to 74 pixels) compared to relative pointing mode (25 to 30 pixels). This suggests that participants had better control in placing the cursor on top of the target with relative pointing mode. This also suggests that Relative input is relatively easier for precise pointing with BoD input.

EXPERIMENT 3: EXPLORING ACCURACY AND REACHABILITY WITH ABSOLUTE POSITIONING

Overall, our results indicate that relative mode provides better precision than absolute mode for BoD input. Absolute mode suffered from input in the lower regions of the trackpad. This concern with reachability has also been noted in one-handed thumb input [8]. Based on this result, we chose to explore ways to improve precise selection with absolute mode to resolve concerns of reachability. To this end, we designed and evaluated two variations of absolute pointing and compared them against relative pointing.

Two new variations of absolute cursor positioning

Inspired by ThumbSpace [6], we implemented *Physical ThumbSpace*. We mapped a region of the trackpad to the entire screen of the device (Figure 9).

Since all areas of the mapped region of the trackpad would be within reach of the index finger, users would be able to reach targets with ease. As in the previous two experiments, we used a modified version of absolute pointing, which upon landing allowed users to move the cursor to attain greater precision.

Apparatus

The apparatus was similar to that in study 1 and 2.

Participants

Twelve participants (11 males) between the ages of 21 and 35 were recruited from a local university to participate in this study. All participants were right-handed, and had at least 1 year of experience with mobile devices.

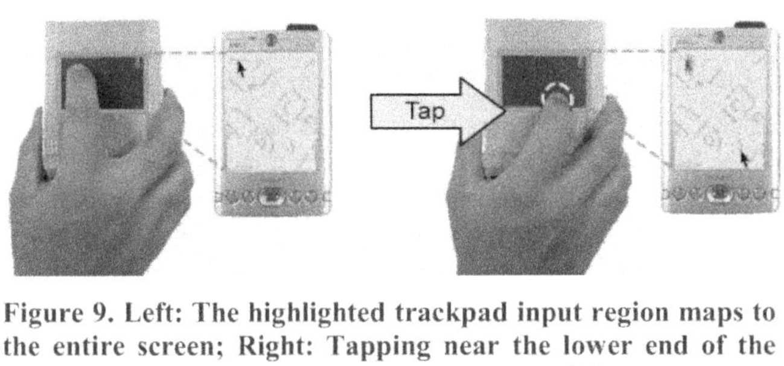

Figure 9. Left: The highlighted trackpad input region maps to the entire screen; Right: Tapping near the lower end of the input region moves the cursor to the bottom of the screen.

Our second enhancement, *SlidingWindow* (Figure 10), was inspired by cursor displacement techniques [14, 17]. *SlidingWindow* divided the display area in two regions of equal sizes, each of which had a 1:1 mapping to the top part of the trackpad. Users could move from one region to the other (by double tapping), and this would allow them to reach targets located in the lower regions with ease.

Tasks and procedure

Participants were asked to perform target selection tasks using Physical Thumbspace, SlidingWindow, Absolute (same as in the previous experiments), and Relative pointing (same as in the previous experiments).

In this experiment, we placed the Start button at the top-middle position on the screen. Targets were placed in two different positions relative to the Start button, *Near* (70 to 90 pxls or15.4 to 19.8 mm) and *Far* (250 to 270 pxls or 55 to 59.4 mm). A trial started after the Start button was selected, and ended if a target was successfully selected or if participants failed to make the selection within 25 seconds.

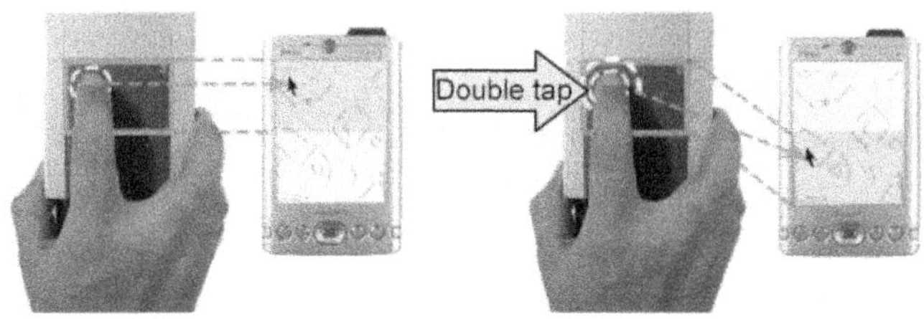

Figure 10. Left: The highlighted input region is mapped to the upper portion of the screen; Right: Double tapping toggles the mapping.

Experimental design

The experiment used a 4×2 within-subject factorial design. The independent variables were *Technique* (*Physical-Thumbspace*, *SlidingWindow*, *Relative* and *Absolute*) and *Target Position* (*Near* and *Far*). Each trial represented a *Techniques* × *Target Position* combination, and was repeated 12 times by each participant. The order of presentation of *Technique* was counterbalanced using a Latin square design. The size of the target was fixed at 30 pixels (6.6 mm), and the selection mechanism was side-button.

Measures

Dependent measures include task completion time and the number of attempts. The task completion time was recorded as the time from when the user selected the Start button to when they successfully selected the targets. The number of attempts was measured by the number of times a participant presses the side button for selection.

Results

Task completion time

We removed outliers, defined by 3 s.d. from the mean. This resulted in 2% of trials being excluded.

We found a significant effect of *Technique* ($F_{3,33}$=5.92, p<0.005) and *Target Position*($F_{1,11}$=88.71, p<0.0001). However, there were no significant interaction effects of *Technique*×*Target Position* ($F_{3,33}$=0.61, p=0.61).

Post-hoc pair-wise comparisons showed no significant differences between *Relative* (M=2977ms, s.e.=167) and *Absolute* pointing (M=3556ms, s.e.=261), but found a trend of Relative outperforming Absolute pointing (p=0.08). However, in Relative pointing, participants were significantly faster than *Physical Thumbspace* (M=3589ms, s.e.=240;

$p<0.05$) and *SlidingWindow* (M=3686ms, s.e.=211; $p<0.001$). There were no significant differences between the Absolute pointing and its two enhancements ($p=1$).

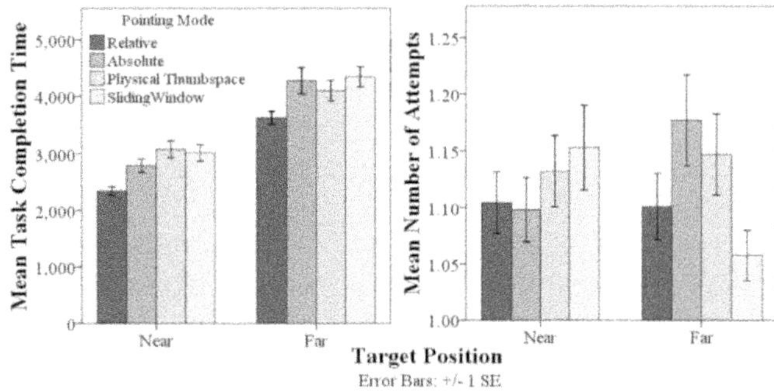

Figure 11. Mean completion time and number of attempts of the 4 techniques based on the target distance.

Post-hoc pair-wise comparisons also revealed significant differences between *Near* (M=2800ms, s.e.=178) and *Far* (M=4105ms, s.e.=227; $p< 0.001$). Participants were fastest with *Relative* (M=2,339ms) than with *Absolute* (M=2786ms), followed by *PhysicalThumbspace* (M=3010ms) and *SlidingWindow* (M=3072ms), when targets were located in *Near* position. For *Far* targets, participants were also faster with *Relative* (M=3,622ms), followed by *PhysicalThumbspace* (M=4,120ms), then *Absolute* (M=4,279ms) and *SlidingWindow* (M=4,347ms).

Number of Attempts

ANOVA tests yielded no significant effects of *Technique* ($F_{3,33}=0.64$, $p=0.6$), *Target Position* ($F_{1,11}=0.002$, $p=0.96$) and *Techniques×Target Position* ($F_{3,33}=2.83$, $p=0.05$) on the number of attempts. For Near targets, Absolute led to fewest attempts, whereas for Far targets it was SlidingWindow.

User preference

In an exit survey, participants ranked the four techniques using a 1-5 Likert scale. They preferred *Relative* the most (M=4.17), followed by *PhysicalThumbSpace* (M=3.75), then *SlidingWindow* (M=3.08), and finally *Absolute* (M=2.33). A similar pattern was observed in terms of ease of control. Participants were also asked to rate the techniques based on how well they supported selecting *Near* and *Far* targets (5=really well; 1=not well at all). Table 1 summarizes the results. *Absolute* was rated the second best, after *Relative*, for *Near* targets, but the worst for *Far* targets. *ThumbSpace* was rated the best for reaching *Far* targets.

	Absolute	Relative	SlidingWindow	Thumbspace
Near	3.92	4.75	3.50	3.58
Far	1.83	3.33	3.33	3.92

Table 1. Participants' rating for selecting targets in different positions and techniques.

DISCUSSION

We first discuss the results of Experiment 3 and then present a general discussion.

Discussion of experiment 3

We found a trend that Relative pointing outperforms Absolute even though with relative pointing, users were required to travel larger distances in this study, requiring additional clutching. Number of clutching can be alleviated by increasing the control-display ratio of the cursor as we had only provided a 1:1 gain. Other techniques are also possible, such as cursor acceleration to increase CD gain as the cursor speed increases.

Figure 12 (right) illustrates the amount of overshooting taking place with the various pointing styles; a lower percentage indicates that participants had more control with a technique. Relative allowed better control. As expected SlidingWindow has less overshooting (thus more control) than Absolute pointing.

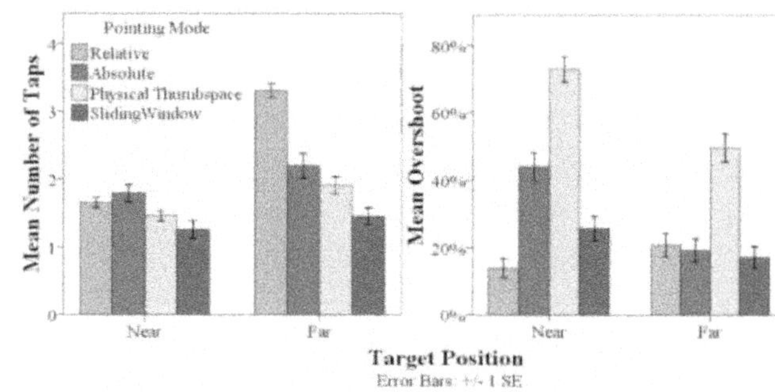

Figure 12. Left: Mean number of taps according to target distance;Right: Average vertical distance ('overshooting') according to target distance.

Physical ThumbSpace used a distorted the mapping between input and screen (a non-1:1 mapping) so that remote objects could be reached with ease. Although this technique did not do as well as we had thought, it allowed us to observe that users were capable of developing motor memory and perform well using a distorted mapping (we only provided minimal training in our study). Physical ThumbSpace allowed participants to rapidly move to a distance location. The flip side of this technique was that it could lead to imprecise movements when reaching a closer region (see Figure 12, right).We could resolve this by introducing non-linear mappings. For example, we could use a 1:1 mapping for nearby regions; and, as we move further away the mapping can gradually scale up. The imprecise movements are also due to the lack of visual feedback—an inherent problem with Absolute pointing. For techniques that distort the 1:1 mapping, it may be necessary to have additional feedback to reduce trial-and-error actions.

SlidingWindow tried to resolve the reachability issue with a different approach. The need to move the window up and down introduced additional cognitive load and taps. We found that participants sometimes accidentally double tapped for some targets located in the Near locations (17%); for targets in Far locations, some participants double tapped more than once (13%). This led to longer completion times. This explicit mode switch made it less efficient for Far targets. However, for Near targets, *SlidingWindow* performed relatively well (slightly better than Physical ThumbSpace) and was less affected by overshooting problems.

General discussion

Summary of findings

The findings from the first experiment show that, among the three tested selection techniques, *Side-button* was most preferred by users and also had the best performance. This is because we designed *Side-button* to take advantage of the thumb position so that selection of targets requires minimal additional movement.

Results from our second experiment indicate that Relative input can be more efficient and accurate for cursor positioning and target selection (see also *Limitations* below). Our results also show that Absolute positioning can be as efficient in tasks that require less accuracy (e.g., positioning inside large targets) and that take place in a reachable region (e.g., top and middle parts of the back). In addition, our results suggest that both Absolute and Relative positioning required almost the same number of attempts (about 1) to select a target. Our third study was mainly exploratory in nature and aimed at finding ways to improve Absolute positioning, especially for targets located in the lower regions. Of the two new techniques, *SlidingWindow* showed better performance, especially in terms of the number of attempts to select Far targets. The other technique, *Physical Thumbspace*, did not do as well due to the additional cognitive effort to use the distorted mapping between the input space and the display. This is apparent in the number of attempts and amount of "overshooting", problems that are exacerbated because of the lack of feedback of where the finger lands in Absolute mode. Overall, we found a trend that Relative input improves performance in comparison to variations of Absolute pointing.

Limitations

Our last two studies show that Relative cursor positioning allows for better overall performance. However, our results are heavily influenced by the target sizes we chose. As target sizes increase, Absolute positioning will have comparable performance to Relative pointing, if the control-display gain is 1:1. As is, our results show that for targets of 30 pixels (6.6mm) or less, Relative positioning is more precise.

Our last two studies also suggest that Relative positioning seem to be a better choice for BoD input. However, in some situations, e.g. with a multi-touch input device, Absolute input can be more natural and intuitive. Similarly, results from the third study suggest that distorting the mapping between the input space and the display does not improve the Absolute input. This is true of the two techniques we tested. However, we have not studied a variety of mapping factors, which could enhance the performance of Relative and/or Absolute positioning.

Lessons for designers

Based on the findings of our experiments, we make the following guidelines when designing for one-handed BoD interaction:

- Regardless of the cursor positioning method, separating selection and cursor control so that one finger is assigned to each function leads to increased performance (Experiment 1);
- With Absolute positioning, targets should be at least 30 pixels in size (6.6 mm) and preferably placed in the top index-reachable part of the display (Experiment 2);
- When using Relative positioning, targets can be as small as 22 pixels (4.8 mm) (Experiment 2);
- For tasks requiring precision, Relative positioning should be provided (all three experiments);
- In Absolute mode, when distorting the 1:1 mapping between the input space and display, consider providing additional visual feedback (Experiment 3).
- Whereas most work on BoD input has considered cursor positioning in absolute mode, our results suggest that designers could consider relative input mode as being effective in a number of different conditions.

Advantages of Relative input over Absolute input

We do not strongly advocate for either type of pointing style as both have their merits. Our studies show a trend toward integrating Relative input for BoD pointing, a finding that has not been previously reported. We have further shown that Relative input allows for higher precision. Therefore relative input is a compelling choice for tasks requiring small targets. Absolute input alleviates the need to clutch and can works well with targets that are at least 6.6 mm in size. Unfortunately, Absolute input is affected by concerns of reachability, as the index finger is limited in its range of movement behind the device.

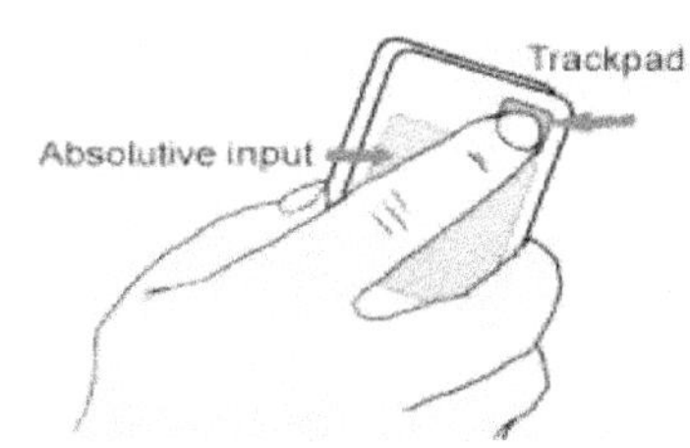

Figure 13. An illustration of the design of relative + absolute input on the back of the device

We did not explore varying the control-display gain for Relative input. This style of interaction can allow for more variety of control and could also benefit from improvements to selection derived for mouse-cursor input on the desktop. Such augmentations can potentially make Relative input a choice technique for BoD interaction. One option might be to place a relative input controller on the back, along with a touch-pad for absolute interaction, such as text-entry. Other combined alternatives could also be designed such that both modes co-exist (Figure 13).

CONCLUSIONS

In this paper, we present the results of three experiments which explore several aspects of one-handed back-of-device interaction. In the first experiment, we examine which selection mechanisms are suitable, with the results suggesting that it may be best to assign selection to one finger and cursor control to another. In the second experiment, we compare the performance of Absolute and Relative cursor positioning modes, and found that Relative is better for tasks requiring high precision, while Absolute may be suitable for tasks for targets located in the top 2/3 of the display. Finally, we used our third study to explore two approaches to solving the reachability issue with Absolute cursor control so that targets located in the lower end of the screen could accessed with ease. We found that distorting the mapping between the input space and the display (e.g., having a smaller input space to control a cursor in a larger display) can be difficult to work with. In addition, enhancements to Absolute control could be based on providing additional visual feedback to users.

REFERENCES

1. Baudisch, P. and Chu, G. (2009). Back-of-device Interaction allows creating very small touch devices. CHI'09. pp. 1923 - 1932.
2. Forlines, C., Wigdor, D., Shen, C., and Balakrishnan, R. (2007). Direct-touch vs. mouse input for tabletop displays. CHI'07. pp. 647-656.
3. Grossman, T. and Balakrishnan, R. (2005). The bubble cursor: enhancing target acquisition by dynamic resizing of the cursor's activation area. CHI'05. pp. 281-290.
4. Irani, P., Gutwin, C., and Yang, X. D. (2006). Improving selection of off-screen targets with hopping. CHI'06. pp. 299-308
5. Kabbash, P. and Buxton, W. (1995). The "Prince" technique: Fitts' law and selection using area cursors. CHI'95. pp. 273-279.
6. Karlson, A. and Bederson, B. (2007). Thumbspace: Generalized one-handed input for touchscreen-based mobile devices. Interact'07. pp. 201-210.
7. Karlson, A. and Bederson, B. (2008). One-handed touchscreen input for legacy applications. CHI'08. pp. 1399-1408.
8. Karlson, A., Bederson, B., and Contreras-Vidal, J. (2006). Understanding Single-Handed Mobile Device Interaction. TechReport HCIL.
9. Karlson, A., Bederson, B., and SanGiovanni, J. (2005). AppLens and launchTile: two designs for one-handed thumb use on small devices. CHI'05. pp. 201-210.
10. Li, K., Baudisch, P., and Hinckley, K. (2008). BlindSight: eyes-free access to mobile phones CHI'08. pp. 1389-1398.
11. MacKenzie, S. (1992). Fitts' Law as a Research and Designtool in Human-computer Interaction. Human-Computer Interaction. v7 (1), pp. 91-139.
12. McCallum, D. C. and Irani, P. (2009). ARC-Pad: absolute+relative cursor positioning for large displays with a mobile touchscreen. UIST'09. pp. 153-156.
13. Parhi, P., Karlson, A. K., and Bederson, B. B. (2006). Target size study for one-handed thumb use on small touch-screen devices. MobileHci'06. pp. 203-210.
14. Potter, R., Weldon, L., and Shneiderman, B. (1988). Improving the accuracy of touch screens: an experimental evaluation of three strategies. CHI'88. pp. 27-32.
15. Schwesig, C., I. Poupyrev, and E. Mori. Gummi: a bendable computer. Proceedings of CHI'2004. 2004: ACM: pp. 263-270
16. Scott, J., Izadi, S., Rezai, L. S., Ruszkowski, D., Bi, X., and Balakrishnan, R. (2010). RearType: Text Entry Using Keys on the Back of a Device. MobileHCI'10. pp. 171-180.
17. Sears, A. and Shneiderman, B. (1991). High precision touchscreens: Design strategies and comparisons with a mouse. IJMMS. v34 (4), pp. 593-613.
18. Sugimoto, M. and Hiroki, K. (2006). HybridTouch: an intuitive manipulation technique for pdas using their front and rear surfaces. Extended Abstracts of MobileHCI'06. pp. 137-140.
19. Vogel, D. and Balakrishnan, R. (2005). Distant Freehand Pointing and Clicking on Very Large, High Resolution Displays. UIST'05. pp. 33-42.
20. Vogel, D. and Baudisch, P. (2007). Shift: a technique for operating pen-based interfaces using touch. CHI'07. pp. 657-666.
21. Wigdor, D., Forlines, C., Baudisch, P., Barnwell, J., and Shen, C. (2007). LucidTouch: A See-through Mobile Device. UIST'07. pp. 269-278.
22. Wigdor, D., Leigh, D., Forlines, C., Shipman, S., Barnwell, J., Balakrishnan, R., and Shen, C. (2006). Under the table interaction. UIST'06. pp. 259-268.
23. Wobbrock, J. O., Myers, B. A., and Aung, H. H. (2008). The performance of hand postures in front- and back-of-device interaction for mobile computing. IJHCS. v66 (12), pp. 857-875.
24. Worden, A., Walker, N., Bharat, K., and Hudson, S. (1997). Making computers easier for older adults to use: area cursors and sticky icons. CHI'97. pp. 266-271.
25. Yang, X. D., Irani, P., Boulanger, P., and Bischof, W. F. (2009). One-handed behind-the-display cursor input on mobile devices. CHI EA '09. pp. 4501-4506.
26. Yang, X. D., Mak, E., Irani, P., and Bischof, W. F. (2009). Dual-Surface Input: Augmenting One-Handed Interaction with Coordinated Front and Behind-the-Screen Input. MobileHCI'09. pp. 1-10
27. Yang, X. D., Mak, E., McCallum, D. C., Irani, P., Cao, X., and Izadi, S. (2010). LensMouse: Augmenting the Mouse with an Interactive Touch Display. CHI '10. pp. 2431-2440.

Soft Trust and mCommerce Shopping Behaviours

Serena Hillman, Carman Neustaedter, John Bowes, and Alissa Antle
School of Interactive Arts and Technology, Simon Fraser University
250-13450 102 Avenue, Surrey, British Columbia, Canada
shillman@sfu.ca, carman_neustaedter@sfu.ca, bowes@sfu.ca, aantle@sfu.ca

ABSTRACT
Recently, there has been widespread growth of shopping and buying on mobile devices, termed mCommerce. With this comes a need to understand how to best design experiences for mobile shopping. To help address this, we conducted a diary and interview study with mCommerce shoppers who have already adopted the technology and shop on their mobile devices regularly. Our study explores typical mCommerce routines and behaviours along with issues of soft trust, given its long-term concern for eCommerce. Our results describe spontaneous purchasing and routine shopping behaviours where people gravitate to their mobile device even if a computer is nearby. We found that participants faced few trust issues because they had limited access to unknown companies. In addition, app marketplaces and recommendations from friends offered a form of brand protection. These findings suggest that companies can decrease trust issues by tying mCommerce designs to friend networks and known marketplaces. The caveat for shoppers, however, is that they can be easily lured into a potentially false sense of trust.

Author Keywords
Mobile; commerce; trust; shopping

ACM Classification Keywords
H.5.2 [User Interfaces]: User-Centered Design

INTRODUCTION

As a culture we are now seeing a large uptake of mobile devices that expand the ways in which people connect with and obtain information. This trend has resulted in an increasing number of opportunities for people to shop for and purchase items online using mobile devices such as smartphones, e-readers, tablets, etc. This activity is called *mobile* Commerce or *mCommerce* for short [20]. The growth of mCommerce is noted by many companies [1,3,12,13]. For example, Paypal reports that it processes up to $10 million dollars in mobile payments a day and predicts $3 billion in mobile payments in 2011 [12]. While there has been a large amount of research on eCommerce [6,8,14] there has been comparatively very little that focuses on understanding mCommerce. This gap is important as mCommerce is not a simple extension of eCommerce. —mCommerce has its own technological infrastructure, new business models and value chain, and new value for consumers. Hence, it requires new thinking for its dissemination and adoption" [11].

Our own interest in the topic was twofold. First, we were interested in understanding the everyday routines of people who perform mCommerce activities to learn what people shop for, when they shop, and how they feel about shopping on mobile devices. Second, we wanted to focus in on the topic of *trust* and explore how mobility and the use of mobile devices affects issues of trust amongst shoppers. In the past, a lack of consumer trust has been cited as a major barrier to the adoption of eCommerce [25] and researchers have even developed trust models to understand and address buyer concerns [8,25]. We wanted to understand how such models might extend to mCommerce, if at all.

To address this, we conducted an exploratory study of mCommerce activities where 17 participants recorded their mobile shopping activities in an online daily journal for three weeks. Following this, we conducted semi-structured interviews with them to further understand their routines and, specifically, issues or moments related to trust in their mCommerce activities. Here we focused on issues of —soft" trust (e.g., willingness to make a transaction, knowledge of companies) [6], as opposed to —hard" trust (e.g., encryption) [6,14], in order to limit the scope of our study. Surprisingly, given the large volume of eCommerce literature on trust issues, our results show that users do *not* often have soft trust issues as it relates to their mCommerce activities. This is because app marketplaces (e.g., the Apple App Store) lend brand protection, users' friends make shopping recommendations, the social web ranks, reviews and policies, and large brands dominate other mediums to provide a level of perceived trust for mobile shoppers. The challenge following from this is that mobile shoppers may be lead into a (potentially) false sense of security.

Our paper unfolds as follows. First, we talk about related work on mobile device usage, eCommerce, and frameworks for understanding trust. Second, we outline our diary and interview study methodology. Third, we detail the main

MobileHCI'12, September 21–24, 2012, San Francisco, CA, USA.

findings from our study. We conclude by discussing the importance of our findings for the design of mCommerce applications and devices to support them.

RELATED WORK

eCommerce and Trust

People commonly shop for any and all things online, though some people are less likely to adopt online shopping behaviours than others [8]. A common assumption is that consumers are vulnerable and likely to expose themselves to loss if they provide personal information during an online purchase transaction [6]. Thus, one of the main focal points of eCommerce research is trust; it is one of the main factors that affect whether or not people engage in eCommerce activities and to what extent [8].

Trust is a complex term. Researchers typically describe trust as being based around: predictability, reliability, fairness, benevolence and integrity [5]. Social exchange theory shows that people make social decisions based on perceived costs and benefits, trying to maximize benefits and minimize costs [8]. For eCommerce, if the perceived risk is low enough, people will purchase products online [8]. Trust is commonly divided into two categories for commerce activities. First, *hard trust* is based around technical solutions and secure interactions with the belief that data will be transmitted and encryption and firewalls can protect customer information [6]. Second, *soft trust*—the focus of our study—is centered around the privacy of personal information and vendors' quality of service [6]. This type of trust normally cannot be resolved through the application of back-end technology such as new encryption methods, data transfer protocols, etc. [9].

There are several factors that make it difficult for online companies to develop trust with their customers as compared to in-person stores. Typically online stores are easier to quickly create; consumers are not able to view a company's investment in buildings and personnel; consumers are unable to physically evaluate products in an online environment; and, online stores often lack human elements and interaction [6].

Zucker developed three types of Trust Production Mechanisms [25] which Luo [8] subsequently extended in eCommerce. First, *characteristic-based trust* relies on similarities between consumers and companies in order to establish trust (e.g., similar sex, ethnicity, or affiliations) [8, 25]. Second, *Process-based trust* refers to trust that is built through a history of past transactions [25]. Luo describes it as a form of gift-giving and sharing of information that is especially important in the business-to-business (B2B) world [8]. For example, companies often create and distribute ‗white papers' to promote their company [8]. Third, *institutional-based trust* is deliberately intended to build trust in the holder's ability, integrity and intentions [5, 25]. This is done through third party guarantors such as universities with certified education, associations with professional conduct standards, and medical and law licenses to guarantee ethical practice [5, 8, 25].

Mobile Device Usage

Turning to mobile device usage, we see that people use mobile devices in a variety of situations and for different purposes. Using a diary and interview study, Nylander et al. [15] explored the use of mobile phones and found that they were most often used in the home (31% of the time), in addition to outdoors (23%), in transit (23%), indoors (16%), and at work (8%). Most surprisingly, more than 50% of their participants used their mobile phones to access the Internet even though they had access to a computer that was close-by [15]. Our study builds on this to understand where and when mCommerce activities occur.

Researchers have also investigated specific instances of mobile device usage that offer important comparisons for our study. Using a voicemail diary, Palen et al. [19] explored the mobile phone practices of new adopters. Results showed that people normally started using mobile phones for reasons of safety, business, or to replace a landline phone; however, usage often migrated to unexpected things such as constant accessibility and microcoordination [19]. O'Hara et al. [16] explored mobile video telephony and found that video calling was often seen as being awkward in public places because other people could easily observe the activity [16]. We explore whether or not the same issue arises for mCommerce activities done in public. O'Hara et al. [19] also explored the consumption of video on mobile devices and found that people would watch videos both in and outside the home despite having computers or televisions nearby [19]. People also watched video on their mobile devices at routine times during their day (e.g., while in transit) and would even turn shared spaces (e.g., a carpool) into a more private place by watching video in a solitary manner [19]. We show how a similar activity occurs for mCommerce. Using a survey and screenshot diary study, Karlson et al. [7] found it was difficult to follow-up (or continue) with uncompleted tasks at a later point, especially if this was done on a different device or computer [7]. Our study builds on this by showing that mCommerce activities do not typically migrate between devices.

The only study that we know of specifically focusing on mCommerce activities was O'Hara and Perry's [18] photo diary and interview study that looked at how users deferred impulsive shopping purchases. Their findings showed that people often needed more information about items before purchase and were unable to get this information. Thus, half of deferred transactions could be further supported by the incorporation of cross-medium information transfer strategies such as QR codes [18]. They also found that deferred transactions resulted because of the social nature of some purchases and a requirement for discussion or asking permission (e.g., asking a partner) before buying.

Thus, they suggest incorporating social networks in mCommerce design.

In summary, the related work provides a backdrop for understanding trust and eCommerce activities. We also see that mobile activities have been studied in a variety of ways, but there is little specific research on mCommerce. We return to these topics in our Discussion to interpret our findings and compare our work to the related literature.

DIARY & INTERVIEW STUDY METHODOLOGY

We conducted a diary and interview study of mobile device shopping and purchasing behaviors and routines, as well as issues of soft trust.

Participants

We recruited 17 adult participants (9 female) who were regular mobile device shoppers (e.g., purchased online at least once every two weeks). We chose this population because their shopping behaviours and trust issues were less likely to be a result of new user adoption or novelty. Our recruitment strategies included advertising in social media applications, to undergraduate classes, and via email forwarding as a form of snowball sampling. All participants but one was from the same metropolitan city within North America. Participants' ages ranged from 19 to 44 and occupations varied heavily (e.g., students, social workers, designers, salespeople, teachers, administrative assistants, marketers). Only four participants were undergraduate students; we purposely chose to move beyond just studying this distinct population. Participants also ranged in terms of their main mobile device: eight people used an iPhone, three used an iTouch, three used a Blackberry, two used an Android device, and one person used an iPad. In all cases but the iPad, the participant carried the device with them nearly all the time.

Method

Our study method was deliberately exploratory, despite there being existing knowledge of mobile device routines, eCommerce activities, and trust frameworks. We wanted to explore mCommerce without preconceived notions of what the activity ―should" entail. Our focus was also specifically on *mobile* shopping and not on providing detailed descriptions of eCommerce practice such that one could properly and deeply compare eCommerce to mCommerce. We recognize, however, that what is or is not mCommerce is a bit of a gray area. Historically, mCommerce was defined as shopping on devices with continuous Internet connectivity [24]. Yet with an increasing number of computational devices available in varying sizes and shapes with different levels of ‗connection,' this definition is dated. For clarity and focus then, our study looks specifically at shopping on devices that are easy to carry and take with a person (e.g., they are mobile), where they may have either continuous or intermittent Internet connectivity. Thus, our study focuses on shopping on smartphones, tablets, e-readers, and mobile music players (e.g., iPods) with shopping capabilities, but not on computers or laptops. Our study method consisted of two distinct stages.

1. Electronic Diary. We recognized that mobile device activities can take place at various times and places and it can be difficult to directly observe these activities as a result [7,15,19]. For this reason, participants first kept an electronic diary of their mCommerce activities over a period of three weeks where we asked them to fill out an online form for each of their mCommerce activities. This included both shopping (without purchasing) and buying. The diary form asked participants to describe their activity, any concerns about trust (where we purposely did not define ‗trust'), and their location when the activity occurred. Participants received a daily reminder via email and SMS, encouraging them to visit the e-diary form and enter their mCommerce activity for the day. Participants were also asked to send in a diary entry even if they did not do any shopping activity that day in order to indicate this was the case. To aid in accessibility, participants were asked to install a shortcut on their computer and mobile devices to the diary webpage.

We recognized that participants might not be able to make a diary entry as soon as they participated in a mCommerce activity due to the mobile and likely spontaneous nature of such activities. It was also apparent during test runs of the study that having memory aids were useful when making diary entries. Because of this, participants were encouraged to take a screenshot of their mCommerce activities as they happened in order to capture an in-the-moment visual that could be later used for recollection; this is similar to [7]. Participants could upload screenshots using the diary form.

2. Semi-Structured Interview. Following the three-week diary period, we conducted a semi-structured interview with each participant. The goal of the interview was to expand on the understanding of the activities recorded in each participant's diary, to check the accuracy of entries, and allow participants to voice any other additional insight. Example questions included: what prompted you to perform the activity; what were you doing before/after the activity, were you familiar with the company you purchased or shopped from, did you have any trust concerns, etc. Participants were paid a total of $40 for both study stages.

Both the diary entries and interviews took place over the summer months of 2011; thus, they did not span any major holidays known for ‗excessive' shopping. As a result, our findings are focused on more ‗normal' everyday shopping.

Data Collection and Analysis

In total, participants completed 161 diary entries that contained mCommerce activities. All participants had at least one activity and the average was 9.5 entries across the three-week span (median 9, range 1 to 20). All interviews were audio recorded in order to review interview data numerous times. We also kept handwritten or typed notes. We inductively analyzed all diary entries along with our interview notes using open, axial, and selective coding to draw out the main themes [21] and compare participants.

Next we outline our results focusing on several main themes found in our data. First, we explore mCommerce shopping and purchasing activities to describe what people commonly shop for and purchase. Second, we describe when and where people shop from and why. Third, we explore in detail the trust concerns (or a lack thereof) that participants experienced and the reasons for this.

SHOPPING AND PURCHASING ACTIVITIES

Participants used their mobile devices for a large variety of mCommerce activities, as shown in Table 1. This was dominated by shopping without purchase (Row 1), followed by the acquisition of software (e.g., apps) (Row 2), the purchase of ‗real world' items (Row 3), and bidding/selling items in auctions (e.g., eBay) (Row 4). Some people performed certain activities more than others, yet we did not notice any trends related to specific demographics.

For ***shopping***, participants were looking for particular item at one or more stores (on their mobile device) or comparing prices of an item. In this case, however, there was no purchase. Items varied and included clothing, housing accessories, shoes, car insurance, cellphone accessories, toys, and pet products. Reasons for not purchasing included: a high price, the item or service was not what they were looking for in terms of location, quality, or they were just browsing for fun and nothing ‗caught-their-eye.' Most shopping was done within apps created and published by specific stores (e.g., eBay, Amazon). To a much lesser extent, some participants would use their mobile device's web browser to shop on a particular company's website.

Software downloads included a large amount of ‗app' downloads for the device itself using the device's marketplace (e.g., Apple App Store) (92%). Others bought a browser download, OS upgrade, and a podcast.

Participants bought a variety of ***real world items*** including movie or sports tickets, food, jewelry, shoes, yoga classes, flowers, ebooks, books, and clothing. 17 participants logged in to a previously created account to make a purchase; this included using Amazon and eBay apps, along with apps made by Social Couponing sites and local food stores. The other 11 participants entered their credit card information from scratch into a web browser page to earn additional credit card points, or because the company did not have an app with recorded payment information.

A breakdown for the cost of items/services/products people shopped for is shown in Table 2. This illustrates that people predominantly shopped for small value items on their mobile devices, but occasionally people did shop for more expensive things. When it came to whether or not people purchased these items, we saw greater than a 76% percent purchase rate for items under $5. Only five of the 25 $30-$100 products were purchased or downloaded. Only two of the $100-$350 were purchased or downloaded.

DAILY ROUTINES AND TIMING

We found that the timing of mobile shopping and purchasing fell into three broad categories. People either shopped spontaneously when the need arose, as a habit or routine, or during fixed time intervals based on schedules.

Spontaneous Mobile Shopping

Close to half of our participants (8 of 17) were highly spontaneous in their shopping habits. In these cases, participants' shopping and purchasing activities were a response to their external environment and other activities. This included triggers from activities both on and off their mobile device. For example, participants were already out shopping in person and needed to compare prices on products, they were told that new software updates were available for their device, or they completed certain activities, such as reading a book, which prompted them to shop for and download a new book to read. Because participants carried their mobile device with them nearly all the time and most had constant Internet connectivity, they were able to act on these stimuli in the moment, regardless of their location or time of day. For example, when asked on the diary form why they engaged in each shopping activity, P2's diary described several points in time were other activities were the trigger, both on and off the mobile device:

Activities	%
Shopping (no purchase)	54%
Software Downloads	39%
"Real World" Items	17%
Auctioning/Selling	3%

Table 1. Activities across diary entries (n=161).

Cost	%
Free	30%
$1-$5	5%
$6-$30	30%
$31-$100	14.5%
$101-$350	14.5%
$350+	6%

Table 2. Cost across diary entries (n=161)

"While in future shop we were about to purchase a laptop when we thought we saw it at London drugs for cheaper"

"Today I received an email that OS Lion was ready to download and purchase"

P9's diary entries also reflected very spontaneous shopping activities. This included browsing for products based on recommendations from friends (both in person and via online messages), going on a vacation to Seattle and looking for a tourist pass, and looking up board games after a night of playing games with friends.

Shopping as a Habit or Routine

Just under half of our participants (6 out of 17) were much more routine in their shopping activities. Routines certainly varied across participants, but the fact that shopping activities occurred in a consistent and repeating pattern was somewhat surprising. That is, participants had a specific time and place where they shopped on their mobile device, they looked for a specific type of item or specific stores' items, and the behaviour repeated regularly. Shopping was either simply for the sake of having something to do, or it was because the participant had a particular interest in a certain type of item.

Routine shopping was most often reported to occur during public transit rides to or from work or school. In these situations, participants often had ‗time to kill' and would shop in these moments of downtime. The mobility of their device and constant Internet connectivity made this possible. For example, 6 of 7 diary entries made by P1 were shopping activities that occurred during the participants' commute from home to work where all occurred within the same two-hour window of time. This is despite the participant feeling that her shopping activities were more spontaneous in nature than routine. While the items purchased may have been spontaneous, the routine nature of the timing of such shopping activities was certainly routine for the participant.

For some participants, the routine act of shopping was tied strongly with checking their email, which was also a routine act done at particular times in the day. For example, P8 recorded eight diary entries, all of which took place while on the train commuting to school in the morning and shortly after the participant checked his email. His diary entries repeated the same scenario over and over:

"I went on the Internet to check my email and saw a daily deal for Groupon"

"While waiting for my train to class, I went on the Internet to check my email and saw the daily deal for Indulge and Groupon"

"Checking email while taking [train] to school this morning. Saw Groupon and Indulge daily deal..."

Other participants were also triggered to shop based on their routine checking of email but these activities occurred at either at home or work where the timing was typically the same each day. This included first thing in the morning, first thing once arriving at work, or in the evening before bed. Email triggers ranged from eBay alerts of daily deals to ‗one off' specialty stores' promotions. For example, P17's 15 diary entries all involved the same routine of checking email:

"every morning I wake up, shower and everything, flip through my emails, either first thing in the morning, before I leave for work or first thing when I get to the office ... that is what I do every day, literally, every day ... if something comes in, in the middle of the night, I want to get jump on it and if there is deals within those I share with my friends."

Two participants used their mobile devices to shop at eBay, Amazon, and specific interest stores for collectable items on a regular basis from their work or homes. Here they were interested in specific items as opposed to simply ‗filling the time.' This illustrates the more targeted nature of some participants' shopping routines. For example, P15 is an avid collector of pens, inks, and flutes and satisfies his interests by frequently browsing eBay for ‗good value' items to add to his collections. The participant talks about shopping during routine times, *"it was my usual browsing time after lunch..."*. P10 was remarkably similar to P15 and frequently shopped on his mobile device on eBay (using its app) and specialty stores. Here the interest was in specialty clothing and occurred at his desk at work (where shopping was done on his mobile device and *not* the computer) or at home with the majority of activity happening late at night. Several diary entries from P10 illustrate this behaviour:

"decided to check on what's new at Macy's for the Sean John Men's line"

"Quickly checked on eBay to see the Sean John auctions as it has been a while since I last checked"

"Went on to Dr. Jay's to check out the Sean John clothes".

In summary, we see several interesting patterns in these results. First, not all participants are restricting themselves to purchasing in the privacy of their own home. This suggests a lack of concern that others might see their shopping activities, in particular, in places of (often) tight quarters such as public transit. Second, we see the strong tie of mCommerce activities to the routine checking of emails from companies as well as friends. We return to this later as one important factor affecting trust. Also, we saw participants engaging in shopping and purchasing over their mobile devices at home or work even when a personal computer was available and nearby. When at home, the most common location for participating in shopping activities was in bed (e.g., late at night). Participants indicated the mobility of the device allowed for greater ease of use in this location.

Shopping During Fixed Time Intervals

We also saw that while not necessarily routine, three participants had fixed time intervals when they would shop. That is, they would shop at a certain time, yet they wouldn't do this on a consistent basis and they weren't looking for specific items. These instances were also not spontaneous in nature.

For example, several participants described being at work and having a few spare minutes where they decided to shop online. Their company policy was such that they were not allowed to ‗surf' certain websites so, instead, they would use their mobile phone for these shopping activities. Thus, the time interval for shopping was during the participants' work hours, but it didn't occur every workday and there was no particular spontaneous trigger for the activity. It was simply out of a desire to shop.

Another participant would similarly shop in the evening when she was at home after work. This too wasn't a recurring routine, but her shopping always occurred at this time and place when it did happen:

"well I suppose I don't really use it to browse (shop) when I am at work, because I just use it for my emails and my work related stuff and then by the time I get home it is about 6:30pm-7:00pm and then by the time I eat it is probably 8pm and that is when I have spare time to mess around and do shopping".

CHARACTERIZING TRUST (AND MISTRUST)

Overall, participants had few trust concerns when shopping and making transactions on their mobile devices. This was surprising given the concerns people often have for eCommerce [8]. We explore the reasons for this next.

Little Risk

First, many participants felt that most of their mCommerce activities presented little actual risk to them. Participants who in particular felt there was little risk were not surprisingly those who: spent very little money, mostly only acquired free products or services, or simply shopped as opposed to purchased. For example, P2 and P4 both told us that they had no trust issues because they did not actually purchased anything. P9 elaborates with a very common reaction from participants who just shopped:

"I was just looking at prices and seeing product descriptions so I don't have trust issues associated with that."

P5 similarly told us he had no trust concerns when downloading a podcast because *"it's free and no cost is involved."* Low cost items were also often regarded as low risk because of the cost of the service or product.

On the other hand, one participant did mention she had trust concerns when buying free or low cost items. P13 only downloaded free applications for her mobile device, but instead of seeing this as little risk she saw it as a potential invasion of privacy. The participant explains her concern:

"I briefly thought about how (the app) now knows about some of the types of music I listen to, after I played a song for the app and they offered me ringtones. Will they now try and market similar types of music/lifestyle products to me?" And during another free download purchase the participant mentions "(it) made me think if this information (is) being accessed and used for marketing."

While seemingly mundane, the above findings show that when people think about ‗trust' in their mCommerce activities, they mostly think about loss of money. Because the cost of many items (e.g., apps for their devices) is low or free, they do not feel trust is a concern. Yet there are certainly many other issues that could arise and pose trust issues for mobile shopping and purchasing such as the reveal or surreptitious use of personal information (e.g., credit card information), the tracking of one's browsing activities, the tracking of one's purchases, poor quality of service, etc. P13's comments begin down this path; however, this line of thinking was rare amongst participants.

When items were expensive, participants never mentioned a heightened level of trust. Instead they would just comment on the cost being too expensive. One participant, who bought car insurance, a $550 purchase, indicated she would have had no problem ordering over her mobile device but the company would not allow her to do so. Instead, she had to migrate from shopping on her phone to purchasing on her computer.

Product and Store Brands

Aside from simply a lack of risk due to little money being exchanged, ‗brand' played the most significant role in trust for mCommerce. By brand we are referring to the actual company that participants engaged with to shop or make purchases (e.g., the eBay app, the Macy's web page). Participants continually stressed their trust in these brands either as a marketplace app or the actual vendor. Only one participant recorded diary entries, which, excluding price comparison activity, had no past experience with the vendor. Some comments around large well-known brands included:

"Amazon is a trustworthy site" – P10

"eBay is a trusted company"- P15

"(Macy's) are the most reputable big department retail store in the U.S., so in terms of security, if that fails I don't know who to trust then" – P10

"[the] Apple App store is an official app for Apple brand and since Apple is a famous brand so I have no problem trusting and purchasing online with them." – P8

In cases where participants had negative feelings towards a brand, the company's app was never downloaded to the person's mobile device. Participants simply knew the companies before they would shop at their stores (via the store's app) on their mobile device.

Several participants commented that they repeatedly purchased from the same places and this history made them feel safer and lead to them trusting the company and their activities with it. When it came to first time shopping with a particular company, participants relied on other indicators to increase the level of trust they felt. These included the overarching approval process of many mCommerce applications and relying on the recommendations of others; we discuss these in the next two sections.

Brand Transfer through the 'App' Approval Process

In addition to trust in store and product brands themselves, participants mentally transferred their trust from larger companies (e.g., Apple) that approved mCommerce applications to the applications themselves. That is, app marketplaces were highly successful in transferring trust from their well-known brands—Android App Market, Amazon's marketplace, Apple's iTunes, and the Apple App

Store—to their affiliates and partners. For example, if participants were using an app on their mobile device for shopping, regardless of which company made the individual app, because the app had been approved through a larger trusted company (e.g., Apple), the trust the participant had with that company transferred to the app itself. A similar phenomenon occurred for purchasing or downloading apps themselves. Because apps were approved by a larger, trusted company, apps themselves were considered to be trustworthy.

For example, many participants said that apps found in the Apple store were trustworthy because, as consumers, they felt they were protected by the Apple brand and the ‗prescreening' that the company does before permitting an app to be present in the store.

"everything is prescreened in the (Apple) app store, so there is no worry about (trust)". – P1

"it just feels like a more cohesive thing when it is under that one umbrella company of Apple... [not using the app store] just feels like you are opening up your phone to all the internet and random companies". – P4

"It was through iTunes so I didn't have any trust issues... I trust the iTunes brand and I believe they really check the quality in products before they release them ..." – P17

We also found that in some cases participants were not even conscious of the mental transfer of trust between brands in this way. For example, during some interviews, participants would first claim that they would not download an app without knowing the company who created it or offered it. However, in subsequent interview questions, they admitted to doing just that.

Recommendations from Friends or Family Members

We also found that participants had few trust concerns because many of their shopping or purchasing activities were based on recommendations by close friends or family. For example, 9 of the 17 participants engaged in mCommerce activities that were initiated by a friend or family member's recommendation, either in person or via an electronic medium (e.g., email). Within these nine, four even engaged in a mCommerce activity directly through a social media platform (e.g., Twitter, Facebook).

The times of items and stores that people received recommendations on varied heavily. For example, P1 downloaded a sports team app for her mobile phone based on a friend's recommendation, P2 downloaded a recipe from a recipe site recommend by her partner, P9 shopped for racquets based on the recommendations of her friend, a tennis ‗pro,' and P13 bought frozen yogurt based on a friend's recommendation. Perhaps the most self-aware of the influence that friends had on his shopping was P17 who said, *"I have a whole shopping network... me and my friends all use Groupon."*

Because of the social influence of others, interactions with particular vendors or products were deemed to be trustworthy, regardless of whether they actually were or not in fact. The sheer act of social recommendation elevated companies, brands, or items to a trustworthy status.

In most cases, social recommendations were just from close friends or family members, yet they did sometimes come from strangers where a person would rely on them if there was a large response from people:

"The seller has 100% positive feedback on eBay and I don't buy from sellers that [have] neutral or negative feedbacks" - P15

Mistrust

In some cases, mistrust did arise but this was rare. Across all 161 diary entries, only 11 entries indicated there was a trust issue. The reasons for why the participants had trust issues often related to the previously discussed reasons for assuming trustworthiness.

Social Recommendations. Four diary entries discussed a lack of trust in the purchasing of a mobile device app because the app had a low rating as recommended by other users. In only one case did the participant continue on to downloading the app. Another participant commented *"I decided not to download even the free version because the comments were all negative."* Together, this further suggests that even if a person doesn't receive advice or recommendations from people they know, if there is a large enough response, they will rely on the advice of strangers.

Brand. In total, four diary entries related to mistrust because of brand. Two diary entries by the same participant reflected instances where he simply did not trust a brand because of a lack of recent history with it. When asked if he had trust issues, he told us in the first case, *"yes, as I have not purchased on this site before,"* and, in the second case, *"yes because I haven't ordered flowers for a long time and I couldn't remember what website I had used before."* In addition to this, we saw two more diary entries where the brand (the company) was not trusted because of the company's location; one was located in Hong Kong and one was in England, which are both a long distance away from the participant.

Hard Trust Issues. Two diary entries related to hard trust concerns. One participant was concerned about a potential virus, while another was worried about the security of the wireless network they were on in a mall.

Other Reasons. In addition to the above, participants cited usability issues (1 entry) and the limited ability to physically evaluate a product (1 entry) as reasons to mistrust mCommerce activities.

Even though the frequency of the above occurrences is small, it further suggests the importance of the aforementioned reasons why people have few trust concerns for their mCommerce activities.

DISCUSSION

The purpose of our study was to explore people's mCommerce routines and activities, identify how people think about trust during these activities, and understand how trust affects their shopping and purchasing behaviours. We now turn to a discussion of our results and reflect back on the related work for mobile device usage along with theories of trust.

Mobile Device Usage

First, our work builds on the related work of mobile device usage. We now know that mCommerce activities occur in a variety of locations, including the home, public transit, and, to a lesser extent, at work. This more specifically builds on Nylander et al.'s location classification for mobile device usage [15] and shows that people turn to their mobile devices for shopping even if computers are located close by. This is because a large amount of mCommerce activities relate to purchases for the mobile device itself, but also because people simply have a preference for shopping in this way. Like the consumption of mobile video and video telephony services [16,17], mCommerce activities also occur in public spaces like transit commutes where the act of shopping represents a private activity in a more public space. We also have found that shopping activities typically stay on the mobile device with little concern about migrating the activity to other computers or devices; this contrasts Karlson et al.'s [7] findings about email-based activities. Palen et al. [19] showed that mobile phones are very much social devices; we extend this to show the impact of social recommendations on mobile shopping activities and trust. Similar to O'Hara and Perry's results [18], we too saw social collaboration as a major theme in user behaviour. However, in our study, social collaboration was just as much a catalyst to spontaneous purchases as a deterrent [18]. Furthermore, we found no participants partook in mCommerce activities that originated from interruptive marketing efforts via mobile, print or television advertising, which is a new finding.

There are certainly many possible design implications from these shopping behaviors. At the most basic level, they suggest that mobile shopping designs could be created to target users based on these routines (or lack of) and optimize their experience. For example, 'fixed time' shoppers could be detected based on their pattern of usage and provided with a more 'browsing'-like experience to fill their time. We encourage others to continue to build on this paradigm of design suggestions and use our study findings as a basis for additional design work.

Trust in mCommerce Activities

Our work has also illustrated the ways that trust is thought about by people participating in mCommerce activities and how trust concerns are largely mitigated.

First, Zucker [25] developed three trust mechanisms—characteristic-based, process-based, and institutional-based trust—that have been used as a lens for eCommerce trust [8]. If we look at these mechanisms in relation to our findings about mCommerce, we see how some of them continue to play a significant role in establishing consumer trust. However, the fulfillment of these mechanisms often took on a new form that was specific to mCommerce when compared to eCommerce or traditional retail shopping.

Characteristic-Based Trust. Characteristic-based trust refers to trust that is developed through similarities between consumers and companies (e.g., similar gender, ethnicities, affiliations) [8,25]. In age of mobile shopping, devoid of much human contact (at least between company employees and consumers), one might think that it would be hard to establish trust in this way. Yet, as our results showed, many participants engaged in mCommerce activities that were initiated by a friend or family member's recommendation. Because of the social recommendation, people placed trust in a site, service, or product, regardless of whether or not it was trustful. Thus, having friends, family, or, to a lesser extent, social networks provide recommendations for shopping makes characteristic-based trust a key component for mCommerce trust.

This is promising for companies; however, if one thinks about targeted advertising, consumers face a challenging future where it will be increasingly difficult to know if social recommendations are valid. For example, social networking sites (e.g., Facebook) are increasingly placing advertising amongst information about one's friends and family. The mere placement of such information in close proximity to one's trusted social network may easily suggest a false sense of security for mCommerce activities.

Process-Based Trust. For process-based trust—trust that is built through a history of past transactions [8,25]—we see that even though participants were experiencing a new medium for shopping (e.g., mobile shopping), they brought notions of trust with them through their prior experiences with eCommerce and retail experiences. For example, they continued to shop with companies that were previously known to them in the non-mobile space, such as eBay, Amazon, etc. For companies that are designing applications to support mCommerce, this suggests that designers should fully integrate their mobile commerce opportunities with existing commerce sites and interactions such that notions of trust will transfer. For example, a company that presents an eCommerce web presence should provide a similar mCommerce presence in look and feel where a person could easily migrate between the two. Some companies already do this to a certain extent (e.g., eBay), yet we now see and understand the importance in doing so as it relates to trust.

Institutional-Based Trust. Institutional-based trust relates to trust that is established by presenting a public presence that is respected and shows integrity [25]. This is commonly done through third-party guarantors, membership in associations with professional codes of conduct, etc. [5,8,25]. The definition of this type of trust mechanism did not historically include distribution models such as app marketplaces, yet these have in essence played the role of third party guarantors when it comes to mCommerce. That is, the (often stringent) approval processes (e.g., Apple's App Store) that mobile apps must go through before they are even placed in the hands of consumers acts as a guarantor of service or products acquired through it. This is regardless of whether or not such approval processes actually do make companies more trustworthy with their apps or shopping services. For consumers, it doesn't matter; they simply assume so.

One could argue that historically this trust role has been associated with search engines in eCommerce. Yet in mCommerce, app marketplaces have now taken over this role. While the actual creator of the app might not get the brand recognition for the experience, in the mobile space this seems to be one of the best ways for companies to get their products in the hands of potential new users. Traditional more obvious eCommerce institutional-based trust mechanisms such as third party seals and security seals were never mentioned or became apparent amongst participants.

Consumer Vulnerability. If we look at Head and Hassanein's [6] factors which make consumers vulnerable in eCommerce transactions—providing their email address, shipping information, credit card numbers, etc.—it is evident that these happen at the time of purchase. For example, a user must input detailed information in order to finalize a purchase on an eCommerce web site. Yet this does not transfer to mCommerce. As our results showed, nearly all purchases occurred through an app marketplace, which means that purchase information went through the larger trusted brand provided by the marketplace and not necessarily at the actual time of purchase. For example, when making a purchase in the Apple App Store, payment information is entered when a user first creates an Apple account. Then, when consumers decide to purchase something through the App Store, they need only enter in an account password in order to make the purchase. This type of ‗automatic' payment eliminates factors of perceived vulnerability. One could compare this to the manner in which PayPal provides assurances for eCommerce.

Retail Shopping. Finally, Head and Hassanien [6] developed a set of factors that describe why it is difficult for eCommerce companies to develop trust as compared to retail stores (e.g., it's easy to create an eCommerce site, etc.). When considering mCommerce, we can see less concern when it comes to establishing a mobile shopping presence as there is typically a rigorous process to create and publish mobile apps. Our participants recognized this and felt increased trust because of it. Similarly, one could argue because of the higher barrier of entrance, having a mobile presence would be a show of longevity similar to that of a physical investment. This would be akin to consumers being able to see a retail store's investment in buildings and personnel. In the case of human interaction, our participants often relied on social recommendations and brand recognition to establish trust; this makes such interactions less of a concern for mCommerce. Yet such social recommendations could easily become problematic if they are based on minimal knowledge.

Limitations. While beneficial, we recognize that our work did not explore all routines and practices that might be experienced by mCommerce users. Our users were all periodic to regular shoppers and, as such, we did not collect any data from people who were new to mobile shopping and purchasing, or even mobile devices for that matter. It is likely the case that such individuals would have different shopping behaviours and increased trust concerns at least initially as they learn how to shop and buy on their mobile device; however, further studies are needed to explore this. Our study is limited to presenting findings on experienced, regular shoppers who have an established understanding of mCommerce and ‗trust' (or mistrust) within it and moves our findings beyond more generic issues of technology adoption.

There are also potential limitations with our study methods. Participants' self-reporting and the diary's focus on mCommerce could have increased their mobile shopping activities; yet, this is likely not the case as we did not see high amounts of shopping activities. We also specifically asked participants about ‗trust' (albeit very generally), which could have made them think about trust more. Given our findings, we feel responses were not biased in any significant way. The results—which showed few trust issues—are strong proof of this. There are also well documented limitations for *in situ* methods [2] hindering the organic experience, however, we chose our method because the benefits of users recording *in the moment* examples and detail were important to the study. We reduced these limitations by providing the participant with convenient ways to capture activity while under mobile and active conditions.

CONCLUSION

Our paper explored the shopping and purchasing behaviours of users on their mobile devices through a diary and interview study. Here we found that mobile commerce activities are a ubiquitous activity that occurs in many places, including home, work, and on transit. For some this spontaneous, and for others it was either part of a routine or during fixed time intervals. In relation to trust, many people had few concerns and this can be attributed to several factors that map at a high level to trust mechanisms established for eCommerce. That is, most of the trust mechanisms/factors that we saw for mCommerce could be translated in some form to those established for eCommerce. However, in each case, mCommerce brought unique nuances in terms of how the trust mechanisms were being applied and thought about by users. Our results suggest that because purchases were made on a mobile device, unlike personal computers, they tended to be made from companies which either already had a strong relationship with users from previous mobile transactions, those done in other mediums, or because of a strong referral by friends (or at the very least a referral in a social space). Compared to eCommerce, mCommerce seems to be more of an extension of the entire ‗brand experience' and less of a starting point in an introduction to a brand. Our findings suggest that the more mCommerce applications tie to existing friend networks or established and known brands, the more likely people will trust them (for good or bad).

Perhaps the most fascinating difference between eCommerce and mCommerce activities and notions of trust was the heavy use of application stores and ‗apps' designed by specific companies. The regular use of these applications is non-existent within the eCommerce literature. Of course, we are now beginning to see companies migrate many strategies from mCommerce to the eCommerce domain where computer-based shopping and purchasing *can* be performed in app marketplaces just like on mobile devices. For example, the Apple App Store can now be used on a Mac computer for buying software (e.g., programs, games). This suggests that commerce activities in the future will further blend between eCommerce and mCommerce. We purposely did not study shopping on computers as our focus, yet future studies should investigate how mCommerce routines translate to this new paradigm of eCommerce shopping, or vice versa.

REFERENCES

1. Amazon.com Announces Second Quarter Sales up 41% to $6.57 Billion, http://phx.corporateir.net/phoenix .zhtml?c=176060&p=irolnewsArticle&ID=1451043&hi ghlight=, Accessed Sept 2011.
2. Brandt, J., Weiss, N., and Klemmer, S.K. txt 4 l8r: lowering the burden for diary studies under mobile conditions. In CHI Extended Abstracts 2007,
3. Bloomberg Business Week, http://www.businessweek .com/news/2011-01-20/ebay-shares-rise-after-2011-forecasts-top-estimates.html, Accessed Sept 2011.
4. comScore, July 2011 U.S. Mobile Subscriber Market Share, http://www.comscore.com/Press_Events/Press_ Releases/2011/8/comScore_Reports_July_2011_U.S._ Mobile_Subscriber_Market_Share, Access Sept 2011.
5. D.H. McKnight, V. Choudhury, and C. Kacmar, Developing and Validating Trust Measures for e-Commerce: An Integrative Typology, Information Systems Research, Vol. 13, (2002), 334-359.
6. Head, M. and Hassanein, "Trust in e-Commerce: Evaluating the Impact of Third-Party Seals", *Quarterly Journal of Electronic Commerce*, 3(3), (2002), 307-325.
7. Karlson, A., Iqbal, S., Meyers, B. Ramos, G., Lee, K., and Tang J., Mobile Taskflow in Context: A Screenshot Study of Smartphones, *Proc. CHI,* ACM Press (2010).
8. Luo, X., Trust Production and Privacy Concerns on the Internet - A Framework Based on Relationship Marketing & Social Exchange Theory, *IMM,* 31,(2002).
9. Lumsden, J., MacKay, L., "How Does Personality Affect Trust in B2C e-Commerce?", National Research Council of Canada, August, (2006).
10. McCabe, L., "What is Mobile Commerce, and Why Should You Care?", Small Business Computing.com, September 13, (2010).
11. Min, Q., Ji, S., and Qu G, Mobile Commerce User Acceptance Study in China: A Revised UTAUT Model, Tsinghua Science Technology, 13(3), (2008).
12. Mobile Commerce Daily, http://www.mobilecomme rcedaily.com/2011/06/27/paypal-predicts-3b-in-mobile-payments-in-2011, Accessed Sept 2011.
13. Mulpuru, S. Mobile Commerce Forecast. Forrester Research, http://forrester.com/rb/Research/mobile_com merce_forecast_2011_to_2016/q/id/58616/t/2 (2011).
14. Ngai, E.W.T., and Gunasekaran, A. A Review for Mobile Commerce Research and Applications, *Decision Support Systems,* 43, Elsevier (2007).
15. Nylander, S., Lundquist, T., and Andreas B. At Home and with Computer Access: Why and Where People Use Cell Phones to Access the Internet, *Proc. CHI*, (2009),
16. O'Hara, K., Black, A., and Lipson, M. Everyday Practices with Mobile Video Telephony, *Proc. CHI,* ACM Press (2006).
17. O'Hara, K., Mitchell, A., and Vorbau, A. Consuming Video on Mobile Devices, *Proc. CHI,* ACM (2007).
18. O'Hara, K., and Perry, M., Shopping Anytime Anywhere, Extended Abstracts Proceedings of the ACM CHI 2001, p. 345-346 (2001).
19. Palen, L., Salzman, M., and Youngs, E. Going Wireless: Behavior & Practice of New Mobile Phone Users, *Proc. CSCW,* ACM Press (2000).
20. Stafford, T., Gillenson. M, Mobile Commerce: What It Is and What It Could Be, *Communications of the ACM*, 46(12), ACM Press (2003).
21. Strauss, A. and Corbin, J. Basics of Qualitative Research, 2nd Edition, Sage Publications (1998).
22. Tammienen, S., Oulasvirta, A., Toiskallio and Kankainen, A., Understanding Mobile Contexts. *Personal & Ubiquitous Computing*, Springer (2004).
23. Tauber, E., "Marketing Notes and Communication: Why Do People Shop?", *Journal of Marketing*, 36, (1972).
24. Tiwari, R. and Buse, S., The Mobile Commerce Prospects, Hamberg University Press, pp. 30-31, (2008).
25. Zucker L. Production of Trust: Institutional Source of Economic Structure: 1804-1920, *Research in Organizational Behavior*, 8, JAI Press (1986), 53-11.

Context-Aware, Technology Enabled Social Contribution for Public Safety using M-Urgency

Shivsubramani Krishnamoorthy
University of Maryland
College Park, MD 20854 USA
shiv@cs.umd.edu

Ashok Agrawala
University of Maryland
College Park, MD 20854 USA
agrawala@cs.umd.edu

ABSTRACT
M-Urgency is a public safety system that (1) redefines how emergency calls are made to a Public Safety Answering Point (PSAP) like the 911 system and (2) is designed to be context-aware of the situation in which it is used. M-Urgency enables mobile users to stream live audio and video from their devices to local PSAP along with the audio stream, the real time location and the relevant context information, enabling appropriate and prompt service. This paper presents a new feature, incorporated in M-Urgency, that enables social contribution whereby users in the vicinity of an emergency event can help operation conducted by the emergency personnel through verbal/visual information useful to them or by providing assistance. Our experiments show a very positive response from the participant to the capabilities of our system. In this paper, we also discuss the social implications such as privacy and security for this system.

Author Keywords
Context, Context-Aware, Social Computing, M-Urgency, Emergency System

ACM Classification Keywords
C.0 Systems Application Architecture; H.5 Information interfaces and presentation

INTRODUCTION
It is usually a difficult task for the emergency personnel to gather information about the situation when an emergency call is made. The dispatcher has to ask a lot of questions to get the precise idea about the situation, which causes delays and also may involve exchange of inaccurate information when the time is critical. M-Urgency is the next generation emergency response system that provides a more efficient and timely service. It is a significant advance in how emergency calls are made to systems such as 911. M-Urgency enables a person to establish an audio and video stream connection with a PSAP (Public Safety Answering Point), to give the dispatcher a precise idea about the situation. More interestingly, it also enables the dispatcher to forward the stream to a responder such as a squad car, nearest to the location of emergency or most appropriate one, to ensure a timely service.

M-Urgency is built over the Rover-II architecture, a context aware framework which caters to the development of mobile applications. As technology is used to augment human capabilities, it is important that the applications should combine the context of the end user, the system and the environment, to provide relevant functions and most appropriate support to the users. Our framework uses a paradigm for handling context information that includes user specific context combined with common context. The framework supports connections to mobile devices using any communications means available and connections to back-end data servers, application servers, and service providers.

We believe that the M-Urgency system could be further effective if more information could be gathered from the point of incident or from the vicinity. Social contribution from other users in the vicinity of the M-Urgency caller can help the emergency personnel understand the situation better and can even provide assistance to the caller, if required. We have extended the M-Urgency application enabling the emergency dispatcher to define a geo-fence around the caller and look for other M-Urgency users in the region. Other than just gathering information from them, the dispatcher could also group the user(s) with the caller establishing a audio/video interaction between them.

We performed experimental studies to analyze our system at two levels, (i) to understand how acceptable and welcomed a system of this kind would be, seeking social contribution from the users in an emergency situation and (ii) a usability study based on usage of our system by a group of users. The results show a very encouraging response to our system and the idea of social contribution in emergency situation as a whole. We have laid a promising foundation in utilizing social contributions in handling emergency situations but certain concerns/issues need to be further more analyzed.

Objective
The objectives of this paper are:

- to present an extension of M-Urgency system that enables social contribution by users when an M-Urgency call made from a location in their proximity,
- to provide the details and results of experimental study, analyzing the effectiveness of the system and assessing how acceptable it is to the participants,

MobileHCI'12, September 21–24, 2012, San Francisco, CA, USA.

- to discuss certain social computing issues/concerns such as privacy, security etc. with regards to our system.

Overview

The rest of the paper is organized in the following way. We first introduce the M-Urgency system in section *M-Urgency System*, explaining the basic functionalities. The central point of the M-Urgency system is Rover-II server that manages the connections, information, a/v streaming etc. which we briefly discuss in section *Rover-II*. We then discuss the features introduced in M-Urgency to enable social contribution, in section *Social Contribution in M-Urgency*. We then explain our experimental design in section *Experiments* and discuss the results in section *Results and Discussion*. We also discuss about some of the concerns regarding social computing with respect to our system in section *Social Concerns*.

RELATED WORK

Handling emergency situations is critical. There have been efforts put forth enhancing the emergency system like 911, reported in the literature. The efforts range from improving the quality of the service to providing better information to the emergency responders. From the spectrum of these efforts, the focus of M-Urgency has been on providing better contextual information to the emergency responders which enables them to be better prepared for the situation and can provide better efficient and effective service.

Connie White et. al. [16] recognize the extreme popularity of social network sites today and that they can be employed in the context of emergency service. Considering the open nature of the social networks, they can be effective in creating awareness, preparedness and sharing of some critical information but contradict the nature of how 911 services work today where maximum confidentiality is maintained. Jiang et al [8] show how gathering, integrating and distributing contextual information enables tacit communication between fire fighters. NG-911 [5], the next generation 911 service operates on Internet protocol enabled emergency service communications network infrastructure. The focus here is to establish better interoperability among the emergency call centres, fire and rescue unit, law enforcement department and other emergency services. A major accomplishment of NG 911 has been in establishing a centralized approach for receiving an emergency from anywhere in the USA and routing the call to the appropriate call center based on the location provided by the mobile vendor. E-911 [4], enhanced 911 has enabled making emergency calls through voice over IP (VoIP), providing the location information and call back number. There has been attempt to make use of video stream to improve situational awareness during emergencies, as presented by Bergstrand et al [3]. The initial study proves the effectiveness of video communication in such situations. Kraut et al [9] have also shown how visual information can be used in effectively accomplishing a collaborative physical task in a given situation. They show how the impact of the amount and the quality of visual information on the performance. There have been other attempts to provide location services during emergency calls as in [14] and [18].

Our efforts align with the overall objectives of 911.gov, where the focus is on forming Community Response Grid (CRG) [15][7][6][17]. The Community Response Grid would enables residents to report and receive information about emergent events such as fires, floods, tornados, hurricanes, community health concerns, and terrorist attacks through web-enabled computers and mobile devices, as well as cell phones providing text messages, photos, or videos that could be shared with community officials and other citizens. The central idea of a CRG is to provide ICT-empowered resident-to-resident (R2R) assistance when it is needed. The Nation of neighbors (http://www.nationofneighbors.com) is another effort in effectively involving social contributions to handle crimes. It's Reporting System enables citizens to report incidents which may go through a member moderation process before it is being broadcast and utilized by law enforcement groups and/or other citizens.

We did not find in the literature efforts taken to handle all the three critical aspects which we try to address through M-Urgency: (1) utilizing technology, enabling social contribution towards public safety, (2) utilizing technology for effective communication (audio, video, real-time location etc.) and more importantly (3) real-time/immediate reporting of the emergency, directly to the PSAP.

M-URGENCY SYSTEM

In this section, we present the basic functionalities of the M-Urgency system [10, 11]. M-Urgency is a public safety system that significantly advances how emergency calls are handled. M-Urgency enables a person to establish and audio and a video stream connection with the Public Safety Answering Point (PSAP), to provide the most precise idea about the situation. The motive behind building the system is to enable effective and efficient emergency handling by providing the right contextual information at the point of decision making and a convenient interface to initiate the required actions/activities.

M-Urgency presents information, in addition to the audio and video, that facilitates time-critical decisions by the dispatcher and responders. The dispatcher and the responder are provided with contextual information such as:

- Relevant information about the user, e.g. disability or special needs, gender etc. so that they can dispatch aid accordingly.
- The user's real time location that is reflected on a map interface even when he or she is mobile.
- Additional information, such as weather and traffic, to gather the context of the incident scene.

There have been attempts to provide location services during emergency calls [13][18]. We attempt to take it a step further by providing real-time location as the incident/user may not be static. As noted above, we consider many variables, in addition to the location, to define context pertaining to the user and the incident. The context can be better defined as more services are added to the service tier of Rover-II.

Since the emergency personnel are provided with all the contextual information, they are in a position to efficiently provide service accordingly. Further, M-Urgency enables the dispatcher to forward the stream and the contextual information to first responders like a police officer, ambulance, fire engine etc., assigned to handle the call, by a gesture as simple as drag and drop. In this way the responder precisely knows the latest situation even before he gets to the incident scene.

Components

There are three main components that build up the M-Urgency system.

Caller Application

It runs on a smart phone, tablets, PDA, laptop, etc., allowing the user to initiate an emergency call by the press of a button. The application communicates with Rover-II and facilitates the location and the streaming service. Thus, an audio/video stream along with the location information is sent to the Public Safety Answering Point (PSAP). Fig 1 shows the screen shots of the caller application before and after an emergency call is initiated.

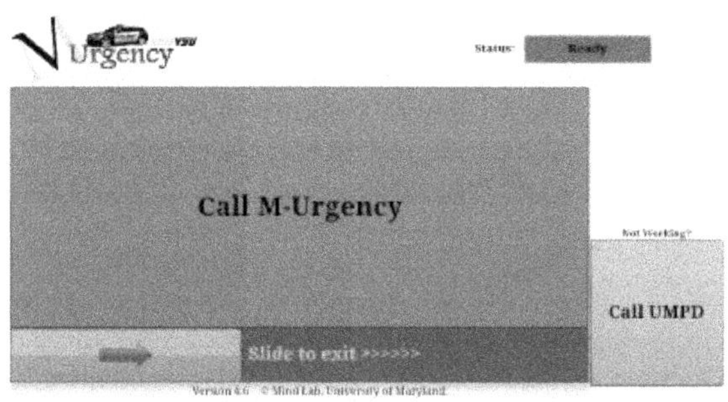

(a) Caller Application

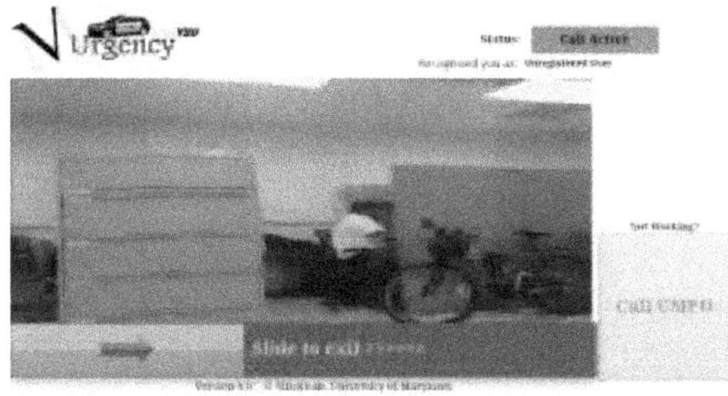

(b) Caller Application after call

Figure 1. Caller Application screenshots before and after initiating a call

Dispatcher Console Application

This is the central part of the M-Urgency system. Used by the PSAP, it runs on a desktop and receives emergency calls with the audio/video feeds. Fig 2 shows the screenshot of the dispatcher console application. It enables the dispatcher to:

- View the incoming calls (on the left) and interact with them using audio selectively as needed,
- View the real time location of the caller on a map interface along with the context information about the caller,

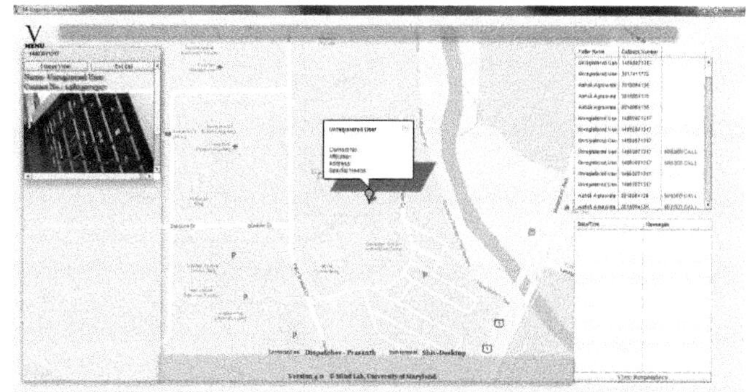

Figure 2. Dispatcher console application screenshot

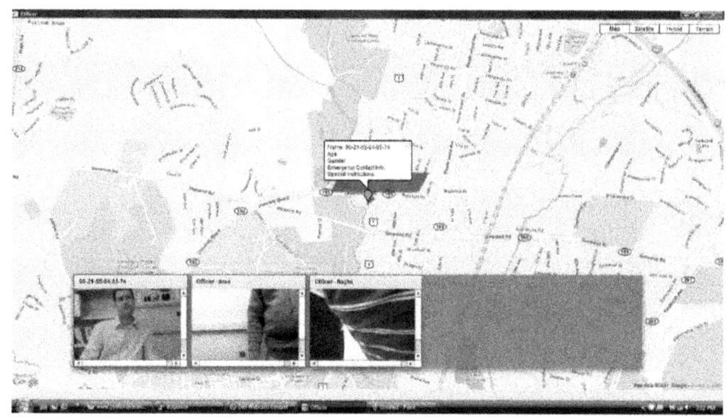

Figure 3. Emergency Responder application screenshot

- View the list of available emergency responders (on the right),
- Group more than one emergency calls together, if so desired,
- Assign responder(s) to the caller/incident through drag and drop operations, etc.

We present the actual sequence of events in the subsequent sections.

Emergency Responder Application

It runs on laptops, typically in the emergency vehicle. Once the dispatcher assigns the responder to an incident/caller, this application receives the forwarded audio/video streams of the assigned caller(s) along with the real time location information of the same. Thus the responder gets the precise information about the emergency situation and can get there prepared accordingly. Fig 3 shows the screen shot of a responder application.

Status

We presented only the basic functionalities of M-Urgency in this section. An M-Urgency pilot, with many more additional functionalities, has been deployed at the University of Maryland Police Department, catering to our campus community of about 44000.

M-Urgency has been developed using Adobe Flex open source framework with Flash Media Server and Flash Media Gateway at the server end for audio/video streaming and

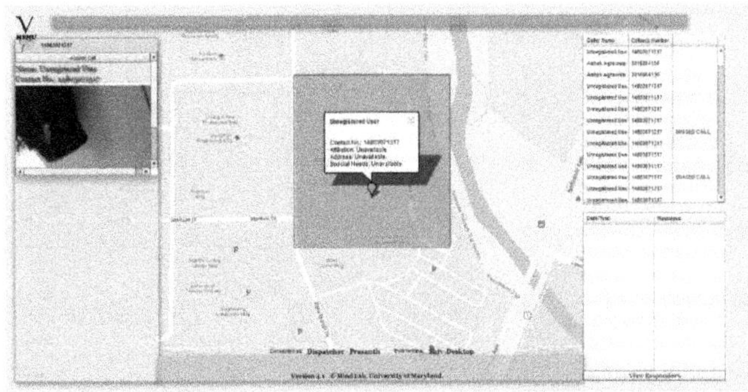

Figure 4. Dispatcher creates a geo-fence around the caller's location and initiates a call to the users within the region

SIP call generation respectively. The dispatcher and responder (officer) modules run on a desktop/laptop computer and the caller applications run on android and iOS platforms.

SOCIAL CONTRIBUTION IN M-URGENCY

We believe that the M-Urgency system could be further effective if more information could be gathered from the point of incident or from the vicinity. Installing additional sensors, security cameras or deploying additional security personnel would be an expensive option. An effective approach would be to utilize the people around, in the vicinity of the emergency incident. Social contribution from other users in the near vicinity of the M-Urgency caller can greatly help the emergency personnel understand the situation better and can even provide assistance to the caller, if required. We have extended the M-Urgency application enabling the emergency dispatcher to define a geo-fence around the caller and look for other M-Urgency users in the region. Other than just gathering information from them, the dispatcher could also group the user(s) with the caller establishing a audio/video interaction between them.

As the emergency dispatcher, at the PSAP, receives an M-Urgency call, the caller's window appears on the left side of the screen and the real time location displayed on the map interface (figure 2). The map is zoomed to the resolution such that all the structures and landmarks of the region can be recognized by the dispatcher. The dispatcher has the provision to mark a rectangular region around the callers' location, defining a geo-fence to look for other users in the region. Figure 4 shows the callers' location from a particular building and the dispatcher geo-fences the whole building looking for other users in the building.

M-Urgency users can opt in to be a good samaritan, ready to help in case of an emergency. When such a user activates the caller application on mobile device, it establishes a connection with Rover-II and runs in the background. The location of the users are provided to the server once every few minutes. Thus, the Rover-II server keeps track of active users and their locations. When the dispatcher defines a region around the caller's location and initiates a call, all the M-Urgency users within the rectangular region are intimated. The user receives an audio alert and the caller application is automatically invoked to the foreground. The interface of the application changes, as shown in figure 5, wherein the user can accept or reject the call. Once the user accepts the call from the dispatcher, an audio/video stream is established with the dispatcher. The windows of such users appear at the bottom of the dispatcher console, as shown in figure 6.

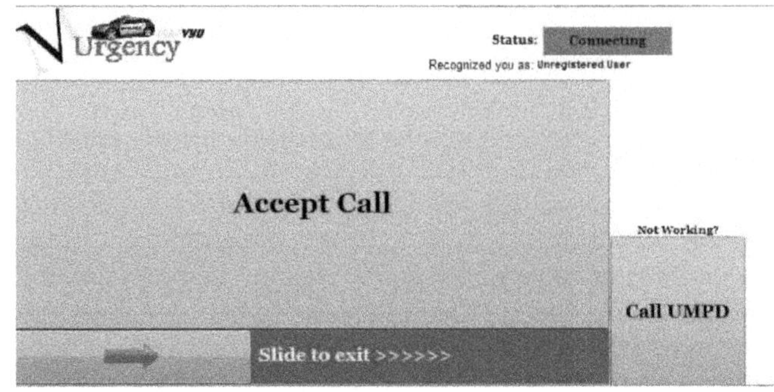

Figure 5. The caller application interface, when a call from the dispatcher is received.

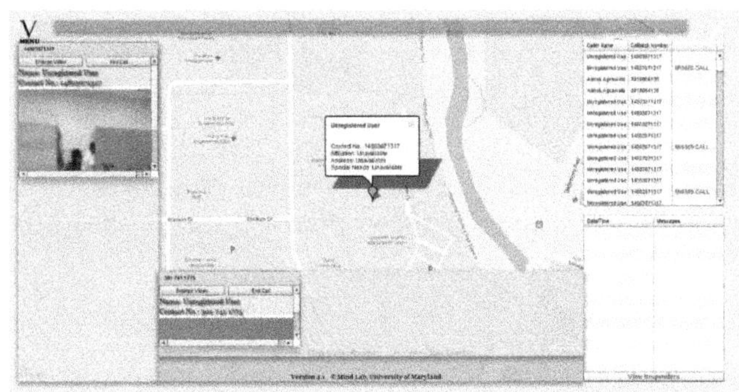

Figure 6. Users who have accepted the call from dispatcher are displayed at the bottom of the dispatcher console.

The dispatcher can interact with each of the users and gather as much information about the situation from them. He could also hook the users up together by grouping them. The users can then interact with each other through a audio/video stream. The caller application interface is shown in figure 7. The caller could tap on each of the other user's window to interact with them and to enlarge their video pane. The dispatcher will be involved in every group and has the ability to add or remove any user to/from the group.

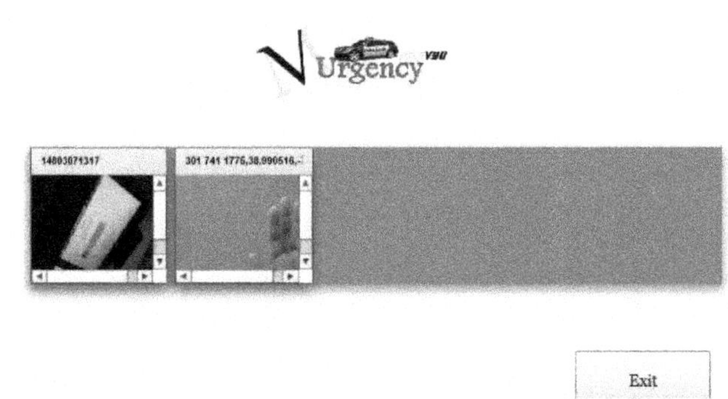

Figure 7. Caller application interface when the users are grouped together by the dispatcher.

Prospective Situations

We believe the new feature in M-Urgency will be effective in many situations, few of which are listed below:

- *Situations demanding immediate additional information*: For instance, there has been an M-Urgency call made from indoors the dispatcher can well gather information from users around the building about the situation around the building. For example, a fallen tree blocking the front entrance or huge snow accumulation on the west side of the building that can hinder the rescue process etc.
- *Situation demanding different angles of view of a location*: In the event of a fire or road accident users around the location can stream videos, providing different angles of views or the users can show the dispatcher the situations on the nearby roads leading to the building.
- *Situation demanding immediate assistance*: In case of a medical emergency, a doctor (and user of M-Urgency) spotted in the same building can be requested for immediate assistance.
- *Situations demanding coordinated response*: In situations of hostage or campus shootout, various users within a building can be grouped together for a coordinated effort.

ROVER-II

Rover [1] is a context-aware server that caters to the development of context-aware mobile applications. Our framework uses a paradigm for handling context information that includes user specific context combined with common context. The next version - Rover-II [12] is in its early development stage. The context model mentioned in the previous section forms the crux of Rover-II

We have designed the architecture of Rover-II keeping three essential features of context-aware systems in mind, namely customization, adaptability and interactivity [1]. The system will support human decision making. Thus, the final decision of taking any action, based on the contextual information provided by Rover-II, rests with the human decision maker.

Rover-II is an integration and fusion platform that seeks to provide a mechanism to aid communication of heterogeneous information sources to all interested and authorized entities. Additionally, entities utilizing Rover add as much information as possible to aid the fusion of information sources, including augmenting information sources with additional contextual information.

Rover-II caters to the development of context-aware applications. It not only provides means to store and retrieve context information, but also facilitates relevant services to the applications so that the context information could be more effectively used. Rover-II implementation is an advance on Rover [1][2], where some aspects of the existing architecture were revisited. Figure 8 provides a high level layout of the Rover-II architecture. This architecture is centered on the information flow between the various sources and the end application or the user. The architecture is organized in three tiers as presented below:

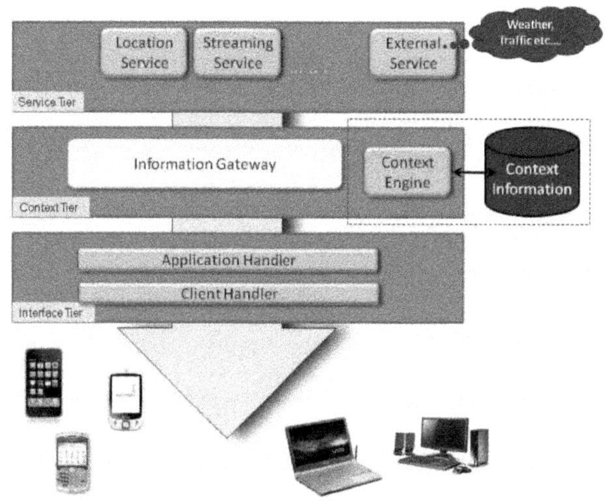

Figure 8. Rover-II ecosystem architecture

- **Service Tier** The service tier is implemented as a collection of service engines and Figure 8 shows some of the service engines that have been implemented in the system to date. The key role of the service engines is to fetch or translate unstructured information, to meaningful and useful form for the user, and provide services as needed. We have implemented three services at this time. The location service plays the role of resolving GPS or Wi-Fi based coordinates to actual physical location; The streaming service enables any application to establish an audio/video stream with the system; The external service enables incorporation of external information to add to the clarity of the context, e.g. the weather information, traffic information etc. We are in the process of adding more services to this tier.
- **Interface Tier** This tier provides a well defined interface for the clients/applications to associate with the system, though API calls.
- **Context Tier** This is the critical part of the system which makes use of the contextual information of each user to mediate the flow of information from the source to the client/user. Based on the context of the user, along with the general context of the environment, the information is filtered, adjoined and/or rearranged, and some services enabled.

EXPERIMENTS

We had to understand two things regarding our system:

1. whether people would be willing to offer some help in case of emergency in their vicinity in form of providing information or by assistance
2. how effective our system is in facilitating this social contribution

We designed two experimental study for this which we explain as the following.

Initial Study

The initial study was just to understand how acceptable is the whole concept of social contribution in the event of an emergency. We selected a group of potential users of our system comprising of six students, two emergency dispatchers and UMPD IT support personnel. We conducted informal interview and discussion sessions with the participants, introducing our idea to them and making note of their reactions. We also recorded their concerns and suggestions expressed during the session.

Detailed Study

Once the social contribution features were implemented and incorporated into the M-Urgency system we conducted a usability study with a group of participants. M-Urgency system is currently being tested by a group of 38, comprising of UMPD staff and members of UMPD auxiliary services including students. We performed our experimental study with the help of the same group. Our study was designed at two levels.

Opt-in Procedure

We initially wanted to learn how many participants would actually volunteer to opt-in to make use of M-Urgency application to provide help/assistance during emergency situations near their vicinity. We communicated with the 38 participant through an email, introducing the new feature in M-Urgency in detail and providing them an option to opt-in for the new feature and download the new version of the mobile application. We also encouraged them to reply to the email expressing any concern or suggestion that they may want to express.

Feedback Session

The second part of our study was based on the usage of the system by the participants. Participants were requested to make at least one M-Urgency call every Monday through Thursday between 9am and 5pm (UMPD has a high rate of actual 911 emergency calls from Thursday evening through the weekend). The participants submitted their feedback on an online system after every call. The dispatchers were also requested to log a feedback after every M-Urgency call received by them. As an M-Urgency call is received by a dispatcher, the dispatcher would look for other M-Urgency users in the vicinity by drawing a geo-fence on the map interface. When another user spotted in the geo-fence answers the call, the dispatcher puts forth simple questions to the user asking about the weather condition, traffic condition in the road nearby, asking the user to focus the camera on a particular object (building, car, display board etc.) in the region. The dispatcher was also suggested to put forth the same question to both the actual M-Urgency caller and the other user in the vicinity and see how consistent the responses were. These questions were to mimic an actual emergency situation and to verify whether this method would be effective in gathering additional useful information from or near the scene of the incident.

The users logged their feedback in two formats - (i) if user initiated the call, the feedback was regarding the call quality and the like and (ii) if the user received a call from the dispatcher, how good/bad was the situation to accept the call, whether the call was burdensome and why was it burdensome and any issue or concern regarding security/privacy that the particular situation raised. The dispatchers on the other hand logged their feedback specifying about the call quality and the like in addition to some specific questions like the following:

- Did you find a user in the vicinity?
- Did the user accept the call?
- Was the user receptive to the questions/tasks put forth? (Did you have difficulties in conveying your questions to the users with respect to audio/video delay, quality, echo etc.)
- Were the responses from the user satisfying and effective?
- Any concerns regarding security or privacy issues that this particular call raised?

RESULTS AND DISCUSSION

Initial Study

In general, the initial study results were very encouraging. From the informal interview/discussion sessions we could understand that the idea of social contribution in an emergency situation nearby was welcomed by the student participants. We received a 100% positive response. The students did not show much concern about privacy and security with some of them stating that it was fine since the whole system was under the direct control of the police. Some of them reserved their comments, regarding the concerns, for after actually they actually used and tested the system.

However, the response from the UMPD side was not totally positive. The dispatchers did seem hesitant in adopting to new technologies and their main concern was regarding the workload in managing the whole scene with additional users. The IT personnel were concerned regarding the 911 standards in handling emergency situation versus involving people from general public in such situations. Their concerns were also in terms of ensuring privacy and security to all the individuals involved with the system in a given situation. But, both the groups strongly agreed with the fact that the method would definitely help gathering more information from the scene and would make the whole process better effective.

Detailed Study

Opt-in procedure

The response through the opt-in procedure was quite positive too. 26 participant responded to our emails. Most of the participants were willing to make use of M-Urgency in providing help/assistance in case of emergencies. As shown in figure 9, 93% of participants were willing to help in case an emergency situation arose near them. About 11% were willing to help or not help depending on the situation they are in that point of time. The rest were willing to help any time. 7% of the participants were not willing to participate in such situations. One participant expressed his willingness to provide help but was not sure because of certain disabilities. Overall, the response was very encouraging.

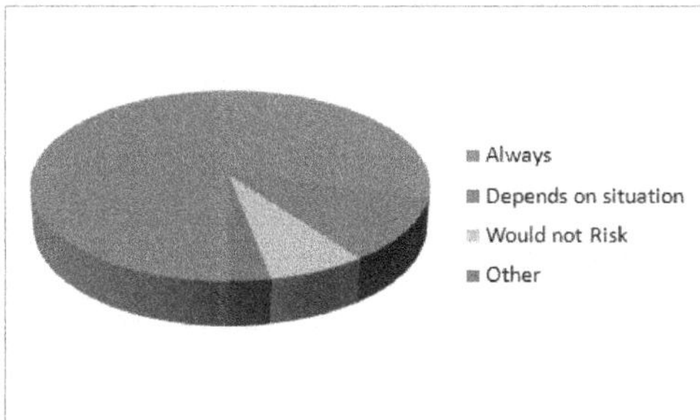

Figure 9. Participant's willingness to provide assistance in the event of an emergency situation near them.

8 participant expressed concerns regarding privacy because of video streams being involved in the process. 5 of the participants also expressed concerns about battery life of their mobile devices as location technology like GPS and WiFi on their devices would be made use of by our system. The caller application picks up the location of the device only once in every few minutes which we believe does not consume too much of battery power.

Feedback Session

The logged feedback data was collected for a period of 16 days. 198 M-Urgency calls were received over this period, as recorded by the dispatchers. Of these calls, 28 calls were such that the concerned dispatcher was able to spot another M-Urgency user within the defined vicinity. 22 calls were answered and 6 were ignored. Four users out of the six who ignored a call from the dispatcher logged their feedback stating they were not in a position to accept the call either being present in a class, meeting etc. when they received the call.

Analyzing the callers' logs, we could not find a significant negative feedback that is worth highlighting. There were a few complaints about the video freezing, choppy audio streams etc, but nothing specific to the social contribution part. We did not ignore these comments since they do affect the efficiency of the system in critical situations and considered them as negative feedback. We had instructed the participants to mark the "concerns" column as *none* if they did not have any concerns. We considered this as a positive response. 76% of the callers mentioned that the situation was good to answer a call from the dispatcher, 3% marked it neutral and the rest ignored the calls. On average, the users who answered the calls were on the call for only few minutes responding to the few queries put forth by the dispatchers. It could be probably because of this that most of the users did not mark the calls being burdensome. Only two users reported the call being burdensome for the reasons like they had to walk out of the building, they were in a noisy environment etc.

We also analyzed the feedback logged by the dispatchers. As noted earlier, from the M-Urgency calls received by the dispatchers, they could spot another user in the vicinity in only 14% of cases and about 11% of the calls being actually answered by the users. We are not very concerned about these figures because only 26 users were actually using M-Urgency altogether. We believe that as M-Urgency is used by more in the university community, the probability of another user existing in the same vicinity will be much higher, as many more users will be using the application.

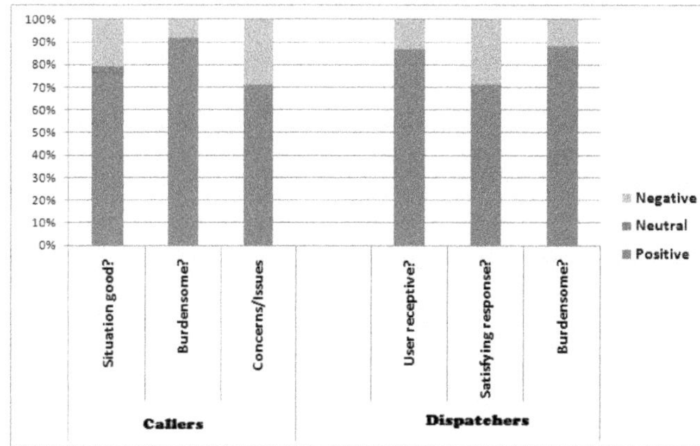

Figure 10. Summarizing the caller's feedback log; being mostly positive.

In 87% of the cases when a call was answered, the dispatchers thought that the users were well receptive to their instructions/queries and the communication happened without much of a hassle. Breaking audio and choppy video streams were reported in the other cases as logged by the users too. All more importantly, in 71% of the cases the dispatchers received satisfying response from the users for their queries; or in other words the interaction was effective and the dispatcher could gather a better idea about the place where the actual caller and the samaritan user were at. However in 12% of the cases the dispatchers felt that involving an additional user turned out to be burdensome. Interestingly, the grouping feature was never used by any of the dispatchers wherein they could group the caller/samaritan users together so that they can interact within themselves through an audio/video stream. The logs did not reveal a reason why this feature was not utilized.

Considering the feedback from the callers (actual callers and samaritan users) and dispatchers and categorizing them as positive, negative and neutral, figure 10 clearly shows that though there were certain issues, the overall response to our system has been very positive.

A dispatcher described one of the calls, specifying how the social contribution was actually effective in the situation. The original caller initiated the call from within one of the buildings in the campus. The dispatcher could interact with the caller for a while when caller lost the connection. The dispatcher could not understand what exactly happened and could spot another user in the same building. Since the dispatcher had managed to roughly understand where in the initial caller was, he requested the samaritan user to go up to the initial caller. Since the samaritan user was connected through WiFi, he could maintain a seamless connection and could reach up to the initial caller. The dispatcher could, then, well understand that the initial caller had totally lost reception from his mobile service provider and therefore got disconnected. The dispatcher noted that this scenario will be very useful in an actual emergency event where the connection with a caller is lost for some such reason.

SOCIAL CONCERNS

An endeavor involving technology enabled social computing understandably raises the concerns regarding *security* and *privacy*. Incorporating social interaction in M-Urgency may make it vulnerable to such issues. In this section we would like to highlight certain features and scenarios that, we believe, would help mitigate these issues:

- We believe, there are four levels of interaction in our system.
  - A user makes an M-Urgency call and interacts with the dispatcher and the officers
  - In addition to that, the dispatcher interacts with other available users near the point of emergency
  - At the third level, the dispatcher groups the caller with the samaritan users nearby and they can interact amongst each other
  - Finally, the dispatcher can reveal the actual precise location of the caller to a samaritan user and request him to go up to the caller to assist him

  We believe that the first two levels of interaction do not significantly raise the issues of privacy and security as the interaction is taking place with a police personnel and is similar to the case of any emergency call. The user makes an M-Urgency call only by choice and the additional video feature only helps the police understand the situation better.
- From the results discussed in this paper, we understand that the dispatchers find our system effective with the first two levels of interaction itself. We believe that the third and fourth level of interaction is not very likely and may be utilized only in very critical cases.
- In case of the third level of interaction, the process is still under the full control of the dispatcher who is the part of formed group and will be involved in the interactions. Breach of privacy or security does not seem likely in this case. It is clear that any misbehavior by any one of the users in the group will be tracked by the dispatcher (all the streams are anyway recorded by the system to serve as proof for further investigation). Moreover, the dispatcher has the provision to add/remove any of the users from the group.
- Assigning a user to assist another can probably be most vulnerable to misuse of the situation. But we would like to highlight some of the features of our system that we believe address this issue:
  - We haven't discussed all the features of Rover-II in detail in this paper. Rover-II is capable of hosting many databases for specific applications. Based on the context of situations, contextual rules could be set to automatically access certain piece of information from the databases. Thus, our system is capable of providing additional information about the user including his/her criminal background, fetched from a police department's database, to the dispatcher before he/she could decide whether or not to request a user for assistance.
  - Moreover, the dispatcher monitors the scene through two connections and respective streams - that of the actual caller and the samaritan user requested to assist. Thus an unfortunate event is unlikely.
  - The dispatcher, as per the protocol, would definitely assign responders to the situation who arrive at the scene at the earliest. With dispatcher monitoring the scene and the short time before the responders arrive, it would definitely be difficult for the user to misbehave with the other.

We do not claim that our system completely addresses the issues of privacy and security, but it does significantly provide the emergency personnel with features wherein such situations can be handled well. Exploring further into these issues remains an open problem.

CONCLUSION

In this paper we presented a new feature incorporated into M-Urgency system that enables social contribution. In an event of emergency, M-Urgency enables users from the near vicinity of the event to contribute to the rescue operation conducted by the emergency personnel by providing verbal or visual information useful to them or by providing assistance. We discussed the results of our experimental study that show a very positive response by the participants to the capabilities of our system. We believe that we have laid a promising foundation in utilizing social contributions in handling emergency situations but certain concerns/issues need to be further analyzed.

REFERENCES

1. Almazan, C. B. *ROVER: Architectural Support for Exposing and Using Context*. PhD thesis, University of Maryland, College Park, 2010.
2. Almazan, C. B., Youssef, M., and Agrawala, A. K. Rover: An integration and fusion platform to enhance situational awareness. In *In proc. IEEE International Conference on Performance, Computing and Communications 2007,*, IEEE (2007), 582–587.
3. Bergstrand, F., and Landgren, J. Using live video for information sharing in emergency response work. *International Journal of Emergency Management 6* (2010), 295–301.
4. Dickinson, R., Marshall, R., and Helme, S. Enhance e911 locaiton information using voice over internet protocol (voip), 2005.
5. Holloway, J., Seeman, E., and oHara, M. State agency and local next generation 911 planning and coordination to implement state ng 911 and ip enabled network policies. *Pittsburgh Journal of Technology Law and Policies 11* (2010).
6. Jaeger, P. T., Fleischmann, K. R., Preece, J., Shneiderman, B., Wu, F. P., and Qu, Y. Community response grids: Facilitating community response to biosecurity and bioterror emergencies through information and communication technologies. *Biosecurity and Bioterrorism 5* (2007), 1–12.

7. Jaeger, P. T., Shneiderman, B., Fleischmann, K. R., Preece, J., Qu, Y., and Wu, F. P. Community response grids: E-government, social networks, and effective emergency response. *Telecommunications Policy 31* (2007), 592–604.

8. Jiang, X., Chen, N. Y., Hong, J. I., Wang, K., Takayama, L., and Landay, J. A. Siren: Context-aware computing for firefighting. *Pervasive Computing 3001/2004* (2004), 87–105.

9. Kraut, R. E., Fussell, S. R., , and Siegel, J. Visual information as a conversational resource in collaborative physical tasks. *Human Computer Interaction 18* (2003), 13–49.

10. Krishnamoorthy, S., and Agrawala, A. A context-aware framework for mobile applications. In *Proceedings of the 9th international conference on Mobile systems, applications, and services*, MobiSys '11, ACM (New York, NY, USA, 2011), 403–404.

11. Krishnamoorthy, S., and Agrawala, A. M-urgency: a next generation, context-aware public safety application. In *Proceedings of the 13th International Conference on Human Computer Interaction with Mobile Devices and Services*, MobileHCI '11, ACM (New York, NY, USA, 2011), 647–652.

12. Krishnamoorthy, S., Bhargava, P., Mah, M., and Agrawala, A. Representing and managing the context of a situation. *The Computer Journal bxs037v1-bxs037.* (2012).

13. Sayed, A., Tarighat, A., and Khajehnouri, N. Network-based wireless location: Challenges faced in developing techniques for accurate wireless location information. *IEEE Signal Processing Magazine 22* (July 2005), 24 40.

14. Sayed, A. H., Tarighat, A., and Khajehnouri, N. Network-based wireless location: Challenges faced in developing techniques for accurate wireless location information. *IEEE Signal Processing Magazine 22* (2004), 24–40.

15. Shneiderman, B., and Preece, J. 911.gov. *Science 315* (2007).

16. White, C., Plotnick, L., Kushma, J., Hiltz, S. R., and Turoff, M. An online social network for emergency management. *International Journal of Emergency Management 6*, 3-4 (2009), 269–382.

17. Wu, P. F., Qu, Y., Preece, J., Fleischmann, K., Golbeck, J., Jaeger, P., and Shneiderman, B. Community response grid (crg) for a university campus: Design requirements and implications. In *Proceedings of the 5th International Conference on Information Systems for Crisis Response and Management* (2008).

18. Zagami, J., Parl, S., Bussgang, J., and Melillo, K. Providing universal location services using a wireless e911 location network. *IEEE Communications Magazine 36* (1998), 66–71.

"There Are No Secrets Here!": Professional Stakeholders' Views on the Use of GPS for Tracking Dementia Patients

Yngve Dahl
SINTEF ICT
NO-7465 Trondheim, Norway
yngve.dahl@sintef.no
+47 905 27 892

Kristine Holbø
SINTEF Technology and Society
NO-7465 Trondheim, Norway
kristine.holbo@sintef.no
+47 402 17 189

ABSTRACT
This paper investigates the attitudes of professional stakeholders involved in dementia care to GPS tracking of dementia patients. Data were gathered via focus groups that met in the context of a field experiment in which patients' spatial activities were tracked using GPS. Four main topics emerged: (1) different perspectives on the purpose of the measure; (2) privacy concerns and underlying premises for employing GPS technology in professional care, including; (3) knowledge about patients; and (4) routines for use.

Our findings highlight the need to consider carefully which aspects of dementia patients' movements a GPS tracking system should provide to care workers, and how positioning information should be presented. We found that the level of detail required is intimately linked to the purpose of use. Positioning data that were regarded as being irrelevant for the immediate situation could be perceived as violations of patient privacy and damaging for the system's efficiency.

Author Keywords
Awareness; autonomy; dementia care; electronic tracking; GPS; privacy.

ACM Classification Keywords
H.5.m [Information interfaces and presentation]: Miscellaneous;
J.3 [Life and Medical Sciences]: Health

INTRODUCTION
Dementia is a syndrome associated with many progressive brain disorders that affect a person's memory, thinking, and behavior. It primarily affects people of 65 years of age and older and its incidence increases with age [21]. Symptoms such as memory loss and disorientation in time and space gradually make it difficult for persons with dementia to perform everyday activities such as outdoor walking on their own without compromising their safety and security. This can lead to increased social isolation and reduced physical activity.

Advances in mobile technology are opening up new means of looking after persons with dementia. In particular, electronic tracking of human activities using the Global Positioning System (GPS) has raised interest among both care providers and in care- and technology-oriented research. The application of GPS technology in dementia care is often envisioned as a tool that could help caregivers maintain an awareness of the safety and security of a person with dementia. By helping caregivers to form a better understanding of when, where and how to intervene, GPS technology could potentially extend the time that a dementia patient can perform unsupervised outdoor activities [6].

Electronic tracking of persons with dementia, however, is a controversial issue. Among the major concerns reported in relevant studies is infringement of privacy and human dignity [1], and reduced human contact between older people and their environment [20]. While family carers have shown strong support for the use for tracking and tagging technologies in the care of persons with dementia, the application of this type of technology is more contentious in the context of professional care [15].

As part of a research project on assistive technologies in Norwegian local authority dementia care, we have explored professional stakeholders' perspectives on the use of GPS for tracking patients with dementia. In this paper, we report on their attitudes to the concept. The goal of this paper is to contribute to a qualitative understanding of professional dementia care as an application of mobile tracking technology, with primary focus on care workers' perceived issues of concern and premises for its successful adoption.

Dementia care by local authorities involves different institutions with different responsibilities. The stakeholders consulted as part of this study included care workers in three different municipal care institutions:

- Nursing homes
- Home care
- Aid call alarm service.

We have also consulted persons involved in the administration of the care services listed above.

To date, few studies have investigated how GPS and other awareness technologies can accommodate the various responsibilities of professionals at relevant institutions.

Data were gathered primarily through focus groups with representatives from the institutions involved. The consultations took place over a five-month period, concurrently with a field experiment. During the field experiment, care workers at the stakeholder institutions tested a GPS tracking system to monitor the movements of dementia patients. The study was exploratory in nature in the sense that we investigated issues that have arisen *from* discussions with professional stakeholders, rather than collecting responses to presupposed issues.

While our focus has been on identifying the attitudes of care professionals to the use of GPS tracking in general, the patients who participated in the field experiment acted as concrete cases for reflection during the focus group discussions. The care personnel interacted with them on a daily basis and their observations of how patients responded to the technology were discussed during the focus group meetings.

BACKGROUND

Dementia; personal, interpersonal and societal effects

The term dementia denotes a set of symptoms that can be caused by a number of irreversible and progressive brain disorders, which may result in memory loss, difficulty in performing familiar tasks, problems with language, disorientation, impaired judgment and capacity for abstract thinking, and changes in mood, behavior, and personality [8, p. 23]. The progress of the disease is highly variable, and depends on the type of dementia involved. Alzheimer's disease is the most common cause of dementia [21].

Deterioration of intellectual faculties gradually makes it difficult for a person to carry out everyday tasks. A high proportion of people with dementia are in need of care, ranging from support with certain activities related to daily living, such as cooking and shopping, to constant supervision. Dementia often places a heavy burden on the close family of the affected person. Close relatives are often affected on multiple levels; personal, emotional, financial and social [21].

Dementia has a significant impact on every health and social care system in the world. The socio-economic burden of Alzheimer's disease and other dementias is considerable, both in terms of direct costs (medical and social care) and indirect costs (unpaid caregiving by families and friends) (ibid.).

The motivation for dementia-assistive technologies

The growing prevalence of dementia

The global prevalence of dementia is expected to grow [8, p. 15]. This has led to rising interest in how information and communications technology can improve the quality of life for persons with dementia and their families, and help to reduce the cost of private and public care. This interest is also evident in the field of Human-Computer Interaction, as reflected in output from important academic conferences including ACM CHI [7, 25] and ACM MobileHCI [9].

Person-centered care

The current focus on the development of technologies aimed at maintaining the autonomy of dementia patients follows in the wake of the reappraisal of dementia that has taken place over the past two or three decades. Studies by Kitwood [12, 13] and others [2, 11] have helped to drive a shift from regarding dementia as a strictly biomedical phenomenon, to focusing on the personhood of the affected individual – the emphasis now being put on his or her perspectives and subjectively defined experiences and needs. Kitwood's paradigm of *person-centered care* has had a major impact on modern dementia care. While the old "culture" of care relied heavily on control techniques, including chemical and physical restraint, warehousing and high levels of medication, the core values of the new paradigm in professional dementia care are independence, wellbeing, and empowerment of individuals and their families [5].

The extent to which the use of GPS for tracking patients with dementia actually contributes to the values of person-centered care has been a matter of debate. Some people regard electronic tracking a means of maintaining the autonomy of patients, since it potentially enables them to perform outdoor activities on their own [6, 24]. Others regard the potential loss of privacy, which remote monitoring of spatial activities opens up for, as a diminution of autonomy and a threat to human dignity [16, 17, 24]. From this perspective, electronic tracking of dementia patients echoes the old-style care regime of control and restraint.

RELATED WORK

The use of awareness technologies such as GPS in dementia care has attracted the attention of several disciplines including computer science, geriatrics, psychiatry and social care. Our brief review of relevant work represents a careful selection of the multidisciplinary literature that addresses stakeholders' attitudes to the management of persons with dementia in formal and informal care, and the use of electronic tracking in these contexts.

One of the most extensive studies of relevance to this work was that of Robinson et al. [23], who performed a systematic review and qualitative investigation of the perspectives of professional caregivers, family caregivers and persons with dementia in the management of wandering[1] in dementia. Based on a comparison of the stakeholders' views, Robinson et al. identified the conflict

[1] Wandering refers to aimless or purposeful walking that can result in the person with dementia getting lost, leaving secure environment, or entering inappropriate places [4].

between prevention of harm on the one side, and the facilitation of an individual's right to autonomy on the other, as a major concern for carers. The study showed that formal carers tended to prioritize prevention from harm, while family carers favored quality of life and independence of the individual over the potential risks.

The tendency in professional dementia care to prioritize prevention of harm has also been reported in other studies. In a study by McShane et al. [18], professionals highlighted the need to balance the autonomy of a person with dementia against the risk of harm.

Landau et al. [15] examined the attitudes of professional and family caregivers to the use of electronic tracking of elderly persons with dementia. The study was based on an analysis of data collected from questionnaires. The study revealed that professionals attached higher value to the respect for the person's autonomy and limited support for electronic tracking.

In a related study, Landau et al. [14] addressed the issue of who should decide on the use of electronic tracking for safety purposes among private caregivers, professional caregivers and persons with dementia. The results showed that the family, and particularly the spouse or most closely involved family members, was perceived as being more important in the decision-making process than non-family members. Persons with dementia were ranked as least important.

Like Landau et al. [15], Müller et al. [19] also addressed stakeholder attitudes to tracking technologies for dealing with wandering by persons with dementia. Their qualitative study focused on the core dilemmas "awareness vs. privacy" and "safety vs. autonomy", and how these were managed in practice. On the basis of a series of interviews, Müller et al. argue that these issues need to be tackled from practice-based views. This implies that location-based systems used in dementia care need to be customizable both for the caregivers who use it for tracking patients and for the individuals being tracked.

Contribution of study

Stakeholders' attitudes to the use of electronic tracking of persons with dementia are also the main focus of this paper. While much earlier work have focused differences between professional caregivers and family caregivers, this study focuses on developing an understanding of the various perspectives held by care personnel who play a variety of roles within the context of professional dementia care.

Our study is also methodologically distinct from the related work described above, particularly with respect to providing care workers with practical experience before collecting data about their viewpoints regarding GPS tracking in dementia care.

PARTICIPATING STAKEHOLDER INSTITUIONS

This section provides a brief description of the responsibility of the care institutions that took part in the study and the roles they play in the care of patients with dementia.

Nursing homes

Nursing homes are primarily for persons who depend on regular supervision or continuous 24/7 assistance. Patients with dementia are often in medium or advanced stages of development of the condition.

Home care

The home care service performs services for persons who prefer to live at home but require full or partial assistance for everyday tasks (personal and practical needs) due to reduced functional capabilities. Services include home nursing, safety-alarm service, and practical assistance in the home (cleaning, laundry, cooking, grocery shopping, banking, post office and other public-sector offices). Home care workers sometimes share the care responsibility with the patient's relatives.

Persons with dementia who receive home care services are typically in the early phases of development.

Aid call service

The aid call service is organized as a special unit of the home care service. It is responsible for responding to aid calls from persons who have home safety alarms and fall detectors. Personnel have direct access to information in patient records from the home care service, in order to be better able to evaluate the severity of each individual alarm call. The aid call service also pays nighttime visits to patients who receive home care.

As an ambulatory service, aid call personnel occasionally take part in searches for missing patients, but this is mainly a police duty.

METHOD

Methodological motivation

The primary objective of the study was to gather stakeholder reflections on the use of GPS tracking in professional dementia care. We performed a field experiment in which a GPS fleet tracker system was employed in the participating care institutions for a period of five months. The regional ethics committee approved the field experiment.

Feedback from relevant stakeholders was collected through a focus group that met throughout the period of the field experiment. The main purpose of this field experiment was thus to act as a catalyst for reflection among the stakeholders. In this sense, there are parallels with the *technomethodology* approach of Button and Dourish [3], where technology becomes a vehicle for social research, the results of which in turn can inform future design.

Field experiment

Description of the GPS tracking system

We employed a commercially available GPS tracking system that supported a range of location-based services, accessible via a web interface or by means of SMS commands sent from predefined mobile phone numbers. The system included a polling service that reported the most recent registered position of a specified tracking module, and a service that notified clients if the tracking module was taken beyond a predefined perimeter (geo-fencing). In addition, the user of a tracking module (the dementia patient) could notify predefined clients about his position via a button on the module. Reported positions for a given period could be visualized on a map in the tracking systems' web interface (Figure 1).

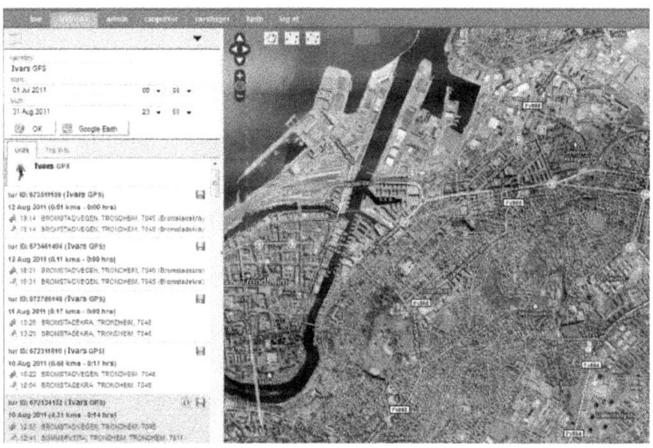

Figure 1. Screenshot of the GPS tracking system's web interface. Spatial activities can be selected from the menu to the left and visualized on the map to the right.

Care workers were given brief instructions in how to use the system.

Recruitment of patients

Workers in the respective institutions initially suggested candidate patients for participation in the experiment. The candidates were persons who were regarded as traffic-safe and still capable of going for walks without supervision. Decisions about participation were made after close dialog with the patient, his or her closest relatives, and professional caregivers. Written consent to participate was obtained from both patients and their close relatives. Routines for practical issues, such as charging tracking units, how to ensure that patients carried the tracking units with them when outdoors, etc., were established for each individual patient.

The field experiment involved five patients. Since the main purpose of the experiment was to help catalyze reflections on the concept of electronic tracking in formal dementia care, a low number of patients was acceptable. Keeping the number of electronically tagged patients low was also a way to accommodate the limited capacity of the participating institutions to handle the practical issues described above.

Ethical and methodological considerations

Every user-centered study where persons with cognitive impairment are stakeholders faces the ethical dilemma of how actively this group should be involved. In accordance with the person-centered care paradigm, there is a need to take into account their perspectives and subjectively defined experiences and needs. At the same time, persons with dementia may be particularly liable to stress. A central ethical concern in the context of research is the extent to which the knowledge acquired in the course of a study is valuable enough to justify or even request the participation of a vulnerable group. It is therefore important that attempts to include persons with dementia are made "by thought" rather than "by rule".

Given the focus of this study and the participating patients' general level of disease severity and dysfunction, we decided to give the patients a more peripheral role. Firstly, our primary focus was on eliciting professional carers' views on the use of GPS in dementia care, and on developing an understanding of related benefits and challenges as perceived against their professional background, their intimate knowledge about dementia and dementia patients, and an institutional context of care. Secondly, we view the current study as a first step in an iterative process towards a more comprehensive understanding of how various dementia stakeholders are affected by awareness technologies, such as GPS. Thirdly, the participating patients showed significant problems with memory, judgment, and abstract thinking, making it challenging to elicit supplementary feedback of value.

In order to ensure that the patients' needs and experiences still were taken into account throughout the investigation, we took the following measures:

- The patients where initially asked about their personal attitudes to allowing care personnel to verify their physical whereabouts before they were recruited as participants. Throughout the experimental period we repeatedly verified with the patients that they were comfortable about being electronically tagged and tracked.
- The care personnel were encouraged to observe and to take note of particular incidents relevant to understanding patients' attitudes towards the technology. These incidents were discussed during the focus groups.

Procedure

During the field experiment, care workers used the tracking system on a daily basis to assess the relative safety of the participating patients. The care workers were encouraged to write down specific events that affected their own or perceivably the patients' experience of and attitudes toward the system. The incidents noted by the care workers formed topics for discussion during focus group meetings.

Focus groups

A total of eleven persons involved in professional dementia care participated in the focus groups that were organized during the study. The participants included three nursing home workers, three home care workers, three aid call service workers, and two workers employed in the municipal administration of care services. The groups included both managers and staff members of the respective institutions.

In the course of the experimental period we arranged two focus groups per stakeholder institution, for a total of six. We also organized a multi-stakeholder focus group towards the end of the experimental period, at which participants from the earlier focus groups, in addition to representatives from the local government care institution administration, were present.

The primary motivation for organizing focus groups that involved only care workers from a specific institution was to collect data on their attitudes to GPS technology while experience from its use was still fresh in their minds. The multi-stakeholder focus group gave us the opportunity to follow up relevant issues, and to encourage debate between the different stakeholders.

During the focus group meetings we used the care workers' noted experiences from use and the patient tracking logs, as these appeared in the tracking systems' web interface (Figure 1), to trigger reflections and encourage discussion.

Figure 2. Focus group at the aid call service central.

Analysis

The focus groups were recorded on video (Figure 2) and transcriptions were made and analyzed in search of recurring issues. Descriptive codes were attached to portions of the text in order to organize the transcriptions into meaningful units. The coding was done in three iterations:

1. The first coding was data-driven and based on themes that emerged in the transcriptions. Each theme was given a main key word, such as "PRIVACY" or "PURPOSE OF USE", and combined with a few words from the quote to capture its meaning.
2. In the second iteration, we verified the consistency of the descriptive codes in order to ensure that they were used in the same way in the different texts. Where different codes had been used to describe the same theme, the most descriptive term was chosen
3. In the third iteration, the quotes were organized so as to reflect the objectives of the investigation.

This process enabled us to identify four wider themes.

EMERGING THEMES

Our analysis of the transcribed focus group discussions revealed the following four recurrent themes: (1) purposes of use, (2) patient privacy, (3) knowledge about patients, and (4) routines for use. The presentation of the results is structured around these four themes. The first two themes primarily concern attitudes to GPS technology in formal dementia care, while the last two relate to what the focus group participants regarded as underlying premises for realizing the potential of GPS technology in this area.

Purposes of use

An issue that arose early, and which dominated much of the discussions, was how GPS technology should be uses by the care services. The focus group participants offered different views on this matter. Some argued that location-based services should be used exclusively as an emergency aid under circumstances where it is reasonable to assume that a patient's safety or security might be at risk. Others argued that services could also be used for safety control purposes. Finally, others argued that location-based services could be utilized to improve the efficiency of patient care.

Emergency aid

Participants who expressed a restrictive view on the application of electronic tracking in dementia care regarded GPS technology an emergency aid that ought to be reserved for safety-critical situations. From their perspective, the main reason for using this technology was to prevent patients from coming to harm. The potential for faster recovery of missing patients was seen as its key benefit.

Participants holding this view pointed to cases when patients had gone missing for a long period of time, especially during the winter, as examples of situations that could justify the use of GPS and location-based services. As such, the technology was seen as particularly relevant for patients who have a habit of wandering.

These participants considered the question of when to make use of location-based services to be part of a continuous risk assessment.

Reassurance

Although all participants agreed that preventing harm was the strongest motivation for employing GPS and location-based services in dementia care, some also suggested how tracking data could used outside of strictly safety-critical situations. One possibility discussed by the focus groups was that care workers might use it for control purposes and to reassure caregivers about the patients' safety. The need for such control mechanisms was typically related to situations in which the care workers might not know the whereabouts of a patient, but had no specific indications that his or her safety may be at risk at risk. The geofencing service offered by the GPS tracking system was one mechanism that was discussed, and found potentially useful for such purposes.

Reflections made by home care workers during one of the individual focus groups exemplify where the need for a control mechanism arises from. In the case of one dementia patient who lived alone, the home care workers often found that the patient was not at home during scheduled visits. According to them, the patient was highly physically and socially active, and enjoyed outdoor walks and visiting friends. The home care workers considered that his high level of mobility was beneficial to the patient's physical and mental health. At the same time, her mobility was a source of concern for the care workers. This concern was particularly caused by occasions on which she was still out after the care workers had paid their last home visit of the day. Although there had been no cases when the patient had been unable to find her own way home, they were often concerned about her safety. Due to the progressive nature of the patient's disease, the care workers were very aware of the possibility that sooner or later, she would have a problem in finding her way home. The care workers explained that, as with many other patients, the patient had difficulties using a telephone. This meant that they had no way of contacting her in order to verify that she was safe. It was pointed out that being able to check the most recent movements of the patient in such situations would help ease the care workers' minds.

The care workers also pointed out that the possibility of unobtrusively reassuring themselves about the wellbeing of patients could help reduce the need to contact their relatives and friends and potentially cause unnecessary stress for them. As such, the GPS tracking system was seen as a substitute for many of the telephone calls they have to make to relatives at present.

Care efficiency

The third purpose that was discussed involved ways in which GPS technology could increase the efficiency of work and help to tailor care services so that they matched the patients' everyday routines.

The high mobility of the patient described above often made it difficult for home care workers to give her her medication. Because she was often out when the health care workers called, many of their visits were futile and regarded as "*wasted time*"; time that could have been used to perform services for other patients.

The care workers who made the home visits found that it could be beneficial to use the GPS tracking system to check ahead of visits whether the patient was at home or not. As such, it was a helpful tool for saving time. They pointed out that the time saved by avoiding unsuccessful visits to patients could benefit the patient group as a whole, as care givers could then spend more time together with each individual patient during visits. The care workers point out that their workload severely limits the time they can afford to spend together with individual patients.

Patients' privacy

Feedback from the focus groups suggested that they were highly mindful about preserving the privacy of patients. Potential violation of patients' privacy was a key concern . The possibility of using the GPS tracking system to examine, in high detail, the movements of patients generally evoked strong negative reactions. One of the participants remarked, "*There are no secrets here!*", in response to what she perceived as an over-exposure of details about patients' movements.

Participants who argued for restrictive use of positioning information were uncomfortable with using location-based services as a basis for performing services that were part of their daily work routines. This was particularly with regard to the use of these services to improve care efficiency, such as home visits to patients. During the plenary focus group, one participant said: *"When I think about GPS, it is about preventing users from getting into risky situations. That is my perspective. If we are to use it in order to save time...that is something different"*.

The fundamental dilemma of using electronic tracking information beyond safety-critical situations, as some participants pointed out, was what they perceived as a lack of direct benefit for the individual patient being electronically tracked. Many agreed that using GPS technology for purposes of control might well be in the best interest of the patient. However, when used to improve efficiency or for the convenience for care personnel, the lack of any evident direct benefit for patients produced many negative reactions. In response to suggestions that location-based services could potentially improve efficiency, one focus group participant remarked *"...then the focus is on our needs, rather than [the patient's]."* Others agreed to a restrictive use of GPS in dementia care: "*[Home care services] are performed on the basis of a formal resolution of need, and if you start using the GPS to get your job done, I feel that that is misuse.*

From this viewpoint, direct benefit for patients was regarded as a fundamental criterion that must be met to compensate both for the privacy that electronically tracked patients renounced and the extra burden of carrying a tracking device.

Concerns regarding patient privacy were another central issue for those who supported the use of tracking information beyond safety-critical incidents. One of the home care workers made the following comment when reflecting over GPS tracking used for control purposes: *"Perhaps it is not necessary to track [the patient's] movements except in situations where [the patient] has not returned home"*.

As described above, home care workers found that tracking information could be helpful, for example, to adapt timing of home visits to better match the daily routines of individual patients. Further reflections made by the home care workers revealed that only parts of the information provided by the tracking system were needed for such purposes. While the tracking system that was used as part of the field experiment could provide a detailed map of where the patient had been over a given period of time, the care workers only found certain aspect of that information, such as whether or not the patient was at home, or time intervals the patient usually was at home, to be relevant to their responsibilities.

In the context making regular home visits, additional information such as patterns of recent movements, were regarded not only as an unintentional invasion of the patients privacy. From the care workers' point of view, it was also irrelevant information, which, as far as they were concerned, made the system less efficient.

Knowledge about patients

The focus group participants emphasized that the effective use of GPS technology in dementia care, for example in cases where the technology is used for control purposes, is highly dependent on *whom* the receiver of the information is.

On several occasions, caregivers stressed the importance of being familiar with a patient and his or her behavioral patterns in order to "make sense" of recorded tracking information, and be able to make decisions, for example, on when to intervene. Knowledge of their patients is an essential component in the continuous risk assessment that professional care workers perform. When we reviewed the tracking logs of patients during the focus groups, we found that the care workers relied heavily on their previous knowledge of the patterns of movement and radius of action of their patients to determine whether the recorded information reflected a type of behavior that they expected from a given patient. The ability to draw such conclusions appeared to build on intimate knowledge of each patient, such as where friends and relatives of the patient live, where the patient does his shopping, and habits with regard to transport. This is knowledge that care workers typically acquire over time as they become more and more familiar with the personality and behavior of each patient. One care worker pointed out that care personnel who share responsibility for a patient over a period of time typically learn to recognize his or her general activity patterns without the use of GPS. In the acquisition of knowledge of their patients, their relatives often act as important sources of information.

Much of the knowledge concerning the activity patterns of patients is not registered in their medical records. It exists mainly in the head of the patient's primary care contact and partially in the heads of other care workers who share responsibility for that patient.

Participants from the aid call service also pointed out that the information provided by the positioning system alone was not sufficient to trigger a search for a patient. Aid call service personnel typically have no first-hand knowledge of the behavior or appearance of the patients for whom they are searching. As such, they tend to be dependent on close collaboration with and information from the primary care taker of the patient.

Routines for use

The fourth and final theme that emerged from the focus group discussions concerned the need for formal routines for GPS patient tracking. In many ways, this need is a synthesis of the other emerging themes; a need for guidelines that take into account the various potential uses of the system, patient privacy issues, and background knowledge about patients.

Key questions that surfaced during the focus group discussions included who is responsible for checking the physical position of a patient, how often should a patient's physical position be checked, how should incidents that need to be followed up be organized? The questions were based on what many of the participants found to be unresolved issues in the course of the field experiment.

Focus group participants regarded formal routines as a key premise not only for successful collaboration among caregivers sharing the responsibility for a patient, but also for having a common policy for handling potential privacy-related issues.

Feedback from the participants emphasized the need for individually adapted routines for each patient. Factors that were identified as affecting the development of patient-specific routines included disease progression, the patient's ability to perform unsupervised outdoor activities, and his or her general level of safety in traffic. Comments from the participants also suggested that there was a clear need to establish routines in close collaboration with the patient's relatives. In particular, focus group participants found it important to decide, in collaboration with a patient's closest family, the extent to which tracking information should be used as a basis for contacting relatives.

Due to the progressive nature of dementia, the participants emphasized the need for regular evaluations of routines for GPS tracking of dementia patients. They also highlighted the need for care workers to document that established routines for use are being followed, just as care workers are required to document that current care plans are being followed.

DISCUSSION

The focus group discussions helped us to identify a wide range of possibilities, concerns, and premises related to the use of GPS for tracking dementia patients under professional care. They also helped to provide deeper insight into the basis of the stakeholders' views.

The question of how tracking technology can be used without compromising patient privacy stood out as a central issue in the focus group discussions. In this section we examine and discuss the nature of privacy issues in formal dementia care and some key implications for the use of GPS tracking systems in this field.

The contextual nature of privacy issues

The focus group discussions highlighted the contextual nature of privacy. The extent to which care workers perceived the use of tracking data to be a violation of a patient's right to privacy, or to serve in the best interest of the patient, was intimately tied to the circumstances of use. Factors of importance include the patient's level of autonomy, traffic safety, time since last observation, and time of the day.

The patient privacy threshold and beneficiary of use.

A fundamental problem regarding the use of awareness technologies is that of finding a balance between what is thought to benefit the patient and preserving his or her right to privacy. The level of detail a that system provides about a person's movements was central in this connection. Applications that were regarded as primarily benefitting the individual patient lowered the privacy threshold, while those that were seen as primarily benefitting care staff raised it. Figure 3 illustrates where the previously discussed applications of GPS can be placed with respect to primary beneficiary and privacy threshold.

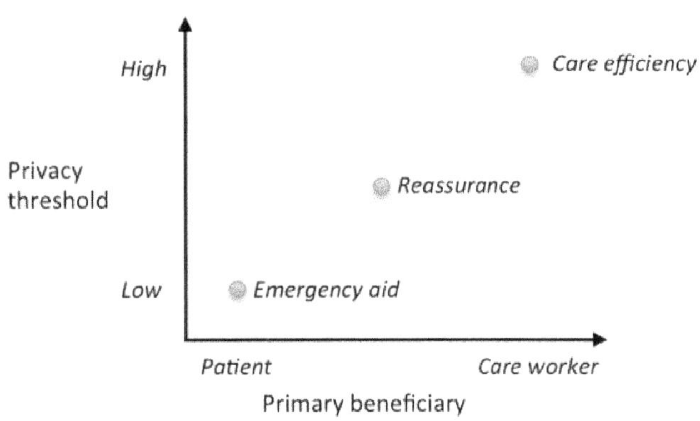

Figure 3. Applications of GPS structured according to primary beneficiary and privacy threshold.

Patient privacy and perceived relevance of tracking data

In accordance with their patient-centered care philosophy [13], the participants emphasized the need for detailed information on the patient's life history, preferences, habits, and interests in order to provide individualized care. Much of the patient knowledge that care workers obtain through their daily work is of a private or personal nature. However, the care workers participating in the focus groups tended to view the acquisition of background knowledge as being in the best interests of the patient. Much of the information provided by the tracking system, on the other hand, was felt to violate patients' right to privacy. While this might appear contradictory, one probable explanation is related to the *relevance* of the two different types of information in the context of care. Solid background information about patients was felt to be necessary in care planning, and in the daily interaction and communication with patients. Much of the information provided by the tracking system, however, was not perceived as beneficial, either for the patient or the care workers (except in safety-critical situations). Instead of *watching over* or safeguarding patients, which is an essential part of care, many participants were more under the impression that they were simply *watching* or spying on patients via the GPS tracking system. In this sense, there appears to be a tight coupling between what care workers consider irrelevant information for care purposes, and what they perceive as violations of a patient's right to privacy.

This discomfort can be seen also to underlie the care workers' expressed need to establish patient-specific routines in order to maintain patient privacy in the context of GPS tracking.

Patient privacy in the view of care responsibilities

There were conflicting perspectives among the participants regarding the use of location-based services beyond potentially safety-critical situations. Although some participants, particularly home care workers, argued for using such services beyond safety-critical situations, for example to verify that patients were at home before conducting visits, we do not consider this an indication of being less concerned with the privacy issues that GPS tracking raise. Essentially, the same participants also pointed out concrete privacy concerns related to the tracking system used in the field experiment and what they perceived as an overexposure of details of the patients' movements. This suggests that care workers' perception of what serves patients' best interests and what is perceived as an intrusion of patient privacy is intimately bound to their care responsibility, and that different responsibilities give grounds for different rationales.

Implications for electronic tracking systems in professional dementia care

The general opinion among the care workers regarding the tracking system was that, except in safety critical situations, the level of detail on the tracking information exceeded their needs. Not only was this regarded as being in conflict with patients' right to privacy, but also as being ineffective as far as the other practical purposes GPS tracking potentially could fulfill (e.g. checking whether or not a patient is at home before an home visit).

We see two implications in particular for the use of electronic tracking systems in dementia care. First, we learned that care workers could benefit from representations of patient tracking data that are better tailored to specific uses. Apart from safety-critical situations, the question that care workers want answered through positioning technology is not: "where is the patient?" or "where is he moving to?" More relevant questions, as seen from the care workers' point of view are: "is the patient at home?" and "how long has he been out of doors?" Although these are questions that conventional GPS tracking systems, such as the one used here, can potentially answer, the way the information is presented to the user does not make it easy to use and efficient in care situations. Purposes of use are likely to differ depending on the responsibilities of the particular care worker; aid call service personnel searching for a missing patient are likely to have different requirements with regard to details of tracking information and how it is presented, than a home care worker who wants to check if a patient is at home before making a scheduled visit.

Secondly, the tension between patient privacy and care worker awareness need to be resolved in a way that incorporate some degree of flexibility with regard to the level of detail about patients' movements. Allowing care workers to modify the level of detail would make a system more adaptable to the changing factors that the awareness needs of the care workers. Changing the frequency of position reports, or the number of positions shown on the user interface are two ways in which requirements for privacy and awareness can be reconciled.

Relating the results to previous studies

Like previous work [15, 19, 23], our study highlights the core dilemma that caregivers face in the context of electronic tracking of persons with dementia; the safety of patients versus preservation of their autonomy. However, we find the reasons given by the different professional stakeholders for their perspectives enriched our understanding of this dilemma and of professional dementia care as a potential application for awareness technologies. The purpose of use, privacy concerns, knowledge about patients, and routines for use were key factors in the care workers' appraisal of the dilemma. Moreover, our analysis revealed a strong link between these issues (e.g. between views on privacy issues and purpose of use, privacy issues and the need for individually adapted routines).

Our results also demonstrate that professional stakeholders have different attitudes towards electronic tracking of dementia patients, depending on their specific responsibilities. To our knowledge, this has not been reported to the same extent in previous studies.

Unlike most work on stakeholder attitudes to electronic tracking of persons with dementia, we gave care workers practical experience of using GPS technology through an extensive field trial. While this produced results that to some extent correspond to findings reported elsewhere, we believe that our technomethodology-inspired approach has improved the credibility of our findings.

Limitations of the study

While we believe that our work has contributed to a better understanding of professional dementia care as an application for tracking technology, we need to acknowledge its limitations. Our study involved a small number of persons from various stakeholder institutions. Although some of the participants' perspectives were obviously based on how they felt that the technology could fit into their everyday work and accommodate their care responsibilities, the question of whether their views are representative of the specific institutions they represented remains open.

We also acknowledge that attitudes are dynamic and likely to be affected by situational variables. If we had been able to involve persons with dementia and their close family in the focus group meetings, the attitudes of the professionals could have been affected for those particular cases, as a result of interplay between possibly different perspectives. Our focus, however, was on formal carer's attitudes towards the use of GPS tracking in dementia care, in light of general professional care values and practices.

Based on studies on attitudes to surveillance technology in other cultural settings [10, 22], we think it is likely that our findings are to a certain extent culture-specific with regard to emerging privacy issues, but also with regard to the organization of care.

SUMMARY AND CONCLUSION

This study investigated the perspectives of professional stakeholders involved in municipal care on the use of GPS for tracking dementia patients. Drawing on experiences gained through a field trial, the stakeholders identified a range of purposes that tracking technology could fulfill, related privacy concerns, and underlying premises for successful use.

Studies of stakeholders' attitudes to tracking technologies employed in dementia care tend to treat the concept of electronic tracking in a very general way. Our findings highlight the need to consider carefully which aspects of dementia patients' movements a GPS tracking system should provide to care workers, and how positioning information should be presented. We found that the level of detail required, as seen from the perspectives of the care workers, is intimately linked to the purpose of its use. Positioning data that were regarded as being irrelevant for the immediate situation could be perceived as violations of a patient's right to privacy and damaging for the system's efficiency.

We found that the stakeholders had nuanced views on the dilemmas related to GPS tracking of patients in professional dementia care. To help drive research on how GPS and other mobile technologies can better accommodate this domain, we need to take into account their nuanced, and sometimes contradictory, views. In light of this, we encourage human-computer interaction research aimed at studying how the tension between patients' right to privacy and the awareness needs of caregivers can be accommodated in future designs of dementia care technologies.

To develop a more complete understanding of stakeholders' attitudes toward GPS technology used in the context of dementia care, future work will explore the attitudes of persons with dementia and their family caregivers.

ACKNOWLEDGEMENTS

This study was financed in part by Telenor ASA and by the Norwegian regional research project *Trygge Spor* (RFFOFJOR 208820).

Special thanks go to Babak Farshchian, Anders Kofod-Petersen and Hugh M. Allen for helpful comments on previous drafts of this paper.

REFERENCES

1. Astell, A. Technology and personhood in dementia care. *Quality in Ageing*, *7* (1). 15-25.
2. Bamford, C. and Bruce, E. Defining the outcomes of community care: the perspectives of older people with dementia and their carers. *Ageing Soc*, *20* (5). 543-570.
3. Button, G. and Dourish, P. Technomethodology: paradoxes and possibilities. Tauber, M.J. ed. *In Proc. of the SIGCHI conf. on Human factors in computing systems: common ground (CHI '96)*, ACM, New York, NY, USA, 1996, 19-26.
4. Cummings, J.L. and Benson, D.F. *Dementia: A clinical approach*. Butterworth-Heinemann, Boston, 1992.
5. Epp, T.D. Person-centred dementia care: A vision to be refined. *The Canadian Alzheimer Disease Review*, *5* (3).
6. Essén, A. The two facets of electronic care surveillance: an exploration of the views of older people who live with monitoring devices. *Soc Sci Med*, *67* (1). 128-136.
7. Gowans, G., Campbell, J., Alm, N., Dye, R., Astell, A. and Ellis, M. Designing a multimedia conversation aid for reminiscence therapy in dementia care environments. *In CHI '04 ext. abstracts on Human factors in computing systems (CHI EA '04)*, ACM, New York, NY, USA, 2004, 825-836.
8. Green, R.C. *Diagnosis and management of Alzheimer's disease and other dementias*. Professional Communications, New York, 2004.
9. Göllner, S., Hurtienne, J., Gollner, U. and Naumann, A.B. Mobile technology keeping people with dementia independent and socially active. *In Proc. of the 13th International Conf. on Human Computer Interaction with Mobile Devices and Services (MobileHCI '11)*, ACM, New York, NY, USA, 2011, 593-598.
10. Harada, T., Ishizaki, F., Nitta, Y., Nitta, K., Shimohara, A., Tsukue, I., Wu, X. and Cheng, W. Microchips will decrease the burden on the family of elderly people with wandering dementia. *International Medical Journal*, *15* (1). 25-27.
11. Killick, J. Communication: a matter of life and death of the mind. *Journal of Dementia Care*, *5* (5). 14-15.
12. Kitwood, T. Cultures of care: tradition and change. in Benson, S. and Kitwood, T. eds. *The New Culture of Dementia Care*, Hawker, London, UK, 1995.
13. Kitwood, T. *Dementia reconsidered: the person comes first*. Open University Press, Buckingham, UK, 1997.
14. Landau, R., Auslander, G.K., Werner, S., Shoval, N. and Heinik, J. Who should make the decision on the use of GPS for people with dementia? *Aging Ment Health*, *15* (1). 78-84.
15. Landau, R., Werner, S., Auslander, G.K., Shoval, N. and Heinik, J. Attitudes of Family and Professional Care-Givers towards the Use of GPS for Tracking Patients with Dementia: An Exploratory Study. *Br J Soc Work*, *39* (4). 670-692.
16. Marr, J. Electronic tagging. *Nursing Standards*, *4* (9).
17. Martin, S., Cunningham, C. and Nugent, C. Ethical Considerations for Integrating Technology Into Community-Based Service Models for Adults With Dementia. *Alzheimer's Care Today*, *8* (3). 251-258.
18. McShane, R., Hope, T. and Wilkinson, J. Tracking patients who wander: Ethics and technology. *The Lancet*, *343* (8908). 1274.
19. Müller, C., Wan, L. and Hrg, D. Dealing with wandering: a case study on caregivers' attitudes towards privacy and autonomy when reflecting the use of LBS *In Proc. of the 16th ACM international conf. on Supporting group work (GROUP '10)*, ACM, New York, NY, USA, 2010, 75-84.
20. O'Neill, D.J. Electronic tagging of people with dementia. Tagging should be reserved for babies, convicted criminals, and animals. *BMJ*, *326* (7383). 281.
21. Prince, M. and Jackson, J. *World Alzheimer Report 2009*. Alzheimer's Disease International, 2009.
22. Rialle, V., Ollivet, C., Guigui, C. and Herve, C. What do family caregivers of Alzheimer's disease patients desire in smart home technologies? *Methods Inf Med*, *47* (1).
23. Robinson, L., Hutchings, D., Corner, L., Finch, T., Hughes, J., Brittain, K. and Bond, J. Balancing rights and risks: Conflicting perspectives in the management of wandering in dementia. *Health Risk Soc*, *9* (4). 389-406.
24. Welsh, S., Hassiotis, A., O'Mahoney, G. and Deahl, M. Big brother is watching you - the ethical implications of electronic surveillance measures in the elderly with dementia and in adults with learning difficulties. *Aging Ment Health*, *7,* (5). 372-375.
25. Wherton, J. and Monk, A. Choosing the right knob *In CHI'09 ext. abstracts on Human factors in computing systems (CHI EA '09)*, ACM, New York, NY, USA, 2009, 3631-3636.

But I Don't Trust my Friends
Ecofriends – An Application for Reflective Grocery Shopping

Jakob Tholander, Anna Ståhl, Mattias Jacobsson, Lisen Schultz, Sara Borgström, Maria Normark, Elsa Kosmack-Vaara
Mobile Life @ SICS/Stockholm University, Stockholm Resilience Centre
Box 1263, SE-164 29 Kista, Sweden, jakobth@dsv.su.se

ABSTRACT
The Ecofriends application was designed to encourage people to reflect on their everyday grocery shopping from social and ecological perspectives. Ecofriends portrays the seasonality of various grocery products as being socially constructed, emphasizing subjective dimensions of what it means for a product to be in season, rather than attempting to communicate it as an established fact. It provides the user with unexpected information (news, weather, blog posts and tweets) about the place where the product was grown, and visualises how the product's popularity shifts throughout the year, among the user's friends, among chefs and other food experts, and the general public. Key findings from users' first encounters with the system are presented. In particular, we discuss aspects of trust, information fragments as catalysts, and how several of the participants were challenged by the system's portrayal of season.

AUTHOR KEYWORDS
Subjectivity; Social Construction; Mobile Interaction; Sustainable Interaction

ACM CLASSIFICATION KEYWORDS
H.5.m. Information interfaces and presentation (e.g., HCI).

INTRODUCTION
The Ecofriends application was designed to engage group of friends to reflect on their everyday grocery consumption behaviours from social and ecological perspectives. Shopping of groceries is nowadays characterized by considerations of a variety of factors such as price, taste, health, habits, social context, availability, and to an increasing extent ethical aspects, such as environmental effects and fair trade.

MobileHCI'12, September 21–24, 2012, San Francisco, CA, USA.

The design aimed for an open-ended style of interaction with the intention to spur reflection, inspire, and challenge people's basic assumptions regarding seasonal aspects of groceries, as well as broader issues of ecological consequences of our daily choices. It is designed to be social but with the twist that a user's group of 'ecofriends' are one of three social media voices about seasonality. The other two are "experts", such as food experts and chefs that are blogging. The last one is local twitter-users that are micro-blogging about a product. The application attempts to encourage users to take the complexity of consumption choices into account, grounding them in a number of personal, social, and informational aspects of their lives. It portrays the subjectivity of season and seasonal purchases rather than attempting to influence people to make "the right choice". Moreover, the application is designed to provide ways for users to relate to the contextual circumstances around the product.

In wealthy parts of the world, it is more or less expected that all products should be available at all times of the year. In reaction to this, it has become increasingly popular to buy food that is 'in season' and locally produced. The reason for this is plenty-fold, including environmental reasons to decrease transportation and to support local farming, as well as to consider natural conditions that maximize taste and nutritional value of fruits and vegetables. In a sense, due to the ubiquitous accessibility of any kind of fruit and vegetables in grocery stores as well as our everyday consumption and shopping of food, some of our sense of a product's natural growing conditions and natural season is lost.

In this paper we discuss the application and the rationale behind it. The application was designed through collaborative efforts in a multi-disciplinary design team consisting of interaction designers, researchers in sustainability and ecosystem management, and experts in visual design. Some key findings from a number of users' first encounters with the system are presented. In particular we discuss aspects of trust, information fragments as catalysts, and how several of the participants often were challenged by the system's portrayal of season.

DESIGN APPROACH – EXPERIENCING SEASONS AS A SOCIAL CONSTRUCTION

Our work draws on a number of design approaches that have recently emerged in HCI. These emphasize subjective and value-based dimensions of experience, and how these are socially constructed phenomena. Approaches such as reflective and critical design [6], openness for interpretation [7], interactional empowerment [5], and ambiguity [5] explore ways of designing technologies that engage users in reflective and subjective experiences. We contribute to expanding these approaches into the area of sustainable interaction [1] by providing further design examples, in a fashion related works like the Prayer companion [3]

These approaches bring up questions regarding the nature of the values that designers deal with as well as their actual sources. Are they contained in the system or are they to be understood as constructed and communicated by the users themselves? Critical and interpretationist approaches explore how values in design can be accounted for as something constructed by users own actions and interpretations, rather than as something that can be contained in, and delivered by a computer system. Values are looked upon as something to be *discovered* by users rather than communicated by a system [2]. Overall, we portray the notion of 'season' as a *social construction* that arises out of people's situated actions with each other and with the environment. From this point of view, what is 'in season' emerges from interactions around aspects such as cooking trends, personal preferences, and political values, rather than from a stipulated set of facts. As discussed above, season as a time-bound phenomenon has largely disappeared from grocery stores. Basically, the same selection of products is available independent of the time of the year. In a sense, groceries have to some degree lost their relation to place, and the 'real' season of that place. As one of the participants in our study put it, *"the origin of a product is more like a label, just like a price tag, it might say Israel or 4.95, but that does not really mean anything"*. The range of different eco labels work in a similar way. In their attempt to simplify choices, they tend to abstract or hide some of the complexity of environmental effects. For example, as pointed out by another participant: *"When I hold two tomatoes in my hand, one labelled as environmentally friendly, but grown far away, and one conventionally farmed, but grown nearby, I don't know whether the label includes the effects of transportation or not, so I don't know which one to choose"*. To broaden this picture we have attempted to give people access to socially and contextually rich material that can create novel reactions and also spur reflection. In addition, it enables users to situate and "embody" themselves in some of the 'real stuff' such as political values, local weather, growth conditions, and environmental influences that socially constructs the notion of season of fruits and vegetables.

To allow for interaction around these aspects, i.e. the values around the notion of season and what constitutes the real places of the fruits and vegetables, the Ecofriends application was designed to mirror seasons, places and their context. Firstly, based on data captured from social media such as Twitter and blogs, the system continuously constructs and portrays three *social voices* of what products are 'in season', the voices of your friends, food experts and chefs, and the general public. Secondly, the system dynamically gathers information about the origin and context of the different products the users are buying. Local news, weather, together with tweets and blogs relating to the product supports users in making a *contextually rich interpretation* of the product and its origin. This data is presented in interaction style, intended to be aesthetically inspiring. In summary, the design aims at providing users with a socially grounded system for inspiration and reflection around everyday food consumption.

THE DESIGN OF ECOFRIENDS

Ecofriends is a mobile application that connects you to other friends. It is designed to work as a scanning device used when grocery shopping at the supermarket. A user's 'ecofriends' are other users that uses the application and are connected through existing social networks. In the current prototype we implemented hard-coded relationships for the sake of keeping the study tight. The application has three visualization views; scanning of groceries the seasonal changes (Fig. 1), and product-related visualization (Fig. 2).

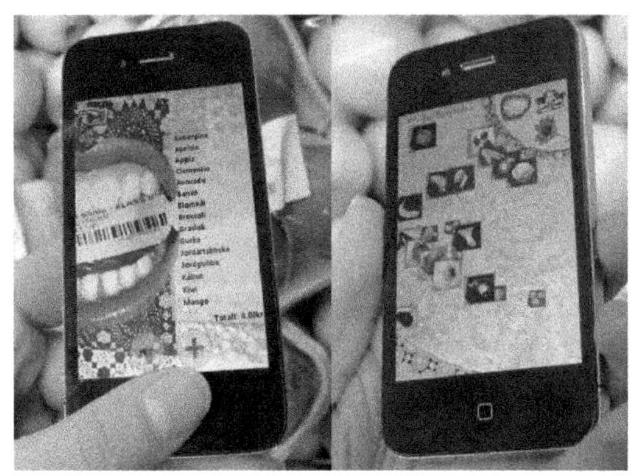

Figure 1. Left: Scanning of groceries. Right: Seasonal changes

The seasonal visualization portrays the three social voices of which products are 'in season'. The voice of your friends is based on the purchases of fruits and vegetables to calculate when a product is 'in season'. The voice of food experts and chefs uses occurrences of particular groceries in social media to calculate when a product is 'in season'. The voice of ordinary people is based on twitter feeds in your local area to calculate the when various products are 'in season'. These three categories have their own expression to let the user distinguish between them. The top 5 fruits and vegetables each week, within each category, are emphasised in the interface. The groceries that are less 'in season' are gradually faded out in the interface. The user can scroll back and forth in time to see how seasons dynamically change from week to week over the last year.

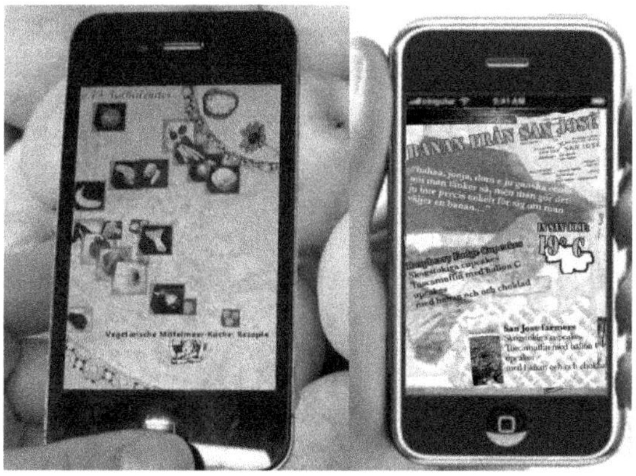

Figure 2. Product related information brought by an angel (left), as a collage (right)

Groceries 'in season' or recently scanned trigger product related messages. These contain information with local news and weather from the origin of the product, together with a tweet and a blog relating to that product.

USER ENCOUNTERS WITH ECOFRIENDS

Our aim was to get insight into people's experiences of using the application in a realistic setting. The study was therefore set up in form of a dinner party among three groups of friends, consisting of four to seven people including two researchers. Each group was asked to use the application to plan a three-course dinner, shop for groceries, and cook the meal together. During the dinner itself we held an open-ended group interview around the participants' experience of the application. The interviews evolved around the following themes: what they found the application to be about, representations and expressions of season and place, how and if the application influenced their understanding and motivations of seasonal shopping. The data was explored through collaborative video analysis sessions in which the authors individually identified key aspects in the interviews. These were collaboratively iterated and discussed to identify critical themes.

Overall, the participants described the application to be about various things. Some described it as an inspirational tool for cooking ingredients, while others saw it as an inspiration for making ecologically grounded choices of what products to buy, or combinations of the two. One participant said it helped him reconnect to nature and reflect on the origin of products. In the following, we discuss two of the themes that emerged from the discussions, along with examples from our data.

1. Trust and the pursuit of 'the truth'
2. Information fragments as catalysts

Trust and the pursuit of *the truth*

Common to the ways that participants described the application was that they got engaged in the trustworthiness of the system. These descriptions regarded the character and form of the information presented. How the notion of season was portrayed was perceived as frustrating, provocative, as well as inspiring. In a similar vein, they also got involved in discussing the sources that were used and their reliability. This way of reflecting upon season as a concept was in line we wanted to achieve with the design.

In all three groups of friends, the system spurred discussions among participants about recipes, environmental issues, and what is actually meant for a product to be 'season'. When scrolling between weeks of the year, participants reflected on the changes in popularity of various products, and how this related to their own ideas of what was 'in season'. Some noted that it was "*actually quite accurate*" whereas others argued for the opposite by claiming that "*bananas should never be in 'season in' Sweden*". As an example of this discussion about the accuracy of the application, one participant said that he simply did not trust it. He described himself as a "*facts*" guy and that he early on had dismissed the information in the application. He called the design and the way information was represented in the application muddled and sometimes confusing. He claimed that the traditional Swedish "Bondepraktika" - a farmers' calendar with seasonal heuristics - would do the job of the application and simplify the whole thing. Another participant would rather have the application based on "*scientific calculations of all the environmental effects*" of various choices. On the contrary, others brought up that they were much aware of the complexity of seasonality, its environmental effects and the specific interests and values of these. Still, they found that the application turned the abstract character, often experienced in this, into something to deal with concretely at particular moments and situations. These users also emphasized that they appreciated the subjectivity of the application, but still felt that it could provide simplified hints for positive or negative choices.

Moreover, several participants elaborated on questions of the kind of sources they would consider reliable. Most of them agreed that it is interesting to know and see what products friends buy and the meals they cook. However, some still claimed that this would not imply that these would be trusted in relation to seasonal shopping. One participant even claimed that "*I don't trust my friends*" in these matters. On the other hand, when we probed him and his friends on what sources they would trust, they brought up a weekly delivery service of groceries for pre-specified recipes as a trustworthy example. When asked for the reason for this they had no clear argument apart from that "*they should know*". On the issue of trusting the 'voices of the experts' of the system, they claimed that they did not know enough about who the experts were and that they wanted to know the exact sources. In relation to this, some suggested a redesign where they themselves could select voices that they already trusted, e.g. eco-chefs and environmentally progressive friends and role models. The variety of ways that the participants talked about these issues points to how the application engaged them in a tension between wanting to know what was the best choice, or *the truth* like someone said. Ecofriends seems to engage participants to reflect on the subjective dimensions and nuances involved in the ecological consequences of different choices. This relates to issues of how individuals and communities handle uncertainties and that we must adapt and act without perfect knowledge in everyday life, e.g. to practically adapt to changing environmental conditions and the role of technology in such processes.

Information Fragments as Catalysts

The participants had a variety of reactions and reflections to the product-related information. Our initial assumption, confirmed by several of our participants, was that people tend to disregard the country of origin of a certain product. Being rather fragmentary in character, the meaning of this information is only loosely coupled to the specific products at hand. It is not selected because of its immediate relevance, but rather because it provided potential seeds for surprise, reflection, and provocation. The participants perceived the fragmentary collection of information in various ways. Some regarded it as irrelevant nonsense that they could not see the point of. However, in cases when specific elements in some way or another talked to their previous experiences or interests, they found it amusing and inspiring in different ways. For instance, when browsing for zucchini one participant said "*Hey, but Lars aren't you from Skara*?". This led to discussions of farming in Skara as well as fun memories of old friends. The information thereby worked like a springboard for further reflection and discussion in playful manners among the participants.

Some participants claimed that this random selection of fragmentary information provided concrete traces back to the actual grocery and made its context and origin more 'alive'. By juxtaposing information about the weather situation with news from the country, the system occasionally allowed for unexpected conclusions, provocations regarding the choice of a specific grocery, as well as opinions about the appropriateness of linking food to politics. E.g., two participants got deeply engaged in the question of actually buying mango when having read about laws that inflicted on women's rights in the area where the mango was from, saying that "*this is the kind of reasons that makes this so hard*", referring to the challenges of making informed choices. Moreover, seeing weather information like persistent sunshine next to news about drought spurred participants to reflect upon relationships between eating habits and the effect they have on the world. In some occasions, participants described how the system's portrayal of place made geographic distance more explicit, which let that place come to life in the here-and-now. Interestingly, the participants that instead claimed this information to be unnecessary and uninteresting, "*What do I care about the weather forecast of San José?*", still told humorous anecdotes inspired by this part of the system.

These ways of interpreting and relating to fragmentary product-related information, points to how unexpectedness and unpredictability can provide ground for surprise, playfulness and provocation. Through the users' own contextualisation and meaning making, this selection of partially unfiltered assemblies of information can become catalysts for a variety of social interactions. It may work as sources for deeply political issues, as springboards for novel topics of discussion, and as inspirations for cooking.

FINAL REMARKS

In reflecting on the design of the Ecofriends application we saw how the leading design rationales that drove the process were mirrored in the kind of interaction users got engaged in. By construing 'season' as a socially constructed phenomenon we have, to some extent, reconnected users back from a disembodied relation to food and groceries. Our studies points to how in situations like these, people often want to know 'the truth' of the consequences of their actions in order to make decisions that they feel are correct. By presenting potentially relevant pieces of information the application invites the user to contextualise the product. The way information is juxtaposed in the application tied the product closer to its origin and social context, in a way, giving it its own agency. Once this agency was established, users could weigh the voices of the experts, friends or general reflections about these voices. Abstract relations between me and what I consume is expressed through concrete informational representations. The immediate connection of the information to the product provided concrete in-the-moment and here-and-now manifestations of the relation. The open-ended design provided users with a space in which to navigate their own conceptualization about seasonality, put it in a broader context.

REFERENCES

1. Blevis, E. Sustainable interaction design: invention & disposal, renewal & reuse. *CHI '07*. 2007
2. Gaver, W., Blythe, M., Boucher, A., Jarvis, N., Bowers, J., and Wright, P. The prayer companion: openness and specificity, materiality and spirituality. *CHI '10*. ACM. 2003.
3. Gaver, W., Beaver, J., & Benford. S. Ambiguity as a resource for design. *CHI '03*. ACM. 2003.
4. Höök, K., Ståhl, A., Sundström, P. and Laaksolaahti, J.. Interactional empowerment. *CHI* '08. ACM. 2008.
5. Le Dantec, C., Shehan Poole, E., and Wyche. S. Values as lived experience: evolving value sensitive design in support of value discovery. *CHI '09*. ACM. 2009.
6. Sengers, P., Boehner, K., David, S., and Kaye, J. 2005. Reflective design. CC '05. ACM. 2005.
7. Sengers, P., and Gaver. W. Staying open to interpretation: engaging multiple meanings in design and evaluation. *DIS'06*. ACM. 2006

A Recognition Safety Net: Bi-Level Threshold Recognition for Mobile Motion Gestures

Matei Negulescu
University of Waterloo
Waterloo, ON, Canada
mnegules@uwaterloo.ca

Jaime Ruiz
Colorado State University
Fort Collins, CO, USA
jgruiz@cs.colostate.edu

Edward Lank
University of Waterloo
Waterloo, ON, Canada
lank@cs.uwaterloo.ca

ABSTRACT
Designers of motion gestures for mobile devices face the difficult challenge of building a recognizer that can separate gestural input from motion noise. A threshold value is often used to classify motion and effectively balances the rates of false positives and false negatives. We present a bi-level threshold recognition technique designed to lower the rate of recognition failures by accepting either a tightly thresholded gesture or two consecutive possible gestures recognized by a relaxed model. Evaluation of the technique demonstrates that the technique can aid in recognition for users who have trouble performing motion gestures. Lastly, we suggest the use of bi-level thresholding to scaffold the learning of gestures.

KEYWORDS
Bi-level thresholding, motion gestures, safety net

ACM CLASSIFICATION KEYWORDS
H.5.2 [Information Interfaces and Presentation]: User Interfaces - Interaction styles.

GENERAL TERMS
Human Factors

INTRODUCTION
Modern sensors such as accelerometers can be leveraged to expand a mobile device's input space by detecting *motion gestures* – gestures that require a user to move and/or translate the entire device in three dimensions. A unique challenge in the design of motion gestures for mobile interaction is the need to develop recognition algorithms that are sufficiently powerful to both recognize a large set of motion gestures and to discriminate intentional gestures from everyday device movement. The focus of this paper is specifically in discriminating intentional motion gestures from everyday motion. Because smartphones are frequently carried in a purse or pocket, the accelerometers and gyroscopes that measure device movement are frequently receiving data. Without careful tuning, unintended commands (i.e. false positives) can be invoked.

There are two possible techniques for segmenting a motion gesture from a smartphone's input stream. The first, and most common, approach is to use an explicit delimiter to discriminate a motion gesture from everyday device movement [6]. Researchers have used hardware buttons, on-screen buttons, and specific, easy-to-discriminate motion gestures as delimiters. However, there are several situations where it is undesirable to use a delimiter. For example, consider using a motion gesture repeatedly to step through a set of objects. Performing an explicit delimiter for each motion gesture may frustrate end-users, particularly if they must repeat a large number of motion gestures within a restricted time. Furthermore, even if delimiters support reliable discrimination from an input stream, it is also important to determine how necessary delimiters are to the design of motion-gesture input.

The second technique for discriminating motion gestures from random device movement is to create a threshold, i.e. a criterion value, that best trades-off between false positives (accidental activations) and false negatives (failed attempts to perform a gesture). If the criterion value is too permissive, many false positives will occur. However, if the criterion value is too restrictive, it may become very difficult for the system to reliably identify intentional user gestures. Designers of systems frequently use visualization techniques like receiver operating characteristic curves to identify the best criterion value for a recognizer (e.g. [1]). Despite this, a majority of the motion gesture research uses delimiters, not criterion values, presumably because of the difficulty of selecting a criterion value that appropriately balances false positives and false negatives [6].

In this paper, we address the challenge of non-activations by creating a novel, bi-level thresholding technique for selecting a criterion value that is appropriately restrictive and while not yielding a prohibitively high number of false negatives. Our bi-level thresholding technique works as follows: if a user-performed gesture does not meet a strict threshold, we then consider the gesture using a relaxed threshold – a more permissive criterion value – and wait to see if a similar motion follows it. Figure 1 displays a Venn diagram that represents our input space. The system recognizes a gesture either if the end-user performs a tightly thresholded motion gesture (i.e. success in the first instance), or if the user performs two relaxed thresholded gestures within a short period of time.

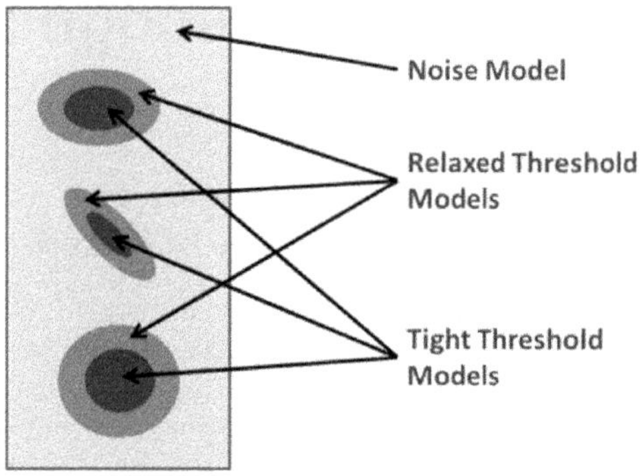

Figure 1. An illustration of the bi-level thresholding model in the allowable input space.

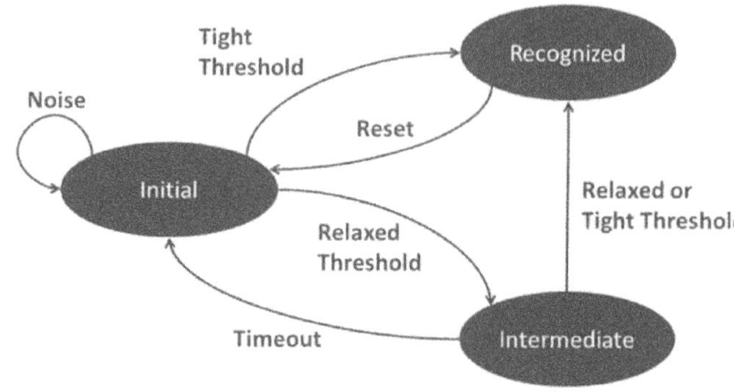

Figure 2. Bi-level thresholding described as a state machine.

RATIONALE FOR BI-LEVEL THRESHOLD RECOGNITION

Our bi-level thresholding technique is based on field notes of typical participant behavior during controlled studies of motion gesture interaction [4]. Participants frequently begin an experiment successfully performing motion gestures. Over time, however, due to the noise within our neurophysiological system, the participant's action may drift from ideal. If a participant does not successfully activate a gesture, their most frequent response is to attempt the gesture again immediately upon recognizing failure. If the gesture succeeds on the second attempt, the cost of missed activation seems quite small. However, participants become frustrated if repeated attempts to activate a gesture also fail. As a result, they begin to alter their input patterns, until they find a gesture profile that is correctly recognized.

We observe that a failure to perform a recognized gesture is often the result of the sensor input falling just outside of the recognition threshold specified by the criterion value. However, adjusting the criterion to recognize these gestures would lead to a prohibitively high rate of false positives.

Our goal in introducing bi-level thresholding was to create a "soft-landing" for users who attempt a gesture and almost succeed at exceeding the criterion value. Rather than requiring the user to repeatedly attempt to match a tight threshold, we noted that the likelihood of observing two sequential gestures at a lower criterion value within a time period is the square of the likelihood of observing one instance of that relaxed-criterion gesture within the time period (e.g., if the odds are 1 in 10 of one relaxed threshold within a time period, the odds of observing two relaxed thresholds within that same time period are 1 in 100). This technique can be seen as a mediation technique that helps to clarify a user's input as outlined by Mankoff et al.[3]. However, in contrast to simple repetition techniques, the goal of bi-level thresholding is adapting to the user's first motion to improve the likelihood of recognition for users who struggle performing motion gestures.

We hypothesized that bi-level thresholding may support successful gesture-from-noise discrimination in situations where a tighter threshold would not. In addition, bi-level thresholding may also provide a mechanism for gradual online learning of the gesture set because users are more likely to succeed at performing correctly recognized gestures.

IMPLEMENTING BI-LEVEL THRESHOLDING

Bi-level thresholding is meant to be recognizer agnostic, applicable to both state based recognizers (e.g. hidden Markov models) and temporal matching algorithms (e.g. Dynamic Time Warping). At a high level, our technique can be visualized as a simple three-state finite state automaton (FSA), as shown in Figure 2. From the *Initial* state, if the recognizer observes a tight-threshold gesture, the system moves to the *Recognized* state and the gesture is recognized. If, in contrast, we observe a relaxed-threshold gesture, the system moves to state the *Intermediate* state. In this state, if the system receives either a tight-threshold or relaxed-threshold input, the system moves to the *Recognized* state and the gesture is recognized. If, instead, a timeout occurs, the system moves back to the *Initial* state.

To evaluate our technique, we implemented bi-level thresholding using a hidden Markov model (HMM) approach [2] due to the input's inherently stochastic nature. The implementation consists of a continuous HMM with four-state models recognizing each gesture. As features, we use time-ordered acceleration (in three dimensions) and orientation readings (three degrees of freedom). Though a full description of hidden Markov models is outside the current scope, we give a brief outline of our gesture models.

The tight-threshold gesture models were built by having six expert users perform each of the gestures in our gesture set 50 times. Though it scales as well as other HMM recognizers, as a proof of concept, our gesture set contains three gestures taken from Ruiz et al.'s consensus gesture set: *Double Flip*, *Next*, and *Previous* (see [5,6]). The HMM was trained using the Baum-Welch algorithm [2] on the pre-segmented gestures performed by our experts. The gesture models comprising our tight threshold were tuned so that three expert users can perform the gestures with greater than 80% accuracy over 20 instances while achieving no more than two false positives when tested with 20 minutes of background walking data.

The relaxed threshold is built by copying the tight-threshold gesture models and loosening the observation distributions for each state by applying a linear Gaussian blur to all features in each observation distribution. This produces three additional HMM models that are more permissive, i.e. that allow a greater range of values. We tune the blur to create an acceptable false positive rate for the gestures. For example, if $R \in (0, 1)$ is an acceptable false positive rate for the single-threshold models, then $R^{1/2}$ is an acceptable false positive rate for the relaxed-threshold models. This ensures that the false positive rate for all gestures is at most R.

Finally, we added a model that represents random device motion, or noise. This model was created by repeatedly performing a random walk of the above six models and using the random state transitions to saturate the entire space of allowable inputs with a random motion recognizer.

As we wish for our recognizer to be always on (as opposed to recognizing pre-delimited content), our implementation links all the gesture and the noise models together with a start state to form a single continuous model, as in [2]. In this method, the Viterbi algorithm is used to consider the most likely sequence of states that generates given sensor observations. A recognized gesture is one where the Viterbi path ends in a gesture model's end state. The interplay of the gesture models and the noise model creates the initial tight threshold that segments noise from gestures.

To guide the reader's intuition of how this recognizer works, consider Figure 1 showing the input space for three gestures. The noise model dominates the background region of the Venn Diagram. However, if the observations from the smartphone sensors lie inside the relaxed threshold, then the relaxed-threshold models have higher probability. Likewise, if the sensor observations lie inside the tight threshold models, then these models dominate. As noted, Figure 2 illustrates how recognition is performed using our relaxed-threshold, tight-threshold, and noise models.

STUDY

We evaluated bi-level thresholding to gauge its feasibility as a safety net for participants who have trouble performing gestures. The study used a within participants design asking eight participants to perform each of three motion gestures, *Double-flip*, *Next*, and *Previous,* 42 times each. A software glitch resulted in the elimination of the first gesture in each set, yielding 125 gestures attempted by eight participants, or 1000 motion gestures in total. A Nexus One smartphone was used to perform and recognize gestures. The order of the gestures was randomized, with the software ensuring that each gesture was performed the same number of times.

The application presented the user with a black screen. In the centre of the screen the word "Double-Flip", "Next", or "Previous" was presented to the user. Once the system detected the given gesture, the screen flashed green, vibrated for 200ms and preceded to the next gesture. If a gesture other than the given gesture was recognized (i.e. a *Recognition Error* occurred), the screen vibrated for 200ms, but did not move on to the next gesture. Instead, it logged the misrecognized attempt and presented the gesture again. If the participant failed to activate the given gesture within 15 seconds, the screen flashed red for 200ms, vibrated, and moved on to the next gesture after logging the instance as a *skipped gesture*.

There are two open questions which we aim to address with our experiment. First, is the bi-level threshold useful in supporting recognition? To analyze this question, we examined at the proportion of gestures recognized using the double relaxed threshold versus the number of gestures recognized using a tight threshold. If you consider the FSA in Figure 2, the tight threshold could successfully recognize gestures from either the *Initial* or *Intermediate* states. In either of these cases, the bi-level threshold provides limited benefit as it does not eliminate gesture attempts. It is unclear how common the bi-level technique will be during recognition. It may be the case that it increases recognition reliability significantly (i.e. it frequently performs the recognition of gestures). On the other hand, participants may hit the tight threshold or fail to hit a double relaxed threshold often enough to improve recognition rates.

Second, we wish to determine whether the rate of skipped gestures can tell us anything about the potential of bi-level thresholding as a mechanism for scaffolding. For example, do users who struggle with motion gestures make increased use of bi-level thresholding?

RESULTS

During our experiment, 93% of gestures were recognized successfully for all users within the timeout period. The other 7% were skipped gestures. Moreover, the recognizer performed at an accuracy of 95.3% (S.D. = 6.4%) with five out of eight participants achieving 99.8% accuracy. Due to the tuned tight threshold and the given task, no false positives were recorded during the session.

We analyze the behavior of our recognizer by examining the various recognition paths taken through the FSA (Figure 2). For each user, we separate the proportion of successes recognized with a) the double relaxed threshold, b) the single tight threshold, and c) those recognized with the relaxed then tightly thresholded models (i.e. tight from the *Intermediate*). We show the various fractions in Figure 3.

We note that 65% of recognized gestures were recognized using the double relaxed gesture model. Another 9% of successful recognitions were flagged by the single tight threshold model while already in the *Intermediate* state, i.e. after an initial relaxed threshold event. The remaining 26% of gestures were recognized using the single tight threshold, from the *Initial* state. The large proportion of successes caught using our bi- threshold gives some promise that the technique acts to improve overall efficiency.

While an average rate of 7% of total gestures attempted using the bi-level threshold recognizer (SD=10.0) were

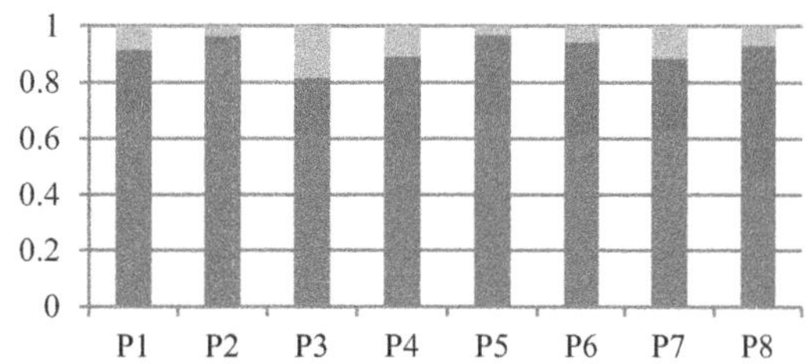

Figure 3. Breakdown of gestures by whether recognition occurred using the double relaxed model (blue), the single tight model (red), or the relaxed then tight model (green).

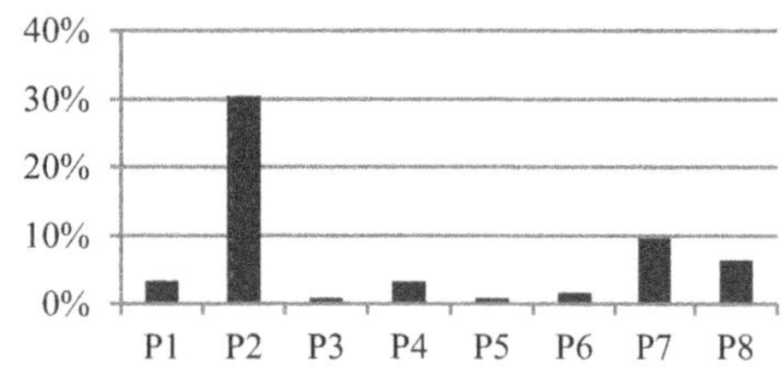

Figure 4. Rate of skipped gestures, per participant

skipped gestures, there is variability among participants. As shown in Figure 4, P2 is an outlier, failing to successfully perform the gesture within the timeout window 30% of the time. P2 provides an interesting case study for our bi-level thresholding technique. P2 only successfully completed 70% of the gestures, compared to over 90% for all other participants. Of P2's successfully recognized gestures, 94% were recognized using our double-relaxed model (Figure 3) versus 50-66% for all other participants. P2 was an outlier in both the failure rate experienced performing motion gestures and in how frequently their successes were recognized using the bi-level thresholding technique. Although care must be taken to generalize from the behavior of this one participant, this participant's case study may indicate the potential use of the lower threshold for users who have trouble completing motion gestures.

DISCUSSION

The results of our experiment indicate that the bi-level thresholding technique for motion gesture recognition can aid in recognition of motion gestures. The recognizer was tuned so that expert users found it easy to use while limiting the number of false positives. However, though recognition rates were high, our novice participants had difficulty in consistently activating the motion gestures. Two-thirds of all gestures recognized during our experiment were recognized as a result of the double-relaxed threshold model of the bi-level thresholding technique. These gestures would need at least another attempt by the participant to be recognized successfully if using a similarly tuned single-tight threshold. The relaxed threshold acted as a safety net for participants who were inexperienced with motion gestures. An open question is whether such a safety net can be used to scaffold learning to perform motion gestures over a long period of time.

We note that, in our experiment, we do not consider delimiters. It is true that, if an effective delimiter is chosen, then the system can use a more permissive criterion function -- one less likely to label movement as noise. However, even with delimiters, criterion functions are still required. To understand why, consider what happens when a delimiter is activated. If, after delimiter activation, the end-user is performing any action at all – walking, driving, looking at the phone, turning in a desk chair, holding the phone, etc. – then the accelerometer and gyroscope in the smartphone will receive data. If the system assumes that all received data constitutes a motion gesture, then a gesture may fire accidentally before the user has any chance to execute a deliberate gesture, solely based on random input. Regardless of whether or not delimiters are used, it is still necessary to create a noise model and to select a criterion value to separate deliberate movement from noise.

Finally, while we focus on motion gestures as the application space for bi-level thresholding, we believe that the technique is applicable to other gestural domains, including surface gestures and stylus interfaces. For example, consider using an always available scratch-out gesture within a stylus program like Windows Journal. If the scratch-out gesture fails initially (something that frequently occurs), a bi-level recognition model could be designed that handles two poorly performed scratch-out gestures, thus aiding reliable recognition.

CONCLUSION

We present a bi-level thresholding technique to support the recognition of motion gestures for smartphone input. Our results show that, when available, the bi-level thresholding technique frequently catches input gestures that an optimized criterion function misses. The end result is that end-users need fewer attempts to successfully activate motion gestures using bi-level thresholding.

ACKNOWLEDGEMENTS

Funding provided by the Natural Science and Engineering Research Council of Canada (NSERC) and the Networks of Centres of Excellence for Graphics, Animation and New Media (NCE-GRAND).

REFERENCES

1. Fogarty, J., Baker, R.S., and Hudson, S.E. Case studies in the use of ROC curve analysis for sensor-based estimates in human computer interaction. *Proc. of GI*, (2005), 129–136.
2. Lee, H.K. and Kim, J.H. An HMM-based threshold model approach for gesture recognition. *IEEER Trans. on Pattern Analysis and Machine Intelligence,* 10 (1999), 961–973.
3. Mankoff, J., Hudson, S.E., and Abowd, G.D. Interaction techniques for ambiguity resolution in recognition-based interfaces. *Proc. of UIST '00*, ACM (2000), 11–20.
4. Negulescu, M., Ruiz, J., Li, Y., and Lank, E. Tap, swipe, or move: attentional demands for distracted smartphone input. *Proc. of the AVI*, ACM (2012), 173–180.
5. Ruiz, J., Li, Y., and Lank, E. User-defined motion gestures for mobile interaction. *Proc. of CHI*, ACM (2011), 197–206.
6. Ruiz, J. and Li, Y. DoubleFlip: a motion gesture delimiter for mobile interaction. *Proc. of CHI.* ACM (2011), 2717–2720.

Extending a Mobile Device's Interaction Space through Body-Centric Interaction

Xiang 'Anthony' Chen, Nicolai Marquardt, Anthony Tang, Sebastian Boring, Saul Greenberg
Department of Computer Science, University of Calgary
2500 University Drive NW, Calgary, AB, T2N 1N4, Canada
xiangchen@acm.org, {nicolai.marquardt, tonyt, sebastian.boring, saul.greenberg}@ucalgary.ca

Figure 1. Body-Centric Interaction anchors digital content & actions on & around the body where one can position/orient the device to navigate multiple objects (left), place/retrieve bookmarks on a virtual canvas (center), select an application control options (right).

ABSTRACT
Modern mobile devices rely on the screen as a primary input modality. Yet the small screen real-estate limits interaction possibilities, motivating researchers to explore alternate input techniques. Within this arena, our goal is to develop *Body-Centric Interaction with Mobile Devices*: a class of input techniques that allow a person to position and orient her mobile device to navigate and manipulate digital content anchored in the space on and around the body. To achieve this goal, we explore such interaction in a bottom-up path of prototypes and implementations. From our experiences, as well as by examining related work, we discuss and present *three recurring themes* that characterize how these interactions can be realized. We illustrate how these themes can inform the design of *Body-Centric Interactions* by applying them to the design of a novel mobile browser application. Overall, we contribute a class of mobile input techniques where interactions are extended beyond the small screen, and are instead driven by a person's movement of the device on and around the body.

Author Keywords
Body-Centric Interaction, mobile device, mobile interaction.

ACM Classification Keywords
H.5.2 [User Interfaces]: Input devices and strategies, Interaction styles.

INTRODUCTION
Modern mobile devices, such as smart phones and PDAs, rely on the screen as their primary input and output modality. For input, these devices rely mostly on direct touch, albeit augmented with a few physical buttons and sensor data. For output, small displays (i.e., between 3.5" and 4" diagonal) provide only a limited view of information displayed by the device. While enabling portability, the problem is that small screen space restricts designers to a limited interaction palette. Consequently, some actions require long sequences of on-screen operations (e.g. navigating through hierarchies, or swiping and searching through 'pages' of content). Interaction tedium is exacerbated as mobile applications increase in both number and complexity.

Prior work has suggested various solutions to address this 'small-screen' problem of mobile devices. For example, some systems allow people to place digital information onto different body parts so it can be easily retrieved later [1,7,24]. Others create virtual workspaces around a person's body [14,28] or more generally in space [6] where one orients the device to 'peep into' and navigate an information space that is significantly larger than the screen. Researchers also envision a wearable mobile device whose functions are shaped by the way it is held or worn on the body [27].

On reflection, we find this body of work shares an important design theme: they all extended the spectrum of interactions to include a person's body and its surroundings. Our own particular focus is on a subset of the above, where we define and develop *Body-Centric Interaction with Mobile Devices* – a class of mobile input techniques that allow people to navigate and manipulate mobile digital content by positioning and orienting the device *on* and *around* their bodies (Figure 1 shows three examples of *Body-Centric Interaction* techniques).

MobileHCI'12, September 21–24, 2012, San Francisco, CA, USA.

While a limited amount of prior work in this area does cover this idea, the problem is that they mostly represent point solutions. A broader view of this design theme has not yet been established. Therefore, it is somewhat difficult to generalize ideas from one implementation, or to systematically leverage ideas found across several point systems, or to distill 'guidelines' that stimulate new mobile interaction designs based on a person's body and the space anchored to it. Consequently, our goal is to explore the breadth of this design theme, where we go beyond point solutions in an attempt to create a network of design ideas.

To attain this goal, we began with a bottom-up path of prototypes and implementations, where each prototype represents a specific body-centric mobile input technique. We then reflected on our designs (as well as others found in the literature), to reveal and extract more general aspects of designing such *Body-Centric Interactions*. These aspects present three recurring themes that encapsulate how the interactions can be realized. In brief, proximal spaces on and around the body are identified and delimited to situate interactions; within these spaces, the spatial relationship between the body and the device serves as 'raw input'; and, given such 'raw input', various considerations will influence the design of interactions to navigate and manipulate the device's on-screen content. We summarize and present these recurring themes as a set of reusable design guidelines, which are further illustrated in our final prototype – the body-centric browser. By taking a body-centric approach, we create new experience of using a mobile browser where one can manipulate multiple tabs, bookmarks and controls on and around her body. Overall, this paper contributes a class of mobile input techniques where interactions are extended beyond the small screen, and are instead driven by a person's movement of the device on and around the body.

PROTOTYPING BODY-CENTRIC INTERACTION

To begin our exploration, we implemented a set of prototypes, each of which represents a specific body-centric mobile input technique. (For clarity, Figures 2-7 use sketches rather than system photographs to illustrate these prototypes; however the accompanying video illustrates several of these in actual operation). During this prototyping process, we focused on three different design directions, each of which assigned a specific role to the body in mobile interaction. As we will shortly show, we considered how our body and its surroundings can afford (1) storing and retrieving digital objects (bookmarks, photos, etc.), (2) triggering digital shortcuts (making a phone call, starting the music player, etc.), and (3) controlling applications (navigating the calendar time line, selecting from a set of tools, etc.). Before presenting these prototypes, we first explain the enabling sensing technologies.

Implementation Technologies

While our prototypes are fully implemented, they are best considered as design sketches that develop and formulate basic ideas. However, we acknowledge that the technology we use is not yet suitable for day to day deployment on consumer mobile devices. This is not a problem for our purposes, as we see this setup as an enabling technology that allows us to explore possible interactions that leverage a device's knowledge of where it is situated and how it is moved in the space relative to a person's body.

When using a mobile device to situate interactions *directly on* the body, we need to identify the body location that the mobile device is referring to. We used two approaches. First, we embedded RFID tags in clothes, which in turn are associated with discrete locations representing the underlying body part. Tags are read by an RFID reader attached to the mobile device. Second, we also used the device's integrated camera to recognize either fiduciary tags or shapes imprinted on clothes via computer vision. Both work to identify body locations. These vision-based approaches provided additional information, where they could also return a continuous stream identifying the device's position relative to particular locations.

When situating interactions in the space *around* the body, we needed to capture the fine-grained changing spatial relationships of the device relative to the body. To do this, we attached reflective markers to both the body and the device. Using infrared cameras and the Proximity Toolkit [15] running atop the Vicon motion capture system[1], we could easily acquire the position and orientation of the device relative to particular body parts.

Body-Centric Digital Content Storage/Retrieval

The first two prototypes concern the storage and retrieval of digital content.

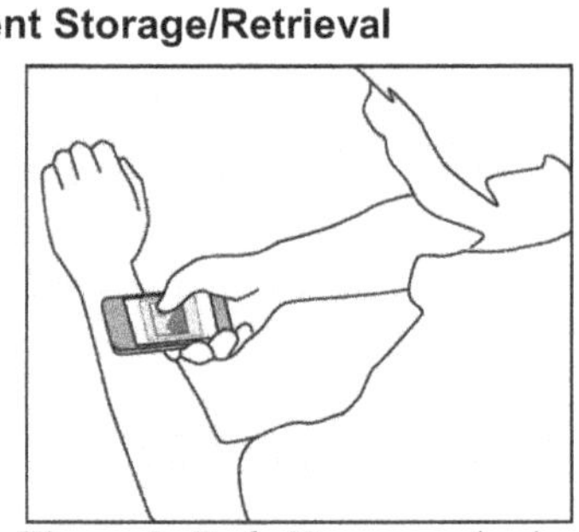

Figure 2. *Body Viewer*: anchoring digital content to the forearm

Body Viewer is an image viewer that allows people to place and retrieve digital content – in this case digital images – by anchoring them on one or more body parts. Figure 2 illustrates a person anchoring the image currently displayed on his device to his forearm: he simply brings the device over the forearm and then taps the screen. When the device is next brought to the forearm, a preview of that image appears: a further tap will retrieve and display it on the screen. If an image was already on display when the device was brought next to the forearm, both images are shown side by side: tapping the unanchored image will anchor it, while tapping the

[1] http://www.vicon.com/

anchored image will retrieve it. This can be repeated on multiple body parts.

Body Cobweb, inspired by Virtual Shelves [14], is a virtual 3D 'cobweb' contained in the space in front of a person's body that, in our prototype, is used to manage web page bookmarks. Figure 3 illustrates this cobweb as consisting of two virtual layers (hemispheres) located at distinct distances from the body, where bookmarks (shown here in black) are scattered upon it. Figure 3 shows a person orienting the device and pointing to a bookmark on the cobweb (see the arrow). Pushing it to the 'retrieving' layer (Figure 3a) picks up that bookmark and displays the web page on the screen. To create a new bookmark, one pushes the device further to the 'placing' layer (Figure 3b) which drops the bookmark on the cobweb. (If there is an existing one on that location, the new bookmark will replace it).

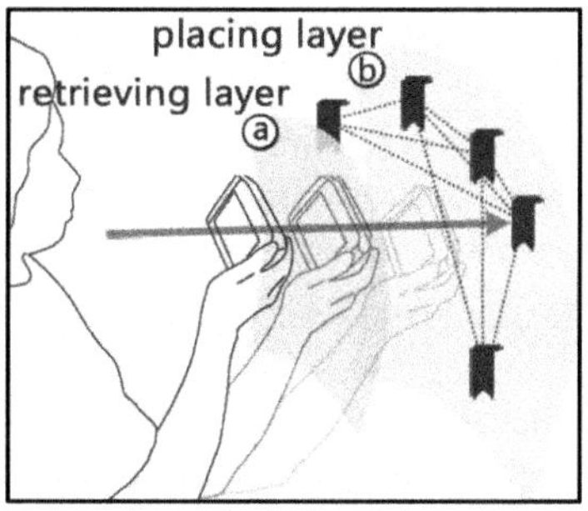

Figure 3. *Body Cobweb* is an imaginary cobweb anchored to a person's body.

Discussion. Both *Body Viewer* and *Body Cobweb* are similar as they use the body and its surroundings as a mobile canvas to extend the mobile device's file storage/access mechanism. They differ in that they appropriate different proximal spaces of the body. *Body Viewer* associates images to discrete marked locations directly on the body's surface. *Body Cobweb* goes beyond the body's surface, where it senses the device's continuous distance and orientation in relation to the space around the entire body, and uses that information to dynamically anchor or retrieve bookmarks from that space. Spatial memory, augmented by visual feedback presented on the mobile device, is a key factor in enabling both interactions [2]. It helps people recall which body part they have associated an image to, or which part of the cobweb holds a bookmark of interest. As well, people's associative experience of how a real cobweb functions helps them understand concepts such as 'layers' and 'sticking a web page on the cobweb'.

Body-Centric Digital Shortcuts

The next two prototypes consider triggering digital actions.

Body Shortcuts, inspired by Guerreiro et al. [7], follows the same interaction style as *Body Viewer* except that we developed associated meanings of body parts to trigger *programmable digital actions*. For example, in Figure 4a a person has associated a calendar application with the wrist, and holding the device close to the wrist opens the calendar. Similarly, a person can also associate his stomach to finding the nearby restaurants (Figure 4b), his knees to searching for walking routes to nearby amenities (Figure 4c), and so on.

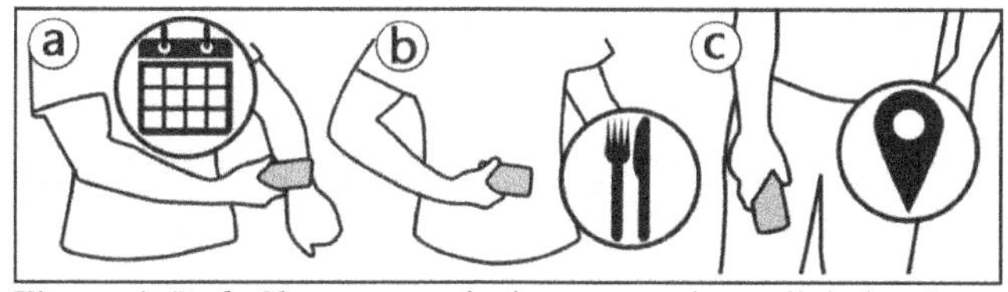

Figure 4. *Body Shortcuts* use body parts to trigger digital actions.

Whereables, inspired by [27], is also designed for triggering programmable actions, but it does this by having a person wear the device at particular locations on the body, which changes to the foreground application mapped to that location. Figure 5a illustrates how the device's currently running application switches to a phone when held close to the ear, while in Figure 5b it automatically switches to a music player when attached to the upper arm (e.g., via a band). This implicit application switching is in sharp contrast to the application juggling that occurs when a person is using on-screen touch controls.

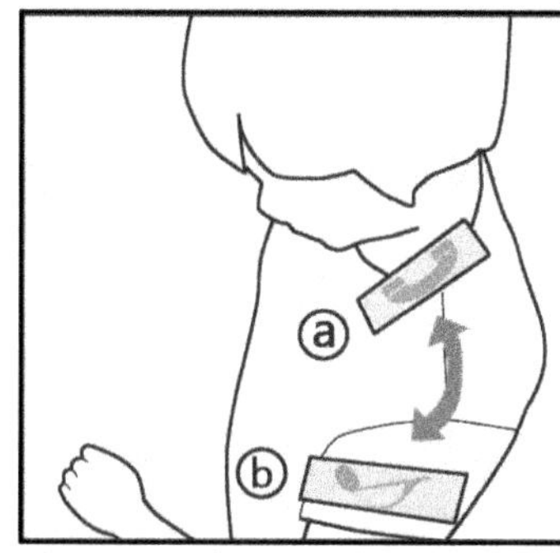

Figure 5. *Whereable* is a device whose functions are triggered by wearing it on different body locations.

Discussion. Both *Body Shortcuts* and *Whereable* use body locations to trigger programmable digital actions, which would otherwise require a sequence of screen navigations. Technically, both perform in quite similar ways, yet they are perceived by a person quite differently: one by temporary moving to a location to activate an action, the other by making the device's function location-dependent.

One important aspect revealed by our examples in this section is that people can apply their associative experience to semantically relate their body parts to certain digital actions. Unlike the cobweb model, body parts are visible and full of meaning. They provide visual cues that help people recall what digital actions are readily available from their body. The wristwatch on the wrist relates to time and thus calendars, the stomach to food and thus restaurants, the ear to listening and thus phones, and so on. People's kinesthetic sense also adds to such interactions [25]. It allows a person to reach their body parts with reduced visual attention. However, physical constraints must be considered. For instance, placing a shortcut on one's back makes it almost impossible (and at times inappropriate) to reach and trigger.

Body-Centric Controls

The next two prototypes concern using the device's location relative to the body as input to control a running application.

Body Toolbar, inspired by Shoemaker et al. [23], allows a person to access virtual tools associated with body

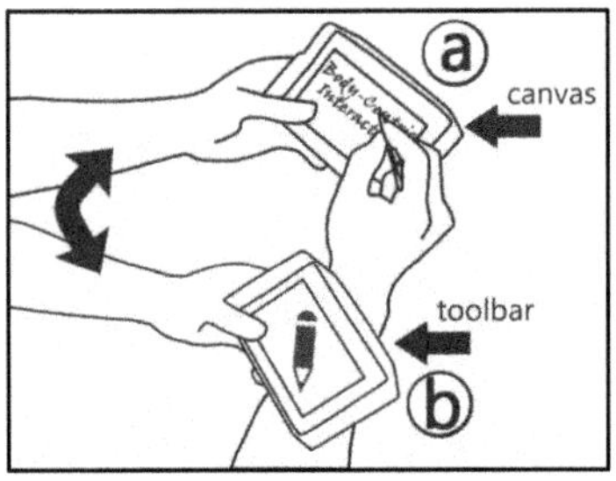

Figure 6. *Body Toolbar* lets one view and select from a palette of tools located on the body

locations. People select a tool by moving the device close to a particular body part. Figure 6 shows our sketch application. The screen only displays the drawing canvas when held in a normal viewing position (Figure 6a). To select different painting tools, a person positions the device along her right arm (Figure 6b), where the screen responds by showing available tools associated with locations along the arm. A person selects the tool by touching the screen. The previously active tool is kept if a person moves the device away without touching the screen. To pick a color, a person would move the device along the left arm instead, which reveals a palette of colors that can be picked as drawing colors.

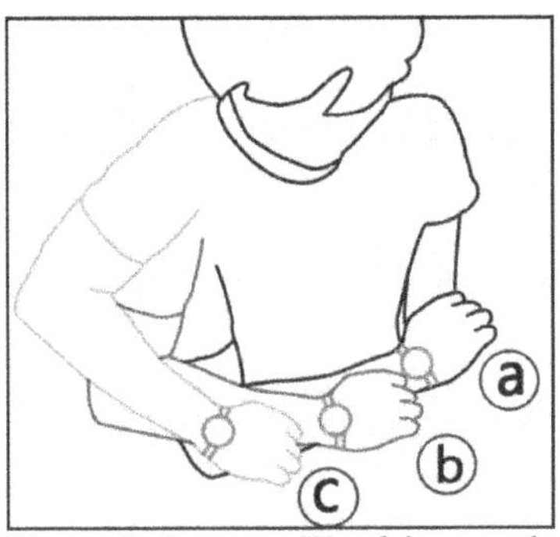

Figure 7. *Rotating Watch* is moved around the body to display scheduled events in a sequence corresponding to particular positions

Rotating Watch is a wristwatch mobile device that shows a person's daily schedule one event at a time. People move the watch around their body to go through their scheduled events (Figure 7). The watch measures its orientation relative to a person's body and maps it to the change of time. The present time is immediately in front (Figure 7a) while future times appear as the arm is rotated to the right (Figure 7b, c), and likewise past events are shown when rotating leftward. The resolution of interaction is decided by a pre-defined arm rotating range, while the time of the calendar is calculated by interpolating between the leftmost and the rightmost orientations.

Discussion. Both *Body Toolbar* and *Rotating Watch* track device-body relationships as input to control a running application. They both reduce the need for conventional on-screen widgets that compete for the limited screen real estate, as well as reducing navigation through hierarchical on-screen menus. Yet both realize this goal differently. *Body Toolbar* extends the canvas of a sketching program naturally to its nearest body parts – people's arms. In contrast, *Rotating Watch* casts the interaction to the arm's rotating range around the body. *Body Toolbar* lets people position the device to specify discrete tools on the body while *Rotating Watch* measures the device's continuous orientation with regards to the entire body. Both leverage a person's associative experience, but do so differently: *Body Toolbar* somewhat mimics a GUI toolbar as a pallet affixed to an arm, while *Rotating Watch* maps orientation to scheduled events in a way that conforms to people's notion of time units (i.e., the hours of a day sweeping from left to right). Further, people's spatial memory and kinesthetic sense also help them understand and make use of these two interaction techniques, e.g., recalling which arm part a tool is associated with (*Body Toolbar*), and guiding the arm to rotate to a specific event (*Rotating Watch*).

REVEALING RECURRING DESIGN THEMES

Having presented a series of prototype systems, we now reflected on the design of each of these prototoypes, as well as the literature, to identify three recurring themes that encapsulate how *Body-Centric Interactions with Mobile Devices* can be realized. First, proximal spaces on and around the body are identified and delimited to situate interactions. Second, within these spaces, the spatial relationship between the body and the device serves as 'raw input'. Third, given such 'raw input', various considerations should be incorporated when designing interactions of navigating and manipulating the device's on-screen content. We consider these three themes as important lessons learnt from our bottom-up prototyping practice. We now articulate them in more detail as well as their implications.

Situating Interactions in the Body's Proximal Spaces

We surveyed neuropsychology theories in order to deepen our understanding of people's perception of the space centered on their bodies. As a result, we found that within the personal space (defined by Hall [10]), most neuropsychologists suggest that our brain builds up multiple representations of space [12] centered on one's corporeal body [5,12] (see Figure 8):

- *Pericutaneous space*: the space immediately outside the body;
- *Peripersonal space*: the space surrounding the body and within easy reach of the hands;
- *Extrapersonal space*: the space far from the body and outside of one's reach.

This neuropsychological understanding of the body has contributed to HCI research as various spatial models, such as Benford and Fahlén's model for mediating interaction between persons and objects inhabiting a virtual space [3], or Shoemaker's model for leveraging the body to interacting with large wall displays [23]. With *Body-Centric Interaction with Mobile Devices*, we specifically focus on and refine two proximal spaces of the body.

- *On-body* space, corresponding to pericutaneous space, hosts interaction where people's actions specify particular body parts (e.g., in *Body Shortcuts*, referring to the wrist to trigger a calendar app).
- *Around-body* space, corresponding to peripersonal space, supports interaction where the people's actions specify a location at an arm-reachable distance from her entire body (e.g., in *Body Cobweb*, pointing to

Figure 8. The perceived proximal spaces on and around the body.

bookmarks and passing through different layers to place or retrieve web pages).

We also realize design possibilities exist in the space far from the body (corresponding to extrapersonal space) [23]. While this is beyond our scope – our focus is the space within immediate reach by the hand holding the device – we recognize extrapersonal space offers fertile grounds for interaction.

Tracking the Device-to-Body Spatial Relationships

The interaction techniques for all our prototypes – on or around the body – are driven by the spatial relationships between the device and the body. However, they differ in how they exploit these spatial relationships.

In the *on-body* proximal space, our prototypes' basic approach is to detect whether the mobile device is spatially located within certain range of a body part. For example, *Body Viewer*, *Body Shortcuts*, '*Whereables*', and *Body Toolbar* develop and track this spatial relationship between the device and the person's wrists, forearms, abdomen, knees, etc. To further explore the richness of interacting with body parts, we can categorize these spatial relationships into the following dimensions: *discrete/continuous position* and *orientation* (captured as the angle of the device relative to the normal of a particular body location). We can alternate these dimensions to expand the richness of interactions. For example, we can extend the original *Body Viewer* to incorporate the continuous changes of position between the device and a body part, thus enabling more interaction possibilities. For example, once an image is retrieved, moving the device up and down over that location zooms in/out that image. Similarly, we can consider *orientation* changes to drive the interaction. For instance, as an extension to *Body Toolbar*, a person can *rotate* the mobile device around the forearm to customize a parameter of the currently selected tool (e.g., adjusting the thickness of the brush).

In the *around-body* proximal space, our prototypes consider the position and orientation relative to the *entire body of a person*. For example, the *Body Cobweb* prototype exploits orientation of the device relative to the body's center to allow a person to navigate across the cobweb for viewing/placing bookmarks, while *Rotating Watch* uses changes in orientation of the device (attached to the arm but still relative to the center of the body) to cycle through calendar events. Similar to the on-body proximal space, other metrics can be extracted, such as device's *position* along a given orientation (i.e., distance to the body). *Body Cobweb* identifies two discrete distance values to demark the retrieving/placing operations of bookmarks. Further, monitoring *continuous* changes of distance allow more interaction possibilities, such as transitioning from an overview of all bookmarks, to gradually 'zooming in' to, and eventually focusing on a particular one.

In short, the device-body spatial relationship can be represented as the device's *position* and *orientation* – measured *discretely* or *continuously* – in relationship either to particular body parts, or to the entire body in the environment. Table 1 compiles examples where these two relationships between a device and the body are driving the types of interaction.

Table 1. Examples for applying discrete or continuous measurements of a device's on-/around-body position and orientation.

Spatial metric / Proximal space	Position		Orientation	
	Discrete	**Continuous**	**Discrete**	**Continuous**
On-body	Moving the device close to the shoulder to trigger an application (see *Body Shortcuts*)	Hovering the device over a forearm location to zoom in/out a retrieved image (see *Body Viewer*)	Rotating the device along the circumference of the forearm to switch between viewing either an image or its properties (see *Body Viewer*)	Rotating the device along the circumference of an arm location to adjust the thickness of the brush tool (see *Body Toolbar*)
Around-body	Placing the device at distinct distances from the body to perform different bookmark operations (see *Body Cobweb*)	Moving the device along a direction from the body to transition between overview and focus of bookmarks (see *Body Cobweb*)	Pointing the device at distinct orientations to place/retrieve a bookmark (see *Body Cobweb*)	Rotating the device around the body to shift the time line of a video (see *Rotating Watch*)

Considerations for Mapping the Interactions

Our prototypes and prior work illustrate a range of different kinds of mappings between the device-body relationship and actual interaction. A number of factors should be considered in deciding on these mappings. For instance, while designers may be limited by physical constraints, they can take advantage of people's kinesthetic sense, visual cues, and even associative experience to create mappings that will be easy to execute (kinesthetic sense), understand (visual cues), or remember (associative experience).

Physical constraints of people's bodies restrict the possible design options (cf. [17] where 'physical constraint' describes situations where some actions are impossible on a GUI). Consider *Body Toolbar*. While it is reasonable to place a tool shortcut on the arm, the interaction becomes cumbersome when placing it, say, under one's knees, where the hand can hardly reach (and where the device would be out of view). Similarly, when mapping the arm to a slider, it is more reasonable to place the control along the arm's length rather than its width as the latter provides very limited sliding range.

Kinesthetic sense is our awareness of body parts' relative positions [19,25], while *spatial memory* is our ability to memorably associate space with information [2]. Through both, it enables people to 'remember' where they have previously placed the digital content. In *Body Viewer*, people can associate an image with an arbitrary body part (say, the arm) as a short-term bookmark.

Visual cues of the body (also combined with kinesthetic sense) further strengthen the association between its space and information [26]. In the *Body Shortcuts* prototype, the visual cues of one's wrists, abdomen, and knees inform people of the digital shortcuts that are readily available from their bodies, while kinesthetic sense allows them to accurately locate these body parts in order to trigger the associated shortcuts. Further, clothes and items worn on the body also serve as visual cues.

Associative experience associates prior experiences, metaphors, uses of the body, and uses of space to the mapping process. One approach builds associations based on conventions [17] developed from the GUI paradigm, where people would use the interface on and around their body in a manner that is similar to using a GUI. For example, people can transfer their knowledge of using a digital calendar to using the *Rotating Watch* where the arm's rotating range maps to how one scrolls the day-view of a calendar application. Another approach creates meaningful, sometimes personalized, body-information association. For example, in '*Whereables*', one can switch the device from 'phone' to 'music player' by moving it from ears to the upper arm. The knowledge of how to make a phone call and the experience of wearing a music player during workout are the underlying motivation for customizing such association.

USING DESIGN THEMES TO REFLECT ON PAST WORK

We now discuss the three recurring themes in relationship to previous related work. For the purpose of illustration, we organize this discussion by the three proximal spaces centered on the body (pericutaneous, peripersonal, and extrapersonal [5]). In each category, we begin with a broader overview of interactions in this body's proximal space; we then narrow to a specific focus on *Body-Centric Interactions with Mobile Devices*. Our goal here is to use reflection to see how others have (perhaps tacitly) considered our design themes, as well as to further understand the interplays between interactions and the body.

Space on the Body

Ishii & Ullmer envisioned that the locus of computation would shift into two directions, one of which was to people's skins and bodies [13]. This vision pointed to the development of wearable computing where the boundaries blurred between everyday clothing and computing devices [18]. Sharing the same interest of the body, physiological interactions exploits the body's biological properties to enable direct interaction with the skin [11], muscle [21], or the entire body [4]. Shoemaker et al. appropriated a person's body as data storage and control surface [23]. Gustafson et al. appropriated the human palm as a phone interface [9].

On-Body Interaction with a Mobile Device

Our work differs from above, as we focus on positioning and orienting a *mobile device* to specific locations on the body, which are then mapped to various digital objects and the interaction with them. Several projects are related to this approach. In *Body Mnemonics* [1], people were asked to describe what kind of information and applications they would associate to particular body locations. A follow-up study generated associative maps of the information associated to the body. *BodySpace* applied this idea to a music player which is controlled by placing the device close to different parts of the body [24]. Similarly, *Mnemonic Body Shortcuts* enabled quick access to applications by moving the device from one's chest to a number of designated body parts [7]; *Snaplet* provided a wearable flexible E-Ink display with varied functions decided by how people hold or wear it [27].

As a whole, this work chose the space on a person's body as the input area. The interactions are primarily driven by the device's *discrete* on-body *positions* where people's associative experience of their body plays an important role in enabling the mapping between pointing to a body part and retrieving a piece of associated digital content.

When considering our identified design themes we find new design opportunities that could extend this prior work. For example, while most projects considered binary body-device relationships, one can add more expressive actions by considering continuous measurements of distance. Orientation, while mostly overlooked in previous work, can be also leveraged to enrich interaction design. To illustrate this, we will shortly showcase a prototype where a location on the arm carries an 'armband' of buttons, reachable by rotating the device and the arm relative to each other.

Space Around and Far From the Body

Interactions can also be extended outward from the body. Shoemaker realized people's ability to manipulate far-away UI objects using a shadow metaphor [22]. *SixthSense* demonstrated a type of gestural input by positioning and moving hands in front of the body [16]. *Imaginary Interface* let people create a virtual interface and point and draw on it in mid-air [8].

Around-Body Interaction with a Mobile Device

Our work differs from above, as we focus on the closer-to-body peripersonal space reachable by the device held in a person's hands. Two projects presented similar focus. Yee's *Peephole Displays* imagined an invisible information space in front of a person who used a handheld device to 'peep' into this space [28]. For example, one can move the device on a horizontal plane in front of her where the screen consistently reveals parts of a subway map. Li et al's *Virtual Shelves* developed a similar idea where they enabled people to trigger programmable shortcuts by spatially orienting their devices within a circular hemisphere in front of them [14]. The interaction carried the metaphor of a 'shelf' wherein one could organize and retrieve the many mobile apps with reduced visual attention.

These two projects both situated interactions *around* a person's body. *Peephole Displays* tracked the device's *continuous positions* and mapped it to the movement of a shifting window over the underlying information space. *Virtual Shelves* tracked the device's *orientation* based on a Spherical coordinate system and mapped it to a number of spatially distributed (*discrete*) shortcuts. Both systems made use of people's spatial memory to maintain a model of the virtual information space (*Peephole Displays*) or the shelves of content in their mind (*Virtual Shelves*).

By again considering our design themes, we can think of their design approaches as complementary. First, *discrete orientation* around the body is useful for sorting many digital objects and retrieving them with reduced visual attention. Once an object is retrieved, tracking the device's *continuous position* on a virtual canvas enables finer-grained manipulation with that object.

The two broad categories above – using space on *vs.* around the body, are not mutually exclusive. Neither are the use of both position and orientation for spatial tracking, and the various mapping considerations. Yet the prior work we are aware of typically considers only a few of the 'parameters' suggested by our themes. By articulating these 'parameters', we can now contemplate how interaction design could benefit from a more holistic view and a spectrum of interaction possibilities suggested by the design themes. As a first step to apply and reflect on these themes, below we showcase a design wherein a body-centric approach leads to new ways of using a mobile application.

DESIGNING THE BODY-CENTRIC BROWSER

While the earlier-mentioned prototypes have developed the fundamental concepts of *Body-Centric Interactions with Mobile Devices*, they only demonstrated parts of the underlying design themes. In this section, we illustrate how to apply these themes as a whole to the design and implementation of a mobile browser application. In particular, we show how a *body-centric* approach has led us to a novel design direction: in a mobile browser, one can manipulate multiple tabs, bookmarks and controls on and around her body.

Interaction Scenario

The following scenario (as well as our video) introduces the kinds of expressive interactions possible with our body-centric browser. Larry is browsing the web on his smart phone where he holds the device in the *viewing zone* – the space with a comfortable eye-reading distance in front of his upper body (Figure 9a, 10a). He has opened a number of tabs, each of which is maintained in a queue located in the *navigating zone* – a virtual circular tab bar around his lower body (Figure 9d). In Figure 10d, Larry is retrieving an earlier-opened tab by simply orienting the device along the navigating zone: the screen reveals the tabs consistent with the device's orientation. To bookmark the page on this tab, Larry goes to the *bookmark zone* – a virtual cylindrical canvas sitting behind the viewing zone – where one can pin or unpin a web page for future reference (Figure 9c). In Figure 10c, we see Larry positioning the device at his eye level, orienting it to the 1 o'clock direction and tapping to pin the page on the canvas. Later Larry wants to share this information with his friend Sally. He goes back to the bookmark zone, positions and orients the device to locate the web page and taps to select it from the canvas. He then orients the device to the *control zone* – an array of virtual buttons aligned on his right wrist (Figure 9b). Figure 10b shows Larry *positions* the device on the wrist, and *orients* them relative to each other (where in this case 'orientation' is done by moving the device around the wrist) to go through a number of buttons until he locates the 'email' option.

Design Details

Tabbed browsing – a useful feature in most desktop browsers – is more difficult to perform in the mobile setting. In designing this prototype, we apply a body-centric approach to enhance the manipulation and navigation of browser tabs. Specifically, our designed body-centric browser has three requirements: displaying and managing opened tabs, bookmarking web pages, and providing controls to work with them. We now describe how our three design themes brought *Body-Centric Interactions* to the implementation of these functional requirements.

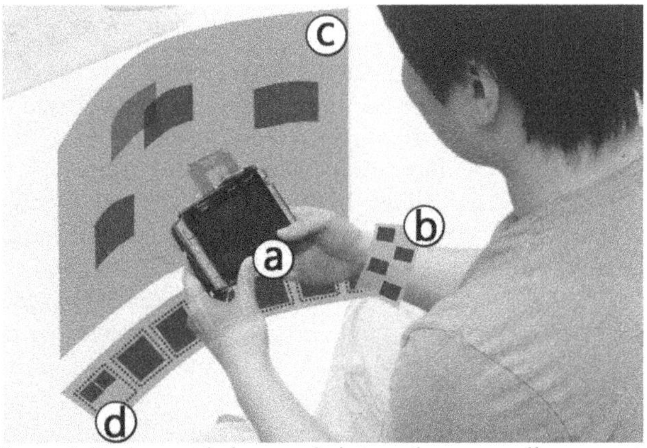

Figure 9. Body-centric browser's interactive zones allow users to (a) view, (b) control, (c) bookmark, and (d) retrieve browser tabs.

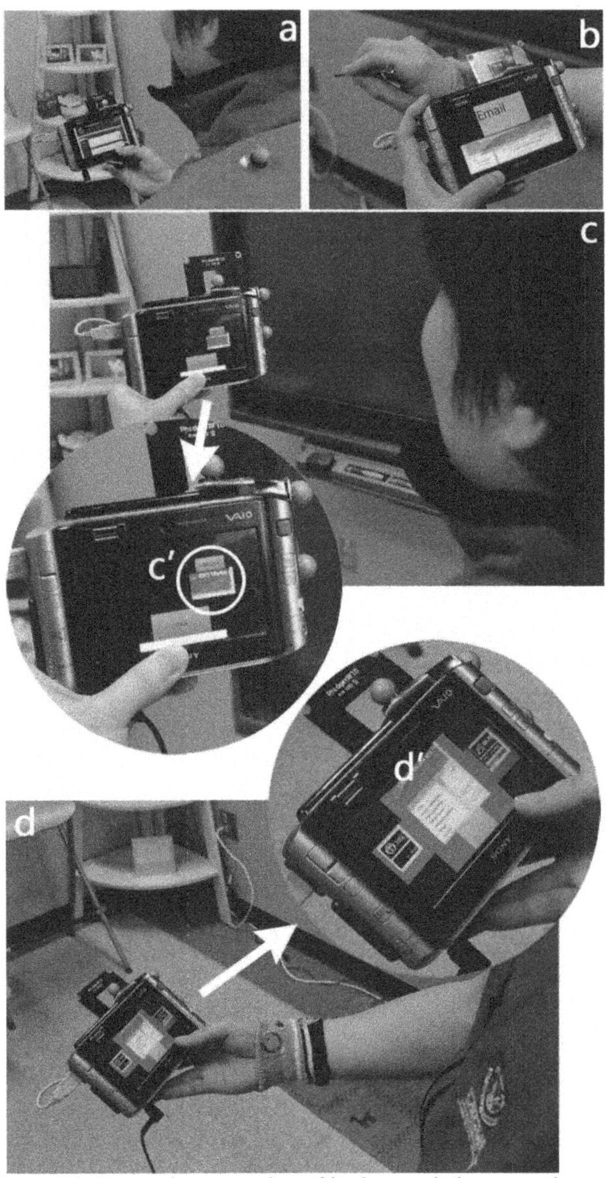

Figure 10. Interaction scenarios of body-centric browser: the user positions/orients the device on and around his body to navigate and manipulate browser tabs.

Displaying and managing opened tabs: the tab navigating zone. To fulfill this requirement, we learned from the browser's design of tab bar where it can be easily seen (usually just atop the web pages) and retrieved by a person. When thinking of potential design ideas, we found people normally hold and view the device in their field of view (i.e., a 'viewing zone' at an eye reading distance in front of their upper body). First, it made sense that our tab navigating zone should be close to this position while not interfering with it. Thus we placed the tabs in front of a person's waist, which is immediately below this 'viewing zone'. One could easily lower the device to reach and switch between these two zones (Figure 10a, d).

Essentially, this layout exploits people's associative experience of the 'tab bar' widget in desktop browsers. Furthermore, we situate this zone *around* the body, where the semi-circular queue of tabs is shaped to match the motor characteristics of the arm (*physical constraints*). Thus the *orientation* of the device maps to parts of the queue that are then displayed on the screen (Figure 10d'). This leverages ideas found in *Rotating Watch*, as the tabs are normally in time-order, and panning around them essentially navigates across time. A further design challenge is how to adapt the layout to an increasing number of tabs. Currently, we fix the number of (discrete) slots in the queue to seven. We allow for more than seven tabs by collecting older tabs within a hierarchy (e.g., as a collage or pile within a slot). Figure 9d shows the two oldest tabs squeezed in the leftmost slot so that the other six newer tabs can have their individual ones. However, this adds interface complexity. Still, as we will talk about shortly, making a modest number of tabs available for rapid access is still valuable.

Bookmarking tabbed web pages: the bookmark zone. We needed to allow people to 'casually' bookmark a tab by 'pinning' it somewhere for future reference. Similar to how we considered tab navigation (and leveraging the *Body Cobweb* design), we chose the space behind the viewing zone (i.e., further in front of one's upper body), as we wanted people to be able to easily bookmark a page immediately after viewing it, where they could freely pin, move, and unpin a web page anywhere within it. Our space is modeled as a cylindrical canvas, matching a cylindrical coordinate system. We measure the device's *continuous orientation* and height (y-axis *position*) to keep track of its location on the canvas (e.g., somewhat similar to [14]). Upon 'touching' the web page when in this bookmark zone, the web page displayed in the device (which perhaps had been previously selected from the tab navigating zone) can be pinned on it by a single tap. It is then anchored to that location and shown as a web page thumbnail (Figure 10c') during navigation. Tapping an existing bookmark (i.e., a web page thumbnail) selects it, after which one can pin it somewhere else or return to the viewing zone to browse the page. Because these bookmarks stay at the same location, interaction with this bookmark zone exploits people's spatial memory to recall the spatial mapping between the canvas and the bookmarks.

Providing control options with tabs: control zone. Our last requirement is to provide basic control options, such as those that operate on the currently web page (e.g., 'email', 'refresh', etc). These controls are used intermittently, so we decided to place them somewhat off the body's main viewing axis, just as a palette of tools in a GUI are typically at the edges of the window rather than its center. As a result (which also leverages ideas in *Body Toolbar*), we designed a band of 'control buttons' that is virtually worn on a person's wrist. To choose a control, a person *positions* the device on the wrist, and *orients* them relative to each other. The changing orientation leads to different control options seen on the screen. A single tap then selects and executes that option.

DESIGN ISSUES AND CHALLENGES

Body-Centric Interactions with Mobile Devices addresses the small screen real-estate problem with a variety of design strategies. Yet this interaction – in and of itself – also raises several issues and challenges, which we briefly outline below.

Scalability

The resolution of *Body-Centric Interaction* is limited by the number of digital items that need to be displayed. For example, in the body-centric browser, as the number of tabs increases, it will become more and more difficult to locate or retrieve a particular tab from the navigating zone. Of course, larger zones can fit more items, but the space for these zones is fairly limited. Consequently, the greatest benefit of *Body-Centric Interaction* comes from reserving that space for a modest number of important items and actions. Examples include quickly placing content for later retrieval, accessing frequently done actions, navigating to favored places, repeating recently done actions or viewing recently visited content (i.e. a history list), and a place to customize favored actions as shortcuts.

Search and Find

Another challenge occurs when a person cannot quite remember where something was placed – how do they search and find digital content on and around the body? Our current designs require them, for instance, to 'scan' the virtual canvas with the device in order to visually locate an item (e.g., a web page thumbnail in the bookmark zone). We can improve this by standard information visualization mechanisms – although we recognize that we are still limited by the small screen of the device. For example, consider an overview mechanism. When moving the device towards the bookmark zone (of the body-centric browser), the screen first shows an overview of the entire canvas, perhaps with items altered to best represent them at their small size (i.e., semantic zoom). As the device gets closer, it gradually zooms in the overview until finally focusing on a particular area.

Social and Cultural Concerns

Finally, *Body-Centric Interaction* should take into account social and cultural concerns. For example, can the body-centric browser be used in public? It might not be socially appropriate to wave the device around one's body (cf. [20]). It may look odd, and might even invade others' personal spaces (e.g., when used in a crowded elevator or a restaurant with cramped seats).

CONCLUSION AND FUTURE WORK

Body-Centric Interaction with Mobile Devices contributes a class of mobile input techniques, where the focus of interaction has shifted from the device's screen to include a person's body. Our goal is to mitigate the 'small screen' problem by enabling beyond-screen interactions mapped from one's actions of holding and moving the device on and around her body.

A bottom-up path of prototypes explored how such interactions can be realized, which in turn revealed several recurring themes reusable for new designs. We showcased one such new design in the body-centric browser prototype. By taking a body-centric approach, we create new experience of using a mobile browser where one can manipulate multiple tabs, bookmarks and controls on and around her body.

This work is just the beginning. As usual in any new interaction paradigm, much is left to do. While our prototypes and techniques seem intuitively appealing, their actual usefulness and usability in practice are yet to be determined: much iterative redesign is likely. Similarly, we need to see how effective our recurring design themes will influence actual designs in terms of inspiring novel mobile interactions. Finally, we need robust and reliable enabling technologies if we are to move beyond proof-of-concept prototypes to actual systems that people can use and enjoy in their daily lives.

ACKNOWLEDGMENTS

Funding was provided by AITF, NSERC, and SMART Technologies, ULC. We thank our colleagues in the Interactions Lab who provided invaluable feedback to our work.

REFERENCES

1. Ängeslevä, J., Oakley, I., Hughes, S., and O'Modhrain, S. Body Mnemonics. *Mobile HCI Conference*, ACM (2003), 15–22.
2. Baddeley, A.D. and Hitch, G.J. Developments in the concept of working memory. *Neuropsychology 8*, 4 (1994), 485–493.
3. Benford, S. and Fahlén, L. *A spatial model of interaction in large virtual environments*. Kluwer Academic, Dordrecht, 1993.
4. Cohn, G., Morris, D., Patel, S.N., and Tan, D.S. Your noise is my command. *Proceedings of the 2011 annual conference on Human factors in computing systems - CHI '11*, (2011), 791.

5. Elias, L.J. and Saucier, D.M. *Neuropsychology : clinical and experimental foundations*. Pearson/Allyn & Bacon, Boston, 2006.
6. Fitzmaurice, G.W. Situated information spaces and spatially aware palmtop computers. *Communications of the ACM 36*, 7 (1993), 39–49.
7. Guerreiro, T., Gamboa, R., and Jorge, J. Mnemonical Body Shortcuts for Interacting with Mobile Devices. In M. Sales Dias, S. Gibet, M.M. Wanderley and R. Bastos, eds., *Gesture-Based Human-Computer Interaction and Simulation*. Springer Berlin Heidelberg, Berlin, Heidelberg, 2009, 261–271.
8. Gustafson, S., Bierwirth, D., and Baudisch, P. Imaginary interfaces. *Proceedings of the 23nd annual ACM symposium on User interface software and technology - UIST '10*, (2010), 3–12.
9. Gustafson, S., Holz, C., and Baudisch, P. Imaginary Phone. *Symposium on User Interface Software and Technology*, (2011), 10–19.
10. Hall, E.T. Proxemics. *Current Anthropology 9, 2/3*, (1968), 83–108.
11. Harrison, C., Tan, D., and Morris, D. Skinput. *Proceedings of the 28th international conference on Human factors in computing systems - CHI '10*, (2010), 453–462.
12. Holmes, N.P. and Spence, C. The body schema and multisensory representation(s) of peripersonal space. *Cognitive Processing 5*, 2 (2004), 94–105.
13. Ishii, H. and Ullmer, B. Tangible bits. *Proceedings of the SIGCHI conference on Human factors in computing systems - CHI '97*, (1997), 234–241.
14. Li, F.C.Y., Dearman, D., and Truong, K.N. Virtual shelves. *Proceedings of the 22nd annual ACM symposium on User interface software and technology - UIST '09*, (2009), 125.
15. Marquardt, N., Diaz-Marino, R., Boring, S., and Greenberg, S. The proximity toolkit. *Proceedings of the 24th annual ACM symposium on User interface software and technology - UIST '11*, ACM Press (2011), 315.
16. Mistry, P. and Maes, P. SixthSense. *ACM SIGGRAPH ASIA 2009 Sketches on - SIGGRAPH ASIA '09*, (2009), 1.
17. Norman, D.A. Affordance, conventions, and design. *interactions 6*, 3 (1999), 38–43.
18. Post, E.R. and Orth, M. Smart fabric, or "wearable clothing."*Digest of Papers. First International Symposium on Wearable Computers*, (1997), 167–168.
19. Proske, U. and Gandevia, S.C. The kinaesthetic senses. *The Journal of Physiology 587*, 17 (2009), 4139–4146.
20. Rico, J. and Brewster, S. Usable gestures for mobile interfaces. ACM Press (2010), 887.
21. Saponas, T.S., Tan, D.S., Morris, D., Balakrishnan, R., Turner, J., and Landay, J.A. Enabling always-available input with muscle-computer interfaces. ACM Press (2009), 167.
22. Shoemaker, G., Tang, A., and Booth, K.S. Shadow reaching. *Proceedings of the 20th annual ACM symposium on User interface software and technology - UIST '07*, (2007), 53.
23. Shoemaker, G., Tsukitani, T., Kitamura, Y., and Booth, K.S. Body-centric interaction techniques for very large wall displays. *Proceedings of the 6th Nordic Conference on Human-Computer Interaction Extending Boundaries - NordiCHI '10*, (2010), 463.
24. Strachan, S., Murray-Smith, R., and O'Modhrain, S. BodySpace. *CHI '07 extended abstracts on Human factors in computing systems - CHI '07*, (2007), 2001.
25. Tan, D.S., Pausch, R., Stefanucci, J.K., and Proffitt, D.R. Kinesthetic cues aid spatial memory. *CHI '02 extended abstracts on Human factors in computing systems - CHI '02*, (2002), 806.
26. Tan, D.S., Stefanucci, J.K., Proffitt, D.R., and Pausch, R. The Infocockpit. *Proceedings of the 2001 workshop on Percetive user interfaces - PUI '01*, (2001), 1.
27. Tarun, A.P., Lahey, B., Girouard, A., Burleson, W., and Vertegaal, R. Snaplet. *Proceedings of the 2011 annual conference extended abstracts on Human factors in computing systems - CHI EA '11*, (2011), 329.
28. Yee, K.-P. Peephole displays. *Proceedings of the conference on Human factors in computing systems - CHI '03*, (2003), 1.

Tilt Displays: Designing Display Surfaces with Multi-axis Tilting and Actuation

Jason Alexander
School of Computing and Communications
Lancaster University, UK
j.alexander@lancaster.ac.uk

Andrés Lucero
Nokia Research Center
Tampere, Finland
andres.lucero@nokia.com

Sriram Subramanian
Department of Computer Science
University of Bristol, UK
sriram@cs.bris.ac.uk

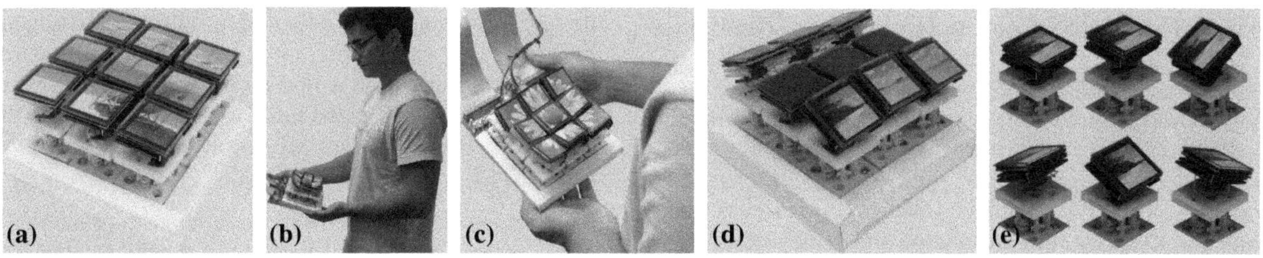

Figure 1. Tilt Displays. (a) Flat screen configuration; (b, c) User holding 12cm×12cm portable prototype; (d) Collaboration Mode; (e) Individual modules in (clockwise from top left) down, up, tilt left, tilt right, tilt forwards and tilt backwards configurations.

ABSTRACT

We present a new type of actuatable display, called Tilt Displays, that provide visual feedback combined with multi-axis tilting and vertical actuation. Their ability to physically mutate provides users with an additional information channel that facilitates a range of new applications including collaboration and tangible entertainment while enhancing familiar applications such as terrain modelling by allowing 3D scenes to be rendered in a physical-3D manner. Through a mobile 3×3 custom built prototype, we examine the design space around Tilt Displays, categorise output modalities and conduct two user studies. The first, an exploratory study examines users' initial impressions of Tilt Displays and probes potential interactions and uses. The second takes a quantitative approach to understand interaction possibilities with such displays, resulting in the production of two user-defined gesture sets: one for manipulating the surface of the Tilt Display, the second for conducting everyday interactions.

Author Keywords

Tilt Displays; actuated displays; physical actuation; non-planar surface interaction.

ACM Classification Keywords

H.5.2 **[Information interfaces and presentation]:** User Interfaces. - Graphical user interfaces.

INTRODUCTION

Innovations in sensors and actuators allow us to explore the design of mobile devices that extend beyond the static flat display surfaces with which we are currently familiar. The next generation mobile devices will instead include actuatable screens that physically mutate themselves to better represent their on-screen content.

Imagine for example, a mobile device that is visually displaying a street map and whose screen has physically mutated to show the hilly terrain and buildings. The device both visually and physically represents the 3D scene. This physical mutation facilitates effective consumption of multi-dimensional data by moving one information layer to another modality. As a step towards realising such a scenario, this paper builds on previous work on actuated surfaces [11, 20] and dynamic displays [9] by presenting Tilt Displays: a new form of display surface whose components not only actuate but also physically tilt.

A Tilt Display (Figure 1) is a display surface about half-the size of a standard tablet (e.g. an iPad). It consists of a collection of individual display components each of which can tilt along one or more axes and move vertically up and down (Figure 1e). This ability to tilt along multiple axes distinguishes them from previous actuatable displays.

Such screen versatility opens a range of opportunities for providing an additional integrated information channel to the user. These opportunities include: collaboration (Figure 1d), terrain modeling (Figure 3a and Figure 3b), 3D video that is beyond auto-stereoscopic 3D and tangible gaming. We can imagine many scenarios that would benefit from the physicality afforded by Tilt Displays; however, we first need to establish whether users can relate to the new experiences and advantages of using such a device. This type of display also raises a number of unique interaction issues, such as the difficulties around applying commonly used multi-touch input techniques.

The primary goal of this paper is to explore the design space around Tilt Displays to understand users' initial impressions and to examine how users may interact with these surfaces. We are especially interested in the use of these displays in mobile contexts, as this domain presents a range of opportunities for exploitation. To do this, we start with a more detailed description of Tilt Displays and situate them within existing literature. We describe our prototype display giving details of our design rationale, identifying factors that influence the design of Tilt Displays and outline example scenarios where they would be beneficial. We then describe our first exploratory user study that gathered initial user impressions of the concept, and possibilities for interaction. A second user study then investigates interactions with Tilt Displays. We finally discuss this concept and its future for construction and deployment.

The contributions of this paper are: 1) The design and implementation of a Tilt Display; 2) A taxonomy of Tilt Display output modalities, with example applications; 3) An exploratory user study probing initial user reactions to applications and interaction possibilities; 4) A study examining user perceptions of interactions with such a display resulting in two user-defined gestures sets for interaction: one for manipulating the display's tilt angle, the second for performing low-level tasks with such a display.

RELATED WORK

Tilt Displays draw their inspiration from actuatable displays, shape displays and deformable displays. They are also an instantiation of a multi-display environment. We summarise previous work in these areas in this section.

Actuatable Displays

Actuatable or 'shape' displays vertically move display surface components. Lumen [20, 21] is a low resolution display where each pixel has a colour value and can vertically actuate. Projection-based systems are used to increase the resolution of the display. Feelex [11] used an actuator array, covered with a flexible screen, to present a physically reconfigurable surface that was augmented with graphics. Force sensors on each actuation rod conveyed presses to the system. Leithinger and Ishii's Relief display [14] used 120 motorised pins (electric slide potentiometers from audio mixing boards), allowing users to push and pull individual rods. A Lycra cover was added to provide a smooth surface when modelling terrain. Top projection provided visual cues. Blackshaw et al. [5] and Leithinger et al. [15] continue this work by conceptually examining the design-space for input control with shape-changing displays, describing touch input, external controller input and mid-air gestural control. Our studies examine user perception of such input methodologies for Tilt Displays.

Implementing Actuation

Researchers have employed a variety of tactics to create vertically actuating visual displays. Pneumatic actuation employs a gas, usually air, to flood or evacuate chambers. Harrison and Hudson [9] used a chamber-based button system to make shapes protrude, lie flat or sink into the display. A latex cover is used to seal over pre-defined cutouts and rear projection provides the display, with diffused illumination used to detect touches and pressure-sensing used for continuously variable parameters.

Mechanical and electromechanical systems actuate by moving rods using either solenoid or motor-based actuation. Pin arrays consist of small cylinders (a few millimetres in diameter) that protrude a few millimetres out of a surface. Actuating these 'pin' sized tubes creates patterns the finger can detect. Pin arrays are most commonly actuated using solenoids [8] or servo motors [25].

Shape Memory Alloys (SMA) are composite materials that maintain their shape until heated. At a critical temperature the alloy flexes in a particular direction. This 'on-demand' flexing is used in devices such as Surflex [6], a foam sheet with embedded SMAs that bends according to the user's input, and Sprout I/O [7] that programmatically represents patterns in a similar manner to when a foot leaves an imprint on carpet. Lumen [20, 21] uses SMA actuation to raise and lower a series of wave guides to provide a height and colour controlled display. SMAs are also being employed in pin-rod actuators to provide increased range of motion and reduced pin intervals [19].

Deformable Displays – Flexing, Bending and Stiffening

An alternative to vertical actuation is to manipulate the properties of a surface to emulate the feel of virtual objects. The viscosity of fluids contained in pouches can be altered by changing the surrounding magnetic field. Particles suspended in the fluid form chains along the flux lines altering the fluid's viscosity. Jansen [12] used magneto-rheological fluid to change the viscosity of their multi-touch display, while Taylor et al. [23] employed electro-rheological fluid under a rubber skin to stiffen a surface.

Adjusting the tension bias of a flexible sheet allows the user to feel the different 'hardness' of virtual objects proportional to the sheet's tension [24]. Placing an LCD below a tension sheet allows the haptic and visual channels to be combined in the same space. Usually, the deformation in these environments cannot be visually inspected.

Flexible displays provide an opportunity for presenting the visual data in an actuatable display. Unfortunately, while flexible displays are capable of bending, they do not stretch. This prevents their use as the display surface on top of vertical actuators as upwards pressure will simply result in a curved surface, rather than one that can display, for example, map relief. However, bend gestures using a flexible display offers insights into alternative methods of input appropriate to Tilt Displays. Schwesig et al's Gummi

[22] suggested a range of non-WIMP interactions using bending, while Lahey et al. [13] produced a bend gesture set for a display tied at two corners.

Multi-Display Environments (MDEs)

Tilt Displays are a type of MDE, with each component a separate display. The MDE literature describes solutions to the 'displayless space' problem: stitching is commonly employed in desktop computing (where the cursor 'jumps' from one monitor to the next), other proposed techniques include mouse ether [3], where the pointer must move the equivalent physical distance between two displays, cursor warping [4] and display selection using head tracking [1]. Studies also show that tilting a secondary display can aid in minimizing the effects of visual separation [27].

Desktop-centric MDEs are generally too cumbersome for spontaneous physical reconfiguration. However, providing the user with the flexibility of reconfiguration has proven beneficial. Siftables [18] allow the user to rearrange small screens into user-defined configurations. They allow direct interaction with digital media, with piling and gathering gestures having a direct connection to the Siftable's content. Although we envisage Tilt Displays to always be attached, their ability to flexibly reconfigure themselves will allow a range of contexts of use.

TILT DISPLAYS

What are Tilt Displays?

Tilt Displays are a new class of physically mutatable visual feedback devices whose display components support multi-axis tilting and vertical actuation. The distinguishing feature of Tilt Displays over previous actuatable systems is their ability to tilt visual components along multiple axes, as illustrated in Figure 1e.

Design Decisions

We made a series of conscious design decisions during development of our prototype Tilt Display. These are described below.

Tilt Component Surface Profile: The surface profile of the actuated components, especially if they are larger than a few millimeters, will influence the raised or lowered shapes that can be conveyed when multiple components are actuated simultaneously. These components may either be identical (e.g. uniform triangles) or non-identical (e.g. circles with space-filling diamonds). Selection of the size and shape will be intertwined with the envisioned applications and the choice of display method. We believe the square 34mm×34mm surface profile of our displays provides an ideal platform for evaluation (sufficiently sized components to expose issues such as the size of bezels and gaps) while supporting our chosen display method (see below).

Display Method: There were three feasible choices for producing the visual output for our Tilt Display: top projection, rear projection and embedded displays. Single source top projection suffers from shadowing issues during user interaction, which can be resolved using multiple projectors [2], although this inhibits use in mobile contexts, and increases the system cost and complexity.

Rear projection does not suffer from shadowing, however, incorporating projection within actuation components is challenging, if mechanical mechanisms are employed. Both top and rear projection systems require pre-processing to reduce distortion when projected onto non-planar surfaces.

We chose to use embedded screens to prevent the issues associated with projection. We selected small (34 mm square) OLED screens—these were the smallest, readily available self-contained commercial display. The additional complexity of actuating a display surface (instead of a projection surface) was further outweighed by the constant non-deforming visual resolution and related experience.

Method of Tilt and Actuation: Having settled on the display method, we examined a number of actuation possibilities, as discussed in the related work section. For simplicity and cost, our prototype uses small actuators, typically used in model aeroplanes—these were inexpensive, robust and easy to control. This model of actuator provides 9.1 mm of stroke—sufficient to differentiate between raised and lowered components and provide approximately 30° of tilt along the x- and y- axes.

Display Surface: When the individual OLED displays tilt, the edges of adjacent screens move apart, exposing the edges of the screens and creating a variable sized gap between the displays (see Figure 1d and Figure 3c). One option is to cover the displays with a stretchable material (such as lycra) to remove the gaps and smooth the surface between displays. We chose not to add such a covering so that we could explore user perceptions and any required coping strategies with variable width gaps in the display.

Input: Tilt Displays, like their mobile device counterparts, can support external key/button input, touchscreen input/gestures and also potentially above-device gestures [15]. Touch/pressure input can be achieved by adding touch-overlays onto the display panels; physical manipulation of the displays can occur by replacing the servo motors with back-drivable models.

Our prototype Tilt Display does not explicitly support input. The literature reports several *possible* methods of input, but does not report user perception of these methods. To solicit uninhibited user suggestions (and to avoid any bias from the implementation), we chose against implementing all possible forms of input.

Prototype Construction

To validate the feasibility of Tilt Displays, to examine users' perceptions and understand how people might interact with such a device, we implemented an initial prototype system. The system is in between the size of a typical mobile-device and a tablet, having a footprint of 120×120 mm. It is light enough to be picked up and held in a similar manner to a mobile phone (see Figures 1b and 1c). The prototype display is illustrated in Figure 1.

Our prototype consists of a 3x3 array of 34mmx34mm OLED screens (4D Systems µOLED-128-G1), with resolution 128×128px, each mounted on three actuators (Spektrum AS2000L) to provide both vertical actuation and tilting along the x- and y-axes (Figure 1e). A single module's construction is illustrated in Figure 2. The actuators have a stroke of 9.1mm. Each module is based around a small, interlocking 3D-printed block. Each of the displays and actuators are individually addressable and independently configurable.

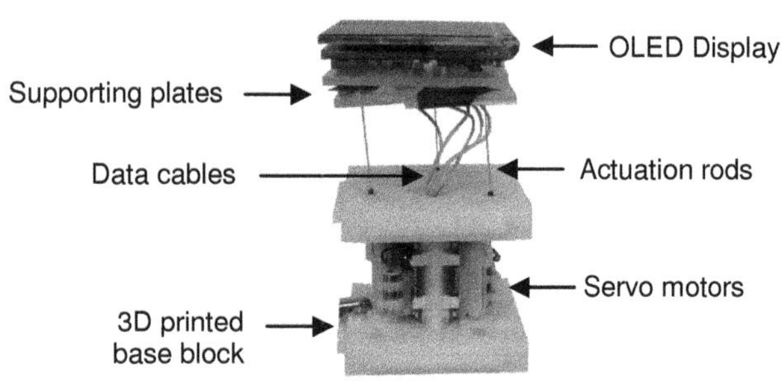

Figure 2: Prototype construction

The prototype Tilt Display is controlled using an XMOS XC-1A microcontroller (www.xmos.com/xc1a), with commands issued via serial control from a PC. The microcontroller continually sends PWM signals with an appropriate duty cycle to each of the 27 actuators. By varying the PWM duty cycle at different rates, the actuators can also move at different speeds, up to a maximum of 20mm/sec. The microcontroller also maintains the appropriate display by instructing each OLED to show images or videos from their on-board micro-SD card.

		Visual display	
		Static	*Dynamic*
Physical movement	*Static*	3D model	3D fixed mode
	Dynamic	3D movement	3D video

Table 1: Tilt Display output modalities

Output Modalities

Tilt displays offer four primary modalities of use, which we classify based on the coupling between the visual display and physical movement. This classification is shown in Table 1 and described, with example applications below.

3D Modelling: Static Physical State/Static Visual State
Once configured, the physical and visual states remain constant. 3D modelling allows physical three-dimensional data to be represented in a physical 3D manner.

3D Terrain modelling provides users with an additional information channel that is difficult to represent using a traditional 2D display. Contour lines are often excluded from electronic street maps to aid clarity and because users may not have sufficient technical understanding to correctly interpret their meaning. Tilt Displays are advantageous over vertical actuation in this scenario as they can easily and more accurately represent sloped surfaces, such as hills and mountains (Figure 3a and Figure 3b). Users can absorb this additional information by passing their hand over the Tilt Display or by visibly observing the peaks and troughs in the terrain. This type of route-finding is particularly useful for wheel-chair users, cyclists, and the elderly who wish to choose an appropriate route based on surface gradient.

Partially sighted persons can also make use of terrain modelling. For example, by illustrating steps and slopes, the physical output can help the user to find a suitable route. Tilt displays provide a mechanism for physically representing a scaled version of the environment, avoiding the need for users to translate crude tactile feedback from vibration motors into visualisations of the environment.

Figure 3: (a, b) Example of terrain modeling, with mountains raised around a lake (c) Four-way colllaboration

3D Fixed Mode: Static Physical State/Dynamic Visual State
This modality pre-sets the physical configuration of the display and then allows user interaction with the visual content. This is useful in collaborative situations.

In mobile contexts, users are often seen rotating or handing their mobile device to a peer to share on-screen content, such as photos or videos. Tilt Displays facilitate sharing by tilting a portion of the screen towards a second viewer (see Figure 1d). A primary user with a 'private' view could then only push selected images or content to the remainder of the display. Four people can also be accommodated by appropriate screen tilting (Figure 3c).

3D Movement: Dynamic Physical State/Static Visual State
Physical movement can play an important role in conveying information. For example, a 2D image of a flower can 'come to life' by a slowly animating the raising of the petals (Figure 1). A sensation of gradient can be created using the same effect: a photograph taken at street level looking up a hill can be animated with slowly tilting forward screens to give the impression of an up-hill slope.

This same physical movement also provides the opportunity to explore a new gaming dimension—that of tangible entertainment in mobile contexts. Tilt Displays would allow users to add simple tangible objects, such as a small foam ball, onto their display and then with careful manipulation of the actuation components the tangible objects will roll or slide across tilted screens.

3D Video: Dynamic Physical State/Dynamic Visual State

3D video couples a continually changing physical movement with dynamic on-screen visuals. The most striking example of this modality is a video stream that incorporates 3D height information. Gathering depth information is becoming more common with 3D cinematography and cheaply available depth cameras. One example is a low level fly-over of a route on a map. As the visual content passes by hills or buildings the physical surface protrudes from the display to show the height of passing objects (see accompanying video figure).

Support of this modality is also crucial for future interactive applications: if a map were panned or zoomed the user will see both the visual and physical representations change.

Concept and Prototype Evaluation

After the Tilt Displays' construction, we informally demonstrated the device to many groups of people, each time receiving comments and suggestions on possible applications and ideas for improvement. For the evolution of Tilt Displays we believe it is important to capture these first impressions and explore users' first reactions using each of the four output modalities described in the previous section. To do this we carried out a user study on initial impressions and applications of Tilt Displays.

EXPLORATORY STUDY 1: IMPRESSIONS AND APPLICATIONS

Following a user-centered design approach, we conducted a study to gather initial impressions and to explore potential uses of Tilt Displays. Participants experienced a range of applications in each of the device's output modalities. We wanted to assess the effect of independently tilting and actuating the screens, investigate how people would interact with Tilt Displays and how they perceived the variable gaps in between the screens, both visually and for interaction.

Participants

We recruited 11 participants who varied in gender (10 male, 1 female), age (25 to 39), and background (8 technical, 3 non-technical). Almost half of these participants (5/11) had previously participated in evaluations of the MindMap [17] or the *pass-them-around* [16] prototypes and had therefore witnessed and interacted with a system that allows people to tile displays together. This mixture of participants ensured we had feedback from early and late technology adopters and from people who had and had not previously encountered new and novel forms of displays.

Method

The study consisted of three parts: an introduction, the prototype's demonstration and a semi-structured interview. We first gathered the participants' background information and explained the primary goal of the study. We then demonstrated a range of applications with the Tilt Display (see Table 2). Finally, we conducted semi-structured interviews with the participants where we asked them a series of open-ended questions and encouraged open discussion regarding both the positive and negative aspects of the prototype display.

1. Flat screen, beach image (Figure 1a) *(3D Model)*
2. Collaboration for 2, 4 and 8 people (Figure 1d, 3c) *(3D Fixed Mode)*
3. Vertical actuation, terrain and buttons *(3D Fixed Mode)*
4. Map terrain (Figure 3a, b) *(3D Model)*
5. Uphill and downhill visualization *(3D Movement)*
6. Flower petals raising ('coming to life') (Figure 1b,c) *(3D Movement)*
7. Terrain flyover *(3D Video)*

Table 2: Tilt Display applications demonstrated

The session was conducted in an open meeting room, with the prototype set on a tall table in the middle of an open space. All 11 participants saw the demonstration at the same time. Each application was shown twice with all participants having the opportunity to experience the demonstration from the 'front on' position. The semi-structured interview was video-recorded. Each participant received a movie ticket to compensate them for their time.

RESULTS

We adapted the standard affinity diagramming method [10] to analyse the data from the semi-structured interviews. We grouped together participants' main reactions to the Tilt Display into four categories. We interleave our discussion with participants' comments (italicised).

Tilt Displays as a New Form of 3D

In general, participants were very positive about the Tilt Display concept. Their first impression was to associate Tilt Displays to a new method of presenting and consuming 3D content: *"For me it's like watching a 3D movie without wearing 3D glasses"* [P7]. Participants immediately valued the advantages of Tilt Displays over other 3D content, *"This visual presentation is very important. (...) When you wear a 3D glass, it takes some time for your brain to (...) get a real feeling. But if you have this kind of display then it's very good"* [P2]. Participants envisioned wide application of the technology, for example in a travel agent: *"You don't need to go to Hawaii, just experience it"* [P8].

Participants immediately linked the Tilt Display to other forms of 3D displays, such as those used in cinemas. Participants liked and noted the reduction in cognitive load that the physical 3D representations required to interpret compared to glasses-based 3D displays. These initial comments confirmed our impressions that Tilt Displays are a viable method for physically presenting 3D information.

Movement Conveys Additional Information

The movement of display components played an important role in conveying an additional information layer. In some scenarios, observing the physical movement conveyed more information that the final rendered position. With reference to the dynamic movement of a flower 'coming to life', one participant said: *"For me, the movement itself conveys more information. (...) The movement itself is compelling for how our vision system works in our minds"* [P9].

For this same reason, participants were positive about the use of vertical actuation to display high priority positions of interest. For example, clickable areas of a map were highlighted by raised tiles. Participants also appreciated and understood the use of movement to inform navigation. One demonstration showed the view of a street looking uphill. Slowly tilting the displays towards the user had the immediate effect of conveying the street's gradient: *"It's a good way to direct yourself and where to go, what are the directions and things like that"* [P4].

Orienting Displays for Collaboration

Participants were positive about the usefulness of the collaboration mode and could easily foresee using it to share content on their device. They discussed several aspects of Tilt Displays that would impact their success for collaboration: size, distance, number of displays and the orientation. At the start of the conversation, participants reflected on the screen size required for effective collaboration, reaching a consensus that a tablet-sized device would be most appropriate: *"I think it's only good on tablets or maybe big screens, because if we have a smartphone with a small screen it's not suitable for [that]. At least 7 or 10-inch screens"* [P1], *"Using tablets for presentation while having 8 people there, that would be really good. It would be fantastic to do that."* [P11]

By the end of the session, participants had also mentioned the distance from the display and the number of Tilt components as important factors that would influence whether Tilt Displays would be suitable for collaboration: *"[The experience]would depend on how far you are looking from"* [P10], *"It depends on the application, but the greater the number of screens, the greater the experience"* [P7].

Participants also concluded that, regardless of the size of the Tilt Display (mobile phone or tablet), they would place the device on a horizontal surface to allow users to sit or stand around. In this way, individual displays (or groups of displays) can be tilted towards different locations.

Three Methods of Interaction with Tilt Displays

The physically dynamic nature of Tilt Displays means that traditional touch-screen interactions will not always be practical, such as when the display is in a convex configuration. Throughout the study we asked participants to consider how they would interact with such a device. Three types of interaction emerged: touch gestures, direct manipulation of the screens and gestures above the display.

Almost all the participants mentioned some kind of touch input, either by performing touch gestures on the screen (e.g. swipe) or by physically pushing the screens down. One participant described the physicality of interaction: *"(I would interact) by tilting the displays, by pushing with different strengths and really doing the tilt as it is now, but with my hands"* [P9].

Participants also discussed the trade-off between performing gestures across all screens, and using a single screen that would control all other screens: *"A swipe could go through several screens (...) sometimes you might just use one screen for swiping, but if you want to exchange pictures then you can do reverse swipes across different screens."* [P9]

The varying size bezels gaps between the screens also influenced opinions on interaction. Some participants foresaw the bezels hindering interaction: *"It's impossible, I think (to swipe uphill or downhill with the gaps)"* [P1]. Other participants saw the bezels as an opportunity for interaction—covering the gaps with a stretchable material (e.g. lycra) would create visual continuity between the screens and also create an interaction surface: *"The stretchable material could also be touch sensitive. For the visuals, the material would smooth the gaps, but it could (...) also become part of the interaction."* [P9]

We believe that the bezels play an important role in Tilt Displays. Participants did not mention the bezels as hindering their perception of the visual display. But, it appears that these gaps play an important role in the perception of movement and thus how we extract the additional (3D) information from Tilt Displays. Before filling the gaps with Lycra for smoother interaction, consideration should be given to the role these gaps play in the perception of movement and direction.

Summary

This user study found participants were positive about Tilt Displays and were enthusiastic about their practical applications. One aspect that induced much discussion was that of (input) interaction. The issue of 'how best to interact' was present from the design stages of our prototype Tilt Display. To examine this issue further we conducted a second user study to explore user perceptions on methods of interaction.

INTERACTING WITH TILT DISPLAYS

There are two fundamental interaction issues that require evaluation before such displays could be deployed in real-world contexts. First, how would users manually manipulate the tilt of actuation components and second, how would users perform commonly required actions, such as panning and zooming on non-flat surfaces. These two issues do not arise in static, flat displays.

We wished to derive user impressions of how such interactions should take place on these types of devices. To do this, we chose a methodology similar to Wobbrock et al. [26] by providing users with a series of *initial* and *end* states and asking them to provide appropriate gestures to achieve the required transformations. This allowed participants to conduct their own interactions, without the restrictions of technical limitations, that they felt appropriate to achieve the goal. To summarise participants' input we derive two user-defined gesture sets. Our full methodology is outlined below.

Participants

We recruited 12 participants (four female), with a mean age 28.3 years. Ten had previous experience with touch-screen based gestures and ten had previous experience with mid-air gestures (e.g., those captured by an XBox Kinect).

Experimental Design and Methodology

We used the same methodology (and participants) to investigate both tilt manipulation and the interaction with tilted surfaces. All participants completed the tilt manipulation tasks first.

We used a series of cardboard mock-ups to allow users to pick-up, feel, push, pull and manipulate in any manner to avoid any limitations or preconceptions that accompanied our prototype. For each task, participants were first shown, using the cardboard mock-ups, the initial state of the screen, followed by the final state of the screen. They were then asked to hold a mock-up device in one hand and perform a single-handed gesture with their other hand. This was to simulate what would be possible in a mobile device context. Users were free to change the hand they held the device with during the study.

For each task we asked participants to perform a contact gesture and then a mid-air gesture. Contact gestures required one or more fingers to be in contact with any part of the device—either on or around any part of the screen. These two classes of gestures align with those expressed in user study one, with contact gestures encompassing both on-screen and screen manipulation gestures.

Participants were asked to consider their gestures independently from other tasks they had performed (i.e. participants did not have to concern themselves with gesture uniqueness). Users were also encouraged to not think about any technical limitations of implementing or detecting their actions. Finally, before moving to the next task, we asked participants to pick which of the two gestures they preferred. All sessions were video recorded.

We used two sets of initial and end states—one set for the tilt manipulations, the other for the tasks that required interaction with a tiltable surface. The following two sections describe these task sets.

#	Start	End	#	Start	End
1.	Flat	Tilt right	6.	Tilted right	Flat
2.	Flat	Tilt left	7.	Tilted left	Flat
3.	Flat	Tilt forward	8.	Tilted forward	Flat
4.	Flat	Tilt backward	9.	Tilted backward	Flat
5.	Flat	Raise	10.	Raised	Flat

Table 3: Physical state change tasks

Tilt Manipulation

This set of tasks required the participants to perform gestures to take the display from one physical state to another (e.g. for configuring a collaborative mode). These tasks assume that an appropriate region of the screen is already selected (selection is investigated in the following set of tasks). The state changes tested are shown in Table 3.

Interaction with Tiltable Surfaces

We also wished to investigate how users might perform common low-level interactions with tilted surfaces. We selected panning, scaling, rotating and area selection as gestures that may require re-designing on non-planar surfaces. We then provided participants with a series of non-flat screen configurations and asked them to perform an appropriate gesture to achieve each of the four required tasks. The screen configurations are described in Table 4.

#	Description	#	Description
1.	Flat screen	6.	Concave
2.	Tilt left	7.	Convex
3.	Tilt right	8.	Vertically raised section
4.	Tilt forward	9.	Vertically lowered section
5.	Tilt backward	10.	Steps

Table 4: Surface configurations for interaction tasks

Results

We analysed of our results by first calculating the between participant agreement of the gesture sets and from that extracting a user-defined gesture set for *tilt manipulations* and *interactions*. We then summarise the participants' subjective preferences.

Tilt Manipulations

Each participant provided a contact and a mid-air gesture for the 10 tilt manipulations, providing a total of 120 observed gestures (12 users × 10 manipulations). Based on the participants' interactions, we extracted a user-defined gesture set for the 10 manipulation tasks in Table 3. This set is depicted in Figure 4. All interactions are mid-air gestures except for tilting the screen backwards, where users preferred an on-screen swipe.

The selected interactions are those that had the greatest agreement between participants for that task—high agreement values indicate many participants selected the same gesture for a task, low agreement indicates a large diversity in the selected interactions. The agreement value, A, is calculated as [26]:

$$A = \frac{\sum_{t \in T} \sum_{P_i \subseteq P_t} \left(\frac{|P_i|}{|P_t|} \right)^2}{|T|}$$

Where t is a task in the set of all tasks, T, P_t is the set of all proposed interactions for task t, P_i is a subset of identical interactions from P_t. An agreement value of 1 indicates complete agreement between all participants.

Figure 5 shows the agreement values between the gestures that participants chose for each task. Many of the mid-air gestures showed strong agreement, while contact-based gestures showed greater diversity.

The gestures that emerged for several of the tasks were identical. For example, a mid-air downward push was the accepted gesture for lowering a raised screen, flattening the screen from a forward tilt and flattening the screen from a backward tilt. Because all of these tasks require the screen to end in a flat state, there is no conflict or ambiguity in using the same gesture for multiple tasks.

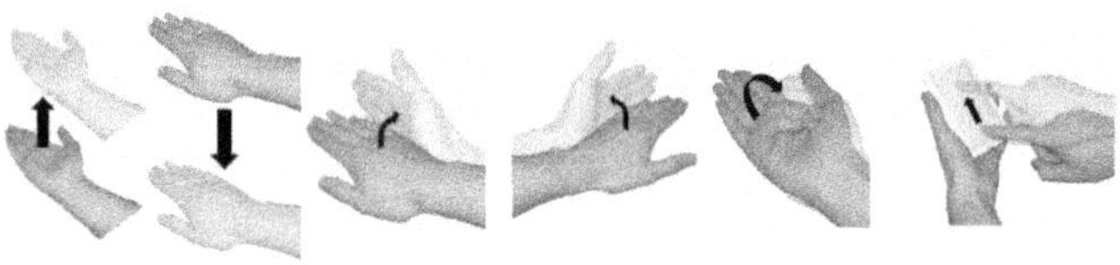

Figure 4: User-defined gesture set for tilt manipulations. Left to right: raise screen; lower screen & flatten from backward or forward tilts; tilt right (right hand) & flatten from left tilt (left hand); tilt left (left hand) & flatten from right tilt (right hand); tilt forward; tilt backwards.

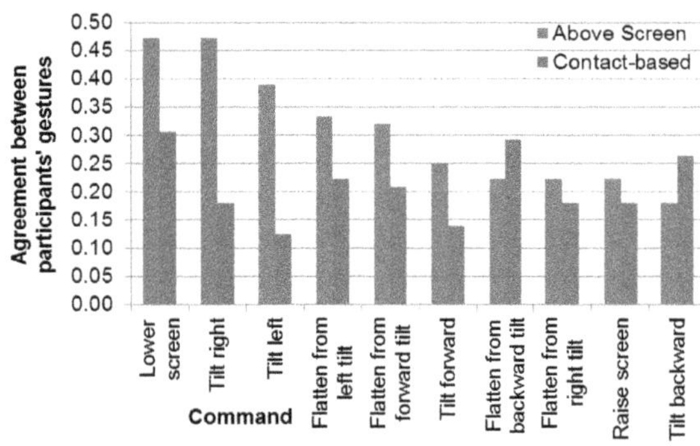

Figure 5: Agreement between participants' gestures for tilt manipulation

	Panning		Scaling		Rotating		Selection	
	CB	Abv.	CB	Abv.	CB	Abv.	CB	Abv.
1. Flat Screen	**FS**	FS	**P**	P	T	**T**	TP	TP
2. Tilted left	**FS**	FS	**P**	P	T	**T**	TP	TP
3. Tilted right	**FS**	FS	**P**	P	**T**	T	**TP**	TP
4. Tilted forward	**FS**	FS	P	P	**T**	T	**TP**	TP
5. Tilted backward	**FS**	FS	**P**	P	**T**	T	**TP**	TP
6. Concave	FS	**FS**	P	**P**	FR	**T**	TP	**TP**
7. Convex	FS	FS	**P**	P	FR	**T**	TP	**TP**
8. Vertically raised section	FS	**FS**	P	**P**	T	**T**	**TP**	TP
9. Vertically lowered section	FS	**FS**	P	P	T	**T**	**TP**	TP
10. Steps	TS	**FS**	P	**P**	VFS	**T**	TP	**TP**

Key: FS=1-Finger Swipe, P=Pinch, T=2-Finger Twist, TP=Trace Path, FR=1-Finger Rotate by dragging corner, TSE=Touch Start, Touch End, VFS=Vertical Finger Swipe.

Table 5: User-defined gestures (CB = Contact Based gesture, Abv = Above screen gesture)

Interactions

Each participant provided a contact-based and a mid-air gesture for the four tasks on 10 different surfaces, giving a total of 960 observed interaction gestures. Gestures took a variety of forms, but were heavily biased towards those that physically acted on the required objects.

For each surface/task pair, we grouped identical interactions and listed the most common in Table 5. We also calculated agreement values between the user-provided interactions for each task on each surface. The interactions with the highest agreement for each surface/task pair are shaded in the table (those pairs without shading had equal agreement values). The interactions in bold show those which had the greater overall user preference (no bolded value indicates preferences were evenly split).

Figure 6 depicts the user-defined gesture set. It contains no overlap in interactions for different tasks; the majority of gestures selected by participants are identical for the same task across different surfaces. The interactions were often identical for both the contact-based and mid-air scenarios.

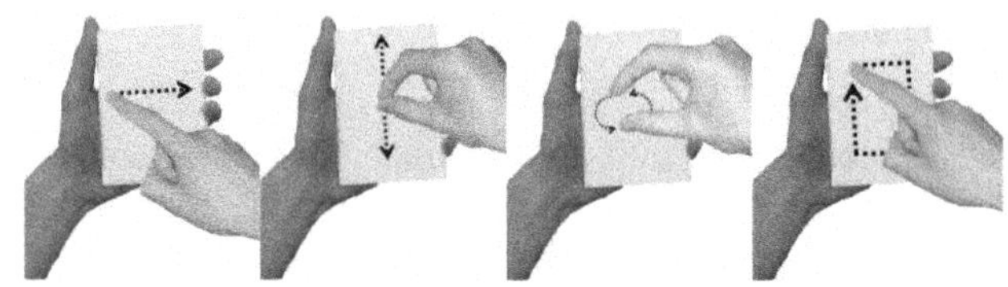

Figure 6: User-defined interaction set. From left, panning, scaling, rotating and selection. Contact-based gestures were used for planar displays, mid-air gestures of the same nature were used for non-planar surfaces.

Regardless of the tilt angle, an identical gesture set emerges for each of the planar surfaces (lines 1–5). On-screen swipe and pinch gestures are preferred and show greatest agreement for panning and scaling respectively, while rotation is performed using two-finger twists and path tracing used for selection (again with preferences and agreement towards contact-based gestures). Participants noted that when either gesture was practical, they tended to prefer on-screen gestures due to the inherent tactile feedback that is present.

When using uneven or non-planar surfaces, participants in general had a greater preference for mid-air gestures (lines 6–10). For panning and scaling, swipe and pinch gestures again showed the greatest agreement, with preferences this time for *above* the screen versions. Participants employed a wide range of contact-based rotation gestures for non-planar surfaces. However, they showed a unanimous preference for an above-screen twist gesture. Path tracing was preferred for non-planar selection, with the particular surface influenced preference of on- or above-screen.

The close correlation between contact-based and above-screen gestures demonstrates users' preferences to extrapolate their knowledge of current on-screen gestures to the mid-air realm. This reduces the users learning and memory requirements and is important for developers of gesture sets for these types of devices.

DISCUSSION

Device Size and Size of Tilt Components

This work focussed on our prototype Tilt Display that is sized between a mobile device and a tablet. We envision this footprint to approximate the ideal size for Tilt Displays.

However, there remains the question of device scalability and the impact that has on the size of tilt components.

Larger, table-scale implementations of these displays might be desirable for some of the applications outlined earlier. This then poses questions about the size of actuatable components (should they also scale in size?) and whether the stroke of the actuators must scale with an enlarged surface. To achieve the same flower effect on a larger surface would require the outside petals to move further away from the originating surface.

All Tilt Displays also lie on a continuum that describes the area of each actuation component. The extreme cases range from each individual pixel tilting and actuating to a single, whole device tilt. Single pixel tilt and actuation would provide high precision and likely come at very high cost. Whole device tilt and actuation opens a range of opportunities for multi-device collaboration: one such example might be for users to place their mobile devices together to form a large Tilt Display.

User Studies

Influence of Prior Knowledge and Familiarity

All but two participants indicated that they had prior experience with multi-touch input and 3D input devices. In the exploration of tilt control, we observed a diverse range of gestures for the required input. In the interaction study, users reverted back to more familiar, already known, gestures. Although we encouraged users to experiment with and employ any kind of gesture participants may have struggled to remove themselves from what they might class as 'common knowledge'. However, we can also interpret these results as the participants believing that these gestures are the most appropriate for the required actions.

Gesture Sets and Compound Gestures

In User Study 2, all gestures were provided using a single hand, based on the assumption that the remaining hand would be used for gripping the device. While all gestures in the interaction set can be performed with either hand, the tilt manipulation set contains two gestures that are most comfortably performed with a particular hand (the tilt right and tilt left gestures using the right and left hands respectively). While in isolation there is little issue with this, when users are performing compound gestures (multiple gestures one after another) then continually swapping the interaction and gripping hands will be tiresome. Further work is needed to address compound gestures and how users perform such actions.

Design Implications

Tilt Displays for 3D Content: Based on the results of the first user study, participants easily related to the Tilt Display concept. Users felt that the actuatable screens created a new form of 3D that was much more evocative than existing 3D displays. A clear advantage that was often mentioned by the participants was that of visualising 3D information without the need to wear 3D glasses. Participants of the first study mentioned that they could see Tilt Displays being used to display 3D images on a mobile phone or to enhance the experience of watching a 3D movie at home using larger and more screens.

Tablet-Sized Tilt Displays: Our first user study also indicates that while mobile phone sized Tilt Displays are suitable to present information to individual users, a larger tablet sized device would be better positioned to support all the interaction modes we created, especially for collaboration. Participants felt that a tablet size Tilt Display would allow subdividing the screen so that four users could comfortably gather around the device and start collaborating and sharing information. By placing the Tilt Display on a horizontal surface, its individual screens would transition between a flat mode where everybody would look at the same tiled display and a collaborative mode with separate views for each user.

Bezels Convey Information: Participants disliked bezels when performing continuous touch gestures (as expected), but surprisingly they did not complain about the bezels visually breaking an image. Instead, they commented on the importance that the gaps and bezels play in the perception of elevation and movement. Participants also suggested that Tilt Displays could be used for navigation as the gaps and the movement could more clearly show which direction you have to go to by taking a quick glance at the display.

Manual Tilt Manipulation: Participants showed a clear preference for 'copy me' style interactions when manually manipulating the display's tilt. Their 3D hand position indicated how the screen should mutate. This interaction style is simple and easy for new users to learn.

Interaction on Non-planar Surfaces: Participants showed a strong preference for alternate interaction for low-level tasks on non-planar surfaces. We derived a user-defined set of mid-air gestures that translated common on-screen interactions to their above-device equivalents. Participants were keen for the same touch actions they applied on planar surfaces to scale to mid-air gestures above non-planar surfaces. Mobile devices will soon contain depth cameras, mean recognition of such gestures will not be a problem.

CONCLUSION

This paper has introduced Tilt Displays, a new type of actuatable display that combines visual feedback with both multi-axis tilting and vertical actuation. We presented an exploration of the design space around Tilt Displays through two user studies. The first found positive user attitudes towards this new type of display, with participants immediately seeing the benefits in the physical 3D output.

The second user study examined interaction possibilities with such a display. It resulted in the generation of two user-defined gesture sets: the first to manipulate the tilt of the display, the second to interact with display. A set of six gestures were employed to control all facets of tilt and actuation. The second set, for the low-level interactions of panning, scaling, rotating and selection, found that users prefer on-screen gestures for planar surfaces, but mid-air versions of the same gestures for non-planar configurations. This demonstrates users' ability to 'scale up' their knowledge of gestures to the domain of Tilt Displays.

ACKNOWLEDGEMENTS

The authors would like to thank all of the study participants for their time and valuable feedback. This work was partially funded by EPSRC (EP/G058334/1) and MobileVCE (www.mobilevce.com) as part of the User Interactions for Breakthrough Services research program.

REFERENCES

1. Ashdown, M., Oka, K., and Sato, Y. *Combining Head Tracking and Mouse Input for a GUI on Multiple Monitors.* in *CHI '05 EA*. Portland, OR, USA: ACM.
2. Audet, S. and Cooperstock, J.R. *Shadow Removal in Front Projection Environments Using Object Tracking.* in *Computer Vision and Pattern Recognition*. 2007.
3. Baudisch, P., Cutrell, E., Hinckley, K., and Gruen, R. *Mouse Ether: Accelerating the Acquisition of Targets Across Multi-Monitor Displays.* in *CHI '04 EA*. Vienna, Austria: ACM.
4. Benko, H. and Feiner, S. *Multi-Monitor Mouse.* in *CHI '05 EA*. Portland, OR, USA: ACM.
5. Blackshaw, M., DeVincenzi, A., Lakatos, D., Leithinger, D., and Ishii, H. *Recompose: Direct and Gestural Interaction with an Actuated Surface.* in *CHI EA '11*: ACM.
6. Coelho, M., Ishii, H., and Maes, P. *Surflex: A Programmable Surface for the Design of Tangible Interfaces.* in *CHI '08 EA*. Florence, Italy: ACM.
7. Coelho, M. and Maes, P. *Sprout I/O: A Texturally Rich Interface.* in *TEI '08*. Bonn, Germany: ACM.
8. Frisken-Gibson, S.F., Bach-y-Rita, P., Tompkins, W.J., and Webster, J.G., *A 64-Solenoid, Four-Level Fingertip Search Display for the Blind.* IEEE Trans on Biomedical Engineering, 1987. **BME-34**(12): p. 963–965.
9. Harrison, C. and Hudson, S.E. *Providing Dynamically Changeable Physical Buttons on A Visual Display.* in *CHI '09*. Boston, MA, USA: ACM.
10. Holtzblatt, K., Wendell, J.B., and Wood, S., *Rapid Contextual Design.* 2005: Morgan Kaufmann.
11. Iwata, H., Yano, H., Nakaizumi, F., and Kawamura, R. *Project FEELEX: Adding Haptic Surface to Graphics.* in *SIGRAPH '01*: ACM.
12. Jansen, Y., Karrer, T., and Borchers, J. *MudPad: Tactile Feedback and Haptic Texture Overlay for Touch Surfaces.* in *ITS '10*. Saarbrücken, Germany: ACM.
13. Lahey, B., Girouard, A., Burleson, W., and Vertegaal, R. *PaperPhone: Understanding the use of Bend Gestures in Mobile Devices with Flexible Electronic Paper Displays.* in *CHI '11*. Vancouver, Canada: ACM.
14. Leithinger, D. and Ishii, H. *Relief: A Scalable Actuated Shape Display.* in *TEI 2010*. Cambridge, Massachusetts, USA: ACM.
15. Leithinger, D., Lakatos, D., DeVincenzi, A., Blackshaw, M., and Ishii, H. *Direct and Gestural Interaction with Relief: A 2.5D Shape Display.* in *UIST '11*. Santa Barbara, CA, USA: ACM.
16. Lucero, A., Holopainen, J., and Jokela, T. *Pass-them-around: Collaborative use of Mobile Phones for Photo Sharing.* in *CHI '11*. Vancouver, BC, Canada: ACM.
17. Lucero, A., Keränen, J., and Korhonen, H. *Collaborative use of Mobile Phones for Brainstorming.* in *MobileHCI '10*. Lisbon, Portugal: ACM.
18. Merrill, D., Kalanithi, J., and Maes, P. *Siftables: Towards Sensor Network User Interfaces.* in *TEI '07*. Baton Rouge, Louisiana: ACM.
19. Nakatani, M., Kajimoto, H., Sekiguchi, D., Kawakami, N., and Tachi, S., *3D Form Display with Shape Memory Alloy.* Proceedings of the Virtual Reality Society of Japan Annual Conference, 2003. **8**: p. 247–248.
20. Poupyrev, I., Nashida, T., Maruyama, S., Rekimoto, J., and Yamaji, Y. *Lumen: Interactive Visual and Shape Display for Calm Computing.* in *ACM SIGGRAPH '04 Emerging technologies*. Los Angeles, California: ACM.
21. Poupyrev, I., Nashida, T., and Okabe, M. *Actuation and Tangible User Interfaces: The Vaucanson Duck, Robots, and Shape Displays.* in *TEI '07*. Baton Rouge, Louisiana: ACM.
22. Schwesig, C., Poupyrev, I., and Mori, E. *Gummi: A Bendable Computer.* in *CHI '04*. Vienna, Austria: ACM.
23. Taylor, P.M., Pollet, D.M., Hosseini-Sianaki, A., and Varley, C.J., *Advances in an Electrorheological Fluid Based Tactile Array.* Displays, 1998. **18**(3): p. 135–141.
24. Uesugi, R., Inoue, K., Sasama, R., Arai, T., and Mae, Y. *See-through Sheet Visual Display for Haptic Device Using Flexible Sheet.* in *ICAT '03*.
25. Wagner, C.R., Howe, R.D., and Lederman, S.J., *A Tactile Shape Display Using RC Servomotors.* HAPTICS '02.
26. Wobbrock, J.O., Morris, M.R., and Wilson, A.D. *User-Defined Gestures for Surface Computing.* in *CHI '09*. Boston, MA, USA: ACM.
27. Yang, X.-D., Mak, E., McCallum, D., Irani, P., Cao, X., and Izadi, S., *LensMouse: Augmenting the Mouse with an Interactive Touch Display*, in *CHI '10*. ACM.

m+pSpaces: Virtual Workspaces in the Spatially-Aware Mobile Environment

Jessica Cauchard*, Markus Löchtefeld‡, Mike Fraser*, Antonio Krüger‡, Sriram Subramanian*

*University of Bristol
Woodland Rd, Bristol UK
{cauchard, fraser, sriram}@cs.bris.ac.uk

‡German Research Center for Artificial Intelligence (DFKI), Saarbrücken, Germany
{markus.loechtefeld, krueger}@dfki.de

ABSTRACT

We introduce spatially-aware virtual workspaces for the mobile environment. The notion of virtual workspaces was initially conceived to alleviate mental workload in desktop environments with limited display real-estate. Using spatial properties of mobile devices, we translate this approach and illustrate that mobile virtual workspaces greatly improve task performance for mobile devices. In a first study, we compare our spatially-aware prototype (*mSpaces*) to existing context switching methods for navigating amongst multiple tasks in the mobile environment. We show that users are faster, make more accurate decisions and require less mental and physical effort when using spatially-aware prototypes. We furthermore prototype *pSpaces* and *m+pSpaces,* two spatially-aware systems equipped with pico-projectors as auxiliary displays to provide dual-display capability to the handheld device. A final study reveals advantages of each of the different configurations and functionalities when comparing all three prototypes. Drawing on these findings, we identify design considerations to create, manipulate and manage spatially-aware virtual workspaces in the mobile environment.

Author Keywords

Mobile virtual workspace; spatially-aware displays; multi-display environments; pico-projectors; m+pSpaces.

ACM Classification Keywords

H.5.2 [Information Interfaces and Presentation]: User Interfaces: Input devices and strategies, Interaction styles.

INTRODUCTION

The use of multiple workspaces is common in desktop computing and integrated into most Operating Systems (OS). Known as *workspaces* on Linux, *spaces* in Mac OS or *virtual desktop* in Windows OS, they allow users to de-clutter their principal workspace and mitigate physical display size limitations by adding virtual display real-estate. For mobile platforms, the concept of virtual display space is quite different; it is often used to store icons but rarely to switch between tasks or activities that have already been started. Users instead go back to the main menu and select an icon to access the corresponding application. Since the use of multiple virtual workspaces was initially recommended as a technique to alleviate some of the mental workload in limited display real-estate [6], it seems natural to use this concept for mobile phone technologies.

Current desktop environments represent virtual workspaces using thumbnails spatially arranged in a line or grid. In mobile environments, since the devices themselves have intrinsic spatial properties, we propose to use these spatial properties instead of using a graphical representation. This will give users a more tangible and direct interaction with virtual workspaces that does not exist in desktop computing thus expanding the capabilities of current systems.

The concept of virtual workspaces as it exists in desktop computing can be translated to the mobile environment. Yet, this is not a straightforward process and the results obtained would be suboptimal if careful consideration was not given to the design, as the two categories of devices have very different characteristics and capabilities.

In this paper, we explore the use of virtual workspaces in mobile environments. We present *mSpaces*, *pSpaces* and *m+pSpaces*, three phone-based user interface prototypes, which allow simple and fast access to multiple virtual workspaces located around the user, drawing on their spatial memory and awareness. With *mSpaces*, the user accesses different workspaces by moving the phone to different physical locations, while *pSpaces* (Figure 1) gives access to multiple virtual workspaces by pointing a pico-projector attached to the phone at the various locations.

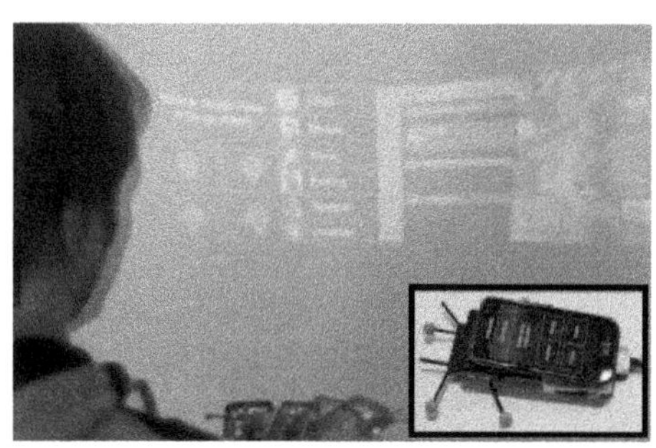

Figure 1: pSpaces: User accesses various virtual workspaces by moving the pico-projector to the associated physical space.

MobileHCI'12, September 21–24, 2012, San Francisco, CA, USA.

This interface makes full use of the user's spatial awareness. Finally *m+pSpaces* makes use of both the screen and pico-projector. The mobile virtual workspaces are always linked to real physical locations relative to the user. In two experiments we compare *mSpaces* to the current use of multiple concurrent applications on a mobile phone and to *p-* and *m+pSpaces*. While this paper explores interaction techniques to access the various workspaces, it does not investigate new interaction techniques for input.

The contributions of this paper are: 1. Findings suggesting that spatially-aware virtual workspaces provide easier and faster switches between applications in the mobile context. 2. We propose three spatially-aware prototypes of mobile virtual workspaces, two of which include the use of mobile projection spaces that capitalizes on the emerging trend of augmenting mobile phones with pico-projectors. 3. Pico-projection improves the capabilities of spatially aware mobile virtual workspaces. 4. We extend our contribution of using mobile workspaces and complete the design of *m-* and *pSpaces* by proposing a set of design considerations to create, manipulate and manage these techniques.

BACKGROUND

Desktop Virtual Workspaces

Virtual workspaces are first introduced by Card and Henderson [6,8], who initially proposed *Rooms*, a system for managing multiple virtual workspaces as a way to cope with limited display real-estate by expanding it into virtual workspaces. Multiple workspaces lower the cognitive overhead created by trying to switch tasks and move windows across a limited physical display real-estate. One of the authors' arguments for virtual workspaces is that they help overcome the limitations of small screen size, which is a highly relevant issue for today's mobile technologies.

Ringel [17] proposes a "taxonomy of organization strategies" for users of multiple virtual workspaces. Five organization strategies emerged from a field study. Participants would consistently use the different workspaces to either: divide tasks, divide subtasks, change context between personal and professional usage, use multiple OS, and classify applications. They also show that virtual workspaces have different uses to multiple displays. It is therefore likely that adding an auxiliary display to a mobile environment would not replace the need for multiple workspaces. Finally, users with smaller displays used "more virtual desktops, on average," [17]. This proves that multiple workspaces will be well suited to mobile environments that traditionally afford smaller displays.

Mobile Virtual Workspaces

We use *mobile devices* to refer to handheld devices such as mobile phones and tablets. Laptops are not considered to be part of this category as they are traditionally used sat down on a flat surface and not handheld. Fitzmaurice [10] presented the Chameleon system in 1993, offering spatially aware interactions with the environment using a palmtop computer. Despite, the concept of virtual workspaces as we know it in desktop environments is seldom implemented in current mobile devices and many mobile phones only offer the possibility of displaying static menu icons on one or more virtual desktops. Moreover while some mobile phones have the capability to display multiple applications at once, they do not exploit advantages offered by virtual workspaces as they exist in the desktop environment. Adapting multiple virtual workspaces to mobile devices will extend the current range of possibilities offered, such as providing users with a task partitioning tool.

While the concept of multiple virtual workspaces can be translated to the mobile domain, the interaction techniques need to be adapted. This is particularly evident since display sizes and interaction techniques are inherently disparate between desktop and mobile environments.

Representation of Virtual Workspaces

In the desktop environment, multiple workspaces are often displayed as a group of thumbnails, each representative of one workspace. They are traditionally organized as a line of thumbnails – such as when pressing ALT+TAB in Windows OS or CMD+TAB in MacOS – or as a 2x2 grid when 4 workspaces are being shown. In early systems, thumbnails were referenced to by numbers. They are now often presented as a thumbnail of the actual workspace with its applications positioned as in the workspace itself.

In existing mobile environments, the main screen can sometimes be extended to display additional static information such as extra application icons. These application launcher spaces can be represented as a line of dots in the main menu where one dot is highlighted, indicating the workspace in view. Some phones also propose solutions close to the concept of multiple workspaces in desktop computing such as the Nokia N900 where multiple applications can be running in additional virtual space. Yet, there is no point of reference to what the user is currently viewing with respect to the virtual space.

In all instances presented above, there is a spatial relationship between the workspaces: one can be represented next to the other, above or below.

Spatial Awareness

The use of spatial awareness to represent and provide users with an understanding of virtual workspaces is to be expected since using spatial memory has proven to be effective for tasks such as the document management technique Data Mountain [18]. Additionally, Tan et al. [20] show that using kinaesthetic cues increases spatial recall. Li et al. build on this theory and propose Virtual Shelves [14], allowing users to orient a mobile phone to trigger shortcuts. They show that the user can "accurately point to 7 regions on the Θ plane and 4 on the Φ plane". A more recent study by Gustafson et al. [12] show that one can interact with mobile devices by transferring the spatial memory of the interaction technique to the palm of their hand.

Earlier, Yee presented Peephole [21], an interaction

technique for a spatially-aware display that "provides a window on a larger virtual workspace". They mention that this window could be used to display several applications on the same workspace where users could draw connections between applications. In *mSpaces*, we take this concept further by mapping the location of each distinct virtual workspace to a physical location, relative to the user. The user can access each workspace by orienting the mobile device in the direction of the workspace, hereby receiving permanent visual feedback to which workspace they are looking at. This technique utilizes the intrinsic properties of a context-aware mobile device, the user's spatial memory, as well as kinaesthetic cues that will ostensibly alleviate some of the user's mental workload.

Besides, Cao and Balakrishnan [5] explore using a handheld projector to access multiple items on a single virtual space. We take a step further by accessing multiple virtual spaces at different physical locations with constant visual feedback. In *m-* and *pSpaces*, each virtual space is linked to a location relative to the user, who then points at the physical location to display the associated virtual space.

In order to determine how virtual workspaces can be displayed in the mobile environment, we conducted a user study comparing various implementations.

USER STUDY 1: MOBILE VIRTUAL WORKSPACES

This study aims to find out the type of interface is suited to implement virtual workspaces in a fully mobile environment. While there are many ways to implement mobile virtual workspaces, we compared the current use of mobile phones to two probable implementations.

Virtual Workspaces

In order to keep the current display paradigm used in mobile phones, each workspace contains one application only. The mobile phone's screen would quickly become cluttered if more than one application was displayed at a time on such a small display. Ringel [17] indicates that the average number of virtual workspaces used in desktop computing is four; we therefore implemented the prototypes with four virtual workspaces and four running applications.

Apparatus

The three conditions for the experiment are: *no virtual workspace*, which corresponds to the current use of mobile phones; *workspace switcher*, which provides a representation of the workspaces, and *mSpaces*, which distributes the workspaces across space. All conditions have been implemented on the same mobile phone, a Samsung Galaxy S running Android 2.3 OS.

No Virtual Workspace

This condition reflects the current usage of mobile phones. To switch applications, the user returns to the main menu by performing a short click on the home button at the bottom of the screen. There, they click on the icon corresponding to the application they want to open.

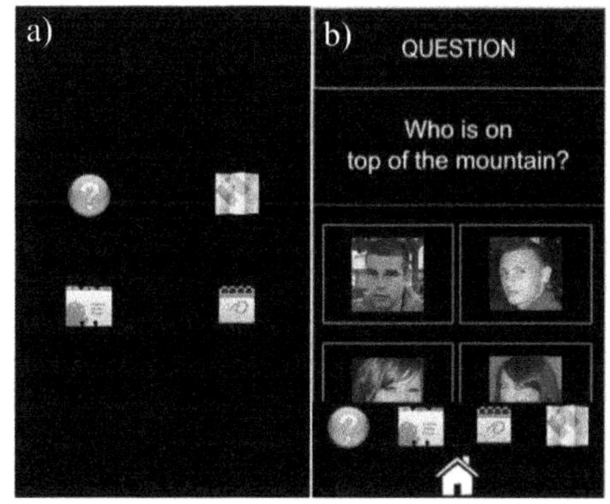

Figure 2: a) No virtual workspace: menu of icons b) Workspace switcher: a bar of icons representing the workspaces appears at the bottom of the screen.

This operation must be performed every time the user wants to switch application. This technique is a typical interaction technique for browsing through applications in mobile phones. The menu displayed consists of a 2x2 grid of icons, each one representing an application (Figure 2a).

Workspace Switcher

This condition simulates the current metaphors for switching workspaces in the desktop environment. The *workspace switcher* is a graphical representation of the available workspaces, consisting of a bar of icons that appears at the bottom of the screen superimposing and partially hiding the current visible workspace (Figure 2b). Each icon represents a workspace as in the *no virtual workspace*'s condition menu. The user performs a long click (500 ms.) on the home button to access the *workspace switcher* as they would typically do for switching context on mobile phones when the functionality is available.

mSpaces

The third condition, *mSpaces*, is a prototype that allows the user to choose which virtual workspace they want to display by moving to its physical space. The technique is in the same idiom as the interaction techniques presented in Imaginary Interfaces [11], Virtual Shelves [14] and Peephole [21]. In *mSpaces* however, kinaesthetic cues are attached to the workspace switches. The user accesses the distinct workspaces with permanent visual feedback; without having to press any button; just by moving the device to a new physical location. *mSpaces* is a spatially-aware device, in which 6 degrees of freedom tracking is

Figure 3: mSpaces: spatially-aware mobile device. Different workspaces appear depending on the device's position.

Figure 4: Screenshots of a type4 trial – To answer Question (a), the participant needs to match the picture with the person's name on the Contact list (b) and use the Agenda (c) to identify what activity they will be doing with this person. The next step is to use the Map (d) to locate the activity. Once the participant has navigated through all workspaces, they can answer the Question.

realized using a NaturalPoint OptiTrack motion-capture system through IR-reflecting markers attached to the prototype (Figure 3). Workspace are separated from one another on the horizontal axis by a 30° angle as is advised in the literature [14]. In the experiment, the workspaces are positioned on a single vertical level but the prototype would in addition support having workspaces at multiple heights.

The position of the workspaces was fixed for the experiments and participants had a chance to become familiar with the system prior to the experiment.

Tasks

To evaluate how virtual workspaces need to be designed for mobile devices, we asked participants to answer questions for which they need to look up information using familiar mobile applications. We used spatial search tasks where participants needed to access multiple workspaces to find the right answer. Since the tasks are spatial, the applications do not require any user interaction, aside from navigating between workspaces and using the touch screen to answer the question. The applications visible to the users are pre-designed screenshots of applications that may contain some clues to answer the trial question. The user can retrieve the clues by perusing the screenshots using the workspace switching technique. This task is representative of a task where a user consults their agenda to give a date or location to a person on the phone or next to them. This task is not designed for "on-the-move" scenario but instead a scenario where the user would stop for a short moment to consult some data on their phone as this is current practice.

For the four workspaces available, four applications are proposed: a question (Figure 4a), contact list (Figure 4b), calendar (Figure 4c) and map (Figure 4d). These applications correspond to everyday tasks commonly undertaken on mobile phones. Four types of tasks were presented to generate different sets of workspace switches. type1 respectively involves looking at the contact list and the map; type2 at the map and the calendar; type3 at the contact list and the agenda; while type4 involves all workspaces and is therefore harder than other types.

The aim of each task is to answer the trial question. The participant doesn't know the type of the task; and for each trial, all four workspaces are available even if they do not all provide clues to answering the question. Once the answer is found, the participant gets back to the initial question workspace to validate their choice by touching an answer out of four choices on the touch screen (Figure 4a).

Procedure

12 volunteers (4 female) aged between 23 and 44 ($\mu = 29.5$) were recruited from our research institution. All were right-handed, familiar with smartphones and touch-screen technologies. We used a within-subjects experimental design where each participant had to answer all questions and the type of virtual workspace was counterbalanced across participants. The task was explained individually to each participant who could try out each condition with a randomly chosen task in their own time. When they felt ready, they pressed the "Start" button to start the experiment and again before each trial. At the end of the experiment, users filled out a NASA TLX survey.

The independent variables were: The *type of virtual workspaces*: No virtual workspace (Nv), workspace switcher (Ws), *mSpaces* (mSp). The *type of task*: type 1 to 4 (t1 to t4). There were 6 questions of 4 different types per condition (i.e. type of workspace), which corresponds to 24 questions for each condition and 72 trials overall per participant. The experiment had: 12 participants x 3 virtual workspaces x 4 tasks types x 6 trials for 864 data points.

Measures

The experimental software recorded trial completion time (MT) and error rate (ER) as dependent variables. MT is the total time taken to complete the task and is defined as the time taken for the user to perform a trial. The counter begins when the user presses "Start" and stops when the user clicks on one of the response buttons. If the user did not select the right answer an error was registered and the user was allowed to progress to the next trial. In an exit questionnaire we asked participants to complete the NASA

TLX questionnaire. This allows assessing on a 7-point Likert scale subjective information for mental, physical and temporal demand; performance; effort and frustration. In addition to the NASA TLX we asked participants to rank the techniques and comment on their personal preferences.

Results

We used the univariate ANOVA with Tamhane post-hoc pairwise (unequal variance) comparisons for our analyses.

Error Rate

There were 59 errors out of 864 trials. With 8 incorrect trials, participants made fewest errors with *mSp* followed by 21 incorrect trials for *Nv* and 30 for *Ws*. All 59 trials with incorrect responses were removed from further analysis.

Completion Time (MT)

The average trial completion time over all tasks and techniques was 16.6s with standard deviation of 4.1s. There was a significant effect of technique on trial completion time ($F_{2,22} = 10.85$, $p<0.01$); *mSpaces* was significantly faster than the other two techniques followed by *No virtual workspace* (Nv) and *Workspace switcher* (Ws). We found no significant difference between Nv and Ws. There was a significant effect of task type on MT ($F_{3,33} = 19.6$, $p<0.01$). Figure 5 Left shows the mean MT with standard error-bars for each technique and task type.

Subjective Evaluation

The NASA TLX questions were analysed separately using non-parametric tests (k-related samples with Freidman Test Type) (Table 1). We found a significant difference for the following pairs: Mental Demand: (Ws,mSp), Performance: (mSp,Ws) and Effort: (mSp,Ws) & (mSp,Nv). All other combinations did not reveal significant differences." Low performance value shows that users felt they performed

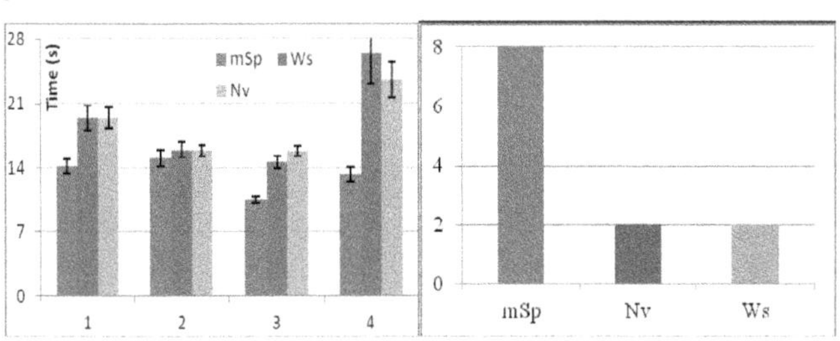

Figure 5: Left: Mean trial completion time for each technique and task. The horizontal axis shows the four task types. Right: Subjective preferences of the different techniques.

Factor	$\chi^2(12)$	P	mSp	Nv	Ws
Physical Demand	4.919	>0.05	1.96	1.62	2.42
Mental Demand	6.645	<0.05	1.54	2.08	2.38
Temporal Demand	0.261	>0.05	1.96	2.08	1.96
Performance	7.0	<0.05	1.67	1.92	2.42
Effort	11.862	<0.05	1.42	2.08	2.50
Frustration	2.606	>0.05	1.75	1.96	2.29

Table 1: Results of NASA TLX questionnaire.

well. Users felt *mSpaces* required the least mental demand and effort. In overall ranking of techniques, 8 out of 12 participants preferred *mSpaces* to the other two conditions (Figure 5 Right).

DISCUSSION

Virtual Workspaces in Mobile Devices

Participants felt that the traditional use of a phone, as in the *no virtual workspace* condition, although it "was already common" and well understood, was "annoying to always start in the menu". Our experiment shows that the use of virtual workspaces to complete tasks requiring serial switching through different applications can be significantly faster and less prone to errors than the traditional use of mobile phones. This is the case when comparing *mSpaces* to the *no virtual workspace* condition.

In the *workspace switcher* condition, the results were very similar to the ones of the *no virtual workspace* condition and slightly better for type3 tasks and worse for type4. This provides evidence that, although virtual workspaces can foster significant improvement over current use of mobile phones, they need to be carefully designed to fully realize their potential.

Spatial Memory to Position Virtual Workspaces

The results show that *mSpaces* improves decision-making accuracy. Additionally, the NASA TLX questionnaire shows that participants felt that they were less frustrated and required less effort to use *mSpaces*. This implies that virtual workspaces can therefore be managed on mobile phones using spatially-aware techniques. With *mSpaces*, people use kinaesthetic cues and spatial memory to intuitively understand the positions of the various workspaces. In addition to being more efficient than the other conditions, *mSpaces* was preferred by 67% of the participants who enjoyed the opportunity to "build a spatial knowledge of the location of apps in space" and were able to "arrange [their] apps around [them]". They found *mSpaces* "faster", "easy to use", "quick and advanced", "very intuitive" and one mentioned that they "could browse everything pretty fast and easily look something up again".

Our implementation of *mSpaces* is built for displaying virtual workspaces, nonetheless the strong results and very positive feedback obtained from the study lead us to believe that the use of spatial awareness and memory to interact with mobile technology is very promising in spite of being under-exploited. It could be used not only to navigate through workspaces (*mSpaces*), menus [11] and shortcuts [14], but also to manage interruptions in mobile technology.

Memory Aids

The results show that using spatial memory only; participants can locate the different workspaces and navigate between them. Participants noted that "after a short learning phase it was easy and comfortable to switch between apps" and "navigational help on the display would be useful". This suggests that *mSpaces* requires some memory aid. This will also be useful as a reminder when users haven't used *mSpaces* in some time. One way to provide a memory aid would be to display a map with the phone's current position compared to the overall position of all workspaces. We therefore implemented a *workspace viewer* and conducted a user study to investigate if this functionality would improve usability.

Home Button Curse

In this experiment, we noticed that imposing an extra click to request the workspace switch is time consuming and frustrating. Participants commented that the "long press was irritating" and that the *no virtual workspace* condition required a "ridiculous amount of clicking". Users should indeed be able to access a different workspace without having to first return to a main menu. One way would be to use a button dedicated to workspace navigation, which could display all workspaces available and allow navigation between them. This notion of a dedicated workspace button is described in more detail in the design considerations section. *mSpaces* obviously does not suffer from the "Home button curse" as the device is simply moved in order to switch to another workspace, neatly avoiding the issue. The current use of mobile phones with a home button to return to a main menu may then not be optimal, especially for tasks requiring several workspaces or application switches.

One-Handed Interaction Technique

We did not instruct participants on how the phone should be held. They could hold it as they felt comfortable and all held it naturally as they would with their own mobile phone. Nonetheless we noticed that for *mSpaces*, 75% of the participants held the device in their dominant hand only and interacted with the dominant thumb, leaving their second hand completely free. Only two held the phone in their dominant hand while interacting with the other hand. Finally one person used both hands after the first three trials as they "[feared] to drop the phone when moving it too fast". For the two other conditions: *workspace switcher* and *no virtual workspace*, 7 out of 12 participants used two hands to hold the prototype. This is despite both techniques being implemented on the same prototype as *mSpaces*.

Number of Workspaces

For a task with a higher number of switches such as type4 tasks, there was a significant difference in time completion across the techniques. *mSpaces* was more efficient and less error prone than the other two conditions. The number of workspaces may well therefore influence which technique is most appropriate. With the number of applications being concurrently used on mobile phones growing, *mSpaces* seems better suited than other techniques that would clutter the phone's screen with extra icons, switches or scroll bars. Yet, *mSpaces* scalability will need to be determined in future work. According to Ringel [17], some users prefer partitioning information on their screens by using external displays rather than virtual workspaces. We are going beyond this statement by proposing to improve the use of *mSpaces* by adding an external display (pico-projector) on the mobile phone and fitting it with our *mSpaces* approach.

USER STUDY 2: EXTENDING MSPACES

We propose to test if we can further improve *mSpaces* by including an external display on the mobile phone as well as a workspace viewer. Since pico-projectors are common external displays used for today's mobile phones, we propose to implement *pSpaces*, a projected version of *mSpaces*. *pSpaces* has the added advantage of displaying the workspaces externally from the device via the projection beam, which may improve the speed and accuracy of users when performing a task. In this study, we also compare both solutions to a hybrid version: *m+pSpaces* where the main workspace is displayed on the phone's screen while other workspaces are being projected one at a time depending on the position of the projection as in *pSpaces*. For both *pSpaces* and *m+pSpaces* prototypes, the user points the projector at the physical space to display the virtual workspace corresponding to the location.

Apparatus

All prototypes used a Samsung Galaxy S and Microvision ShowWX+ pico-projector, of size 14mm and weight 122g. To guarantee the comparability of results the *mSpaces* prototype used in this experiment uses the same hardware as *pSpaces* and *m+pSpaces* with the projector turned off.

pSpaces

We implement *mSpaces* on a pico-projector connected to a phone where the user can point at the virtual workspace to display it. The pico-projector is fixed to the phone and the participant moves the projector-phone to different locations to display different content. The motion-capture system used is the same as for the *mSpaces* prototype described in the first user study. The computer determines which workspace to display depending on the prototype's position.

All workspaces are accessible and displayed via the projection. In *pSpaces*, a spatial representation of the virtual workspaces, *workspace viewer* (Figure 6), is displayed on the phone's screen. Workspaces are represented by a thumbnail and not an icon, as in current mobile phones displays; allowing users to benefit from both their visual

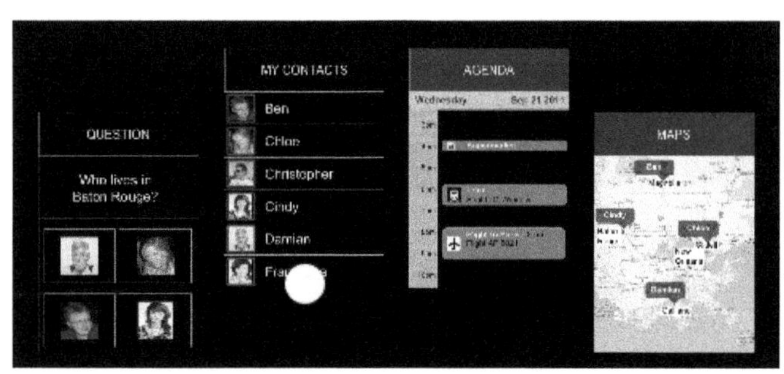

Figure 6: Workspace Viewer: Spatial representation of the virtual workspaces on the top part of the phone's screen. The phone's position is represented by a white dot.

and spatial memory [13]. The *workspace viewer* provides constant information on users' location in the environment compared to other workspaces. This answers some of the concerns addressed by participants in user study 1 where some felt that they couldn't remember the exact physical location of workspaces: "you first had to discover and "save" [remember] the positions of the apps". In order for participants to complete the task and to not introduce a new interaction technique, participants used the touch screen to answer the question as for *mSpaces*. Participants needed to return to the question workspace for the answer buttons to appear on the screen below the *workspace viewer*.

m+pSpaces

This condition is a hybrid version of *mSpaces* and *pSpaces* where the main workspace in use is displayed on the phone's screen while the other workspaces are accessible by projecting towards their physical locations (as for *pSpaces*). As the only input needed from the user is on the question workspace, the latter is defined as main workspace, constantly displayed on the phone's screen. Since the screen will be occupied by the main workspace, the *workspace viewer* will not be displayed or made available. We discuss in the design considerations section some interaction techniques that can be used to define what workspace to display on the phone's screen.

Procedures

The tasks used for this experiment are the same as for the previous experiment. We recruited 12 new participants (3 female) for this study aged between 23 and 45 ($\mu = 31.3$), all but one right-handed and all but two smartphone owners. While all participants were familiar with touch screens, only two had used a pico-projector prior to the study.

We used a within-subjects experimental design where all participants had to answer all questions and prototypes were counterbalanced across participants. The tasks were explained individually to each participant who could try out the prototypes with a randomly chosen task in their own time. When they felt ready, they pressed a "Start" button to begin the experiment and again to initiate each trial. After the experiment, users filled out a NASA TLX survey.

The independent variables were: The *virtual workspaces prototype*: mSpaces (m), m+pSpaces (m+p) and pSpaces (p). The *type of task*: type 1 to 4 (t1 to t4).

There were 6 questions of 4 types per prototype corresponding to 24 questions for each prototype and 72 trials overall per participant. In summary the experimental design was: 12 participants x 3 virtual workspace prototypes x 4 types of tasks x 6 trials = 864 data points.

Measures

The experimental software recorded trial completion time (MT) and error rate (ER). In addition, the number of switches between workspaces (SW) was recorded as dependent variable. SW corresponds to the number of times (switches) the user stops on a workspace during a trial. We measure this data to ensure that visual separation effects [7] in the *m+p* and *pSpaces* conditions do not hinder the results. We count a switch each time the user spends at least 300 consecutive ms on a workspace. There is no maximum number of switches as users can change workspaces as many times as they want until they find the answer to the question. Since *m+pSpaces* has one workspace displayed on the screen, SW is recorded as the actual number of switches per task minus the minimum number of switches required to perform this type of task with a given prototype. We gathered the same qualitative data as for user study 1.

RESULTS

We used the univariate ANOVA with Tamhane post-hoc pairwise (unequal variance) comparisons for our analyses.

Error Rate

There were a total of 43 errors out of 864 trials (Figure 7 Left). With 9 incorrect trials, participants made fewest errors with the *pSpaces* technique followed by 16 incorrect trials for *mSpaces* and 18 for *m+pSpaces*. The 43 trials with incorrect responses were removed from further analysis.

Completion Time (MT)

The average trial completion time overall was 14.4s with standard deviation of 2.6s. There was a significant effect of type of task on trial completion time ($F_{3,33}=17.09$, $p<0.001$). Yet, we found no significant effect of workspace prototype.

Switches Between Workspaces (SW)

The average number of switches overall was 4.2 with standard deviation of 0.2. There was a significant effect of prototype used on number of switches ($F_{2,22}=5.83$, $p<0.05$). *mSpaces* (m) and *m+pSpaces* (m+p) resulted in significantly less switches than *pSpaces* (p) (Figure 8). There was also a significant effect of type of task on trial number of switches ($F_{3,33} = 67.9$, $p<0.001$)

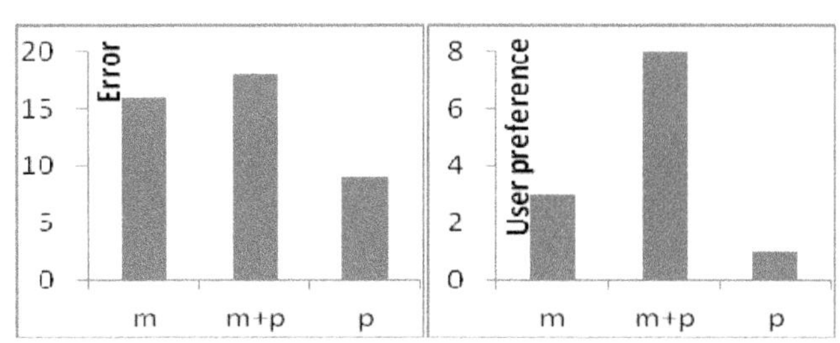

Figure 7: Left: Mean number of errors for each type of workspace prototype – Right: User favorite prototype.

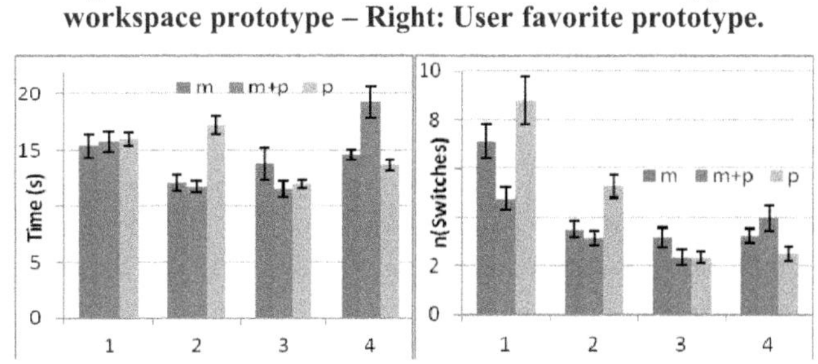

Figure 8: Mean trial completion time (left) and switches between workspaces (right) for each technique and task.

Subjective Evaluation

The NASA TLX questions were analysed separately using non-parametric tests (k-related samples with Freidman Test Type). We found no statistical difference between the different prototypes on any of the NASA TLX factors. In terms of preferences, 8 out of 12 participants preferred *m+pSpaces*, 2 *mSpaces* and 1 *pSpaces*. (Figure 7 Right)

DISCUSSION

Spatially Aware Virtual Workspaces

In this experiment, we did not find any significant difference in the overall task completion time over the three spatially-aware virtual workspaces prototypes. In the first study, for the same tasks, we found that using spatially aware workspaces was significantly faster than current usages of mobile devices. We conclude that while using spatial awareness greatly improves current usages, the way in which the spatially aware system is designed does not seem to influence the system's pace. This further reinforces our first user study finding that virtual workspaces need to be designed with considerations to users' spatial awareness.

Memory Aids

During the first study where *mSpaces* is compared to current usage of mobile phones, users have reported needing time to learn the position of the workspaces and mentioned that "navigational help on the display would be useful". We decided to provide users with a workspace viewer in the *pSpaces* condition since all workspaces were projected and the phone's screen could then be used for displaying the workspace viewer. The idea was to provide users with a constant reference to their position in the environment. This technique also relates well to current existing techniques for switching workspaces in the desktop environment. To our surprise, when we asked users if they found the workspace viewer helpful and if they used it, the 10 out of 12 participants who answered, unanimously replyed that not using it nor finding it useful. The reasons they provided were that "it was quite easy to spot the projections" and "easy to remember the positions". They mentioned they "concentrated on the projection", "knew the arrangement already from the task [they] did before" and "that the other screens were sufficient".

This suggests that with *pSpaces*, users are able to remember the position of the workspaces without needing any workspace viewer. Projection onto the external space has rich spatial cues that, when combined with the kinesthetic cues of moving the device, help users remember the location of the workspace. Additionally, no participant mentioned struggling with finding the position of the workspaces across all conditions, contrary to the first study. Furthermore, in the second study, contrary to the first, all conditions expect users to remember the physical locations of the workspaces so it is possible that the nature of the task condition people to remember the workspaces locations better than in the first study. This leads us to think that when there is no reference to other types of interaction; people feel comfortable and lose their apprehension towards using such interfaces.

Workspaces Switches

The number of workspace switches is significantly higher for *pSpaces* than for both *mSpaces* and *m+pSpaces* (Figure 8 right) while there is no significant difference in the average time needed to perform the trials; which shows that users switched between workspaces in a faster way using *pSpaces*. At the same time, the NASA TLX shows that participants did not find *pSpaces* more mentally or physically demanding or even more frustrating than the other two prototypes. Since we found that participants had no issue finding the position of the workspaces, we can conclude that participants chose, whether consciously or not, to switch more often betwen workspaces in the *pSpaces* condition. This is also very likely to be the reason why users made considerably less errors in performing the task with *pSpaces*. This higher number of switches seems to indicate that *pSpaces* provide an easy avenue to externalize users' thoughts as in [7]".

One Handed vs. Two-Handed Interaction

In this experiment, only two participants held the prototypes in their dominant hand; while all others always held the prototypes with both hands. We hoped that the projector would be small and light enough to not affect the interaction technique. Unfortunately, the device was bigger and heavier than in the first study and that affected the interaction. Since this *mSpaces* prototype was held in both hands instead of one for the first study prototype, we believe that there is a potential for *pSpaces* and *m+pSpaces* to also be one handed techniques provided a smaller embodiment of pico-projection technology inside phones.

Projected Virtual Workspaces

In terms of performance, *pSpaces* appears to be the best technique as users answered more accurately for the same completion time and swap workspaces more often, probably as a way to externalize their thoughts. Nonetheless, *m+pSpaces* was preferred by 75% of the participants and for performances similar to *mSpaces*. Participants preferred *mSpaces* as "it [is] useful to have the task visible all the time while working on it" and as it was "interesting to have one workspace always in sight". Some participants also liked "having the screens in [a] big size on the wall and at the same time to have the question at hand" and finally one mentioned that "it somehow "divided" the task and space".

In summary, whether due to performances (*pSpaces*) or user preferences (*m+pSpaces*), external projection improves the capabilities of spatially aware virtual workspaces.

DESIGN CONSIDERATIONS

Our experiments show that virtual workspaces have the potential to improve the usability of mobile environments. In this section we would like to propose some design considerations for *m-* and *pSpaces*.

Creating Virtual Workspaces & Managing Applications

There are different aspects to take into consideration when designing virtual workspaces. The workspace needs to be created and an application needs to be allocated to this particular workspace. The virtual workspace also has some attributes such as size and position that need to be defined. We present this set of design considerations below.

Creating & Positioning New Workspaces

There are two strategies for creating workspaces in the space around the user. The first consists of creating an empty workspace and moving applications inside it in separate actions. The second consists in directly positioning an application and creating the workspace at the same time. The latter strategy is the most efficient when there is only one application per workspace. We advise no more than one application per workspace to keep the current mobile device interaction paradigm, and due to the small amount of screen real-estate available for phone handsets.

We propose to introduce a specific button – software or hardware – to trigger and control the workspaces management. This will preserve the one-handedness of the interaction technique while keeping it intuitive for the user. The interaction can be "hold and release" based where the user holds the button, moves the device to a physical location and releases the button to complete the operation. This technique allows a direct allocation of the application in view to the newly created workspace.

Another solution is to implement a drag-and-drop approach similar to Boring et al. [3]. For *pSpaces*, an application launcher could be displayed on the mobile screen for the selected application to open up on the actual external projection at the current pointing direction of the device. The workspace position can then be directly controlled by pointing or moving the device to the physical location corresponding to where the workspace will be residing.

Workspaces Dimension

While in *mSpaces* the workspace size is limited to the size of the mobile phone's screen, as discussed in the previous section, in *pSpaces* the corners and size of the workspaces could directly be defined by manipulating the projection area in the environment through an appropriate gesture via the device itself. We could envisage having a virtual workspace larger than the size of the phone's screen in *mSpaces*, similarly to the concept of Peephole displays [21], but this would require a set-up stage via the touch screen or some movement recognition technique and incur additional interaction controls to scroll through the virtual workspace.

Moving Applications Across Workspaces

When moving applications across workspaces we need to differentiate between *m-* and *pSpaces*. In *mSpaces* we propose to use a similar approach to the way applications are already organized on a smartphone application launcher space. In *pSpaces* we can take advantage of the mobile device screen to "grab" an application and "drop" it on an arbitrary workspace after having "pointed" at it. We propose a special "grab" gesture (such as quickly tilting towards the user, as in Boring's Tilt interface [4]) to copy the actual projected workspace to the screen in *m+pSpaces* so the user can provide touch input to an application.

Repositioning Workspaces

The thumbnails representing workspaces or applications can be rearranged on the *workspaces viewer* on the mobile device's screen to rearrange the actual physical location of workspaces. The spatial alignment of the thumbnails and their sizes on the screen will directly translate into the spatial alignment and actual sizes of the workspaces surrounding the user in an appropriate manner – such as by inserting at least 30 degree separation angles between workspaces. The rearrangement of thumbnails on the screen will then lead to the corresponding spatial realignment of the workspaces themselves. In the case of *m+pSpaces*, the same technique is used for ad-hoc selection and modification of which workspace is to be displayed on the screen and respectively the projection.

Finding Virtual Workspaces

We show that users get shortly accustomed to their current workspaces' spatial configuration and do not need memory aid. Yet, this will be useful when people move workspaces around or create new ones and disturb the established spatial arrangement. Similarly, it will benefit users who have high numbers of workspaces or haven't used the system in a long time. An overview of the arrangement of the workspaces on the device screen is needed as well as a finding function which allows rapid access to a workspace. We can use a graphical representation of space like Nacenta's [16] work on MDEs of the positions and shapes of all available displays – virtual workspaces in our case –. Finding a particular workspace could be done by displaying arrows on the screen pointing to the direction of the workspace's location. Haptic feedback could be used to indicate the position of a workspace, which would allow users to simply wave the device until they receive the haptic feedback (similar to Sweep-Shake [19]).

Favourite Configuration

Storing favourite configurations would allow for the configuration of different arrangements based on context as Böhmer [2] proposes for icons. In fact, when the phone is used in different contexts – e.g. personal or profesional – or when used by more than one person, different favorite configurations may exist. For multi-users, it is equivalent to starting one's own session on a shared computer.

Applications & Tasks Awareness

To be used for more effective task management, we can provide awareness that a task in another virtual workspace requires a user's attention by adding some visual feedback. We could display a coloured bar on one side of the display (reflective of the position of the other workspace) and for example changing its colour [15] to indicate the status of the task. Another possibility is to use a halo technique [1] or an off-screen visualization pointing triangle [9]; and haptic feedback could also be used. For example, a light vibration would indicate an alert on a workspace which is currently not visible associated to a stronger vibration when the user hovers over the workspace in question – as we describe in the 'creating virtual workspaces' section above.

Deleting a Virtual Workspace

A gesture, such as drawing a cross while pointing at the workspace could be used to delete it. Alternatively, a specific button could indicate deletion of the workspace. This may require a confirmation click or movement. If the deletion is not linked to the deletion of the application on the workspace, then the confirmation is not compulsary as the effects of a mistake will only be minimal.

CONCLUSION

We investigated virtual workspaces in mobile environments. We started with existing techniques for workspace management in the desktop environment with the view to translate them to mobile settings. We show that extra spatial awareness, that is possible in the mobile context, vastly enhances users' performance. We have presented *mSpaces*, a spatially aware prototype for virtual workspaces, which allows workspace switching by moving the phone to various physical locations, providing users with rich spatio-kinesthetic cues. To determine if using external projection spaces further enhances users' performance, we designed the *m+p* and *pSpaces* prototypes. In a final user study we compare the three techniques to show that projection enhances users' abilities to switch between workspaces, potentially encouraging them to use such methods. We conclude with design considerations to create, manipulate and manage virtual workspaces in the spatially-aware mobile environment.

REFERENCES

1. Baudisch, P. and Rosenholtz, R. Halo: a technique for visualizing off-screen objects. In *CHI'03*,ACM,481-488.
2. Boehmer, M. and Bauer, G. Exploiting the icon arrangement on mobile devices as information source for context-awareness. In *MobileHCI'10*, ACM,195-198.
3. Boring, S., Baur, D., Butz, A., Gustafson, S. and Baudisch, P. Touch Projector: Mobile Interaction Through Video. In *CHI '10*, ACM Press, 2287-2296.
4. Boring, S., Jurmu, M. and Butz, A. Scroll, tilt or move it: using mobile phones to continuously control pointers on large public displays. In *OZCHI SIG: Design: Open 24/7*, ACM Press (2009), 161-168.
5. Cao, X. and Balakrishnan, R. Interacting with dynamically defined information spaces using a handheld projector and a pen. In *UIST'06*, 225-234.
6. Card, S. K. and Austin Henderson, J. A multiple, virtual-workspace interface to support user task switching. *SIGCHI Bull.* 17, (1986), 53-59.
7. Cauchard, J., Löchtefeld, M., Irani, P., Schöning, J., Krüger, A., Fraser, M. and Subramanian, S. Visual Separation in Mobile Multi-Display Environments. In *UIST 2011*, ACM Press (2011), 451-460.
8. D. Austin Henderson, J. and Card, S. Rooms: the use of multiple virtual workspaces to reduce space contention in a window-based graphical user interface. *ACM Trans. Graph.* 5, (1986), 211-243.
9. Ens, B., Ahlström, D., Cockburn, A. and Irani, P. Characterizing User Performance with Assisted Direct Off-Screen Pointing. In *MobileHCI '11*, ACM, 485-494.
10. Fitzmaurice, G. W. Situated information spaces and spatially aware palmtop computers. *Commun. ACM* 36, ACM (1993), 39-49.
11. Gustafson, S., Bierwirth, D. and Baudisch, P. Imaginary interfaces: spatial interaction with empty hands and without visual feedback. In *UIST'10*, ACM (2010), 3-12.
12. Gustafson, S., Holz, C. and Baudisch, P. Imaginary Phone: Learning Imaginary Interfaces by Transferring Spatial Memory from a Familiar Device. In *UIST '11*, ACM Press (2011), 283-292.
13. Lewis, J. P., Rosenholtz, R., Fong, N. and Neumann, U. VisualIDs: automatic distinctive icons for desktop interfaces. In *SIGGRAPH'04*, ACM (2004), 416-423.
14. Li, F. C. Y., Dearman, D. and Truong, K. N. Virtual shelves: interactions with orientation aware devices. In *UIST'09*, ACM Press (2009), 125-128.
15. Matthews, T., Czerwinski, M., Robertson, G. and Tan, D. Clipping lists and change borders: improving multitasking efficiency with peripheral information design. In *CHI'06*, ACM Press (2006), 989-998.
16. Nacenta, M., Gutwin, C., Aliakseyeu, D. and Subramanian, S. There and Back again: Cross-Display Object Movement in Multi-Display Environments. *Journal of HCI* 24, (2009), 170-229.
17. Ringel, M. When one isn't enough: an analysis of virtual desktop usage strategies and their implications for design. In *CHI '03 EA*, ACM Press (2003), 762-763.
18. Robertson, G., Czerwinski, M., Larson, K., Robbins, D. C., Thiel, D. and Dantzich, M. v. Data mountain: using spatial memory for document management. In *UIST'98*, ACM Press (1998), 153-162.
19. Robinson, S., Eslambolchilar, P. and Jones, M. Sweep-Shake: Finding Digital Resources in Physical Environments. In *MobileHCI '09,* ACM, (2009), 1-10.
20. Tan, D. S., Pausch, R., Stefanucci, J. K. and Proffitt, D. R. Kinesthetic cues aid spatial memory. In *CHI '02 EA*, ACM (2002), 806-807.
21. Yee, K.-P. Peephole displays: pen interaction on spatially aware handheld computers. In *CHI'03*,ACM Press (2003),1-8.

Creative Cameraphone Use in Rural Developing Regions

David Frohlich,[1] **Simon Robinson,**[2] **Kristen Eglinton,**[1] **Matt Jones,**[2] **Elina Vartiainen,**[2]

[1] Digital World Research Centre
University of Surrey,
Guildford, GU2 7XH, UK
{ d.frohlich, k.eglinton } @surrey.ac.uk

[2] Future Interaction Technology Lab
Swansea University, SA2 8PP, UK
{ s.n.w.robinson, matt.jones,
e.vartiainen } @swan.ac.uk

ABSTRACT

In this paper we consider the current and future use of cameraphones in the context of rural South Africa, where many people do not have access to the latest models and ICT infrastructure is poor. We report a new study of cameraphone use in this setting, and the design and testing of a novel application for creating rich multimedia narratives and materials. We argue for better creative media applications on mobile platforms in this region, and greater attention to their local use.

Author Keywords

Mobile; storytelling; cameraphone; development.

ACM Classification Keywords

H.5.m [**Information interfaces and presentation**]: Misc.

INTRODUCTION

Recent developments in mobile computing often assume an always-on infrastructure in which devices can connect to each other and the web. For example, portable navigation systems and location-based services rely on GPS coordinates being available from a satellite and usable in remote web searches. However in many parts of the world this infrastructure assumption is not true [27]. Although the use of mobile phones is increasing exponentially in so-called developing countries, many of these phones cannot connect to the internet, and for those that can, the cost of using a connection may be unaffordable by large parts of the population. Even when users can afford to connect, further barriers to use include language diversity and low textual literacy. Web-based information may not be available in local languages, and low textual literacy will inhibit the kinds of interactions that users can undertake on a mobile phone, using textual menus, textual content and free-text entry. In these circumstances, it is important to consider the value of cheaper services running over more restricted forms of infrastructure, as well as more localised uses of the mobile phone platform that are less reliant on text.

In this paper we report further results from the Community Generated Media project that has been addressing these issues in Mankosi, a rural region of the Eastern Cape in South Africa. The focus of the project is on mobile digital media sharing in a community context, building on previous work by members of the project team in India and South Africa [3, 10, 11]. The sharing of multiple forms of media in pictures, sound, video and text is something that is already enabled on a wide variety of cameraphones, and does not necessarily rely on a mobile internet connection. It also extends existing practices of analogue media sharing represented by community radio, theatre, newspapers and television. These are more popular and valuable than internet use in many parts of the world, and stand to gain enormously from digitisation in various forms, not least in the area of mobile production and consumption.

Previous research in the Mankosi community has reported on the use of free 'callback' services on low-end phones to save money on text messages [2], and the deployment of an asynchronous audio sharing system [29]. In this paper we trace the development and early use of a 'MultiMedia Narrative' (MMN) application, based on insights from a study of cameraphone use in the region. The aim of this paper is to reveal the many ways in which local people derive benefit from their existing cameraphones, and how these effects can be accentuated by the provision of simple multimedia narrative capabilities in future phones.

We begin by outlining related work and the community context before describing the cameraphone study in brief. This leads onto an explanation of the design of the MMN application itself and the way it was received and used in a series of 'storytelling' workshops with local community groups. The paper ends with a discussion of the implications of our findings for mobile computing in this and similar contexts. We will argue that the cameraphone has the status of a multimedia entertainment and communication device in developing communities, and would benefit from additional facilities for locally archiving and remixing content in creative ways.

RELATED WORK

In a review of over 200 studies of mobile phone use in developing regions, Donner [7] provides a framework for mapping out differences between them. This can also be applied to studies in other parts of the world and is useful here for understanding work related to the current study. Donner distinguishes between studies concerned with the use of the mobile phone to aid social and economic development (Information and Communication Technologies for Development; ICT4D studies) and those concerned with the more general use of mobiles in society (non-ICT4D studies). In each category,

MobileHCI '12, September 21–24, 2012, San Francisco, CA, USA.

he points to studies of mobile adoption, mobile impact and mobile interrelationships with everyday life. Our work falls into the latter area, since it seeks to understand and then enhance the use of cameraphones for both personal (non-ICT4D) and community (ICT4D) benefit. In fact, we begin by conducting a study of personal cameraphone use in order to take a step back from our previous work on community media for development. We then seek to use the findings to design an application for community media sharing that is better fitted to what individuals are already doing on their mobile phones.

One reason for starting with a more general view of cameraphone use in rural South Africa is that there are few non-ICT4D studies of cameraphones in this geography compared with those in the US and UK. Donner lists many studies of the non-ICT4D use of mobiles across the world, but these often focus on patterns of calls and text communication rather than photographs or media sharing (e.g., Horst and Miller [14]; see also [5, 16]). Other studies have examined the use of mobiles in sharing pre-recorded audio and video media [19, 26, 30]. In contrast, there have been several non-ICT4D studies of cameraphone use in the West, where the devices are used in conjunction with other technologies such as computers, photowebsites and social networking sites.

For example, Kindberg et al. [17], in a study of 19 UK and 11 US participants, show how the cameraphone is used to take familiar snapshots for remembering special events, but also to exchange more playful images to enhance or share live gatherings and to capture functional image reminders or items for a shared task. A more recent series of studies illustrate a variety of 'downstream' activities from cameraphone use involving uploading, tagging, sending and archiving images [1]. In contexts where other receiving technologies are reduced or absent we wondered whether the same uses of images would still apply. Other studies in the West have also found evidence of 'lightweight' and 'heavyweight' video capture and sharing, albeit on a smaller scale compared to photo sharing (e.g., [18, 22]). Comparable studies in developing communities have looked at more facilitated forms of multimedia content creation and sharing for development. We mention this now as a final backdrop to our current design and evaluation work.

Community media production has long been a part of development work, and is thought to give communities a stronger voice in the development process (e.g., [32]). This effect has been accentuated recently by attempts to apply a digital storytelling approach to development contexts. This refers to the creation of short two-minute personal stories in photographs and voiceover, originating in California in the late 1990s [20]. Facilitation of digital story creation in community workshops using scanners, cameras, dictaphones and multimedia computers has been tried in a number of contexts around the world [12]. One value appears to be the expression of community issues and information in a more sharable and accessible form [13].

This approach has been condensed into the provision of digital storytelling software on mobile phones, which are a cheaper and more pervasive technology in development contexts. Thus Frohlich et al. [10, 11] developed a 'story phone' as part of the StoryBank project in rural India. This allowed the creation of short audiophoto narratives comprising up to six images with up to two minutes of synchronised voiceover. Stories could be uploaded and downloaded from a community library and touch screen display, and were useful for sharing both practical and cultural information of local interest. A similar approach was used in a multimedia phone application developed in rural South Africa by Bidwell et al. [3]. This used a more flexible 'carousel' of images with associated sound clips to support the capture of both contemporary and heritage stories, and indigenous knowledge. Both these prototypes had their own usability issues and excluded the use of text and video. They also resulted in stories that were not easily shared or exported. Related prototype story-phones in the West (e.g., [15, 21]) result in standard MMS messages or MP4 video files which would be expensive or impractical to share in developing areas.

Figure 1. The landscape of the Mankosi region.

In the work that follows, we examine the naturalistic use of cameraphones in a rural South African setting to re-consider the design of a story-phone for that region. By looking at existing practices of cameraphone use in this area we hope to fill a gap in the literature whilst identifying more precise requirements for mobile media sharing in general.

COMMUNITY CONTEXT

Mankosi is a district in Nyandeni, Eastern Cape, South Africa. The community has a population of approximately 11000, spread over twelve separate villages. Villages are formed primarily of scattered rural settlements, most of which consist of small groups of rondavels (see Fig. 1).

Infrastructure and services are very limited, and community members do not have domestic access to mains electricity, water or sanitation. There are high levels of poverty, and the majority of the residents of the Nyadeni municipality have either no income (36 %) or less than 800 Rand per month (41 %; $120 approx.) [24]. Electricity availability is very low, and generators and solar panels are uncommon due to their expense and the risk of theft. Two solar-powered mobile phone charging stations, sited here as a separate part of this project, provide some access to power for mobile phones, however.

Literacy levels in the community are low, but Mankosi people have a rich oral isiXhosa-speaking culture, and mobile phones have become an important part of this. Mobiles are the main method of long-distance communication, but due to the expense of airtime many people make use of free text-based services such as 'callback' [2]. The majority of the mobiles used locally are low-end keypad-based models. An increasing number of phone owners use their device to take and view photos and listen to music, and a smaller number use their phones to record audio. Bluetooth sharing of media between mobile phones is reasonably common, due to the great expense of network-based sharing methods.

Access to the community was facilitated through a partner organisation by a member of the project team living full time in the area. TransCape was founded in 2004 initially to help with HIV/AIDS problems, and now runs a variety of health, education and microfinance programmes to counteract poverty in the region. Nicola Bidwell lived as a situated researcher in this area for four years, conducting ethnographic action research on local technology use and design. With a team of local researcher/translators Bidwell helped set up many of the interviews and workshops, hosted us on visits, and advised on local customs and lifestyles whilst leading a parallel project strand of research on a MXit[1]-based media sharing system.

CAMERAPHONE STUDY

In April 2011 we travelled to Mankosi to get a better understanding of the ways in which community members were producing, consuming, and sharing audio and visual material on their phones. To get at these processes we conducted a small-scale qualitative study which employed ethnographic observation, individual and group interviews, as well as two salient digital methods we called *mobile media-elicitation* and *multimedia portraits*. These digital methods were used during both group and individual interviews. Mobile media-elicitation was based on photo-elicitation techniques, but contextualised for a region with no electricity or venues to develop photos. It included asking participants to talk about (and when possible show) media stored on their phones. Participants were asked about their favourite images and other media such as voice recordings and music on their phones, as well as media that they would 'never delete.' The multimedia portraits included engaging participants in getting their photo taken and then, with the help of a local researcher, recording 'why the phone is important to them.' These audio recordings were later layered on top of the image as a kind of audio-photograph (cf. [10]).

Arriving in the community in early April, time was spent in the villages learning about the context, and recruiting participants. The central criterion for participant selection was ownership of a phone which had a camera built in. Overall, 28 people aged between 18 and 60 participated in one of the 17 individual or group interviews. The majority of participants were female, and aged between 18 and 30.

Using mobile media-elicitation all participants were asked to show us or to talk about their 'favourite' content on their phone. Taking out their phones many people shared images of themselves and of the community; images of friends, family, and distant relatives were common. However, it was just as common for them to show us favourite music clips and other media stored on their phones. For example, people spoke about the importance of conversations with friends recorded on their phones. Others referred to video clips of their children singing and dancing. In the remainder of this section we describe several of these findings, beginning with photos, and followed by sound and video. A more detailed account of the findings is also in preparation (see [8]).

Figure 2. An example portrait photo from one of our participants.

This was a favourite photo of one young woman, marking a time before she got married. As she put it, the photo was taken at a "time when [she] was young single, nice and beautiful."

Images of self, family and community life were often shared with us by most participants. However, unlike the casual and spontaneous images found on cameraphones in the West (e.g., [17]), many of the photographs were stylised and posed. In fact they were typified by *portraits* of individuals taken at significant moments or simply when subjects were looking their best. Many were self-portraits or portraits of the phone owner taken by others (see, for example, Fig. 2). Multiple participants, particularly female participants, told us how they took photos of themselves to share via Bluetooth with their husbands so their husbands could have the images before they left for work outside of the villages. Images of children, family, partners and friends were also shared with us. These images were captured for various reasons including people asking to have their photograph taken, marking an event, or to share with others often as a means of managing long distance relationships. Friends and family asked to be photographed so the picture taker could both remember them and share the image with others. Finally, others spoke about how they take images of friends and family, images which later trigger memories. One young woman spoke about her favourite picture on her phone; it was of her best friend she met at boarding school who lived far from the village. As she told us:

> *"This picture reminds me a lot of things because the first time I met this girl it was like, we didn't plan to be the friends but it just happened like that because we were in the school last year [. . .] we started to talk, started to ask where we live, where we come from, then it just, it was the first day that we start to be the friends. So this picture I like it a lot because it reminds me everything."*

The propensity to dress up for special portrait photographs was also illustrated by reactions to our method of taking a multimedia portrait of participants with their phones. This was treated with intense engagement and often resulted in elaborate preparations, a change of clothes and a large audience gathering to watch. Consequently the resulting photographs were highly valued and participants asked to keep them on their phones as souvenirs from the study. This behaviour is also consistent with participants experiences of interaction with a local 'cameraman' who could be hired to take individual printed photographs delivered the next day.

[1] An SA-based instant messaging and chat platform: www.mxit.com.

Although more casual photographs were also captured on phones, their use may have been curtailed by another issue specific to the developing community context. Most participants had no other devices to backup their photographs to. This underscores the lack of other common technologies taken for granted in the West, such as home computers, laptops and other storage devices that were entirely absent from the Mankosi region. Consequently, participants in our study had to constantly juggle with the tension of capturing media on their phones and deleting it to make room for new material. This meant that more casual and transient event-based photographs may be captured, shared and deleted, in favour of archiving more stable portrait representations of self and others.

People's favourite media on their phones went beyond still images. Sound or audio and video were oft-cited media people captured and shared. Sound included both voice and music. Looking closer at this, many participants spoke about using the voice recorder on their phone to capture and later listen to friends talking, joking, or singing. One young man who sang in the choir told us how he would use the voice recorder to record and then listen to himself singing when he was alone. A young woman spoke about recording herself singing on her phone and then playing it back to *"see how [she] sounded."* The voice recorder was used to capture community and conversations with friends. One of the young men told us how he recorded himself and his friends *"speaking about the soccer ball"* (i.e. football). He said he recorded the conversation so that he could *"re-listen to news of the ball"* when he returned home that evening. A young woman spoke about recording her children's voices, and another told us how she likes to use the voice recorder to capture people talking about *"good news."*

Within the theme of sound or audio, music was of central importance. Every participant referred to capturing and sharing music on their phones. Asking one young woman to share the most important media on her phone, she immediately played us a reggae song, and told us how her husband is a *"rasta man."* Others spoke about the capture and, often more important, the sharing of music as one of the most important capabilities of their phones. The importance of music cut across all ages. Even Elders cited *"listening to music"* as an important part of their phone. Gospel music, followed by R&B and pop music were the most highly consumed genres. The sources of this music varied. Some participants spoke about using the voice recorder to capture music from the radio they played in their home; many got their music from other people's phones via Bluetooth. Several young male participants went to the nearest town and bought songs downloaded from the internet. These songs were then brought back to the community and shared from phone to phone. Depending on the battery life, music was listened to on the phones intermittently throughout the day. Music was sometimes consumed using headphones, but more often it was shared *"into the air."* Many participants told us how they would share their Gospel music with their children by playing the music through the speakers of their phone. As one young male put it: *"sometimes when we are actually all together with kids and stuff like that we play the phone and the kids will dance and have fun."* Indeed, the phone sometimes operated as the family stereo, where music was played as people went about their housework or entertained visitors.

This idea of the phone as a site of multimedia entertainment or multimedia production and consumption is also threaded through participants' use of video. Video capture was often referred to as *"videolising."* Video usage included the production of video content from the community, as well as the capture of video from popular culture sources. For example, one young woman spoke about how on her last visit to the nearest city she used the video recorder on her phone to record a football match from a TV. In particular, she described how she recorded the match by holding her phone up to the TV for the length of the game. She later shared this match with a friend who, she claimed, asked her to record it for him. Local football games were also captured on video using phones. One young man told us about videoing the local team playing football, and sharing the footage with friends. Numerous women spoke about videoing community life, including church services and the choir. An older woman described how she uses the video and the voice recorder on her phone to capture *"pictures in church when the choir is singing."* She then shares the content with friends and neighbours who cannot make the long journey to church by foot. In another example, a younger woman used her phone to record people in the local shebeen (informal bar); she would then play the recordings back to other patrons.

MULTIMEDIA NARRATIVE APPLICATION

These findings on the existing use of pictures, sound recordings and video clips on cameraphones, suggest a number of enhancements that might be made to the cameraphone platform as well as an opportunity to combine media into a richer narrative format.

Greater attention might be given to sound and image quality to enhance recording and playback on the device itself. Methods of docking, relaying or projecting content for presentation to larger audiences should be considered, as well as capture via Bluetooth or the internet. A reverse camera would improve the taking of self-portraits, while a line-in socket would support the capture of audio from other sources, such as radios. Media mixing might allow different combinations of sound and image with judicious use of text by which to index the results. Lightweight text annotation fits with 'callback' activity observed in low end phones of the region [2]. Media formats should be extensible to allow social commentary and responses to media. Local memory and battery capacity should be large enough to support long-term storage and long-duration playback, but software designs should take into account these limitations. Oral and musical traditions suggest particular attention to sound design which might support the layering and concatenation of multiple sound channels.

In short, the findings suggest a design transition from cameraphone to 'mediaphone' in this region, to support and extend the mobile media practices already in play. This might not necessarily have all the facilities of a smartphone to access the internet continuously, but it would have better media handling facilities and, in addition, would support more creative capture and mixing of multiple media forms for audiovisual entertainment and communication.

With these requirements in mind we developed a MultiMedia Narrative (MMN) application for both cameraphones and

Figure 3. The MMN application. Left: a stack of narratives on the main MMN screen. Users can scroll up and down between narratives, and left to right between frames. The '+' button inserts a new narrative at the top of the stack; an identical button is shown at the end (far right) of existing recordings to allow users to append a new frame to any narrative. Holding down on two consecutive frames inserts a new frame between them. Centre: options for recording a multimedia frame. This example frame currently contains a picture (top), three simultaneous audio tracks (centre) and text (bottom, centre). From this screen users can also delete the frame (bottom, right), or return to the main narratives screen (bottom, left). Right: playback of a narrative. When playing, text content is overlaid on imagery, and audio tracks are played automatically. From this screen users can also export the narrative in the SMIL multimedia format, sending to other devices via Bluetooth.

smartphones. The application allows currently separate media streams to be combined creatively into multimedia narrative clips, thus extending the expressive properties of the phone for information, entertainment and communication. In the rest of this paper we concentrate on describing and testing the high-end smartphone version of the application, in anticipation of the future affordability of smartphones in developing regions, and because this affords greater capabilities for high-quality media creation, playback and sharing. However, both versions will be released as part of a free open source community media toolkit in the summer of 2012. Although the application was developed for this rural South African region, it relates to key aspects of storytelling in general. We therefore hope it will have a more universal appeal outside this context and be taken up by a variety of groups around the world.

The high-end application runs on a standard Android phone, has a fluid touchscreen interface, and allows users to record images, audio and text along a flexible and extensible timeline structure. Our aim was to allow people to create sophisticated narratives, combining any of these three media elements using a simple interface. This comprises a narrative 'storyboard' of frames on which sound, image and text elements can be built up into a 'story', and exported to a variety of different devices and platforms. The application supports multiple layered audio streams such that the user can record several audio tracks, each of which will be played simultaneously when the story is replayed. After some deliberation we excluded video from the media mix because many phones support separate video capture, and we wanted to preserve the economical storage requirements and expressive quality of audiophoto narratives.

This approach is distinctly different from more conventional video editing applications for mobile phones, then, allowing users to easily capture, edit, append, insert or retake media at any point of the narrative. Our choice of the frame metaphor is intended to prompt users to take photos or record sound during an event, but move beyond simple archiving of raw media elements by prompting later editing and combining of media into narratives. We also focus on generating small file sizes that can be shared with the low-end devices that are common in Mankosi and similar contexts.

Figure 3, left, shows the application's main interface. When the user first opens the application they are presented with a scrollable canvas of existing narratives, ordered by creation date. Dragging up or down navigates through narratives; scrolling left to right moves between the components of a single narrative – individual frames. Each narrative can be made up of any number of frames, and each frame can contain any combination of: an image (via the front or back camera); text; and, any number of concurrent audio recordings. This novel layered audio approach is designed to allow mixing with, for example, speech overlaid on background music.

The interface for capturing the media elements of each frame is shown in Fig. 3, centre. This design focuses around audio and photos, with less graphical emphasis given to text content. From this screen, pressing the camera button allows the user to take a picture, and pressing the audio button begins recording. While recording, pressing the same button again stops recording. Further audio layers can be added by repeating the process. At the bottom of the screen, users can return to the main narrative browser, add text, or delete the frame. We refrained from adding more complex recording and editing features (moving or merging audio recordings, for example) in order to keep the interface as simple as possible.

The system uses a timeline-based approach, but is completely flexible with regards to the components and length of each narrative. For example, a user could choose to compose a story entirely of audio and without visuals – an important consideration in Mankosi and similar communities [3]. Our application does not restrict the duration of individual frames, nor of narratives, and any element can be returned to, edited or extended at any time after creation. We imagine this feature as an enabler for extended conversations, allowing back-and-forth, minuted discussion between two or more parties where, for example, each could take a self portrait photo and then add their own views on a theme.

The application avoids the use of text in menus and icons, preferring an icon-based interface to support the literacy levels of the Mankosi community. Unlike some previous designs, however, we do not aim to prevent the use of text – we feel that text can be an important element in stories if people choose to incorporate it.

Recorded narratives can be played on the phone itself (full-screen), or shared with others by using the application's export feature. Stories are exported (and imported) using the SMIL multimedia format. This choice of format has two benefits. It allows for particularly small file sizes – especially important for further sharing and to cope with storage space limitations on other local devices. A typical exported three-minute MMN narrative with five photos, continuous audio throughout, and text on the first and last frames is approximately 560 kB in size. Secondly, this choice ensures that all the narrative's components are separate and therefore viewable on any platform, even if SMIL playback itself is unavailable.

While the phone application is self-contained, we also designed it to be compatible with two existing media browser tablet PCs that are attached to mobile phone charging stations situated in the community. The MMN application can send stories to a media browser via Bluetooth, and these appear as stories for public viewing. In contrast to other previous media sharing approaches (StoryBank [10], for example), with our approach, in addition to the narrative itself each of the story elements themselves are shared individually, and can therefore be repurposed by other users in their own sharing and storytelling.

MANKOSI STORIES

In October 2011 we returned to the Mankosi region to carry out workshops in which we showed the new MMN application to various community groups for feedback and use. Groups were chosen with the local situated researcher to represent important social institutions or collectives in the area, who already acted as information hubs and might benefit from multimedia information. They included two groups of voluntary home care workers who visited sick people at their homes, a group of tourist guides and hostel owners working with local tourists, members of a local church choir and volunteer staff from our NGO partners TransCape. Groups were asked to consider the use of the MMN mobile phone application for both community and personal use.

A series of five one-day workshops were held on consecutive days of the week with a total of 32 participants. Six or seven participants were present on each day, together with three representatives of the UK project team and one or two local researchers, who acted as translators. All sessions were held in the local isiXhosa language, except for those with TransCape staff who spoke English. Mornings were taken up with a discussion of group activity and a demonstration of the MMN application for feedback and discussion. After lunch, groups split into two halves to create narrative content of their own, facilitated by a UK project team member. Sessions culminated in the joint viewing and discussion of mobile narrative content downloaded onto a laptop for playback.

A thematic analysis of group discussions and created narratives was carried out to identify common themes regarding MMN value and use. It is important to note that these are hypothesised values and uses offered as part of an initial reaction to the technology, which may change in actual practice. This will be addressed in future publications dealing with subsequent use of the phones, which were left in situ in the community after we left, and managed by local researchers and our situated project researcher. Moreover, with the release of the MMN application as part of an open source toolkit we will learn a great deal about how communities react to and use the technology in their everyday lives. For now we report briefly on five potential uses which emerged from the analysis of workshop data alone. These uses cut across the personal and community dimensions which participants found hard to distinguish from each other in discussion. They include: advertising; multimedia letters; documentation; learning resources; and, healthcare advice.

Using multimedia narratives for **advertising** local services or events emerged first in the tourist guide group, where participants saw them as a way of communicating with tourists themselves. They wanted to make narrative films of local attractions and put them up on the internet for tourists to see – despite having no access to the internet themselves: *"We can record the caves and cultural practices here so that when tourists are coming here they must know what the expectations are [. . .] they can see the videos and get interested."* Subsequent content creation tried to realise this by building a narrative around a photograph of a printed advert for local kayaking trips along the river. Members of the choir suggested using the application to advertise church events and services. They also made an evangelical narrative for a forthcoming youth event comprising six frames. The narrative started with a picture of three girls singing a gospel song and went on to feature short testimonial talks by each girl in turn (to a profile

Figure 4. A short hymn recording, intended to be played to and left with a sick person. The initial title frame (not shown) says 'Singing.'

Figure 5. A multilingual flashcard showing the isiXhosa word for 'fork.' The words are also spoken three times on each frame.

picture) before closing with a picture of the bible with spoken appeal and final song to textual credits. When the elders of the group saw this later they were so impressed that they discussed showing it at the planned event. This raised issues of how to transfer narrative content made on the phones to other devices such as computers and televisions.

The tourist group were also forthright in suggesting a use of the MMN application for writing **multimedia letters** to government authorities. This was seen to give a new voice to those who could not handwrite conventional letters, and resulted in the creation of a single narrative comprising the spoken complaints of three tourist group members, set to their own portrait pictures. An opening text frame was entitled simply *"Mankosi (Tshani) Tourism Needs."* Complaints included descriptions of poor roads, sanitation and litter, with appeals for electricity, toilets and running water to boost tourism in the area. TransCape staff also mentioned the possibility of creating multimedia messages highlighting local issues, and made a similar narrative in text and audio, dealing with poor schooling, beach safety, forced marriage and the value of sport.

A logical development of the multimedia letter ideas was manifest in a very large category of suggestions relating to the **documentation** of community life. The mobile phone application was seen as tool for recording both personal and community events either as an enriched record to be shared with those not present, or as a kind of legal evidence that could be shared with authorities of various kinds. For example, narrative recordings were suggested for personal, family and cultural events like Xhosa weddings, dances and initiation ceremonies, as well as for recording meetings for live or later consumption: *"Maybe in a meeting I can share to the other person who is not in the meeting. If you are to take a decision you must also accommodate that person."* More serious uses of documentation included the proposed recording of crime or abuse to report to the police later: *"you can use it in cases of rape to take the evidence."* Several mentions were made of recording sports events, church services and musical performances to share with others or simply enjoy as a form of entertainment later. This was manifest in one short narrative recorded by four women from the choir group. After an opening title frame they sang a song in harmony, which culminated in a prayer (see Fig. 4). They suggested recording this on a visit to a sick person and leaving it as a gift of hope.

Discussion of recording some community events suggested using MMN content as a **learning resource**. This was true in the case of recording school lessons or church sermons which participants felt could be recycled in their own right to larger audiences. Recorded football and netball games were also thought to be useful for training players and referees: *"it can help us in the netball club because the rules are changing."* Some narratives for providing specific advice to children by elders were suggested and made in the home care worker and choir groups. These were thought to overcome the embarrassment of talking about difficult subjects such as sex or violence. In a similar vein, mini-dramas were made to provide a more vivid kind of advice or instruction on health or other issues (see healthcare advice below). In a non-healthcare example, a short drama was made to explain farming cooperatives using a textual title slide, two sketches and a picture of two people tending a garden together.

The scanning and circulation of printed materials such as school books or posters was also mentioned as a kind of learning resource, and the local creation of audio-photo books was suggested in the TransCape group as a reading aid: *"We don't have a reading culture but that could grow. You could make an illustrated book that's got voice with text. It could be a tool to educate people to read and write."* Another creative idea to emerge in this group was the ad hoc production of talking flash cards for language learning. Several were made very quickly in the afternoon session. A picture of an object was taken and annotated with the English and Xhosa words in text and speech. These were placed side by side in a two-frame narrative, as shown in Fig. 5.

The creation of multimedia narratives for **healthcare advice** was enthusiastically recommended by the home care worker groups. A very natural use was seen to be the recording of short dramas illustrating HIV/AIDS experiences and treatments, or those for other health-related conditions such as diabetes or domestic violence. These were felt to provide practical advice

Figure 6. A talking pill packet.

The voiceover explains that the pill "gives you energy, it makes appetite to make you eat more and more food. It is good to take these pills because if you are sick you have that power you want to eat more food. It gives you energy to get strong."

as well as bringing hidden topics into the open, to encourage discussion and self-revelation: *"it would be helpful to use the pictures, because people don't open up, so maybe when they see the pictures they say I am also suffering from this disease."* Participants were familiar with seeing live dramas about these subjects and took immediately to the creation of their own dramas in the afternoon sessions. These were the longest narratives recorded in the workshops comprising up to 11 pictorial frames with spoken dialogue lasting for up to nine minutes. For this reason they are the most difficult to illustrate here. Other contexts for recording health advice included remote diagnosis of emergency conditions, the capture of advice given by doctors and nurses in consultations, and the recording of verbal medicine instructions around pictures of medical packaging or patient record cards. A simple example of the latter use is shown in Fig. 6 which was a single-frame narrative describing the purpose of a packet of pills.

SECOND MMN PROTOTYPE

Feedback from the storytelling workshops highlighted several improvements to the application; consequently we have developed a second version. This supports inserting frames at the start of a story, and the recording of a single verbal narrative or music track against which to set individual frames (recently highlighted in [28]). This second version also limits the number of simultaneous audio recordings to three separate layers, allowing us to both explicitly highlight this feature and to allow users to easily re-record or delete individual layers.

The updated MMN2 application allows users to export their stories in an additional, more future-proof format. It uses an HTML5-based container with media components base64-encoded and embedded in a single file. While this adds 20 % to 30 % to the size of an exported file (the three-minute example given earlier is around 120 kB larger, typically), we think this choice is necessary to extend compatibility and allow more widespread sharing of stories. This export format still preserves the open nature of individual media components, however, to ensure recipients and viewers are free to adapt and remix stories. We have also added the ability to export movie files that could be shared on services such as YouTube.

Perhaps the most exciting aspect for NGOs and other similar organisations is the ability of our new design to create story templates that could prompt, say, discussions about current issues, or act as a flexible multimedia-capable community survey. Any existing story can now be used as a template, and later loaded to be edited to incorporate new content in the same sequential format. The high- and low-end versions of the application will be made available as elements of an open source toolkit for mobile digital storytelling in mid-2012.

DISCUSSION

The aim of this work has been to consider the range of personal and community benefits of cameraphones in a rural South African setting, and how these might be enhanced. We reflect now on what we have learned in this respect from our two studies, which broadly addressed each issue in turn.

The study of cameraphone use delivered findings that were initially reminiscent of those from other studies reported in the literature from US and UK settings. The phones themselves were used for keeping in touch with family and friends, and photographs were taken to mark special events and relationships. However, the taking or staging of self-portraits was much more prevalent in this context, and seemed to indicate a strong interest in personal identity and its performance through images (cf. [31]). At first sight this appears to contradict lay notions of what it might be to live in a less individualistic and more community-centred culture, but is actually consistent with cultures in which pride is taken in clothing and physical appearance (e.g., [23]). In fact the whole question of whether aspects of phone use were for personal or community benefit appeared to confuse participants, as they thought of themselves as both community members and individuals who benefited personally in both roles. This was illustrated more dramatically in the second study where community activities such as advertising tourist sites or writing to authorities were seen to be of potential benefit to everyone.

The use of sound recording was another distinctive feature of cameraphone use in this region that was not reported in early studies of cameraphone use in the West. Local recordings made up the majority of clips and comprised local music performances, everyday conversations including jokes and stories, and commentaries on live events such as football matches. In addition, participants reported capturing popular and folk music clips from the radio and collecting other pre-recorded music from visits to urban centres where they could access the internet or receive downloaded content from intermediaries. These findings echo those of Kumar et al. [19] in India and contrast with specific studies of mobile sound capture in the West, which have shown a preference for ambient sound recording to support memory for events [6, 9, 25]. They also contrast with mobile music practices in the West involving direct downloading of internet content or synchronisation of mobile devices with digital music archives on a home PC (e.g., [4]). Entertainment appears to be the dominant motivation for sound recording and capture here, but the mechanisms for realising it are different. They reflect a bias towards the local recording of self-made media and transient audio broadcasts, over the direct downloading of internet content from mobile handsets themselves.

Some propensity for video recording was also evident in the study, but this was further constrained by the limited storage capacity of phones in the absence of backup facilities, and the time taken to transfer video between devices via Bluetooth. All this suggests the need for greater attention to sound as well as image recording on phones designed for regions like Mankosi, with local playback from the phones themselves. Our MMN application was designed with this in mind and provides new facilities for the combination of three separate media types: image, sound and text. This amounts to a kind of 'annotated audiophotography' application, oriented more to the creation of multimedia narrative items, than the capture of audio-augmented photographs.

Our second study showed that local people perceived many possible benefits of this approach, some of which they tried to realise in the narratives they made. The ability to combine media appeared to stimulate a creative imagination in many participants who got excited about what new media could be made and shared for different purposes. In general, people were impressed by how quickly short films could be put together in a series of simple frames, and were able to make two or more examples in a short space of time (with some assistance from a member of the project team). Although some of the suggested uses, such as documentation, could have been achieved by the capture of individual media, others could not. For example, the whole category of learning resource examples were based on the ability to combine oral and visual media in new ways, as in the language flash cards. Furthermore, there was something appealing to participants about the form of various combinations, compared with single media recordings. For example, although a football or netball match could be video recorded for playback to referees, it was the ability to highlight and comment on particular moves that was seen to be the attraction of the MMN application. This is similar to the argument used in digital storytelling, which is said to encourage people to go beyond the archiving of raw media elements such as photographs or sound recordings. The possibility of assembling particular sets of photographs and audio into a narrative structure invites authors to reflect on their personal meaning in a new way [20].

The findings were similar to those on the StoryBank project, where a multimedia story-phone application was trialled in rural India. A variety of cultural and development stories were created by different sections of the community, depending on their own interests and job responsibilities [11]. The stories suggested in our content creation workshops were similarly shaped by the background and interests of participants, and also began to show a diversity of content types and media forms. These related to health, education and advertising purposes as well as more personal ones such as sport and music. The biggest difference seemed to result from the lack of constraints on the length of media clips or narratives created with the MMN application. This resulted in some very long monologue recordings (within multimedia letters) and dramas of up to nine minutes duration. Again the distinctions between content created for personal and community use, entertainment and 'development' purposes, were challenged by our findings. As in other studies we found a strong motivation and practice of creating multiple media for personal and community entertainment, alongside a strong interest and aptitude for multimedia creation for professional use [26, 30].

In general, the findings point to some special features of mobile media sharing in rural developing regions which distinguish them from the kind of urban contexts examined by Smyth et al. [30]. At the simplest level, participants in Smyth et al.'s study lived in the busy metropolis of Bangalore, India, with access not only to cheaper 'Chinese set' featurephones with removable MicroSD cards, but also a ready supply of electricity and proximity to cybercafés and mobile shops offering low cost media downloads. Our participants often had to walk many miles simply to charge their phones, which varied greatly in age and facilities. Consequently, the default mode of media capture was local and self-made on the phone itself. Photographs, sounds and video clips were recorded in situ, juggled within the internal memory of the phone, and Bluetoothed to others in the region via face-to-face transactions. Pre-recorded media capture was limited to live recording of radio broadcasts, unless someone travelled to a town. In that case, music and video content could be brought back into the region by the traveller and shared with others in the community. Hence the sharing of pre-recorded media turns up in our study, but mainly as a by-product of human mobility and connectivity

The question of connectivity is a key one for rural South Africa, and other places in the world where ICT infrastructure is poor or patchy. Internet connectivity and cloud computing only really makes sense if devices have reliable connections to remote machines and data, and users can afford to upload and download content between them. Neither assumption was true in this region, yet users extolled the virtues of creating and sharing multiple forms of information on their mobile phones. If such phones are the only pervasive devices in the community, more attention should be paid to their local use and interaction so that they can substitute for other devices taken for granted elsewhere, such as televisions, radios, DVD players, computers, photo displays and the rest. For example, community meeting points could house app stores and libraries of shared content, accessed over a cheaper to operate local wireless network. Content might be refreshed and updated by human travellers moving between rural and urban regions and donating both collected and self-made media to the community. When mobile data services become more affordable, these local access points might be supplemented by remote providers. Elsewhere in the project we have begun to think about alternative architectures for this kind of situated media computing, which are asynchronous, intermittently connected and self-powering. This, in turn, may have implications for ubiquitous computing in the West, and how to make it more accessible and sociable, and sustainable in the face of disturbances in the infrastructure due to natural or man-made disasters or fluctuating costs.

ACKNOWLEDGEMENTS

This work is funded by EPSRC project EP/H042857/1. We would like to thank Gary Marsden (UCT) for hosting us in Cape Town, Bill Tucker (UWC) for building the original link to the community and Nic Bidwell (CSIR-Meraka) for facilitating, training local researchers and interfacing with the Mankosi community. We are deeply grateful to local researchers Masbulele, Mvuzo, Nomphello, Roico, Senzo and

Thomeka, to Transcape for their partnership in this project, and to the local residents who participated in our workshops.

REFERENCES

1. Ames, M., Eckles, D., Naaman, M., Spasojevic, M. and House, N. Requirements for mobile photoware. *Personal and Ubiquitous Computing* 14.2 (2010), 95–109.
2. Bidwell, N., Lalmas, M., Marsden, G., Dlutu, B., Ntlangano, S., Manjingolo, A., Tucker, W., Jones, M., Robinson, S., Vartiainen, E. and Klampanos, I. Please call ME.N.U.4EVER: designing for 'callback' in rural Africa. In *Proc. IWIPS '11*, Product and Systems Internationalisation, Inc. (2011), 117–138.
3. Bidwell, N., Reitmaier, T., Marsden, G. and Hansen, S. Designing with mobile digital storytelling in rural Africa. In *Proc. CHI '10*, ACM (2010), 1593–1602.
4. Bull, M. Sound Moves: iPod Culture and Urban Experience. Routledge (2008).
5. Castells, M., Fernández-Ardèvol, M., Qiu, J. and Sey, A. Mobile Communication and Society: A Global Perspective. The MIT Press (2007).
6. Dib, L., Petrelli, D. and Whittaker, S. Sonic souvenirs: exploring the paradoxes of recorded sound for family remembering. In *Proc. CSCW '10*, ACM (2010), 391–400.
7. Donner, J. Research approaches to mobile use in the developing world: a review of the literature. *The Information Society* 24.3 (2008), 140–159.
8. Eglinton, K., Frohlich, D., Robinson, S., Jones, M., Vartiainen, E. and Bidwell, N. Mobile Media Production, Consumption, and Sharing in Rural South Africa. *[Unpublished manuscript currently in preparation]*.
9. Frohlich, D. Audiophotography: Bringing photos to life with sounds. Springer (2004).
10. Frohlich, D., Rachovides, D., Riga, K., Bhat, R., Frank, M., Edirisinghe, E., Wickramanayaka, D., Jones, M. and Harwood, W. StoryBank: mobile digital storytelling in a development context. In *Proc. CHI '09*, ACM (2009), 1761–1770.
11. Frohlich, D., Bhat, R., Jones, M., Lalmas, M., Frank, M., Rachovides, D., Tucker, R. and Riga, K. Democracy, design, and development in community content creation: lessons from the StoryBank project. *ITID* 5.4 (2009), 19–35.
12. Hartley, J. and McWilliam, K. Story Circle: Digital Storytelling Around the World. Wiley-Blackwell (2009).
13. Hearn, G., Tacchi, J., Foth, M. and Lennie, J. Action Research and New Media: Concepts, Methods and Cases. Hampton Press (2008).
14. Horst, H. and Miller, D. The Cell Phone: An Anthropology of Communication. Berg Publishers (2006).
15. Jokela, T., Lehikoinen, J. and Korhonen, H. Mobile multimedia presentation editor: enabling creation of audio-visual stories on mobile devices. In *Proc. CHI '08*, ACM (2008), 63–72.
16. J. Katz, ed. Handbook of Mobile Communication Studies. The MIT Press (2008).
17. Kindberg, T., Spasojevic, M., Fleck, R. and Sellen, A. I saw this and thought of you: some social uses of camera phones. In *Proc. CHI '05: Extended Abstracts*, ACM (2005), 1545–1548.
18. Kirk, D., Sellen, A., Harper, R. and Wood, K. Understanding videowork. In *Proc. CHI '07*, ACM (2007), 61–70.
19. Kumar, N., Chouhan, G. and Parikh, T. Folk music goes digital in India. In *Proc. CHI '11*, ACM (2011), 1423–1432.
20. Lambert, J. Digital Storytelling: Capturing Lives, Creating Community. Life on the Water Inc. (2002).
21. Landry, B. and Guzdial, M. iTell: supporting retrospective storytelling with digital photos. In *Proc. DIS '06*, ACM (2006), 160–168.
22. Lehmuskallio, A. and Sarvas, R. Snapshot video: everyday photographers taking short video-clips. In *Proc. NordiCHI '08*, ACM (2008), 257–265.
23. Miller, D. Stuff. Polity (2009).
24. Nyandeni Local Municipality. Nyandeni Integrated Development Plan: Review 2010/2011. URL: `http://goo.gl/ijTy1` (visited on 12/04/2011).
25. Oleksik, G. and Brown, L. M. Sonic gems: exploring the potential of audio recording as a form of sentimental memory capture. In *Proc. BCS-HCI '08*, British Computer Society (2008), 163–172.
26. Rangaswamy, N. and Cutrell, E. Anthropology, development and ICTs: slums, youth and the mobile internet in urban India. In *Proc. ICTD '12*, ACM (2012), 85–93.
27. Rangaswamy, N. and Sambasivan, N. Cutting chai, jugaad, and here pheri: towards ubicomp for a global community. *Personal and Ubiquitous Computing* 15.6 (2011), 553–564.
28. Reitmaier, T., Bidwell, N. and Marsden, G. Situating digital storytelling within African communities. *International Journal of Human-Computer Studies* 69.10 (2011), 658–668.
29. Reitmaier, T., Bidwell, N., Siya, M., Marsden, G. and Tucker, W. Communicating in designing an oral repository for rural African villages. In *Proc. IST-Africa*, 2012.
30. Smyth, T., Kumar, S., Medhi, I. and Toyama, K. Where there's a will there's a way: mobile media sharing in urban India. In *Proc. CHI '10*, ACM (2010), 753–762.
31. Thrift, N. and Dewsbury, J.-D. Dead geographies—and how to make them live. *Environment and Planning D: Society and Space* 18.4 (2000), 411–432.
32. Watkins, J. and Tacchi, J. Finding a voice through content creation. In *Participatory Content Creation for Development: Principles and Practices*, UNESCO (2008), 13–20.

AutoWeb: Automatic Classification of Mobile Web Pages for Revisitation

Jie Liu **Wenchang Xu** **Yuanchun Shi**
Key Laboratory of Pervasive Computing, Ministry of Education
Department of Computer Science and Technology, Tsinghua University, China
{liujiejesse, wencxu}@gmail.com, shiyc@tsinghua.edu.cn

ABSTRACT
Revisitation in mobile Web browsers takes more time than that in desktop browsers due to the limitations of mobile phones. In this paper, we propose AutoWeb, a novel approach to speed up revisitation in mobile Web browsing. In AutoWeb, opened Web pages are automatically classified into different groups based on their contents. Users can more quickly revisit an opened Web page by narrowing down search scope into a group of pages that share the same topic. We evaluated the classification accuracy and the accuracy is 92.4%. Three experiments were conducted to investigate revisitation performance in three specific tasks. Results show AutoWeb can save significant time for revisitation by 29.5%, especially for long time Web browsing, and that it improves overall mobile Web revisitation experience. We also compare automatic classification with other revisitation methods.

Author Keywords
Mobile Web; automatic classification; revisitation.

ACM Classification Keywords
H.5.2 **[Information Interfaces and Presentation]**: User Interfaces – Graphical User Interfaces.

General Terms
Human Factors, Design, Algorithms

INTRODUCTION
With the popularity of smart phones and the improvement of wireless connection, people tend to spend more time surfing the Internet on mobile devices. Mobile Web browsing experience is affected by many factors, such as small screens, low CPU performance and variable latency of wireless networks [21].

Small screen makes it difficult to get a normal view of what is displayed and it also affects the accuracy of input via pen taps or direct finger touches [4]. When users want to revisit an opened Web page, they scroll history lists or bookmarks back and forth or just tap back button several times. It takes extensive scrolling to target an intended Web page if many pages are opened. Users can also type related characters in the URL field to locate previous page in the pull-down suggestion list. But this search-based revisitation only applies to the pages that can be recalled clearly, such as frequently or recently accessed pages.

To get an overview of opened Web pages quickly, representation of history list should be re-designed. Mobile browsers can not show as many entries of history list in one screen as desktop browsers. To solve this problem, we can narrow down search scope in history list. If opened Web pages are classified into different groups based on their content, users can view all groups quickly on small screens. When a user wants to revisit a previous Web page, s/he can first choose the group that shares the same topic with the intended Web page, and then in this group find the target. Revisitation becomes topic-specific and needs less movements and scrolling. In addition, navigation pattern changes from one level to two levels.

If we apply classification to mobile browsers in the same way as desktop browsers [15, 16, 27], users have to classify opened Web pages manually, which in turn increase the input complexity on users' side. Classification can be performed by browsers themselves instead. We design AutoWeb (Figure 1) to automatically classify opened Web pages into different groups according to their contents.

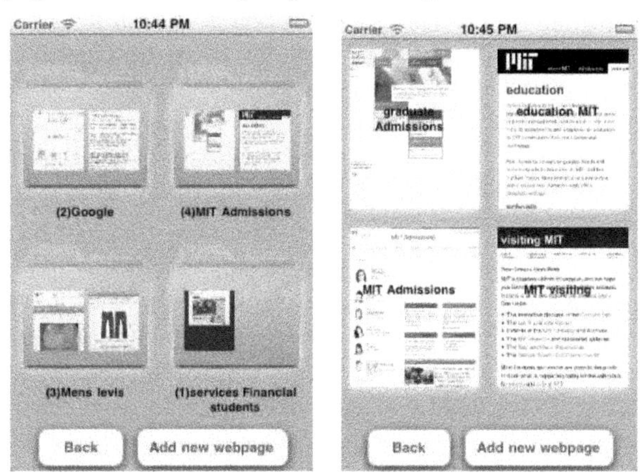

Figure 1. Revisitation in AutoWeb
(Left: Groups Level, Web pages are classified into groups. Right: In-Group Level, similar Web pages are in one group)

The rest of paper is organized as follows. Following a review of relevant literature, we describe a pilot survey to find out the frequency, methods and other aspects of mobile Web revisitation. Then we explain the design and evaluation of AutoWeb. After that, we give a detailed explanation about three experiments to investigate revisitation experience in three tasks in comparison with traditional history list and search-based revisitation. We conclude the paper with discussion and future work.

RELATED WORK

Various studies have been conducted to investigate mobile Web browsing and revisitation. We discuss related work from both human and technique aspects.

Human Factors in Mobile Web Browsing

Performing tasks on mobile browsers place heavy cognitive demands on users' short-term memory because of limited screen size, scrolling capabilities, and slower processing [2]. Shrestha [21] found that participants had frustrating experience using mobile browsers as they spent significant time in navigation by extensive scrolling and full concentration on browsing rather than actual content. Scrolling the long history or bookmark list also takes much time for revisitation.

Users form mental models to help them make connections among disparate bits of information [19]. With a small screen size, users have difficulty in activating a mental model for interpreting the information and in placing information within the existing mental model [2]. Besides the screen size constraint, AutoWeb also introduces another mental model issue. Since AutoWeb automatically classifies Web pages into several groups without users' intervention, how to guide users to match their mental models to the right group needs much consideration. In later sections, we'll discuss some approaches to address it.

Mobile Web Browsing Activities

For active mobile Internet users, mobile Web browsing and searching are the dominant information access methods [10] and are intended to support task-specific usage [2]. Church *et al.* [6] conducted a large-scale study of mobile Web use and indicated that browsing accounts for the majority of information access activities.

As with the content of mobile Web browsing, Sohn *et al.* [22] did a diary study and claimed that *trivia*, *directions (navigation)* and *point of interest (local services)* are the most cited information needs. Church *et al.* [5] classified Web content by topics and found that the most popular mobile topics were *local services* and *travel & commuting*. Heimonen [10] came up with a similar result, which *trivia*, *work/studies/hobbies*, *public transportation (navigation)* were top three frequent categories. Considering the proportions of each kinds of Web content, we design several sets of tasks and simulate usage scenarios in daily life to evaluate AutoWeb's revisitation performance.

Revisitation Methods

Revisitation occurs frequently when users browse Web pages. Early studies show that from 58% [23] to 81% [7] Web pages visited by users have been previously accessed. Recently, Weinreich [28] suggested revisitation frequency dropped to 43.7%. Zhang *et al.* [30] measure revisitation in tabbed browsing and rated the effective revisitation frequency at 59.6%. All the researches above are about conventional revisitation on desktop browsers. To our knowledge, there is no similar research on mobile Web browsing. Hence, we conduct a pilot survey to find out revisitation frequency on mobile Web browsing.

Usually, users resort to history lists, back button and bookmark for revisitation. But these tools can only help to revisit Web pages in a specific context. Many studies [3, 7, 13] show that users seldom use Web history to visit Web pages for lack of clear description of entries. The back button comprised 30% [24] of revisitation action. But it is only useful for short-term revisitation. Up to 94% of users [1] utilized bookmarks to revisit and organize information over several Web pages. Users have to manage bookmarks themselves, and more efforts are taken as bookmarks increase.

Users can also use search-based methods for mobile Web revisitation. Users can directly type related characters in the URL fields to locate previous Web pages in the pull-down list, or use a search engine to find the information again. These methods put a heavy burden on users' cognition and memory. They only apply to the Web pages that can be recalled clearly, such as frequently or recently accessed pages. Moreover, extensive typing is needed, which is not efficient for software keyboards on small screens.

Many novel tools try to facilitate revisitation. Thumbnail images of Web pages tend to reduce contained text beyond readability and have visual cues to remind users of the Web pages they accessed previously. Session Highlights [11] arranged thumbnails in chronological order besides browser. Visual Snippets [25] presented a compact representation of Web pages to support both the identification of new relevant Web pages and the re-finding of previously viewed pages. AutoWeb also uses thumbnails to help users recall opened Web pages. MacKay *et al.* [15, 16] and Wang *et al.* [27] designed browser plugins to support multi-session tasks. Users create a task group, add several Web pages related to a specific task to this task group and manage the tasks manually. This method costs lots of operations on users' side, so it's inappropriate for mobile browsing.

Automatic Classification Algorithms

Many algorithms have been proposed for automatic classification in information retrieval field. These algorithms can be categorized into two types, link-based analysis algorithms and content-based analysis algorithms. Link-based analysis algorithms use hyperlink information inside Web page source. If one page has a link to another page, these algorithms infer that these two Web pages are relevant to each other. But linkage information cannot show the sematic meaning of Web pages [9]. Content-based analysis algorithms employ information retrieval methods to extract keywords from a set of Web pages and calculate the similarity among them. It is more accurate than the link-based analysis algorithms [17]. Hence, we adopt the content-based analysis algorithm for automatic classification in AutoWeb.

In consideration of constrained resources on mobile phones, complex classification algorithms are not appropriate for slow CPU frequency and small amount of RAM. It also introduces noticeable latency that affects browsing experience. TF-IDF algorithm [14, 26] only uses simple mathematical operations and consumes acceptable computing resources. We customize TF-IDF algorithm to achieve satisfactory classification accuracy and speed.

PILOT SURVEY

Before we design AutoWeb, some prerequisite facts need to be confirmed. The frequency may not fall in line with that on conventional desktop browsing. We should know whether users revisit Web pages often on mobile devices like that on PCs. Unfortunately, to our knowledge, previous researches mainly focus on desktop Web browsing and no available reference we can refer to. Hence, we conduct a pilot survey to find the answer.

We recruited 45 paid participants from our university and a residential area nearby, in which 31 participants (68.9%) were male. Ages ranged from 19 to 35 years (*mean*=23.5, *SD*=4.1). They took different occupations, including undergraduates, graduates, teachers, businessmen, managers and IT employees. All participants used smart phones like iPhone or Android phones in daily life. They were all experienced mobile Web users with at least one year for mobile Web browsing.

The browsing events on their phones were captured for one week with their consent. We measure revisitation frequency by using a traditional approach. It is rated by using the number of repeated page loading events divided by the total number of page loading events [24, 30]. The methods used for revisitation were also logged. In total, 33750 loading events were logged. One Web browsing session is defined as a continuous browsing phase in which no intervals between two consecutive loading events exceed one hour. Revisitation span is the number of page loading events before the last revisitation.

The number of opened Web pages for each browsing session is 27.6 on average (SD=15.3). Revisitation frequency on mobile browsing is 45.8% (SD = 14.3%) with 15458 repeated loading events. It means that users revisit about 13 Web pages during one browsing session. It is relatively high. The acceleration of revisitation introduced by AutoWeb will contribute to improving mobile browsing experience.

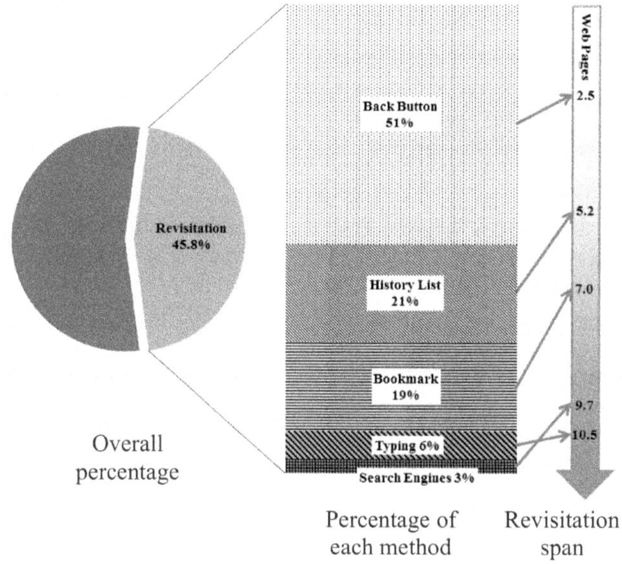

Figure 2. Revisitation Frequencies and Spans in Mobile Web Browsing

We also present the usage frequencies and revisitation spans of bookmark, history list, back button, typing in the URL field and search engines in Figure 2. Participants relied heavily on back button for revisitation, and the frequency of using bookmark and history list is similar. It differs with previous study results on desktop browsers as mentioned in *Revisitation Methods* section, in which back button comprised 30% of revisitation action and history list is seldom used. In the informal interview after the survey, some participants said that they thought back button was an easy tool to re-find Web pages that were recently accessed. So they used back buttons often.

Typing in the URL field and search engines were rarely used. Some participants said they could remember only a few frequently used URLs and mainly typed homepages' URLs. If they typed some other keywords in the URL field, they need to scroll the long suggestion list and pay much attention to find the target link.

From the perspective of revisitation span, we can find a rough negative correlation between revisitation frequency and span. The more often a revisitation method is used, the less revisitation span it has. It indicates that users tend to use simple operation and less taps or touches in mobile Web revisitation. We suggest the reason why mobile Web revisitation differs with that on desktop is the inherent limitations of mobile devices, which are slow input speed and low accuracy, small display size and etc.

AUTOWEB

We design AutoWeb to achieve the goal of speeding up revisitation in one browsing session. In AutoWeb, we use two levels to represent opened Web pages. Groups Level holds all groups of topics, and In-Group Level contains opened Web pages in each group sharing the same topic.

Considerations in Design

We choose iPhone as the platform. A recent report in May, 2011 reveals that iPhone tops first in mobile phones' network traffic in 10 out of 13 main countries [8]. In addition to iPhone's popularity in mobile Web browsing, it is easy for development using Xcode and distribution via App Store.

To help users identify Web pages quickly with less mental effort, an appropriate page representation is necessary. As mentioned in *RELATED WORK*, thumbnails are helpful for supporting re-finding Web pages [25]. We use a hybrid way by combining thumbnails and texts. Thumbnails give users visual cues and provide large touch areas for selection. Keywords used for classification are also displayed on thumbnails to help users match their mental models. In Group Level, we use the folder as the metaphor for a group of classified Web pages. Smaller thumbnails also appear in the folder to indicate the content of this group.

As with the order of each opened Web page, some alternatives are based on alphabet, recency and frequency of visits [29]. Recency is a strong reuse pattern [23] for Web browsing. It requires less cognitive efforts when users search for newly visited sites on top of the list [12]. Therefore, we adopt the recency-based approach to sort groups and Web pages in each group.

To guide users match their mental models with automatic classification results, several methods are introduced to help address this issue. When a Web page is loaded, a pop-up window will show the keywords of this Web page for one second to give users first expression (see part ① in Figure 4). At Groups Level, Web page thumbnails in the folder icons and the keywords below provide cues for recall. At In-Group Level, larger thumbnails with keywords in the center also help to match users' mental models (in Figure 1).

Clustering Algorithm in AutoWeb

Clustering is a computation intensive task. In consideration of limited computing resources on mobile phones, an efficient clustering algorithm is necessary.

We use vector-space model (VSM) to represent each Web page source as vectors in a multidimensional Euclidean space. The frequency of each word is counted. AutoWeb uses TF-IDF algorithm [26]. Term frequency $TF(d,t)$ is the number of times term t occurs in document d, which is $n(d,t)$. So, $TF(d,t)=\frac{n(d,t)}{\sum_{\tau} n(d,\tau)}$.

For Inverse document frequency $IDF(t)$, if D is the document collection and D_t is the set of documents containing t, $IDF(t)=\log\frac{|D|}{1+|D_t|}$.

Web page source is in a relatively structured format. HTML tags and metatags indicate different significance of terms. So we assign weights to them. Title, keywords and description in metatags weigh the highest. The first level headings have a medium weight, and bold words, headings in second level and below weigh the lowest. Hence, in vector space, the coordinate of document d in axis term t is given by $d_t = w_t TF(d,t) IDF(t)$, where w_t is the weight of t. Let $\vec{d}$ represent document d in vector space, then each Web page can be represented as $\vec{d}=\{i : w_i TF(d,i) IDF(i)\}$.

After calculating TF-IDF value of an incoming Web page source, we apply single-pass incremental clustering to it. Although for each calculated Web page, its D and D_t may change by 1. This doesn't affect the clustering result greatly. So we don't re-calculate IDF values for the consideration of efficiency. The similarity of incoming Web page with existing pages in each cluster is computed. We calculate inter-document similarity $s(\vec{d}_i,\vec{d}_j)$ using cosine measure, which is $s(\vec{d}_i,\vec{d}_j)=\frac{\vec{d}_i \vec{d}_j}{|\vec{d}_i||\vec{d}_j|}$.

If the similarity value is above a given threshold, this Web page belongs to this cluster. If more than one cluster pass the threshold, all these clusters will contain this Web page so as to increase the hit rate of revisitation. A new cluster will be created when no existing clusters go beyond the threshold.

Classification Procedure

When users input a URL or touch a link, a request for a Web page is issued. After getting the requested Web page, AutoWeb extract Web source and parse it in several steps.

Figure 3 shows the detailed procedure of clustering. We parse the source for text components using Document Object Model (DOM). Given the limited computing resources on mobile phones, we choose the most significant parts of text components, which are titles, keywords,

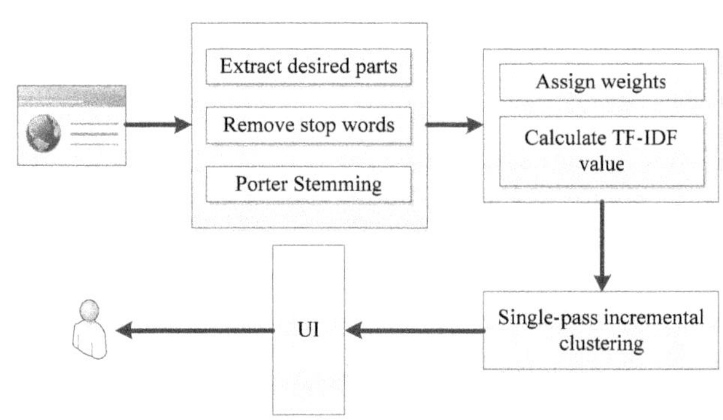

Figure 3. The Procedure of Clustering Web Pages

description, bold words and headings. We remove stop words in these components. Porter Stemming algorithm [18] is employed to map words to the same stem. Then we assigned different weights to different components and calculate TF-IDF values for each selected terms in this Web page. After single-pass clustering, results are stored and ready for revisitation. Users interact with the system by a designed UI as illustrated in Figure 1.

User Interface

We also take the UI design into account. Since AutoWeb features automatic classification, at the bottom of the main window there are two buttons, one for viewing current Web page in the same group of topic and the other one for viewing all groups. Figure 4 illustrates the user interface of AutoWeb. When a user wants to revisit a previous Web page sharing the same topic, s/he just simply touches the same-topic button to enter In-Group Level and view all the Web pages that belong to the same group. If more than one group hold this Web page, all Web pages in these groups will be shown. The user can select the desired Web page to revisit by touching the thumbnail image. If a user wants to shift to a different topic performed earlier, s/he touches the all-topics button and enters Groups Level. AutoWeb shows all groups with one folder for one group. Below the folder shows the keywords this group holds. By picking a folder with the desired topic, the user steps into that folder and choose a specific Web page. So at most three steps are taken to target a desired Web page and no extra interaction such as text input is necessary.

Accuracy of Automatic Classification

We evaluated the system by processing Web pages related to four kinds of most frequent activities [5, 10], that is *local services*, *travel*, *trivia* and *work/studies/hobbies (shopping)*.

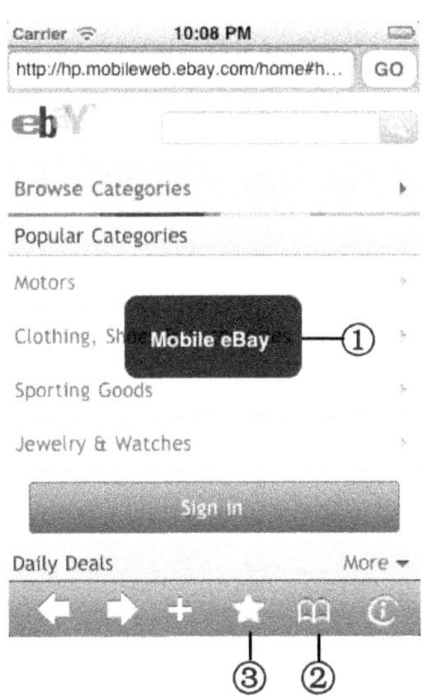

Figure 4. UI of AutoWeb.
(①Pop-up Window, lasts for 1 second ② Same-Topic Button, ③All-Topics Button)

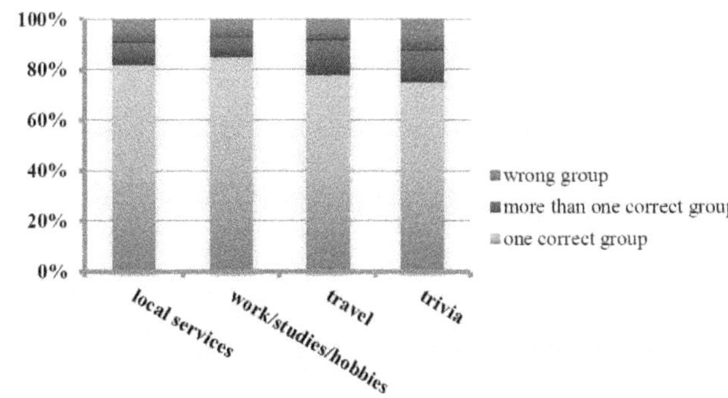

Figure 5. Classification Accuracy in Each Activity

We did these activities in AutoWeb with at least 50 related Web pages opened for each activity independently. We recorded the numbers of Web pages that were classified into one correct group, more than one correct group, and wrong group in each activity. In the case that the Web page was classified into several groups but not all these groups should hold this Web page, we considered it was classified into wrong group. We measured classification accuracy from users' perspective rather than using F-measure, Purity or other theoretical measures. Since in AutoWeb, it's users that judge whether previous Web pages are classified into correct group. For each opened Web page, if a user can find it in a folder at a time, it is regarded as a time of correct classification.

Figure 5 shows the results of evaluation. In every activity, about 80% of Web pages can be correctly classified into one group of topic. Plus more than one correct group classification, the accuracy is 92.4%. Still there are 7.6% of Web pages that were not placed into correct groups. We analyzed these Web pages and found that they contained few feature keywords and less descriptive titles, which were difficult for classification. This is the drawback suffered by content-based analysis algorithms. We'll study the effect on revisitation caused by classification missing in experiment 2 of the user study.

USER STUDY SETUP

The goal of our user study is to find out whether AutoWeb is helpful, in what condition, to what extent AutoWeb facilitates the revisitation and the difference between other methods. We conducted three experiments.

Study Design

We compare AutoWeb with a conventional mobile browser. Elapsed time of each revisitation in AutoWeb starts from touching revisitation button, goes on by stepping into Groups Level and In-Group Level (maybe some iterations for classification miss), ends by choosing an intended Web page. The times that participants step into wrong groups were also logged. We define Miss Ratio as the rate that the times of entering wrong In-Group Level divided by the total times of entering In-Group Level.

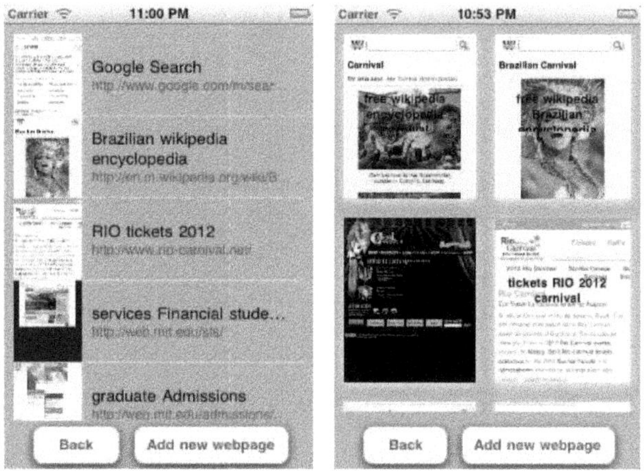

Figure 6. Two Representations of Opened Web Pages (Left: PlainWeb, Right: AutoWeb, In-Group Level)

Mobile Safari is a built-in browser in iOS devices. But due to the limitation of software authority, browsing events in Mobile Safari cannot be logged. So we also implement a traditional mobile browser called PlainWeb to log events (in Figure 6, left picture), which only has back button and traditional history list for revisitation. History list in PlainWeb also adopts recency order and a hybrid Web page representation with thumbnails and texts. The elapsed time of revisitation begins with touching the history button and ends with finishing finding a target Web page.

Participants

We recruited 26 participants (9 females). They all took part in previous pilot survey. Ages ranged from 21 to 32 years (*mean* = 22.4, *SD* = 4.5). 12 participants were students affiliated with computer science, 4 with electronic engineer and 3 with economics. Other participants were 2 teachers, 2 salesmen and 3 IT employees. They are active mobile Web users with iPhone. Before experiments, all participants were instructed how to use AutoWeb and PlainWeb. They practiced browsing Web pages with these browsers for at least half an hour until they got used to them.

EXPERIMENT 1

Tasks Design

Web content varies so greatly that it affects the results of automatic classification. To conduct the experiment in a controlled way, we design three typical sets of tasks according to existing studies about mobile browsing content [5, 10] to simulate the daily use of mobile browsing. These tasks are about *local services*, *shopping*, *trivia* and *travel*, which are the most frequent activities in mobile browsing.

All participants fulfilled these three tasks in sequence using both AutoWeb and PlainWeb. Web pages accumulate over each task. 13 participants used AutoWeb first, and the others used PlainWeb first to receive counterbalanced results.

Task 1 Make a Shopping Plan

This task focuses on local services and shopping. We design a scenario where participants make a shopping plan for this weekend.

First, participants required to find the latest fashion trends (such as jeans, suits) using Google. Then they searched it in the on-line shopping sites (such as amazon, eBay) to find the price and discount. After that, they searched shopping centers in New York, compared them and chose the favorite one. After finishing the previous steps, they should write down the name and price of desired clothing, the shopping center's location and other related information.

Task 2 Answer Questions

This task is to perform trivial information retrieval activities. There are eight questions focusing on the worldwide mobile network and iPhone, such as the most recent mobile network traffic in America, the market share of iPhone, the quantity of apps that had download from App Store, the number of countries had deployed 3G wireless network, and iPhone's share of mobile network traffic.

Task 3 Create a Travel Itinerary

This task is about travel. We put participants in the scenario that they are planning a trip to Rio, Brazil.

First, they should find the price of flight from New York to Rio on different airlines, compare and choose a proper one. And then, they searched for hotels in Rio and booked a room. There would be an annual carnival held in Rio during the stay. So they wanted to learn more about the carnival on Google and Wikipedia. After that, they decided to prepare a costume for the carnival. So they modified the shopping plan to buy a costume. After finishing previous steps, they should write down the information of flight, hotel and carnival, name and price of costume, shopping center's location and other related information.

Results

After participants accomplished all tasks using AutoWeb and PlainWeb, we transferred log files from phones to a desktop computer for analysis. We measure the average revisitation time. Classification accuracy differs in a small range, which is 91.1%-91.7%. The average revisitation times for each participant is 44.2 (*SD* = 7.5) in AutoWeb, and 38.4 (*SD* = 8.1) in PlainWeb. We use two-way ANOVA to analyze which factor may affect revisitation performance. We also interviewed several participants for their comments.

We investigate the average revisitation time in different tasks and browsers. The average revisitation time is the average time participants spent in re-finding one opened Web page. We explore each participant's average revisitation time using AutoWeb and PlainWeb. The hypothesis is: Participants revisited Web pages faster when using AutoWeb.

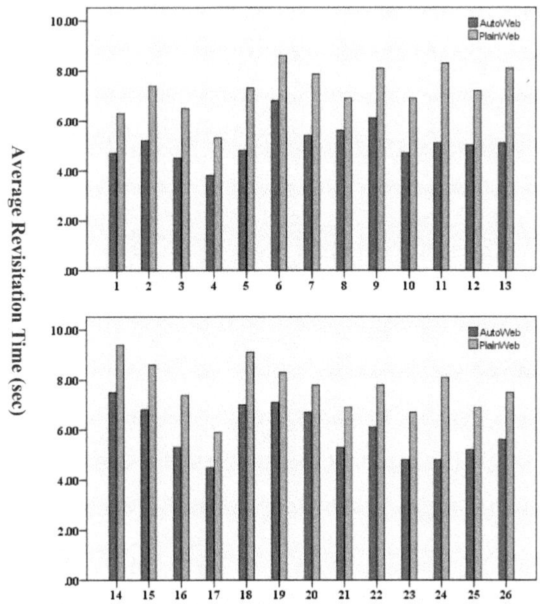

Figure 7. Average Revisitation Time for Each Participant

Figure 7 illustrated every participant's average revisitation time in two passes. There is a significant difference in AutoWeb and PlainWeb in terms of average revisitation time ($F(1, 24)=6.53$; $p<.001$). It conforms to the hypothesis. The result suggests that participants were able to revisit previous Web pages more quickly using AutoWeb. The average revisitation time of AutoWeb is 5.52sec (SD=.96sec), while the average revisitation time of PlainWeb is 7.83sec (SD=1.10sec). AutoWeb saves up to overall 29.5% revisitation time.

User Experience

We also investigated participants' browsing experience with AutoWeb and PlainWeb. After finishing these three tasks, Participants filled out a questionnaire to rate some aspects of AutoWeb and PlainWeb in Likert scale[1]. We collected and calculated the ratings for each browser. Standard t-test comparison cannot be used because Likert scale responses are not normally distributed. We use Mann-Whitney U Test to make pairwise comparisons between AutoWeb and PlainWeb.

As with ease of use, AutoWeb received a mean rating of 4.13, while PlainWeb received 4.08. There is no obvious difference in ease of use between these two browsers. As with the question, "Which browser do you like", AutoWeb received a mean rating of 4.50, and PlainWeb receive 3.12. Mann-Whitney U Test show a significant differences between AutoWeb and PlainWeb (z=4.13, $p<.001$). It reveals that participants prefer AutoWeb.

Discussion

In the informal interview, we want to explore how participants felt about revisitation during browsing and how their mental model works when they use AutoWeb.

Several participants mentioned that, at the beginning of each pass, "I didn't find the benefit of AutoWeb. I can easily revisit a Web page use PlainWeb with the cue of thumbnails (at the beginning)." When participants opened more Web pages, "When I began to write down the results, I came to realize that AutoWeb is helpful. Because by PlainWeb, I had to scroll up and down several times in the history list to find my target. Especially in Task 3, when I have to go back to Web pages opened in Task 1, it took great pains to scroll down so many times to find them.". "Using AutoWeb, I only scroll down few times to find the folder, and in the folder, find the page at once." Their browsing experience in different browsing stages falls in line with the revisitation time in different stages. AutoWeb can easily manage a large number of opened Web pages and speed up revisitation.

As with the mental model, we are interested in the way how participants find the target with the help of the cues we provide. Some participants said, "The pop-up window gave an overview of the Web page and I got an idea of keywords in this page." When searching in the Groups Level, "I first skimmed over the thumbnails in the folder icon. If folder icon didn't contain all the thumbnails, I would look at the text below." One participant said, "After several times of revisitation, I almost remembered the folders' names and locations. So before I began to find a Web page, I knew where to find it."

EXPERIMENT 2

AutoWeb relies on automatic classification to facilitate revisitation. Classification accuracy is crucial to reducing revisitation time and improving browsing experience. AutoWeb proves to be faster for revisitation at a relatively high accuracy in experiment 1. In this experiment, we want to discover the relationship between classification accuracy and revisitation time in a quantitative way. Furthermore, how different classification accuracies affect browsing experience will be discussed.

Experiment Setup

23 out of 26 participants who took Experiment 1 took this experiment. Participants were not instructed to open specified Web pages. They can access any Web pages related to these topics. They surfed the Internet for at least one hour.

Results

By analysis of log files, we calculated miss ratio (MR) and corresponding average revisitation time (ART). The overall trend is that ART increases as MR increases (Figure 8). In the experiment, MR ranged from 7.4% to 14.1% while ART ranged from 4.5 sec to 8.7 sec. In previous experiment 1,

---

[1] Likert scale responses range from 1 to 5, where 1 stands for strongly disagree and 5 stands for strongly agree

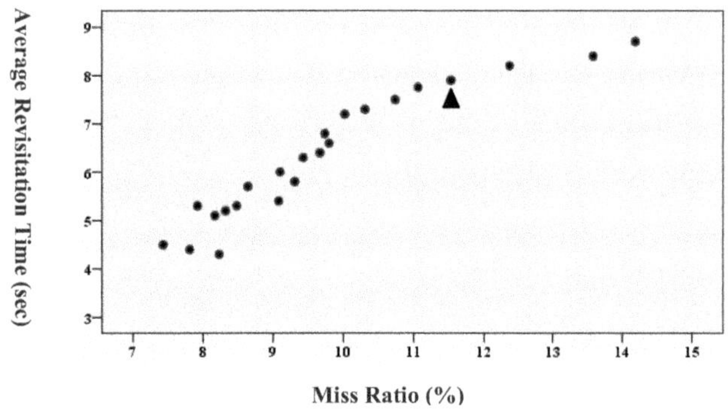

Figure 8. Average Revisitation Time at Different Miss Ratio

ART in PlainWeb is 7.83sec. In Figure 8, when MR is 11.53%, ART is 7.9 sec (marked by a triangle). Hence, we can get an empirical conclusion that to keep ART in AutoWeb lower than that in PlainWeb, we should control MR fewer than 11.53%. 74% participants are under 11.53% about MR. In most conditions, AutoWeb can speed up the revisitation in daily use.

Interview and Discussion

In the informal interview after experiment, we wanted to know what measures participants would adopt if a classification miss occurred and how they felt about this more freely browsing.

The measures taken by participants to handle miss issues differed. Some participants told that they just went back to the Groups Level and found another proper folder, stepped into it. There would be some iteration to find a target Web page. One participant said, "When I didn't find the Web page, sometimes I would scroll up and use a similar one or one that can lead me to the target." Someone said, "If I didn't' find it at the second time, I would give up and open a new Web page instead".

A participant said that when using traditional mobile browsers before, in order to narrow down the search scope in history list, he would recall approximately the last accessed time. AutoWeb released him from memory burden. He could just choose one group of Web pages by the hints to find an intended Web page.

AutoWeb also changes the way of mobile browsing. A participant told us that when using AutoWeb, she paid more attention to the topic of Web pages. The whole procedure of browsing became more topic-specific. She would sometimes touch same-topic button to enter In-Groups Level and see Web pages that shared the same topic. It could remind her of the pages that she didn't pay much attention to before. She would also step into Group Level to get a whole view of topics.

During the experiment, we noticed that there was some difference in the pattern of browsing using two browsers. In PlainWeb, when searching for information by search engines, participants would touched one link in the search result Web page, stepped in and browsed it. In current Web page, they would follow another link to other pages. After tracing down several pages, they went back to the search results page, touched a second link and browsed it. They searched information in depth. In AutoWeb, a number of participants opened several link pages continuously. Then they browsed them one by one. They searched information in width. They said that in this way they would focus on the topic and make comparison between similar Web pages more quickly.

EXPERIMENT 3

In order to compare automatic classification with other revisitation methods such as search-based navigation, we conduct another experiment to investigate the difference.

We integrate other revisitation methods, namely back button, history list, bookmark, typing in the URL field and search engines, into AutoWeb and installed the software in participants' own iPhones for daily use. We recruited 12 participants from experiment 2 and conducted a one-week log study. After collecting log files, we calculated the revisitation frequency of each method for each participant (in Figure 9).

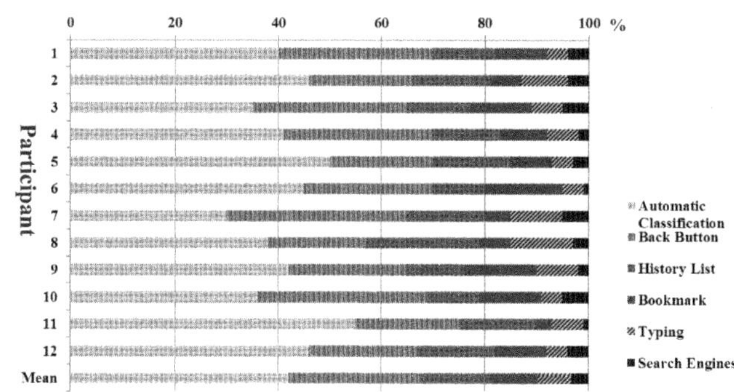

Figure 9. Comparison of Each Revisitation Method

In the experiment, participants preferred to use the automatic classification method to revisit Web pages at the frequency 42.0% (*SD* = 6.6%). Back button (*mean* = 25.4%, *SD* = 5.5%), history list (*mean* = 13.8%, *SD* = 3.1%), and bookmark (*mean* = 9.2%, *SD* = 3.6%) were used less than those in previous plot survey. Interestingly, typing in the URL field (*mean* = 6.4%, *SD* = 2.6%) and using search engines (*mean* = 3.2%, *SD* = 1.4%) were similar with those in pilot survey. This indicates that automatic classification replaces about half of the usage of back button, history list and bookmark, while has little effect on the long revisitation span methods, like typing in the URL field and search engines.

Back button is the second most frequent revisitation method. Some participants said that back button is indispensable since it takes only few operations to find the Web pages which are one or two pages before the current one. But sometimes they might touch the same-topic button instead if these consecutive pages share the same topic. Similarly, they would touch the all-topics button instead of history list or bookmark to find a Web page that is in a relatively longer revisitation span.

We also investigate the difference that participants use the same-topic button and all-topics button. The majority of participants (10 people) would like to click on the all-topics button and navigate to previous Web pages, but two participants prefer to search for a related page first and then touch the same-topic button to find similar pages. They said this method can save time in choosing the topic folder.

DISCUSSION

Results presented in user study confirm that AutoWeb is easy to use and facilitates the revisitation for browsing mobile Web pages. AutoWeb introduces the concept of automatic classification according to Web contents into mobile browsers. This method proves effective and conducive to revisitation.

The essence of automatic classification in AutoWeb is to narrow down the searching scope of opened Web pages. However, in some extreme situations, AutoWeb won't work well. If all Web pages share the same keywords, all of them will be classified into one group. Users can only search in one folder for a desired Web page. Then AutoWeb degenerates to a traditional mobile browser that uses history list to hold accessed entries. If every Web page doesn't share the same keyword with each other, one topic group will hold only one opened Web page. In this worst case, AutoWeb won't speed up the revisitation. Users will take more steps in revisitation on the contrary. But in practice, for a relatively long time browsing and common activities, these extreme situations seldom happen in our evaluation and user study.

As to classification algorithm itself, to our knowledge, there is no algorithm that can automatically classify all Web pages correctly. Taking the limited computing resources of mobile phones into consideration as well, the efficiency of algorithms is more crucial. In the design of AutoWeb, we got an idea to design client/server architecture. If we move the heavy computing burden to a powerful server and adopt more complicated and accurate algorithm, we can get a better classification result. But the communication latency will increase so as to affect user experience. Moreover, the server gets every request from users, so privacy will be another issue. The practical method is to provide some remedy tools when automatic classification fails to put Web pages into right groups. Our goal is to speed up the revisitation on the whole and make the loss of classification miss at the very least.

We use two levels to represent classification results. If AutoWeb also support long-term revisit, many Web pages would be classified into one group. So Web pages at In-Group Level may also need to be classified into different groups. Two levels may not be enough. But the increase of levels also increase the complexity of guide and navigation, it also increase recognition burden on users' side. How to strike a balance between the number of levels and ease of use needs further study.

The user study also has some limitations. Firstly, we only implement AutoWeb on iPhone due to its dominance in mobile network traffic [8]. Other platforms, such as Android and Symbian should be implemented in future. Secondly, since each participant only took hours to finish experiments, experiment time was relatively short. Hawthorne Effect[2] may exist. So we need carry out a long-term study to verify the result.

CONCLUSION AND FUTURE WORK

We have introduced a novel approach for revisitation on mobile browser by automatic classification of Web pages. Due to the limitations on mobile devices, revisitation takes more time than that on desktop computers. We use automatic classification method to classify opened Web pages into different topics of groups. It helps users to narrow down searching scope and to reduce extensive scrolling.

We have presented results from a pilot survey to find that revisitation occurs frequently on mobile Web browsing. We have described the design and implementation of AutoWeb. The consideration in design was explained in detail. We also described the UI design and the process of operation. We evaluated classification accuracy of the system. The results proved satisfactory. In most cases, AutoWeb can classify Web pages correctly at the rate of 92.4%.

We have presented a user study in detail. In the controlled experiment, we design three tasks which are most frequent activities on mobile browsing. We found that AutoWeb can facilitate revisitation a lot and save up to overall 29.5% revisitation time. Users also got a better revisitation experience and preferred AutoWeb other than PlainWeb. In the semi-open experiment, how classification accuracy and miss rate affect revisitation was discussed. We find average revisitation time increases as miss ration increases. In most conditions, AutoWeb can facilitate the revisitation in daily use. We also conducted an experiment to find the difference between automatic classifications with other revisitation methods.

Future work includes adding the features that users can intervene in classification process for more satisfactory results such as manually adding or moving an opened Web page to a desired group. The system should learn from users' choice and adjust the classification results accordingly. More practical remedy tools in case of classification miss should be

---

[2] Hawthorne effect is a form of reactivity whereby subjects improve or modify an aspect of their behavior being experimentally measured simply in response to the fact that they are being studied, not in response to any particular experimental manipulation.(Wikipedia.org)

provided in AutoWeb. Besides, an appropriate number of levels for representation should be investigated.

ACKNOWLEDGMENTS

This work is supported by the University Doctorial Research Foundation, No. 20100002110052 and the Nokia - Tsinghua University Joint Research Funding.

REFERENCES

1. Abrams, D., Baecker, R. and Chignell, M. Information archiving with bookmarks: Personal web space construction and organization. *Proc. CHI 98*, pp. 41-48
2. Albers, M.J. and Kim, L. User web browsing characteristics using palm handhelds for information retrieval. *In Proc. IPCC/SIGDOC 2000*, pp. 125-135.
3. Aula, A., Jhaveri, N., and Käki, M. Information Search and Re-access Strategies of Experienced Web Users, In *Proc. WWW 2005*, pp. 583-592.
4. Borodin, Y., Mahmud, J., and Ramakrishnan, I.V. Context Browsing with Mobiles - When Less is More. In *Proc. MobiSys 2007*, pp. 3-15
5. Church, K., and Smyth, B. Understanding the Intent Behind Mobile Information Needs. In *Proc. IUI 2009*, pp. 247-256
6. Church, K., Smyth, B., Cotter, P., and Bradley, K. Mobile information access: A study of emerging search behavior on the mobile Internet. In *ACM Trans. Web, 2007, 1(1).*
7. Cockburn, A. and McKenzie, B. What do Web Users do? An Empirical Analysis of Web Use. In *International Journal of Human-Computer Studies, 2001(54)*, pp.903-922.
8. Device Essentials. http://www.comscore.com/Press_Events/Press_Releases/2011/6/comScore_Introduces_Device_Essentials
9. Dourisboure, Y., Geraci, F., and Pellegrini, M. Extraction and classification of dense implicit communities in the Web graph. In *ACM Trans. Web 2009;3(2)*
10. Heimonen, T. Information Needs and Practices of Active Mobile Internet Users. In *Proc. Mobility 2009.*
11. Jhaveri, N. and Räihä, K. The Advantages of a Cross-Session Web Workspace. In Proc. *CHI extended abstracts on Human factors in computing systems, 2005,* pp. 1949-1952
12. Kaasten, S. and Greenberg, S. Designing an integrated bookmark/history system for web browsing. *In Proc. WCGS, 2000.*
13. Kellar, M., Watters, C. and Shepherd, M. A Goal-Based Classification of Web Information Tasks. In *Proc. the American Society for Information Science and Technology, 2006, 43(1),* pp. 1–22.
14. Liu, J., Yu, C., Xu, W and Shi. Y. Clustering web pages to facilitate revisitation on mobile devices. In *Proc. IUI 2012*, pp. 249-252
15. MacKay, B. and Watters, C. Building support for multi-session tasks. *In Proc. CHI 2009*, pp. 4273-4278.
16. MacKay, B. and Watters, C. Exploring multi-session web tasks. *In Proc. CHI 2008*, pp. 1187-1196.
17. Nikolaev, K., Zudina, E., and Gorshkov. A. Combining anchor text categorization and graph analysis for paid link detection, In *Proc. WWW 2009.*
18. Porter, M., An algorithm for suffix stripping. 1980 http://tartarus.org/~martin/PorterStemmer/
19. Redish, J., C. Understanding Readers. In *Techniques for Technical Communicators. 1994*. pp. 15-41
20. Setlur, V., Rossoff, S., and Gooch, B. Wish I Hadn't Clicked That: Context Based Icons for Mobile Web Navigation and Directed Search Tasks. In *Proc. IUI 2011*, pp. 165-174
21. Shrestha, S. Mobile Web Browsing: Usability Study. *In Proc. Mobility 2007*, pp. 187-194
22. Sohn, T., Li, K., Griswold, W. and Hollan. J. A diary study of mobile information needs. In *Proc. CHI 2008*, pp. 433-442.
23. Tauscher, L., and Greenberg, S. How People Revisit Web Pages: Empirical Findings and Implications for the Design of History Systems, *International Journal of Human-Computer Studies, 1997, 47(1),* pp.97-137.
24. Tauscher, L. and Greenberg, S. Revisitation patterns in World Wide Web navigation. In *Proc. CHI 1997*, pp. *99-106.*
25. Teevan, J., Cutrell, E., Fisher, D., Drucker, M. S., Ramos, G. Visual Snippets: Summarizing Web Pages for Search and Revisitation. In *Proc. CHI 2009*, pp. 2023-2032.
26. TF-IDF algorithm. http://en.wikipedia.org/wiki/TF-IDF
27. Wang, Q., and Chang H. Multitasking Bar: Prototype and Evaluation of Introducing the Task Concept into a *Browser, In Proc. CHI 2010, pp. 103-11.2*
28. Weinreich, H., Obendorf, H., Herder, E. and Mayer, M. Not Quite the Average: An Empirical Study of Web Use. In Trans. Web 2008; 2(1).
29. Yoong-En, T., and Seong, D.S.K. Visual History Mechanism on Mobile Internet Browser. In *Proc. Mobility, 2007*, pp. 372-379.
30. Zhang, H. and Zhao, S. Measuring Web Page Revisitation in Tabbed Browsing. In *Proc. CHI 2011*, pp. 1831-1834.

Enough Power to Move: Dimensions for Representing Energy Availability

Anders Lundström[1], Cristian Bogdan[1], Filip Kis[1], Ingvar Olsson[3], and Lennart Fahlén[2]

[1)] Royal Institute of Technology
Media Technology and Interaction Design
Lindstedtsvägen 5, SE-100 44
Stockholm, Sweden
{andelund, cristi, fkis}@kth.se

[2)] Swedish Institute for Computer Science
ICE-lab
Box 1263, SE-164 29
Kista, Sweden
lef@sics.se

[3)] Tritech Technology AB
P O Box 1094, SE-172 22
Sundbyberg, Sweden
ingvar,olsson@tritech.se

ABSTRACT

Energy and design of energy-feedback are becoming increasingly important in the mobile HCI community. Our application area concerns electric vehicles. We thus depart from home and workplace appliances and address range and energy anxiety caused by short driving distance capabilities and long charging times in mobile settings. While some research has been done on energy management of mobile devices, less has been done on mobility devices like electric vehicles. We explore this topic by letting conventional fuel car drivers reflect on their current driving habits through an exploration tool that we developed. Our results demonstrate three dimensions related to energy availability to consider for design of energy dependent mobility devices and provide explanations on how these dimensions could be utilize in our design through energy visualizations. With this we contributed not only by demonstrating aspects of energy availability and mobility, but also through opening up for new interesting possibilities and inquires in our and possibly other domains.

Author Keywords

Electric Vehicle; Mobility; Sustainability; Energy; Energy Availability; Range Anxiety; Interaction Design; Information Visualization.

ACM Classification Keywords

H.5.m. Information interfaces and presentation (e.g., HCI): Miscellaneous.

INTRODUCTION

Energy and design of energy-feedback are becoming increasingly important in the mobile HCI community, out of both sustainability and practical usability reasons. Several recent studies have for instance addressed how users deal with limited battery lifetime when using mobile phones in what is refered to as human-battery interaction [3, 24, 25]. In mainstream HCI, a related topic has been concerned for some years with ways to visualize and materialize energy consumption with regard to home or workplace consumption to provide energy-feedback [2, 10, 12, 15, 21, 27], sometimes using mobile devices for feedback [1]. Energy as such is a peculiar material that is invisible, undifferentiated and intangible [23], and making it easy to understand this material is therefore a challenge that demands more focus from designers and researchers.

One application area that is becoming increasingly relevant to the this problem domain concerns the visualization and maintenance of energy in battery-only driven electric vehicles (EVs), i.e. without alternative fossil fuel extension units such as in hybrid electric vehicles. In this domain, energy maintenance takes place in a mobile setting, in which loss of power has very strong and direct consequences for the mobility of the user.

Our aim with this paper is to contribute to the energy discussions in HCI through a research-through design approach inspired by Fällman [11] and Zimmerman et al [30]. This means that we are constantly reframing the problem through an iterative process in order to achieve a better result. Additionally we believe in the importance of gaining new insight about the peculiar energy material [23], as well as our users, through the use of prototypes. Our prototypes are of varying natures through the design process, from exploration and reflection tools such as EVERT presented here, to in-car and mobile driving and trip-planning support tools.

Figure 1. Study setup of using EVERT as a technology probe for exploring understandings of range and energy in scenarios and real world cases of driving electric vehicles.

Through illustrated examples, we present different forms of energy visualizations, beginning with a high-tech range exploration tool (EVERT) developed in the process to support understanding of energy, EV technology and planning of driving sessions. EVERT can be regarded as a technology probe [14] for increased understanding of the design space through users and designers exploring properties of the problem domain and materials. In what follows we will introduce EVERT and the results from the design exploration conducted using EVERT. The results are then discussed from an energy availability perspective and three aspects to consider when designing energy dependent mobile applications are presented. These dimensions are then used to re-design the initially presented design, as a demonstration on how this perspective could be used in our domain for a better design.

BACKGROUND

The previous studies on human-battery interaction in Mobile HCI are relevant to the problem space of interacting in EV use settings in the sense that they are concerned with energy management. However, even though research focusing on improving battery lifetime is important and relevant for EV technology, mobility in a mobile phone setting is very different to our case. This is since poor energy management in EVs have more severe impact on mobility, and therefore other aspects become more prominent in this context. But there are also studies looking solely on how users interact with batteries in mobile phones and laptops without a specific focus on battery lifetime [3]. To make things clear and emphasize the difference, these efforts focus on energy management using *mobile devices*, while we focus on energy management of *mobility devices*.

For the case of mobile applications, a lot of research has been done on in-car information systems, in particular on navigation systems [17, 22, 26, 28, 29], but usually not in relation to any form of representation of energy.

In the EV use context, where energy is tightly coupled with range, energy awareness manifest itself through the phenomenon referred to as *range anxiety* [8, 19]. Range anxiety is an anxiety or fear that one may not reach a target before the battery is empty, which can occur while driving or prior to driving as the user worries about later planned trips. The main cause for this problem is that EVs have a more limited driving range (e.g. Nissan Leaf have a claimed range of about 160 (100 miles)) in combination with charging times of approximately 8 hours in normal power plugs and a minimum of about 2 hours in fast charging stations for a fully charged battery. This is due to available battery technology and limitations of the electrical grid. This means that it might take hours to correct a trip-planning mistake, or even make the driver stuck if the mistake is discovered too late. While there is hope for improving battery technology in the future, current knowledge does not offer cheap manageable solutions for improving battery performance. We address this problem by interaction design in the energy representation area, thereby contributing to this research topic by specific designs focused on maps.

Figure 2. Typical in-car display showing the approximate distance left before the tank is empty.

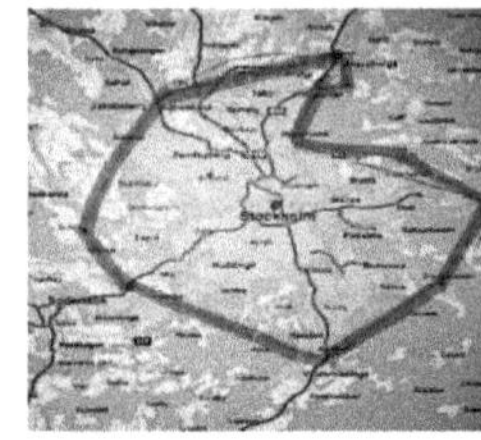

Figure 3. A mockup showing the reachable area based on a fixed distance.

Translucency and Unfamiliar Technology

EV technology is new and unfamiliar to most car drivers, which in itself may cause anxiety and distrust. This anxiety regarding range might be possible to ease with the use of better energy feedback [7].

An alternative approach to interaction design for electric vehicles, rather than simply capitalizing on familiar user interface elements and hide technological details beyond them, is to treat the user interface as more than a set of levers that help manipulate the vehicle, but also as an explanatory guide for the (unfamiliar) technology and its limitations. In other words, a specific kind of visibility, which is termed by Dourish and Button, as *translucency* [8]:

"By revealing more of what lies behind them, 'translucent' interfaces provide cues as to not only what the system was doing, but why it was being done. A view onto the mechanism can provide a context to make system activity rationalizable, and to do so within the circumstances of its activity rather than outside of it (as, say, manuals might do)" (p. 16)

To follow this rationale and familiarize users with EV technology with regards to range, we need to provide users with a more translucent view of EV range properties. In earlier work we showed how other novel technologies like presence sensors could be made translucent to users [5]. The typical way of expressing driving range used today is a "distance left to empty" meter, similar to the one illustrated in Figure 2. However, this representation is rather abstract and lacks direct mapping to the physical world, and might therefore be hard to grasp. In this sense, a reachable area mapped onto a representation of physical space (maps), might provide a more graspable and understandable picture of range properties in terms of realistic driving distance. As an example, the Nissan Leaf presents a circular reachable area to the user. However, as we will demonstrate later, the reachable area is not a circle and needs to be computed 360 degrees around the EV, than the circle would start to take the form of a polygon, like in Figure 3.

EVERT – ELECTRIC VEHICLE EXPLORATION OF RANGE TOOL

EVERT (Figure 4) is a tool for users to explore their own reality when driving an EV – to elaborate on driving plans and to test whether various trips are possible given their own context. The tool could also be used as a basis for discussion and articulation, as well as for shaping meaningful activities and routes within pre-given scenarios. In that sense, EVERT might initially be considered a 'translator of thought' between us as designers and the presumptive or novice EV drivers [2]. However, the end result is expected to be something useful and meaningful for EV driving in situ (i.e. a tool for driving and planning). Our current design is intentionally slightly more informative in its nature to raise questions through retrospection among the participants [16].

Design scope: Who said something about a straight, flat and windless road?

Many aspects can influence energy consumption and driving range, some affect driving range in all directions, other only apply to certain roads and directions. Imagine that you enter an EV with a charging level that should be sufficient for driving 100 km (60 miles). It is easy to imagine a perfectly round circle on a map displaying the reachable area (as in the Nissan Leaf). This is however never the case since roads are rarely straight and the reachable area therefore need to be computed using the actual roads rather then the straight-line distance (Figure 3). This is perhaps not anything new and not that groundbreaking either. In fact, we can probably deal with this when it concerns locations that are important to us, for instance we often hear statements as "it is about 40 km (25 miles) to my parents' place", these types of statements are clear indicators that we are aware of the actual road distance, rather than the straight-line distance between different points, at least to our most important locations. However, something that is rarely mentioned is how factors like speed, elevation, slope of road, air resistance, rolling resistance, traffic, driver profile, carload and wind affect energy consumption and the reachable area. For example, a Nissan Leaf range chart drawn up by the Nissan Leaf driver community [20] demonstrate how driving range varies with speed under the following condition: *"Level Road, No Heating or Air Conditioning, Battery Temperature 70F/20C, Windows Closed"*. With all this in mind, it becomes important to explore how richer information than the usual "distance left to empty" meter (Figure 2) might be displayed to ease driver anxiety and understanding of the situation, as well as how these factors affect everyday driving. One way of doing this is by visualizing the reachable area on a map, based on approximations of energy consumption (using these factors) while driving in any possible direction. The outer edge of this area then takes the shape of a polygon rather than a circle (Figure 3).

Overview of current functionality and implementation

EVERT is cloud-based and implemented for browsers using HTML, JavaScript, jQuery and the Google Maps API. In its current implementation EVERT is distance-based and calculates the reachable area based on remaining energy in the battery (i.e. for now without taking into account wind,

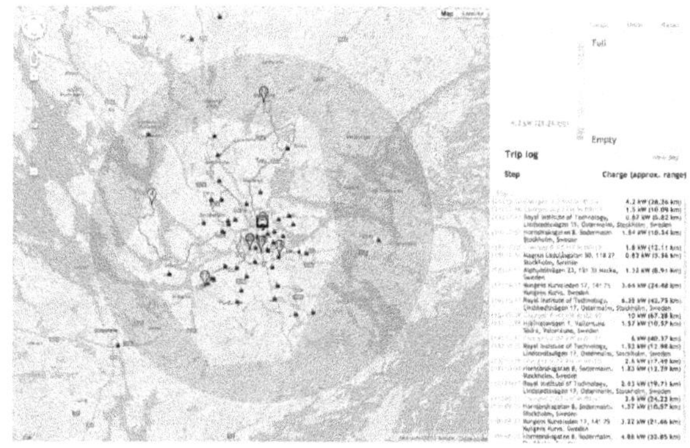

Figure 4. Overview of EVERT running in a browser, the left is the map displaying the reachable area, and to the right charging level and trip log.

temperature, traffic, etc.). The reachable area takes the shape of a polygon on the map, and an outer circle shows the straight-line distance range for comparison (Figure 4). The user can select to go to a new location by clicking within the reachable area. The tool also displays historical paths and locations. Another part of the tool shows the current charging level in the form of a slider, which is reduced while driving (clicking) to new locations. There is also a trip log, as a resource for reflection. The user can increase the charging level by moving the slider up, and EVERT will display how long charging time is required for that operation. It is also possible to discharge to be able to set up tricky scenarios for the user or to simulate accidental battery discharge. All logs and previous location markers on the map are color coded with the remaining charging level at that particular point. The prototype also displays all available charging stations in Scandinavia to provide infrastructural awareness [13].

METHOD AND DESIGN OF STUDY

A study was conducted to provide an extended understanding of current driving practices among ordinary fuel car drivers, explore mobility aspects, identify future challenges in EV usage, get feedback on our design concept, and explore new potentials and hatch new ideas and challenges. To do this we used EVERT as a probe.

There are many ways to interpret probes in the HCI community [4]. For this study the notion of probe is used mainly as a technology probe [14] in an experience prototyping [6] manner, as an attempt to realize opportunities for design through the use of interactive equipment. The purpose is to inspire and inform the design process, as well as to create a dialogue, meanwhile taking interaction and interactive experience into account, based on the drivers personal context and perceptions [18].

There are many reasons for choosing this approach, the most prominent is the time required to explore typical scenarios in real life, in our case, 7-13 whole days with each participant, which was practically impossible since we did not have either have EVs or drivers for that type of activity. Another reason for choosing this is that it allowed us to explore the application area much earlier than we could have done if aiming for a in-car prototype, which would not only require extensive access to an EV, but also more time for integrating the tool with the EV.

There were 5 participants (P1-P5) with varying levels of knowledge of EV technology, aged between 30 and 60 with 5-45 years of driving experience, and living in urban or suburban areas in major cities in Europe (Sweden and Croatia).

Each session lasted for 30-90 minutes and was structured in 4 parts: (i) basic questions about their life situation, the car they use, everyday driving practices and knowledge about EVs, (ii) basic information about EVs and a demo of the tool followed by a session (iii) trying out 4 different predefined scenarios based on their own driving practices in a think-aloud fashion, ending with (iv) open ended questions concerning how they believe an EV would function in their life, attitudes towards EVs and reflections regarding EVERT. All session were conducted using a laptop and were recorded (Figure 1).

The briefs for the 4 scenarios presented to the participants are shown below. They were chosen with the intention of covering a variety of usual driving situations, over a spectrum of possible travel lengths, ranging from everyday driving (often), to more driving intense weekend activities (common) and longer holiday trips (rare). Briefs B-C were specifically chosen to simulate critical situations:

A. An ordinary day in life, follow your everyday routine, your EV is fully charged.

B. Same as scenario A, except you forgot to plug in your EV last night and the charging level is low.

C. Make up a possible weekend that is more complex with regards to activities and driving needs; you start with a fully charged EV.

D. Pick a far away spot that you might want to go to for holiday using your vehicle for transportation. Try to manage to reach your destination using available charging stations.

All scenarios were carried out with the following rule: The EV can only be charged at home, at friends, at charging stations and at other suitable charging locations that they can motivate that it is was possible to charge at.

General opinions about EVERT

All participants were positive to EVs, both before and after they had explored their everyday driving habits with EVERT, and stated that they would like to own one for everyday driving in *"the city area"* (P3) or *"in Stockholm"* (P1) mainly for environmental and economical reasons, given that the EV was not too expensive in comparison to a regular car with combustion engine. More demanding weekend activities seemed to be manageable as long as the driver started the weekend with a fully charged EV.

"good for exploring how driving electric cars would be" (P2)

"gave me a good perspective on using electric cars" (P3)

Longer holiday trips were problematic for all participants; in some cases the desired destination was or seemed impossible to reach because of available charging infrastructure or problems finding alternative routes with sufficient infrastructure.

"holidays are impossible, I would rather rent a car" (P1)

For one participant (P5), the chosen holiday destination was barely reachable and the tool than provided valuable information for taking a more informed decision:

"I would not do this trip, I would not take that risk" (P5)

Overall the participants thought that the information on the map was useful for planning, although the outer circle representing the straight-line distance was questioned as not very useful. On a question regarding whether the tool would be helpful for planning, one participant with good knowledge about battery technology said:

"Yeah, somehow yeas, yeah definitely...if the tool is cleaver enough to take into account weather, traffic and things like that, then I would feel quite safe...I would not depend on that if there was traffic... it would probably take about 1,5 hour to get home...then light and heating would probably consume all the energy...probably this estimation of the driving range should also contain data about traffic" (P4)

Even though EVs are more efficient than fossil fuel cars, information about traffic might be crucial as traffic jams might drain a lot energy on heating, cooling etc., particularly if the battery level is low.

ENERGY AVAILABILITY IN MOBILE SETTINGS

Below is a summary of the most relevant results that were brought up in this study relating to energy in mobile settings. First, we argue that range anxiety is a particular form of energy availability anxiety, and we consider the reasons why it is important to address energy availability when dealing with energy matters in mobile settings. Second, we consider how our notion of energy availability relates to and is supported by findings from an interview study made by Nilsson [19], and how our study alters some of the recommendations given from that study. Finally, we propose dimensions to consider when designing energy availability dependent applications in mobile settings.

In home or workplace appliances, reducing energy consumption is often the main goal for energy designs and representations. But in the mobile context, this seems to be of less interest for the user of energy intense mobile technology. This was for instance highlighted when participants in our study were selecting suitable charging stations while exploring scenarios that required charging:

"..is the charging station unoccupied when I reach it? How many plugs are there at the station?.. I need to drive to a charging station I know I will be able to charge at". (P1)

"there are no charging stations...it is impossible" (P2)

This clearly stresses the need to focus on energy availability in mobile contexts.

When it comes to possibilities and constraints for the mobile energy consumer, statements like the ones made by our informants clearly demonstrate that it is not sufficient enough to simply know the locations of energy resources, like charging stations or the private power plug on a relative's driveway. The mobile energy consumer also needs to know whether or not the resources are occupied at the time of arrival, if they are functional on arrival, if the power grid will be able to deliver enough energy for fast charging at arrival time, but also, how the resources could be utilized to extend range.

None of our participants had problems managing their everyday routine using the tool, not even when they were forced into tricky scenarios when we intentionally reduced the charging level to a problematic level. In these scenarios, all of our participants used private energy resources and still did not appear to, or consider themselves to, have any problems regarding range. These energy resources have probably been available to them for many years and it is likely that they have learned to trust them, as these resources are likely to be functional and available at any time. This is interesting, since it indicates that the anxiety often mentioned as *range anxiety*, is not necessarily about range, but rather a particular form or derivative of *energy availability anxiety*. In the same way, when using laptop computers or other mobile devices, *charge anxiety* might be a form of energy availability anxiety when lacking available resources for charging, or when locations or availability of charging options are somewhat uncertain.

With this in mind, focusing on forms of energy availability, in our case *range anxiety,* might be misleading when addressing design issues concerning energy in mobile settings, as it focuses only on particular forms, or symptoms, of an underlying cause. In the EV case, this might lead to a focus on making the design and technology translucent with regard to the temporality of current reachable area, rather than on anxiety-free comfort zones that are offering a sufficient level of energy availability, which the driver could travel freely within.

The longer trips were problematic to all participants, not only because they took a lot of time and planning, but also, because participants tended to end up in dead ends along the planned path. As an example, one participant (P1) made a quite serious attempt to drive 460 km (285 miles) to his destination of choice. During the trip, he needed to do some serious re-planning and was forced to completely change the planed route several times. Half way through, he got stuck because he lacked 23 km (14 miles) to reach the next charging station. He tried to find a solution to the unfortunate situation, without success. Another participant (P3) succeeded with a similar trip, but due to the many required stops for charging, and the total estimated required time of 32 hours he commented:

"it is too much trouble for something like that (referring to the trip)" (P3)

Another example demonstrating a similar problem was when a participant (P2) had decided to drive to a golf course located about 90 km (56 miles) from home, which was a usual activity during the summer. The decision to proceed with the trip was based on the fact that the destination was reachable given the information from the tool. But, when the participant reached the golf course, it became obvious in EVERT that it was impossible to reach home on the current charging level (20 km (12 miles) were missing) and no charging options appeared available, after some consideration and exploration of the map, the participant figured out a work-around:

"I have to go and visit my mother and charge there" (P2)

Other participants also spoke about and utilized alternative none public charging spots not visible on the map:

"I have a friend here on the way" (P5)

"I could charge at work" (P2)

However, both the "long trip" and the "golf course" scenarios demonstrated above show serious problems linked to the underlying problem of energy availability, and not directly on the particular form, as in range. The drivers needed to know the extended range that could be achieved using energy resources (charging) for the different steps in the plan, in other words the zones or areas offering sufficient energy availability at the beginning of the trip, rather than just the current state of the reachable area. This stresses the need to design for the broader notion of energy availability, which clearly includes range, rather than on only the particular form.

Our design, had focused on making range properties translucent to address range anxiety, in that, we were quite successful as many participants stated that the range visualization was valuable.

"It is excellent, if I had an electric car with this tool I would feel more relaxed because I have an estimation of what I can do" (P4)

"good for planning and quickly test if a trip is manageable" (P1)

These finding also seem to be inline with findings from an interview study [19] conducted by Nilsson on EV users, where it is concluded that:

"Range anxiety is manifested as a constant awareness of current available resources"

This clearly focuses the problem on the underlying problem of energy availability, even though Nilsson does not explicitly phrase it as a particular form of energy availability anxiety. Furthermore, Nilsson also continues with some recommendations connected to the finding:

1. The driver should be able to understand the current state of the vehicle.
2. The driver should be able to understand the future state of the vehicle.
3. The driver should be able to understand the effect of their current actions.

Recommendation 1 is handled in our design, as the driver at any time has full view of the reachable area on a map, current charging level, and history as feedback for understanding the reasons for the current state of the vehicle. Recommendation 2 is partially lacking in our design since it is not possible to fully grasp the state using a sequence of charging stations. This recommendation have a strong connection to availability, although one might discuss on what level the driver needs to know the future state; on an 'exact' level, or is it 'good enough' to know that any future state within an energy availability *comfort zone* might be manageable? Our attitude is probably more towards the latter, that driving in these types of zones might be enough to overcome anxiety, partially based on the anxiety free travelling within the home area. On recommendation 3, we have provided a design offering some translucency on the effects of current actions, at least within some proximity. However, this is also connected to recommendation 2, when driving into the "unknown", how does current action or current plan effect or work out in the future undiscovered territory? Nilsson also comes to the conclusion:

"Range anxiety exists due to the uncertainty in the existing solutions to limited range incidents"

While this is arguably true and a consequence of the underlying problem of energy availability anxiety, we have found that the recommendation provided to address the finding is not enough in practice:

"The driver should be able to judge where the possible charging stations are located."

Even though this is correct, the driver also needs to know what these charging stations could offer in terms of extended range and availability, as argued earlier.

Three Dimensions of Energy Availability

From the argumentation above and the results from the study, we have identified the following dimensions to consider when designing energy availability dependent applications in mobile settings.

- Public and private resources
- Current and future states
- Energy forecasts

We will briefly discuss some important aspects of these dimensions to consider when designing applications relying on energy availability.

Public and Private Resources

It is important to distinguish between public and private when considering energy availability. There are some differences between public and private resources. Private resources might be somewhat trustworthier, as people have been living with them for many years and in that sense know that they work and they are available when needed. In particular resources that are controlled or "owned", but also friends or relatives energy resources might be more reliable as we probably know whether or not we are allowed to use them, and if we decide to use them we probably call and check if they are home and if it is okay that we stop by. All these resources are probably owned and controlled by oneself or somebody we know, which means that we could personally check their "status" using normal known communication channels. But also, private resources might involve social activities that could make them more attractive for use, as they might be merged with other socially important activities, and in that sense cover some of the possible downsides of using remote located energy resources, i.e. time aspects.

Public resources on the other hand, are available to all, which means that they are affected by other unknown people's actions, therefore they might be occupied when we need them, or out of order due to misuse. Furthermore, it might not be as easy to check the status of the resource, i.e. check if it will be available tomorrow at 17:00 pm from a remote location, as with the private resources. This might make them harder to trust or count on. But also, using public resources might also mean spending time on an unwanted location, in other words waiting. In the EV case, this could take several hours, but it is easy to imagine that other mobile devices might claim similar amounts of time. These aspects might make public resources harder to trust or rely on and less socially acceptable, if they are not designed to ensure such aspects. Therefore, they may be less attractive to mobile energy users. However, over time, society might change to ensure social aspects at energy resources making them more attractive. Charging stations might for instance become natural meeting places providing food and lesiure, architects might build nice attractions, wifi hotspots might be combined with the energy resources so that energy users could socialize, work or pass time on the internet and so on.

Current and Future States

In our design, we display the current state of the EV in terms of providing a visual view of the reachable area at a particular place and time. However, for anxiety free mobility and planning, it is also important to bring some translucency to possible future states, or the sum of a chain of states. For instance, if the EV driver decides to go to a

Figure 5a,b. (a) Visualization of one-way energy coverage using public charging stations and computed with the properties of a brand new Nissan Leaf. (b) A richer visualization of the reachable area based on public charging stations. Light turquoise displays return-trip range and the dark gray one-way reachable area. Red circles highlights areas that are impossible to cross.

particular location, it is important to be able to both determine if it is possible to reach, regardless of being in the close proximity or a distant location, and have an understanding on how the state would be at that particular location. But, as argued earlier, the level or details of this information might not need to provide "full" translucency, it might be enough to know that it is possible, and that the driver will be in a manageable situation at arrival. The need to know the possible space of future states was observed among all participants in scenario C and D as they struggle with finding routes to their target; one participant summarized the problem quite well:

"I need a sequence for the whole route, so I know it is safe" (P5)

Energy Forecasts
Other factors might also influence energy availability, like weather, traffic, status of energy plants, maintenance of infrastructure, occupancy of charging stations, and other events in society. Some were obvious concerns for our participants, as mentioned earlier, others less obvious but still of the same character. This might be important information in some application areas (ours), as it might make some scenarios impossible at times. For instance, a cold and windy day, or a traffic jam, might make an otherwise normal trip unmanageable. But also the opposite, a tailwind might make an otherwise impossible trip suddenly possible. With this in mind, it becomes relevant to talk about *energy forecast* as a way to inform and shape energy availability based on estimations, probable condition or known events, as these factors might both constrain and improve mobility for the EV driver.

VISUALIZING ENERGY AVAILABILITY
To get a sense and explore how the coverage of energy availability might look like for EVs, we decided to use our range computation algorithm (used in EVERT) to calculate how charging station covers the landscape (Figure 5a). The visualization is generated by computing the one-way reachable area starting from each individual public energy resource (charging stations) in Sweden, using our algorithm and the properties of a particular vehicle as input. In our case, we use the properties of a Nissan Leaf under good condition. The visualization reveals the one-way energy availability coverage using publicly available charging stations, in other words the outer bounds of mobility, with a particular vehicle in a particular condition. Another interesting aspect with this visualization is that all covered areas are drawn with varying levels of opacity so that areas with more charging stations become more intense green, which makes it easier to see the *density of energy availability*.

Even though the visualization in Figure 5a helps to display reachable and unreachable areas, as well as, the intensity of available energy resources, there are still problematic areas hidden in the visualization since the calculation is based on the one-way trip. This means that somewhere halfway from the charging station to the outer bounds, the driver crosses a line when it is no longer possible to return to the charging station that the driver started from. To address this problem we generated a new visualization that layered the one-way reachable areas and the return-trip reachable areas (Figure 5b). When this is generated for all the energy resources, the areas start to connect and overlap each other if the charging stations are close enough. This combined return-trip area represents the maximum area that is possible to travel within while keeping the possibility to return to an energy resource. We refer to this larger or extended reachable area as the *comfort zone* of the EV driver. Furthermore, the visualization also displays whether it is possible to cross areas and reach energy resources, some areas turn out to be directly un-crossable, even though they could be crossed through a detour, while other areas are revealed to be unreachable as the comfort zones of the areas are disconnected.

DISCUSSION THROUGH DESIGN
Representations of energy in interaction design are a growing topic in interaction design nowadays, with concerns such as sustainability and energy feedback [2, 10, 12, 15, 21, 27], and human-battery interaction in the mobile domain [3, 24, 25]. In our case, we contribute to this body of work through designing energy feedback appliances in a mobile context of use, were we focus on availability of energy rather than on saving energy by making energy aspects EVs more translucent [7] through visualizations.

We will now discuss our paper by showing how these dimensions of energy availability can inform the design of energy feedback on the move. We will thus show how the

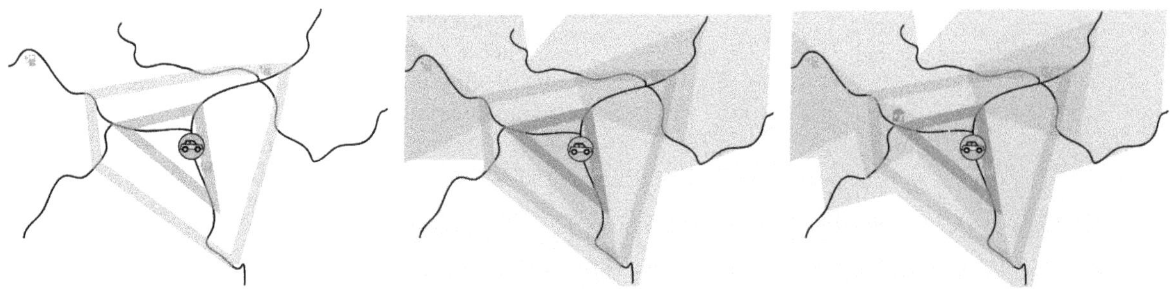

Figure 6a,b,c. (a) Identical to the design in EVERT, except that the return-trip area is added. (b) In this design the visualization of energy availability in Figure 5b is added as a layer. (c) In this design the home has been added as private energy resource.

dimensions of *Public and Private resources*, *Current and Future States* and *Energy Forecast* could be used in design. The resulting re-design is a fusion between well-known representation of the physical world (maps) and lesser-known representation of energy (range), in combination with our visualizations of energy availability. In this context, we suggest energy availability visualizations, as a way to display implications for mobility in terms of possibilities and constraints, as these aspects are often important for effective use and management of energy-intense *mobility devices*, in our case EVs. The resulting designs are not meant to be final, but just initial results of ideation that help us illustrate how the Energy Availability dimensions can be used in design.

In our initial design (EVERT), we only displayed the one-way outer bounds as the reachable area. As discussed earlier, this means that the driver accidentally might aim to go to locations were it is impossible to return to the current location. To improve this it might be a good idea to also indicate the return-trip area within the one-way reachable area, so that the driver quickly could get a feel for how far away it is possible to drive and then return. This is depicted by the inner polygon in Figure 6a.

One of the dimensions we introduced is *Current and Future States*, and we will now show how our design could take it into account. Following our idea that it might be "good enough" to know the area where future state of the vehicle are in some sense manageable (the *comfort zone*), the visualization in Figure 5b actually becomes a good representation of the maximum bounds of possible manageable future states. As long as the driver wants to travel within this area, it is always possible to solve and manage energy availability. Since the driver is given a better view of the bounds or possibilities and constraints for their mobility, beyond the current state (reachable area) and location, they could also immediately tell whether or not a trip is possible and if it requires a detour. An incorporation of this representation in our initial designed is illustrated in Figure 6b where we have added the energy availability visualization (Figure 5b) to the initial design (EVERT) as a new layer. The grey area represents the one-way reachable area, and the brown area the return-trip reachable area. Please note that as long as the driver only uses energy resources included in the visualization, the one-way reachable area marked with red, can never reach outside the grey area. This is since the visualization of energy availability is computed using the properties of the vehicle itself, and represents the personal energy availability with a particular vehicle in a particular condition. In the similar way, the return-trip reachable area of the vehicle, could never reach outside the brown area.

Let us turn to the *Public and Private Resources* dimension. The visualizations in Figure 5 only incorporate the publicly available energy resources. As discussed earlier, private resource might be even more important in users everyday life for trust, practical or social reasons. This dimension is therefore also important to incorporate to open up the possibilities with locations directly connected to the drivers' life and travel patterns. In the visualization (Figure 6c), we have added the drivers' home resource, which widens the comfort zone, outer bounds and possibilities. In the example, this opens up the possibility to safely travel to a new area that previously (Figure 6b) seemed unavailable. In our design, it could also be possible to add or turn on or off the locations of energy resources available from friends and relatives, to be able to get a more accurate view based on knowledge about the world and social conditions (e.g. a friend could be abroad and therefore the driver could not use that friends otherwise available energy resource).

Infrastructure could be designed to provide a way of reserving public energy resources at a specific time and place so that this could be reflected in all users individual energy visualizations. For instance, if a charging station were occupied, a "hole" would appear at that location and time in others' energy visualizations. If reservation of infrastructure would be possible, this would probably also reflect larger societal events and patterns as well. Energy companies could also begin to feed maintenance, load and disturbance information into the system so that it could be included in the visualization as well.

As mentioned earlier, *Energy Forecast* has many components of various complexities ranging from weather and traffic to infrastructure and energy production. To be able to support planning and driving with regards to these aspects, one needs to access the forecast in the tool, much like the weather report, but focused on energy. To calculate the forecast, estimations of the future need to be available in the system and be reflected in energy visualizations. For instance, the design could provide an interactive function enabling the possibility to scroll the map into the future and see how these aspects are reflected.

To provide accurate energy forecasts, temperature can be applied by adjusting the range calculations in each energy visualization centered on each energy resource, taking temperature properties of the particular EVs battery and the forecasted temperature at the energy resource into account (Figure 7). A cold day might for instance reduce the comfort zone due to the need for extra energy for heating and the behavior of battery technology under cold conditions.

We have found that some aspects that need to be included in the visualization are more problematic than temperature and infrastructure. In its current format, the visualization is calculated from the center of each energy resource without taking into account the location of the EV and therefore we only present a general estimation of the energy availability. This is problematic, as we have argued earlier that some aspects are directional, like wind and elevation. While we have recently started to investigate these aspects and their application, we are still looking for a good way of visualizing them.

An interesting feature that could be added with this type of energy visualization is an interactive element that lets the driver adjust desired charging time, in other words let the driver interactively affect the *Current and Future States* using *Public and Private Resources*. For instance, if the driver just wants to charge for 30 minutes, then the visualization in Figure 5b is computed to utilize only the amount of energy possible to charge during 30 minutes, which will make the reachable area and comfort zone shrink in comparison with how it is computed now (based on full charging time). This would be a particularly interesting feature in cities, as it would more accurately display the comfort zone and limits given the time the driver is prepared to spend on charging. This could even be set to zero if no charging at all is preferable.

Having shown how the energy availability dimensions can be used in design, there are some considerations to make on the design that resulted. One problem with our design is that it requires many layers of information in the spatial plane. This could make things muddy and dense if not designed carefully. Colors and opacity of layers need to be chosen carefully to emphasize the most important aspects. Another way might be to add additional interactive elements to the design so that it is possible to turn on and off the different features. This might be beneficial, as some scenarios might not require some of the layers to the same extent as others. To utilize the concept in driving practice, we are aware that safety aspects of driving a vehicle need to be considered, as well as usability aspects in general.

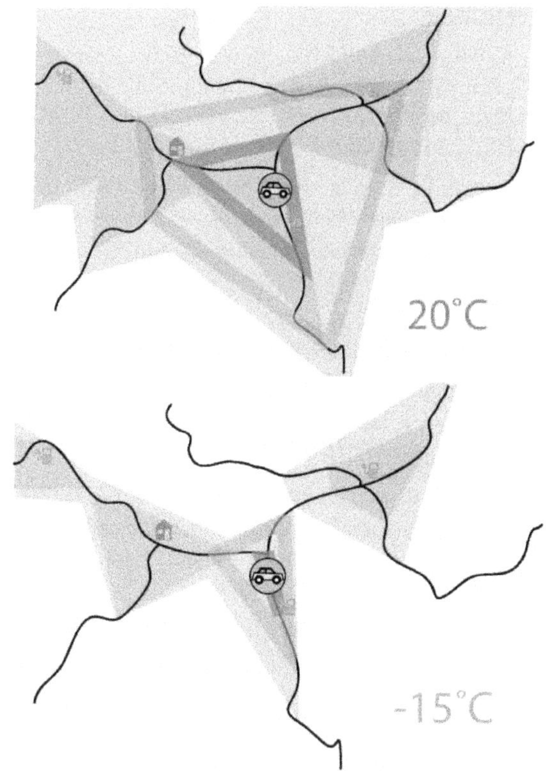

Figure 7. Displaying how temperature might affect the energy availability visualization.

CONCLUDING REMARKS

In this paper, we have explored and argued for a focus on energy availability in mobile settings and demonstrated that it might be more prominent to address energy and mobility related subjects from that perspective rather than on various symptoms of energy availability, such as range anxiety.

Within the argument, and based on the data of our study, we identify three dimensions that we believe are important to consider when designing energy availability dependent applications in mobile context. Namely, *Current and Future States*, *Public and Private Resources,* and *Energy Forecasts.* Furthermore, we demonstrate our dimensions by making design considerations on how these dimensions could be utilized to improve the design of our EV application. This is done by incorporating and modifying a visualization of energy availability into our initial design. This may work as a starting point or inspiration to others working with similar or related topics. To the EV domain we believe it to be a leap forward with regards to energy management and the discussed problem of range anxiety.

Finally, we conclude that we have contributed by demonstrating important aspects of energy availability and mobility in the still quite unexplored area of energy matters concerning *mobility devices*. With this we hope that we have opened up for new interesting possibilities and inquires, at least for the EV domain, but hopefully also for other domains.

REFERENCES

[1] Acharya, K. and Mikkonen, J. 2010. Energy usage responsive space and personal mobile devices. *Proc. MobileHCI '10* (New York, New York, USA, 2010), 407.

[2] Backlund, S. et al. 2007. Static! The aesthetics of energy in everyday things. *Proc. Design Research Society Wonderground International Conference* (2007), 1-4.

[3] Banerjee, N. et al. 2007. Users and batteries: Interactions and adaptive energy management in mobile systems. *UbiComp 2007*. (2007), 217–234.

[4] Boehner, K. et al. 2007. How HCI interprets the probes. *Proc. CHI '07*. (2007), 1077-1086.

[5] Bogdan, C. and Eklundh, K.S. 2004. FingerPrint: supporting social awareness in a translucent sensor-mediated cue-based environment. *CHI'04 extended abstracts* (2004), 1263-1266.

[6] Buchenau, M. and Suri, J.F. 2000. Experience prototyping. *Proc. DIS '00*, 424–433.

[7] Darby, S. 2006. *The Effectiveness of Feedback on Energy Consumption: A Review for DEFRA of the Literature on Metering, Billing and Direct Displays*. Environmental Change Institute, University of Oxford.

[8] Dourish, P. and Button, G. 1998. On "Technomethodology": foundational relationships between ethnomethodology and system design. *Human-Computer Interaction*. 13, 4 (1998), 1-28.

[9] Eberle, D.U. and von Helmolt, D.R. 2010. Sustainable transportation based on electric vehicle concepts: a brief overview. *Energy & Environmental Science*. 3, 6 (2010), 689-699.

[10] Froehlich, J. 2009. Promoting energy efficient behaviors in the home through feedback: The role of human-computer interaction. *Proc. HCIC Workshop* (2009).

[11] Fällman, D. 2003. *In Romance with the Materials of Mobile Interaction: A Phenomenological Approach to the Design of Mobile Information Technology*. Doctoral Thesis. Umea University, Sweden: Larsson & Co:s Tryckeri.

[12] Grevet, C. and Mankoff, J. 2009. Motivating Sustainable Behavior through Social Comparison on Online Social Visualization. *HCI conference 2009* (2009), 1-5.

[13] Hincapi, J.D. and Bardram, J. 2010. Designing for the Invisible — User-Centered Design of Infrastructure Awareness Systems. *Interfaces*. (2010), 9-12.

[14] Hutchinson, H. et al. 2003. Technology Probes: Inspiring Design for and with Families. *Proc. CHI '03* (2003), 17-24.

[15] Jönsson, L. et al. 2010. Watt-Lite: energy statistics made tangible. *Proc. DIS '10* (2010), 240–243.

[16] Kim, T. et al. 2010. Design requirements for ambient display that supports sustainable lifestyle. *Proc. DIS '10* (2010), 103–112.

[17] Mahmud, A.A. and Mubin, O. 2009. User Experience with in-car GPS Navigation Systems : Comparing the Young and Elderly Drivers. *Information Sciences*. (2009), 1-2.

[18] Mattelmäki, T. 2006. Design probes. Unpublished doctoral dissertation, University of Art and Design Helsinki, Helsinki, Finland.

[19] Nilsson, M. 2011. *ELECTRIC VEHICLES: An interview study investigating the phenomenon of range anxiety*.

[20] Nissan Leaf range chart: 2012. *http://www.mynissanleaf.com/viewtopic.php?p=101293*. Accessed: 2012-06-14.

[21] Odom, W. and Pierce, J. 2008. Social Incentive & Eco-Visualization Displays: Toward Persuading Greater Change in Dormitory Communities. *Workshop Proc. Of OZCHI* (2008).

[22] Oliver, K.J. and Burnett, G.E. 2008. Learning-oriented vehicle navigation systems: a preliminary investigation in a driving simulator. *Proc. MobileHCI '08* (2008), 119–126.

[23] Pierce, J. and Paulos, E. 2010. Materializing energy. *Proc. DIS '10* (2010), 113–122.

[24] Rahmati, A. et al. 2007. Understanding human-battery interaction on mobile phones. *Proc. MobileHCI '07* (New York, New York, USA, 2007), 265-272.

[25] Rahmati, A. and Zhong, L. 2009. Human–battery interaction on mobile phones. *Pervasive and Mobile Computing*. 5, 5 (Oct. 2009), 465-477.

[26] Schreiber, J. 2009. Bridging the gap between useful and aesthetic maps in car navigation systems. *Proc. MobileHCI '09* (2009).

[27] Shrubsole, P. et al. 2011. Flo: raising family awareness about electricity use. *Proc. CHI '11* (2011), 669-672.

[28] Smets, N.J.J.M. et al. 2008. Effects of mobile map orientation and tactile feedback on navigation speed and situation awareness. *Proc. MobileHCI '08* (2008), 73–80.

[29] Williamson, J. et al. 2006. It's a long way to Monte Carlo: probabilistic display in GPS navigation. *Proc. MobileHCI '06* (2006), 89–96.

[30] Zimmerman, J. et al. 2007. Research through design as a method for interaction design research in HCI. *Proc. CHI '07* (2007), 493–502.

Revisiting Peephole Pointing: A Study of Target Acquisition with a Handheld Projector

Bonifaz Kaufmann and David Ahlström
Department of Informatics Systems, Alpen-Adria-Universität Klagenfurt
Universitätsstraße 65-67, 9020 Klagenfurt, Austria
{bonifaz.kaufmann | david.ahlstroem}@aau.at

ABSTRACT

Peephole pointing is a promising interaction technique for large workspaces that contain more information than can be appropriately displayed on a single screen. In peephole pointing a window to the virtual workspace is moved in space to reveal additional content. In 2008, two different models for peephole pointing were discussed. Cao, Li and Balakrishnan proposed a two-component model, whereas Rohs and Oulasvirta investigated a similar model, but concluded that Fitts' law is sufficient for predicting peephole pointing performance. We present a user study performed with a handheld projector showing that Cao et al.'s model only outperforms Fitts' law in prediction accuracy when different peephole sizes are used and users have no prior knowledge of target location. Nevertheless, Fitts' law succeeds under the conditions most likely to occur. Additionally, we show that target overshooting is a key characteristic of peephole pointing and present the implementation of an orientation aware handheld projector that enables peephole interaction without instrumenting the environment.

Author Keywords

Peephole pointing; pico projector; Fitts' law; modeling.

ACM Classification Keywords

H5.2. Information interfaces and presentation (e.g., HCI): User Interfaces, Theory and methods.

INTRODUCTION

In most graphical user interfaces, an application window is used as a viewport to the underlying virtual workspace with its information and interactive objects. In situations where the viewport is smaller than the underlying virtual workspace, the user can navigate the workspace by moving it (e.g., by scrolling, panning or paging operations) until the desired part is visible through the viewport. In 1993, Fitzmaurice [13] explored the opposite navigation concept and introduced the idea of 'peephole' interaction. A spatially aware display serves as a viewport that is moved across a stationary workspace, as depicted in Figure 1. In more recent years – with the rapid development of mobile devices, motion sensors and handheld projectors – peephole interaction has gained increased attention as a promising basis for emerging mobile interaction scenarios and applications. Peephole interfaces have now been implemented using small-size computing devices such as PDAs [31], tablet PCs [29], and camera phones [25], and also using wrist-worn [4] or handheld projectors [3, 5, 17, 24].

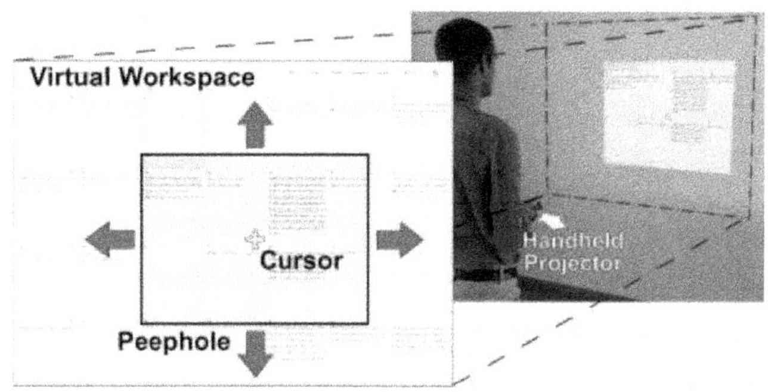

Figure 1. A peephole is moved to reveal content of a larger virtual workspace and a centered cursor is used for selection.

Many of the peephole scenarios presented in the literature [3, 5, 8, 17, 22, 23] require the user to point at and select objects that are revealed by the peephole as it is moved across the workspace. A common way to implement pointing operations in peephole systems is to have a cursor fixated in the center of the peephole. When the cursor is positioned over an object, the object can be selected. Although pointing is fundamental for many peephole applications, few projects have investigated user performance in peephole pointing tasks and little is known about the human factors that influence user performance and peephole interface design.

Given the inherit characteristic of peephole pointing, target acquisition can be divided into two consecutive discriminative interactions: at first the peephole is moved in order to reveal the target, and then the cursor is positioned over the target to select it. Cao, Li and Balakrishnan [7], hereafter CLB, proposed and tested a target acquisition model for peephole pointing that incorporates this characteristic and the size of the peephole. Their analysis indicates that the suggested model predicts movement time more accurately than Fitts' law [12]. Independent from CLB, Rohs and Oulasvirta [26], hereafter RO, investigated yet another model for peephole pointing. In contrast to CLB, RO report that peephole pointing is well described by

MobileHCI'12, September 21–24, 2012, San Francisco, CA, USA.

Fitts' law. CLB and RO published their results simultaneously in the proceedings of CHI 2008.

In this paper, we present a user experiment aimed at clarifying this discrepancy and to gain further insights in peephole pointing with handheld projectors. We make three specific contributions. (1) We show that both CLB's and RO's model is superior to Fitts' law in modeling one-dimensional pointing task performance, under some conditions (so long as results are aggregated across different peephole sizes and users have only limited knowledge of target location). Fitts' law is more suitable when different peephole sizes are treated separately or when the user has already gained more knowledge of the target's location through a previous visit. (2) We show that target overshooting is one key characteristic of peephole pointing that relates largely to prior knowledge of target location. (3) We demonstrate how to implement an orientation aware handheld projector prototype using off-the-shelf hardware that enables peephole interaction without instrumentation of the environment.

RELATED WORK

Our work builds on recent explorative work using handheld projectors as interaction devices and on user performance modeling of target acquisition in constrained situations where the target is not immediately visible.

Peephole Interaction with Handheld Projectors

Three different methods have been published that implement peephole interaction with a handheld projector: (1) a camera mounted to a projector that recognizes optical markers or laser dots at the projection surface in order to calculate the projector's location and orientation relative to the projection surface [3, 22], (2) using a camera-based tracking system with passive markers attached to the projector [5], or (3) solely utilizing inertial sensors [24]. Each method aims at generating a virtual workspace that appears to be fixed on the projection surface. This way, movement or rotation of the projector can be used to reveal content of a much larger virtual workspace, just as a flashlight would turn real world objects in a dark room visible when they are illuminated. Although the third method (inertial sensors only) cannot calculate the location of the projector, it is self-contained and not constrained to a specific environment as is the case for the other two approaches. On the downside, the projected content moves with the projector, thus rotation must be used to move the peephole. The effect is akin to using a flashlight to look around a dark room without entering.

Spatially aware camera phones and tablet PCs have also been used as 'peepholes' or 'magic lenses'. They reveal virtual or physical workspaces to provide additional information during map navigation [16, 25] or city walks [27], magnify image content in large scale drawing programs [29] or allow viewing and annotation of 3D models in design applications [30]. Demonstrated and conceived applications for projector-based peephole interaction include warehouse inventory scenarios [22], ad hoc information spaces for collaborative purposes [5], game playing [8], multi-user interaction [6], and the operation of traditional desktop applications [3, 14, 23].

One issue that arises with handheld pointing devices is hand jitter. Davis and Chen [11] reduced hand jitter by applying a Kalman filter to pointer position data. Pavlovych and Stuerzlinger [21] studied the effect on task performance and error rate when trading jitter for latency. Forlines et al. [14] propose an interaction technique called *zoom-and-pick* to cope with jitter, enabling accurate per-pixel pointing with handheld pointing devices.

Rukzio et al. [28] provide a survey of different interaction concepts for personal projectors followed by a discussion of sensing and tracking issues and potential application domains. Dao et al. [10] present a comprehensive method that uses inertial sensors to produce undistorted images in real-time with a handheld projector.

Other interaction techniques exist for displaying information that does not fit onto a single screen. For example *overview+detail*, zooming, *focus+context* or cue-based techniques [9], like Halos [1] and Wedges [15].

Modeling Peephole Pointing

Fitts' law [17] is an established model for directed pointing movement. Given a target of width W at distance A (amplitude), the movement time MT can be predicted by the following formula:

$$MT = a + b \log_2\left(\frac{A}{W} + 1\right) \quad (1)$$

where a and b are experimentally determined constants and $log_2(A/W+1)$ describes the task difficulty, ID (index of difficulty). More recently, CLB [7] and RO [26] proposed extended models of Fitts' law that take the peephole size S into account as an influencing factor for pointing performance in target acquisition tasks through peepholes.

Besides the peephole size S, CLB's model (Eq. 2) also introduces a new constant n, having a value between 0 and 1, that describes the influence S has on movement time in relation to W.

$$MT = a + b\left(n \log_2\left(\frac{A}{S} + 1\right) + (1-n)\log_2\left(\frac{A}{W} + 1\right)\right) \quad (2)$$

CLB argue that peephole pointing can be seen as an interaction sequence consisting of two parts: searching the target by moving the peephole until the target is visible, $log_2(A/S + 1)$, then moving the cursor to finally acquire the target, $log_2(A/W + 1)$. Since a target can be found more easily with a larger S, the task difficulty decreases with increasing S. As S approaches infinity, the influence of S decreases and n approaches 0. With a sufficiently large S the peephole pointing task turns into a standard pointing task which is described by Fitts' law, as reflected in CLB's model.

RO aimed at modeling pointing with a 'magic lens' and proposed Eq. (3) as a model to predict target acquisition time. In contrast to peephole pointing, which operates only on virtual workspaces with content outside the peephole being invisible, magic lens interaction augments real world surfaces (e.g., a map) by moving a display (e.g., a camera phone) over the observable background.

$$MT = a + b \log_2\left(\frac{A}{S} + 1\right) + c \log_2\left(\frac{S/2}{W} + 1\right) \quad (3)$$

RO's model also consists of two components describing the interaction involved in magic lens pointing. First, the magic lens is moved to the directly observable target position until the target becomes visible inside the magic lens, $a + b\ log_2(A/S + 1)$, followed by precise aiming when looking though the magic lens, $c\ log_2((S/2)/W + 1)$.

RO applied their model to both interaction variants (magic lens and peephole pointing) and found a good match. Fitts' law did not predict magic lens pointing well, but predicted peephole pointing just as well as their two component model. Thus, unlike CLB, they recommend Fitts' law to predict movement time in peephole pointing tasks. RO argue that the different results relate to a significant difference within the first interaction phase: while the target position in magic lens pointing is constantly observable, in peephole pointing the target position must either be searched or be recovered by spatial memory when the target location is known due to previous visits.

In 2011, Rohs et al. [27] validated the model for magic lens interaction (Eq. 3) by conducting a user study involving real world augmented reality tasks with a camera phone. CLB's model (Eq. 2) has not been validated with a handheld projector so far and there is still confusion whether target acquisition performance in peephole interaction is sufficiently described by Fitts' law or not. CLB proved their model by simulating peephole pointing with different peephole sizes on a desktop computer with a tablet and a stylus as input devices. RO, on the other hand, conducted their experiments on a spatially aware display testing one particular peephole size only. Zooming by moving the display farther away from the background surface enabled participants to gather information about the location of the circularly arranged targets, hence all target positions were known prior to the task. In order to produce comprehensive data about peephole pointing we performed our experiment on a handheld projector, testing a large range of peephole sizes on tasks with prior and without prior knowledge of target locations.

HANDHELD PROJECTOR PROTOTYPE

In order to test a large range of different peephole sizes and to gain insights into handheld projector interaction we developed an orientation aware handheld projector based solely on inertial sensors. Although a spatially aware projector with an accurate tracking would provide a richer peephole pointing interaction compared to an orientation aware projector, it would also require external reference information which is not feasible for a handheld projector that should be usable outside of prepared test environments.

Our interactive handheld projector prototype, shown in Figure 2, consists of three parts: a Samsung Nexus S smartphone running Android 2.3.4, a MicroVision SHOWWX+ laser pico projector, and a laptop computer running the Java-based test application. The smartphone is mounted on top of the projector with the touchscreen facing up. The projector is connected via a VGA cable to the laptop. The native resolution of the projector is 848×480 pixels and the mass of the prototype (phone and projector) is 262 grams.

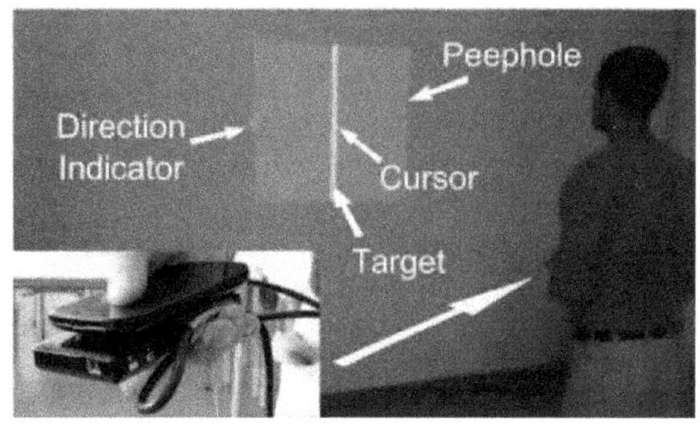

Figure 2. Experiment setup and projector prototype.

The smartphone maintains a wireless connection to the laptop in order to transmit touchscreen events and gyroscopic data from its built-in gyroscope sensor. The entire touchscreen is listening for touch events; hence it works as one big touch button. Hand pointing devices suffer from a 'dip down' effect [20] where pressing a button displaces the cursor. We used the touch-down event for selection as suggested in [20]. Orientation data is sent at a rate of 50 Hz over wireless LAN to the laptop where the data is filtered and the position of the peephole is calculated. The algorithm used to calculate the orientation of the device is based on gyroscopic data only. It works as follows:

1. On the phone gyroscopic samples are collected as fast as possible (on a Nexus S this is about 800 Hz) and integrated over time to convert the data from angular speed to orientation angles. Mathematically, integrating noisy gyroscopic data over time causes sensor drift. Since the amount of drift is quite predictable we can reduce it to 5 to 15 pixels per minute. As a result of the drift, the entire virtual workspace shifted very slowly in space; which means that after 10 minutes of operation, the virtual workspace was displaced by about 10 to 30cm. Because of the minimal drift and since users had no reference point for the virtual workspace, after about five minutes drift started to become recognizable. Since targets were placed randomly and sequences of pointing tasks only lasted for a few seconds this did not influence the experiment. Because of the accumulated drift the workspace was re-centered manually every five to ten minutes.

2. The orientation angles are sent to the laptop where the data is smoothed. First a moving average filter over three samples is applied, and then a weighted average is calculated between the averaged sample and the orientation data that has been calculated during the previous loop.
3. Next the smoothed orientation angles are linearly mapped to screen coordinates.
4. Finally a moving average filter over three screen coordinate samples is applied.

With the described algorithm we are able to reduce jitter to ±2 pixels. Smoothing slightly increases latency which has a negative impact on pointing throughput. However, reducing jitter increases pointing accuracy and so might lead to an increased overall interaction performance due to a reduction in error correction time [21]. Although filters are applied to reduce noise and jitter, latency is kept below the level where it would be noticeable. In fact, no participant mentioned that they felt a delay or found the pointing inaccurate when using our prototype. It is remarkable that our inertial-sensor-only prototype allowed all participants to select 3.2cm wide targets (16 pixels) from two meters distance with ease and high performance.

Applying image distortion correction was not necessary for our study purposes since our pointing experiments only included one-colored rectangular targets (effective distortion correction procedures are described by Dao et al. [10]).

EXPERIMENT

The purpose of our experiment was two-fold: (1) to shed light on the conflicting conclusions reported by CLB and RO (which model, Fitts' law, CLB's or RO's, best describes peephole pointing?); and (2) to model peephole pointing performance using an orientation aware handheld projector. We decided to design a close replication of CLB's experiment in order to get comparable results.

Terminology

We first introduce terms and briefly explain their meaning within the context of our paper.

Virtual workspace: Defines the region where targets can appear. The content of the virtual workspace can only be seen and accessed through the movable peephole. Parts of the workspace that lie outside the peephole are invisible.

Peephole: The visible portion of the virtual workspace. Selections are made with a cross-hair cursor fixed in the center of the peephole. The peephole (and the cursor) is moved by pointing the projector.

Trial: Moving from one target to select a second target is denoted a trial.

Sequence: A sequence involves two targets and consists of two trials, Trial 1 and Trial 2. Trial 1 starts when the first target is hit and ends as soon as the second target is selected. Ending Trial 1 immediately starts Trial 2 which ends when the first target is hit again.

Block: A block has 60 sequences, respectively 120 trials.

Participants and Apparatus

Sixteen volunteers (three females) aged 17 to 48 years (mean 30.9, SD 8.2) participated. All were daily computer users but none had previous experience with peephole pointing or using a handheld projector. The prototype described in the previous section was used.

Setup and Task

The experiment took place in a dimmed room with the participant standing two meters from a white projection surface (Figure 2). When the projector was pointed orthogonally to the wall, a 512 pixels wide peephole revealed roughly one meter of a one-dimensional 1600 pixels wide workspace that spanned over approximately 3.2 meters. A projected pixel corresponded to approximately 2mm. Since a participant was standing two meters in front of the projection wall, the proportion between a pixel and its size on the wall did not change during the test. Pointing the projector left and right moved the peephole like a flashlight beam and allowed the participant to access the entire workspace which appeared to be stationary on the wall. The cursor was a yellow cross-hair anchored in the center of the peephole, so that moving the peephole moved the cursor.

The background of the workspace was dark gray with a red border denoting either end, as shown in Figure 3. Since the horizontal resolution of the projector was larger than the tested peephole sizes, the remaining border left and right of the peephole was set to black, so as it would not be part of the projection. As a result, targets were only visible within the peephole.

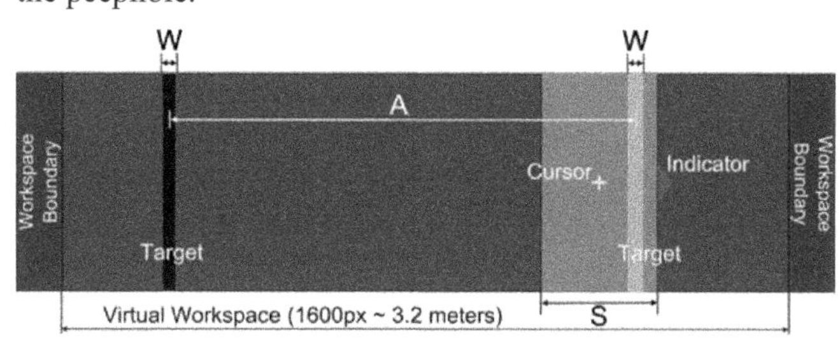

Figure 3. Experiment setup (here A=1024, S=256, W=32).

The task was a non-conventional reciprocal one-dimensional pointing task, in which the participant moved the cursor back and forth between two targets, which is denoted as a sequence. Targets and the peephole appeared as bars and were virtually of infinite height stretching from the bottom to the top of the projected image (Figure 3). The distance A between targets, the target width W, and the peephole size S stayed the same during each sequence.

In order to start a sequence the participant had to locate the first target. The black border of the peephole was set to semi-translucent to ease searching. The actual position of the first target was randomly chosen after each sequence but evenly balanced between the left and the right half of the workspace. If the first target was placed within the left half, the participant could expect the second target to be right of it and vice versa. Trial 1 in a sequence started upon selection of the first target, the semi-translucent border became opaque and a blue arrow appeared next to the border of the peephole to indicate in which direction to search for the second target. Note that the blue arrow did not change when the second target was overshot; it aided participants only by indicating the direction for searching.

Selections were made by touching the display on the smartphone. After the first target was hit, the second target was placed at distance A and the participant had to find and select it. In cases when the peephole size was at least twice as large as the distance ($A>=2S$), the second target appeared inside the peephole and was immediately visible. Otherwise, the participant had to search for the second target by moving the peephole in the indicated direction. Since the participant did not know the location of the second target before selecting the first target, Trial 1 in a sequence is called pointing *without prior knowledge*. Selecting the second target completed the first trial. Trial 2 started as Trial 1 ended. In Trial 2 the participant had to return to the first target. The position of the first target had not changed since it was clicked initially to start Trial 1. Thus, Trial 2 is called pointing *with prior knowledge* and differs in this respect significantly from Trial 1. Selecting the first target ends Trial 2 and the sequence is completed.

Successfully selecting a target turned its color from green to light gray while a short click-sound was played for positive feedback. The first target before Trial 1 was blue instead of green designating the beginning of a sequence. Missing a target counted as an error and triggered an error sound. Erroneous sequences had to be completed before the next sequence was started but were put back into the queue of uncompleted sequences at a random position. Participants were asked to complete sequences as fast as possible while trying to keep the error rate below five percent.

Design

We used a 4×3×5×2 within-subjects design with the following independent variables: target distance A (128, 256, 512, 1024 pixels), target width W (16, 32, 64 pixels), peephole size S (32, 64, 128, 256, 512 pixels) and *prior knowledge of target position* (yes, no). Each participant completed three blocks of 120 trials (60 sequences), one sequence for each A-W-S combination in random order, resulting in a total of 3×120=360 trials per participant. There was a 3-minute break between blocks. A training set of 40 trials had to be completed before the first block was started. A session lasted about 50 minutes and ended with a short briefing and a questionnaire about subjective impressions.

The experiment is a close replication of CLB's experiment with the following modifications. CLB performed the experiment on a desktop computer and tested two different *cursor control mechanisms*, 'coupled' and 'decoupled', but for a handheld projector a coupled cursor, which stays at the center of the peephole and cannot be moved separately, is more suitable, thus we removed this factor. CLB also used an additional target width of 8 pixels which we omitted, since pilots showed that these targets were too difficult to select due to hand jitter.

Results

Non-parametric Friedman tests and Wilcoxon Sign-Rank tests for post-hoc pairwise comparisons were used for error data. Movement time analyses were done using repeated measures ANOVAs with post-hoc pairwise comparisons (Greenhouse-Geisser corrections are marked GGc). For all analyses we used an alpha level of 0.01 and all post-hocs were Bonferroni adjusted. Since pre-analyses indicated learning effects with most participants performing significantly better in the last two blocks, we removed all trials from the first block. The following analyses include 4166 trials (326 erroneous and 3840 error free trials).

Errors

With 326 erroneous trials, the overall error rate was 7.8%. Having prior knowledge of a target's position did not influence participants pointing accuracy, nor did the amplitude A. Target size W did ($\chi^2_{(2,N=16)}=26.00$, $p<.01$), and post-hoc pairwise comparisons showed that the accuracy increased with increasing target size (240, 69 and 17 errors for $W=16$, $W=32$ and $W=64$, respectively; all post-hocs were significant, each $p<.0032$). This is consistent with our pilot-observations – and with CLB's results – and can be explained through the increased task difficulty as W decreases.

Also peephole size S influenced participants selection accuracy ($\chi^2_{(4,N=16)}=13.51$, $p<.01$): 50, 52, 66, 99 and 59 errors were made with $S=32$, $S=64$, $S=128$, $S=256$, and $S=512$, respectively. However, post-hocs showed that the only significant difference was between the second largest peephole (which had the most errors) and the two smallest peepholes (256 vs. 32: $Z=2.84$, $p=.0009$; 256 vs. 64: $Z=3.07$, $p=.0008$). All other comparisons were not significant. This result is also similar to CLB's findings. They found the lowest error rate with the smallest peephole and the highest error rate with the largest. CLB point out that this is somewhat counterintuitive and they speculate that the reason for more errors with large peepholes might be that participants were 'over-careful' with the small peepholes and 'over-relaxed' with the larger ones. Based on our observations we support CLB's argument.

Movement time

We discarded 24 trials as outliers (0.6%, with a movement time more than 3 SD from the mean for any A-W-S combination). The mean movement time for the remaining 3816 trials was 1767ms. We found the same main effects in our data as CLB did. Movement time was significantly influenced by all four independent factors: *Prior*

Knowledge ($F_{1,15}$=548.4, p<.01), *A* (GGc: $F_{1.14,17.04}$=170.9, p<.01), *W* ($F_{2,30}$=279.1, p<.01), and *S* ($F_{4,60}$=233.1, p<.01). Trials without prior knowledge were 37% slower than trials with prior knowledge (1488 vs. 2045ms). Post-hoc comparisons between all levels of factors *A*, *W*, and *S* all showed significant differences (for *A*, all p's<.0025; for *W*, all p's<.003; for *S*, all p's<.002). That is, we see a monotonic increase in movement time as *A* increases and monotonic decreases with increases of both *W* and *S*.

However, these results should be considered in light of the interplay between factors *prior knowledge*, *A* and *S*, as expressed through three significant 2-way interactions and one 3-way interaction. We first turn to the *prior knowledge×A* interaction (GGc, $F_{1.60,23.9}$=25.0, p<.01), plotted in Figure 4a. We see that the performance gain of having prior knowledge of target location is about similar for targets at low amplitudes (roughly 500ms). It seems as though the advantage of prior knowledge can be fully exploited when the area to search for an unknown target location becomes large enough. This allows a strategy of traveling long distances at high 'non-searching' pace. Unfortunately, with 1024 pixels as the largest amplitude used in the experiment, we cannot confirm our speculations that the benefit of prior knowledge grows as the amplitude extends beyond 1024 pixels. We have put such an investigation on our agenda for future work. Since, CLB did not detect a similar trend in their stylus data; we suspect it might be a device-related issue.

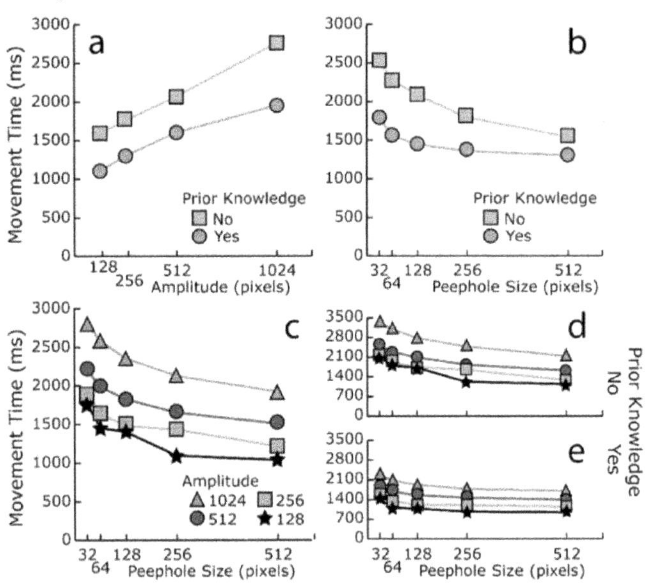

Figure 4. Interactions: (a) Prior knowledge×A, (b) Prior knowledge×S, (c) A×S, and (d+e) Prior knowledge×A×S.

Prior knowledge also interacted with *S* ($F_{4,60}$=70.5, p<.01), as plotted in Figure 4b. This interaction is also reported by CLB and we see that the positive effect of having prior knowledge of a target's location grows larger as the size of the peephole decreases; the smaller the peephole the greater the benefit. In fact, if the peephole is large enough to render the target visible (*S>=A/2*), the added knowledge would have no considerable effect and the task becomes a standard pointing task.

We also point out that with the tested values of *S* and *A* there were indeed trials in both CLB's and in our experiment where the target was visible inside the peephole throughout the whole task. Namely, in trials with *A <= S/2* (*A*=128 with *S*=256, *A*=128 with *S*=512, and *A*=256 with *S*=512). Accordingly, with large peepholes more trials included visible targets. Since visible targets render prior knowledge less important, we see how the value of prior knowledge increases with decreasing peephole size.

The influence of these 'visible' trials are also manifested in our third interaction, *A×S* ($F_{12,100}$=3.84, p<.01), which were not present in CLB's data, and which we show in Figure 4c. We see an irregular drop in movement time for targets at amplitude 128 when the peephole size changes from 128 to 256 pixels, i.e., these targets are now visible within the larger peephole, and can thus be selected more rapidly. Likewise, the data for trials at amplitude 256 exhibits a similar drop. But here, movement time irregularly falls first when the peephole is enlarged from 256 to 512 pixels, i.e., when the trials at amplitude 256 turn into 'visible' trials.

If we now split the data in Figure 4c according to prior knowledge we end up with plot d and e in Figure 4. Together they visualize our significant *prior knowledge×A×S* interaction ($F_{12,180}$=2.33, p<.01). After close inspection we see that both the irregularity for *A*=128 at *S*=256 and for *A=256* at *S*=512 are seen in plot d, but not in plot e. The absence of the drops in plot e is interesting since it might further demonstrate the viability of peephole pointing. If the user has acquired some information about target location, adding more location knowledge in terms of target visibility does not seem to significantly improve pointing performance. This was demonstrated when larger peepholes made both targets visible during Trial 2. However, we should be careful not to underestimate the role motor-memory plays in rapid reciprocal tasks such as ours.

Model fitting

To recap, we have three main candidate models for our peephole pointing tasks: the traditional Fitts' law model (Eq. 1), the two-stage model proposed by CLB (Eq. 2), and RO's model (Eq. 3). As CLB did, we perform separate analyses for trials with and without prior knowledge, as this factor significantly influenced the movement time. We first ignore (as CLB did in their analyses) the fact that with nine of the sixty different *A*-*W*-*S* combinations participants were arguably not doing peephole pointing since the targets were visible inside the peephole throughout these tasks. We use least square regressions, non-linear for CLB's and RO's models and linear for Fitts' law.

The top section of Table 1 (Non-visible and visible combined) shows the parameter estimates and R^2 values from the corresponding regressions. With either CLB's or RO's model, we find R^2 values close to or above 0.9, both with (white columns) and without prior knowledge (gray columns). With Fitts' law we found markedly lower values, demonstrating the need to account for the peephole size when modeling peephole pointing. Removing the nine visible targets from the analyses (middle section) has the most negative impact on the Fitts' law results, which further supports the other two models. Using only visible targets (bottom section), provide similar results for all three models. Again, this confirms CLB's model as it suggests that when the peephole is sufficiently large (visible targets) the peephole task becomes a standard Fitts' law task.

	CLB's Model		RO's Model		Fitts' Law	
	Prior Knowl.		Prior Knowl.		Prior Knowl.	
	Yes	No	Yes	No	Yes	No
Non-visible and visible combined (60 *A-W-S* combinations)						
n/c	0.361	0.577	314	259	–	–
a	279	537	13	384	319	627
b	388	541	429	562	319	386
R^2	0.949	0.920	0.909	0.873	0.822	0.604
Non-visible (51 *A-W-S* combinations)						
n/c	0.376	0.569	332	286	–	–
a	268	625	57	476	413	913
b	393	515	408	522	300	332
R^2	0.938	0.890	0.910	0.858	0.791	0.557
Visible (9 *A-W-S* combinations)						
n/c	0	0.159	297	246	–	–
a	225	512	-297	72	225	531
b	304	303	918	842	304	256
R^2	0.977	0.845	0.980	0.836	0.977	0.844

Table 1. Model fitting results.

As we would expect a suitable model to accurately describe data for each peephole size independent from other instances of *S*, we are also interested in knowing how the three candidate models fit the data in such situations. Neither RO, who only used one peephole size, nor CLB, who only present results aggregated across *S*, provide any information on this matter.

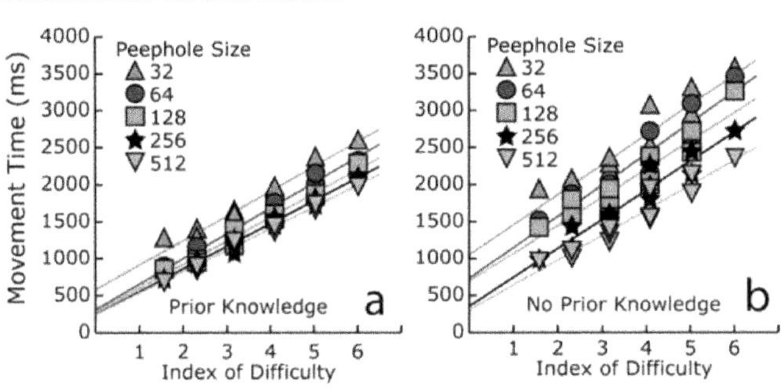

Figure 5. Fitts' law prediction trends for each S.

However, plotting the data against Fitts' index of difficulty for each *S*, as in Figure 5, clearly shows why Fitts' law makes a poor job when applied on data aggregated across different peephole sizes (cf. top section two rightmost columns of Table 1): we end up with different intercept and slope values for each peephole size, causing a vertically spread of the nearly parallel trend lines (most pronounced in Figure 5b for *no prior knowledge*). This also explains why CLB, who only analyzed data aggregated across *S*, found a poor fit for Fitts' law and why RO, who only used one peephole size, argue for Fitts' law.

Table 2 shows the model fitting results of the three candidate models when each *S* is treated separately (for brevity, we refrain from reporting *a* and *b* parameters).

	CLB's Model		RO's Model		Fitts' Law	
	Prior Knowl.		Prior Knowl.		Prior Knowl.	
	Yes	No	Yes	No	Yes	No
Non-visible and visible combined						
***S*=256**, 12 *A-W* combinations (9 non-visible + 3 visible)						
n/c	0	0.443	360	340	–	–
R^2	0.992	0.961	0.993	0.966	0.992	0.929
***S*=512**, 12 *A-W* combinations (6 non-visible + 6 visible)						
n/c	0	0.571	321	259	–	–
R^2	0.990	0.970	0.993	0.986	0.990	0.927
Non-visible						
***S*=32**, 12 *A-W* combinations						
n/c	0	0.262	881	857	–	–
R^2	0.950	0.900	0.950	0.898	0.950	0.883
***S*=64**, 12 *A-W* combinations						
n/c	0.131	0.392	556	537	–	–
R^2	0.990	0.913	0.985	0.912	0.986	0.876
***S*=128**, 12 *A-W* combinations						
n/c	0.046	0.209	430	466	–	–
R^2	0.969	0.883	0.981	0.898	0.969	0.876
***S*=256**, 9 *A-W* combinations						
n/c	0	0.465	371	338	–	–
R^2	0.990	0.930	0.994	0.946	0.990	0.881
***S*=512**, 6 *A-W* combinations						
n/c	0.104	0.684	327	255	–	–
R^2	0.989	0.994	0.991	0.996	0.988	0.836
Visible						
***S*=32, *S*=64, *S*=128** no targets were visible						
***S*=256**, 3 *A-W* combinations, no meaningful regression possible						
***S*=512**, 6 *A-W* combinations						
n/c	0	0	314	263	–	–
R^2	0.985	0.921	0.997	0.928	0.985	0.921

Table 2. Model fitting results with separated peephole sizes.

We note that for each *S* in cases with prior knowledge (white columns), either model yields an exceptionally high R^2 value and that CLB's model often predicts a standard pointing task. We suspect that participants had gained enough position knowledge through the previous target visit and could perform a rapid and accurate movement toward the target area without any pronounced 'target-searching' movements, probably capitalizing on motor-memory.

In cases without prior knowledge (gray columns), CLB's and RO's model yield slightly better fits than Fitts' law, in particular for non-visible targets. This indicates that the effect the peephole size has on pointing performance is more pronounced when targets are not visible and the user has no prior knowledge of target location.

Movement characteristics

Figure 6 shows the pointer movement data of all the participants under one exemplarily *A-W-S* condition. A dot represents the cursor position at a certain time. The cursor position was sampled every 50ms. The bottom plot visualizes the first trial in each sequence (without prior knowledge) and the upper plot the second trial (with prior knowledge). Each plot has 32 horizontal lines (2 blocks × 16 participants) with each line representing one trial. For better comparison, the direction of movement is normalized so that each path can be read from left (trial starts) to right (trial ends). As Figure 6 indicates, overshooting was more pronounced when participants had no prior knowledge of target location. This characteristic was relatively uniform over different *A*-*W*-*S* conditions.

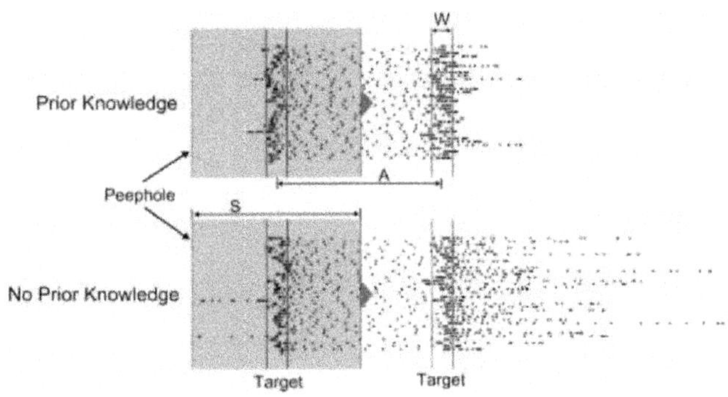

Figure 6. Pointer movement sample that shows the path of all participants at A=256, W=32, S=256.

Overall, participants overshot the target in 66.3% of the trials. Overshooting was more frequent in trials without prior knowledge (83.3%) than with prior knowledge (49.2%).

In relation to the overall movement time, we found that, when either *S* or *A* increases, overshoot time decreases (Figure 7). Overshoot time started when the cursor moved beyond the target, and ended when the target was selected.

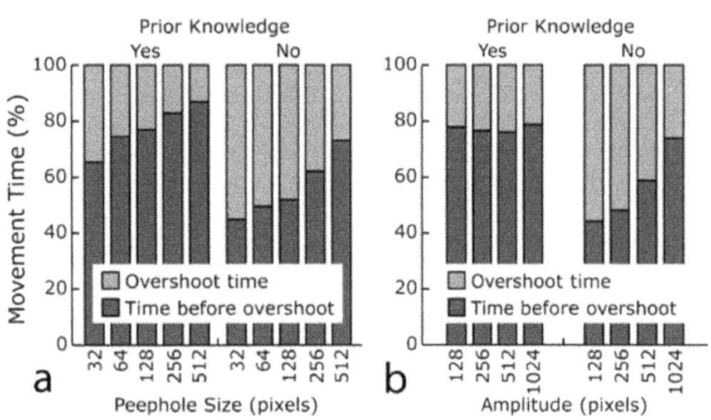

Figure 7. Overshoot time in relation to movement time.

When participants started searching for a target, they accelerated quickly in the search direction. With larger peepholes, the targets could be observed earlier. This allowed for more time to slow down, and so resulted in less overshoot time (Figure 7a). With short *A* and no prior knowledge (Figure 7b, right), it happened frequently that participants rushed past the target resulting in more than 50% overshoot time. At greater amplitude participants started to "suspect" the target to appear soon when they came close to the workspace border, and so decelerated earlier. A comparison of different amplitudes in prior knowledge trials (Figure 7b, left) showed that overshoot time stayed constant at about 25% of the overall pointing time, since users knew roughly when to slow down.

Figure 8 reveals an interesting fact: users searched at a slower pace when the peephole was large (S>=256). We think this happened because users were more relaxed when looking through a larger peephole which probably provided more confidence that the target can be acquired without overshooting. With small peepholes, participants were eager to uncover the target location by scanning the workspace as quickly as possible; accepting that they would overshoot. The length and amount of overshoot is surprisingly high. One would expect that participants are over careful with small peepholes not to oversee the target, but it seems as if they were trading search time for overshoot recovery time.

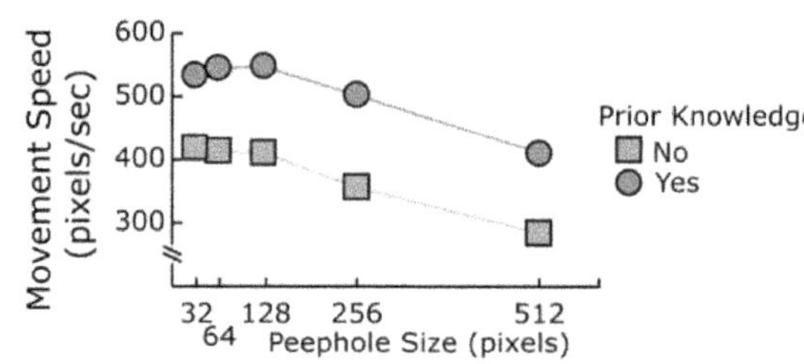

Figure 8. Pointer movement speed in pixels/sec for each peephole size S.

Subjective impressions

In a post-experiment questionnaire participants rated peephole pointing as an intuitive interaction technique for handheld projectors, giving it an average of 4.3 (5 is highest) on a Likert-scale. One participant mentioned that targets close to the border were more difficult to hit due to image distortion.

Although most participants started out holding the device with one hand, after a few sequences all participants used both hands for better stabilization and accuracy. In general, participants found the handheld projector prototype easy to use and very accurate.

DISCUSSION

The experiment provided a good understanding of modeling peephole pointing and pointing characteristics. However, two-dimensional tasks are closer to real world scenarios. In our ongoing work we have already experimented with two-dimensional tasks during a pilot study. Preliminary results suggest that our findings from the 1D experiment hold for 2D tasks as well. The next logical step will be to conduct a comprehensive experiment with 2D tasks to prove our hypothesis.

Our model fitting results shows that in most cases Fitts' law succeeds in predicting peephole pointing performance.

Only under three certain conditions, Fitts' law performs slightly worse than CLB's and RO's model:

1) when data with significantly different peephole sizes are aggregated,
2) when users do not have prior knowledge of target location, and
3) when at least one of the aggregated peephole sizes is below a certain threshold.

Although CLB's and RO's models have slightly higher prediction accuracy under the listed circumstances, it is very unlikely that these circumstances will be present in real world peephole interfaces. First of all, a peephole device, whether it is a projector or a handheld display, will only support one peephole size: the largest possible. It is hard to imagine a use case in which the peephole size changes during interaction. Secondly, peephole interfaces most likely will offer some information about a target's location (e.g., Halos or Wedges [2, 15]) otherwise selecting targets becomes an extensive search task. Thirdly, there is certainly a maximum speed at which participants can search for a target. Above a certain peephole size, users are able to search with maximum speed while still being able to decelerate when the target becomes visible. In this way, overshooting is less pronounced and peephole pointing becomes a standard pointing task. Unfortunately, with our experiment we could not determine the threshold above which peephole pointing can always be modeled as a standard pointing task. A test with several large peephole sizes would have been necessary. According to our analysis we suspect the threshold to be between 512 and 1024 pixels.

After all, Fitts' model provides well enough estimates for almost all situations most likely to occur in peephole pointing interfaces and there is no real benefit in applying one of the more specific models. Additionally, proponents of the principle of parsimony (Ockham's razor) would teach us to favor the simplest candidate model – in our case the Fitts' law model.

Overshoot time accounted for 43.8% of the overall movement time when users had no prior knowledge of target location and 25.8% otherwise. Therefore, pointing performance could be noticeable increased by reducing overshoot; either by providing more information about the target location or by using techniques such as force fields [1] or expanding targets [17]. On the other hand, knowing that no participant had ever used a handheld projector before, they were surprisingly fast in completing tasks. The mean movement time of 1767ms measured in our experiment is even slightly better than the movement time of 1884ms reported by CLB (note that they had also 8px targets). Considering that we had a close replication of CLB's experiment but used a handheld projector instead of a tablet and stylus, our results are very promising for peephole pointing with projectors.

Additionally, error rate was low compared to laser pointer interaction [20]. It could have been even lower, but the touch screen was extremely sensitive and participants occasionally touched it accidently causing an erroneous trial. Using a hardware button might have solved this issue, but would have caused a stronger 'dip down' effect reducing pointing accuracy. As an improvement, only a portion of the screen should be defined as a button, ideally positioned over the device's center of gravity, as this would reduce unintentional touches and in addition further reduce the 'dip down' effect.

CONCLUSION AND FUTURE WORK

We presented and analyzed the results of an experimental target acquisition study of peephole pointing with a handheld projector. We pointed out that three main candidate models exist for predicting peephole pointing task performance: the Fitts' law model [17], the two-stage model proposed by Cao et al. [7], and the model presented by Rohs and Oulasvirta [26]. Cao et al. found their model to perform better than Fitts' law, whereas Rohs and Oulasvirta suggested Fitts' law for modeling peephole pointing tasks.

We showed that under most conditions all three models provide good estimates. However, the other two models slightly outperform Fitts' law in prediction accuracy when significantly different peephole sizes are used and users have no prior knowledge of target location. Since these conditions are very unlikely to occur in peephole interfaces we suggest Fitts' law over the two other models. In addition, we found indications that the benefit of the other two models only pays off when peephole sizes are below a certain threshold. We plan to conduct further studies in order to specify the threshold. We discovered that target overshoot is a key characteristic of peephole pointing and that it relates strongly to prior knowledge of target location.

For future work we would like to investigate applicability of techniques like force fields [1] and expanding targets [19] to reduce overshoot in peephole pointing situations. Moreover, a 2D study with a handheld projector should be conducted to prove that our results also hold for 2D targets and to gain insights into other possible peephole interaction techniques such as steering, dragging, and crossing. Design guidelines for peephole interfaces might be worth exploring as well as design and interaction implications when dealing with much larger virtual workspaces (e.g., 360 degrees) or workspaces that span over an entire room including ceiling and floor.

REFERENCES

1. Ahlström, D. Modeling and improving selection in cascading pull-down menus using Fitts' law, the steering law and force fields. In *Proc. CHI 2005*, ACM Press (2005), 61-70.
2. Baudisch, P. and Rosenholtz, R. Halo: a technique for visualizing off-screen objects. In *Proc. CHI 2003*, ACM Press (2003), 481-488.

3. Beardsley, P., van Baar, J., Raskar, R., and Forlines, C. Interaction using a handheld projector. *IEEE Computer Graphics and Applications 25*, 1 (2005), 39-43.
4. Blask, G. and Coriand, F. Exploring interaction with a simulated wrist-worn projection display. In *Proc. ISWC 2005*, IEEE Computer Society (2005), 2-9.
5. Cao, X. and Balakrishnan, R. Interacting with dynamically defined information spaces using a handheld projector and a pen. In *Proc. UIST 2006*, ACM Press (2006), 225-234.
6. Cao, X., Forlines, C., and Balakrishnan, R. Multi-user interaction using handheld projectors. In *Proc. UIST 2007*, ACM Press (2007), 43-52.
7. Cao, X., Li, J.J., and Balakrishnan, R. Peephole pointing: modeling acquisition of dynamically revealed targets. In *Proc. CHI 2008*, ACM (2008), 1699-1708.
8. Cao, X., Massimi, M., and Balakrishnan, R. Flashlight jigsaw: an exploratory study of an ad-hoc multi-player game on public displays. In *Proc. CSCW 2008*, ACM Press (2008), 77–86.
9. Cockburn, A., Karlson, A. and Bederson, B.B. A review of Overview+Detail, Zooming, and Focus+Context interfaces. *ACM Computing Surveys 41*, 1 (2008), 1-31.
10. Dao, V.N., Hosoi, K., and Sugimoto, M. A semi-automatic realtime calibration technique for a handheld projector. In *Proc. VRST 2007*, ACM (2007), 43-46.
11. Davis, J. and Chen, X. Lumipoint: multi-user laser-based interaction on large tiled displays. *Displays 23*, 5 (2002), 205-211.
12. Fitts, P.M. The information capacity of the human motor system in controlling the amplitude of movement. *Journal of Exp. Psychology 47* (1954), 381-391.
13. Fitzmaurice, W.G. Situated information spaces and spatially aware palmtop computers. *Communications of the ACM 36*, 7 (1993), 39-49.
14. Forlines, C., Balakrishnan, R., Beardsley, P., Baar, J. Van, and Raskar, R. Zoom-and-pick: facilitating visual zooming and precision pointing with interactive handheld projectors. In *Proc. UIST 2005*, ACM Press (2005), 73-82.
15. Gustafson, S., Baudisch, P., Gutwin, C., and Irani, P. Wedge: clutter-free visualization of off-screen locations. In *Proc. CHI 2008*, ACM Press (2008), 787-796.
16. Henze, N. and Boll, S. Evaluation of an off-screen visualization for magic lens and dynamic peephole interfaces. In *Proc. MobileHCI 2010*, ACM Press (2010), 191-194.
17. Löchtefeld, M., Gehring, S. and Krüger, A. Distributed user interfaces for projector phones. Book chapter in distributed user interfaces: designing interfaces for the distributed ecosystem, Springer (2011), 113-123.
18. MacKenzie, I. S. Fitts' law as a research and design tool in human-computer interaction. *Human-Computer Interaction 7*, 1 (1992), 91-139.
19. McGuffin, M. and Balakrishnan, R. Acquisition of expanding targets. In *Proc. CHI 2002*, ACM Press (2002), 57-64.
20. Oh, J.-Y. and Stuerzlinger, W. Laser pointers as collaborative pointing devices. In *Proc. GI 2002*, 141-149.
21. Pavlovych, A. and Stuerzlinger, W. The tradeoff between spatial jitter and latency in pointing tasks. In *Proc. EICS 2009*, ACM Press (2009), 187-196.
22. Raskar, R., Beardsley, P., Van Baar, J., Wang, Y., Dietz, P., Lee, J., Leigh, D., and Willwacher, T. RFIG lamps: interacting with a self-describing world via photosensing wireless tags and projectors. *ACM Transactions on Graphics 23* (2004), 406-415.
23. Rapp, S. Spotlight Navigation: a pioneering user interface for mobile projection. In *Proc. Ubiprojection, Workshop on personal projection at Pervasive 2010.*
24. Rapp, S., Michelitsch, G., Osen, M., Williams, J., Barbisch, M., Bohan, R., Valsan, Z., and Emele, M. Spotlight Navigation: Interaction with a handheld projection device. *Pervasive Conference*, Video paper, (2004).
25. Rohs, M., Schöning, J., Raubal, M., Essl, G., and Krüger, A. Map navigation with mobile devices: virtual versus physical movement with and without visual context. In *Proc. ICMI 2007*, ACM Press (2007), 146-153.
26. Rohs, M. and Oulasvirta, A. Target acquisition with camera phones when used as magic lenses. In *Proc. CHI 2008*, ACM Press (2008), 1409-1418.
27. Rohs, M., Oulasvirta, A., and Suomalainen, T. Interaction with Magic Lenses: real-world validation of a Fitts' law model. In *Proc. CHI 2011*, ACM Press (2011), 2725-2728.
28. Rukzio, E., Holleis, P., and Gellersen, H. Personal projectors for pervasive computing. *IEEE Pervasive Computing 11*, 2 (2011), 30-37.
29. Sanneblad, J. and Holmquist, L.E. Ubiquitous Graphics: combining hand-held and wall-size displays to interact with large images. In *Proc. AVI 2006*, ACM Press (2006), 373-377.
30. Tsang, M., Fitzmaurice, G.W., Kurtenbach, G., Khan, A., and Buxton, B. Boom Chameleon: simultaneous capture of 3D viewpoint, voice and gesture annotations on a spatially-aware display. In *Proc. UIST 2002*, ACM Press (2002), 111-120.
31. Yee, K. Peephole Displays: Pen interaction on spatially aware handheld computers. In *Proc. CHI 2003*, ACM Press (2003), 1-8.

Mobile Augmented Reality: Exploring Design and Prototyping Techniques

Marco de Sa
Yahoo! Research
4401 Great America Pkwy, Santa Clara, CA, USA
marcodesa@acm.org

Elizabeth F. Churchill
Yahoo! Research
4401 Great America Pkwy, Santa Clara, CA, USA
churchill@acm.org

ABSTRACT
As mobile devices are enhanced with more sensors, powerful embedded cameras, and increased processing power and features, new user experiences become possible. A good example is the recent emergence of Augmented Reality (AR) applications that are designed for personal use while people are on-the-go. However, designing effective and usable AR experiences for mobile devices poses challenges for the design process. In this paper we outline reasons why simulating a compelling, mobile AR experience with sufficient veracity for effective formative design is a challenge, and present our work on prototyping and evaluation techniques for mobile AR. An experiment within the context of an ongoing design project (Friend Radar) is presented along with resulting findings and guidelines. We reflect on the benefits and drawbacks of low, mixed and high fidelity prototypes for mobile AR by framing them into a set of analytic categories extracted from the existing literature on prototyping and design.

Author Keywords
Mobile; Mobile HCI Augmented Reality (AR); design; design process; prototyping; experiment; interview; methodology; service design.

ACM Classification Keywords
H.5.2. Information interfaces and presentation (e.g., HCI): User Interfaces, Prototyping.

INTRODUCTION
As mobile devices grow in power, capabilities and features, doors open for designers and engineers to create new experiences and applications. Augmented Reality (AR) applications are expanding in terms of function, not least because of the growing capture, sensor and location-sensing capabilities of emerging mobile devices. As a result, mobile AR applications are increasingly useful and appealing. Recent research suggests that mobile AR could be responsible for amassing an enormous amount of profit in advertising, games and applications in general as it becomes increasingly feasible and popular [12].

MobileHCI'12, September 21–24, 2012, San Francisco, CA, USA.

Early experiments with mobile AR required considerable amounts of equipment in their creation [1, 29], equipment that arguably produced decrements in the user experience and therefore in the user's assessments of the benefits of such applications. By contrast, current smart-phones can easily support this type of experience in real world settings. In addition, utilizing GPS and integrated compasses, the combination of AR and location-enabled and positioning services [17, 15] means that it is now possible provide users with ways to use AR and gain easy access information about their surroundings while on-the-go.

Nevertheless, significant design challenges are posed by the ever-evolving hardware, features and capabilities of mobile devices and the services they utilize. While assessment of the usability of specific interface or interaction design features yield well to laboratory-based evaluation of static of minimally interactive mock-ups (e.g., is the target area large enough to be selected?, is the font readable and in what lighting conditions?, is the image occluding other content?), full service ecosystem design, such as those imagined for mobile AR applications do not yield so well to such methods. Therefore, designers are required to come up with new ways to convey their visions and test their concepts when designing new services, services that draw on real-time information from multiple sources using interaction methods that are often unfamiliar to users. To prototype the envisioned, fully-fledged service is obviously costly and will result in premature, often non-retractable, commitments within the service design; such premature commitments are precisely what iterative design and evaluation are aimed at circumventing. However, these are rarely applied to AR [28] and, to get useful feedback from users, it is necessary to create an experience that is 'realistic' or provocative enough of the envisioned scenario of use such that users are able to give meaningful and actionable feedback. Herein lies the tension we address in this paper: *how to create a user experience that is sufficiently "realistic" and provocative for users to envisage the final service experience and thus give meaningful and actionable feedback without building the whole service ecosystem?*

In this paper we illustrate our design methodology, through description of our approach to designing a mobile augmented reality application called Friend Radar. We utilized three different techniques to prototype our concept: (1) a low-fidelity prototype (i.e., mock-up and Wizard of

OZ); (2) a mixed-fidelity prototype using video and (3) a high-fidelity working prototype used on an actual smart phone. Using these three prototypes, we conducted a set of in-situ evaluation sessions, gathering feedback from users in real life scenarios. Our application focuses on allowing users to find whom of their friends are in the local vicinity by displaying icons and avatars overlaid on the current camera-rendered location, showing distance and direction in relation to the user.

Our contribution emerges from the findings on the use of the three different prototyping techniques for mobile AR. In particular, we detail the benefits and drawbacks of each approach and the settings, scenarios and phases of the design process (such as during early ideation or later stage evaluation) in which they may be best used.

BACKGROUND AND RELATED WORK

Recently, with the growing proliferation of smart-phones, mobile HCI researchers have been not only focusing on interface usability and user experience but also on tackling the growing design challenges that come along with new technologies and services [10, 28]. In particular, dealing (1) with the multiplicity of contexts, (2) the real world settings, (3) simulating real-time services or location-based services and (4) the newer features and modalities that mobile devices support, have been major challenges. To overcome these challenges, new techniques have emerged that cope with these issues, providing new design guidelines [9], prototyping [5] and evaluation techniques [30, 6].

Design Methodologies and Prototyping Techniques

In particular, motivated by the new form factor and usage paradigm that mobile devices afford, strong emphasis has been placed on how to effectively create prototypes that can be used to validate concepts at early stages and, preferably, during out of the lab field tests. This offers users a better perspective of how the system will be used thus resulting in better feedback for the design process. However, for mobile AR, given the tight coupling with context and, for visual-based AR, the real world view through the camera feed, simulating windows, menus and icons is not sufficient [5].

From the HCI and prototyping literature [31] and more recent mobile related experiments [5, 14, 18, 19, 32] two main prototyping approaches can be found: (1) low-fidelity and (2) high-fidelity prototypes. While the former are usually easily and quickly built, using mock-up and paper to simulate a working system (e.g., Wizard-of-Oz), the latter generally offer an experience closer to that of the final product, allowing users to interact with working software, at least to some extent. More recently, experiments have been trying to understand the value of the middle ground between these two approaches, using mixed-fidelity prototypes [22]. These aim at bridging the gap between low- and high-fidelity prototypes by introducing the flexibility of the former but still providing means to increase the degree of visual refinement or interactivity [22], adjusting the prototype to the desired goals.

Nevertheless, very few accounts of prototyping for mobile AR are available in the literature [8].

Mobile Augmented Reality Channels and Trends

Augmented reality and mixed reality are concepts that have been used around technology for more than 20 years [1,3, 20, 21, 25]. However, their coupling with mobile devices has only been made possible more recently with the advent of powerful smart-phones and new and smaller sensors (e.g., GPS, cameras). Consequently, cumbersome, intrusive equipment is no longer required to create these experiences. Moreover, as previous work has shown, augmented reality provides new affordances and visualization options that enhance experiences by providing additional information combined with the real world surroundings of the users [29, 1, 25, 15]. By placing virtual objects over reality users are provided access to information that is typically not available to them using their own senses [1]. Naturally, this gains further relevance with mobile technology as users move around and are able to explore what is around them freely within real world settings [2][25].

With technological advances in the field of sensors (e.g., GPS, Accelerometers, Gyroscopes, Cameras) a number of mobile AR trends have recently emerged. Visual-based AR is the most common trend and represents the majority of existing applications like Yelp's Monocle[1] or Layar[2]. With visual mobile AR, applications typically overlay additional information on top of what the smart-phone's camera captures, displaying a combination of the real world with added information on top of what is around the user. The majority of such applications are strongly based on location services, providing information on the user's surrounding [2]. Within these we can find a wide variety of services that are oriented mostly towards search, entertainment, gaming, daily life support applications, advertising and shopping.

The two other trends within mobile AR, far less popular and very much underexplored, make use of the additional feedback channels available on most smart-phones – haptics and sound [11, 33]. A traditional example is the common eyes-free turn-by-turn navigation system that uses speech to provide directions to its user. However, more recently, some research efforts have been combining the use of haptics and sound to augment reality at specific locations, providing context-awareness of additional information used both in gaming apps (e.g., treasure hunts) and commercial or advertising applications (e.g., play a jingle/song when close to a certain shop).

Challenges

However, despite the new opportunities they provide, these new features and capabilities now available on most smart-phones present new challenges, especially when creating such rich interactive experiences [5]. Specifically, AR on mobile devices is still very new and few guidelines or

[1] Yelp – http://www.yelp.com
[2] Layar – http://www.layar.com

documented accounts on how to design such rich experiences are available [5, 27]. Furthermore, despite the highly enthusiastic projections for its adoption in the near future, the majority of users, even savvy smart-phone aficionados are not aware of the existence of AR for mobile devices, nor what the concept means. Therefore, designers are faced with the challenge of how to test and validate their ideas at initial stages of the design process.

Although some reports on designing mobile AR can be found, most refer to highly complex settings and infrastructures, defined for very specific purposes [1, 1, 17, 15] or are strongly focused on the hardware constraints [4, 1]. Still, despite being a medium that serves as a window to the user's reality, amplifying actions or activities and changing the user's perception of the world, studies on design or from a user-centered perspective are scarce [5] and accounts on prototyping are almost non-existent [8]. As a consequence methods and techniques for the design of mobile AR are yet rarely studied or defined but increasingly needed.

THE FRIEND RADAR CONCEPT

The Friend Radar concept merges social networks, messaging tools and location-based services, and makes use of AR. Information is presented in a way that allows users access to friends' information without losing the current, local, physical context around them.

The Friend Radar concept draws data from existing technologies such as social networks like Facebook[3] and Google+[4], location based apps/services such as Foursquare[5] and similar check-in tools and previous experiments designed specifically for mobile devices like DodgeBall Social. However, the Friend Radar aims at enhancing the experience by providing an enriched visual display of friends overlaid on the users' surroundings. In particular it provides added affordances that allow users to see where friends are situated in relation to him/her and their distance. It also presents details such as preferred friends, directions where groups of friends are located and their availability meshed with the real world. In opposition to map-based radars, this AR based concept does not require users to translate two-dimensional views into their surroundings, which is especially relevant at non-familiar locations.

Our goals with this concept, in this initial stage, are to show friends' positions in relation to the user, including details such as proximity and availability. Friends' location and status can be retrieved from various sources (e.g., Messenger apps, Social networks) and their avatars configured, being overlaid over the locations to which the user is pointing his/her camera/device (Figures 3 and 4). In addition, tapping on a friend's icon displays his/her profile with information from the service they are using at that moment and allows for some types of communication (e.g., sending a message or alert) – Fig. 1. Overall, it merges the social network experience with the real world, enhancing it with additional, contextually relevant, information.

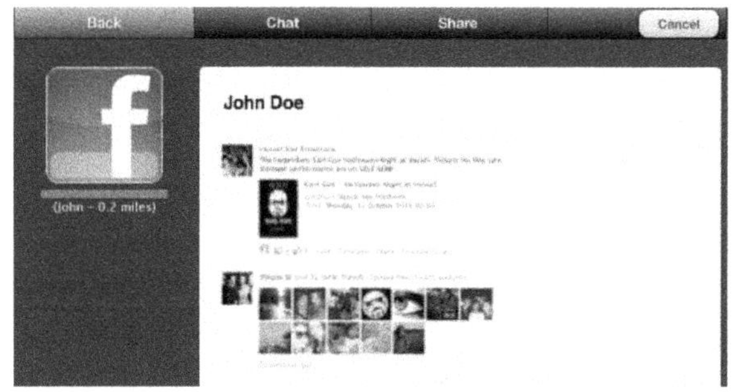

Figure 1. In addition to the AR interface, users can retrieve detailed information on distance and friends' activities.

Design Approach

The design process we are following is focused on users. Our aim is to understand the best way to provide users with realistic experiences at early stages of the design process and, from a methodological perspective, understand which are the best approaches to prototype for mobile AR. In an area that is growing so rapidly, it is crucial to understand what it means to prototype for mobile AR and to be able to create the experiences for end-users, without committing to costly development processes.

In particular, some of the techniques used for the initial design stages are based on previous experiments for mobile interaction design [6]. As suggested by recent literature, better results can be achieved while designing mobile interaction when immersing users within realistic scenarios, including prototypes and in-situ tests [6, 30, 24]. In order to do so for AR, our goal was to approach the design process by experimenting with different prototyping techniques and exploring the benefits and drawbacks of each.

PROTOYPES

Three different mocks/prototypes for the Friend Radar concept were created. To build these we used three significantly different approaches – low-, high- and mixed-fidelity - but following the same philosophy: to create a prototype as close to the real experience as possible in terms of form factor and weight. Our hypothesis was that each prototype would yield different advantages but, given the highly interactive nature and rich experience that mobile AR presents, best results would come from the higher fidelity prototypes.

Low-fidelity mocks

The lowest fidelity prototype used for this study was built using a dummy/non-functional device (e.g., a product design mockups that was created typically to illustrate a form factor design). The dummy phone mimicked a common Android device with a 3.5-inch screen (Figures 2 a) and b). In order to simulate the camera feed, the screen

3 Facebook – http://www.facebook.com
4 Google+ - http://plus.google.com
5 Foursquare - https://foursquare.com/

was removed and a hole was cut on the back cover of the phone (the inside of the dummy phone is hollow). A transparent screen was placed on top of this hole to simulate the device's screen (e.g., reflection) and to allow users to easily use it as a touch input device, while maintaining the ability to see through (see Figure 2a). In addition, this screen was also used to allow for an easier use of the Wizard-of-Oz technique, where small icons were glued to the screen to simulate the augmented reality. For the moving avatars longer pieces of paper were used. This facilitated their movement by the "wizard" simulating the actual location-based interaction.

Figure 2. a) Low-fidelity mock. The see-through hole allows users to see what is behind the device, simulating the camera.

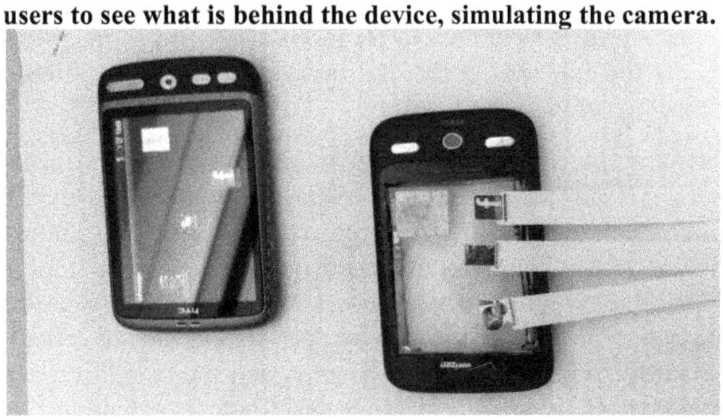

Figure 2. b) Low fidelity mock and used icons (right) next to an actual working device with the hi-fidelity prototype (left).

A small amount of clay was also added to the fake phone to slightly increase its weight and make it identical to an actual functioning device. The building process lasted approximately one hour, including the creation of the attachable icons (e.g., map, avatars) and weight add-ons.

Mixed-Fidelity Videos

For the second prototype, a mixed-fidelity prototyping approach was used, combining aspects from both low and high fidelity prototypes. In particular, for this case, and following the categories defined by McCurdy et al [22], the degree of visual and aesthetic fidelity was high while the interactivity remained low. Our hypothesis was that using video would be an adequate approach to simulate a realistic in-situ experience at a very early stage, as it allows simulating movement and including additional content over captured footage, displaying it directly on mobile devices.

Figure 3. Video of the mixed-fi being played on a smart-phone.

To create the prototype, two different locations were selected. Videos were shot beforehand. For the first location, a public park with a few people sitting down and walking around was selected (Figure 3). The second set of videos was shot in a busy square with shops, buildings and people walking and standing in different areas (Figure 5). Both locations were selected because they represent places where friends usually meet-up, seek encounters and congregate. Each video had an approximate duration of 30 seconds and included light panning and some jitter to emulate a realistic usage scenario (i.e., scanning the area for friends).

Figure 4. High-fidelity prototype. The icons are overlaid on the camera feed and move with the phone's movement.

Once the videos were captured, they were edited and the friends' icons were overlaid using a video editing software. This process took around one hour for each of the videos. Icons were placed hovering above people's heads. Those placed over people that were walking followed that person around, simulating a connection between the person and the avatar (Figure 3). The videos were exported to a phone, used during the evaluation sessions.

High-Fidelity Prototype

The high-fidelity prototype was developed using the Android Development Kit. The prototype uses the camera feed, displaying it live and showing whatever the camera is capturing. On top of this feed, shown on full screen mode, a set of icons and avatars is also displayed on semi-fixed positions. Using the accelerometer and compass sensors, whenever the device is rotated, the icons and avatars will maintain their position in relation to the surrounding environment. They will be occluded when the device is not facing the icon's position. This offers an accurate rendering of mobile augmented reality (Figure 4).

In addition to the interactive view, this prototype also includes the possibility of interacting with some of the icons. Once an icon is tapped, a second screen displaying detailed information about that person will be shown (see Figure 1). The working prototype required approximately 2 working days to be fully developed. We note that the icons had already been designed for the previous prototypes.

EXPERIMENT

Our goal with this experiment was to assess the benefits and drawbacks for each approach–the low-fi, the mixed-fi and the high fidelity prototypes–evaluating the trade-offs and adequacy of each technique to different scenarios.

	Development Time	Skills and tools	Location Dependent
Low-Fidelity	30 minutes	Wizard of Oz	No
Mixed-Fidelity	1 hour (per location)	Video editing	Yes
High-Fidelity	2 Days	Programming knowledge	No

Table 1. Summary of requirements and development time for each prototyping approach.

When compared with storyboards or simply describing scenarios to users, we felt this in-situ approach, using artifacts that could be seen and touched by the users, would be much more beneficial to the design process. Accordingly, we set up a short experiment where we used all the prototypes for users to experiment in-situ, simulating a real life situation. As a result, we expected participants to (1) clearly understand the concept without any explanation; (2) detect some of the features presented through the prototype; (3) validate some of the idealized functionalities; (4) assess the concept's usability and (5) use it as an exploratory tool regarding users' expectations for such an application.

Evaluation Sessions

The experiment was conducted following a *guerrilla* approach [23]. The overall idea on this approach is to rely on methods that are not strict and can be easily adjusted to situations where costs (both financial and effort wise) have to be kept very low. It assumes that a simple scenario is set and, using a prototype, a set of quick tests with a small group of users take place, producing highly valuable results when compared to the effort the approach takes.

For our study, participants were approached directly, while relaxing or idling, at the same locations where the videos were shot. These locations were selected for all the three prototypes in order to avoid any bias that the location and environment could introduce into the study but also to fake reality. Participants were approached and were selected randomly. Each participant was invited to participate by one of the researchers while another researcher filmed the experiment.

A total of 24 users participated in these sessions and interacted with or visualized prototypes. Much in line with similar exploratory and detailed experiments, and field studies [24, 1, 16, 30], a group of 8 participants interacted with each type of prototype. Participants for each prototype were divided into two groups (one per location). Each session took around 1 hour, in addition to the time spent interacting with the prototypes and responding to the questionnaire (detailed on the following sections). No gratuities were provided and participants authorized the filming. The goals of the experiment were not explained beforehand.

For the low-fidelity prototype, participants were only explained what technique would be used and requested to imagine it as a functioning application. One of the researchers involved in this experiment played the Wizard and held the icons in front of the device at different locations, allowing the participant to see these icons whenever pointing the device at them.

For the video prototype, participants were only requested to visualize the prototype for the duration of the video. Each participant was handed the smart-phone immediately after one of the researchers had pressed play. Participants were also allowed to review the video again if so desired.

Finally, for the high-fidelity prototype, participants were handed the phone and requested to play and interact with an application that was being developed.

Once again, we emphasize that no explanation on the type of applications or its goals was provided to any user. We intentionally omitted this information to test how easy it would be for users to understand what they were doing based on the prototype alone.

Once finished interacting (or visualizing) the prototypes, participants were asked to provide their opinion through a short set of questions during a follow-up interview. Most sessions were filmed for additional analysis.

Figure 5. User testing the video (mixed-fidelity) prototype on a busy urban location.

Post-experiment

Follow-up interviews took place immediately after the participants used the prototypes. Tests lasted around 5 minutes for the low-fidelity prototypes, from 1 to 2 minutes for the video prototypes (depending on the number of times the participant watched the videos) and approximately 3 minutes for the high-fidelity prototypes. The interviews took from 5 to 10 minutes on the questionnaires and from

30 minutes to one hour for follow-up comments and discussion (here participants were allowed to freely explore the prototypes). The goal was to establish a comfortable conversational setting for participants from which we could gather data and understand their motivations and responses in as much detail as possible.

The majority of the questions were pre-defined on a script while others emerged during the interview and follow-up conversations. On the questionnaire, participants were requested to rate the prototypes and experiment using a 7-point Likert scale (1 – strongly disagree; 7 – strongly agree) with regards to realism, ability to convey the concept and easiness to understand. Again, the goal was to focus on each prototype's ability to convey a concept, its features and support early stage identification of issues and advantages. A set of questions regarding the application per se (e.g., user interest in using it, privacy) was also included.

RESULTS

Participants who interacted or visualized the prototypes were aged between 17 and 48 years. Their professions ranged from students (14), customer service representatives (2), teachers (2), attorneys (2), strategists (1), and financial advisors (1) to unemployed (2). From the 24 participants, only 5 stated not owning a smart-phone. Only three in 24 participants had any previous contact with AR applications while 6 knew what the expression meant and could explain what the concept was. Once again, the sample size for our study followed the standard for in-situ mobile evaluation available throughout the literature [24, 1, 28, 16, 30], allowing for rich, interactive and highly detailed sessions.

As expected, there are some significant differences between the three approaches. The following sections detail the results for each type of prototype.

Low-Fidelity Mocks

The low-fidelity mock-ups, using the dummy phone and the Wizard-of-Oz approach produced the poorest results. As shown on the chart on Figure 6, the majority of users had difficulties understanding the concept just by holding and panning the mock. Six out of 8 participants disagreed that it was easy to understand the goal of the app or what they were looking at. Interestingly, given that the Wizard promptly showed the avatars/icons whenever the participant pointed the phone to the right direction, 5 of the 8 participants stated that it was easy to understand how it would work, despite not comprehending the goal of the app or the content being shown.

Regarding the prototype's realism, all users were adamant that the prototype did not feel real or look real in any way, that it was clearly just an experiment and that should not be taken very seriously.

Finally, once the questionnaire had been completed, our concept for the applications was explained. After receiving the explanation, all participants understood the concept and application functionality, and all replied positively when enquired on whether they would use the app (Figure 9).

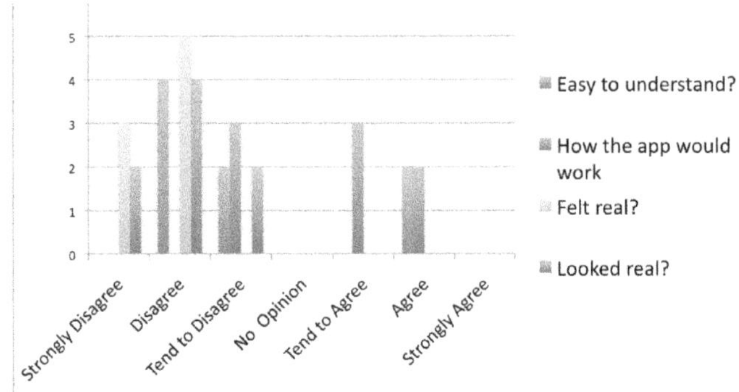

Figure 6. Results from the tests with the low-fidelity prototype. Users had trouble understanding the concept.

During the interviews that followed the tests, but prior to the explanation of the concept, most people did not understand the concept:

> "I just don't get it. I just see a fake phone and someone showing me pieces of paper."

There was one exception to this:

> "I get what is happening. As I move the phone different things are shown. I'm seeing on the device things that could or should be there but that I don't see by myself, right? I just don't know what those things are!"

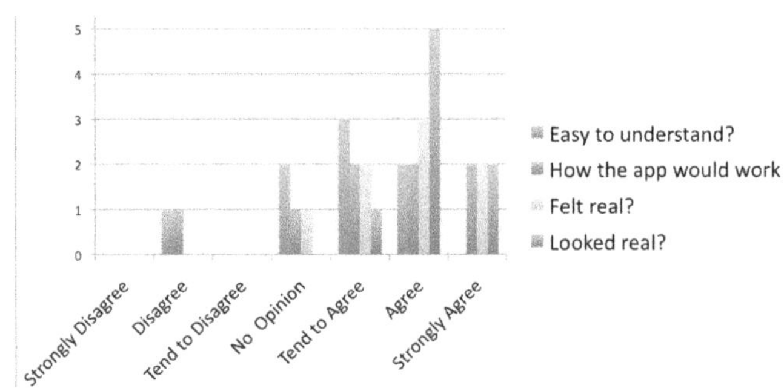

Figure 7. Results from the tests with the video prototype.

Mixed-Fidelity Videos

Results for the video (mixed-fidelity) prototypes can be seen on the chart (Figure 7). Five out 8 participants thought it was easy or very easy to understand the concept just by viewing the 30 seconds video. The majority also stated being able to understand how it would work (6 out of 8) and that the prototype felt and looked real (7 out of 8). Six out 8 users showed great interest in the concept and stated they would use the application. No further explanation on what the concept was or which features would be available was given before enquiring about participants' interest in the Friend Radar app.

From the post-test interviews, some of the participants, having understood both the concept and interaction mechanisms, mentioned:

"It would be cool to touch the icons and see something happen like showing that user's Facebook profile"

One participant had some trouble understanding the basic interactive features stating that:

"I think it works great to show how the app would work or look like but it's not the best way to see how I would use it."

In regards to the actual concept and their interest in the application, most users were excited about the possibility of using it. In particular, one user said:

"When will it be available? I would love to have this app!"

High-Fidelity Prototype

Surprisingly, results from the high-fidelity prototype were less positive than those from the mixed-fidelity prototype (Figure 8). Only half of the participants (4 out of 8) tended to agree, agreed or strongly agreed that the concept was easy to understand by interacting with or using the prototype. However, as shown on Figure 9 the majority of participants replied positively when asked if it was easy to understand how the application would work. On this question, only one participant (who never owned a smart-phone) strongly disagreed and another tended to disagree. With respect to realism, results were substantially better and the majority of users (6 out of 8) were positive about whether the prototype felt and looked real.

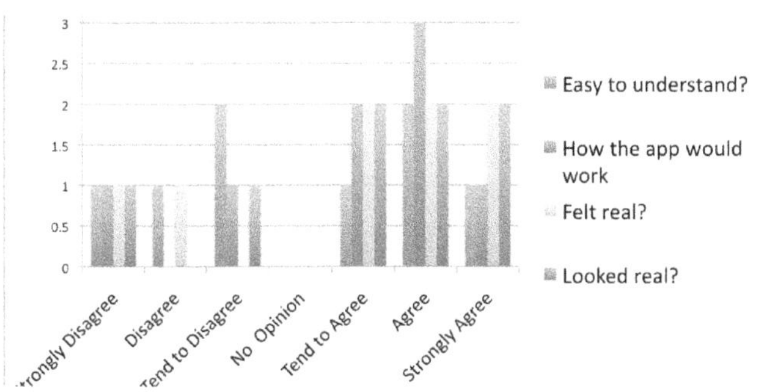

Figure 8. Results from the high-fidelity prototype tests.

During the interviews, some participants commented on the responsiveness and interactivity of the prototype:

"It's a bit slow and it doesn't do much. Is it this all it does?"

Another participant mentioned the icons were too small:

"It's difficult to hit the buttons on this tiny screen when they are always moving!"

Interest and acceptance

Once the questionnaire had been completed, the concept and features for each prototype were explained to participants. As noted above, when asked about whether they would be interested in using such an application post this explanation, people were largely positive (Figure 9).

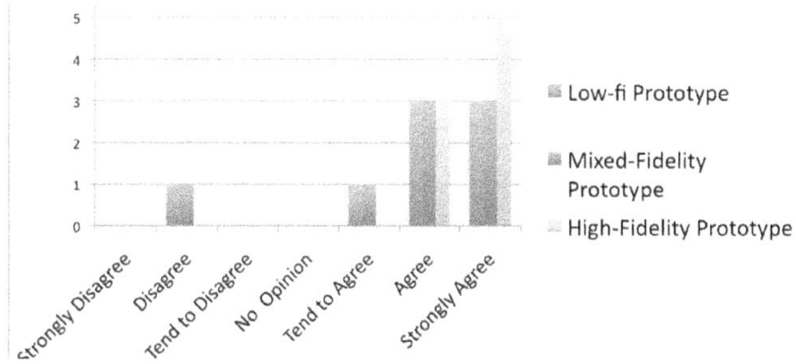

Figure 9. Results from the final question. The vast majority of participants stated being very interested or interested in using the Friend Radar application.

DISCUSSION

Our goal in this investigation was to explore the extent to which different kinds of prototype can be provocative and inspire a sense of an envisioned end-user experience in order to get feedback that would be valuable for the design process. The value of role-playing is well established but our concern was that for AR, effective props would be necessary to make the role-playing realistic and engaging enough to get useful feedback.

Each of the three prototyping techniques showed some potential benefits for application/service evaluation. Two in particular easily conveyed the idea that was being tested, without any explanation and to users who had no previous knowledge of what mobile AR means.

In analyzing our results, we derived a number of analytic categories–these were inspired in part from previous literature on prototyping and evaluation. We use these categories to reflect on users' reactions to our prototypes.

These categories are shown in Table 2, and are as follows:

- Probing – triggering users imagination in a provocative way and using the prototypes to explore new applications, concepts and usages for technology being studied [13, 26].
- Concept Validation – addressing the concept in general, the overall idea of the application and its goals, by presenting it to end-users and requesting their feedback.
- Feature Validation – validating the different features and functionalities that compose the application in more detail.
- Usability Testing – addressing interface usability issues and breakdowns and assessing efficiency and ease of use [23].
- User Experience Evaluation – understanding users' feelings, opinions, expectations, acceptance, pleasure and deeper emotions regarding the experience of use.

	Probing	Concept Validation	Feature Validation	Usability Testing	User Experience Evaluation
Low-Fidelity (Mock-ups and WOz)	Good for probing as it allows to easily add features.	Not very good to demonstrate the concept or interaction flow.	Difficult to demonstrate features but easy to include new ones in-situ.	Not great to test usability issues, but enough to validate icon size and readability.	Not adequate to evaluate more complex dimensions such as excitement, aesthetics, etc.
Mixed-Fidelity (Video)	Not great for probing as it is non-interactive and non-flexible.	Very good for concept validation as it shows features and interaction flow very easily.	Good for simple features. Difficult to demonstrate more complex features as it is non-interactive.	Not ideal for usability testing but still allows for the detection of some issues.	Good to assess some aspects of user experience (e.g., aesthetics, flow).
High-Fidelity (Functional Prototype)	Supports probing to some extent but does not allow for in-situ add-ons.	Good for concept validation mainly because it is interactive.	Good for feature validation as it allows users to explore them in detail.	Very good for usability testing as it supports interaction and functionality.	Good for experience evaluation, if care is taken to polish the interactivity.

Table 2. Summary of benefits and drawbacks from the different approaches.

Low-fidelity

Throughout the tests conducted with the low-fidelity mock-ups and using the Wizard-of-Oz technique, it became clear that there were significant challenges to applying this approach for such a rich and novel experience as augmented reality. Nevertheless, despite the difficulties in applying this technique in-situ (which, from our perspective might generalize to all mobile design in general), the low-fidelity prototype showed the greatest flexibility. The possibility of maneuvering the icons according to the situation, adapting features and behaviors on the fly had a positive impact on the study (Table 2). It's easy to update format yields very well to probing purposes as it is easy to quickly create new icons and add features on-the-fly. Although the prototype did not look or feel real, it allowed participants to understand how it would work (i.e., being aware that they would be able to see information added to the world through phone's). In addition, the low-fi approach benefits from being location independent (i.e., can be used at any location). Finally, the relatively easy building process is also a major advantage of this approach.

However, although low-fidelity prototypes are great tools for initial stages of design, for the particular case of mobile AR, as already mentioned, their evaluation and use during in-situ tests is both difficult to achieve and cumbersome. The process itself becomes distracting to users and detracts from the validity of the experiment, making it difficult to validate an unknown concept with end users. Moreover, it requires an additional person to act as the Wizard, further increasing the effort to experiment these prototypes on the field. Finally, as our results clearly show, the low-fidelity prototype provided the poorest results and was the least successful in conveying our idea and concept to participants and for the detection of some usability problems (see Figure 7 and Table 2).

Mixed-fidelity

The second approach used in this experiment, video based mixed-fidelity prototypes showed some interesting benefits. They provided a realistic way to convey the concept to users, even at very early stages. Results showed that users understood the concept without any previous explanation, even those without smart-phone and AR experience.

Crucial to these results was the ability to visualize the video prototypes on the same location where the videos were captured. This allows users with no experience or knowledge of AR applications to quickly grasp the idea and understand the concept (as shown in Table 2). An interesting finding that emerged from the experiment was that some of the participants started following the video movement (e.g., accompanying the pre-set panning from the captured footage), reenacting the actual scene, without any suggestion to do so. This leads us to believe that users quickly gain awareness of what is happening on the video and how the prototype would be used in real-life allowing the validation of the concept and simple features (Table 2).

Another benefit, which is common to other types of prototypes, especially when used in-situ, video for AR design promoted user participation and triggered their imagination for features and usages. When interviewed, several users suggested different usage possibilities for some of the icons and UI details as well as the app's goals (e.g., discovering what the others are wearing). The greatest advantage of this approach, however, is the degree of realism and level of fidelity it provides for the effort and time it takes to build. Simulating mobile AR with video is a quick process that requires no coding or programming knowledge yet has several benefits (Table 2).

Despite the positive results in terms of providing a good idea of the experience and showing users the concept of what is being designed, there were some shortcomings on using video as a prototype. In general, the majority of the experiment's participants felt the need to experience interactivity. Several participants tried to interact with the icons on the videos without any feedback in return, which caused some confusion and frustration. Moreover, it is possible that video prototypes require similar conditions when testing to those that were available when filming the initial videos. Further tests will be conducted to validate this hypothesis. However, although weather conditions were slightly different (e.g., sunny morning vs. grey afternoon) from video to test, both locations provided similar results. It is also noteworthy that some affordances and features are not easily perceived through video (e.g., the use of gestures) – see Table 2. Usability testing.

Overall, these results show that to make this approach more ecologically valid, further work is required, especially in regards to how interactive the prototypes are. As used, the video was clearly a very provocative experience that triggered users interest and clearly demonstrated the concept. However, some of the features and the lack of different affordances and interactivity were clearly a drawback and merit further research.

High-fidelity

From the three approaches, the high-fidelity prototype was expected to show the best results, as it is closest to an actual working application. Unsurprisingly, our test showed that this was, in fact, the best approach in terms of realism, feeling and looking real for the majority of users. In particular, the ability to immediately match the surroundings (including passers by) with what is being displayed is a determinant factor to support this result. Furthermore, the interactivity that can be achieved with a developed and functioning prototype is far greater than that which can be achieved with the two previous approaches, making it especially adequate to explore available features and assess user experience (Table 2). This also facilitates usability testing, as users are able to interact with the various elements of the user interface, allowing for the detection of functional and interaction issues (see Table 2). Finally, the ability to display the camera feed also makes this a location independent approach.

However, despite the clear advantages that creating a working prototype has over video or low-fidelity mock-ups, there are important drawbacks to this approach, very noticeable on our experiment's results. One of the main reasons behind these less than optimal results comes from the fact that, when users interact with an actual device and notice the live video feed, expectations are raised to much higher levels. Even when faced with a working set of features and a higher degree of interactivity, participants stated that the prototype did not look real merely because of the response time to some of their actions (e.g., tapping the icons) or because of the resolution of some of the icons. Some of the comments and reactions during these tests suggest that results from our questionnaire might not match reality, especially if compared to the other approaches. Future experiments will address this issue by presenting different approaches to the same participants at different stages of the design process.

The major drawback from this approach, however, is the effort and knowledge it required to be developed, in comparison with low-fi and mixed-fi prototypes. Moreover, the ability to update and adjust prototypes on the fly is also unavailable and new prototypes have to be developed for different platforms (i.e., iOS, Android, Windows Phone).

CONCLUSIONS AND FUTURE WORK

Mobile devices now afford extremely rich experiences that have yet to fulfill their full potential. Mobile Augmented Reality in particular is expected to have a significant impact on the mobile world, providing a new and exciting way to interact and observe the world.

However, currently, mobile AR is still barely known by most mobile device users and presents a difficult design challenge for developers and designers. The combination of sensors and the new interaction paradigm that combines the surrounding 'real world' context with interactive visual elements and real-time data sourcing and presentation, makes it especially difficult to test with users at early stages in the design process. Designers are required to come up with new ways to convey their visions and test their concepts when designing new services in order to get useful feedback from users. In this paper we have presented three forms of prototype for a social, mobile augmented reality application, the Friend Radar, and have evaluated user reception of those prototypes to assess their ability to convey a complex, novel interaction scenario. We presented results from an experiment that assessed three different, low time requirement prototyping approaches for mobile AR – embodied as a low, a mixed and a high-fidelity prototype.

Our results have shown that all possess strengths and weaknesses but, surprisingly, the mixed-fidelity approach is the one that seems to provide the best trade-off. Not only were users able to understand the concept that was being shown very quickly, but this approach also afforded the detection of usability and design issues, triggering users imagination at the same time. Naturally, this last factor is highly valuable as it allows designers to get feedback at a very early stage. This combined with the easiness to create the video prototypes demonstrated the value of this approach. That said, high-fidelity prototypes provide even more realistic experiences, and can, at early design stages, offer results that are similar to those offered by mixed-fidelity prototypes. However, users' expectations are raised to higher levels, requiring care with the fidelity of some of the features and the fluidity of the interactive elements.

These results provide a significant contribution to the mobile interaction design community, which, with the rapid evolution of mobile devices, will soon embrace the potential of mobile AR.

REFERENCES

1. Balcisoy, S. et al. 2000. A framework for rapid evaluation of prototypes with augmented reality. In Procs. of VRST '00. ACM, 61-66.
2. Barrie P., et al. 2009. A pervasive gesture-driven augmented reality prototype using wireless sensor body area networks. In Procs of Mobility '09. ACM, 4 pages.
3. Crabtree, A., et al. 2004. Orchestrating a mixed reality game 'on the ground'. In CHI '04. ACM, USA, 391-398.
4. Damala, A., Cubaud, P., Bationo, A., Houlier, P. and Marchal, I. 2008. Bridging the gap between the digital and the physical: design and evaluation of a mobile augmented reality guide for the museum visit. In Procs of DIMEA '08. ACM, NY, USA, 120-127.
5. de Sá, M., Antin, J., Shamma, D., and Churchill, E. 2011. Mobile augmented reality: video prototyping. In CHI EA '11. ACM, NY, USA, 1897-1902.
6. de Sá, M. and Carriço, L. 2008. Lessons from early stages design of mobile applications. In MobileHCI '08. ACM, NY, USA, 127-136.
7. Dunser, A., et al. (2011) Handheld AR for Outdoor Navigation, Procs of 1st Workshop on Mobile AR, MobileHCI'11, Stockholm, Sweden, 2011.
8. Gabbard, J., and Swan II, J. 2008. Usability Engineering for Augmented Reality: Employing User-Based Studies to Inform Design. IEEE TVCG 14, 3 (2008), 513-525.
9. Hakkila J. and Mantijarvi, J. 2006. Developing design guidelines for context-aware mobile applications. In Proceedings of Mobility '06. ACM, NY, USA, 24.
10. Hagen, P., Robertson, T., Kan, M. and Sadler, K. 2005. Emerging research methods for understanding mobile technology use. In Procs of OZCHI '05, Australia, 1-10.
11. Heller, F., and Brochers, J. (2011) Corona: Audio Augmented Reality in Historic Sites, Procs 1st Workshop on Mobile AR, MobileHCI, Sweden, 2011.
12. Holden, W. Augmented Reality on the Mobile to Generate $732 million by 2014(2009) Juniper Research, http://juniperresearch.com/viewpressrelease.php?pr=166
13. Hulkko, S., et al. 2004. Mobile probes. In Proceedings of NordiCHI '04. ACM, NY, USA, 43-51.
14. Jones, M. and Marsden, G. 2006. Mobile Inter-action Design. John Wiley & Sons.
15. Karlsson, J., Rehman, S., and Li, H. 2010. Augmented reality to enhance visitors experience in a digital zoo. In Procs. of MUM '10. ACM, 4 pages.
16. Kjeldskov J., and Stage, J. 2003. Designing the handheld maritime communicator. In Proceedings DUX '03. ACM, NY, USA, 1-15.
17. Lee, G., et al. 2009. Freeze-Set-Go interaction method for handheld mobile augmented reality environments. In VRST '09, ACM, 143-146.
18. Lim, Y., et al. 2006. Comparative analysis of high- and low-fidelity prototypes for more valid usability evaluations of mobile devices. In Procs. of NordiCHI '06 ACM, New York, NY, USA, 291-300.
19. Lim, Y., Stolterman, E., and Tenenberg, J. 2008. The anatomy of prototypes: Prototypes as filters, prototypes as manifestations of design ideas. ACM Trans. Comput.-Hum. Interact. 15, 2, Art. 7 (2008), 27 pages.
20. Mackay, W., et al. 1993. Augmenting reality: adding computational dimensions to paper. Commun. ACM 36, 7 (1993), 96-97.
21. Milgram, P., and Kishino, F. 1994. A taxonomy of mixed reality visual displays. IEICE Transactions On Information And Systems E77-D, 12 (January).
22. McCurdy M., et al. 2006. Breaking the fidelity barrier: an examination of our current characterization of prototypes and an example of a mixed-fidelity success. In Procs of CHI '06, ACM, NY, USA, 1233-1242.
23. Nielsen, J. 1994. Guerrilla HCI: using discount usability engineering to penetrate the intimidation barrier. Cost-justifying usability, Academic Press, USA 245-272.
24. Nielsen, C., Overgaard, M., Bach Pedersen, M., Stage, J. and Stenild, S. 2006. It's worth the hassle!: the added value of evaluating the usability of mobile systems in the field. In Procs of NordiCHI '06, ACM, NY, 272-280.
25. Nilsson, S. and Johansson, B. 2007. Fun and usable: augmented reality instructions in a hospital setting. In OZCHI'07,ACM, 123-30.
26. O'Brien, S. and Mueller, F. 2006. Holding hands over a distance: technology probes in an intimate, mobile context. In OZCHI '06, ACM, NY, USA, 293-296.
27. Olsson, T., Soronen, H, and Vaananen-Vainio-Mattila, K. 2008. User needs and design guidelines for mobile services for sharing digital life memories. In Procs of MobileHCI '08. ACM, NY, USA, 273-282.
28. Paay J., and Kjeldskov, J. 2008. Understanding the user experience of location-based services. J. Locat. Based Serv. 2, 4, 267-286.
29. Piekarski, W. et al. 2004. Designing Backpacks for High Fidelity Mobile Outdoor Augmented Reality. In Procs of ISMAR '04. IEEE, Washington, USA, 280-281.
30. Rogers, Y., et al., "Why it's worth the hassle: The value of in-situ studies when designing ubicomp," in Ubicomp 2007, Innsbruck, Austria: ACM, September 2007.
31. Virzi, R., Sokolov, J., and Karis, D. 1996. Usability problem identification using both low- and high-fidelity prototypes. In Procs. CHI '96, ACM, NY,USA, 236-243.
32. Weiss, S. 2002. Handheld Usability. John Wiley & Sons, Inc., New York, NY, USA.
33. Xu, Y., and MacIntyre, B. (2011) Theory-driven Design for Social Play with Mobile AR Games, Procs of 1st Workshop on Mobile AR, MobileHCI'11, 2011.

Playing it Real: Magic Lens and Static Peephole Interfaces for Games in a Public Space

Jens Grubert[1], Ann Morrison[2], Helmut Munz[3], Gerhard Reitmayr[1]

[1]Institute for Computer Graphics and Vision
Graz University of Technology, Austria
[grubert | reitmayr]@icg.tugraz.at

[2]Department of Architecture, Design
and Media Technology
Aalborg University
DK-9220 Aalborg Øst
ann.morrison@acm.org

[3]haellmuth@gmail.com

ABSTRACT

Magic lens and static peephole interfaces are used in numerous consumer mobile phone applications such as Augmented Reality browsers, games or digital map applications in a variety of contexts including public spaces. Interface performance has been evaluated for various interaction tasks involving spatial relationships in a scene. However, interface usage outside laboratory conditions has not been considered in depth in the evaluation of these interfaces.

We present findings about the usage of magic lens and static peephole interfaces for playing a find-and-select game in a public space and report on the reactions of the public audience to participants' interactions.

Contrary to our expectations participants favored the magic lens over a static peephole interface despite tracking errors, fatigue and potentially conspicuous gestures. Most passersby did not pay attention to the participants and vice versa. A comparative laboratory experiment revealed only few differences in system usage.

Author Keywords

Augmented Reality; Static Peephole; Magic Lens; Field Trial

ACM Classification Keywords

H5.m [Information interfaces and presentation (e.g., HCI)]: Miscellaneous; H.5.2 [Interfaces and Presentation]: User Interfaces - Benchmarking

General Terms

Performance; Design; Experimentation; Human Factors

INTRODUCTION

The increasing processing power of sensor equipped smartphones along with the increasing usage of state of the art vision and machine learning algorithms in mobile phone applications give rise to mobile users being confronted with relatively novel interface metaphors such as gestural [19], speech [9] or magic lens (ML) interfaces [2]. Specifically in mobile handheld Augmented Reality (AR) systems the ML metaphor is employed by relating information to physical objects or locations on the screen of the mobile device.

Static peephole (SP) [16] [31] interfaces are integrated into various map-based applications on mobile devices for years. On multi-touch enabled smartphones they make use of surface gestures such as drag-to-pan and pinch-to-zoom to navigate in a virtual space. With SP interfaces users can hold the phone proximate to their bodies, allowing use in a variety of situations while walking, standing or sitting. In contrast, ML interfaces require users to align the orientation of the device with the physical object (reference frame) to be augmented during the whole time of interaction.

While performance comparisons between ML, SP and dynamic peephole (DP) interfaces have been carried out in laboratory settings relatively few studies investigated user adoption of these interfaces in public contexts [17] [18]. For example, it is not yet well explored how potentially more visible gestures that are part of ML usage (while still unfamiliar to the general public) influence the adoption of this interface.

Within this paper our main research interests are to explore *if and how* people would use a ML interface for a mobile game in a public location when a SP interface is available as alternative, to gauge the *reactions from the general public* and to determine the *impact of location and audience on task performance*.

Therefore, we designed a mobile phone game that could be played at a poster mounted at a public building in a transit area or on the smartphone alone but at the same location. We complemented the observations at the public space with observations of a separate group conducting the same tasks in a controlled laboratory setting.

With this work we add insights about user and audience behavior when using a ML interface outside the laboratory and complement existing studies that investigated collaborative use of mobile AR systems in the wild.

RELATED WORK

The performance of ML, SP and DP interfaces was thoroughly investigated under laboratory conditions in various works. Rohs et al. compared users' performance in a find-and-select task for ML, DP and SP interfaces [26] and showed that ML and DP pointing outperformed joystick-based SP pointing. They also investigated the impact of item density and visual context [23] on ML and DP pointing and proposed a two-phase adaption to Fitt's law which they evaluated in laboratory [24] and real world settings [25].

Due to the limited screen space on mobile devices various off-screen visualization techniques have been proposed for SP interfaces [1] [4] [8]. Off-screen visualization for ML interfaces can be split into ones indicating target regions if the reference frame is a planar target in front of the user [10] and ones that indicate a target around users that is inside the same reference frame as the users [3]. While we do not use off-screen visualizations in our system, the trends to conduct studies in the field [11] [28] encouraged us to study potential effects that might not be observed in laboratory settings such as the influence of the audience on system usage.

Social interactions at public displays or interactive installations have been investigated in several approaches (e.g., [13] [14] [21]). The combination of private and public displays was also examined for example, by looking at how to initiate connections between devices [15]. However, relatively few approaches considered social aspects when interacting with novel gestures and postures on handheld devices in public spaces.

One of the first works that evaluated a handheld ML interface in a museum setting was described in [27]. While the authors concentrated on the technical feasibility of the system they also investigated the use of handheld AR systems for short games (2-3 min each). In particular the authors found that while the motivation of children was generally high, tasks involving AR had to be explained in detail.

In an online survey Rico and Brewster evaluated the social acceptability of device and body based gestures [22] for different locations and audiences and complemented it with field trials in a private and a public setting. However, they did not specifically consider the use of ML and peephole interfaces.

Morrison et al. conducted field trials on the collaborative use of handheld ML and SP interaction with a single device in each group [18] and later expanded to synchronous use of multiple mobile devices [17]. One observation from these trials was that users of ML concentrated more on the interface and the game whereas SP users were more aware of their environment. In contrast to these studies we are focusing on single user adoption of ML and SP interfaces in a public setting in a non-collaborative task while taking into account reactions from the public.

We add to previous studies by investigating how people would use a ML and SP interface with a vertical reference frame (poster) in a public setting and what the influence of location and audience is on task performance.

GAME DESIGN AND IMPLEMENTATION

Find-and-select tasks are common in mobile AR games. Users are required to physically translate (pan and zoom) and eventually rotate their phones in order to detect targets; selection is typically accomplished through touching the screen. While mobile AR games often employ only a ML interface to solve the task, mobile AR browsers offer alternative list and SP views on the data. SP interfaces for smartphones allow navigation through dragging (pan) and pinching (zoom).

We wanted to observe how users would adapt to ML and SP interfaces if they can solve a task with either interface in a public space. We decided on a simple find-and-select task similar to previous performance-centric studies [10]. To engage people over an extended period of time at one location, we designed a game-like experience with background music, audio, graphical effects and challenges. Each level lasted approximately one to two minutes; playing 8 consecutive levels could eventually lead to fatigue. The game could be played with a ML and with a SP interface (see Figure 1) that showed similar views on the game to lower the mental gap when switching between them. The interaction methods to find the targets were different between the interfaces (physical pointing in ML, drag-to-pan and pinch-to-zoom in SP). Selection was accomplished by clicking in either interface. The poster as reference frame for the game was available in both interfaces (physical for ML, virtual for the SP). The field of view of the virtual camera was set to match the one of the physical camera. For the game we did not focus on collaborative activities. Instead, the game tasks required the players to repeatedly find a 'moving worm' that could appear at one of 20 locations (apples on a tree) in two possible sizes. Individual targets had to be selected three times before appearing elsewhere.

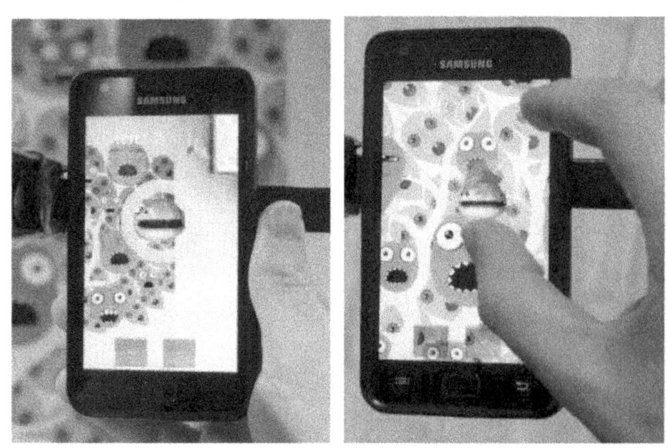

Figure 1. A large target within selection distance (indicated by orange ring) in the magic lens view (left). User pinching to zoom in to a small target in the static peephole view (right).

Figure 2. A participant playing the game in front of the poster at the public transit place in Graz, Austria.

Figure 3: Participant playing the game in the laboratory.

To select the targets, users had to be in a minimum distance in front of the target (ca. 30 cm for a small target, ca. 60 cm for a large one) forcing them to physically move back and forth with the ML interface or to pinch in and out in the SP interface.

Users could explicitly switch between the interfaces by pressing buttons at the bottom of the screen which would show the closest orthogonal view of the virtual poster when switching from ML to SP. When users pointed their phone down they implicitly switched into a standard view (showing approximately 2/3 of the virtual poster.)

The levels did not increase in difficulty to observe possible learning and fatigue effects; only the positions and sizes of the worms were varied randomly. There were 8 levels in total, each with 15 targets to be played. Through pre-experiments we adopted parameters for dragging and pinching speeds, the default scale for the virtual poster and the minimum distances for target selection to ensure comparable times in both interfaces for a trained user.

The game was implemented in Unity with Qualcomm's Vuforia toolkit and deployed on a Samsung Galaxy SII smartphone running Android 2.3.

STUDY DESIGN

We designed an outdoor study and replicated a comparative indoor study to act as a control group. The outdoor study took place at a building below a large video wall on a central place in Graz, Austria (see Figure 2). The place serves as the main transit zone of the town to change public transportation lines and acts as a waiting area. In addition, musicians or advertisers can often be found here. Participants conducted the study in front of a DIN A0 sized poster that was mounted vertically at a height of 2 m. The control study took place inside a laboratory at Graz University of Technology (see Figure 3). Both the laboratory and outdoor studies took approximately one hour per participant and all participants were taken through the sequences by the same one researcher in the interests of consistency.

There were 6 phases: introduction (5 min), training (5-10 min), demographic questionnaire (5 min), main game (15-20 min), interviews and questions (10-15 min) and performance (10-15 min). In the initial training phase the participants were made comfortable with both interfaces to a level where they could explicitly and implicitly switch between the two. They also learnt how to easily recover from tracking failures that could appear in the ML condition (e.g., due to fast movements or being too close to the poster, see Figure 4, left). As it was very cold (at times even down to -10°C, regardless, we witnessed people standing outside waiting for friends) after the training phase, participants filled out a demographic questionnaire in a nearby café.

In the main phase they were asked to select fifteen worms in 8 levels each. Participants were free to choose their preferred interaction technique. This was explained clearly in the training phase and again in the transition to the main phase. In addition, it was made clear they could switch interfaces as often as they liked, there were no restrictions on this. Participants were asked to complete the tasks but we clearly emphasized that their target focus was not speed or precision. Participants could set their own pace, taking breaks between the levels as they wished, with warm tea on hand.

The main phase was followed by a questionnaire and interview session in the same café where the demographic questionnaire was filled out. Finally, a performance phase was conducted at the poster similar to the one described by Henze et al. [10]. Participants had to find-and-select the bluest out of 12 boxes ranging from green to blue by panning and touching at a fixed distance (showing approximately 1/4 of the search area) 15 times in 4 repetitions resulting in 480 measurements per group and interface (see Figure 4, right). Participants were checked for color blindness before starting this test. This time they could only use *either* the SP or the ML interface at any one time. This meant that half of the participants started with the ML mode and then conducted the task in the SP mode, while the other half started with SP and then used the ML mode to ensure a balanced sample.

Figure 4. Tracking errors indicated by black circle in the middle of the screen (left). Overview of one configuration of colored target boxes in the performance phase (right).

Further, a control group of eight participants conducted the exact same procedure from beginning to end, including the initial training and performance phases, but in an indoor laboratory setting. The laboratory setting did not have passersby, only each participant and the experimenter were present. The poster was mounted on the same height as in the public condition.

Participants

There were 16 participants in total (8 female, 8 male) evenly distributed between the study at the laboratory and at the outdoor location. In both groups participants were aged between 21 and 30 years. All of them had either a university degree or were studying. Five people in the public location group had a computer science, two a design and one a social science background. In the laboratory group four people had a computer science, three a design, and one a mathematical background. Thirteen of 16 participants were familiar with the idea of AR, or had used AR at least once, regularly or professionally. All but one participant never to rarely (at most 1 hour per week) played video games and all but one never played video games on mobile devices.

Hypotheses

We followed an exploratory approach for the main part of the study to obtain insights into how the participants would employ the system and how the public would react to the interactions of the participants, specifically with the ML interface. Nonetheless, we had the following two hypotheses: *H1*: *ML will be used less often in the public setting than in the laboratory*. We suspected that playing the game in the ML interface would cause more attention from the public and that participants would feel exposed and watched, eventually switching to the less obtrusive SP interface in the public setting. *H2*: *ML will be used less as the game progresses*. As the game levels were repetitive and the main phase was expected to last for 15-20 minutes we suspected that as arm fatigue increases and the novelty of the ML interface decreases participants would eventually switch to SP.

Data Collection

We collected video, survey and device logging data, complemented with notes, stills and additional videos taken by one observer. Quantitative data was analyzed with Microsoft Excel and the R statistical package. Null hypothesis significance testing (NHST) was carried out with the 0.05 level.

Video Data

A small camera with a wide angle lens (100° diagonal field of view) was vertically mounted next to the poster (behind a pillar in the public condition), which recorded participants' actions and the reactions from the public during the main task. In addition an observer took notes and additional footage with another camera. In total 2 hours of video footage (only for the main game phase) was collected for the public condition and processed by a single coder.

Survey Data

We employed questions that are based on Flow [30], Presence [29] and Intrinsic Motivation [5] research and were adapted through a series of studies [13, 17, 18]. We customized them for this study to capture reactions on the system and tasks in the environment using a 5-point Likert scale. A multiple choice questionnaire similar to [22] about location and audience was used and followed by a semi-structured interview focusing on how participants used the system and how they would use it in other settings.

Device Data

The position of the real camera (in ML) or the virtual camera (SP) mode was sampled at 10 Hz. Additionally, events such as touches, interface switches, task completion times (TCTs) interface were logged on the device. The timing data was not normal distributed so non-parametric NHST was applied. One participant in the public location had to abort the main phase after 6 of 8 levels but eventually continued with the performance phase.

Limitations

While we employ NHST, we stress that with our limited sample size the results are particular to this situated instance. Further exploration with a larger sample in a wider variety of settings is required prior to being able to make any generalizations from our findings. As with many mobile trials conducted in a public space, the setting and tasks are generally somewhat contrived with participants aware that they are taking part in a study where they are accountable to the researcher team while doing tasks designed to test unknown (to them) research-related criteria.

FINDINGS

We report on our observations combining quantitative and qualitative results as well as findings from the public and the laboratory setting where appropriate for our limited sample size.

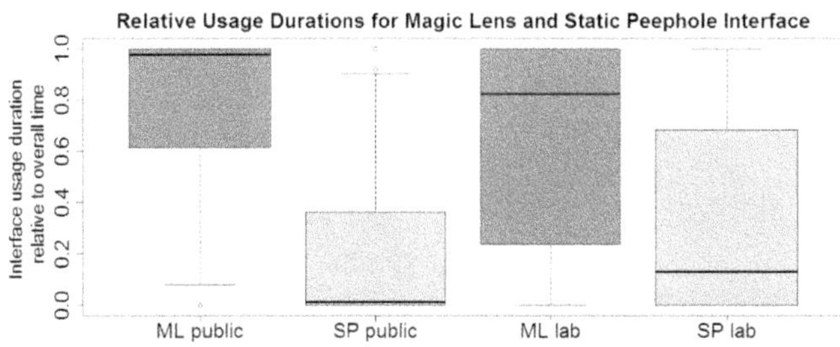

Figure 5. Relative usage duration for the magic lens (blue) and static peephole (green) interface in the public and lab condition.

Magic Lens was used most of the Time

The ML interface was used 72% of the time (76% in the public setting, 68% in the lab) as illustrated by Figure 5. The ML interface was used weak significantly longer in the public setting than in the lab condition as indicated by a Mann-Whitney U test ($p = 0.056$, $Z = -1.59$). The significant difference is due to one participant playing solely in SP mode in the lab condition. But even with considering this one participant as an outlier (resulting in no significant difference in usage time of ML between both locations) our hypothesis *H1* that the ML interface would be used less in the public setting is contradicted. Figure 6 shows boxplots of the absolute TCTs over all levels.

A Mann-Whitney U test indicated no significant differences for completion times over all levels between the groups. In addition, a Friedman rank sum test did not reveal significant differences for ML usage duration between the 8 levels for the public location and for the lab group, thus contradicting hypothesis *H2 that the ML interface would be used less as the game progresses*. Figure 7 shows the relative usage duration of the ML interface over 8 levels in the public location group.

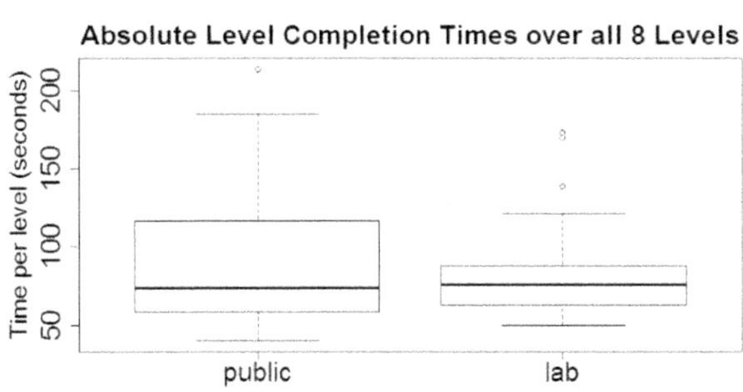

Figure 6. Absolute level completion times for the public and lab group.

Spatial Configurations for Magic Lens Usage

Generally, participants switched between a position in which they could get an overview about the whole poster to identify the target and then moved in to select the target.

We observed diverse ways of how participants handled the fact that they needed to move back and forth during the game and the holding of the phone itself. All but one participant used a relative fixed arm pose and moved using their feet, stretching their arms only for the last few inches towards the poster.

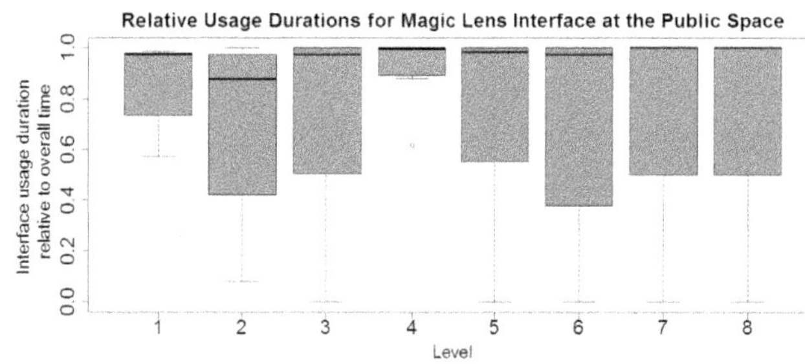

Figure 7. Relative usage duration for the magic lens interface over individual levels in the public setting.

As the mounting of the poster should reflect a possible real-world scene its height was not adjusted to match participants' height. Two small participants held the phone above their heads to reach targets at the top of the poster, one of them eventually switched to the SP mode after 4 levels. Three participants bent their knees regularly to hit targets at the lower half of the poster (see Figure 8).

The phone itself was held in various ways (see Figure 9). One participant switched from portrait to landscape mode to get an overview of the scene and stabilize tracking. Two participants held the phone on the long edge as the phone was more stable when touching it and subsequently tracking errors would be reduced; six held it on the short edge. Six participants held the phone mainly one handed, two used both hands. Two participants eventually used their gloves to hold the phone and changed them between levels due to the weather condition. We could not reliably identify fatigue as a single cause for changing hand poses. The tracking system failed regularly and participants adapted to the tracking system throughout the game. Three participants explicitly mentioned they had changed their hand poses to address tracking errors.

Reasons for Using Magic Lens

A Wilcoxon signed rank test indicated significantly higher ratings for the ML over the SP interface for enjoyment and preference for the public location group (see Table 1).

Questionnaire item	Result	p-value	Z-score
I enjoyed using the ML (MD=5) | SP (MD=3) view in the environment	ML>SP	0.036	1.80
I would rather do the task with the ML (MD=5) | SP (MD=2) view only	ML>SP	0.029	1.90

Table 1. Questionnaire items that were rated significantly higher for the ML over the SP interface in the public group.

When being asked why the participants who played the game mostly in the ML mode chose to do so, four participants replied that they "liked it more", found it more "groovy", "fun" or just "novel" and "much more interesting". One participant mentioned "I wanted to try out Augmented Reality [ML], as I can use the map [SP] view all the time".

Figure 8. Participant using solely his arms to move back and forth (a, b), bending knees to hit a target at the lower half of the poster (c, d), holding the phone above the head to reach targets at the top of the poster (e, f).

Another participant who used the ML mode exclusively said "I would probably not use it if it would be commonly available". Two participants explicitly mentioned that they felt being faster in the ML mode. One felt that the music was too attention grabbing in the environment and distracting, turned it off, and continued to play in the ML mode. Another mentioned that with the ML interface "you are much more in the game". One participant said that she had a better overview in the ML mode and felt it was easier to step back and forth than to pinch-to-zoom. Similarly, another participant said the ML mode was "more intuitive".

Reasons for Using Static Peephole

While the ML interface was used almost exclusively by 6 of 8 participants in the public setting, two female participants eventually switched to the SP interface completely after 4 and respectively 5 levels. One of them mentioned "I liked that [ML] mode more but switched due to the cold and eventually my hand felt more relaxed". In the lab condition one participant used the SP interface exclusively as it was "more comfortable" and "not as shaky" as the ML interface. If tracking recovery did not work as expected or took too long participants tended to switch to the SP interface.

Figure 9. Various ways to hold the phone in the magic lens condition: Switching from portrait to landscape mode (a, b), holding the phone across the short or long edge (c, d), using gloves to cope with the cold (e, f, g).

One participant who switched back and forth between the interfaces said: "I wanted to use that [ML] mode but the system [tracking] did not work so I eventually switched to the other [SP] mode and tried again later". Six participants switched back to the ML interface after playing one level of the game in SP latest. Two participants used ML as overview SP for quickly zooming in and two tried the SP mode to see whether they could be as fast as in ML mode.

Reactions from the Public

We observed reactions from 691 people, who passed by in a half circle of ca. 10 meters around the poster. Approximately every 5 minutes a larger group of 5-10 people simultaneously passed by to change lines. The majority of the passersby did not notice the participants, the poster or the recording equipment at all (68%).

Figure 10. Passersby not noticing the participants interacting with magic lens (left) and static peephole interfaces (right).

Thirty percent of the passersby had short glimpses of less than a second and kept on walking (Figure 11, a). It was not possible to differentiate between the reasons for glimpsing, i.e. whether people looked primarily at the poster, the participant interacting or the wall mounted camera.

Figure 11. Passersby glimpsing (a), watching from a distance (b) and approaching a participant (c).

Ten people (1.5%) stopped and watched for more than 5 seconds (Figure 11, b). In three occasions (0.5%) participants were approached (by one elderly adult, one young adult, group of two boys) and asked what they were doing at the poster. In one occasion the participant explained the game to the children (Figure 11, c).

Detachment from the Environment

The ratings of following items indicated that participants concentrated on the system and tasks (see Figure 12) and did not focus on their environment:

q1: *I concentrated on the system.*

q2: *The tasks took most of my attention.*

Participants also indicated that the environment did not distract them much by rating following items:

q3: *It was hard to concentrate on some targets as I was distracted with the environment.*

q6: *I did not pay attention to the environment when using the ML interface.*

q11: *I was not as aware of time passing or of other people when using the system to complete the tasks, as I feel I would usually be.*

q13: *I felt nervous while using the system.*

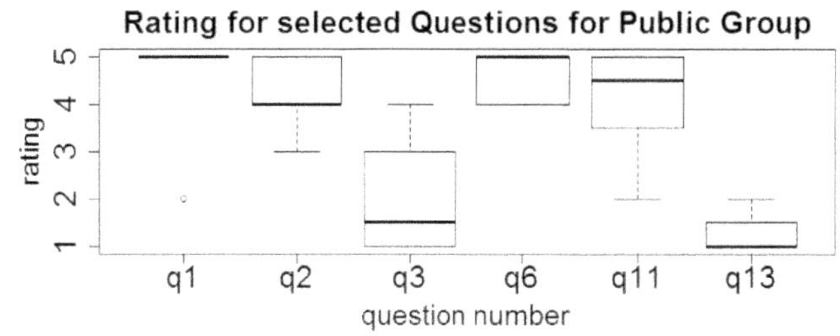

Figure 12. Ratings for selected questions concerning concentration on system and task and distraction by environment (5-point Likert scale, 1: totally disagree, 5: totally agree).

In addition, a Mann-Whitney U test indicated significant differences between the public location and lab group for questionnaire items listed in Table 2. The ratings to the first two items might indicate that even though participants in the public condition were aware of their different role in the environment they did not care about the actions of the surrounding audience. This is also reflected in participants' comments stating that they knew people were around but they did not care about it. The significant lower ratings to the social presence questionnaire item in the last two rows might eventually highlight the fact that users in the public condition played the game in a low temperature environment.

Questionnaire item	Result	p-value	Z-score
I did not pay attention to the environment when using the ML view. (P: MD=5, L: MD=4)	L<P	0.042	-1.72
I was aware that I had a different role in being there than most people in the environment. (P: MD=5, L: MD=4)	L<P	0.002	-2.91
I would rather do the task with the ML view only (P: MD=5, L: MD=3)	L<P	0.039	-1.77
I had to look away from the screen to perform the task (P: MD=1, L: MD=2)	L>P	0.013	2.24
How did you feel using the system in the environment? Cold ... Warm (P: MD=2, L: MD=4)	L>P	<.0001	3.24
How did you feel using the system in the environment? Insensitive ... Sensitive (P: MD=4, L: MD=2, 3)	L<P	0.035	-1.81

Table 2. Questionnaire items that were rated significantly different between the public location (P) and lab (L) group.

During the interviews one participant described the gaming experience as "asocial". She felt "totally focused on the game" and did not pay attention to passersby at all as she "did not care about anything else". Another comment was: "The people watch and see that you are doing something – but actually you are completely passive to your environment"

No Significant Differences in Performance between Lab and Public Group

We included an experimental phase similar to the one described in [10]. We wanted to investigate possible effects of location and audience on task performance. This separate phase was conducted as participants had the free choice on interface usage in the main game phase. The main game phase was not used to analyze task performance. Mann-Whitney U tests indicated no significant differences between the groups for the TCTs or error rates in ML and SP mode (see Table 3 and Table 4).

	Public	Lab
ML	M=50.2 SD=22.3	M=58.5 SD=22.6
SP	M=43.3 SD=10.3	M=43.0 SD=11.1

Table 3. Task completion times (seconds) over 4 levels in performance phase.

	Public	Lab
ML	M=0.31 SD=0.53	M=0.78 SD=1.18
SP	M=0.38 SD=0.71	M=0.31 SD=0.64

Table 4. Selection errors over 4 levels in performance phase.

Using the Interfaces Outside of the Study Setting

Only half of the participants at the public location indicated that they would use the ML interface outside of the study setting at a public transportation stop (see Figure 13). Figure 14 shows in front of which audience the participant would use the interfaces. The questionnaire is similar to the one employed in [22]. According to pairwise Chi-Squared tests of independence there were no significant differences between groups for location or audience ratings. The public group would use the SP interface in public transportation significantly more often (χ^2=6.25, p=0.012).

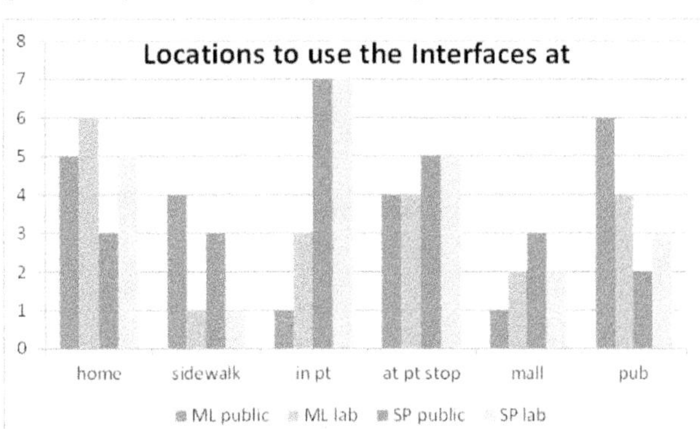

Figure 13. Number of participants who would use the interfaces at various locations (pt: public transportation).

While Yate's continuity correction was applied for adressing the low expected cell count the sample size of 16 items in a 2x2 table should be taken into account when interpreting these results. During the interviews participants further explained their decisions and two mentioned that they would use the interface specifically with friends around.

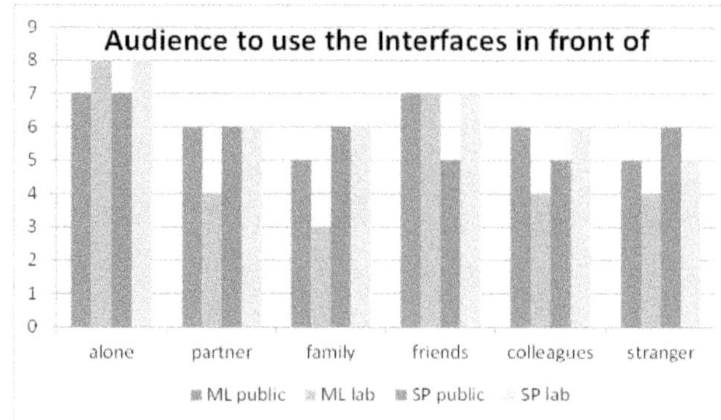

Figure 14. Number of participants who would use the interfaces in front of various audiences.

DISCUSSION

The study demonstrated that, contrary to our expectations, the ML interface was used in the field most of the time; with only few significant differences when compared to laboratory usage. The use of the ML interface was at least partly driven by curiosity as most participants were already familiar with the SP interface and perceived the study as an opportunity to "try out" a new mobile AR game. The novelty of the interface was also indicated by the diverse ways participants handled the phone.

The SP interface was mainly used when the system could not recover from tracking errors fast enough or when participants did not want to move closer to the poster but rather zoomed in to hit the small targets. The levels did not increase in difficulty to ensure we could study fatigue and learning effects. However, we could not uniquely identify individual causes for changing user behavior (especially hand poses). This might be partly due to reoccurring tracking errors being a confounding factor in this study and needs further consideration. Contrary to previous studies about the use of ML and SP interfaces in handheld systems outside the laboratory [17] we used a game design that demanded the attention of single users and had no collaborative aspects. In this study we found no significant effects of location and audience on user behavior and task performance. Participants concentrated mostly on the game task and did not pay attention to passersby and activities going on around them in the street. This finding is supported by other studies where for example, mobile AR users bump into lampposts while engrossed in the screen interface [18] and is a commonly identified problem with pedestrians using their mobile phones and walking out into traffic.

While the ML interface was used by participants most of the time during the study, only half of them indicated they would continue to do so if they had the opportunity to play a game at an augmented poster at a public transport stop in the future. However, the indicated non-game-playing attitudes of the participants need to be taken into account when considering these responses.

Despite confounding factors such as a public space, cold weather and a repetitive task, most users continued to use the ML interface. While the two interfaces were designed to balance the achievable performance and ease the mental gap when switching views, participants' comments indicated that the game could just be less engaging in the SP interface. Overall, the fact that the ML interface was used for an overwhelming percentage of the interaction time requires more exploration.

The majority of passersby did not pay attention to the participants interacting with the poster; if they did then only for a short period of time. As one participant mentioned playing the game in ML mode "is comparable of hearing loud music in public transportation. ... If users do not care about that they might probably also use this [ML] interface". Our observations within this study indicate that for a public transit place interacting with a ML interface does to a large extent not result in socially conspicuous behavior. The observations complement recent online surveys that indicate a small but growing number of users adapting to novel interactive systems, such as QR code equipped products [6] or mobile AR browsers [7] [20] through their smartphones in public spaces.

An open question concerning well-designed augmented posters might be: would people continue to use the ML interface once they become familiar and the novelty has worn off? Our study indicates that at least reactions from the public might not inhibit the initiation of ML usage. Furthermore, "Playing with friends" was a motivating factor mentioned in the interviews to use a ML interface in public when participants would not use that interface alone. Therefore, enabling group activities on augmented posters might lower the barrier for initiating interactions with the ML interface further.

CONCLUSION

We presented a field study on the use of magic lens and static peephole interfaces in a game-like setting at a public transit place. The magic lens interface was used significantly longer and was preferred by participants over the static peephole interface. The audience on the public space mainly did not pay attention to the participants interacting and participants themselves did feel isolated from their environment. A comparison to a control group in a laboratory setting did reveal only few differences despite extenuating circumstances such as weather conditions and the transit nature of the space itself.

In future work we want to conduct the same study at more public locations, particularly those that afford social interactions (e.g., mall, train station) and distribute mobile Augmented Reality games through advertising campaigns in our local cities. We would then collect system usage data remotely, similar to the approach of Henze et al. described in [12]. Further, we want to develop a mobile Augmented Reality game that invites multiple players to collaboratively solve tasks at public posters to investigate potential effects of and on the audience. Finally, we want to examine how to combine complementary views in the magic lens and static peephole interfaces and switch readily between these in transitional interfaces to enable useful and engaging interfaces depending on the users' context.

ACKNOWLEDGMENTS

This work is made possible by the Austrian National Research Funding Agency FFG in the SmartReality project.

REFERENCES

1. Baudisch, P., and Rosenholtz, R. Halo: a technique for visualizing off-screen objects. *Proc. CHI 2003*, ACM Press, 481–488.
2. Bier, E. A., Stone, M. C., Pier, K., Buxton, W., and DeRose, T. D. Toolglass and magic lenses: the see-through interface. *Proc. SIGGRAPH 1993*, ACM Press, 73–80.
3. Biocca, F., Tang, A., Owen, C., and Xiao, F. Attention funnel: omnidirectional 3d cursor for mobile augmented reality platforms. *Proc. CHI 2006*, ACM Press, 1115–1122.
4. Burigat, S., Chittaro, L., and Gabrielli, S. Visualizing locations of off-screen objects on mobile devices: a comparative evaluation of three approaches. *Proc. MobileHCI 2006*, ACM Press, 239–246.
5. Deci, E. L., and Ryan, R. M. The "what" and "why" of goal pursuits: Human needs and the self-determination of behavior. *Psychological Inquiry 11*, 4 (2000), 227–268.
6. Econsultancy. 19% of uk consumers have scanned a qr code. http://econsultancy.com/uk/blog/8118-19-of-uk-consumers-have-scanned-a-qr-code-survey.
7. Grubert, J., Langlotz, T., and Grasset, R. Augmented reality browser survey. *Tech. rep. 1101*, ICG, University of Technology Graz, Austria, 2011. http://www.icg.tugraz.at/publications/augmented-reality-browser-survey
8. Gustafson, S., Baudisch, P., Gutwin, C., and Irani, P. Wedge: clutter-free visualization of off-screen locations. *Proc. CHI 2008*, ACM Press, 787–796.
9. Hearst, M. A. 'natural' search user interfaces. *Commun. ACM 54*, 11 (Nov. 2011), 60–67.
10. Henze, N., and Boll, S. Evaluation of an off-screen visualization for magic lens and dynamic peephole interfaces. *Proc. MobileHCI '10*, ACM (New York, NY, USA, 2010), 191–194.
11. Henze, N., Poppinga, B., and Boll, S. Experiments in the wild: public evaluation of off-screen visualizations in the android market. *Proc. NordiCHI 2010*, ACM Press, 675–678.
12. Henze, N., Rukzio, E., and Boll, S. 100,000,000 taps: analysis and improvement of touch performance in the large. *Proc. MobileHCI 2011*, ACM Press, 133–142.
13. Jacucci, G., Morrison, A., Richard, G. T., Kleimola, J., Peltonen, P., Parisi, L., and Laitinen, T. Worlds of

information: designing for engagement at a public multi-touch display. *Proc. CHI 2010*, ACM Press, 2267–2276.

14. Jacucci, G., Spagnolli, A., Chalambalakis, A., Morrison, A., Liikkanen, L., Roveda, S., and Bertoncini, M. Bodily explorations in space: Social experience of a multimodal art installation. *INTERACT 2009*, Springer, 62–75.

15. Kray, C., Nesbitt, D., Dawson, J., and Rohs, M. User-defined gestures for connecting mobile phones, public displays, and tabletops. *Proc. MobileHCI* 2010, ACM Press, 239–248.

16. Mehra, S., Werkhoven, P., and Worring, M. Navigating on handheld displays: Dynamic versus static peephole navigation. *ACM Trans. Comput.-Hum. Interact. 13*, 448–457.

17. Morrison, A., Mulloni, A., Lemmelä, S., Oulasvirta, A., Jacucci, G., Peltonen, P., Schmalstieg, D., and Regenbrecht, H. Mobile augmented reality: Collaborative use of mobile augmented reality with paper maps. *Comput. Graph. 35*, 789–799.

18. Morrison, A., Oulasvirta, A., Peltonen, P., Lemmela, S., Jacucci, G., Reitmayr, G., Näsänen, J., and Juustila, A. Like bees around the hive: a comparative study of a mobile augmented reality map. *Proc. CHI 2009*, ACM Press, 1889–1898.

19. Norman, D. A., and Nielsen, J. Gestural interfaces: a step backward in usability. *Interactions 17*, ACM Press 46–49.

20. Olsson, T., and Salo, M. Online user survey on current mobile augmented reality applications. *ISMAR 2011*, IEEE, 75 –84.

21. Peltonen, P., Kurvinen, E., Salovaara, A., Jacucci, G., Ilmonen, T., Evans, J., Oulasvirta, A., and Saarikko, P. It's mine, don't touch!: interactions at a large multi-touch display in a city centre. *Proc. CHI 2008,* ACM Press 1285–1294.

22. Rico, J., and Brewster, S. Usable gestures for mobile interfaces: evaluating social acceptability. *Proc. CHI 2010*, ACM Press, 887–896.

23. Rohs, M., Essl, G., Schöning, J., Naumann, A., Schleicher, R., and Krüger, A. Impact of item density on magic lens interactions. *Proc. MobileHCI 2009*, ACM Press 38:1–38:4.

24. Rohs, M., and Oulasvirta, A. Target acquisition with camera phones when used as magic lenses. *Proc. CHI 2008,* ACM Press, 1409–1418.

25. Rohs, M., Oulasvirta, A., and Suomalainen, T. Interaction with magic lenses: real-world validation of a fitts' law model. *Proc. CHI 2011,* ACM Press, 2725–2728.

26. Rohs, M., Schöning, J., Raubal, M., Essl, G., and Krüger, A. Map navigation with mobile devices: virtual versus physical movement with and without visual context. *Proc* ICMI 2007, ACM Press, 146–153.

27. Schmalstieg, D., and Wagner, D. Experiences with handheld augmented reality. In *Mixed and Augmented Reality, 2007. ISMAR 2007.* IEEE, 3 –18.

28. Schwerdtfeger, B., Reif, R., Günthner, W. A., and Klinker, G. Pick-by-vision: there is something to pick at the end of the augmented tunnel. *Virtual Real. 15* (June 2011), 213–223.

29. Short, J., Williams, E., and Christie, B. *The Social Psychology of Telecommunications*. Wiley, Sept. 1976.

30. Sweetser, P., and Wyeth, P. Gameflow: a model for evaluating player enjoyment in games. *Comput. Entertain. 3* (July 2005), 3–3.

31. Yee, K.-P. Peephole displays: pen interaction on spatially aware handheld computers. *Proc. CHI 2003*, ACM Press, 1–8.

Integrating the Physical Environment into Mobile Remote Collaboration

Steffen Gauglitz **Cha Lee** **Matthew Turk** **Tobias Höllerer**
Department of Computer Science, University of California, Santa Barbara
{sgauglitz, chalee21, mturk, holl}@cs.ucsb.edu

ABSTRACT
We describe a framework and prototype implementation for unobtrusive mobile remote collaboration on tasks that involve the physical environment. Our system uses the Augmented Reality paradigm and model-free, markerless visual tracking to facilitate decoupled, live updated views of the environment and world-stabilized annotations while supporting a moving camera and unknown, unprepared environments. In order to evaluate our concept and prototype, we conducted a user study with 48 participants in which a remote expert instructed a local user to operate a mock-up airplane cockpit. Users performed significantly better with our prototype (40.8 tasks completed on average) as well as with static annotations (37.3) than without annotations (28.9). 79% of the users preferred our prototype despite noticeably imperfect tracking.

Author Keywords
telecollaboration; video-mediated communication; Augmented Reality; markerless visual tracking; user study

ACM Classification Keywords
H.5.2 Information Interf. and Presentation: User Interfaces

INTRODUCTION
With the widespread deployment of fast data connections and availability of a variety of sensors for different modalities, the potential of remote collaboration has greatly increased. While the now ubiquitous video conferencing applications take advantage of some of these capabilities, the use of video between remote and local users is limited largely to watching disjoint video feeds, leaving much to be desired regarding direct interaction with the remote environment. Thus, teleconference-like applications have been largely successful when the matter at hand can be discussed verbally or with the help of purely digital data (such as presentations slides), but they hit severe limitations when real-world objects or environments are involved.

Gesturing and pointing are very natural and effective parts of human communication, without which communication can be ineffective and frustrating ("If I could just point to it, its right there!" [8]). To incorporate these means of communication, researchers have explored various ways to support remote pointing. However, previous studies use indirect [8] or counter-intuitive [3] means to display the pointers, or require specialized hardware [11, 21] or prepared environments [7]. Most notably, most of these systems assume a static camera as otherwise the pointers lose their referents.

Advances in computer vision facilitate applications which are to some degree able to understand where mobile cameras are pointed and what is being seen. These new capabilities should be exploited to enable the remote user to interact with what she[1] sees, instead of forcing her to passively watch whatever is viewed by the local user's camera. Further, we suggest that mobile Augmented Reality (AR) provides a natural and user-friendly paradigm to communicate spatial information about the scene and to browse an environment remotely. While many enabling technologies for AR still have deficiencies (such as limited robustness of visual tracking), we show that visual tracking has advanced to the point that it can significantly improve telecollaboration systems.

The contributions presented in this paper fall into three areas:

- We describe a system framework for unobtrusive mobile telecollaboration that integrates the physical environment. Our framework is compatible with a wide range of hardware configurations, including systems that are already ubiquitous (e.g., smartphones) as well as more advanced immersive systems.
- We designed a prototype that implements this framework and features several novel interface elements for unobtrusive mobile telecollaboration in unprepared environments. Our system uses *model-free, markerless, expanding visual tracking and modeling* to enable a remote user to provide visual/spatial feedback by means of *world-stabilized annotations* that are displayed to a local user with AR. Further, our system enables *decoupling* of the local user's view from the remote user's view while maintaining live updates. This gives the remote user some control over her viewpoint as well as allowing her to point at objects not currently in the field of view of the local user.
- We conducted a user study with 48 participants to evaluate the benefits of our prototype interface over an interface

[1]For ease of readability, we will assume a *female* remote user and a *male* local user in this text.

MobileHCI'12, September 21–24, 2012, San Francisco, CA, USA.

without annotations as well as an interface with static annotations, and we discuss both quantitative results and qualitative observations in detail. To our knowledge, our study is among the first formal user studies overall to purely rely on markerless, model-free visual tracking.

RELATED WORK

Video-mediated communication of remote collaborators has been studied in detail, including various video configurations [10,20] and support for pointing or gesturing [8,18].

Further research has been done on increasing the level of immersion of teleconferences [22,30,33], for example, by transferring live three-dimensional or perspectively corrected imagery of the participants. These setups typically require static hardware installations. Collaboration is possible on purely virtual data [22,30,33], but spatial references to the physical world are not supported.

There are several AR frameworks that focus on collaborative work and more mobile infrastructure [4,5,6,31]. However, they also facilitate collaboration on virtual data only and have not been able to reduce the gap between virtual data and the remote physical environment. On the other hand, "VideoDraw" [34] and the "DoubleDigitalDesk" [37] are noteworthy early examples of integration of the remote physical space, but are limited to a static setup.

While many of the above systems focus on symmetric setups (i.e., both participants have the same equipment and share their own environment to the same degree), further work has been done on asymmetric local worker/remote expert scenarios [1,3,7,8,18,21,29]. These systems tend to focus on tasks involving objects in the local worker's physical environment ("collaborative physical tasks" [18]). Various ways to support the visual/spatial referencing have been studied, for example remote pointers or markers [3,7,8], laserpointers [21], the ability to draw onto the video stream [17,29], or directly transferring videos of hand gestures [1,17,18].

With respect to the use of remotely controlled pointers or markers in a user study and the local worker/remote expert scenario, our work is most closely related to the studies by Fussell et al. [8], Bauer et al. [3], and Chastine et al. [7]. In [8], the local user had to assemble a toy robot with guidance from the remote user. The remote user saw the local user's workspace by means of a static camera looking over the local user's shoulder, while the local user saw the same view on a separate monitor in front of him. The remote user controlled a cursor which was visible on both screens.

In [3], the local user was wearing a video-see-through head-worn display (HWD) and had to solve a puzzle-like task. The remote expert saw the video and controlled a pointer visible to both of them. To be able to accurately reference objects despite movement of the local camera, the remote expert could freeze the video. However, they did not employ any kind of tracking and thus had to freeze the local worker's view simultaneously to be able to display the pointer. This appears to be a suboptimal user interface especially for an HWD, where the user expects the video to respond to his head movement.

In [7], the local user was asked to build a structure of wooden blocks, for which the remote user sees a virtual model in AR. Fiducial marker-based tracking was used to establish a shared coordinate system for both the virtual model (on the remote user's side) and the physical model (to be built on the local user's side), and the remote user could place pointers by placing additional fiducial markers around the virtual object. (Note that here, the virtual model serves not only as "expert knowledge," but additionally as surrogate for the physical model when placing the markers around it.)

However, all of these systems either assume a static camera, since otherwise virtual annotations lose their referents [1, 3, 8, 11, 17, 18, 21], or require extensive equipment and prepared environments to track and thus maintain the annotations' locations [7]. Furthermore, in all of these systems, the remote user's view into the local environment is either restricted to a static camera [8, 17] or tightly coupled to the local user's head or body movement [1,3,7,21], thus forcing the remote user to constantly re-orient and ask the local user to hold still (or, in the case of [3], enforcing this by freezing both users' views) while pointing at an object.

In contrast, our system is able to support a *moving camera* by leveraging visual tracking. Annotations are displayed in AR, which provides a very natural alternative to Fussell et al.'s indirect third person view. Further, tracking the camera allows to *decouple* the views of local and remote user, thus allowing for accurate pointing and correct "anchoring" of annotations while avoiding Bauer et al.'s frozen HWD view.

The idea of using model-free, markerless visual tracking for the purpose of remote collaboration has previously been conceptualized by Lee and Höllerer [25] and Ladikos et al. [24].

One alternative to a wearable setup is to use a camera and projective device mounted to a robot which is controlled by the remote user [11,23]. However, this requires specialized hardware which needs to be carried around and put in place, and the range and speed of operation are limited by the robot.

Our work is further related to studies of pointing [16] and collaboration [26] in virtual environments, as well as support for pointing in groupware applications [13, 15], although these systems do not reference the physical environment.

A FRAMEWORK FOR MOBILE TELECOLLABORATION THAT INTEGRATES THE PHYSICAL ENVIRONMENT

Fig. 1 describes the proposed framework which enables the remote user to explore a physical environment by means of live imagery from a camera that the local user holds or wears. The remote user is able to interact with the model fused from these images by creating virtual annotations in it or transferring live imagery (e.g., of gestures) back.

The crucial and, with respect to live mobile telecollaboration systems, novel component of this framework is the tracking and modeling core, which enables the system to (1) synthesize novel views of the environment and thus decouple the remote user's viewpoint from that of the local user, giving her some control over her viewpoint, and (2) correctly register virtual annotations to their real world referents.

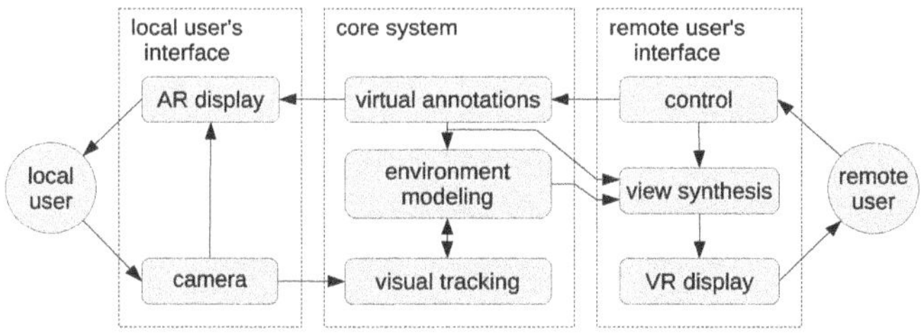

Figure 1. Overview of the proposed framework for unobtrusive, mobile telecollaboration that includes the physical environment. This figure depicts the situation that the user on the left is situated in the physical task environment and thus assumes the role of the local user, while the user on the right assumes the role of the remote user.

This framework is compatible with hardware systems that are already ubiquitous (e.g., smartphones), but scales to more advanced high-end systems as well. In particular, it is compatible with various types of displays for the local user, including projector-based setups [11].

Local User's Interface

The local user is assumed to hold or wear a device that integrates a camera and a display system (e.g., hand-held tablet or HWD with camera), which is used to both sense the environment and display visual/spatial feedback from the remote user correctly registered to the real world. In the case of a hand-held device, it acts as a *magic lens* (i.e., showing the live camera feed plus virtual annotations). Since a collaboration system has to aid the user in his or her actual task rather than distract from it, an interface which is simple and easy to comprehend is essential. It must facilitate an active user who may be looking at and working in multiple areas.

Remote User's Interface

The remote user is presented with a view into the local user's environment, rendered from images obtained by the local user's camera. The remote user can place annotations that will be displayed to both users, correctly registered to their real-world referents from their respective point of views. Annotations may include point-based markers, more complex three-dimensional annotations, drawings, or live imagery (e.g., of hand gestures).

In the simplest case, the remote user's viewpoint may be restricted to being identical to the local user's current camera view. In this case, no further image synthesis is needed. Ideally, however, the remote user should be able to decouple her viewpoint and control it independently, as far as supported by the available imagery of the environment.

If the system allows for decoupled views, it is important that only the *viewpoint* is decoupled; the video is still synthesized and updated from live images in order to enable consistent communication. (In the case of our prototype system, the effect of this can be observed in Fig. 2(c): although the viewpoints are different, the remote user sees how the local user is pointing to a control element on the panel in front of him.)

Visual Tracking & Environment Modeling

We assume that the environment may be completely unknown prior to the start of the system, that is, we do not require any model information. While using model information bears the potential to make the system more robust, any kind of model information has to be collected in some way prior to the task, which either severely limits the generality of the system or puts a burden on the user.

Instead, we assume that the system starts with no prior knowledge about the scene and builds up an internal representation on the fly, which automatically expands to include new areas as the camera moves. Our framework is compatible with environment modeling systems of different levels of flexibility and generality, including panorama mappers [35] and Simultaneous Localization and Mapping (SLAM) [19]. If admissible for the application, other sensors such as active depth cameras could also be used [28].

PROTOTYPE IMPLEMENTATION

We designed a prototype system which implements the framework described in the previous section. Our prototype is fully functional, but in several ways the simplest or least immersive implementation of our framework. With the user study discussed in the next section, we show that it nevertheless provides significant benefits in a telecollaboration task.

Our current prototype is limited in generality in one particular aspect: its tracking and modeling capabilities are restricted to homographic warps, that is, it is compatible with planar scenes or rotation-only movements, but not with general camera motion in general environments. (While state-of-the-art SLAM-like systems [19, 27] have demonstrated impressive robustness, they still require the user to move the camera in a certain way especially during initialization. We thus consciously decided to not use a SLAM system for this study.) This is flexible enough for our study setup and serves as proof of concept for both the framework and the interfaces described in the following. We plan to address this restriction in future work.

User Interfaces

As hardware interface for the local user, we decided to use a hand-held tablet screen, since we wanted to show that benefits can be achieved using hardware setups that are already in widespread deployment. In the current prototype, for ease of implementation and flexibility with respect to the hardware components to be used, we use a USB-driven screen with a camera mounted on the back (Fig. 2(a)) instead of a stand-alone tablet computer, and all computations are executed on the connected PC. However, we do not make use of a GPU and the computation-intensive part (i.e., the tracking with the template matching core, cf. details below) is very similar to the tracking system by Wagner et al. [36], which operates in real time on a 2009 smart phone. Thus, our system could be implemented on a mobile device (such as a light-weight tablet or smartphone) given appropriate optimizations.

When tracking is lost and needs to be recovered, the local user sees a large red 'X' across the screen to indicate that tracking is lost and hence virtual annotations cannot be drawn. By pointing back to a previously seen location, the user can help the system to recover tracking (cf. section on recovery below).

(a) hand-held device for local user (b) view for local user (c) view for remote user

Figure 2. (a) Hand-held device for local user: 10" USB tablet screen with camera mounted on back; (b,c) view for local and remote user. The remote user's viewpoint is frozen, but the live video frame is – correctly registered with the frozen frame – blended in, such that the remote user can still observe the local user's actions. The remote user has set three markers in her view. Two are inside the local user's current field of view, the third lies outside his view on the left, as indicated by the (accordingly colored) arrow on the left. Note that the visual tracking works fine (as apparent from the correctly registered frames and markers) despite significant occlusion from the local user's hand.

Even if tracking is lost, the live video feed is not interrupted and the local user may continue to work.

As virtual annotations, our prototype supports point-based markers which the remote user controls. They are displayed to both users in their respective views as an 'X' anchored to the real world, with a number attached to it and additionally color coded to disambiguate between multiple markers. When a marker is set outside the current view or moves outside the current view, a correspondingly colored arrow appears on the border of the screen pointing towards the marker's location (see Fig. 2(b)). (Cf. [2, 12] for other visualizations of off-screen objects.)

The remote user is presented with a view of the local user's environment and can place markers by clicking into this view (Fig. 2(c)).

We provided one particular feature that allows control over the remote user's viewpoint: the remote user can "freeze" (and un-freeze) her viewpoint at any time. Despite its simplicity, this feature allows decoupling of the remote view from local movement, and thus enables for example precise clicking on objects despite the movement of the camera on the local user's side. (Cf. Güven et al.'s "Frame & Freeze" [14]; the difference is that they developed their technique for a mobile user to interact with his own view.)

In contrast to the setup by Bauer et al. [3], the local user's screen is *not* affected by this and remains "live" at all times. Using visual tracking, the remote user's view is still registered to the local user's live view. Therefore, when markers are set, they immediately appear at the correct position with respect to the world on both the local and remote views. The remote user can return to the live view at any time by right-clicking again, and the view "zooms back" to the live view, animated by interpolating a few frames between the two viewpoints.

Note that not the remote user's *frame* is frozen — this would have the crucial disadvantage that the remote user would not receive any visual updates and could not observe the local user's action. Instead, we only freeze the *viewpoint* of the remote user and display a transparent image of the live stream on top of the remote user's frozen view, correctly registered with the frozen viewpoint. This creates the effect that, when the local user points to something within his camera's field of view, the remote user sees a half-transparent hand correctly indicating the object of interest. Blending the two frames rather than displaying only the warped live frame has the advantage that the initial frozen frame remains visible and stable even if the warped view becomes jittery or blurry (due to jittery tracking, motion blur, or extreme warping angles), and it reduces artifacts along the border of the live frame. The blended view with the local user's half-transparent hand (Fig. 2(c)) bears noteworthy resemblance to the blended video feeds in [17, 34, 37], but these systems require a static setup with known camera pose.

Visual Tracking & Environment Modeling

We used a multi-level, active search patch tracker with normalized cross-correlation (NCC)-based template matching and keyframe-based recovery, inspired by the systems of Wagner et al. [36] and Klein and Murray [19]. In preliminary investigations, this algorithm was found to perform favorably in terms of speed/robustness trade-off compared to several image alignment- and other feature-based algorithms.

As postulated by our framework, we do not use any model information; that is, the environment is completely unknown prior to the start of the system. Instead, our system builds up an internal representation on the fly which automatically expands to include new areas as the camera moves.

The tracking system could enable further features that may improve the collaboration. Most notably, it could effectively increase the field of view of the remote user by displaying the entire map collected by a panning camera. However, we decided to make only minimal use of the tracking by only world-referencing annotations and the remote user's viewpoint, to allow evaluation of these features in particular.

Details of the Tracking Algorithm

From the first frame, the tracker creates an image pyramid by half-sampling the image twice. On each level, keypoints are detected with the FAST corner detector [32], and a subset that is spatially well-distributed across the image is selected as described in [9]. Those keypoints constitute the features that are tracked and based on which the camera viewpoint (modeled as homography) is estimated for each frame.

Each incoming frame is projected back to the initial viewpoint, taking the previous frame's estimated homography as prior estimate (such that the patch tracker has to be robust to the distortion between two subsequent frames only). Then, each feature's new position is established by NCC-based template matching of an 11×11 pixel image patch. This is done for the top-most (smallest) image level first, then the homography is re-estimated from the putative feature correspondences using RANSAC and used to project the features into the next level. This ensures robustness to relatively large inter-frame movements despite a small template matching area. We used a radius of 5 pixels on the top-most level, resulting in tolerable movements of 20 pixels between two frames.

As new areas come into view, features are detected in those areas as well and added to the internal map by storing their position and NCC template with respect to the initial frame's coordinate system.

Tracking Loss & Recovery

We implemented a recovery algorithm similar to that of Klein and Murray [19]. In certain intervals and if tracking quality is deemed good (as determined by the fraction of inliers found by RANSAC), the system creates a keyframe by downsampling the current frame to 80×60 pixels, blurring it with a Gaussian kernel ($\sigma = 1.5$), and storing it together with the current pose information.

The system declares tracking to be lost if RANSAC fails to find a certain fraction of visible features (25%) that agree on one pose estimate. If tracking is lost, each new frame is also downsampled and blurred, and the NCC score between this frame and all stored keyframes is computed. The keyframe with the highest score is then aligned to the downsampled current frame. During this image alignment step, the homography is restricted to be affine, which increases both the speed and the convergence rate. The refined pose of the stored keyframe is then fed back into the tracking algorithm. If RANSAC is able to again find a sufficiently large fraction of inliers among the feature correspondences, tracking is assumed to be restored successfully; otherwise, the recovery algorithm is run again with the next frame.

When It Is Not Necessary to Recover Tracking

Unless tracking recovery succeeds quasi-instantaneously and thus fully automatically, the user has to help out by pointing towards a previously seen location. This is a distraction from his actual task, and thus should only be done if necessary. Therefore, it is important to understand when recovery is dispensable and design the system appropriately.

In our system, tracking is needed in two cases: when annotations (markers) are present, and when the remote user has frozen her viewpoint. If neither is the case, tracking is not currently needed and hence the user should not be bothered with requests to recover it. In this case, recovery is attempted only for a maximum of 10 frames. If unsuccessful, tracking is simply reset and re-initialized with the current frame. If, however, tracking is needed to maintain currently active markers or the registration with the remote user's frozen viewpoint, recovery is attempted for much longer, asking the user to help with recovery by displaying the red 'X' if needed. If recovery is not successful after 240 frames, it is assumed that the user does not want or is unable to recover tracking, and the tracking is reset.

local user	female	female	male	male
remote user	female	male	female	male
# of teams	6	4	5	9

Table 1. Gender distribution and participant teams.

Real-time Performance

Overall, this system is fast enough to operate in real time — the framerate is limited by the camera (30 Hz) and not by the tracking algorithms — and robust enough to be used by our study participants without any specific instructions, while coping with (or successfully recovering from) free camera movement, motion blur, specular reflections, and significant occlusion (e.g., due to the user's hand, cf. Figs. 2(c) and 4(b)).

EVALUATING THE EFFECTIVENESS OF LIVE ANNOTATIONS IN A COLLABORATIVE TASK

To evaluate the effectiveness of world-stabilized markers, we designed a user study comparing our interface using world-stabilized markers against one interface without any annotations and one interface with static markers. The study's scenario was that of a remote expert instructing and directing a novice local user in operating an airplane.

Various parameters of the study as reported below were refined during several pilot study trials with a total of 12 users.

Participants

We had a total of 48 participants in the main study, 18 to 39 years old (average 23.3), 27 male and 21 female, who worked together on 24 teams as detailed in Table 1.

All participants had normal or corrected vision. 40 reported they did not know the other participant, 4 had "met before," and 4 "knew each other well." 93% stated they had at least 10 years of experience speaking English. Each user was compensated for their time commitment of about one hour with a nominal amount of US $10. We had two further participant teams whose data we did not include in the analysis. In one team, one individual had a form of color-blindness; in the other team, one participant did not adequately follow the study administrator's instructions during the training period.

Physical Setup

We created a mock-up airplane cockpit by printing a high-resolution image of the interior of an airplane cockpit (Fig. 3) on 3'×4' paper and mounting it to a metal panel on the wall. To simulate a remote user in another location, we placed a room divider next to the poster and placed the remote user's

Figure 3. Our testbed: view of a Boeing 737 cockpit. This image was printed in size 3'×4' and mounted to a metal panel on the wall. The resolution is high enough that most of the control element labels are readable. Original image file obtained from iStockphoto.com/Smaglov.

station on the other side. This allowed both users to communicate verbally by simply talking out loud while blocking any direct visual communication.

The device for the local user consisted of a MIMO 10.1" "iMo Monster" Touchscreen (used as display only, touch disabled) with a Point Grey Firefly (34° horizontal field of view) mounted on the back to deliver 640×480 Bayer images at 30 Hz. To make the tablet more comfortable to hold, we added some rubber padding on both sides of the tablet and a strap to go around the user's hand (cf. Fig. 2(a)).

The remote participant used a standard desktop PC interface with monitor, keyboard, and mouse. The system ran on a standard PC with an Intel i7 Core with 4 GB RAM running Ubuntu 10.10. All interfaces and further system components were implemented in C++, making use of the OpenCV and libCVD libraries for the vision system.

Task

The task that each pair of participants performed was to identify and "operate" a series of control elements in our mock-up cockpit, in order to, e.g., "safely land the airplane." The local user was assumed to be a novice, not knowing which elements to operate, and had to be instructed by the remote expert. "Operating" an element was simulated by placing a magnetic pin onto it. The pins were numbered so that the study administrator could later verify the correct placement and order. We chose the testbed such that it would neither be too easy nor too difficult to reference the control elements verbally. Many of the elements had readable labels, visually distinguishable features, and/or could be described by their relative position in the cockpit. However, labels were rel-

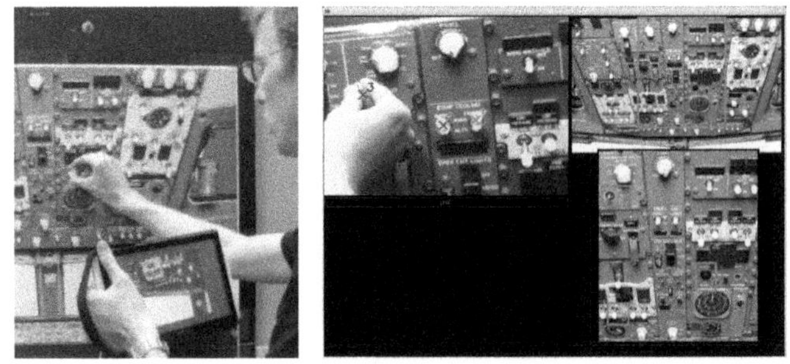

(a) local user (b) remote user's interface

Figure 4. (a) Local user with tablet, putting a magnetic pin on one of the "buttons." (b) Overview of the remote user's interface with live video view on the top left and "expert knowledge" information (consisting of overview image on the top and detail on the bottom) on the right.

atively small, and some switches were in a series of alike-looking elements. It would be easy to design a testbed that would be much easier or much harder, but through pilot studies we arrived at this setup as a reasonable and, in particular, realistic compromise between the two extremes.

One participant played the role of the local user. This participant stood in front of the poster with the display device (as seen in Fig. 4(a)) and was instructed by the remote user as to which control elements to "operate," i.e., place a pin onto.

The other participant played the role of the remote expert and was responsible for directing the local user as to which control element to operate. The remote user sat in front of a desktop monitor which showed the camera feed from the local user on the left side. On the right side, the remote user saw a detail of the cockpit with a sequence of buttons clearly marked and, above, an overview image in which the location of the detail was indicated (Fig. 4(b)). These images simulated the "expert knowledge" that the remote user was assumed to possess. The remote user then communicated the locations of each element to the local user verbally and via the interface functions. In addition to directing the local user, she was asked to monitor correct pin placement. (Users were allowed to remove and re-place incorrectly placed pins, and the remote user was instructed to inform the local user accordingly if she observed an error.)

Each page of the expert knowledge information indicated a sequence of five random buttons. When completed, the remote user could press a key to proceed to the next page. After five pages (25 buttons), we introduced a brief break in which the study administrator would take down the pins, comparing them with a control sheet and noting down errors (if any).

Conditions

With all interfaces, the participants were able to talk to each other without restriction.

Interface A: video only

In this interface, the live video from the tablet's camera is streamed to the remote user's screen (i.e., one-way video), but the remote user does not have any means of providing visual feedback. This is similar to using a current tablet PC with rear-facing camera and standard video conferencing software.

Interface B: video + static markers

In this interface, the remote user can click into the video view to create a marker — a colored 'X' — that is visible on both screens (the remote user's screen as well as the local user's tablet screen). However, the marker is static within image coordinates, so it appears to "swim away" from its original position if the tablet's camera is moved. The remote user can set up to five of those markers, and clear them by pressing the space bar at any time. By pressing a number key between 1 and 5, the user can select the next marker to be set; without pressing number keys, the system rotates through markers 1 to 5. The next marker to be set is indicated by a small white number next to the mouse cursor. This condition is similar to the pointing in [8] in that it assumes a stationary camera.

Interface C: video + world-stabilized markers

This interface is using our prototype system as described in the previous section. As with interface B, the remote user can set up to five markers by clicking into the video view (space bar to clear, number keys to select marker as in B). However, now the markers are stored in world-stabilized coordinates and thus stick to their original positions despite movement of the camera. With a right-click, the remote user can freeze her viewpoint as described in the previous section.

Experimental Design

We used a within-subjects design with a single independent variable (interface type A, B, C) and a single dependent variable (total number of tasks completed). We also recorded the number of errors. The order of the interfaces was completely balanced for all six possible orderings, with each possible ordering traversed by four teams, and the tasks were randomly selected for each interface from a set of tasks.

Our hypotheses about the study's outcome were as follows:

H1 Users will complete more tasks with both interface B and C than with interface A.

H2 Users will complete more tasks with C than with B.

H3 Users will prefer interface C over both A and B.

H4 Users will feel more confident about their task performance with interface C.

Procedure

At the beginning of the study, each participant was given a color blind test and filled out a pre-study questionnaire with demographic and background information. The study administrator then verbally explained the scenario and the roles each participant would play. Next, the local user was given the hand-held display and adjustments to the strap were made so that the user was comfortable holding the device in one hand.

For each interface, the administrator explained the respective interface. The administrator was careful to only explain the individual features and to not recommend any particular strategy; instead, the users were explicitly told that it was up to them to determine how exactly they would make use of the features. Next, the users were given a training session of five minutes to get accustomed to the interface and develop a strategy for using it. During this training session, the administrator would correct any mistakes made by either user, and would also encourage the users to try out the different features if they had not already done so. After the training session, a measured session of seven minutes was started. Before starting this session, the administrator gave the stipulation that selecting the correct elements in the correct order was important and that participants should confirm with each other if in doubt, but that within that, users should work as fast as possible.

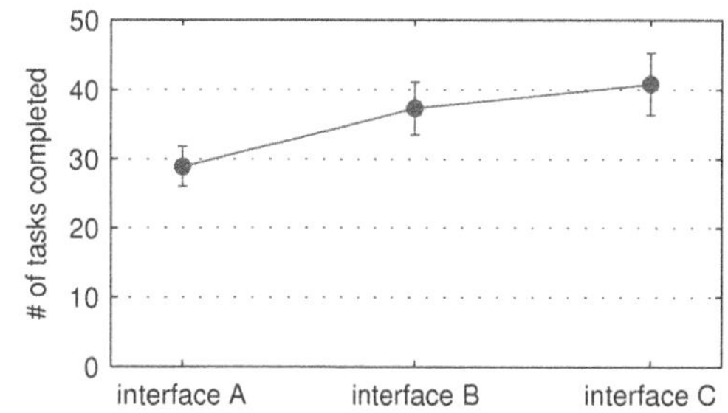

Figure 5. Main quantitative result: number of tasks completed as a function of the three different interfaces, shown are mean and 95% confidence intervals. Users were significantly faster with B than with A, and significantly faster with C than with A (cf. Table 2).

After each interface, users filled out a brief questionnaire asking about their experience with the interface and any physical discomfort they may have felt. While some local users indicated that their arms got tired, all of them explicitly confirmed verbally that they did not have any concerns about continuing the study.

Finally, the participants were asked to fill out a post-study questionnaire, asking them to compare the interfaces and to note any further comments on the study.

RESULTS

Task Performance

The stipulation to not make mistakes and confirm with each other when in doubt worked very well: 16 out of 24 teams completed all three trials without a single error, and only two teams made more than one error in one trial (in which users would select around 20 to 60 buttons). The errors were spread evenly among the three interfaces.

Participants were able to complete the most tasks with Interface C, averaging 40.8 tasks. Participants averaged 37.3 tasks with Interface B and 28.9 tasks with Interface A (Fig. 5). Analyzing our results, Mauchly's test did not show a violation of sphericity against interface ($W(2) = 0.94$, $p = 0.49$). With a one-way repeated measures ANOVA, we found a significant effect of interface on the number of tasks completed with $F(2,46) = 23.45$, $P < 0.001$, and $\eta^2_{\text{partial}} = 0.50$. Using Tukey's posthoc analysis (Table 2), we found that users completed significantly more tasks with both interfaces B and C than with interface A, thus confirming hypothesis H1. We did not find a significant difference between B and C, hence hypothesis H2 could not be confirmed despite the slightly higher average number of completed tasks with interface C.

Interfaces	Difference	Lower	Upper	P Adj.	
B – A	8.42	4.08	12.75	< 0.001	*
C – A	11.92	7.58	16.25	< 0.001	*
C – B	3.50	-0.83	7.83	0.135	

Table 2. Tukey's posthoc analysis for all pairwise comparisons with a 95% family confidence interval. * indicates significant differences.

Questionnaires

In the post-study questionnaire, users were asked to rate and rank the three interfaces. The results are aggregated in Fig. 6. Overall, users clearly preferred interface C: 72% 'strongly agreed' to the statement "Interface C helped me to solve this task," compared to 8.5% for A and 23% for B; 68% 'strongly agreed' to the statement "Interface C made me feel confident that I was doing the task correctly," compared to 17% for A and 11% for B. When asked "Which of the interfaces did you like best/would you choose to use for a real task?," 79% selected interface C as their first choice. Many users further confirmed their preference with comments: "The interface with vision tracking was better and easier." — "I was very impressed with the tracking capabilities. The interface was very easy to understand" — "This interface is an order of magnitude better than the others" — "The tracked markers [were] much eas[ier] to give direction[s] with."

When mapped to a linear scale and analyzed with ANOVA, the ratings for interface C are significantly better than the ratings for both A and B for all of the above questions (in above order: $F(2,90) = 32.7$, $F(2,90) = 14.6$, $F(2,90) = 32.6$, with $P < 0.001$ for all). There were no significant differences in the answers to "I had difficulties using this interface."

These data confirm hypotheses H3 and H4.

Very few users seemed to be distracted by the additional features and the multimodality of the task or commented to that effect: "It was actually easier to just talk it [out] rather than worry about clicking the mouse which left me distracted."

DISCUSSION

Overall, most participants seemed very engaged with the task, and many explicitly commented that they liked the experience. With both interfaces B and C, most teams effectively used multimodal communication, by indicating control elements with markers as well as visually describing them at the same time. However, it was apparent that with interface C, many teams needed very little verbal communication, largely relying on the markers (however, users did add verbal descriptions for "difficult" markers or to confirm if needed). With interface B, more verbal communication and more corrections were needed ("Is it this one?" — "No, no, the one next to it!"). This is a possible explanation for why users felt more confident when using interface C (cf. Fig. 6).

Use of Features

Use of the interface features varied among participants. Almost all used markers for the overwhelming majority of cases; most used the freeze function, though frequency and strategy varied. Only a few people used the number keys to change the sequence of markers.

Task Performance with Interface C vs. Interface B

Given the overall very good user ratings of interface C and few usability problems, the question remains why the study did not show a significant difference between C and B in terms of the number of tasks completed. It is possible that for this task, both interfaces are equivalent. However, we observed indications for other possible explanations:

- One very frequently employed strategy with interface C was to first navigate the local user to the general area, then freeze, mark several buttons, then observe the local user's actions. If the local user started to put the pins down while the remote user would mark the next elements (i.e., they would work in parallel, for which the decoupling of views is essential), this strategy seemed to achieve the best performances, which could not be reached with the other interfaces. However, a few local users waited until all markers would be selected (sometimes encouraged to do so by the remote user, even though her view was frozen and thus not affected by his movement) before putting down pins, which negatively impacted the performance.
- Since the local user had to wait for instructions from the remote expert for each step, it was relatively easy (although, as some users commented, more strenuous) for him to hold the tablet still while she pointed out the elements to be marked. A task that required more autonomous work from the local user would likely show a greater benefit of the decoupling of views.
- Due to our use of a "magic lens" tablet, our AR experience was indirect. Some users explicitly commented on this: "I had to see where the X was on the screen then find it again in 'real life.' That transition added a non-trivial delay." Due to this indirection and since they could hold the tablet in one hand, putting down pins with the other, interfaces B and C are effectively more similar to each other than with a direct view (e.g., with an HWD or projective display).
- Loss of time due to tracking loss: although not perceived as a large problem by most users (61% of the users reported 'no' or 'at most a little' impact on task performance, another 29% 'some' impact), it is clear that occasional or more frequent tracking loss impacted the task performance. One noteworthy circumstance is that tracking got lost if users moved very close to the poster (due to fewer trackable features in the field of view and interpolation/sampling artifacts when matching across scales), so that users had to step back a little to recover tracking: "I found that when I [...] needed to 'zoom in' to physically put the push pins in the correct spots, the tracking marks sometimes did not show up [...] until I zoomed out again... this slowed things down a bit." Improving tracking for this condition in particular would be beneficial.
- Since interface C offers more functions, it is slightly more complex, which may have counteracted potential benefits. Although the data shows that in general, users did not find interface C more difficult to use (cf. Fig. 6), individual users commented that C might benefit from longer-term use: "I would utilize B [...]. However, with more time to

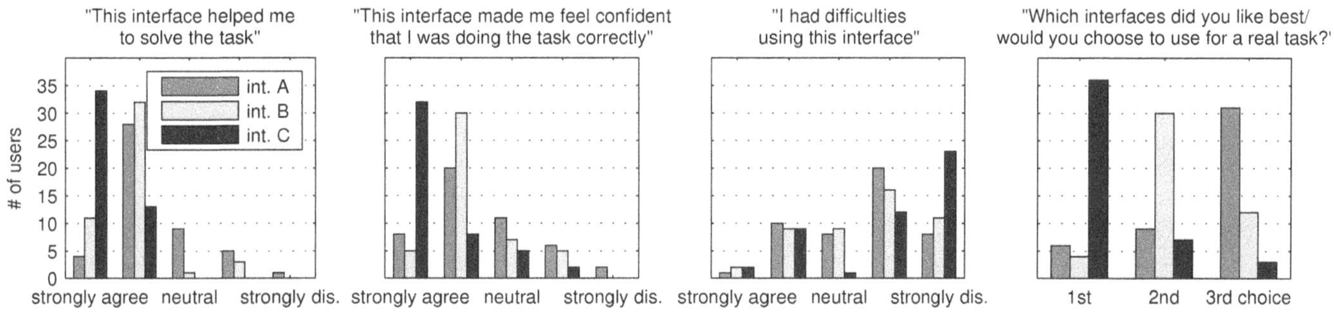

Figure 6. User responses from post-study questionnaire.

adapt, I probably would utilize C"; "I thought using the markers and the freeze was more difficult [...]. I think with another trial's worth of practice it would have less effect."

CONCLUSIONS AND FUTURE WORK

We described a system framework which uses computer vision and AR to facilitate better integration of the physical environment for unobtrusive mobile telecollaboration. We designed one particular prototype that implements this framework, featuring several novel interface elements. We then provided empirical evidence in the form of a user study that our framework can provide significant benefits for a remote collaborative task: Even though our current visual tracking is noticeably imperfect and our prototype is not the most immersive implementation of our framework, the task performance was significantly better compared to a video-only reference interface, and our prototype was much preferred by users over both compared interfaces.

We conclude that the proposed framework is promising and has the potential of significantly improving telecollaboration interfaces. We suggest that this requires neither futuristic, fully immersive hardware interfaces nor perfect tracking, but that current computer vision and AR technologies can be used effectively for collaboration without any special training.

The most obvious extension of our work is to remove the tracking and modeling system's restriction to homographic warps. A potential remedy is to integrate SLAM-like modeling [19, 27] or use active depth sensors [28].

Further, our prototype implementation does not exhaust the potential of the proposed framework: Guided by Fig. 1, several components may be substituted with more flexible, more powerful, or more immersive components. This includes more flexible viewpoint control for the remote user, support for more complex virtual annotations, and use of more immersive display systems. For example, one could use the feature-rich annotation tool and pico projector-based setup by Gurevich et al. [11] as interfaces in Fig. 1 (note that they mention the use of visual tracking for future work, thus arriving at a similar vision), or directly overlay hand gestures (as in [18, 29], but now for a moving camera). When using more complex annotation or gesture interfaces, existing work on the design of shared visual spaces and gesture support [10, 18, 20] will be very valuable. All of these aspects deserve further investigation and bear the potential to further increase the applicability of mobile interactive telecollaboration interfaces.

ACKNOWLEDGMENTS

We thank Andy Beall (Dept. of Psychology, UCSB) for helpful discussions and suggestions on the design of the study, Daniel Sheinson (Dept. of Statistics and Applied Probability, UCSB) for his help in conducting the statistical analysis, and our anonymous reviewers for several suggestions that helped to improve our manuscript. This work was partially supported by a fellowship from UCSB, NSF CAREER grant IIS-0747520 and ONR grant N00014-09-1-1113.

REFERENCES

1. Alem, L., Tecchia, F., and Huang, W. HandsOnVideo: Towards a gesture based mobile AR system for remote collaboration. In *Recent Trends of Mobile Collaborative Augmented Reality Systems*, L. Alem and W. Huang, Eds. Springer New York, 2011, 135–148.
2. Baudisch, P., and Rosenholtz, R. Halo: a technique for visualizing off-screen objects. In *Proc. ACM SIGCHI Conf. on Human Factors in Computing Systems (CHI)*, 2003, 481–488.
3. Bauer, M., Kortuem, G., and Segall, Z. "Where are you pointing at?" a study of remote collaboration in a wearable videoconference system. In *Proc. Intl. Symp. on Wearable Computers (ISWC)*, 1999, 151 –158.
4. Billinghurst, M., Bowskill, J., Jessop, M., and Morphett, J. A wearable spatial conferencing space. In *Proc. Intl. Symp. on Wearable Computers (ISWC)*, 1998, 76 –83.
5. Billinghurst, M., Weghorst, S., and Furness, T. Shared space: An augmented reality approach for computer supported collaborative work. *Virtual Reality 3* (1998), 25–36.
6. Butz, A., Höllerer, T., Feiner, S., MacIntyre, B., and Beshers, C. Enveloping users and computers in a collaborative 3D augmented reality. In *Proc. IEEE/ACM Intl. Workshop on Augmented Reality*, 1999, 35–44.
7. Chastine, J., Nagel, K., Zhu, Y., and Hudachek-Buswell, M. Studies on the effectiveness of virtual pointers in collaborative augmented reality. In *Proc. IEEE Symp. on 3D User Interfaces (3DUI)*, 2008, 117 –124.
8. Fussell, S. R., Setlock, L. D., Yang, J., Ou, J., Mauer, E., and Kramer, A. D. I. Gestures over video streams to

support remote collaboration on physical tasks. *Hum.-Comput. Interact. 19* (Sept. 2004), 273–309.

9. Gauglitz, S., Foschini, L., Turk, M., and Höllerer, T. Efficiently selecting spatially distributed keypoints for visual tracking. In *Proc. IEEE Intl. Conf. on Image Processing (ICIP)*, 2011.
10. Gergle, D., Kraut, R., and Fussell, S. Action as language in a shared visual space. In *Proc. ACM Conf. on Computer Supported Cooperative Work*, 2004, 487–496.
11. Gurevich, P., Lanir, J., Cohen, B., and Stone, R. TeleAdvisor: a versatile augmented reality tool for remote assistance. In *Proc. ACM SIGCHI Conf. on Human Factors in Computing Systems*, 2012, 619–622.
12. Gustafson, S., Baudisch, P., Gutwin, C., and Irani, P. Wedge: clutter-free visualization of off-screen locations. In *Proc. ACM SIGCHI Conf. on Human Factors in Computing Systems*, 2008, 787–796.
13. Gutwin, C., and Penner, R. Improving interpretation of remote gestures with telepointer traces. In *Proc. ACM Conf. on Computer Supported Cooperative Work*, 2002, 49–57.
14. Güven, S., Feiner, S., and Oda, O. Mobile augmented reality interaction techniques for authoring situated media on-site. In *Proc. IEEE/ACM Intl. Symp. on Mixed and Augmented Reality (ISMAR)*, 2006, 235–236.
15. Hayne, S., Pendergast, M., and Greenberg, S. Implementing gesturing with cursors in group support systems. *J. Manag. Informat. Syst.* (1993), 43–61.
16. Hindmarsh, J., Fraser, M., Heath, C., Benford, S., and Greenhalgh, C. Fragmented interaction: establishing mutual orientation in virtual environments. In *Proc. ACM Conf. on Computer Supported Cooperative Work*, 1998, 217–226.
17. Kirk, D., and Stanton Fraser, D. Comparing remote gesture technologies for supporting collaborative physical tasks. In *Proc. SIGCHI Conf. on Human Factors in Computing Systems (CHI)*, 2006, 1191–1200.
18. Kirk, D. S. *Turn It This Way: Remote Gesturing in Video-Mediated Communication*. PhD thesis, University of Nottingham, 2006.
19. Klein, G., and Murray, D. Improving the agility of keyframe-based SLAM. In *Proc. European Conf. on Computer Vision (ECCV)*, 2008, 802–815.
20. Kraut, R., Miller, M., and Siegel, J. Collaboration in performance of physical tasks: Effects on outcomes and communication. In *Proc. ACM Conf. on Computer Supported Cooperative Work*, 1996, 57–66.
21. Kurata, T., Sakata, N., Kourogi, M., Kuzuoka, H., and Billinghurst, M. Remote collaboration using a shoulder-worn active camera/laser. In *Proc. Intl. Symp. on Wearable Computers (ISWC)*, 2004, 62–69.
22. Kurillo, G., Bajcsy, R., Nahrsted, K., and Kreylos, O. Immersive 3D environment for remote collaboration and training of physical activities. In *Proc. IEEE Virtual Reality*, 2008, 269 –270.
23. Kuzuoka, H., Oyama, S., Yamazaki, K., Suzuki, K., and Mitsuishi, M. Gestureman: a mobile robot that embodies a remote instructor's actions. In *Proc. ACM Conf. on Computer Supported Cooperative Work*, 2000, 155–162.
24. Ladikos, A., Benhimane, S., Appel, M., and Navab, N. Model-free markerless tracking for remote support in unknown environments. In *Proc. Intl. Conf. on Computer Vision Theory and Applications*, 2008.
25. Lee, T., and Höllerer, T. Viewpoint stabilization for live collaborative video augmentations. In *Proc. IEEE/ACM Intl. Symp. on Mixed and Augmented Reality*, 2006, 241–242.
26. Mortensen, J., Vinayagamoorthy, V., Slater, M., Steed, A., Lok, B., and Whitton, M. Collaboration in tele-immersive environments. In *Proc. Workshop on Virtual environments*, 2002, 93–101.
27. Newcombe, R., Lovegrove, S., and Davison, A. Dtam: Dense tracking and mapping in real-time. In *Proc. IEEE Intl. Conf. on Computer Vision*, 2011, 2320–2327.
28. Newcombe, R. A., Izadi, S., Hilliges, O., Molyneaux, D., Kim, D., Davison, A. J., Kohli, P., Shotton, J., Hodges, S., and Fitzgibbon, A. KinectFusion: Real-time dense surface mapping and tracking. In *Proc. IEEE Intl. Symp. on Mixed and Augmented Reality*, 2011.
29. Ou, J., Fussell, S. R., Chen, X., Setlock, L. D., and Yang, J. Gestural communication over video stream: supporting multimodal interaction for remote collaborative physical tasks. In *Proc. Intl. Conf. on Multimodal Interfaces (ICMI)*, 2003, 242–249.
30. Regenbrecht, H., Lum, T., Kohler, P., Ott, C., Wagner, M., Wilke, W., and Mueller, E. Using augmented virtuality for remote collaboration. *Presence: Teleoper. Virtual Environ. 13* (July 2004), 338–354.
31. Reitmayr, G., and Schmalstieg, D. Mobile collaborative augmented reality. In *Proc. IEEE/ACM Intl. Symp. on Augmented Reality*, 2001, 114 –123.
32. Rosten, E., and Drummond, T. Machine learning for high-speed corner detection. In *Proc. IEEE European Conf. on Computer Vision*, 2006, 430–443.
33. Sadagic, A., Towles, H., Holden, L., Daniilidis, K., and Zeleznik, B. Tele-immersion portal: Towards an ultimate systhesis of Computer Graphics and Computer Vision Systems. In *Proc. Intl. Workshop on Presence*, 2001.
34. Tang, J. C., and Minneman, S. L. VideoDraw: a video interface for collaborative drawing. *ACM Trans. Inf. Syst. 9* (April 1991), 170–184.
35. Wagner, D., Mulloni, A., Langlotz, T., and Schmalstieg, D. Real-time panoramic mapping and tracking on mobile phones. In *Proc. IEEE Virtual Reality*, 2010.
36. Wagner, D., Schmalstieg, D., and Bischof, H. Multiple target detection and tracking with guaranteed framerates on mobile phones. In *Proc. IEEE Intl. Symp. on Mixed and Augmented Reality (ISMAR)*, 2009, 57–64.
37. Wellner, P., and Freeman, S. The DoubleDigitalDesk: Shared editing of paper documents. Tech. Rep. EPC-93-108, EuroPARC, 1993.

Touch Behavior with Different Postures on Soft Smartphone Keyboards

Shiri Azenkot
Computer Science & Engineering | DUB Group
University of Washington
Seattle, WA 98195 USA
shiri@cs.washington.edu

Shumin Zhai
Google Inc.
1600 Amphitheatre Parkway
Mountain View, CA 94043
zhai@google.com

ABSTRACT
Text entry on smartphones is far slower and more error-prone than on traditional desktop keyboards, despite sophisticated detection and auto-correct algorithms. To strengthen the empirical and modeling foundation of smartphone text input improvements, we explore touch behavior on soft QWERTY keyboards when used with two thumbs, an index finger, and one thumb. We collected text entry data from 32 participants in a lab study and describe touch accuracy and precision for different keys. We found that distinct patterns exist for input among the three hand postures, suggesting that keyboards should adapt to different postures. We also discovered that participants' touch precision was relatively high given typical key dimensions, but there were pronounced and consistent touch offsets that can be leveraged by keyboard algorithms to correct errors. We identify patterns in our empirical findings and discuss implications for design and improvements of soft keyboards.

Author Keywords
Mobile text entry, touch interfaces.

ACM Classification Keywords
H.5.2. [Information interfaces and presentation]: User interfaces—input devices and strategies.

INTRODUCTION
Text entry on small devices remains slower and more error-prone than on traditional computer keyboards [10]. In recent years, the soft QWERTY keyboard (Figure 1) has emerged as a standard smartphone text entry method, offered as the default keyboard on millions of Android phones, iPhones, and Windows phones. These keyboards are commonly designed for finger (as opposed to stylus) input, and have sophisticated algorithms to mitigate user error.

Understanding touch behavior is critical for improving keyboard algorithms. While prior research on touch keyboards has made progress in understanding users' speed and aggregate error rate [2,3,18,19,21], our work focuses on *where* users touch when targeting specific keys. Patterns in touch locations can help automatically prevent and correct errors. For example, if we find that users commonly hit below target keys, a keyboard algorithm can compensate by adding the typical pixel offset to the input touch's screen coordinates, preventing errors caused by this tendency. We identify such patterns with the goal of providing a foundation for improving soft keyboard algorithms.

Figure 1. A user prepares to enter text on a smartphone.

Conceivably, users' touch patterns may vary according to hand posture (i.e., how they hold the mobile phone and type on it). We observed that people have different preferences in hand posture and may change hand posture depending on the use situation. When holding a cup of coffee, for example, one may enter text with a single thumb since only one hand is available. In other situations, one may use an index finger or two thumbs to type. We therefore compare three common hand postures in our analysis, showing distinct trends among them. To our knowledge, this is the first systematic investigation of touch patterns in relation to these three postures.

In this work, we analyze text entry data we collected from 32 participants who entered text using two thumbs, an index finger, and a thumb. We report the traditional text entry measures of words per minute (WPM) and error rates, but focus our discussion on touch patterns particularly in terms of offsets and spreads for different keys. An offset is the distance between the user's touch point and the target key center. The spread of touch points refers to their distribution for a specific key. Large spreads and offsets both increase the chance to touch outside key boundaries, causing errors by the conventional definition. It is important to understand what the natural tendencies of these parameters are when

MobileHCI'12, September 21–24, 2012, San Francisco, CA, USA.

the user is unencumbered by current error correction algorithms and how these parameters change with different hand postures.

Our contributions include (1) the analysis of touch behavior for text entry with three common postures, and (2) a discussion of how future keyboards can be improved based on the patterns we identify. We hope this work will serve as a foundation for improving touch keyboards.

RELATED WORK

The current work is situated in the growing body of literature of touch screen interfaces and text input. We can only briefly highlight three basic categories of work most related to the current study: investigations of touch performance in general, efforts to model and understand text entry performance, and improvements in key detection and auto-correction algorithms.

Understanding Touch Performance

Several papers, reviewed in this section, have explored human touch performance on capacitive touch screens, but not in the context of text entry. Continuous text entry has higher cognitive and motor demands than pointing tasks with a single target, so text entry behavior may be different.

Lee and Zhai [16] investigated soft button user performance in comparison to hard buttons and as a function of implement (finger vs. stylus), feedback (auditory and tactile-vibrato), and button size.

Henze et al. [8] analyzed a wealth of touch data collected from a smartphone game that was deployed in the field. Game players hit targets across the screen and Henze et al. identifyed patterns in their touch offsets. We draw inspiration from their analysis and visualizations, and compare their results to ours. While we collected a smaller amount of data through lab studies rather than field deployment, we had more control and were able to compare differences among hand postures.

Like Henze et al., Holz and Baudisch [11] also found that users touched a surface with consistent offsets from a target. Their subsequent studies show that a user's perceived contact point was approximated by the center of the fingernail, which was above the actual contact point along the finger's axis [12].

Wang and Ren [23] compared touch offsets among all five fingers, reporting that the thumb and pinky finger were less accurate than the others.

Understanding Text Entry Performance

Several papers aim to better understand touch performance during text entry. Findlater et al. [4] presented an analysis of 10-finger typing on large touch surfaces that is parallel to our work on smartphones. Other papers have focused on modeling time rather than understanding causes of errors. MacKenzie and Zhang [19] present a model based on Fitts' Law for predicting expert speed on pen-based soft keyboards. In subsequent work, MacKenzie and Soukoreff [18] presented a model for two-thumb entry which is empirically validated and adjusted by Clarkson et al. [2]. These models predict the words per minute (WPM) of expert typists and do not consider error patterns as we do.

Improving Key Detection and Auto-Correct Algorithms

Our work provides a foundation for improving key detection and auto-correct algorithms, so we also consider work that aims to improve these techniques.

Soft keyboards can in effect dynamically change the underlying key size according to context in order to correct touch error. Goodman et al. [6] used character probabilities along with observed touch point distributions for keys to correct user error. They made several general observations about touch point distributions. Gunawardana et al. [7] proposed a less aggressive approach to key-target resizing that does not prevent users from typing their desired text. In later work, key-target resizing algorithms were personalized through the Text Text Revolution game [21], which collected users' touch data to train the key-target resizing algorithm.

Kristensson and Zhai [13] used geometric pattern matching to do word level error correction. Both Goodman et al. [6] and Kristensson and Zhai [13] focused on stylus input on early generations of touch screen products.

Other work identified errors on physical mini-QWERTY keyboards using timing [3], or on number pad keyboards with nine soft buttons [22]. Gong et al. [5] aimed to improve auto-correct systems by rearranging the order of corrected word candidates that were displayed to the user.

A relatively new error tolerant method of text entry is the gesture keyboard that first appeared in the academic literature in 2003 [14,27,28]. We limit our investigation to point touch only, although previous work has shown gesture keyboards and touch keyboards can be linked in their underlying algorithms [13].

USE OF DIFFERENT HAND POSTURES IN TEXT ENTRY

To base our touch behavior study on empirical facts with regard to hand postures, we conducted a survey to determine how often people used two thumbs, one thumb, and one finger to enter text on touch screen phones.

Method

Seventy-five participants completed our survey, all of whom had touch screen phones. There were 58 (77%) males and 17 (23%) females, with an average age of 32 (*SD* = 9). Participants were Google employees and were recruited via an internal mailing list.

The survey included three questions about the frequency in which participants used two thumbs, one thumb, or one finger to enter text. An example of this type of question was:

> How often do you enter text on your phone with two thumbs?

- Almost always
- Often
- Sometimes
- Almost never

Participants were able to select one response per question.

Results

Participants reported relatively high proficiency levels with smartphone text entry. The mean level of proficiency was 5.05 (*SD* = 1.27), on a 7-point scale where 1 indicated the user had no experience and 7 indicated the user was an expert at entering text on soft smartphones keyboards.

As shown in Figure 2, each of the three postures was used at least "sometimes" by about 60% of the participants. On the other hand, no single method was used by all participants. Two thumbs, one thumb, and one finger were "almost never" used by 37%, 35% and 41% of the participants, respectively.

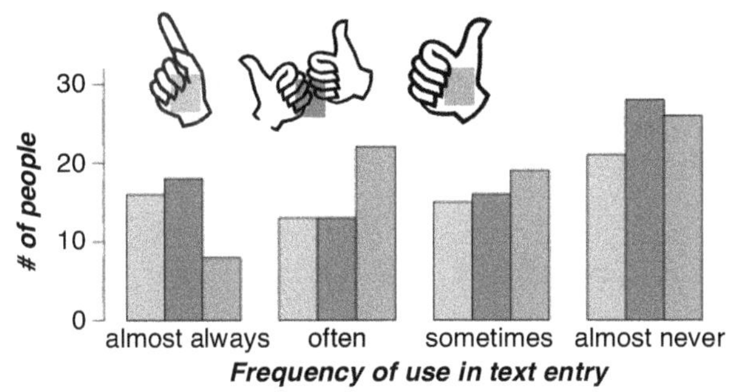

Figure 2. Use of an index finger, two thumbs, and one thumb during text entry on smartphones.

A deeper exploration of the contexts in which each posture is preferred would provide further insight into our survey results. Yet these preliminary findings do suggest that touch behavior with all three postures should be considered when designing improved soft keyboards.

COLLECTING TOUCH POINT DATA

We conducted a study to collect the touch point data that we explore in this work. Our goal was to collect and analyze data that reflected fundamental human behavior, with minimal bias towards a particular keyboard design.

Participants

We recruited 32 participants (15 females and 17 males) with an average age of 27 (*SD* = 6). Participants were required to have experience with text entry on a touch screen phone. Only two participants were left-handed and the rest were right-handed. All participants were Google employees and were recruited through an internal mailing list. The same recruitment process was used for this study and the survey that was described in the previous section.

Apparatus

Participants completed the study by typing phrases on a custom Android application, which we call the Keyboard Touch Collector (KTC). This application displayed a series of phrases and a minimal keyboard as shown in Figure 3. We designed the KTC to achieve two goals:

1. To capture fundamental user behavior on soft keyboards that is unaffected by the design (and potential shortcomings) of current keyboards.
2. To align touch points with target letters. We needed to reliably label touch points with the key the user targeted. If we did not know which key the user intended to hit, a touch point provided little information about the user's performance.

The KTC keyboard dimensions were the same as those of the default Android keyboard. We chose a minimal design to prevent more complex visual elements from affecting the user's behavior either positively or negatively. In other words, we wanted to collect *baseline* touch patterns and performance measures.

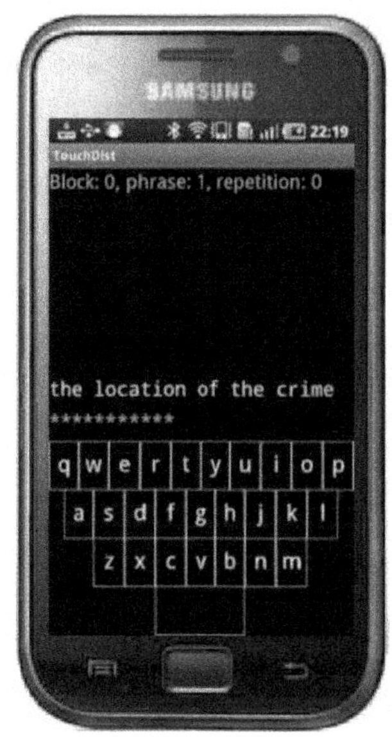

Figure 3. The Keyboard Touch Collector application used for collecting touch data in our study.

The application logged the x and y pixel coordinates of each keyboard touch along with the aligned character in the presented phrase. Touch points were logged on "touch down" events.

When a user touched the KTC keyboard, an asterisk appeared on the screen. We chose to provide limited feedback because displaying the input character would involve using a particular character detection algorithm that may affect the user's behavior. Even a naïve algorithm, where the selected key is the one that visually bounds the touch (without key-target resizing), may cause the user to slow down her input rate to prevent errors. Another naïve algorithm, where the "right" character is displayed regardless of the touch input, may give the user a false sense of confidence and cause unusually erroneous input. Thus, we do not inform the user whether her touch was "correct" to observe natural performance that is independent of keyboard algorithms.

The KTC did not have a BACKSPACE key and users were unable to correct errors. Correcting errors takes time: the user must enter the BACKSPACE key in addition to reentering the deleted character. An ideal keyboard, therefore, would tolerate imprecision and automatically correct the user's errors instead of requiring her to manually correct them. We wanted to capture the natural variance and biases in touch behavior without the assistance or limitations of the current generation of soft keyboards. We thus decided that analyzing human performance without error correction is essential for guiding improved keyboard design.

Users were asked to input short and shortened phrases that were randomly selected from the phrase set designed by MacKenzie and Soukoreff (M&S) [17,24]. There are a number of studies on phrase set selection for text input testing, e.g., [15,20]. Some of these studies question whether the M&S phrase set represents mobile text input with new technologies that use language models in predictive text input. However, at this time there is still no universally agreed standard set that considers all the factors involved in text input testing, such as memorability, mutual-information between test and application, and fun factor for the participants. For the purpose of the current study that focuses on touch patterns around individual characters, the M&S phrase set seemed appropriate since it has a good correlation with common English text at a letter frequency level [17].

We used a Samsung Galaxy S phone running Android 3.2 for all sessions, with a screen size of 60 by 100 mm with a resolution of 480 by 800 pixels. The keyboard dimensions were 60 by 37.5 mm.

Study Procedure

Each participant completed one 30 minute session where he or she answered a short questionnaire and then entered phrases on the KTC. The first ten phrases served as a warm-up and participants were able to take short breaks after each set of 10 phrases. We instructed them to type "as accurately and as naturally" as possible.

Participants completed the study while seated in an office environment. We instructed each participant to enter text with "two thumbs," "one index finger," or "one thumb." For the latter two postures, we asked participants to choose one hand and use it throughout the study. No further specification was given in order to capture participants' natural hand posture inclinations.

Experiment Design and Analysis

Our experiment was designed with the between-subjects factor Posture with three levels: Two-thumbs, One-thumb, and One-finger. Postures were randomly assigned to each participant and balanced, such that 11 participants entered text with two thumbs, 11 entered text with one thumb, and 10 entered text with one finger. While a 32 participants study is not large for a between-subject design, it is on par with or larger than most perceptual-motor skill tests.

Statistical results are reported with a significance level of $\alpha = 0.05$.

Amount of Data Collected

We collected a total of 86,888 labeled touch points, not including warm-up phrases; 35,124 labeled touch points were entered with two thumbs, 27,628 were entered with one thumb, and 24,126 were entered with one finger. On average, each participant entered 117 phrases.

Labeling Touch Points

Reliably labeling touch points was important in most of our analysis, yet our data included some points that seemed to be mislabeled, lying far from their labeled keys. Such points were probably a result of omission, insertion, or transposition of characters. We removed points that were more than 1.5 times the key height away from their labeled key center (see Figure 4), resulting in the removal of 3.19% of the data.

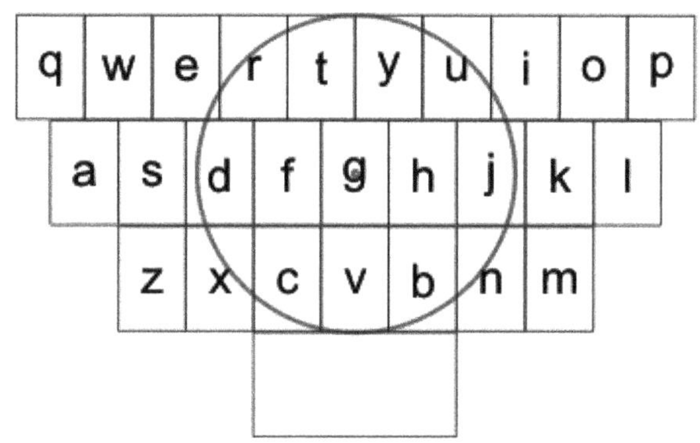

Figure 4. The blue circle marks the region that defines outliers for the "g" key. All points outside the blue circle were not included in parts of our analysis that required labeled points.

WORDS PER MINUTE

Our goal in this section was to compare the text entry speeds for the three hand postures. The KTC offered a baseline upper bound for smartphone keyboards because entry rates were unhindered by error correction. Such an upper bound baseline simulates the performance of a "perfect" smart touch keyboard whose algorithms would correct all of a user's errors automatically, enabling her to achieve unhindered entry rates. To our knowledge, our results are the first empirical estimates of upper bound smartphone touch tapping performance.

The average entry speed for all participants was 41.01 WPM (SD = 13.43), similar to the higher speeds achieved by Rudchenko et al. [21]. When calculating WPM, every 5 characters (including the SPACE character) were counted as one word. As seen in Figure 5, entry with two thumbs was fastest, at 50.03 WPM (SD = 13.57). One-finger input rates were far lower, averaging only 36.34 WPM (SD = 11.28).

Entry rates with one thumb were 33.78 WPM (*SD* = 6.87), slightly lower than with one finger.

We found that the differences in speed among postures were statistically significant. WPM measures for phrases were not normally distributed (Kolmogorov-Smirnov D = 0.111, $p < 0.0001$), so we ran a Kruskal Wallis test that revealed a significant effect of Posture on WPM ($x^2_{(2)}$ = 1101.4; $p < 0.001$). A post-hoc test using Mann-Whitney tests with Bonferroni correction showed that there were significant differences between all pairs of postures.

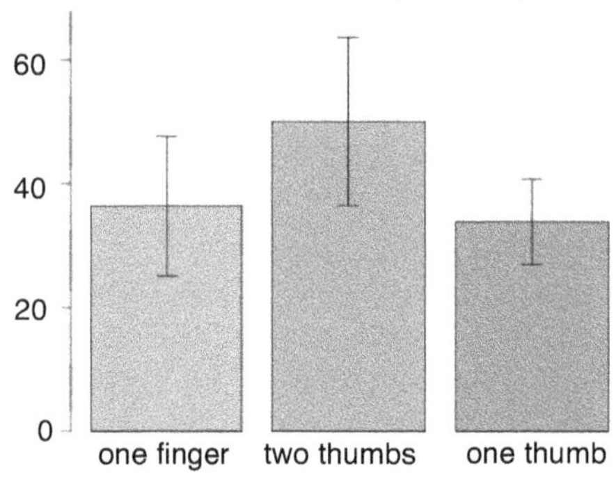

Figure 5. Words per minute vs. hand posture. Entering text with two thumbs was significantly faster than entering text with one finger or one thumb.

We expected two-thumb entry to be faster than the other postures. Since each thumb only moves within one half of the keyboard, less time is required to move from one key to the next. Furthermore, a user can move one thumb towards its next target while the other thumb is active, parallelizing movement from key to key. Frequent left and right alternation, a property of the QWERTY layout, was originally designed to minimize mechanical jamming but later became a major advantage for two-handed typing [26]. Such a property still gives a time advantage to two-thumb typing as is shown in our results.

It is surprising that one-thumb entry was only slightly slower than one-finger entry. The index finger seems far more dexterous than the thumb, and one-thumb entry was not as commonly used as one-finger entry according to our survey results. Entering text with one thumb offers the advantage of being one-handed, since using an index finger requires one to hold the phone with the other hand. It may also have the advantage of being more stable since the thumb movement is relative to the same hand that holds the phone.

ERROR RATE

Along with words per minute, the mean phrase error rate is traditionally reported in text entry studies. Our goal in this section was to compute baseline error rates for the three postures that may help keyboard designers assess keyboard improvements that aim to reduce the overall error rate.

For this purpose we use a narrow definition for error that follows from the hard key analogy, where a touch that lies outside of the visual boundary of its target key is considered an error. Reasonable key detection or auto-correct algorithms would use probabilistic inference to decide which key a user targeted given a touch point and its context (*e.g.*, a language model, a user's past behavior) and the visual boundaries would not necessarily matter. Our error rates thus provide an upper bound that can serve as a point of comparison for better keyboard algorithms.

The error rates among postures reflected a speed-accuracy trade-off, as seen in Figure 6. Overall, the mean error rate (number of errors in a phrase divided by the total phrase length) was 8.87% (*SD* = 10.51). The highest error rate was obtained with the two-thumb posture at 10.80% (*SD* = 12.46). The error rate for one-finger input was lower, at 8.17% (*SD* = 9.57), and the error rate for one-thumb input was the lowest, at 7.00% (*SD* = 7.84).

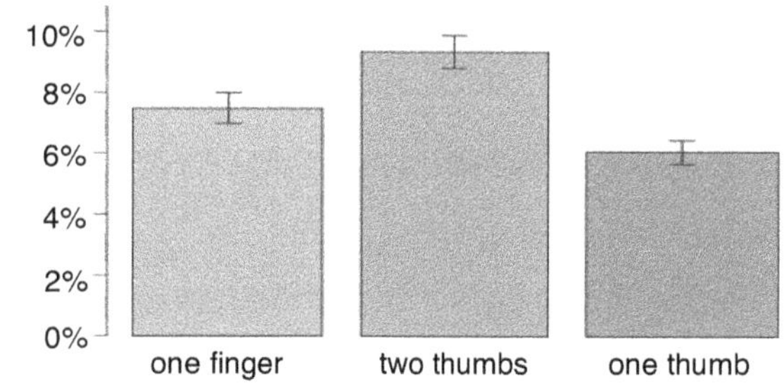

Figure 6. Error rate vs. hand posture. The lines and whiskers mark the 95% confidence intervals for the mean error rates.

Differences between postures were mostly statistically significant. As is typical, the distributions of error rates per phrase were not normal (Kolmogorov-Smirnov D = 0.200, $p < 0.0001$), so we ran a Kruskal-Wallis test that showed there was a significant effect of Posture on Error Rate ($x^2_{(2)}$ = 65.1, $p < 0.001$). A post-hoc test using Mann Whitney tests with Bonferroni correction showed that there were significant differences between error rates with two thumbs and one thumb ($p < 0.001$) and between input with two thumbs and one finger ($p < 0.001$). There was no significant difference between error rates with one-thumb and one-finger input.

We expected the error rate for one-thumb input to be higher than for one-finger input. Prior work found a thumb to be less accurate in touch screen pointing [23], but it seemed digit width did not yield more errors in our context of soft keyboarding. Note that in this context the one-thumb condition differed from the one-finger condition in two aspects: different touching digit and different holding hand. With one thumb keyboarding, the same hand holds the device and activates the key presses.

In the following sections, we explore the distributions of touches for keys, which provide far more information about the kinds of errors that users make than traditional text entry measures.

TOUCH POINT DISTRIBUTIONS

To better understand touch performance, we explore touch point patterns for keys that are input using the three hand postures. Previously, we presented measures that were computed for phrases entered by the user. We now take a different approach, where we group input touches by target key rather than phrase, examining touch locations relative to their target key areas.

As expected, the distribution of touch points per key was roughly a bivariate Gaussian, confirming previous findings [6,23]. The keyboards on the left in Figure 7, Figure 8, and Figure 9 show the collected touch points for each of the three postures over an outline of the keys (see Figure 4 for key labels). There is overlap between keys, however, so many of the points are occluded. Also, some keys have substantially more data points than others, so it is difficult to detect trends in these plots.

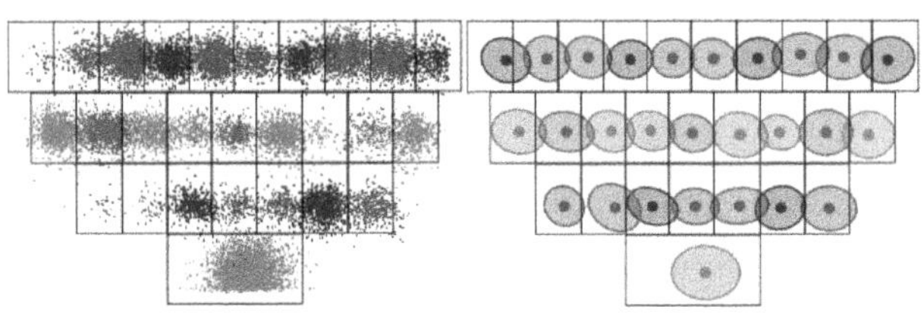

Figure 7. Touch points (left) and 95% confidence ellipses (right) for text entered with one finger.

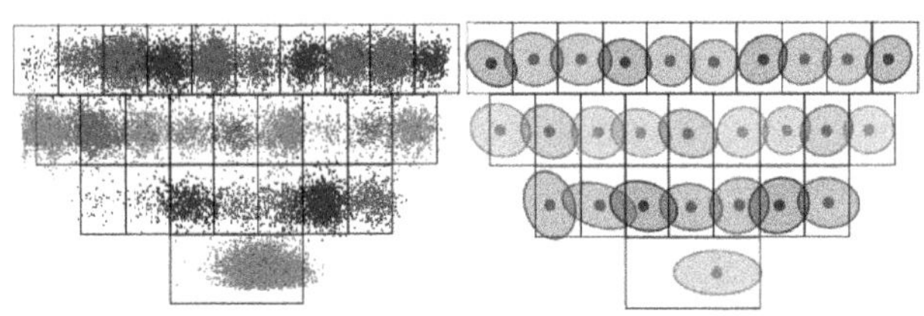

Figure 8. Touch points (left) and 95% confidence ellipses (right) for text entered with two thumbs.

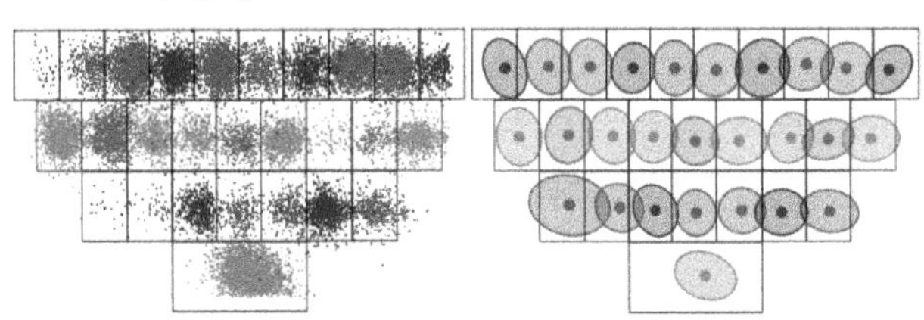

Figure 9. Touch points (left) and 95% confidence ellipses (right) for text entered with one thumb.

For a more informative visualization, we plotted the 95% confidence ellipses for the points of each key, shown on the right of Figure 7, Figure 8, and Figure 9. The centers of the ellipses mark the mean of the touches for a key, showing how accurate they were. The closer the ellipse center is to its key center, the higher the accuracy for that key. The size of the ellipses reflect the collective spread of the points, showing how precise they were. The smaller the ellipse, the more precise the touch points were for the key.

In addition to accuracy and precision, the ellipses also show the shape of the spreads. While the keys are tall rectangles, the touch spreads are ellipses that are often wider than they are tall. Some ellipses are stretched along the diagonal. The orientation of the major axis of each ellipse corresponds to the covariance, or correlation, between the x and y coordinates of the points. Early work on stylus keyboards also found that covariance varies among keys [6], but no further discussion was provided.

We believe the covariance is determined by the context of touches for the key: the direction whence the digit came and possibly also the direction in which the digit is headed. Plotting the touches of particular bigrams or trigrams may be useful for understanding how the shapes of the ellipses form. We defer this analysis to future work.

VERTICAL TOUCH POINT OFFSETS

In this section, we explore the vertical offsets of touch points for keys in different postures. The vertical offset of a point is the difference between the y coordinate of a touch point and the y coordinate of the key center. The mean offsets indicate whether there is a tendency to hit below (a positive offset) or above (a negative offset) the key.

There is an overall trend that touches tended to land below key centers. Figure 10 shows the vertical offset for each key in every posture. There are only a handful of keys with positive vertical offsets, all of which are negligible. The patterns and magnitudes of vertical offsets varied among postures. The mean vertical offset for keys in the one-finger posture is largest, at 4.69 pixels (SD = 2.92), the mean for keys in the two-thumb posture is 2.16 pixels (SD = 2.06), and the mean for keys in the one-thumb posture is 3.25 pixels (SD = 2.37). Note that the height of each alphabetical key is 75 pixels.

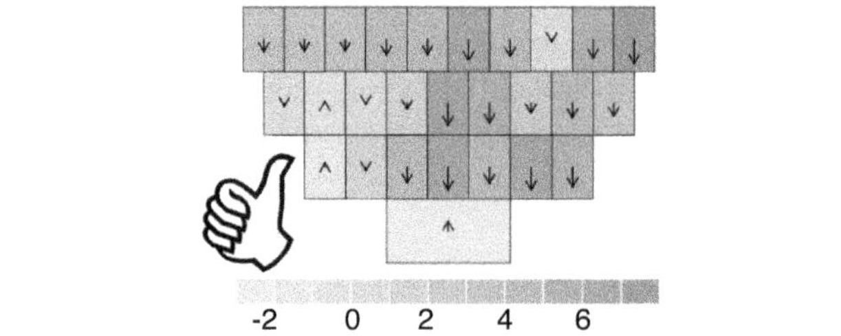

Figure 10. Vertical offsets for touch points in all three postures. The color gradient of each key indicates the value of the offset. The arrows show relative offset sizes among keys, but are not drawn in the scale of the keyboard outline.

Our findings are generally in agreement with findings in the context of touch pointing at single targets. Holz and Baudisch [12] show that the actual contact point lies below the user's perceived contact point for a touch along the fingertip. However, Henze et al. [8] found that targets that lie roughly in the bottom 10% of the screen induced touch points with high negative vertical offsets (i.e., the contact points were above the targets). Henze et al. collected hit data for targets that appeared across the entire screen, however, and our participants hit targets that were only within the bottom portion of the screen. On average, it seems the touch point data from Henze et al.'s experiments had a positive vertical offset, similar to our findings, despite the different use context (keyboarding vs. single target pointing).

As the top left keyboard in Figure 10 shows, one-finger touch data exhibits a striking trend across the key rows. Offsets of keys nearly double from one row to the next. The mean vertical offset for keys in the top row is 2.13 pixels (*SD* = 1.80); for the second row from the top the mean vertical offset is 4.89 pixels (*SD* = 1.87), and for the third row, it is 8.10 pixels (*SD* = 1.20), which was more than 10% of the key height.

It seems that the thumb is not as likely to hit below the target as the index finger, as the two-thumb and one-thumb postures do not exhibit such strong trends in vertical offsets. Keys in the center of the keyboard have slightly higher vertical offsets for two-thumb entry while keys on the right side of the one-thumb keyboard tend to have slightly higher vertical offsets than keys on the left side.

HORIZONTAL TOUCH POINT OFFSETS

We explore horizontal offsets, or the difference in the *x* coordinates of touch points and their target key centers, in this section. A positive offset indicates that the touch lies to the right of the key center. Horizontal offsets revealed more surprising trends than vertical offsets.

Horizontal offsets were more pronounced than vertical offsets. The horizontal locations of the ellipses in Figure 7, Figure 8, and Figure 9 clearly show that the touch points are not centered within their target keys along the *x* axis. In some cases, such as the "q" key in the one-thumb posture, the center of touch points is almost at the right key boundary. Figure 11 shows the mean horizontal offsets for keys in all three postures.

The SPACE key in all three postures has large positive horizontal offsets. We discuss this in a later section and focus on trends among the alphabetical keys in this section.

For all three postures, offsets were greater in magnitude on the left side of the keyboard than on the right. For two-thumb entry, it seems that participants were more accurate with their right thumbs. Recall that we only had two left-handed participants, so participants appear to be more accurate with their dominant hand. For one-finger and one-thumb entry, it seems participants were less accurate when reaching for keys across the keyboard.

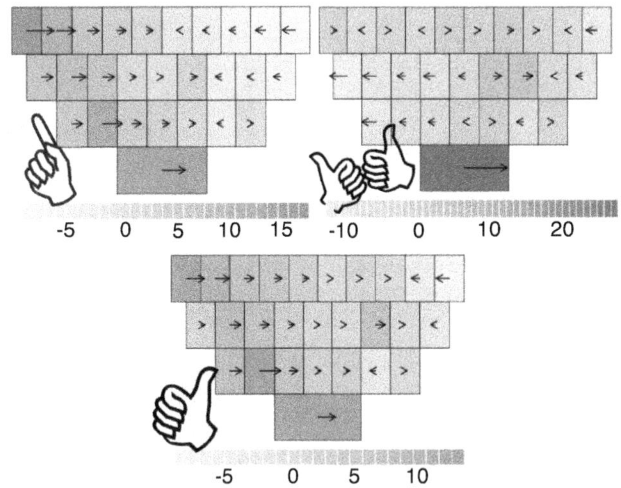

Figure 11. Horizontal offsets for touch points in all three postures. As in Figure 10, the color gradient of each key reflects the value of the offset. The arrows show relative offset sizes among keys, but are not drawn to the scale of the keyboard outline.

The trends in horizontal offsets on the left side of the keyboard were strikingly different among postures. Keys in this region had negative offsets with two-thumb entry and positive offsets with one-thumb and one-finger entry. This suggests participants try to minimize the distance their thumb or finger must travel and in many cases, they did not reach far enough across the keyboard.

As with vertical offsets in our data, horizontal offset patterns for the single-digit postures support prior work [6,8]. Henze et al. [8] also found (1) larger horizontal offsets on the left side of the screen (although their study involved discrete target pointing) and (2) smaller negative horizontal offsets on the right side of the screen. While Henze et al. conducted unsupervised field deployments where hand posture was not known, we conjecture that many participants used one finger or one thumb to play their game.

TOUCH POINT SPREADS

We observe the sizes of touch spreads, comparing the precision of user hits for different keys. To measure the spread size, we compute the standard deviation of touch points, which is the expected distance of an observed touch from the mean.

Figure 12 shows average spreads for the collective data and for the individual participants (the spread of points per key per participant). A large collective spread can emerge in two ways. Participants may have large spreads of touch points, showing high imprecision when targeting keys. Alternatively, participants may be fairly precise, but have largely differing offsets which result in large spreads of the collective data. Both cases are important to explore. Individual trends have implications on the design of adaptive or personalized keyboards, while spreads in the collective data have implications for keyboards that are designed to support all users.

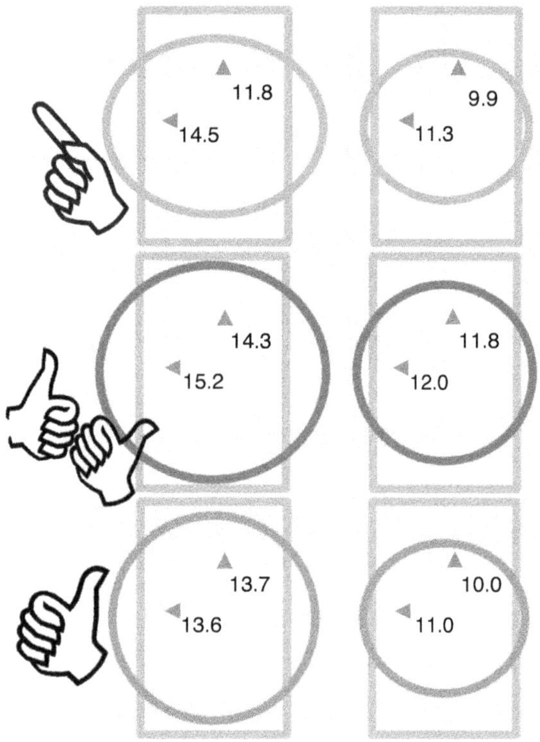

Figure 12. Collective (left) and average participant (right) touch spreads, marked by 95% confidence ellipses relative to a key outline. The ellipses are drawn to scale. The standard deviation (SD) is reported in pixels for each dimension, indicated by an arrow.

For two-thumb and one-finger entry, touch point spreads for keys are larger in the x dimension than in the y dimension, even though keys are much taller than they are wide. The differences between dimensions are more noticeable in the one-finger posture, as seen in Figure 12. Current keyboard dimensions are probably a result of the key height being less constrained than key width, which is limited to 1/10 of the total screen width. Our data suggests that the key height may be reduced if it is desirable to have the keyboard occupy a smaller portion of the screen. Further research is needed to ensure there is no coupling effect between the vertical and horizontal dimensions. More constrained vertical dimension may lead to overall more cautious user behavior.

Data collected during one-thumb entry showed a distinct pattern in spread height across the keyboard. The spreads for keys in the top left of the keyboard were taller than they are wide, unlike the spreads in the other two postures. Surprisingly, we did not observe these trends within the points of individuals; it seems the large overall spreads were a result of varying offsets among participants, possibly due to different thumb sizes. For example, the standard deviation in the y dimension of all one-thumb entry points for the 'q' key was 14.26 pixels. The mean standard deviation for the points of individual participants, however, was just 8.88 pixels ($SD = 4.66$).

Individual participants were more precise than the collective data suggested, with spreads that were only slightly larger than the key widths. Small keys thus do not appear to be a major cause of error; different offsets among participants produced large overall spreads and seem to be a more compelling source of errors.

THE SPACE KEY

We explore touch points for the SPACE key separately, since this key is different than the alphabetical keys in form and function. While all keys have the same height, the width of the SPACE key is typically at least three times the width of an alphabetical key on mainstream smartphone keyboards, as shown in Figure 13. The SPACE key is functionally different because it delimits words and triggers auto-correct modifications.

Figure 13. The iPhone's keyboard (top-left) SPACE key spans five alphabetical keys, the Windows Phone 7 keyboard (top-right) SPACE key spans four alphabetical keys, and the Android keyboard (bottom) SPACE key spans three keys.

As seen in Figure 7, Figure 8, and Figure 9, the spreads of touch points for the SPACE key mostly lay to the right of the key center. Horizontal offsets were large, especially for the two-thumb posture. It seems that participants mostly hit the SPACE key with their right thumb. Findlater et al. [10] also found that participants often hit the space key with their right thumbs when typing with 10 fingers. Our one left-handed participant who entered text with two thumbs in the study tended to hit to the right of the SPACE key center as well. It would be interesting to gather data from other left-handed people to see if they used their right thumbs.

In addition to being shifted, the spreads of points on the SPACE key were small compared with the width of the key. The spread in the two-thumb data were largest among the postures, and yet the 95% confidence ellipse only covered two-thirds of he key's width. This suggests that the space key may not need to be as wide (but perhaps moved to the right), yet it is even wider on other common keyboards.

DISCUSSION AND IMPLICATIONS FOR DESIGN

Our empirical findings show distinct patterns among three common hand postures used to enter text on mobile phones.

This suggests that researchers and practitioners should consider hand posture when designing and evaluating keyboards. We argue that keyboards should therefore detect, automatically or with user input, which posture is being used to support a large number of people in different mobile computing contexts. We distill our findings and discuss their implications for design, following the idea that hand posture should be considered.

Touch points tend to land below key centers. There should be a small (several pixels) vertical correction subtracted from each touch point.

One-finger input has the highest vertical offsets, which increases along the top three rows of the keyboard. Vertical corrections should be larger in one-finger input, and should depend on the key row.

Touch points for one-finger and one-thumb input tend to hit towards the center of the right half of the keyboard. Horizontal corrections should be added to touch points accordingly, effectively shifting the centers of the keys in the left side of the keyboard to the right.

Touch points on the left side of the keyboard are largely offset to the left for two-thumb entry. The affected key centers should be shifted to the left to accommodate. Also, automatic corrections in general should be more aggressive for keys in this region and posture because their high negative offsets cause many points to land outside of key boundaries.

Spreads of points are wider than they are long for one-finger and two-thumb input. Keys may not need to be as tall as those we tested, since the vertical space is not utilized.

Spreads of points are relatively small among participants, but collective spreads are larger, and they vary by key and posture. Participants were relatively precise, but their offsets differed. This suggests that adaptable keyboards that adjust for key offsets according to the individual (personalization) and the hand posture (adaptation) would perform well.

The spreads of points on the space key were shifted to the right and did not span the full width of the key. The space key can be made smaller and moved to the right of the bottom row.

These implications for design should be viewed as suggestions for future experiments. It is likely that any of the changes we recommend will affect user behavior. For example, if a vertical correction was added for each key, participants may adapt to this change and produce even greater vertical offsets in their touches. Since participants received minimal feedback from the Keyboard Touch Collector in our study, we believe our data does show raw, intrinsic, and in some ways optimal, performance for a keyboard in the given layout. More importantly, the value of the touch patterns we presented is not limited to the outlined design implications. Designers may draw their own conclusions according to their design goals and constraints from our well controlled empirical findings.

LIMITATIONS AND FUTURE WORK

Our analysis has several limitations, which we view as opportunities for future work.

First, we plan to determine the effect of visual design elements on touch behavior. We collected data on a basic keyboard which served as a baseline. It would be interesting to compare our data to data collected on keyboards with varying key gutters, color gradients, label sizes, etc. We tested and collected our data on one device size. A larger or smaller physical size of the keyboard may impact the touch patterns significantly.

Second, we hope to collect additional data and explore the speed-accuracy trade-off. By observing touch data for specific bigrams, we can control the distance moved and compare accuracy for different movement speeds.

Third, it would be interesting to analyze error across the dimension of time and order. We have focused on touch location, i.e., imprecision and inaccuracy, as a cause of error and our criteria (the same number of taps as characters in the target phrase) eliminated most other types of errors. However, transposition of inputs, as found in prior work on physical keyboards [3], and other timing patterns may account for and help us correct errors as well.

Fourth, in our study we instructed participants to enter data "as accurately and as naturally" as possible. This could have encouraged them to be unusually cautious. It is an open question if participant behavior would significantly change if the goal was to type as fast as possible.

Finally, we have only studied touch tapping as a way of entering text on soft keyboards. Understanding the fundamental motor control behavior and patterns in gesture keyboards [13,14,28] is another future research direction.

CONCLUSION

We have explored touch performance on soft QWERTY keyboards that are used by millions of people on their smartphones. We found that an index finger, two thumbs, and one thumb are all common hand postures used for entering text, and they induce different touch patterns and overall performance. Our empirical findings and implications for design may serve as a foundation for keyboard researchers, designers, and developers to improve keyboard layouts and algorithms. Understanding touch performance is an important step in advancing soft keyboards on small screens so they can ultimately out-perform traditional hard keyboards, continuing to expand the potential of mobile computing.

ACKNOWLEDGMENTS

This research was conducted at Google Research where the first author was a graduate intern. We thank Zhiwei Guan, Pernilla Qvarfordt, and Jacob O. Wobbrock for sharing their experimental research and data analysis experience with us.

REFERENCES

1. Bao, P., Pierce, P., Whittaker, S., and Zhai, S. (2011). Smart phone use by non-mobile business users. *Proc. MobileHCI '11*, 445-454.
2. Clarkson, E., Lyons, K., Clawson, J., and Starner, T. (2007). Revisiting and validating a model of two-thumb text entry. *Proc. CHI '07*, 163-166.
3. Clawson, J., Lyons, K., Rudnick, A., Iannucci, Jr., R., and Starner, T. (2008). Automatic whiteout++: correcting mini-QWERTY typing errors using keypress timing. *Proc. CHI '08*, 573-582.
4. Findlater, L., Wobbrock, J. O., and Wigdor, D. (2011). Typing on flat glass: examining ten-finger expert typing patterns on touch surfaces. *Proc. CHI '11*, 2453-2462.
5. Gong, J., Tarasewich, P., and MacKenzie, I. S. (2008). Improved word list ordering for text entry on ambiguous keypads. *Proc. NordiCHI '08*, 152-161.
6. Goodman, J., Venolia, G., Steury, K., Parker, C. 2002. Language modeling for soft keyboards. *Proc. IUI '02*, 194-195
7. Gunawardana, A., Paek, T., and Meek, C. (2010). Usability guided key-target resizing for soft keyboards. *Proc. IUI '10*, 111-118.
8. Henze, N., Rukzio, E., and Boll, S. (2011). 100,000,000 taps: analysis and improvement of touch performance in the large. *Proc. MobileHCI '11*, 133-142.
9. Himberg, J., Häkkilä, J., Kangas, P., and Mäntyjärvi, J. (2003). On-line personalization of a touch screen based keyboard. *Proc. IUI '03*, 77-84.
10. Hoggan, E., Brewster, S., & Johnston, J. (2008). Investigating the effectiveness of tactile feedback for mobile touchscreens. *Proc. of CHI '08*, 1573-1582.
11. Holz, C. and Baudisch, P. (2010). The Generalized Perceived Input Point Model and How to Double Touch Accuracy by Extracting Fingerprints. *Proc. CHI '10*, 581-590.
12. Holz, C. and Baudisch, P. (2011). Understanding Touch. *Proc. CHI '11*, 2501-2510.
13. Kristensson, P-O., Zhai, S. (2005). Relaxing Stylus Typing Precision by Geometric Pattern Matching. *Proc. IUI '05*, 151-158.
14. Kristensson, P.O. and Zhai, S. (2004). SHARK2: A Large Vocabulary Shorthand Writing System for Pen-based Computers. *Proc. UIST '04*, 43-52.
15. Kristensson, P. O., and Vertanen, K. (2012). Performance comparisons of phrase sets and presentation styles for text entry evaluations. *Proc. IUI '12*, 29-32.
16. Lee, S., Zhai, S. (2009). The performance of touch screen soft buttons. *Proc. CHI '09*, 309-318.
17. MacKenzie, I. S. and Soukoreff, R. W. (2003). Phrase Sets for Evaluating Text Entry Techniques. *Proc. EACHI '03*. 754–755
18. MacKenzie, I. S. and Soukoreff, R. W. (2002). A Model of Two–Thumb Text Entry. *Proc. GI '02*, 117–124
19. MacKenzie, I. S., Zhang, S. X. (1999) The design and evaluation of a high-performance soft keyboard. *Proc. CHI '99*, 25-31.
20. Paek, T., and Hsu, B.-J. P. (2011). Sampling representative phrase sets for text entry experiments: a procedure and public resource. *Proc. CHI '11*, 2477-2480.
21. Rudchenko, D., Paek, T., and Badger, E. (2011). Text Text Revolution: A game that improves text entry on mobile touchscreen keyboards. *Proc. Pervasive '11*, 206-213
22. Kumiko Tanaka-ishii. (2007). Word-based predictive text entry using adaptive language models. Nat. Lang. Eng. 13, 1 51-74.
23. Wang, F. and Ren, X. (2009). Empirical evaluation for finger input properties in multi-touch interaction. *Proc. CHI '09*, 1063-1072.
24. Wobbrock, J. O., and Myers, B.A. (2006). Analyzing the input stream for character-level errors in unconstrained text entry evaluations. *ACM TOCHI* 13 (4), pp. 458-489.
25. Wobbrock, J. O., Myers, B. A., and Aung, H. H. (2008) The performance of hand postures in front- and back-of-device interaction for mobile computing. Int. J. Hum.-Comput. Stud. 66, 12, 857-875.
26. Yamada, H. (1980). A historical study of typewriters and typing methods: from the position of planning Japanese parallels. Journal of Information Processing, 1980. 2(4): 175-20.
27. Zhai, S. and Kristensson, P.-O. (2003). Shorthand Writing on Stylus Keyboard. *Proc. CHI '03*, 97-104.
28. Zhai, S. and Kristensson, P.O. (2006). Introduction to Shape Writing. IBM Research Report RJ10393 (also as Chapter 7 of I. S. MacKenzie and K. Tanaka-Ishii (eds), Text Entry Systems: Mobility, Accessibility, Universality, Morgan Kaufmann Publishers, 139-158.

Digging Unintentional Displacement for One-Handed Thumb Use on Touchscreen-Based Mobile Devices

Wenchang Xu **Jie Liu** **Chun Yu** **Yuanchun Shi**

Key Laboratory of Pervasive Computing, Ministry of Education

Department of Computer Science and Technology, Tsinghua University, China

{wencxu, liujiejesse, yc2pcg}@gmail.com, shiyc@tsinghua.edu.cn

ABSTRACT

There is usually an unaware screen distance between initial contact and final lift-off when users tap on touchscreen-based mobile devices with their fingers, which may affect users' target selection accuracy, gesture performance, etc. In this paper, we summarize such case as unintentional displacement and give its models under both static and dynamic scenarios. We then conducted two user studies to understand unintentional displacement for the widely-adopted one-handed thumb use on touchscreen-based mobile devices under both scenarios respectively. Our findings shed light on the following four questions: 1) what are the factors that affect unintentional displacement; 2) what is the distance range of the displacement; 3) how is the distance varying over time; 4) how are the unintentional points distributed around the initial contact point. These results not only explain certain touch inaccuracy, but also provide important reference for optimization and future design of UI components, gestures, input techniques, etc.

Author Keywords

Unintentional displacement, thumb use, touch screen, mobile device, user study.

ACM Classification Keywords

H.5.2 User Interfaces: evaluation/methodology, user-centered design.

General Terms

Human Factors.

INTRODUCTION

Mobile devices with touchscreens are becoming increasingly popular, on which people select the target using their fingers. However, as generally assumed, the touch input cannot be accurate due to the *fat finger problem* [25], i.e., the occlusion of the target by the user's finger as well as the ambiguity about which part of the finger generates the contact point. As a result, a number of techniques were designed to enhance target selection on touchscreen-based mobile devices, of which *Shift* [25] is a typical representative. Although *Shift* overcomes the *fat finger problem* by providing a callout showing the occluded area and the contact point, its mean error rate is still higher than 30% if the target's size is around or smaller than 1 mm, as indicated by [14, 31]. An important factor for it is that there is usually an unaware screen distance between initial contact and final lift-off when users tap on touchscreen-based mobile devices with their fingers, which we summarize as unintentional displacement. In fact, unintentional displacement almost occurs every time when touch happens and may affect the results of target selection, gesture performance, etc.

In current mobile applications, most on-click events are triggered when the user's finger is lifted, which brings the slide-lift selection mode, i.e., pressing on a certain position of the screen, sliding towards some direction and lifting until the desired target is reached. A typical example is the virtual keyboard input. As shown in Figure 1, in order to select a character, a user can either perform direct touch with slight moving adjustment (Figure 1 (a)), or use the slide-lift selection mode without concerning where the finger is put initially (Figure 1 (b)). Based on the two selection modes, we give our models of unintentional displacement under static and dynamic scenarios respectively. For the static scenario, unintentional displacement denotes displacement between the moments of initial contact and final lift-off, while for the dynamic scenario, unintentional displacement starts when the desired

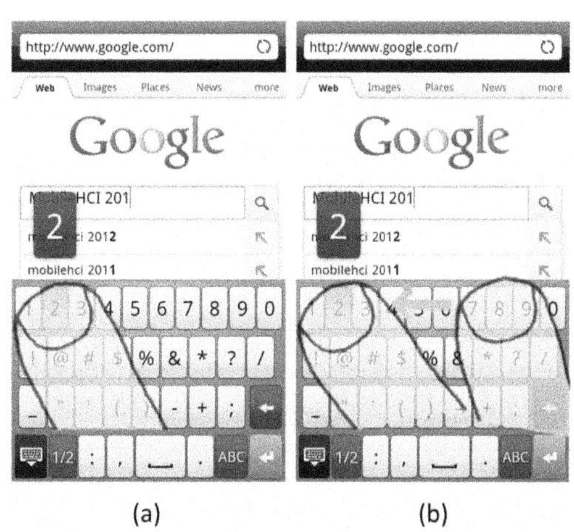

Figure 1. Two selection modes of virtual keyboard input: (a) direct touch; (b) slide-lift selection.

target is initially reached and ends until the finger is lifted. The unintentional displacement may be caused by several reasons, e.g. finger slipping, deformation, etc. However, we will focus on measuring the displacement instead of extracting the exact reasons in this paper.

Given the unintentional displacement models, we then conducted two user studies to understand unintentional displacement for one-handed thumb use, the prevalence of which has been confirmed through the study of device users under mobile scenarios [13]. We were trying to answer the following four questions:

(Q1) What are the factors that affect unintentional displacement; **(Q2)** what is the distance range of the displacement; **(Q3)** how is the distance varying over time; **(Q4)** how are the unintentional points distributed around the initial contact point.

In the first user study, we selected finger pitch, roll and duration as factors and gave the answers of the questions under the static scenario. In the second user study, we considered two more factors – sliding direction and distance for the dynamic scenario, finding out more interesting results that are different from the static scenario. The results of both scenarios coincide with our daily experiences. These results not only explain certain touch inaccuracy, but also provide important reference for optimization and future design of UI components, gestures, input techniques, etc.

The rest of the paper is organized as follows. First, we review existing research related to our work. We then introduce the unintentional displacement models for both static and dynamic scenarios. Next, we detail the design of the two user studies and the analysis of the results. We then describe potential usages of the interesting findings. Finally, we discuss future work and draw conclusion.

RELATED WORK

Unintentional displacement is related to touch technologies, impact of finger posture, target size and location studies as well as target selection techniques.

Touch Technologies

The goal of touch technologies is to determine input coordinates. There are generally three types of touch technologies, including electric induction (e.g. *resistive sensing*, *capacitive sensing* [4]), *FTIR* [7, 24] and camera-based technologies. Electric induction is widely used in existing touchscreen-based mobile phones, pads and interactive screens. Nowadays, *capacitive sensing* is more frequently adopted than *resistive sensing* as it is more sensitive to finger touch and interaction. *FTIR*, short for *frustrated total internal reflection*, is a typical optical technology that is widely adopted in multi-touch tables. Users' input precision on such an optical system was examined by [27]. The computer vision technique is often used in camera-based technologies [28]. Malik and Laszlo [15] identified users' fingertips and determined finger yaw using two cameras, while Agarwal et al. [1] recognized fingertips and distinguished touching or hovering using machine learning with stereo cameras above the user's hands. Wilson [30] derived touch input from the distance between the user's fingers and shadows they cast with a camera above at an angle. In fact, unintentional displacement exists and has different effects on all these touch technologies. Here we focus on touchscreen-based mobile devices on which the *capacitive sensing* is adopted.

Impact of Finger Posture

Finger posture indicates the angle between the finger and the touch surface, which contains finger pitch, roll, yaw, etc [8]. It is an important factor that we think will affect unintentional displacement on touchscreen-based mobile devices. Researchers have shown how finger posture affects touch accuracy. Forlines et al. [5] found that a flatter finger pitch would cause a larger contact area, which led to an offset input location. Wang and Ren [27] also presented the impact of finger posture and motion on the size of contact area. Holz and Baudisch investigated the impact of finger posture (roll and pitch) on accuracy of traditional touch [8] and verified their suggested models through varying the finger posture [9].

Some research is also aimed at extracting certain subsets of finger posture. *Microsoft Surface* [16] detects finger orientation by analyzing the diffuse reflection of the hovering hand, while the *FingerWorks iGesture* pad [4] estimates finger orientation based on the eccentricity of the contact area. Wang et al. [26] proposed hand orientation-aware gesture processing, which detected finger yaw by observing the changes in contact area over time. Roudaut et al. [22] proposed finger roll as the basis for a new gesture language and distinguished rolling from dragging.

Target Size and Location Studies

Researchers have also studied how target size and location affect users' target selection accuracy and efficiency [13, 17, 18, 19], which provides helpful guidance to our unintentional displacement study. Parhi et al. [17] designed a two-phase study including both discrete pointing tasks and serial pointing tasks that varied 5 target sizes and 9 locations in the selected area. Park et al. [18] investigated the target selection accuracy with 3 target sizes and 25 locations while Perry et al. [19] chose 5 target sizes and 25 locations. A similar conclusion was drawn that target size around 9.6 mm was large enough for maintaining both high selection accuracy and short movement time. They also indicated that targets near the center of the screen were easier to reach than those close to the screen edge. These results provide useful guidance for target design on mobile devices with touchscreens.

Target Selection Techniques

As generally assumed, the touch input cannot be accurate due to the *fat finger problem* [25]. As a result, a number of techniques were designed to enhance target selection on touchscreen-based mobile devices. A series of them address the problem by avoiding occlusion and enhancing accessibility, e.g., *Offset Cursor* [10, 20, 23], *Shift* [25], *ThumbSpace* [11, 12], *Barrier Pointing* [6], *MagStick* [21], etc. Specifically, *LucidTouch* [29] allows the user to control the application by touching the back of the device through pseudo-transparency. Others improve target selection accuracy by expanding or changing the target selection region, e.g., *TapTap* [21], *Escape* [31], *Gesture Avatar* [14], *Starburst* [3], etc. Holz and Baudisch [8] proposed the *perceived input point* model to replace the *fat finger problem* and introduced their approach of doubling touch accuracy by extracting fingerprints. Although the *fat finger problem* is reduced or overcome by these techniques, some of their mean error rate is still high under certain conditions. For example, the mean error rate of *Shift* is higher than 30% if the target's size is around or smaller than 1 mm [14, 31]. Fortunately, we can explain some of the inaccuracy with unintentional displacement and potentially provide important reference for input technique design with full understanding of this phenomenon. Next, we will give the models of unintentional displacement and answer the questions we raised at the beginning through user studies.

UNINTENTIONAL DISPLACEMENT

Continuing with the two selection modes (direct touch and slide-lift selection) presented in the introduction, we then give the models of unintentional displacement under static and dynamic scenarios respectively.

Model under the Static Scenario

In the static scenario, unintentional displacement denotes displacement between the moments of initial contact and final lift-off. Figure 2 (a) shows the two crucial moments as well as the initial contact point P_0 and the lifting point P generated in the two moments respectively. Therefore, $|P - P_0|$ denotes the final unintentional displacement distance. However, there may be some other contact points generated between the two moments due to users' natural finger shaking, so the unintentional displacement distance may be changing before the final lift-off.

This model applies to conditions when there is no intentional finger movement performed by users on the screen during the whole touch process. A specific target may not even be necessary. Typical scenarios include direct touch selection of a certain target or long press on any part of the screen to generate pop-up menus, etc.

Model under the Dynamic Scenario

In the dynamic scenario, the major difference from the former model is that there is an intentional prior sliding before the desired target is reached. In this case, unintentional displacement starts when the desired target is initially reached and ends until the finger is lifted. Figure 2 (b) shows the three crucial moments from the initial contact

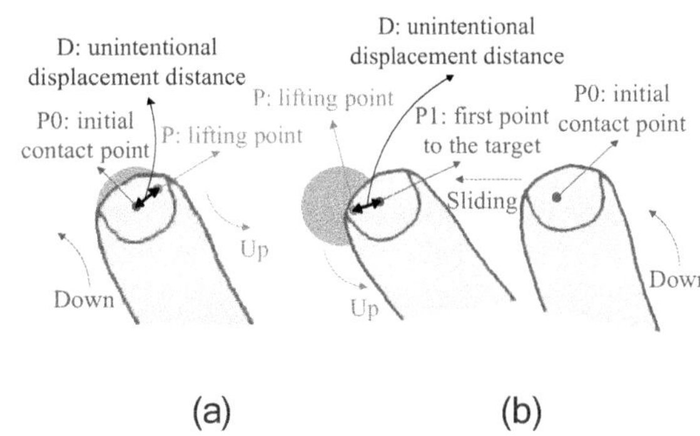

Figure 2. Unintentional displacement models: (a) static scenario; (b) dynamic scenario.

to the final lift-off, which generate the initial contact point P_0, the first point to the target P_1 and the lifting point P respectively. Therefore, the selection process is divided into two parts, the prior sliding from P_0 to P_1 and the unintentional displacement, whose final distance is denoted by $| P - P_1|$. Similar to the static scenario, the unintentional displacement distance may be changing before the final lift-off. However, unintentional displacement here is not only caused by the natural finger shaking, but also affected by the inertia of the prior sliding.

The model under the dynamic scenario applies to conditions when a specific target is displayed and the intentional prior sliding exists. Typical scenarios include the slide-lift selection of the virtual keyboard input (Figure 1 (b)) and the action of connecting targets in certain applications or games, etc.

INTERVIEW

Before the user studies, we recruited 20 participants (14 males and 6 females) from our department, all of whom were between 20 and 28 years old. They were all accustomed to operating touchscreen-based mobile devices with one-handed thumb use. We interviewed them about their finger postures of touch input on touchscreen-based mobile devices in order to determine the range of finger posture parameters (pitch, roll and yaw) in our user studies.

To help participants become aware of their finger postures of touch input, we asked them to acquire targets of three different sizes (8 mm, 5 mm and 2 mm) in the four corners, the center and five other random positions on an HTC Desire with their commonly-used hand thumbs. Then, to answer our questions about their finger postures, they were given enough time and were allowed to tap on any position of the mobile phone to make sure of their replies. Based on the participants' statements and our observation, we concluded the results as follows:

1) The finger posture of touch input was a combination of pitch, roll and yaw. **2)** The pitch angle could vary between 0° and 90°. Specifically, 15 participants said they were used to adjusting their pitch angles to acquire targets of different positions. In addition, they tended to put their thumbs straight down when acquiring small targets. The angle could be up to 90°. However, other 5 participants were inclined to adjust their postures of holding the mobile phone in order to keep a static pitch angle. One of them even kept his thumb horizontal (0°). **3)** The roll angle could vary between -45° and 45°. Specifically, 13 participants said their roll angle changed within a range to both sides when acquiring targets of different positions. We summarized the range as -45° and 45° based on our observation and discussion with the participants. However, other 7 participants said they would keep the roll angle 0° (nail horizontal) or varying within 5°. **4)** The yaw angle could vary between 0° and 90°, which was supported by all participants. **5)** 8 participants said that they were accustomed to adjusting their postures of holding the mobile phone to acquire targets of different positions. The rest participants didn't adjust the posture so often, but none of them objected to do the adjustment when necessary.

With the results as guidance, we will next introduce the apparatus and participants of our experiments, and describe the user studies we conducted to understand unintentional displacement of the two models for the widely-adopted one-handed thumb use on touchscreen-based mobile devices.

APPARATUS

The user studies were deployed on an HTC Desire with Android 2.2 platform, whose screen size is 4.8×8.0 cm and display resolution is 480×800 pixels with 0.1 mm dot pitch. The study interfaces and control software were developed using Android SDK 2.2 [2]. Specifically, it can record users' finger movements by keeping track of screen coordinates of real-time finger down, move and up actions during the whole touch process.

PARTICIPANTS

We recruited 18 participants including 13 males and 5 females, 15 of whom were right-handed while 3 were left-handed. 14 of them were graduate students from our department, 2 worked in finance companies and 2 were public servants. The age of the participants varied between 22 and 38 years, with a mean of 27.2 years old. They had no physical movement disease (e.g. Parkinsonism) and were familiar with one-handed thumb use on touchscreen-based mobile devices. During the user studies, they were all required to finish the tasks with their commonly-used hand thumbs.

USER STUDY 1: UNDERSTANDING UNINTENTIONAL DISPLACEMENT UNDER THE STATIC SCENARIO

The first user study was conducted to understand the model of unintentional displacement under the static scenario.

Design

The first step of the design was to determine the factors to be used in the user study. As described in the model, unintentional displacement denotes displacement between the moments of initial contact and final lift-off in the static scenario. Therefore, we need to consider factors related to both users and targets.

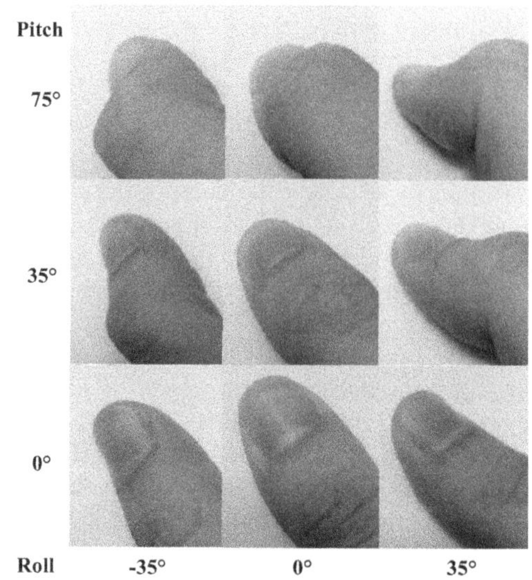

Figure 3. Finger postures used in user study 1. Pitch: 0°, 35°, 75°; roll: -35°, 0°, 35°; yaw: 45°.

Finger posture: roll, pitch and yaw. Finger posture indicates the angle between the finger and the touch surface, which has been concluded to include roll, pitch and yaw [8], and proved to affect touch input [5, 8, 9, 27]. Therefore, it is the most straightforward factor that is supposed to have an effect on unintentional displacement.

We provided three different levels of pitch and three different levels of roll. We varied pitch among "horizontal" (0°), "moderate tilted" (35°) and "almost straight down" (75°), and roll among "rolled left" (-35°), "nail horizontal" (0°) and "rolled right" (35°). According to the results of our interview, the range of the pitch angle was between 0° and 90°, while the range of the roll angle was between -45° and 45°. For the roll angle, we didn't select the range value 45° because not everyone could roll his/her thumb to such an angle. 35° was a reasonable trade-off that was still close to the range value. In the actual experiment, it was enough for the participants to roll their thumbs to a non-zero angle within the range between 30° and 45°. For the pitch angle, we didn't select the range value 90° because it was difficult to keep the thumb completely straight down while rolling it to a certain side. So we selected the "almost straight down" value 75° as an alternative. In the actual experiment, a miss angle of 10° was tolerated for the levels 35° and 75°.

While we varied pitch and roll, the variation of yaw was unnecessary because yaw took place in the flat screen of the mobile phone. When pitch and roll were fixed, we could rotate the contact points to generate the approximate results of different yaw angles. Therefore, in our experiment, we fixed the yaw angle as 45° with a 10°'s error toleration. As a result, there were 9 combinations of finger postures in user study 1, as shown in Figure 3.

Target: size and location. Target size and location have been proved to affect users' target selection accuracy and efficiency [13, 17, 18, 19]. Therefore, they may also have an effect on unintentional displacement. However, as indicated in the results of the interview, users' target selection of a certain size and location firmly corresponds to a finger posture, in other words, a combination of finger pitch, roll and yaw. Therefore, we would ignore target size and location, and focus on the study of finger posture.

Duration. In the static scenario, unintentional displacement starts when the user presses on the screen and ends until lifting. During this period of time, the user may perform natural finger shaking, thus affecting the unintentional displacement distance. Therefore, duration is also an important factor that is supposed to have an effect on unintentional displacement. In user study 1, we defined the parameter duration as the period between the initial contact and the reminding of lifting, specifically the screen's turning green, which was varied among 0, 500ms, 1000ms and 2000ms. However, as there was an extra period of reaction time, the actual touch time was a little bit longer.

User. We have introduced that the participants had no physical movement disease (e.g. Parkinsonism). However, different users may still generate different unintentional displacement results due to their different natural finger shaking habits, even though the same finger posture and duration are applied. Therefore, we would consider the effects of users in user study 1. Despite our 15 right-handed and 3 left-handed participants, the use of left or right hand doesn't matter. In fact, we can simply do an axial symmetrical transformation of the results of left-handed participants so as to combine them with the results of right-handed participants.

Once the factors had been fixed, the study process was quite simple. For a single task, a green circle with a radius of 50px was rendered in the center of the screen initially. Then the participants were asked to press on the circle using their commonly-used hand thumbs with the required pitch, roll and yaw until the whole screen turned green, reminding them of lifting their thumbs after the time duration. Touch process with initial point out of the circle was invalid and would be redone. The size and position of the circle were fixed, so participants were allowed to adjust their postures of holding the mobile phone so as to perform the required pitch, roll and yaw in comfort. We recorded the screen coordinates of participants' real-time finger down, move and up actions during the whole touch process.

A within-subjects factorial user study was used in this experiment. Before the formal study, each participant was asked to practice the experimental task for different finger pitch, roll, duration and the fixed yaw. They were allowed to practice until they were familiar and felt comfortable with it. In the formal study, we varied the finger pitch, roll and the duration, which were the independent variables of our experiment. We carefully examined participants' postures and asked them to redo it if certain posture was considered to be performed beyond our error toleration. For each (*Pitch*, *Roll*, *Duration*) combination, we assigned 10 repetitive tasks. Therefore, the experimental design was 18 *Users* × 3 *Pitch* (0°, 35°, 75°) × 3 *Roll* (-35°, 0°, 35°) × 1 *Yaw* (45°) × 4 *Duration* (0, 500, 1000, 2000ms) × 10 *Repetitive Tasks* = 6480 tasks. We randomized the order of the tasks to counterbalance the effect of the order.

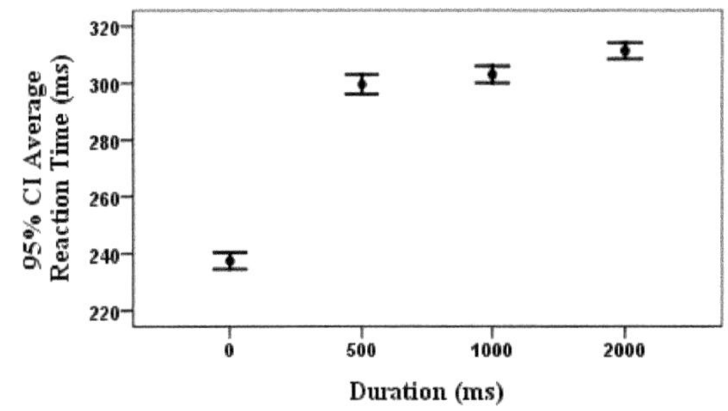

Figure 4. Average reaction time for user study 1. Error bars represent 95% confidence intervals.

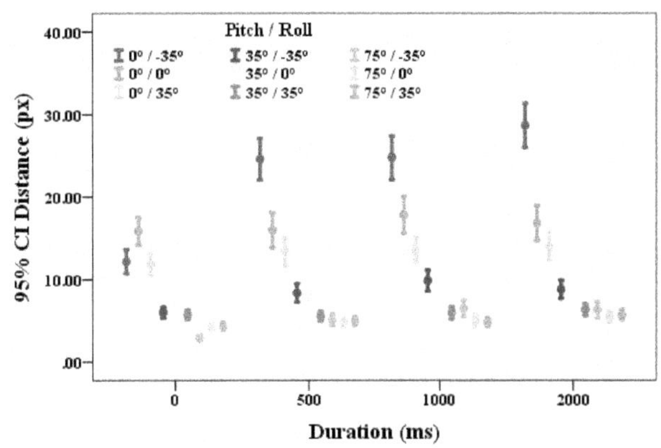

Figure 5. Mean unintentional displacement distance at the moment of final lift-off for user study 1. Error bars represent 95% confidence intervals.

Results

In user study 1, the actual touch time was the sum of the parameter duration and the reaction time. Figure 4 shows the average reaction time of different durations for user study 1. We will next answer Q1-Q4 for the static scenario through the following results.

Result 1: Mean Unintentional Displacement Distance at the Moment of Final Lift-Off

Result 1 answered the questions (Q1) what are the factors that affect unintentional displacement and (Q2) what is the distance range of the displacement in the static scenario. Figure 5 shows the mean unintentional displacement distance at the moment of final lift-off with different finger pitch, roll and durations for user study 1. Generally speaking, finger pitch and roll angles as well as the duration all had a great effect on the unintentional displacement distance. In addition, as shown in Figure 5, the range of the unintentional displacement distance was around 30px (3mm) with the pitch angle 0°, the roll angle -35° and the duration 2000ms, which explained the reason why certain target selection techniques cannot be accurate when the target's size is small (e.g. *Shift* [25]).

We performed a within-subjects analysis of variance (ANOVA) for *Users* × *Pitch* ×*Roll* × *Duration*. A main effect was found for *Users* ($F_{17,6462}$=26.741, p<0.001), *Pitch* ($F_{2,6477}$=477.653, p<0.001), *Roll* ($F_{2,6477}$=133.425, p<0.001) and *Duration* ($F_{3,6476}$=54.578, p<0.001). *Pitch* × *Roll* ($F_{4,6471}$=64.986, p<0.001), *Pitch* × *Duration* ($F_{6,6468}$=12.781, p<0.001), *Roll* × *Duration* ($F_{6,6468}$=23.758, p<0.001) and *Pitch* × *Roll* × *Duration* ($F_{12,6444}$=9.300, p<0.001) were significant interactions. Tukey's post-hoc pair-wise comparison showed that the unintentional displacement distance of pitch angle 0° was significantly larger than that of pitch angles 35°and 75° for all roll angles and durations. For pitch angle 0° and durations longer than 500ms, the unintentional displacement distance was significantly smaller when the roll angle was larger. For pitch angles 35°and 75°, there was no significant difference of the unintentional displacement distance on the roll angle for all durations.

Result 2: Mean Unintentional Displacement Distance over the Process of Touch

Result 2 answered (Q3) how the unintentional displacement distance varied over the process of touch in the static scenario. However, the graphical representation of such process was a little bit tricky, since the actual touch time and unintentional displacement point number of the same (*Pitch, Roll, Duration*) combination were different among participants and even different tasks of the same participant. Therefore, we calculated the mean actual touch time for all tasks with the same (*Pitch, Roll, Duration*) combination, and then fitted the distance curves of these tasks to one curve with the time range equal to the closed interval between 0 and the mean actual touch time. As a result, we got Figure 6, which could reflect the mean unintentional displacement distance over the process of touch.

The end of each curve in Figure 6 represented the mean unintentional displacement distance at the moment of final lift-off, which coincided with the results in Figure 5. Comparing the four sub-charts of different durations in Figure 6, we could easily find their similarities in value distribution and variation trend of the curves. For pitch angles 35° and 75°, the unintentional displacement distances of the whole touch process stayed small and changed little. For the pitch angle 0°, the curves rose rapidly to an approximate maximum value, and then remained stable for a period of time until a sudden drop to the end. We will explain how the curves were generated in the actual situation in result 3. But one fact we could infer was that the stable interval

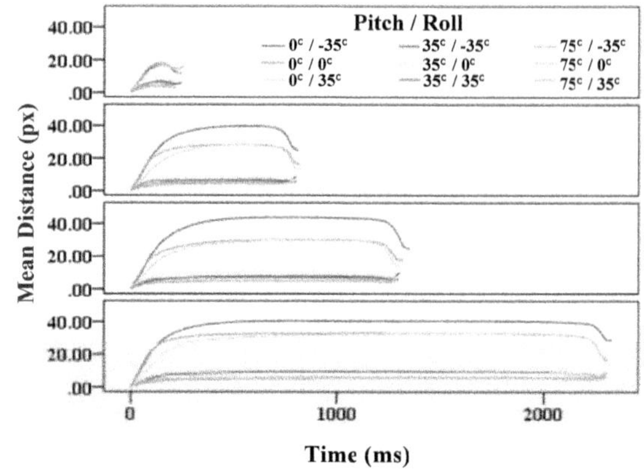

Figure 6. Mean unintentional displacement distance over the process of touch for user study 1.

represented the period of time when the participant held the screen and the point of the sudden drop represented the moment when the participant started to lift the thumb. This explained why curves dropped directly after reaching the peak in the first sub-chart with duration equal to 0 in Figure 6.

Result 3: Distribution of Unintentional Displacement Points around the Initial Contact Point

Result 3 answered (Q4) how the unintentional displacement points were distributed around the initial contact point. To unify the distribution, we relocated the coordinates of all initial contact points to (0, 0) and plotted the unintentional displacement points according to their relative positions to the corresponding initial contact points. For left-handed participants, the generated points were axisymmetric with those of right-handed participants under the same finger pitch, roll and yaw. So we simply performed an axial symmetrical transformation of the results of left-handed participants to combine them with the results of right-handed participants.

Figure 7 shows the distribution of unintentional displacement points in the static scenario, in which the blue, green and yellow dots represent the points of initial contact, displacement over the touch process and final lift-off respectively. An obvious conclusion was that the unintentional displacement ranges of pitch angles 35° and 75° were much smaller than that of pitch angle 0°. It was easy to explain in the actual situation that a flatter pitch angle would cause a larger contact area, which led to more natural finger shaking or deformation and a larger unintentional displacement range. This coincided with results in [5] and explained why the unintentional displacement distances of the whole touch process stayed small for pitch angles 35° and 75° in result 2. For pitch angle 0°, the four-direction distributions (top-left, bottom-left, top-right, bottom-right) of unintentional displacement points over the touch process were shown in Table 1, which indicated that participants tended to slip or deform to the left for roll angles -35° (rolled left) and 0° (nail horizontal), while tended to slip or deform to the bottom-right for roll angle 35° (rolled right). However,

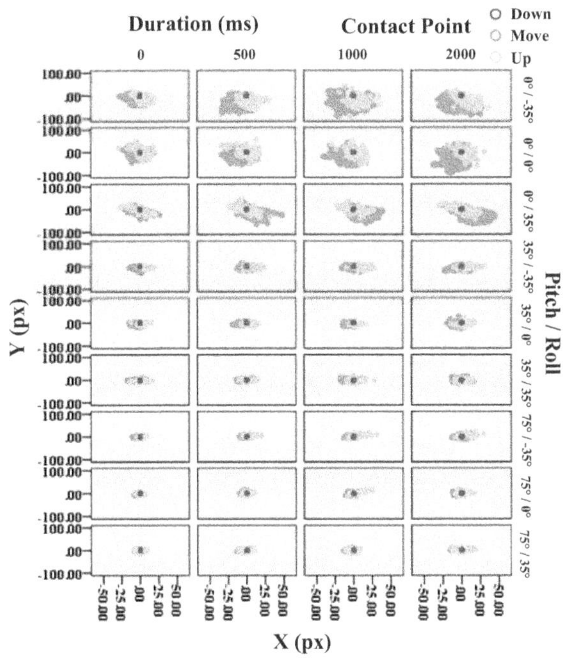

Figure 7. Distribution of unintentional displacement points for user study 1.

the lifting points were distributed closer to the initial contact points, which indicated the process that participants would restore from the rolling actions before lifting their thumbs. This also explained why the curves dropped before the final lift-off for pitch angle 0° in result 2.

Direction / Roll angle	Top left	Bottom left	Top right	Bottom right
-35°	12.3%	51.8%	9.7%	26.2%
0°	20.4%	37.5%	17.3%	24.8%
35°	15.9%	8.6%	13.2%	61.3%

Table 1. The four-direction distributions of unintentional displacement points over the touch process for pitch angle 0°.

USER STUDY 2: UNDERSTANDING UNINTENTIONAL DISPLACEMENT UNDER THE DYNAMIC SCENARIO

The second user study was conducted to understand the model of unintentional displacement under the dynamic scenario.

Design

The similarity of the dynamic scenario and the static scenario is that users acquire the target using their thumbs with specific postures. Therefore, we can infer from user study 1 that the finger posture (pitch, roll and yaw) also plays an important part in unintentional displacement under the dynamic scenario. However, different from the static scenario, there is an intentional prior sliding before the desired target is reached in the dynamic scenario. On one hand, users' finger postures may be changing all the time during the prior sliding, which makes the study of finger postures rather complicated. On the other hand, unintentional displacement may be affected significantly by the prior sliding due to users' inertial motion. Therefore, we will focus on how the intentional prior sliding, specifically the prior sliding direction and distance, affects unintentional displacement in the dynamic scenario. For the prior sliding direction, we performed the prior sliding to eight directions including left, bottom-left, bottom, bottom-right, right, top-right, top and top-left. For the prior sliding distance, we simply adopted two distances including 100px (10mm) and 200px (20mm).

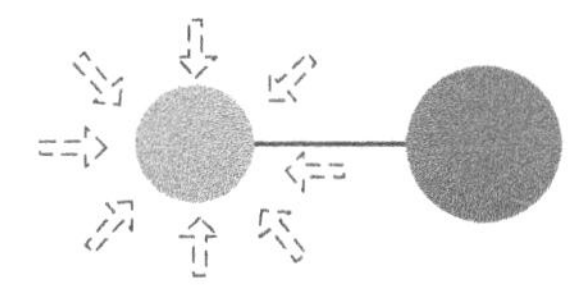

Figure 8. Process of user study 2.

In the dynamic scenario, unintentional displacement starts when the desired target is initially reached and ends until the finger is lifted. Therefore, our study process was designed as Figure 8. For a single task, a green target circle with a radius of 25px and a red assistant circle with a radius of 40px as well as their connecting line were rendered in a random position of the screen initially. The distance between the two circle centers was the prior sliding distance and the connecting line indicated the prior sliding direction. Then the participants were asked to slide from the red circle (start point out of the red circle was invalid) to the green circle using their commonly-used hand thumbs and their natural postures until the whole screen turned green, reminding them of lifting their thumbs when the green target circle was initially reached. We recorded the screen coordinates of participants' real-time finger down, move and up actions during the whole touch process.

A within-subjects factorial user study was used in this experiment. Before the formal study, each participant was asked to practice the experimental task for different prior sliding directions and distances. They were allowed to practice until they were familiar and felt comfortable with it. In the formal study, we varied the prior sliding direction and distance, which were the independent variables of our experiment. For each (*Direction, Distance*) combination, we assigned 10 repetitive tasks. Therefore, the experimental design was 18 *Users* × 8 *Directions* × 2 *Distances (100px, 200px)* × 10 *Repetitive Tasks* = 2880 tasks. We randomized the position of the targets and the order of the tasks to counterbalance their effects.

Results

In user study 2, we defined the effective touch time as the period between the reminding of lifting, specifically the screen's turning green when the green target circle was initially reached, and final lift-off. We will next answer Q1-Q4 for the dynamic scenario through the following results.

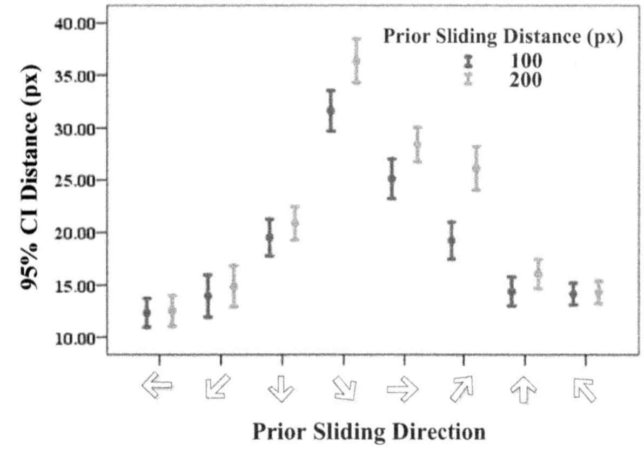

Figure 9. Mean unintentional displacement distance at the moment of final lift-off for user study 2. Error bars represent 95% confidence intervals.

Result 1: Mean Unintentional Displacement Distance at the Moment of Final Lift-Off

Result 1 answered the questions (Q1) what are the factors that affect unintentional displacement and (Q2) what is the distance range of the displacement in the dynamic scenario. Figure 9 shows the mean unintentional displacement distance at the moment of final lift-off with different prior sliding directions and distances for user study 2. Generally speaking, the prior sliding direction and distance both had a great effect on the unintentional displacement distance. The effect of the prior sliding distance could be explained by the motion inertial. We will further reveal the effect of the prior sliding direction in result 3. In addition, as shown in Figure 9, the range of the unintentional displacement distance was around 35px (3.5mm) with the prior sliding direction to the bottom-right, which was a little bit larger than the range of the unintentional displacement distance under the static scenario. This indicated that the design of target selection techniques should take more consideration of unintentional displacement in the dynamic scenario.

We performed a within-subjects analysis of variance (ANOVA) for *Users* × *Directions* × *Distances*. A main effect was found for *Users* ($F_{17,2862}$=23.006, p<0.001), *Directions* ($F_{7,2872}$=196.443, p<0.001) and *Distances* ($F_{1,2878}$=40.345, p<0.001). *Directions* × *Distances* ($F_{7,2864}$=5.006, p<0.001) was a significant interaction. Tukey's post-hoc pair-wise comparison showed that the unintentional displacement distances to the bottom, bottom-right, right and top-right directions were significantly larger than other directions for both prior sliding distances. In addition, the unintentional displacement distance of prior sliding distance 200px was significantly larger than that of prior sliding distance 100px for directions to the bottom-right, right and top-right.

Result 2: Mean Unintentional Displacement Distance over the Process of Touch

We also studied (Q3) how the unintentional displacement distance varied over the process of touch in the dynamic scenario. Since the effective touch time and unintentional displacement point number of the same (*Direction*, *Distance*) combination were different among participants and even different tasks of the same participant, we did similar preprocessing as user study 1. We calculated the mean effective touch time after the green target circle was initially reached for all tasks with the same (*Direction, Distance*) combination, and then fitted the distance curves of these tasks to one curve with the time range equal to the closed interval between 0 and the mean effective touch time. As a result, we got Figure 10, which could reflect the mean unintentional displacement distance over the process of touch in the dynamic scenario.

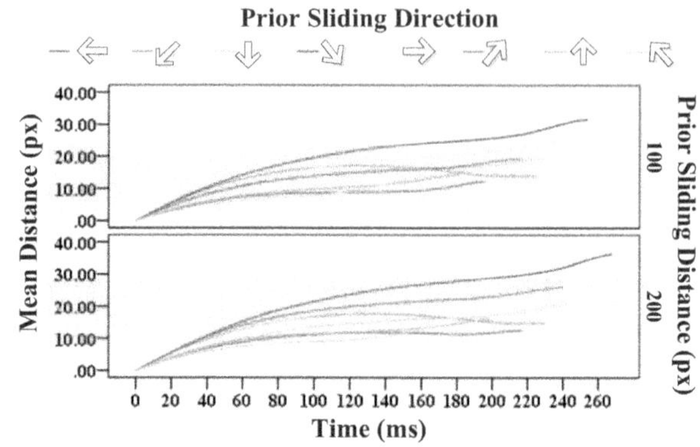

Figure 10. Mean unintentional displacement distance over the process of touch for user study 2.

Similarly, the end of each curve in Figure 10 represented the mean unintentional displacement distance at the moment of final lift-off, which coincided with the results in Figure 9. The curves of directions with a larger unintentional displacement distance at the moment of final lift-off also kept a larger unintentional displacement distance over the process of touch. The variation trend of the curves in the two sub-charts of different prior sliding distances in Figure 10 was similar. The curves were generally rising slowly as the time went on until the participants lifted their thumbs. This was understandable since the participants would perform the inertial motion for a short period of time due to the intentional prior sliding.

Result 3: Distribution of Unintentional Displacement Points around the Initial Point to the Target

We further studied (Q4) how the unintentional displacement points were distributed around the initial point to the target under the dynamic scenario. We would like to emphasize that the initial point here was not the initial contact point but the first point to the target. To unify the distribution, we relocated the coordinates of all initial points to (0, 0) and plotted the unintentional displacement points according to their relative positions to the corresponding initial points. For left-handed participants, the generated points were axisymmetric with those of right-handed participants under the same prior sliding direction and distance. So we simply performed an axial symmetrical transformation of the results

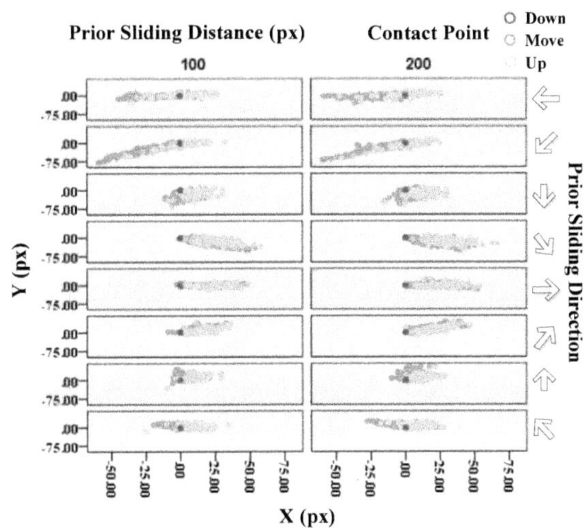

Figure 11. Distribution of unintentional displacement points for user study 2.

of left-handed participants to combine them with the results of right-handed participants.

Figure 11 shows the distribution of unintentional displacement points in the dynamic scenario, in which the blue, yellow and green dots represent the points of initially sliding to the target, final lift-off and displacement between the first two moments respectively. An intuitive conclusion was that the point distribution of each (*Direction*, *Distance*) combination was in line with the prior sliding direction, which accorded with the commonly-accepted inertia law. For left-related directions (left, top-left and bottom-left), the left and right distributions were 68.3%, 31.7% for the displacement (green) points and 23.2%, 76.8% for the lifting (yellow) points. In other words, the lifting action with the opposite direction would counteract the unintentional displacement to a certain extent, which reduced the unintentional displacement distance of the final lift-off. For other directions, especially the right-related directions, the displacement points and the lifting points were mostly distributed at the right side, which accumulated to a larger final unintentional displacement distance. This indicated that right-handed (left-handed) participants tended to lift their thumbs to the right (left) side in the dynamic scenario. It also explained why different prior sliding directions led to different unintentional displacement distances in result 1.

DISCUSSION

With a comprehensive understanding of unintentional displacement, we will next discuss how the results explain certain touch inaccuracy and indicate design of UI components, gestures, input techniques, etc.

Explain Touch Inaccuracy

Now with the results of our user studies, we can explain the inaccuracy of certain target selection techniques with unintentional displacement. Both *Offset Cursor* and *Shift* avoid finger occlusion by providing a cursor at a fixed distance above the contact point or a callout showing a copy of the occluded screen area in a non-occluded location. Even though a user presses right on the target with the help of the offset cursor or the callout, he/she may still perform unintentional displacement with a distance up to 3-4mm. Therefore, there is a high probability that the final lifting point is off the target if the target size is small. In fact, unintentional displacement may even become the bottleneck of touch-based target selection techniques. Another type of touch inaccuracy is related to gestures. We may have the experience that when we are pressing on the screen to generate certain pop-up menu, the content may scroll slightly as if we are performing a scrolling gesture. In fact, an unintentional displacement distance of 3-4mm is not a small offset on mobile devices. So it is not surprising that some gestures may be performed by mistake due to unintentional displacement.

Indicate Optimization and Design of UI Components, Gestures and Input Techniques

Our results can also contribute to the improvement of input efficiency and accuracy by providing important reference for optimization and future design of UI components, gestures, input techniques, etc.

Firstly, our results indicate the minimum size (3-4mm) of UI components to be acquired accurately with existing touch-based target selection techniques (e.g. *Offset Cursor* and *Shift*). We also indicate that for positions where the user may perform a flatter pitch angle and a larger roll angle (e.g. the top-left corner for right-handed users), the target should be designed larger. In addition, according to the point distribution of unintentional displacement and users' accustomed postures of holding the mobile phone, the target's orientation can also be considered in the design to increase the target selection accuracy, especially when the target may be acquired in the dynamic scenario. Secondly, the parameters of recognizing gestures should be carefully designed. Specifically, with our results about unintentional displacement distances and point distribution, we should design more strict approaches to distinguish different gestures and touch actions (e.g. long press and slight scrolling gesture). Thirdly, given the bottleneck of touch-based target selection techniques, we should design new approaches that bypass the bottleneck to complement the inaccuracy of touch input for target sized smaller than the range of unintentional displacement distances. In fact, some gesture-based target selection techniques are good choices, such as *Gesture Avatar* [14] and *Escape* [31].

CONCLUSION

In this paper, we studied the unintentional displacement, a novel concept concluded from the common phenomenon that there is usually an unaware screen distance between initial contact and final lift-off when users tap on touchscreen-based mobile devices with their fingers. We described its models under both static and dynamic scenarios and conducted two user studies to understand unintentional displacement for the widely-adopted one-handed thumb use on touchscreen-based mobile devices under both scenarios respectively. We provided a detailed understanding of unintentional displacement in both scenarios, which can be used to explain certain touch inaccuracy and indicate potential optimization and design of UI components, gestures as well as input techniques.

ACKNOWLEDGMENTS

This research was supported by the University Doctorial Research Foundation No. 20100002110052 and the Nokia - Tsinghua University Joint Research Funding.

REFERENCES

1. Agarwal, A. et al. High Precision Multi-Touch Sensing on Surfaces using Overhead Cameras. In *Proc. Tabletop 2007*, pp. 197-200.
2. Android SDK. http://developer.android.com/sdk.
3. Baudisch, P. et al. Starburst: a Target Expansion Algorithm for Non-Uniform Target Distributions. In *Proc. AVI 2008*, pp. 129-137.
4. FingerWorks SDK. http://fingerworks.com.
5. Forlines, C. et al. Direct-Touch vs. Mouse Input for Tabletop Displays. In *Proc. CHI 2007*, pp. 647-656.
6. Froehlich, J. et al. Pointing: Using Physical Edges to Assist Target Acquisition on Mobile Device Touch Screens. In *Proc. ASSETS 2007*, pp. 19-26.
7. Han, J. Y. Low-Cost Multi-Touch Sensing through Frustrated Total Internal Reflection. In *Proc. UIST 2005*, pp. 115-118.
8. Holz, C. and Baudisch, P. The Generalized Perceived Input Point Model and How to Double Touch Accuracy by Extracting Fingerprints. In *Proc. CHI 2010*, pp. 581-590.
9. Holz, C. and Baudisch, P. Understanding Touch. In *Proc. CHI 2011*, pp. 2501-2510.
10. Huot, S. and Lecolinet, E. Focus+Context Visualization Techniques for Displaying Large Lists with Multiple Points of Interest on Small Tactile Screens. In *Proc. Interact 2007*, pp. 219-233.
11. Karlson, A. K. and Bederson, B. B. One-Handed Touchscreen Input for Legacy Applications. In *Proc. CHI 2008*, pp. 1399-1408.
12. Karlson, A. K. and Bederson, B. B. ThumbSpace: Generalized One-Handed Input for Touchscreen-Based Mobile Devices. In *Proc. INTERACT 2007*, pp. 324-338.
13. Karlson, A. K. and Bederson, B. B. Understanding Single-Handed Mobile Device Interaction. In *Proc. HCIL 2006*.
14. Lü, H. and Li, Y. Gesture Avatar: A Technique for Operating Mobile User Interfaces Using Gestures. In *Proc. CHI 2011*, pp. 207-216.
15. Malik, S. and Laszlo, J. Visual Touchpad: a Two-Handed Gestural Input Device. In *Proc. ICMI 2004*, pp. 289-296.
16. Microsoft Surface. http://www.microsoft.com/surface.
17. Parhi, P. et al. Target Size Study for One-Handed Thumb Use on Small Touchscreen Devices. In *Proc. MobileHCI 2006*, pp. 203-210.
18. Park, Y. S. et al. Touch Key Design for Target Selection on a Mobile Phone. In *Proc. MobileHCI 2008*, pp. 423-426.
19. Perry, K. B. and Hourcade, J. P. Evaluating One Handed Thumb Tapping on Mobile Touchscreen Devices. In *Proc. GI 2008*, pp. 57-64.
20. Potter, R. et al. Improving the Accuracy of Touchscreens: An Experimental Evaluation of Three Strategies. In *Proc. CHI 1988*, pp. 27-32.
21. Roudaut, A. et al. TapTap and MagStick: Improving One-Handed Target Acquisition on Small Touch-Screens. In *Proc. AVI 2008*, pp. 146-153.
22. Roudaut, A. et al. MicroRolls: Expending Touch-Screen Input Vocabulary by Distinguishing Rolls vs. Slides of the thumb. In *Proc. CHI 2009*, pp. 927-936.
23. Sears, A. and Shneiderman, B. High Precision Touchscreens: Design Strategies and Comparisons with a Mouse. *Int. J. Man-Mach. Stud.* 34(4): 593-613. 1991.
24. Smart Tables, SmartTech. http://www.smarttech.com.
25. Vogel, D. and Baudisch, P. Shift: A Technique for Operating Pen-Based Interfaces Using Touch. In *Proc. CHI 2007*, pp. 657-666.
26. Wang, F. et al. Detecting and Leveraging Finger Orientation for Interaction with Direct-Touch Surfaces. In *Proc. UIST 2009*, pp. 23-32.
27. Wang, F. and Ren, X. Empirical Evaluation for Finger Input Properties in Multi-Touch Interaction. In *Proc. CHI 2009*, pp. 1063-1072.
28. Wellner, P. Interacting with Paper on the DigitalDesk. In *Commun. ACM 36, 7(Jul. 1993)*. pp. 87-96.
29. Wigdor, D. et al. LucidTouch: A See-Through Mobile Device. In *Proc. UIST 2007*, pp. 269-278.
30. Wilson, A. D. PlayAnywhere: A Compact Interactive Tabletop Projection-Vision System. In *Proc. UIST 2005*, pp. 83-92.
31. Yatani, K. et al. Escape: A Target Selection Technique Using Visually-cued Gestures. In *Proc. CHI 2008*, pp. 285-294.

PinyinPie: A Pie Menu Augmented Soft Keyboard for Chinese Pinyin Input Methods

Ying Liu[1], Xiantao Chen[1], Lingzhi Wang[1], Hequan Zhang[2], Shen Li[3]

[1]Nokia Research Center Beijing
No. 5 Donghuan Zhonglu, BDA
Area, Beijing 100176, China

[2]China Mobile Research Center
No. 53, Xi Bian Men Nei Da
Jie, Beijing 100053, China

[3]Academy of Art & Design
Tsinghua University
Beijing 100084, China

Ying.y.liu, ext-xiantao.chen, ext-lingzhi.2.wang@nokia.com;
zhanghequan@chinamobile.com;shen.li@me.com

ABSTRACT

Soft keyboard for Chinese pinyin input methods are rarely studied although it is one of the default methods on devices with touch screens. Via an analysis of the digraph frequency of the pinyin system, we discovered a unique characteristic of the pinyin system: only 10 Roman letters are needed for the subsequent characters in a pinyin syllable after the leading letter. Making use of this feature and existing knowledge on layout optimization of soft keyboard, pie menu and ShapeWriter, we designed a pie menu augmented keyboard. We conducted a user study to compare user performance to test if the pie menu can help to increase user performance with a working prototype. We found that after about 2 hours' use of the pie menu augmented quasi-QWERTY keyboard, users can reach a speed of 25 Chinese characters per minute with slightly lower error rate. Moreover, users can well remember the layout of the pie menu after about two hours' use of it.

Author Keywords

Chinese; text input; soft keyboard; pie menu; pinyin.

ACM Classification Keywords

H.5.m [Information Interfaces and Presentation]: Miscellaneous.

INTRODUCTION

Mobile phones and tablet computers that incorporate capacitive touch screens are becoming popular among users. Entering texts is one of the key challenges of using such devices, which is also the case for Chinese users. Chinese text entry methods on such devices are of critical importance considering the large number of Chinese speakers worldwide. There are generally two types of Chinese text entry methods available on devices with touch screens: pinyin soft keyboard methods and Chinese handwriting recognition methods.

MobileHCI'12, September 21–24, 2012, San Francisco, CA, USA.

The pinyin system was proposed by Zhou et al in 1950s based on Mandarin (aka Northern China) pronunciations of the Chinese language [31]. It is now the standard Romanization system for Chinese characters. Pinyin-based keyboards are the most often used methods with both computers and mobile phones by hundreds of millions of users in mainland China [13, 14]. However, academic studies of pinyin soft keyboard designs are rare despite its huge amount of users and broad explorations done on keyboard layout for English input. Although it is understood that any new keyboard layout need to overcome significant learning cost, various explorations on optimizing user performance with soft keyboard have been done for English [2, 15, 16, 24, 25, 26, 27, 28, 29, 30] based on the assumption that once learned, the optimized layouts would pay off in greater efficiency in the long run. Different approaches have been applied to seek optimal layout for soft keyboard.

A pinyin syllable corresponds to a Chinese character, including minimally 1 pinyin letter (e.g. "*a*" for 阿) and maximally 6 Roman letters (e.g. "*shuang*" for 双). There are a total of 418 pinyin syllables in the pinyin system [14]. In our study, we discovered a surprising pinyin phenomenon: while 23 of the 26 Roman letters can appear as the leading character of a pinyin syllable, only 10 Roman letters (*"e, r, u, i, o, a, g, h, v, n"*) can appear as subsequent characters in a pinyin syllable. This is the case for all 418 syllables in the pinyin system.

We designed a pie-menu augmented soft keyboard for Chinese pinyin input based on the unique feature of the pinyin system, and existing knowledge on layout optimization of soft keyboard, pie menu and ShapeWriter. An 8-cell pie menu accommodating the 10 Roman letters for all other characters except the leading character in pinyin syllables were integrated on top of a quasi-QWERTY keyboard. Once users click the leading character on the quasi-QWERTY keyboard, the pie menu will pop up and users can draw a multi-stroke gesture to enter the subsequent characters to complete a pinyin syllable. Advanced features like phrasal input were also supported in the design. We built a prototype on a mobile device and conducted a user study to compare its user performance with the keyboard without the pie menu.

The user study results show both positive and negative areas of the pie menu augmented keyboard design. After two hours' use of the pie augmented keyboard, users can reach a speed of 25 Chinese characters per minute. However, the speeds are still a few characters slower than those with the keyboard without a pie menu although participants can well remember the layout of the pie menu after using the pie menu for about two hours. We discussed the user study results with our assumptions and identified the areas for future work.

The rest of the paper is organized as follows. First, we review relevant works. Second, we present the unique feature of the pinyin system and design of the pie menu augmented soft keyboard for pinyin methods. Third, we present the user study and results. Finally, we discuss the results and identify the future working areas.

RELATED WORKS

The Pinyin System and Related Works

A pinyin syllable usually consists of a consonant and a vowel, with the exception of a few syllables that consist of vowels alone [12, 13, 14, 31]. Table 1 shows the 23 consonants and the 33 vowels.

23 consonants	b p m f d t n l g k h j q x zh ch sh r z c s y w
33 vowels	a e i o u v(ü) ai an ao ei en er ia ie in iu ou ua ue ui un uo ang eng ian iao ing ong uai uan iang iong uang

Table 1. The consonants and vowels in the pinyin system

Entering Chinese characters with a QWERTY keyboard requires two steps. First, users type in the pinyin syllable. Second, the system provides a list of matching Chinese characters sharing the same pinyin syllable and users select the target character. Wang, Zhai, and Su conducted an anatomical study of a QWERTY-based pinyin method and found that the selection process takes 52% of the total time when users enter texts with a desktop keyboard in a PC character by character [22]. Liu and Räihä found that with the T9 pinyin method for the 12-key keypad, selecting the target Chinese character takes more than 65% of the whole input time with a predictive user model [14]. Thus both sub-processes, which are the entry of pinyin syllables and the selection of target character from a list of options, are important for improvement of user performance when users enter Chinese texts character by character with pinyin methods.

Some advanced features are essential and normally integrated in pinyin input methods, for example, predictive input and phrasal input. After users enter a Chinese character, system would provide predictions for the next character and users can select the target character from it without entering its pinyin syllable. Phrasal input enables users to enter a phrase including more than one character at a time by typing the pinyin syllables of associated characters. Entering pinyin syllables of a phrase would decrease the number of matching options for Chinese characters.

Studies on pinyin input methods with soft keyboards is rare. Liu et al. conducted a user study to understand performance of novice users with a QWERTY soft keyboard and a consonant plus vowel keyboard designed for pinyin methods when users used a stylus to interact with both keyboards [12]. In the study, they reported user speeds of 14.32 and 9.66 Chinese characters per minute with respective QWERTY keyboard and the consonant plus vowel keyboard. Error rates reported were quite low as about 5%. Other that the study mentioned above, we did not find any other studies on soft keyboard of pinyin methods.

Pie (Marking) Menu

Pie menu is a menu format that all menu items are laid around a central point (see Figure 1) [3]. In the few years after pie menu was studied by Callahan et al., pie menu had been heavily studied in HCI field due to its potential to increase user performance on menu selection tasks [3, 5, 7, 8, 9, 10, 20, 21, 23]. Since movement distance to reach a menu item is decreased and the width of a menu item is comparatively enlarged with a pie menu, user performance with it is supposed to be better than pull down menus according to Fitts' law [16, 17, 19]. Marking menu is another name for pie menu. Marking menu enables users to quickly choose an item from a pie menu via a stroke gesture before shown of all menu items. It was believed that marking menus can assist users to transfer from a novice to an expert of pie menus [8, 9].

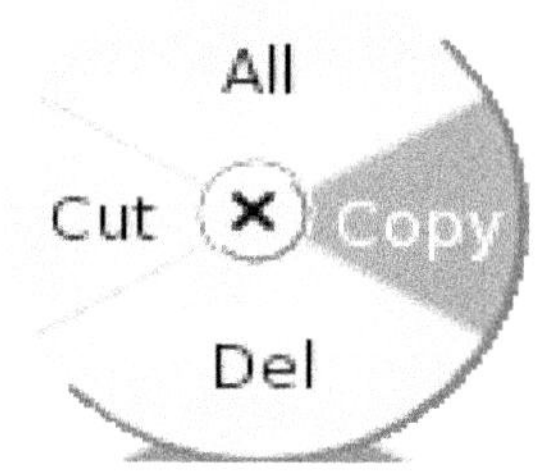

Figure 1. A pie menu

There are challenges to apply a pie menu in user interface design. First, the round shape does not take a full advantage of display spaces, for example, the mismatch between the two-dimensional texts for labeling menu items and the wedge shape for a menu item often requires a bigger space than normal pull down menus. To avoid such limitations of pie menus, some researchers removed the menu edges [19]. Second, a pie menu cannot accommodate too many items. It was suggested that even numbers of menu items including 4 to 8 items would be better for a pie menu. And a pie menu can maximally include 12 menu items [19]. Some new forms of menus are also designed to expand the number of menu items a pie like menu can accommodate [1, 5]. Third, how pie menus could support two or more hierarchies of menu items and how feedbacks can be designed for pie menus are also challenging [8].

Pie menu has also been studied with different pointing devices including stylus and mouse. Clicks and stroke gestures (from the central point to the target menu item) are two common ways to interact with pie menus. New interaction methods had also been proposed by different researchers. For example, Guimbretiere and Winograd proposed the Flowmenu applying the stroke gesture from Quickwriting (starting from the central point and ending at the central point too) on a pie menu to enable users to access deeper hierarchies of menu items [5, 18]. Pie menu or marking menu were recognized as a good form for contextual menus and was widely applied or studied within many different applications. Pie menu has been implemented in multimedia content editing applications (e.g. [5]), for text entry purposes (e.g. [6]), together with gesture interactions (e.g. [23]). A recent study by Kin, Hartmann and Agrawala also reported their observations on user performance while marking menu was applied on small touch devices [7].

Perhaps the most relevant past works to the current study were the following. Isokoski (2004) proposed a pie menu augmented soft keyboard [6]. In his proposal, an 8-cell pie menu was integrated with a QWERTY keyboard to enhance user performance of text entry. Users can quickly draw a stroke with the pie menu to enter the next possible letter after clicking a key in the QWERTY keyboard. Venolia and Neiberg proposed a design combining an 8-cell pie menu with stroke gestures and enabled users to enter texts, alphabets and symbols [18].

Layout Optimization and ShapeWriter-like Gesture

Soft keyboard is easy to change. Thus many explorations on how to improve user performance with soft keyboards have been conducted. Decreasing motor movements is the most common approach to optimize soft keyboard layouts. For example, MacKenzie, Zhang and Soukoreff proposed two new layouts of OPTI I and OPTI II, minimizing the overall motor movement distance according to Fitts' law and the relative frequency of bigrams [15, 16, 17]. The Metropolis algorithms were also applied to propose optimized soft keyboard layouts and quasi-QWERTY layouts [2, 27].

Another key inspiration to our work is ShapeWriter, which was proposed by Zhai and Kristensson in 2003 [28, 29]. With ShapeWriter, users can draw a multi-stroke gesture on a soft keyboard along the alphabets of an English word or a short hand stroke with similar shape to enter the word [4, 28, 29]. We call such a gesture on soft keyboard a "ShapeWriter-like" gesture, or simply gesture, in the rest of the paper. Moreover, ShapeWriter enables users to transfer from novice users who draw the stroke across all alphabets of a word to expert users who draw short hand stroke for the word [4, 28, 29]. In this paper, we propose to combine pie menu with the ShapeWriter-like gestures within the pie menu to enable users to complete pinyin syllables more efficiently. However, short hand gestures are not supported in our implementation for the pie menu augmented pinyin soft keyboard.

THE DESIGN

A Unique Feature of the Pinyin System

The pinyin coding system is a man-made system. Via an analysis of the digraph frequency for the pinyin system based on a Chinese short message corpus[1], we discovered a unique characteristic of the pinyin system: 23 of the 26 letters from "*a*" to "*z*" can be the leading letter for all pinyin syllables in the pinyin system ("*a*" to "*z*" excluding "*i*", "*u*" and "*v*"), but only 10 letters are needed for subsequent characters except the leading one in pinyin syllables.

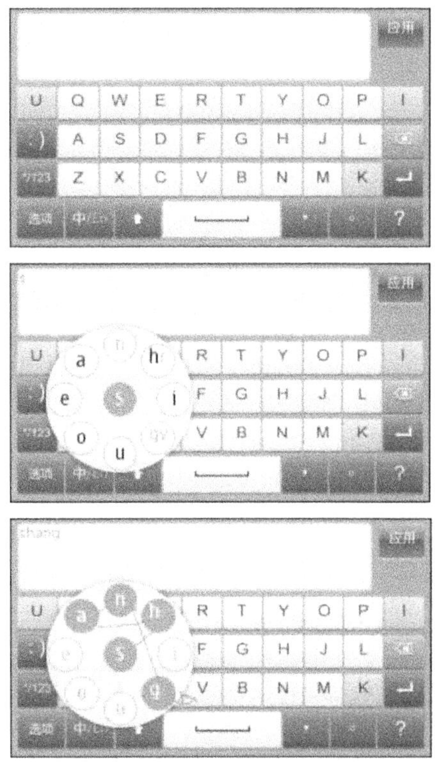

a) The underlying quasi-QWERTY keyboard: three keys were moved ("*u*", "*i*" and "*k*")

b) A click on "s" pops up the pie menu accommodating the 10 letters for subsequent characters

c) Users draw a multi-stroke gesture on the pie menu along "h-a-n-g" to enter "shang"

Figure 2. Screen shots of the pie soft keyboard for Chinese pinyin method: quasi-QWERTY keyboard and the pie menu with a fixed layout covering 10 letters

For comparison, language like English does not have such a feature according to analysis by Soukoreff and MacKenzie on digraph frequency for English [19]. Although an alphabet may be more likely to follow some alphabets and never follow some others in English, there is no clear pattern on the following relationship as in Pinyin.

[1] The corpus includes 630,000 text messages, which was mainly licensed from a third party.

First Letter	Second Letter																										
	A	B	C	D	E	F	G	H	I	J	K	L	M	N	O	P	Q	R	S	T	U	V	W	X	Y	Z	Total
A	-	-	-	-	-	-	-	-	186319	-	-	-	-	545926	414159	-	-	-	-	-	-	-	-	-	-	-	1146404
B	84842	-	-	-	17267	-	-	-	31573	-	-	-	-	-	1637	-	-	-	-	-	100583	-	-	-	-	-	235902
C	12492	-	-	-	718	-	-	67381	4717	-	-	-	-	-	2973	-	-	-	-	-	4844	-	-	-	-	-	93125
D	88800	-	-	-	117034	-	-	-	55871	-	-	-	-	-	9693	-	-	-	-	-	51122	-	-	-	-	-	322520
E	-	-	-	-	-	-	-	-	112106	-	-	-	-	207008	-	-	-	18336	-	-	-	-	-	-	-	-	337450
F	38064	-	-	-	11854	-	-	-	-	-	-	-	-	-	1388	-	-	-	-	-	9785	-	-	-	-	-	61091
G	40958	-	-	-	61700	-	-	-	-	-	-	-	-	-	15518	-	-	-	-	-	44879	-	-	-	-	-	163055
H	140063	-	-	-	145117	-	-	-	168529	-	-	-	-	-	47800	-	-	-	-	-	226875	-	-	-	-	-	728384
I	419155	-	-	-	51513	-	-	-	-	-	-	-	-	156243	1124	-	-	-	-	-	54906	-	-	-	-	-	682941
J	-	-	-	-	-	-	-	-	185336	-	-	-	-	-	-	-	-	-	-	-	16034	-	-	-	-	-	201370
K	30118	-	-	-	22539	-	-	-	-	-	-	-	-	-	4546	-	-	-	-	-	17030	-	-	-	-	-	74233
L	56750	-	-	-	11469	-	-	-	174933	-	-	-	-	-	2890	-	-	-	-	-	6860	1169	-	-	-	-	254071
M	75422	-	-	-	68171	-	-	-	27254	-	-	-	-	-	2039	-	-	-	-	-	1978	-	-	-	-	-	174864
N	50566	-	-	-	38291	-	389905		191330	-	-	-	-	-	228	-	-	-	-	-	1453	3342	-	-	-	-	675115
O	-	-	-	-	-	-	-		-	-	-	-	-	65138	-	-	-	-	-	-	107634	-	-	-	-	-	172772
P	8747	-	-	-	7791	-	-		9825	-	-	-	-	-	7842	-	-	-	-	-	757	-	-	-	-	-	34962
Q	-	-	-	-	-	-	-		61899	-	-	-	-	-	-	-	-	-	-	-	38236	-	-	-	-	-	100135
R	14257	-	-	-	24494	-	-		2661	-	-	-	-	-	2072	-	-	-	-	-	7709	-	-	-	-	-	51193
S	9945	-	-	-	885	-	-	273531	14525	-	-	-	-	-	2958	-	-	-	-	-	16753	-	-	-	-	-	318597
T	39344	-	-	-	4712	-	-		59233	-	-	-	-	-	11506	-	-	-	-	-	3825	-	-	-	-	-	118620
U	121534	-	-	-	23088	-	-		89651	-	-	-	-	17256	111198	-	-	-	-	-	-	-	-	-	-	-	362727
V	-	-	-	-	-	-	-		-	-	-	-	-	-	-	-	-	-	-	-	-	-	-	-	-	-	4511
W	40625	-	-	-	26362	-	-		-	-	-	-	-	-	213879	-	-	-	-	-	18930	-	-	-	-	-	299796
X	-	-	-	-	-	-	-		185387	-	-	-	-	-	-	-	-	-	-	-	12055	-	-	-	-	-	197442
Y	107410	-	-	-	24896	-	-		91259	-	-	-	-	-	62332	-	-	-	-	-	23007	-	-	-	-	-	308904
Z	77193	-	-	-	14182	-	-	128079	18176	-	-	-	-	-	7478	-	-	-	-	-	22484	-	-	-	-	-	267592
Total	1456285	-	-	-	672083	-	389905	468991	1670584	-	-	-	-	991571	923260	-	-	-	-	-	787739	4511	-	-	-	-	11276685

Table 2. The digraph frequency of pinyin based on a Chinese short message corpus

Concept design

The unique feature of the pinyin system seems not fully utilized in design of current pinyin input methods. The most relevant feature now available might be the predictive input. To better leverage this unique feature of the pinyin system, we proposed a pie menu augmented soft keyboard as a pinyin input method. Our goal is to improve the efficiency of entering pinyin syllables (see Figure 2).

The pie menu augmented soft keyboard includes two parts: an underlying soft keyboard covering the 26 "*a*" to "*z*" alphabets and a pop-up pie menu with 8 cells including all 10 alphabets that can appear as second or subsequent letters in a pinyin syllable. In the next section, we will explain how the layouts for both elements are specified as they are. Two types of user interactions are supported with the design solution: a multi-stroke gesture on the pie menu and key clicks on the underlying keyboard.

The interaction process with the proposed keyboard is as follows: first, users click a key on the underlying keyboard to enter the leading character of a pinyin syllable (See Figure 2a); then a pie menu pops up accommodating all ten alphabets that are needed for subsequent characters of a pinyin syllable; finally, after the popping up of the pie menu, users can move the finger from the clicked key to subsequent letters on the pie menu without lifting the finger until the target syllable is complete (See Figure 2b). Proper candidates for Chinese characters are shown after pinyin syllables are entered. When users draw gestures on the pie menu, if users touched a wrong cell to enter a wrong letter, they can draw back to the letter again (if a user's finger is already outside of this cell) or touch the key for a pre-defined timeout (if a user's finger is still in the cell) to unselect it. This way, users can correct errors while drawing a gesture. We also considered including a backspace key in the pie menu for error corrections. But since a backspace key in the pie menu may be too easy to be touched accidently by users and causes more errors, we finally give up the idea.

During the process of drawing a gesture on the pie menu, any time when users lift their fingers, the pie menu will disappear. If users don't want to draw the gestures on the pie menu, they have the flexibility to turn it off or just click the keys on the underlying keyboard by ignoring the popping up menu. Detailed layout designs for the underlying keyboard and the pie menu will be explained in the next session.

The design has the following potential benefits:

1) It can potentially improve user performance of completing a pinyin syllable by decreasing the movement distance of a hand. All needed letters for subsequent characters in pinyin syllables are covered on the pie menu and gathered around the first clicked key. Users don't need to move their finger across the whole keyboard so the overall motor movement distance may be decreased. This concept may work better on a device with large touch screens like a tablet PC. Users don't need to move their fingers or arms to enter full pinyin syllables.

2) The design can potentially enable users to transfer from novice users to experts if short-hand gestures are supported in future. The pie menu includes 8 slices. After some practice, users might be able to memorize the positions of all 10 alphabets on both cognitive and motor levels. In such

circumstances, users can draw the strokes without waiting for the appearance of the pie menu.

3) The pie menu is also a flexible user interface element that can be integrated on top of any underlying keyboards including a standard QWERTY soft keyboard or a 12-key soft keyboard. And the combination of a gesture stroke with key clicks may bring a fun experience.

Layout Design

Based on the concept, we specified the layouts for the underlying keyboard and the pie menu. For the underlying keyboard, the QWERTY layout is a natural choice since it is the most common layout for keyboards. However, with the QWERTY layout, letters such as "*q*", "*p*" and "*a*" that are close to the edges of a display. If users want to complete a pinyin syllable whose first letter is e.g. "*q*", after they click it, half of the pop-up pie menu would outreach the display and become invisible for users.

To address the challenge and keep the pie inside the display, we proposed a quasi-QWERTY layout for the underlying keyboard. In the layout, two of the three letters that never appear as the leading character in pinyin syllables, i.e. "*i*" and "*u*", were moved to the edge of the keyboard but kept in the same row as they are in the QWERTY layout. The letter "*k*" was also moved from the second row to the third row to keep the three rows of keys balanced. We moved "*k*" instead of other letters for two reasons: first, "*k*" is not the positioning letters like "*f*" and "*j*", which are used to indicating finger positions on a hard keyboard; second, "*k*" is also one of the less frequently used alphabets in the second line in pinyin system. All letters that were moved are indicated in different colors (See Figure 2a).

The design of the pie menu faced a few challenges: how to accommodate the 10 letters in a pie menu? How to define an optimal layout for the pie menu? How to decrease the impacts of the fat finger problems including the interaction accuracy and possible hide of letters from fingers?

To enable a quick learning of the layout of the pie menu by users, the layout of the pie menu should be fixed. Past studies on pie menu already indicated that a pie menu preferably include even number of cells and its maximum cell number is 12 [20]. We decided to utilize an 8-cell menu. To accommodate the 10 letters in an 8-cell pie menu, some menu cells need to cover more than one letter. We finally decided to put "*g*" and "*v*" into one cell and "*h*" and "*r*" together in another cell in the pie menu. There are two reasons behind: first, among all 10 letters, the four letter of "*g*", "*v*", "*h*" and "*r*" are comparatively less frequently used than the other 6 letters. Second, in a pinyin syllable, "*g*" and "*v*" has no overlaps on their appearing positions and "*h*" and "*r*" will not follow the same alphabets in pinyin syllables. Besides the leading position in pinyin syllables, "g" only appears at the third to sixth positions and "v" only appears as the second character in a pinyin syllable. Thus once users move their fingers to "*gv*" for the second character, the entered character should be "*v*" instead of "*g*".

To avoid possible errors for drawing the gesture stroke on the small pie menu, we calculated possible layouts for the pie menu to meet one principle: the next legal alphabets are not adjacent to the previously entered alphabet in a pinyin symbol. We didn't get a layout fully meeting the principle but we got a few layout options that only two cells adjacent to each other may appear next to each other in pinyin symbols. We decided to design the layout based on such layout options.

Another problem we try to address was the hide from fingers when draw a gesture on the pie menu. We considered the problem together with the frequencies of the 8 letter or letter pairs as shown in Table 3. We put the least used letters or pair of letters on positions that may be easy to hide by a finger. Considering Chinese users are often right handed [11], we put "*gv*" in the southeast cell of the pie menu. The final layout for the pie menu is shown in Figure 1. No matter which key is clicked in the underlying quasi-QWERTY keyboard, the layout of the popping-up pie menu keeps to be fixed as Figure 1 shows. Thus users can probably learn and memorize the layout of the pie menu and draw relevant gestures more efficiently after some use of the soft keyboard.

Alphabets	Frequency	Alphabets	Frequency
i	4203307	u	1783062
a	3224587	e	1602150
n	2289843	hr	1206050
o	1963079	gv	954998

Table 3. The frequencies of alphabet or alphabet pairs in the 8-cell pie menu

Other Features and the Implementation

Based on the layout designs, we implemented a working prototype on a Nokia N8 with an engine of the pinyin method. The user interface is developed with Qt[2] on the Symbian platform. Figure 2 and 3 show the screen shots of the prototype.

Advanced pinyin input features like the predictive input of pinyin and Chinese characters, the phrasal input including the phrasal input with either full pinyin or initial letters only are also supported (See Figure 3) so as to accommodate different user habits while using pinyin soft keyboards.

---

[2] Qt is a cross-platform application framework that is widely used for developing application software with a graphical user interface.

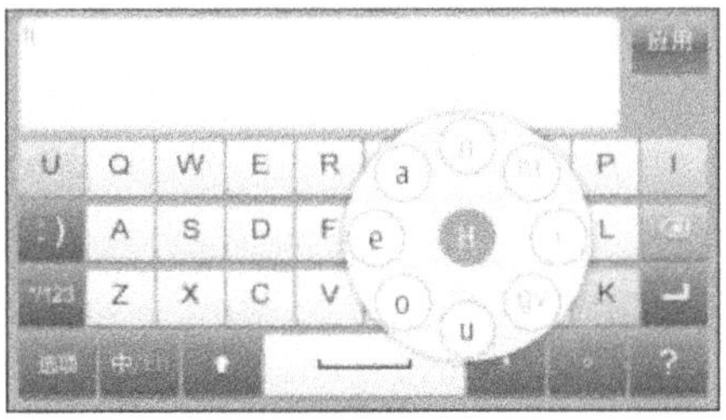

a) After "h" is clicked, legal letters that can follow it are shown in the pie menu in black. Illegal ones become dim.

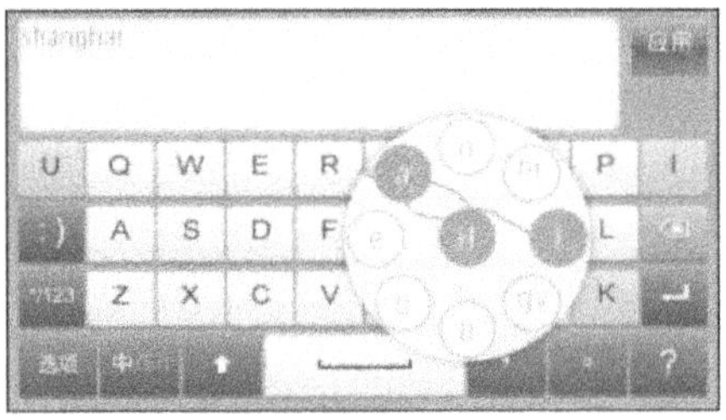

b) Phrasal input is supported: users can enter pinyin of "shang" and "hai" to enter the phrase of "上海".

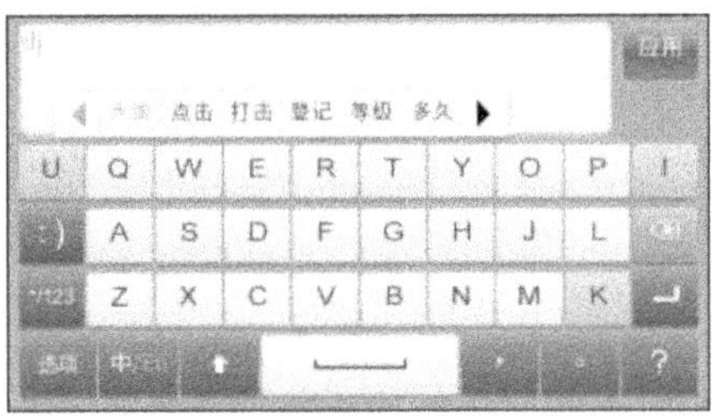

c) Users click the initial letters of two pinyin syllables to enter a phrase.

Figure 3. Screen shots of the prototype showing the predictive input and phrasal input

USER STUDY

Objectives

We conducted a user study with the working prototype to test a few key hypotheses in the design of the pie menu augmented soft keyboard. Following is a summary of the hypotheses:

1) The soft keyboard design with the pie menu may increase user performance for entering Chinese characters with pinyin methods;

2) After some period of use, we assumed that users can both explicitly and implicitly remember the layout of the pie menu.

3) With the working prototype, users can use either thumbs of both hands (See Figure 4c) or the index finger of the dominant hand (See Figure 4d) to draw the multi-stroke gestures on the pie menu. It would be valuable to learn if the design brings advantages to any of interaction methods. Before the study, our assumption is that the keyboard design with the pie menu may be favorable for the interaction with the index finger of the dominant hand than with thumbs of both hands. There are two reasons behind the assumption: on one hand, since the layout is fixed for the pie menu, when users draw gestures with both thumbs, there is a conflict about remembering a gesture path because both thumbs are respectively controlled by different sides of our brain. On the other hand, the keys on both the quasi-QWERTY keyboard and the pie menu are small, which is again favorable for index fingers that are often smaller than thumbs.

Methods

Design

The study was a within-subject design. All 12 participants used both types of keyboards (the Quasi-QWERTY keyboard with a pie menu and the Quasi-QWERTY keyboard without a pie menu) to complete text entry tasks specified in the study. Participants can choose to use either thumbs in both hands or the index finger of their dominant hand to draw gestures on the pie menu (see examples in Figure 4d). But once they chose the interaction method with the keyboards, participants were asked to keep using the same interaction method across keyboards and study sessions.

a. Using the quasi-Qwerty keyboard with both thumbs

c. Using the pie menu augmented keyboard with both thumbs

b. Using the quasi-Qwerty keyboard with the index finger of the dominant hand

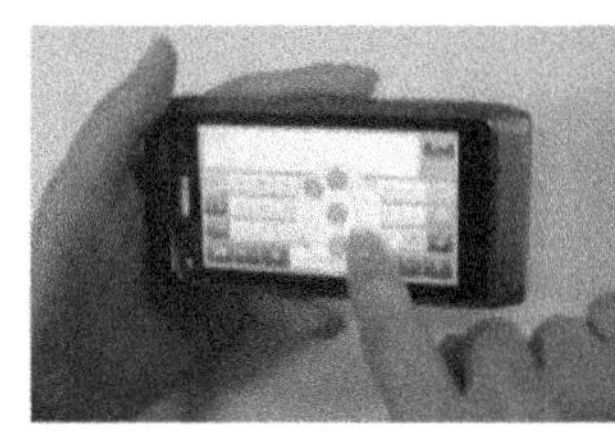

d. Using the pie menu augmented keyboard with the index finger of the dominant hand

Figure 4. Examples of using both keyboards with both thumbs and the index finger of the dominant hand

The study took about three hours for each participant. To avoid fatigue, each participant completed the study in 5 sessions with one session per day. Between any two adjacent sessions for a participant, a maximum gap would be two days. Each session included two blocks for respectively two keyboards with and without the pie menu. In each block, a participant will type texts with a specified keyboard for about 30 minutes. And in a session, a participant can take breaks as s/he wants to. The orders of methods are balanced among users. After 5 sessions, a participant has used both keyboards with and without a pie menu for two and half hours.

Participants

Twelve participants, half male and half female, volunteered to take part in the study. All are right handed. Their average age was 24.0 ($SD = 1.68$). All participants are either student interns or researchers in Nokia Research Center in Beijing. All are everyday users of the QWERTY keyboard and can blindly type texts with a hard QWERTY keyboard on PCs. All are daily users of pinyin methods on both their PCs and mobile phones.

Tasks and Materials

In this study, we instructed participants to copy texts printed on paper to mobile devices with both methods with and without the pie menu. And the advantages of such texts copy tasks had been discussed in previous publications so will not be covered here again [17]. In each session, participants were asked to enter texts as fast and accurately as they can. Time tags for key clicks, drawing gestures and UI changes e.g. pie menu popping up while user enter texts were automatically logged into a file in the mobile phone for data analysis afterwards.

Texts materials that users entered in the study were selected Chinese messages from a short message corpus. The letter level correlations of the selected messages with the Chinese short message corpus are all above .90 [17]. Table 4 shows an example of the used messages in this study.

An example of the used message	Letter level correlation [17]
老刘，很久不见了，最近忙什么呢，找个时间出来聚一下吧，明天一起去吃海底捞怎么样？	.902
Pinyin: lao liu, hen jiu bu jian le, zui jin mang shen me ne, zhao ge shi jian chu lai jv yi xia ba, ming tian yi qi qu chi hai di lao zen me yang?	
Translation: Laoliu, we haven't met each other for long! What are you busy with? When do you have time to meet me? How about meeting at the restaurant of Haidilao tomorrow?	

Table 4. An example of Chinese message used in the study

Apparatus

Nokia N8 (See Figure 4), that integrates a capacitive touch screen, was used as the test device in this study. We developed two prototypes respectively for the quasi-QWERTY keyboard with a pie menu and the quasi-QWERTY keyboard without a pie menu. The same pinyin recognition engine was utilized in both prototypes to avoid involvements of any other factors in the study. With the quasi-QWERTY keyboard without a pie menu, users just need to click the associated alphabets for pinyin syllables to enter Chinese characters. We also record the study sessions with a video camera with permissions of participants.

Procedure

The study was conducted with a participant and a coordinator in a quiet lab environment. Besides the text entry tasks, the first session include two other processes: first, the coordinator welcomed the participant and explained the study objectives to the participant; second, the coordinator asked the participants to try the pie menu augmented keyboard, observed how they interact with the new design and collected their comments. In all sessions, participants were asked to complete specified text entry tasks as quickly and accurately as they can. During a session, participants can take breaks as they want to.

After the 5th session, we conducted a memory "test" to see if participants can implicitly and explicitly memorize the layout of the pie menu. We did not tell participants about the test before so they cannot intentionally prepare for it. The memory test includes two simple tasks: first, we presented participants tens of 8-cell empty pie menus on an iPad and asked them to draw gestures for 31 Chinese characters; second, we present an empty 8-cell empty pie menu on a piece of paper and asked them to fill the alphabets or alphabet pairs based on their memory. In the end, all participants were presented with a gift.

Figure 5. The setting of the user study

Results

Text entry rates

We calculated user performance results based on the collected user data in the last sessions i.e. after about two hours' use of both methods. We use Chinese characters per minute (CCPM) to present the text entry rate results. Time for making and correcting errors were removed from the task completion time when we calculated results of text entry rate. And two punctuations were counted equaling to one Chinese character when we calculate the text entry rate. Figure 6 shows the results of text entry rate with both methods. The average text entry rates for the quasi-QWERTY keyboard only and the quasi-QWERTY keyboard with a pie menu were respectively 30.65 CCPM ($SD = 6.53$) and 24.95 CCPM ($SD = 4.11$). After using both methods for about two hours, participants achieved better speeds with the Quasi-QWERTY keyboard without the pie menu.

A paired t test on text entry rates was conducted. The analysis indicated that user speed with the quasi-QWERTY keyboard without the pie menu is significantly faster than that with the quasi-QWERTY keyboard with the pie menu after about two hour's use of both keyboards ($t = 4.23$, $p < .05$).

Error rate and error categories

We counted all errors based on the logged data and calculated the total error rate by dividing all errors by total characters. Figure 7 shows the average error rate results. The average error rates with the pie menu augmented quasi-QWERTY keyboard and the quasi-QWERTY keyboard only are respectively 6.68% (SD=0.028) and 6.82% (SD=0.025). Participants made slightly more errors with the quasi-QWERTY keyboard than that with the pie menu augmented quasi-QWERTY keyboard.

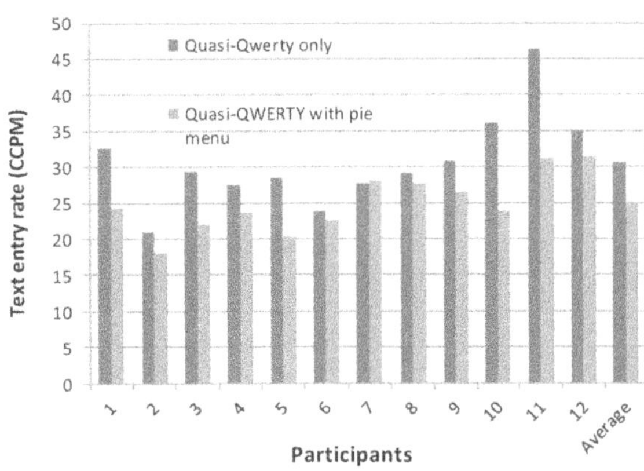

Figure 6. Text entry rates with keyboards with a pie menu and without a pie menu

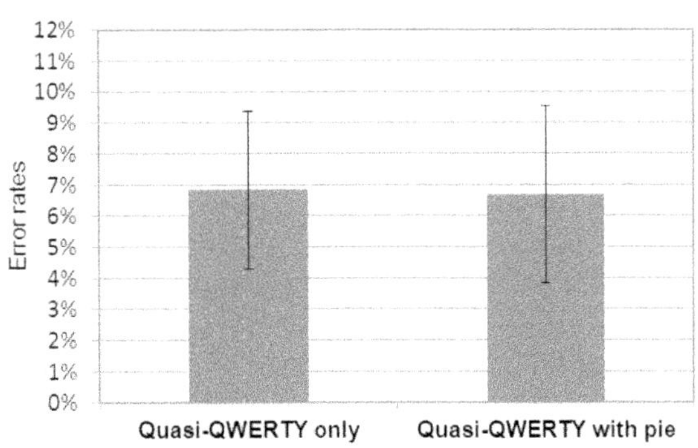

Figure 7. Average error rate results

We conducted a paired t test on the total error rate and the results indicated that there is no significant difference between the two types of keyboards on error rate ($t = .636$, ns).

We also analyzed the category of errors that participants made during the study. Two types of errors are more often to appear: touch errors and spell errors (or draw a wrong gesture on the pie menu). Touch errors are caused by participants by missing touching an intended soft key or touching a wrong key that is often physically close to the intended key. For example, participants intend to click "*n*" but miss touching it or accidently click "*m*" that is next to "*n*". A spelling error is made by participants by missing an alphabet or entering a wrong or an extra alphabet in a pinyin syllable. But those errors are not caused by wrongly touching physically close buttons. For example, users intend to type a pinyin syllable of "zhuang" but instead they enter "zhuan". We analyzed the distribution of error types with both type of keyboards and found that with only the quasi-QWERTY keyboard, participants made more touch errors and with the quasi-QWERTY keyboard with a pie menu, users made comparatively more spell errors.

Memory of the Layout of the Pie Menu

Figure 9 shows two pictures from the memory test. The left figure shows a gesture drawn by one participant on an open 8-cell pie menu. The right figure shows a filled pie menu by one participant based on his memory. Figure 10 shows the results for the memory test of the 12 participants. On average, participants can explicitly and correctly remember more than 90% of the cells in the pie menu.

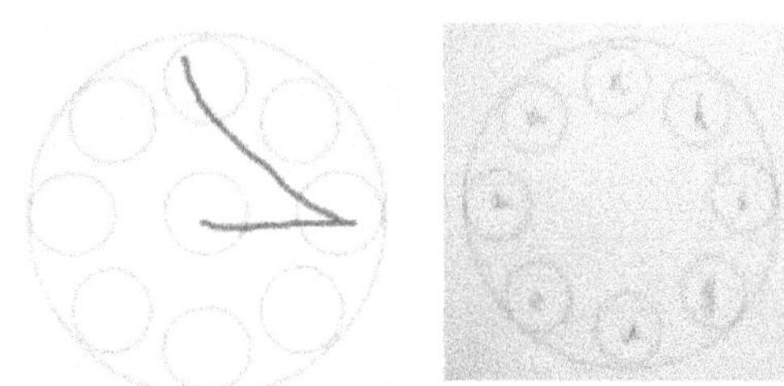

a) Gesture drawn by a participant on an empty pie menu

b) Filled empty pie menu on a piece of paper

Figure 9. Two pieces of fill pie menu by participants of the study

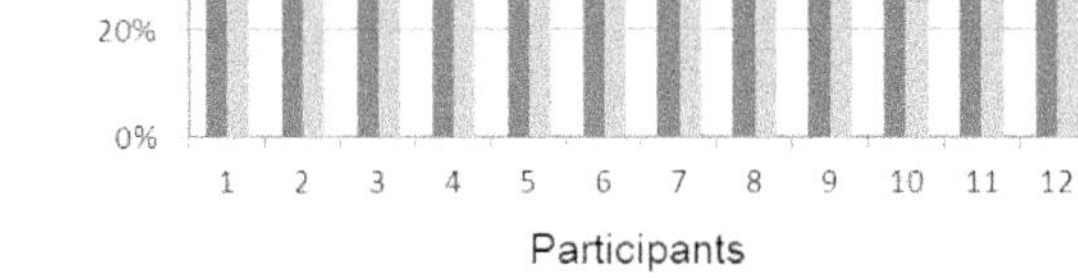

Figure 10. Results from the memory test

Effect of interaction method on user performance

Among the 12 participants, 6 participants chose to use their thumbs to interact with both keyboards while holding the phone with both hands. The other 6 participants chose to use the index finger of their dominant hand to interact with both keyboards while holding the phone in the non-dominant hand. Due to the limited samples, we conducted a non-parametric Mann-Whitney test on both text entry and error rate results. The results indicated that interaction method did not significantly affect user performance including text entry rate and error rate with both types of keyboards (see results in Table 5).

	Quasi-Qwerty without a pie menu		Quasi-Qwerty with a pie menu	
	Text entry rate	Error rate	Text entry rate	Error rate
U scores	14	14	22	10
p	.758	.758	.294	.910

Table 5. Mann-Whitney tests results on effect of interaction methods

DISCUSSIONS

The text entry rate results show that after about two hours use of the pie augmented quasi-QWERTY keyboard, user speed reached about 25 CCPM with an average total error rate of around 6.68%. When a pie menu is not there, the average user text entry rate can reach 30 CCPM with an error rate of around 6.90%. The user performance results are better than those reported in [12], in which immediate user performance with a pen and two types of pinyin soft keyboard was more focused on.

The results also indicated that the pie menu does not help to improve user speed. There might be a few reasons behind:

First, entering Chinese texts with pinyin soft keyboard includes two sub-processes: entering pinyin syllables and choosing target Chinese characters. Optimizing only one sub-process may not help to improve the overall user speed significantly. Past studies on pinyin input process indicated that the sub-process of selecting target Chinese characters take more than half of whole input time with pinyin method [14, 22]. Wang, Zhai and Su found that selecting target Chinese characters takes about 52% of the whole input time when users enter Chinese characters with a pinyin method without phrasal input using QWERTY keyboard of a PC [22]. Liu and Räihä found that with the T9 pinyin method for the 12-key keypad, selecting the target Chinese character takes more than 65% of the whole input time with a predictive user model [14]. Our exploration in this study focused on optimizing the sub-process of entering pinyin syllables. We suggest future works in the field consider optimizing both sub-processes of entering pinyin syllables and selecting target characters.

Second, via an analysis of a short message corpus, Liu and Räihä found that the average numbers of alphabets included by pinyin syllables are respectively 2.88 and 3.24 when frequencies of Chinese characters were taken into account or not [14]. Thus on average, our approach just decreased motor movement distances from the first alphabet to the second then to the third one. The decrease of motor movements may not be tremendous enough. Moreover, the interaction method in our new design changed to ShapeWriter-like gestures, which may be slower than key clicks [4].

Third, shorthand gestures were not supported in our implementation. Accurate touch of an alphabet cell was needed to enter an alphabet. The tradeoff in our design is not more prone to speed over error rate without supporting shorthand gestures although the good memory of the layout by users proved the short hand gestures are applicable.

The exploration is not so successful in terms of improving user performance. However, we hope that our work presented in this paper is able to draw more explorations in the field and serve as a useful start.

CONCLUSION

Soft keyboard for Chinese pinyin input methods are rarely studied although it is already one of the default methods on devices with touch screens. Via an analysis of the digraph frequency of the pinyin system, we discovered a unique characteristic of it: 23 Roman letters can be the leading letter in pinyin syllables but only 10 Roman letters are needed for subsequent characters of a pinyin syllable. Making use of this feature and existing knowledge on layout optimization of soft keyboard, pie menu and ShapeWriter-like gesture, we proposed a pie menu augmented keyboard. Once users click a key on a Quasi-QWERTY keyboard, an 8-cell pie menu covering the 10 alphabets would pop up and users can enter a pinyin syllable via drawing a multi-stroke gesture on the pie menu. We conducted a comparative user study on it and found after about 2 hours' use of the method, users can reach a speed of 25 Chinese characters per minute with slightly lower error rate. Although user speeds is still slower than the keyboard without a pie menu, participants can well remember the layout of the pie menu.

ACKNOWLEDGMENTS

The work presented in the paper was done during the internship of the 4th and 5th authors in Nokia Research Center in Beijing. We thank Dr. Shumin Zhai for share of his knowledge, his comments and revisions of the paper. We thank to Dr. Zhen Liu for his sponsor of the work.

REFERENCES

1. Bailly, G., Lecolinet, E., Nigay, L. Flower menus: a new type of marking menu with large meth breadth, within groups and efficient expert mode memorization. In *Proceeding of AVI 2008*, 15-22.

2. Bi, X., Smith, B.A., Zhai, S., Quasi-Qwerty soft keyboard optimization. In *Proc. of CHI 2010*, ACM Press (2010), 283-286.

3. Callahan, J., Hopkins, D., Weiser, M., Shneiderman, B., An empirical comparison of pie vs. linear menus. In *Proc. of CHI 1988*, ACM Press (1988), 95-100.

4. Castellucci, S. J., & MacKenzie, I. S. Gathering text entry metrics on Android devices. In *Extended Abstracts of CHI 2011*, ACM Press, 1507-1512.

5. Guimbretiere, F., and Winograd, T. FlowMenu: combining command, text, and data entry. In *Proceeding of UIST 2000*, ACM Press (2000), 213-216.

6. Isokoski, P. Performance of menu-augmented soft keyboards. In *Proceedings of CHI '04*, ACM Press (2004), 423–430.

7. Kin, K., Hartmann, B., and Agrawala, M., Two-handed marking menus for multitouch devices. In *ACM Transaction on Computer-Human Interaction*, 18 (3), 16.

8. Kurtenbach, G., Buxton, W., The limits of expert performance using hierarchic marking menus. In *Proc. of CHI 1993*, ACM Press (1993), 482-487.

9. Kurtenbach, G., Buxton, W., User learning and performance with marking menus. In *Proc. of CHI 1994,* ACM Press (1994), 258-264.

10. Kurtenbach, G., Fitzmaurice, G. W., Owen, R. N., Baudel, T. The hotbox: efficient access to a large number of menu-items. In *Proceeding of CHI 1999*, ACM Press (1999), 231-237.

11. Li, X.-T. The distribution of left and right handedness in Chinese people. In *Acta Psychological Sinica, 1983 (3),* 268-276.

12. Liu, Y., Ding., K., & Liu, N. Immediate user performances with touch Chinese text entry solutions on handheld devices. In *Proceedings of Mobile HCI 2009*, ACM Press (2009), 56–57.

13. Liu, Y., & Räihä, K.-J. (2008). RotaTxt: Chinese pinyin input with a rotator. In *Proceedings of International Conference on Human-Computer Interaction with Mobile Devices and Services (Mobile HCI '08)*, ACM Press, 225–233.

14. Liu, Y., & Räihä, K.-J. (2010). Predicting Chinese text entry speeds on mobile phones. In *Proc. of CHI 2010,* ACM Press,

15. MacKenzie, I. S., Zhang, S. X., & Soukoreff, R. W. (1999). Text entry using soft keyboards. *Behaviour and Information Technology*, 18, 235–244.

16. MacKenzie, I. S. and Zhang, S. X., The design and evaluation of a high-performance soft keyboard. In *Proc. of CHI 1999*, ACM Press, (1999) 25-31.

17. MacKenzie, I. S., & Soukoreff, R. W. Text entry for mobile computing: models and methods, theory and practice. *Human-Computer Interaction*, (2002), 17, 147–198.

18. Perlin, K. Quickwriting: continuous stylus-based text entry. In *Proceeding of UIST 1998*, ACM Press (1998), 215-216.

19. Soukoreff, R. W., & MacKenzie, I. S. Theoretical upper and lower bounds on typing speed using a stylus and soft keyboard. *Behaviour & Information Technology*, (1995), 14, 370-379.

20. Tapia, M. A., Kurtenbach, G. Some design refinements and principles on the appearance and behaviors of marking menu. In *Proc. of UIST 1995,* ACM Press (1995), 189-195.

21. Venolia, D., Neiberg, F., T-cube: a fast self-disclosing pen based alphabet. In *Proc. of CHI 1994*, ACM Press (1994), 265-270.

22. Wang, J., Zhai, S., & Su, H. (2001). Chinese input with keyboard and eye-tracking: an anatomical study. In *Proceedings of CHI 2001*, ACM Press (2001), 349–356.

23. Wu, M., Balakrishnan, R., Multi-finger and whole hand gestural interaction techniques for multi-user tabletop displays. In *Proceeding of UIST*, ACM Press (2003), 193-202.

24. Zhai, S., A. Sue, and J. Accot. Movement model, hits distribution and learning in virtual keyboarding. In *Proc.of CHI 2002*, ACM Press (2002), 17-24.

25. Zhai, S., B.A. Smith, and M. Hunter, Performance optimization of virtual keyboards. *Human-Computer Interaction*, 17(2&3) (2002), 229-270.

26. Zhai, S., Hunter, M., and Smith, B.A., The metropolis keyboard – an exploration of quantitative techniques for virtual keyboard design. In *Proc. of UIST 2000*, ACM Press (2000), 119-128.

27. Zhai, S., Kristensson, P.- O., Shorthand writing on stylus keyboard. In *Proc. of CHI 2003*, ACM Press (2003), 97-104.

28. Zhai, S., & Kristensson, P.-O. Introduction to Shape Writing. In: MacKenzie, I. S. & Tanaka-Ishii, K. (Eds.), *Text Entry Systems: Mobility, Accessibility, Universality*, Morgan Kaufmann (2007), 139–158.

29. Zhai, S., Kristensson, P.-O., & Smith, B. A. In search of effective text input interfaces for off the desktop computing. *Interacting with Computers*, (2005), 17, 229–250.

30. Zhai, S., Smith, B. A., & Hunter, M. Performance optimization of virtual keyboards. *Human–Computer Interaction*, (2002), 17 (2,3), 89–129.

31. Zhou, Y. Research on Chinese Pinyin. Shanghai East Bookstore (1953).

An Empirical Investigation into How Users Adapt to Mobile Phone Auto-Locks in a Multitask Setting

Duncan P. Brumby, Vahab Seyedi
UCL Interaction Centre
University College London
London WC1E 6BT UK
Brumby@cs.ucl.ac.uk, Vahab5@yahoo.co.uk

ABSTRACT

Auto-locks are a necessary feature on many modern day mobile devices, but can they sometimes have detrimental consequences? In this paper we investigate how auto-locks can affect behavior in a demanding multitasking scenario. A study is conducted in which participants had to enter text using a touch-screen interface while driving a simulated vehicle in a lab setting. Different auto-lock mechanisms were implemented on the secondary device, manipulating both the duration of the lockout threshold (i.e., the period of inactivity before the auto-lock was initiated) and the complexity of the unlock procedure (i.e., how easy it was for the user to unlock the device once it had locked). Results showed that lane-keeping performance on the primary driving task was worse when there was a shorter lockout threshold. The reason for this was two-fold: (1) participants took fewer long pauses between typing actions, so as to avoid being locked out of the device, and (2) when the device did lock, unlocking it took time and further distracted the driver. In support of this latter finding, we also found that a more complex unlock procedure, which required a pin code to be entered, resulted in worse lane-keeping performance than when the device could be unlocked by making a simple button press. These findings suggest that auto-locks can dissuade users from regularly interleaving attention between other ongoing activities. Designers should keep this in mind when incorporating auto-locks in mobile devices.

Author Keywords

Multitasking, mobile phone use, driving, driver distraction.

ACM Classification Keywords

H.1.2 User/Machine Systems: human factors; H.5.2 User Interfaces: evaluation/methodology, interaction styles; H.5.m. Information interfaces and presentation (e.g., HCI): Miscellaneous.

MobileHCI'12, September 21–24, 2012, San Francisco, CA, USA.
Copyright 2012 ACM 978-1-4503-1105-2/12/09...$10.00.

INTRODUCTION

Consider for a moment a user composing a text message while walking down a busy street. In a mobile context like this one, our interactions with technology are often fragmented [18,21,22], meaning that tasks are often completed in small bursts of activity, lasting only a few seconds each, before attention is directed elsewhere. For our user this might mean that they have to momentarily suspend their interactions with the phone partway through composing their text message in order to focus on what is going on around them. After a short pause, the user might continue interacting with their phone. However, there is a problem with this vision of mobile use. Should the user wait too long before resuming their interactions they will typically find themselves locked out of their phone. While auto-locks are a critical feature of current generation smartphones, we wonder what impact they might have on how users choose to interact with their device in a demanding multitasking environment. In particular, whether auto-locks might sometimes put pressure on the user to return their attention to their phone sooner than they might normally have done in order to avoid being locked out.

The auto-lock mechanism is a vital feature of current generation smartphones. It extends the battery life of the phone by having the phone's display enter a sleep mode when it is not needed. Auto-locks are usually time-based, such that they are initiated after a specified period has passed in which there has not been any input from the user. For instance, on the Android operating system the default option is for the auto-lock to be initiated after one minute of inactivity, though the user may choose to set lockout threshold as short as 15-seconds should they wish.

To unlock the phone there are a variety of common methods. In the simplest case, the user simply swipes their finger from one area of the screen to another to unlock it. However, many users choose to enable stronger security features, which require a password or pin to be entered to unlock the phone. This makes sense. Mobile devices are valuable and often contain personal data. Karlson, Bush and Schechter [16] have shown that people are often unwilling to share their phone with other people who they know because of concerns that their personal data might be accessed. Given these concerns it is therefore of little surprise that many users choose to enable security features that are designed to make it difficult for unauthorized users to access their phone should it be misplaced or stolen. Moreover, there is external pressure to enable such security features, particularly in the form of security policies that employers often want their employees to adhere to [1,3].

So while the auto-lock seems like an important and necessary feature of current generation smartphones, they can sometimes be frustrating to deal with. Given the fragmented nature of mobile interactions [18], where tasks are started, interrupted, and then later returned to partway through, it seems inevitable that many users will have had the experience of their phone locking on them while they were busy attending to something else. In these situations unlocking the phone can be a nuisance, since it takes time to deal with and sidetracks the user from their primary task. We wonder whether users might therefore sometimes feel pressure to return their attention to their phone sooner than they might normally have done in order to avoid the auto-lock.

In this paper, we examine the impact that the auto-lock feature can have on how users choose to interact with a mobile device in a demanding multitasking environment. The multitasking scenario that we focus on here is that of a user interacting with a device while driving. We choose to focus on this scenario given reports that some people choose to interact with their mobile phone while driving, for instance, updating their Twitter feed from behind the wheel [7]. This is clearly a dangerous and reckless activity to perform and one that we would not condone. Research has consistently demonstrated that performing a secondary task while driving impairs performance and increases the likelihood of a collision (e.g., [2,4,8,12,13,14,15,19,23]). For example, Horrey and Wickens [12] review a large number of studies demonstrating the negative effects that mobile phone use can have on driving performance.

Despite the abundance of research demonstrating the dangers of using a phone while driving, some people persist. The reason for this might in part be because many of us have come to rely on our smartphone to support our daily activities, such as navigating to a novel destination or sending an urgent message to a colleague. As a result some people possibly choose to remain switched on while on the road and are then tempted to interact with their phone (or other in-car technology) while driving. While we do not endorse this behavior, we do wonder whether the auto-lock features used in many modern day smartphones might exacerbate this already dangerous situation by putting pressure on the user to keep their attention on the phone rather than the road ahead.

To tackle this question we choose to focus on a text entry task performed while driving. A number of recent studies have demonstrated that texting while driving is distracting and can have a negative impact on driving performance [8,14,19]. However, to the best of our knowledge no research has yet considered the potential impact that having an auto-lock mechanism might have on how drivers choose to interleave attention between texting and driving. Text entry is interesting because it is a task that can be easily suspended partway through and returned to later. In this way it seems likely that this activity could be susceptible to the timeout characteristics of an auto-lock. To investigate this question we designed a study that varied the way that the auto-lock mechanism is setup to see what kind of impact this has on driving performance.

The contribution that this paper seeks to make to mobile HCI is an empirical one. We report the results from a study in which participants had to enter text on a touch-screen while driving a simulated vehicle. We considered several different auto-lock settings in our study. In particular, we varied the lockout threshold, such that the phone locked either after a very brief 5-second period of inactivity or after a longer 15-second period of inactivity. We also considered two different forms of unlock mechanisms: an easy method that simply required the user to press a button on the screen to unlock the device, and a more complex method that required the user to first recall and then enter a pin code. What effect might these various auto-lock settings have on the user's behavior and on their driving performance?

In order to enter text while driving, participants in our study would need to make decisions about how to interleave their attention between the two tasks [4]. Driving is a dynamic task that requires frequent glances of attention from the user, without which driving performance declines rapidly [21,24]. In contrast, a text entry task can normally be completed in a more discretionary fashion at the user's own pace. For instance, the user might choose to enter a single character, and then pause before entering another character. With the introduction of an auto-lock mechanism, a time pressure is introduced to return to the text entry task before it locks. The reason for this pressure is that unlocking the device incurs additional time costs to the user. We know that users often work to minimize the time costs associated with interactions [9,10]. So given that locks are costly to open, we might therefore expect users to avoid them if they can. It follows that when there is a shorter lockout threshold, users will choose to return their attention to the phone sooner than they might normally do in order to stop it from locking. Presumably any effect here would also be sensitive to the complexity of the unlock procedure; in that, users might be even more motivated to avoid being locked out if they have to go through a long and complex unlock procedure. Such decisions, if made, would presumably have severe consequences for the primary driving task in terms of a decline in lane-keeping performance. We address this below.

Figure 1. Screen shots showing the secondary text entry interface and driving simulator environment.

METHOD

Participants

Fourteen participants (6 female) took part in the study. Participants were aged between 22- and 36-years. All had a valid driver's license and at least two years of driving experience. All participants were highly proficient at reading and speaking in English (i.e., to the standard set by the university's admissions criteria), and regularly sent and received text messages using their mobile phone. The study took about 60 minutes to complete and participants were paid £4 ($6) for their time.

Materials

In the study participants had to enter text using a touch-screen interface while steering a simulated vehicle. The driving simulation environment was displayed on a 30-inch monitor and was controlled by a Logitech G25 Racing Wheel. The secondary task was presented on a 7-inch touch-screen display. Figure 1 shows screen shots of the text entry interface and the driving simulator environment.

The driving task required participants to steer a simulated vehicle along a three-lane highway environment. The participant was only required to steer the vehicle and maintain a central lane position. The driving simulator added noise to the vehicle dynamics causing it to gradually drift about in the lane. This meant that the participant had to actively control and monitor the vehicle's lateral position and heading to maintain a central lane position. To reinforce safe lane keeping, safety cones were placed at either side of the driver's central lane. A lead vehicle was placed at a fixed distance in front of the participant's vehicle. This driving set-up is similar to that used in a number of other studies [5,6,15,17,20].

The driving environment was made up of alternating sections of curved and straight road (see Fig. 2). The vehicle's speed was held at a constant 60 mph (97 km/h). This meant that the driver alternated between each section of road at a constant rate: 9-seconds of driving around the curved section of road followed by 5-seconds of driving along a straight section of road. The motivation for having these alternating sections of road was to create distinct periods of high and of low driving demand so as to consider whether this had any effect on when participants choose to engage in the secondary text entry task. Previous research has shown that participants tend to pause secondary task interactions while navigating a corner section of road [17]. We therefore wanted to see whether participants would suspend typing while navigating the curved sections of road.

The secondary task required participants to copy and enter a target word using a touch-screen interface. Figure 1 shows the interface that was used for this task. On a given trial, participants were 'notified' of a new target word by a short auditory alert. The to-be-entered target word was then displayed in the 'target text' area on the display. The participant was to enter the target word into the 'entered text' area using the virtual keyboard. Target words were

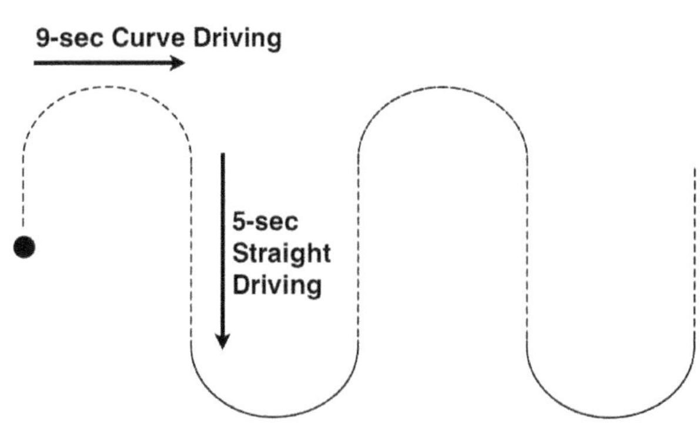

Figure 2. Schematic representation of the layout of the driving simulator test track. The vehicle's speed was held at a constant 60 mph (97 km/h). This meant that the driver alternated between each section of road at a constant rate.

natural category labels, such as 'airplane', 'apartment', and 'bluebird'. These category labels were taken from [11], originally reported in [25]. We choose to use these category labels as they represented common English words. All words were between 7 and 9 characters.

Once the target word for a given trial was entered, the participant had to press the 'send' button on the display (see Fig. 1). If there were any text entry errors (i.e., the text in the 'entered text' area did not match the text in the 'target text' area), then an error message was displayed notifying the participant that they had to correct the error (by pressing the 'Del' button) and re-enter the target word correctly. Once entered correctly, all content information was removed from the display and it was reset for the next trial.

The secondary task interface implemented an auto-lock system. The general idea was to mimic the way that many smartphones lock after a period of inactivity. To implement this functionality, the text interface would lock if participants paused for too long while entering the target word. The system logged the time period between consecutive keypresses, and would lock after either a short 5-second period of inactivity or a longer 15-sec period of inactivity. When in the locked mode, the 'send' button was greyed out and all input to the keyboard was ignored, except for the '.?123' button.

Two unlock procedures were implemented, one easy and one more complex. The easy unlock procedure required the participant to simply press the 'unlock' button on the interface. We refer to this as the 'press-to-unlock' method. The more complex unlock procedure required the participant to press the '.?123' button. This changed the virtual alphabetical keyboard to a numerical keyboard. Participants then entered a 4-digit pin. After entering the pin, participants had to press the 'unlock' button. We refer to this as the 'enter-pin-to-unlock' method. Regardless of the unlock procedure, once unlocked the interface returned to its pre-locked state and the participants was free to continue entering the target word.

Design

The purpose of the study was to investigate whether features of the auto-lock mechanism would affect multitasking behavior and performance. To address this question, the study used a 2x2 within-subjects design in which we varied the lockout-threshold (5-seconds vs. 15-seconds) as well as the complexity of the unlock procedure (press-to-unlock vs. enter-pin-to-unlock).

We consider a number of measures to gain a detailed understanding of how the different lockout conditions affected performance and participants' multitasking strategy. The main dependent variables of interest were:

1. Proportion of dual-task trials in which the lockout mechanism was activated. This gives us a sense of how often participants were letting the secondary task device lock.
2. Lane-keeping performance: The driving simulator logged the lateral distance of the vehicle from center of the lane at a rate of 200 Hz. We consider the variability (standard deviation) of these lateral deviation samples for a given trial to determine how well the participant was able to maintain a stable lane position. We also consider the root mean square error (RMSE) of these lateral deviation samples to get an idea of how far the vehicle was from the center of the lane. We found that these two performance measures were highly correlated with each other.
3. Task time: The time taken to correctly enter the target text in dual-task trials.
4. Inter-Action-Interval: The time between consecutive keypress actions made for the secondary text entry task. This gives us a sense of how participants were choosing to interact with the secondary task while driving.
5. Proportion of secondary task interactions that occurred while the vehicle was in the curved section of the road. Driving around a bend in the road requires constant visual feedback [24], and we were interested to know whether participants would continue to enter text during these periods of heavy demand from the primary driving task.

Procedure

Participants were informed that they would be required to enter text using a touch-screen device while steering a simulated vehicle. The experimenter explained the general setup and showed the participant how to use the steering wheel and secondary task interface. Once familiar with the equipment, participants completed a series of practice trials before completing the main experimental trials. The whole experiment took about an hour to complete, after which participants were debriefed and paid £4 ($6) for their time.

The experiment was separated into four distinct stages. We explain each in turn:

1. Single-task driving practice trials

Participants completed two single-task driving practice trials. For each of these practice trials, participants drove for a period of 30-seconds along the simulated highway environment described above (see Fig. 2). Participants were instructed to keep the vehicle as close to the center of the lane as possible throughout. This practice period gave the participant ample opportunity to familiarize themselves with the driving simulator and the way that the vehicle handled, particularly around the curved sections of road. At the end of every 30-second trial, participants received feedback on their lane-keeping performance (as RMSE lateral deviation). Participants were instructed to minimize this value (i.e., this gave the participant a clear understanding of what 'good' driving performance represented within the context of our lab study).

2. Single-task text entry practice trials

Participants completed five single-task text entry practice trials. For each of these practice trials, participants were instructed to type a target word into the entry text area on the secondary task interface using the virtual touch-screen keyboard. Participants were asked to enter the word as quickly as possible. Participants were informed that they should press the 'send' button, once they had entered the target word into the entry text area. Participants were told that they could press the 'Del' key to delete the previously entered character from the text entry area of the display to correct any typing errors that were made. During these single-task practice trials, the auto-lock mechanism was disabled.

3. Dual-task practice trials

Participants completed eight practice dual-task trials (two trials for each of the four experimental conditions). Before completing the dual-task practice trials, participants were told about the auto-lock mechanism and the different ways in which it could operate. The operation of each of the different conditions was explained to the participant in detail, that is, the duration of time before which the lockout would become activated would be either 5-seconds or 15-seconds, and that to unlock the device they would either need to press the 'unlock' button or enter a pin number followed by the 'unlock' button. Participants were told the pin number and given ample time to memorize it.

Once familiar with the auto-lock system, participants completed four dual-task practice trials. For each of these practice trials, participants were instructed to enter the target word while driving. Participants drove the vehicle as in the single-task driving trials (see Fig. 2). After a short period of time, participants were alerted to the need to complete the secondary text entry task by a brief audio alert. The trial ended once the target text had been correctly entered and the 'send' button pressed. Participants were told that they were to prioritize the steering task at all times and keep the vehicle as close to the lane center as possible while still completing the secondary text entry task. To reinforce this safety-orientated instruction, participants received feedback about the vehicle's RMSE lateral deviation at the end of every trial and told to minimize this value. Again, the intention of providing this feedback was to give participants a clear understanding of what 'good' driving performance represented within the context of the study.

4. Main experimental dual-task trials

In the main part of the experiment, participants completed four blocks of 10 experimental trials (one block for each of the experimental conditions). The experimental dual-task trials followed the same procedure as that used for the dual-task practice trials (described above). The order in which each condition was experienced was counter-balanced across participants. Participants received a short 30-second break in between each block of trials.

RESULTS

In this section we report on a number of measures to gain a detailed understanding how the different conditions affected performance and participants' multitasking strategy. For statistical analysis we use a 2x2 (lockout-threshold x unlock-procedure) repeated measures analysis of variance (ANOVA). Effects were judged significant if they reached a .05 significance level.

Outlier removal

We noticed that on some very rare occasions participants irreparably lost control of the vehicle to the point that it left the simulated roadway, and that it then took participants a significant amount of time to return it to the lane. While these situations are interesting, the extreme lateral deviation samples generated would disproportionality skew any mean values reported here. Hence we chose to exclude from our analysis any trials in which the observed RMSE lateral deviation was greater than five meters from lane center. This value was based on two standard deviations of the overall participant mean. Using this method six (out of 560) trials were excluded from this analysis.

How often did the lockouts occur?

We first consider the proportion of dual-task trials in which the lockout mechanism came into effect. As might be expected, increasing the lockout threshold had an effect on the frequency with which the lockout occurred. In particular, it was found that the lockout came in to effect on far more trials when there was a shorter 5-second lockout threshold (M=19%, SD=15%) compared to when there was a longer 15-second threshold (M=1%, SD=2%). This difference between the two lockout-threshold conditions was significant, $F(1,13)=22.45, p<.001, \eta_p^2=.63$. In terms of the unlock procedure, it was found that the lockout occurred on more trials when participants had to use the 'enter-pin-to-unlock' method (M=13%, SD=15%) than when they used the 'press-to-unlock' method (M=7%, SD=6%). However, statistical analysis showed this difference to be non-significant, $F(1,13)=1.99, p=.18, \eta_p^2=.13$. The interaction between lockout-threshold and unlock-procedure was also not significant, $F(1,13)=2.48, p=.14, \eta_p^2=.16$.

Did the duration of the lockout-threshold affect lane-keeping performance?

We next report on lane keeping performance during dual-task trials. Recall that the simulator logged the vehicle's lateral distance from the center of the lane at a rate of 200 Hz. We calculated both the distance from center (RMSE) and the variability (standard deviation) of these samples for each dual-task trial. We found that these two measures correlated highly with one another and yielded an identical pattern of statistical results. Thus, we choose to report data from the analysis of participants' variability (standard deviation) in lane keeping performance during dual-task trials because this measure gives an indication of how well the participant was able to maintain a stable position in the lane (regardless of absolute distance from center).

Figure 3 shows the variability in lane keeping for the different lockout conditions. It can be seen that lane-keeping was worse when there was a 5-second lockout threshold (*M*=0.97 m, *SD*=0.56 m) compared to when there was a longer 15-second threshold (*M*=0.77 m, *SD*=0.34 m). Consistent with this observation, a significant main effect of lockout-threshold was observed, $F(1,13)=9.23$, $p=0.01$, $\eta_p^2=.42$.

Did the complexity of the unlock procedure affect lane-keeping performance?

We next consider whether there is any evidence that the difficulty of the unlock procedure affected lane-keeping performance. It can be seen in Figure 3 that there is some indication that driving performance is marginally worse when participants had to use the more complex 'enter-pin-to-unlock' method (*M*=0.83 m, *SD*=0.40 m) than when they used the easier 'press-to-unlock' method (*M*=0.91 m, *SD*=0.50 m). However, statistical analysis showed that there was no significant main effect of unlock method on lane-keeping performance, $F(1,13)=2.79$, $p=.12$, $\eta_p^2=.18$, nor was there a significant interaction, $F(1,13)=2.12$, $p=.17$, $\eta_p^2=.14$. This would suggest that overall there is not strong evidence to suggest that the difficulty of the unlock procedure had an effect on lane-keeping performance.

However, we know from the proceeding analysis that the lockout almost never came into effect when there was a 15-second lockout threshold; in fact, it occurred on only 1% of trials. It is therefore of little surprise that there is no difference in lane-keeping performance between the two unlock conditions: when there was a 15-second lockout threshold, the lockout was almost never experienced! In contrast, the lockout occurred reasonably frequently when there was a 5-second lockout (20% of trials). Hence, data from this condition provides a more reliable assessment of the impact of using each of the different unlock procedures would have on lane-keeping performance, since it often occurred in this condition.

We therefore conducted a test of the *simple main effects* of unlock procedure on data from the 5-second lockout condition. As can been seen in Figure 3, the results of this simple main effects analysis showed that participants had significantly worse lane-keeping performance when using the more complex 'enter-pin-to-unlock' method than when using the easier 'press-to-unlock' method in the 5-second lockout condition, $F(1,13)=6.81$, $p=.02$, $\eta_p^2=.34$.

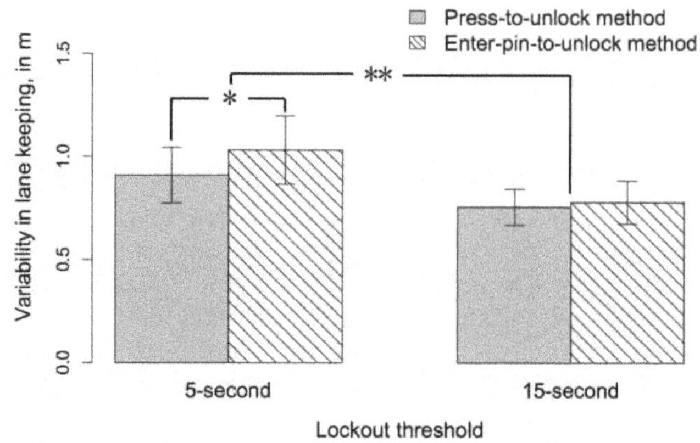

Figure 3. Mean lane-keeping performance across various auto-lock manipulations. Error bars depict standard errors. * $p < 0.5$. ** $p < 0.01$.

Furthermore, if we focus on what was happening during the period of time that the secondary task interface was locked, then we find further evidence that the more complex 'enter-pin-to-unlock' method was more distracting than the easier 'press-to-unlock' method. It was found that the 'enter-pin-to-unlock' took far more time to unlock (*M*=14.66 sec, *SD*=4.64 sec) than the 'press-to-unlock' method (*M*=7.52 sec, *SD*=7.41 sec). As a result, lane-keeping performance during these unlock periods was worse when the participant was dealing with the 'enter-pin-to-unlock' method (*M*=1.12 m, *SD*=0.46 m) than with the 'press-to-unlock' method (*M*=0.57 m, *SD*=0.46 m). (Note that statistical analysis is not feasible here because of missing cells owing to the fact that even in the short 5-second lockout condition, the lockout did not occur in both conditions for every participant.)

What was the effect of lockouts on how participants interacted with the secondary device?

Participants took on average 28.06 seconds (*SD*=4.11 sec) to complete a dual-task trial and enter the target word correctly. There were no significant effects of any of the experimental manipulations on task time. Similarly there were no effects on the frequency of typing errors. This suggests that across conditions participants were trying to enter the target word accurately.

To gain a more detailed view of how and when participants were choosing to pace their interactions with the secondary device, we consider the average time between two consecutive keying actions on the secondary task, that is, the inter-keypress interval (IKI). Results showed that IKIs between secondary task typing actions were shorter when there was a 5-second lockout threshold (*M*=2.04 sec, *SD*=0.52 sec) than when there was a 15-second threshold (*M*=2.36 sec, *SD*=0.46 sec). Consistent with this observation, a significant main effect of lockout-threshold was observed, $F(1,13)=8.70$, $p=.01$, $\eta_p^2=.40$. Changing the demand of the unlock procedure did not have any noticeable impact on IKI (easy unlock: *M*=2.19 sec, *SD*=0.49 sec; hard unlock: *M*=2.21 sec, *SD*=0.44 sec).

Results of statistical analysis showed that there was no effect of unlock condition on IKI, nor a significant interaction (both *F*'s < 1).

The data above suggests that with a shorter lockout threshold participants chose to interact with the device more frequently to stop it from locking. To further investigate this, Figure 4 shows a series of histograms showing the distribution of IKIs across the two lockout conditions. Interestingly there is only a very small shift in the peak of the IKI distribution between conditions. This would suggest that participants had a tendency to 'chunk' many of their typing actions to the secondary task into busts of activity, regardless of condition, and only occasionally took longer pauses when needed.

However, it can clearly be seen that the duration of the lockout threshold had an effect on the frequency of these longer pauses between typing actions. When there was a longer 15-second lockout threshold, there were more long pauses (in the 5- to 15-second IKI range) than in the 5-second lockout condition. Losing these longer pauses in the 5-second lockout condition is what presumably underlies the declines in lane-keeping performance reported above.

When did participants choose to interact with the secondary device?

Finally, we consider at which points along the test track participants choose to interact with the secondary task. Recall that the test track had alternating sections of straight and curved road. Previous research has shown that drivers tend to pause secondary task interactions while driving around a curved section of road [17]. If this is the case here then the duration of the lockout threshold should influence this behavior. Given that each curved section of road took 9-seconds to travel around, participants would have to interact with the secondary device while in the curved section of road to stop it from locking when there was a short 5-second lockout threshold. In contrast, when there was a 15-second threshold, participants could more easily suspend secondary task interactions while navigating each curved section of road without the device locking.

We therefore consider the proportion of keypresses that were made while the vehicle was in the curved section of the road and whether the duration of the lockout threshold had any effect on this measure. Results show that when there was a shorter 5-second lockout threshold significantly more keypresses were made while the vehicle was in the curved section of the road (*M*=53%, *SD*=8%) compared to when there was a longer 15-second threshold (*M*=46%, *SD*=11%), $F(1,13)=12.42$, $p=.005$, $\eta_p^2=.49$. This suggests that the shorter lockout threshold was overtly affecting participants' decisions about when to interact with the secondary task. There was no significant main effect of unlock procedure, $F(1,13)=2.04$, $p=.17$, $\eta_p^2=.14$, nor a significant interaction, $F(1,13)=1.44$, $p=.25$, $\eta_p^2=.10$.

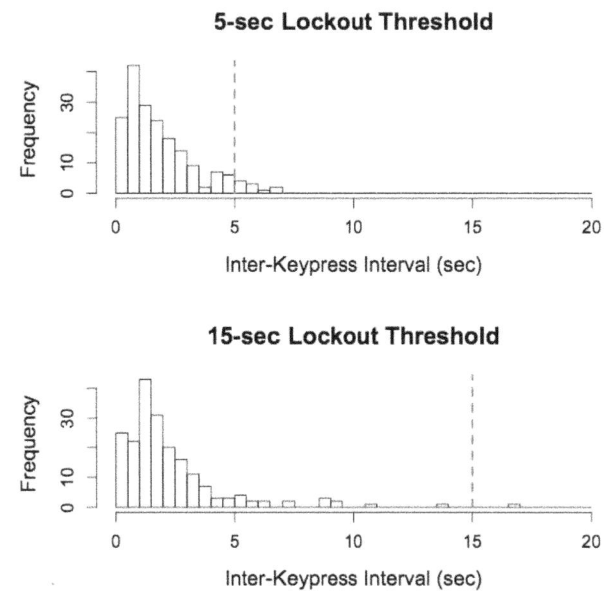

Figure 4. Histograms showing the distribution of inter-keypress intervals between secondary task typing actions across the two lockout threshold conditions.

DISCUSSION

This paper investigated the potential impact that auto-locks, which are a common feature on current generation smartphones, can have on user behavior in a demanding multitask setting. A study was conducted in which participants had to enter text using a touch-screen interface while driving a simulated vehicle. Different auto-lock mechanisms were implemented. When the auto-lock was setup so that it would activate after just 5-seconds of inactivity from the user, participants changed their behavior in such a way as to avoid being locked out from the phone. As can be seen in Figure 4, participants took fewer longer pauses between typing actions when there was a 5-second lockout threshold. These longer pauses were critical for the driving task, and failing to take them resulted in a significant decline in lane-keeping performance (see Fig. 3). This finding suggests that auto-locks can have serious consequences for user behavior in mobile settings in which the user is engaged in multiple tasks or activities at the same time [18,21,22].

A second major finding from the study concerns how the complexity of the unlock mechanism affected lane-keeping performance on the primary driving task. Results showed that dealing with a more complex unlock procedure, which required a pin to be entered, had a greater negative impact on driving performance than when the device could be unlocked by making a simple button press. This finding suggests that the added interaction time required to unlock a device in a mobile setting can potentially affect the users ability to attend to other important tasks that are going on around them. In the remainder of this paper, the limitations and implications of this research for mobile HCI are discussed.

Limitations

We discuss two potential issues with our study. The first centers on the very brief nature of the lockout thresholds that we choose to use, while the second concerns the simplicity of the driving task that we used. We consider the implications of each for thinking about how our results might generalize to other contexts.

For the purposes of our study we choose to implement a very short lockout threshold of just 5-seconds. This value is clearly very low compared to the default timeout values of many mobile phones. For instance, on the Android operating system the default option is for the auto-lock to be initiated after one minute. The primary reason that we adopted this very short lockout threshold is because in the context of the lab environment, multitasking is safe, easy and predictable. Participants did the same kind of tasks, in the same way, many times, and there were no unexpected events or surprises. If we had used more realistic lockout thresholds, say of up to one minute, it would seem likely to us that we would have learnt nothing about the effect that auto-locks can have on behavior because our participants would never have experienced the lockout in our lab setting. Indeed, when there was a lockout threshold of just 15-seconds, the lockout almost never occurred. Hence, we believe that while our lockout threshold values were clearly not representative of the values used on real phones, they were suitable to explore the effect that they have on behavior in the context of our lab study.

The critical question then is does the kind of tension that we have begun to explore in this paper exist with real world mobile interactions? We would argue that it does. Text entry done in-the-wild on a busy street or from behind the wheel of a car would be sensitive to many things that might grab the users attention for a sustained length of time such that the user would find themselves locked out of their device on returning to it. Hence we argue that while the precise scaling involved might be different, we do believe that users out in the wild would be sensitive to the kind of pressures to return their attention to their phone before it locked in just the kind of way that we have begun to explore here. Further research is clearly needed to address this question in detail, however.

A second concern with generalizing the findings reported in this paper to real-world mobile contexts is that we were limited to using a low-fidelity driving simulator. Our driving task required participants only to control the steering of a vehicle as it travelled at a constant speed down a straight highway environment. This lane keeping performance measure can serve as a useful proxy for assessing drivers' attention, since steering control is an open-loop process that requires constant visual input [24]. However, this setup clearly does not allow us to investigate the full complexity of driver behavior. Varying the demands of the driving environment between straight and curved sections of roads did at least give us an insight into how people might adapt their behavior to changing driving conditions. Despite the above limitations and concerns that could be expressed about this research, we believe that the results give some insight into how people likely interact with their phones in mobile environments.

Implications and future directions

The results of this study suggest that longer auto-lock settings are clearly better suited for mobile device use. With a longer auto-lock threshold, participants in our study felt less pressure to return their attention to the phone sooner. This was shown in two ways: (1) participants took more long pauses between keypress actions to the phone and (2) fewer keypresses were made while the vehicle was in the curved section of the road. Together these resulted in better lane-keeping performance in the context of our driving simulator study. In the broader context one would imagine that a longer lockout threshold would carry similar benefits. However, there is a tradeoff to be had, in that, while a longer lockout threshold might make a device more usable in a mobile setting, this defeats the very reasons for having them in the first place: energy conservation and security. Striking a balance between these tradeoffs would be an important practical concern and something that improved design solutions should work to tackle.

Beyond auto-locks, there are other features of mobile devices that are sensitive to the timing of user interactions. For instance, many text entry systems use pauses in user input to guide auto-complete suggestions. The nature of these timings would presumably raise similar issues to those explored here.

CONCLUSION

The results of this study suggest that auto-locks can sometimes have unintended consequences in mobile contexts in which users are engaged in multiple tasks. We provide data from a controlled lab study, which was designed to investigate how users might adapt their behavior to the presence of an auto-lock feature on a mobile phone used in a multitask setting. We found that auto-locks might sometimes put pressure on the user to return their attention to their phone sooner than they might normally have done in order to avoid being locked out. We believe that this is an important empirical phenomenon for mobile HCI to understand given the ubiquity of auto-locks and other timeout features within the current generation of smartphones on the market.

ACKNOWLEDGMENTS

The study reported here was undertaken as part of the second author's MSc research project, and was in part supported by EPSRC grant EP/G043507/1. We thank Dario Salvucci for providing the initial code for the driving simulator. Finally, we thank our reviewers and also Chris Janssen for their constructive feedback and comments to help us improve this paper.

REFERENCES

1. Adams, A. & Sasse, M.A. Users are not the enemy: Why users compromise security mechanisms and how to take remedial measures. *Communications of the ACM, 42*, (1999), 40-46.
2. Alm, H. & Nilsson, L. The effects of a mobile telephone task on driver behaviour in a car following situation. *Accident Analysis & Prevention, 27*, (1995), 707-715.
3. Beautement, A. & Sasse, M.A. The economics of user effort in information security. *Computer Fraud & Security, 10*, (2009), 8-12.
4. Brumby, D.P., Salvucci, D.D., & Howes, A. Focus on driving: How cognitive constraints shape the adaptation of strategy when dialing while driving. In *Proc. CHI 2009*, ACM Press (2009), 1629-1638.
5. Brumby, D.P., Del Rosario, N., & Janssen, C.P. When to switch? Understanding how performance tradeoffs shape dual-task strategy. In *Proc. ICCM 2010*, Drexel University (2010), 19-24.
6. Brumby, D.P., Davies, S.C.E., Janssen, C.P., & Grace, J.J., Fast or safe? How performance objectives determine modality output choices while interacting on the move. In *Proc. CHI 2011*, ACM Press (2011), 473-482.
7. Crowd Science. Social media insights – twitter. http://www.crowdscience.com/blog/article/social_media_study_twitter_while_driving/, September 4th 2009.
8. Drews, F.A., Yazdani, H., Godfrey, C.N., Cooper, J.M., & Strayer, D.L. Text messaging during simulated driving. *Human Factors, 51*, (2009), 762-770.
9. Gray, W.D. & Boehm-Davis, D.A. Milliseconds matter: An introduction to microstrategies and to their use in describing and predicting interactive behavior. *Journal of Experimental Psychology: Applied, 6*, (2000), 322-335.
10. Gray, W.D., Sims, C.R., Fu, W.T., & Schoelles, M.J. The soft constraints hypothesis: A rational analysis approach to resource allocation for interactive behavior. *Psychological Review, 113*, (2006), 461-482.
11. Halverson, T., *An "active vision" computational model of visual search for human-computer interaction.* Doctoral dissertation, Department of Computer and Information Science, The University of Oregon (2008).
12. Horrey, W. & Wickens, C.D. Examining the impact of cell phone conversations on driving using meta-analytic techniques. *Human Factors, 48*, (2006), 196-205.
13. Horrey, W.J. & Lesch, M.F. Driver-initiated distractions: Examining strategic adaptation for in-vehicle task initiation. *Accident Analysis and Prevention, 41*, (2009), 115-122.
14. Hosking, S.G., Young, K.L., & Regan, M.A. The effects of text messaging on young drivers. *Human Factors, 51*, (2009), 582-592.
15. Janssen, C.P., Brumby, D.P., & Garnett, R. Natural break points: The influence of priorities and cognitive and motor cues on dual-task interleaving. *Journal of Cognitive Engineering and Decision Making*, 6, (2012), 5-29.
16. Karlson, A.K., Brush, A.J.B., & Schechter, S., Can i borrow your phone? Understanding concerns when sharing mobile phones. In *Proc. CHI 2009*, ACM Press (2009), 1647-1650.
17. Kuganesan, A., *Would a change in driving demand or secondary task difficult affect a person's modality choice whilst driving?* Bachelor's dissertation, Department of Computer Science. University College London (2011).
18. Oulasvirta, A., Tamminen, S., Roto, V., & Kuorelahti, J., Interaction in 4-second bursts: The fragmented nature of attentional resources in mobile HCI. In *Proc. CHI 2005*, ACM Press (2005), 919-928.
19. Reed, N. & Robbins, R., *The effect of text messaging on driver behaviour: A simulator study*. Transport Research Lab Report, 2008.
20. Salvucci, D.D. & Beltowska, J. Effects of memory rehearsal on driver performance: Experiment and theoretical account. *Human Factors, 50*, (2008), 834-44.
21. Salvucci, D.D. & Taatgen, N.A., *The Multitasking Mind.* Oxford University Press, 2011.
22. Salvucci, D.D., Taatgen, N.A., & Borst, J.P., Toward a unified theory of the multitasking continuum: From concurrent performance to task switching, interruption, and resumption. In *Proc. CHI 2009*, ACM Press (2009), 1819-1828.
23. Strayer, D., Drews, F., & Johnston, W. Cell phone-induced failures of visual attention during simulated driving. *Journal of Experimental Psychology Applied, 9*, (2003), 23-32.
24. Wallis, G., Chatziastros, A., & Bülthoff, H. An unexpected role for visual feedback in vehicle steering control. *Current Biology, 12*, (2002), 295-299.
25. Yoon, C., Feinberg, F., Hu, P., et al. Category norms as a function of culture and age: Comparisons of item responses to 105 categories by American and Chinese adults. *Psychology and Aging, 19*, (2004), 379-393.

Back to the App:
The Costs of Mobile Application Interruptions

Luis A. Leiva[1,*] **Matthias Böhmer**[2] **Sven Gehring**[2] **Antonio Krüger**[2]
[1]ITI/DSIC, Universitat Politècnica de València (Spain) [2]DFKI GmbH, Saarbrücken (Germany)
llt@acm.org, {matthias.boehmer, sven.gehring, krueger}@dfki.de

ABSTRACT
Smartphone users might be interrupted while interacting with an application, either by intended or unintended circumstances. In this paper, we report on a large-scale observational study that investigated mobile application interruptions in two scenarios: (1) intended back and forth switching between applications and (2) unintended interruptions caused by incoming phone calls. Our findings reveal that these interruptions rarely happen (at most 10% of the daily application usage), but when they do, they may introduce a significant overhead (can delay completion of a task by up to 4 times). We conclude with a discussion of the results, their limitations, and a series of implications for the design of mobile phones.

Author Keywords
Interruptions; Application Switching; Task Interleaving; Task Deferral; Resumption Lags; Large-scale Study

ACM Classification Keywords
H.5.m. Information Interfaces and Presentation (e.g. HCI)

INTRODUCTION
Nowadays, smartphones have emerged as multipurpose devices. Besides calls and text messages, smartphones offer the possibility of installing multiple applications for a variety of purposes, e.g., gaming, browsing, listening to music, editing pictures, etc. Hence, the role of smartphones has changed from pure communication appliances to multifunctional toolsets.

So far, the amount of functionalities that are supported by mobile applications is steadily increasing. At the same time, due to the limited capabilities of smartphones and the security restrictions imposed by the manufacturers, current operating systems for smartphones lack possibilities for interplay between individual apps. As a result, instead of using a separate task-dedicated appliance, users have to switch between applications; and more elementally, applications are interrupted when unintended events like phone calls occur.

*Work done while visiting the DFKI institute.

MobileHCI'12, September 21–24, 2012, San Francisco, CA, USA.

From the perspective of interaction, being mobile is cognitively costly [5]. Although task interruption is an inherent problem in smartphones, little is known about the phenomenon at the fine-grained level of application usage. Yet it remains an open question how often such interruptions appear, what impact they have on the user's performance and, especially, what costs they impose on task completion times.

Researchers have investigated task interruption in the desktop domain (see next section). In this paper, we extend findings of previous in-lab studies to the domain of smartphones. We conducted a large scale observational study "in the wild" that investigated mobile application interruptions in two scenarios: (1) intended back and forth switching between applications, and (2) unintended interruptions caused by incoming phone calls. Concretely, we looked into the cost of these interruptions on task completion time. Therefore, in the context of this work, and acknowledging its limitations, we consider task completion as the time spent using an application.

We present a framework that can easily assist researchers to detect application interruptions on mobile phones at a large scale. Our findings show that interruptions caused either by incoming phone calls or by application switching rarely happen on smartphones but, as soon as they do, they might cause a significant impact on the interrupted activity. We conclude with a discussion on preventive and curative strategies, and their implications for the design of mobile phones.

RELATED WORK
Task interruptions have been extensively studied on stationary PCs (see, e.g., [1, 3, 4, 7, 8]), but little has been reported for mobile users and their unique set of difficulties. It is clear that mobility imposes cognitive restrictions and continuous interruptions on application usage; however, to the best of our knowledge, there is no previous research that focuses *exclusively* on the application level. Moreover, other studies in a similar vein [5, 6] have been performed in carefully controlled settings. Our main aim is to investigate the costs of mobile application interruptions "in the wild", i.e., in a natural, general environment *and* at scale.

Oulasvirta et al. [6] carried out a study (28 subjects) on mobile Web search tasks while moving, and observed that continuous attention to the mobile device is fragmented, mostly due to environmental distraction, and broke down into short time spans. Karlson et al. [5] focused on the tasks as a whole, including switching to a PC, if necessary, to complete them. They carried out a 2-week diary study mostly focused on email management (24 subjects), characterizing how problematic interruptions are to mobile users and identifying primary sources of frustration. In addition, Böhmer et al. [2]

looked into unconstrained mobile application usage, reporting descriptive statistics on what is probably one of the largest datasets in mobile HCI today. However, they did not study how often interruptions happen and what their real impact is on the user's productivity.

STUDY

We analyzed the *AppSensor* dataset provided by Böhmer et al. [2]. *AppSensor* is an Android background service that indicates the currently used (foreground) application at a sampling rate of 2 Hz. It also provides data related to phone usage such as runtimes or timestamps of screen on/standby. *AppSensor* collapses measured values into single data samples, with one sample denoting which application was launched at what point in time and for how long it was used; e.g., the phone application was launched at 6:30 PM and then was used for 32 minutes. A detailed description of this corpus as well as the *AppSensor* tool can be found in [2].

The dataset contained around 5.5M data samples, corresponding to 15.7K different applications used for one year and a half (from August 2010 to January 2012, Table 1) by 3.6K unique users who were geographically distributed worldwide.

Data samples	Days of study	Applications	Users
5,495,815	532	15,756	3,611

Table 1: Features of the analyzed dataset.

Method

Detecting Interruptions

As observed in Figure 1, an interruption is considered when the foreground activity changes from application x to y ($x \neq y$) and then returns to x. Additionally, as indicated in the figure, we impose the following restrictions: *1)* Launcher/dialer applications (L) and calls (C) are not considered to be interrupted. *2)* An application cannot be interrupted by L. More formally, $L \neq x \neq C$ and $y \neq L$. This way, applications can be deferred (i.e., *interrupted on purpose*) or interrupted by an *incoming* phone call. For the sake of brevity, we will refer to the former case as **internal** interruptions, and will use **external** for the latter.

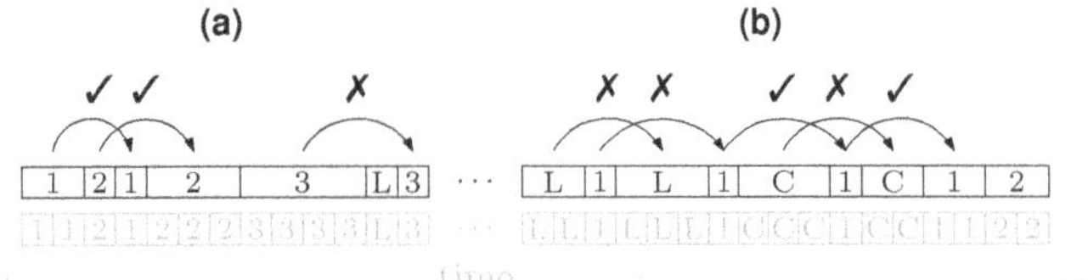

Figure 1: Light-gray boxes illustrate app identifiers from the data samples, which were used to recompose the sequences of each user's activity (black boxes) and detect **internal** [1a] and **external** [1b] interruption patterns.

It is worth noting that applications can be deferred for a long time because of environmental distractions not related to mobile phone usage (e.g., being prompted by a friend to chat for a while), in which case the device switches to stand-by mode. Because of this, to avoid misleading results, we use a time window of 1 minute; so that if a series of consecutive data samples were found for the same user + day + app, such application was considered as a different activity if the time between data samples exceeded 1 min.[1] We chose this specific duration for the time window based on the average application usage length according to the literature [2, 10].

Measuring Interruptions

Let T_n be the runtime of an application in *normal* operating condition (i.e., without interruptions) and let $T_r = T_b + T_a$ be the runtime of the same application when it is interrupted, which is decomposed into the runtime *before* the interruption T_b and the runtime *after* the interruption T_a (until the application is closed, or another interruption is detected). As shown in Figure 2, $T_o = T_r - T_n$ is the overhead imposed on the application as a consequence of the interruption T_i. Overheads are also cited as "resumption lags" in the literature [3, 8], and usually lead to a decrease in primary-task performance. However, notice that, while $\{T_a, T_b, T_i, T_n\} \in \mathbb{R}_0^+$, $T_o \in \mathbb{R}$, i.e., overheads can be either positive or negative, since an application that is used in normal conditions for a very long time might not be resumed when the user recovers from an interruption, yielding $T_r < T_n$ and hence $T_o < 0$.

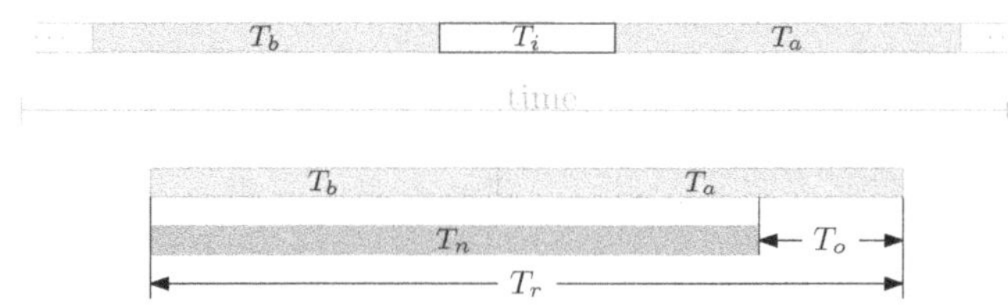

Figure 2: Computing an application overhead when interrupted.

Notice also that overheads can only be fairly computed for paired cases, i.e., one needs to compare the time an application is interrupted against its normal usage time for a given user. Nonetheless, while mining the dataset we computed all possible cases (including unpaired conditions), in order to quantify precisely how often interruptions did happen (Table 2). Then, unpaired cases were filtered and dropped from the subsequent analysis (Table 3 and Results section).

Procedure

Logs were sequentially grouped per day per user. Then we processed all interaction sessions, which are summarized in Table 2, and computed a series of descriptive statistics, depicted in Table 3. These values were macro-averaged, to give equal weight to each user and their applications. Outliers were considered when the mean exceeded 1.5 the interquantile range. To highlight the differences between both types of interruptions, we carried out different hypothesis tests. Interaction effects were considered at the $p < .05$ level.

RESULTS

As previously mentioned, we report here the results of our study for **external** vs. **internal** interruptions after removing

[1] Concretely when $t_j - (t_{j-1} + r_{j-1}) > 1$min, where t_j is the jth log timestamp and r_{j-1} is the application runtime.

	external	internal
Interruption data samples	776,922	970,543
Interrupted users	1,929 [1,676]	2,926 [2,609]
Interrupted applications	1,373 [487]	4,626 [1,043]

Table 2: Dataset summary after processing the logs, showing in brackets the number of balanced (paired) cases.

outliers and unpaired cases (final sample sizes are denoted in brackets in Table 2).

	external	internal
Daily interruptions (% usage)	3.2 (2.2)	8.3 (5.3)
Interrupted applications	3.3 (2.6)	8.7 (7.2)
Regular app. runtime (s)	24.8 (31.8)	18.9 (24.4)
Runtime when interrupted (s)	107.1 (121.1)	87.9 (75.5)
Interruption duration (s)	12.5 (8.1)	23.7 (19.3)
Overhead duration (s)	43.2 (65.9)	34.4 (40.7)

Table 3: Mean (and SD) values per user (first 2-rows) and per app.

Since data could not be considered as normally distributed[2], we used the Kolmogorov-Smirnov test, which is non-parametric[3] and hence does not make assumptions about data distribution.

Unsurprisingly, **internal** interruptions are more frequent ($D^+ = 0.50, p < .0001, \text{Cohen's } d = 1.24$) and involve more applications ($D^+ = 0.36, p < .0001, d = 0.98$) in comparison to when users are interrupted by phone calls, as shown in the first 2 rows of Table 3. These differences were found to be statistically significant.

Overall, applications interrupted by phone calls take more time to complete than switched applications ($D^+ = 0.06, p = .04, d = 0.18$). Notice the differences on application runtime when compared to its normal usage ($D = 0.09, p = .003, d = 0.20$). The duration of phone calls was found to be significantly smaller than the duration of the switched applications ($D^- = 0.31, p < .0001, d = 0.75$), however phone calls produce a significantly higher overhead time on the interrupted application compared to the **internal** pattern ($D^- = 0.08, p = .006, d = 0.17$). These results suggest that people usually engage more when using applications, and that **external** interruptions are more disruptive regarding task recall.

We computed the correlations between these measurements, and they were found to be mostly weak/moderate (Figure 3). The most consistent correlations found both in the **external** and **internal** groups were, as expected, those of *1)* the runtime of an interrupted application vs. its overhead; and *2)* number of daily interruptions vs. number of interrupted applications.

In sum, it was interesting to observe that, overall, mobile interruptions at the application level do not happen often: around 3% of daily usage in case of phone calls, 8% when

[2]Verified by previous Shapiro-Wilk tests ($p < .0001$ in all cases).

[3]Kolmogorov's D statistic refers to two-tailed comparisons, while D^+ and D^- refer to one-tailed comparisons.

	n_i	n_a
n_i	–	0.26***
n_a	0.27***	–

(a) Per user.

	T_r	T_i	T_o
T_r	–	0.12**	0.68***
T_i	0.09*	–	0.13**
T_o	0.51***	0.22***	–

(b) Per user applications.

Figure 3: Correlation study. Above main diagonal: ρ for **external** interruptions. Below main diagonal: ρ for **internal** interruptions. [3a] n_i: number of daily interruptions, n_a: number of interrupted applications. [3b] T_r: interrupted application runtime, T_i: interruption time, T_o: overhead time. Statistical significance: $^*p < .05$, $^{**}p < .01$, $^{***}p < .001$.

switching back and forth between applications; but, when they do, the resumption cost may be exceedingly high.

DISCUSSION

The extent to which an interruption occurs can be a helpful means for designing smartphone interaction. Also, knowing both the duration of the interruption and the resulting overhead can help to improve the design of applications that are aimed to support multitasking to a greater or a lesser degree.

An obvious approach to reach these goals is helping the user regain the context of the deferred application when it is resumed. On the desktop arena, when this happens, pertinent visual cues are given as a help for easing the recovery from the interruption; however, this is usually not applied to smartphones [5]. Iqbal and Horvitz [3] offered two directions for recovering from interruptions on the desktop: reminding users of unfinished tasks and assisting them in efficiently recalling task context. We believe that, in the mobile domain, the key factor is reducing the overhead time that is introduced by an application interruption. To do so, we suggest either helping the user to maintain the context while switching to another application, or to support regaining context when returning to the interrupted application. Next, we describe design considerations that can support these recommendations.

Design Implications

Our results entail a series of interventions for designing mobile interaction to reduce the overhead that is introduced by application interruptions. In general, inspired by previous approaches in the field of desktop interruptions, we distinguish between *preventive* (preparing the user for being interrupted, cf. [9]) and *curative* (supporting the user after being interrupted, cf. [3]) strategies.

Preventive: Preparation for Being Interrupted

When a task interruption occurs, the user could be prepared to leave the current task. For instance, for incoming phone calls the caller usually waits on the line for some seconds. Postponing the call a bit more (say, 500 ms) might provide time to give the user an auditory/visual/haptic signal that soon the phone application will pop-up. This way, the user would be able to save a mental state and keep in mind the recently interrupted application before he is interrupted. Further, currently users receive a full-screen visual notification of incoming calls on most smartphones. We believe that gradually overlaying this notification onto the currently used application would also provide the user with the possibility to take a subconscious snapshot of his most recent action. This particular approach may apply equally to the **internal** interruptions.

Curative: Guidance for Going Back into Tasks
When the user resumes a previously interrupted application, she has to reallocate cognitive resources, which becomes increasingly difficult if the resource demands were high to begin with [3]. Therefore, she should be given some help to be able to immediately (and easily) continue with it. For example, this could be achieved by automatically replaying the last N milliseconds of UI interactions, to give a hint of what she was doing before the interruption. The system could also leave a visual on-screen cue such that the user could remember at any time to which task she is switching back. Alternatively, when returning to the interrupted application, the canvas of the foreground application could vanish into the direction of the last focus of interaction, in order to guide the user to the screen position before the interruption took place.

Limitations of the Study

First, our results are dependent on the quality of the dataset. As previously pointed out, there exist many disruption contenders apart from mobile application usage itself that lead people to change tasks and applications [1]. In addition, while the overhead measure has been used in the literature for routine tasks, it is ideally suited to resumption where there is little re-encoding of the primary task required (see [7]). These facts and other environmental factors are an important source of indeterminism that we were unfortunately not able to measure within the data. Although we can report that interruptions *do* happen at the application level and that their cost is significant, our observational study was non-controlled, based on pure data mining. Hence, a line of future work will be enriching the data collection process with additional experience sampling approaches. This would provide us with deeper insights about tasks being interrupted.

Furthermore, we acknowledge that a direct mapping between tasks and applications is hard to convey, as a task can involve a single application (e.g., reading a document) or many (e.g., to prepare a meeting one can usually check the calendar, consult a web page, and take some notes). As such, it is not clear to what extent the ecological impact of mobile application interruptions would align with user's cognitive load and higher-level goals; e.g., one cannot guarantee if a 2-minute phone call would really significantly interrupt a user preparing a meeting.

Finally, another observation associated with this analysis is that, besides having used a large population with different backgrounds in a realistic context, the analyzed user sample comes from one of the mainstream mobile ecosystems. As such, further research would be needed to understand application interruptions in other platforms and verify whether our findings still hold.

CONCLUSION

In this paper, we replicated findings of previous lab studies on desktop interruptions and extended them to the mobile domain, by exploiting a large-scale dataset of mobile application usage. We have observed that app-switching behavior as well as incoming phone calls are a non-negligible source of disruption and therefore should be mitigated. Our study reveals three general findings:

1. Application interruptions rarely happen on smartphones, but when they do, they can be really costly for the user. This poses a wealth of new challenges for mobile designers and smartphone vendors.
2. App-switching behavior does not happen as often as it is presumed. While smartphones allow changing the focus of interaction, users are reluctant to do so. One reason might be that there are no mechanisms or suitable interaction techniques (yet) to support regaining context after switching between mobile applications.
3. Phone call interruptions add a significantly high overhead on the interrupted application in comparison to those of app-switching. This was expected, as incoming calls potentially can happen anytime. However, it was surprising to note the cost on the interrupted application: the runtime could be increased by up to four times.

Furthermore, we have discussed possible approaches to reduce the overhead caused by application interruptions and to help users resume task flow. Aside from the limitations of the study, it is our belief that our observations can lead to helpful guidelines for mobile interaction design.

ACKNOWLEDGMENTS

We thank Duncan Brumby and our reviewers for their valuable suggestions to strengthen this paper. We also thank Antti Oulasvirta for providing initial feedback. This work is partially supported by the MIPRCV project (CSD2007-00018).

REFERENCES

1. Benbunan-Fich, R., Adler, R. F., and Mavlanova, T. Measuring multitasking behavior with activity-based metrics. *ACM TOCHI 18*, 2 (2011), 7:1–7:22.
2. Böhmer, M., Hecht, B., Schöning, J., Krüger, A., and Bauer, G. Falling asleep with Angry Birds, Facebook and Kindle – A large scale study on mobile application usage. In *Proc. MobileHCI* (2011), 47–56.
3. Iqbal, S. T., and Horvitz, E. Disruption and recovery of computing tasks: field study, analysis, and directions. In *Proc. CHI* (2007), 677–686.
4. Jin, J., and Dabbish, L. A. Self-interruption on the computer: a typology of discretionary task interleaving. In *Proc. CHI* (2009), 1799–1808.
5. Karlson, A. K., Iqbal, S. T., Meyers, B., Ramos, G., Lee, K., and Tang, J. C. Mobile taskflow in context: A screenshot study of smartphone usage. In *Proc. CHI* (2010), 2009–2018.
6. Oulasvirta, A., Tamminen, S., Roto, V., and Kuorelahti, J. Interaction in 4-second bursts: the fragmented nature of attentional resources in mobile HCI. In *Proc. CHI* (2005).
7. Salvucci, D. D. On reconstruction of task context after interruption. In *Proc. CHI* (2010), 89–92.
8. Salvucci, D. D., and Bogunovich, P. Multitasking and monotasking: The effects of mental workload on deferred task interruptions. In *Proc. CHI* (2010), 85–88.
9. Trafton, J. G., Altmann, E. M., Brock, D. P., and Mintz, F. E. Preparing to resume an interrupted task: effects of prospective goal encoding and retrospective rehearsal. *Int. J. Hum.-Comput. Stud. 58*, 5 (2003), 583–603.
10. Vaz De Melo, P. O. S., Akoglu, L., Faloutsos, C., and Loureiro, A. A. F. Surprising patterns for the call duration distribution of mobile phone users. In *Proc. ECML PKDD* (2010), 354–369.

Visual Search on a Mobile Device while Walking

Ji Jung Lim
San José State University
San José, CA, USA
innoixdesign@gmail.com

Cary Feria
San José State University
San José, CA, USA
cary.feria@sjsu.edu

ABSTRACT

As smartphone usage increases, safety concerns have arisen. Previous research suggested cognitive impairments while using mobile devices in walking conditions. Mobile user interfaces that are designed in ways not to require users' full attention may mitigate the safety concerns. Primary focus of this research was on the perception process during visual search rather than the physical target selection by finger tapping, which most previous research focused on. The effects of object size, contrast, and target location on mobile devices while walking and standing were examined. A serial visual search using "T" and "L" shapes on a mobile device was conducted, which controlled for the physical target selection involvement. The results showed that walking, bigger object size, and the target position in the outer area of the mobile device display slowed the visual search reaction time. This suggests mobile interface improvement possibilities by proper object sizing and placement.

Author Keywords
Human Factors; mobile interaction; mobile user interface; visual search; walking; target acquisition

ACM Classification Keywords
H.5.2 [Information Interfaces and Presentation]: User Interfaces - Interaction styles

General Terms
Design; Experimentation; Human Factors; Performance; Verification

INTRODUCTION

Smartphones that support multi-touch screens have become ubiquitous as hand-held computing devices as well as mobile phones since the iPhone was released to the market in 2007 [10]. The smartphone market has been the fastest growing segment in the mobile phone market for the last 3 to 4 years. According to a mobile market research report by ComScore, in 2010, there were 45.5 million smartphone subscribers out of a total of 234 million cell phone subscribers in the United States [4]. Moreover, a digital media research firm, Berg Insight, reported in 2011 that global shipments of smartphones had increased 74% from 2009 to 2010 [3]. Berg Insight also predicted that there would be 2.8 billion smartphone users globally by 2015.

Smartphones and 3G / 4G (fast) mobile wireless networks have increased the usage of advanced functions (i.e., web surfing, emailing, text messaging, taking picture and videos, etc.) on smartphones that used to be major functions on PCs, and these mobile wireless networks have enabled even faster communication among smartphone users. Because of the new, fast communication trends, immediate responses using a smartphone are generally expected nowadays. Thus, advanced function usages (i.e., web surfing, emailing, text messaging, taking picture and videos, etc.) on the smartphone while walking are easily witnessed on the street and have become common practice. This trend has raised a safety concern. Running into objects or people, or falling into manholes or puddles has caused injuries and the numbers of instances often are reported in the media [21]. According to Richtel, the amount of injuries associated with pedestrian cell phone usage has increased over recent years. More than 1000 pedestrians visited the emergency room in 2008 because of cell phone usage related injuries. In 2007, the number of pedestrian emergency room visits for the same reason doubled compared to the previous year, and that happened again in 2008. Hatfield & Murphy [9] reported that pedestrians who crossed the street talking on the phone walked much slower and were much less attentive to the road situation or traffic, compared to pedestrians who crossed without using a mobile phone. Hatfield & Murphy's research suggested that using a mobile phone whilst crossing roads creates unsafe pedestrian behaviors.

Numerous studies after Hatfield and Murphy's study have confirmed that there is significant cognitive distraction of mobile phone users who cross oncoming traffic. This cognitive distraction of mobile phone users on roads increases situation unawareness, unsafe behaviors, and more risk for accidents or injuries regardless of pedestrian gender or age [11, 19, 25].

In spite of this astonishing growth of smartphone usage and safety issues, not much has been studied in the way of mobile user interface design solutions to reduce cognitive workload and enable successful multi-tasking on a mobile device while walking. Presumably in a walking condition, information-processing abilities would be decreased, and cognitive workload would be increased because of dual tasking (i.e. reading while walking or searching while

MobileHCI'12, September 21–24, 2012, San Francisco, CA, USA.

walking) or multitasking (i.e. reading, searching, selecting a target while walking) [20].

Well-designed mobile interfaces using effective visual search attributes, such as color, brightness, size, etc. may improve the visual search performance on mobile devices as well as abilities to walk. In the present study, the performance of visual searches (i.e. searching for targets among distracters) is examined. Visual search, which consists of perceiving and searching information on the display, would be the very first task among any other major tasks, such as menu navigation, text input, etc. A more efficient visual search process may reduce user's cognitive workload for the tasks on a mobile device and mitigate the safety concerns. To measure mobile users' information processing abilities while walking, a conventional serial visual search paradigm [29] was used; participants were instructed to search for a target ("T" shape) among distracters ("L" shapes) in different rotated orientations. This visual search paradigm was used to reduce effects of other variables that are not relevant to this study such as reading abilities, color preference, etc. The differences in cognitive workload between mobile device users in a walking condition versus a standing condition were measured using the workload self-assessment based on the NASA Task Load Index (TLX) [18].

Visual search accuracy per target location on a mobile device was also evaluated to understand the effects of the target location on visual search performance. Mobile user interface designs with the optimal target location should reduce visual search time and increase accuracy. Understanding the effects of object size, object contrast, and location on a mobile device is expected to lead to mobile user interface design solutions that reduce cognitive workloads, allow for efficient task completion on mobile devices, and alleviate safety issues while using mobile devices in walking conditions.

RELATED WORK

Smartphone use while walking
Many studies have evidenced a negative performance effect on target selection and reading on a mobile device while walking. Schildbach & Rukzio [24] found negative performance effects of walking on reading and selecting targets on a mobile phone. The negative performance effect of walking can be caused by many different environmental factors, such as vibration, light, glare, noise, weather, temperature, uneven terrain, etc. To compensate for the negative performance effects of mobile phone usage while walking, mobile user interface design solutions (i.e. adding bigger buttons, providing a walking mode of user interface, etc.) have been suggested in previous studies [12, 24].

Reading while walking
Vadas et al. [27] investigated reading performance on a mobile device while walking. The results indicated that walking led to decreases in reading accuracy, increases in mental workload, and increases in stress levels compared to stationary usage. Studies by Schildbach & Rukzio [24] found that increasing target size could not compensate for the negative performance effect of walking on a reading task. This was because larger text requires more scrolling on a mobile phone.

Visual search on mobile device
Nowadays, there are many features to interact with on mobile devices, and there is so much information to read on mobile phones. Activities of visually searching, reading, and selecting the target on a mobile screen while walking have increased accordingly. Previous studies [12, 24, 27] have examined reading and comprehension performance using text and paragraphs on the screen. However, on mobile devices, people perform not only reading, but also visually searching objects, such as icons, photos, and videos, in a grid view or list view. In the current study, a conventional visual search paradigm (i.e., searching for the target ("T" shape) among distracters ("L" shapes) was used. The conventional visual search paradigm is a suitable fit for the current study in order to examine the effects of visual search attributes during mobile device usage and to reduce irrelevant factor effects, such as reading and comprehension abilities.

Target size on mobile device while walking
Hasegawa et al. [8] examined the effect of text font size on the legibility on a mobile display and reported that legibility was higher with larger characters (2.5 mm height) than medium (2.0 mm height) and small (1mm height) characters. Decreasing the character sizes resulted in an increase of subject evaluation of legibility and error rate, and a decrease of viewing distance.

Lin et al. [14] examined the effects of target size, walking speed, and walking difficulties on stylus-based tapping performance and validated the effectiveness of Fitts' Law [7] on a mobile phone usage while walking. Fitts' Law is a classic human computer interaction principle, which defines the correlation between selection time, target size, and distance between the starting point to the center of the target. That is, the reaction time increases when the target size decreases and when the distance to the target increases. Lin et al. [14] also reported that walking increased the task completion time, error rates and cognitive workloads of target selection tasks on mobile phones. They also examined the effect of target sizes 1.9mm to 6.4 mm in diameter, and found that a larger target size decreased the error rate and the selection time in all the following conditions: seated, slow walking, fast walking, and obstacle course.

In Lin et al.'s study, a single target was displayed at a time and participants needed to select the actual target by tapping on it in the display. This task involved not only visual perception but also physical targeting activities. In the current study, the primary focus of the study is the visual perception and cognitive activities of users on a mobile device display. To avoid the physical targeting process, which is unrelated to the focus of the study, the selection buttons were separated from the actual visual search display (target and distracters) and remained at the same location.

Lin et al. [14] used a wide range of target sizes (1.9mm to 6.4 mm). In the current study, two different target sizes were used, 6.74mm and 9.5 mm, which are larger than the target sizes Lin et al. used in their study and are now commonly used in mobile phone user interfaces. The object sizes used in the current study are the actual size of application icons and menu icons on the Android phones and iPhones [1, 2]. Lin et al. [14] found that the target size 6.4mm condition maintained an error rate of less than 10% for the obstacle course condition, and Park et al. [21] reported that 7mm and 10mm target size performed better than 4mm in their target selection study. The two object sizes used in the current study are thus good object sizes to examine the interaction between object size, object contrast, target location, and the walking condition on a mobile user interface.

Target contrast during visual search on mobile device

Schaik and Ling [23] studied the effect of contrast during a visual search on a computer display. Black (#000, hexadecimal color code in HTML and CSS) on grey (#BBB) with a contrast ratio of 10.94:1 and white (#FFF) on grey (#BBB) with a contrast ratio of 1.92:1 were compared, but were not found to differ. Hasegawa et al. [8] examined the effect of display contrast on legibility on mobile phone screens, however, there was no effect found. In Hasegawa et al.'s [8] study, meaningless text was used to measure legibility, and the task was performed only in a sitting condition. Although the previous studies did not find an effect of contrast either on a computer display nor a mobile device while sitting, it is unknown whether contrast has an effect on a mobile device display while walking. In the current study, the effect of contrast on a mobile display while walking is investigated with a conventional visual search paradigm, which controls for irrelevant factors such as reading ability and character familiarity.

Visual attention during visual search on mobile device

Many studies regarding eye tracking on desktop computers have been done to understand users' visual attention movement and gazing dwell time while interacting with the computer user interface and to apply the findings to user interface design strategies. However, eye tracking on mobile phones has not often been done. One of the reasons for this is that the history of smartphone usage is relatively much shorter than the history of desktop computer usage. Another reason is that it is very difficult to measure users' fixation points and eye movements accurately on mobile phones because of the small sized display, the frequent head movement, and the jitter of the eye fixation while holding the mobile phone [5, 17]. In the current study, a visual search paradigm was used to measure users' visual attention on a mobile device display, which avoids the issues with eye tracking measurement. The cell location of the target on a 4 by 6 grid display was manipulated to examine which area of the display got more attention and accuracy on target detection. To avoid the physical targeting aspect of visual search activities and measure the perception process only on a mobile device display, selection buttons are located in a constant location rather than physically pressing on the target location.

Target location during visual search on mobile device

Lin et al. [14] found that, consistent with Fitt's Law [7], target size and distance to the target affect target selection, as measured by tapping on a mobile display, while walking in the obstacle course condition. Park et al. [21] recommended using the center area of a mobile display for the general input elements because the results of their target selection performance study suggested that the center area of the mobile display provides higher pressing convenience, higher success rate, and fewer errors than the outer areas of the display.

According to Fitts' Law, the farther the distance to the target, the greater the reaction time. Since attention begins at the previous target location, the distance from the previous target to the subsequent target may affect the reaction time. The center (inner) area of display is more likely closer to the previous target location than the outer area of the display. Thus, better performance (shorter reaction time and lower error rate) in the center (inner) area of the mobile display was expected in the current study, consistent with the findings of the study by Park et al. [21].

Discussion of related work

Previous studies have found visual information processing impairments while walking; however, comprehensive user interface design solutions for mobile devices have not yet been proposed much. In the present study, mobile device usage performance while walking was compared with stationary usage. Effects of the visual search attributes of object contrast and size were examined on a mobile user interface while walking to assess whether and which attributes can compensate for the negative performance effect of the mobile device usage performance in a realistic walking simulation. In addition the target location on the user interface was investigated to understand the mobile user's visual focus of attention on a mobile device display.

HYPOTHESES

H1. Smaller object size will result in lower visual search performance on a mobile device.

H2. Walking will result in lower visual search performance on a mobile device.

H3. Targets in locations near the center (inner area) of the display will result in better search performance than targets in outer locations.

METHOD

The current study aimed to understand the effects of object size and object contrast during visual search performance while using a mobile phone in walking and standing conditions. In addition, the study aimed to examine the effects of the target location. The experiment was conducted on an indoor test track.

Participants

29 participants (females and males) participated in the study for university class credit. Participants were at least 18 years old. Participants who owned a mobile phone (either feature phone or smartphone) and do not have a visual impairment were recruited. During recruitment, there were no restrictions on right handed or left handed participants.

Experimental design

A within-subjects design was used. The experiment was divided into two blocks.

Visual search task

A visual search performance task using the shapes "T" and "L" was conducted (See Figure 1).

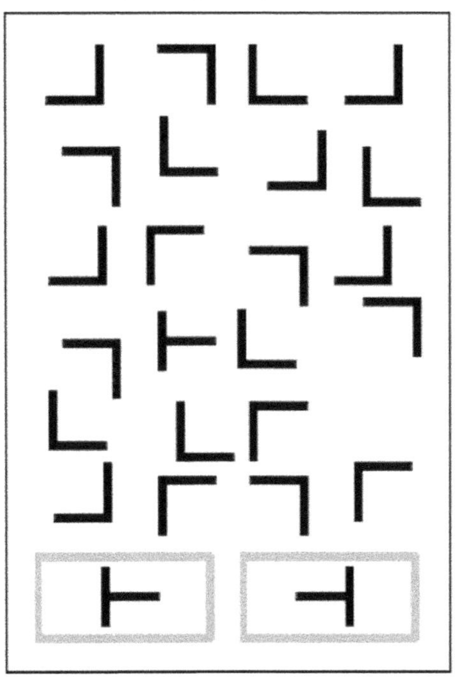

Figure 1. Example of the target and distracters shown on the mobile phone screen for the visual search performance task.

The mobile phone screen displayed the target "T" shape in two different orientations: the top of the "T" shape faced either right or left. There were multiple "L" shapes as distracters in four different orientations: the top of the "L" shapes faced top, right, bottom, and left. Combinations of one target and between 20 and 23 distracters were displayed in a 4 by 6 grid. The number of "L" shapes and their orientation were randomly chosen on each trial. Participants performed the visual search tasks by searching for the target "T" and selecting either the 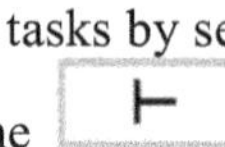 or 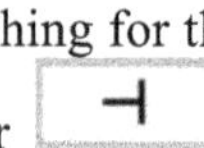 button based on the orientation of the target on the screen.

Independent variables

The first independent variable, ***object*** (target and distracters) ***size***, had two levels, small and large. The small target font size was 6.74 x 6.74 mm. The large object size was 40% larger in height and width, 9.50 x 9.50 mm, than the small object size. (See Figure 2.) The cell size of the 4 by 6 grid remained the same.

Figure 2. Two different object font sizes.

The second independent variable, ***object contrast,*** had two levels "high" and "low." High contrast (contrast ratio: 21.00:1) showed a black (Web color: #000) object on a white (Web color: #FFF) background and low contrast (contrast ratio: 2.85:1) showed a light gray (Web color: #999) object on a white (Web color: #FFF) background. (See Figure 3.)

Figure 3. Two different object contrasts.

In each trial, the mobile screen displayed one of the four different array types in a random order. Four different array types were Type A: Large font size and High contrast, Type B: Large font size and Low contrast, Type C: Small font size and High contrast, and Type D: Small font size and Low contrast. (See Figure 4 for screen samples.) On any given trial, the target and all the distracters had the same size and contrast.

A single object (either a target or a distracter) was presented in each cell of the 4 by 6 grid. A jitter, between 0 to 3 pixels in 4 different directions (top, down, left, and right), was randomly applied for each object.

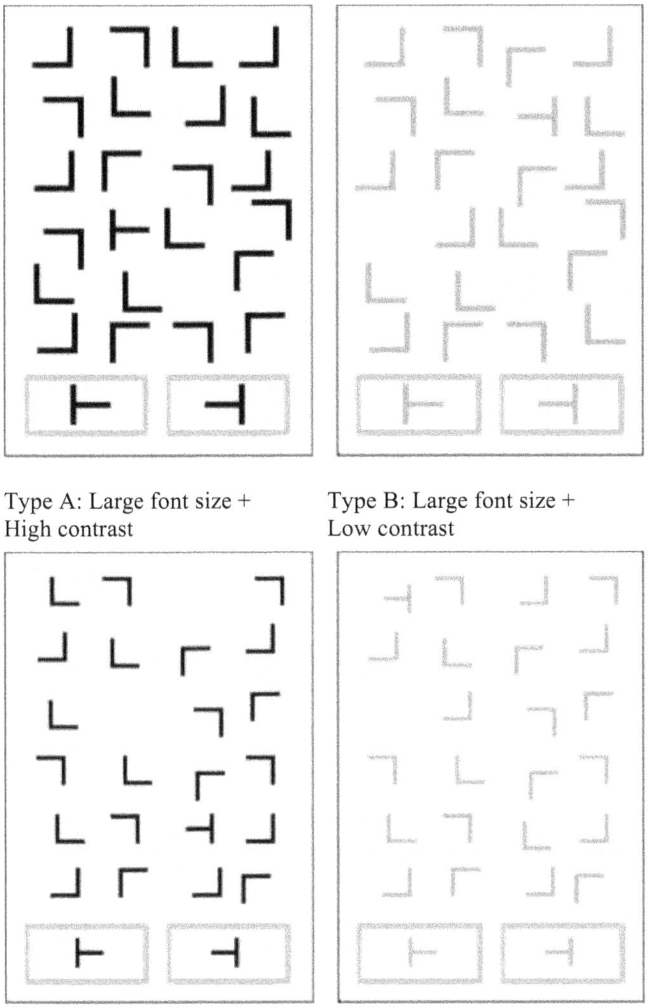

Type A: Large font size + High contrast

Type B: Large font size + Low contrast

Type C: Small font size + High contrast

Type D: Small font size + Low contrast

Figure 4. The four different array types.

The third independent variable was *walking* condition. Half of the participants were walking while performing the visual search performance test on a mobile phone in the first block, and standing while performing the trials in the second block. The other half of the participants were standing while performing the trials in the first block and then walking in the second block to counterbalance the order of walking and standing conditions. To measure the walking speed difference, participants were asked to walk at their comfortable (normal) walking speed for 1 lap before the beginning of the block of the walking condition. The walking speed while performing the trials for 1 lap were compared with the comfortable (normal) walking speed.

The fourth independent variable was *target location*. A single target was randomly presented in one of the 24 grid cells on each trial. Each cell was assigned a unique id (see Figure 5). The center (inner) area of the display was defined as ID 6, 7, 10, 11, 14, 15, 18, and 19, which were the 2nd and 3rd columns in the 2nd through 5th row in the 4 by 6 grid.

1	2	3	4
5	6	7	8
9	10	11	12
13	14	15	16
17	18	19	20
21	22	23	24

Figure 5. 4x6 grid locations on the mobile display, with the inner area colored gray and the outer area colored white.

Materials

A Motorola Droid 2 phone with a resistive touch-screen and Android operation system was used during the study. The visual search prototype application was implemented using Flex and Adobe Air.

Test track

To simulate the real life visual searching situation while walking, a non-linear, circular shaped track around obstacles was designed in a 7.93m x 16.98m indoor lab. (See Figure 6.)

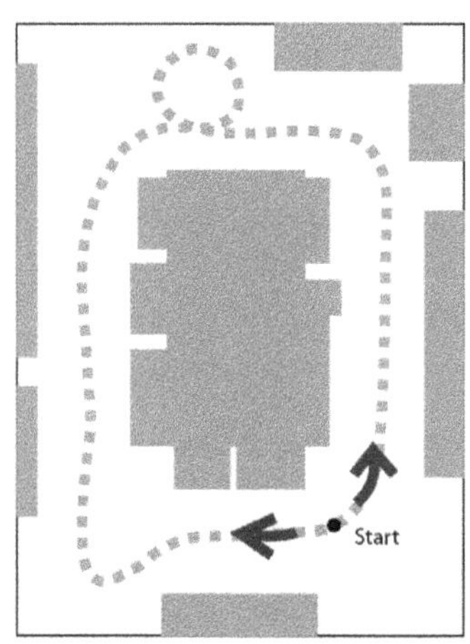

Figure 6. The test track layout in the indoor lab with obstacles marked with solid sections and the test track marked with a dotted line.

To reduce learning of the environment, participants were asked to walk on the track in two different directions, clockwise and then counter-clockwise around obstacles (i.e., machines, chairs, etc.) until the block was completed. The 46.08m-length track was drawn on the lab floor around the obstacles. (See Figure 6.)

To avoid possible injuries during the experiment, all obstacles' corners were padded, and participants were allowed to walk around the track before the experiment to get acquainted with the environment.

Dependent measures

To measure the visual search performance, reaction time (RT) and error rate (ER) were measured. The data of the target selection (correct and wrong), and reaction time (ms) were recorded automatically. There were 300 trials, including 1 practice trial in each block.

To assess participants' workload, participants were asked to fill out a questionnaire after each block. The questionnaire included a workload self-assessment based on the NASA Task Load Index (TLX) [18] (See Figure 7) and self-assessment questions regarding visual search performance and emotional response while walking and while standing. In the workload self-assessment questionnaire, mental demand, physical demand, temporal demand, performance, effort, and frustration were measured on 5-point scales.

Mental Demand	Very low 5–4–3–2–1 Very high
Physical Demand	Very low 5–4–3–2–1 Very high
Temporal Demand	Very low 5–4–3–2–1 Very high
Performance	Perfect 5–4–3–2–1 Failure
Effort	Very low 5–4–3–2–1 Very high
Frustration	Very low 5–4–3–2–1 Very high

Figure 7. Workload self-assessment based on NASA TLX 5-point scale.

The experimenter also recorded participants' walking errors, such as bumping into the obstacles or having to readjust direction, in order to observe any walking performance changes.

Procedure

Prior to the experiment, participants confirmed their normal vision and mobile phone ownership. Participants listened to the visual search task instructions and the track layout details. The instructions included walking directions details (alternating direction: clockwise and then counter-clockwise) and walking speed (walking at a normal walking speed) for the walking block. Participants were also instructed to use two hands: one hand for holding the phone and the other hand for selecting one of the buttons. The auto-rotation feature on the mobile phone was turned off during the study to ensure that the screen displayed in a vertical orientation only. Before the walking block, participants were asked to walk around the track once in their normal walking speed, to compare their normal walking speed with their walking speed during the visual search trials for one randomly chosen lap in the walking block.

In the first block, participants performed the visual search trials either while walking or standing. In the second block, participants performed the visual search trials in the opposite condition.

After each block, participants filled out a post-block questionnaire, including the workload self-assessment questionnaire based on the NASA Task Load Index (TLX). Participants also filled out a post-experiment questionnaire regarding daily personal phone usage at the end of the experiment.

RESULTS

Reaction time

The mean reaction time was calculated for each participant in each of the sixteen conditions and was submitted to a 2 (walking condition) x 2 (object size) x 2 (contrast ratio) x 2 (location) repeated measure analysis of variance (ANOVA). Trials with incorrect responses were excluded from the data.

There was a significant main effect of the walking condition on the reaction time, $F(1, 28) = 20.02$, $p < .001$. The mean reaction time of the walking condition (M = 1957.29 ms, SD = 398.44 ms) increased by 19.29% over the standing condition (M = 1640.78 ms, SD = 334.22 ms).

There was a significant main effect of the object size on the reaction time, $F(1, 28) = 14.02$, $p < .01$ (see Figure 8). On average, the reaction time of the bigger object size (M = 1827.70 ms, SD = 333.22 ms) increased by 3.24% over the reaction time of the smaller object size (M = 1770.37 ms, SD = 304.65 ms). The results showed the opposite effect of the hypothesis (that the reaction time would decrease when object size increases). The spacing between objects might have affected the results. Bigger objects (target and distractors) in the given 4x6 grid space decreased the size of the spacing between objects, thereby creating a higher density in the display.

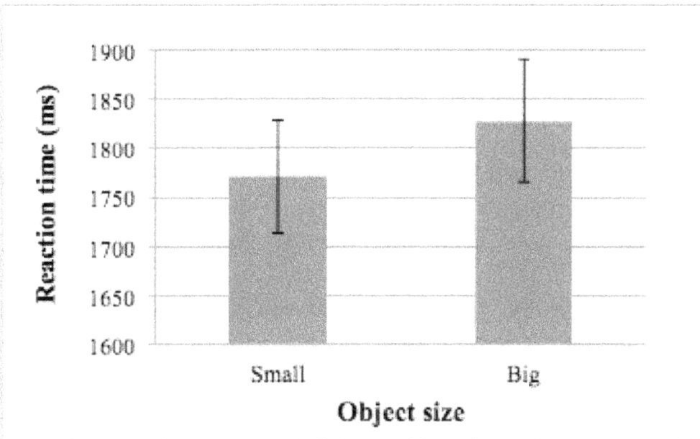

Figure 8. Object size main effect on reaction time. Error bars represent standard errors.

The effect of density on visual search tasks has been reported in many previous studies [6, 26, 28], and the effect of density might interfere with the object-size effect in the current study.

There was no significant main effect of the contrast ratio on the reaction time, $F(1, 28) = 0.20, p > .05$.

As hypothesized, a significant main effect of the target location on the reaction time was found, $F(1, 28) = 47.82, p < .001$. On average, the reaction time when a target was presented in the inner area (M = 1727.77 ms, SD = 300.21 ms) decreased by 7.62% over the reaction time when a target was presented in the outer area (M = 1870.30 ms, SD = 340.94 ms) of the mobile device screen.

There was a significant interaction between the target location and the walking condition, $F(1, 28) = 6.77, p < .05$ (see Figure 9). The difference in reaction time between the inner area and the outer area was smaller in the walking condition than in the standing condition.

No other 2-way, 3-way, and 4-way interactions were significant.

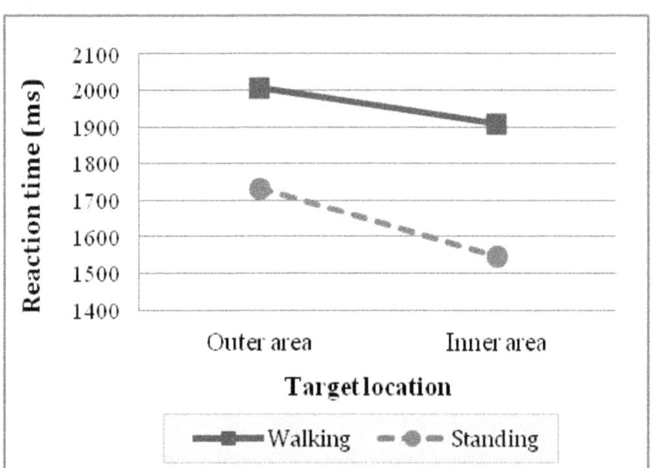

Figure 9. Interaction between walking condition and target location on reaction time

Error rate

The mean error rate was calculated for each participant in each of the sixteen conditions and was submitted to a 2 (walking condition) x 2 (object size) x 2 (contrast ratio) x 2 (location) repeated measures ANOVA. The error rate was calculated by dividing the number of trials with incorrect responses by the total number of trials in each condition.

There was a significant main effect of contrast ratio on the error rate, $F(1, 28) = 4.82, p < .05$. The error rate of the high contrast ratio condition (M = 0.008, SD = 0.011) was significantly higher than the error rate of the low contrast ratio condition (M = 0.005, SD = 0.005). However, both error rates were less than 1%, and the effect could be trivial. The error rate data did not produce any other significant main effects or interactions.

Walking speed

To measure the walking speed changes between the normal walking speed and the walking speed while using a mobile device, participants were asked to walk around the track for one lap in their normal walking speed and the time for one lap was logged prior to the trials. In addition, participants were instructed to keep their normal walking speed during the trials and the walking time during the trials for one randomly chosen lap was logged. A dependent samples t-test was conducted to test for a difference between the participants' normal walking time and their walking time while performing the visual search trials on the mobile device. Results showed that walking time during the visual search trials on the mobile device (M = 5400.35 ms, SD = 665.39 ms) was significantly longer than the normal walking time (M = 4419.04 ms, SD = 394.73 ms), $t(28) = -10.405$, p<.001. On average, the walking speed during the visual search trials took 22.21% longer than the normal walking speed.

Workload self-assessment based on NASA TLX

Participants assessed their mental demand, physical demand, temporal demand, performance, effort, and frustration for the trials based on their subjective judgment after each block: one block for the walking condition and the other block for the standing condition. In the workload self-assessment based on the NASA TLX, 5-point scales (Very low 5–4–3–2–1 Very high) were used. To compare workload self-assessment ratings between the walking condition and the standing condition, dependent samples t-tests were used.

The mental demand of the standing condition (M = 3.62, SD = 1.115) was significantly less than the walking condition (M = 2.90, SD = 1.081), $t(28) = 4.638, p < .001$. The physical demand of the standing condition (M = 4.17, SD = 0.966) was significantly less than the walking condition (M = 3.38, SD = 1.015), $t(28) = 4.075, p < .001$. The effort of the standing condition (M = 3.48, SD = 1.184) was significantly less than the walking condition (M = 2.83, SD = 1.002), $t(28) = 3.494, p < .01$. There was no significant difference between the temporal demand of the standing condition ($M = 3.24$, $SD = 0.951$) and the walking condition ($M = 3.17$, $SD = 1.002$), $t(28) = 0.338$, $p > .05$. Prior to the trials, participants were instructed to focus on the visual search task primarily and that might have led the participants to not rush on the trials regardless of being in the walking or standing conditions. There was no significant difference between the participants' perception of their visual search task performance between the standing condition ($M = 4.21$, $SD = 0.774$) and the walking condition ($M = 4.07$, $SD = 0.704$), $t(28) = 0.891$, $p > .05$. There was no significant difference between the frustration during the visual search tasks while standing ($M = 4.17$, $SD = 1.037$) and while walking ($M = 3.86$, $SD = 1.156$), $t(28) = 1.470$, $p > .05$. These results suggest that participants perceived that the trials in the walking condition required more mental demand, physical demand, and effort than the trials in the standing condition.

The overall workload self-assessment score based on NASA TLX was calculated by summing all 6 ratings of each participant for the walking condition and for the standing condition. The overall workload self-assessment scores of the walking and standing conditions were compared using a dependent samples t-test. Overall workload self-assessment ratings in the standing condition ($M = 22.90$, $SD = 4.186$) were significantly less than in the walking condition ($M = 20.21$, $SD = 3.913$), $t(28) = 3.941$, $p < .001$.

DISCUSSION

Although several previous studies have examined the effects of mobile user interface attributes on target search performance while walking, the focus of the previous studies was physical target selection performance [14, 21, 24]. Few studies have investigated the effects of mobile user interface attributes in the perception process during mobile interface use. The current study aimed to examine the perceptual processes that facilitate visual search tasks during mobile use while excluding physical target selection aspects. The visual search process is required in many activities on the mobile user interface. The current study revealed that walking, object size, and target location had significant effects on the visual search reaction time.

As hypothesized, walking slowed visual search, and this is consistent with the results of previous studies using related tasks. Mizobuchi, Chignell, and Newton [16] reported that text input while walking was slower than while standing during their mobile text entry performance research. Schildbach and Rukzio [24] examined the effect of walking on target acquisition and text reading task performance and confirmed the negative effect of walking for both tasks. Lin et al. [14] examined the task of tapping on predefined targets on a PDA and found that the obstacle course condition had a slower task completion time than the seated condition. In these previous studies, physical target selection with finger tapping on a target displayed on a mobile device was examined. The current study revealed that negative performance effects happened not only in physical tasks but also in the visual perception process during visual search on a mobile device.

The workload self-assessment rating of the current study showed that mental demand, physical demand, and effort in the walking condition were greater than in the standing condition. This is consistent with Lin et al.'s [14] target acquisition study, which showed that the obstacle course condition had a higher perceived workload rating than the seated condition. The finding that workload is increased for a visual search while walking suggests a need for future work to design user interfaces for mobile devices that can reduce the user's mental and physical workload while walking.

In the current study, large object size was expected to lead to better visual search performance, but interestingly the large object size slowed the visual search completion. There was no significant effect of object size on the error rate. These results contrasted with previous findings [8, 14, 24]. The difference in results between the current study and previous studies might be due to the inter-object spacing difference between the larger object display and the smaller object display. In the current study, unlike the previous studies, larger object size reduced the spacing between objects in the display, and the reduced spacing between objects may have made the visual search more difficult. Hasegawa et al. [8] increased spacing between letters as the letter size increased in the display. In the study of Lin et al. [14], the spacing effect between objects was not applicable because they displayed one target at a time.

The current result that visual search is slowed with the smaller spacing between objects along with larger object size is consistent with some previous studies on the effect of inter-object spacing. Ling and Schaik [15] and Lee, Chao, Ko, and Shen [13] used letters to find the effect of inter-object spacing and found that high density increased the visual search time, in agreement with the current study's results. However, Everett and Byrne [6] and Tseng and Howes [26] used icons and image thumbnails to find the effect of inter-object spacing and found that a higher density decreased the visual search time. The range of inter-object spacing also might cause the inconsistent results. Vlaskamp et al. [28] found that the inter-object spacing effect varied over different inter-object spacing ranges. Decreasing inter-object spacing decreased the search time in the inter-object spacing range from 7.1° to 3.4°. There was no inter-object spacing effect in the inter-object spacing range from 3.2° to 1.5°. Decreasing inter-object spacing increased the search time for inter-object spacing smaller than 1.5°. In the current study as well as the studies of Ling and Schaik [15] and Lee et al. [13], a smaller inter-object spacing range might have been used unlike the studies of Everett and Byrne [6] and Tseng and Howes [26]. This supports the idea of inter-object spacing involvement in the unexpected results of the object size effect investigation in the current study. This also suggests a need for further investigation on the effect of inter-object spacing in a mobile display.

In the current study, there was no difference in reaction times between the low contrast ratio (2.85:1) and the high contrast ratio (21.00:1), similar to the results of the previous studies. Schaik and Ling [23] studied the effects of background contrast on visual search performance in web pages, and they did not find an effect of contrast on either accuracy or speed. Similarly, Hasegawa et al. [8] evaluated the legibility of characters on a mobile phone display and did not find effects of contrast ratio on letter search time. Zuffi, Brambilla, Beretta, and Scala [31] studied the effects of contrast on readability, and they recommended at least 3:1 as a minimum contrast ratio for good visual performance. The World Wide Web Consortium (W3C) also recommended 3:1 contrast ratio as a minimum contrast ratio in large-scale texts (at least 18 point [6.77 mm] regular or 14 point [5.26mm] bold) [30]. In the current study, the low contrast ratio (2.85:1) used was very close to the industry minimum contrast ratio recommendation (3:1 for large scale texts) and the object sizes used were close to the size of large-scale texts. That might have led to the lack of a significant effect of the contrast ratio on the visual search performance. The current results suggest that the contrast ratio has little effect on a visual search on a mobile device at least for contrasts that are near or above the W3C suggested ratios.

The results showed that visual search was completed more quickly when the target was in the inner area of the mobile device screen than when it was in the outer area. This was expected because the distance between the target location on the previous trial and on the current trial is likely to be less for a target in the inner area than for a target in the outer area. Park et al. [21] examined the effect of location on physical target selection task performance on a mobile device and found improved performance near the center of the display. Unlike Park et al.'s study, the current study isolated the effects of target location on the perceptual processes in visual search. To control for the physical aspect of target selection, selection buttons were separated from the target display area. The current study showed that the target location affects not only physical target selection but also visual perception processes during mobile use. This result has important implications for mobile device user interface design. It suggests that placing targets such as contents to read, or call-to-action buttons, in the inner area of the display is likely to facilitate perceptual task performance on a mobile device.

SUMMARY AND FUTURE DIRECTIONS

Along with the exponential increase of smartphone and tablet use, mobile device usage while walking has increased followed by the increase of safety concerns. Many previous studies have reported a negative performance effect of walking during physical target selection tasks on a mobile device. Unlike the previous studies, the current study aimed to examine the visual perception and attention processes during visual search tasks on a mobile device by controlling for physical target selection aspects.

In the current study, the results confirmed the negative performance effect of walking and found effects of the object size and the target location during visual search tasks. Small (6.74mm) object size resulted in faster reaction time than larger (9.5mm) object size. When the target appeared in the inner area of the mobile device, the visual search was faster than when it appeared in the outer area of the mobile device screen. This suggests that placing major content and call-to-action items in the inner area of the display would likely facilitate task performance on a mobile device. The effect of target location found in the current study merits further investigation. In future studies, the optimal location and the treatment of specific mobile user interface elements, like alerts and call-to-action buttons, should be examined in an ecological approach.

REFERENCES

1. Android user interface guidelines. Retrieved from http://developer.android.com/guide/practices/ui_guidelines/icon_design.html
2. Apple iPhone human Interface guidelines. Retrieved from http://developer.apple.com/library/ios/documentation/userexperience/conceptual/mobilehig/MobileHIG.pdf
3. BergInsight: Smartphone markets and technologies (2nd ed.). (2011). Retrieved from http://berginsight.com
4. ComScore Report: Smartphone market share. (2010). Retrieved from http://www.comscore.com/Press_Events/Press_Releases
5. Drewes, H., Luca, A. D., & Schmidt, A. (2007). Eye-gaze interaction for mobile phones. *Mobility: Proc. of 4th International Conference on Mobile Technology, Applications and Systems* (pp. 364-371). New York: ACM Press.
6. Everett, S. P., & Byrne, M. D. (2004). Unintended effects: Varying icon spacing changes users' visual search strategy. *Human Factors in Computing Systems: Proc. of CHI 2004* (pp. 695-702). New York: ACM Press.
7. Fitts, P. M. (1954). The information capacity of the human motor system in controlling the amplitude of movement. *Journal of Experimental Psychology, 47*(6), 381-391.
8. Hasegawa, S., Miyao, M., Matsunuma, S., Fujikake, K., & Omori, M. (2008). Effects of aging and display contrast on the legibility of characters on mobile phone screens. *21st Symposium on Human Factors in Telecommunication*, *2*(4), 7-12.
9. Hatfield, J., & Murphy, S. (2007). The effects of mobile phone use on pedestrian crossing behavior at

signalised and unsignalised intersections. *Accident Analysis and Prevention*, *39*, 197–205.

10. Honan, M. (2007). Apple unveils iPhone. Macworld. Retrieved from http://www.macworld.com/article/54769/2007/01/iphone.html
11. Hyman, I. E., Boss S. M., Wise, B. M., McKenzie, K. E., & Caggiano, J. M. (2010). Did you see the unicycling clown? Inattentional blindness while walking and talking on a cell phone. *Applied Cognitive Psychology*, *24*, 597-607.
12. Kane, S. K., Wobbrock, J. O., and Smith, I. E. (2008). Getting off the treadmill: Evaluating walking user interfaces for mobile devices in public spaces. *Proc. of MobileHCI 2008 (pp.* 109-188). New York: ACM Press.
13. Lee, D., Chao, C., Ko, Y., & Shen, I. (2011). Effect of light source, ambient illumination, character size and interline spacing on visual performance and visual fatigue with electronic paper displays. *Displays*, *32*(1), 1-7.
14. Lin, M., Goldman, R., Price, K. J., Sears, A., & Jacko, J. (2007). How do people tap when walking? An empirical investigation of nomadic data entry. *International Journal of Human-Computer Studies*, *65*(9), 759-769.
15. Ling, J., & Schaik, P. (2006). The influence of line spacing and text alignment on visual search of web pages. *Displays*, *8*(2), 60-67.
16. Mizobuchi, S., Chignell, M., and Newton, D. (2005). Mobile text entry: relationship between walking speed and text input task difficulty. *Proc. of MobileHCI 2005 (pp.* 122-128). New York: ACM Press.
17. Nagamatsu, T., Yamamoto, M., & Sato, H. (2010). MobiGaze: Development of a gaze interface for handheld mobile devices. *Human Factors in Computing Systems: Proc. of the 28th of the International conference extended abstracts* (pp. 3349-3354). New York: ACM Press.
18. NASA Ames Research Center: Manual of NASA Task Load Index (TLX), v 1.0. (1987). Retrieved from http://human-factors.arc.nasa.gov/groups/TLX/index.html
19. Nasar, J., Hecht, P., & Wener, R. (2008). Mobile telephones, distracted attention, and pedestrian safety. *Accident Analysis and Prevention*, *40*, 69-75.
20. Ophir, E., Nass, C., & Wagner, A. D. (2009). Cognitive control in media multitaskers. *Proc. of the National Academy of Sciences, USA*, *106*, 15583-15587. doi: 10.1073/pnas0903620106
21. Park, Y. S., Han, S. H., Park, J., & Cho, Y. (2008). Touch key design for target selection on a mobile phone. *Proc. of MobileHCI 2008 (pp.* 423-426). New York: ACM Press.
22. Richtel, M. (2010). Forget gum. Walking and using phone is risky. *New York Times.* Retrieved from http://www.nytimes.com/2010/01/17/technology/17distracted.html
23. Schaik, P. V., & Ling, J. (2001). The effects of frame layout and differential background contrast on visual search performance in web pages. *Interacting with Computers*, *13*, 513-525.
24. Schildbach, B., & Rukzio, E. (2010). Investigating selection and reading performance on a mobile phone while walking. *Proc. of MobileHCI 2010 (pp.* 93-102). New York: ACM Press.
25. Stavrinos, D., Byington, K. W., & Schwebel, D. C. (2009). Effect of cell phone distraction on pediatric pedestrian injury risk. *Pediatrics*, *123*, 179-185.
26. Tseng,Y., & Howes, A. (2008). The adaptation of visual search strategy to expected information gain. *Proc. of CHI* 2008 *(pp.* 1075-1084). New York: ACM Press.
27. Vadas, K., Patel, N., Lyons, K., Starner, T., & Jacko, J. (2006). Reading on-the-go: a comparison of audio and hand-held displays. *Proc. of MobileHCI 2006 (pp.* 221-226). New York: ACM Press.
28. Vlaskamp, B. N. S., Over, E. A. B., & Hooge, I. T. (2005). Saccadic search performance: the effect of element spacing. *Experimental Brain Research*, *167*(2), 246-259.
29. Wolfe, J. M., & Horowitz, T. S. (2004). What attributes guide the deployment of visual attention and how do they do it? *Nature Review Neuroscience*, *5*, 1-7.
30. World Wide Web Consortium (W3C), Web content accessibility guidelines (WCAG) 2.0 Retrieved from http://www.w3.org/TR/WCAG/
31. Zuffi, S., Brambilla, C., Beretta, G., & Scala, P. (2007). Human computer interaction: legibility and contrast. In R. Cucchiara (Ed.), *Proc. of International Conference on Image Analysis and Processing 2007 (pp.* 241-246). New York: IEEE.

Bridging Waiting Times on Web Pages

Florian Alt, Alireza Sahami Shirazi, Albrecht Schmidt
University of Stuttgart
Institute for Visualization and Interactive Systems
{firstname.lastname}@vis.uni-stuttgart.de

Richard Atterer
Google Zurich
atterer@google.com

ABSTRACT
High-speed Internet connectivity makes browsing a convenient task. However, there are many situations in which surfing the web is still slow due to limited bandwidth, slow servers, or complex queries. As a result, loading web pages can take several seconds, making (mobile) browsing cumbersome. We present an approach which makes use of the time spent on waiting for the next page, by bridging the wait with extra cached or preloaded content. We show how the content (e.g., news, Twitter) can be adapted to the user's interests and to the context of use, hence making mobile surfing more comfortable. We compare two approaches: in *time-multiplex* mode, the entire screen displays bridging content until the loading is finished. In *space-multiplex* mode, content is displayed alongside the requested content while it loads. We use an HTTP proxy to intercept requests and add JavaScript code, which allows the bridging content from websites of our choice to be inserted. The approach was evaluated with 15 participants, assessing suitable content and usability.

Author Keywords
WWW; mobile device; waiting time

ACM Classification Keywords
H.5.4 **Information Interfaces and Presentation**: Hypertext/ Hypermedia – *User issues*

INTRODUCTION
Non-digital natives still remember the early days of the Internet when surfing the web was slow and the page loading time often exceeded the time spent reading it. Today, exponential growth in network bandwidth and computational power, as well as cloud computing, have made this problem much less pronounced. Especially in developed countries, broadband connections with good connectivity are pervasive, allowing web pages to be loaded very fast. Nevertheless, there are still complex operations, such as querying large databases, that are time-consuming. Many websites try to fill the gap between the user's request and the system's response by presenting system feedback or ads in order to keep the user's attention towards the website and to prevent them from clicking 'reload'.

MobileHCI'12, September 21–24, 2012, San Francisco, CA, USA.

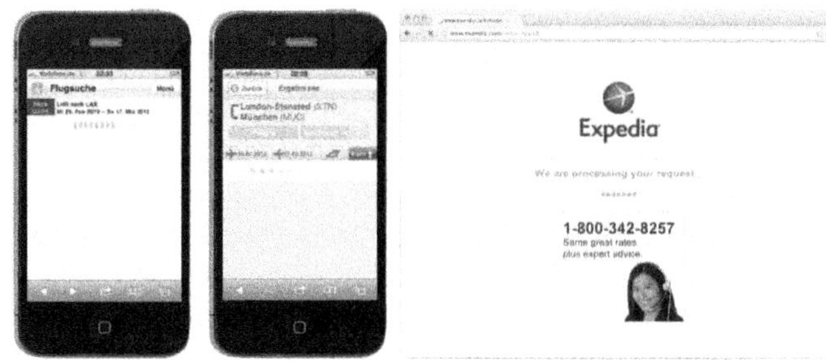

Figure 1: Websites that query large databases have to bridge waiting times. Current practice includes progress animations (left) and advertisements (right).

This problem is even more pronounced for the mobile Internet. Wireless connections strongly depend on the supported connection type (WiFi, UMTS, HSDPA, GPRS, EDGE) and on the number of people that simultaneously use the network. Hence, on average, data rates are lower during peak hours and in situations when we are moving (e.g., on the train). As a consequence, browsing on mobile devices is often cumbersome and the experience of surfing the Internet on a mobile device is very different from that on a PC or laptop [10].

A traditional approach of reducing waiting times is prefetching content that is linked from the current page. However, with highly linked pages and low bandwidth, this approach is not feasible on mobile devices. In this work, we aim at making Internet surfing on mobile phone more convenient by bridging the waiting time with useful content. In order to achieve this, we make use of the fact that the Internet connection is idle as soon as a webpage has been loaded and the user starts reading it. We use this time to preload content which can later be displayed when the next requested page is being loaded. However, the major challenge we are confronted with is the selection and presentation of appropriate content. Such content needs to require only little bandwidth to avoid affecting the overall performance. It should also not distract the user from his primary task and it should be tailored to the user's interests. Furthermore, it should be presented in such a way that the user's experience and the system's usability during Internet browsing is not negatively affected.

The contribution of this paper is twofold: (1) We present a prototype implementation based on an HTTP proxy that allows the preferred content to be inserted into web pages. Furthermore, we identify suitable content. (2) In a qualitative evaluation with 15 participants, we examine the usability of our solution when surfing on mobile devices, focussing on the impact of the loading time, the content, and its presentation.

RELATED WORK

Modifying webpages for different purposes has been subject to research for many years. Atterer et al. employed UsaProxy to monitor the user's browsing behavior and enable collaborative browsing [3]. Alt et al. extended UsaProxy to allow arbitrary applications to be deployed on top of existing web pages [2]. Approaches that deal with transforming a website's appearance are mainly browser extensions (e.g., Greasemonkey, Platypus). WBI is a pre-Web 2.0 approach that observes user interactions by using different kinds of agents [5]. Chickenfoot [6] and WebL [11] provide a language to ease the manipulation of web pages. *Intermediaries* like proxies can modify the information flow between the provider and the consumer by adapting content based on user profiles and histories [12].

A lot of research has been conducted on enhancing mobile surfing. Buyukkokten et al. looked at browsing on a PDA with low bandwidth, small display, and slow CPU [8]. Efficiently downloading content on mobile devices was investigated by Vartiainen et al. [15]. Kim et al. explored use contexts and usability problems of the mobile Internet [10]. Ways to more effectively use small displays and to enhance their usability were presented by Buchanan et al. [7]. It was found that simplicity of content, navigation, and easy and well-arranged controls are most important factors.

Ultimately, researchers have investigated the cost of task interruptions. Mark et al. found that people compensate for interruptions by working faster [13]. Iqbal et al. reported that the visibility of suspended application fosters faster recovery and suggest to provide easy access to the suspended task [9].

Our approach builds on previous findings. Keeping users updated on the current status of the web page is not new. Some existing websites that include lengthy processes or querying large databases to prepare responses attempt to make the waiting time more interesting by showing progress animations or promotions (Figure 1). The purpose is to keep the user focused and to lower the risk that he leaves the page due to the long loading time. Furthermore, it prevents him from reloading the page as he thinks the page is unresponsive. These solutions are successful, but limited to individual websites. We are not aware of any existing work that universally applied this approach to arbitrary websites. As we believe that our work can unfold its full potential on mobile devices, due to the aforementioned limitation, we focus on mobile surfing.

BRIDGING THE WAITING TIME

Assuming the user surfs web page A and clicks a link leading to web page B, bridging content can technically be realized in various ways. We sketch three different alternatives.

A. Showing Bridging Content on Page A Bridging content can be loaded in the background while the user is surfing page A. As the user clicks on the link to page B, the bridging content is displayed. The bridging content is directly replaced with B's content by the browser once page B has completely loaded. No extra effort is required by the user to skip the bridging content. The idle time between the click and completely loading page B can be optimally used. There is no control over how long the content is shown.

B. Showing Bridging Content on Page B Bridging content can be loaded on page B prior to loading the rest of the page. For this approach, the bridging content needs to be small to be pre-loaded as quickly as possible. This has the advantage of having full control over how long the bridging content is shown. This is especially useful if the content on page B loads more quickly than expected. As a consequence, the time the bridging content is shown can be extended in order to allow it to be perceived by the user.

C. Hybrid Solution By setting HTTP headers, it is possible to preload content on page A so that it will be fetched from the browser cache on page B without further network access. Alternatively, the JavaScript history API can be used to make the browser display page B's URL and load the content of B while the JavaScript used to load the bridging content continues to run. From the view of the browser, no page load happens. Instead content from A is replaced with content from B via manipulating the DOM tree.

Suitable Content

Arbitrary content can be used as a gap filler between clicking a link and displaying the requested web page. However, in practice the possible types of bridging content depend on the envisioned time the user stays on a web page, as this has a direct impact on the amount of data that can be fetched. For instance, the user is likely to stay longer on a news website than on a search results page. In general, brief, non-complex information that can be quickly perceived and does not distract users from the main browsing task is most suitable. Furthermore, to succeed in displaying interesting information in an unobtrusive and non-distracting way, the user's interests and the context of the website should be taken into consideration.

Alt et al. [1] identified news, weather, and entertaining content (cartoons, etc.) as most promising forms of micro entertainment based on a web survey with 127 participants. In times of social networks, we also see potential in displaying the latest feeds from networks such as Facebook or Twitter. Ads as the most obvious business model might also be considered. With knowledge about user interests, ads can be personalized to fit the viewer's interest. For our prototype we opted to support the following types of information: weather, RSS news feeds, Facebook news feeds, and contextual ads.

Presentation of Content

Finally, we reflected on the *presentation* of the content. We implemented two visualization modes. First, in *time-multiplex mode*, we use the entire screen to display the content during the idle time while the requested page is loading. As soon as the requested page has been completely loaded, the bridging content disappears and the requested content becomes visible. In *space-multiplex mode*, content is displayed alongside the requested content as it is loading (see Figure 2).

PROTOTYPE

We use an *HTTP proxy* to intercept HTTP requests that occur when the browser loads a web page, and insert JavaScript into the HTML code to provide the required functionality. At the same time, a *Content Creator* module handles choosing and requesting the bridging content, inserting it into the

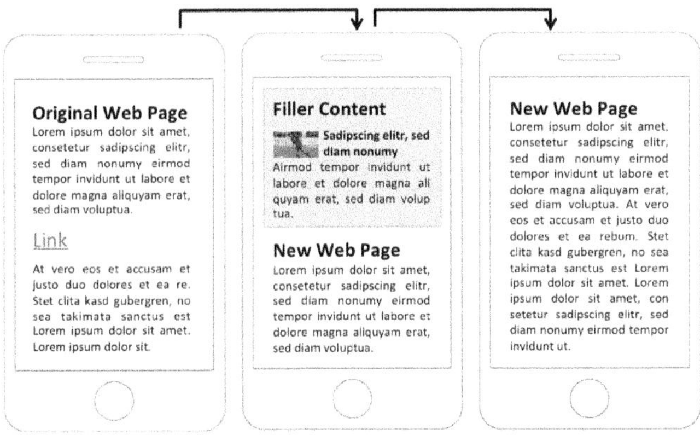

Figure 2: In space-multiplex, the bridging content is displayed alongside the new page as it is loading.

HTTP response together with the associated JavaScript code. Furthermore, an *administration (web) interface* is provided that allows the bridging content to be personalized. In the client (browser), the JavaScript is responsible for displaying the bridging content in time- or space-multiplexing mode.

For the prototype implementation, we used four different types of content: weather (from WorldWeatherOnline.com based on the IP address), RSS new feeds, Facebook news feeds, and contextual ads. Content is shortened to 100 characters due to the limited display size on mobile devices. Each content title is a hyperlink which points to the full article.

The prototype allows each user to specify (a) the content type, (b) the RSS feed category, and (c) the multiplexing mode via an admin interface. For each type of *content* the user can select whether the respective type of content should be displayed at all. Furthermore, he can specify a priority, which affects how frequently it occurs. Similarly, the user can choose his preferred *RSS feed category* (sports, computers, etc.). Based on this, content from the associated RSS feeds is used. Finally, the *multiplexing mode* can be selected.

EVALUATION

In a lab study with 15 participants, we were interested in (a) how suitable the approach is for different devices (smartphones, tablets), (b) whether there is an effect of the loading time on the perceived usability, and (c) the preferred presentation mode. We used a within subject design. The users had to perform search tasks for products on the Amazon web page (e.g., "What is the price of the iPad 16GB?"). The users performed the search tasks on two mobile devices – a Samsung GalaxyTab and an HTC Desire HD smartphone – and for each device in time-multiplex, space-multiplex, and a baseline mode (no bridging content). This resulted in 6 conditions that we counter-balanced between the participants. The search tasks were read aloud by the experimenter. As soon as participants found the answer, they informed the experimenter. The search tasks were performed for 5 minutes per condition. To reduce the complexity, we only used non-personalized RSS feeds in the study. We selected 200 RSS feeds and separated them into 20 categories prior to the study. Ten categories were used in each mode.

As our prototype loads the bridging content on the requested page, we were not only able to control how long the content was shown, but also to measure how long it was visible to the participants (e.g., when they scrolled away or clicked to close it). During the study, we logged user interaction (user ID, current website, device, loading time of the website). Additionally, for space-multiplex mode, we logged the time until users scrolled away from the bridging content. For time-multiplex mode, we recorded whether content was closed prior to the page being loaded or if content was brought back. Usability was measured using an SUS questionnaire [4] for each condition. Finally, a semi-structured interview was conducted.

FINDINGS

In total, 15 people participated in the study (11 male, avg. age 25.8 years). All were students, 12 owned a touchscreen phone and 8 had unlimited data access on their phone. Note that despite the limited demographics, our sample of young people nevertheless represents one of the main target groups.

The analysis focuses on the mobile phone as we assumed the surfing experience on the tablet to be more similar to the PC. In order to assess the perceived *usability*, we compared the SUS scores for all conditions. For the phone, the baseline condition (86.9) was rated slightly higher than space-multiplex (85.2) and time-multiplex mode (79.6). Further analysis revealed no significant differences between all conditions, which suggests that our approach does not have any negative influence on usability for mobile surfing.

We were also interested in the effect of the *loading time*. The analysis of the log file showed that the average loading time on the mobile phone (avg.=4.5s, STD=5.09s) was much higher than on the tablet (avg.=1.9s, STD=2.03s). A Pearson correlation analysis revealed a negative correlation between the loading time and the SUS score for the phone in the baseline condition ($r=-.56$, $p<.04$). This is a strong indicator that for long loading times, browsing on a mobile device was perceived to be less usable. Interestingly, no significant correlation was found for time-multiplex and space-multiplex mode. Consequently, we believe that our approach has the potential to overcome the perceived low usability of mobile surfing. For the tablet we did not find any significant correlation between the conditions and the SUS scores.

With regard to the *content*, we were interested in how much time people would spend with the bridging content. For space-multiplex mode, we logged the time until users scrolled away from the content (which was possible at any time). On the phone, this happened on average after 5.05s (STD=9.38s), on the tablet after 2.9s (STD=3.9s). When subtracting the average loading time, participants spent 2.43s longer with the content on the phone than in the baseline condition, on the tablet 2.27s. These results are interesting, e.g., for advertisers, as there is a high chance that users indeed perceived the content. Also, these values are likely to increase if the content is tailored to the users' interests. In time-multiplex mode, users were able to hide the content before the page finished loading in the background, and they were able to redisplay the content after it had been closed. On the phone, the bridging content was never hidden, but in 8 cases it was redisplayed and perceived for 8.22s on average before closing it again. On the tablet, the bridging content was closed 23 times. In 8 cases, content was redisplayed and perceived 15.9s on average.

The *qualitative feedback* showed that the system was very intuitive and usable. For the time-multiplex mode, participants felt that more feedback on the current loading status would be useful. All would be interested to get personalized content.

DISCUSSION AND CONCLUSION

We presented an approach for bridging loading times on web pages based on personalized content. We described 3 approaches on preloading content and discussed advantages and disadvantages. Our prototype embeds the bridging content either in a time- or space-multiplexed manner. Findings from our evaluation suggest that both approaches are most suitable if the connection speed is low and the screen is small. No negative experience or impact on usability were observed. Yet, no conclusion can be drawn as to which approach is more usable: space-multiplexing gives the user more control as she can immediately perceive a partially loaded page, whereas time-multiplexing only notifies her as the page is loaded.

We should mention that the study design was *not* in favor of our approach. First, the users had a directed task. Hence, a rather low interest in the additional information can be assumed. Nevertheless, the additional content was explicitly followed in 16 cases. We believe that the full potential of the approach will only become evident for activities where users do not follow a certain goal, such as reading news websites. In these cases, they will be more open to follow and perceive the additional content and links. Second, in order to reduce complexity and not to bias the participants, we did not exploit the adaptive capabilities of the system. However, we see a lot of potential in tailoring content to the users' interests.

Qualitative feedback revealed that the participants' primary concern was the distraction from the primary task. As mentioned above, this was probably due to the directed search task. We believe that this could be improved by considering the main content of the website when choosing the bridging content. Bridging content that aligns well with the requested web page is likely to minimize distraction (e.g., showing links to related articles as the user browses a news site). A future version could tailor the bridging content based on semantic information from the current page. Future research could investigate cases in which users find personalized content so interesting that they abandon their current task and whether this potentially leads to loss-of-activation or description errors [14].

Though our approach can be universally applied, we nevertheless see potential in incorporating it with certain websites, especially when facing long loading times. This way, the type of information can be tailored to the site. For instance, an online store like Amazon might choose to display ads related to the products the user looked at, and a travel site like Expedia might show a checklist where the user ticks off "hotel booked", "flight booked", or "car rented".

ACKNOWLEDGEMENTS

We would like to thank Markus Stumvoll for his help with extending the UsaProxy and during the study. The research leading to these results has received funding from the European Union Seventh Framework Program (FP7/ 2007-2013) under grant agreement no. 244011.

REFERENCES

1. Alt, F., Kern, D., Schulte, F., Pfleging, B., Shirazi, A. S., and Schmidt, A. Enabling micro-entertainment in vehicles based on context information. In *Proc. of AutomotiveUI '10*, ACM (2010), 117–124.
2. Alt, F., Schmidt, A., Atterer, R., and Holleis, P. Bringing web 2.0 to the old web: A platform for parasitic applications. In *Proc. of Interact '09*, Springer-Verlag (Berlin, Heidelberg, 2009), 405–418.
3. Atterer, R., Wnuk, M., and Schmidt, A. Knowing the user's every move: user activity tracking for website usability evaluation and implicit interaction. In *Proc. of WWW '06*, ACM (2006), 203–212.
4. Bangor, A., Kortum, P., and Miller, J. An empirical evaluation of the system usability scale. *International Journal of HCI 24*, 6 (2008), 574–594.
5. Barrett, R., Maglio, P. P., and Kellem, D. C. How to personalize the web. In *Proc. of CHI '97*, ACM (1997).
6. Bolin, M., Webber, M., Rha, P., Wilson, T., and Miller, R. C. Automation and customization of rendered web pages. In *Proc. of UIST '05*, ACM (2005), 163–172.
7. Buchanan, G., Farrant, S., Jones, M., Thimbleby, H., Marsden, G., and Pazzani, M. Improving mobile internet usability. In *Proc. of WWW '01*, ACM (2001), 673–680.
8. Buyukkokten, O., Garcia-Molina, H., Paepcke, A., and Winograd, T. Power browser: efficient web browsing for pdas. In *Proc. of CHI '00*, ACM (2000), 430–437.
9. Iqbal, S. T., and Horvitz, E. Disruption and recovery of computing tasks: field study, analysis, and directions. In *Proc. of CHI '07*, CHI '07, ACM (2007), 677–686.
10. Kim, H., Kim, J., Lee, Y., Chae, M., and Choi, Y. An empirical study of the use contexts and usability problems in mobile internet. *Proc. of HICSS* (2002).
11. Kistler, T., and Marais, H. Webl - a programming language for the web. In *Proc. of WWW '98*, Elsevier (1998), 259–270.
12. Maglio, P., and Barrett, R. Intermediaries personalize information streams. *Commun. ACM 43* (2000).
13. Mark, G., Gudith, D., and Klocke, U. The cost of interrupted work: more speed and stress. In *Proc. of CHI '08*, ACM (2008), 107–110.
14. Norman, D. A. *The Design of Everyday things*, 1 ed. Basic Books, Dec. 2002.
15. Vartiainen, E., Roto, V., and Popescu, A. Auto-update: a concept for automatic downloading of web content to a mobile device. In *Proc. of Mobility '07*, ACM (New York, NY, USA, 2007), 683–689.

Thermal Icons: Evaluating Structured Thermal Feedback for Mobile Interaction

Graham Wilson, Stephen A. Brewster
School of Computing Science,
University of Glasgow,
Glasgow G12 8QQ, UK
gawilson@dcs.gla.ac.uk;
stephen.brewster@glasgow.ac.uk

Martin Halvey
Glasgow Caledonian
University,
Glasgow G4 0BA, UK
martin.halvey@gcu.ac.uk

Stephen A. Hughes
SAMH Engineering
1 Leopardstown Drive,
Blackrock, Dublin Ireland
stephenahughes@gmail.com

ABSTRACT

This paper expands the repertoire of non-visual feedback for mobile interaction, established through Earcons and Tactons, by designing structured thermal cues for conveying information. Research into the use of thermal feedback for HCI has not looked beyond basic 'yes-no' detection of stimuli to the unique identification of those stimuli. We first designed thermal icons that varied along two parameters to convey two pieces of information. We also designed intramodal tactile icons, combining one thermal and one vibrotactile parameter, to test perception of different tactile cues and so evaluate the possibility of augmenting vibrotactile displays with thermal feedback. Thermal icons were identified with 82.8% accuracy, while intramodal icons had 96.9% accuracy, suggesting thermal icons are a viable means of conveying information in mobile HCI, for when audio and/or vibrotactile feedback is not suitable or desired.

Author Keywords

Thermal feedback; mobile interaction; non-visual feedback.

ACM Classification Keywords

H.5.2 User Interfaces: Haptic IO

INTRODUCTION

The small and cramped GUIs of mobile phones have motivated the design of non-visual cues to display information and free visual attention. Examples include Earcons [1, 2] and Tactons [3], structured auditory or vibrotactile stimuli that can convey two or three pieces of information to the user, mapped to the icon's structural parameters such as rhythm or timbre/roughness. Thermal stimulation is a rich, emotive and entirely silent information source, which could be used as an alternative mobile feedback channel when required, as it is silent for quiet environments and potentially more salient for bumpy environments. It may also provide hedonic meaning not necessarily present in vibrotactile patterns [8]. While we have a finely tuned thermal sense in terms of detecting changes, it is yet to be fully established whether identification of unique thermal stimuli is possible and if they can be used in mobile HCI to convey information. It is also possible that thermal feedback could be used to augment existing vibrotactile feedback, either replacing less distinct or feasible Tacton parameters (such as spatial location) or by adding an extra thermal parameter to vibrotactile feedback.

MobileHCI'12, September 21–24, 2012, San Francisco, CA, USA.

Therefore, we tested the identification of specific forms of thermal stimulation. Following in the footsteps of Tactons we began with two parameters, *direction of change* (warm and cool) and *subjective intensity of change* (moderate and strong) in order to convey the Source ("Personal" and "Work") and Importance ("Standard" and "Important") of a message. In a separate condition, we also used one thermal parameter (*direction of change*) and one vibrotactile parameter (*rhythm*) together to convey the same information. The purpose was to test interpretation of two different tactile feedback channels simultaneously, to judge if thermal feedback could successfully augment or replace Tacton parameters. We use the term 'intramodal' to refer to this use of two channels (vibration and thermal) of the same modality (tactile), in contrast to 'bimodal', which refers to the use of more than one modality (e.g. tactile + audio). The research described in this paper was conducted with participants sat indoors and so serves as an initial baseline investigation.

BACKGROUND

Audio and Tactile Icons

Earcons [2] are structured, abstract non-speech sounds used to convey information about an interface non-visually. Information is encoded in the sound's auditory parameters, such as the timbre, rhythm and pitch. In this way a single Earcon can convey up to three pieces of information [2]. Using Earcon design as a basis, Brown *et al.* [3] developed Tactons to convey information through vibrotactile stimulation of the skin. Manipulating the rhythm and roughness parameters of Tactons provides reliable identification of two pieces of information, with spatial location providing a potential third parameter.

Because some environments are not suitable for audio or tactile feedback, and because user preference varies regarding which modality is desirable when, Hoggan and colleagues developed crossmodal audio and tactile icons which can be interchanged to suit the user's current environment or preference [6]. While vibrotactile feedback is commonly used for private notifications, it is not entirely private, as the vibration is often audible to, or even felt by, others. Thermal icons could provide an entirely silent means of conveying information, or provide a replacement parameter for less reliable (e.g. roughness) or less feasible (spatial location) Tacton parameters [3].

Thermal Perception

There are myriad influences on thermal perception; only those most relevant to the current study are included here. Thermal perception can be highly precise, with experts able to detect changes less than 0.2°C above/below skin temperature in ideal laboratory conditions [9]. The skin sits at a neutral temperature of 30-36°C, depending on the individual [7]. Detection of changes within this range is dependent more on the rate of change (ROC) of the stimulus than the actual extent of the change itself [8]. Faster changes feel stronger and are felt sooner than slow changes. Outside of this range, we become more sensitive to changes that move further away from neutrality towards the pain threshold [8].

Thermal HCI

Wettach *et al.* [10] designed a Peltier-based thermal feedback device for mobile interaction and tested users' abilities to differentiate three different stimulus temperatures (32°C, 37°C and 42°C). Error rates remained at 25% even after long-term training. None of these temperatures would be considered 'cool', so although the error rate was relatively high, this study suggests that individuals may be able to identify absolute degrees of warmth, given the right stimuli. Wilson *et al.* [12] tested the effects of various factors on detection rates of stimuli as well as subjective perceptions of the stimuli (intensity and comfort). They found that the Thenar eminence (bulbous area of palm adjoining the thumb) was the most sensitive location, cold stimuli were easier and faster to detect and that manipulating both the extent of thermal change (Wilson *et al.* use the term "intensity") as well as the ROC created different subjective intensity ratings. Therefore, subjective stimulus intensity is not solely based on the extent that the stimulator changes from skin temperature. For example, the same extent of change (e.g. 6°C) felt subjectively less intense when warmed or cooled at the slower ROC of 1°C/sec, compared to the faster 3°C/sec. This suggests that manipulating both extent of change and ROC can create perceptually distinct stimuli.

EVALUATION

We used an updated design of the hardware used by Wilson *et al.* [12], with ours shown in Figure 1. The same Peltier module was used, but it was attached to a larger heat sink for more effective heat dissipation. The Peltiers connected to a MacBook Pro running Windows 7 via a Bluetooth microcontroller and were powered by 4xAA batteries. For the vibrotactile feedback, an EAI C2 Tactor was used (www.eaiinfo.com), which converts audio files to vibration. This is the same device used in other Tacton research [3].

The task closely resembled that used by Brown *et al.* [3] for identifying multidimensional Tactons. Four thermal icons and four intramodal thermal + vibrotactile icons were used to represent the arrival of four different text/email message types. The messages varied along two dimensions: message Source and message Importance. The Source was either "Personal" or "Work", and the Importance either "Standard" or "Important", giving Standard Personal, Important Personal, Standard Work and Important Work messages.

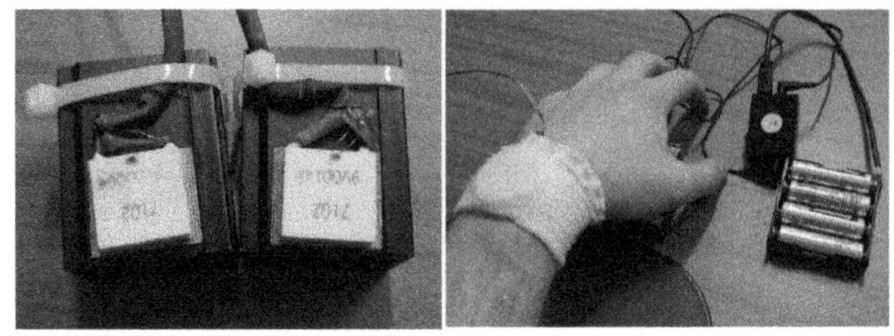

Figure 1: Peltier modules used to produce thermal stimuli (left); experiment apparatus with Peltiers under palm (right).

Thermal Icon Design

The design of the thermal icons was guided by the recommendations in Wilson *et al.* [12]. Because the icons are intended for use in mobile HCI, we also took into account the effects of mobility [12] and outdoor environments [5] to choose stimuli that should be perceivable in mobile situations. We chose two of the most salient parameters of thermal stimulation to create the thermal icons: *direction of thermal change* and *subjective intensity of change*. Each of these had two levels: 'warming' and 'cooling' for *direction of change* and 'moderate' and 'strong' for *subjective intensity*, giving four thermal icons: Moderate Warmth, Strong Warmth, Moderate Cooling and Strong Cooling. The mappings between icon and message type are shown in Table 1. For *direction of Change* we began at a neutral skin temperature of 32°C [7], warming and cooling from there. Warmth was chosen to represent personal messages, as there is evidence of an innate association between physical warmth and interpersonal warmth/trust [11]. Work messages are an alternative to personal messages and so were mapped to cold changes. More important messages were mapped to subjectively stronger changes as they are more attention-grabbing [8].

	Thermal	Intramodal
"Source" Parameter	*Direction of Change*	*Direction of Change*
Personal	Warm	Warm
Work	Cool	Cool
"Importance" Parameter	*Subjective Intensity*	*Tactile Rhythm*
Standard	Moderate	Slow Rhythm
Important	Strong	Fast Rhythm

Table 1: Mappings of thermal and tactile parameters to Source and Importance of a message.

Wilson *et al.* [12] used the term "intensity" to refer to the number of degrees by which the stimulator changed from 32°C neutral. To avoid confusion with the *subjective intensity* parameter, we use the term "extent of change" here instead. Therefore, the *subjective intensity* parameter used two extents of change which have received different subjective intensity ratings [12]: 3°C and 6°C (warming to 35°C and 38°C and cooling to 29°C and 26°C respectively). To make the two extents more perceptually different, we used a slow ROC (1°C/sec) for the 3°C changes and a fast ROC (3°C/sec) for the 6°C changes. We avoided smaller changes in temperature, as these are far less likely to be detected, especially when walking [12] or when outdoors [5].

Intramodal Icon Design

The thermal parameter chosen was *direction of change* as it is particularly salient, while the vibrotactile parameter chosen was *rhythm* as this is one of the most easily identifiable parameters of Tactons [3]. Again we used warming and cooling for the two levels of *direction*, in this case warming or cooling by 6°C at 3°C/sec, the large extent of change from the thermal icons. As identification of different vibrotactile rhythms is easier when they contain different numbers of notes [3], we used two 3-second rhythms, one "slow" with three long notes and one "fast" with nine short notes. The *rhythms* are shown in musical notation in Figure 2. The four intramodal icons were: warming + slow rhythm, warming + fast rhythm, cooling + slow rhythm, cooling + fast rhythm. The mappings to message type are shown in Table 1. Rhythms lasted 3 seconds, as this length of time was required to reach the full extent of warming/cooling. We were interested in how well the thermal and vibrotactile stimuli could be processed when presented simultaneously, as skin temperature influences vibrotactile perception [4].

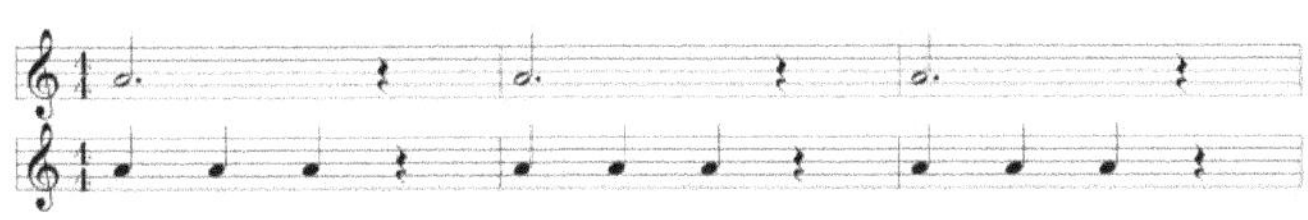

Figure 2: Slow (top) & fast (bottom) Intramodal icon rhythms.

Design & Procedure

Twelve participants took part (7 male, 5 female), aged from 18 to 43 (mean 25.08). All were from within the University and were paid £6 for participation. The evaluation had two conditions: one identifying thermal icons (Thermal condition) and one identifying intramodal thermal+vibrotactile icons (Intramodal condition). The procedure was the same for both conditions and participants took part in both, with the order counterbalanced. The Thenar eminence/lower palm was chosen as the site for thermal stimuli as it is highly sensitive [12] and directly contacts a mobile device held in the hand. Participants laid the palm of the non-dominant hand on top of two Peltiers, with the arm supported by a padded rest (see Figure 1), while the other hand operated a PC mouse. During the Intramodal condition, they also had the C2 contacting with the top of the non-dominant wrist, secured by an elastic strap (white band in Figure 1). Although it was important to present both stimuli (thermal and tactile) at the same location (mimicking presentation from the mobile device itself), it was not feasible in this case to have both presented to the palm, due to the size and placement of the Peltiers.

Both conditions started with adaptation of the palm to 32°C, by resting the palm on the Peltiers for 60 sec. Participants first completed a 10-minute training session where they could feel each icon several times. During this time, four buttons were shown on the PC screen corresponding to each of the four message types. When clicked, the corresponding icon feedback was produced, and participants had to learn to associate the feedback with the message type. In both conditions, the Peltiers changed to the relevant temperature and remained there for 10 sec, before returning to 32°C for 30 sec. In the Intramodal condition, the tactile rhythm and thermal change began simultaneously. Headphones were worn so the vibrations were inaudible.

For the full task, all four stimuli/message types were presented four times in a random order, giving 16 icons per condition. The same four button interface screen was shown as soon as the icon was initiated and the participants were asked to click the button corresponding to which message type they interpreted the icon as representing. As soon as a button was clicked, the Peltiers were returned to 32°C for 30 seconds, after which the next random icon was presented. This repeated until all icons were judged four times. The dependent variables were: *accuracy* (whether the right message type was identified) and *identification time* (IDT, the time taken to choose a message type). IDT indicates the time required to become confident in identifying an icon.

RESULTS

The overall mean accuracy for two-parameter thermal icons was 82.8% (SD=37.8). Mean accuracy for the two thermal parameters individually was 85.4% for *subjective intensity* and 97.4% for *direction of change*. The confusion matrix for thermal icons is shown in Table 2. The median IDT for each Thermal icon was 5.40s, 5.34s, 5.61s and 4.29s for the moderate warm, strong warm, moderate cool and strong cool icons respectively. A Friedman's analysis of the data indicated a significant effect of icon on IDT ($\chi^2(3)=11.075$, $p<.05$), with the two cool icons being significantly different from each other (Wilcoxon T=854, p=0.006) with an adjusted alpha (p-value) of 0.008.

		Perceived Icon			
		Mod Warm	Strong Warm	Mod Cool	Strong Cool
Actual Icon	Mod Warm	46	1	1	0
	Strong Warm	11	35	1	1
	Mod Cool	0	1	38	9
	Strong Cool	0	1	7	40

Table 2: Thermal Icons confusion matrix: the icons presented and the number of each icon they were perceived as.

The overall mean accuracy for two-parameter Intramodal icons was 96.9% (SD=17.4). Mean accuracy for the two Intramodal parameters was 97.4% for *rhythm* and 99.5% for *direction of change*. A Wilcoxon *T* test showed that participants identified significantly more Intramodal icons than Thermal icons (T=558.0, p<0.001). The median IDT for each Intramodal icon was 4.12s, 3.77s, 3.63s and 3.91s for the warm+slow, warm+fast, cool+slow and cool+fast icons respectively. A Friedman's test indicated a significant effect of icon on IDT ($\chi^2(3)=11.275$, p=0.01), but no Wilcoxon *T* tests reached the adjusted level of significance (p=0.008).

DISCUSSION AND CONCLUSIONS

The mean identification rate for thermal icons is high, with 82.9% accuracy in identifying two pieces of information, suggesting thermal icons are a promising method of conveying information. This figure is higher than the 71% identification rate for two-parameter Tactons [3], although we only used two levels per parameter and Brown *et al.* used three. While the results are promising, future revisions should address the slightly more error-prone parameter of *subjective intensity (SI)*. Of the 33 errors, 28 confused the *SI* of the icon, resulting in 85% accuracy for that parameter. The other 5 (of 33) errors confused warm for cold or *vice versa*, giving *direction of change* a much higher accuracy of 97%.

As seen in Table 2, a roughly equal number of *SI* errors occurred within both warming (12) and cooling (16), however the pattern of confusion was different. All but 1 of the warm confusions felt subjectively less intense than was intended (i.e. Important Personal was interpreted as Standard Personal). In contrast, roughly equal numbers of cold confusions were perceived as less (7) or more (9) intense than intended. Participants reported believing that either they became "less sensitive" to changes over time or simply that the stimuli became harder to differentiate. Looking at the frequency of errors over the course of the Thermal condition showed no pattern of increasing error with time so, even if the ability to identify the *SI* depreciated, it did not do so enough to make them indistinguishable. However, given the frequency of such comments, it will be necessary to test this temporal effect on perception fully. One way of increasing the subjective difference between stimuli would be to decrease the extent of change of the moderate warmth/cold and increase the extent of strong cold. Increasing the strong warmth may move too close to the pain threshold, so this is not recommended.

The intramodal icons had a significantly higher mean identification rate than the thermal icons, at 97%, with 99% accuracy for *direction of change* and 97% accuracy for *rhythm*, a figure similar to rhythm identification in Tactons (96.9%) [3]. Therefore, presenting thermal and vibrotactile stimuli together does not appear to significantly hinder interpretation of either, and so thermal changes may be a useful addition to Tactons.

The identification time (IDT) of thermal icons showed that, in line with previous research [5, 12], the coldest icon (strong cool/Important Work) was the fastest to be identified, but only compared to the moderate cool, otherwise the times were comparable. However, overall the IDT were quite high, at 5-6 seconds. Because the two *subjective intensities* varied in their rate of change, they took different lengths of time to reach their extents. Participants may have waited a length of time to see how far the Peltiers changed temperature. In contrast, the amount of thermal change was irrelevant in the intramodal icons, and so identification was 1-2 seconds faster than thermal.

This paper has presented the first examination of thermal icon design and identification, as well as the first study of intramodal thermal+vibrotactile presentation. Results from both are encouraging, as identifying two pieces of information from thermal icons was easy and could be improved with adjusted designs. Presenting two different tactile stimuli simultaneously does not seem to produce confusion. While a necessary next step is testing identification while the user is walking and in outdoor environments, these initial results show thermal icons to be similarly effective in conveying information as Earcons and Tactons.

ACKNOWLEDGEMENTS

This research was funded by EPSRC grant EP/G063427/1.

REFERENCES

1. Brewster, S. Overcoming the lack of screen space on mobile computers. *Personal and Ubiquitous Computing*, 2002. **6**: p. 188-205.
2. Brewster, S., P. Wright, and A. Edwards. A detailed investigation into the effectiveness of earcons. *Proc. of ICAD 1994*. 471-498.
3. Brown, L., S. Brewster, and H. Purchase. Multidimensional Tactons for Non-Visual Information Presentation in Mobile Devices. *Proc. of MobileHCI 2006*, p. 231-238.
4. Green, B. The Effect of Skin Temperature on Vibrotactile Sensitivity. *Perception & Psychophysics*, 1977. 21(3): p. 243-248.
5. Halvey, M., G. Wilson, S. Brewster, and S. Hughes. "Baby It's Cold Outside": The Influence of Ambient Temperature and Humidity on Thermal Feedback. *Proc. of ACM CHI 2012*, p. 715-724.
6. Hoggan, E. and S. Brewster. Designing audio and tactile crossmodal icons for mobile devices. *Proc. of ICMI 2007*, p. 162-169.
7. Jones, L.A. and M. Berris. The Psychophysics of Temperature Perception and Thermal-Interface Design. *Proc. of IEEE HAPTICS 2002*, p. 137-142.
8. Stevens, J.C. Thermal Sensibility, in *The Psychology of Touch*, M.A. Heller and W. Schiff, Editors. 1991, Lawrence Erlbaum: New Jersey.
9. Stevens, J.C. and K. Choo. Temperature sensitivity of the body surface over the life span. *Somatosensory & Motor Research*, 1998. 15(1): p. 13-28.
10. Wettach, R., C. Behrens, A. Danielsson, and T. Ness. A thermal information display for mobile applications. *Proc. of MobileHCI 2007*, p. 182-185.
11. Williams, L. and J. Bargh. Experiencing physical warmth promotes interpersonal warmth. *Science*, 2008. 322: p. 606-607.
12. Wilson, G., M. Halvey, S. Brewster, and S. Hughes. Some Like it Hot? Thermal Feedback for Mobile Devices. *Proc. of ACM CHI 2011*: p. 2555-2564.

Touching the Micron: Tactile Interactions with an Optical Tweezer

Stuart Lamont[1] stuartalamont@gmail.com

Richard Bowman[2] r.bowman@physics.gla.ac.uk

Matthias Rath[1] matthias.rath@tu-berlin.de

John Williamson[1] jhw@dcs.gla.ac.uk

Roderick Murray-Smith[1] rod@dcs.gla.ac.uk

Miles Padgett[2] Miles.Padgett@glasgow.ac.uk

1. School of Computing Science, 2. School of Physics, University of Glasgow, G12 8QQ, Scotland.

ABSTRACT

A tablet interface for manipulating microscopic particles is augmented with vibrotactile and audio feedback.The feedback is generated using a novel real-time synthesis library based on approximations to physical processes, and is efficient enough to run on mobile devices, despite their limited computational power. The feedback design and usability testing was done with a realistic simulator on appropriate tasks, allowing users to control objects more rapidly, with fewer errors and applying more consistent forces. The feedback makes the interaction more tangible, giving the user more awareness of changes in the characteristics of the optical tweezers as the number of optical traps changes.

ACM Classification Keywords

H.5.2 User Interfaces: Input devices and strategies

Author Keywords

Tactile feedback; optical tweezers; real-time synthesis.

INTRODUCTION

We apply developments in mobile multimodal feedback design [3, 12] to augment the tablet controller of an Optical Tweezer, described in [2], by augmenting the visual and touch-based interaction with vibrotactile and audio feedback. These feedback the level of force control users have over the microscopic objects being manipulated, allowing them to better control their finger movements. We also introduce an optical tweezer simulation for training and interaction design.

Optical Tweezers

Many areas of science and engineering are increasingly concerned with micro- and nanometre length scales. The ability to manipulate microscopic objects is, therefore, an important tool in fields ranging from biology to nanofabrication. This can be achieved by passing a tightly focussed laser beam through a small transparent object, where any deflection of the light results in a change in the momentum carried by the beam. This change in momentum results in a force which, for most objects, acts to pull the object towards the focal point of the beam (hence the name 'trap'), and was first used to manipulate micron-sized objects by Ashkin [1]. This technique has been extended and refined to make precise force and displacement measurements [7], providing important insights into biophysical problems such as muscle motors and DNA dynamics [7]. Holographic Optical Tweezers (HOT) [9], provide an extension of this technique which uses diffractive optics to provide interactive 3D control over multiple particles [5].

MobileHCI'12, September 21-24, 2012, San Francisco, CA, USA.

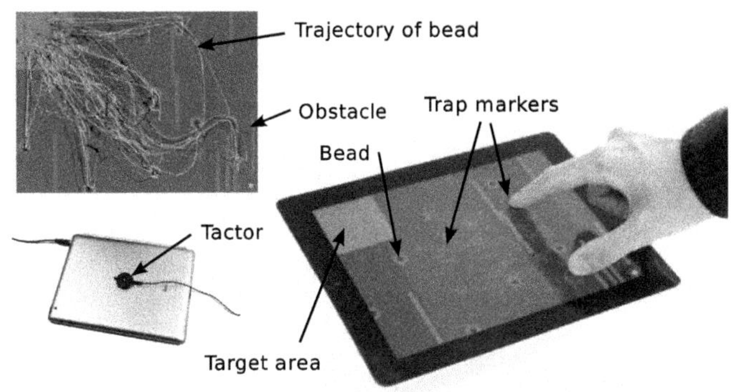

Figure 1: a) Running an experiment with the simulator on a tablet, with a user manipulating particles. b) Plots indicating user behaviour in one of the experiments.

Interaction challenges

Guiding several particles dynamically, simultaneously along trajectories is a non-trivial problem, not easily solved with a mouse or joystick based interface. Multi-touch tablets or surfaces allow the user to simultaneously manipulate multiple particles, overcoming a limitation of mouse-based interfaces. The tablet form factor used here is more convenient and affordable than the previously-used table [4]. However, as the number of optical traps increases, each trap becomes weaker, leading to an increased lag in movement, and an increased likelihood of dropping the trapped object, if moved too rapidly. As the tablet's touch interface is an absolute position interface, where the finger obscures the object in the trap, it is important to consider designs which provide appropriate feedback to the user to allow them to control the system efficiently.

The issue of occlusion in touch interaction is well-known in mobile HCI, e.g. [11], but the challenges in this application differ from the typical occlusion problems in HCI. In the optical tweezer application, users are often dragging several objects in traps to a particular location, in order to create a specific geometric structure, where they are focussed on the goal, and potentially on avoiding obstructions on the way. The dynamics of the individual traps varies rapidly as the number of traps changes, and it is relatively easy for the user to pull too fast and drop the contents of one of the traps, but only to discover this several seconds later, when they arrive at the goal. Offsetting the selected trap would not improve the matter.

FEEDBACK DESIGN

The feedback design is aimed at making the system easier to learn, reducing the number of errors occurring in use, and speeding up performance. When a user has trapped an object on the tablet, their finger obscures the visual feedback, making it difficult for them to control their behaviour as they move to drag the object away. To support the user, we generate audio and vibrotactile feedback that are a function of the user's movement velocity, the strength of trap, and the relationship between trap and objects, i.e. it is modelled around the physical attributes of the particles during manipulation. If multiple traps are controlled, the sounds are the same for each, in this implementation. The audio and vibrotactile feedback is presented via an EAI C2 Tactor[1] taped to the centre of the back of the tablet, and a stereo line splitter allows the separation of audio and tactile signals. Users could hold the device in their hands as normal. The physical insight of the equations of motion of particles affected by traps informed the design of the vibrotactile and audio feedback. In fig. 2 we show the time-series of states, and the vibrotactile response.

Feedback is only provided when a user-controlled trap is interacting with a particle. The feedback is based on all three dimensions. Three different real-time sound models were used to supply the user of the tablet interface with auditory feedback while controlling the optical probe. When objects are moved on the screen a sliding/scratching sound is generated, as of a small solid object sliding on a rough hard surface. This sound depends in every instant on the velocity with which the object is being moved. If the user has tried to move an object too quickly so that it drops, the sound of a falling object such as a light plastic cup is synthesized. The velocity of the user's movement in the moment of the "accident" is mapped to the height or, equivalently, initial velocity of the modelled falling object such that faster movements result in sounds of a cup falling from larger heights (or larger initial impulse).

It is likely that prior to a user's attempt at manipulating the system, they will have a poor intuition about the laser's capabilities in terms of manipulation potential (as this depends on the number of traps already selected), resulting in attempts to move a particle too quickly, with the consequence of dropped particles. They tend to move slower than optimal, wasting resources and reducing work throughput. To persuade users to stay within a safe speed range, while still maintaining the highest possible throughput, a third type of feedback is used. When the user taps on an object on the tablet a short ringing sound, as of a small metal bell, is synthesized, and the tone is adjusted as a function of trap strength. As more traps are added to the interface, the strength of each trap weakens. This feedback is generated regardless of the presence of a particle

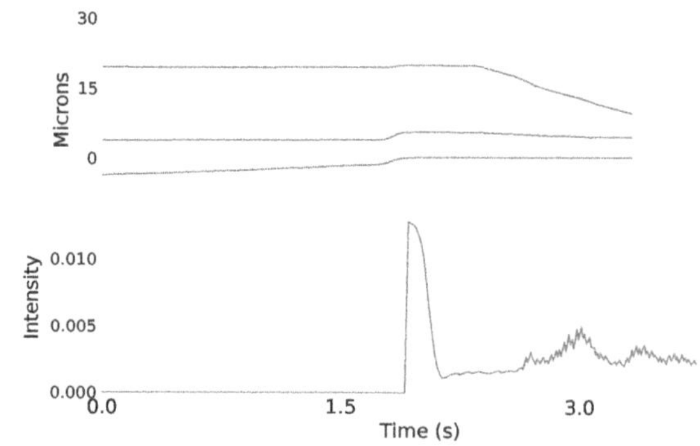

Figure 2: State evolution (x, y, z) of a particle being trapped, then at 2.25s following as the user drags the trap. The lower plot shows the intensity of the vibrotactile response.

in the trap or not, so before the user performs any action on the particles, they are inherently aware of the laser's current particle manipulation capabilitites.

SYNTHESIS OF FRICTION AND IMPACT EFFECTS

All auditory feedback in this tablet interface is generated by means of a real-time sound synthesis engine which can generate everyday impact and friction responses, rather than by playing back recorded sound files. The use of real-time synthesis was chosen, as it provides the potential to provide rich real-time feedback about the continuous states of the controlled system. The main technique used in synthesising the sound feedback is known as "modal synthesis" and has been used for the modelling of environmental sounds [6, 10, 8]. It allows us to characterise resonant behaviours, e.g. of vibrating solid objects such as the metal bell or the sounding cup used in the tablet interface in this paper, by means of a set of resonant frequencies and according decay times, or, equivalently, Q-factors. Implementation takes the form of a second-order IIR filter for each considered mode of vibration. For simple but efficient sound behaviours, such as the ones used in the present interface, even a couple of modes can be sufficient. The overall computational cost of these sound models is therefore relatively low.

While modal description can often be used very successfully to model vibration around an equilibrium, such as for elastic deformation of a solid object that is not extremely and enduringly deformed, generally additional techniques are needed to model interactions between two or more objects. In the present sound models, the contact forces in sliding, dropping and hitting are generated as statistical patterns of impulses; in the case of sliding contact the interaction force also includes a continuous component of bandlimited noise. This approach is very similar to the one used in *Phya* [6] where, however, the impulse patterns are for the most part generated by (or an the basis of information from) a game physics engine external to the sound engine. For mobile devices, as the use of such physics engines is neither inherently necessary nor appropriate, interaction forces have to be modelled "from scratch" as part of the sound engine. The generation of the impulse and noise patterns adds only minimal computational effort so that the overall sound generation algorithm remains

[1] http://www.eaiinfo.com/PDF Documents/C-2 tactor.pdf

sufficiently lightweight to be used as part of a user interface on a mobile device. Synthesising sound feedback in real-time generates more richly varied feedback and saves memory and sample acquisition effort when parameterising a wide range of responses.

The key aspect of the synthesis approach is that it inherently supports instantaneous reactivity of sounds reflecting the dynamics of the control interaction. In the current case, the sliding sound directly reflects the momentary velocity of the user's control movement, which cannot be perceived due to the occluded target, and the perceived height of the dropping sound provides the user with feedback about the excessive speed of movement that lead to the error. The ringing sound on acquiring a trap provides feedback about the potential force that can be applied by that trap.

SIMULATION ENVIRONMENT FOR DESIGN

The tablet interface is usually coupled directly to a microscope, but one innovation in this paper is the development of a realistic simulation environment as a convenient way of training new users, and testing the interface in a consistent manner. Optical tweezers are typically used to manipulate micron-sized particles in a fluid, and thus the motion of a trapped object is usually governed by three forces: the spring-like force pulling it towards the trap, viscous drag from the fluid and random thermal motion caused by collisions with the molecules of the fluid. Inertia is not an important effect at this length scale, thus the system is overdamped by the fluid (usually water) in which the particles are manipulated. Simulating the behaviour of optically trapped particles is thus relatively simple.

The important quantities are the positions of the beads and optical traps; we denote the position of the ith bead as x_i and the jth trap as $x_{\mathrm{T}j}$. The collisions of molecules of the fluid with our particle give rise to a fluctuating force ζ which, on millisecond timescales, is a Gaussian random variable, independent and identically distributed for each particle and timestep. The force from an optical trap is proportional to the displacement of the bead from that trap $x_i - x_{\mathrm{T}j}$, giving a force $-\kappa(x_i - x_{\mathrm{T}j})$, where κ is the spring constant of a trap. Finally, viscous drag gives rise to a force proportional to velocity $-\gamma\dot{x}_i$ where $\dot{x}$ represents the first derivative with respect to time and γ is the friction coefficient. These can be combined in the Langevin equation for a trapped particle $-\kappa\sum_j(x_i - x_{\mathrm{T}j}) - \gamma\dot{x}_i = \zeta$. Solving this for the motion of a particle over a time δ and explicitly showing the dependence of x_i on time, we find $x_i(t+\delta) = x_i(t) + R - \alpha\sum_j(x_i(t) - x_{\mathrm{T}j}(t))$, where $\alpha = 1 - \exp(\kappa\delta/\gamma)$ is related to the rate at which the particle returns to the centre of the trap following a displacement and R is a Gaussian random variable representing Brownian motion. However, the linear force-displacement relationship is only valid for small displacements. We therefore introduce a cubic term such that the force falls to zero at the "capture radius" r_c (i.e. the maximum distance at which the particle experiences a force), which is around one particle diameter.

We typically measure the positions of all particles which are in (or near) optical traps with image analysis. HOTs position the traps in an extremely repeatable way, so it is not necessary to directly measure the trap positions $x_{\mathrm{T}j}$ in order to infer the forces $\kappa(x - x_{\mathrm{T}})$. At each simulation step, we add the random displacement R to each particle's position, then we add the displacement for each trap closer than r_c; $x_i = x_i - \alpha(x_i - x_{\mathrm{T}j})\left(1 - d_{ij}^2/r_c\right)$, where d_{ij} is the 3D distance between bead i and trap j. We then add in the "scattering force" from the laser, which we approximate as an upwards force on each particle in a trap (causing particles to sit slightly above the trap positions) and also add in a small downwards force on each bead to represent gravity $z_i = z_i - v_{\mathrm{s}}\delta$ where v_{s} is set such that the particles sediment to the bottom of the simulation volume in a few seconds. Experienced users validated that interacting with the simulator was close enough to the real system.

EXPERIMENT DESIGN

To test the impact of the multimodal feedback we compared the original iTweezers application with the new application with the additional vibration and audio feedback enabled. All twelve participants were considered novice users, as they had never used optical tweezers or similar systems before. The task design for each trial involved ten particles being placed at random coordinates on the screen, as illustrated in Fig.1. Users were told to collect all the particles and deposit them in a target area, which is shown as a blue square on the interface, avoiding varying numbers of obstacles. Each trial run had a different layout and required path, but the experiment was constant across all participants. Users were split evenly into two groups, with one group performing evenly-numbered tasks with multimodal feedback and odd-numbered tasks with just visual feedback, and the other group performing the reverse. Each trial run contains specific obstacles around which the user had to navigate. If a particle comes into contact with one of these obstacles, an error is logged by the system. Likewise, if the user attempts to move a particle too quickly, and the particle is dropped, an error is logged. These reported errors, along with the overall time to complete each task, provide a performance measure of the completed task.

Early experiments with a single trap showed negligible differences between the feedback modes, due to the ease of control, so in order to challenge the users appropriately, three traps were provided to pick up the particles. This meant that the overall power of each trap was divided by a third, making it much more easy to drop a particle. This made the task of moving a particle with a trap require greater concentration. As the participants progressed through the trials, the skill required to complete them error-free increased. Each sequential task involved one additional obstacle placed at random coordinates, meaning users must deviate their path in order to avoid them while increasing the risk of causing errors. In all tasks, all finger contacts were logged. This information provides us with a descriptive metric of the user behaviour differences between the original system and the feedback enabled one. Each user performed 15 trials, but we ignored the data from the first trial for each user. Two performance metrics were used: Time to completion, t_c, Number of errors N_e. The particle trajectories were also recorded for analysis.

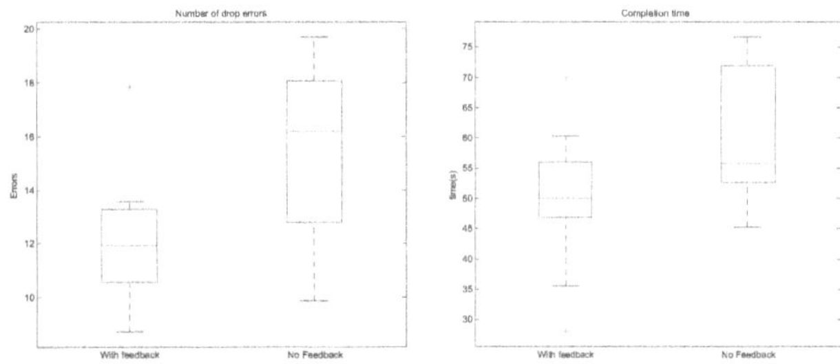

Figure 3: a) Box plots comparing error rates (N_e) and time to completion (t_c). With feedback, t_c was ($\mu = 50.01s, \sigma = 10.91$), Without feedback t_c was ($\mu = 60.04s, \sigma = 11.11$). With feedback N_e was ($\mu = 12.14, \sigma = 2.34$), Without feedback N_e was ($\mu = 15.39, \sigma = 3.45$).

A separate experiment was included to evaluate force control ability, a task with a circular obstacle around which users had to drag a bead at a constant force. This involved three expert users (physicists who were experienced in particle manipulation in microscopes using the iTweezer system, and who were generally faster and less error prone than naive users), and 12 naive users (graduate students in their 20s) who had never worked with the system, randomly allocated to multimodal or visual conditions.

RESULTS

Users with multimodal feedback performed significantly more quickly (on a Wilcoxon paired two-sided signed rank test at $p = 0.0005$), taking only 83% of the time, averaged over all three-trap trials. Despite the increased speed, users did this with significantly fewer drop errors (on a Wilcoxon paired two-sided rank test at $p = 0.0132$), an average of 3.25 fewer per trial, 78% of the error rate without feedback. The distribution of these data are summarised in Boxplots in figure 3 for the 12 naive users. The force variability experiment also showed a difference between visual and multimodal cases, where users with multimodal feedback had less variability in the distance of the trap from the bead during the circumnavigation of the circle $\sigma_f = 16.09$ compared to $\sigma_f = 26.86$, so users were better able to apply constant force on an object, while moving around the perimeter of the object's boundaries. However this result is not significant, with a $p = 0.1213$ on a Kruskal-Wallis test.

CONCLUSIONS

A combination of vibrotactile and audio feedback improved the usability of a tablet application for control of optical tweezers at the micron scale. The experiments demonstrate that the use of real-time synthesised multimodal feedback improved task performance in a touch-controlled, tablet-based optical tweezers application, significantly increasing speed and decreasing error rates in object placement tasks. In terms of subjective feedback, most users commented on the multimodal feedback making them aware of dropping the ball more rapidly without having to devote too much visual attention to each trapped object. Several said that after using the multimodal condition, they found the effort increased when they moved to visual-only. Professional users (who were not part of the experiment) were faster than naive users in all conditions, but they still commented on how surprised they were about the added value of the multimodal feedback. The fact that users have the sensation of direct physical contact with micron-sized objects which they could never normally perceive is also something that excited even professional scientists, and suggests potential applications of this in teaching and public engagement situations.

ACKNOWLEDGEMENTS

Support from the Scottish Informatics and Computing Science Alliance (SICSA), SUPA | Physics Scotland, EPSRC, Nokia and a University of Glasgow summer studentship.

REFERENCES

1. A. Ashkin, J. M. Dziedzic, J. E. Bjorkholm, and S. Chu. Observation of a single-beam gradient force optical trap for dielectric particles. *Opt. Lett.*, 11(5):288–290, 1986.
2. R. W. Bowman, G. Gibson, D. Carberry, L. Picco, M. Miles, and M. J. Padgett. iTweezers: optical micromanipulation controlled by an Apple iPad. *Journal of Optics*, 13(044002), 2011.
3. S. Brewster, F. Chohan, and L. Brown. Tactile feedback for mobile interactions. In *Proc. SIGCHI*, pages 159–162, New York, NY, USA, 2007. ACM.
4. J. A. Grieve, A. Ulcinas, S. Subramanian, G. M. Gibson, M. J. Padgett, D. M. Carberry, and M. J. Miles. Hands-on with optical tweezers: a multitouch interface for holographic optical trapping. *Optics Express*, 17(5):3595–3602, 2009.
5. J. Leach, K. Wulff, G. Sinclair, P. Jordan, J. Courtial, L. Thomson, G. Gibson, K. Karunwi, J. Cooper, Z. J. Laczik, and M. Padgett. Interactive approach to optical tweezers control. *Appl. Opt.*, 45(5):897–903, 2006.
6. D. Menzies. Physical audio for virtual environments, phya in review. In *ICAD'07*, pages 197–202, 2007.
7. J. E. Molloy, J. E. Burns, J. Kendrick-jones, R. T. Tregear, and D. C. S. White. Movement and force produced by a single myosin head. *Nature*, 378(6553):209–212, 1995.
8. M. Rath. Energy-stable modelling of contacting modal objects with piece-wise linear interaction force. In *DAFx-08*, Espoo, Finland, 2008.
9. M. Reicherter, T. Haist, E. Wagemann, and H. Tiziani. Optical particle trapping with computer-generated holograms written on a liquid-crystal display. *Opt. Lett.*, 24(9):608–610, 1999.
10. K. van del Doel, P. G. Kry, and D. K. Pai. Foleyautomatic: Physically-based sound effects for interactive simulation and animation. In *Siggraph'01*, 2001.
11. D. Vogel and R. Balakrishnan. Occlusion-aware interfaces. In *SIGCHI'10*, pages 263–272. ACM, 2010.
12. J. Williamson, R. Murray-Smith, and S. Hughes. Shoogle: Multimodal excitatory interaction on mobile devices. In *CHI '07*, pages 121–124. ACM Press, 2007.

An Evaluation of BrailleTouch: Mobile Touchscreen Text Entry for the Visually Impaired

Caleb Southern[1], James Clawson[1], Brian Frey[2], Gregory D. Abowd[1], Mario Romero[1]

[1]Georgia Institute of Technology
85 Fifth Street NW, Atlanta, GA 30332, USA
caleb.southern@gatech.edu, jamer@cc.gatech.edu,
abowd@gatech.edu, mario@gatech.edu

[2]University of Maryland, Baltimore County
1000 Hilltop Circle, ITE Building, Suite 415
Baltimore, MD 21250, USA
frey1@umbc.edu

ABSTRACT

We present the evaluation of BrailleTouch, an accessible keyboard for blind users on touchscreen smartphones. Based on the standard Perkins Brailler, BrailleTouch implements a six-key chorded braille soft keyboard. Eleven blind participants typed for 165 twenty-minute sessions on three mobile devices: 1) BrailleTouch on a smartphone; 2) a soft braille keyboard on a touchscreen tablet; and 3) a commercial braille keyboard with physical keys. Expert blind users averaged 23.2 words per minute (wpm) on the BrailleTouch smartphone. The fastest participant, a touchscreen novice, achieved 32.1 wpm during his first session. Overall, participants were able to transfer their existing braille typing skills to a touchscreen device within an hour of practice. We report the speed for braille text entry on three mobile devices, an in depth error analysis, and the lessons learned for the design and evaluation of accessible and eyes-free soft keyboards.

Author Keywords

Accessibility; text entry; blindness; mobile devices; touchscreens; multi-touch interaction; chording; gestures.

ACM Classification Keywords

H.5.2. [Information Interfaces and Presentation]: User Interfaces – Input devices and strategies, Voice I/O.

K.4.2. [Computers and Society]: Social issues – assistive technologies for persons with disabilities.

INTRODUCTION

While volunteering at a local vision rehabilitation center, we observed a teenager using a mysterious portable device with six buttons. Although bulky and awkward, it was entirely effective at making her giggle at what we realized were text messages from a friend. She was like any other teenager with a smartphone, an expert at texting. The only difference was that she was doing it on the braille keyboard of a Braille Sense Plus. Upon researching this device, we were shocked to discover that it cost $6000. We recognized a potential cause for a profound digital divide, and a significant design challenge: *How can we support affordable text entry for the visually impaired on inexpensive commodity mobile devices?*

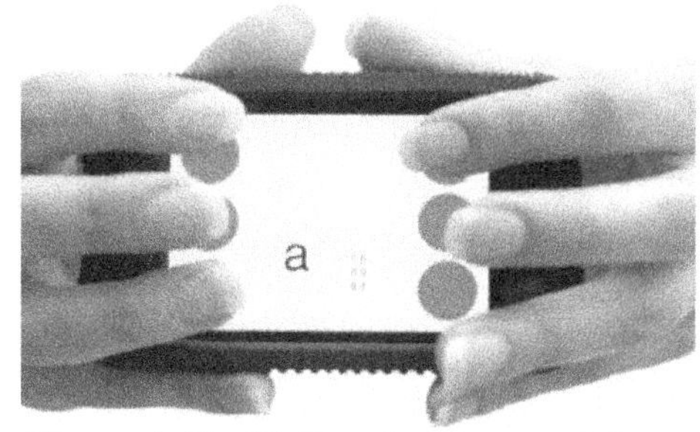

Figure 1. BrailleTouch on a smartphone.

As evidenced by today's young adults, texting is a dominant form of mobile communication and connectivity. American cell owners between the ages of 18 and 24 send or receive, on average, 109.5 text messages compared to 17.1 calls per day [23]. Today's technologies support mobile text entry poorly due to the size constraints of mobile devices. Phones have too many buttons, physical or virtual, that are too small. Most users have no option but to look at their device while typing. This problem is particularly limiting for the visually impaired. With 284 million visually impaired people worldwide [26], it is imperative to create affordable forms of accessible text entry.

Previously, we presented the design of BrailleTouch, an eyes-free text entry system for mobile devices (see Figure 1) [7, 22]. The contributions of the evaluation reported here are: 1) the first formal measure of English text entry speed and accuracy on a standard braille keyboard; and 2) an analysis of typing speed and accuracy across three experimental conditions: a traditional electronic braille keyboard; a soft braille keyboard on a touchscreen tablet; and the BrailleTouch soft keyboard on a smartphone.

RELATED WORK

In this section, we tell the history of manual, mechanical, and electronic braille writing and the most relevant methods for eyes-free mobile text entry.

MobileHCI'12, September 21–24, 2012, San Francisco, CA, USA.

Device Name	Braille Display	Price (USD 2012)
GW Micro Braille Sense Plus	Yes	6000
GW Micro Voice Sense	No	2000
Humanware VoiceNote BT	No	2000
Freedom Scientific PACmate BX 400	No	1500
AFB Braille+ Mobile Manager	No	1400
Humanware Maestro	No	1300
EmpTech Nano Braille PDA	No	1000

Table 1. Common commercial braille notetakers.

A Brief History of Braille Writing

In 1821, twelve-year-old Louis Braille witnessed Barbier's tactile writing system demonstration [16]. Deeply inspired, he optimized the raised-dot system to a cell that fits under a single fingertip and encodes 63 (2^6–1) characters on a 3×2 binary matrix, with dots numbered one through six in column-major order (see Figure 2) [3].

In 1829, Braille and Barbier introduced the slate and stylus, the analog to pen and paper for sighted people [25]. Until the advent of electronic braille "notetakers", the slate and stylus was the only portable device for blind people to write and read notes. Still in use, it consists of a hinged guide for dot-by-dot manual input with an awl. A person writes braille characters on the back of the page from right to left in mirror image, and turns the page over to read from the front.

Frank Hall invented the first mechanical braillewriter in 1895, which introduced the standard six-key chorded keyboard [25]. The keyboard unfolds the braille cell using dots 1 and 4 as hinges, resulting in the key arrangement of (3, 2, 1) and (4, 5, 6). The Perkins Brailler adopted the Hall keyboard and remains the standard today. In addition to the six main keys, the Perkins has a spacebar, a backspace key on the far right, and a paper advance key on the far left (see Figure 3).

In 1986, predating the PDA by a decade, Dean Blazie introduced the Braille 'n Speak, the world's first portable electronic braille note taking device [10]. Featuring the Perkins-style keyboard and speech output, it became the first alternative to the slate and stylus for taking braille notes while on-the-go. Today there are many braille notetakers, unfortunately all expensive (see Table 1).

While there are many studies of braille reading performance, there exist only two studies measuring braille writing performance on the six-key keyboard, none in English. Lee et al. measured the speed of a commercial braille keyboard for Korean text entry at 27.9 words per minute (wpm) with 2.8% error [15]. Oliveira et al. measured the speed of Portuguese text entry on a Perkins Brailler at 16.7 wpm [20].

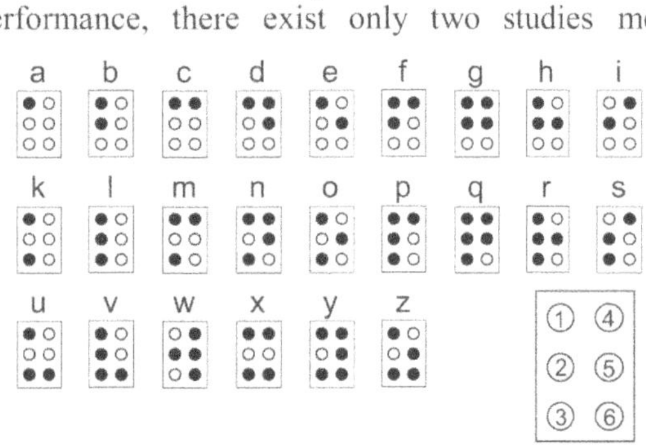

Figure 2. The braille cell and code for English.

Eyes-Free Mobile Text Entry

Although portable, most braille notetakers are too large to be considered mobile devices. We discuss a range of eyes-free mobile keyboards designed for the visually impaired.

Touchscreen Braille Keyboards

Kane et al. presented *Slide Rule*, an interface to control mobile devices with multi-touch input and audio feedback [12]. While Slide Rule employs a soft QWERTY keyboard for text entry, the authors suggested a soft braille chorded keyboard as future work. Fard et al. presented a design for such a device, but did not implement it [6]. Although not mobile, Keles developed a braille keyboard on the IMPAD touch input surface [14].

Oliveira et al. presented *BrailleType*, where the user sequentially enters one dot at a time and signals the end of the braille character with a double tap [21]. Its speed was 1.45 wpm with 9.7% error. Mascetti et al. presented *TypeInBraille*, in which the user types the braille cell one row (2 dots) at a time and enters `space` with a flick gesture [18]. TypeInBraille's speed was 6.3 wpm with 3% error. Azenkot et al. presented *Perkinput*, a chorded input for touchscreens where the braille cell is typed one column (3 dots) at a time [1]. Perkinput's speed was 6.1 wpm with an uncorrected error rate of 3.5%. After the date of our evaluation, Radomir Bruder, a visually impaired hobbyist from Slovakia, released but did not evaluate the *Type Brailler Learn Braille* app for the iPhone [4]. The user can chord all six braille dots simultaneously with the screen facing away, in a similar manner to BrailleTouch.

Other Mobile Keyboards for the Blind

Oliveira et al. and Azenkot et al. both evaluated accessible soft QWERTY keyboards, similar to Apple's *VoiceOver* split-tap keyboard for the iPhone [1, 21]. In the split-tap interaction, the first tap produces a voiced output of the character under the finger and a second tap

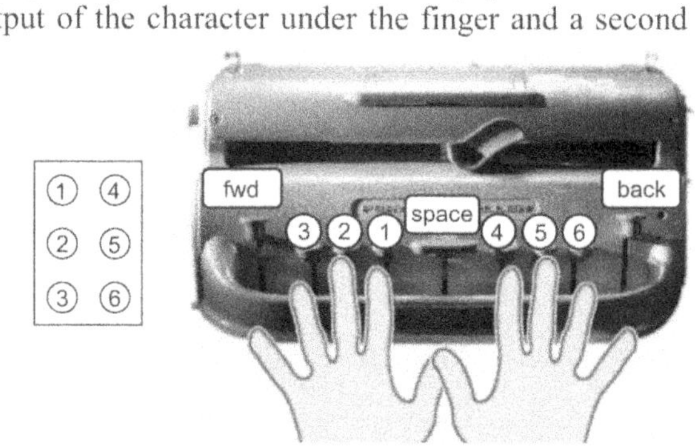

Figure 3. Mapping braille on to the Perkins Brailler.

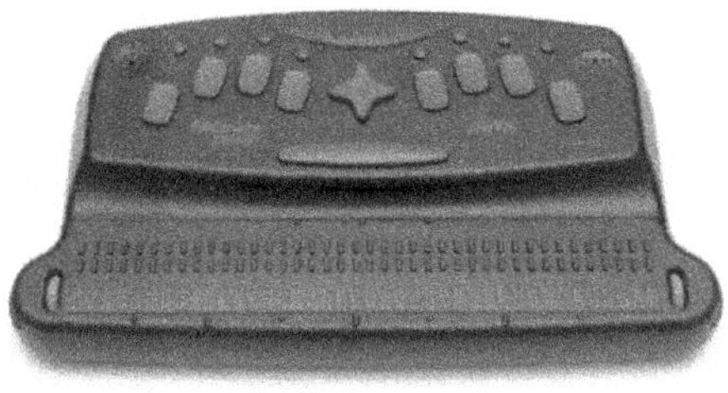

Figure 4. Freedom Scientific PACmate BX400.

Figure 5. Perkins-style keyboard on a tablet.

selects the character. The speed of split-tap text entry was 2.11 to 3.99 wpm with 5.2% to 6.4% error.

Bonner et al. presented *No-Look-Notes*, a multi-touch eyes-free text entry system that divides the touchscreen into eight pie segments for a first-level selection of character sets and provides a second-level menu for individual character selection [2]. No-Look-Notes' speed was 1.33 wpm with 11% error.

Guerreiro et al. measured three eyes-free text-entry techniques for the standard physical 3×4 numeric keypad on a mobile phone: *Multi-tap*, *NavTap*, and *BrailleTap* [11]. Multi-tap assigns groups of characters to keys 2 through 9. For instance, users press key 2 once for A, twice for B, and three times for C. Guerreiro et al. measured multi-tap's speed at 0.88 wpm with 15.28% error. NavTap provides a navigation interface for a 5×6 virtual table of the alphabet where vowels occupy the first column. Its speed was 1.37 wpm with 9.87% error. BrailleTap maps the 3×2 braille cell to the six keys on the upper right corner of the 4×3 keypad. Users input a character one dot a time, and signal the end of the dot sequence by pressing key 4. BrailleTap's speed was 3.6 wpm with 6.55% error.

Lee et al. presented a braille text entry glove [15]. The typing speed for their experimental braille glove was 24.3 wpm with 5.2% error. Similarly Miele et al. developed but have not evaluated an accelerometer glove that allows the user to chord braille on any flat surface, such as a desk [19].

BrailleTouch Design

The design goal for BrailleTouch was to provide affordable and accessible text entry for the visually impaired on commodity smartphones [7, 22]. Our initial challenge was to accommodate six fingers simultaneously on the limited screen area of a multi-touch smartphone. To solve this challenge, we designed BrailleTouch to be held with two hands, with the screen facing *away* from the user (see Figure 1), similar to the Lucid Touch see-through interaction [27]. The rationale was that blind users need not see the screen. The index, middle, and ring fingers of each hand wrap around the edges of the phone and land on a 3×2 keyboard with the same finger-to-key convention used on standard braille keyboards. We implemented the `space`, `backspace`, and `enter` control keys through gestures: right-flick, left-flick, and two-finger right-flick, respectively.

STUDY DESIGN

We investigated the typing performance of blind users on three experimental braille keyboards: 1) BrailleTouch on a touchscreen smartphone; 2) a soft braille keyboard on a touchscreen tablet; and 3) the PACmate, a commercial braille keyboard with physical buttons. We describe the participants, apparatus, methodology, and procedure.

Participants

We recruited eleven visually impaired participants (4 male) through a newsletter circulated by the Center for the Visually Impaired in Atlanta, GA, USA, and through the Georgia Radio Reading Service (GaRRS) statewide radio broadcast. Additional volunteers contacted us through referrals from other participants. The average age was 47.4 (SD=14.1, range: 28 – 65). Nine participants were blind from birth. All participants were self-described as "proficient with the six-key braille typing system." We did not require or assume prior experience with touchscreen devices; only three owned an iPhone (see Table 2).

P	Age	Sex	CVL	Handed	Br	Job	Ed	iPhone
A1	57	M	0	R	5	N	16	
A2	57	F	0	R	7	N	16	
A3	65	F	0	L	7	N	18	
A4	30	F	0	R	4	N	16	
A5	58	F	0	R	7	Y	13	Y
A6	49	F	0	L	6	Y	19	Y
B1	46	M	32	R	29	Y	17	Y
B2	38	M	0	R	5	N	12	
B3	29	F	27	R	11	Y	12	
C1	28	F	0	L	5	Y	12	
C2	64	M	35	A	7	N	12	

Table 2: Participants. CVL = current vision level since age; Br = age learned braille; Ed = education level (grades).

Apparatus

Our study apparatus consisted of the three experimental braille input devices networked with a PC which ran the typing test software, presented uniform audio feedback for all devices, and recorded performance logs.

For the control condition, we used a Freedom Scientific PACmate BX400 braille notetaker (see Figure 4). For the tablet experimental condition, we implemented a soft braille keyboard on an Apple iPad, based on the PACmate keyboard layout (see Figure 5). The PACmate is a commercial braille notetaker with six physical keys in the standard Perkins arrangement, plus a space bar, `backspace` on the left, and `enter` on the right. The PACmate's keyboard design is comparable to that of other braille notetakers (see Table 1). On the tablet, the user initially defines a comfortable keyboard location on the screen through an eight-finger press-and-hold gesture, an then types. The smartphone experimental condition was BrailleTouch on an Apple iPod Touch (see Figure 1).

Each of the three braille input devices wirelessly transmitted typed characters to a central PC, which provided uniform audio feedback for all three typing conditions and ran the typing test software. Therefore, the input interaction on each of the three braille keyboards was the only independent variable that differed between the experimental conditions during the typing task.

Methodology

We modified the standard text entry study methodology to accommodate visually impaired participants.

From Transcription to Dictation

In traditional text entry studies, sighted participants read short phrases from a screen and transcribe them on the experimental keyboard. Because visually impaired participants cannot use visual phrase stimuli, we presented phrases to the participants through audio for a dictation task. We employed a speech synthesizer, the American English voice in Google's online language translation utility, to ensure uniform delivery [9]. Dictation, in the form of taking notes on a braille keyboard, is a common real-world task for blind users, hence the name "braille notetaker" for the class of devices including the PACmate.

Phrase Set

MacKenzie and Soukoreff developed a standard set of 500 English phrases commonly used in text entry studies [17]. These phrases approximate the letter frequency of the English language. As is typical in text entry studies, we asked our participants to only input lower-case letters and spaces, with no numbers or punctuation.

A dictation-based text entry study introduces three auditory confounds not present in visual transcription tasks: 1) phrases can be aurally ambiguous; 2) users may not know the spelling of a word; and 3) users may not comprehend the delivered speech. We mitigated aural ambiguity by removing problematic phrases from the standard MacKenzie-Soukoreff phrase set. Criteria for removing phrases included homophones, compound words, and mondegreens (phrases aurally similar to others). We removed 65 of the 500 phrases from the standard phrase set. MacKenzie and Soukoreff provide software for analyzing the correlation of a phrase set to English [17]. The correlation for their original phrase set is .954, and for our modified set is .952.

Typing Test Software

We modified the Twidor typing test software, freely available at [8], by adding speech synthesis to present the phrases and audio feedback for the keyboard input. For each character typed, Twidor played a typewriter click sound effect, similar to the mechanical Perkins brailler. When the user backspaced, the system played a *swoosh* sound effect, in addition to the speech of the letter erased. Finally, we played a distinct sound effect when the user pressed `enter` to submit a phrase.

Unlike with sighted users who can see presented phrases on the screen, the visually impaired might not know how to spell a word, might not remember the entire phrase while typing, or may not comprehend the delivered speech. In an effort to address these challenges we implemented two hints in our typing test software to mitigate these factors. The first hint (chord 4-5-6) spelled out the entire phrase, letter by letter, before the timer started. The second hint (chord 1-4-5-6) repeated the entire phrase.

Experimental Procedure

We structured our study as a 3×5 within-subjects design with two independent variables: *Device* (PACmate, tablet, smartphone) and *Session* (1 to 5). During each session, participants performed a 20-minute typing test on each of the three devices, separated by a short break. Sessions lasted approximately 90 minutes. Each session was separated by at least 90 minutes and no more than three days. We counterbalanced the three conditions across participants and sessions to control for ordering effects.

During each typing test, participants typed as many blocks of ten phrases from dictation as they could start within a 20-minute period (see Video Figure 1). We instructed them to type the phrases "as quickly and accurately as possible." After each block of ten phrases, we provided verbal feedback on their most recent speed (wpm) and accuracy, and encouraged participants to briefly rest their hands.

At the beginning of the study, we trained participants and gave them the opportunity to practice on the three devices. To avoid contaminating participants with actual test phrases, we presented them with phrases from an alternative corpus, the Children's Phrase Set [13]. Before each typing test, we allowed participants time to briefly warm up with two practice phrases: (1) the alphabet; and (2) "this is a practice sentence".

We compensated participants at the rate of \$0.125 × wpm × accuracy for each 20-minute typing test, with a floor of \$2.00 per test. In addition, we offered a \$5 bonus for completing the entire study. This is a similar scheme to other text entry evaluations [5]. Therefore, all participants whose results are presented here earned at least \$35 (5 sessions × 3 conditions × \$2 + \$5 bonus). Our rationale for rewarding performance was to motivate participants to

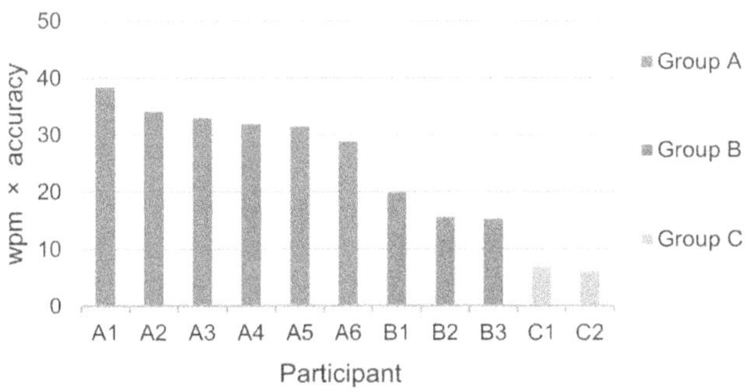

Figure 6: Participant groups clustered on typing Speed×Accuracy on the first session on the PACmate.

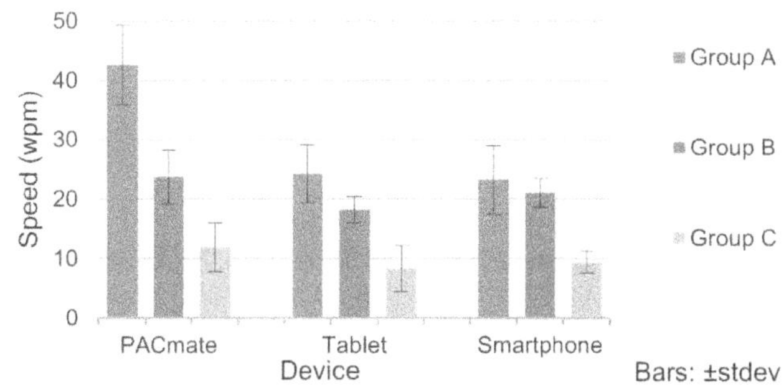

Figure 7: Speed per group per device on last session.

continue to type as quickly and accurately as possible throughout the study.

RESULTS

The eleven participants typed a total of 9092 phrases across 165 twenty-minute typing tests on three braille keyboards. We shall discuss: 1) braille typing performance on a standard keyboard; 2) effects of device and session; 3) performance-based groups of participants; 4) typing speed; and 5) typing accuracy.

Standard Braille Typing Performance

We present the first formal evaluation of English text entry on a standard physical braille keyboard, the PACmate. In the final session, participants averaged 32.9 wpm (SD=14.1), which is consistent with Lee's study in Korea which reported typing speeds of 27.9 wpm on a Perkins-style keyboard [15]. The Total Error Rate (described below) for the PACmate on the final session was 9.41% (SD=6.12%).

Device and Session

There was no significant effect on the touchscreen devices between *Session* 3 and either 4 or 5, indicating that people who know the braille keyboard can transfer their typing skills to a touchscreen within an hour of practice. Surprisingly, we found no significant effect on speed between the tablet and the smartphone, despite their different interaction techniques.

We analyzed the data using a mixed model analysis of variance with fixed effects for *Device* and *Session* and a random effect for *Participant*. We also included *Order* in the model to test for ordering effects. Our counterbalanced order of testing layouts achieved the desired outcome, as the main effect and interactions for *Order* were not statistically significant.

We found a main effect of *Device* on speed ($F_{2,20}$ = 19.968, $p < .001$) as well as a main effect of *Session* on speed ($F_{4,40}$ = 22.369, $p < .001$). To analyze these effects further, we conducted post-hoc pairwise comparisons using Bonferroni correction. The post-hoc test for *Device* shows a significant effect on speed between the PACmate and the tablet (t_{10} = 4.739, $p < .001$) and a significant effect on speed between the PACmate and the smartphone (t_{10} = 4.767, $p < .001$).

The post-hoc test for *Session* shows a significant effect on speed between Sessions 1 and 3 (t_{10} = -5.709, $p < .001$), Sessions 1 and 4 (t_{10} = -4.834, $p < .001$), Sessions 1 and 5 (t_{10} = -6.326, $p < .001$), Sessions 2 and 3 (t_{10} = -4.237, $p < .002$), Sessions 2 and 4 (t_{10} = -5.772, $p < .001$), and Sessions 2 and 5 (t_{10} = -6.780, $p < .001$). No other statistically significant effects on speed were found for *Session*, indicating that from session 3 on, significant learning did not occur. However, due to a significant effect between the first and last session, we use Session 5 for the speed and error analyses below.

Participant Groups

Similar to [20], we observed a wide variance between participants' individual braille typing abilities on the PACmate control device. These skill differences appeared to be related to participants' success in adapting to the touchscreen braille keyboards. As such, using k-means clustering on their performance, we classified participants into three groups (see Figure 6). We determined three groups to be the best clustering set based on the minimum inconsistent clustering coefficients for a hierarchical cluster tree. The classification was based on speed × accuracy (the same metric used to compute compensation) from the first typing session on the PACmate control device. Group A consists of six expert participants (A1-A6); Group B is three participants with moderate performance (B1-B3); and Group C is two participants with poor performance (C1-C2).

Speed

On the PACmate in the fifth session (see Figure 7), Group A averaged 42.6 wpm (SD = 6.7); Group B averaged 23.7 wpm (SD = 4.5); and Group C averaged 11.9 wpm (SD = 4.1). Participants in Groups A and B both typed quickly on the two touchscreen devices. Group A averaged 24.2 and 23.2 wpm on the tablet and smartphone, respectively. Group B averaged 18.2 and 21.0 wpm on the tablet and smartphone, respectively. Group C did not achieve comparable speeds, averaging 8.3 and 9.4 wpm on the

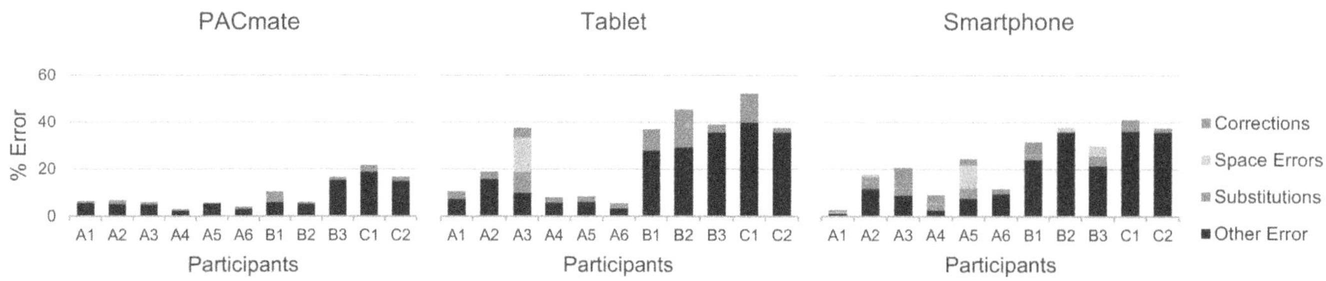

Figure 8: Four error types per participant per device: corrections, space errors, substitutions, other errors.

tablet and smartphone, though this is not much slower than their 11.9 wpm on the PACmate control device.

Accuracy

We first calculated accuracy using MacKenzie and Soukoreff's Total Error Rate, which reflects insertion, deletion, substitution errors, as well as the keystrokes needed to make corrections (i.e. backspaces) [24]. Total error combines the number of errors made and corrected (IF), the number of errors made but not corrected (INF), the number of keystrokes invested in error correction (F), and the number of correct keystrokes (C), such that,

$$Total\ Error\ Rate = \frac{INF+IF}{C+INF+IF} \times 100\%.$$

We report the total error rates for the final session. The expert braille typists in Group A averaged 14.8% and 14.5% error on the tablet and smartphone, respectively. These figures are roughly three times the 5.3% total error on PACmate Session 5. The five participants in Groups B and C completed the study continuing to exhibit error rates on the touchscreen devices prohibitive for real-world usage. Group B averaged 40.5% and 33.1% total error on the tablet and touchscreen, respectively, as compared with 11.0% error on the PACmate. Group C averaged 45.0% and 39.3% total error on the tablet and touchscreen, respectively, compared to19.3% error on the PACmate.

Deconstructing the Error

To better understand errors, we examined the logs of the typing tests and identified three common patterns of errors: *Corrections*; *Substitutions*; and *Space Errors*. Figures 8 and 9 show the contributions of these three classes of error, along with the remaining *Other Error*. The full height of the stacked bars represents the Total Error.

Minimum String Distance (MSD)

Correction errors occur when the user backspaces over a character and then types a replacement character. These are captured in the Total Error Rate. We observed that, for some participants, the final corrected input strings they submitted were much more accurate than what was reflected in their Total Error scores. To quantify this observation, we employed another error metric, the Minimum String Distance (MSD) [24].

MSD captures three types of errors that represent the difference between the presented string and the transcribed string: insertions, deletions, and substitutions. The Levenshtein distance, or MSD, between two character strings is the minimum number of insertion, deletion, and substitution operations necessary to transform one string into another. Oliveira et al. report MSD error in their study of blind text entry [20]. By subtracting the MSD Error from the Total Error for each of the 165 typing sessions, we were able to measure the portion of the Total Error that was due to participants backspacing and correcting their text input.

In order to identify specific instances of substitutions, or input characters being substituted for presented characters, we implemented software to walk through the pairs of strings in the typing logs and line up the pairs of substitution characters, by accounting for insertion and deletion errors.

Below, the bottom line is a string transcribed by participant A5. The underscore represents a deletion error, or omitted character. The top line is the presented string. The underscore represents an input insertion error. By aligning the two strings, accounting for insertions and deletions, we identify character pairs in substitution errors, indicated by the carets on the third row.

```
just what the doctor_ ordered
dofg _f`t the doctor` o"de"ed
^^^^  ^^               ^   ^
```

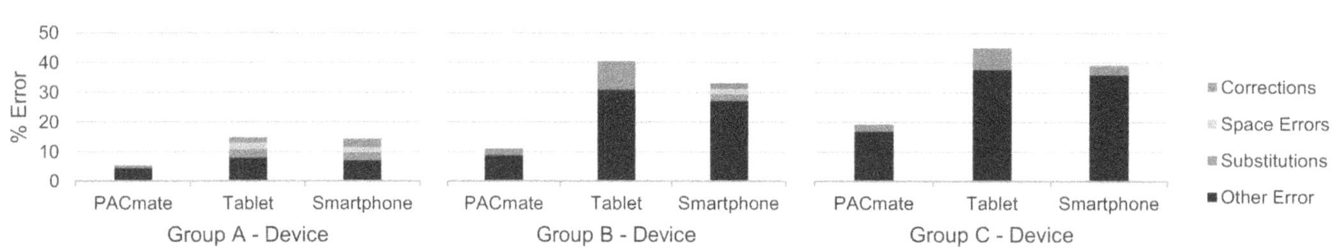

Figure 9: Four average error types per participant group per device.

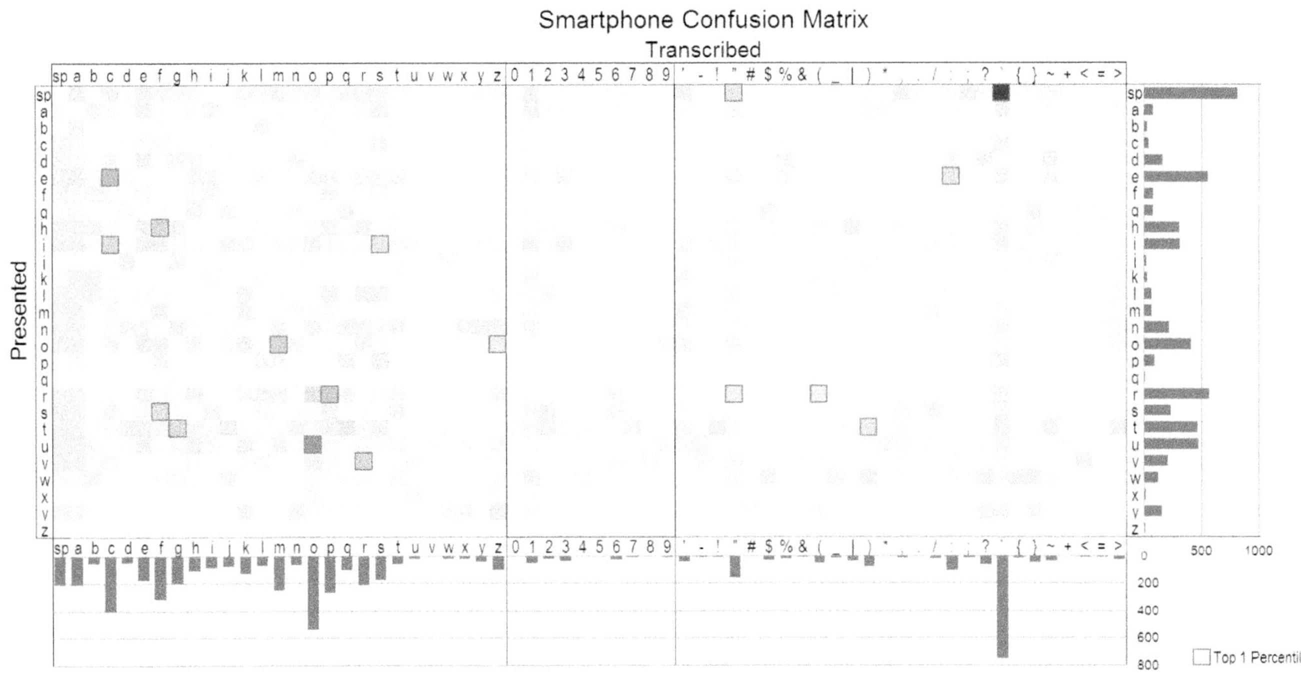

Figure 10: Confusion matrix for substitution errors for Brailletouch on smartphone.

The MSD algorithm calculates an $m \times n$ matrix, where m and n are the lengths of the two strings being compared.The operations to transpose one string into the other can be determined by walking backward through the MSD matrix from the bottom-right to the top left.

One of the most frequent substitutions we observed was `space ← grave accent (`)`. We broke out *Space Errors* as a special case of substitution errors. On the smartphone, the `space` character is typed with a flick gesture to the right. Most participants performed this gesture with their right index fingers. On the braille keyboard, the right index finger falls over dot-4, which represents the grave accent character. Thus, our software failed to accurately recognize the flick gesture for many participants, instead interpreting the touch event as a tap on dot-4. We also observed this same substitution error pair on the tablet soft braille keyboard. While some participants hit the soft space bar with their thumb, as our design anticipated, others moved their right index finger down from dot-4 to tap the spacebar. Thus the same substitution error occurred frequently on both the smartphone and the tablet, although with different causes.

Confusion Matrices

In order to quantify the effect on the error rate from substitution errors, we identified each substitution character pair from the presented and transcribed strings and populated a confusion matrix with the total number of errors for that character pair (see Figure 10). The rows in the matrix represent the 27 presented characters (*a* to *z* plus *space*). The columns represent the 64 possible characters in the transcribed input string typed by the user (63 binary combinations of the six braille dots, plus *space*).

We identified the top 1 percentile of substitution errors for each of the three devices from the confusion matrices (see Table 3). This first percentile accounts for 47% of the total error. Most of these substitution errors could be explained by a 1-dot difference in the corresponding braille chords. For example, in the substitution pair `v ← r`, our software interpreted a dot-5 where the adjacent dot-6 should be. We shall examine this in detail in the Discussion section.

DISCUSSION

We first compare the speed and accuracy of our BrailleTouch system in the context of comparable technologies. We then discuss the design implications of this study for our system, especially in regard to automatic error correction to improve accuracy. Finally, we discuss lessons learned for conducting text entry research with the visually impaired.

Speed and Accuracy

Our touchscreen braille keyboards offer a significant speed advantage over other touchscreen braille keyboards for the visually impaired, all of which report participants' typing speeds of less than 7 wpm. Users with expert and moderate braille typing ability were able to type at approximately 18-24 wpm on both the tablet and smartphone.

One surprising result is that there is no statistically significant effect on speed or accuracy between the two touchscreen devices. We expected to see an effect between each of the three devices. The PACmate and tablet differ in that one has physical buttons, while the other has virtual buttons on flat glass. The tablet and the smartphone differ ergonomically and in the keyboard orientation. Our analysis shows that moving from physical buttons to a touchscreen matters, but rotating one's hand position (tablet vs. smartphone) does not.

Our expert participants' average touchscreen error rate of ~15% was in line with results from other assistive technology text entry evaluations, such as MultiTap (15%) and BrailleType (8%) for the visually impaired [20] and Edgewrite for people with motor disabilities (29.56%) [28]. Concerned with the prohibitive error rates we observed from Groups B and C, we further examined what types of errors the participants were committing, and how we could change our touchscreen designs to improve accuracy.

	Presented Character	Transcribed character	Presented braille	Transcribed braille	Dot-level analysis	Gesture-level interpretation
1.	sp	`	swipe	⠈	4-insertion	Missed swipe
2.	u	o	⠥	⠕	5-del + 6-ins	R. F2 drift down
3.	e	c	⠑	⠉	5-de l+ 4-ins	R. F2 drift up
4.	r	p	⠗	⠏	5-del + 4-ins	R. F2 drift up
5.	o	m	⠕	⠍	5-del + 4-ins	R. F2 drift up
6.	v	r	⠧	⠗	6-del + 5-ins	R. F2 drift up
7.	h	f	⠓	⠋	5-del + 4-ins	R. F2 drift up
8.	t	g	⠞	⠛	3-del + 1-ins	L. F1 F2 drift up
9.	i	c	⠊	⠉	2-del + 1-ins	L. F2 drift up
10.	s	f	⠎	⠋	3-del + 1-ins	L. F1 F2 drift up
11.	e	:	⠑	⠱	6-ins	
12.	r	o	⠗	⠕	2-del	
13.	sp	“	swipe	⠐	5-ins	Missed swipe
14.	i	s	⠊	⠎	3-ins	
15.	t	)	⠞	⠾	6-ins	
16.	o	z	⠕	⠵	6-ins	
17.	r	“	⠗	⠐	(1+2+3)-del	
18.	r	(	⠗	⠾	1-d + (4+6)i	

Table 3: Top 1% substitution errors on BrailleTouch. Ins=insertions; Del=deletions; R=right. F# = finger number.

Automatic Error Correction

In our analysis, we classified four components of the Total Error rate*:* *Corrections*; *Substitutions*; *Space Errors*; and *Other Errors*. The corrections represent user edits by backspacing, and thus do not need automatic solutions; rather they show an attention to accuracy by the participants. We shall discuss strategies for automatic correction of the *Space* and *Substitution Errors*, in order to improve accuracy in future design iterations.

Space Errors

The misinterpretation of `space` gestures can be addressed by adjusting constants in our software. On the smartphone, the space character is a flick gesture to the right. It was frequently misinterpreted as a dot-4, or a tap by the right index finger. Our gesture recognizer was based on two constants: the minimum distance and the maximum time between the touch down and touch up events on the screen. Through empirical analysis of raw touch position and timestamp data from blind users, we can determine better values for these two constants, which we believe will greatly reduce these space substitution errors. On the tablet, the spacebar was defined as any touch greater than a constant distance below the main soft braille buttons. Similarly, we can adjust this constant through empirical analysis of the actual touch positions of users.

Substitutions

We identified the most common substitution errors for each device (see Table 3). These data can inform two types of real-time automatic error correction in future design iterations. First, we can compare the typed characters to real words in a dictionary. If the input string does not match a real word, we can iterate through permutations of the input string that reflect the most frequent substitution errors.

Second, most of the common substitution errors reflect a single dot error within the braille cell. In other words, the user either deleted a dot (left out finger), inserted an extra dot (by pressing an extra finger), or substituted a finger (e.g. pressed dot 3 instead of adjacent dot 2). Insertions and deletions of dots can inform the dictionary approach described above. The finger substitutions suggest we should improve our spatial algorithms that assign an (x, y) position on the screen to one of the six braille soft buttons. This is effectively a classification problem. Future analysis of raw touch positions may provide simple heuristics that will improve soft braille key recognition, and therefore accuracy.

We observed that blind users' hands tend to drift across the touchscreen over time, given the lack of tactile landmarks. The constrained size of the smartphone mitigated the drift issue, while drift was more pronounced on the tablet due to its larger screen area. We believe that this drift across the screen is related to some of the substitution errors that involve adjacent braille dots. In future work, we will investigate the use of a Kalman filter to correct for users' hand drift over time.

Methodology

We designed our study to produce quantitative results that could be compared with other text entry research in the literature. However, we had to modify several practices that have become standards in the text entry research community because our subjects were visually impaired.

Audio Feedback

In our study, we provided participants with only keyclick audio feedback for each character entered. We chose this over having the system speak each character entered because the Google speech synthesizer we employed could not keep up with the high text entry speeds we observed in our pilot studies. However, many users complained of the lack of voice feedback, as they had difficulty determining if they had entered the correct character. Screen reader accessibility software can speak individual characters fast enough to match high text entry speeds, and in a manner that is familiar to many visually impaired users. In future studies we will employ character- and word-based auditory feedback.

Dictation Phrase Set

Although we removed 65 aurally ambiguous phrases from the standard Mackenzie-Soukoreff text entry phrase set, some remaining phrases were still problematic for our participants. The best solution is to create a new phrase set optimized for dictation typing tests.

Braille and the Blind Community

The significance of braille literacy in the blind community is a hotly discussed topic. Indeed fewer people may be reading tactile braille than were a generation ago, due in part to text-to-speech technology. However braille writing, which is the application for BrailleTouch, is a different matter than braille reading. Since we published the initial design of BrailleTouch, the authors have been personally contacted by hundreds of enthusiastic people from all over the world who want this technology. One study participant was so excited about the potential of BrailleTouch that she donated her $4000 PACmate to the research team. Furthermore, the six-key Perkins-style braille keyboard is much easier to learn than tactile braille reading. With no prior knowledge of braille, the authors were able to learn the alphabet within several hours and soon after achieve 12-16 wpm typing speeds.

Most blind people who know braille are accustomed to both reading and writing in Grade 2, or contracted, braille, a shorthand which requires fewer characters than the printed form of the same text. Similar to other braille text entry studies [1, 18, 21], we employed Grade 1 braille, which uses one braille chord for each character. While we initially thought that contracted braille was just convenient shorthand, our participants informed us that contracted braille has the significance of a language within the blind community. As a result, many participants reported translating dictated phrases into Grade 1 braille (which they never use) in their heads before typing the characters. One described this as "like hearing English and having to type French." It is essential that future braille text entry research employs contracted braille in order to be relevant to the blind community.

CONCLUSIONS AND FUTURE WORK

We presented the evaluation of BrailleTouch, an eyes-free text entry system for mobile touchscreen smartphones, with eleven blind participants. The six expert braille typists averaged speeds of 23.2 wpm with 14.5% error on a smartphone. In response to the high Total Error rates we observed, especially in Groups B and C, we classified three common types of errors and presented strategies to improve accuracy in future design iterations. BrailleTouch has the potential to revolutionize mobile text entry for the visually impaired by replacing assistive technology that costs $1000s with an application on a commodity smartphone. Sighted users may also benefit from the design lessons learned for eyes-free typing on a touchscreen. In future work, we will evaluate BrailleTouch in real-world scenarios by deploying it on the smartphones of blind users.

ACKNOWLEDGMENTS

We thank the Atlanta Center for the Visually Impaired, the Georgia Radio Reading Service, the Atlanta Vision Loss Center, and especially the study volunteers. We also gratefully acknowledge support from a Nokia University Research Award.

REFERENCES

1. Azenkot, S., Wobbrock, J. O., Prasain, S., and Ladner, R. E., Input Finger Detection for Nonvisual Touch Screen Text Entry in Perkinput, in *Proc. Graphics Interface*. Canadian Information Processing Society, Toronto, (2012).
2. Bonner, M., Brudvik, J., Abowd, G., and Edwards, K., No-Look Notes: Accessible Eyes-Free Multi-Touch Text Entry, in *Proc. Eighth International Conference on Pervasive Computing* Springer: Heidelberg, (2010), 409-426.
3. Braille, L., *Procedure for Writing Words, Music and Plain-song Using Dots for the Use of the Blind and Made Available to Them*, Institut National des Jeunes Aveugles (Royal Institution Of Blind Youth): Paris, (1829).
4. Bruder, R. *Type Brailler Learn Braille Lite*. (2012) May 7, 2012 [cited 2012 June 14]; Available from: http://itunes.apple.com/app/type-brailler-learn-braille/id509166743?mt=8.
5. Clawson, J., Lyons, K., Starner, T., and Clarkson, E., The Impacts of Limited Visual Feedback on Mobile Text Entry for the Twiddler and Mini-QWERTY Keyboards, in *Proc. Ninth IEEE International Symposium on Wearable Computers*, IEEE Computer Society, (2005), 170-177.
6. Fard, H. G. and Chuangjun, B., Braille-based Text Input for Multi-touch Screen Mobile Phones, in *School of Computing*, Blekinge Institute of Technology, (2011), 68.

7. Frey, B., Southern, C. and Romero, M. BrailleTouch: Mobile Texting for the Visually Impaired., in *Proc. HCII.* Springer Berlin / Heidelberg, (2011).
8. Fusia, J. *Twidor - The Twiddler Tutor.* (2005) [September 20, 2011]; Available from: http://wearables.cc.gatech.edu/projects/twidor/download.html.
9. Google. *Google Translate.* [September 19, 2011]; Available from: http://translate.google.com/translate_tts?tl=en&q=google+voice.
10. Gordon, G., The Past, Present, and Future of Portable Note-takers, in *Technology And Persons With Disabilities Conference*, Center On Disabilities - California State University Northridge: Los Angeles, (2002).
11. Guerreiro, T., Lagoá, P., Santana, P., Gonçalves, D., and Jorge, J., NavTap and BrailleTap: Non-Visual Texting Interfaces, in *Proc. Rehabilitation Engineering and Assistive Technology Society of North America Conference (Resna)*: Washington, D.C., (2008).
12. Kane, S. K., Bigham, J. P., and Wobbrock, J. O., Slide rule: Making Mobile Touch Screens Accessible to Blind People Using Multi-touch Interaction Techniques, in *Proc. 10th International ACM SIGACCESS Conference on Computers and Accessibility*, ACM: Halifax, Nova Scotia, Canada, (2008), 73-80.
13. Kano, A., Read, J. C., and Dix, A., Children's Phrase Set for Text Input Method Evaluations, in *Proc. 4th Nordic Conference on Human-Computer Interaction: Changing Roles*, ACM: Oslo, Norway, (2006).
14. Keles, M., INEXPENSIVE BRAILLER: Writing Braille Using IMPAD, in *Department of Computer Science*, New York University: New York, (2009), 40.
15. Lee, S., Hong, S. H., Jeon, J. W., Choi, H. G., and Choi, H., Design of Chording Gloves as a Text Input Device, in *Computer Human Interaction - Lecture Notes in Computer Science*, 3101/2004 (2004), 201-210.
16. Lorimer, P., Origins of Braille, in *Braille: Into the Next Millenium*, J. M. Dixon, Editor. National Library Service for the Blind and Physically Handicapped of the Library of Congress: Washington D.C.,18-39, 2000.
17. MacKenzie, I. S. and Soukoreff, R. W., Phrase Sets for Evaluating Text Entry Techniques, in *CHI '03 Extended Abstracts on Human Factors in Computing Systems*, ACM: Ft. Lauderdale, FL, (2003), 754-755.
18. Mascetti, S., Bernareggi, C., and Belotti, M., TypeInBraille: Quick Typing on Smart Phones by Blind Users, in *Universitá Degli Studi Di Milano*: Milan, Italy, (2011).
19. Miele, J. A. and Edwards, O. R., WearaBraille: Development of a Wireless, Virtual, Braille Keyboard, The Smith-Kettlewell Eye Research Institute: San Francisco, CA, (2011).
20. Oliveira, J., Guerreiro, T., Nicolau, H., Jorge, J., and Gonçalves, D., Blind People and Mobile Touch-based Text-entry: Acknowledging the Need for Different Flavors, in *Proc. 13th international ACM SIGACCESS Conference on Computers and Accessibility*, ACM: Dundee, Scotland, UK, (2011), 179-186.
21. Oliveira, J., Guerreiro, T., Nicolau, H., Jorge, J., and Gonçalves, D., BrailleType: Unleashing Braille over Touch Screen Mobile Phones, in *Human-Computer Interaction – INTERACT 2011*, P. Campos, et al., Editors, Springer Berlin / Heidelberg: Lisbon, Portugal, (2011), 100-107.
22. Romero, M., Frey, B., Southern, C., and Abowd, G., BrailleTouch: Designing a Mobile Eyes-Free Soft Keyboard, in *MobileHCI 2011*: Stockholm, Sweden, (2011), 707-709.
23. Smith, A., Americans and Text Messaging, in *Pew Internet & American Life Project*, Pew Research Center: Washington, D.C., (2011).
24. Soukoreff, R. W. and MacKenzie, I. S., Metrics for Text Entry Research: An Evaluation of MSD and KSPC, and a New Unified Error Metric, in *Proc. SIGCHI Conference on Human Factors in Computing Systems*, ACM: Ft. Lauderdale, FL, (2003), 113-120.
25. Tobe, C. B., Callahan, E., and Callahan, M., Embossed Printing in the United States, in *Braille: Into the Next Millennium*, J. M. Dixon, Editor. National Library Service for the Blind and Physically Handicapped of the Library of Congress: Washington, D.C., (2000), 41-71.
26. W.H.O. *World Health Organization Fact Sheet N°282 on Visual impairment and blindness.* (2011); Available from: http://www.who.int/mediacentre/factsheets/fs282/en/.
27. Wigdor, D., Forlines, C., Baudisch, P., Barnwell, J., and Shen, C., Lucid Touch: A See-through Mobile Device, in *Proc. 20th Annual ACM Symposium on User Interface Software and Technology*, ACM: Newport, Rhode Island, USA, (2007).
28. Wobbrock, J. O., Myers, B. A., Aung, H. H., and LoPresti, E. F., Text Entry from Power Wheelchairs: Edgewrite for Joysticks and Touchpads, in *Proc. 6th international ACM SIGACCESS Conference on Computers and Accessibility*, ACM: Atlanta, GA, USA, (2004), 110-117.

PocketMenu: Non-Visual Menus for Touch Screen Devices

Martin Pielot, Tobias Hesselmann, Wilko Heuten
OFFIS Institute for Information Technology
Oldenburg, Germany
pielot;hesselmann;heuten@offis.de

Anastasia Kazakova, Susanne Boll
University of Oldenburg
Oldenburg, Germany
anastasia.kazakova@uni-oldenburg.de
boll@informatik.uni-oldenburg.de

ABSTRACT
We present PocketMenu, a menu optimized for non-visual, in-pocket interaction with menus on handheld devices with touch screens. By laying out menu items along the border of the touch screen its tactile features guide the interaction. Additional vibro-tactile feedback and speech allows identifying the individual menu items non-visually. In an experiment, we compared PocketMenu with iPhone's VoiceOver. Participants had to control an MP3 player while walking down a road with the device in the pocket. The results provide evidence that in the above context the PocketMenu outperforms VoiceOver in terms of completion time, selection errors, and subjective usability. Hence, it enables usage of touch screen apps in mobile contexts (e.g. walking, hiking, or skiing) and limited interaction spaces (e.g. device resting in a pocket).

ACM Classification Keywords
H.5.2 User Interfaces: Haptic I/O

Author Keywords
Handheld Devices and Mobile Computing; Input and Interaction Technologies; Tactile & Haptic UIs

INTRODUCTION
Regarding mobile devices, there is a clear trend towards removing physical buttons in favor of a large touch screen. The best example is the iPhone, which offers a single "home" key on its front while all the other interaction is done via the touch screen. The advantage over hardware interfaces is that the interactive elements on touch screens allow to better adapt the interface to each application.

However, interacting with touch screens places heavy visual load on the user. Even if the user learns the layout of the user interface – which often happens with physical interfaces – it still would be close to impossible to hit the correct item blindly. This problem increases when additionally the user is on the move (e.g. walking, cycling, or skying) or using the device in constraint spaces, such as the jacket pocket.

While many approaches existing to make touch screens accessible for non-visual use [1, 2, 3, 4, 5, 6, 10, 11], they might not cope well with the limited interaction space and the not-so-well-known orientation of the device when the device rests in a pocket. The PocketMenu[1] exploits the fact that most handheld's screen borders have tactile features and thus can be felt. Menu items are laid out along the border so it provides a means of orientation. By adding vibro-tactile feedback when crossing the border of an item, it enables users to navigate a menu purely through touch.

MobileHCI'12, September 21–24, 2012, San Francisco, CA, USA.

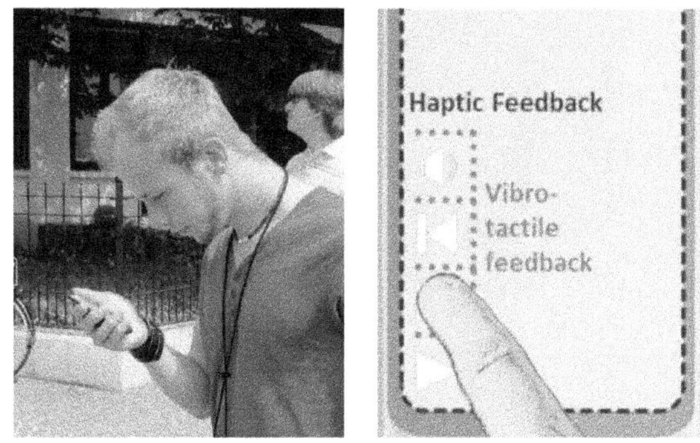

Figure 1. To avoid having to look at touch screen for interacting with them (left) we propose the PocketMenu (right).

In a field experiment we compared the PocketMenu against iPhone's VoiceOver. The results suggest that the concept of the PocketMenu has significant positive advantages when used eyes-free and in the pocket.

RELATED WORK
Several novel input techniques have been proposed to allow eyes-free interaction with touch screens. For example, PieMenus allow users to spawn a menu at any point on the touch screen. Its items appear around the touch points. Items are selected by swiping towards them. Combined with audio feedback, PieMenus even allow blind people to enter text on a touch screen [1]. SlideRule [6] combines gestures with audio feedback to enable blind users to interact with touch screens. Compared to a button-based system it was faster but more error prone. Recently, Wilson et al. [9] proposed pressure-based menus and showed that these are well suited for eyes-free interaction on the move.

Another approach to improve the accessibility of touch screens is to use haptic feedback. EdgeWrite [10] uses a plastic template with a small hole to limit the movement of a stylus used for gesture-based character input. Wobbrock et al.

[1] `https://play.google.com/store/apps/details?id=org.pielot.pocketmp3`

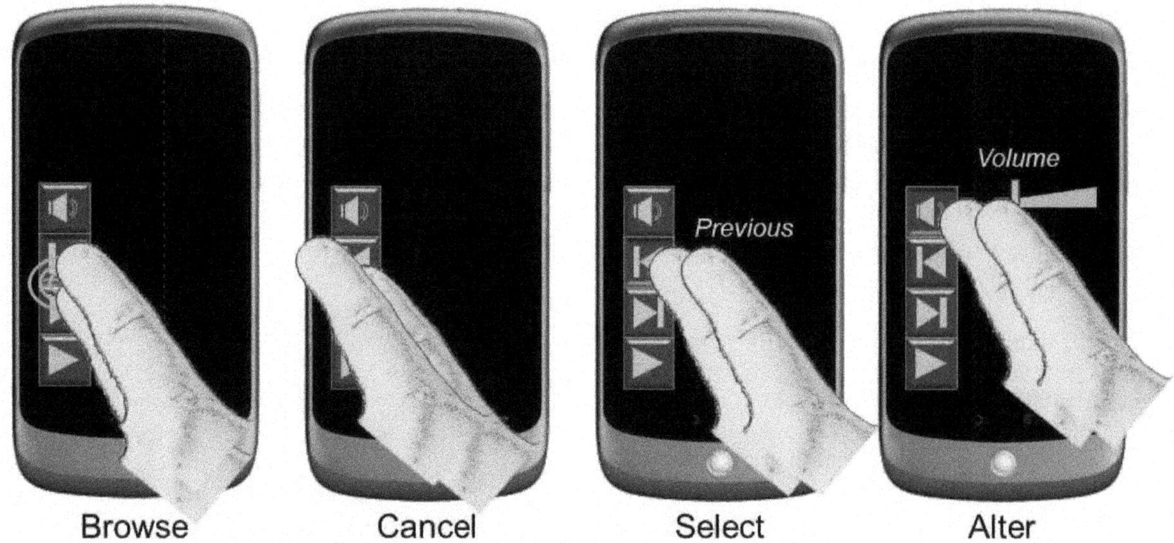

Figure 2. The four main functions of the PocketMenu: browse, cancel, select, and adjust.

show that text entry with EdgeWrite is faster than free letter recognition. Barrier Pointing [4] aims at making stylus-based touch screen interaction more accessible for motor impaired users by utilizing the raised borders of the screen that can be found in some devices. The menu is arranged along the border of the screen. The raised border is used to restrict and guide the stylus input. McGookin et al. [8] used raised paper to make touch screens accessible for the blind. These previous world show that haptic feedback can effectively increase the accessibility of touch screens.

A related approach is using vibro-tactile feedback. T-Bars [5] introduce stroke-formed menu items which trigger vibration when being touched. To select an item the user slides along the stroke until its end. Pilot evaluations showed that this feedback helps users to keep their fingers on the line more accurately. Rich tactile feedback is used by SemFeel [11] to not only indicate the presence of an item on the touch screen but also to convey the item's type.

DESIGN

While previous work shows how to facilitate non-visual access to touch screens, PocketMenu specifically aims at supporting interaction on the move with the device in the pocket. These constraints make it difficult to directly apply previous approaches. The unknown orientation of the device impedes hitting the desired element on the screen. Restricted space for physical interactions hinders performing gestures.

Layout. As a solution, PocketMenu (see Fig. 2) combines previous approaches into a new concept. The menu items are laid out along the screen's border. Similar to EdgeWrite [10], the screen border serves as tactile reference, guiding the user's finger when browsing the menu's items. Vibro-tactile feedback, as e.g. used in T-Bars [5], is used to indicate the border between menu items. The lower-left edge of the touch screen serves as the menu's origin, as edges are physical forms that are identified easily by the sense of touch [7].

Browse Items. To browse the menu, the user slides her/his finger along the screen's border. A short tactile pulse of 100 ms indicates that the finger crosses the border between two items. Menu items can be identified in two ways. First, when the finger enters a menu item the associated action is announced via text-to-speech. Second, when the users start building a mental model of the menu, they can just remember the items' position and count the number of vibro-tactile pulses when sliding along the screen border, which allows to use the menu without speech output if desired.

Cancel Browsing. Browsing the menu can be aborted by simply releasing the finger. In the related work, e.g. SemFeel [11], releasing the finger has been used to trigger the last selected item. However, due to the constraints we were afraid that users too often might lift the finger by accident. Our release-to-cancel approach avoids these accidents.

Select and Alter. The PocketMenu offers two kinds of items: button-like items that trigger associated actions (e.g. Play or Pause) and slider-like items that allow to continuously adjust a value (e.g. Volume). The selection of button items is inspired by the classic PieMenu [2]: by swiping the finger towards the middle of the screen the associated action is executed. A short tactile pulse ($100ms$) confirms that the button item has been 'pressed'. Slider items are selected in a similar way. The associated value can be adjusted by swiping more or less far away from the menu border before lifting the finger. A series of short tactile pulses ($< 10ms$) issued when moving the finger indicate that the associated value is altered.

USER STUDY

To study how well PocketMenu enables in-pocket-use on the move, we conducted a field experiment, where we compared it with a replica of VoiceOver available on iPhone 3GS and later models.

Methodology

Material. We implemented a simple MP3 player as test application. It offers five different functions: start/pause, next, prev, volume up, volume down. As baseline for the study we replicated the relevant interaction concepts of the iPhone's *VoiceOver* functionality and implemented menu that resembled a typical MP3 player control (see Fig. 3). Using the VoiceOver clone users can explore the screen elements by moving the finger over the screen elements. When hitting an element a short click sound is played the associated action function is announced via speech. To execute the action of the recently touched element the user has to perform a double-tap anywhere on the screen. To alter adjustable elements, such as the volume slider, the finger needs to remain on the screen after the second tap hit the screen. Then the element can be continuously be altered by swiping left or right. Alternatively, the user can double-tap onto the slide to jump the cursor to the tapped position.

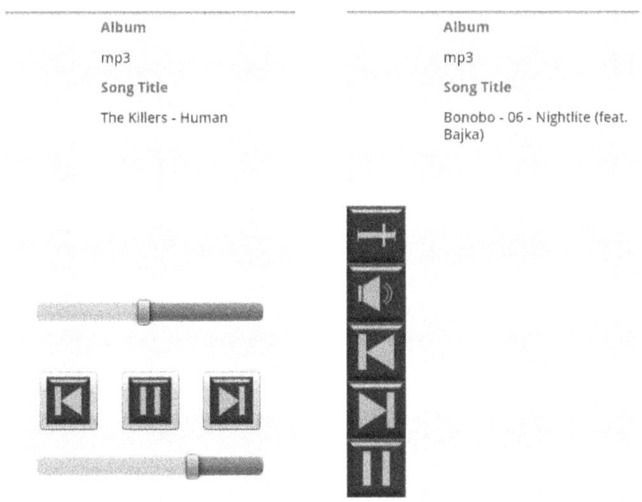

Figure 3. Two screenshots of the evaluated menus. On the left the layout of the *VoiceOver* enhanced menu is shown (control condition), The right screenshot shows the layout of the *PocketMenu* (experimental condition).

Participants. Ten participants (4 female) with an average age of 25.4 (SD 2.95) took part in the study. The average experience with touch screens was rated above average with a considerable spread (3.40, SD 1.58, on a five-point Likert-scale, 1=low, 5=high).

Design. The menu type served as independent variable with two levels: VoiceOver, PocketMenu. We used a within-subject design with a counter-balanced order of conditions. As performance measures, the software automatically recorded the *completion time* (the time it takes the participants to execute a given command) and the *selection errors* (number of times the participants execute the wrong action). Furthermore, we noted the number of *breakdowns* (participant has to take device out of the pocket to execute command) and we approximated the cognitive workload by measuring the *effective walking speed*. The standardized SUS questionnaire was used to quantify the menus' *subjective usability*.

Procedure. At the beginning of each session, the participants could familiarize themselves with both menus. This typically took 10 to 15 minutes. Afterwards, the evaluation was continued outside. The participants were asked to walk down a pedestrian a sidewalk with the phone in the pocket of their jacket. The software announced the action to be executed (e.g. "press play" or "change the volume"). The participants repeated the announcement, so the experimenter had the chance to correct any misunderstanding. Then, the participants tried to execute the action as fast as possible while avoiding mistakes. 13 items had to be selected with each menu. The interaction with the menu (*completion time* & *selection errors*) was logged automatically by the application. The *breakdowns* and the walked distance, which was used to infer the *effective walking speed*, were noted by the experimenter. Afterwards, the participants were asked to fill out two SUS questionnaires, one for each menu. Finally, a short open interview was conducted to learn about the participants' impressions and thoughts on both designs.

Results

Table 1 summarizes mean and standard deviation for each dependent measure.

Table 1. Quantitative Results

	VoiceOver	*PocketMenu*
Completion Time (s) ***	18.13 (22.33)	11.12 (12.28)
Selection Errors (#) **	1.68 (5.84)	0.51 (1.67)
Breakdowns (#)	1.80 (1.81)	1.00 (1.70)
Walk. Speed (km/h)	3.21 (2.06)	3.44 (1.47)
Usability (SUS) **	50 (28.6)	78.5 (19.7)

PocketMenu users selected items significantly faster (*completion time*) ($p < .001$), made significantly fewer *selection errors* ($p < .01$), and provided significantly higher *subjective usability* ratings ($p < .001$). No significant effects could be found on the number of *breakdowns* between the conditions ($p = .10$) and the *effective walking speed* ($p = .27$).

The participants appreciated that for the PocketMenu the screen's border provided orientation. Not knowing about the tests aims they proposed to rotate the VoiceOver menu's content by 90 so the two sliders would be next to the screen's border to simplify the interaction with them.

The PocketMenu's swipe technique was preferred over the VoiceOver's double-click to execute menu items. The main point of criticism about the VoiceOver menu was that it was found difficult to perform double-clicks in the pocket. However, it was also appreciated that the double-click selection made it easier to perform repeated selection of the same item.

When browsing the PocketMenu, many participants appreciated the tactile feedback. The speech output, in contrast, was often considered annoying after repeated usage. VoiceOver also added an auditory click whenever a button was touched, which was found to be adding to the "cacophony of sounds". Two participants reported to have browsed the PocketMenu based on the tactile feedback only and ignored the speech announcements altogether. Suggestions were to allow the user to turn off the speech output or replace it by more subtle non-speech audio or tactile feedback.

Discussions

In summary, the PocketMenu allowed the participants to execute actions in less time and with fewer errors. The participants appreciated the haptic feedback and rated its usability higher.

There are three design difference between the PocketMenu and the VoiceOver menu, which are potential causes for these observed effects: (1) in the PocketMenu the screen border guides the interaction by providing tactile feedback, (2) buttons provide speech + vibro-tactile instead of speech + auditory feedback, and (3) elements are executed by a swipe gesture instead of a double-click.

From the participants' feedback we learned that the haptic feedback provided by the border, as suggested by Wobbrock et al. [10] for stylus-based touch screen interaction can successfully be transferred to finger-based interaction. According to the qualitative feedback, this was the key design element to support usage on the move.

Our study's results confirms that vibro-tactile feedback, as proposed by Hall et al. [5] or by Yatani and Truong [11], is a highly efficient feedback mechanism. Unlike the auditory feedback, it did not become annoying. For the PocketMenu, some participants suggested to allow turning of the speech output completely, since they felt able to find the right button via vibration feedback only. Other participants suggested replacing speech announcements through vibration patterns, which has been found useful in previous work [11]. We conclude that tactile feedback has the potential to replace annoying audio feedback. On the basis of these findings, we informally tested replacing the VoiceOver's click with a vibro-tactile buzz and believe to have observed a notable performance boost.

With respect to the executing of menu items our results support the guideline established by McGookin et al. [8] to avoid double clicks in non-visual touch screen interaction. Further, the results support the findings by Ecker et al. [3] and Bonner et al. [1] that swiping is an effective and efficient gesture for interacting non-visual with touch screens.

CONCLUSIONS

With the PocketMenu, we introduced a menu design that enables eyes-free, in-pocket use of handheld touch screen devices on the move. It guides the interaction by haptic feedback from the raised border of the screen and vibration pulses created by the internal pager motor. In a field study with 10 participants, who had to control an MP3 player on the move and with the device in their pocket, we experimentally compared the PocketMenu with a replica of iPhone's VoiceOver solution. The results provide evidence that the added tactile feedback allows faster interaction with fewer errors and improves the subjective usability.

The PocketMenu enables designing touch screen applications that users can controls without dedicating visual attention to it. This applies to all applications that convey their information in non-visual formats and that are used in mobile situations where the visual attention is desired/required elsewhere, such as walking, driving, cycling, or skiing. Since many countries discuss legislative approaches to discourage mobile phone use in traffic due to visual distraction, enabling eyes-free usage of touch screen UIs may even become mandatory in some contexts, such as information systems in cars.

ACKNOWLEDGMENTS

The authors are grateful to the European Commission which co-funds the IP HaptiMap (FP7-ICT-224675).

REFERENCES

1. Bonner, M. N., Brudvik, J. T., Abowd, G. D., and Edwards, W. K. No-look notes: Accessible eyes-free multi-touch text entry. In *Pervasive* (2010).
2. Callahan, J., Hopkins, D., Weiser, M., and Shneiderman, B. An empirical comparison of pie vs. linear menus. In *Proc. CHI* (1988).
3. Ecker, R., Broy, V., Butz, A., and De Luca, A. pietouch: a direct touch gesture interface for interacting with in-vehicle information systems. In *Proc. MobileHCI* (2009).
4. Froehlich, J., Wobbrock, J. O., and Kane, S. K. Barrier pointing: using physical edges to assist target acquisition on mobile device touch screens. In *Proc. ASSETS* (2007).
5. Hall, M., Hoggan, E., and Brewster, S. T-bars: towards tactile user interfaces for mobile touchscreens. In *Proc. MobileHCI* (2008).
6. Kane, S. K., Bigham, J. P., and Wobbrock, J. O. Slide rule: making mobile touch screens accessible to blind people using multi-touch interaction techniques. In *Proc. ASSETS* (2008).
7. Lederman, S. J., and Klatzky, R. L. Haptic identification of common objects: effects of constraining the manual exploration process. *Percept Psychophys. 66*, 4 (2004), 618–628.
8. McGookin, D., Brewster, S., and Jiang, W. Investigating touchscreen accessibility for people with visual impairments. In *Proc. NordiCHI* (2008).
9. Wilson, G., Brewster, S. A., Halvey, M., Crossan, A., and Stewart, C. The effects of walking, feedback and control method on pressure-based interaction. In *Proc. MobileHCI* (2011).
10. Wobbrock, J. O., Myers, B. A., and Kembel, J. A. Edgewrite: a stylus-based text entry method designed for high accuracy and stability of motion. In *Proc. UIST* (2003).
11. Yatani, K., and Truong, K. N. Semfeel: a user interface with semantic tactile feedback for mobile touch-screen devices. In *Proc. UIST* (2009).

Clicking Blindly: Using Spatial Correspondence to Select Targets in Multi-Device Environments

Krzysztof Pietroszek
University of Waterloo
200 University Ave. West, Waterloo, ON, CA
kmpietro@uwaterloo.ca

Edward Lank
University of Waterloo
200 University Ave. West, Waterloo, ON, CA
lank@uwaterloo.ca

ABSTRACT
We propose *spatial correspondence targeting* to support interaction between devices in multi-device environments when network connectivity fails. In spatial correspondence targeting, for a given target on surface A, an end-user envisions the relative position of that target on surface B and interacts on surface B without any visual depiction of the target on surface B. The targeting task relies on human spatial visualization ability, i.e. the ability to relate the spatial position of objects on one display to their scale-invariant position on another display. We provide experimental evidence that demonstrates that users may be able to target up to 25 discrete targets using a smartphone screen even in the absence of a depiction of the target on the smartphone screen. We argue that the accuracy of spatial correspondence targeting is sufficient for the technique to have many practical applications.

Author Keywords
Mobile human-computer interaction; target acquisition; touchscreen interface

ACM Classification Keywords
H.5.2 [User Interfaces]: Input devices and strategies

General Terms
Human Factors

INTRODUCTION
One opportunistic way to enable interaction with public digital displays is to leverage mobile devices as a personal interface to the public display. Classrooms, movie theatres, shopping malls, airports, and research conferences are all environments that could benefit from leveraging mobile devices to support public interaction with content displayed on public displays. Usually, interaction between devices in these multi-device environments requires some form of communication channel, such as Wi-Fi, IR, Bluetooth, or 3G. However, there exist many common contexts where interaction is desired but a communication channel is unavailable (e.g. no network coverage), too expensive (e.g. data roaming), or bandwidth-limited (e.g. overloaded access points). The specific question we address here is whether some graceful mechanism could be identified to support interaction despite the challenges associated with network failures and bandwidth limitations.

MobileHCI'12, September 21–24, 2012, San Francisco, CA, USA.

Figure 1. Landscape painting as spatial correspondence targeting task

Our approach has been to explore strategies where users interact without connectivity and then either wait for connectivity or use an alternative channel (e.g. text messages) to transmit interaction data. The challenge, of course, is that, without a data channel, the end-user will be required to target content on their smartphone that may only be displayed on a large, shared screen embedded in their surroundings. In other words, they must mentally align the viewport on their phone with the public display they wish to target. We call this interaction technique *spatial correspondence targeting*.

Spatial correspondence targeting relies on our natural ability to relate spatial position of objects in a viewport to their relative position within a second viewport, i.e. our spatial visualization ability. For a given target visible on surface A (called the ***targeted** surface*) humans are able to find the imagined corresponding position of that target on surface B (the *targe**ting** surface*). Artists, architects, interior designers, and engineers all engage in spatial correspondence targeting when beginning to create a painting, floor plan, or technical drawing (Figure 1).

However, it is not clear how accurately non-artists and non-engineers can perform a spatial correspondence targeting task. How large of an error is introduced in the targeting task when targeting through spatial correspondence? How does this error compare to traditional targeting, where a user clicks on a target on the display on, for example, a smartphone?

In this paper we show that, for our experimental configuration, a set of smartphone owners can target an area to within less than 4% of the area of the display. Stated another way, we show that end-users are capable of targeting, with 90% reliability, up to 25 distinct on-screen targets using only spatial correspondence to identify the location of the target. This result has implications for the design of multi-display applications that degrade gracefully in the presence of network delays and interruptions.

RELATED WORK

Spatial correspondence targeting leverages end-users spatial visualization ability, a component of spatial reasoning. Because of the importance of spatial visualization and spatial reasoning to science, technology, engineering, and mathematics (STEM) disciplines, a number of researchers have explored various factors that affect spatial reasoning ability [1,2] and ways to design instruction to enhance spatial visualization [4].

Within the domain of multi-device environments, significant research has made de facto use of *spatial correspondence* targeting, i.e. targeting content based on relative positions in the presence of visual feedback. Carnegie Mellon University's BARN Project (http://www.cmu.edu/barn/) allowed the use of personal computers in conjunction with a large display. Users were required to virtually reposition their device's input window to a corresponding region of the large display to interact with content at that location. However, the handheld computer displayed the content at its present location and the large screen displayed a pointer representing the location of the handheld computer within the larger display space. Ka Ping Yee's peephole system [7] used spatially aware handheld computers to access an information space much larger than the device display, but, again, the handheld computer displayed the information located at the peephole. Efficiently pointing at display screens from a distance with devices like the "wiimote" requires spatial correspondence targeting to map wiimote displacement onto on-screen cursor positions [6], but a cursor is typically displayed on the large screen. A technique resembling spatial correspondence targeting is explored by Baudish, but he proposes using an *imaginary* targeting surface [5]. Finally, digitizer tablets, the computer mouse, trackpoints and touchpad all make use of spatial correspondence targeting to all their users to control the amplitude and direction of input device displacement, again using a pointer to indicate the current location and instantaneous movement of the input device.

EXAMPLE APPLICATIONS: CLASSROOM POLLING

Figure 2 depicts two instances of a classroom polling application, one with the network active and a second without network connectivity. Our goal is to determine whether spatial correspondence targeting is sufficiently accurate to support delayed participation in in-class polls. Perhaps, for example, students are given participation points for polls they participate in and answer correctly.

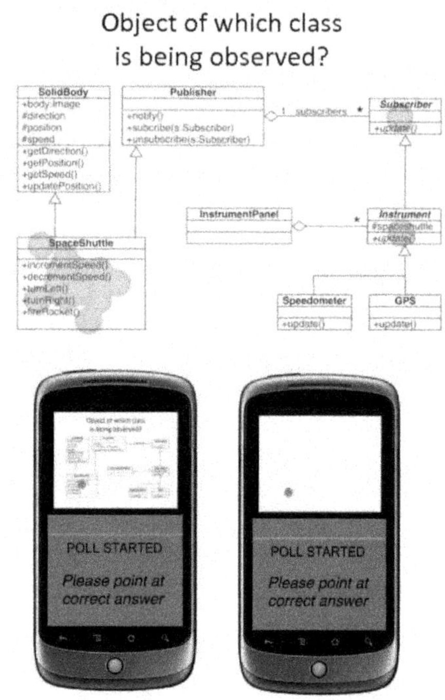

Figure 2. Heatmap of students' responses to instructor's question about Observer Design Pattern.

More generally, whether cost or the availability of bandwidth limit connectivity, we wish to determine the relative accuracy of spatial correspondence targeting to correspondence targeting with visual feedback. Thus, in the remainder of this paper we provide experimental results on accuracy of spatial correspondence targeting. In particular, we are interested in investigating:

1. What is an accuracy error of spatial correspondence targeting?
2. How does the accuracy of spatial correspondence targeting compares to the accuracy of target acquisition, when the miniature of a target is visible on the input device (called *traditional targeting*).

EXPERIMENT

Interface and Equipment

Our experiment uses an interface similar to the interface depicted in Figure 2. Participants used an HTC Nexus One Smartphone to select targets in two different conditions: traditional targeting, where the desired target was displayed on the screen; and spatial correspondence targeting, where participants used spatial visualization to select a target without any visual cues on the smartphone screen. Targets were circular regions displayed on a large external screen and on a smartphone. The external large display screen was a 2.5m X 2m rear projection screen projected at 960 X 720 pixels. The nexus one phones have a screen resolution of 480 X 800 pixels. However, to preserve aspect ratio mapping, we used a rectangular region of size 480 X 360 pixels (48mm X 36mm) at the top of the screen when the device was held in portrait mode. Auto-switching to landscape mode was disabled.

Experimental Variables

There are two factors that we explore that may affect spatial correspondence targeting. First, the presence or absence of the target on the smartphone should alter accuracy. Without a target, accuracy should decrease. However, our specific goal is to characterize what that decrease is.

Second, the size and position of the target may influence accuracy. For size, while small targets will be harder to acquire in both the spatial and traditional targeting tasks, small targets may encourage more precision. To evaluate this, we varied the size of the on-screen targets between 5% and 25% of display width in increments of 5%. For position, we varied positions pseudo-randomly on the display to ensure good coverage of all quadrants.

Finally, we acknowledge that screen sizes and screen resolutions may also cause variations in accuracy, but, for the purposes of our present study, we consider these nuisance variables. We did not vary screen size and resolution in the current study.

Participants

Ten university students (6 males) with a mean age of 25 years participated. Participants did not receive any payment for their involvement.

Method

Participants stood in front of the projection screen in a distance between 2 and 3 meters. A participant's view angle onto the projection screen was no more than 20 degrees to prevent the targeting accuracy error resulting from perspective distortion of view on target position. A short training session for the targeting task was conducted. Each participant then performed 200 spatial correspondence targeting tasks (no target visible on smartphone) and 200 traditional targeting tasks (target visible on the smartphone). In both conditions, the target was visible on the large display. Spatial correspondence and traditional targeting were counterbalanced. Target size and target location was drawn, in pseudo-random order, for a set of fixed target size/location pairs.

Participants P4, P5, and P6 participated as a group using three smartphones. All other participants completed the experiment individually.

Measures

We report targeting accuracy as a percentage of screen width. We also report the error rate of the targeting task, i.e. number of clicks within target, for both conditions.

RESULTS

Figure 3 depicts the results of our study. As expected, the traditional targeting task (shown on the right) was significantly more accurate than spatial correspondence targeting. We also find, somewhat counter-intuitively, that the size of the target had no effect on the distribution of taps.

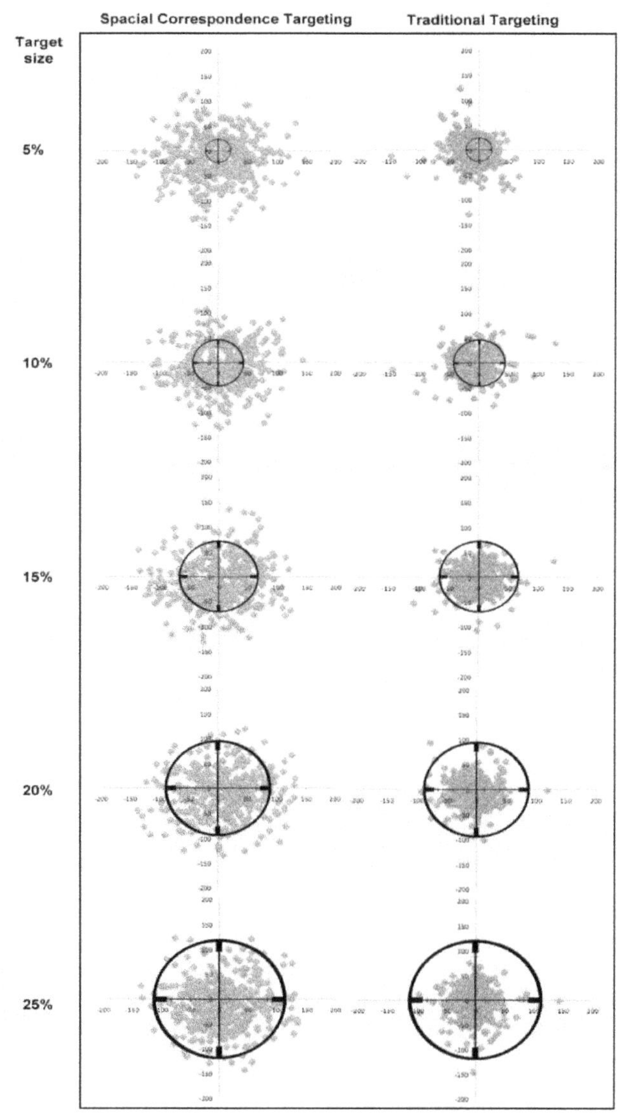

Figure 3. Accuracy of spatial correspondence targeting vs. traditional pointing for a targeted screen 960x720

In absolute accuracy, we find that error almost exactly doubles when moving from the traditional to the spatial correspondence task (table 1). For the traditional targeting task, error was 3.5% of screen width (mean = 34 pixels, standard deviation = 25 pixels). In the spatial correspondence task, error was 6.4% of screen width or 62 pixels (standard deviation = 32 pixels).

	Spatial Correspondence mean error in targetted screen pixels (960x720)	Spatial Correspondence error's Standard Deviation in pixels	Traditional targetting mean error in targetted screen pixels	Traditional targetting error's Standard Deviation in pixels
All Participants	**62**	**32**	**34**	**25**
Participant 1	62	32	26	13
Participant 2	56	30	35	20
Participant 3	62	31	35	20
Participant 4	65	36	45	28
Participant 5	71	34	41	25
Participant 6	67	32	27	21
Participant 7	57	30	24	13
Participant 8	51	25	28	18
Participant 9	62	31	26	15
Participant 10	63	31	25	15
Group (P11,P12,P13, P14,P15,P16)	60	32	34	24

Table 1. Our error vs. traditional targeting error

DISCUSSION

Recall that the motivation for this work was to support interaction in situations where unavailability, high cost, or low bandwidth may prevent connectivity. In these situations, our goal was to explore whether participants might be able to use spatial correspondence to interact with content, and then take advantage of alternative communication channels (e.g. texting) or latency (e.g. wait until connectivity is restored or WiFi access exists) to send and/or receive data. To support this style of interaction, we are particularly interested in the magnitude of the error for spatial correspondence targeting.

In our study, we found that spatial correspondence targeting had an error rate of approximately 6% of screen width, almost exactly twice the error observed for traditional targeting when the target is displayed on the screen. The high level of accuracy for targeting without on-screen visual cues was quite surprising to us. When we examined the standard deviation, we found that over 90% of targeting tasks fell within a radius of 10% of the display width. Stated another way, users were able to localize their targeting task to within 4% of the display area.

Standing Versus Sitting, Groups Versus Singles

Two lingering areas of concern we had were whether or not groups might have characteristics that differ from individuals (perhaps because of the need to spread out more to view content), and whether standing might have an effect on accuracy. The first concern arose because of our small group of subjects comprised of P4, P5 and P6. We noted that all of these participants had higher error rate than the average.

To verify this, we conducted a final experimental trial with six participants simultaneously (P11 – P16) seated around a table. However, we found virtually identical numbers for error rate (3.5% versus 6.2% for traditional versus spatial correspondence targeting).

Limitations

We report the error of traditional targeting as 3.5% of screen width using the standard point of contact on our smartphone devices. Additional evaluation is needed for non-matching aspect ratio, thus the result is an upper bound of precision. We are aware this naïve interpretation of contact point has been shown to be inferior to models that take advantage of an awareness of finger position relative to onscreen location [3]. Making use of more accurate models of contact location may enhance both the traditional and the spatial correspondence targeting tasks. However, we believe that the basic results presented here, specifically that targets can be localized to an area corresponding to approximately 4% of display area, will be affected in only minor ways.

CONCLUSION

The results of our experiment allow us to conclude, first that spatial correspondence targeting supports reasonably high accuracy. For a generic smartphone + large screen configuration, we found that participants can target with over 90% accuracy a region corresponding to 4% of the display. This corresponds to an end-user targeting one of 25 distinct targets on a large screen display without any visual feedback on their smartphone device.

REFERENCES

1. Deno, J., "The Relationship of Previous Experiences to Spatial Visualization Ability," Engineering Design Graphics Journal, 59:3, 1995, pp. 5-17.
2. Fennema E., and Sherman, J., "Sex-Related Differences in Mathematics Achievement, Spatial Visualization and Affective Factors," American Educational Research Journal, Vol. 14 (1977), pp. 51-71.
3. Holz, C and Baudisch, P., "The Generalized Perceived Input Point Model and How to Double Touch Accuracy by Extracting Fingerprints", Proceedings of CHI 2010, pp. 581-590.
4. Hsi, S., M.C. Linn, and J.E. Bell, "The Role of Spatial Reasoning in Engineering and the Design of Spatial Instruction", Journal of Engineering Education, 86:2, 1997, pp. 151–158.
5. Gustafson, S., Holz, C., and Baudisch, P. "Imaginary Phone: Learning Imaginary Interfaces by Transfer of Spatial Memory from a Familiar Screen Device," Proc. of UIST 2011, pp. 283-292.
6. McArthur, V., Castellucci, S., and MacKenzie, I.S., "An empirical comparison of "wiimote" gun attachments for pointing tasks", Proc. of ACM SIGCHI Symposium on Engineering Interactive Computing Systems (EICS '09), pp. 203-208
7. Yee, KP, "Peephole displays: pen interaction on spatially aware handheld computers", Proceedings of CHI 2003, pp. 1-8.

A Real-World Study of an Audio-Tactile Tourist Guide

Delphine Szymczak **Kirsten Rassmus-Gröhn** **Charlotte Magnusson** **Per-Olof Hedvall**
Department of Design Sciences, Lund University
P.O. Box 118, 22100 Lund, Sweden
(delphine.szymczak, kirre, charlotte, per-olof.hedvall)@certec.lth.se

ABSTRACT
This paper reports on the in-context evaluation of an audio-tactile interactive tourist guide – one test was done in a medieval city center, and the other was done at an archaeological site. The activity theory framework was used as a perspective to guide design, field-study and analysis. The evaluation shows that the guide allows users to experience an augmented reality, while keeping the environment in focus (in contrast with the common key-hole like experience that on-screen augmented reality generates). The evaluation also confirms the usefulness of extending the vibrational feedback to convey also distance information as well as directional information.

Author Keywords
Navigation; multimodal; augmented reality; non-visual; inclusive

ACM Classification Keywords
H.5.2 User Interfaces: Auditory (non-speech) feedback; Haptic I/O; Evaluation/methodology

General Terms
Design; Human Factors

INTRODUCTION
The small screen on mobile devices poses a well known problem. By making better use of additional (non-visual) modalities, it is possible to create applications where the user can keep attention on the environment even when being "on the go". More modalities also help users who have problems accessing information through a specific channel – a design relying only on visual on-screen information will not be possible to use for persons with vision problems.

In the present paper we describe an inclusive tourist application (the Lund Time Machine) which allows users to be guided along a historical trail and experience sounds from the past. We also report the results from a qualitative outdoor study.

STATE OF THE ART / PREVIOUS WORK
Current navigation systems in mobile phones are based on screen interaction. The user is usually expected to look at the map to find where to go (e.g. Google Maps). The interest in non-visual modalities to guide navigation is increasing in the research community, explained in part by the need to reduce the load on visual attention in mobile situations [21]. Several systems have been devised using sound as guidance. An early attempt was the Audio GPS [7]. The Swan project [32] gives auditory feedback about routes and contexts aimed at visually impaired people. The ONTRACK [9] system uses 3D audio and music to guide the user, while Soundcrumbs [13] uses chosen audio tracks of varying volume according to the user's phone bearing. Audio Bubbles [17] gives auditory feedback about nearby landmarks. Others have explored vibrations to convey information. Sweep-Shake [24] for example uses vibration feedback instead to let users get information on points of interest close-by. It was then evolved to support users' navigation as described in "I did it my way" [25]. The Tactile Wayfinder [22] explores the use of a vibrating belt to give directional information. PointNav [12] gives both orientation and navigation support through vibrations and speech feedback. For more exploratory navigation, different kinds of soundscapes have been created by communities or artists. The Urban Sound Garden [30] and the Tactical Sound Garden [28] are two examples.

When designing for mobile usage, the context in which the application or device is used will impact drastically on the user experience. To cover this explicitly, the concept of "situation induced disabilities" has been introduced [26, 27]. When an augmented reality application is intended to be used "on the go" it is clear that one situation induced disability is the difficulty looking at and attending to the screen (since you have to attend to/look at your environment in order to avoid obstacles, people etc). Not attending to your environment may even be dangerous [31]. Despite this, the bulk of mobile augmented reality applications developed rely primarily on screen-based presentations. That this is not unproblematic is exemplified by [2] where the authors report "Paradoxically the game encourages looking at the screen more than the surroundings". Even "Backseat playground" [1] which makes use of audio for most of its interaction use on-screen visual elements for feedback, and the authors report that this drew the eyes of its users towards the screen rather than to the surrounding environment. Another problem often occurring in visual augmented reality is the difficulty of having a smooth juxtaposition of virtual elements on the real world image. GPS, compass and other sensor inaccuracies causes the virtual parts of the image to move around in an unconvincing way [2, 31].

Concerning mobile observation, there has been a number of evaluations done in the wild or in the field, outside of the controlled laboratory, in mobile contexts of use. Diverse methods have been described for example in [14]. Their pros and cons are worth taking into account when choosing a method of evaluation. Direct observation by following the participants is a way to see what really happens, and let the observer get a full sense of the meaningful events during the test. However, the observer's presence can disturb the users and a human observer can miss quite a lot of what is really happening. Logging and recording, to recreate the experience later on can be used as in [8]. Those methods give a perfect but partial rendering of the experience, and they still require a long time to be analyzed afterwards, and much equipment and organization during the evaluation. Those methods, complemented by traditional interviewing, would give a quite complete picture of the experience. Usually, a trade-off between available equipment, participants and time need to be done in order to get a good understanding while keeping the evaluation manageable. It has been shown that It's worth the hassle [19].

DESCRIPTION OF THE LUND TIME MACHINE

The "Lund Time Machine" (LTM) is a tourist guide application developed for Android 2.2. It uses GPS positioning and compass orientation to guide a tourist along a trail by tactile guiding (vibrations), and displays relevant information at the points of interest. The information given is of the kind a human tourist guide could tell about specific points of interest in a city. During navigation, one tab with a map of all points (Figure 1, left picture) and another with the list of points was displayed. The current distance to the points was also displayed for each point in the list. When arriving within 15 meters of a point of interest, an information screen was displayed and a sound file with recorded speech was played automatically. A picture of the place was also displayed on the screen (Figure 1, right). Along the trail, ambient sound sources were played back at specified locations. At some of the points of interest, users could choose to answer a multiple choice question. The questions were related to the place and the results were given at the end of the trail.

By using the mobile phone as a scanner (pointing with it in different directions), the participant will get feedback in which direction to walk. When the phone is pointing in the direction of the next point of interest, within an angle of 60 degrees as recommended in [15], the phone vibrates with 3 short bursts. As the user gets closer to the target, the pulse trains of 3 bursts are repeated more often. The pattern of 3 bursts is always played until its end, to avoid getting borderline effects when exiting the 60 degree target angle. The pattern starts anew when the user goes outside the target angle and then re-enters it again. The calculations of the frequency of bursts is based on the actual distance to target, but also on a distance zone, so that the frequency increase in part becomes "stepwise" (see Figure 2). The vibration pattern design was iteratively and systematically evaluated before the contextual evaluation reported here.

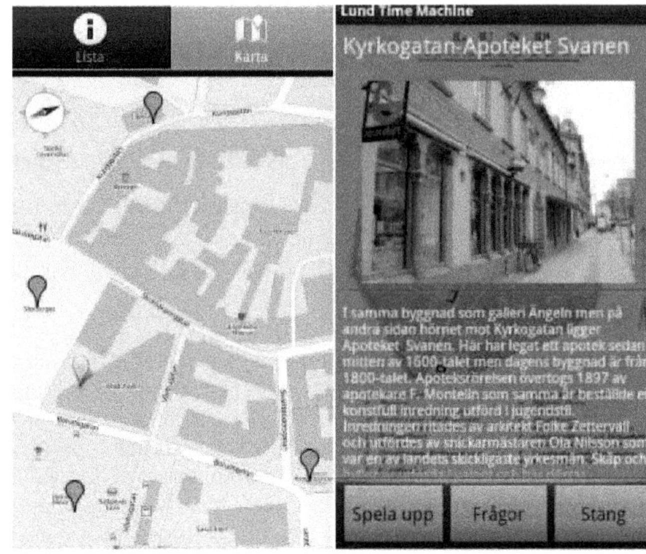

Figure 1: Screen shots from the tourist guide

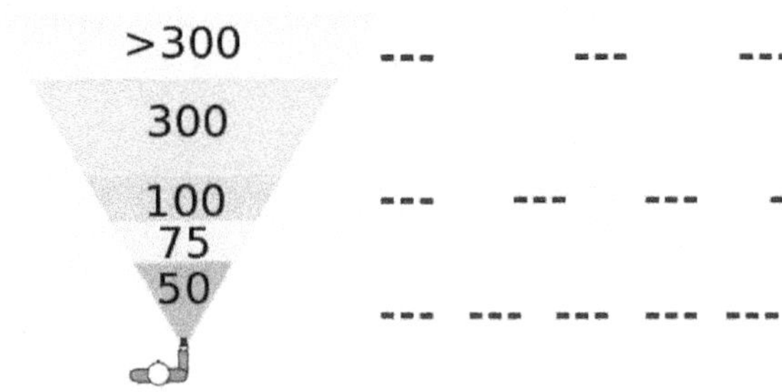

Figure 2: Haptic patterns and distance zones

An alternative guiding behavior can be chosen by the user: the tourist guide incorporates an audio Geiger, that plays sounds with different timbre and volume, as is described in [16]. To let the users benefit fully of the ambient sound, only the vibration Geiger (described more fully in [29] was used during the reported evaluation.

Sound Windows from the Past

In this application, the main purpose of the location based sounds was to communicate context. The sounds that could be heard were like "open windows from the past" being sound clips with sounds that could have been heard at this location in the past. On the medieval market place, the user would hear animal sounds; when passing by a house, where in medieval times there was a pub, pub noise and music could be heard. In the streets, different horse and carriage sounds would be heard. The sounds were played back in mono, but were location based, which meant that they would increase in volume when nearing the sound window. Playback in mono was deliberately chosen, to allow users to use only one earphone, and to possibly lessen sound artifacts from GPS instability. The volume increased from 0% at a radius of 10 meters from the GPS location in the archaeological site and 30 meters in the city to 100% at a radius of 6 meters.

METHODOLOGY OF THE STUDY

The evaluation was carried out in multiple steps. As a first proof-of-concept, informal tests were conducted in the area near the lab in the late stages of development where at least 5 different persons were involved in the tests. Then, three pilot tests were conducted in the city center of Lund. The final evaluation took place in the city center in Lund, where the participants walked one of two trails or on an archaeological excavation site from Viking times – Uppåkra, which lies just south of Lund. In the first location, the participants were 6 elderly persons (68 to 74 years), and 2 visual impairment experts, one of whom had a visual impairment. On the second location 5 elderly persons (67 to 78 years) and a school class of 24 10-year-old children were involved. For each test, the participants were given an introduction to the demonstrator. The participants were instructed how to use the demonstrator, by scanning, following the vibrations and answering questions (see description of demonstrator above). The users had a phone each (in all cases but the test with the school children, where they were walking in pairs), and earphones to hear the sound clearly.

Activity Theory in Evaluation Procedure

To guide the observations and strengthen the rigor of the analysis, we decided to make use of the activity theory framework. Activity theory as described in [10] considers the human action in the context of his or her interactions with the surrounding world and the other humans. When acting towards a goal, the person is mediating his or her action with artifacts or elements of the world, as well as with other humans.

Usually when evaluating interaction, the focus is on the device and how the user interacts with the device. Since what users do in a concrete activity is not limited to the interaction with the device, we tried to take the interactions with the surrounding world and the human context into account. The evaluation had as one of its aim to apply activity theory into the iterative design and evaluation of our navigation application. To achieve this, The Activity Diamond [5] was used as a conceptual model when designing the research activities and later on as an analytical construct guiding the analysis of the results.

The Activity Diamond is a conceptual model that portrays a human activity system [3], where the subject-object relation is mediated and thus influenced by the artifactual, natural, and human environments. The model is based on four interrelated sets of factors and is situated in time and place. Conceptually, the Activity Diamond captures an activity system that is changing and developing over time. This means that it can cover both historical development and instantaneous snapshots of an activity system.

The four sets of factors are:

1. **The subject** in the model, which is often an acting individual, but can also be a group of people such as a family. In our case, the subject was a test participant.
2. **The object** of an *activity*, which is related to the will and needs of the subject. It is determined by the motive behind the activity [10], such as getting better grades, learning to read, or developing and producing a multimodal tourist guide. In our study, the motive was slightly artificial for the participants, and differed between several of them. The envisioned activity was to follow a guided tour with the device. As a real guided tour, the users would follow a trail and get information on points of interest along the way.

   It is possible to distinguish a *hierarchical structure* in human activity: "Activities are composed of actions, which are, in turn, composed of operations. These three levels correspond, respectively, to the motive, goals, and conditions." (figure 3.4 p.64 in [10]) We did not enforce a motive, but the participants were all given the same goal - to follow the trail and get information at the points of interests. This sequence of actions was assumed to be the same for real tourists in Lund, whatever their motives might be. The hypothesis was that with several people having a common goal, it was possible to evaluate how the device can be adapted to better mediate the interaction with the environment, in a way that was adaptable to different motives.

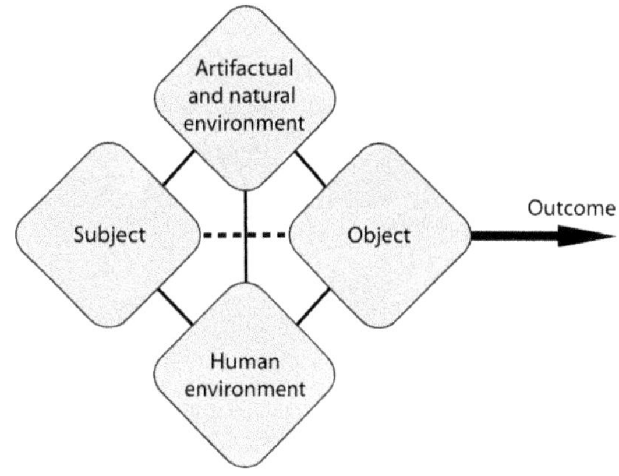

Figure 3: The Activity Diamond : The participant's activity mediated by human and artifactual environments

3. **The artifactual and natural environment**, which consists of material and immaterial artifacts and nature. Artifacts are everything human-made, such as computers, languages, symbols, legislation, along with their respective affordances [20], and resistances (i.e., the ways in which the artifact may enhance or impede functioning). An example of a factor in the natural environment is sunshine, which sometimes can make it hard to see what is on the screen of a computer or phone. A busy street environment that people have to attend to, as well as points of interest, are also part of the artifactual and natural environment. The impact of the artifactual and natural environment is described in more detail in the result section.
4. **The human environment**, which is the people or groups of people influencing the activity at hand: family, personal assistants, work colleagues; larger sectors of the population that are involved in or otherwise affect attitudes, norms, and expectations associated with an activity. Here, the human environment consisted of the other participants, the

Figure 4: Testing at the archaeological site in Uppåkra

observer and the other people wandering in the city. Considering the whole activity required to observe not only the interaction with the device, as is often the focus in such an evaluation, but also what happened around it in the real world. We thus chose to conduct the evaluation in a real environment with a diversity of users, so that the actions of the users were as similar as possible to the targeted tourist experience.

Town and Field, Real-Life Context

The evaluation took place in context. The Lund city environment is a small scale city, with a medieval city center. The tests were carried out during the day in a normal busy city environment. Cars and people were passing by, forcing the participants to pay attention to their surroundings. In the second site, Uppåkra, there was on the contrary no distraction, except the other participants. There were no remains in the field, and the participants could only discover the points of interest through the device that was handed to them. The content of the tourist guide in both cases – historical city and archaeological finds – had been collected and narrated by archaeologists.

The content consisted of 2 different city trails based on sculptures as points of interest, and the historical information about people or places connected to this sculpture. By choosing less prominent sights, also test participants living in Lund could discover something new. In the archaeology field, only one trail was created, with a collection of finds.

Observation and Recording

During the test, one observer followed the participants, part as a technical support, while also ensuring the safety of the participants, in case the device use would have made them unaware of the surroundings. The main task was to observe the participants and what happened during the interaction, as well as to do the video-recording. During the trail following, various recording occurred. In the city evaluation, the participants were walking either alone or in pairs. The participants were video filmed from a distance and the conversation between participants was recorded. The participants were asked to walk in pairs in order to get natural "think aloud" from their conversation. In the field evaluation (Uppåkra), the participants did not get audio-recorded, because the group was too large. Usually three to six participants would walk in the field at the same time, making it difficult to follow each one individually. In those cases, the interviews were most helpful to gain insights into the participants' experience. The main observations gathered from in-person observation as well as video and audio recording are described in the results.

Interviews

The interviews were conducted after the evaluation in Swedish. The quotes reproduced here are translated by the authors. The interviews always started with a NASA RTLX subjective workload rating (without pairwise comparisons) [4, 18]. As the navigation method (scanning with the mobile phone) was new to participants, it was used as a measure to assess whether users experienced a high amount of cognitive load or annoyance using it. A questionnaire, designed to determine the visual, hearing and mobility abilities of the participants, as well as their previous experience with smartphones and GPS devices was also issued. If time allowed, a Santa Barbara Sense of Direction Scale (SBSOD) [6] was answered by participants, in order to get a more precise rating of their sense of direction. The main interview consisted in structured and semi-structured questions to elicit participants view on the tourist guide application. The different user groups were asked the same set of basic questions, but the elderly user group had a more detailed interview, as the children were expected to tire faster. The common questions were:

- What are your general/spontaneous comments to the tourist guide?
- What (parts) were easy to use?
- What (parts) were hard to use?
- What was the one most difficult part to use?
- Is there anything you would like to add? What?
- Is there something you would want to remove? What?
- Did you experience any problems and how did you solve them?

The additional questions for the elderly participants consisted of qualitative questions, also asking them e.g. about how much they focused on the surroundings compared to how much they focused on the tourist guide application. An additional question in the city was added, asking the user to compare the Lund Time Machine with their previous experience of tourist trails with paper maps or tourist guides. Those questions and specifically the comparison one were chosen with the help of the Activity Checklist [11].

Due to slight differences in the set-up and the number of questions, the three different user groups (8 in the city, 5 elderly in the archeology field and 24 children in the archeology field), have been treated separately in the analysis. Additionally, the recordings from the semi-structured interviews were partially transcribed and used alongside the notes from the interviewer to extract the most important subjective results. The observations from the observer together with the video recordings were used to obtain a better understanding of what happened during the trail. When the technical recordings allowed, the video from behind and the sound from the participant's speech were merged. In that way, the observer could reconstruct the dialogs of the participants while seeing what happened. The reconstructed video was then analyzed using Lignes de Temps [23] to mark important events in the time-line. Those observations were correlated to the interview results.

RESULTS

In this section we will present the results of our evaluation. First we present the information on the test participants gotten through a detailed questionnaire, reflecting their diversity. Then a section on the global results given by the inspiration of Activity Theory that framed our analysis follows. After this, the detailed results are given in several sections.

A Diversity of Users

The participants were asked to give some details about their visual, hearing and sensory-motor abilities, as well as their previous mobile phone and GPS usage. The scales were from 1 for normal ability to 4 or 5 for no ability (e.g. complete blindness) As the guide was aimed at a diversified population, the age span was deliberately chosen. The declared visual ability of elderly people is to be contrasted with the declarations of school-children. The sight decreases normally with age, and some problems that seem to be normal when being older might not be seen as vision problems, and thus still rated under "full vision" by the older participants. When asked about a rating of their vision, while answering the best item "complete vision" one older participant stated: "It is quite good, for my age."

Participants Sense of Direction

In addition to the basic questionnaire, six out of the ten adult participants filled in the Santa Barbara sense-of-direction scale, and all of them were asked a single question about self-assessment of their sense-of-direction.

Overall, people did not use the lowest ratings for their sense-of-direction, but we find that the participants are quite well distributed between the highest rating (very good sense-of-direction) and the neutral rating (neither good nor bad). When comparing these data to the requests for specific help (for example routing) expressed in the interviews, no correlation between routing preference and good/bad sense-of-direction rating was found.

Activity Diamond Framing Results and Analysis

The observer and the video from behind enabled us to have an understanding of what happens on a moment-to-moment basis. It was possible during the analysis to look at the videos and pick up moments when the participants made use of the surrounding artifacts (for example the street names) to mediate their actions toward the goal of following the trail. Activity theory was used during the analysis, in order to guide the interpretation of the data.

The audio-recorded conversation of the participants, in the case of the city evaluation, was especially helpful in understanding how participants used the human and artifactual environment to mediate their actions toward the goal, since they would discuss about what they were currently doing or trying to do. For example, a participant who couldn't read the questions and text on the screen repeatedly asked the accompanying participant (human environment) to read to her what was on the screen. In another case, a participant was pointing to something, and the audio recording made possible to hear the participant say the street name (artifactual environment) she was pointing to, thus explaining what video alone could not have.

Group	1 – Adults	2 – Schoolchildren
Gender	4 male - 40% – 6 female - 60%	9 male - 37.5% – 15 female - 62.5%
Average age	66.8	9.5
Age span	43 to 78	9 to 11
Highest completed education (average & spread)	From high school to 4 years university education. Most had a specialized education for their diverse professions.	All in the same school class. Primary education – 10 years-old.
Visual ability (1 to 5 scale)	Mean 1.4 ; no color blind	Mean 1.04 ; one color blind
Hearing ability (1 to 5 scale)	Mean 1.6 ; 60% with musical exp.	Mean 1 ; 52% with musical experience
Motor ability (1 to 4 scale)	Mean 1.2 ; 90% right-handed	Mean 1.13 ; 77% right-handed
Mobile phone experience	80% had one for more than 2 years. Half of those had used touch screens.	92% had a mobile phone. Only 2 declared using a touch screen.
GPS experience	60% never used a GPS. Otherwise, it was mainly used for unknown routes in cars.	71% never used a GPS. Among the other, it was mainly used by their parents in cars.

Table 1: Demographic information of test participants

The trails and content of the tourist guide was devised to appeal to the participants, even if they were not regular tourists, so that their experience could reflect more one of a tourist in the activity of visiting than one of a test participant testing an application or discovering a new technology. In most of the cases, the interviews and observations showed that we succeeded.

Participant 7 (adult in the city) : "I found out things I had no idea about!"

Only two participants seem to have clearly had their main motive (driving their activity) to test the application. In one case, this was reflected in their behavior by an increased scrutiny of the application. This was obvious in the interview when the participant had a tendency to answer not with their own experience, but with general statements. When asked about the importance of a component of the application, the participant said :

> Participant 4 (adult in the city) : So it is... for whom? [. . .]
>
> Interviewer : It is always for you.
>
> P4: It is always for me? Yes, for me... It is then not so important. But I can see, for people- that there is an advantage. It must not only be for me...

In another case, a participant, that had already discovered the content earlier, walked the trail without stopping at any point to listen to the information.

The users were also diverse in their previous experience with GPS and smartphones, and were recruited mostly following their age group (elderly people and school-children), so that their motives could match more those of a diversity of tourists. Unlike a guided tour with a guide, you could take as long as needed and do the circuit independently, but you could obviously not have a human interaction with its full flexibility with a human guide. On the contrary, participant 8 (adult in the city) told us : "You get the info without effort - the guide tells you – like having a personal guide that you can ask to repeat [. . .] instead of rushing on to the next thing."

Interaction Without Occlusion – Participants' Focus

In visual augmented reality, the user needs to look at the screen to get the additional information. An audio and tactile modality lets the user interact more freely, since the device is not a barrier between you and the world. Through both the interview and the observation, we tried to get a sense of where the focus of participants was directed, so that we could confirm this hypothesis about non-visual augmented reality. All users but one expressed to have focus on the environment, reflecting that the object of their activity was not mainly the LTM. Here are quotes from two adult participants (P1 and P2) in the city :

"I had time to look in the shop windows" / "I looked at the ducks on the big square. And the alcoholics on the bench by the art museum..."

Although one user (who unfortunately also suffered from technical problems with the GPS) said:

P4 : "You focus quite a lot on the vibrations. If you walk with a map you look around more to identify buildings on the map – so you have to look around more than you did with the vibrations... but at the same time you can think about other things – I remembered that I had forgotten my library card..."

From the observer point of view, it was possible to see where the participants directed their gaze. In Uppåkra, where the environment was poor in content (a field of grass), the participants had naturally more focus on the device. In the city environment, they were alternating between the screen and the buildings and roads. At a POI most participants could look at the real building when one was present. When in pairs, the participants could also interact with each other while following the vibrations. In the Figure 5, the participant was walking and he stopped to focus on a man-hole cover decorated as

(a) Man hole cover (b) Participants walking

Figure 5: User focusing on an element of the real environment

Figure 6: User holding the phone lightly and pointing

a Swedish coin. This was not at all something mentioned in the application, and this focus was a spontaneous observation made by the participant. Some participants would rely more on the environment than on the guiding vibrations. One participant even walked along the street in a wrong direction for one or two minutes before changing and coming back after checking the vibrating angle with the device.

Some users focused more on the screen than expected. One user particularly used the written distance information to understand better if she was nearing the target or not. Despite the guiding voice, which read exactly the text on the screen, some users preferred to read themselves also. The interviews gave us a more global view on this matter. When asked directly, all except one of the participants in the city-environment evaluation answered that their focus was equally on the device and the surroundings or more on the surroundings (and other people) as opposed to focus on the device. Participant 2 (adult in the city) stated clearly : "The vibrations allowed you to look around."

Trail Following through Vibration

The participants could all follow the trail and complete the visit of all the points of interest. In the archaeological site, the participants could only rely on the vibrations. In the city interviews, when asked about the easiest to use parts of the application, the vibrations were cited by all participants. Overall in the interviews, the participants rated the vibrations to be both very important and fun or easy to use. The additional question on comparison of the same activity without the LTM also elicited interesting comments, this question was specifically formulated because we focused the evaluation on a tourist activity. Here are some quotes from the adult participants in the city :

(P5) "It was easy to find the direction" / (P7) "The vibration guiding was practical – and pleasurable" / (P1) "The vibrations felt good... in Lund it feels natural to point like this." / (P2) "If you turn a paper map upside down you will walk in the wrong direction. A paper map doesn't vibrate. [to show you where to go]" / (P1) "Good if you are alone in an unknown city - more discreet than a big paper map."

Only one participant found the vibrations of less importance, but she felt the distance coding was appropriate. (P4) "It "burns" when you are near. (it is) good."

The in-context field evaluations of the LTM demonstrator took between 10 minutes and 45 minutes for the completion of the tourist trail. The time differences are explained in part by the fact that the tracks were different in length. Another factor for the difference in time is the length between two points, and the varying time spent listening to information and answering questions at the points of interest.

Sound Windows

The reception of ambient sounds was also positive, although seen as less important than the vibrations :

(P1) "It was a little strange with all the animals." / (P3) "Cozy sounds – nice to listen to! I liked the horse sounds." / "I liked that the sounds were so real – when I heard the cows I started looking around to see where they were..."

Some felt the historical dimension of the sounds :

(P8) "You feel a bit as if you are moved to the middle ages" / (P7-8) "The sounds are important for the experience. You get a feeling of the history."

Comments showed another rather important effect: the sound windows could also be used to enhance the awareness of the current reality:

(P7) "It was good there was horse [and carriages] sounds– they reminded me that there could be traffic"

Those comments show a working mediation through the LTM toward the enjoyment of a medieval Lund tourist experience.

Low Effort/Cognitive Load

To assess the level of cognitive load and general effort required by this type of navigation, we asked the participants to rate their effort through a NASA-TLX test, with a 7-point scale (from low = 1 to high = 7). All tests were given within 15 minutes of the actual walking with the phones.

The tests were given just after the evaluations in the center city. On the field, it was not possible to fill them in between the two tested applications. The adults were asked to distinguish their answers to relate only to the Lund Time Machine evaluation, and thus given two NASA-TLX tests. The children were asked the questions for the two evaluations as a whole, rating the effort for the global experience.

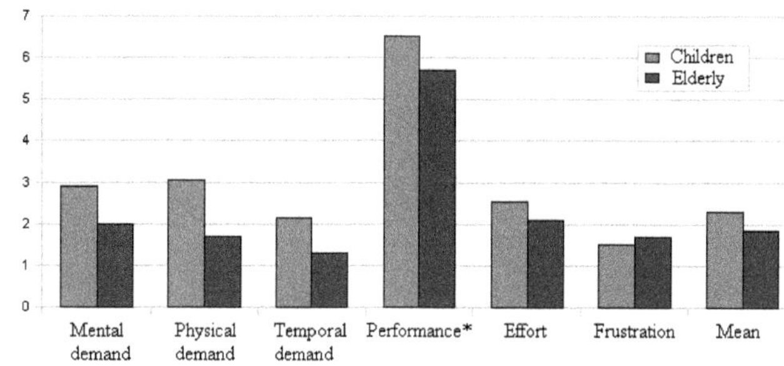

Figure 7: NASA-TLX aggregated answers

The performance question was reversed (indicated by * in figure 7), but the mean takes this into account. The mean adapted to a 100-scale is of 32.73 for the schoolchildren and of 26.37 for the adults. Globally, the values indicate a low demand related to the time dedicated to the demonstrator use. This low effort can be correlated with the possibility to focus on the environment, which both indicates that the Lund Time Machine enables to be guided with less effort and more freedom to explore the surroundings.

Some comments also confirm this: (P2) "I didn't think it was hard at all." / (P3) "This was just fun!"

Possible Improvements

Directions and Routing

In the Lund Time Machine, the direction to follow is given without routing, as the crow flies, to the next point of interest. This means that in a constructed environment, the LTM vibrations might guide you toward a wall, part of the artifactual and natural environment.

In the city environment evaluations, we have observed two different reactions toward the guiding behavior :

> P8 : You had to think one step further – aha – it may be on the other side of the house. You feel the impulses pointing you in a direction, but when you look there is a wall.
>
> P7 : No, I had no problems with that – I am used to think around corners.

Some people will naturally go around the buildings that are in the way, having no problems understanding the given directions. This kind of guiding allows the participants to walk different routes to reach the same points, encouraging free exploration of the city.

For some other participants, this lack of routing was seen as a difficulty. In several occasions, the participants would walk as close to the wall as possible, before turning to the observer and ask for what to do - thus taking advantage of the mediation through the human environment. Maybe embedding the distance information in the LTM might have helped here, since repeating that the target might be far away and that it was possible to go around buildings seemed enough to help the participants to continue walking in those cases. Obviously, this problem doesn't appear in an empty field.

Figure 8: Seeking shade to read screen

Soft Keys and Touch Screen Interaction Problems
The reactions to the screen interaction were a little different for the two different age groups. The school-children rated the use of buttons and the information on screen as both important and satisfying, positioning them just behind the vibrations in terms of preference.

For the elderly, the screen interaction revealed several difficulties. The most frequent comment was that the text presented on screen was too small. Usually it was also read aloud, but the questions were only displayed on screen, and were identified as one non-accessible element.

We were using a Nexus One with Android 2.2.1. When confronted with a dry environment, pressing and clicking the buttons seemed to become harder: (P1) "The screen was not very responsive". The problem was exacerbated with the group of elderly persons. The soft buttons below the screen were also problematic, because they were too close to buttons on screen, and were not giving feedback when pressed by mistake, which lead to unexpected changes of focus outside of the application. Getting back from this was not always easy: (P7) "The back button is not obvious, if you are not used to it."

We took care to note the features of the natural and artifactual environment that could be influence the activity. Most tests were conducted in a very sunny weather natural environment). Some participants had difficulties : (P8) "To read on the screen was hard – I had to go and stand in the shade" (Figure 8).

However, some users seemed to like to read on the screen, also while listening to the text. For example: (P2) "The images were quite important when you were unfamiliar with the place". The users used it: (P1) "I looked at the screen to compare the images to the houses."

DISCUSSION

The main non-visual interface components (the vibration interaction and the sound windows) proved to be both usable and satisfactory to the majority of the users. Although the using a pointing gesture in combination with vibration feedback is not new [24, 25, 22, 12] the distance coding was novel – and the results of the test shows that not only direction but also distance is important.

For the elderly group, the use of the touch screen was the main problem, but they could still follow the guide and get access to the historical and cultural information within the guide. Taking into account the different preferences by users, this calls for a stricter adherence to the cross-modal ideal. One the one hand, we need to communicate that the product is usable without the screen, while making all parts of the application usable through gestures, audio and vibrations. On the other hand, we would also need to redesign to make use of the screen in the best possible way, allowing users to zoom and scroll text and pictures and to use good contrast. Varying the placement of application specific buttons to avoid accidental soft key activation may also be one way of improving the functionality.

Half of the participants in the city requested routing as an addition to the application. At the same time there are participants who prefer to explore and discover alternative routes - there are after all users who do not like to use a GPS because it is "no challenge" (as one person said in the interviews). We interpret this as a sign that both possibilities should be made available to the user. An intermediated position could also be to design the trails using so called "via-points" without historical information. Displaying the distance information in a more obvious way – maybe by speech - could also help.

Most of our users were able to keep their focus on the environment – in contrast with [2] our users are looking at ducks, houses, manhole covers, alcoholics etc. Although the screen is still useful, our results indicate that anyone interested in enhancing (and not occluding) the reality needs to carefully consider which modalities to use. One unexpected effect was the fact that the sound windows also could be used to alert users to current day dangers (such as traffic) – this is something which should be considered explicitly in future designs.

Another positive result from using sound windows is that these are less sensitive to signal jitter/disturbances. In contrast with [31, 2] we had no complains about jumping virtual elements.

When observing how the users relied on the outside environment to follow the trail, we noticed that some users were focusing on specific information like the street signs around them. One aim of this application was to be more accessible for visually-impaired people. Integrating the elements that are not visible to them in the world – like street signs, high buildings in the far as point of reference – could give them this missing information that has been useful for users in the present evaluation.

In this evaluation, an activity theoretical approach through the Activity Diamond was used to coherently analyze the human, computer-mediated, interaction taking place in the participants' real-world human, artifactual and natural environments. Activity theory has been largely and fruitfully applied to the domain of Computer Supported Cooperative Work (CSCW) (p.85 in [10]), but to a lesser degree in other domains of Human-Computer Interaction. Our results show that it is a framework also useful for the design and analysis also of augmented reality applications.

Although we took steps to ensure that the participants' would have motives close to those of real tourists, the envisioned motive of visiting the town as a tourist was slightly artificial for our users. In a future study, we would aim at taking real tourists maybe from the tourist office, who already have this motive, and propose to them to test our application while doing as they had planned.

CONCLUSION

The interaction method using scanning and pointing to navigate proved useful to follow the trail while still enjoying the tour. We add to the previous work [24, 25, 22, 12] by providing a vibration coding that gives both direction and distance information.

The Lund Time Machine was successfully used to guide users in their navigation in both a town and field environment, enabling the users to enjoy an augmented city environment without too much distraction from the device (in contrast with [2]). Looking at our results we suggest that for interaction "on the go" the kind of non-visual designs we have tested are particularly useful and that on screen elements are more suited for interaction where the user is standing or sitting (as is indicated by users having to go to specific locations to be able to read on the screen at all). We hope our results will encourage a more wide spread use of non-visual interaction within the augmented reality community.

The results indicate that activity theory is a useful framework also outside of the cooperative domain – and suggest that it is fruitful for the design and analysis of augmented reality applications, where there is a need to consider real-world human, artifactual and natural environments. Other elements of the interaction have been identified through the activity-based evaluation as sources of improvement. We see that both routing and "as the crow flies" has advantages – and suggest that future tourist applications allow users to choose. Other elements that support the interaction in the real world, like street names, could also be considered.

Our issues with the touch screen finally, shows that possible alternative modes of input should be made available. The application implements some limited gesture recognition (allowing users to shake the device to press the "next button"), but this should be extended in future versions of the application and is something that needs to be considered by anyone designing for a wider range of users.

ACKNOWLEDGMENTS

The authors are grateful to the European Commission which co-funds the IP HaptiMap (FP7-ICT- 224675). We also want to thank VINNOVA for additional support.

REFERENCES

1. John Bichard, Liselott Brunnberg, Marco Combetto, Anton Gustafsson, and Oskar Juhlin. Backseat playgrounds: Pervasive storytelling in vast location based games. In *Entertainment Computing - ICEC 2006*, volume 4161 of *Lecture Notes in Computer Science*, pages 117–122. Springer Berlin - Heidelberg, 2006.
2. Tara Carrigy, Katsiaryna Naliuka, Natasa Paterson, and Mads Haahr. Design and evaluation of player experience of a location-based mobile game. In *Proceedings of the 6th Nordic Conference on Human-Computer Interaction: Extending Boundaries*, NordiCHI '10, pages 92–101. ACM, 2010.
3. Yrjö Engeström. *Learning by Expanding: An Activity-Theoretical Approach to Developmental Research*. Orienta-Konsultit Oy, 1987.
4. Sandra G. Hart and Lowell E. Staveland. Development of nasa-tlx (task load index): Results of empirical and theoretical research. In Peter A. Hancock and Najmedin Meshkati, editors, *Human Mental Workload*, volume 52 of *Advances in Psychology*, pages 139 – 183. North-Holland, 1988.
5. Per-Olof Hedvall. *The Activity Diamond - Modeling an Enhanced Accessibility*. PhD thesis, Lund University, 2009.
6. Mary Hegarty, Anthony E. Richardson, Daniel R. Montello, Kristin Lovelace, and Ilavanil Subbiah. Development of a self-report measure of environmental spatial ability. *Intelligence*, 30(5):425–447, 2002.
7. Simon Holland, David R. Morse, and Henrik Gedenryd. Audiogps: Spatial audio navigation with a minimal attention interface. *Personal and Ubiquitous Computing*, 6:253–259, 2002.
8. Francis Jambon and Brigitte Meillon. User experience evaluation in the wild. In *Proceedings of the 27th international conference extended abstracts on Human factors in computing systems*, CHI EA '09, pages 4069–4074. ACM, 2009.
9. Matt Jones, Steve Jones, Gareth Bradley, Nigel Warren, David Bainbridge, and Geoff Holmes. ONTRACK: Dynamically adapting music playback to support navigation. *Personal Ubiquitous Comput.*, 12(7):513–525, 2008.
10. Victor Kaptelinin and Bonnie A. Nardi. *Acting with Technology: Activity Theory and Interaction Design*, chapter Activity Theory in Interaction Design, pages 1–134. The MIT Press, Boston, MA, USA, 2006.
11. Victor Kaptelinin, Bonnie A. Nardi, and Catriona Macaulay. Methods & tools: The activity checklist: a tool for representing the "space" of context. *interactions*, 6:27–39, July 1999.
12. Charlotte Magnusson, Miguel Molina, Kirsten Rassmus-Gröhn, and Delphine Szymczak. Pointing for non-visual orientation and navigation. In *Proceedings of the 6th Nordic Conference on Human-Computer Interaction: Extending Boundaries*, NordiCHI '10, pages 735–738. ACM, 2010.

13. Charlotte Magnusson, Kirsten Rassmus-Gröhn, and Björn Breidegard. Soundcrumbs - Hansel and Gretel in the 21st century. In *Proceedings of the 4th international workshop on Haptic and Audio Interaction Design*, HAID '09. Springer-Verlag, 2009.

14. Charlotte Magnusson, Kirsten Rassmus-Gröhn, and Delphine Szymczak. Methods for understanding the mobile user experience. In *Proceedings of the 1st International OMUE Workshop. Held in Conjunction with NordiCHI.*, Observing the Mobile User Experience, pages 1–4, October 2010.

15. Charlotte Magnusson, Kirsten Rassmus-Gröhn, and Delphine Szymczak. Scanning angles for directional pointing. In *Proceedings of the 12th international conference on Human Computer Interaction with Mobile devices and services*, MobileHCI '10, pages 399–400. ACM, 2010.

16. Charlotte Magnusson, Annika Waern, Kirsten Rassmus-Gröhn, Åse Bjernryd, Helen Bernhardsson, Ann Jakobsson, Johan Salo, Magnus Wallon, and Per-Olof Hedvall. Navigating the world and learning to like it: mobility training through a pervasive game. In *Proceedings of the 13th International Conference on Human Computer Interaction with Mobile Devices and Services*, MobileHCI '11, pages 285–294. ACM, 2011.

17. David McGookin, Stephen Brewster, and Pablo Priego. Audio bubbles: Employing non-speech audio to support tourist wayfinding. In *Proceedings of the 4th International Conference on Haptic and Audio Interaction Design*, HAID '09, pages 41–50. Springer-Verlag, 2009.

18. W.F. Moroney, D.W. Biers, F.T. Eggemeier, and J.A. Mitchell. A comparison of two scoring procedures with the nasa task load index in a simulated flight task. In *Aerospace and Electronics Conference, 1992. NAECON 1992., Proceedings of the IEEE 1992 National*, pages 734 –740 vol.2, may 1992.

19. Christian Monrad Nielsen, Michael Overgaard, Michael Bach Pedersen, Jan Stage, and Sigge Stenild. It's worth the hassle!: the added value of evaluating the usability of mobile systems in the field. In *Proceedings of the 4th Nordic conference on Human-computer interaction: changing roles*, NordiCHI '06, pages 272–280. ACM, 2006.

20. D.A. Norman. *The psychology of everyday things*. Basic Books, 1988.

21. Antti Oulasvirta, Sakari Tamminen, Virpi Roto, and Jaana Kuorelahti. Interaction in 4-second bursts: the fragmented nature of attentional resources in mobile HCI. In *Proceedings of the SIGCHI conference on Human factors in computing systems*, CHI'05, pages 919–928. ACM, 2005.

22. Martin Pielot and Susanne Boll. Tactile wayfinder: Comparison of tactile waypoint navigation with commercial pedestrian navigation systems. In *Pervasive Computing*, volume 6030 of *Lecture Notes in Computer Science*, pages 76–93. Springer, 2010.

23. Vincent Puig. Lignes de temps, un logiciel pour l'annotation de films. *Culture et Recherche*, 112(t 2007):25–26, 2007.

24. Simon Robinson, Parisa Eslambolchilar, and Matt Jones. Sweep-Shake: finding digital resources in physical environments. In *Proceedings of the 11th International Conference on Human-Computer Interaction with Mobile Devices and Services*, MobileHCI '09, pages 1–10. ACM, 2009.

25. Simon Robinson, Matt Jones, Parisa Eslambolchilar, Roderick Murray-Smith, and Mads Lindborg. "I did it my way": moving away from the tyranny of turn-by-turn pedestrian navigation. In *Proceedings of the 12th international conference on Human Computer Interaction with Mobile devices and services*, MobileHCI '10, pages 341–344. ACM, 2010.

26. A Sears, M Lin, J Jacko, and Y Xiao. When computers fade pervasive computing and situationally-induced impairments and disabilities. *HCI International*, 2:1298–1302, 2003.

27. Andrew Sears and Mark Young. The human-computer interaction handbook. chapter Physical disabilities and computing technologies: an analysis of impairments, pages 482–503. L. Erlbaum Associates Inc., Hillsdale, NJ, USA, 2003.

28. Mark Shepard. Tactical sound garden toolkit. In *ACM SIGGRAPH 2007 art gallery*, SIGGRAPH '07, pages 219–219. ACM, 2007.

29. Delphine Szymczak, Charlotte Magnusson, and Kirsten Rassmus-Gröhn. Guiding Tourists through Haptic Interaction: Vibration Feedback in the Lund Time Machine. In *Proceedings, Part II of the 8th International Conference on Haptics: Perception, Devices, Mobility, and Communication*, EuroHaptics '12, pages 157–162. Springer, 2012.

30. Yolanda Vazquez-Alvarez, Ian Oakley, and Stephen Brewster. Urban sound gardens: Supporting overlapping audio landmarks in exploratory environments. In *Proceedings of Multimodal Location Based Techniques for Extreme Navigation workshop*, Pervasive 2010, 2010.

31. Richard Wetzel, Lisa Blum, Wolfgang Broll, and Leif Oppermann. Designing mobile augmented reality games. In Borko Furht, editor, *Handbook of Augmented Reality*, pages 513–539. Springer New York, 2011.

32. Jeff Wilson, Bruce N. Walker, Jeffrey Lindsay, Craig Cambias, and Frank Dellaert. SWAN: System for wearable audio navigation. In *Proceedings of the 2007 11th IEEE International Symposium on Wearable Computers*, pages 91–98. IEEE Computer Society, 11-13 Oct. 2007.

TraceViz: "Brushing" for Location Based Services

Yung-Ju Chang, Pei-Yao Hung, and Mark W. Newman
School of Information, University of Michigan
Ann Arbor, 48109
{yuchang,peiyaoh,mwnewman}@umich.edu

ABSTRACT
The popularization of Location Based Services (LBS) has created new challenges for interaction designers in validating the design of their applications. Existing tools designed to play back GPS location traces data streams have shown potential for testing LBS applications and for supporting rapid and reflective prototyping. However, selecting a useful set of location traces from among a large collection remains a difficult task. In this paper, we present TraceViz, the first system that is aimed specifically at supporting LBS designers in exploring, filtering, and selecting location traces. TraceViz employs dynamic queries and "brushing" to allow LBS designers to flexibly adjust their trajectory filter criteria to find location traces of interest. An evaluation performed with eight LBS designers and developers indicates that TraceViz is helpful for rapidly locating useful traces and also highlights areas for future improvement.

Author Keywords
Location-based services; design tools; information visualization; direct manipulation; capture and playback

ACM Classification Keywords
D.2.2 [Design Tools and Techniques]: User interfaces; H.5.2 [User Interfaces]: Interaction styles

INTRODUCTION

Commercial location-based services (LBS) have been popular on many mobile platforms in recent years because of the low cost of sensors and widespread high-speed mobile Internet access. In addition to these commercial LBSes, many researchers have sought to develop a variety of LBSes for mobile guides, transport support, mobile gaming, and assistive technology and health [7]. However, to develop a high-quality LBS, testing and evaluation are essential tasks during development. Because an LBS is meant to provide information based on location context—i.e., a user's current location, trajectory, speed, or direction—it is critical that the designers examine and evaluate their LBS's design and behavior in realistic situations by testing with real location data. While field testing is an important technique for evaluating application behavior under realistic conditions, it can be expensive, time consuming, and infeasible early in the design process. An alternative approach is to *bring the field into the lab* by capturing naturalistic location data to "play back" during development time to enable rapid iterative design and testing [6].

Several widely used LBS development tools such as the Dalvik Debug Monitor Server (DDMS)[1] for Android and the location simulator of Xcode[2] for iOS development both provide a location testing feature that allows LBS designers to examine how application prototypes behave with actual GPS location data traces. Thanks to the prevalence of mobile GPS recording applications, it has become increasingly easy and economical for designers to capture a large collection of location traces. However, as an increasing amount of GPS location data has been captured and aggregated, it becomes difficult to select particular location traces for testing. While general-purpose geovisualization tools like Google Earth Desktop[3] can be used to visualize location traces on a map, it remains challenging to explore, filter, and select individual location traces when presented with a large set of data.

Consequently, a tool that can effectively filter and highlight relevant location traces is needed. To address these needs, we developed a trace filter and selection tool called TraceViz to allow LBS designers to filter by *brushing* to directly indicate geographical regions and trajectories of interest. TraceViz provides three brush modes—*Reselect*, *Intersect*, and *Union*—to allow designers to flexibly narrow down or expand filter criteria. When a brush stroke is drawn, the system calculates the similarity score of nearby traces and adjusts their visual saliency: only highly similar traces remain salient on the map to make it easier to highlight and select those relevant traces. After selecting traces of interest, the designer can import the selected traces from into their chosen playback tool.

MobileHCI'12, September 21–24, 2012, San Francisco, CA, USA.

[1] http://developer.android.com/guide/developing/debugging/ddms.html

[2] http://developer.apple.com/xcode/

[3] http://www.google.com/earth/explore/products/desktop.html

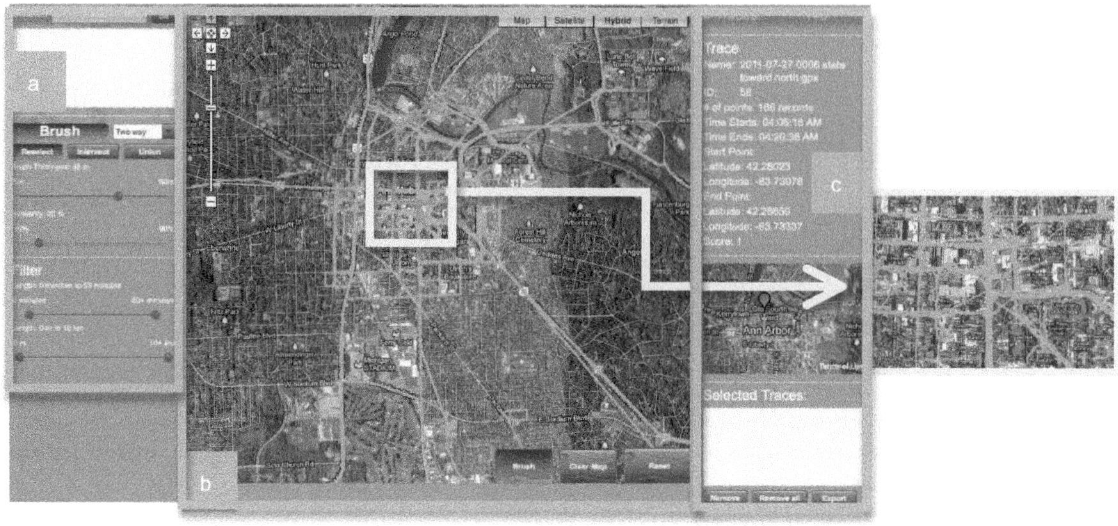

Figure 1. (Left) The main interface of TraceViz consists of three components. The Control Panel (a) contains a search box for geographical queries, brush related controls, and generic filtering controls. The TraceViewer (b) allows users to view traces and filter them by brushing. The Trace Info Panel (c) displays detailed information about a currently highlighted trace. (Right) With a large number of overlapping traces it is difficult it is to distinguish one location trace from others.

TraceViz is the first tool to leverage *brushing* to help LBS designers explore, filter, and select location traces for testing LBSes. By making it easier to find and select relevant traces, TraceViz can potentially encourage LBS designers and researchers to validate the design of their location-aware applications with a greater variety of location traces, in turn producing higher-quality systems. In the remainder of this paper we discuss related work, describe the TraceViz system with a focus on the implementation of brush-based filtering, and present the results of a preliminary evaluation.

RELATED WORK

A number of geovisualization systems have been developed for supporting movement analysis, identifying trajectory patterns and path summarization (e.g.[1,3]). These systems, however, have not focused on supporting the selection of specific examples for application testing. Brushing has been proposed in GIS systems for data linking and highlighting (e.g. [5]), as well as for specifying queries. de Silva and Aizawa [2], implemented a system for users to sketch a path or an area on a map to query linked multimedia data related to that path or area. FromDady [4] employs brushing to support iterative queries for helping visual analysis of aircraft trajectories. TraceViz is unique from these prior systems in that: a) brushing is used as a way for specifying *trajectory as a filter criterion* rather than simply for querying data in a brushed area, and b) it is the first work dedicated to supporting LBS designers in exploring, filtering, and selecting specific location traces for playback and application testing.

A SCENARIO OF USING TRACEVIZ

Here, we describe a scenario in which a LBS designer would like to use TraceViz to find particular location traces.

David is a LBS designer who is developing an application that recommends promotions to a user based on their current location and recent trajectory. Knowing that such an application would need to intensively respond to location updates at various places in the downtown area, David's team recruits prospective users to collect a large collection of location traces for testing. As the application prototype evolves, David wants to test the prototype with a number of test cases that involve a traveler passing by specific promotions. To find traces that travel specific routes will require David to review all of the traces his team has collected, so he turns to TraceViz.

David launches TraceViz and uses the search box to center the map on a certain restaurant. He enables the brush mode and brushes a route along a street on which a promotion is located. This results in only five traces that pass through the area he brushed on the map. David selects one location trace from this set, and uses it for testing the application.

THE TRACEVIZ INTERFACE

TraceViz consists of three major components, as shown in Figure 1. The *TraceViewer* (Figure 1b) visualizes location traces and allows users to brush to filter traces. Traces are color-coded based on whether they are highlighted, selected, or brushed. Users can hover over a trace to view detailed information in the *TraceInfo Panel* (Figure 1c), and they can click on the trace to select it. The *Control Panel* (Figure 1a) allows filtering based on trace duration and distance, and additionally provides controls for users to select brush modes, adjust brush thickness, and set a brush tolerance threshold. Users can utilize the time and physical length filters location traces by time duration and physical length of the traces in addition to brushing. The brush thickness slider allows users to adjust the coverage of a brush stroke. The tolerance threshold slider controls whether a brushed trace should be displayed based upon its similarity to the brush stroke. The brush mode buttons allow users to switch among the Reselect, Intersect, and Union modes (described below). Once one has selected a set of location traces, the selected traces can be downloaded in a preferred file format (e.g., GPX) or loaded directly into RePlay [6], a dedicated capture and playback tool.

TraceViz was built using the Flex 4.1 SDK and uses the Google Map API for Flash. It can run on any browser with Flash Player 10 installed. It connects to a MySQL database that contains the traces, and has the ability to import traces in standard file formats such as GPX.

BRUSHING TO EXPLORE AND FILTER TRACES

Brushing is a direct manipulation technique that TraceViz employs to allow users to specify trajectories on a map to filter traces that are "similar" to the brushed stroke. When a brush stroke is drawn on the TraceViewer, we determine which traces are "similar" to the stroke as follows:

1. We identify a set of *candidate traces* by including all traces that have at least one point within the stroke's *candidate area*, which we define as a rectangular area around the stroke that is *2 * brush thickness* pixels larger than the stroke bounds in all directions. The goal of this step is to reduce the number of traces that are subsequently considered while retaining enough information about each trace to be able to determine the degree to which it is aligned with the brush stroke.
2. For each *candidate trace,* we compute the *brush-to-trace similarity* by computing the proportion of *brush points* that are *near* (i.e., within *brush thickness* of) at least one *trace point*. This gives a higher score to traces that are well aligned with the brush stroke throughout the stroke's entire length. It also penalizes traces that have few points that fall within the brush stroke, whether due to misalignment or due to sparse data.
3. We also compute the *trace-to-brush similarity* for each trace by computing the proportion of *trace points* that are *near* at least one *brush point.* This gives a higher score to traces whose nearby points lie mostly within the brush area and penalizes traces whose trajectories diverge from that of the stroke. While in most cases the *brush-to-trace* and *trace-to-brush* scores are redundant, both are needed to deal with cases where the trace and brush point densities differ.
4. Finally, we compute the *overall similarity* by averaging the *trace-to-brush* and *brush-to-trace* similarity scores. Note that all traces that lie outside the *candidate area* are assigned an *overall similarity* of zero.

Each trace is then rendered on the map according to its similarity score: first, all traces with similarity scores below the user-defined *tolerance threshold* are given alpha values of zero, and all other traces are given alpha values proportional to their similarity score.

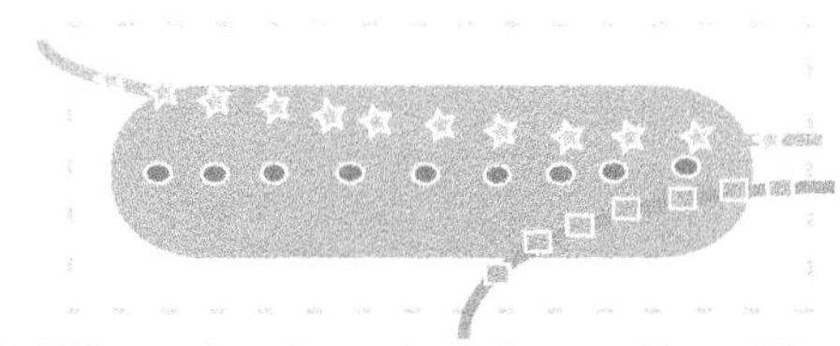

Figure 2. When a brush stroke is drawn, TraceViz computes the "similarity" of all nearby traces to the stroke. Here, two *candidate traces* intersect the *candidate area* (dashed yellow line). The top trace (green stars) is found to be more similar than the bottom trace (blue squares) because more of its points lie within the brush stroke region (pink oval).

As an example, consider the situation depicted in Figure 2. Trace 1 (green stars) is assigned a *brush-to-trace* similarity of 1 since all of the *brush points* are near to at least one *trace point.* It receives a *trace-to-brush* similarity of 0.83 since 10 of 12 *candidate points* are near at least one *brush point.* The *overall similarity* is therefore 0.92. Trace 2 (blue squares), on the other hand, receives a *brush-to-trace* similarity of 0.44 since 4 of 9 *brush points* are *near* at least one *trace point,* and a *trace-to-brush* similarity of 0.71 since 5 of 7 *trace points* are near a *brush point.* Trace 2's *overall similarity* is thus 0.58.

In order to give LBS designers additional control, TraceViz provides three brush modes—*Reselect, Intersect,* and *Union.* In Reselect mode, every stroke generates a new result. In Intersect mode (shown in Figure 3), each stroke after the first refines the filter to show only traces that pass through all strokes, whereas in Union mode each stroke widens the filter to include traces that pass through *any* stroke. As an example, we return to our earlier scenario to illustrate the use of Intersect mode:

David wants to find a trace passing by both a coffee house and a bookstore that are on two different streets. He uses the Intersect mode to brush two strokes near the coffee house and the bookstore, respectively. However, he finds that the filtered traces are still many and overlap one another. As a result, he brushes the third stroke on another street to refine the filtered results. Now David can easily distinguish the traces and select them for testing.

USER STUDY

To observe whether and to what extent TraceViz can help LBS designers efficiently select location traces, we conducted a preliminary usability evaluation. We recruited eight people with experience in designing or developing mobile applications to participate and asked them to use TraceViz to perform four tasks in which they selected traces to load into RePlay [6]. Their goal was to test aspects of a sample LBS called Here & Now (H&N), which is a location-based advertising application we developed for the purpose of testing TraceViz and related tools. H&N allows merchants to create promotions that are delivered to mobile customers and allows customers to see the promotions nearby their current location. Customers can adjust the "notification range" within which they receive information

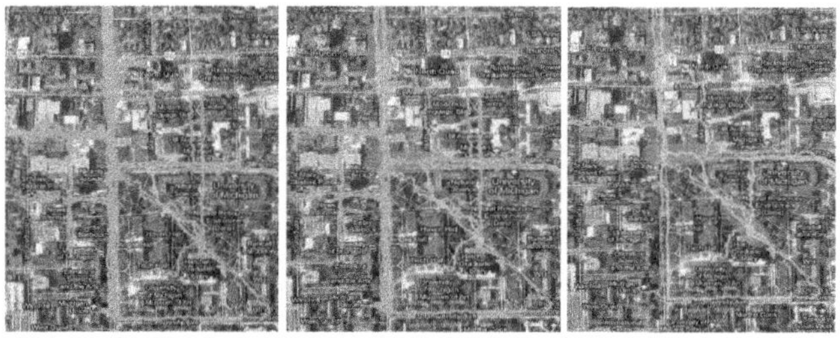

Figure 3. The Intersect brush mode allows an LBS developer to refine a filter by adding additional brush strokes, as shown here from left to right.

about promotions. Our tasks were all based on finding traces that would be suitable for testing this feature.

In the first task, participants were asked to practice selecting a trace by brushing. In the second task, they needed to find a trace that allowed testing different display ranges (0.5 km, 1km, and 2km) and show that H&N respected users' preferences in all cases. In the third task, participants had to find traces that passed by at least two active promotions. Finally, in task 4, participants needed to find two traces that approached a promotion from different directions in order to show H&N working with multiple simultaneous users. We provided each participant with 200 GPS traces collected in Ann Arbor, Michigan, USA (the city where our study took place). All participants received a demonstration of TraceViz, RePlay, and H&N at the beginning of the session. Upon completing the tasks they were asked about their reflections on using TraceViz. Participants were encouraged to solve the tasks in any way they wished, and were not directed to use particular features of TraceViz. Video and audio for all sessions was captured, along with detailed session notes, and these data were reviewed to assess and interpret task success, critical incidents, and participant satisfaction.

Seven of the eight participants were able to finish all four tasks with little or no assistance. Most participants were able to find suitable traces within one or two attempts for each task. This suggests that TraceViz as a whole is able to support LBS designers' in efficiently finding and selecting traces for testing a LBS. Moreover, participants developed several different strategies of using brushing for finding suitable traces. For example, while some participants used the Intersect mode for finding traces passing by two specific areas, other participants used it simply for reducing the number of traces on the map.

However, we also uncovered several shortcomings to be addressed in future versions of TraceViz. Some shortcomings were basic usability problems, such as confusion about the brush mode names and difficulties switching between brushing, selecting traces, and panning the map. Additionally, most participants struggled when choosing a trace with unexpected characteristics, including changes in direction and speed or poor signal quality. For instance, P2 selected a trace with sparse location records (probably due to poor GPS signal), and it took her a long time to accomplish one of the tasks as a result. Improving TraceViz to provide more detailed information about traces, such as speed, signal quality, and direction of travel would likely help with this problem. We also observed that participants had trouble understanding a trace's overall trajectory once they had zoomed the map in too far. Better overviews in the TraceInfo Panel could help here. Finally, sometimes participants still encountered difficulties selecting overlapping traces even after brushing and using other filter controls. This suggests that more precise selection capabilities may be needed for especially dense data sets. We plan to address these issues in future work.

CONCLUSION

In this paper we have presented and evaluated TraceViz, a novel tool that employs "brushing" to support LBS designers in exploring, filtering and selecting GPS location traces from large data sets. TraceViz supports Reselect, Intersect, and Union modes to enable LBS designers to more flexibly explore and filter location traces based on trajectories in order to meet various testing requirements. We believe that with the support of TraceViz, LBS designers will have more incentive to test their LBS with a larger variety of location traces, which will in turn help the designers produce higher quality designs.

ACKNOWLEDGMENTS

We thank Eytan Adar, Mark Ackerman, and members of the Interaction Ecologies group for helpful comments on this work. We also thank our study participants.

REFERENCES

1. Andrienko, G., et al. Interactive visual clustering of large collections of trajectories. In Proc. *VAST 2009*, 3-10.
2. de Silva, G.C., Yamasaki, T., and Aizawa, K. Sketch-based spatial queries for retrieving human locomotion patterns from continuously archived GPS data. *IEEE Transactions on Multimedia 11*, 7 (2009), 1240 -1253.
3. Girardin, F., et al. Digital Footprinting: Uncovering Tourists with User-Generated Content. *IEEE Pervasive Computing 7*, 4 (2008), 36-43.
4. Hurter, C., Tissoires, B., and Conversy, S. FromDaDy: Spreading aircraft trajectories across views to support iterative queries. *IEEE Transactions on Visualization and Computer Graphics 15*, 6 (2009), 1017–1024.
5. Monmonier, M. Geographic brushing: Enhancing exploratory analysis of the scatterplot matrix. *Geographical Analysis 21*, 1 (1989), 81–84.
6. Newman, M.W., et al. Bringing the field into the lab: supporting capture and replay of contextual data for the design of context-aware applications. In Proc. *UIST 2010*, 105-108.
7. Raper, J., et al. Applications of location–based services: a selected review. *Journal of Location Based Services 1*, 2 (2007), 89–111.

Urban Exploration Using Audio Scents

Andreas Komninos, Peter Barrie
Glasgow Caledonian University
70 Cowcaddens Rd., Glasgow G4 0BA, UK
[andreas.komninos, peter.barrie]@gcu.ac.uk

Vasilios Stefanis, Athanasios Plessas
University of Patras / RACTI
Rion, Patras, Greece
[stefanis, plessas]@ceid.upatras.gr

ABSTRACT
We describe the design and evaluation of an audio-based mixed reality navigation system that uses the concept of *audio scents* for the implicit guidance of tourists and visitors of urban areas, as an alternative to turn-by-turn guidance systems. A field trial of our prototype uncovers great potential for this type of implicit navigation and is received positively by our participants. We discuss the technical implementation of our prototype, detailed findings from quantitative and subjective evaluation data gathered during the field trial and highlight possible strands for further research and development.

Author Keywords
Audio mixed reality, implicit navigation, urban environments

ACM Classification Keywords
H.5.m Information interfaces and presentation (e.g., HCI): Miscellaneous. H.5.2 User Interfaces - Auditory (non-speech) feedback and User-centered design. H.5.5 Sound and Music Computing - systems

General Terms
Design, Experimentation, Human Factors,

INTRODUCTION
Turn-by-turn (TbT) GPS navigation for pedestrians is a technology that many tourists have found to be a valuable aid for navigating unfamiliar urban environments. However the experience of tourism is not just about getting from A to B. Assimilation of the surroundings, sights, sounds and smells is a critical factor in the visit experience. When attention is shifted away from the surroundings (e.g. through close following of turn-by-turn instructions or through constant consultation of a mobile screen), the visitor experience suffers greatly. Krüger et al [1] and Aslan et al. [2] found that turn-by-turn systems often fail to help users assimilate and form an impression of the navigated environment. Seager [3] also discusses many of the challenges in screen-based pedestrian navigation, while Pielot & Boll [4] found that users often feel "bossed around" by the explicit commands issued by TbT systems.

Since visual distraction is the most detrimental factor in a user's visiting experience, researchers have attempted to examine solutions using other interaction modes, such as audio and haptic feedback. Jones et al. [5] and Strachan et al. [6, 7] examined systems that dynamically adapt the music that a user is listening to, in order to guide them in a certain direction, by controlling the left and right audio channel volume. Route finding applications, such as the AudioGPS system [8], Mediascapes [9], Audio Bubbles [10] and Soundcrumbs [11], have used abstract sounds as an auditory beacon to support navigation tasks and guide users to points of interest. These beacons alert users of their proximity to a location of interest through a brief repeating sound such as an Earcon (a structured non-verbal audio message, e.g. a trumpet sound to indicate the discovery of a location), or an Auditory Icon (a familiar sound mapped onto an event to which it clearly relates e.g. water noises to indicate the presence of a river). Auditory beacons are generally presented within proximity and activation zones around the landmarks.

Other applications like the Roaring Navigator [12] estimated the position and orientation of the listener's head by means of a GPS receiver and magnetometer and also used stereo panning to indicate the direction of a navigational goal, i.e. animal sounds, located at the various enclosures in a zoo in both a navigational and an exploratory scenario. Vazquez-Alvarez et al. [13] examined the use of Earcons as auditory landmarks and 3D audio spatialisation, aiming to test the user experience of unguided exploration of an environment populated with multiple simultaneous sound sources. They showed that spatial audio together with Earcons allowed users to explore multiple simultaneous sources and had the added benefit of increasing the level of immersion in the experience. In addition, spatial audio encouraged a more exploratory and playful response to the environment. While these approaches have shown promise, related early work has found that many users are reluctant to use headphones for this type of task [14], citing concerns about being recognised as tourists, or a feeling of isolation from the environment [12]. Additionally, Harma et al. [15] show that 3D audio spatialisation suffers from users' lack of

MobileHCI'12, September 21–24, 2012, San Francisco, CA, USA.

ability to clearly distinguish between front and rear sound placement.

Robinson et al. [16] discussed the concept of navigation by removing turn-by-turn instructions, so as to prompt users to explore, rather than hurry through their surroundings. Their approach helps to minimise the effects of strict TbT audio feedback, using vibrotactile feedback to allow a less restrictive interaction style, in which users point their device towards their navigation goal and appropriate feedback is given through vibration-encoded information from their mobile. A similar concept is also discussed in [17], using multiple track points to guide users using a mobile device, while significant advantages in using a non-visual vibrotactile belt interface for navigation were found in [4].

Further from the aspect of navigation, mobile location-based audio offers excellent opportunities to deliver guided tours, or information relevant to sights for tourists. The Hear & There system [18] was able to determine the location and head position of the user using the information from GPS and a digital compass. This system used "customizable collections of sounds that could be placed in the space" consisting of "a single primary sound, with other audio braided in the periphery". In [19], Reid et al. describe the use of location-based audio in order to provide a mixed reality experience in the form of a play, which is acted out as the user walks through the streets of Bristol. The system was implemented with the use of a PDA with a GPS receiver so that audio could be triggered at appropriate locations, and the user was required to wear headphones. The experience could also be shared with a companion, through the use of headphone splitters. The experience was found to be compelling and immersive for users, though immersion was found to be a transitive state and often delivered in short bursts, due to the continuous interleaving of real and virtual world events. Rowland also recorded positive user experience outcomes from delivering location-based stories to cyclists [20].

The findings of research in mobile aids to assist pedestrian navigation and exploration can be summarised as follows:

- TbT systems deliver performance and security in navigation, but at the detriment of the overall visitor experience.
- Earcons and 3D spatialisation can perform well for navigation but front/back sound placement is not clear to users
- Location-based delivery of audio narratives can provide a very immersive experience
- Users express issues and worries over headphone usage in respect of safety implications and isolation from fellow travellers
- Research has focused on the individual user, with little consideration for the support of tourist groups

FOLLOWING THE TRAILS OF AUDIO SCENTS

To escape the "tyranny" of turn-by-turn navigation, we considered the concept of audio scent trails to encourage exploration in an urban environment while giving a sense of direction and security. Much like a trail of scent that can be picked up by an animal with enhanced olfactory perception, an audio scent is a trail generated artificially by a navigation system that augments a user's perceptive experience with *continuous* (compared to *discrete*) cues for navigating through the environment. Just as the animal following a scent trail is free to explore different directions of travel in order to pick up the scent and able to return to previous locations where the scent was stronger, a pedestrian following an audio scent is encouraged to explore their surroundings in order to figure out where the audio scent is stronger. However, in contrast to the goal-driven animal, for our pedestrian the exploratory experience *is* the goal. The freedom to roam about, albeit within the confines of the safety zone within which users can pick up the audio scent, is the distinguishing feature of our concept and its main advantage in improving a visitor's experience in exploring an urban environment. To illustrate the concept by example, one might split the reviewed literature in three main categories:

1. Navigation systems such as [4-7] and [16,17] appropriate for the type of tourist that simply wants to go from A to B without obeying specific verbal commands,
2. Exploratory systems such as [10-13] appropriate for a tourist that wants to just "roam about" without a clear navigation goal and
3. Audio mixed reality experience systems such as [18-20] appropriate for the delivery of meta-information about an environment without navigation support as a goal.

Our audio scent concept sits somewhere between categories 1 and 2. Our user is a tourist that would like to go from A to B, but is not in a hurry and does not want to just take the shortest route. They want to head towards B and explore along the way until they eventually get to their destination.

The SoNav prototype

We developed a prototype system called SoNav, which can become a promising platform for addressing the issues identified by the preceding survey of the state of the art. SoNav uses 3D spatialised audio on a mobile device to deliver feedback about a user's position compared to a pre-determined path. Our prototype is built on the Android platform and requires a device with a GPS and magnetic compass sensor. Internet connectivity is desirable, as it allows the UI to display local maps (Fig. 1) and dynamically compute a route between any chosen start and end points, but is non-essential - as will be shown below.

The mode of operation is as follows: The user selects a start and end point from a map-interface on their device. A path between selected points is calculated using the Google directions service and is drawn on the map (Fig. 2). Alternatively, a user can load a pre-defined path stored locally on the device. The waypoints of each path are drawn as small orange blobs. Each path is thus divided into appropriate segments, which are later used to determine user distance and azimuth to the path. The user then puts on their headphones, places the phone in their pocket and starts to walk toward their destination and along that path.

As discussed previously, to materialize our concept of an audio scent emanating from the path, we use the following approach: A thread of execution plays back a constant sound (the audio scent) through the user's headphones, which can be music or a looping Auditory icon. At the moment, we use the sound of a couple of people walking in a city environment, which gives a deeply immersive experience, as if the user is walking with a virtual group. This thread utilizes a port of the OpenAL 3D audio library for Android and thus has the ability to control the sound source distance and orientation during playback. A second thread of execution is responsible for updating the user's current position using the device location sensors (A/GPS). A final thread monitors the user's current orientation (magnetic compass).

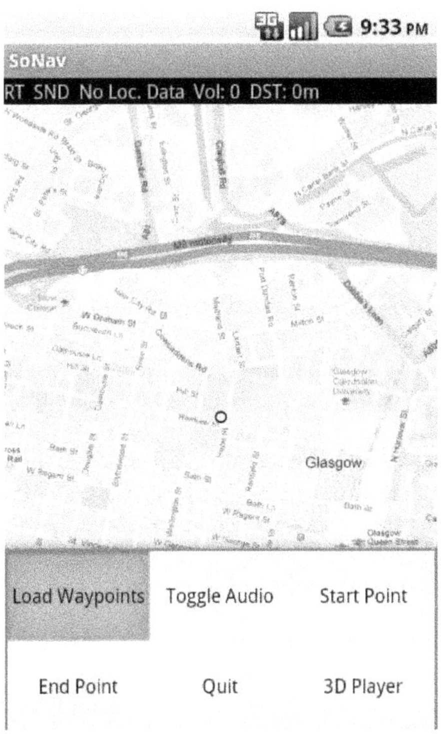

Figure 1 The SoNav user interface and basic options menu

At every orientation update, we calculate the distance of the user to the nearest segment of the path and also the relative azimuth of the user to that of the nearest path segment, using the magnetic north as reference. This information is then passed to the audio player thread, which is responsible for changing the sound source orientation in such a manner so it would seem to the user that the sound is emanating from the direction of the nearest path segment.

As the user places themselves at different angles to the left or right of the path, the sound shifts in 3D around them to indicate the relative position of the path. Additionally, the further away the user is from the path, the lower the sound volume becomes, giving a sense of moving far away from the path, or, in the case of our prototype, to convey a sense of having veered away from the path. Additionally, multiple sound sources can be placed within the soundscape, to act as virtual sound beacons, perhaps marking the location and direction of a point of interest, or the end point of a route.

Technically, the main differences between the audio scent concept and other exploratory or navigation systems which are based on audio beacons (e.g. [9-13]) is that in lieu of having fixed audio beacons at certain positions, our user experiences a moving beacon (placed on the optimal route). The user does essentially have to travel towards the beacon. As long as they hear it at a constant level from some direction, they are effectively travelling in parallel to it. Hence they can explore by taking alternative routes, without pressure to move towards a certain direction.

To better demonstrate our concept, consider the following simple use case: Our pedestrian is placed away from the path in the position marked by the blue marker in Figure 3 and pointing towards the north-west (as indicated by the pointed end of the marker). In this position, the path is to the user's right at approximately 45 degrees, and as such, the audio balance is shifted mostly (but not fully) towards the right headphone. The user understands that the path they should follow is somewhere to their right, so at the next junction, they take a right turn. As they turn, the sound starts to shift towards their left ear. Given the fact they are now closer to the path, the sound volume becomes higher, indicating their increasing proximity. As the user reaches the position marked by the orange marker, the path is directly to their left, hence the sound shifts to play exclusively in their left headphone.

The user keeps walking until they finally reach the path, in which case the sound equalizes on both ears, as they stand directly on top of the path (actually we do allow a certain radius to account for street and pavement width for this change). Now the user has a choice, whether to turn left or right. Turning left will keep them on the path. A further right turn will gradually take them further away from the path. The sound source will now be behind the user and the sound volume will attenuate as the user walks increasingly further from the path, indicating that they have taken a wrong turn. One might ask, what would have happened if the user had not turned right at the junction after the blue marker but continued straight ahead? This is precisely the point - SoNav leaves the user free to explore an area as they desire, with constant and reassuring feedback given to them at all times, as long as they remain within a certain distance from the path. There is no right or wrong path to follow. The feedback is continuous and there is no need to wait for a turn-by-turn system to recalculate or to issue the next command, which could well not be issued for several hundred meters from the previous one (e.g. walking in a straight line).

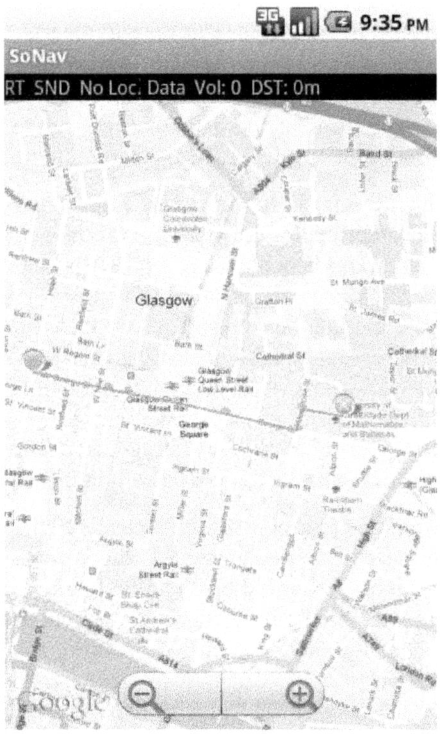

Figure 2 A user has selected a random start (green bubble) and end (grey bubble) point. The route drawn in green is retrieved using the Google directions API

This means that the user can place their focus on the environment without a need to constantly check a screen or interact with the device for instructions. The user can also choose to wear their headphones occasionally, so as to better focus on the environment or interact with their group. Finally, because we use organic city sounds with intermittent volume peaks (e.g. the sound of a walking person's heels) and let external sounds filter through, the user is at much less of a danger while navigating than they would be with a constant isolating sound like music.

USER TRIALS

We were keen to explore the effect of SoNav with real participants, and designed an experiment to navigate an urban environment. We felt that it was important that we carry out our experiment in a realistic environment. Most literature reports on experiments in relatively quiet and safe areas, such as parks, university campuses or quiet parts of town. Since our system is geared towards exploring urban environments, we felt that an experiment in any other setting would detract from our findings. However, using actual tourists for an experiment in a busy urban setting would have been dangerous. We did not want to follow them so as not to interfere with their behaviour; at the same time, we could not afford to have participants getting lost or straying too far from the experiment area. A further factor to consider was that the experiment was carried out in a right-hand driving country, a system which many overseas tourists would be unfamiliar with and would thus require additional attention on the road from them.

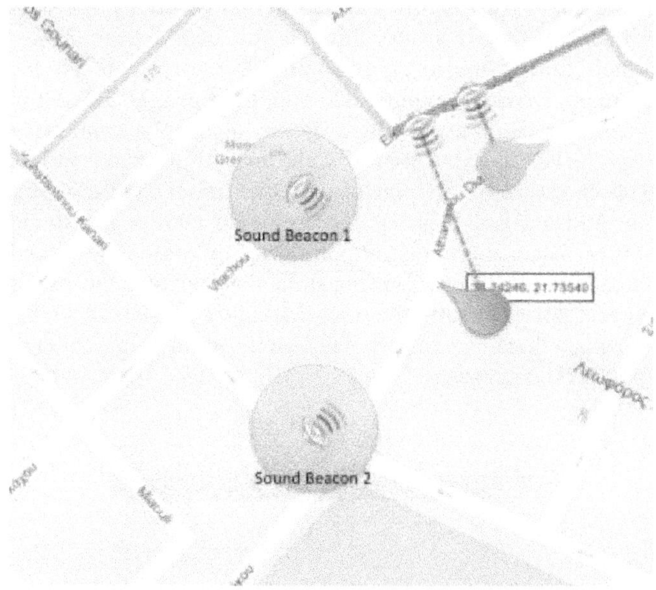

Figure 3. A simplified visualisation of the audio scent principle, auxiliary beacons and their corresponding range

Bearing in mind the safety of participants, we decided to conduct an experiment whereby the participants would be reasonably familiar with the experiment area. To simulate the effect of being a tourist and thus generally unsure of where to go, we asked our participants to navigate to a destination which remained unknown to them for the duration of the experiment. As such, they would be forced to explore the area, in order to discover the actual destination. We recruited a total of 16 participants (15 male, 1 female) with an age range between 18 and 35 (one user being older than 40). Two participants were members of staff in our university in the areas of Audio and Interactive Media while the rest were postgraduate and undergraduate students with varied discipline backgrounds (Computing, Business, Engineering). Most of the participants (9) had made use of a GPS turn-by-turn system in the past while the rest had experienced and understood the function of such systems (e.g. as passengers in cars with such systems in operation), although they had never used one themselves.

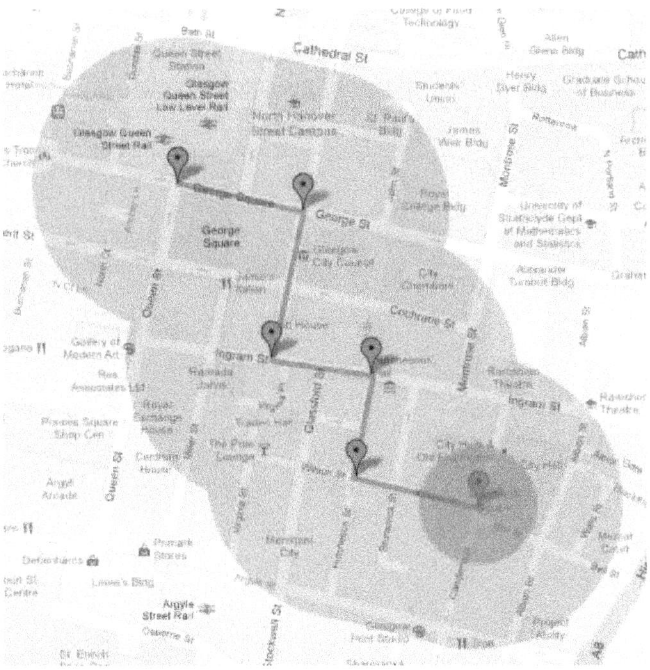

Figure 4. The experiment route, starting at a busy railway station and ending at a popular visitor attraction. The shaded area shows the audio scent coverage. The red shaded area shows the coverage of the target audio beacon.

We chose a route for our experiment that was reasonably varied in direction in order to present several decision points for our participants (Fig. 4). The route of our experiment began at the entrance of a busy railway station, right at the heart of the city. In contrast, the end point was a relatively quiet part of town as shown in Fig. 6. This allowed us to explore user behaviour in areas with both heavy traffic and low traffic density. The route was also quite rich in shortcuts that participants could take, including a square and three pedestrian pathways, in order to maximize the possible variability of the routes. Our participants were briefed about the system and its general mode of operation and were informed of the general direction of their destination (just as a local would tend to point a tourist towards the general direction of a destination). We told participants that their route was approximately 5 minutes away by foot if they knew exactly where to go and to take as much time as they liked with their exploration. We also told them to come back to the starting point if they started to feel lost or if they felt the experiment was taking too long.

Each participant was given a mobile device with the route pre-loaded and a pair of in-ear headphones. The device was hung around the participants' neck and kept relatively still by tucking the device into the participants' jackets (Fig. 8). This ensured that the device orientation would remain parallel to the users' body throughout the experiment and thus provide consistent orientation information.

Figure 5. The starting point of our experiment simulated a tourist's arrival at a busy railway station whose entrance is in a noisy heavy traffic area

Figure 6. The end point of the experiment route was in a quiet part of the city and represented a popular visitor attraction

.

Configuration of the prototype

The prototype was configured to produce sound at a radius of 160m from any path segment. We chose this radius as being roughly equivalent to the size of two blocks in the city where the experiment was carried out. Additionally, we set up a "buffer zone" of 12m (typical width of a city street and pavements) around the path where the orientation of the sound was disabled. This was in order to prevent erratic sound shifts as the path runs through the middle of the street and it is not reasonable to provide a directional cue when the participant is on either pavement beside the path. Additionally, we set up a sound beacon at the target at a range of 80m (one average block). The audio scent used for the path was a recording of a woman walking in heels, in an urban environment (Fig. 7). The sound clip contained organic urban sound artefacts in the background, such as the sound of cars driving by or pedestrian random chatter. This sound clip was selected primarily for two reasons. First, the background artefacts were low in volume, and the walking heels sound is effectively represented by short duration volume spikes. This allows external sound to filter through the headphones, even if these are of the in-ear type. This makes the experience both more realistic (enhancing the mixed reality immersion) and safer for the user as they can still hear sounds such as oncoming traffic.

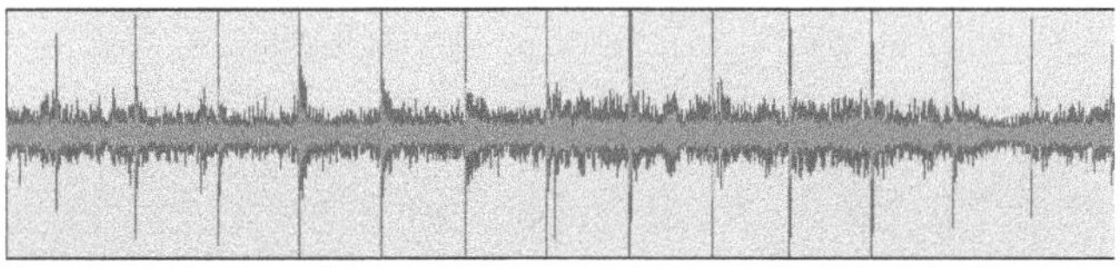

Figure 7. The audio clip used to represent the audio scent. The sound of walking heels (spikes) is clearly distinguishable from the constant background noise (organic urban sounds). This choice gives constant feedback while allowing external sound to filter through, enhancing the mixing of reality.

The target audio beacon was represented by a simple looping music clip, to create the sense that one is arriving a point of interest (just as one can hear the muffled music when heading towards a bar that they intend to go to).

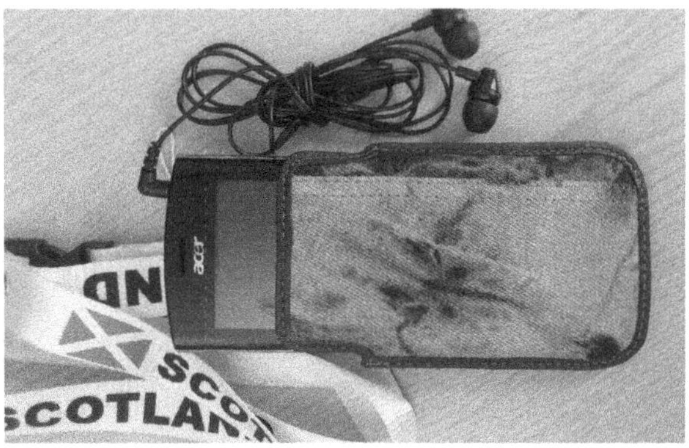

Figure 8. The equipment worn by participants. It consists of an Acer Liquid Metal Android device with integrated GPS & magnetic compass, a soft fabric case, neck strap and in-ear Sony headphones.

We were keen to obtain both qualitative and quantitative data from our users. At the end of the experiment, we asked the participants to fill in a short questionnaire with several limited-option questions and a final open-ended comments box at the end. Our prototype applications also recorded the GPS location of the users during the trial, their speed, bearing, location provider (GPS/Network) and time. In this paper we present an analysis of the GPS location.

FINDINGS

User exploratory behaviour

We used Seth Golub's heat map generator[1] to plot the GPS traces recorded during our experiment. As can be seen from the heat maps produced by the logging of GPS data, the users stayed reasonably close to the route preloaded into the system. In most cases, the participants remained within the zone of the audio scent, with the exception of one person who clearly went outside the zone, realized they were not hearing any sound and return soon after (right side of Figure 9). We note that our users, as a group, explored most of the possible routes to the target. This behaviour is also observable for each individual user, with the average number of route segments visited exceeding the number of route segments laid out by our pre-planned route.

Figure 9. Heat map of all participants' GPS traces. The blue arrow indicates the start point; the black arrow is the end point.

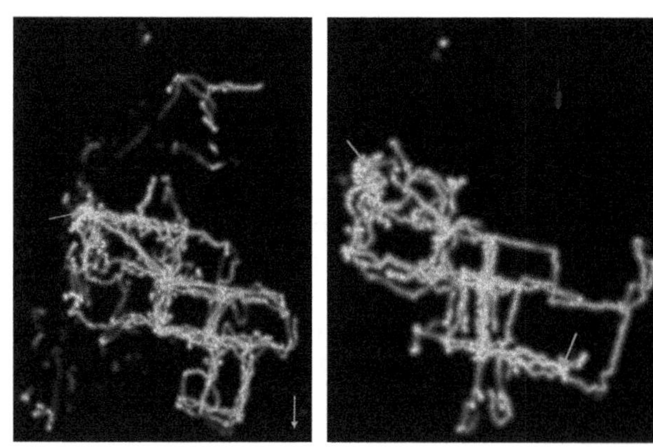

Figure 10. Breakdown of participant GPS traces in failed (left) and successful (right) task completion. The blue arrows denote the start and end points of the route.

Several disconnected islands of GPS traces appear in our heat maps. These are attributable to GPS errors, which are expectable within an urban environment. This highlights a need for our system to "filter out" such erroneous data,

[1] http://sethoscope.net/heatmap/ [accessed 10/2/2012]

which in some cases caused erratic jumps in the directional cues given to participants. The participants highlighted this behaviour in their comments, and we can see this explained by the GPS errors (verified from application log files).

Overall, 7 participants managed to navigate to the target destination, while 9 participants failed to find the target. Upon splitting their GPS traces and analysing them separately (Figure 10), it can be seen that failing participants actually got rather close to the target (approximately one block away). Unfortunately, this distance was just out of range for our target beacon (the block preceding the destination was slightly larger than the average block size of 80m). This highlights a need for our system to perhaps offer more help and guided direction near the target destination for users.

The average walking speed in our experiment was 2.313Km/h (1.437mph), indicating a rather leisurely style of walking considering that in the UK, pedestrian crossing traffic light timings are calculated using a standard pedestrian average speed of 4.32Km/h (1.2 m/sec) [21]. This can be attributed to the low stress factor reported by our participants (see qualitative results below) and also the fact that they were mostly exploring, thus the cognitive load of following the audio scent could be an attributing factor to the lowering of their speed.

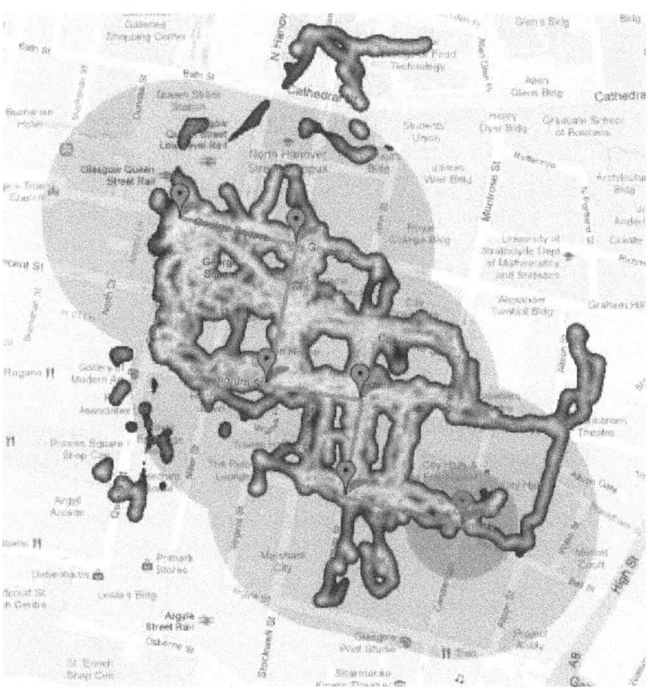

Figure 11. Heat map of all participants' GPS traces superimposed on the audio scent zone of coverage (shaded grey area), clearly showing the islands of GPS data (errors)

User subjective evaluations

At the end of our experiment, we asked participants to fill in a short questionnaire to capture their subjective evaluation of the prototype. Not all participants agreed to provide a questionnaire response; hence we gathered 14 questionnaires from our 16 participants. We asked a total of 10 questions with pre-defined answers and provided a final comments box for free entry at the end of the questionnaire. The first three questions we asked were related to the participants' sex, age and previous experience with turn-by-turn guidance systems. The remaining seven were focused on the affective impact of SoNav on the participants, in terms of feeling lost, ability to re-gain orientation, overall enjoyment and preference of music vs. the walking sound for navigation. In this paper we shall focus on the responses to the two most interesting questions, starting with the sentiment of participants during use.

This question included a list of 12 experience state descriptions, split equally between positive and negative axes. We note from the participants response that the positive states gathered 31 responses while the negative states gathered 15. Particularly noteworthy is that despite a feeling of being lost and distracted, participants nevertheless felt free, relaxed and having fun, while a sense of exploration was highly present amongst the group of participants.

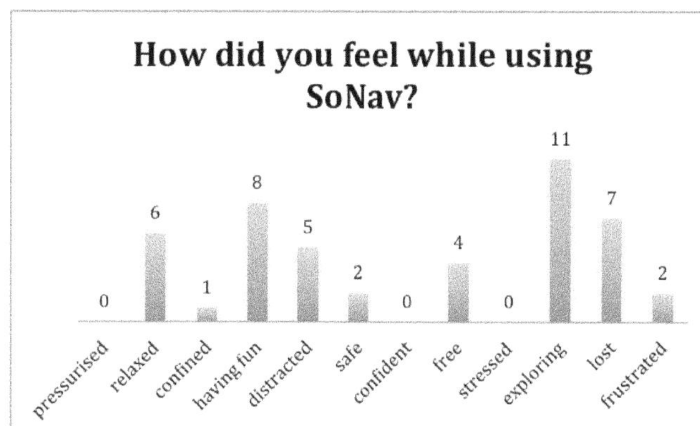

Figure 12. Participants' subjective perception of experience states while using SoNav

We asked our participants to rate our prototype against traditional turn-by-turn systems. In summary, we noted that participants felt that overall a turn-by-turn system was better for guidance in an unfamiliar urban environment, more accurate, able to guide from A to B quicker, being less stressful to use, easier to understand and safer. However, our prototype scored very highly in being more enjoyable to use, allowing a person to focus more on their environments and it was felt that overall it was better for exploring a new area.

We also asked the participants if there were features within the prototype that they would like to be improved or added. Two participants indicated that the addition of a head-mounted digital compass sensor would lead to a more natural searching motion where only the the head (rather than torso) need be rotated to allow the user to sense the target direction. This technique has been utilised by [12] and [13], where the sensing equipment (GPS and magnetometer) was worn on the head of participants (mounted on earcup headphones and a baseball cap respectively). However, in our prototype, we wanted to explore a more realistic solution that would not involve hardware or wearable items not currently available on the market. Three participants indicated that they would welcome some improvement to the directional focus of the audio scents to more clearly indicate target direction. There were also some conflicting requests from participants in relation to audio volume. Although four participants indicated that they would like increased volume in order to overcome ambient noise levels, three of the participants indicated that the audio scent used within the trial (walking with heels sound) actually merged-with and "blurred" the ambient soundscape to the extent that they felt uncertain of the degree of disconnect of the virtual from the external real environment; one participant highlighted this as a potential safety issue. Other uses indicated that a hybrid system, with user-selectable periods of directed turn-by-turn navigation, would instill more confidence in the use of this technology. This is an obvious area for further investigation.

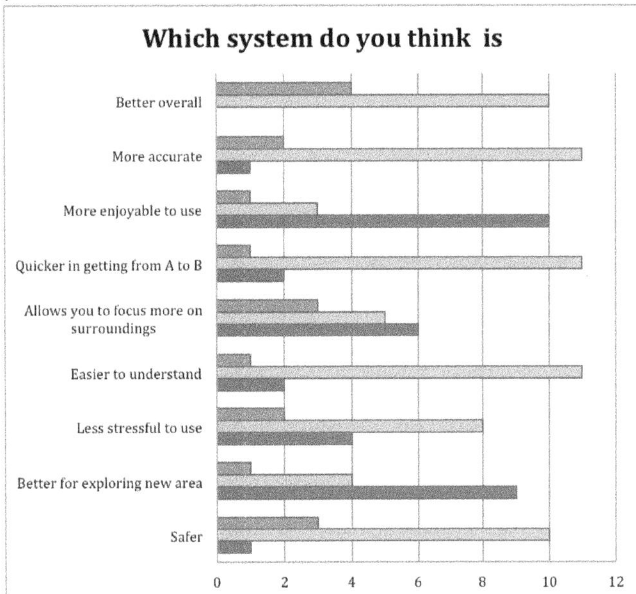

	Safer	Better for exploring new area	Less stressful to use	Easier to understand	Allows you to focus more on surroundings	Quicker in getting from A to B	More enjoyable to use	More accurate	Better overall
No Preference	3	1	2	1	3	1	1	2	4
Turn-By-Turn	10	4	8	11	5	11	3	11	10
SoNav	1	9	4	2	6	2	10	1	0

Figure 13. Participants subjective evaluation of SoNav compared to turn-by-turn guidance systems

Two of our users indicated that the system would sometimes provide directional feedback changes at times when they were crossing a street and highlighted this as safety concern, as their attention would be partially diverted from the task of crossing a street to interpreting the new directional cues. Finally, most users reported a general sense of confusion at the start of the experiment, which subsided as they walked nearer the destination. They reported that this was partly due to the high noise levels and traffic caused by buses and heavy car traffic at the starting point. This is a natural observation – any tourist that has ever arrived at a busy station in a new city is often confounded with "arrival stress" [22] which relates to the sudden intake of large volumes of information and a need to orient one's self towards their destination. The increased load of traffic and noise at the starting point added to the uncertaintly of choosing a direction of travel and thus it might be assumed that our system could benefit from deterministic and explicit instructions to get people started on their journey, and revert to implicit navigation shortly afterwards.

The system that we have designed has as a fundamental tenet the use of subtle intervention rather than a directed navigational experience. There is an indication that users may find difficulties in separating the virtual-reality world (the ambient soundscape overlaid with the *walking* or other organic urban audio scents) from the ambient audio reality around them. There are clearly further questions in relation to the following aspects: How merged or separated should reality be from virtual reality? Should we use audio scents that are obviously distinct from the ambient soundscape and would this lead to better separation of real and virtual? Amongst the participants who succeeded in finding the destination, a strong preference for the musical guidance was shown over the walking sound. However, music is a continuous stream of audio which effectively blocks most external sounds, hence is more likely to impact on pedestrian safety. There are clearly design tradeoffs in relation to these that bear further investigation.

CONCLUSIONS AND FURTHER WORK

We developed a prototype that implicitly guides visitors of urban environments towards a destination of their choice. We used the concept of an audio scent that continuously "emanates" from a pre-determined route towards a target. Instead of giving explicit directions to users, our prototype allows them to freely roam while attempting to understand the direction that the audio scent is coming from. In contrast with turn-by-turn guidance systems, our prototype encourages and promotes exploration of the urban environment. It was shown during our trials that participants visited a greater area of a city than the area covered by a pre-determined route. The concept of the audio scent was effective in keeping participants within a certain area, allowing them to explore without straying too far away. While our participants perceived a turn-by-turn system to be more efficient for navigation, they indicated high levels of enjoyment from using our system and felt it would be better for exploring a new area and assimilating as much of their environment as possible.

Our participants highlighted the need for further research along two main axes: Firstly, there is a clear need to investigate the balance of perception between real and virtual in our mixed audio reality system. This is a crucial direction of research, as the safety implications as highlighted by our participants can be significant. A better ability to distinguish real and virtual information might also lead to improved performance in navigation.

Secondly, though there is a strong positive perception of implicit navigation for exploring a new area, it is clear that implicit navigation alone cannot adequately support the needs of tourists in urban environments. A hybrid implicit / turn-by-turn approach, particularly for guiding people during the initial segments of a route, is possibly a better design approach. A hybrid approach that allows a tourist to fall back to turn-by-turn guidance might also increase the perceived levels of safety and stress during the exploration of new environments.

We are also keen to explore new ways of extending our prototype further in order to incorporate spoken narratives alongside the implicit navigation element, and also investigate social and group aspects in navigation, orientation and POI discovery. Our prototype can accommodate the incorporation of sound beacons, to represent points of interest along a route. We are especially interested in examining whether the use of 3D audio can help with points of interest on the vertical axis (e.g. architectural features in tall buildings), as our system currently only uses the horizontal plane (left and right). We are also very keen to investigate the playback of seamlessly integrating context-relevant narratives near beacons, which will serve as both informational and direction-finding clues, thus creating themed navigation experiences. Additionally, looping Earcon or musical layers can be incorporated in the system to give various "feels" to certain areas of the environment (e.g. appropriate music to indicate a dangerous part of the city, or a historic/modern/shopping area of a city). Our prototype can be easily extended to accommodate groups of tourists, by sharing locations of individuals so that one "group" can hear where other groups are in the city, in relation to it. Finally our system can possibly benefit from the integration of data from social media (e.g. Foursquare check-ins) to mine for socially popular locations (e.g. good restaurants) and portray these to the users as they walk along an unfamiliar road.

ACKNOWLEDGMENTS

This work is inspired by early work from S. Strachan and M. Jones to whom we would like to extend special thanks. Additional thanks are extended to M. Dunlop for his feedback and enthusiastic support. Finally we would also like to particularly thank M. Pielot for openly releasing his port of the OpenAL library to the Android platform, without which this work would not have been possible.

REFERENCES

1. Kruger A, Aslan I, Zimmer H The effects of mobile pedestrian navigation systems on the concurrent acquisition of route and survey knowledge. *In: MobileHCI '04, volume 3160 of LNCS. Springer, Berlin , pp 446–450* (2004)
2. Aslan I, Schwalm M, Baus J, Kru¨ger A, Schwartz T Acquisition of spatial knowledge in location aware mobile pedestrian navigation systems. *In: Proceedings of CHI '06, ACM, pp 105–108* (2006)
3. Seager W The usability of map-based applications for pedestrian navigation. *PhD thesis, Nottingham University* (2007)
4. Pielot M., Boll S. C. J. Tactile Wayfinder: Comparison of tactile waypoint navigation with commercial pedestrian navigation systems. *In The Eighth International Conference on Pervasive Computing, Helsinki, Finland* (2010)
5. Jones M, Jones S, Bradley G, Warren N, Bainbridge D, Holmes G ONTRACK: dynamically adapting music playback to support navigation. *Personal & Ubiquitous Computing 12(7):513–525* (2008)
6. Strachan S, Eslambolchilar P, Murray-Smith R, Hughes S, O'Modhrain S gpsTunes: controlling navigation via audio feedback. *In: Proceedings of MobileHCI '05, ACM, pp 275–278* (2005)
7. Strachan S, Murray-Smith R Bearing-based selection in mobile spatial interaction. *Personal & Ubiquitous Computing 13(4):265–280* (2009)
8. Holland S, Morse DR, Gedenryd H AudioGPS: spatial audio navigation with a minimal attention interface. *Personal & Ubiquitous Computing 6(4):253–259* (2002)
9. Cater K, Hull R, O'Hara K, Melamed T, Clayton B The potential of spatialised audio for location based services on mobile devices: Mediascapes. *SAMD: Workshop on Spatialised Audio for Mobile Devices, MobileHCI 2007* (2007)
10. McGookin D, Brewster S, Priego P Audio Bubbles. Employing non-speech audio to support tourist wayfinding. *In: Altinsoy ME, Jekosch U, Brewster S (eds) HAID 2009, LNCS, vol 5763, pp 41–50* (2009)
11. Magnusson C, Breidegard B, Rassmus-Gröhn K Sound- crumbs-Hansel and Gretel in the 21st century. *In: HAID 2009, LNCS. Springer* (2009)
12. Stahl C The roaring navigator: a group guide for the zoo with shared auditory landmark display. *In:*

Proceedings of MobileHCI 2007. ACM Press, New York, pp 282–386 (2007)

13. Vazquez-Alvarez Y., Oakley I., Brewster S. A. Auditory display design for exploration in mobile audio-augmented reality, *Personal & Ubiquitous Computing, Online First* (2011)
14. Borntrager C, Cheverst K, Davies N, Dix A, Friday A, Seitz J Experiments with multi-modal interfaces in a context- aware city guide. *In: MobileHCI '03, volume 2795 of LNCS. Springer, Berlin, pp 116–130* (2003)
15. Härmä A., Jakka J., Tikander M., Karjalainen M., Lokki T., Hiipakka J., Lorho G. Augmented reality audio for mobile and wearable appliances *J. Audio Engineering Society 52: 6. 618-639* (2004)
16. Robinson, S. Matt Jones, John Williamson, Roderick Murray-Smith, Parisa Eslambolchilar and Mads Lindborg Navigation your way: from spontaneous independent exploration to dynamic social journeys. *Personal & Ubiquitous Computing, Online First* (2011).
17. Magnusson, C., Rassmus-Gröhn, K. & Szymczak, D.. Navigation by pointing to GPS locations. *Personal and Ubiquitous Computing Online First* (2011)
18. Rozier J, Karahalios K, Donath J Hear & There: an augmented reality system of linked audio. *In: Proceedings of the international conference on auditory display—ICAD 2000* (2000)
19. Reid, J., Geelhoed, E., Hull, R., Carter, K., Clayton, B. Parallel worlds: Immersion in location-based experiences. *In: CHI 2005, Portland, Oregon, vol. 2, pp. 1733– 1736. ACM Press, New York* (2005)
20. Rowland D., Flintham M., Oppermann L., Marshall J., Chamberlain A., Koleva B., Benford S., Perez C. Ubikequitous computing: designing interactive experiences for cyclists. *In Proceedings of the 11th International Conference on Human-Computer Interaction with Mobile Devices and Services (MobileHCI '09). ACM, New York, NY, USA* (2009)
21. Kennedy J., Sexton B. Literature review of road safety at traffic signals and signalised crossings, *Transport Research Laboratory, ISBN 978-1-84608-859-9* (2009)
22. Cole S. Information needs of the independent traveller on public transport, *Wales Transport Centre ISBN 1-840540-87-7* (2003)

iFitQuest: A School Based Study of a Mobile Location-Aware Exergame for Adolescents

Andrew Macvean
School of Mathematical and Computer Sciences
Heriot-Watt University
apm8@hw.ac.uk

Judy Robertson
School of Mathematical and Computer Sciences
Heriot-Watt University
judy.robertson@hw.ac.uk

ABSTRACT
Exergames, games that encourage and facilitate physical exercise, are growing in popularity thanks to progressions in ubiquitous technologies. While initial findings have confirmed the potential of such games, little research has been done on systems which target the needs of adolescent children. In this paper we introduce iFitQuest, a mobile location-aware exergame designed with adolescent children in mind. In an attempt to understand how exergames can be used to target adolescent children, and whether they can be effective for this demographic, we outline the results of a school based field study conducted within a P.E. class. Through a detailed analysis of our results, we conclude that iFitQuest appeals to twelve to fifteen year olds and causes them to exercise at moderate to vigorous levels. However, in order to develop effective systems that can dynamically adapt to the adolescent users, further research into different categories of users' behavior is required.

Author Keywords
Exergames; location-aware games; serious games for health

ACM Classification Keywords
K.8 [**Personal Computing**]: General - *games*

General Terms
Design, Human Factors

INTRODUCTION

The World Health Organisation recently announced that the world was witnessing an obesity epidemic [35]. Overweight and obesity issues are particularly concerning with regards to children. First of all, "obesity in childhood, particularly in adolescence, is a key predictor for obesity in adulthood" [4, p.239], which in turn increases their chances of developing chronic conditions such as type 2 diabetes and abnormalities in the heart [12]. Further to the physical health concerns, obesity can be linked to psychological issues [27,34], as well poorer academic performance [5,17] and absenteeism from school [31].

Thus, the motivation for addressing weight issues is clear. However, while the problem is not a straightforward one, due to a complex interaction of many socio-economic factors [28], adopting a sedentary lifestyle and failing to participate in physical activity have been strongly linked to obesity [16]. With adolescents regularly experiencing what is known as the "adolescent slump", a dramatic downturn in physical activity around the age of 12 [29], adolescent children remain a prime target for physical activity interventions.

Recently, thanks to progressions in ubiquitous technologies, a new genre of gaming has emerged with the potential to address the problem. *Exergames* are video games which also incorporate an exercise, in an attempt to facilitate physical activity and positive behavioral change within a fun and enjoyable environment. Killi and Merilampi state "Exergames involve physical activity as a means of interacting with the game and have evolved to facilitate the physical health of the players" [11, p.103].

While exergaming remains a relatively young genre, there has already been evidence to suggest its potential to facilitate physical activity [19,22,26]. However, very few exergames have explicitly targeted adolescents, with their unique demands and needs. As young people are a prime demographic for traditional video games [7], and their parents are happy to support them in using exergames [37] we must build upon prior work on exergames to understand how to build effective exergame interventions for this age group.

In this paper we report on the attitudes and behavior of adolescent users of a location-aware exergame called *iFitQuest*. iFitQuest contains a prototype suite of mini-games designed to encourage physical activity in an enjoyable and motivating context. An important perspective underlying our work is the notion of inclusion; it is important that exergames can appeal to players of different demographics (both genders and novice to expert gamers) as well as those with different initial finesses and attitudes towards exercise. We consider throughout how different demographics react to the game, in an attempt to understand how best to design exergames for a diverse audience.

In developing our system we draw from, and build upon the existing body of literature on exergame physical activity interventions. We discuss the success of exergames, as well as the gaps in current understanding which motivate our work. A user-centered design approach is then explained along with the design of our location-aware exergame,

MobileHCI'12, September 21–24, 2012, San Francisco, CA, USA.

iFitQuest. The results of a school based field study are then discussed along with the conclusions we have drawn from our work.

RELATED WORK

Exergames

Exergames are a relatively new concept afforded by progressions in ubiquitous technologies. Exergames aim to take the enjoyable and motivating nature of traditional video games, and combine this with the beneficial nature of physical activity. While the genre remains in its infancy, there already exists tentative research highlighting its potential. Dance Dance Revolution, while not initially developed as an exergame, has been found to increase aerobic fitness [19] as well as promote teamwork, creativity, cooperation and fair-play [36]. Another commercial example, WiiFit has been found to be more enjoyable than traditional exercise [9], as well as increasing lower limb strength and balance [22], making it a positive modification to traditional video game play.

Mobile Exergaming

For many, console based exergames fail to utilize the pervasive nature afforded by modern ubiquitous devices. Building upon the notion of *pervasive games,* where "games are no longer confined to the virtual world domain of the computer but integrate the physical and social aspects of the real world" [15, p.2], mobile exergames aim to bring a new dimension to the genre, by allowing play out in the real world where new and different exercise can be performed and the experience is more socially rich.

Many mobile exergames have looked at using pedometers to increase the wearer's daily step count, with the emphasis placed on continuous low intensity exercise rather than shorter, higher intensity, dedicated sessions. The American Horsepower Challenge is one such example which focused on a school based pedometer intervention. The game encouraged inter-scholastic competition and was found to increase the daily step count of those children taking part [26]. On a similar note Fish'n'Steps [13], and NEAT-o-Games [6] have used body worn sensors to track the activity level of the user and use this as an input into a competition style game, both with relative success.

Mobile geo-location enabled devices, with their ability to track the real world location of the user, form an interesting area known as *location-aware exergaming*. By using GPS data as an input into the game, players can be encouraged to travel in the real world in order to interact with the game. One such example used GPS technology to augment traditional playground style games, putting a modern twist on successful, well established play types [18].

Limitations of Current Research

However, while these early results appear positive, exergames are not simply a ready-made solution to increasing a child's activity levels. 'Novelty effects' have been observed where by initial excitement and effort quickly dwindles [13]. In some cases, researchers have also found that exergames such as the WiiFit are not physically demanding enough to facilitate the type of exercise that may be required [10, 22].

Therefore as researchers, we must carefully consider a complicated design task. Games must be made to be both enjoyable and physically demanding; these are potentially conflicting requirements (depending on the user). Further to this, exergames must be designed such that they can adapt to the unique needs of the user, pushing them in such a way that is suitable for their own fitness, goals and motivation. By catering games to the unique needs of the user, and adapting to their own situation, we hope that we can begin to combat the novelty effects and miss-calibrated exercises previously reported.

While researchers have begun looking at how the design of exergames should be approached [1, 2], few have looked at how we can model users, and as such begin to create games which can be catered to the individual's unique needs. When considering a demographic like adolescent children, we are dealing with a diverse population with unique wants and needs. While in this section we have highlighted a few examples of exergames designed for children, there exists a gap in the understanding of how different children will react to exergames. It is naive to think that exergames can appeal to all, but by understanding how different players from different demographics experience a game, we can begin to model players and take a first step towards developing adaptive exergames, capable of catering themselves to a player's unique wants and needs.

DEVELOPMENT PROCESS

The development of exergames provides an interesting problem for researchers, full of conflicting and contrasting requirements from different stakeholders. Exergames are still games and therefore they must be fun to play. As Sinclair et al. state, exergames must be fun if we want the players to return and play the game frequently [32]. However, often in contrast to this, the game must be physically demanding and facilitate physical activity. In addition, the context in which the game will be played, and the technical feasibility must all be considered.

We chose to develop our exergame to be played within a school context. Prior research on health promotion programs has found the context of the intervention is critical to the design of the program [33]. Schools have been selected as the chosen space for many health interventions due to their ability at reaching the majority of youths, the existence of appropriate facilities, as well as having existing programs for physical activity [26]. Due to these factors, as well as the success of previous ubiquitous computing health interventions in schools [26], we chose to develop our system for this context.

We chose to approach the development process using a user-centered, prototype driven approach with teenagers

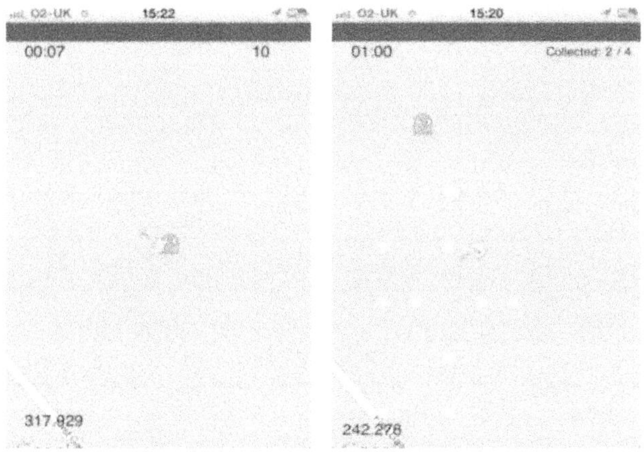

Figure 1. Overview of the Escape the Ghost (left) and Collect the Coins (right) visual interface.

and teachers as design informants [8], building upon the previously published exergames design requirements [1, 2]. In this educational context, the view of a physical education teacher on exercise demands was as important as consulting teenagers about motivating aspects of games. Our design process therefore included an expert interview with a physical education (P.E.) teacher at a local secondary school, an observation of a routine P.E. class on the sports field, a focus group with six 13 year olds on their favorite games, and a session in which the same adolescents tried and critiqued off the shelf exergames available for the Wii Fit. Through this process, the adolescents provided the inspiration for the themes, content and style of the game, and the P.E. teacher provided details on the exercise requirements and contextual constraints.

IFITQUEST

iFitQuest is a location-aware mobile exergame designed to target adolescent children. The game is made up of a number of 'mini-games' each designed to target a different type of fitness, or different game mechanic.

iFitQuest uses GPS and compass data to track the real world location of the player, using this as the primary input into the game. The player's real world physical movements are used to control their virtual character. By moving in the real world, the player can interact with Non Player Characters (NPCs), visit landmarks and collect items. Figure 1 shows two example screenshots from the game.

The game is played on the iPhone, and uses Google Maps to provide the in game representation of the player, NPCs and landmarks. All virtual game items are not pre-programmed, but dynamically generated based on the current location of the user. Thus, the game can be played anywhere, at any time. Although the game was developed for in school use, due to the procedurally generated content, as well as single player gameplay, the games could be played outwith the school context. In the next two sections we describe two of the mini-games that make up the iFitQuest suite. The following two games provided the focus of our field study.

Escape the Ghost

Escape the Ghost is a simple exergame inspired by the traditional children's playground game of chase and catch. The user must try to escape capture from the ghost for a predefined period of time, moving in the real world in order to steer their virtual character away from the virtual ghost pursuing their character. This type of game mechanic was found to be effective in location-aware exergames for children [18]. Figure 1 shows a screenshot of the game.

The game difficulty can be altered in one of two ways. The time in which the player must 'survive' away from the ghost can be increased or decreased in order to alter the length of time the child is exercising. Alternatively, the speed at which the ghost will chase the child can be altered, resulting in a higher or lower intensity of exercise. Difficulty is automatically increased after a player wins a game, and is decreased after the player loses. The player may also choose to override the difficulty setting manually.

The game was designed to mirror that of sprint training, in which the athlete undertakes repetitions of high intensity bursts of speed for a short period of time. Audio and vibro-tactile cues are used to alert the player when they have been captured by the ghost or won the mini-game.

Collect the Coins

Collect the Coins was derived from the traditional Pac-Man game [20]. The user must try to collect the designated number of coins while simultaneously avoiding the patrolling ghost – which does not actively chase the player like in the Escape the Ghost game, but rather patrols around the play area. In this game there is no predefined time limit, however the aim of the player is to collect the coins in as short a time as possible. Figure 1 shows a screenshot of the game.

The game difficulty can be altered in one primary way. The number of coins the player is required to collect can be changed, in order to have them exercise for a greater or shorter length of time. As before, changes in difficulty can be triggered automatically or by the user.

The game was designed to comply with the P.E. teacher's request of 'short sharp bursts' of exercise with agility training through directional changes. The idea is that the players use the visual output on the screen to orientate themselves towards a coin, before they sprint in that direction. An audio cue and vibro-tactile output signals to the player that they have collected a coin and that they should return to the visual output in order to decide what direction to run next.

RESEARCH GOALS

In order to produce adaptable exergames, capable of targeting the specific needs of our users, we need a basic level of understanding about how different people interact with iFitQuest. Our research questions are as follows:

- *What are adolescents' opinions of the pilot games, and how much exertion do they expend in playing them?* Although previous research has indicated that exergames in general can be effective, iFitQuest requires user evaluation to establish whether the design is effective in terms of enjoyment and physical exertion.
- *How do gender and prior gaming experience affect users' attitudes towards the game?* It is known that girls and boys have different motivations and preferences for playing computer games [23]. Further, although both boys and girls enjoy games and spend a lot of time playing them, boys are more likely to devote more leisure time to gaming and are therefore usually more experienced gamers [14]. As it is also known that adolescent girls can be more at risk from obesity related illnesses than boys [24], it is particularly important to establish whether the game is sufficiently appealing to encourage them to exercise.
- *To what extent and in what way do users configure the challenge level of the game to tailor it to their fitness needs?* As any group of children will have a range of fitness levels and speed, the default settings for iFitQuest will not be calibrated correctly for all users. A simple way to achieve this is to enable users to change the difficulty level of the game (e.g. by altering the speed at which they must run to succeed in the game objectives). However, the extent to which teenaged users are willing and able to adjust challenge levels appropriately in this context is an open question which requires exploration.
- *How does winning or losing a game affect users' enjoyment of the game? Does success or failure have an impact on user alterations to difficulty levels?* Is the phrase often used by P.E. teachers "it's the taking part that counts" true in this context? Or do users play exergames motivated by a desire to win, as in competitive sports? Do users use feedback from success or failure in a game level to further personalize the difficulty setting of the game?

SCHOOL BASED FIELD STUDY

In order to begin answering these research questions we conducted a school based field study using 25 participants. Due to the exploratory nature of the work, no preconceived hypotheses had been formed.

Videogame Play Background	Frequency	Exergame play background	Frequency
Never	1	Never	8
Once or twice per week	9	Once or twice per week	16
Most days	9	Most days	1
Every day	6	Every day	0

Table 1. Overview of the evaluation participants gaming background.

Method

Participants

We recruited 25 participants from a local high school. All participants had volunteered based on an invitation from one of their subject teachers. The participant's age ranged between 12 and 15, with the average age 12.9 and modal age 13. Of the 25 participants, 15 were male while 10 were female. As this was an open invitation, we did not preselect participants in terms of exercise or video game background. Table 1 provides an overview of our participants' gaming and exergaming preferences.

Our participants were asked to numerically self report their fitness and enjoyment of exercise with values between 1 and 10. They were on the fitter end of the spectrum (*avg.*=7.84, *SD*=1.197) and enjoyed exercise (*avg.*=8.66, *SD*=1.434).

Data Gathering

All participants completed a pre-test background questionnaire, and a post-test evaluation questionnaire. The post-test questionnaire asked the participants to numerically rate their enjoyment and exertion between 1 and 5, as well as open ended questions in order to establish the reasoning behind their ratings. As well as the questionnaires, in-game log-files were collected during play, allowing us to analyse how enjoyment/exertion changed over time, how successful the players were in the game, as well as how far, and at what speed the participants were travelling for an assessment of their activity levels. In-game ratings were collected at the completion of each level of a mini-game, users were asked to numerically rate their exertion and enjoyment between 1 and 10. Finally, an expert P.E. teacher observed the session in order to comment on the level and type of exercise being done by the participants as well as levels of effort and enjoyment in comparison to a 'traditional' P.E. lesson. Following the session, an experienced researcher interviewed the P.E. teacher in order to document her opinion.

Procedure

The evaluation consisted of two separate 3-hour sessions, with 17 participants taking part in the first session, and 8 in the second. Each session was organized as follows:

- Initial briefing by P.E. teacher and researcher.
- Time to complete pre-test background questionnaire.
- Non game warm-up conducted by the P.E. teacher.
- Short in-situ demonstration of the game.
- Free time to play the game within a designated area.
- Time to complete post-test evaluation questionnaire.
- Short informal focus groups to clarify questionnaire answers and de-brief participants.

During the free play of the game, the participants were given 30 minutes to play each of the two mini-games, 15 minutes per game. They were asked to play each game as many times as they could / wanted in that time. After each play of a mini-game, they were given an in-game rating screen where they were asked to rate their current level of enjoyment and exertion. They could also increase or decrease the difficulty level of the game, as they desired for their next playthrough. This formed the basis of the log-file analysis previously described.

RESULTS

In this section we report upon the results from our preliminary evaluation. It should be noted that log-file analysis could only be completed for 20 of the 25 participants, due to a failure in the logging system on certain devices.

General

Overall, our participants reacted positively to the experience, rating the game favorably for both enjoyment and exertion. The P.E. teacher reported that her class worked "as hard, if not more so" than her average P.E. lessons in terms of physical exertion, and that their enjoyment was greater than normal. Using the post-session questionnaire, participants were asked to rate their overall enjoyment, and overall level of exertion out of 5. Our participants gave the game an average score of 4.12 for enjoyment (*SD*=0.44) and 3.76 for exertion (*SD*=0.52). Further to this 21 of our 25 participants (84%) said they would want to play the game again. Thus, at a high level, we appear to have met our goals of developing an enjoyable and physically demanding game.

Escape the Ghost Vs. Collect the Coins

As we begin to decipher how different game mechanics appeal to different players, the first item for consideration is the way players reacted to our two mini-games. As specified in the previous section, both games were designed with different exercise types in mind, containing different game mechanisms. Escape the Ghost focuses on very simple, playground style gameplay, while Collect the Coins contains a more advanced and slow paced game in which the player must focus more carefully on their movements and balance collecting items with avoiding capture.

You got more exercise	7
It was more fun	7
You had to run more	4
It was more exciting	3
Collecting the coins was too challenging	2
It was an easier concept	2
More involving	1

Table 2. The reasons given by the children when discussing their preference of the Escape the Ghost game.

Of our 25 participants, 22 preferred the 'Escape the Ghost' game (88%). In Table 2 we present the reasons given by the participants when asked why they stated this preference. Participants were allowed to give multiple responses.

Discussion

It is interesting to note that our participants rated both the exercise aspects, and the fun aspects as the two most prevalent reasons for preference of the Escape the Ghost game. As these are the two most valuable considerations for an exergame, and often thought of as being in contrast to one another within traditional exercise, this represents a large success for this particular mini-game. As exercise and running were both mentioned as primary reasons of preference, it would be interesting to see how children with a lower preference for exercise reacted to such a game.

The simple and familiar mechanics associated with the favoured game raise the important consideration of simplicity. It is easy to over complicate a game, and by expecting the child to do too much, the important purpose of the game can be lost. These findings mirror those reported by Misund et al. who discuss the merits of simple, traditional playground game mechanics [18].

Log-File Analysis

In order to better understand the way in which the participants behaved during the session, and the way in which the play experience changed over time, a log-file analysis of the in-game recordings is required. This paper focuses on an analysis of the Escape the Ghost game, as the gaming sessions were longer for this game than for the Collect the Coins game and gave richer data.

There were a total 106 game levels played across participants. Participants played on average 5.3 levels within a session.

Enjoyment

Using the in-game reporting of our participants and the resultant log-files, we were able to analyse how the players' experience changed over the course of the session. By looking at the way in which the participants rated the first level of the mini-game and comparing that with their rating of the last level of the mini-game, we can begin to garner an understanding of how our players experienced the game.

The average numerical rating after playing one level was 7.89 (*SD*=2.33), and the average rating after the last level was 8.59 (*SD*=2.24). Of the 20 participants, 7 increased their rating between first and last levels, 2 decreased it, and 11 made no change.

These results highlights the following: a) the in-game ratings confirm the post-test scores, highlighting the high level of enjoyment of our participants; b) the players' enjoyment generally increased or stayed the same over the course of the session; and c) generally, the players' initial opinion of the game was accurate.

Discussion

Further to the general enjoyment scores, it was very positive to note the findings of our log-file analysis. Prior research has confirmed the importance of exergames having a 'pick up and play' mentality [32] as well as the importance of avoiding novelty effects [13] Although our results come from a single session, it is none the less positive to note that the participants very quickly reacted positively to the game, and this was maintained or improved upon over the course of the session. This confirms our intuition to use simple, easy to master game mechanics, which can then be built upon in order to provide a sustained experience.

Exertion

Log-file analysis indicates that the average distance travelled while playing Escape the Ghost was 349 metres (*SD*=117, range = 153-567). The average speed for a level was 5.98 (*SD*=1.17) mph. According to [21] this equates to "vigorous" aerobic activity. The entire group had a speed representing "moderate to vigorous" activity. Similar to the enjoyment discussion above, we can assess using the in game log-files the way in which a participant's level of exertion changes whilst playing our game.

Participants altered their exertion rating between their first and last level as follows: 12 increased their exertion rating, 2 decreased it, and 6 made no change. On average, the initial level of exertion having completed one game was 6.06 (*SD*=3.03), this increased to an average exertion level of 7.85 (*SD*=2.81) following the last game. Note that the P.E. teacher explained that the users had previously been taught to use self-reported exertion levels in this way for other P.E. activities. This form of self-reporting has been found to be consistent with data from heart rate monitors [30]. With the average exertion level increasing, and the majority of our participants (90%) maintaining or increasing their exertion levels, this can be viewed as a success for the system.

In Figure 2 we present a state transition diagram showing the odds after each game that a participant will alter their exertion level in comparison to the previous game. After 3 games, the player's exertion level is variable, with a 0.55 chance that it will change. However, after the 4th game this drops to a 0.33 chance of changing, and after the 5th game it drops again to a 0.29 change of changing. This shows that after an initial variable period, the level of exertion of our participants settled down to a stable level.

Discussion

It is pleasing to observe that our participants generally increased their level of exertion whilst playing the game, a rudimentary requirement of exergames. It was also interesting to observe that our participants experienced changes to their exertion during the initial games, which then settled down by the 4th or 5th level.

This is a favourable observation as it is important to work up to the desired exertion level so as to avoid injury from overworking, and then maintain this level in order to feel the physical benefits. The pick up and play aspects of our game meant that the participants could quickly begin working, while the ability to customize difficulty settings meant that the participants could begin to challenge themselves and work at an appropriately high level.

Boys Vs. Girls

With gender a key aspect of consideration, we wanted to compare how boys and girls experienced our game. Boys and girls both enjoyed our exergames, with boys giving an average rating of 4.27 (*SD*=0.46) out of 5, and girls giving an average rating of 3.90 (*SD*=0.32). However, an

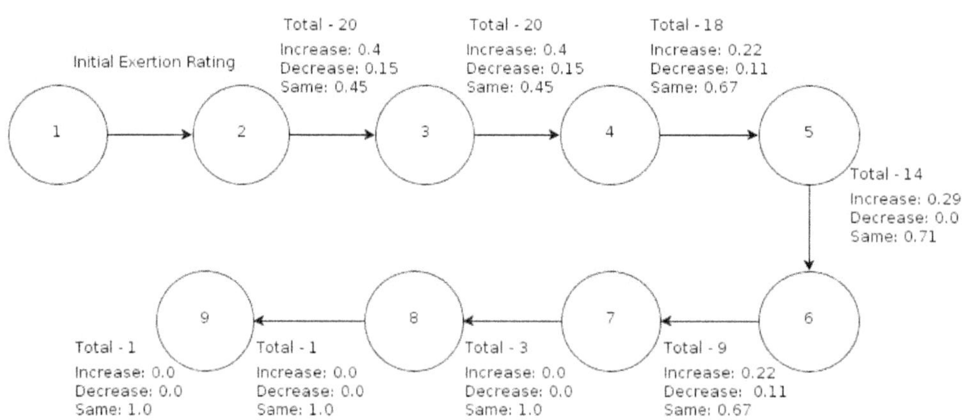

Figure 2. State diagram showing the odds of a participant altering their previous exertion score after each game.

independent sample t-test indicates that boys enjoyed the game significantly more than girls ($t(23)$=2.37, $p<0.05$). The effect size for gender was large (Cohen's d=0.94).

Discussion

By adopting a user-centred design approach and seeking the opinions of both males and females, it was disappointing to note that there was a significant difference in the experience linked to the gender of the individual. This result is not wholly unsurprising when we consider what is known about the preferences and game playing habits of both genders. A fuller analysis of more game mechanics will be done to establish whether the 'type' of game could be affecting enjoyment ratings. Character skins will also be investigated, to establish whether something as simple as using ghosts, rather than say, animals, could affect enjoyment. The issue is not however overly concerning as despite the significance findings and large effect size, girls still enjoyed the experience and indicated that they wanted to play the game again.

Gamers Vs. Non Gamers

In Table 1 we presented the frequency with which our participants played videogames. Using these four categories, we did a between groups one way ANOVA in order to establish whether there were any differences between the participants' enjoyment of our game, or the amount of exercise they got while playing the game, according to gaming experience.

Our results showed that there was no significant difference between the gaming background groups and the participants' enjoyment score ($F(3,21)$=0.401, $p=0.75$) or their exertion rating ($F(3,21)$=0.725, $p=0.55$).

Discussion

As the hope is for exergames to encourage new demographics into exercise, it is important that exergames do not solely appeal to those with an existing interest in traditional video games. Prior exergame research has highlighted the way in which game experience can influence the way in which a participant benefits from an exergame [38], however little has been reported on how a general gaming background influences the experience.

It is pleasing to report that in our game, both avid gamers and less frequent gamers displayed no distinction in their level of enjoyment and physical benefit. By mixing traditional video game mechanics with physical activity, as well as the novel interactions afforded by location-aware games, it is possible to develop a genre of gaming with equal appeal to a wide variety of gamer. This finding supports the claim that exergames will be capable of appealing to new demographics. While it is encouraging to note the regular gamers could not be distinguished from less frequent gamers, due to a lack of non-gamers in our study, further consideration must be made to this aspect during future evaluations in order to fully validate our claims.

	Increase	Decrease	No Change
Win	26	13	20
Lose	6	12	9

Table 3. The frequency with which players altered the game difficulty following a win or loss.

Success Vs. Failure

We wanted to investigate how user enjoyment was affected by the participant's success in the game. Of the 106 levels played, 68% were won by the player. By looking at each of the levels played, and the way in which a success or failure in the game affected the resultant enjoyment rating, results from a point biserial co-efficient show that there was no significant relationship ($r_{pb}=+0.17$, $t=+1.71$, $df=104$) between game outcome and enjoyment score.

Discussion

One interesting aspect of exergames is the way in which success and failure influence the experience. Players expect a certain amount of failure in a traditional video game; in fact very challenging aspects may provide the greatest motivation to certain players. However, this balance must be carefully managed in an exergame. It is important not to de-motivate people by setting unattainable goals. Difficulty levels must be carefully managed with regards to exercise levels as well as game aspects, it is important not to work people too hard too soon.

It is positive to note that in our game, the players experience is in no way influenced by their success in the game. By taking the focus away from simply winning and losing, and moving towards enjoyable gameplay with an active twist, players are less likely to place focus on actual success.

Difficulty Changes

Another interesting question with regards to the psychology of exercise is the way in which success in the game influences a person's behavior with regards to altering the difficulty levels.

We wanted to know whether we could see a correlation between success and failure in the game and the way in which a player altered the challenge level of the game. Did participants keep difficulty levels low to maintain success, or did they manually increase it to keep themselves exercising at a high level?

There were 86 opportunities to change the challenge setting presented across all users, and 57 changes were made (66%). There was an average of 2.85 manual changes to the challenge setting per user. Of the 57 changes, 32 increased the difficulty (56%) and 25 decreased it. In Table 3 we present the way in which players manually altered the games difficulty following a success or failure in the preceding game.

As a case study we consider the behavior of a sample of our participants. P4, who completed 6 game levels, appeared motivated by success within the game. After winning the first two games, P4 found the difficulty level they wanted to play at. Despite winning the next 3 games, P4 overrode automatic difficulty increases in order to keep the difficulty level constant. Similarly, P7 appeared motivated by in game success. Despite winning their first 3 levels, they continually lowered the difficulty such that each new level was easier than the last. On their fourth game they increased the difficulty to a high level, however a resultant loss meant that they lowered the difficulty back to the level they knew they could be successful at.

Conversely, we see examples of players willing to challenge themselves further through increases to difficulty levels. P17 won only one of their 5 games, however they chose to maintain or in two cases increase the difficulty level despite their failure on the current level. P8 increased the difficulty after success in a level, but then maintained the difficulty on a level they failed at until they could succeed, only then increasing the difficulty level. P17 is an example of someone not affected by in game success, while P8 is someone who wanted to beat the difficulty levels that had caused them problems, rather than let the system take them to an easier difficulty.

Despite the very different behaviour of the participants highlighted, each of the examples came from a player who worked within the 'vigorous' exercise category. Thus, the examples are not of players trying to 'cheat' or simply explore, rather they highlight the different ways in which players can be motivated within an exergame.

Discussion

Possibly the most interesting finding is the way in which players altered the difficulty of the game. As we speculated in the early sections, exergames must be carefully tailored to the individuals needs, not only through setting activity at the correct level, but also through setting goals which appropriately motivate the player. What we see in our findings is a wide range of behaviours, from those that seek greater challenge after a success, to those that would rather succeed consistently.

These results highlight the needs for an understanding of the user's motivation and attitude towards exercise. Where as it may seem appropriate to increase difficulty following a success in traditional video games, it is important here to consider how much challenge a participant really needs. As long as they are exercising at the appropriate level, it is not necessarily appropriate to keep increasing difficulty levels. Where as some children will be motivated by the challenge, others will be motivated by success, understanding these differences will be key to the development of a successful exergame.

LESSONS LEARNED

The results of this field study illustrate that it is possible to facilitate moderate to vigorous - yet enjoyable - exercise in adolescents using a pervasive exercise game. The user-centred design process was successful in balancing the requirements of the P.E. teacher and the adolescents, resulting in a game which motivates adolescents during out of doors physical exercise.

The results and experiences from this study lead us to the following observations.

For a game to work within the tight constraints of a school P.E. lesson, it should have a shallow learning curve.

Our observations of the P.E. class and our field study indicate that there is very little time for exercise, given the constraints of the school timetable and the time it takes to change clothing at the start and end of a lesson. For this reason, time spent using the game should be in pursuit of fitness goals rather than learning game mechanics.

Challenge may work differently for exergames.

Consider how challenge is structured in a traditional computer game. Typically, the difficulty of the game increases as the player successfully completes tasks [25]. Even after several hours of gaming, the player will have increased competence through practice and will be performing more demanding tasks. In contrast, players of exergames cannot keep increasing their level of physical effort indefinitely due to physical exhaustion. Further, as they get more tired, they have to expend more effort to maintain their initial performance. Often the goal of an exercise session is to maintain (rather than increase) performance over a short, bounded time period. If the game mechanics are tightly coupled to the exertion level of the game, difficulty level cannot keep increasing. On the other hand, non-exertion related game mechanics (such as puzzle solving) could increase in difficulty while exertion levels were maintained at a constant level. Flow theory suggests that players would value the sense of accomplishment which comes from an upwards challenge trajectory [3]. A successful design could perhaps be one in which the exertion mechanics involved repetitions of a task interspersed with rest periods but an additional mechanic increased the cognitive challenge for the player during the rests. If not, designers will need to develop a set of game mechanics designed around satisfying the player as they keep their performance constant. An additional complication comes from the fact that physical exercise causes pleasurable chemical changes in the brain (such as endorphin release) which are likely to increase motivation in a way which even the most zealous of sofa-bound gamers are unlikely to experience.

Further work is necessary to further understand the interaction between a constellation of player attributes and player behaviour when playing the game. Although the P.E. teacher described the lack of physical fitness of her pupils in general, it transpired that the learners who took part in the field study reported themselves as already fit, and by and large had positive attitudes towards exercise. This is a shortcoming in our evaluation because we are unable to compare the experience of unfit individuals to fit individuals, or those with low opinion to exercise to those with high. We also lacked the number of participants which would have been necessary to conduct an analysis for interaction effects between gender and gaming background.

In our next study, we will deliberately attempt to work with learners who are less fit and less inclined towards exercise in order to investigate whether their attitudes to the game, and behaviour while using it are different. For example, it is likely to be the case that users who do not enjoy exercise and have poor self-efficacy in this area will enjoy the game less, and exert themselves less than the users from the current study. It is also possible that their behaviour during the games will be different; such users are arguably less likely to increase the difficulty level during the game, and their enjoyment may decrease if they lose a level. Ideally, enjoyment of the game and exertion levels should increase after winning a level if the game truly does have a motivating effect. These effects may be mediated by the gaming background of the user: it is likely that users who do not typically enjoy exercise but who are avid gamers are more inclined to enjoy the game than users who like neither exercise nor games. Following on from this study, we will conduct an eight week longitudinal intervention to establish how players' attitudes to exercise and physical fitness change once the use of the game becomes a routine part of P.E. class. Using the results of these studies, we aim to design an adaptive exergame which can generate personalised exergame programmes for individuals based on their fitness, their attitude towards exercise and their previous performance with the game.

CONCLUSIONS

What are adolescents' opinions of the pilot games, and how much exertion do they expend in playing them? Results from a school based field study with 25 users which indicate that iFitQuest is enjoyable for 12-15 year olds, and it facilitates moderate to vigorous exercise.

How do gender and prior gaming experience affect users' attitudes towards the game? Girls and boys both enjoyed the game and would like to use it again. There is a significant difference with a large effect size between genders; boys are more likely to rate the game more highly. There was no significant difference in attitudes towards the game among groups with different prior gaming experience.

To what extent and in what way do users configure the challenge level of the game to tailor it to their fitness needs? Users accepted the opportunity to change the difficulty level of the game 66% of the time. As 56% of these changes were to increase the difficulty, this suggests that the users were attempting appropriate changes rather than simply 'cheating' by making the game easier.

How does winning or losing a game affect users' enjoyment of the game? Does success or failure have an impact on user alterations to difficulty levels? The users' enjoyment ratings did not appear to be influenced by success or failure in the game, suggesting that their motivation was not affected by their performance. This result may not hold for less fit users or those with low self-efficacy as they may become demoralized after losing a game. After losing a level, the players were most likely to decrease the difficulty level, presumably trying to make the challenge more appropriate. After winning a level, players were most likely to increase the difficulty, indicating an appropriate desire to increase challenge and exertion.

The above answers to these research questions provide the first steps towards developing exergames which appropriately tailor physical activity to user characteristics, highlighting the different ways in which a particular demographic group experiences an exergame, and the way in which an accurate player model will be required to create effective adaptive exergames.

REFERENCES

1. Campbell, T., Ngo, B., and Fogarty, J. Game design principles in everyday fitness applications. In *Proc. CSCW 2008*, ACM Press (2008), 249-252.
2. Consolvo, S., Everitt, K., Smith, I., and Landay, J. Design requirements for technologies that encourage physical activity. In *Proc. CHI 2006*, ACM Press (2006), 457-466.
3. Csikszentmihalyi, M. *Flow: The psychology of optimal experience*. Harper Perenial (1990).
4. Deckelbaum, R., and Williams, C. Childhood obesity: the health issue. *Obesity Research 9*, 4 (2001) 239-243.
5. Falkner, N., Neumark-Sztainer, D., Story, M., Jeffery, R., Beuhring, T., and Resnick, M. Social, educational, and psychological correlates of weight status in adolescents. *Obesity Research 9* (2001), 32-42.
6. Fujiki, Y., Kazakos, K., Puri, C., Buddharaju, P., Pavlidis, I., and Levine, J. NEAT-o-Games: Blending physical activity and fun in the daily routine. *Computers in Entertainment 6*, 2 (2008).
7. Gentile, D., Choo, H., Liau, A., Sim, T., Li, D., Fung, D., and Khoo, A. Pathological video game use among youths: A two-year longitudinal study. *Pediatrics 127*, 2 (2011), 319-329.
8. Good, J., & Robertson, J. CARSS: A framework for learner-centred design with children. *International Journal of Artificial Intelligence in Education16*, 4 (2006), 381-413.
9. Graves, L., Ridgers, N., Williams, K., Stratton, G., Atkinson, G., and Cable, N. The physiological cost and enjoyment of wii fit in adolescents, young adults, and older adults. *Journal of Physical Activity and Health 7*, 3 (2010), 393–401.
10. Graves, L., Stratton, G., Ridgers, N., and Cable, N. Comparison of energy expenditure in adolescents when playing new generation and sedentary computer games:

cross sectional study. *British Medical Journal 335*, 7633 (2007).

11. Killi, K., and Merilampi, S. Developing engaging exergames with simple motion detection. In *Proc. MindTrek 2010*, ACM Press (2010), 103-110.

12. Krauss, R., Winston, M., Fletcher, B., and Grundy, S. Obesity: Impact on cardiovascular disease. *Circulation, 98* (1998), 1472-1476.

13. Lin, J., Mamykina, L., Lindtner, S., Delajoux, G., and Strub, H. Fish'n'steps: Encouraging physical activity with an interactive computer game. In *Proc. UbiComp 2006*, ACM Press (2006), 261–278.

14. Lenhart, A., and Kahne, J. *Teens, video games, and civics*. Pew Internet and American Life Project Report (2008).

15. Magerkurth, C., Cheok, A., Mandryk, R., and Nilsen, T. 2005. Pervasive games: bringing computer entertainment back to the real world. *Computers in Entertainment 3*, 3 (2005).

16. Marshall, S., Biddle, S., Gorley, T., Cameron, N., and Murdey, I. Relationships between media use, body fatness and physical activity in children and youth: a meta analysis. *International Journal of Obesity 28* (2004), 1238-1246.

17. Mikkila, V., Lahti-Koski, M., Pietinen, P., Virtanen, S., and Rimpela, M. Associates of obesity and weight dissatisfaction among Finnish adolescents. *Journal of Public Health and Nutrition 6,* 1 (2003), 49-56.

18. Misund, G., Holone, H., Karlsen, J., and Tolsby, H. Chase and catch – Simple as that? Old-fashioned fun of traditional playground games revitalized with Location-aware mobile phones. In *Proc. ACE 2009.* ACM Press (2009), 73-80.

19. Murphy, E., Carson, L., Neal, W.,Baylis, C., Donley, D., and Yeater, R. Effects of an exercise intervention using dance dance revolution on endothelial function and other risk factors in overweight children. *International Journal of Pediatric Obesity 4*, 4 (2009) 205–214.

20. Namco's Pac-Man. http://www.namcogames.com/mobile/pacman_27.html

21. NHS Physical Activity Guidelines for Children and Young People. http://www.nhs.uk/Livewell/fitness/Pages/physical-activity-guidelines-for-young-people.aspx.

22. Nitz, J., Kuys, S., Isles, R., and Fu, S. Is the wiifit a new-generation tool for improving balance, health and well-being? A pilot study. *Climacteric 13*, 5 (2010) 487-491.

23. Olson, C. Children's motivations for video game play in the context of normal development. *Review of General Psychology 14*, 2 (2010), 180-187.

24. Ortiz, R., Rodriguez, R., Aleman, A., and Weffer, S. Relationships between body mass category and systolic blood pressure in rural adolescents. In *Proc. 2011 APS Conference: Physiology of Cardiovascular Diseases: Gender Disparities*, (2011).

25. Oxland, K. *Gameplay and Design.* Harlow: Addison-Wesley (2004).

26. Poole, E., Miller, A., Xu, Y., Eiriksdottir, E., Catrambone, R., and Mynatt, E. The place for ubiquitous computing in schools: Lessons learned from a school-based intervention for youth physical Activity. In *Proc. UbiComp 2011.* ACM Press (2011), 395-404.

27. Puhl, R., and Heuer, C. The stigma of obesity: A review and update. *Obesity 17*, 5 (2008), 941-964.

28. Reilly, J., Armstrong, J., Dorosty, A., Emmett, P., Ness, A., Rogers, I., Steer, C., and Sherriff, A. Early life risk factors for obesity in childhood: Cohort study. *British Medical Journal, 330*, (2005).

29. Rotwein-Pivnick, R. Getting kids and adolescents exited about exercise. *IDEA Fitness Journal 3*, 2 (2006).

30. Sallis, J., Bruno, M., Roby, J., Micale, F., and Nelson, J. Seven-day recall and other physical activity self-reports in children and adolescents.*Medicine and Science in Sports and Exercise 25,1 (1993), 99-108.*

31. Schwimmer, J., Burwinkle, T., and Varni, J. Health related quality of life of severely obese children and adolescents. *Journal of the American Medical Association 289,* 14 (2003), 1813-1819.

32. Sinclair, J., Hingston, P., and Masek, M. Considerations for the design of exergames. In *Proc. GRAPHITE 2007.* ACM Press (2007), 289-295.

33. Stokols, D. Translating social ecological theory into guidelines for community health promotion. *American Journal of Health Promotion 10*(1996), 282-298.

34. Stunkard, A., and Wadden, T. Psychological aspects of severe obesity. *American Journal of Clinical Nutrition 55* (1992), 524-532.

35. The World Health Organization Obesity Factsheet. http://www.who.int/mediacentre/factsheets/fs311/en/

36. Trout, J., and Zamora, K. Using dance dance revolution in physical education. *Teaching Elementary Physical Education 16,* 5 (2005), 22–25.

37. Ulicsak, M., and Crammer, S. *Gaming in families*. Technical report, Future Lab, March 2010.

38. Whitehead, A., Johnston, H., Nixon, N., and Welch, J. Exergame effectiveness: What the numbers can tell us. In *Proc. SIGGRAPH SandBox 2010*. ACM Press (2010), 55–62.

Tacticycle: Supporting Exploratory Bicycle Trips

Martin Pielot, Benjamin Poppinga
OFFIS Institute for Information Technology
Oldenburg, Germany
pielot;poppinga@offis.de

Wilko Heuten
OFFIS Institute for Information Technology
Oldenburg, Germany
heuten@offis.de

Susanne Boll
University of Oldenburg
Oldenburg, Germany
boll@informatik.uni-oldenburg.de

ABSTRACT
Going on excursions to explore unfamiliar environments by bike is a popular activity in many places in this world. To investigate the nature of exploratory bicycle trips, we studied tourists on their excursions on a famous vacation island. We found that existing navigation systems are either not helpful or discourage exploration. We therefore propose Tacticycle, a conceptual prototype of a user interface for a bicycle navigation system. Relying on a minimal set of navigation cues, it helps staying oriented while supporting spontaneous navigation and exploration at the same time. In cooperation with a bike rental, we rented the Tacticycle prototype to tourists who took it on their actual excursions. The results show that they always felt oriented and encouraged to playfully explore the island, providing a rich, yet relaxed travel experience. On the basis of these findings, we argue that exploratory trips can be very well supported by providing minimal navigation cues only.

ACM Classification Keywords
H.5.2 User Interfaces: Haptic I/O

Author Keywords
Handheld Devices and Mobile Computing; Tactile & Haptic UIs; Navigation Systems; Cycling; Exploration; Tourists

INTRODUCTION
Bicycling is a famous vacation activity in many Europe. Individuals, families, and groups often use their bicycle to explore their vacation environment as recreational activity. In this scenario, reaching a specific place is much less important compared to e.g. the daily commute to work. Although one typically choses a destination a little deviation from the route here and there is not a problem. In fact, these deviations can be a vital part of the excursion, as they promote serendipitous discoveries.

However, the fear of getting lost can harm this experience. With the advent of portable navigation systems, it seems that the problem is solved: we just enter the address of the destination and turn-by-turn navigation instructions will guide us there. The problem is that turn-by-turn instructions are known to disengage users from the environment [6] and lead to a significantly worse understanding of the environment [1]. Also, these systems guide travelers along the shortest or fastest route, missing out all the beautiful alternatives that might lie left and right of the optimal path—the opposite of what comprises an interesting and engaging excursion.

Figure 1. Our prototype: a smartphone attached to the handle bar provides the visual feedback. The yellow fabrics wrapped around the handles house the vibration motors.

We set out to explore alternative ways of navigation support for tourists on bicycle trips. Following the philosophy of user centered-design, we initially investigated the nature of exploratory bicycle trips by studying tourists on the island of *Borkum*. We found that these tourists often exhibit a rather errant and spontaneous form of navigation. While they often specify an area as destination, they not always reach it – which is not considered a big problem – and often loose orientation during their trips.

On the basis of our findings, we propose Tacticycle, a prototype of a navigation system that provides a minimal set of navigation information only. On a map, we highlight the available points of interest (POIs), so travelers can quickly browse potential travel destinations. When the user selects a POI as travel destination, the Tacticycle does not provide turn-by-turn instructions. Instead, it conveys the POI's general direction "as the crow flies". To not distract users from the environment, the direction is presented via vibration motors attached to the bicycle's handle bar. The relative intensity of the vibration is used to cue the direction in relation to the bicycle's heading. In addition, vibration is used to notify the user about nearby POIs to encourage spontaneous exploration and deviation from the planned route.

On the island of *Borkum*, we rented the prototype to tourists for their actual excursions. We used GPS tracking, experience sampling (ESM), the SenseCam, and post-hoc interviews to collect data, and found mixed results. While the Tacticycle helped the tourists to remain oriented, some of them initially struggled with the idea of not receiving turn-by-turn instructions. Others, who embraced the paradigm change, highly appreciated the freedom to shape their trip, as they like.

RELATED WORK

Today, navigation support is usually provided in the form of turn-by-turn instructions, such as "In fifty meters turn left into Old Street". While this has proven to be successful in practice in cars, a number of studies highlight the disadvantages of this approach. For example, when people describe routes they rarely use distances and street names. They rather tie their navigation instruction to landmarks, such as "turn left at the shop with the huge red neon sign." [8, 11]. People also are less engaged with the environment [6] and develop less spatial knowledge about it [1]. As a countermeasure Leshed et al. [6] propose i. a. to introduce ambiguity into the navigation instructions to "provoke independent assessment". One solution to navigate by ambiguous information has been around for about a decade: instead of providing instructions on each turn only the general direction of the destination is presented "as the crow flies". This means, on each turn the navigator has to make her own decision about which path might lead to the destination.

On the basis of the observation of tourists who navigated with a map, Brown and Laurier [3] found that tourists tend to "*head in a 'roughly correct' direction, rather than along a specific route.*" They conclude that "*map use involves activities that are not goal-oriented [...] we must be careful to hold on to the image of wandering tourists rather than the lone optimizing tourist*".

Allowing people to freely explore the environment has been proposed to address this issue. Hornecker et al. [5] proposed the Serendipity City Guide, location-based service that provides proximity alerts tourists to make its users aware of nearby POIs. Rider Spoke by Rowland et al. [12] went even one step further. Riders were allowed to freely explore the city and encouraged to record their thoughts about locations they went by. At the same time, riders could listen to previous recordings, which contributed to intensive experiences. Nevertheless, Rowland et al. also found that more than half of the participants lost their orientation at some point. As a consequence, many participants stayed close to "close to home".

This finding suggests that navigation support is still required to support serendipitous exploration. On the basis of Brown's and Laurier's observation that tourists *head in a 'roughly correct' direction*, we believe that cueing the general direction of a travel destination or an orientation landmark is therefore a viable approach. However, unlike turn-by-turn instructions, a general direction has to be available at all time, so navigators can orient themselves at all times. The challenge in implementing this paradigm into a user interface is to avoid distracting the user, e.g. by requiring her to frequently check the display of a handheld device, as this may be considered contradictory to the idea of enjoying a touristic trip.

In previous work, several ways of presenting general directions non-visually have been proposed already. Holland et al. [4] proposed AudioGPS, an auditory user interface that using the panning of an audio signal to encode general directions. In this approach the direction of the sound's panning corresponds to the direction of the destination. The system was found effective in pilot field trials, but due to its rather "sluggish" reaction times (according to the authors) no claims were made about its usability. Strachan et al. [14] investigated a more advanced version of that approach and showed that it enables users to reach "virtual" destinations only by following the panning of the auditory cue. Only recently, Zwindermann et al. [18] showed that this approach also works for cyclists in a city.

However, in a touristic scenario listening the environment, such as singing birds or ocean waves rolling on the shore, may be an integral part of the experience. Also, as observed in [5], auditory notifications may become inaudible in a noisy environment. The sense of touch offers a viable alternative for the information presentation in such situations. As long as the tactile stimuli do not become obtrusive they won't supposedly interfere with the experience of the trip.

An intuitive way of providing general directions with tactile displays is exciting locations around the torso with vibrotactile stimuli [13]. This can done with the help of tactile belts, such as the ActiveBelt [15]. Vibration motors are sewn into flexible fabrics and equally distribute them around the torso. Activating a motor e.g. at the navel is intuitively considered as pointing forward. Van Erp et al. [16] have shown that this kind of information presentation can be used to guide users along a set of waypoints by always pointing into the direction of the next waypoint.

With the increasing prevalence of orientation sensors in Smartphone, researchers have investigated using pointing gestures to convey navigation information [7, 10, 17], such as the location of a travel destination. When the pointing device, e.g. a mobile phone, points into the direction of the travel destination it vibrates. This technique has been found to enable pedestrians to effectively reach the cued location.

Yet, neither a belt nor pointing gestures might be suitable for cycling. The belt needs to be attached and worn all the time, which might be considered disrupting the experience. Pointing gestures can be dangerous to perform on the bicycle and should therefore not be encourage. In our previous work [9], we therefore proposed integrating the tactile display into the handle bars of the bicycle, so it is automatically available when users are riding, but the tourists do not have to worry about an external display. Following a similar approach, Bial et al. [2] have investigated providing turn-by-turn instructions via tactile displays integrated into the gloves of a motorcy-

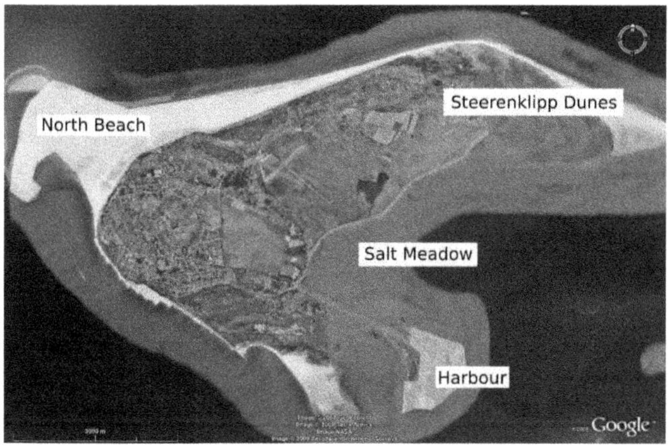

Figure 2. Popular areas that were named by informants of the survey as destinations for their trips.

clist. They found that the tactile signals can be recognized most of the time (87.4%) under real driving conditions.

What is currently missing is evidence that the concept of cueing general directions as orientation cues for serendipitous exploration is helpful for actual tourists. We will advance related work by investigating this concept in-situ with tourists on vacation on their bicycle trips.

ANALYSIS OF EXPLORATORY BICYCLE TRIPS

Following a user centered design approach, we initially conducted user studies to understand tourists on bicycle trips. In this section, we report our findings from these studies. We argue that tourists exploring confined areas, such as an island, are not well supported by predominant forms of navigation aids.

The studies took place at the island of *Borkum*. *Borkum* has about 5300 inhabitants, is about $30km^2$ wide, and has lots of visitor attractions to offer. Typical tourists are families with small children and people with chronic respiratory diseases, who are patients in one of the numerous clinics. Due to the size and the infrastructure of the island, it is very well suited for exploring it by bicycle.

We approached the requirements analysis from two angles. First, we assessed how tourists plan and conduct their bicycle trips through a survey. Second, we shadowed tourist on their trips to learn about the context of use.

Survey

For the survey, a local bicycle renter agreed to issue a questionnaire to tourists renting a bicycle. The tourists were asked to return it together with the bicycle. The questionnaire was split into three sections: the first section asked the tourists about their plans regarding the bicycle trip; the second section focused on the experiences during the planned trip; the third section gathered relevant demographic details.

Ten people completed and returned questionnaire. These people were either tourists or patients of one of the clinics. All of them had stayed at least two weeks on the island. Eight of these informants reported that they used a navigation aid on their trip. These were mostly paper maps and public overview maps. None of the participants used electronic navigation aids. Although eight informants had reported that their excursion had a concrete destination, only five of them stated that they had actually reached that destination. One informant summed it up as: *That's no problem, I am on vacation.* The destinations often described larger areas rather than landmarks, places, or points of interest. The most popular destinations of the area of the study are marked in Figure 2. Seven informants stated that they had lost orientation at least once during the trip. Nevertheless, they still expressed that they found the navigation aids they used to be helpful.

Field Observation

In order to complement the findings from the survey, we additionally shadowed tourists during their actual trips. We randomly picked tourists and more or less secretly shadowed them. We did not attract attention, since, around the time the study took place, the island was full of other cyclists. The tourists were mostly only observed for a part of their route and only in public places. Once they left public space, e.g. when having a break at a cafe, we discontinued the observation for ethical reasons. Findings were noted directly after the observation from the observer's memory. No personally identifiable information was recorded.

Six groups and four single travelers were observed during the study. Eight of them never used any navigation aid; two used a map. In order to read the map they all stopped. Route choices often seemed intuitive and spontaneous. Sometimes they were heavily discussed within the group. At other times, it did not seem to be much of a deal, which route was actually taken. One family, for example, turned around three times during the observation. They appeared to make those decisions based on how much they liked the environment. Overhearing conversations between the members of these groups, we discovered that sometimes there were no definite destinations for the trips, or that the destination was changed during the trip. People seemed to decide spontaneously to stop at a visitor's attraction or at restaurants.

Findings

Map is most prevalent navigation aid

In the survey, eight of ten informants reported to have brought a map. When we shadowed tourists, however, maps were used two times only. The use of other navigation aids was neither reported nor observed. Therefore, we conclude that for our sample maps are the most used navigation aid, though they are not used a lot. The inconvenience of having to stop in order to read the map might be one of the reasons for that.

Loss of orientation occurs frequently

Seven of ten survey participants reported to have lost orientation at least once. During the field observation at least five tourists/groups appeared to have lost orientation, as they stopped for a longer time, turned around, or mentioned this in discussions amongst each other. These results indicate that on *Borkum* loosing one's orientation is a frequent issue for tourists on bicycle trips.

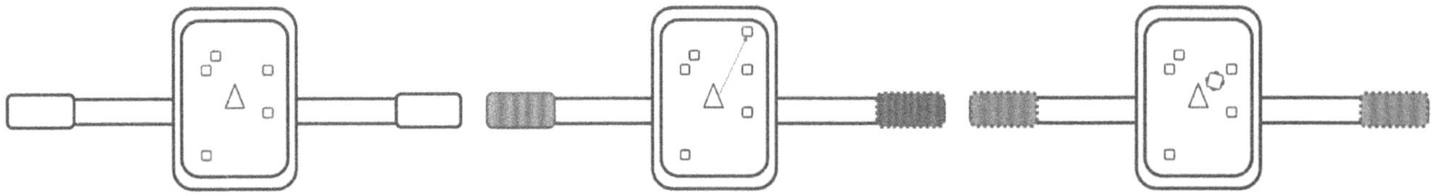

(a) Spontaneous navigation is supported by showing potential travel destinations (POIs) all the time on the display.

(b) Orientation support is provided by cueing the general direction of a POI through directional tactile vibration of the handlebar, here on the right side.

(c) Exploration and spontaneous navigation is supported by highlighting the presence of POIs nearby through visual and tactile alerts on both sides of the handlebar.

Figure 3. Illustration of the three main design concepts.

Reaching the destination is not mandatory
While eight of ten survey participants specified a destination for their trip, only five actually reached that place during their trip. Additionally, most destinations were not specific places but larger areas. From the observed tourists only three of ten seemed to have a specific destination. Therefore, reaching specific places does not seem to be a high priority for tourists. It also shows that those tourists were willing to alter their plans spontaneously.

Spontaneous navigation prevails
The observation showed that if people were uncertain at decision points, they often spontaneously decided how to proceed. From the survey we learned that it did not matter too much if a destination was not reached. We believe that happens because of the relaxed mood people have during their holidays.

TACTICYCLE DESIGN

Our requirements studies showed that tourists on bicycle trips on the island of *Borkum* in general use - if any navigation aid - maps, frequently lose their orientation, navigate spontaneously, and do not consider it crucial to reach their destination if any is specified. In this section we argue that neither maps nor turn-by-turn navigation systems are suited to support the serendipitous, exploratory nature of these trips. On the basis of these findings we propose the Tacticycle, an electronic navigation system for bicycles that focuses on supporting exploratory trips.

Design Implications from Requirements Analysis

From the requirements analysis we learned that efficiency is not a primary requirement for navigation systems for tourists. Rather than guiding the traveler from A to B as fast as possible, a navigation system for cyclists on *Borkum* should have the following properties:

Support spontaneous trips
Trips are rarely planned in advanced. Instead, travelers typically keep heading in the direction of a certain area or point-of-interest, and reaching this place is not always mandatory. Hence, the system should provide the possibility to quickly browse and select alternative travel destinations. To encourage spontaneous exploration, the system should also make the user aware of interesting sights nearby.

Provide orientation support
We also found that the majority of the travelers had lost orientation at least once during their trips. Although this was not considered critical, we believe that a loss of orientation is rather a stressful experience than a positive one. However, providing turn-by-turn direction might contrast the idea of an engaging trip [1, 6]. Instead the system should try to prevent the user from feeling lost in the first place, e.g. by providing the user with simple orientation hints, such as cardinal directions or the directions of relevant landmarks. This approach allows users to keep exploring and to choose whatever route they like without getting lost.

Be simple and easy to learn
In an environment such as *Borkum*, not all of the potential users of the Tacticycle are experienced with technology. Therefore, the system should be kept simple and easy to learn.

Do not require to constantly check a screen
As the observed tourists rarely checked the maps, we assume that the system should not rely too much on visual information presentation. If e.g. a visual display is used it should not require the user to frequently have a look at it. This is also important considering that distracting the user from traffic might lead to dangerous situations.

Design

In order to fulfill above requirements we implemented the Tacticycle along the following three design concepts.

Quick access to potential travel destinations
In order to make the Tacticycle easy to use for beginners, we make the selection of the destination as simple as possible. Instead of having to search for a destination via text-entry, we show all points of interests of the categories amenity, leisure, tourism, and historic (from OpenStreetMap) on a map (see Figure b).

The rationale behind that design decision is twofold: first, tourists from our requirement studies often selected general areas as destination. Thus, if users would like to visit a certain area, they can just select a POI from this area. Thus, the location of the POI is important context information, which a list, rather than a map, might not provide. Second, maps were the only navigation aid we saw being used. Hence, we believed that users would desire having a map for their trips.

The left screenshot in Figure shows the user interface that implements this concept. For the technical implementation, we use a mobile device (Android Smartphone), which gets attached to the bicycle's handle bar. By default the map is centered to the user and rotated head-up, meaning that the "up"

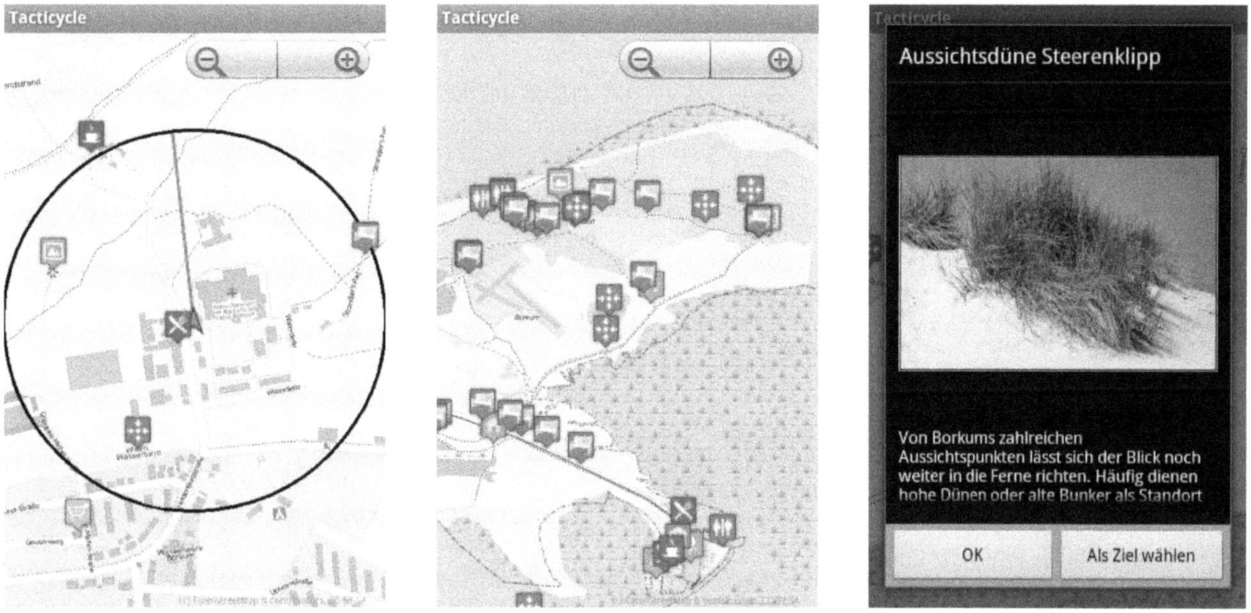

(a) In general, the map centers on the user's position and rotates so that "up" corresponds to the driving direction.

(b) To browse the environment and select a travel destination users can scroll and zoom the map.

(c) Descriptions for each POI can be obtained by long-clicking an icon.

Figure 4. Screenshots of the application.

on the map corresponds to the driving direction. The map can be scrolled and zoomed to browse the island. Colored icons indicate the locations of points of interest prominently. Users can select a point of interest as travel destination by simply clicking on it. By long-clicking on an icon the application shows details about the point of interest, which consists of the POI's name, an image, and a textual description.

Convey direction of travel destination for orientation

In order to provide orientation support, we assumed that providing simple hints, such as the direction of a landmark as point of reference, would be sufficient. We therefore designed the Tacticycle to convey the general direction of the POI selected as destination.

To not require the user to constantly check the mobile device's screen, we chose to communicate the direction via the sense of touch. By attaching one vibration motor to each handle bar, we turned the Tacticycle's handle bar into a tactile user interface. We used vibro-tactile actuators, because these are best studied and most robust. The rationale behind using the handle bar is that these - alongside the seat - are the only parts of a bicycle that the rider constantly touches during the ride. We decided against using wearable tactile displays, since tourists often interrupt their ride and would have to stow away and setup up the wearable display in such cases. When a point of interest is selected, the vibration motors start indicating its general direction. As showing in Figure b, the direction is encoded in the relative intensity of the vibration in the two handles. If the destination is 0 degree / straight ahead both handles vibrate with the same intensity. If the destination is to the left, e.g. 45 degrees, the intensity in the right handle increases and the intensity in the left handle decreases. This allows encoding the full 180-degree spectrum of directions ahead of the cyclist. When the cyclist moves away from the destination the vibration remains silent. The handles vibrate constantly in pulses. The length of a pulse is 500ms followed by a 2000ms pause. These timings were chosen, because they continuously convey the direction of the selected POI without reducing the sensitivity of the skin, which would be caused by constant vibration.

Unlike car navigation systems, this design does not provide turn-by-turn instructions. It rather just gives the direction like a compass "as the crow flies", such as "the selected point of interest is 30 degrees to the right-hand side". This can also mean that the system points forward, but there are obstacles (e.g. a lake) in the way. Thus, users may have to find their way around obstacles by themselves. While this renders the navigation support less effective we presumed that it would encourage exploration.

Highlight nearby POIs to encourage spontaneous navigation

To support spontaneous navigation and serendipitous exploration, we aimed at informing the user about nearby points of interest. We used the tactile user interface to deliver tactile alerts, so the user does not have to check the display frequently. Whenever the user passes by a POI in a distance of 50m or less, the handle bars will alert the rider by delivering four short pulses, each with a duration of 500ms followed by a 250ms pause. If a POI is selected as travel destination at the same time, the presentation of its directions through vibration is paused for the alert. Through pilot tests we found out that both patterns can be very well discriminated.

At the same time, the icon of the POI that is highlighted by the tactile interface is briefly enlarged and starts rotating. Hence, even when the display is difficult to read, the icon stands out clearly.

Pilot Study

To ensure that the Tacticycle is sufficiently usable, in particular its tactile user interface, we conducted a pilot study. Six participants, three female and three male, aged between 20 and 26 years (M 23.33, SD 2.32) took part in the study. None of the participants had previous experiences with the tactile or visual information presentation methods described.

Method

The pilot study was divided into two tasks. In the first task, the participants were asked to interpret directions presented by the tactile user interface. Thirteen random angles had to be recognized. Since different sources of vibration can interfere with each other, and the bicycle itself also vibrates while riding, we conducted the study outdoors. The participants were asked to ride back and forth in an empty parking area. A mobile device monitored the driving speed via GPS. Once the bicycle started moving, a direction was presented via the tactile interface. Once the participants had covered a distance of about 50 meters, they had to stop and estimate the perceived angle on a clock face. The vibration stopped when the bicycle stopped, so the participants could not "cheat" and listen to the vibration while standing still. The system did not provide any feedback about the correctness of the judgment.

In the second task, we asked the participants to reach a given destination. We therefore selected a POI, which was about 2 km away from the parking area, and asked the participant to ride there. None of the participants was familiar with the streets between the destination and the parking area. Hence, they had to rely on the visual and the tactile feedback given by the application. One experimenter followed the participants on another bicycle to make observations and to listen to any in-situ comments of the participants.

Results

The results of the first task (identifying given directions on a clock face) show that users struggle with giving a correct estimate. As shown in Figure 5 users can best identify the cardinal directions (left/right/ ahead = 9/12/3 o'clock). 12 o'clock was recognized in 44.4% of the trials. Left and right (9 and 3 o'clock) were recognized in 58.3% of the trials. The intermediate directions (10/11/1/2 o'clock were recognized in only about 10 to 20% of the trials. The majority of misjudgments were adjacent angles.

In the second tasks (reach a given destination) all participants arrived at the destination without difficulties. One participant primarily used the visual display to find his way (the application had a visual cue which we removed later: a line drawn from the own position to the location of the POI). Five of the six participants mainly relied on the tactile feedback. They explicitly appreciated the increased awareness for the environment or the decreased need to check the handheld device's screen.

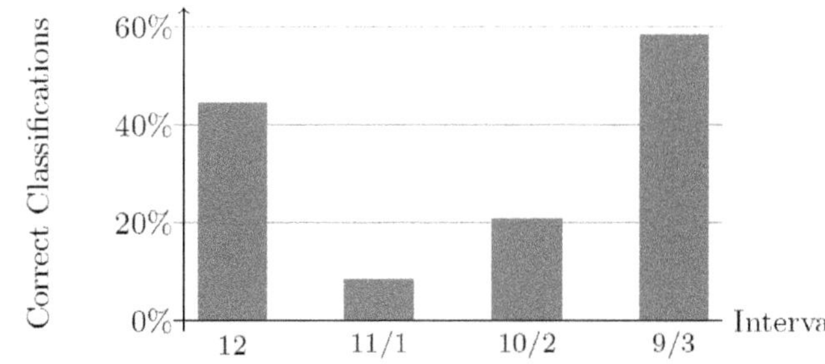

Figure 5. Recognition rates by presented direction.

Discussion

The pilot test indicates that cueing general directions in vibration intensities, although being quite coarse, resembles an effective and usable navigation and orientation aid. The participants reported no difficulties in understanding the general concept of mapping vibration intensities to directions, though their estimates were only roughly correct. Nevertheless, the results from the second task hint that these rough directional cues are sufficient to guide cyclists to a given destination in an unfamiliar environment.

IN-SITU FIELD STUDY

To study the prototype in-situ we conducted a field study. During a period of seven days we gave it for free to tourists to use it for leisure time trips. The aim was to investigate whether the underlying concepts are useful, usable, and whether they match the desires of tourists to improve the experience of the trip.

Method

Venue & Participants

For the study we received support from a local bicycle rental attached to a rehabilitation clinic for respiratory and dermatological diseases. Patients usually stay at the clinic for two to four weeks. Many of them rent a bicycle for their whole stay, so they can run errands, explore the island, or go on trips. The owner had arranged that all newly arriving patients found a handout in their rooms informing them about the opportunity to take part in the study. We set up an info booth at the bicycle rental where interested patients could approach us to arrange an appointment for their participation.

Eleven patients decided to take part in the study. Their age ranged from approx. 20 to 55 (M 43.18, SD 10.55) years. Seven of them were female, four male. All of them had just arrived to the island in the past few days and were not yet familiar with the area. They all rented a bicycle for their whole stay. For our study, we asked them to use our prototype instead of the rented bicycle on one of their trips they would be doing anyway.

Material

To be able to reconstruct the trips and understand how participants used the Tacticycle we implemented a set of logging methods. First, the application logged the route via GPS. Second, we used a SenseCam to get pictures of the trip. The *SenseCam* is camera developed by Microsoft Research with the size of a cigarette box. It is worn by a cord around the

Figure 6. Cyclists exploring the island with the Tacticycle (2nd bicycle).

neck. For the study we configured it to take one picture every five seconds. Third, we used the experienced sampling method (ESM) to acquire in-situ feedback. Every 30 minutes a dialog popped up and asked the participants to rate how much they agree two on of the following statements: *I feel oriented and know where I am*, *I feel distracted by the system*, or *I feel relaxed*, and were randomly selected. The statements were chosen randomly and the rating was entered using a five-point Likert scale.

These three data sets, namely the GPS track, the SenseCam photos, and the ESM responses, could be imported into a custom made application that called *Context Player*. Timestamps in all three data sets allowed the Context Player to synchronize the data. The Context Player (see Fig. 7) allows to play back the route and to browse back and forth, similar to a video player. For each point in time of the trip it shows the participant's position on a map, the recent picture taken by the SenseCam, and the recent ESM statement along with the recorded response (or the message that the statement had been ignored or discarded).

Figure 7. The Context Player application that was used to play back the trials to the study participants.

Procedure

Initially, we gave the participants a quick introduction to the background of the study. Then, we explained the Tacticycle to the participants by giving them a guided walkthrough. We asked them to browse the map, select different POIs, and test the tactile feedback. We asked them to select a POI so they could experience the vibration feedback. We explicitly mentioned that the system does not work like common turn-by-turn navigation systems, but that it only displays the general direction of the POI. We stressed that it even might happen that they approach an intersection where the system tells them to go straight while the streets only lead left and right. We told them that they would have to find their own route in such cases. To avoid accidents, the participants were instructed to only interact with the mobile device when halting. We also informed them about the logging methods. We explained that the GPS track would be recorded, that the SenseCam would take pictures every few seconds, and demonstrated an ESM dialog. We said that responding to an ESM dialog was encouraged, but it also was allowed close them or ignore them. We also told the participants to not depend on the system and always carry a map or similar as fallback. All participants signed an informed consent form. They were informed that all personally identifiable information, if recorded at all, would be treated confidential and that they could stop their participation at any time.

After the instruction they departed on their trips. Eight participants went alone, three together with another person. For 7 participants we conducted the interview directly after they returned. The others made an appointment and came back for the interview within 24 hours. During the interview we first asked the participants to reconstruct the trip by indicating visited places on a timeline (see Fig. 8). Second, we asked how they had used the Tacticycle and what their impressions on the different features were. In the meantime, we had imported the log data to the Context Player. Once finished we showed the Context Player to the participants and used it to replay the route to trigger additional feedback.

As a reward, each participant received a USB stick with the SenseCam photos from their trip after the interview. They also received a discount worth about $10 on the fee for the "ordinary" bicycle they had rented.

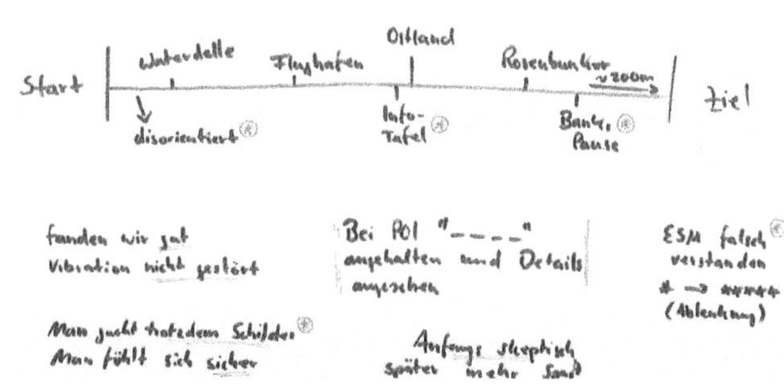

Figure 8. Snippet of a timeline sketched during the post-hoc interview to reconstruct the trip.

Characteristics of the Trips

Figure 9 shows the routes travel by our participants. The trips took between 20 minutes and 2.5 hours (M 74.6 min, SD 46.0 min). The distance covered ranged from 1.7 to 17.8 (M 9.77, SD 5.34) km.

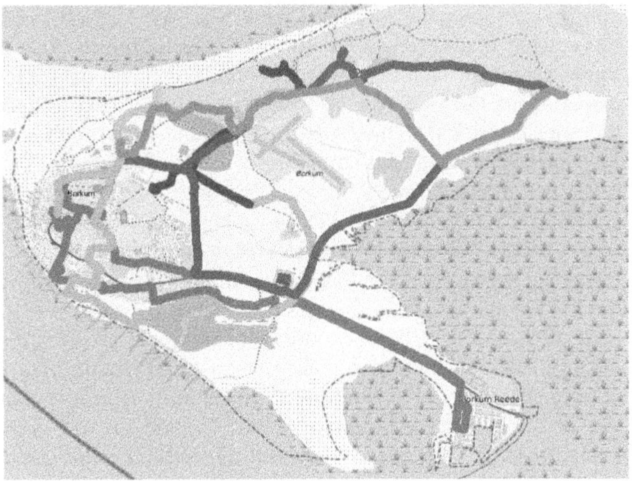

Figure 9. Plot of the recorded GPS tracks.

Multiple Destinations Visited

23 destinations (2.3 per traveler) have been specified. 17 of these were reached. There were two types of trip destinations: the countryside and the city center. 6 participants visited the almost uninhabited east side of the island, 1 participant went to the harbor on the south side of the island. On 5 tours participants visited destinations in the city center, including the tourist info, a supermarket, an official beach, a light house, and a war memorial. The system highlighted 63 POIs (5.7 per traveler) of which 2 were visited.

Participants Felt Relaxed and Oriented

43 statements were prompted via the Experience Sampling Method (ESM). 20 were answered, 19 were overseen/ignored, and 4 were actively dismissed. In average, the participants did not feel disoriented (2), were neutral about the level of distraction (2.8), felt supported in their exploration (4.25), and relaxed (4.5).

All values are means. The ESM questions were answered via 5-point Likert scales, where 1 = strongly disagree and 5 = strongly agree.

Interview Results

In the following we report our findings from the interviews. We only report these aspects that were spontaneously mentioned by the participants. So, if for example we report that 2 participants disliked the system, this might mean that all others did, too, but they did not mention this by themselves.

Vibration Needs Short Learning Period

7 participants found the vibration odd in the beginning. But once they got used to it 5 named it unobtrusive and 4 said that it boosted their confidence. 3 participants considered positively that it was unnecessary to watch the map.

Direction "as the crow flies" Considered Controversial

4 participants appreciated that presenting the direction "as the crow flies" allowed them to choose the route freely, e.g. decide between paved road and forest trail depending on the situation. 2 participants found the concept of presenting the direction "as the crow flies" to odd and rather expect navigation systems to present turn-by-turn instructions. In particular, one participant desired detailed guidance in the case of getting lost. 2 participants mentioned that they found it annoying when the system pointed to the side for a long time, but there was not path leading into that direction.

No Loss of Orientation with Tactile Feedback

None of the participants reported to have felt disoriented. Also, the play back of the trips with the context player showed no signs of a loss of orientation when the tactile display showed the direction of a POI. However, P9 failed to enter a proper POI on her way back, so she received no vibration feedback. Playing back the route on the Context Player it was obviously that she was lost at that time, since she desired to come back to the home base but took a detour of about 30 minutes and had to turn around.

Situation-induced impairments occurred frequently

6 participants reported from problems reading the display due to different reasons. Two complained that it impossible to read the display when sunshine was reflecting on the display. Another participant faced a rainstorm, which made it also impossible to read the display. Two participants mentioned that they were not able to read the map on the move, since it was too small for them. One participant mentioned that on rough roads the device would shake so much that it became difficult to read the display.

Spontaneous Navigation only Observed at Some Trips

7 participants only used the POI radar to specify the initial destination, but not anymore afterwards. 4 participants used it in a playful way, i.e. they went to an area with a lot of POIs and visited a large number of them in a short period of time. 1 of these participants noted that offering only a limited number of potential destinations helped in deciding for a new destination.

Paper Map Considered Less Helpful

All but 2 participants said that they would usually keep a paper map with them. In contrast to the paper map, 3 participants appreciated that the Tacticycle allowed faster orientation and did not require stops. 5 participants said that maps can be difficult to read at times, e.g. when there are no landmarks to determine one's location. In these situations, an egocentric cue as provided by the Tacticycle would be most helpful.

Navigation System Considered Overkill

All participants had experience with car navigation systems. Only one participant had been using a bicycle navigation system as well. 5 participants stated that a navigation system providing turn-by-turn instructions would be overkill and annoying for such tours, since they did not find it important to reach a specific destination quickly.One participant appreciated that he was more conscious about the environment compared to a navigation system. However, 2 participants pointed out that turn-by-turn instructions might become handy when getting lost.

Discussion

In brief, all participants were able to use the Tacticycle in a meaningful way. Although many participants had no previous experience with Smartphones and touch screens, all were able to browse and select POIs. The tactile direction cueing was in general well received and proofed to be understandable and effective. None of the participants lost orientation as long as haptic feedback was provided. Our findings suggest that it helped overcoming situational impairments and improved the user experience.

Tactile Direction Cueing

The tactile direction cueing was perceived as the most helpful and exciting feature. All participants tried to follow the navigation instructions delivered by the tactile user interface. Most participants appreciated receiving directional cues throughout the ride. It boosted the confidence, in particular of those who believed in having a bad sense of orientation. In general the tactile cues were described as unobtrusive or even too weak. We could confirm the findings from the pilot study that the accuracy of the display was rather coarse, but we could also confirm that this hardly leads to any notable difficulties in the navigation. In brief, the study provides evidence that cueing the direction of a destination in vibration patterns works well for longer tours in unfamiliar environments, and with people that are not necessarily experienced with smartphones and similar technology.

Our findings confirm the motivation for using a tactile display. For example, the participants mostly stopped to read the map, since they found it too small. When it was sunny or raining they struggled with reading the display at all. We also received the feedback that it was easy to stay aware of the environment compared.

One issue we found is that many people today are used to turn-by-turn car navigation systems and find it difficult to understand and/or accept another concept than turning instructions. During the explanation, we very explicitly stated that the system would show directions "as the crow flies", we illustrated this with examples, and we said that the system might tell to go ahead when there is actually a huge obstacle (e.g. a lake) ahead. Nevertheless, some participants found this very hard to grasps and presumably still expected to receive turning instructions. We still received complaints that "the system did not show that turn". Yet, even those who did not grasp the concept still were able to navigate by the tactile cues. They obviously explained unexpected turning instructions as system malfunctions and otherwise followed the tactile cues if they found them to be logical.

Spontanous Navigation

Providing quick access to potential travel destinations was most helpful in the beginning, when the participants needed to select their initial destination. Two third of the participants only used it to be guided to their trip destination and back to the bicycle rental. The remaining third used it for spontaneous navigation and exploration. They reported to have developed a game-like attitude and selected POIs nearby "just for fun" or out of curiosity. These results show that the POI selection method can assist spontaneous navigation and exploration, but is only used by a minority of the users.

As no experimenter was present during the study and the study equipment was not found to be obtrusive, our participants were not constantly reminded that they were part of a study. However, to achieve this we had to refrain from accompanying and observing them on their trips. Instead we had to rely on the collected data and the post-hoc interviews. The quality of interviews, however, depends on the ability of the participants to recall important events and thoughts. Being able to replay the tour (GPS, SenseCam, Experience Sampling Questions) via our application was indispensable to elicit rich feedback. It helped to uncover a lot of events the participants "forgot" to report. Hence, we believe that not shadowing participants was the right choice, since this increases the ecological validity of our findings.

Limitations

The study took place in an environment that had a lot of alternative paths and that was geographically constraint. Thus, our participants would usually find a way to their destination as long as they kept going roughly into the right direction, and they did not have to be afraid of getting lost by going into the wrong direction for too long. This might raise the question, to what extent the results can be applied to other environments. Yet, we believe that these limitations can be addressed by technology. Constraining the exploration environment can be achieved virtually by using boundary notifications, as proposed by Hornecker et al. [5]. In areas with few alternative paths intermediate landmarks could be used to guide the users through the bottlenecks. For example, if the selected destination is on the other side of a river, the system could automatically place an intermediate destination at the nearest bridge.

The study offers no baseline. Thus, we cannot be sure to what extent our findings are caused by the Tacticycle or by other factors. Yet, our findings show that the novel concept of cueing directions "as the crow flies" through vibrating handle bars is sufficiently easy to use for non-tech-savvy people and that it is highly appreciated for not requiring to stop to check the map and for allowing to freely chose the actual route. Therefore, the study provides important evidence for the emerging approach of cueing directions "as the crow flies" as navigation aids, to eventually overcome the *tyranny of turn-by-turn navigation* [10].

CONCLUSIONS

This paper reports from the user-centered development of the Tacticycle, a navigation system that specifically targets the needs of tourists exploring constraint environments, such as an island. The contribution of this paper is three-fold:

- We argue that maps and navigation systems are not always the right tools to provide navigation support, in particular if the goal is to explore confined areas as a tourist. We base our argument on related work, a survey, and a field study.

- To fill this gap, we propose the Tacticycle, the concept of a minimal set of navigation cues for cyclists on exploratory bicycle trips. For quick browsing of potential travel destinations is shows POIs on a map. Further, it uses a tactile display to convey the general direction of the travel destination as orientation guide and highlight nearby POIs to encourage spontaneous exploration.
- From a field study with actual tourists we provide evidence that with the Tacticycle cyclists feel oriented and encouraged to explore the environment. They also appreciate the eyes-free use and have a relaxed travel experience.

Our findings suggest that a minimal set of navigation instructions is sufficient if exploration rather than reaching a destination as fast as possible is the traveler's goal. They show that cueing general directions is a powerful and elegant, yet effective complement to providing turn-by-turn instructions for cyclists. The work shows that instead of only striving for the most accurate and detailed navigation aid only we should not easily neglect how to leverage the human's inherent navigation skills. We should allow for "mistakes" and encourage exploration, as many roads ultimately lead to Rome. Nevertheless, many situations will still require the efficiency of turn-by-turn navigation or the overview that a map provides. However, we have shown that a third way is possible and can be beneficial.

Future work needs to clarify, which of the concepts are superior in which situations. Our participants had surprisingly few problems with the information presentation, which makes us wonder to what extend this concept can keep up with turn-by-turn instructions when efficient navigation is desired.

ACKNOWLEDGMENTS

The authors are grateful to the European Commission which co-funds the IP HaptiMap (FP7-ICT-224675). We thank Antje and Georg Poppinga for allowing us to conduct the study in their bicycle rental.

REFERENCES

1. Aslan, I., Schwalm, M., Baus, J., Krüger, A., and Schwartz, T. Acquisition of spatial knowledge in location aware mobile pedestrian navigation systems. In *Proc. MobileHCI '06* (2006).
2. Bial, D., Kern, D., Alt, F., and Schmidt, A. Enhancing outdoor navigation systems through vibrotactile feedback. In *Proc. CHI '11* (2011).
3. Brown, B., and Laurier, E. Maps and journeys: an ethnomethodological investigation. *Cartographica 4*, 3 (2005), 17–33.
4. Holland, S., Morse, D. R., and Gedenryd, H. Audiogps: Spatial audio navigation with a minimal attention interface. *Personal and Ubiquitous Computing 6*, 4 (2002), 253–259.
5. Hornecker, E., Swindells, S., and Dunlop, M. A mobile guide for serendipitous exploration of cities. In *Proc. MobileHCI '11* (2011).
6. Leshed, G., Velden, T., Rieger, O., Kot, B., and Sengers, P. In-car gps navigation: engagement with and disengagement from the environment. In *Proc. CHI '08* (2008).
7. Magnusson, C., Rassmus-Grhn, K., and Szymczak, D. The influence of angle size in navigation applications using pointing gestures. In *Proc. HAID '10* (2010).
8. May, A. J., Ross, T., Bayer, S. H., and Tarkiainen, M. J. Pedestrian navigation aids: information requirements and design implications. *Personal and Ubiquitous Computing 7*, 6 (2003), 331–338.
9. Poppinga, B., Pielot, M., and Boll, S. Tacticycle: a tactile display for supporting tourists on a bicycle trip. In *Proc. MobileHCI '09* (2009).
10. Robinson, S., Jones, M., Eslambolchilar, P., Murray-Smith, R., and Lindborg, M. "I Did It My Way": Moving away from the tyranny of turn-by-turn pedestrian navigation. In *Proc. MobileHCI '10* (2010).
11. Ross, T., May, A., and Thompson, S. The use of landmarks in pedestrian navigation instructions and the effects of context. In *Proc. MobileHCI '04* (2004).
12. Rowland, D., Flintham, M., Oppermann, L., Marshall, J., Chamberlain, A., Koleva, B., Benford, S., and Perez, C. Ubikequitous computing: designing interactive experiences for cyclists. In *Proc. MobileHCI '09* (2009).
13. Srikulwong, M., and O'Neill, E. A comparison of two wearable tactile interfaces with a complementary display in two orientations. In *Proc. HAID '10* (2010).
14. Strachan, S., Eslambolchilar, P., Murray-Smith, R., Hughes, S., and O'Modhrain, S. Gpstunes: controlling navigation via audio feedback. In *Proc. MobileHCI '05* (2005).
15. Tsukada, and Yasumura. Activebelt: Belt-type wearable tactile display for directional navigation. In *Proc. UbiComp '04* (2004).
16. van Erp, J. B. F., van Veen, H. A. H. C., Jansen, C., and Dobbins, T. Waypoint navigation with a vibrotactile waist belt. *ACM Transactions on Applied Perception 2*, 2 (2005), 106–117.
17. Williamson, J., Robinson, S., Stewart, C., Murray-Smith, R., Jones, M., and Brewster, S. Social gravity: A virtual elastic tether for casual, privacy-preserving pedestrian rendezvous. In *Proc. CHI '10* (2010).
18. Zwinderman, M., Zavialova, T., Tetteroo, D., and Lehouck, P. Oh music, where art thou? In *Proc. MobileHCI '11* (2011).

Displaying Mobile Feedback during a Presentation

Jaime Teevan, Daniel J. Liebling, Ann Paradiso,
Carlos Garcia Jurado Suarez, Curtis von Veh, Darren Gehring
Microsoft Research, Redmond, WA USA
{teevan, danl, annpar, cgarcia, curtisvv, darrenge}@microsoft.com

ABSTRACT
Smartphone use in presentations is often seen as distracting to the audience and speaker. However, phones can encourage people participate more fully in what is going on around them and build stronger ties with their companions. In this paper, we describe a smartphone interface designed to help audience members engage fully in a presentation by providing real-time mobile feedback. This feedback is then aggregated and reflected back to the group via a projected visualization, with notifications provided to the presenter and the audience on interesting feedback events. We deployed this system in a large enterprise meeting, and collected information about the attendees' experiences with it via surveys and interaction logs. Participants report that providing mobile feedback was convenient, helped them pay close attention to the presentation, and enabled them to feel connected with other audience members.

Author Keywords
Mobile, meetings, feedback, presentations.

ACM Classification Keywords
H.5.2 [Information Interfaces and Presentation (e.g., HCI)]: Miscellaneous.

INTRODUCTION
People attending a presentation typically provide feedback to the presenter throughout the course of the presentation. They nod and smile, look perplexed, raise their hands, and check their email. However, much of this feedback in unintentional, and it can be challenging for the presenter to fully synthesize and understand audience sentiment, particularly when presenting to large groups. It is even harder for audience members to know the reactions of the people around them as they focus on the presentation.

There have been a number of tools built to allow people to provide feedback to presenters, particularly in a classroom setting [1, 3, 9, 10]. For example, Chamillard [3] explored using a clicker-based system to engage students in the flow of a lecture. However, most of this work has focused on providing audience feedback solely to the presenter, which the presenter can then use for assessment and pedagogical purposes. In this paper we explore how feedback can be provided directly to the audience to further engage them with each other and the presentation.

MobileHCI'12, September 21–24, 2012, San Francisco, CA, USA.

The most common existing technological way for audience members to engage with each other during a presentation is via a textual backchannel. For example, audience members can associate short snippets of text on Twitter with a shared hashtag to communicate with other people in the room. Yardi [10] describes a backchannel employed by university students in a classroom setting. Sometimes backchannel content will be projected during a talk for all to see. However, backchannel communication can be distracting for participants [10], and typically excludes the presenter, at times with significant social cost [2, 10]. Lighter-weight methods for providing [7] and visualizing [4] feedback have been shown to be more inclusive and engaging.

Crowd Feedback is a mobile phone based system designed to make presentation feedback explicit in a way that engages attendees without distracting them, and provides real-time benefit to the presenter without excluding them. During a presentation, audience members use their mobile phones to "like" or "dislike" what has just been presented. This feedback is then aggregated and displayed on a sidebar projected beside the presentation slides. When interesting feedback events occur, a badge appears on the sidebar and the presenter's mobile phone vibrates. In addition to being fun for the audience, badges let the presenter know that it is worth checking in with how the audience is responding.

We deployed the Crowd Feedback system in a large enterprise meeting, and collected information about the attendees' experiences with it via a survey and interaction logs. After a description of the deployment, we describe how the system was used. We find people who provided feedback felt engaged with the presentation and other audience members, while experiencing minimal distraction. We discuss the unexpected ways feedback was used during the meeting, and suggest ways feedback might be used after a presentation to help attendees recall presentation content.

THE CROWD FEEDBACK SYSTEM
The Crowd Feedback system has three components: a mobile client for providing feedback, a shared visualization of the feedback, and badges designed to include the speaker in the feedback. Each is described in greater detail below.

Crowd Feedback Mobile Client
The Crowd Feedback mobile client is shown in Figure 1. Audience members can provide positive feedback using a green *thumbs up* button, and negative feedback using a red

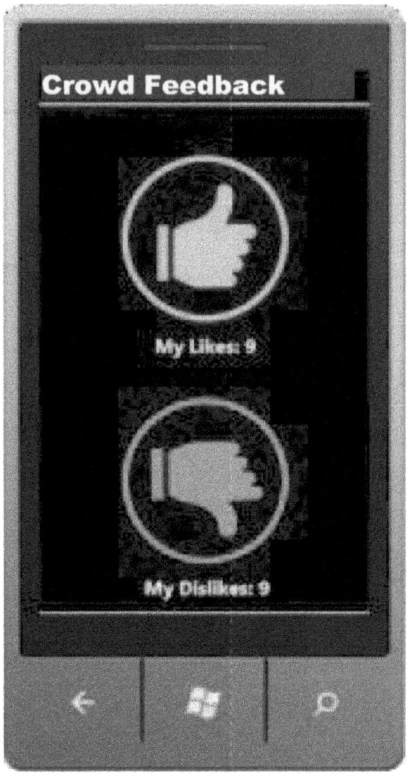

Figure 1. The Crowd Feedback mobile client.

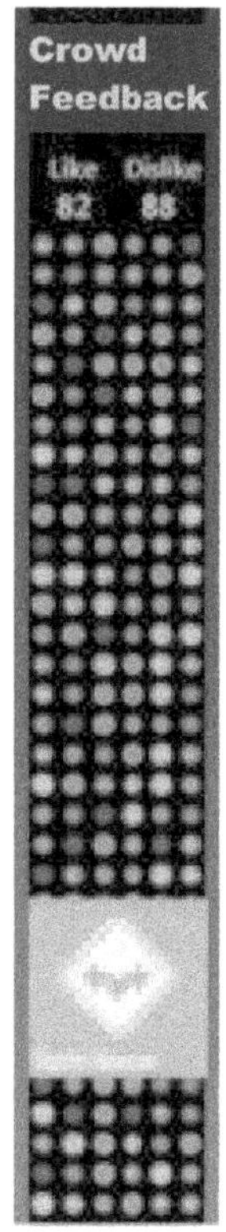

Figure 2. The presentation sidebar

thumbs down button. We targeted mobile phones rather than building a special purpose clicker device [3, 9] or a laptop or tablet-based system [1, 7]. Our approach is similar to classroom-based feedback systems that have used mobile phones for electronic voting [5] and note-taking [8]. Studies have shown that phones are an attractive alternative to other devices because of their prevalence, functionality, and size.

To encourage adoption of the Crowd Feedback client, it is implemented as a webpage optimized for smartphones, rather than as an application that must be installed. To join a meeting, participants merely type, click, or follow a tag to a URL with the active meeting ID. As a result, audience members can also choose to provide feedback via any device with a Web browser, including laptops and tablets.

Crowd Feedback Presentation Sidebar

The feedback provided by audience members is aggregated and represented in the Crowd Feedback Sidebar, shown in Figure 2. The sidebar is a stand-alone executable. When a PowerPoint presentation uses a specially designed template, the active sidebar can be positioned to float above the blank region on the template so that it appears immediately adjacent to the slide content, as shown in Figure 3.

Each audience member is represented as a colored dot in the sidebar. Individuals are identified via a cookie stored on their device, so that it is possible for them to temporarily close their Web browser and still be mapped to the same dot upon returning. As new people join the meeting, a new grey dot appears, and the dot then turns red or green as a function of the feedback provided. The intensity of the dot shows how recently the feedback has been provided. New feedback is shown in Figure 2 as bright dots, while older feedback is shown as faded dots. To quickly summarize the feedback, a count at the top shows the number of people who have recently provided positive and negative feedback.

Figure 3. Crowd Feedback being used by 179 people in an enterprise All Hands meeting.

Crowd Feedback Badges

On interesting feedback events, a badge triggers. Feedback events that trigger badges include the presence of a large number of participants, a lot of positive, negative, or split feedback, and periods of inactivity. The inactivity badge was designed to remind audience members to provide feedback. When a badge triggers, an icon such as the one shown in Figure 2 appears at the bottom of the sidebar and floats slowly to the top. This animation ensures the badge is visible for an extended period of time, while not obscuring any one portion of the sidebar for very long.

It can be hard for a presenter to keep track of what is going on in the sidebar while talking. For this reason, when a badge triggers the presenter's mobile phone vibrates to provide awareness that an interesting feedback event has occurred. The badge speed is designed to provide the presenter with enough time to receive the buzz and look at the sidebar to learn which badge has triggered.

CROWD FEEDBACK IN USE

We deployed Crowd Feedback during a large presentation and studied how people used it. Here we describe the study methodology, people's reactions, and the feedback data.

Study Methodology

Crowd Feedback was deployed at an All Hands meeting at Microsoft, a large software company (see Figure 3). Several hundred people were invited to the meeting. Approximately 250 people were present for the presentation, and 179 used the Crowd Feedback Client to provide feedback. People attending the meeting received the link to the client in the meeting invitation and were asked to bring their mobile phones with them. The client URL and a QR code-like tag were also posted in the meeting room. The presenter provided a brief overview of the system at the beginning of the meeting. During the meeting, the feedback and badges were logged, and the presentation was video recorded.

Following the meeting, a survey about Crowd Feedback was sent to the meeting attendees. In addition to collecting basic demographic information, the survey consisted of two sections, one about viewing the sidebar and the other about providing feedback. Most questions were answered using a 5-point Likert scale. Fifty-one people completed the survey; 40 were male and almost all filled technical roles, which is consistent with attendee demographics.

Survey Responses

In this section, using the survey responses, we describe how mobile phones were the most popular and least distracting device used for providing feedback, show that providing feedback created engagement with the presentation and other audience members, and discuss some of the unexpected ways that feedback was used.

Mobile Phones Popular for Feedback and Less Distracting

Attendees were asked to answer the survey regardless of whether they had provided feedback during the meeting. However, a majority (84%) reported having used the Crowd Feedback client. Most of those who did not provide feedback said it was because they did not have a mobile device with them. Most (79%) of the people providing feedback used their mobile phones; 12% used laptops, and, in the case of remote participants, 7% used desktop computers. About half of the respondents agreed that they would have used the device in question during the presentation even if not providing feedback. This confirms our expectations that mobile phones are already commonly used by audience members in presentations.

Not requiring specialized hardware makes participation easy, but also makes it more likely people will be distracted by using the feedback device in other ways. The use of a laptop while attending a presentation, for example, has been shown to cause the user to miss useful information [6]. Respondents were evenly split as to whether the Crowd Feedback sidebar was distracting, but, consistent with previous work [7], found the process of providing feedback to be relatively less distracting. Having a multi-purpose device out to provide feedback did not appear to encourage people to disengage from the presentation. Only 23% of respondents agreed that they used the feedback device to do activities not related to providing feedback more than they might have otherwise, while 56% disagreed. Phone users were much less likely to agree with the statement (18%) than computer users (44%), perhaps because phones are small and do not support multi-tasking well.

Feedback Creates Engagement with Presentation, Audience

We now look at whether the Crowd Feedback system helped participants engage with the presentation and other audience members. A summary of these results can be seen in Table 1. Because respondents found the sidebar somewhat distracting, they generally did not believe that it helped them pay closer attention to the presentation. In contrast, however, providing feedback made respondents feel more engaged in the presentation.

		Agree	Neutral	Disagree
Sidebar	Helped me pay closer attention	18%	24%	59%
	Helped me know other's reactions	63%	20%	18%
	I felt closer to the audience	55%	33%	12%
	Was easy to see group feedback	67%	16%	18%
FB	Engaged me with presentation	60%	23%	16%
	Engaged me with the audience	72%	21%	7%

Table 1. Agreement with statements related to the sidebar and providing feedback (FB). Maximum value highlighted per row.

Additionally, both viewing and providing feedback helped audience members feel closer to each other. People viewing feedback reported that doing so helped them understand other's reactions, feel closer to other audience members, and easily see other's feedback. Even more strikingly, 72% of people providing feedback said doing so made them feel closer to other audience members. Overall, seeing feedback appears to have helped people understand the audience, while giving it also helped draw them in to the presentation.

Feedback Sometimes Used in Unexpected Ways

Respondents generally felt comfortable providing feedback, although they were somewhat less comfortable providing negative feedback than positive; 21% agreed they felt uncomfortable giving negative feedback, compared with only 5% for positive. Respondents were asked to provide a free-text description of the sentiment behind their feedback. The most common words used to describe positive feedback were "agree", "good", and "yeah", and to describe negative feedback were "boo", "bad", and "disagree". The words "bored" or "boring" were also used, suggesting the negative feedback button may have been overloaded.

Half of those who provided feedback (21 respondents) reported having done so at some point for reasons other than to convey positive or negative feedback. The most common other reason cited was to find their dot on the sidebar. One person also reported conceptually using the feedback mark interesting locations, similar to the Hotspots approach explored by Kalnikaite et al. [7]. The most commonly requested additional type of feedback to provide related to presentation speed (e.g., "move on" or "too fast").

Feedback Collected

In addition to collecting people's subjective experiences with Crowd Feedback, we also logged the feedback people provided. Figure 4 shows these data as a function of time. Positive feedback is shown in green, and negative in red. Consistent with the fact that people were more comfortable providing positive feedback, a majority (71%) was positive.

The large spike at the beginning of the meeting (at about 10 minutes) and the end (at about 75 minutes) indicate times the presenter actively solicited feedback. In this way he incorporated the feedback system into his presentation in a manner for which it had not explicitly designed. In an interview with the speaker following the presentation, he suggested an explicit voting mechanism could be useful. For example, the speaker could click a button to clear the

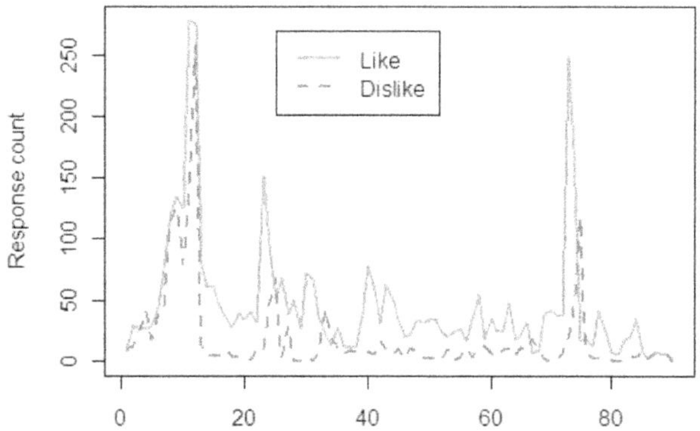

Figure 4. Log data as a function of minutes into the meeting.

existing feedback and enter a voting state where a badge triggers showing the color of the majority vote.

We were somewhat surprised to see that feedback was provided consistently throughout the entire 90 minute presentation, as we had expected people to forget about the system after initially playing with it. In our survey, most people (63%) reported forgetting to provide feedback at some point. Things that reminded them included directed questions by the speaker, new slides, and new topics.

Negative feedback appears to spike fewer times than positive feedback, and to lag positive feedback spikes when they occur. This lag may be because people are emboldened to provide negative feedback after a significant positive feedback event. One survey participant reported that feedback from others sometimes inspired that person to provide feedback. In this way the system may be providing a voice to the minority viewpoint [4]. People also appeared to be more emphatic when providing negative feedback. The mean time between two negative feedback clicks by the same person was only 29 seconds, while the mean time between two positive feedback clicks was 80 seconds.

Badges triggered primarily during the early part of the meeting. The inactivity badge, cued when total feedback activity is low, triggered 24 minutes in and precedes the third largest spike shown in Figure 4. Around 11 minutes in, positive and negative feedback peak within a very short time window, triggering the divisive badge. Reviewing the video shows that the speaker asked a question that divided the audience. When the badge appeared, it elicited laughter.

CONCLUSION AND FUTURE WORK

We have described the Crowd Feedback system, and shown that the ability to share data between ad-hoc, location-based groups of mobile phones can foster rich face-to-face social interactions centered around presentations. Our participants reported that phones were a popular and focused device for providing feedback, and that the process increased audience engagement with the presentation content and with other audience members. Feedback was sometimes used in unexpected ways, and we look forward to supporting richer types of feedback in the future, including polling by the presenter [5] and question asking by audience members [1].

The feedback data collected during a presentation has the potential to have significant value for attendees. Kalnikaite et al. [7] found that when people pressed a button to indicate they had heard something important in a meeting, they were able to use these annotations to recall the meeting several months later. Likewise, we expect the aggregate group feedback to be useful not only during a presentation, but also afterwards, for recall and summarization.

We are particularly interested in exploring how the unique capabilities of mobile phones can improve the feedback experience. Using the touch screen and accelerometer, the phone could recognize gestures and make it possible to provide feedback without attending to the device at all. For example, we observed some users pointed their phones at the sidebar when providing feedback, and this behavior could be used to intelligently target feedback. Likewise, a phone could identify hand raising or clapping, and use that information for feedback. In addition to supporting low-attention input, phones can provide low-attention haptic output via vibration. Just as the presenter's phone vibrates when a badge is triggered, so, too, could audience members', creating communal awareness of feedback events and re-engaging people in the feedback experience.

REFERENCES

1. Anderson, R., Anderson, R., Davis, K.M., Linnell, N., Prince, C. and Razmov, V. Supporting active learning and example based instruction with classroom technology. In *Proc. of SIGCSE*, 2007.
2. boyd, d. Spectacle at Web2.0 Expo... from my perspective. http://zephoria.org, retrieved Feb. 2012.
3. Chamillard, A.T. Using a student response system in CS1 and CS2. In *Proc. of SIGCSE*, 2011.
4. DiMicco, J.M., Pandolfo, A. and Bender, W. Influencing group participation with a shared display. In *Proc. of CSCW*, 2004.
5. Esponda, M. Electronic voting on-the-fly with mobile devices. In *Proc. of ITiCSE*, 2008.
6. Iqbal, S.T., Grudin, J. and Horvitz, E. Peripheral computing during presentations: Perspectives on costs and preferences. In *Proc. of CHI*, 2011.
7. Kalnikaite, V., Ehlen, P. and Whittaker, S. Markup as you talk: Establishing effective memory cues while still contributing to a meeting. In *Proc. of CSCW*, 2012.
8. Lindquist, D., Denning, T., Kelly, M., Malani, R., Griswold, W.G. and Simon, B. Exploring the potential of mobile phones for active learning in the classroom. In *Proc. of SIGCSE*, 2007.
9. Patry, M. Clickers in large classes: From student perceptions towards an understanding of best practices. *International Journal for the Scholarship of Teaching and Learning*, 3:2, July 2009.
10. Yardi, S. Whispers in the classroom. In *Digital Youth, Innovation, and the Unexpected* (ed. McPherson, T.). Cambridge, MA: The MIT Press, 2008, 143-164.

MobiComics: Collaborative Use of Mobile Phones and Large Displays for Public Expression

Andrés Lucero, Jussi Holopainen, Tero Jokela
Nokia Research Center
P.O. Box 1000, FI-33721 Tampere, Finland
{andres.lucero, jussi.holopainen, tero.jokela}@nokia.com

ABSTRACT

We explore shared collocated interactions with mobile phones and public displays in an indoor public place. We introduce *MobiComics,* an application that allows a group of collocated persons to flexibly create and edit comic strip panels using their mobile phones. The prototype supports *ad hoc* sharing of comic strip panels between people and onto two public displays by taking the spatial arrangement of people into account, measured with a radio tracking technology integrated in their mobile phones. *MobiComics* also includes game-like elements to foster social interaction between participants. Our evaluations show that people enjoyed creating panels collaboratively and sharing content using the proposed interaction techniques. The included game-like features positively influenced social interaction.

Author Keywords

Collocated Interaction; Handheld Devices; Public Displays.

ACM Classification Keywords

H.5.m. Information interfaces and presentation (e.g., HCI): Miscellaneous.

INTRODUCTION

Mobile devices have traditionally been very personal devices targeted at individual use. However, over the last years there has been growing interest in systems that couple several mobile devices together and combine them with larger display devices to create broader ecosystems of interaction. Such ecosystems allow groups of collocated users to engage in collaborative activities, thus shifting from *personal-individual* towards *shared-multi-user* interactions. From the designer's point of view, systems involving complex and dynamic geometries of interaction present many challenges over conventional ones. In their taxonomy of multi-person-display ecosystems, Terrenghi *et al.* [32] identify the physical scale of the ecosystem and the nature of the social interaction as their two main attributes.

MobileHCI'12, September 21–24, 2012, San Francisco, CA, USA.

In this paper, we are concerned with collaborative interactions within medium-size groups of approximately 8 to 25 persons in semi-public or public environments such as small cafés or pubs. According to Terrenghi *et al.* [32] such environments can be described as perch-scale ecosystems and the number of users falls between few and many. While some of the persons may be actively engaged in interaction with the system, there may be others with varying levels of awareness of the system and the interaction taking place [24]. As the scale of the system and the number of users increases, not all users can perceive the displays of the mobile devices in the system. Therefore, larger yard-scale public displays must be added to create a common display space. As there typically are far fewer public displays than users, access to the public displays may become a factor limiting the interactions within the system. On the other hand, risk of social embarrassment (e.g., due to making an error in using the system in front of a large audience) may become a deterrent for users to engage in complex interactions on public displays [3,25,29]. Therefore, the role of public displays must be carefully considered in the system design to encourage their fair and efficient use as well as to reduce their irritating or even offending use.

As a practical example of a system supporting rich collaborative interactions within medium-sized groups in (semi-) public places, we present the design and evaluation of *MobiComics*, an application that: 1) allows people to collaboratively create comic strips with their mobile devices, 2) supports different ways to share comic strip panels, including private sharing between devices and sharing with more people over public screens, and 3) features a variety of playful elements to foster social interactions between the participants. In order to allow users to work effectively in parallel without being constrained by limited access to the public displays and to enable different levels of privacy, *MobiComics* supports interactions on three different scales, based on Terrenghi *et al.* [32]. First, two users may couple their devices *ad hoc* to create an inch-scale ecosystem for direct one-to-one interactions. Second, a small number of users can bind their devices together into a yard-scale ecosystem to support collaborative creation of comic strips. Third, all users are part of a perch-scale ecosystem covering the entire physical space (i.e., pub or café) and allowing the sharing of panels on public screens to everybody. In addition to publishing, the users may also pull panels from public displays to their devices, making the public displays a two-way distribution channel. For interactions, the system features extensive use of gestures and spatial interactions, supported by a radio tracking system capable of measuring the positions of the devices relative to each other and to the environment. During a series of evaluations of *MobiComics* in authentic settings, the participants made a versatile use of the different system features, illustrating different strategies for creating and sharing content.

The rest of this paper is organized as follows. We begin by reviewing the relevant related work. Then, we describe the design principles and interaction techniques of *MobiComics* in detail. Finally, we report the results of a series of user evaluations, followed by discussion and conclusions.

RELATED WORK

A large body of related work has influenced the design of *MobiComics*. We have identified three main related-work areas: mobile collocated interactions, interacting with public displays, and applications for public expression.

Mobile Collocated Interactions

One group of applications has supported *ad hoc* collocated collaborative work using mobile devices. In Luyten *et al.* [18], personal displays are tracked and used to share a common information space (i.e., a map), providing peepholes to the data set. Their setup requires external equipment in the form of three infrared towers to track the positions of the devices. Siftables [19] consist of a group of compact display devices that communicate wirelessly and form a sensor network. Although they were conceived with a single user in mind, Siftables have the potential to support mobile collaborative interactions. One limitation of this system is that the positions of the Siftables can only be detected when placed adjacently one next to the other.

Another group of applications has specifically provided support for collocated photo sharing. Ah Kun *et al.* [1] propose a network of PDAs that allows any user of a group to broadcast images on the other devices in that group. Images are transferred wirelessly using Wi-Fi. Their prototype incorporates a series of floor-control policies or software locks that determine who can control the show and when, in order to study how to best manage social interaction. Mobiphos [5] supports capturing and real-time sharing of photos among members of a collocated group using cameraphones. The application presents users with an updated stream of picture thumbnails made by the group. The display is used both as a viewfinder and a thumbnail gallery. Data is transferred between devices using Wi-Fi. Disc-O-Share [14] allows browsing and transferring photos between mobile phones by creating three distal regions around mobile phones. Particular actions are triggered in response to entering or leaving these regions. An external camera tracks the position of the phones by reading visual markers displayed at the top of each device's screen.

Many of the previously described systems require a dedicated infrastructure (e.g., infrared tracking or camera) for position tracking. In *MobiComics,* we provide a 3D tracking solution that is built in the phone, which allows us to detect where the phones are with respect to each other without external equipment. We have demonstrated this technology earlier for an application that supports photo sharing [17]. In addition, studies of the systems discussed here have been limited to small groups of people from two to six persons. In this paper, we study collocated interactions for a group of nine persons.

Interacting with Public Displays

In recent years, there has been an increasing interest within the HCI community in designing, deploying, and studying the use of large interactive displays. In the following review, we focus on findings that stem from user studies of public displays, especially ones that relate to supporting collocated interactions in (semi-) public settings. BlueBoard [27] is an augmented noticeboard that supports lightweight walk up and use interactions. Identified users can quickly retrieve personal information stored on a network, display it on the board, and share it with others via, e.g., email. The authors found that collocated people interacting at the board were able to coordinate their joint actions and thus complex floor control policies were not necessary. Dynamo [12] is a set of large multi-user interactive surfaces that support sharing and exchanging media content. Whenever participants' actions overlapped, people would often speak aloud to make others aware of the overlap or to apologize for their own actions. Similar to what Russell *et al.* noticed with the BlueBoard [27], emerging social protocols allowed resolving the overlaps easily. More recently, CityWall [23] is a large multi-touch interactive display installed in Helsinki's city center that serves as an open platform for passers-by to play around and explore public photos. The authors describe the importance of repurposing existing elements in the available space (i.e., a shop window) to avoid changing how people move.

Although most of these systems have concentrated on large interactive displays, others have considered adding personal mobile devices as part of the interaction [20,25,29,31]. The Pebbles system [20] was one of the first to explore multi-user interactive displays by connecting PDAs that provide concurrent input to a large shared display. The authors suggested that the PDAs could be used as a private space whenever users feel like composing content before sharing it with the group on a public display. The MAGICBoard [31] is a public display deployed in a university setting that solicits votes and opinions on trivial topics from bystanders via SMS or from a laptop. Users post text-based items on the display, which persist until newer items push them off-screen. The authors found that users posting messages from their phones (instead of the laptop) tended to leave longer, more thoughtful messages.

Applications for Public Expression

In Schminky [25], users play together a spontaneous, networked sound-based game using mobile devices (iPAQs) and public displays. The system was evaluated during a weeklong field trial in a café. The game increased the social interaction at the bar by acting as a spur for people to find out who the Schminky players at other tables were. The authors also reported that due to the small size of the device, players were able to interleave playing Schminky with other activities such as gesturing, holding food, or drinking. MobiLenin [29] allows multi-user interaction with a multi-track music video shown on a public display. People can direct the outcome of the video in real time by voting for one of six video tracks from their personal mobile phones. The authors found that empowering people with the joint ownership of the contents motivated users to interact with the public display. During a one-session evaluation in a pub, the authors found that the system had a positive effect on the social interactions that took place at the pub. We deployed *MobiComics* in an *indoor public place* (i.e., at a pub and two social events) to study how people experience the prototype in a situation that is as realistic as possible.

DESIGN OF MOBICOMICS

Based on the relevant literature, we decided to design and implement the *MobiComics* prototype that: 1) allows a group of collocated people to flexibly create and edit comic strips from their mobile phones, 2) supports *ad-hoc* sharing of comic strip panels onto two public displays by taking the spatial arrangement of people into account, and 3) includes game-like elements to foster social interactions between the participants. In other words, *MobiComics* combines a mobile application as a creative tool, a public display as a sharing device, direct social interaction between the participants, and the use of photos from the situation, all as part of an integrated experience.

Creating Content from the Privacy of a Mobile Phone

Studies have identified social embarrassment as a core deterrent to users interacting with a public display in front of an audience [3,25,29]. For example, when typing a message in real time on a public display people feel self-conscious about making and correcting spelling mistakes, taking too long to write an entry, or formulating something inappropriate for the current social situation [3].

To help people cope with social pressure, we support creating and editing comic strips from the privacy of their mobile phones [20]. Sub-group members can discuss panels face-to-face and correct potential mistakes before sending them onto the public displays. Once published on a large display, it is possible for the others to identify which sub-group created a panel but not its individual author, thus supporting anonymous participation.

Flexible Sharing onto and from Public Displays

We extend the existing work on mobile collocated interactions by incorporating public displays. In doing so, we introduce a series of 2D and 3D gestures that allow people to physically throw panels in a given physical space (i.e., inside the pub) as opposed to requiring them to concentrate on the mobile user interface (UI) to select contents and recipients (e.g., from a pull-down menu). We include 2D and 3D gesture-based aesthetic interactions (i.e., flicking, holding, tilting, shaking, picking up) by fully exploiting the affordances of touch UIs and accelerometers in contemporary smartphones.

We support *ad-hoc* sharing of comic strip panels using devices enhanced with radio tracking technology [2], which allows tracking the relative positions of the devices (and the two public displays). The sensors embedded in the mobile phones allow us to know where each sub-group (member) is located inside the pub. In this way, we are able to send panels from one sub-group to another, as well as to send panels onto and receive panels from a public display even when sub-group members are moving in the environment.

Game-Like Elements to Foster Social Interactions

The combination of collocated use of mobile phones and public displays generates interesting possibilities for sharing information and media, as well as for socializing. Besides supporting collaboration between sub-team members, we are interested in studying social interactions as part of the larger interaction with the prototype.

We include game-like elements to stimulate social interactions between sub-groups. For example, a voting system is included as part of the interaction to motivate people to participate by creating a competitive situation between sub-groups. Public displays play a double role of allowing members of the audience to first discover the application and then potentially voice their opinions on the published comics during voting.

INTERACTION

With *MobiComics,* three sub-groups of people (hereafter teams) use their mobile phones to create and edit comic strips, as well as to publish panels onto two public displays.

Creating and Editing Panels

At the start of the interaction, nine people are split into three teams: cyan, magenta, and yellow. After starting the application, each team member is presented with their team's empty panel collection. Each team member can then start creating panels from their device. To create a panel, users must first take a photo with their cameraphone. Users must open the lens cover, which activates the viewfinder, and take a photo. After closing the lens cover, the captured photo can be used as background for a panel. Each captured photo is automatically shared to the team's panel collection, which can be browsed by flicking the panels left or right.

Figure 1. Panel Creation with the different speech bubble types. (a) A red bubble in *edit mode*, and (b) a black bubble currently being edited by another team member.

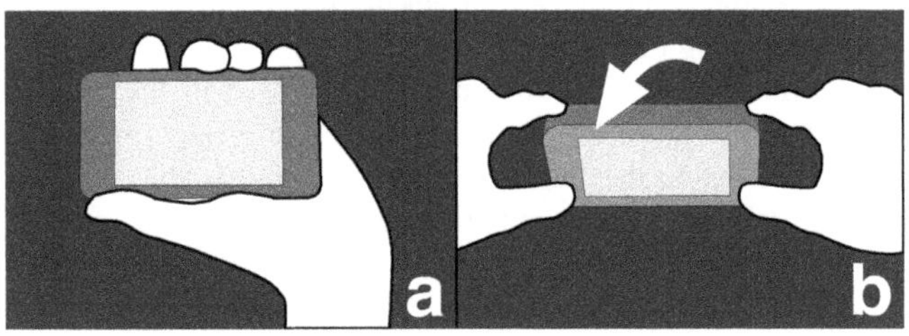

Figure 2. (a) Holding the device up in the air to receive a panel from another team, and (b) tilting vertically towards oneself to take a panel from a public display.

By tapping on a panel from the collection, people are able to edit the panel. Users can add speech bubbles to the panel by performing a long press anywhere on the panel. A red bubble is displayed under the user's finger, indicating that it is in *edit mode* (Figure 1a). Using the physical flip keyboard, users can directly type text onto the bubble, which dynamically changes its shape to accommodate text. To change the shape of the speech bubble users must shake the device, which results in cycling through three bubble types: speech, thought or text box. Users can also modify the position of the bubble and of the bubble tip by dragging either of them with their finger on the touchscreen. While still in *edit mode*, speech bubbles can be deleted by flipping the device upside down. As the screen is no longer visible, a trashcan sound effect provides feedback. To end the *edit mode*, users must tap outside the speech bubble, which then goes back to white. *MobiComics* supports creating panels collaboratively. Team members can edit the same panel simultaneously, but only one person can edit a given bubble at a time. Users can then see in real time when another team member is editing a bubble, which is shown in black (Figure 1b). Other systems such as Comeks [28], the mobile multimedia presentation editor [13] and Automics [6] provide similar ways to annotate photographs in a comic-strip style. However, these systems only allow sharing panels to one other person or to other users of the system.

Sharing Panels onto the Public Displays (Throwing)

MobiComics supports different ways to share panels. First, users can send a panel from their own collection to one of two public displays available in the room (Figure 3.1). The public displays are positioned so that members of the three teams and the crowd members are able to get a clear view of them. To share a panel to a public display, users first select a panel from the team's panel collection and perform a long press on that panel. A thumbnail of the panel is displayed under the user's finger, which can be moved around by dragging the finger on the touchscreen. The panel can then be thrown in the direction of the desired public display by flicking the thumbnail. The devices are fitted with a radio tracking technology to detect the relative positions of the other devices and the two public displays. If no public display is found in the direction the panel was thrown, then the panel briefly shakes back and forth on the sender's device. However, if a public display is located in the direction the panel was thrown, the panel is shown on the public display. The new panel fills up the public display and is shown on top of any other existing panel until a new panel is shared by any of the three teams. An animation shows the direction the new panel is coming from. Throwing panels to public displays makes use of existing multi-display reaching techniques [21].

Sharing Panels with Another Team (Send to Me)

Second, users can send a panel from their own collection to another team (Figure 3.2). To achieve this, one team member on the receiving side must first verbally ask for a panel and then hold the phone up in the air pointing towards the other team, thus expressing the intention to receive a panel (Figure 2a). As the user can no longer see the screen, a subtle vibration is triggered to confirm the device is ready to receive a panel. The screen on that device displays a scrolling *"send to me"* on top of the receiving team's color. With this interaction technique we are exploring the use of mobile phones to display information in public. Once a member from the sending team has spotted this cue, they can then flick a panel to the group that is holding one of their devices up. The throwing mechanism includes the same actions and visual feedback described in the previous section. Additionally, a strong vibration is triggered on both ends to confirm the panel was successfully received. The received panel is automatically shared to the team's panel collection.

Taking Panels from the Public Displays (Retrieving)

Third, users can take a panel from a public display and add it to their team's panel collection (Figure 3.3). To achieve this, users must point with their device towards a public display and tilt [4] the device vertically towards themselves by performing a quick upward movement and bringing it back to the starting position (Figure 2b). An animation showing how the panel taken from the public display is added to the team's collection together with a strong vibration provide feedback to the user.

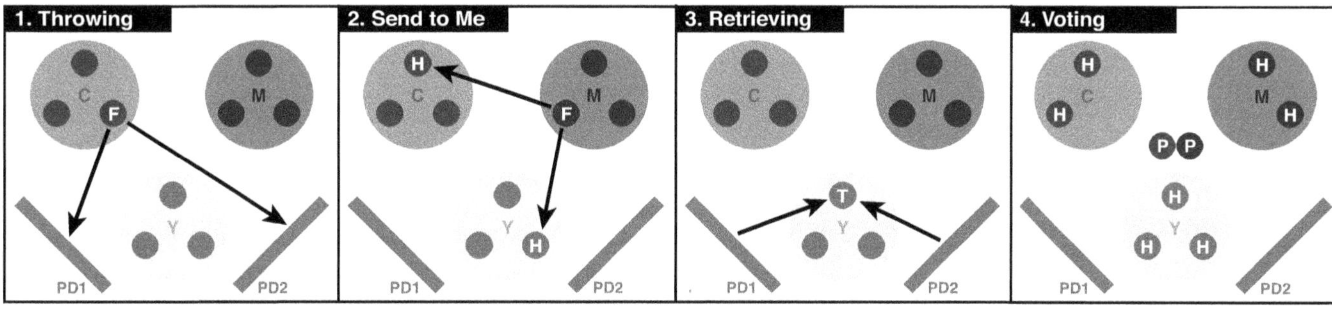

Figure 3. Interaction techniques in *MobiComics*. Nine participants split into three groups: cyan (C), magenta (M) and yellow (Y). 1) Throwing: flicking (F) panels to either public displays (PD1 or PD2). 2) Send to me: flicking (F) a panel while a member from another group holds a device up (H). 3) Retrieving: taking a panel by pointing towards PD1 or PD2 and tilting (T) the device towards thems. 4) Voting: two members, each from a different team, pinch (P) vertically and hold their devices up in the air (H).

Viewing All Panels Shown on the Public Displays

The contents of the public displays are constantly changing depending on how actively participants are throwing panels onto them. As a result, users may miss some of the public display panels. To solve this, each team can access the public display contents locally. Two members of the same team must align their devices horizontally on the short edge and then pinch their devices together [16]. Alternative ways to connect two devices together include: knocking devices together to detect synchronized sounds [26], bumping devices together using accelerometer data [8], and performing pen gestures on touch-enabled devices [9]. When two devices are successfully tiled together, a collection of public panels or panels that have been shown on the public display is presented on the tiled displays. Users can simply browse the public panels by flicking the collection left or right. This composite version of the collection spans both devices allowing users to see the public panels in greater detail. Devices can be disconnected from the tiled view by physically picking them up.

Picking the Best Panels from the Session (Voting)

In an attempt to involve all three teams (and potentially the members of the crowd) in the interaction, *MobiComics* allows people to publicly vote for the best panel of the session (Figure 3.4). To trigger the voting mode, two members, each from a different team, must align their devices, this time vertically on the long edge, and pinch them together (Figure 4a). Requiring two teams to trigger voting prevents having one team dominating the situation, e.g., by continuously pushing new panels for voting. When voting is triggered, an overview of all the panels that have been shown on the public displays is presented both on the tiled devices and on the public displays, thus providing feedback for the members of the crowd. Flicking the public panels up or down results in browsing the overview. This overview is shown on the public displays to create an opportunity for other team members and potentially the audience to influence which panel they would like users to vote on. Meanwhile, the seven remaining participants (see Figure 3.4 for those participants marked with an H) are invited to join the vote by displaying a blinking *"voting ongoing"* inside a large white hand with its thumb sticking up on top of the corresponding team's color.

When a panel is selected from the tiled devices, all remaining team members are prompted to vote. The large white hand starts slowly blinking together with a gentle vibration to encourage users to cast their votes from their devices in favor or against the currently displayed panel. To vote, users must briefly hold the device in the air with the image of the hand pointing its thumb up or down for a positive or negative vote respectively (Figure 4b). This is a second interaction technique that we implemented to explore the use of mobile phones to display information in public. To provide feedback, a strong vibration is triggered on the device, *"Positive/Negative vote cast"* is shown on the device's display, and the number of positive and negative votes is updated on the public display. Voting continues when the next panel is selected, triggering a new voting round. Users can only cast one vote per round, however it is possible to have more than one round per panel. To stop the voting mode, users must physically pick up the connected devices. The remaining participants can then resume the activity they were on when voting started.

EVALUATION

In order to assess the proposed interaction techniques and study how people experience the *MobiComics* prototype, we arranged four evaluation sessions in authentic settings. We collected qualitative data both during the interaction with *MobiComics* and later during semi-structured interviews. Quantitative data was collected by means of a validated questionnaire after a task related to the prototype.

Figure 4. (a) Pinching two devices vertically to trigger voting, and (b) holding a device upright to cast a positive vote.

Figure 5. Evaluation setup. Members of the yellow team creating panels (left), two pub guests conversing (center), a public display showing a panel from the magenta team (right).

Participants

The evaluation was conducted with 36 participants. Each of the four sessions included nine people (i.e., three groups of three friends). We recruited groups of friends, rather than isolated individuals, so participants would feel comfortable expressing themselves around one another. In each session, there were two groups of three friends who knew each other well and at least one acquaintance in common in the third group. The participants were chosen to represent a variety of user types, including parents, international students and professionals. The participants varied in gender (27 male, 9 female), age (between 20 and 43), and background (26 technical, 10 non-technical). All of them owned a mobile phone, different from the one used in the study. Most participants often went to pubs and cafés.

Method

Each two-hour session consisted of four parts: introduction, exploration, task, and semi-structured interview. First, we gathered participants' background information and we explained the purpose of the evaluation to them (10 min). Second, we briefly explained participants how to interact with the *MobiComics* prototype. We then allowed them to explore the available functionality and get acquainted with the application (20 min.). Third, participants freely used *MobiComics* to create and share comic strip panels between teams and onto the public displays (30 min.). At the end of the session, we asked participants to fill-out the AttrakDiff [7] questionnaire to quantitatively measure pragmatic and hedonic aspects of the prototype. AttrakDiff measures the attractiveness of interactive products along four dimensions. Pragmatic quality (PQ) refers to the product's ability to support the achievement of behavioral goals (i.e., usability). Hedonic quality refers to the users' self: stimulation (HQ-S) is the product's ability to stimulate and enable personal growth (i.e., aspirations), and identification (HQ-I), is the product's ability to address the need of expressing one's self through objects one owns (i.e., social aspects of product ownership). Both HQ-S and HQ-I have been found to contribute to perceived attractiveness (ATT), which describes a global value of the product based on the quality perception. Participants indicate their perception of the product by rating 28 pairs of opposite adjectives that relate to the four dimensions on a 7-point scale (-3 to 3). Finally, we had semi-structured interviews with each group in which we asked a consistent set of open-ended questions, prompting participants to reflect back on some of their interaction experiences with the prototype (60 min.). All sessions including the semi-structured interviews were recorded on video using three stationary cameras, one for each group. After the interviews, participants were given one movie ticket each to compensate them for their time.

The four sessions were conducted in three different indoor locations. The first session was conducted in the common room area of the Game Research Laboratory at the University of Tampere during a social event of an international research seminar. The second and third sessions took place at The Dog's Home pub in the city center of Tampere (Figure 5). The fourth session was done in a common room area of the Innovation Center, a facility for cooperation between local universities and companies. Despite the differences between these three locations (i.e., *semi-public* vs. *public* places), the four sessions had many things in common. There was roughly the same amount of people at each location (less than 30 persons, including the nine participants), creating a natural and quiet atmosphere. The two pub sessions were conducted in the evening to ensure that there would be enough guests. In all sessions, there was music playing in the background, people were chatting and drinking. Each participant was provided with one device running the prototype. Participants were either sitting or standing around three tables. The tables were (as much as possible) evenly spaced from one another, in a triangle formation. The two public displays (i.e., projection displays or large LCD screens) were placed on opposite sides of the rooms. By maintaining this spatial structure, we hoped that the interaction would be smoothly balanced both across teams and with the respective public displays.

Affinity diagramming [11] was used to analyze data from the observations of use and the semi-structured interviews. Two researchers independently made notes as they watched the videos for each session. The qualitative data was then collaboratively analyzed through several interpretation rounds. The affinity diagram supported categorization and visualization of the main themes emerging from the data. These themes form the heart of our findings section.

Implementation

We developed a prototype of *MobiComics* on Nokia N900 mobile devices running the Maemo Linux operating system. The prototype was built on top of the Social and Spatial Interactions (SSI) software platform [15] that provides reusable components for rapid development of mobile applications that support rich local collaborative interactions. The SSI software platform was implemented in C++ using the Qt 4.7 software framework. The user interface was developed with Qt Quick and OpenGL ES 2.0 rendering was used for fluent user interface graphics, e.g., animations for moving, rotating, and zooming the panels. A local Wi-Fi network was used to connect the devices to each other and coordinate the application state between the devices. In order to display events across different devices, the devices' clocks were synchronized.

The N900's internal accelerometer was used to detect when a device was picked up from the table, when it was tilted, or when it was held up in the air. When the sensor showed a constant pull toward the back of the device, it was deduced that the device was on the table. When there was a constant and distinguishable pull in a given direction, it was recognized as a tilt or as holding the device up in the air in a certain position. In all other cases, the device was considered to be in free manipulation in the user's hands.

To detect the positions of other devices and the public displays inside the room (e.g., to flick a panel to another device or to a public display), we utilized N900 devices enhanced with radio tracking technology [2]. This particular technology tracks the angular position and distance between devices by embedding multi-antenna receivers under the devices' screen and running sensor array signal processing algorithms on each device. This allows the technology to track multiple emitters such as active RF tags for the public displays or mobile phones.

FINDINGS

Different Panel Creation Strategies

People used different strategies to create panels within each team. All participants were able to create panels by taking a photo and adding speech bubbles. In general, participants considered adding and editing speech bubbles an important part of creating panels and thus took their time to carefully craft each panel. The within-team collaboration created a safe environment for people to freely express themselves before exposing the content to a wider audience. In that sense, working from the mobile devices and checking the panel contents before making them public helped reduce the embarrassment reported in other studies [3].

The device gestures introduced during panel creation (i.e., *shaking* to change bubble shape and *flipping upside down* to delete a bubble) were often used and described as *"natural and logical."* Most participants (32/36) were positive about *shaking* to change bubble shape due to a combination of clear visual feedback and a familiar interaction style: *"Shaking the bubble was really clear, the feedback was quite fast and you see the bubble changing."* (P8) Deleting a speech bubble by *flipping the device upside down* was often used and was well received by the participants. However, two participants commented that the trashcan sound was strange: *"Deleting is really nice. If (panel creation is) only based on touch, then people will feel bored."* (P30) *"But the sound is weird."* (P31)

We observed three main panel creation strategies, which evenly occurred during the four sessions. First, in some teams, members worked individually taking their own photos and editing their own panels. Although some social interaction was observed between team members (i.e., showing panels to other team members from their own devices, helping each other out), these participants spent most of their time focusing on their own devices during panel creation. There was a sense of ownership to the panels made within these teams as a single person created them. Due to this, some participants were unsure about editing someone else's panel: *"I think I added something to the pictures created by others, but there was a barrier to start tampering with somebody else's work."* (P25)

Second, other teams more openly collaborated during panel creation. Some groups planned how to create panels within the team and coordinated their actions accordingly. These groups used the real-time editing possibilities offered by *MobiComics* to create panels collaboratively, which provided clues to what other team members were doing: *"It was fun that you could see the bubbles that the others were editing in real time on your own display."* (P27) The team members in these groups flexibly changed between tasks and thus there were no fixed roles for each team member.

Finally, a third strategy consisted of having fixed complementary roles throughout the session. Similarly to the second group, the members of these teams collaborated during panel creation, however in this case they had a clear role division. As a result, one person took photos, another was in charge of adding and editing speech bubbles, and the last dealt with sharing and retrieving panels: *"It was kind of fun to create collaborative panels: one takes pictures, one adds the bubbles, and one sends it."* (P8)

Regarding the panel contents, participants mainly captured objects found in their immediate surroundings. They did not intentionally manipulate the environment much. The other source of content for the panels was people, including team members and members of the other teams. A few participants (4/36) raised their concerns about taking photos of other people as the subject for the panels, especially if they were members of the audience. From the participants' point of view, the main motivation to create panels was to make something funny and creative: *"We were trying to make funny stuff; maybe some arty or creative stuff."* (P8)

Different Panel Sharing Strategies

We introduced three main methods to share panels onto and retrieve panels from the public displays (i.e., *throwing, send to me,* and *retrieving*). First, participants could *share panels onto the public displays*. All participants were able to share their individual panels by throwing them across the room to one of the two public displays available. Participants created and shared a total of 150 panels onto the public displays during the four sessions (Mean=37.5, SD=5.5). Each team created on average 12.5 panels per session (SD=4.75). A new panel was shared on either of the public displays every 48 seconds. This provides a rough estimate of how often the contents were changing on the public displays. As mentioned previously, participants took their time to carefully craft each panel, which partly explains why participants did not create and share panels more often. Out of the total number of panels, 23% of the panels were direct responses to a panel that had previously been shared on the public display (35/150). Some of those responses were made by members of the same team (19/150), and the rest came from other teams (16/150). The longest chain of direct responses published on the public displays was four panels long. Participants said the use of the spatial arrangement of people inside the pub or social event allowed them to easily share panels to the public displays and other teams. *Throwing* was an intuitive gesture to share panels onto the public displays and the other people in the pub. *"It is really nice, it makes it easier to send something to a person or just aim wherever you want."* (P14) On the AttrakDiff questionnaire (Figure 6), the prototype is located in the above-average region on the attractiveness (ATT) dimension and thus the overall impression of the prototype is very attractive. These high ratings indicate that the participants perceive the prototype as motivating and appealing. Members of a same team successfully but only occasionally tiled two of their devices together to browse the collection of public panels.

Second, participants shared panels with other teams by holding a device up in the air in all four sessions. The gesture itself was often used and was perceived as *"fun and unique."* On stimulation (HQ-S), the first hedonic quality dimension of AttrakDiff (Figure 6), the prototype is clearly in the above-average region implying that people think the prototype is creative and inventive. Most participants referred to the two interaction techniques that explore the use of mobile phones to display information in public (i.e., *'send to me'* and *voting*) as fun and novel, and this rating on the AttrakDiff questionnaire supports that notion. The gesture was originally designed so that if a user would spot a member of another team taking an interesting photo (e.g., a person making a funny face), the user would be able to request that photo immediately (*'send to me'*) without having to wait for the panel to show up on a public display. A few participants (9/36) explicitly commented that the initiation to share panels should come from the sending side: *"It's almost as if it should be the other way round. 'Oh, I've got a cool photo, I want to send it to you.'"* (P30) However, as the users on the receiving side were unable to see the panel contents beforehand, in some cases they requested the sending team to share the panel to the public display first, and after checking the quality of the panel, they retrieved it to their own collection from the public display. In practice, we observed that members of both the sending and the receiving ends had genuine reasons to initiate the sharing of panels. Regarding the device gesture (i.e., holding the device up in the air), some participants (9/36) raised their concerns about performing large, visible gestures while holding their mobile phones in public, which can be socially awkward [22]. Since the use of mobile phones to display information in public is not widespread, a few participants thought the crowd might start wondering what that person holding the device in the air in the middle of the pub is up to: *"It might look strange to hold the phone up if not everyone is in on what I am doing."* (P17)

Third, participants again described the gesture for *retrieving* panels from the public display as *"natural."* Participants retrieved panels several times during each session, although less frequently than they sent panels directly to another team. Participants used this gesture mostly to directly respond to another team's panel or when they saw something interesting on the public displays. *"When I saw something cool up there, I asked P28 to grab it."* (P30)

One additional sharing strategy consisted of showing panels directly from the devices. Participants shared information about panels by showing their devices' screen to one or two other members of the same team. As an example, in session three one participant (P26) took her device to show everyone in her team a panel that she had just made, while she explained her intentions to them.

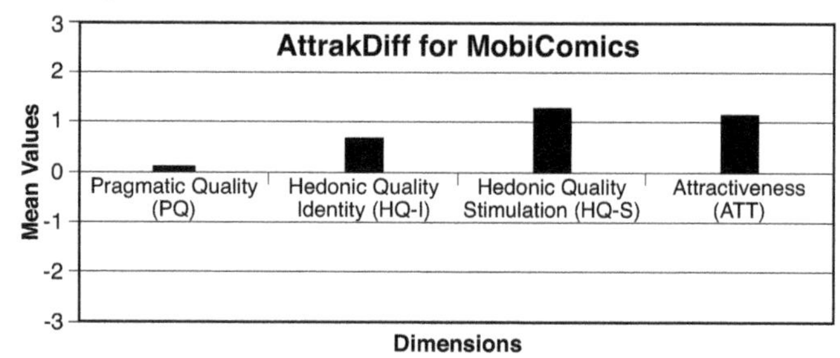

Figure 6. Mean values along the four AttrakDiff dimensions.

Social Interaction Between Groups

As previously mentioned, *voting* was created to involve all three teams and the audience in the interaction by means of a public vote. Voting was triggered between one and three times per session. Each voting session lasted between one and four minutes. It took the teams approximately one minute to select a panel, open the voting, cast the votes and close the voting to select a new panel. Therefore, between one and four panels were voted upon in each voting session. In MobiLenin [29] voting also took one minute, which gives participants a chance to contemplate, celebrate and prepare before the next voting round takes place. During voting, the social interaction between team members was at its peak with lively discussions and laughter. On the other hedonic quality dimension of AttrakDiff, i.e., identity (HQ-I), the prototype is located in the average region, which means that people think the prototype is connective and integrating, but at the same time is not stylish enough for users to fully identify with it. However, this rating confirms the prototype encourages social interaction between people.

Initiating voting required a team member from one team to move to another team's table and connect their devices. All participants were able to successfully tile the displays together by performing the pinch gesture. However, some participants (13/36) commented that this procedure felt artificial and that it broke the flow of interaction. Participants would have preferred to be able to start the vote from within their teams: *"It would've been nice to initiate voting without having to go to another group but having the three of us and we want to vote on this."* (P30) When voting is triggered using two devices, all ongoing activities are interrupted on the remaining seven devices. Although users can later resume the activity where they left it off at the end of the vote, participants felt it was distracting: *"The whole system shut down when there was voting. I would like to continue taking pictures and (then vote) whenever it says 'vote now.'"* (P6) On the AttrakDiff questionnaire (Figure 6), the prototype was only rated as average on the pragmatic quality (PQ) dimension, which means there is room for improvement in terms of usability. Forcing participants to join voting while in the middle of another activity may have impacted the ratings on this dimension.

With voting we were also trying to study the use of mobile phones to display information in public. To cast a vote, users had to briefly hold their device in the air showing an image of a hand pointing its thumb up or down. This gesture was highly visible due to a combination of holding the device up in the air and the bright graphics displayed on the screen. Members of the crowd were easily able to identify whether people were giving a panel a thumbs up or down from a distance (i.e., from anywhere at the pub or social event). In that respect, the mobile phones were successfully used to display information in public. This is further confirmed by the comments from a few participants (6/36) who felt the pressure of publicly revealing their vote to others: *"I have the desire to vote in secret, especially when voting thumbs down."* (P25) Some participants even cheated the system by either doing a small secretive gesture that was not visible to others, by turning the screen away from the crowd (i.e., when located near a wall), or by physically faking a thumbs-up gesture while the image on the screen is displaying a thumbs-down.

DISCUSSION

Collocated Interactions Using Personal Mobile Phones

Participants were positive about using their personal devices to create a common interaction space, but some of them (8/36) were more specific and said they would share their devices with people they know and trust, rather than with complete strangers. One limitation of the *MobiComics* evaluation is that participants were not using their personal mobile phones during the interaction. Participants were using N900 devices enhanced with position tracking, and thus we are unable to fully answer whether they would actually lend their personal phones. In spite of this, the evaluation setup provided a realistic enough situation for us to study. For example, participants were able to raise some privacy concerns regarding taking pictures of strangers at the pub (18/36) and keeping *MobiComics* panels at the end of the session (10/36). For more details on privacy while people interacted with *MobiComics* see [10].

Overall Impression

We have presented the AttrakDiff results by mapping its four dimensions to the different interaction strategies used by the participants. We will now discuss these results in more depth. On the AttrakDiff questionnaire (Figure 6), *MobiComics* was rated in the above-average region on the hedonic quality stimulation (HQ-S) and attractiveness (ATT) dimensions, and as average on the hedonic quality identification (HQ-I) and pragmatic quality (PQ). In other words, the pragmatic value is considered as average while hedonic values are high. *MobiComics* includes 2D and 3D gesture-based aesthetic interactions (i.e., flicking, tilting, shaking) by maximizing the affordances of touch UIs and accelerometers. Participants found these interaction techniques to be novel and fun, but at the same time the interaction techniques were not particularly better in terms of helping participants achieve their goals. Some of the proposed interaction techniques could indeed be simplified and make use of more conventional (mobile) interaction techniques to improve the overall usability of *MobiComics*.

Mobile Devices as Public Displays

MobiComics makes use of users' mobile phone displays to show information in public. Both *send to me* and *voting* display a large scrolling text and an animated hand that are visible to any user from a distance of several meters. All people in the room, including the users not actively engaged with the system, can easily observe these large animations. These uses of mobile device displays lead us to consider the more general idea of using mobile devices as public displays to share information among larger groups of people. While the physical size of a mobile device display is small, it can still be observed from long distances – only the resolution of the display will decrease as the distance increases due to the limited resolution of the human eye. Even if the mobile device display only allows low-resolution images to be shown, larger amounts of information could be presented by using animations, e.g., scrolling text. Ultimately, with increasing distance, the mobile device display would become a one-pixel display. Knowing the relative positions of the devices would allow creating more complex visualizations [30]. The idea of utilizing mobile device displays as public displays offers an interesting line of research for further study.

CONCLUSION

The *MobiComics* prototype allows a medium-sized group of people to create, edit, and share comic strip panels. The prototype encourages people to create panels from the privacy of their mobile device and with the help of their team members by discussing face-to-face. Using devices fitted with radio tracking technology to detect their current location, people are able to share panels to other team members and onto two public displays. Playful elements are included in the prototype to foster social interactions between the participants. Evaluations in authentic settings (i.e., at a pub and at two social events) showed that people enjoyed creating and sharing their panels using our interaction techniques. The game-like elements of the prototype positively influenced social interactions, but at the same time raised some concerns about the visibility of some gestures in public settings.

REFERENCES

1. Ah Kun L. M. and Marsden, G. Co-present photo sharing on mobile devices. *Proc. MobileHCI '07,* ACM, 277-284.
2. Belloni, F., Kainulainen, A., Richter, A. and Koivunen, V. Direction Finding Based Multi-Emitter Tracking System for Mobile Phones. *ICASSP '09 Show&Tell.*
3. Brignull, H. and Rogers, Y. Enticing people to interact with large public displays in public spaces. *Proc. Interact '03*, IOS Press (2003), Amsterdam, 17–24.
4. Cho, S., Murray-Smith, R. and Kim, Y. Multi-context photo browsing on mobile devices based on tilt dynamics. *Proc. MobileHCI '07,* ACM Press (2007), 190-197.
5. Clawson, J., Voida, A., Patel, N. and Lyons, K. Mobiphos: a collocated-synchronous mobile photo sharing application. *Proc. MobileHCI '08,* ACM Press (2008), 187-195.
6. Durrant, A., Rowland, D., Kirk, D.S., Benford, S., Fischer, J.E. and McAuley, D. Automics: souvenir generating photoware for theme parks. *Proc. CHI '11,* ACM Press (2011), 1767-1776.
7. Hassenzahl, M. The interplay of beauty, goodness, and usability in interactive products. *Human-Computer Interaction 19,* 4 (2004), 319-349.
8. Hinckley, K. Synchronous gestures for multiple persons and computers. *Proc. UIST '03,* ACM (2003), 149-158.
9. Hinckley, K., Ramos, G., Guimbretiere, F., Baudisch, P. and Smith, M. Stitching: pen gestures that span multiple displays. *Proc. AVI '04,* ACM Press (2004), 23-31.
10. Holopainen, J., Lucero, A., Saarenpää, H., Nummenmaa, T., El Ali, A. and Jokela, T. Social and privacy aspects of a system for collaborative public expression. *Proc. ACE '11*, ACM Press (2011), Article 23, 8 pages.
11. Holtzblatt, K., Wendell, J.B. and Wood, S. *Rapid Contextual Design.* Morgan Kaufmann, 2005.
12. Izadi, S., Brignull, H., Rodden, T., Rogers, Y. and Underwood, M. Dynamo: a public interactive surface supporting the cooperative sharing and exchange of media. *Proc. UIST '03*, ACM Press (2003), 159-168.
13. Jokela, T., Lehikoinen, J.T. and Korhonen, H. Mobile Multimedia Presentation Editor: Enabling Creation of Audio-Visual Stories on Mobile Devices. *Proc. CHI '08,* ACM Press (2008), 63-72.
14. Kray, C., Rohs, M., Hook, J. and Kratz, S. Bridging the gap between the Kodak and the Flickr generations: A novel interaction technique for collocated photo sharing. *Int. J. Hum.-Comput. Stud. 67,* 12 (2009), 1060-1072.
15. Lucero, A., Keränen, J. and Jokela, T. Social and spatial interactions: shared co-located mobile phone use. *Proc. CHI EA '10*, ACM Press (2010), 3223-3228.
16. Lucero, A., Keränen, J. and Korhonen, H. Collaborative use of mobile phones for brainstorming. *Proc. MobileHCI '10*, ACM Press (2010), 337-340.
17. Lucero, A., Holopainen, J. and Jokela, T. Pass-them-around: collaborative use of mobile phones for photo sharing. *Proc. CHI '11*, ACM Press (2011), 1787-1796.
18. Luyten, K., Verpoorten, K. and Coninx, K. Ad-hoc co-located collaborative work with mobile devices. *Proc. MobileHCI '07*, ACM Press (2007), 507-514.
19. Merrill, D., Kalanithi, J. and Maes, P. Siftables: towards sensor network user interfaces. *Proc. TEI '07,* ACM, 75-78.
20. Myers, B., Stiel, H. and Gargiulo, R. Collaboration using multiple PDAs connected to a PC. *Proc. CSCW '98*, ACM Press (1998), 285-294.
21. Nacenta, M., Aliakseyeu, D., Subramanian, S. and Gutwin, C. A comparison of techniques for multi-display reaching. *Proc. CHI '05,* ACM Press (2005), 371-380.
22. O'Hara, K., Glancy, M. and Robertshaw, S. Understanding collective play in an urban screen game. *Proc. CSCW '08*, ACM Press (2008), 67-76.
23. Peltonen, P., Kurvinen, E., Salovaara, A., Jacucci, G., Ilmonen, T., Evans, J., Oulasvirta, A. and Saarikko, P. It's Mine, Don't Touch!: interactions at a large multi-touch display in a city centre. *Proc. CHI '08,* ACM, 1285-1294.
24. Reeves, S. *Designing Interfaces in Public Settings: Understanding the Role of the Spectator in Human-Computer Interaction.* Springer, 2011.
25. Reid, J., Hyams, J., Shaw, K. and Lipson, M. "Fancy a Schmink?": a novel networked game in a cafe. *Comput. Entertain. 2,* 3 (July 2004), 1-12.
26. Rekimoto, J., Ayatsuka, Y. and Kohno, M. SyncTap: an interaction technique for mobile networking. *Proc. MobileHCI '03,* Springer LNCS 2795 (2003), 104-115.
27. Russell, D.M., Drews, D. and Sue, A. Social Aspects of Using Large Public Interactive Displays for Collaboration. *Proc. UbiComp 2002*, Springer (2002), Berlin, 229-236.
28. Salovaara, A. Appropriation of a MMS-based comic creator: from system functionalities to resources for action. *Proc. CHI '07,* ACM Press (2007), 1117-1126.
29. Scheible, J. and Ojala, T. MobiLenin combining a multi-track music video, personal mobile phones and a public display into multi-user interactive entertainment. *Proc. Multimedia '05,* ACM Press (2005), 199-208.
30. Schwarz, J., Klionsky, D., Harrison, C., Dietz, P. and Wilson, A. Phone as a pixel: enabling ad-hoc, large-scale displays using mobile devices. *Proc. CHI '12*, ACM Press (2012), 2235-2238.
31. Tang, A., Finke, M., Blackstock, M., Leung, R., Deutscher, M. and Lea, R. Designing for bystanders: reflections on building a public digital forum. *Proc. CHI '08*, ACM Press (2008), 879-882.
32. Terrenghi, L., Quigley, A. and Dix, A. A taxonomy for and analysis of multi-person-display ecosystems. *Personal Ubiquitous Comput. 13*, 8 (2009), 583-598.

I Wanted to Settle a Bet! - Understanding Why and How People Use Mobile Search in Social Settings

Karen Church
Telefonica Research
Pl. de Ernest Lluch i Martn, 5
08019 Barcelona - Spain
karen@tid.es

Antony Cousin
University of Nottingham
University Park, NG7 2RD
Nottingham - UK
psxawjc1@nottingham.ac.uk

Nuria Oliver
Telefonica Research
Pl. de Ernest Lluch i Martn, 5
08019 Barcelona - Spain
nuriao@tid.es

ABSTRACT
Recent work in mobile computing has highlighted that conversations and social interactions have a significant impact on mobile Web and mobile search behaviours. To date, however, this social element has not been explored fully and little is known about why and how mobile users search for information in social settings. The goal of this work is to provide a deeper understanding of *social* mobile search behaviours so that we may improve future mobile search experiences that involve a social component. To this end we present the results of two studies: a survey involving almost 200 users and a two-week diary and follow-up interview study of 20 users. Our results extend past research in the mobile search space, by exploring the motivations, circumstances and experiences of using mobile search in social settings to satisfy group information needs. Our findings point to a number of open research challenges and implications for enriching the search experiences of mobile users.

Author Keywords
Mobile search; social mobile search; shared mobile search; search behaviour; collaborative search; survey; diary study

ACM Classification Keywords
H.5.m Information Interfaces and Presentation: Miscellaneous

General Terms
Measurement, Design, Experimentation, Human Factors

INTRODUCTION
Year after year, mobile Web usage has continued to grow at a staggering pace. The number of users accessing the mobile Web has quadrupled in the US and tripled in Western Europe in the past four years[1]. Given that usage and adoption of the mobile Internet is growing at a much faster rate than the desktop ever did, many believe that the mobile Web will inevitably overtake the desktop as the primary means of searching and accessing online content[2].

Search engines remain the main gateway to finding information on the Web — over 18 billion search queries were submitted in December 2011 to the leading search engines[3]. While mobile search has not yet reached the same levels of usage, it is quickly gaining on desktop search. Nearly one in seven of all search queries is now conducted via mobile, compared to just one in fifteen in 2010[4]. And the rapid adoption of smartphones looks set to drive further increases.

As mobile Internet usage has increased, there has been a growing body of research aimed at understanding why and how mobile users search and browse the Web via their mobile handsets. Some of this research has subsequently pointed to an interesting social element in mobile search. For example, it has been shown that mobile search is a social act, often conducted in the presence of others [3]. Recent research has also shown that conversations have a significant impact on the types of information needs that arise while mobile and how those needs are addressed [4, 9, 11, 20]. To date, however, this social component has not been fully explored and little is known about why and how mobile users search for information in social settings. A deeper understanding of this social dynamic will help improve future mobile search experiences.

As such, the focus of this paper is on *Social Mobile Search*, which we define as the *use of mobile search in co-located group settings to satisfy a shared information need.* In this paper we describe two studies examining why and how people use mobile search in co-located social groups to satisfy a shared need for information: (i) a survey (N=193) to gather some initial insights into different aspects of social mobile search behaviour; and (ii) a two-week diary study and follow-up interviews (N=20) to probe more deeply into the dynamics of using mobile search in social settings. We conclude with a comprehensive discussion of our findings and outline a number of open research challenges and design implications.

RELATED WORK
In this section we discuss two areas of related work:(1) studies aimed at understanding mobile Web behaviours, and (2) research focused on the social dimension of mobile search.

[1] *Mobile Internet Usage Rising; Android Users Catching Up with iPhone Counterparts* See http://bit.ly/gl0vA1

[2] *The Mobile Internet Report* See http://bit.ly/4JJDq4

[3] *comScore December 2011 U.S. Search Engine Rankings*, See http://bit.ly/A5nXeG

[4] *1 in 7 Search Queries is on Mobile*, See http://bit.ly/oztn5R

MobileHCI'12, September 21–24, 2012, San Francisco, CA, USA.

Understanding Mobile Web and Search Behaviours

The first set of studies aimed at capturing qualitative insights into mobile Web experiences involve large-scale surveys, contextual inquiries, interviews and in-situ diary-based studies [7, 10, 12, 18, 21]. These studies have highlighted the contexts in which mobile Web access is most useful [18], the main motivations of mobile Web usage (*i.e.* staying aware and up-to-date) [7, 21] as well as key usability issues compared to desktop-based Web access [10, 12].

Researchers have begun to explore and identify changes in mobile Web behaviours as the mobile space has evolved. For example, it has been shown that mobile Web access is occurring in more stationary, familiar environments rather than on-the-move [19]. In fact, most recently, Church & Oliver [3] found that over 70% of mobile Web accesses are conducted at home or at work.

Other work has focused on understanding location-based mobile search [1, 22]. In a recent large-scale survey of local mobile search, Teevan *et al.* [22] found that just 12% of local mobile searches were conducted at home compared to 64% while on-the-move.

The second set of studies aimed at understanding mobile Web behaviour involves analyzing the usage patterns of real mobile subscribers available in search logs [2, 5, 6, 13, 14, 15, 23, 24]. These studies show that mobile users issue few queries per session when compared to desktop users, mobile queries are short, and adult content is popular. Recent studies show that mobile queries have become more diverse over the past few years and that device type impacts on mobile search behaviour, *i.e.* iPhone users search in very similar ways to desktop users [15].

The Social Dimension of Mobile Search

Several studies of mobile information needs have identified that social interactions have an impact on the types of information needs that arise, *e.g.* [4, 9, 11, 20]. For example, Sohn *et al.* [20] found that conversation prompted information seeking behaviour in 27% of cases.

The user-centric studies of mobile Web behaviour mentioned earlier have also hinted at the influence of social interactions on mobile Web use in particular as a *conversation enhancer* [7]. Mobile search has been found to be a social act, often conducted in the presence of other people. For example, Church & Oliver found that in > 65% of cases, mobile search was carried out in the presence of others [3]. Amin *et al.* [1] found that 76% of the local mobile searches where conducted whilst co-located with other people. According to a recent study by Teevan *et al.* [22], local mobile searches are more *social* when the searcher is in-transit than stationary (67% vs. 53% for stationary searches) . Despite the fact that previous work hints at a definite social element in the mobile search space, this dimension has not been explored fully and little is known about the use of mobile search in such social settings.

Finally, there has been some recent research aimed at addressing the various design challenges for co-located collaborative mobile search [16, 17]. In [16], features such as clipping, ranking and sharing of search results between mobile devices is supported via a proof-of-concept prototype. Meanwhile in [17], evaluations of sharing, comparing and analyzing mobile search results within a group of co-searchers is described. However, both works involve lab-based evaluations, with few participants and a narrow range of search tasks. While such research provides initial insights into how collaborative mobile search experiences can be improved, the fact remains that very little is understood about the situations and the dynamics that lead to the use of mobile search in social settings. Before designing new tools and services to help mobile users in such settings, we must first understand the intricacies of such social behaviours.

Hence, the primary contribution of this paper is that we show, both qualitatively and quantitatively, how, why and in what situations people use mobile search in social settings for shared information needs. Our work extends the results of past research by exploring the motivations, circumstances and experiences of using mobile search in social settings for group information needs. And our findings point to a number of open challenges and implications for the design of future social mobile search services. In the following sections we describe the methodology we employed and key results from our study.

STUDY METHODOLOGY

We employed a mixed-method approach in our study consisting of (i) a survey and (ii) an online diary & interview study.

Study 1: Survey

We first carried out a survey to gather initial insights into different aspects of social mobile search behaviour. The survey comprised of three main parts. Part 1 included a series of questions related to demographics and mobile phone usage. In part 2, users were asked to recall their most recent social mobile search experience. That is, carrying out a Web search on their mobile phone in the physical presence of at least one other person in order to satisfy a shared need for information. After recalling this experience, users were asked to answer a series of questions related to that experience including: what they searched for, their information need, their motivation, who they were with, their relationship(s) to the people present, where they were located, what they were doing before and after the search activity, if and how they shared the search results, and if the search had any effect on their future plans. In part 3 of the survey participants were asked about their general mobile search experiences and behaviours whilst in co-located group settings. The survey included a mix of closed and open-ended questions so that we could capture a rich set of data points related to their social mobile search experiences, while minimizing the time burden on the respondents.

Our survey resulted in 193 responses gathered between October and November 2011. Survey participants were recruited from external mailing lists, online social networks such as Facebook as well as online discussion forums. A prerequisite to the survey was that all participants must own an Internet-enabled mobile phone and must perform mobile Web searches at least a few times per month. This pre-requisite was used to ensure at least some level of familiarity with mobile search engines. Survey participants ranged in age between 18–61, with an average age of 31 (SD: 6.9). Responses were provided by 134 men (69.4%) and 59 women (30.6%). The users came from a diverse range of backgrounds (*e.g.*, IT, engineering, sales, telecommunications, education, customer service, etc.). The majority of our participants were residents of Spain (68%), Ireland (17%) or the UK (10%). Respondents primarily used Android (40.4%) to perform their searches, followed by iPhone (30.6%), Blackberry (10.9%), Nokia (6.7%) and other types (11.4%) of mobile devices. Finally we found that the majority of participants (87%) stated that they used mobile search in social settings at least once per week, with 54.9% of participants using it at least once per day. In terms of search engines used, 183 participants (95%) responded using Google's mobile search service.

Study 2: Online Diary & Interview Study

While the first study allowed us to capture a single social mobile search experience from each participant (i.e. their most recent experience), we designed the second study so that we could investigate multiple social mobile search experiences over a longer time period and in more depth. In particular the second study was designed to help us understand *why* mobile users engage in such behaviours. For this second phase, we conducted an online diary and follow-up interview study. Users were asked to share details of their mobile searches carried out in co-located, group settings. Instead of asking users to carry around a notebook, users accessed an easy to use, online diary tool. We employed follow-up interviews to clarify entries and elaborate on their experiences. We focused on *active* mobile search users so that we could draw interesting insights from this user group. We define *active mobile search users* as those who use mobile search on their smartphones daily or multiple times per day[5].

Participants

Diary study participants were recruited from the 193 users who took part in the survey phase of the study. Participants were selected based on the frequency at which they engage in mobile search behavior (as reported by them), in particular in group settings for satisfying *shared* information needs. In total 20 participants were chosen (11 male and 9 female) who actively search for mobile Web content. Participants ranged in age between 22-52, with an average age of 30.5 (standard deviation: 6.5).

Procedure

The diary study ran for a period of 2 weeks in November 2011. Participants were asked to report all of their social mobile search sessions in an online diary tool that was accessible via a Web browser in both mobile and desktop environments. The survey included a mix of open and closed questions so that we could record the motivations, circumstances and experiences of social mobile search while limited the effort required by the participants. Below is a list of the questions we asked each user to answer along with a flag indicating whether the question was open/closed[6].

1. Approximate date and time of the social mobile search *[closed]*
2. The information need they were trying to address *[open]*
3. Their motivation for using mobile search in the given social setting *[open]*
4. Their location at the time of the mobile search *[closed]*
5. How many people were in their group? *[closed]*
6. What was their relationship to each member of the group? *[closed]*
7. What they were doing just before the mobile search? *[open]*
8. What they did immediately after the mobile search? *[open]*
9. What search engine was used? *[closed]*
10. What query did they submit to the search engine? *[open]*.
11. Did the search have any effect on future plans for group activity? *[open]*
12. Was their information need satisfied? *[closed]*
13. If their need was left unsatisfied, why was this the case? *[open]*

Users were asked to submit a single diary entry for every social mobile search session they conducted over the 2-week period and to do so (1) as soon after the mobile search as possible and (2) as accurately as possible. Each participant was sent a daily SMS reminder for the duration of the study and the time at which the reminder was sent was varied so that we could gather a diverse range of social mobile search experiences. At the end of the study, each participant took part in a semi-structured interview (approx. 30 minutes in duration) in which we delved into their experiences, focusing in particular on what they feel are the most positive and negative aspects of using mobile search in social settings and what would improve their social mobile search experiences. We also used these interviews to clarify any issues with the previously recorded diary entries. Each user was given a 25 euro voucher for taking part and we also raffled three 100 euro prizes to three participants.

Data Collected

Over the 2-week period the 20 participants generated 123 diary entries, with an average of 6.2 social mobile search experiences per user (min=2, max=15, standard deviation=3.3). Only 14 of the diary entries (11.4%) were generated from a mobile handset, with the remaining entries submitted via a desktop/laptop. Of the 123 diary entries, 111 (90%) were searches issued via Google's mobile search engine.

RESULTS

In this section we analyze the data collected in both studies and provide a characterization of social mobile search behaviours. We focus on the types of needs that arise in these social settings, the contextual factors that play a role, how these mobile search interactions are shared and the effects of social mobile search experiences on the future behaviours and plans of the group. Note that across both studies, the reported social mobile search instances typically involve ONE member of the group (i.e. the instigator of the search) carrying out the search while the others are waiting for the answer or continuing the conversation. The findings of the survey and diary study are reported alongside each other for comparison.

[5]We focused on smartphone users to avoid any bias that may have been introduced by users of less sophisticated phones

[6]Aside from the questions listed, users were also free to provide additional comments on their experience.

Some differences in patterns emerged from these two studies and as such are highlighted where applicable. However, we found common trends across both studies and the main findings presented within this section reinforce these common behaviours.

Where Do People Use Social Mobile Search?

While recent research shows that the majority of mobile Internet usage occurs in stationary, familiar settings like at home or at work [19, 3], investigations of mobile search behaviour highlights a different trend. For example, mobile users are often away from familiar contexts while searching and at times they search for information about a geographic location [22]. A recent study by Church & Oliver [3] shows that 42% of mobile searches occur when users are away from familiar environments. While we find a similar trend, our results show that *location* seems to play a more important role in social mobile search (see Table 1). In the survey we found that 56.5% of searches were issued when users were away from their home and their work. In the diary study this percentage dropped to 47%. Note that social environments like bars, cafe's, restaurants as well as other people's homes (*i.e.* the homes of friends) account for a significant percentage of search experiences in both the survey (11.4%) and diary study (12.2%) responses. We also found the presence of an *other* category, which includes locations related to (1) shopping, *i.e.* supermarkets, shopping malls, book stores, (2) leisure, *i.e.* in a hotel, on holidays, etc. or (3) general errands, *i.e.* at the doctors, in a meeting, etc.

Table 1. Total number and percentage of mobile searches per location for both the survey and the diary study.

	Survey		Diary Study	
Location	**# num**	**% perc**	**# num**	**% perc**
Home	51	26.4	36	29.3
Work	33	17.1	29	23.6
Walking	27	14	11	8.9
Other persons home	25	13	7	5.7
Commuting	24	12.4	16	13
Bar/Restaurant/Café	22	11.4	15	12.2
Other	11	5.7	9	7.3
Total	**193**	**100**	**123**	**100**

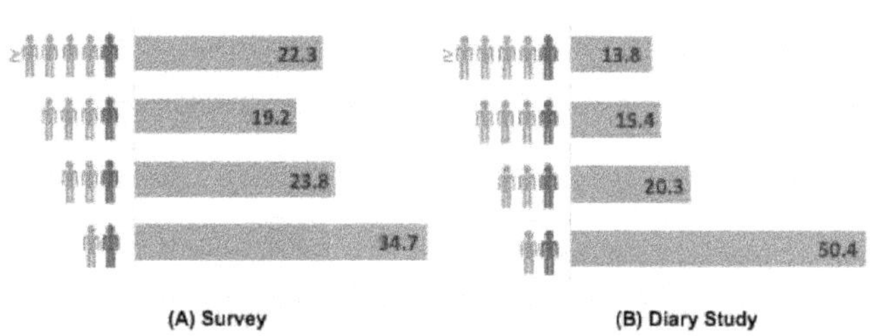

Figure 1. Percentage of social mobile searches in both the survey and the diary study along with the associated number of people present in the group at the time of the search. Note that red person icon represents the instigator of the social mobile search.

Who Do People Search With?

When it comes to who users interact with, we find that group sizes are varied and dynamic and *relationships* appear to play an important role. Figure 1 shows the number of co-located group members (including the instigator of the search) during the recorded social mobile search instances for the survey (A) and the diary study (B). The instigator of the mobile search is highlighted in red while the remaining group members are shown in grey. We find that social mobile search is most often conducted within groups of 2 people, that is, the searcher and one other person (approx. 35-50%). However, at times, group sizes are quite large with >= 4 people (approx. 29-41%).

In terms of relationships (See Table 2), friends were by far the most common group type accounting for 60% of search instances in the survey and 41% of search instances for the diary study. Family (26% vs. 33%) and partners/spouses (15% vs. 29%) were also popular in social mobile search instances. Interestingly, in approximately 30% of cases for both the survey and diary study, two or more relationship types were reported. That is 30% of the time, users searched while with family and friends, or friends and partners, etc. While social mobile search does occur among work colleagues, it appears to occur more often with people with whom users have a closer, more intimate relationship. Note that the *other* category listed in the set of relationships includes items like *taxi driver* and *tourists asking for help/directions*. Therefore in a small number of cases, social mobile search is used with people the user does not actually know.

Table 2. Total number and percentage of mobile searches for both the survey and the diary study and the associated relationship with people present in the group. Given that multiple relationship types could be present in a single social mobile search experience, the percentages extend beyond 100%.

	Survey		Diary Study	
Relationship	# num	% perc	# num	% perc
Friends	115	59.6	50	41.0
Family	50	25.6	41	33.3
Partner	56	29.0	19	15.4
Colleagues	41	21.2	27	22.0
Other	5	2.6	4	3.3
Total	**267**	**138**	**141**	**115.0**

Why Is Social Mobile Search Used?

In this section we investigate the motivations behind conducting mobile searches within social groups. Past work by Taylor *et al.* [21] has shown *awareness* is the key motivations for mobile Web usage. Awareness is defined as the desire to stay current and up to date. Using a similar methodology to Taylor *et al.* we manually classified all social mobile search instances reported in both the survey and diary study according to one of four key motivators, shown in Table 3: (1) Curiosity, (2) Assisting an activity/a task, (3) Staying informed generally (awareness) and (4) Alleviating boredom. Note that two of the authors manually classified the dataset so that total agreement was reached.

In contrast to past work we find the top motivators behind social mobile search are *Curiosity* and *Assisting an activity / task*, as opposed to *Awareness*. Curiosity, as defined by Taylor *et al.* [21], reflects the user's interest in an unfamiliar topic, which normally occurs by chance, *e.g.* conversing with a friend and wanting to settle a friendly bet, watching a movie, wanting more information about an actor, etc. Approximately 47% of survey responses and almost 37% of diary entries belonged to this category. This motivation is primarily driven by conversations and brief chance encounters. Some real examples from the diary study include: ***P1:*** *"The name of the beer from Zaragoza — All of us were thinking about it and nobody remembered"*, ***P7:*** *"New actress in Gossip Girl — who is the new character?"* and ***P14:*** *"The length of Dun Laoghaire West pier — Someone said it was a mile long and others thought it was half that"*.

Table 3. The main motivations for using mobile search in social settings.

	Survey		Diary Study	
Motivation Classification	**# num**	**% perc**	**# num**	**% perc**
Curiosity / fact-finding	91	47.2	45	36.6
Assisting an activity / a task	76	39.4	74	60.2
Staying informed generally	22	11.4	4	3.3
Alleviating boredom	4	2.1	0	0.0
Total	**193**	**100**	**123**	**100**

In contrast, the *Assisting an Activity or Task* category reflects the desire to be more efficient, to plan for things and to get things done. These can relate to work or study, to finding directions, contact and address details or to planning activities/making decisions. We found approx. 39% of survey responses and 60% of diary entries belonged to this category. Some real examples from the diary study include: ***P17:*** *"Palau Sant Jordi — We wanted the best route to reach a specific location. We decided the best route and means of transport and the entire group moved on to the concert"*, ***P2:*** *"Timetable cathedral Salamanca — We were planning a trip"* and ***P10:*** *"What time the car boot sale was on in the pavillion bar in Cork — We wanted to go along to the car boot sale"*.

What do People Search for in Social Settings?

In this section we highlight the information needs associated with the recorded social mobile search instances. Dearman *et al.* [8] previously explored the information needs of average mobile users and devised a comprehensive taxonomy of information needs. To help us assess what types of information needs lead to social mobile search behaviours, we used the original Dearman *et al.* high-level categorization as a basis and manually classified both the diary study entries and survey responses according to one of 10 categories, shown in Table 4[7]. For space reasons, we focus on the top 4 categories which account for > 70% of survey and diary study responses, however, we refer the interested reader to the Dearman *et al.* paper for a full description of all the information need categories [8] . Furthermore, given that Dearman *et al.* provide results of mobile-specific needs we provide comparisons where possible.

The most popular information need is *Trivia & Pop Culture* accounting for approx. 31% of survey responses and 37% of diary study entries. This need type relates to random thought references, factual knowledge, popular culture, definitions, translations and meanings of foreign words; as well as news queries. Some diary study examples include: ***P7:*** *"The writer Patrick Rothfuss"*, ***P9:*** *"What lake was Greenville close to?"*, and ***P3:*** *"Videos and music from Elvis"*. Interestingly, in a study of mobile information needs by Sohn *et al.*, trivia was also the most popular need type, however the volume of such needs was much lower (18.5%) [20]. In the Dearman *et al.* study the volume of trivia-related needs generated while mobile was just 5.4% [8].

Next in popularity is *Finding*, which accounts for 28% of survey responses and 22% of diary entries. This category relates to finding the name or location of a company, service or person; the distance between two points or different routes to a given destination; as well as the time it takes to travel form one point to another. Examples from the diary study include: ***P6:*** *"Hotel dazzler buenos aires"*, ***P17:*** *"Finding the location of a restaurant"*, and ***P7:*** *"Where to get the DVD of Pulp Fiction?"*. The occurrence of this need type appears to be in line with findings of [20] which shows that *Directions* and *Points of Interests* account for 25.7% of mobile information needs. However, *Finding* type needs were more prevalent in the Dearman *et al.* study (41.9% for mobile users) [8].

Guidance type needs relate to instructions, advice, opinion or recommendations. For example, ***P1:*** *"Recipe for risotto with mushrooms.*, ***P7:*** *"How to get rid of a computer virus"* and ***P14:*** *"Best chip shop in Dublin"*. This category of needs account for 8.3% of survey responses and 10.5% of diary study entries. Dearman *et al.* found a similar trend for mobile users (10.6%).

Finally, the *Establishments & Organizations* category includes information about a specific business, association, organization, etc. Most queries associated with this category relate to finding contact details or resource information for a given business or service. For example, ***P12:*** *"Morrison BMW. I was looking for their contact details as I needed to ring them to confirm an appointment time"* and ***P5:*** *"Guinness storehouse — I needed to find out if there are parking facilities at the Guinness brewery"*.

Overall our results show that many of the information needs that arise in social mobile search sessions are comparable with general mobile information needs. However, a significant difference exists when it comes to the volume of *trivia*-type needs. This is perhaps due to the fact that social mobile search tends to occur quite randomly and is sparked by chance conversations. This phenomenon is more apparent when analyzing the mobile queries submitted by our users. Past research on mobile search has shown that although mobile queries are evolving and are becoming less homogeneous, high levels of query repetition still exist among mobile users [6, 5, 24]. However, when it comes to social mobile queries, we that found that there is far less repetition among the queries issued. In fact query repetition rates across the diary and survey study was <1%. This means that diversity among the search queries recorded during both studies was very high and in terms of the queries/keywords entered, users searched for very different things.

[7]We made some small modifications to the original Dearman *et al.* classification: (1) We associated news items with the *trivia & pop culture* category, (2) we added a *learning* category which reflects the desire to learn something new, (3) needs related to distances, the time it takes to get from one point to another point and locating intangible/virtual items such locating a group on LinkedIn to the *finding* category. Again two authors manually classified the dataset so that total agreement was reached.

Table 4. The information needs behind the social mobile searches.

	Survey		Diary Study	
Information Need	# num	% perc	# num	% perc
Trivia & Pop culture	72	37.3	38	30.9
Finding	54	28.0	27	22.0
Guidance	16	8.3	13	10.6
Establishments & Organisations	12	6.2	13	10.6
Offerings	11	5.7	10	8.1
Availability	9	4.7	11	8.9
Unknown	8	4.1	3	2.4
Events	4	2.1	4	3.3
Environmental Conditions	3	1.6	2	1.6
Learning	2	1.0	2	1.6
Persons	2	1.0	0	0.0
Total	**193**	**100**	**123**	**100**

How are Social Mobile Search Experiences Shared?

In both the survey and diary study, users were asked if and how they shared the search experience and results with the members of their group. In our study, one person was typically carrying our the search on behalf of the group. The reporter of the social mobile search instance was the person who conducted the search. Given that the search was issued to address a shared information need, we wanted to understand how the resulting information was shared amongst the group and how many different methods of sharing were employed in a given search session. We provided 4 default sharing modes for users to choose from: (1) Speaking aloud, (2) Showing the screen whilst holding the phone, (3) Handing over the phone, and (4) Sending electronically phone-to-phone (*e.g.* via email, SMS, Bluetooth, etc.). Users were also given the option of specifying *other* sharing means.

Table 5. Total number and percentage of social mobile searches along with how users chose to share the results with members of their group. Given that multiple share types could be present in a single social mobile search experience, the percentages extend beyond 100%.

	Survey		Diary Study	
Sharing Classification	# num	% perc	# num	% perc
Speaking aloud	134	69.4	94	76.4
Showing screen whilst holding	89	46.1	36	29.3
Handing over the phone	27	14.0	20	1.6
Sending electronically	20	10.4	6	4.9
Other	6	3.1	6	4.9
Total	**276**	**143.0**	**162**	**117.1**

Table 5 shows the results of this analysis. In the survey, 69% of search results were communicated by speaking aloud, 46% by the user showing the device screen to other members of the group, 14% handed the phone to another member of the group, whilst 10% of search results were sent electronically. In the diary study we found that speaking the results aloud was even more common with 76% of diary entries. We also found much lower occurrences of showing the device screen to group members (29%) and sending the search results electronically (5%). Interestingly $<$ 2% of diary entries corresponded to users relinquishing control of their device to show the search results to someone else in the group.

It was common for more than one method of sharing to be used in a single search session. In the survey, 23% of searches involved two methods – most commonly (in 70% of these cases) speaking and showing the screen; meanwhile 8% of all search episodes saw three different methods used. Similar results were found in the diary study: 28.5% of diary entries reported at least two sharing methods.

Although the 4 default modes of sharing account for the vast majority of recorded behaviours, users reported using other somewhat surprising means at times. The *other* category of sharing was reported in 3.1% of cases in the survey and almost 5% of cases in the diary study. These other means included: writing the information down on paper, using *Whatsapp* (which is related to sending the information electronically but somehow participants felt it required a separate category) and finally telephone calls. Phone calls were employed when users wanted to share the search results with people not physically present.

It is clear from these results that users generally share results by speaking aloud or showing their phone. Users rarely hand over their phone or send the results electronically. We will show in the discussion section that both the private nature of mobile phones and the type of content being shared have an impact on how information is shared and with whom.

What is the Impact on Future Plans?

In both the survey and diary study, participants were asked if the social mobile searches they conducted had an effect on the future plans or decisions of their group. 34% of survey responses and 25% of diary responses indicated that the reported social mobile search did have an impact on the future plans of the group. Across both studies, the information need type that most often had an impact on future plans was the *Finding* category (47% of the survey responses that impacted on plans and 23% of diary study entries that impacted on plans). *Guidance* and *Availability* needs also had a strong impact on future plans (12.9 vs. 13.7% and 7.6 vs 22.6% respectively).

When asked what effect the search had on their future plans, a diverse range of responses were provided by users. For example[8]: (1) Decisions: ***P9D:*** *"We decided not to take the car"*, ***P16D:*** *"We decided our next stop"*, (2) Plans: ***P2S:*** *"We agreed on a plan"*, ***P7D:*** *"We will read the book"*, (3) Actions: ***P1S:*** *"We went to the cinema"*, ***P16S:*** *"We booked the travel"* and (4) Purchases: ***P2S:*** *"We had to buy an umbrella"*, ***P80S:*** *"We bought flight tickets"*.

DISCUSSION

When compared to prior work on understanding general mobile search behaviour, our results show that social mobile search behaviour is *different* across a number of dimensions: it tends to occur in more unfamiliar and mobile-specific locations, it tends to happen among tightly knit social groups of mixed sizes, it is motivated mainly by curiosity or assisting an activity and it is dominated by trivia and finding information need types. Social mobile search is primarily sparked from conversations and is used primarily to engage or enrich those conversations. In this section we turn our attention to more qualitative data and delve into three insights related to social

[8]The 'S' and 'D' in the participant number listings refer to S: survey participants and D: diary study participants.

mobile search: (1) the pros and cons of social mobile search highlighting mixed feelings in using this technology, (2) the perceptions towards sharing search results with peers and (3) the role of time in the activity planning tasks derived from these social search scenarios.

The Pros and Cons of Social Mobile Search

Through the survey, diary study and follow-up interviews with participants, the general perception towards using mobile search in social settings was deemed to be a very positive experience by our users. One of the key goals of this study was to assess what value users gain from using social mobile search and what is lacking from their current experiences. In the survey, the 193 participants were asked to describe what they liked and disliked most about using mobile search in social environments. Based on their responses we identified 4 benefits and 6 drawbacks of using social mobile search[9].

Perceived Benefits to the User

In terms of value, the first benefit was convenience. That is fast, easy access to a wealth of information anytime, anywhere. Some user comments related to this benefit include: ***P3:*** *"Information is always at your fingertips"*, ***P5:*** *"It's so easy and useful"* and ***P30:*** *"I can get a fast answer without opening/starting/moving to my computer"*.

A second benefit was that it enhances conversations. Many users were able to learn something new, to provide new insights to conversations and to settle friendly bets and debates with friends. For example: ***P39:*** *"It solves a lot of arguments in the group :)"*, ***P151:*** *"The possibility to answer a question that has arisen some discussion in the group. You can settle the discussion having learned something and knowing that it is true."*, and ***P82:*** *"It complement interests and provides random tips that enrich conversation"*.

A third advantage was the means to make well-informed decisions using accurate, real-time information, thus leaving nothing to chance. For example, ***P182:*** *"You can take right decisions in realtime"*, ***P79:*** *"Allow groups take decisions all together every time."*, and ***P71:*** *"It helps us make fast well informed decisions"*.

Interestingly users also indicated that social mobile search enabled a form of *personal empowerment*, i.e, it helped them show initiative and made participants feel in control and independent. Users expressed feeling good when being the first to find the answer to a question and sharing that answer with their peers. For example ***P37:*** *"Always getting the info gives me better visibility in the group and allows me to interact"*, ***P45:*** *"I like to be helpful"*, ***P175:*** *"Being the first to know the answer"*, ***P173:*** *"There's a little phone pride and snobbery about it too when you race with someone to get the info first"*, ***P70:*** *"I like to feel Independent even if I am in a place that I don't know well"*, and ***P80:*** *"To show initiative and technical ability to find information"*.

Perceived Drawbacks to the User

The first downside to social mobile search is that it can be deemed rude and antisocial. For example, ***P50:*** *"It's very impersonal."*, ***P67:*** *"It's rude, just like making a call"* and ***P147:*** *"It can be deemed impolite"*.

Other users expressed that while social mobile search is used as a conversation enhancer, the act of searching in such situations resulted in them feeling removed from the conversation, e.g. ***P115:*** *"You stop talking and can be out of the conversation."*, ***P97:*** *"It can make you feel removed socially as you are fully immersed in getting the information"* and ***P100:*** *"It can be a distraction of the natural flow in a group situation"*.

Another negative aspect of social mobile search is that at times it ended conversations that might have continued if the search had not taken place, e.g. ***P3:*** *"I also feel like it puts an end to fun and friendly debates"*, ***P105:*** *"Sometimes, it's the end of a interesting discussion"*, ***P138:*** *"It can stop the flow of conversation as the focus is taken away from the conversation itself"*.

Some users hinted that it creates a mobile dependency. For example, ***P47:*** *"You get dependent. I feel that I'm using my memory less so I tend to easily forget simple concepts"*.

Contradictory to the *personal empowerment* benefit mentioned earlier, other participants felt that the act of searching reflected poorly on them, leading to a negative reaction from the group, e.g. ***P4:*** *"I feel like I'm acting like a know-it-all when I look things up."*, ***P163:*** *"Some people do find it annoying and might roll their eyes, like 'oh great, they're searching for it on their phone to prove a point and be right'. You have to be conscious of this and sometimes not search for some thing."*, and ***P56:*** *"You can be accused of pedantry"*.

And finally, we were surprised to discover that some users thought that searching for answers in these social situations felt like cheating. For example, ***P172:*** *"It kills the surprise"*, ***P192:*** *"Instead of more discussion we 'cheat' and find the answers"*, and ***P40:*** *"It removes the challenge"*.

Along with the caveats mentioned above, common mobile device usability issues were reported by users — *e.g.* poor coverage, bad speeds, cumbersome input, etc. — however, surprinsingly none of the aforementioned drawbacks were seen as a barrier towards using mobile search in social settings.

Sharing Mobile Search Experiences

One of the research questions we aimed to address in this work is how do people *share* mobile search experiences with their group. Our previous results show that users rarely handed over their phone (14% of survey responses and only 2% of diary entries).Sending the results electronically was also used infrequently (10% of survey responses and 5% of diary entries), mainly because it was too difficult for most users, e.g., ***P1:*** *"It takes a while to do Bluetooth. You have to wait a few minutes to have an image which is ridiculous for something that's not critical"*. In the follow-up interviews with diary study participants, we probed these sharing behaviours in more detail[10].

Sharing the Input

One of the first questions we asked interviewees was whether they shared the query input phase of the mobile search. While

[9] Note that all user comments quoted in this section are from the survey part of our study.

[10] Note that all user comments quoted in this section are from the interview phase of our study.

one user pointed that a group-based search could lead to more engagement, ***P15:*** *"If there was a way to actively group search the discussion would stay on the topic at hand"*, socializing the search input process appears to be an undesirable feature in general. For example: ***P4:*** *"I do not see any point in any social activity for something as simple as entering a search"* and ***P10:*** *"If everyone is looking for info at once it kind of defeats the purpose"*.

Sharing the Results

In terms of sharing the results of the search process, the decision about how to share the results appears to be a consequence of multiple factors, *e.g.* who the recipient is, the type of information being shared, the task at hand, the physical environment and the personal, private nature of mobile handsets. All in all, the decision about how and what to share varies greatly based on personal feelings and preferences. As can be seen from the user comments below, there are contrasting attitudes in terms of what is shared and with whom.

P11: *"If it's short, small bits of information, maps or photos I show. For longer pieces of information I may speak"*, ***P13:*** *"If it's something simple I can say aloud, if it's difficult then I show the phone"*, ***P2:*** *"With family I show and maybe hand over the phone. With friends I generally just speak what's on the screen. It depends how well you know them (i.e. the people you are with). I rarely hand over my phone due to privacy and practical/protective issues"* and ***P13:*** *"With friends I speak it aloud, with colleagues I usually show the phone to share the information"*.

Furthermore, when the search results related to persistent, task-related information, sharing effectively becomes more complex. Maps or navigation type results in particular appear to create significant complications and overhead in terms of sharing. In these cases speaking a word/phrase aloud or showing the screen does not satisfy user needs. For example, ***P10:*** *"In London on a college trip and I was the only person with an iPhone so I used Google maps a lot. I was constantly reading directions. A massive printout of Google maps would have be handy"*.

Finally, the inherent usability issues of mobile phones also have an impact, *e.g.* ***P2:*** *"The problem with giving them my phone is they tend to knock the search off"* and ***P9:*** *"Showing something to someone on a tiny screen on a mobile doesn't make much sense. I don't find it very practical"*.

Group-based Activity Planning

We found that a significant proportion of searches had a real impact on the future plans of the group (34% of survey responses and 25% of diary entries). After exploring this effect in more detail we found that the resulting activity planning had a strong temporal component: *group plans* were spread across the *now+next*, *soon* and *later* time frames.

Most of the activity planning relates to immediate and near-term planning. A number of users mentioned that it was quite common with friends when making in-the-moment decisions about immediate activities, e.g. going to the cinema, deciding on a restaurant for lunch, etc. However, there were also cases of social mobile searches which led to plans in the coming weeks or months ahead. Examples from the survey participants highlight this fact: ***P109:*** *"We are going to that place in December"*, ***P155:*** *"Next weekend we decided to go to St Anton Market"*, and ***P117:*** *"We'll probably go to Zurich next year"*. When the interview participants were asked about their use of social mobile search for planning, they offered a range of responses that not only confirm the existence of these temporal elements but also showed the value of using mobile search in social settings for finding new activities or confirming group plans. For example: ***P11:*** *"When it is related to activities/plans, it's usually just to confirm places or find the way"* , ***P16:*** *"I have been using it a lot to find activities to do in the city where I am"*, ***P1:*** *"Most of the time it's making plans to go out to restaurants, travel, etc"* and ***P15:*** *"My father has his 50th birthday next year so we're thinking about going to Barcelona for the grand prix. So I looked up tickets, etc. I do use it a lot for planning"*.

Interestingly based on feedback in the interviews it appears that certain roles within the group appear to influence this behavior. For example, the *organizers* within the group tend to conduct the majority of these types of searches, e.g. ***P1:*** *"Generally with a group I'm always searching for something we're going to do or thinking of doing."* and ***P10:*** *"I am the organizer of the group so I do searches for these."*

IMPLICATIONS FOR DESIGN

Overall our findings imply that there are a number of caveats in terms of engagement, interaction and sharing during social mobile search usage. In this section we describe a number of open challenges and design opportunities for enriching shared, social mobile search.

Enhancing Sharing

As highlighted earlier, we found that personal preferences, information type, group relationships and privacy/trust concerns all have a role to play in who shares what and with whom. In both the survey and follow-up interviews we asked users what would improve their current experiences and many users pointed to wanting an *easier means of sharing results* with their peers. For example, ***P2:*** *"If you could send, not so much a link, just a screenshot of what you've found. If you could just flick the info onto their phone"*, ***P15:*** *"A lot of people I hang around with are also smartphone users, if somehow they could see the results on their screen"* and ***P16:*** *"it would be nice to have a quick way to share results, so people can also look at them"*.

However we also found that the private, personal nature of mobile phones makes the act of sharing through these devices a complex and sensitive task. For example one user commented. ***P2:*** *"I wouldn't like to share my phone or information from the phone. My phone is always used for work as well so I'm always paranoid that something can happen. Smartphones tend to be expensive, that is a factor"*.

As such it appears that future social mobile search tools will benefit users if they can support easier sharing between devices. However, any future advances in this research space will need to consider user privacy and control as a top priority. And striking a balance between easy to use sharing modes and privacy/control will be a challenging task.

Group Creation & Engagement

Group identification and creation remains an open challenge in social environments, let alone in dynamic mobile environments. In order to increase sharing and engagement in social mobile search settings, users need an easy, fun and privacy-preserving means of identifying group members. While being physically close to a person might be some indication of participation in a group, it's unlikely to work successfully in crowded, public spaces such as bars and restaurants where such behaviors emerge quite frequently. Furthermore, there may be instances where users want to connect and engage with sub-groups rather than the entire group. For example, one participant commented that he wanted to allow his friends to see the search results he discovered, however, in certain circumstances he didn't want to share that information with everyone in the group. While interaction among sub-groups was not reported very often, it's likely that future social mobile search services will need to consider a complex set of group structures and dynamics, especially when facilitating group creation and interaction.

Finally, while all of our participants were smartphones users, a few users expressed a desire to share and engage with friends across a range of devices, *e.g. not specifically an iphone*. One user pointed to using blackberry messenger to share content quickly and at no cost but was restricted to sharing with colleagues that also had blackberry devices. Given the diverse range of mobile handsets on the market today, and the fact that within a given group its likely that multiple handset types are present, any future applications aimed at engaging groups will need to be inclusive and cater for multiple device types.

As described earlier we found mixed user perceptions towards using mobile search in social settings. Users indicated that a fine line exists between appearing rude and showing-off versus using mobile search to facilitate a conversation and engage with the group. At times the act of mobile search in social settings was deemed annoying and anti-social to group members. Sometimes the act of executing the search was distracting and left the searcher isolated and withdrawn from the conversation. We believe that some of the negative connotations associated with social mobile search could subside by developing inclusive services that engage the entire group during the social mobile search activity.

Beyond Co-location

In both the survey and diary study we focused on exploring the use of mobile search in *co-located* group settings to satisfy a shared information need, that is were all group members were physically located in the same place. While the majority of recorded social mobile search instances focused on co-located group members, we did find that some users opted to share search results with group members not physically present either via WhatsApp or via phone calls. While these modes of sharing account for a low percentage of overall usage (3.1% and 4.9% for the survey and diary study respectively), future social mobile search applications may need to facilitate group interaction across multiple locations. Extending location boundaries in this manner is likely to make group creation, interaction and sharing more challenging.

Overall, these qualitative insights suggest that a more engaging, shared mobile search experience *aimed at the entire group* might help in waining the negative aspects and in turn enrich user experiences. There is definite scope to support richer, more collaborative mobile search experiences among groups of mobile users. As pointed out in the related work section, there have been some initial attempts by researchers to support collaborative mobile search for group activity planning tasks [16, 17]. However, given that curiosity motivations and trivia information needs were prominent in our study, it is likely that alternative techniques will need to be explored to support a range of social mobile search behaviours. Furthermore, as outlined in this section, developing richer, shared mobile search experiences is a non-trivial task which we believe will lead to new interaction and design challenges for mobile researchers. We hope that the challenges outlined in this paper inspire other researchers in their future endeavors and that our findings can help inform improvements in future social mobile search services.

STUDY LIMITATIONS

While significant effort was spent to ensure validity of our user study and our results, there are three limitations to our current approach which we would like to discuss. Firstly, the study was conducted in November 2011 and as such there may be seasonal effects in terms of the behaviours that emerged. For example, perhaps users would engage/search differently in summer months. Secondly, while we tried to ensure a balanced sample, we received more responses from male participants for the survey portion of the study. This may also have an impact on findings. Finally, both the survey and diary study relied on self-reported data from users, which could be incomplete or contain inaccuracies. In designing the study, we took these limitation into consideration and decided to combine the survey with a more longitudinal diary study so that we could capture a diverse range of behaviours that may have not emerged in the survey alone. We sent daily reminders to users via SMS to limit missing entries and we conducted in-depth interviews with each of the diary study participants so that we could augment the quantitative findings with more subjective responses. We feel that this combination resulted in a rich dataset which has allowed us to draw a number of insights into how and why mobile users engage in social mobile search.

CONCLUSIONS

In this paper we have presented the results of a survey and diary study investigating why and how people use mobile search in co-located social groups to satisfy a shared need for information. Our results highlight significant differences when compared to prior work on understanding mobile search behaviour. Mostly sparked by random conversations, we have found that social mobile search is more likely to occur in unfamiliar and mobile-specific locations (56.5 % and 47.1 % for survey and diary study respectively), it happens among tightly knit social groups, it is motivated by curiosity or assisting an activity or task and it is dominated by trivia and finding information need types. We have also discovered that a non-negligible proportion of social mobile searches have an impact on the future plans and activities of the groups in question.

In addition to characterizing social mobile search behaviour, we have highlighted key user perceptions towards using mobile search in social settings. Our findings point to a number of open research challenges and opportunities to enrich the future experiences of mobile Web users, in particular related to improving content sharing and group interaction. In terms of future work, we would like to explore social mobile search behaviour *in-situ* through both log analysis and field studies to validate our findings and determine if new trends emerge in-the-wild. There might also be opportunities to explore if demographic, seasonal and cultural differences exist in social mobile search behaviour.

ACKNOWLEDGMENTS

This work is funded as part of a Marie Curie Intra European Fellowship for Career Development (FMIA, PIEF-GA-2009-255625) award held by Karen Church. Thanks to the reviewers for their useful comments and valuable feedback.

REFERENCES

1. Amin, A., Townsend, S., Ossenbruggen, J., and Hardman, L. Fancy a drink in canary wharf?: A user study on location-based mobile search. In *Proceedings of INTERACT '09*, Springer-Verlag (2009), 736–749.
2. Baeza-yates, R., Dupret, G., and Velasco, J. A study of mobile search queries in japan. In *Query Log Analysis: Social and Technological Challenges, WWW 2007 Workshop* (2007).
3. Church, K., and Oliver, N. Understanding mobile web and mobile search use in today's dynamic mobile landscape. In *Proceedings of MobileHCI '11*, ACM (2011), 67–76.
4. Church, K., and Smyth, B. Understanding the intent behind mobile information needs. In *Proceedings of IUI '09*, ACM (2009), 247–256.
5. Church, K., Smyth, B., Bradley, K., and Cotter, P. A large scale study of european mobile search behaviour. In *Proceedings of the MobileHCI '08*, ACM (2008), 13–22.
6. Church, K., Smyth, B., Cotter, P., and Bradley, K. Mobile information access: A study of emerging search behavior on the mobile internet. *ACM Transactions on the Web 1* (May 2007).
7. Cui, Y., and Roto, V. How people use the web on mobile devices. In *Proceedings of WWW '08*, ACM (2008), 905–914.
8. Dearman, D., Kellar, M., and Truong, K. N. An examination of daily information needs and sharing opportunities. In *Proceedings of CSCW '08*, ACM (2008), 679–688.
9. Heimonen, T. Information needs and practices of active mobile internet users. In *Proceedings of Mobility '09*, ACM (2009), 50:1–50:8.
10. Hinman, R., Spasojevic, M., and Isomursu, P. They call it surfing for a reason: identifying mobile internet needs through pc internet deprivation. In *CHI '08 extended abstracts on Human factors in computing systems*, CHI EA '08, ACM (2008), 2195–2208.
11. Hinze, A., Chang, C., and Nichols, D. M. Contextual queries express mobile information needs. In *Proceedings of MobileHCI '10* (2010), 327–336.
12. Kaikkonen, A. Full or tailored mobile web- where and how do people browse on their mobiles? In *Proceedings of Mobility '08*, ACM (2008), 28:1–28:8.
13. Kamvar, M., and Baluja, S. A large scale study of wireless search behavior: Google mobile search. In *Proceedings of CHI '06*, ACM (2006), 701–709.
14. Kamvar, M., and Baluja, S. Deciphering trends in mobile search. *Computer 40* (August 2007), 58–62.
15. Kamvar, M., Kellar, M., Patel, R., and Xu, Y. Computers and iphones and mobile phones, oh my!: a logs-based comparison of search users on different devices. In *Proceedings of WWW '09*, ACM (2009), 801–810.
16. Komaki, D., Oku, A., Arase, Y., Hara, T., Uemukai, T., Hattori, G., and Nishio, S. Content comparison functions for mobile co-located collaborative web search. *Journal of Ambient Intelligence and Humanized Computing 2* (2011), 239–248.
17. Kotani, D., Nakamura, S., and Tanaka, K. Supporting sharing of browsing information and search results in mobile collaborative searches. In *Web Information System Engineering WISE 2011*, vol. 6997. Springer Berlin / Heidelberg, 2011, 298–305.
18. Lee, I., Kim, J., and Kim, J. Use contexts for the mobile internet: A longitudinal study monitoring actual use of mobile internet services. *International Journal of Human-Computer Interaction 18*, 3 (2005), 269–292.
19. Nylander, S., Lundquist, T., and Brännström, A. At home and with computer access: why and where people use cell phones to access the internet. In *Proceedings of CHI '09*, ACM (2009), 1639–1642.
20. Sohn, T., Li, K. A., Griswold, W. G., and Hollan, J. D. A diary study of mobile information needs. In *Proceedings of CHI '08*, ACM (2008), 433–442.
21. Taylor, C. A., Anicello, O., Somohano, S., Samuels, N., Whitaker, L., and Ramey, J. A. A framework for understanding mobile internet motivations and behaviors. In *CHI '08 extended abstracts*, ACM (2008), 2679–2684.
22. Teevan, J., Karlson, A., Amini, S., Brush, A. J., and Krumm, J. Understanding the importance of location, time and people in mobile local search behavior. In *Proceedings of the MobileHCI '11* (2011), 77–80.
23. Vojnovic, M. On mobile user behaviour patterns. In *Communications, 2008 IEEE International Zurich Seminar on* (march 2008), 26 –29.
24. Yi, J., Maghoul, F., and Pedersen, J. Deciphering mobile search patterns: a study of yahoo! mobile search queries. In *Proceeding of WWW '08*, ACM (2008), 257–266.

Degrees of Sharing: Proximate Media Sharing and Messaging by Young People in Khayelitsha

Marion Walton, Silke Haßreiter
Centre for Film and Media Studies
University of Cape Town
Rondebosch, 7700
marion.walton@uct.ac.za, Hassreiter.S@nhtv.nl

Gary Marsden, Sena Allen
Department of Computer Science
University of Cape Town
Rondebosch, 7700
gary.marsden@uct.ac.za, sena.allen@gmail.com

This paper explores the phone and mobile media sharing relationships of a group of young mobile phone users in Khayelitsha, South Africa. Intensive sharing took place within peer and intimate relationships, while resource sharing characterized relationships with a more extensive circle, including members of the older generation. Phones were kept open to others to avoid inferences of stinginess, disrespect, or secretiveness and the use of privacy features (such as passwords) was complicated by conflicts between an ethos of mutual support and the protection of individual property and privacy. Collocated phone use trumped online sharing but media on phones constituted public personae similar to social media 'profiles'. Proximate sharing within close relationships allowed social display, relationship-building and deference to authority. We suggest changes to current file-based interfaces for Bluetooth pairing, media 'galleries', and peer-to-peer text communication to better support such proximate exchanges of media and messaging.

Author Keywords
Mobile phone sharing; privacy; security; Bluetooth; mobile media; mobile photography.

ACM Classification Keywords
H.5.3 User Interface; user centered design.

INTRODUCTION

Mobile phones are central artifacts of global youth culture [5]. For many young people in developed countries, smartphones are fully-fledged channels of sociality and 'networked individualism'[31]. In such contexts, phones extend practices of media use and participation that rely on affordable Internet access and extensive use of computers [10]. This paper explores how mobile media supports sociality among young people in Makhaza, Khayelitsha, in South Africa. Here phones are often shared and computers are scarce. Despite the availability of mobile Internet access, airtime is expensive and so free methods of 'peripheral networking' such as Bluetooth transfers or cheap instant messaging via MXit are popular [13, 29]. Like phone users in Bangalore [23] and other contexts of low income use, young people in Makhaza find ingenious uses for Bluetooth as interface for mobile entertainment and peer-to-peer sharing.

In this paper we introduce a group of twenty young people from Makhaza and explore their use of Nokia feature phones for media sharing. In this context, phones are often semi-public shared resources, and this creates a mismatch with the default values embodied in phone designs and interfaces. The research was driven by a desire to understand how well current mobile devices met the needs of this new group of users and whether existing handset designs could better support their needs. The study was conducted in two phases; phase one studied existing practices whilst phase two introduced new handsets with a more extensive range of features.

Whilst current handset designs do not necessarily assume that a handset is used by only one individual, they do make several questionable assumptions when considered in the light of young people's practices. First, measures creating individual privacy are assumed to be socially desirable (as metaphors such as 'protection' or 'security' reveal), rather than potentially creating conflict or signaling an anti-social refusal to share, or an admission of something to hide. Second, proximate networking via Bluetooth is primarily represented as file transfer between devices and not as a channel for interpersonal messaging. These assumptions did not always hold for the participants in this study, and in fact the designs of devices sometimes actively obstructed use.

Sharing phones

Initial research into mobile phone use in developed countries led researchers to believe that, unlike landlines, which are often shared in domestic contexts, mobile phones play an individualising role [12]. Studies of young people's phone use later revealed intricate sharing and ritual exchanges being used to demonstrate status and rivalry as well as affiliation [26]. Around the world, young people share phone conversations between co-present friends [30], include absent participants in a social gathering [9], and use shared cameraphone images to extend everyday self-authoring into an ambient awareness of absent intimates [17]. Smartphone use has become mainstream among

MobileHCI'12, September 21–24, 2012, San Francisco, CA, USA.

middle class adults, encouraging media display and sharing and requiring more nuanced models of privacy [11]. Features such as rapid access to 'guest' profiles or sensor-activated spheres have been suggested to support privacy or data security [20],[11]. File-sharing or media 'trafficking' practices support various social interactions [8].

Researchers working outside affluent Northern contexts noticed equally complex practices of proximate and distant sharing in developing countries [25]. For impoverished families using a single phone, shared access often overrides mobility and convenience [28]. The complex dynamics of sharing arrangements suggest that, even under circumstances of poverty, 'sharing is not simply a response to scarcity' [3]. Even where phones are initially adopted by individuals, communities (such as fisherfolk in Kerala) may later appropriate them by establishing new modes of cooperation [24]. Such sharing practices are not evidence of undifferentiated or utopian communalism, since a range of important distinctions and power relationships can underlie roles of purchase, ownership, access and control [3]. In Uganda, local anxieties about the 'secrets' in phones and the influence of familial hierarchies and values play an important role in the 'moral economy' [21] into which phones are incorporated, often excluding women from sharing [3]. Finally, studies of cyberbullying in South Africa have shown the prevalence of practices such as 'trickery', where deception leads to the revelation of shared secrets or images, 'outing', where they are passed on to people with whom they were not intended to be shared, or ostracism, when young people are hurtfully excluded from the shared spaces of their peers [4, 27]. This study investigates the pressures on sharing which arise in a South African context when the (often asymmetrical) obligations and conveniences of sharing in families and low income neighbourhoods intersect with the pleasures, status and pressures associated with young people's media sharing in intimate relationships and peer groups. Reliance on free collocated media sharing on phones (rather than social network sites) creates more complex needs for nuanced models of sharing and privacy as dynamic continua.

METHODS

Research site – Makhaza, Khayelitsha

Khayelitsha is a large, generally low-income settlement on the urban periphery of Cape Town. Mobile communication is used extensively here to create social, economic and symbolic capital which helps maintain and support households and social networks encompassing other parts of Cape Town and rural homesteads in the Eastern Cape [22]. Young people in this area were early adopters of mobile-centric [13] Internet, primarily for cheap instant messaging [7]. Like many residents of Khayelitsha, the participants in this study experienced chronic insecurity because of high crime rates, and their mobile phones were often targeted in petty theft and more serious crimes.

Study participants - the video producers

Study participants were a group of twenty young people (ages fifteen to eighteen) who attended an after-school program run by a non-profit youth development organization in Makhaza. In the role of participant observer, one of the researchers, Silke Haßreiter, offered an optional six month course in mobile video production to this group during June to November in 2010. All those attending the course were also invited to participate in the research (subject to parental consent). Names are anonymised throughout to protect privacy.

Interviews and video production

In-depth interviews were conducted at the start and end of the project The first phase of the project documented the research participants' existing mobile phone and mobile media use, focusing on production and exchange of visual media such as photos and videos. The second phase of the project introduced twenty Nokia feature phone handsets, the Nokia 5530 and Nokia X3 (chosen for their multimedia and data capabilities) which were donated to the organisation for use by the twenty video producers, and became the property of the organisation at the end of the project. While using the phones to make their videos for class, these young people had fulltime use of the handsets, storing media on them and customising them extensively. This helped us understand their media-sharing practices on a relatively high-end handset.

Mind maps of close relationships

The video producers were also asked to complete a network diagram (or 'mind map') of their seven closest relationships. These ego-centric network diagrams included a total of 133 relationships with alters. The participants answered twenty three questions about their phone and media-sharing in each relationship, including the directionality of the sharing (giving or receiving) in each case. The total number of affirmative answers was used as a 'sharing score' (Figure 1). A high score suggests that the relationship is characterized by a wide range of sharing practices or intensive sharing. We did not attempt to measure to what extent or how frequently sharing happened. Alters were categorized according to their relationship with the participant and mean sharing scores determined for each type of relationship (Figure 2). The percentage of all relationships in which specific phone features and media were shared served as a 'sharability score' for that feature or media type (Figure 2).

Phone content analysis

At the end of each phase of the project, participants were asked whether they wanted to give the researchers copies of the media stored on their phones. A total of 2125 images were collected and the content of filenames and images was coded and analysed. Not all participants chose to share, and some elected to delete media which was considered private.

Questionnaire

A questionnaire investigating technology access, mobile media usage, and phone sharing was completed by a larger convenience sample (N=46) of 32 young women and fourteen young men. This group included the twenty video producers as well as older teens from the same after-school program.

FINDINGS

Technology and mobile media use

According to questionnaire responses of the larger group (N=46) only a small minority owned a desktop computer (13%) or laptop (4%). Almost all (94%) owned a mobile phone and many (40%) also shared someone else's phone. Almost all (94%) reported that they felt safe using their phones at home, while only a very small number felt safe using phones at school (6%), on the street (2%) or in public transport (2%).

Overall, 77% of participants had taken a photo or video with a cellphone on the previous day. Almost as many (73%) said that they had used Bluetooth to share a photo, music or video. By contrast, only 27% had downloaded media from the Internet using a computer. The majority had access to the mobile Internet (64%), and 30% reported that they used phones and computers equally often to access the Internet. The group were active on Facebook and MXit (a South African mobile chat service).

Cost-saving strategies

Almost half of the survey participants reported that they 'never' or 'rarely' made voice calls. The cost-saving strategy of missed calls or 'buzzing' [6] was used several times per day by about a third, while considerably cheaper MXit messaging was preferred to SMS. Most sent free 'please call me' messages frequently (57% sent them 'several times a day'). In interviews, participants explained how these strategies helped them get by on limited airtime of about R5 ($ 0,71) to R15 ($ 2,14) per week. This was not enough to call, send text messages or even to spend much time on the mobile Internet.

Financial constraints also necessitated a great deal of SIM swapping (to share airtime or media). SIM swapping was hampered by tiny flaps and participants used objects such as feathers or sticks to pry open the flaps. This sometimes damaged the handsets.

Despite the social status of the 5530 and the X3 phones, few participants made extensive use of all the phone's features because, while online activities were easy and accessible, they were also a drain on finances. For example, Lerato (f, 17) used school lunch money to buy the extra airtime needed to pay for her increased Internet use.

Shared images

Images collected from handsets reveal certain media sharing practices which took place between the twenty video producers. Interconnections between their individual collections of images were estimated by identifying the number of duplicate images in the collection, (cases where the same image file appeared on more than one phone). These included 178 image files, or just over 8% of the images in the collection. In the case of the most widely shared images, duplicate files appeared in four separate collections. In most cases only two or three copies of an image appeared in the collection.

A detailed content analysis of these images is beyond the scope of this paper, but one subset of images which made up about 12% of the collection is of particular importance as shared media. Known as 'photo cards', these images were used to transfer a verbal message in visual form and featured decorative and expressive uses of typefaces and other graphics. They often appeared in animated GIF format and were downloaded from WAP sites. Apart from such stock messages, custom edits and annotations were added to photos using the phones' editing functions.

While some annotations involved the addition of labels such as names and nicknames to images, others resembled status updates, witty comments, or were messages addressed to the recipient of a picture. In essence, young people were appropriating the tools on the handset to create a form of asynchronous, peer-to-peer, rich messaging service that would not incur network costs.

Sharing relationships

Network diagrams, along with the 'sharing score' for each relationship and the 'sharability' of different types of media gave us a more detailed picture of how twenty participants shared various kinds of media in their close relationships (N=133). The sharing score was broken down into scores for (i) sharing pictures, (ii) shared use of handset, airtime and other resources, (iii) sharing of passwords and PIN codes, and (iv) other sharing.

Phones were shared in more than half of the 133 close relationships documented in the network diagrams. Participants were more likely to give someone else their handset than to receive a handset from someone else, and were more likely to play games on someone else's phone than to allow someone to play their games. All other sharing relationships were roughly reciprocal.

Participants were most likely to share free phone features such as listening to music, taking pictures with the phone's camera, and looking at pictures. Cameras on phones were shared more often than any other phone feature (52%). Airtime was also highly sharable. Participants reported sharing airtime in almost half of their close relationships (49%). Photos and pictures on cellphones were shared in 50% of the relationships, games in 40%. 'Romantic and sexy' pictures were considered more private but were nonetheless shared in 38% of relationships. Pictures were shared by Bluetooth in 46% of the relationships (music was shared in 45% and videos in 41%). Images were thus considerably more likely to be shared via Bluetooth than via MXit (34%) or Facebook (29%). In 20% of the relationships MXit and Facebook passwords or handset pin numbers were shared. SIM cards were also shared in 20% of these close relationships.

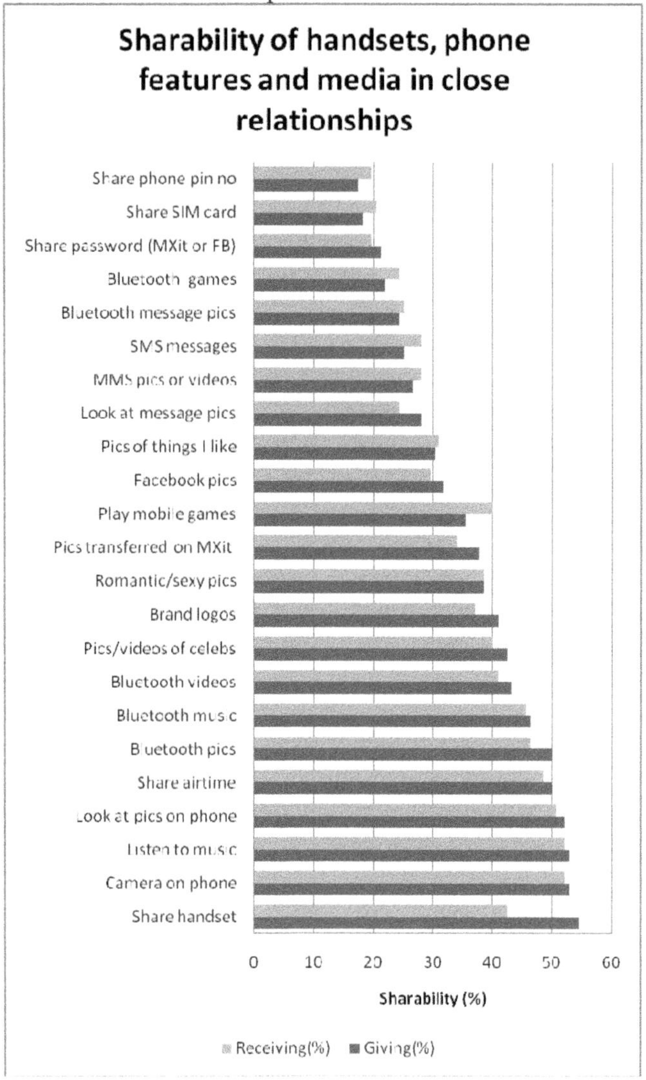

Figure 1: Sharability of media, handsets and phone features in participants' closest relationships (N=133).

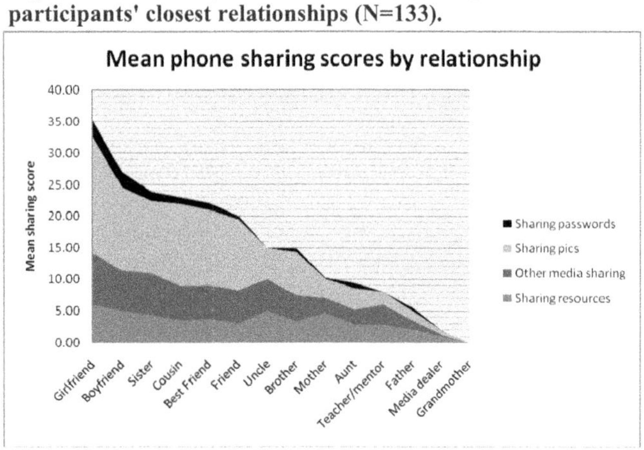

Figure 2: Scores for media and phone sharing in participants' closest relationships (N=133).

Shared resources, shared access and shared culture

Analysis of the network diagrams revealed a small negative correlation between sharing scores and age of alter [r = –.290, n=133, p<0.01]. High overall sharing scores were associated, to a small extent, with relationships with younger alters. There was a medium negative correlation between picture sharing scores and age of alter [r =–.357, n=133, p<0.01]. High picture sharing was thus associated, to a moderate extent with relationships with younger alters. There was a smaller negative correlation between presence of shared access arrangements such as shared passwords and pin codes and age of alter [r (133) = -.179, p <0.05]. Shared access arrangements were associated, to a very small extent with younger alters. There was no correlation between shared use of handsets, airtime, or other resources and age of alters [r (133) = .056, p >0.05] and these forms of sharing appeared in relationships with alters of all ages.

Figure 2 shows intensive sharing behaviors found most often in romantic relationships. Several male participants were outliers who reported extravagant levels of sharing in relationships with their girlfriends, who (they claimed) shared everything with them. In contrast, and particularly in relation to photo sharing, female participants reported somewhat more circumspect sharing relationships with boyfriends. Shared peer culture found expression in the relatively high levels of media sharing among peers. Passwords and pin codes were shared primarily in romantic relationships but also between siblings and friends. Shared use of resources such as airtime and handsets was reported in most of the documented relationships.

DISCUSSION

Network diagrams showed the importance of collocated media use (where two people in close spatial proximity look at the same image) and media sharing via Bluetooth in close relationships. These forms of proximate media sharing were more prevalent than media sharing via social networks such as Facebook. The existence of a relatively large number of duplicate images in the collection further indicates the importance of Bluetooth.

As found in other contexts intensive sharing cements intimate friendships or romantic relationships, semi-public display of media and friends on phones establishes status in the peer group while threatening secrets, much as social network sites do. We found that hiding secrets from adults and more distant peers is made particularly difficult in this context where mutuality is valued and resource sharing often required or expected.

Shared by default

In the first set of interviews, most young people did not initially report that they shared their phones since local norms did not even mark many everyday co-use practices as phone sharing. In fact, resource sharing took place across a range of relationships. Phones and airtime were shared both with the older generation and with peers in extensive support networks. Peer networks were marked by intensive sharing and intimate shared access relationships. Several tensions around sharing emerged from the different social contexts associated with these networks.

Extensive sharing

These young people often lived in households with extended family. Neighborliness demanded many kinds of sharing, including childcare, taps, toilets, and consumer goods, including phones. Without suggesting that an idealized collectivism or *ubuntu* prevailed, coexistence and interdependence [16] were emphasized and an ethos of sharing and mutual support could be called upon [15], albeit at the cost of privacy. Uneasiness around sharing and privacy outlined generational and gender-based hierarchies which gave the older generation rights to access younger people's private spaces, and where media sharing had different meanings for young men and women.

Phone sharing relationships with the older generation centered around resource sharing in this context of shared support. Uncles and mothers shared most, highlighting the relative absence of fathers from this group's social networks. Airtime was considered a shared resource within most of the close relationships reported by the group.

As Bongani (m, 17) explained, when sharing, reciprocal gifts of emotional support and solidarity are expressed. These are just as important to the sharing relationship as the material or economic assistance accessed through sharing:

Sharing is very important. Because if you don't share, if you don't talk to people, you don't feel the pain of someone, if you are in trouble, no one will help you (*Bongani, m, 17*).

In the second set of interviews, Bongani discussed his experience of having had the new Nokia phone for three months. He commented that it was somewhat uncomfortable to allow others to pick up his phone and search through its contents:

Here people like to take your phones and search [through] them. Actually it is a private device, but here you constantly run the risk that someone picks your phone up and looks through it. That is not good. But you cannot do anything.

He accepted, though, that this form of surveillance was a cost of being able to participate in the local gift economy of phones, functionality and mobile media: *'Plus if you want to borrow a phone from someone you cannot refuse [to give] your phone to him the very next day'*.

Most participants responded to local unwritten rules and handed over their phones to others when requested. If they did not share, they were seen as being selfish, or as outsiders. Thus the default orientation towards a phone in this context was that it is a public, rather than a private artifact, available for inspection by anyone in one's circle of acquaintances. This public status was underpinned by reciprocity, a complex and socially regulated form of gift exchange: *If you take some other person's phone, then you have to share yours too. That is law* (Mandla, m, 18).

Phones left unattended were seen as fair game. Young people had their own rules for whose phone they would pick up and inspect, in most cases saying that although they would pick up the phones of anyone they knew, even a phone belonging to one of their parents, and look at its contents; they would not do the same thing with the phone of someone they didn't know: *I don't know the person, I don't take it.* (Zukiswa, f, 17)

Intensive sharing

Other forms of sharing were found in peer networks, including intensive media sharing and intimate shared access relationships.

The intimacy of some of the intensive phone-sharing relationships is apparent from Yola and Lindelwa, who explained that they switched phones for the weekend, holidays, or when they were hanging out together after school. On the day of the interview, Lindelwa was using Yola's phone, in order to help her with a game, while Yola used MXit on Lindelwa's phone, which had more available memory than her own phone did. At other times they would simply switch SIM cards.

By creating Bluetooth connections or 'pairing' phones, young people were able to browse the media stored on their friends' handsets and select images of their friends to download and store on their own phones:

I take pictures from their phones, when they are happy and smiling, laughing. (Sibongile, f, 17)

Lindelwa explained that because Bluetooth transfers were so slow, switching phones or storage media was an easier way to share mobile video clips (recorded from television) with her good friends.

Refusal to share

In the questionnaire, participants were asked how they would respond if a friend did not want to share the media on his or her phone with them. (Responses were anonymized.) The scenario was met with disbelief in some cases: *'She is pretending, why should she not give me her phone?'* A refusal to share phones or media proved that the friendship was faulty: *'if they are friends they must share almost everything of theirs with me'*, revealed a serious lack of trust: *'they don't trust me at all and there's no friendship without trust'*. It might even call into question the relationship itself (*'I'm not really as important to her/him as I was thinking'*). Other interpretations were that the person had something shameful to hide on the phone, was jealous of the friend, or was excessively selfish. In contrast, a reciprocated sharing relationship was a source of delight, evidence of trust, love, inclusion (*'wants me to be a part of her life'*), intimacy (*'keeps us close'*) and the strength of the relationship with the peer (*'real buddies share everything'*).

Legalistic perspectives might view media sharing as theft of intellectual property, but this view was not shared by participants, since their sharing did not deprive anyone else of the ability to use the resource: *'music/media is something that you can share'*, they explained: *'it's not eaten'.*

Sharing, power, generation and gender

Sharing practices articulated with changing peer and romantic relationships, but also resonated with gender, class and consumerist hierarchies which stigmatize the signifiers of poverty [3].

For example, young people such as Bongani who did not have their own phones experienced the pressure of asymmetrical relationships which subjected them to unpleasant forms of dependency in the peer group:

When you don't have [a phone], they always look at you. [He is] boring. He does not have anything, he wants to borrow from us. (Bongani, m, 17)

Unequal relations between generations and genders meant that non-reciprocal sharing was expected from young people and young women in particular.

On the one hand, young people were expected to make their phones available for parental use and surveillance. This applied particularly to mothers and was confirmed by the high sharing scores which characterized many maternal relationships.

On the other hand, the negative correlations between age of alter and sharing suggest that pictures in general and erotic or sexual pictures in particular were kept private from the older generation. Like many of their peers [29], the young men and women who participated in our study valued MXit and mobile phones in general as a space for romantic and sexually focused exploration and play, allowing transgression and intimacy but discreet enough to allow the maintenance of '*ukuhlonipha*' (to respect), a concept which encompasses respectful relationships towards elders, involving deference, politeness and non-confrontational disagreement [2].

Consequently sharing phones with parents was particularly complex. Key complicating factors arose because intergenerational talk about sexuality and romance were taboo: *'Our parents ... don't talk about girls with us'* (Mandla, m, 18).

For example, Mandla reported that when the phone drew his parents' attention to his relationship with a girlfriend (by means of the text of messages or audible message alerts from his girlfriends) he could expect recriminations and admonitions to stay away from the opposite sex and focus on schoolwork. In his experience this kind of talk was intensely uncomfortable, and being subjected to it was a punishment in itself: *'talking about it is already horrible enough'.*

The differential levels of picture sharing with boyfriends and girlfriends (see Figure 1) suggests the existence of a gender-based double standard which influences both sharing and reporting. Girlfriends who share 'too much' according to local norms lose face, while their boyfriends gain bragging rights. These gender differences are confirmed by the use of girlfriends' pictures in status games among male peers, which we discuss below.

Inconspicuous consumption

The first set of interviews reflected the fact that in this teen peer group at least, Makhaza was a roughly homogenous community with relatively egalitarian sharing relationships. These relationships were disrupted by the arrival of the Nokia feature phones. Network diagrams showed that the participants were more likely to give than to receive phones in their sharing relationships (Figure 1), possibly because of their access to the Nokia phones. Exotic and disproportionately valuable, the phones restricted certain kinds of sharing behaviors while amplifying others.

Nolizwe (17, f) pointed out that phones which did not have desirable features such as Bluetooth were less likely to be stolen. Researchers, parents, and teens were all highly aware of the risk of theft, or of being attacked for a phone, and so a good deal of time was spent discussing ways to prioritise safety and use strategies which would make the phones look older or not attract attention to their desirability. As in other South African townships, [19] the risk of theft was simply too great in many parts of Khayelitsha, with the result that these 'mobile' phones were effectively immobilized. Andile (m, 17) commented that unless he knew most of the people in a particular place he could no longer risk going there with the Nokia handset:

There are some places where I cannot go ... You have to know most of the people that are around and then you can go there.

Mandla responded to the responsibility of having to take care of the new handset by restricting the circle of people with whom he would share. He limited its use to trusted family members, such as his mother, who could use it *'as long as she wants'*. He would only allow schoolmates to use the phone in his presence *'Love them all, but don't trust anyone'*. At the NGO more mutual sharing relationships were possible, since he could share with others from the class who also had Nokia phones:

When they have airtime and I not, then we swap phones. He is using my new games and I use his airtime for MXit. Like this we are both happy. (Mandla, m, 18)

Siyabulele (16, m) had a similar dilemma. His previous phone was the ubiquitous Samsung E250, which was unremarkable and yet functional, thus allowing him considerable freedom in managing sharing relationships: *'I used to share a lot'*. Now he could no longer allow his friends to use his phone in his absence. Siyabulele was concerned that one of his peers could remove the memory cards from the side of the phone: *'you don't even see it and they can steal it. So you have to trust people that you give the phone'.*

Mobile profiles

Young people carefully chose and edited the content they stored on their mobile phones, managing impressions, and representing individual identities and social relations. Their major objective was to create and maintain a 'cool' image of themselves, and their overall modus operandi was reminiscent of how teens in other more connected and well-resourced environments created and maintained profiles on online social network sites [1]. Mobile photographs were central to self-presentation during peer interactions:

Most of the time you spend time with your friends to look at photos on your phone and to show other people what you have on your phone. And you also spend a lot of time in choosing what pics and songs that you have on your phone, because you choose your style. You choose what you want others to see about you. (Mandla, m, 18)

Bongani pointed out that phones functioned as a complex accessory signifying young people's identities, which they assembled from the various possibilities available within local youth and consumer culture:

If you have a lot of hip hop pictures on, then you are a hip hop person. When most of the pictures are from cars, then you like cars. When you have a lot of girls, then you are a playboy.

When called upon to share phones as resources in their extensive networks, young people were also sharing access to the content associated with intensive sharing relationships. Unwritten rules of sharing governed such interactions, but they were not foolproof. When giving the phone away for a longer time, the phone owner lost oversight and control of his or her device, and participants were aware that unknown people might view their phone's content while it was being used by someone else.

Just as users of social network sites intentionally place content on their profile to be seen by others [1], participants displayed certain content prominently if they felt it might enhance their status. They deleted or hid certain content which was perceived as too private.

Secrets, messaging, stealth and surveillance

Peers shared unwritten rules about managing shared phone use. It was generally agreed that messages were more private than pictures or videos. *They know that they are not allowed to look at my messages. I trust them. They would not go there. (Andile, m, 17)*

As Andile (m, 17) explained, certain images could be freely shared because of their ambiguity:

Maybe if I have two girlfriends and their photos on my phone, then I can still lie and say that is my classmate – so no problem.

Mutually agreed sharing could shift into inter-personal surveillance if the phone owner's messages were read and disputes arose if airtime was used without permission. Zukiswa (f, 17) accepted that her phone would be picked up and inspected by others (and indeed she did the same thing to others in return), despite her discomfort with such scrutiny.

The problems associated with surveillance of messages was particularly acute given the fact that the phone protects not only its owner's secrets, but also those entrusted to him or her by others:

Messages are most private. There is personal stuff, maybe someone sends something and tells me his or her problem and then there is a secret between me and him and then I don't want anyone to see it. Because then it is all over the place and everyone is talking about it and then the friend thinks I said something and I betrayed him and then we fight. Even if it happened by mistake (Siyabulele, 16, m).

A different set of pressures were apparent in relation to parental surveillance of phone content, which set up an additional audience for young people to consider. boyd [1] identifies the dilemma online teens face when their online profiles, which must be cool enough for peers, are also checked by their parents. In response, some opened a second profile or 'mirror' network. The Makhaza teens tried to create similar private spaces through PINcodes, passwords and hidden folder systems.

A few used password-protection (PIN codes) to protect certain content that was classified as too private, such as text messages, erotic pictures and videos. Lerato (17, f) said that she kept her messages and games password-protected (messages for privacy, games because excessive use quickly used up the battery). Other young people mentioned knowing friends who used passwords to protect pornographic images or videos stored on their phones. This did not mean that they would not share the protected content, but it was a way to ensure that sharing required their consent: *When someone wants to do something then they have to ask for permission* (Lerato, 17, f).

Only best friends or lovers had access to these private spaces, but passwords could backfire if discovered by someone else, since they drew attention to the fact of limitations on sharing. In a context where shared access to phones is the default *modus operandi*, an attempt to establish privacy, or to protect secrets can itself be stigmatized or considered a sign of the transgressive or shameful nature of whatever is being protected. To some extent, collectivist values are in conflict with Western notions of the 'private' and autonomous individual, whose personal integrity and information are be protected from intrusion or surveillance, whether by the state or corporations. According to philosophies such as *ubuntu* something 'private' might be seen as collective property appropriated by an individual rather than individual property protected from the intrusion of others [18].

Thus, in this Makhaza peer group, attempts to establish privacy were likely to be seen as attempts to maintain 'secrecy'. For example, Yolena (f 16) suggested that someone who tried to protect content with a password was suspected by peers of wanting to conceal nude images or pornography. Others said they could get into trouble for even trying to restrict their parents or other carers from seeing their mobile phone content and that a password would in itself be reason enough for punishment.

Instead, as in Bangalore [23], secret folder systems were used to hide content and create a little bit of private space. Parents didn't know about these folders and most were not savvy enough to discover the folders when scrolling through the phones in search of forbidden content. But more than half of the participants reported that most of the time they would not even take the risk. If they received mobile phone content which was too private or which might get them into trouble, they deleted it immediately.

Shared use created additional complications for a password-based security model. Security features are available to all users and so peers of Neo (m, 17) were able to use a PIN code to lock one of the memory cards on the Nokia phone he used. The only way to recover use of the card was to format it, which meant he lost all the media.

Collectors' items

Other content was hidden for different reasons - the latest media (music, games, celebrity pictures and music videos) was often hidden so that the phone's owner could benefit from a period of exclusive ownership. Several of the young men explained that they limited sharing in order to monopolize newly released (and thus fashionable) media. A new hip hop song could be 'displayed' to others (they could listen to it), but it would not be (willingly) shared via Bluetooth.

You want to be the first person to know the lyrics of the song. It makes you special when you are the only one who is an insider. It is a hard competition. Everyone tries to be first. This is a boys thing more than a girls thing.(Bongani, m, 17)

Pictures of friends were also collectible items, and played a role in young people's self-presentation strategies within peer groups:

If you have lot of pictures of friends on your phone, then you are a popular person. If you don't have, then someone is shy and doesn't have any friends. So it is our goal to have a lot of photos on the cell phone. (Bongani, m, 17)

Andile (m, 17) explained that his phone's picture gallery helped to communicate his status and identity: '*I show other people that these are my friends'*. In this way the picture gallery functioned much like a friends list on Facebook might function for other young people where the internet was more accessible and part of everyday life. For the young men, messages and pictures of girls had particular currency and Bongani and Lerato (f, 17) commented that some people 'stole' photographs from other people's phones to appear to have more girlfriends, or to pretend that they knew popular good-looking people. Bongani explained that the young men used pictures and messages from girls to 'show off', establishing their masculinity in the eyes of their peers, as playboys. Mandla explained that young women's pictures and messages would not be put on display in cases where the young man had romantic feelings about the woman: *If it is real love then [you do not use them to show off]. But for the rest yes. (Mandla,m,18)*

Thus, in summary, images associated with romantic or sexual relationships can mark intensive sharing or intimacy which must be concealed from the older generation. Alternatively such images function as reified tokens in a collecting game where an extensive network of peers compete for status, or engage in the aggressive forms of 'outing' associated with cyberbullying.

DESIGN CONCERNS

Media sharing by young people raises complex design-related, legal and ethical challenges. Apart from intellectual property issues, surveillance, and public sharing of mobile media all have implications for parental and state regulation, and, potentially be related to cyberbullying or other forms of abuse. These considerations are particularly acute in the context of young people's vulnerablility and their sometimes short-lived relationships. Nonetheless, we feel it is important to prioritize the concerns of the young people who participated in our study. Our conclusions reflect the high value they attached to participating extensively in phone sharing practices while still having a more precise control over what they shared.

Privacy

Relationships with peers (best friends, friends, romantic partners and brothers and sisters) often involved intensive cellphone and media sharing. Relationships with the older generation (fathers, mothers, uncles and aunts) or a more extensive network of peers were considerably less open, but phones needed to remain accessible to allow resource sharing. These complex arrangements did not respect traditional Western boundaries around the privacy of the individual, or the home/work division. They were dynamic and sometimes shifted disconcertingly as peer relationships deepened, fizzled out or ended abruptly.

To better support young people's attempts to create and manage their own spaces for discreet sharing or privacy, manufacturers could offer 'hidden' profiles which are not visible but can be unlocked by their creator. Currently no handset we surveyed provides this kind of privacy. Such spaces could also implement a relational model of file-sharing, where shared access to media could be granted and later withdrawn if necessary. Another approach would be to support the creation of identities on external memory cards, supporting privacy practices also documented by researchers in India [23]. In the same way that a computer can boot into different modes, it might help if handsets booted an identity off an external card.

Media sharing

Bluetooth presents users with many obstacles to usability[23]. Despite its popularity, Bluetooth functionality is often buried deep in the menus, or users need to enter a file browser, navigate to the file, and choose a Bluetooth sharing option. None of the participants were even aware of the existence of the "mass send" option provided by most Bluetooth implementations. To avoid slow Bluetooth transfers, memory cards were frequently transferred between friend's phones. This raises file compatibility issues, and also an alarming tendency by some handsets to automatically reformat an unrecognized memory card. Memory cards are also not designed to be carried around, and their miniaturised size meant that they were easily lost. Although there now exist multiple-SIM handsets for the developing world, these support a single user with multiple SIMs – current designs make it unnecessarily complex for users to swap a SIM between handsets. Again, handsets should support easier access and more robust forms of card swapping, or provide multiple slots for card copying.

File-sharing or messaging

Other researchers have noted that usability of Bluetooth sharing is improved when transfers are announced via messaging interfaces [8]. Our study goes beyond this to show how extensively Bluetooth has been appropriated for synchronous and spatially proximate messaging. Using Bluetooth (which has an interface designed for file-sharing) to convey interpersonal messages reveals the existence of at least three distinct problems. First, Bluetooth is popular at least in part because of the high cost of airtime, which limits online sharing. Semi-public interfaces could enhance the usefulness of public Bluetooth-based public displays [14], by allowing more affordable uploads to social network sites via cheaper broadband connections. Second, in the case of phone 'pairing', where paired devices can gain access to all the content on another device, local Bluetooth practices highlight the inadequacies of absolute all-or-nothing privacy models. Third, the photo cards reveal the difficulties associated with sharing short text messages via Bluetooth, since even simple texts had to be laboriously created with image-editing software. The absence of any methods for transferring simple verbal messages (or lengthier texts) via Bluetooth is a distinct limitation of current feature phones. An expansion of Bluetooth functionality could allow free text-based messaging and commenting between collocated users. The popular decorative visual features of the cards would likely also be welcomed in other forms of text messaging.

CONCLUSION

While young people around the world use phones to share media and construct digital identities, various local contexts, resources and norms shape practices differently. In this paper we have reported on existing practices in one context and show how current handset designs still make erroneous assumptions based on the behavior and values of wealthier consumers. We believe that with a small effort in design, it is possible to create handsets that better serve the needs of the young people who participated in this study and, perhaps, other teens throughout the developing world.

ACKNOWLEDGMENTS

We thank the young people who participated and Nokia Research Kenya for funding the project.

REFERENCES

[1] boyd, d. Why youth (heart) Social Network Sites: The role of networked publics in teenage social life. In Buckingham, D. ed. *Youth, identity, and digital media.* MIT Press, Cambridge, 2007, 119-142.

[2] Bray, R., Gooskens, I., Moses, S., Kahn, L. and Seekings, J. *Growing up In the new South Africa: Childhood and adolescence in post-apartheid Cape Town.* Human Sciences Research Council Press, Cape Town, 2010.

[3] Burrell, J. Evaluating Shared Access: social equality and the circulation of mobile phones in rural Uganda. , Journal of Computer-Mediated Communication, 15, 2 (2010), 230-250.

[4] Burton, P. and Mutongwizo, T. *Inescapable violence: Cyber bullying and electronic violence against young people in South Africa.* Centre for Justice and Crime Prevention, 2009.

[5] Castells, M., Fernandez-Ardevol, M., Qiu, J. L. and Sey, A. *Mobile communication and society : a global perspective.* MIT Press, Cambridge, Mass., 2007.

[6] Donner, J. The rules of beeping: Exchanging messages via intentional "missed calls□ on mobile phones. Journal of Computer-Mediated Communication, 13, 1 (2007).

[7] Donner, J., Gitau, S. and Marsden, G. Exploring mobile-only internet use: results of a training study in urban South Africa. International Journal of Communication, 5(2011), 574-597.

[8] Harper, R., Regan, T., Izadi, S., Mosawi, K. A., Rouncefield, M. and Rubens, S. Trafficking: design for the viral exchange of TV content on mobile phones. In *Proceedings of the 9th international conference on Human computer interaction with mobile devices and services.* (Singapore,). ACM, New York, NY, USA, 2007, 249-256.

[9] Ito, M. and Okabe, D. Technosocial Situations: Emergent Structurings of Mobile Email Use. Jan 18 2003.

[10] Ito, M. *Hanging out, messing around, and geeking out: kids living and learning with new media.* MIT Press, Cambridge, Mass., 2010.

[11] Karlson, A. K., Brush, A. J. B. and Schechter, S. Can I borrow your phone?: understanding concerns when sharing mobile phones. In *Proceedings of the 27th international conference on Human factors in computing systems.* (Boston, MA, USA,). ACM, New York, NY, USA, 2009, 1647-1650.

[12] Katz, J. and Aakhus, M. eds. *Perpetual contact: mobile communication, private talk, public performance.* Cambridge University Press, Cambridge, 2002.

[13] Kreutzer, T. Generation mobile: online and digital media usage on mobile phones among low-income urban youth in South Africa. MA Diss, University of Cape Town, 2009.

[14] Maunder, A., Marsden, G. and Harper, R. Creating and sharing multi-media packages using large situated public displays and mobile phones. In *Proceedings of the 9th international conference on Human computer interaction with mobile devices and services.* (Singapore,). ACM, New York, NY, USA, 2007, 222-225.

[15] Mosoetsa, S. *Eating from one pot: The dynamics of survival in poor South African households..* Wits U.P., Johannesburg, 2011.

[16] Nyamnjoh, F. *Africa's Media, Democracy and the Politics of Belonging. .* Zed Books, London, 2005.

[17] Okabe, D. Emergent social practices, situations and relations through everyday camera phone use.. In *International Conference on Mobile Communication, October 18-19.* (Seoul, Korea,). , 2004.

[18] Olinger, H., Britz, J. and Olivier, M. Western privacy and/or Ubuntu? Some critical comments on the influences in the forthcoming data privacy bill in South Africa. The International Information & Library Review, 39, 1 (2007), 31-43.

[19] Schoon, A. Raw Phones: The Domestication of Mobile Phones amongst Young Adults in Hooggenoeg, Grahamstown. MA diss., Rhodes University (2012).

[20] Seifert, J., De Luca, A. and Conradi, B. A context-sensitive security model for privacy protection on mobile phones. In *Proceedings of the 11th International Conference on Human-Computer Interaction with Mobile Devices and Services.* (Bonn, Germany,). ACM, New York, NY, USA, 2009, 68:1-68:2.

[21] Silverstone, M., Hirsch, E. and Morley, R. Information and Communication Technologies and the Moral Economy of the Household. In Silverstone, R. and Hirsch, E. eds.*Consuming Technologies.* Routledge, London, 1992.

[22] Skuse, A. and Cousins, T. Spaces of Resistance: Informal Settlement, Communication and Community Organisation in a Cape Town Township. Urban Studies, 44, 5/6 (2007), 979-995.

[23] Smyth, T. N., Kumar, S., Medhi, I. and Toyama, K. Where there's a will there's a way: mobile media sharing in urban india. In *Proceedings of the 28th international conference on Human factors in computing systems.* (Atlanta, Georgia, USA,). ACM, New York, NY, USA, 2010, 753-762.

[24] Sreekumar, T. T. Mobile Phones and the Cultural Ecology of Fishing in Kerala, India. The Information Society, 27, 3 (2011), 172-180.

[25] Steenson, M. and Donner, J. Beyond the personal and private: Modes of mobile phone sharing in urban India. In Campbell, S. W. and Ling, R. eds.*The Reconstruction of Space and Time: Mobile Communication Practices (Vol. 1).* Transaction Books, . Piscataway, NJ, 2009, 231-250.

[26] Taylor, A. and Harper, R. Age-old practices in the 'new world': a study of gift-giving between teenage mobile phone users. In *Proceedings of the SIGCHI conference on Human factors in computing systems:*(Minneapolis, Minnesota, USA,). ACM, New York, NY, USA, 2002, 439-446.

[27] Unicef, Beger, G., Hoveyda, K. P. and Sinha, A. *From 'What's your ASLR' to 'Do You Wanna Go Private?'.* The United Nations Children's Fund, , 2011.

[28] Ureta, S. Mobilising Poverty? Mobile Phone Use and Everyday Spatial Mobility Among Low-Income Families in Santiago, Chile. The Information Society, 24(2008), 83-92.

[29] Walton, M. and Kreutzer, T. A phone that has life has Internet': Mobile-only Internet access and media use by teens in Khayelitsha, South Africa.Annual Conference of the International Association for Media & Communication Research IAMCR, July 21–24 Mexico City.

[30] Weilenmann, A. and Larsson, C. Local use and sharing of mobile phones. In Brown, B., Green, N. and Harper, R. eds.*Wireless World: Social and Interactional Aspects of the Mobile Age.* Springer, London, 2001, 92-107.

[31] Wellman, B., Quan-Haase, A., Boase, J., Chen, W., Hampton, K., DÃaz, I. and Miyata, K. The Social Affordances of the Internet for Networked Individualism. Journal of Computer-Mediated Communication, 8, 3 (2003).

Investigating Collaborative Annotation on Slate PCs

[1] Jennifer Pearson, [2] George Buchanan, [1] Harold Thimbleby

[1]Swansea University, Swansea
csjen@swan.ac.uk, csharold@swan.ac.uk

[2]City University, London
george.buchanan.1@city.ac.uk

ABSTRACT

Mobile reading is becoming evermore popular with the introduction of eInk devices such as the Kindle, as well as the many reading applications available on slate PCs and cellular handsets. The portable nature and large storage capacity of these modern mobile devices is making reading a more technology orientated activity. One aspect of mobile reading that has been given surprisingly little attention is collective reading — which is a common activity with paper documents. We investigate the support of group reading using slate PCs, focussing on collective annotation. In the past, desktop PCs have proved inferior in many ways for reading, when compared to paper. Notably, user evaluations of our new system, *BuddyBooks*, demonstrate that the slate PC form factor can, in contrast, provide advantages for group reading. While annotation practices change with the new format, coordinating within the group can be improved when touch-interaction is carefully exploited.

Author Keywords

Documents, Annotation, Collaboration, Slate PCs

ACM Classification Keywords

H.5.2 [**User Interfaces**]: input devices and strategies; interaction styles; prototyping

INTRODUCTION AND BACKGROUND

While twenty years ago it was the norm to read on paper, now it is a common sight to see people reading from portable devices such as eReaders, slate PCs, and even cellphones. There has been a large body of work dedicated to reading from both mobile and desktop devices. Reading on small screens was investigated as far back as the early 80s [3], and the popularization of online web browsing and reading led to an initial surge in mobile reading over a decade ago [2]. In that context, the main focus was on web content, much of which is relatively brief. Research has demonstrated that both back-lit displays (of all sizes), and small displays are associated with shorter spans of reading. In general close, attentive reading is rare on digital media, even on larger displays [5].

MobileHCI '12, September 21–24, 2012, San Francisco, CA, USA.

There has also been an interest in devices that support prolonged attentive reading. Researchers in "appliance design" investigated the usability of reading appliances [6] – the forerunners of contemporary reading devices, such as the Kindle and iPad. A recent resurgence in reading devices has resulted in research on their legibility and general usability (e.g. [9]). However, this has tended to focus on display technology, rather than interaction design. Another question has emerged around input technology; prototype reading appliances used a stylus, whereas modern devices often adopt touch. The different affordances of the two technologies have provoked a question about their relative merits for different tasks. Annotation is a central task to attentive reading, and the suitability of touch-sensitive devices for annotation [4] has emerged as a key research question.

Research has often focussed on the solitary reader [5]. That emphasis is repeated in the initial designs of reading devices. While reading can be alone, reading with others is surprisingly pervasive: e.g., when school children are encouraged to read in groups. In a mobile context, web content can be shared and read among friends by passing around a smartphone. There are also more structured examples of group reading, such as acting rehearsals, book clubs and research groups.

It seems to be an appropriate time to investigate *collaborative reading* on mobile devices, particularly those devices that are frequently used for longer spans of reading. While social annotations have started to emerge in the Apple iBooks and Kindle Reader software, reading that is shared in the same time and place is not directly supported, despite it being a commonplace activity. There is limited support for multiple screens, shared mark-ups or group coordination within a document. Some commercial whiteboard applications let users work in real-time, on multiple devices making changes to a common document, but these (often being aimed at classroom lecturing) are not reading focused and do not address the problem of coordination.

Electronic media have proved ineffective for certain styles of reading. In collaborative group reading, multiple paper documents remain a popular choice as paper is easily manipulated, and the physical form allows users to sit wherever space is available and interact with each other without being constrained by bulky technology. Individual copies faciliitate personal notes – which would prove difficult if several people shared one single copy.

In this paper, we focus on co-located collaborative reading, as opposed to remote reading, in consequence of initial research [8] that investigated the social context of that activity in detail, drawing a contrast between digital and printed media. The study of users' current behaviour allowed us to narrow and focus the scope of the work undertaken here. However, we also drew on a range of prior research from mobile HCI.

Social and public annotation is a popular topic of research in the mobile context [1], but typically the focus lies outside the specific activity of reading (e.g., photos). In contrast, investigations into the annotation of text have focussed on the use of both desktop PCs and paper, and overlooked mobile devices [5]. Annotations created during reading often contain a high proportion of text. It is well known that typing is a problem on mobile devices, though much improved in recent years. The impact of reduced screen size and the heightened cost of typing on annotation behaviour has received minimal attention, though differences would certainly be expected.

BUDDYBOOKS: A COLLABORATIVE READING SYSTEM

This paper describes *BuddyBooks*, a mobile-based real-time application for collaborative reading in groups. Each member of the group uses their the BuddyBooks app on a personal iPad, mimicking the way groups work together using multiple paper documents. The slate PC form factor allows users to sit near each other, while giving each a personal document view, and providing an intimate social interaction in the shared task. Our software allows each group member to mark-up their own copy of the document while simultaneously viewing the notes of other members. The new interface includes a tool that allows users to quickly and easily 'point out' specific parts of a document to others, helping the group coordinate its reading. Figure 1 shows examples of the tools available within the BuddyBooks application.

System Architecture

To use BuddyBooks, each client iPad must first connect to the host server sending it their IP address and nickname. The server allocates each user a unique color which is used to distinguish between the activity of the readers. The server receives notifications of any mark-ups made, and forwards that information to all the other devices. The document itself is stored locally on the iPads, but the server also keeps a record of the document as well as all the changes made to it for late joining group members to receive all the information. The purpose of BuddyBooks is to allow users to collaboratively *read* a common document. It is not therefore, concerned with the collective editing of a document but rather as an aid to mark-up and co-ordination on content where the original text remains constant.

Annotation Tools

Our goal for BuddyBooks was to allow users the same freedom to mark-up that paper offers while simultaneously overcoming paper's limitations. With this in mind, we opted to include a set of document annotation tools for use within the BuddyBooks interface. The three main objectives we had in mind for these tools were: they should have the same key functions of paper (i.e., users must be able to highlight, bookmark and make notes); they notes of all group members must be visible in real-time by every other group member; and different member's notes must be distinguishable. As a first cut implementation then, we included three main annotation tools in our interface (see Figure 1) : a bookmark tool (shown as ribbons on the top of a page - four are visible in this example); a note-taking annotation tool (shown as small squares on the document view); and a highlighter tool (shown as semi-transparent colored lines). These are all activated by touch gestures. Clicking anywhere on the page when in bookmark mode adds or removes a bookmark for the current page. When an annotation box is clicked, an on-screen keyboard is made visible to add, edit or delete annotations. When highlighting, dragging across the document page leaves a colored trail. All marks made on the working document are sent immediately to every iPad in the group. Each member's marks is distinguished by a unique color.

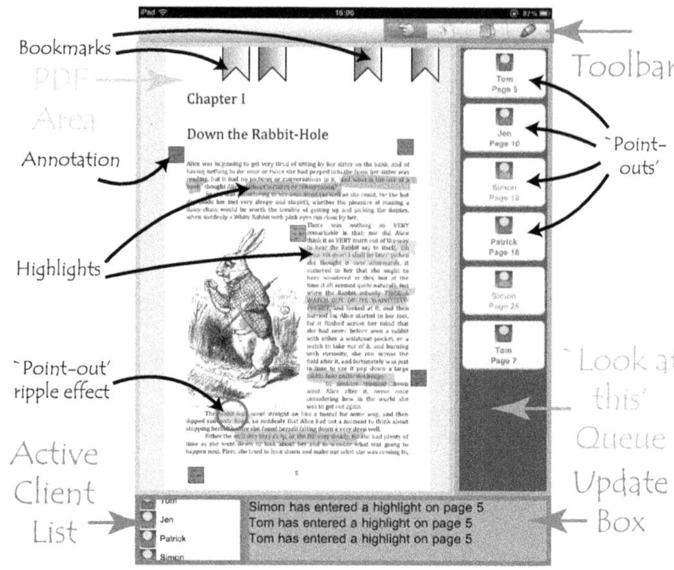

Figure 1. Screen shot from BuddyBooks

'Look at This' Queue

Often in a group collaboration session, users will want to indicate items and locations to other group members, (e.g., "look here on page 10, paragraph 2"); something which we call *mutual navigation*. If all members of the working group have their own copy of the document, it can sometimes be tricky and time consuming for everyone to locate the exact spot in the document, which can consequently cause a break in attention.

To support this, BuddyBooks has a 'look-at-this' queue that allows users to 'point out' specific areas of the original document to other members of the group. Essentially then, the look-at-this queue is a list of temporary placeholders that allows group members to quickly and easily navigate to a specific area of the working document.

To point out a location in the document, a user must simply select the tool and touch on the spot they wish the others to look at. This then automatically sends a point-out to the top of all group members look-at-this queue along with the color and nickname of its creator. Other group members are now aware they are being summoned to another part of the document but can wait to click on the hyperlinked point-out until it is convenient for them. Clicking on an entry in the queue navigates the user to the correct document page and animates a ripple effect (a circle outline that pulses in and out around the co-ordinate point for several seconds) to indicate to the user the exact page and location the point-out was made.

EVALUATION

To evaluate how well BuddyBooks performs compared to traditional paper-based group reading, we performed a comparison study using 18 participants (10M, 8F) aged between 22 and 61. These participants were selected from a cohort of staff and students from Swansea University who have previously undertaken collaborative reading in groups. We split these participants into groups of 3 and 4 providing us with 5 reading groups who then performed reading tasks interactively together. The purpose of the study was to observe participant behaviour while completing each of the group reading tasks and to obtain subjective feedback on each of the methods. These reading sessions took on average, around an hour and a half to complete and each participant was given a £10 gift voucher in return for their time.

Each group session began with the participants completing a questionnaire on their current group reading practices. This was followed by a comprehension-style reading task on a set of paper-based documents (one per participant). Readers were encouraged to discuss and mark-up their documents and were given a range of stationary with which to do so. The goal of the group reading task was to identify weaknesses and errors in the text, to mark these on the document along with a short summary at the end. Immediately following this task, the users then performed a similar task on a different document using BuddyBooks.

We used two documents, of a similar length and complexity, but differing in topic to avoid learning effects. To ensure an unbiased experimental design, we alternated the order these documents were presented to each group. Finally, after the study, each participant was asked to fill out a second questionnaire to gather subjective information regarding each of the respective systems.

The pre-study questionnaire revealed that 11 of the 18 users regularly participated in collaborative reading sessions (the remainder do it occasionally), and the primary medium for 14 participants was paper. The other 4 reported using a computer as their primary medium; none made use of mobile devices such as iPads or Kindles. Given the current popularity of portable reading devices, we feel this statistic highlights the lack of support available for using them for collaborative reading.

The documents used by the participants were two current affairs issues of social concern, with these being used in a balanced pattern between groups for the two different media - i.e. paper and BuddyBooks. None required specific domain knowledge, but each included detailed and complex argument, and was intended for an audience with strong reasoning skills. The groups were asked to critique each paper, and mark key points as they individually saw fit.

	Paper		BuddyBooks		Mann-Whitney
	Avg	SD	Avg	SD	
Q1: How easy was it to view notes made by other members of the group?	4.5	2.4	8.6	1.5	$p<0.0005$ $U=298.5$
Q2: How easy was it to create notes?	8.2	2.3	7.9	1.7	X
Q3: How easy was it to highlight a section of a document and share it with all members in the group?	5.3	2.4	9.1	1.1	$p<0.0005$ $U=297.5$
Q4: How easily could you point out bits of information to one another?	5.06	2.29	8.17	1.62	$p<0.0005$ $U=281.5$
Q5: What score would you give each system overall?	5.67	2.25	8.56	1.34	$p<0.0005$ $U=283$

Table 1. Average subjective ratings (out of 10). X indicates a non-significant result.

Results

We asked the participants to rate each system (paper and BuddyBooks) out of 10 (10 being highest) for a range of attributes relating to group reading. Table 1 shows a selection of these ratings.

The participants' subjective responses show a strong preference for BuddyBooks compared with paper with average overall ratings (Q5) producing significant (Mann-Whitney) results of 5.67 and 8.56. These promising results were also supported by participants' comments:

> "Real time, multiple people editing is major plus point. I would love to adopt this over the reams of paper"

> "It's good to see new system/technology and to see something working well, and how it could one day help me in my job"

We asked users to rate how easy it was to view notes made by other members of the group (Q1), how easy it was to create notes of their own (Q2) and how easy it was to create highlights and share them with all other group members (Q3). Q1 and Q3 here, both yielded highly significant subjective scores in favour of BuddyBooks, suggesting it provides a marked improvement over paper for collaborative reading. Some of the reasons as stated by the participants as why they preferred BuddyBooks included: more legible notes, real-time updates, variety of easy functions and it doesn't require pens. Of these reasons, the ability to see other's notes on their own document seemed to be the most popular feature prompting comments such as:

> "It's very easy to see what others are doing with their annotations/highlights."

> "It was good that I could see other's highlights of spelling mistakes then there was no need for me to mark it too. Saves us all doing the same job."

> "Being able to see everyone's notes in their own color helped a lot I knew that blue comments we made by someone else than the red ones, I could directly ask people in case of any questions."

Though participants did not find it significantly easier to *create* notes using BuddyBooks, the results for this were relatively high for both systems, indicating that the new interface did not add any novel problems.

With regards to the form factor of slate-PCs, participants' comments were generally positive in terms of their wireless form, size, shape which allows them to be used much in the same way as a clipboard and pen.

Turning our attention to mutual navigation, which, as already noted, can be problematic during group reading on paper, Q4 shows that users found it easier to point out content to each other using BuddyBooks rather than paper. The observed behaviour of the participants also uncovered a surprising difference between the two interfaces. Specifically, there was a lot less time spent discussing *where* in the document to look in BuddyBooks than they did on paper (i.e., in the paper task, all five groups were heard describing where to look - e.g., *"over here on page 10, half way down paragraph 2"*). Thus, a much larger number of comments were being made about the content of the text itself in BuddyBooks, and when using paper a large amount of discussion concerned where in the document to focus. BuddyBooks appears to encourage discussion within collaborative working groups – a valuable contribution that demonstrates the value of slate PCs for digital collaborative reading.

One issue that particularly concerns us is the relative use of different styles of annotation when using this form-factor. Highlighting was used extensively (just under 75% of all marks), and annotations and bookmarks only minimally (5% and 3% respectively). The novel point-out tool accounted for the remaining 17%. For example, group 1 used 13 point-outs, 66 highlights, 5 annotations and 2 bookmarks. The use of these different methods on paper and desktop PCs is well documented. Typical values on paper would usually have *at least* double (10% to 35%) the number of textual notes [5] – and thus it appears participants reduced their use of written notes.

The volume of markups between our paper and iPad modes was similar, and both corresponded with documented paper behaviours. Nonetheless, there remains some caution about the iPad form factor for a number of participants, prompting comments such as:

"you can write corrections more easily [on paper]."

"sometimes its nice to do things by hand."

In digital reading the volume of annotations of all types is typically low – a sixth to a third of the number found on paper. In contrast, the volume of markup was consistent between paper and BuddyBooks. We thus have overall annotation behaviours that mirror the volume of paper, and exceeds that of desktop work, but which emphasises non-textual marks over written notes.

CONCLUSIONS

Seymour Papert [7] commented that a primary school teacher 'teleported' from a thousand years ago would notice hardly any difference. Had he used the term "collaborative reading" this would be one of the things that has not changed noticeably. As this paper emphasizes, today's technology can change how collaborative reading is performed – it can enhance mobility and coordination.

The BuddyBooks prototype has shown the utility of slate PC devices for collaborative group reading. When using a mid-sized touch-screen device, the participants in our experiment demonstrated a high level of annotation – a contrast to the normal characteristics of electronic reading on the desktop. Using a PC results in few annotations and a low level of interaction with the text. However, there were changes and adjustments to the participants' use of annotation facilities – textual annotations were infrequent, while highlighting was commonplace.

We have also demonstrated the specific advantages of mobile devices to enhance reading together. Our support for coordinating reading, which avoids the verbose description of document content and locations, demonstrated the potential of mobile technology to expand the scope of reading beyond traditional media. This work is a companion paper to another body of research into collaborative reading [8].

ACKNOWLEDGEMENTS

This work was supported by Microsoft Research Cambridge, and EPSRC grants EP/F041217 and EP/G003971/1.

REFERENCES

1. M. Ames and M. Naaman. Why we tag: motivations for annotation in mobile and online media. In *Procs CHI '07*, pages 971–980. ACM, 2007.
2. G. Buchanan, S. Farrant, M. Jones, H. Thimbleby, G. Marsden, and M. Pazzani. Improving mobile internet usability. In *Procs WWW '01*, pages 673–680. ACM, 2001.
3. R. L. Duchnicky and P. A. Kolers. Readability of text scrolled on visual display terminals as a function of window size. *Human Factors*, 25:683–692, 1983.
4. G. Golovchinsky, S. Carter, and A. Dunnigan. Ara: the active reading application. In *Procs MM '11*, pages 799–800. ACM, 2011.
5. C. C. Marshall. *Reading and Writing the Electronic Book.* Synthesis Lectures on Information Concepts, Retrieval, and Services. Morgan & Claypool Publishers, 2009.
6. C. C. Marshall, M. N. Price, G. Golovchinsky, and B. N. Schilit. Introducing a digital library reading appliance into a reading group. In *Proc. DL '99*, pages 77–84. ACM, 1999.
7. S. Papert. *The children's machine: rethinking school in the age of the computer*. Basic Books, Inc., New York, NY, USA, 1993.
8. J. Pearson, T. Owen, H. Thimbleby, and G. Buchanan. Co-reading: Investigating collaborative group reading. In *Procs of JCDL '12*, page In Print. ACM, 2012.
9. E. Siegenthaler, P. Wurtz, and R. Groner. Improving the usability of e-book readers. *J. Usability Studies*, 6:3:25–3:38, November 2010.

An Investigation into the Use of Tactile Instructions in Snowboarding

Daniel Spelmezan
INRIA; Univ Paris-Sud & CNRS (LRI)
F-91405 Orsay, France
spelmezan@lri.fr

ABSTRACT

In many sports, athletes are spatially separated from their coach while practicing an exercise. This spatial separation makes learning new skills arduous because the coach cannot give instructions or feedback on performance. We present the findings of an in the wild study that demonstrate the potential for teaching sport skills with realtime tactile instructions. We focused on snowboard training. Ten amateurs learned a riding technique with a wearable system that automatically provided tactile instructions during descents. These instructions were in sync with the movements of the snowboard and signaled how to move the body. We found that tactile instructions could help snowboarders to improve their skills. We report insights into the snowboarders' opinion and give recommendations for teaching sport skills with tactile instructions. Our findings help to identify the conditions under which tactile instructions can support athletes in sports training.

Author Keywords

Tactile instructions; vibrotactile feedback; sports training; motor skill learning; snowboarding; wearable computing

ACM Classification Keywords

H.5.2 Information Interfaces and Presentation: User Interfaces—*Evaluation/methodology, Haptic I/O*

INTRODUCTION

For acquiring motor skills, such as in sports training, it is important that the learner frequently receives instructions on how to perform the skill and feedback on the performance. Coaches typically give instructions and feedback before and after a trial, and concurrently during the execution of the movements (Figure 1, left). Yet in many sports the coach cannot correct the learner during an exercise. A good case in point is snowboarding. Snowboarders receive instructions before descending the slope and *delayed* feedback after the ride. During the ride, they are spatially separated from their coach. They have to rely on their own perception of what is right or wrong (Figure 1, right).

Figure 1. Left: The tennis student receives instructions and feedback while practicing an exercise. The coach can also guide her movements to demonstrate the correct technique. Right: The snowboard student is spatially separated from his coach during the ride. He typically does not receive instructions nor feedback while descending the slope. (Image on the left courtesy of Cooper Aerobics Center.)

For instructing snowboarders during the ride, the coach could descend alongside the student to call out instructions. Even so, snowboarders could miss these spoken messages in the noisy environment. Spoken messages could also block environmental audio cues on which snowboarders rely on.

Artificial tactile stimuli are an alternative means to give realtime instructions or feedback without these drawbacks. These stimuli can be generated by actuators, such as vibration motors that are sewn into the sportswear. Tactile stimuli have been proposed as application in sports for instructing athletes where to move to, how to move, and when to move [20]. Their advantage is that they directly stimulate the body, like a coach who guides the student's movements (Figure 1, left).

The findings of several studies indicate that artificial tactile stimuli could be beneficial for learning motor skills, such as dancing [14], rowing [20], and karate moves [3]. There is also evidence that tactile stimuli can facilitate the learning of musical instruments [9, 10, 21]. Even so, this previous work [14, 20, 3] did not consider realistic training scenarios but focused on laboratory settings, nor did it focus on sports training [9, 10, 21]. To better understand the potential and pitfalls of using tactile stimuli for teaching sport skills, it is important to consider a broad range of physical activities, user groups, learning conditions, and real-world scenarios.

We are specifically interested in instructing snowboarders during the ride. Snowboarders experience physical strain and tactile sensations that occur naturally while moving their body. These natural sensations could interfere with artificial sensations that actuators evoke on the skin. Snowboarders also focus their attention on the sport, on their body movements, and on the environment. Thus, they can pay less attention to messages that they receive over the tactile sense. Our challenge is to find tactile stimuli that snowboarders can perceive and attend to in active situations. These instructions should not increase the snowboarders' cognitive load. Moreover, we have to determine the teaching and learning conditions under which realtime tactile instructions are effective.

Our work addresses several questions: Can snowboarders perceive tactile instructions when they practice a new riding technique in a realistic scenario? Can they attend to these instructions? How helpful do they consider these instructions? Under which learning conditions do tactile instructions support snowboarders in acquiring new skills, and which conditions should be avoided during training?

To find answers to these questions, we conducted a field study with ten snowboarders who participated in a snowboarding course for one day. These snowboarders learned an unfamiliar riding technique with traditional lessons where the coach provided spoken instructions and feedback before and after the ride, and with lessons where they additionally received tactile instructions while descending the slope. A custom-built wearable system automatically instructed the snowboarders during the ride. This system sensed the movements of the snowboard and provided tactile instructions at the point in time when the snowboarders had to perform body movements that were essential to their riding technique.

This work investigates the use of realtime tactile instructions for snowboard training in a realistic scenario. We first discuss related work and our research goals. We then describe our wearable snowboard training system and the coach's opinion, who tested the system on the slope. After describing the snowboarding course, we discuss our findings on the effectiveness of tactile instructions and the snowboarders' opinion. We conclude with recommendations for applying tactile instructions during training.

RELATED WORK

Sport technologies use embedded and wearable sensors for measuring physiological aspects and muscle movements that can help coaches to understand and to improve the performance of athletes. Chi et al. [4] gave an introduction to this topic and described that these technologies could help to improve sports performance and learning, to encourage more exercises, and to make sports more entertaining.

Besides assisting coaches, sport technologies could also support athletes with realtime instructions on how to move the body or with immediate feedback on their performance. This information could be presented as artificial tactile stimuli, as sound, or visually on a display.

Tactile Instructions

When the athlete needs only a hint at how to adjust the posture, a tactile stimulus can nudge the body in the right direction. Van Erp et al. [20] described that tactile stimuli could signal to athletes *where* to move to, *how* to move, and *when* to move. Van Erp et al. [20] also reported that the first two application scenarios—where and how to move—were tested with elite athletes in soccer training, cycling, and speed skating. Furthermore, van Erp et al. [20] conducted a laboratory study where rowers received tactile instructions when to move the legs and the back while exercising with a rowing machine. The findings of their study indicated that tactile instructions can help athletes to maintain a high performance level.

Several studies suggest that tactile instructions can support the learner in acquiring motor skills. Bloomfield et al. [3] reported that tactile stimuli at the arm help novices to learn karate arm movements in a virtual reality setup. Nakamura et al. [14] applied tactile stimuli at the wrist to instruct dance beginners when to perform a movement. In general, the participants were able to increase the number of correct movements and to perform these movements faster compared to dancing without tactile cues. Tactile stimuli were also shown to be effective for learning to play musical instruments. For example, Holland et al. [9] used tactile stimuli at the wrists and ankles for teaching drum patterns. Huang et al. [10] used tactile stimuli at the fingers for teaching piano melodies.

In our previous work [16], we focused on designing tactile stimuli that could intuitively represent body movements. We also reported that snowboarders were able to perceive and to identify tactile instructions while descending a slope. We did not, however, consider a realistic training scenario.

Tactile Feedback

Besides instructing when and how to perform a movement, a tactile stimulus can also act as *feedback* when the movement is wrong. In general, feedback does not instruct the learner how to perform a movement but it can implicitly indicate the direction to move in order to correct the error. For example, Lieberman et al. [13] asked participants to mimic an arm movement that was shown on a computer display. A motion capture system tracked and analyzed the performed movements. Realtime tactile feedback at the arm represented the deviations from the target movements. This feedback resembled a force-field around the correct movement path and indicated the intended movement direction. According to the findings of their laboratory study, Lieberman et al. reported that the addition of tactile feedback to motor training could improve performance and could support learning.

Van der Linden et al. [21] conducted a two-months study where tactile feedback supported children in playing the violin in a realistic teaching scenario. Similar to [13], they used a motion capture suit for tracking the children's movements and posture while bowing. They found that realtime tactile feedback at the arms and torso enabled the children to improve the holding of the violin and straight bowing. Moreover, both the teachers and the children used the system in new ways to achieve their own objectives.

Finally, haptic devices that generate force feedback have been used for motor skill training in virtual environments. For example, Feygin et al. [6] reported that haptic guidance helped users to learn the temporal aspects of the motor skill, whereas visual training was better for learning the motion shape.

Audio and Visual Feedback

For elite sports training, Baca et al. [1] explored *rapid feedback systems* for rowing, table tennis, and shooting. These systems sensed relevant performance data and visualized this data as graphs on a computer display shortly after motion execution. For martial arts training, Kwon et al. [12] combined data from accelerometers with video analysis for visualizing the power of punches as circles of different sizes. Takahata et al. [18] used accelerometers for analyzing the timing and the forces of wrist, waist, and ankle movements. These measurements were mapped to sound patterns that enabled novices to hear and to compare the characteristics of their movements to the instructor's movements while punching.

A similar training tool is the *Sonic Golf Club* (see sonicgolf.com). This club measures the speed of the swing with built-in accelerometers, and maps the speed to a sound pattern that is played back over earplugs. The *interactive throwing sleeve* is a high tech-armband with sensors at the wrist and elbow [19]. Intended for sports such as basketball, this tool measures the athlete's arm movements. A remote computer analyzes the data and maps the result to musical cues. Both tools provide instant feedback that enables athletes to hear the characteristics of their movements and to recognize movements that lead to successful shots.

Realtime sound feedback on performance has also been applied to skiing. A common mistake in skiing is to tip the shoulders during turns. The *Ski Coach* (see theskicoach.com) is a mechanical device that generates an audible clink when the skier performs turns without tipping the shoulders.

Although these training tools give athletes immediate feedback on their performance, audio and visual feedback can have disadvantages. Sound can be difficult to perceive in noisy environments and can also block environmental audio cues. Computer displays typically restrict training to laboratory settings and require athletes to divide their attention between the sport and interpreting the displayed data.

RESEARCH GOALS

The aforementioned findings on using tactile instructions and tactile feedback for motor skill learning suggest that artificial tactile stimuli can assist learners in acquiring motor skills. These findings, however, cannot be generalized to sports training because the application domain and the movement tasks are different. Moreover, only a few studies were conducted under real-world conditions. Van der Linden et al. [21] stressed the importance of conducting studies in the wild, as the experiences of a lesson under laboratory conditions differ from the experiences in realistic scenarios.

An important aspect to consider is that physical exertion and cognitive load can degrade the learner's ability to perceive and to attend to tactile stimuli. For example, Bhargava et al. [2] reported that young adults who floated freely during zero-gravity flights in an airplane were not able to reliably identify the location of tactile stimuli on their body. Van der Linden et al. [21] reported that children did not notice tactile feedback in situations where they experienced high cognitive load. Also, Hoggan et al. [8] reported that tactile feedback

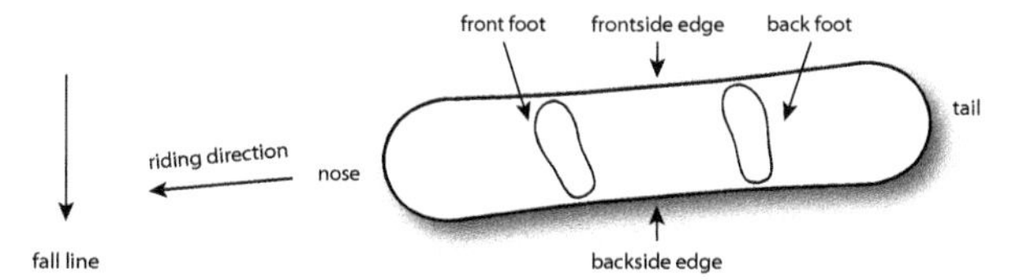

Figure 2. Snowboard terminology and typical stance when the left foot points forward. Alternatively, some snowboarders prefer to descend with the right foot pointing forward. The fall line is the most direct path that a ball would roll down the hill.

for a touchscreen typing task becomes ineffective in an environment with high background vibration levels. Although the findings of several studies indicate that the participants were able to perceive and to respond to tactile stimuli under cognitive load and in active situations [9, 21, 16, 20], it is not known under which conditions tactile stimuli will become ineffective as instructions in sports training.

Finally, it is not known what athletes and coaches think about teaching sport skills with tactile instructions. To give first insights into these issues, we focused on a realistic training scenario. We chose snowboarding as example activity because this sport requires athletes to continuously adjust their movements and posture, instead of performing repetitive movements with a fixed movement range. Snowboarders also perform open skills [22], which involves body movements that they have to execute under time-pressure, without planning them, and in an environment that can change during the execution of the movements. We expected to identify conditions under which tactile instructions should be applied during training, and to gain insights into their use that could also benefit other sports and physical activities.

THE SNOWBOARD TRAINING SYSTEM

To illustrate the aspects of snowboarding that we addressed with tactile instructions, we will briefly introduce the basic technique for descending the slope and two typical riding mistakes. We will then describe the wearable system and the tactile instructions that we used in our study.

Fundamentals of Snowboarding

A snowboard has two edges and resembles a wide ski. Both feet are fixed to the snowboard such that the stance is transverse to the direction of travel (Figure 2). During the ride, the weight is distributed evenly between the feet. The shoulders and hips are in line with the feet's stance. Snowboard coaches refer to this posture as *neutral position* [5].

Descending the slope involves a sequence of turns that alternate between riding on the frontside edge and riding on the backside edge. To switch from one edge to the other edge, the rider points the snowboard downhill and pivots across the fall line. The basic technique for pivoting the snowboard is called *basic turn*. This turn involves a sequence of body movements. Assuming that the left foot points forward during the descent (Figure 2), the rider shifts the weight to the front foot and rotates the upper body to the left, towards the new riding direction. The resulting posture leads the snowboard to follow these movements, to align to the fall line, and to pivot to the backside edge. After pivoting the snowboard,

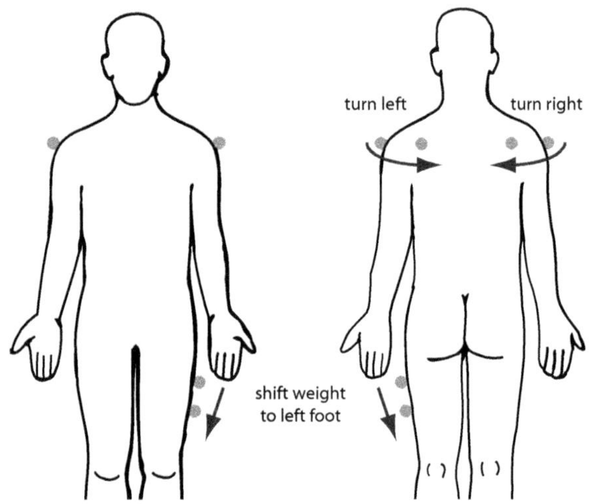

Figure 3. Two vibration motors were placed around each shoulder and laterally at the thigh that pointed forward during the ride. The arrows illustrate the direction of the stimuli on the skin. The labels describe the messages that the stimuli represented.

the rider adopts a neutral position: he redistributes the weight evenly between the feet and aligns the upper body parallel to the snowboard. For the next turn, in order to pivot the snowboard to the frontside edge, the rider shifts the weight to the front foot and rotates the upper body to the right.

This movement sequence challenges snowboard beginners and can lead to two typical mistakes: *incorrect weight distribution* and *counter-rotation* [5]. Facing downhill, many snowboarders tend to shift their weight to the back foot. This posture feels safer but makes it difficult to pivot the snowboard and can lead to falls. Also, they do not properly align the upper body towards the new riding direction. Instead, they counter-rotate the torso in the opposite direction.

Tactile Instructions for Basic Turns

We used two tactile instructions to address these mistakes. These instructions signaled which body movements to perform in order to pivot the snowboard with a basic turn. The first instruction stimulated the thigh and prompted the rider to shift the weight to the front foot. The second instruction stimulated either the left shoulder or the right shoulder, which depended on the direction of the new turn (Figure 3).

We based these instructions on the findings of our previous study [16], which focused on the intuitive interpretation of tactile stimuli. We reported that users preferred directional lines as instructions because they could often associate these lines with body movements. Therefore, we used the sensory saltation phenomenon [7] to draw directional lines on the skin [17]. The motors were sequentially activated. Each motor was pulsed three times for 100 ms with pauses of 50 ms.

For motor skill learning, instructions on how to move the body should guide the learner's attention to the effects of body movements (external focus) instead of to the body (internal focus) [22]. For this reason, we worded the meaning of the tactile instructions to promote an external focus of attention, as noted in [16]. This wording was based on the spoken instructions that coaches use during training. The stimuli at the thigh, which signaled to shift the weight to the front foot, represented the message *Increase the pressure towards the nose of the snowboard.* The stimuli at the shoulder, which signaled to turn left or right, represented the message *Hello mountain* or *Hello valley*. This message depended on the riding direction after pivoting across the fall line, when the rider faced either the mountain or the valley.

Hardware Setup for Automatic Tactile Instructions

A custom-built wearable system automatically triggered the two tactile instructions during the ride. This system was based on an Arduino BT (see arduino.cc) and a Nokia N70 mobile phone as host device. We programmed the system to detect the point in time when the rider pivoted the snowboard from one edge to the other edge, as described in [15].

To sense the riding edge, we used four pressure sensors that measured the rider's weight distribution on the snowboard. One sensor was placed under each heel. Another sensor was placed under the toes. The difference between the pressure that was measured under the toes and under the heels yielded the riding edge. When the weight was towards the toes, the rider descended on the frontside edge (Figure 2). When the weight was towards the heels, the rider descended on the backside edge. Transitions between the frontside edge and the backside edge corresponded to pivoting the snowboard.

This sensing technique could not detect whether the snowboarder's posture was correct or wrong. For this reason, the system automatically provided the two tactile instructions whenever the rider pivoted the snowboard. Thus, the snowboarder received instructions for every turn.

We used off-the-shelf cylindrical vibration motors for mobile phones as actuators (type Nokia 3270). These motors vibrated at a frequency around 180 Hz when powered by four AA batteries. The motors were fixated under a tight T-shirt that had small pouches for inserting actuators.

PILOT TEST AND THE COACH'S OPINION

A snowboard instructor from RWTH Aachen University's sports center volunteered to conduct a snowboarding course for our study. Before the course took place, he tested the wearable system on the slope. To experience when the system triggered tactile instructions and what the evoked sensations felt like, he varied his speed and riding techniques, including basic turns, wide and short turns, riding switch, and carving. He confirmed that the system functioned as intended and that he received instructions whenever he started a new turn.

He suggested, however, to use shorter tactile stimuli because the compound instructions were too long (1750 ms). During short turns at high speed, the two instructions could interfere with body movements that the rider has to perform in order to return to neutral position after pivoting the snowboard. He also noticed that the onset of the instructions was sometimes slightly delayed when pivoting to the backside edge. Ideally, the instructions should occur at the very moment when the rider has to perform the body movements. This is while initiating a new turn before pivoting the snowboard, and while

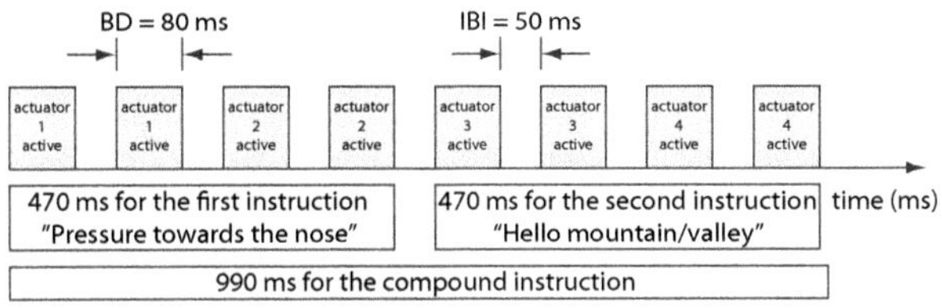

Figure 4. The tactile instructions were based on stimuli with a burst duration BD = 80 ms and an inter-burst interval IBI = 50 ms.

pivoting across the fall line. Even so, our coach considered this delay to be less critical with shorter tactile stimuli.

To shorten the length of the instructions, we experimented with shorter timing values and agreed to pulse each motor twice for 80 ms. These values reduced the length of the compound instruction from 1750 ms to 990 ms (Figure 4).

THE SNOWBOARDING COURSE

Our goal was to explore if tactile instructions can support snowboarders in improving their riding skills. We were also interested in the snowboarders' opinion on receiving tactile instructions during the ride.

The Task

We decided to teach how to ride basic turns switch. This technique required the snowboarders to descend in an unfamiliar posture: the foot that normally pointed backward on the snowboard pointed forward. This entailed that snowboarders who preferred to descend with the left (right) foot pointing forward had to descend with the right (left) foot pointing forward (Figure 2). Riding switch makes snowboarders feel clumsy like beginners and is difficult to master even if they can descend the slope in their preferred stance.

The Participants

Ten university students volunteered (aged 21–29 years, two women). They were snowboarders at advanced beginner level who had basic snowboarding skills but who needed more focused sessions to refine their technique. On a scale ranging from level one (beginner) to level five (expert), three participants rated their snowboarding skills as level one, four as level two (advanced beginner), and three as level three (advanced). Six snowboarders had previously tried to ride switch. One participant was a first-time snowboarder. Before the course started, she received an one-hour introductory lesson to practice the basics of snowboarding.

The Lessons

The study took place in an indoor ski resort. We repeated the snowboarding course on five days with two participants per day. Donning and calibrating the wearable system lasted one hour. The lessons started in the morning and ended in the afternoon. A break of 45 minutes was scheduled at noon.

To allow all participants to experience lessons without tactile instructions and lessons with tactile instructions, we chose a within-subjects design with two conditions:

1. Traditional lessons where the coach provided spoken instructions before and spoken feedback after the descent.
2. Traditional lessons that were accompanied by tactile instructions when the rider pivoted the snowboard.

The order of the conditions was counterbalanced. In the morning, the experimenter randomly chose one participant ($P1$) to descend without tactile instructions (condition 1). The other participant ($P2$) descended with tactile instructions (condition 2). The conditions were reversed after the break. $P1$ received tactile instructions (condition 2), whereas $P2$ did not receive tactile instructions (condition 1).

We conducted a blind study to prevent bias on the coach's part. The coach did not know if his students received tactile instructions during the ride. This setup ensured that he treated all students alike when explaining exercises and when providing feedback on their performance after the ride. The participants carried the wearable system in a pouch and were asked not to reveal if they received tactile instructions.

The slope was 520 m (1700 ft) long. All participants descended ten times in this order:

- One descent for reference
- Four descents for one condition
- Four descents for the other condition
- One descent for reference

The coach used the first descent in the morning and the final descent in the afternoon for rating the participants' skills in riding switch before the course and after the course. The participants did not receive spoken instructions before nor spoken feedback after these reference trials. Neither did they receive tactile instructions while descending the slope.

The course started after the initial descent. The coach explained that tactile instructions during the ride indicate the body movements to perform in order to pivot the snowboard. The experimenter manually triggered the instructions to allow the participants to learn the meaning of the stimuli. This procedure was repeated after the break.

For each of the four descents in the morning and in the afternoon, the coach issued an exercise that his students had to practice. He explained and demonstrated the required movements on level ground at the top of the slope. Then, he slowly descended the first half of the slope to demonstrate this exercise. From the middle of the slope, he signaled the first candidate to descend up to the location where he was waiting. After informing this participant how to improve the riding technique, he observed and advised the second participant. Lastly, the group descended the remaining half of the slope. This time the coach did not correct his students after the ride, which was similar to real courses where the coach cannot give feedback after every run. Even so, the participant who was chosen to descend with tactile instructions did receive these instructions until the end of the slope.

The coach issued exercises as he considered appropriate for teaching basic turns. All participants practiced the same exercises in the morning. Some of these exercises, however, were less appropriate for the skilled snowboarders who quickly

Participant	C	D	E	F	G	H	J
Recognized turns (%)	100	87.0	100	100	51.6	100	100

Table 1. Percentage of turns where the system provided instructions while pivoting (incomplete sensor recordings for participants A, B, I).

progressed during the course. Therefore, the coach also issued more demanding exercises in the afternoon. He asked the advanced snowboarders to increase the edging angle of the snowboard and to carve the turns. Carving requires the rider to descend at higher speed, to adopt a posture that resembles the neutral position, and to pivot the snowboard before passing the fall line. As we did not design the tactile instructions for carving, they were reinterpreted to indicate possible riding mistakes. In this case, the coach asked his students to regard the tactile stimuli as a reminder for avoiding incorrect weight distribution and incorrect upper body rotation because these mistakes could also occur in carving.

Data Acquisition and Analysis

We recorded the course on footage in order to assess the snowboarders' performance off-line. For videoing the participants, the experimenter used a location at the edge of the slope, 230 meters away from the top. This location was above the coach's observation point, who observed his students from the middle of the slope. To evaluate the footage, we recruited another snowboard instructor who did not know about the objective of our study. In addition, the wearable system logged the sensor recordings. We evaluated these recordings off-line in order to assess how accurately the system recognized the pivoting process. This analysis allowed us to identify potential problems with the technology that could have influenced the participants' opinion on tactile instructions. Finally, we interviewed the participants after the course in order to gain insights into their learning experience.

FINDINGS AND DISCUSSION

The Snowboard Training System

The proper functioning of the wearable system was essential for instructing the snowboarders during the ride. We analyzed the sensor recordings and the footage in order to evaluate how accurately the system detected the point in time when the participants pivoted the snowboard.

The footage revealed that the participants performed on average 7.2 turns ($SD = 1.54$, min = 5, max = 11) when descending the first half of the slope with tactile instructions. The system recognized the pivoting of the snowboard on average in 90.7% of these turns. The system worked less accurately for the participants D and G (Table 1). We surmise that the recognition accuracy could improve with additional sensors and with a different sensor setup. For example, sensors could be integrated into the edges of the snowboard or inside the soles of the boots in order to avoid sensor displacement. This setup could also speed-up donning and simplify calibration.

To estimate the period when the system triggered tactile instructions, we marked on footage the turning points on the participants' riding paths (Figure 5 (a)). Based on the timestamps of the footage and of the sensor recordings, we calculated the offset between the time when the snowboarders

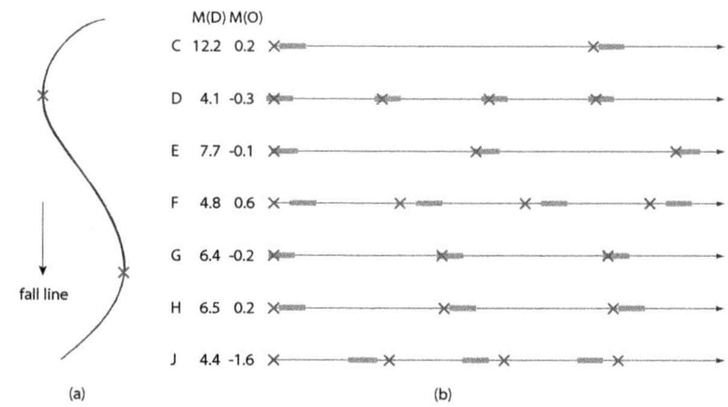

Figure 5. (a) The crosses indicate the turning points on the riding path when the snowboarders passed the fall line. (b) The rectangles show when they perceived the compound instructions (990 ms long) (M(D) = average duration of turns, M(O) = average time offset between passing the fall line and the onset of tactile instructions (in second)).

Participant	A	B	**C**	D	**E**	**F**	**G**	**H**	**I**	J
Previous riding experience	y	y	n	y	y	y	n	n	n	y
Rating before the course	4	7	2	6	2	2	3	2	2	5
Rating after the course	6	8	4	7	4	5	6	4	5	7

Table 2. The participants' previous experience in riding switch (yes/no). The coach's rating of their skills (1 = very bad, 10 = very good; participants with initially poor riding skills are shown in bold font).

passed the fall line and the onset of the instructions. Figure 5 (b) illustrates the average duration between turning points and the time when the system provided the instructions.

On average, the onset of tactile instructions coincided with the time when the snowboarders passed the fall line ($M(O) = -.16, SD(O) = 1.24$ second). Yet, the time offsets varied across the participants. The instructions were most delayed for participant F. He received instructions on average 0.56 second after passing turning points. This indicates that he skidded the snowboard. The system recognized the pivoting process when he exerted more pressure on the new riding edge after passing the fall line. The instructions were also delayed for participant I who commented that he noticed the instruction at the shoulder toward the end of a turn. These delayed instructions could have interfered with the body movements that these snowboarders had to perform in order to return to neutral position. Despite the delay, both F and I considered the instructions to be helpful for riding switch.

Participant J received instructions on average 1.61 second before passing turning points. This strongly suggests that he carved the turns at high speed, otherwise he could not have pivoted the snowboard as early before passing the fall line. In fact, J was an advanced snowboarder who practiced carving in the afternoon. The questionnaire revealed that J did not consider the instructions to be helpful.

The Snowboarders' Skills in Riding Switch

Table 2 shows whether or not the participants had tried to ride switch before the course. The table also shows the course instructor's rating of their initial and final riding skills. Six participants (C, E, F, G, H, I) had poor riding skills at the beginning (rating ≤ 3).

The snowboard instructor who reviewed the footage did not know that the snowboarders had participated in a course. Nei-

Tactile instructions	Participant	A	B	C	D	E	F	G	H	I	J
	Time of day	m	a	m	a	m	a	m	a	m	a
Descents in the morning	Wrong upper body rotation	**42.9**	46.7	**23.8**	12.5	**15.4**	35.7	**14.8**	38.7	**65.8**	45.2
	Wrong weight distribution	**28.6**	0.0	**52.4**	25.0	**26.9**	28.6	**18.5**	29.0	**42.1**	22.6
Descents in the afternoon	Wrong upper body rotation	40.7	**25.0**	20.0	**10.7**	43.5	**26.9**	33.3	**18.9**	48.1	**25.0**
	Wrong weight distribution	29.6	**16.7**	50.0	**7.1**	26.1	**11.5**	37.0	**16.2**	40.7	**32.1**

Table 3. The instructions were provided during descents in the morning or in the afternoon (m/a). Percentage of riding mistakes when riding without tactile instructions (normal font) and with tactile instructions (bold font).

ther did he know that they had learned to ride switch with tactile instructions. He assessed the participants' skills based on the number of riding mistakes. Table 3 shows the average percentage of wrong upper body rotation and weight distribution for descents without and with tactile instructions.

The participants A, C, E, G and I received tactile instructions during lessons in the morning (Table 3). E and G most benefitted from these instructions. They descended more often with correct upper body posture (E, G) and with correct weight distribution (G) in the morning than when riding without tactile instructions in the afternoon. A and C had similar riding skills throughout the day. Participant I improved his upper body posture in the afternoon.

The participants B, D, F, H and J received tactile instructions during lessons in the afternoon (Table 3). D, F and H made fewer mistakes during these rides, but their improved performance could also be attributed to the practice trials in the morning. B and J made fewer upper body mistakes, but they rode more often with wrong weight distribution in the afternoon than in the morning. The reason for these additional mistakes could be the more demanding carving technique that these snowboarders practiced in the afternoon.

For further data analysis we performed a repeated measures ANOVA with *RidingCondition* and *Time* as factors. Regarding the percentage of incorrect upper body rotation, there was no significant main effect of *Time*, no significant main effect of *RidingCondition*, and no significant interaction effect.

For weight distribution, there was no significant main effect of *Time* and no significant main effect of *RidingCondition*. There was a significant interaction effect of *Time x RidingCondition* ($F_{1,8} = 7.96, p = .023, r = .70$). The post-hoc t-test showed some significant effects with large effect sizes: in the afternoon the traditional lessons lead to more mistakes ($M = 36.7, SE = 4.22$) than riding with tactile instructions ($M = 16.7, SE = 4.22, t(14.46) = 2.81, p = .014, r = .59$); lessons with tactile instructions lead to more mistakes in the morning ($M = 33.7, SE = 6.01$) than in the afternoon ($M = 16.7, SE = 4.22, t(14.46) = 2.39, p = .031, r = .53$); traditional lessons lead to fewer mistakes in the morning ($M = 21.0, SE = 5.39$) than in the afternoon ($M = 36.7, SE = 4.22, t(14.46) = -2.20, p = .044, r = .50$).

Overall, it seems that traditional lessons were effective in the morning, whereas lessons with tactile instructions were effective in the afternoon. If we consider the participants' comments (see next section), one reason for these results could be that spoken instructions outweighed tactile instructions when practicing new exercises, whereas tactile instructions were considered to be helpful when advancing in the course.

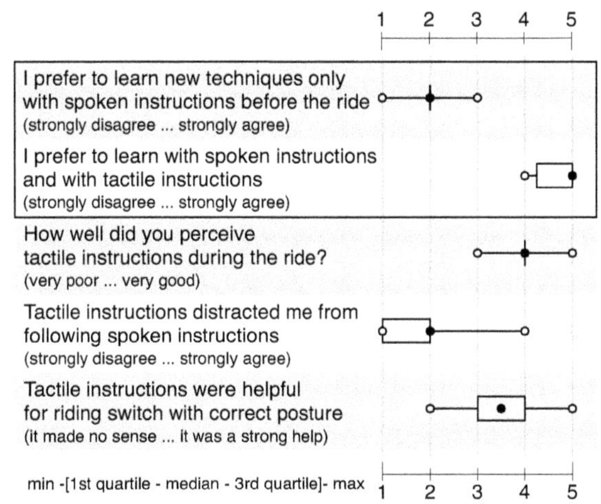

Figure 6. Likert-scale ratings of tactile instructions.

Although the main effect of *RidingCondition* was not significant, tactile instructions had a different effect on the type of riding mistakes, considering all descents and ignoring *Time*. For upper body rotation, there is a noticeable difference between riding with tactile instructions ($M = 26.9, SE = 5.15$) and traditional lessons ($M = 36.4, SE = 3.72$). The post-hoc t-test shows a marginal significance with a large effect size ($t(8) = 2.09, p = .070, r = .59$). For weight distribution the difference between tactile ($M = 25.2, SE = 4.47$) and traditional lessons ($M = 28.9, SE = 4.15$) is small and has a small effect size ($t(8) = .89, p = .40, r = 0.30$).

This observation indicates that the instruction for upper body posture was more effective than the instruction for weight distribution. The reason for this deviation could be that maintaining proper weight distribution requires lots of practice to overcome the feeling of unease when leaning towards the fall line. Another reason could be that paying attention to two riding mistakes and to two tactile instructions is too demanding. It might be beneficial to address only one mistake at a time. In fact, participant I commented that he could not attend to both tactile instructions. He focused on the instruction that was applied either to the shoulder or to the thigh.

The Snowboarders' Opinion on Tactile Instructions

The questionnaire revealed that all participants uniformly agreed to have much improved their skills in riding switch. Half of the group (B, F, H, I, J) considered this riding technique to be difficult to learn.

Figure 6 shows the participants' rating of tactile instructions. Overall, they preferred lessons with tactile instructions over traditional lessons (Wilcoxon signed-ranks test for the framed

Participant	A	**B**	C	**D**	E	F	G	**H**	I	**J**
Instructions were helpful	y	**u**	**u**	**n**	y	y	y	**u**	y	**n**
T. i. corresponded to s. i.	y	**s**	y	**s**	y	y	y	**s**	y	**s**

Table 4. The participants' individual comments on tactile instructions (negative comments are shown in bold font): The instructions were helpful for riding switch (yes/no/undecided). The instructions corresponded to spoken instructions (yes/somewhat).

questions: $T = 0, n = 10, p < .01, r = -.64$). Moreover, they reported that they did not have difficulty in perceiving the instructions. Nine participants agreed that the tactile instructions did not distract them from carrying out the spoken instructions, which the coach gave before the ride.

Eight participants explained why they valued tactile instructions: (A) *"Direct feedback during the ride."*; (B) *"Quite accurate."*; (C) *"Clear enough to notice and locate, but not too strong to distract."*; (D, F, I) *"The feedback at the thigh reminded me of correct position and kept me thinking about the weight distribution."*; (I) *"It was great fun and I would recommend it for snowboard students very much!"*; (E) *"The feedback reminded me of correct basic posture when advancing in the course."*; (H) *"The feedback was an additional clue to activate involved body parts."*

Although all participants favored lessons with tactile instructions, they had different opinions whether or not these instructions were helpful for riding switch in our training scenario (Figure 6). Half of the group considered the instructions to be helpful (Table 4, row 1). The other participants were undecided (B, C, H), or they stated that the instructions did not help (D, J). We can clarify these different opinions if we consider the participants riding skills (Table 2), the exercises that they practiced, and their individual comments.

The following comments illustrate the participants' experiences with tactile instructions: (B) *"It was hard to process this information while trying to follow the spoken instructions."*; (C) *"Since riding switch was completely new to me, I was very concentrated on not falling (in the beginning) and tried to follow the spoken instructions. I did not really react to the tactile instructions, although I noticed them, because there were so many other things to think about. I guess it would have been easier for me to regard them as additional instructions after some time of practice, once the basic way of riding was familiar to me, and when I could spend attention on more exact riding, e.g., at the end of the day."*; (D) *"I was so concentrating on the speed and movements and didn't actually keep my attention on the tactile feedback. I felt the feedback, but didn't actually follow it. I tried more to follow the instructions of the teacher."*; (H) *"When trying to follow the spoken instructions, it was hard to pay active attention to the tactile feedback."*; (J) *"I could not really pay attention to the tactile instructions because I was so concentrating on doing what the teacher told me to do."*

The comments show that these participants focused on the coach's instructions, i.e., the spoken instructions outweighed the tactile instructions. This focus on spoken instructions is understandable because they practiced new exercises: C and H rode switch for the first time; B, D and J practiced carving. Moreover, these exercises caused higher cognitive load. The participants had difficulty attending to tactile instructions while focusing on spoken instructions. In contrast, the participants who had some experience in riding switch and who did not practice carving did not mention having any difficulties paying attention to tactile instructions in addition to spoken instructions. In this case, the task was not too demanding.

These comments suggest that tactile instructions should be introduced later on during training. In fact, J mentioned that tactile instructions could help snowboarders to correct and maintain proper posture at a later stage during training when they can ride better. E shared his point of view: "When I was trying something new the extra feedback was a bit too much, but later, when repeating what I learned, it was very helpful." For this reason, we argue that B, C, D, H and J would have been able to attend to tactile instructions in a different training scenario, for example with less difficult exercises, or without receiving spoken instructions before descending the slope.

Another reason why B, D and J did not consider tactile instructions to be helpful could relate to carving. These participants practiced carving with tactile instructions that represented possible riding mistakes. They stated that the instructions somewhat corresponded to the coach's instructions (Table 4, row 2). Apparently, this use of tactile stimuli was not helpful in our training scenario.

We also found that the participants had a different opinion on how often the system should give instructions. Three inexperienced snowboarders (E, H, I) preferred to receive tactile instructions for every turn. All other snowboarders stated that the system should only give instructions if they make a mistake. This dissent could indicate that the coach should also consider individual learning preferences for adjusting the amount of realtime instructions.

Some participants commented on the wearable system. Their main critique addressed the sensor cables inside the snowboard pants and the fact that the system triggered tactile instructions even while pausing on the slope. Ideally, a wearable training system should perform activity recognition in order to discriminate between riding and pausing [15].

Study Limitations

The results presented in this work have to be interpreted with caution because there are many variables that we could not control in our field study, for example, the participants' fatigue and motivation during the course, and the difficult exercises that the instructor issued to advanced snowboarders during lessons in the afternoon. Moreover, snowboarding is difficult to learn. A short-term study with few participants and with few descents can only provide initial insights into the use of tactile instructions in sports training.

There are several other issues that are difficult to deal with in field studies. For example, it is often difficult for coaches to assess a snowboarder's posture and performance from a distance. For this reason, our results are biased towards the viewpoint of the coach who conducted the course and the instructor who analyzed the footage. In addition, the snowboarders could have intentionally paid more attention to riding with correct posture because they were videoed.

The technology also has to be considered. Our wearable system did not detect snowboarding mistakes. The participants received instructions for every turn, even if their posture was correct. The system also missed some turns. In this case, the snowboarders did not receive instructions. Furthermore, the participants' different riding skills and the exercises that they practiced influenced the way that the system responded to the movements of the snowboard. In particular, the time differed when the participants received instructions while pivoting.

The novelty of the technology is another aspect that could have influenced the participants' opinion. All snowboarders experienced for the first time tactile instructions. The benefits that these instructions could offer during training might not have been obvious to all of them. The experiences that users make with new technology can change over time, and the usefulness and long-term usability of the technology might become apparent only after prolonged use [11].

IMPLICATIONS FOR SPORTS TRAINING

The goal of this work was to identify conditions under which tactile instructions can support snowboarders in acquiring new skills, and conditions that should be avoided. In our training scenario, in addition to spoken instructions, amateur snowboarders received tactile instructions for learning a new riding technique. These tactile instructions were provided for every trial independent of whether the snowboarders made a mistake or not.

Our findings suggest that tactile instructions could potentially help snowboarders to reduce the number of riding mistakes and to improve their skills. Even so, our findings also revealed that it is important to consider the difficulty of the task that the learner performs, the learner's needs during training, and also the learner's preferences. Regarding our research questions, we can summarize our findings as follows:

Can snowboarders perceive tactile instructions when they practice a new riding technique in a realistic scenario? All snowboarders reported that they perceived the tactile instructions, even though their riding skills and the difficulty of the exercises differed. This result is surprising because it contrasts with the findings of other studies where the participants could not reliably locate [2] or could not perceive [21] tactile stimuli in situations where they experienced high cognitive load. We surmise that this could relate to the characteristics of our stimuli. In contrast to [2, 21], which used localized pulses, our stimuli were based on directional lines that stimulated a larger area of the skin. These spatiotemporal patterns could have promoted the perception of the tactile stimuli. Future studies should investigate if such patterns are indeed beneficial in situations of higher cognitive load.

Can they attend to these instructions? The snowboarders who did not have previous experience in riding switch and the snowboarders who practiced new exercises focused on the coach's instructions. This focus on spoken instructions, and the cognitive load participants experienced because they practiced new exercises, made it difficult to pay attention to tactile instructions during the ride. Unlike these participants, the snowboarders who already had some experience in riding switch were able to attend to tactile instructions in addition to spoken instructions. Overall, this finding corresponds to findings of other studies that investigated tactile instructions for teaching motor skills. For example, van der Linden et al. [21] pointed out that the attentional demands of the performed task can influence if the learner can attend to vibrotactile feedback. In our case, however, the results also indicate that some participants received too many instructions. The combination of spoken instructions and tactile instructions made it difficult for some participants to also attend to tactile instructions when they experienced high cognitive load, although perceiving the tactile instructions was not problematic. Thus, besides finding stimuli that learners can perceive and attend to under high cognitive load, it is also important to find the right balance between spoken instructions and tactile instructions.

How helpful do they consider these instructions? All snowboarders stated to prefer lessons with tactile instructions to traditional lessons where the coach gave only spoken instructions before the ride and feedback after the ride. This strongly suggests that they considered tactile instructions to be potentially useful during training. Even so, only the snowboarders who practiced exercises that were not too difficult benefitted from tactile instructions and considered these instructions to be helpful for learning to snowboard.

Furthermore, some advanced snowboarders practiced exercises where tactile instructions signaled possible riding mistakes. Apparently, these instructions were not helpful in our training scenario. This could indicate that tactile stimuli should not signal riding mistakes. A better approach could be to guide the snowboarder how to move correctly during the next trial. This is what coaches do. They do not say that movements are wrong. They say how to improve the posture.

Based on our findings, we conclude that tactile instructions should not be applied during the first lessons or when the coach introduces new exercises. In these cases, spoken instructions before the ride could outweigh tactile instructions even if tactile instructions are provided concurrently during the execution of the movements. Moreover, the learner will experience higher cognitive load when practicing new body movements and might not be able to attend to tactile instructions in addition to spoken instructions. Therefore, tactile instructions should be introduced after the learner has acquired the basic skills in performing the new task. At this stage during training, the cognitive load on the learner will be lower. Tactile instructions could support the learner in practicing and fine-tuning the previously learned movements.

To conclude, we propose a training scenario where tactile instructions will be gradually introduced: The coach gives spoken instructions for a new exercise as usual. After the learner acquires the basic skills for performing the exercise, the coach will introduce one tactile instruction to correct the body movement that he considers most important for improving the learner's skills. The wearable training system will provide this instruction frequently for every trial in order to allow the learner to focus on this particular movement. The frequency of this instruction will be reduced when the learner becomes more proficient in performing the exercise, and will be eventually omitted when the performance becomes stable. If the learner makes the mistake again later on, however, the tactile instruction will be reintroduced as a reminder.

A coach who observes a particular riding mistake could manually trigger a tactile instruction in the aforementioned scenario. Even so, we surmise that this instruction could be delayed. As the timing of the instruction is important, a sensing system may be more precise in providing realtime instructions, in particular if the system can accurately classify a specific body movement or riding mistake. Besides assisting snowboarders during courses and when riding alone, coaches could also benefit from such a system because they cannot always observe and correct every student separately. Moreover, coaches could miss some incorrect body movements when observing students from a distance.

CONCLUSIONS

This work explored the use of realtime tactile instructions for teaching sport skills in a realistic scenario. We conducted a snowboarding course with amateur snowboarders who received tactile instructions while descending the slope. These instructions signaled which body movements to perform. A wearable system automatically provided these instructions for every trial, in addition to the spoken instructions and the feedback that the coach gave before and after the ride. The tactile instructions were most effective when the exercises that the snowboarders practiced were not too difficult. When the snowboarders practiced new and difficult exercises, however, they focused on the coach's instructions and had difficulty paying attention to tactile instructions. Overall, our findings indicate that tactile instructions could support snowboarders in improving their performance. Moreover, our participants considered these instructions to be potentially useful during training. Based on our findings, we can conclude that tactile instructions are a viable approach for supporting learners in acquiring sport skills if these instructions are tailored to meet the learners' needs during training.

As future work, we would like to validate our findings in other training settings and for other physical activities. We intend to conduct a long-term study where tactile instructions are gradually introduced during training. Furthermore, we plan to investigate realtime spoken instructions that are provided over earplugs. Finally, we would like to develop a wearable system that can recognize snowboarding mistakes and that can support snowboarders in learning different riding techniques.

REFERENCES

1. Baca, A., Kornfeind, P. Rapid Feedback Systems for Elite Sports Training. *IEEE Pervasive Computing 5*, 4, (2006), 70–76.
2. Bhargava, A., Scott, M., Traylor, R., Chung, R., Mrozek, K., Wolter, J., Tan, H. Z. Effect of Cognitive Load on Tactor Location Identification in Zero-g. *Proc. WHC 2005*, IEEE Computer Society, 56–62.
3. Bloomfield, A., Badler, N. I. Virtual Training via Vibrotactile Arrays. *Presence: Teleoperators and Virtual Environments 17*, 2, (2008), 103–120.
4. Chi, E. H., Borriello, G., Hunt, G., Davies, N. Guest Editors' Introduction: Pervasive Computing in Sports Technologies. *IEEE Pervasive Computing 4*, 3, (2005), 22–25.
5. Dt. Verband f. d. Skilehrwesen, Interski Deutschland. *Snowboard-Lehrplan.* BLV Buchverlag, München. 2003.
6. Feygin, D., Keehner, M., Tendick, F. Haptic Guidance: Experimental Evaluation of a Haptic Training Method for a Perceptual Motor Skill. *Proc. HAPTICS 2002*, IEEE Computer Society, 40–47.
7. Geldard, F. A. *Sensory Saltation: Metastability in the Perceptual World.* Lawrence Erlbaum Associates. 1975.
8. Hoggan, E., Crossan, A, Brewster, S. A., Kaaresoja, T. Audio or Tactile Feedback: Which Modality When? *Proc. CHI 2009*, ACM Press, 2253–2256.
9. Holland, S., Bouwer, A. J., Dalgelish, M., Hurtig, T. M. Feeling the Beat Where it Counts: Fostering Multi-Limb Rhythm Skills with the Haptic Drum Kit. *Proc. TEI 2010*, ACM Press, 21–28.
10. Huang, K., Starner, T., Do, E., Weiberg, G., Kohlsdorf, D., Ahlrichs, C., Leibrandt, R. Mobile Music Touch: Mobile Tactile Stimulation for Passive Learning. *Proc. CHI 2010*, ACM Press, 791–800.
11. Karapanos, E., Zimmerman, J., Forlizzi, J., Martens, J.B. User Experience Over Time: An Initial Framework. *Proc. CHI 2009*, ACM Press, 729–738.
12. Kwon, D. Y., Gross, M. Combining Body Sensors and Visual Sensors for Motion Tracking. *Proc. Advances in Computer Entertainment Technology, 2005* ACM Press, 94–101.
13. Lieberman, J., Breazeal, C. TIKL: Development of a Wearable Vibrotactile Feedback Suit for Improved Human Motor Learning. *IEEE Transactions on Robotics*, (2007), 919–926.
14. Nakamura, A., Tabata, S. Ueda, T. Kiyofuji, S., Kuno, Y. Multimodal Presentation Method for a Dance Training System. *Proc. CHI 2005 Extended Abstracts*, ACM Press, 1685–1688.
15. Spelmezan, D., Schanowski, A., Borchers, J. Wearable Automatic Feedback Devices for Physical Activities. *Proc. BodyNets 2009*, ICST, 1–8.
16. Spelmezan, D., Jacobs, M., Hilgers, A., Borchers, J. Tactile Motion Instructions for Physical Activities. *Proc. CHI 2009*, ACM Press, 2243–2252.
17. Tan, H., Lim, A., Traylor, R. A Psychophysical Study of Sensory Saltation with an Open Response Paradigm. *Proc. ASME 2000*, 1109–1115.
18. Takahata, M., Shiraki, K., Sakane, Y., Takebayashi, Y. Sound Feedback for Powerful Karate Training. *Proc. NIME 2004*, National University of Singapore, 13–18.
19. Athletic Harmony. News Track in Communications of the ACM 51, 6, (2008), 7.
20. van Erp. J. B. F., Saturday, I., Jansen, C. Application of tactile displays in sports: where to, how and when to move. *Proc. EuroHaptics 2006*, 90–95.
21. van der Linden, J., Johnson, R., Bird, J., Rogers, Y., Schoonderwaldt, E. Buzzing to Play: Lessons Learned From an In the Wild Study of Real-time Vibrotactile Feedback. *Proc. CHI 2011*, ACM Press, 533–542.
22. Wulf, G. *Attention and Motor Skill Learning.* Human Kinetics. 2007.

Tip Tap Tones: Mobile Microtraining of Mandarin Sounds

Darren Edge[1], Kai-Yin Cheng[1,2], Michael Whitney[1,3], Yao Qian[1], Zhijie Yan[1], Frank Soong[1]
[1] Microsoft Research Asia, Beijing, China
[2] National Taiwan University, Taipei, Taiwan
[3] University of North Carolina Charlotte, Charlotte, NC, USA
{firstname.lastname}@microsoft.com, keynes.z@gmail.com, mwhitne6@uncc.edu

ABSTRACT

Learning a second language is hard, especially when the learner's brain must be retrained to identify sounds not present in his or her native language. It also requires regular practice, but many learners struggle to find the time and motivation. Our solution is to break down the challenge of mastering a foreign sound system into minute-long episodes of "microtraining" delivered through mobile gaming. We present the example of Tip Tap Tones – a mobile game with the purpose of helping learners acquire the tonal sound system of Mandarin Chinese. In a 3-week, 12-user study of this system, we found that an average of 71 minutes' gameplay significantly improved tone identification by around 25%, regardless of whether the underlying sounds had been used to train tone perception. Overall, results suggest that mobile microtraining is an efficient, effective, and enjoyable way to master the sounds of Mandarin Chinese, with applications to other languages and domains.

Author Keywords

Mobile Gaming; Microtraining; Language Learning

ACM Classification Keywords

H.5 Information interfaces and presentation: User Interfaces

General Terms

Design; Experimentation; Human Factors

INTRODUCTION & RELATED WORK

For a second language learner, the primary difficulty in understanding ongoing speech is the perception of words. This difficulty is especially pronounced for learners of tonal languages such as Mandarin Chinese, in which the meaning of a sound is inferred from both its changing pitch and its context of use. Since most people who learn Mandarin do so from non-tonal native languages and lack sufficient vocabulary to establish linguistic context, they often find the four tones to be the hardest part of language acquisition [8]. Within the four Mandarin tones (Figure 1), new learners often cannot differentiate between the *first* and *fourth* tones because of the unfamiliar pitch range, and the *second* and *third* tones because both end in a rising pitch.

MobileHCI'12, September 21–24, 2012, San Francisco, CA, USA.

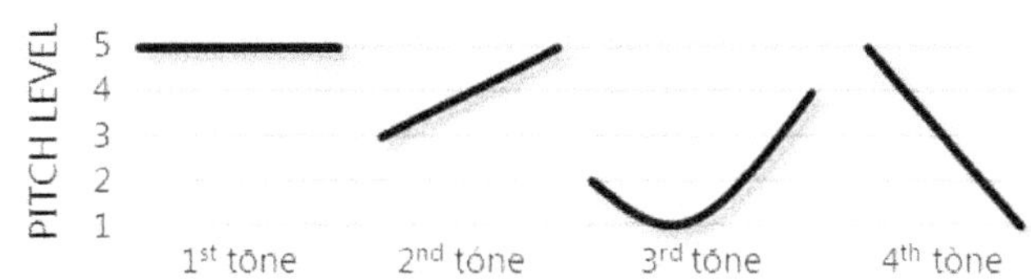

Figure 1. Mandarin Chinese tones on a pitch scale of 1–5.

Tones are not the only difficulty, however. Each syllable is segmented into an *initial* consonant sound followed by a *final* sound which itself can be one or two vowel sounds ending in an optional consonant. There are 23 initials and 34 finals, forming around 1600 tonal syllables in Mandarin Chinese. The importance of understanding this tonal sound system is highlighted in the example of "ma", which when spoken in the first thorough fourth tones "mā", "má", "mǎ", and "mà" (as indicated by the diacritic marks), can refer to the words of mother, hemp, horse, and scold. To complicate further, the Romanized *pinyin* script for pronunciation is idiosyncratic and inconsistent; e.g., "di" and "ci" are pronounced "dee" and "tser" respectively.

As a result of such challenges, the first 2–6 weeks of traditional university-level courses in Chinese are almost exclusively dedicated to the sound system [8]. Since there is no way in which casual language learners can make such commitments, there is a need to support more convenient and accessible learning of the Mandarin sound system.

The standard approach to Mandarin sound instruction is to teach tones, initials, and finals through aural and oral differentiation of minimal pairs (e.g., lā vs. là, zī vs. cī, guǎn vs. guǎng), triplets (e.g., jī, qī, xī), and quadruplets (e.g., mā, má, mǎ, mà). This is grounded in the Speech Learning Model [2], which claims a new phonetic category can only be established if the learner discerns a difference between it and the closest category in their native language. Moreover, adults can only learn novel phonetic contrasts if they re-allocate attention to previously unattended acoustic-phonetic dimensions (i.e., pitch, amplitude, or duration) [3].

Aural perceptual training is effective however, especially when learners are forced to develop and use phonetic codes in short-term memory [3], and the effects have been shown to generalize to novel words and speakers as well as from aural perception to oral production [7]. Recent studies have confirmed that aural training significantly alters brain activation during Mandarin tone perception, showing promising neural plasticity in adult language learners [6].

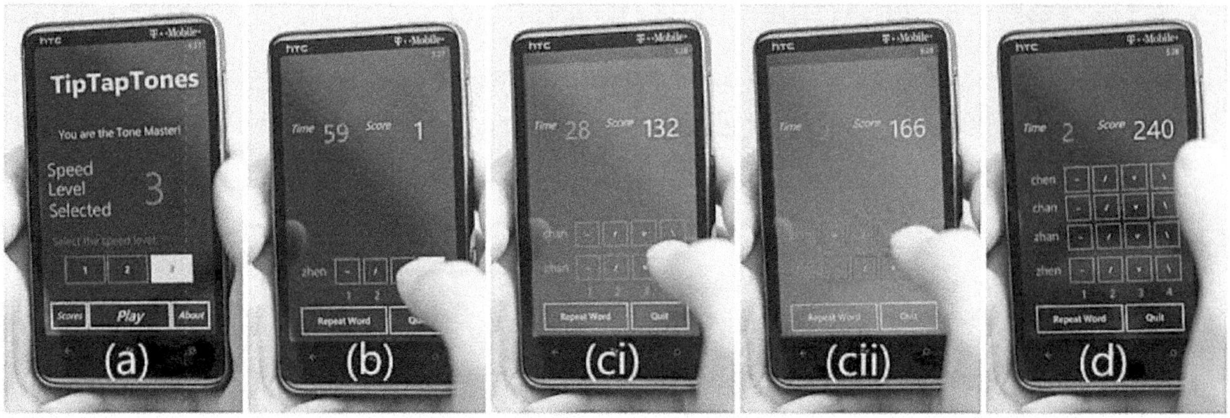

Figure 2. Tip Tap Tones example: (a) Set speed; (b) *zhen* screen (followed by *zhan*, *chen*, and *chan* screens); (ci). *chan* vs. *zhan* screen with "correct" green flash; (cii) *zhen* vs. *chen* screen with "incorrect" red flash; (d) *chen* vs *chan* vs *zhan* vs *zhen* screen.

MOBILE GAME DESIGN

Inspired by casual mobile games, mobile games for learning Chinese characters [5], and mobile microlearning of location-based language [1], we decided to create a mobile "microtraining" game to help learners master the sound system of Mandarin Chinese in short fragments of free time spread throughout the day.

In crafting the game experience, we drew inspiration from the rhythmic tapping of Tap Tap Revolution and the steadily increasing challenge of Tetris[1]. Both use time pressure and repeated actions to facilitate the kind of concentrated attention that leads to skill development.

TIP TAP TONES GAME

The design of our "Tip Tap Tones" game employs a "press your luck" game mechanic: accurate responses are required to complete a level, but more points are awarded for fast level completion. The game screens are shown in Figure 2:

(a) The learner selects a Mandarin sound playback speed of 1, 2, or 3, with sounds of 1s, 0.5s and 0.25s respectively.
(b) In Level 1, the learner hears a Mandarin sound and must press the button corresponding to the correct tone. The learner must give three correct answers for each sound to progress to a similar sound on the next screen. This repeats for four screens before moving to Level 2.
(c) In Level 2, the learner hears a Mandarin sound and must press the button corresponding to both the correct tone and the correct syllable. The choice is between a minimal pair of syllables from the first level; the learner must give three correct answers for each pair of syllables to progress to the next screen. This repeats for four screens of similar pairs before moving to Level 3.
(d) Level 3 is the same as Level 2, but with a choice between four tones and two minimal pairs of syllables. Six correct answers complete the level and the game.

[1] See www.tapulous.com and www.tetris.com respectively.

Game Mechanic

At a minimum, the learner must give 12 correct answers (from 4 options) over 4 screens to complete Level 1, 12 correct answers (from 8 options) over a further 4 screens to complete Level 2, and 6 correct answers (from 16 options) on the final screen to complete Level 3. A total of 30 correct answers over 9 screens in 60 seconds are thus necessary to complete the game. However, this is not always sufficient. If the learner gives an incorrect response, they have one further chance to give the correct answer and continue their progression. If the learner ever gives two incorrect responses in succession, their *correct count* for the current screen is reset to zero and a new sound is selected at random to start the screen again. Learning is facilitated by replaying sounds using the *repeat* button and by feedback, with a correct response followed by a green flash of the screen and an incorrect response followed by a red flash and "punishing" tactile vibration (Figure 2ci–ii).

Points awarded for correct responses in Levels 1, 2, and 3 are 1, 2, and 3 respectively. In Levels 1 and 2, an additional 5 and 10 points respectively are awarded for completion of each screen. A time bonus is also awarded on completion of each level, calculated as *speed factor* × *time remaining* × *level bonus*. The playback speed factors are 1, 1.5, and 2 respectively for speeds 1, 2, and 3, and the level bonuses are 1, 4, and 16 respectively for Levels 1, 2, and 3.

Rationale

Our design of the core game mechanic draws on established guidelines for educational mobile games [4]. It incorporates *adaptation* by varying the game experience according to performance. Learners who consistently give successive incorrect answers will remain in the screens of Level 1, which provide fewer options and thus support initial tone acquisition. Learners who reach Level 2 must demonstrate an additional awareness of the differences between syllables and their spellings in pinyin. Completing Level 3 requires even finer discrimination of sounds while maintaining both accuracy and speed. Since points increase dramatically with the speed of game completion, we provide integrated game and learning *goals* that offer a dynamic *challenge* curve leading towards *mastery* [4].

The decision to limit the duration of each game to a short time period was jointly motivated by the mobile context of use and the natural structure of the minimal-difference identification task. In early experimentation, a game duration of one-minute was found to provide novices with sufficient time to complete at least one game screen successfully (unlike a 30 second version), while allowing sustained concentration from more advanced learners without noticeable fatigue (unlike a 2 minute version).

IMPLEMENTATION

We developed the Tip Tap Tones game in Silverlight for Windows Phone 7 devices, in particular the large-screen HTC HD7 shown in Figure 2. Offline processing was used both to generate the sound files played in the game and to create sets of similar syllables requiring differentiation.

Sound Generation

Synthesized speech is easy to produce but has noticeable artifacts. We therefore recorded sounds from a professional, "golden" speaker reading simplified Chinese characters representing all legal tonal syllables in Mandarin. To create both slower and faster versions of these sounds, we performed Pitch Synchronous Overlap Add (PSOLA) timescale modification after tracking the fundamental frequency and marking the pitch epochs of voiced speech. A panel of native Mandarin speakers determined the time-scaled sounds to be natural and free from artifacts, as would be expected from the limited extent of the transformation.

Syllable Selection

Sounds are perceived as similar if they share phonetic components that are the same or similar in their production. For initial sounds in Mandarin, similarity can arise from articulation (position of the tongue) or aspiration (passage of air) or both. Mandarin finals can also share medial semivowels, nucleus vowels, or coda consonants or vowels.

To create pairs of minimal syllable pairs as required by the game mechanic, for each initial and final we crafted the set of other initials and finals that differed in only one phonetic dimension. For each pairwise product of these initial and final sets, we generated lists of all lexical (i.e., meaning carrying) syllable combinations. From these variable length lists, we first removed the syllables that can only take one or two tones. We then extracted all unique "lattices" of four syllables such that two pairs differed only in their initial sound, and two pairs only in their final sound. This resulted in 100 chains covering 1009 tonal syllables, each used to create the four minimal pairs of syllables used in Level 2 of the game. Each game uses a randomly selected lattice. During gameplay, syllable selection is also random as is the selection of tones from those yet to be used on that screen.

EVALUATION

The evaluation of Tip Tap Tones was based on 3 questions:

1. Can we create a *test* of tone and syllable differentiation on which native speakers achieve near-perfect scores?
2. Does the *game* encourage repeat play and facilitate steady improvement for a range of learner abilities?
3. Does *gameplay* improve *test scores* on the identification of tonal syllables that (a) were trained in the game, and (b) were not trained, indicating phonetic generalization?

To answer question 1, we created a test of Mandarin aural perception using the recordings of the golden speaker. This 10 minute test played a series of non-repeatable Mandarin sounds, with the learner identifying either the correct tone or syllable from four similar options. To address research questions 3(a) and 3(b), both sections included not just all syllables trained in the game, but also the special set of syllables that lack an initial sound (but whose pinyin uses *w* and *y* as prefixes for finals beginning with *u* and *i* respectively). Improvements on these syllables would indicate that training through gameplay results in not just the creation of new phonetic categories, but also their generalization to novel contexts. No feedback was given. Validation with native speakers gave near-perfect scores.

To answer questions 2 and 3, we recruited 12 learners of Mandarin Chinese, drawn from both our lab and the local expatriate community (mean age 30, 2 female). All had lived in China for at least several months prior to commencing our study, but none had reached the level of holding basic conversations. Over the course of a 3-week user study, these participants were free to play Tip Tap Tones on a HTC HD7 Windows Phone 7 as much or as little as they desired. We recommended 3–5 minutes of play per weekday, corresponding to 45–75 minutes in total, but compensation (a small gift) did not depend on this.

Participants completed our test at the beginning and end of the study and did not engage in any additional aural training for its duration (aside from occasional pronunciation feedback in weekly Chinese lessons). We validated our test with Mandarin learners of similar background to the study participants, observing stable scores over the course of a week. We concluded that a control group was therefore unnecessary for the study design, which follows that of [3].

Results

Table 1 shows a breakdown of participant performance. Since tests only measure accuracy and not speed, differences can be observed between advanced learners who focus on accuracy with speed (e.g., *P2*, *P9*) and novice learners who focus on accuracy only (e.g., *P1*, *P7*).

Planned two-tailed paired-sample t-tests comparing pre-test and post-test results indicated that tone accuracy increased significantly by 25% for tones trained in the game, with $t_{11} = 4.7$, $p < 0.01$ from means of 57% (*sd* 24%) and 82% (*sd* 13%). A similar 24% improvement in tone accuracy was also observed for syllables that were not trained in the game, with $t_{11} = 4.6$, $p < 0.01$ from means of 58% (*sd* 23%) and 82% (*sd* 17%). Syllable identification also improved by a significant 12% for syllables trained in the game, with $t_{11} = 3.9$, $p < 0.01$ from means of 68% (*sd* 19%) and 80% (*sd* 17%). Identification of initial-less syllables not trained in the game did not improve, potentially due to their irregular spelling (e.g., the final sound *-ui* becomes the syllable *wei*).

User ID	Game Count	Max Score	Mean Score	CAS Linear Regression		Tone %				Syllable %			
						pre-test		post-test		pre-test		post-test	
				b	R^2	in	not	in	not	in	not	in	not
P1	169	458	157	0.7	0.99	25	29	80	54	52	65	77	75
P2	134	1430	715	4.3	0.88	76	87	82	79	84	90	97	85
P3	104	494	203	1.2	0.92	68	66	86	75	54	80	86	80
P4	78	970	335	3.6	0.98	58	45	95	100	40	60	63	70
P5	66	513	190	1.9	0.93	65	54	88	83	93	75	100	75
P6	60	1042	343	3.8	0.92	89	91	98	95	84	75	100	80
P7	51	152	71	0.7	0.94	17	33	59	62	52	65	56	65
P8	49	1156	350	5.8	0.98	43	70	91	95	84	90	90	85
P9	43	1114	535	10.3	0.85	88	91	95	100	79	80	93	85
P10	39	374	128	1.7	0.86	49	54	77	100	88	80	81	85
P11	33	114	79	1.9	0.95	35	33	59	62	43	80	56	65
P12	22	264	108	1.8	0.43	72	42	70	75	60	66	61	85
mean (*sd*)	71 (44)	673 (444)	268 (198)	3.1 (2.7)	0.89 (0.15)	57 (24)	58 (23)	82 (13)	82 (17)	68 (19)	76 (10)	80 (17)	80 (8)

Table 1. User study game use, cumulative average score (CAS) linear regression (coefficient *b* and adjusted R^2), and pre/post test result for sounds trained "in" the game and "not"

Figure 3 shows a rising *cumulative average score* (CAS) for all learners, indicating improvements in accuracy and speed across sessions. Linear regression gave a strong fit (adjusted $R^2 > 0.85$) for 11/12 learners (see Table 1).

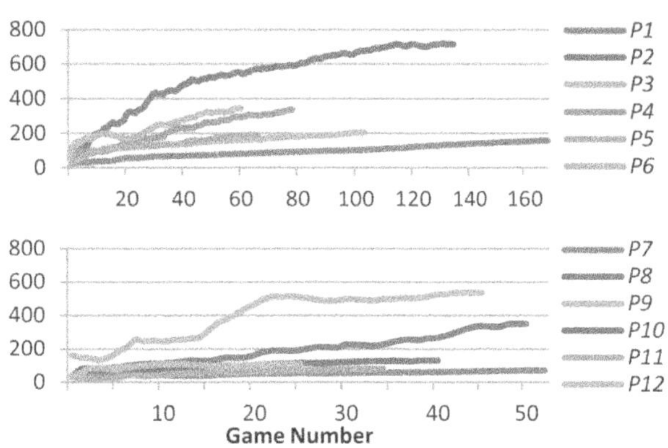

Figure 3 Cumulative average scores over all games played

Qualitative analysis of post-study interviews confirmed tones as the "hardest part" [*P3*] of learning Chinese. All participants thought they had improved, being able to "hear the difference" [*P4*] and "listen quicker" [*P8*]. The minute duration was "great for casual learners" [*P6*], keeping them focused [*P3*] and filling free time [*P1*]. Combined with the feeling of being rewarded [*P6*] by rising scores [*P4*], this time pressure made the game addictive [*P2*]. The increasing "levels of complexity" [*P11*] also made learners pay attention to details they would otherwise miss [*P3*].

Beyond the game, learners reported being better able to listen to tones by "thinking in terms of the Tip Tap Tones screen" [*P8*], read pinyin by "mapping to sounds" [*P10*], and speak by picking out native speaker tones and reproducing them "right away, in the right way" [*P4*].

DISCUSSION & CONCLUSION

Overall, results show that Tip Tap Tones is effective at training learners to correctly identify Mandarin sounds. Large gains in test accuracies and game scores from small time investments suggest mobile microtraining can support efficient and convenient skill development on the move.

Future directions for second-language training include expanding to a "high variability paradigm" with voices from many native speakers (as in [3] and [7]), employing phonetic analysis to mine minimal sound sets in all languages (tonal and otherwise), and using speech analysis for oral pronunciation training. Similar game mechanics could also be useful in domains beyond aural language training (e.g., aural identification of notes for musicians, visual identification of colors for designers, or haptic identification of Braille codes for the visually impaired).

The broadest contribution of this paper is as a case study of how mobile HCI can transform traditional activities by transporting them to new contexts. In particular, we have shown how our design of mobile microtraining has transformed a slow-paced, low-feedback drill into a fast-paced, high-feedback, learner-driven game playable anywhere. Tip Tap Tones is available as a free Microsoft Research application on the Windows Phone marketplace.

ACKNOWLEDGMENTS

We thank all of our testers, participants, and reviewers.

REFERENCES

1. Edge, D., Searle, E., Chiu, K., Zhao, J. & Landay, J. (2010). MicroMandarin: Mobile Language Learning in Context. CHI 2011, 3169–3178
2. Flege, J.E. (2007). Language contact in bilingualism: phonetic system interactions. Laboratory phonology, 9, 353–382
3. Logan, J.S., Lively, S.E., & Pisoni, D.B. (1991). Training Japanese listeners to identify English /r/ and /l/: A first report. Journal of the Acoustical Society of America, 89(2), 874–886
4. Thomas, S., Schott, G. and Kambouri, M. (2003). Designing for Learning or Designing for Fun? Setting Usability Guidelines for Mobile Educational Games. MLEARN 2003
5. Tian, F., Lv, F., Wang, J., Wang, H., Luo, W., Kam, M., Setlur, V., Dai, G. & Canny, J. (2010). Let's play chinese characters: mobile learning approaches via culturally inspired group games. CHI 2010, 1603–1612
6. Wang, Y., Sereno, J., Jongman, A. & Hirsch, J. (2000). Cortical reorganization associated with the acquisition of Mandarin tones by American learners: An fMRI study. Proc. 6th Int. Conf. on Spoken Language Processing, II, 511–514
7. Wang, Y., Spence, M.M., Jongman, A., & Sereno, J.A. (1999). Training American listeners to perceive Mandarin tones. J. of The Acoustical Society of America, 106(6), 3649–3658
8. Xing, J.Z. (2006). Teaching and Learning Chinese as a Foreign Languge. Hong Kong University Press

MemReflex: Adaptive Flashcards for Mobile Microlearning

Darren Edge[1]
[1] Microsoft Research Asia
Beijing, China

Stephen Fitchett[1,2]
[2] University of Canterbury
New Zealand

Michael Whitney[1,3]
[3] University of North Carolina Charlotte
USA

James Landay[1,4]
[4] University of Washington
USA

darren.edge@microsoft.com, stephen.fitchett@pg.canterbury.ac.nz, mwhitne6@uncc.edu, landay@cs.washington.edu

ABSTRACT

Flashcard systems typically help students learn facts (e.g., definitions, names, and dates), relying on intense initial memoriztion with subsequent tests delayed up to days later. This approach does not exploit the short, sparse, and mobile opportunities for microlearning throughout the day, nor does it support learners who need the motivation that comes from successful study sessions. In contrast, our MemReflex system of adaptive flashcards gives fast-feedback by retesting new items in quick succession, dynamically scheduling future tests according to a model of the learner's memory. We evaluate MemReflex across three user studies. In the first two studies, we demonstrate its effectiveness for both audio and text modalities, even while walking and distracted. In the third study of second-language vocabulary learning, we show how MemReflex enhanced learner accuracy, confidence, and perceptions of control and success. Overall, the work suggests new directions for mobile microlearning and "micro activities" in general.

Author Keywords

Mobile Flashcards; Adaptive Systems; Language Learning

ACM Classification Keywords

H.5 Information interfaces and presentation: User Interfaces

General Terms

Algorithms; Design; Experimentation; Human Factors

INTRODUCTION

The mobile phone is the ideal platform for long-term learning, being portable, individual, unobtrusive, available, adaptable, persistent, and useful [22]. In particular, mobile phones can support *microlearning* [13] in fragments of free time throughout the day. Previous work in HCI has examined how flashcards can support mobile microlearning of second-language phrases presented in context, investigating *what* material should be studied *where* [12]. However, relatively little attention has been paid to *when* items should be introduced and reviewed based on *how* the learner has performed in past microlearning sessions, especially in terms of how this relates to learner motivation.

MobileHCI'12, September 21–24, 2012, San Francisco, CA, USA.

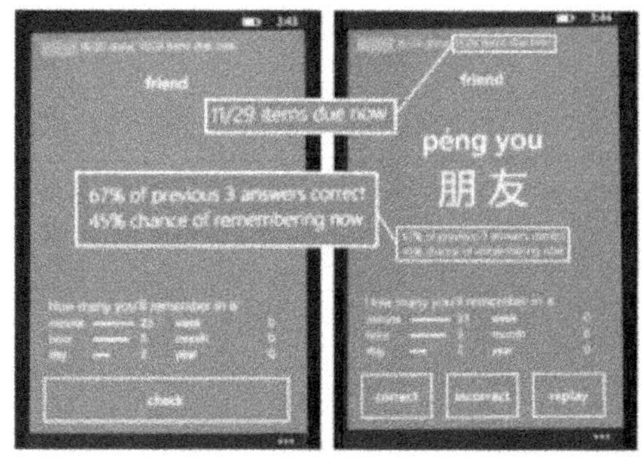

Figure 1. Adaptive flashcards. A cue (left) triggers recall of target information (right). Adaptive scheduling of cued recall tests raises response accuracies towards a goal level, e.g., 90%.

We believe mobile learning should be context-aware in a broad sense – sensitive to learner history as well as the immediate cues of time, location, and motion. We also believe that both text and audio interaction modalities are important to engage learners with different learning styles, as well as learners who move between contexts where different modalities are most appropriate (for example, it might be safer to listen via headphones when navigating busy public spaces, but politer to read from the screen in social situations where some conversation is anticipated).

This paper presents a systematic investigation of how learner *motivation* for microlearning using mobile flashcards is affected by adaptation to past performances, as well as how learner performance "on the move" is affected by the selection of interaction *modality*. The contribution to mobile HCI is a demonstration of how adaptive flashcards can support text and audio-based mobile learning even when walking, and how such adaptation helps drive learner motivation both in the moment and over the longer-term.

We begin with a literature review that motivates system features, before illustrating how existing flashcard systems do not account for the special characteristics of mobile microlearning. Next, we present the algorithm and interface design of our adaptive flashcard system, which we call MemReflex. These flashcards present cues from which learners attempt to recall the target information, with tests scheduled according to a model of the learner's memory (see Figure 1). We end with three user studies that show the effectiveness of MemReflex from the immediate to the longer-term, using either audio or text modalities, even while distracted by the demands of learning on the move.

RELATED WORK

In this section, we survey both the findings of learning research and the learning systems that aim to exploit them. Although we focus on approaches to learning that can be exploited in mobile contexts, our contribution itself is to the larger body of work on mobile learning or m-learning[1].

Learning Research

Learning is not a single process, but a hierarchy of processes reflecting progressive orders of change [2]. Zero order learning is characterized by responses without correction; first order learning by correction of errors within sets of alternatives; and second order learning by a change in the sets of alternatives or the distribution of first order learning over time (also known as "learning to learn").

Reviewing a physical flashcard is an example of first order learning: the front side of the card acts as a cue for the target on the reverse. When a learner attempts to recall the target given such a cue, the learning style is called *cued recall* and has been studied extensively in the learning literature. In contrast, our investigation of how to motivate learners to appropriate time for microlearning is a question of second order learning that has yet to be fully explored.

The testing effect

Much research into learning investigates and exploits the *testing effect* – that tests strengthen memory more than extra opportunities to study, even when mental retrieval is not accompanied by an outward response. Such test-directed learning can therefore take place in contexts where it is undesirable to produce overt responses, such as in public places. Moreover, it has been demonstrated across a variety of domains, including the learning of vocabulary in native and second languages, face–name associations, general facts, text passages, word lists, and even maps [6]. Cued recall tests of the form A→? have also been shown to enhance retention in the opposite direction B→?, as well as enhancing free recall of all cues (As) and targets (Bs) [7].

The spacing effect

The *spacing effect* is that when learning a set of items, superior retention results from multiple shorter presentations than from a single "massed" presentation. The time separating different study episodes of the same material is known as the inter-study interval or ISI. Studies of the spacing effect typically manipulate the ISI of two study episodes, and compare their effect on a later test that occurs after a fixed retention interval. In a review of 427 articles on cued recall learning, it was found that the optimal ISI increases as the retention interval increases [8]. For example, the optimum ISI for a 1-minute retention interval was less than 1 minute, whereas for retention intervals of 6 months or more it was at least 1 month. The implication is that multiple study episodes are needed for continuous retention, as shown in Figure 2.

[1] See the m-learning website at http://www.m-learning.org/.

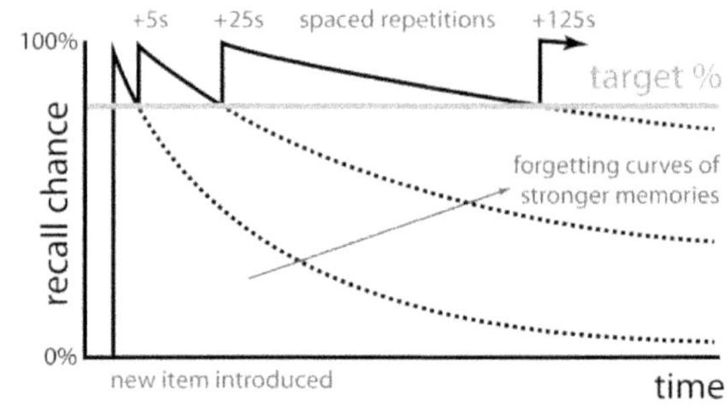

Figure 2. Adaptive spaced-repetition learning

The forgetting curve

The *forgetting curve*, discovered in 1885 [11], describes the inverse exponential nature of forgetting. In the presence of repeated, *spaced repetitions* as described above, the strength of a memory is increased, resulting in a more gradual process of forgetting. The most sophisticated psychological modeling of this process is derived from the ACT-R activation-based model of declarative memory, with each test of an item introducing a new memory trace whose decay rate is a power law function of all traces for the item at the time of the test [17]. In this model, the higher an item's activation, the smaller the effect any additional tests will have on its long-term retention.

Overlearning

Once a learner correctly recalls an item using cued recall, any further testing of the same item in the same session is described as *overlearning*. In two experiments and a review of the overlearning literature, Rohrer et al. [20] show that within a single learning session, doubling the number of tests for each item typically more than doubles the percentage of correct responses when tested again one week later. They suggest that such overlearning is necessary for short-term retention in situations such as preparing for an exam later in the day or learning foreign language vocabulary in advance of planned conversations. However, these benefits diminish for longer retention intervals.

Learning Systems

Since 1967, the dominant approach to audio language learning has been the Pimsleur System [19]. This is a series of 30-minute audio lessons in which basic vocabulary and phrases are introduced and reviewed in cued-recall fashion according to a schedule of *graduated interval recall*. This is a progressive series of exponentially expanding intervals (repetitions after 5^1s = 5 seconds, 5^2s = 25 seconds, 5^3s ≈ 2 minutes, 5^4s ≈ 10 minutes) both within and (roughly) across lessons. The advantages are that it uses deliberate overlearning to breed confidence and support immediate language use. The disadvantages of such lessons, however, are that repetitions are not scheduled in real-time, there is no adaptation to user feedback, lesson-length chunks of free time must be available, and ultimately the learner will run out of lessons. This latter difficulty is addressed by Gradint [14], which allows learners to make their own Pimsleur-like recordings using text-to-speech.

Developed at the same time as the Pimsleur system, the Leitner System [15] for physical flashcards is also based on spaced repetition. Using numbered flashcard piles P_1–P_N, each subsequent pile represents flashcards of both increasing memory strength and increasing inter-study intervals (e.g., on day D of study, test all flashcards in pile P_X where D is a multiple of X). Cards are promoted one pile if correct or else returned to the first pile for relearning. The advantage of this approach is that more difficult items are reviewed more often. The disadvantages are that there is no support for deciding when to introduce new flashcards into the first pile, and that the volumes of flashcards scheduled for review can quickly become unmanageable.

A computer-assisted approach to managing and scheduling the review of digital flashcards was popularized by the SuperMemo algorithm that targets a fixed retention rate [24]. In SuperMemo, the optimum interval I_R following a repetition R of an item is calculated as the product of I_{R-1} and the "optimum factor" for items of that "easiness" at repetition R. The table of optimum factors is updated over time, in response to achieved recall rates, aiming to converge on a long-term recall rate of 95%. Self-assessment on a 6-point scale updates the easiness of the current item and in the case of a low score, resets the repetition count of the item to be relearned. The advantage of adaptive spaced repetition in SuperMemo is that it evolves according to the learner's performance over time. The disadvantage is that it does not support initial learning, with the first test following item introduction not typically occurring for at least 5 days.

SuperMemo has inspired a whole family of algorithms, including the currently popular Anki system [1]. Anki has three distinguishing features: cards support multiple directions of cued recall between multi-attribute "facts" (e.g., the meaning, pronunciation, and appearance of a Chinese character); tests are scheduled each day at a fixed learner-specified rate; and after being tested on a card the learner selects one of four options indicating when they want to be tested on it next. These all increase learner load in terms of deciding which attributes to test, keeping up with scheduled sessions, and judging recall performance.

Finally, the FaCT system for Fact and Concept Training [18] uses the ACT-R cognitive model to predict the best item to test at any point in time, introducing new items when no existing items are near their optimum point for review. This aims to maximize the long-term recall gains of each review, rather than to keep the recall likelihood of all items above a threshold level. This system also incorporates structural models of the domains being studied; e.g., cued recall in one direction can have a calculated carryover on the probability of recall in the opposite direction. As with SuperMemo, however, the primarily visual content leads to a distinction between initial "study" trials – massed presentations of items to learn – and subsequent "drills" of cued recall tests. As such, it takes no account of shorter-term learner experience or of study for immediate use.

Summary

Cued recall learning is a powerful tool for acquiring the kind of domain knowledge that is often fundamental for participation in higher-level activities (e.g., in the domain of second language learning, vocabulary is a prerequisite for conversation). Since spaced repetition of cued recall tests enhances learner performance, cued recall is an ideal candidate for distributed sessions of microlearning.

Flashcards are the prototypical medium for cued recall, but existing systems impose time or structural constraints that do not satisfy the demands of mobile microlearning. Adaptive systems help, since matching perceived challenged to perceived skills can result in a psychological state of *flow* [10,16] as well as enhance learner motivation in the moment and over the long-term [3]. However, learner adaptation has typically focused on long-term retention rather than short-term experience, with little consideration for learners struggling to learn new items (e.g., a microlearning session could easily be dominated by failed attempts to correctly recall new items for the first time).

A more "micro" form of adaptation is thus required to facilitate positive experiences in even the shortest learning sessions, without requiring intense visual "memorization" of new items. The next section describes how we designed a system to support such adaptive mobile microlearning.

ALGORITHM DESIGN

The foundation of our algorithm is the exponential intervals (5 seconds, 25 seconds, 2 minutes, etc.) of the Pimsleur language system because of the uniform emphasis they place on short-term overlearning and long-term retention.

Our first refinement is to incorporate Leitner-style binary feedback from the user after a cue has been presented, indicating whether the target was recalled correctly or not. Such binary feedback is more suitable for lightweight mobile input than the more numerous choices used by SuperMemo and Anki and the text input used by FaCT.

Our second refinement, following SuperMemo, is to adaptively manipulate inter-test intervals according to learner performance, attempting to converge on a goal recall success rate of 90% at all stages of retention for any given item (as shown in Figure 2). In any session, given sufficient learning ability and appropriately spaced prior sessions, the learner should therefore be expected to correctly recall 90% of the items tested. This adaptive matching of challenges to demonstrated skills should help facilitate the short-term experience of flow. The corollary of this for longer-term motivation is that whenever the learner needs to, they should also be able to correctly recall and use 90% of all items they have ever studied.

Our third refinement, as in the FaCT system, is to identify opportune moments to introduce new items when there are no other items due for review. In our algorithm, such moments occur when there are no items with less than a 90% chance of being remembered at that point in time, according to our model of the learner's memory.

Our hypothesis is that this design will be successful at motivating learners through high recall accuracies whatever the learning modality, even when mobile microlearning.

Adaptive Spaced Repetition Algorithm

Our algorithm models a learner's knowledge of a set of items represented as cue-target pairs. For each item, a learnedness value l reflects the algorithm's estimate of the strength of the association of the cue-target pair at the time immediately following the learner's last response.

Exponentially-expanding inter-study intervals

The inter-study interval t_l is calculated based on l :

$$t_l = 5^{10l}$$

When the next item is required, the algorithm selects the most overdue item according to the ratio of actual time elapsed to ideal inter-study interval. If no items are due, a new item is introduced from a queue of items to learn.

For correct responses, l is incremented by a base increase value b. In our algorithm, we initially set b to 0.1 to replicate the Pimsleur intervals of 5s, 25s, 125s, etc. For incorrect responses, l is reset to this initial value of 0.1.

The human forgetting curve [11] models retention as:

$$E(recall) = e^{-t/s}$$

where t is the time that has elapsed since the last presentation of the item and s is the strength of the learner's memory for that item directly following its presentation. We can rewrite this equation to represent memory strength as a fixed scaling of the inter-study interval t_l as follows:

$$E(recall) = e^{-\frac{t}{t_l/\ln(10/9)}} = 0.9^{\frac{t}{t_l}}$$

The scale factor was chosen such that when items are tested on time ($t = t_l$), they have a 90% probability of success. Substituting another base in the final expression above adjusts the goal success rate (e.g., 0.95 would target 95%).

Adapting inter-study intervals to reach goal accuracies

The algorithm adjusts base increase values according to a learner's history across all items of similar learnedness. First, responses are grouped into buckets of size 0.1 based on their item's learnedness, each with their own base increase value. After a response to an item in a particular bucket, we compare the actual proportion of correct responses in that bucket to the goal proportion of 90%. If the correct responses for a bucket fall below this goal, it means the last increases in learnedness for items in that bucket were too large, resulting in excess forgetting. Conversely, a proportion of correct responses above this goal indicates that the last increases in learnedness were too small, resulting in insufficient forgetting and over-practice. To adapt to the learner's history following a response to an item, we therefore update the base increase value of the item's *previous bucket* in the direction and degree that would, *in retrospect*, have resulted in the 90% goal accuracy if it had been used after the last response.

To safeguard against inappropriate adaption in various instances, we set the following requirements for adaptation:

1. The item must have had at least a 60% recall probability (to adapt to forgetting, not delays between sessions).
2. The item's bucket must contain at least five responses (to provide a solid initial basis for adaptation).
3. The base increase value b of a bucket is confined by flexible bounds within the range [0, 0.2] (to avoid over-adjustment of b in the case of unusual response history).

Such stratified adjustments do not account for variations in item difficulty. We therefore added two refinements: first, "hard" items that have received multiple incorrect responses appear more frequently; second, "easy" items recalled many times before an error quickly return to their prior level if subsequent recall attempts are successful.

Simulations

We ran several stochastic discrete-event simulations of our learning algorithm. Results indicated that learning efficiency would increase with more and longer sessions, but with minimal gains after 40 repetitions per session or 4 sessions per day. Given a fixed number of daily repetitions, efficiency was highest when they were broken up into multiple sessions, supporting the strategy of microlearning.

MEMREFLEX FLASHCARDS

The interface design of our MemReflex mobile application communicates the underlying memory modeling of our novel adaptive algorithm. Figure 1 illustrates the primary interaction mechanic using second-language vocabulary taken from our third study: the learner attempts to recall the Chinese translation of "friend" before pressing "check" (left); On seeing and hearing the correct answer of "péng you", the learner indicates whether they were *correct*, *incorrect*, or would like to *replay* the audio pronunciation (right). They also see several key pieces of feedback:

1. The number of items due for review now, or else a countdown of when the next item will become due.
2. The learner's response history for the current item.
3. The estimated chance of the learner correctly recalling the current item, calculated from a memory model.
4. The estimated number of items that will be remembered in a minute, hour, day, week, month, and year.

This feedback, which updates in real-time, helps the learner understand how past interactions have helped to build up his or her memory and how this will be retained into the future. As they study, learners can see their knowledge shifting from shorter- to longer-term memory. When they are not studying, however, the same feedback shows the extent of forgetting that is expected to have occurred. Every 20 flashcard repetitions, the learner sees summary statistics of both that "microlearning" session and overall.

EVALUATION

In this section, we describe how we systematically broke down and validated the concept of adaptive flashcards for mobile microlearning. Our research questions were:

1. Do short, sparse microlearning sessions result in retention beyond the sessions themselves?
2. How does fixed progression, Pimsleur-like learning compare to adaptive learning?
3. Are both screen-text and eyes-free audio appropriate interaction modalities for mobile microlearning?
4. Does adaptive microlearning create new opportunities for short-term mobile learning, such as while walking?
5. How does mobile microlearning support motivation in the longer-term, e.g., for second language learning?

We addressed these five research questions with three user studies tackling questions 1–3, 3–4, and 1–5 respectively. In the first two studies, we use dates and ages as learning material to support controlled testing of precision recall for facts that are interesting but previously unknown. Since numbers are typically difficult to remember, reported results are potentially lower than what might be expected in non-numeric domains. In the third and final study we evaluate real use of the system for language learning.

Participants were recruited from international visitors to our lab as well as the local expatriate community. Backgrounds included engineering, design, teaching, PR, and admin.

All statistical analysis was conducted at significance level $p < 0.05$, with the Bonferroni correction applied to planned post-hoc comparisons. For clarity, we present results using the notation *sample-mean units* (*standard-deviation*) and show standard error bars on charts highlighting results. We also predefine the common measures used across studies:

1. *Items Introduced*. The total number of new items introduced to the learner by the learning algorithm.
2. *Repetition Accuracy*. The percentage of correct responses given by the learner during system use.
3. *Items Retained*. The total number of items correctly recalled on the post-test following system use.
4. *Retention Accuracy*. The percentage of items introduced during system use correctly recalled on the post-test.

STUDY 1: NON-MOBILE AUDIO MICROLEARNING

Our first study tested two hypotheses: that a generalization of the audio-only Pimsleur system could work for audio learning beyond second languages and that our adaptive algorithm could successfully adjust the spacing between repetitions to raise the accuracy of a learner's responses. For this initial study, we used a desktop rather than a mobile system so we could focus on algorithm performance and reduce variation due to differences in learning context.

Study Design

We recruited 14 participants (4 females) with a mean age of 25 for our study. Participants used a desktop application on Windows 7 to learn the years of inventions of technologies through audio-only cued recall. Sounds were synthesized using text-to-speech and on hearing the target, participants clicked a button indicating whether they had recalled it correctly. A *replay* button repeated the last sound.

Each participant used three algorithms but did not know multiple algorithms were being tested. The mapping of data to algorithm across users and algorithm order across users and sessions were counterbalanced. The algorithms were:

1. *Progressive*. Used a fixed progression of exponentially increasing intervals as in the Pimsleur system.
2. *Responsive*. As progressive, but with item relearning on incorrect responses (returning to the first interval).
3. *Adaptive*. Used adaptive intervals as described previously to raise success rates towards 90%.

Participants completed one session per weekday, resulting in 9 sessions over 11 days. Each took about 10 minutes and comprised 60 repetitions. We scheduled only 20 repetitions (around 2 or 3 minutes) per algorithm per day to induce the kind of forgetting and relearning that might be expected in real use. One week after the final session, participants were each given a post-test of all items introduced to them.

Results

Results are shown in Figure 3. We ran one-way repeated-measures ANOVA analyses over the factor of *Algorithm* (with *Progressive*, *Responsive*, and *Adaptive* levels) for the dependent measures of *Items Introduced*, *Repetition Accuracy*, *Items Retained*, and *Retention Accuracy*.

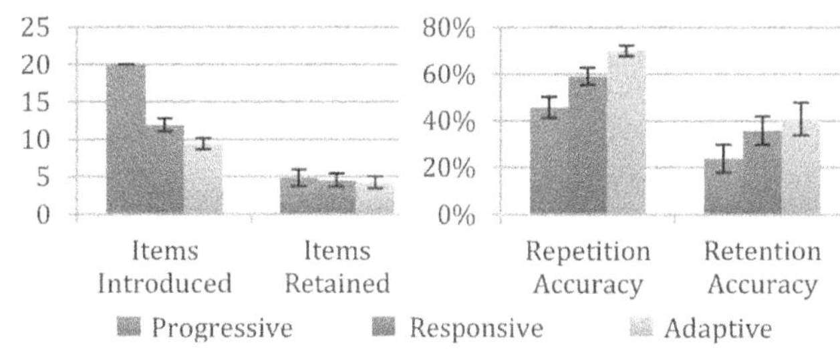

Figure 3. Main Results of Study 1

There were significant differences ($F_{2,26} = 91.8$, $p < 0.001$) in the numbers of *Items Introduced*, with means of 20 (0), 11.9 (3.2), and 9.4 (2.7) for the *Progressive*, *Responsive* and *Adaptive* algorithms respectively. There were also significant differences in *Repetition Accuracy* ($F_{2,26} = 38.0$, $p < 0.001$) with means of 45.7% (15.4), 59.0% (13.0) and 70.0% (7.9) for the *Progressive*, *Responsive* and *Adaptive* algorithms. In both cases, post-hoc tests showed pairwise differences between all three algorithms.

In the post-test 1-week after system use had ended, there were no significant differences in *Items Retained* with means of 4.8 (4.2), 4.5 (3.3) and 4.2 (3.0) for the *Progressive*, *Responsive* and *Adaptive* algorithms. There was a significant difference in *Retention Accuracy* ($F_{2,26} = 4.61$, $p < 0.05$), with means of 23.9% (20.9), 35.9% (20.9) and 40.9% (23.9). Post-hoc comparisons showed an advantage of *Adaptive* over *Progressive*.

Discussion

This first study validated our generalization of Pimsleur-like audio learning to other domains. It also demonstrated the ability of an *Adaptive* system to raise recall success rates beyond those resulting from fixed progression along a series of expanding intervals (*Progressive*) or progression with relearning (*Responsive*). Although there was no significant difference between algorithms for the number of items recalled after the one-week retention interval, the fact that participants could precisely recall facts studied using all methods shows clear potential for the strategy of microlearning even when sessions are sparse.

STUDY 2: MOBILE LEARNING IN MOTION

An important faculty of mobile devices is their ability to support interaction "on the move" [23], and many opportunities for microlearning are likely to occur while the learner is walking. However, previous studies in mobile HCI have shown the negative effects of walking on visual selection and reading performance [21]. The trade-off between walking speed and interaction performance has also been investigated, with the finding that visual target acquisition plateaus at 40–80% of the user's preferred walking speed [4]. As an alternative to visual feedback, audio feedback while walking has been shown to result in higher interaction accuracy as well as lower mental and physical demands [23]. However, no prior work has investigated the effects of motion and modality on the effectiveness of mobile *learning*, rather than selection.

In this second study, we tested hypotheses about mobile microlearning with adaptive flashcards: that they can support high recall accuracy in both text and audio modalities, even while the learner is walking and distracted.

Study Design

We recruited 12 participants (5 females) with a mean age of 28 for our study. Participants used a Windows Phone 7 mobile application on an HTC HD7 to learn animal lifespans through either audio-only or text-only cued recall, with audio recordings provided by a native English speaker.

Data were divided into two sets balanced for complexity and paired with interaction modalities for each user. These pairings and the order of modalities between participants were counterbalanced. The two modalities were:

1. *Audio*. Participants hear audio cues and targets though headphones but see no item text on the screen.
2. *Text*. Participants see text cues and targets on the phone screen but hear no item audio.

The *Adaptive* algorithm from the first study was used for both because of its confirmed ability to control the rate of introduction of new items according to demonstrated learner performance. To support eyes-free interaction using audio, we implemented a button-free, gestural interaction style: *tap* to play the target of a cue, *flick left* if the learner could not recall or incorrectly recalled the target, *flick right* if the learner recalled the target correctly, and *flick down* to replay the last sound heard. For consistency, the same method was also used for text-only interaction.

The study began with a guided walk of an approximately 280 meter lap around an office floor, pointing out the 65 desk and room nameplates that are used in the experiment. This was followed by an introduction to learning through cued recall, using invention dates from the first study.

The first *Continuous* task for each interaction modality was to use it for 5 minutes of learning while walking in a 15m length figure-of-eight path around two pairs of adjacent chairs (a standard setup for interaction-while-walking tasks, e.g., as in [23]). Participants were instructed to focus on learning continuously, walking as fast as this would allow.

The second *Interrupted* task for each interaction modality was 5 minutes of learning while walking 280m laps around an office floor, performing the dual task of checking nameplates for a glanceable but unfamiliar property (colored dots attached to nameplates). By replicating the kind of cognitive load that might be experienced in a highly distracting environment, we could examine how this influenced interaction strategies and learning outcomes across the two modalities. Ten colored dots were added to randomly spaced nameplates, alternating between blue and green. Participants were instructed to check as many nameplates as possible in 5 minutes, always pointing out dots of a particular color and learning as continuously as this would allow. Colors were assigned randomly and switched for the second interaction modality. Each modality condition began with the learner training to proficiency in that modality. The first task, second task, and post-test then followed, each separated by a two-minute break.

Results

We ran repeated measures ANOVA analyses over the two factors of *Modality* (*Audio* and *Text*) and *Task* (*Continuous* and *Interrupted*) for each of the dependent measures *Items Introduced*, *Repetition Accuracy*, *Mean Repetition Duration*, and *Walking Speed*. *Mean Repetition Duration* was calculated by dividing the task time by the total number of repetitions, and *Walking Speed* by dividing the total distance travelled by the task time. We also used paired, two-tailed t-tests to compare the number of *Items Retained* and the *Retention Accuracy* as measured in the post-tests.

There were significant main effects of *Task* for all dependent measures. From the *Continuous* task to the *Interrupted* task, this represents fewer *Items Introduced* with $F_{1,44} = 145$, $p < 0.001$ from means of 10.8 (2.7) and 3.3 (1.5), longer *Mean Repetition Durations* with $F_{1,44} = 15.9$, $p < 0.001$ from means of 5.8s (2.1) and 8.5s (2.7), lower *Repetition Accuracy* with $F_{1,44} = 13.3$, $p < 0.001$ from means of 81.2% (9.2) and 70.5% (12.0), and slower *Walking Speed* with $F_{1,44} = 15.2$, $p < 0.001$ from means of 4.41km/h (0.64) and 3.82km/h (0.55).

For *Items Introduced*, there were no significant main effects for *Modality* or any interaction effects. For *Mean Repetition Durations*, there was a significant main effect for *Modality* with longer repetitions for *Audio* than *Text*, with $F_{1,44} =$

4.20, $p < 0.05$ from means of 7.8s (2.3) and 6.4s (3.0), but no interaction effect. For *Repetition Accuracy*, there was no significant main effect for *Modality* but there was a significant interaction effect ($F_{1,44} = 4.64$, $p < 0.05$). Post-hoc tests revealed that *Continuous Audio* learning with mean 86.3% (5.2) had significantly higher accuracy levels than *Continuous Text* learning with mean 76.2% (9.7), *Interrupted Audio* learning with mean 69.2% (14.7), and *Interrupted Text* learning with a mean of 71.8% (9.0). There was a significant main effect of *Modality* for *Walking Speed*, with *Audio* faster than *Text* ($F_{1,44} = 14.3$, $p < 0.001$) from means of 4.40km/h (0.66) and 3.83km/h (0.55). These results best highlight the characteristics of mobile microlearning across modalities and are shown in Figure 4.

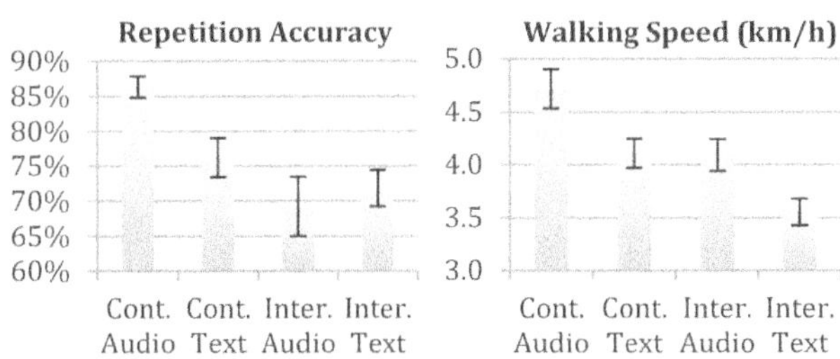

Figure 4. Main Results of Study 2

There was no significant difference in the *Items Retained* or the *Retention Accuracy* on the *Audio* and *Text* post-tests, with *Items Retained* means of 11.6 (3.7) and 11.7 (3.1) and *Retention Accuracy* means of 83.8% (19.4) and 83.6% (12.3). These accuracies represent the small amounts of forgetting below the 90% goal that would be expected during the 2-minute delay that preceded the post-tests.

Discussion

This second study demonstrated a substantial effect of interaction modality on the walking speeds of mobile learners, with eyes-free audio learning increasing walking speeds by 15% over text-based learning. The implication is that audiogestural interaction creates new opportunities for mobile learning while walking when compared with visual flashcard interaction, which typically requires many more repetitions for the same overall level of retention. This is supported by the fact that in our *Continuous* walking task, the mean walking speed with audio learning was as high as 88% of the benchmark 5km/h adult walking speed even while maintaining a mean repetition accuracy level of 86% (compared to 73% and 76% with text-based learning).

In the presence of visual distractions, audio learning maintains its advantage in terms of walking speed but loses its accuracy advantage since it becomes more difficult to regain audio context (by issuing a command to repeat the last sound) than text context (by glancing at the phone). Given that the need to pay visual attention to the environment is typically greater and more persistent than the need to listen, our *Interrupted* task was more representative of mobile navigation "in the wild". However, there is a relatively greater drop in *Repetition Accuracy* for *Audio* than for *Text* when moving from *Continuous* to *Interrupted* tasks (Figure 4), indicating a crossover point at which competing stimuli result in too much cognitive interference for productive audio learning. The conclusion is that we should allow real-time switching between modalities according to contextual demands.

Overall, the high levels of repetition and retention accuracy across both modalities in this second study suggest that adaptive flashcards can support short-term learning using either text or audio, even while attending to the demands of real-world navigation. Even in these sub-optimal learning conditions, especially when using audio-only in the absence of visual distractions, several participants remarked that they "got in the zone". Understanding how similar microlearning experiences can sustain motivation in long-term, high-value activities such as language learning is the question we address with the third and final user study.

STUDY 3: SELF-DIRECTED LANGUAGE LEARNING

Our third study tested hypotheses regarding longer-term, learner-directed system use for second language vocabulary learning: that adaptive flashcards can support high recall accuracy in this more challenging context; that such high accuracies are motivating; and that mobile microlearning is an effective strategy for second language learning.

Study Design

We recruited 12 Mandarin Chinese learners (3 females) with a mean age of 28 from our local expatriate community to participate in a 3-week long user study. Participants used a mobile application on an HTC HC7 Windows Phone 7 to learn Chinese words mined from the Web.

The vocabulary data were taken from the top 2000 two-character Chinese words online, divided into two sets balanced for frequency. To assess the value of adapting to learners' memories in ways that facilitate high recall accuracies, we compared the *Progressive* and *Adaptive* algorithms from study one. To support learner speech and exploit the fast flipping of text flashcards observed in study two, we used text flashcards with English definition cues and Chinese translation targets. To exploit focused attention to audio flashcards, we also played the pronunciation of Chinese words automatically when they appeared, as well as any time the learner pressed a button to replay the word.

Learners alternate between *Progressive* and *Adaptive* every 20 repetitions, which do not include the display of flashcard candidates whenever there are no items due. In such cases, the next most frequent word in the current set is presented as both definition and translation. The learner then chooses one of three options: to *learn* the word using the current algorithm, to indicate that they already *know* the word, or to *skip* the word if it is unappealing. At the end of each session of 20 repetitions, learners see a feedback screen of session statistics as well as overall statistics for both algorithms (simply called "A" and "B"). These are the statistics of

Items Introduced, *Test Repetitions*, and *Repetition Accuracy*. On this screen, learners give a subjective *Session Rating* of how the session felt on a scale of 1 (bad) to 5 (great). The mapping of dataset to algorithm and algorithm order were both counterbalanced across participants.

The *Progressive* and *Adaptive* interfaces shared the same basic elements: the session repetition count (out of 20), the number of items due or the time until an item will become due; the English definition cue and Chinese translation target; the item history as "X% of previous Y answers correct"; and the *check*, *correct*, *incorrect*, and *replay* buttons. The *Adaptive* interface (Figure 1) added two extra elements: an "X% chance of remembering now" estimate from the learner model and visualized estimates of how many words the learner should remember for how long.

Participants were free to use the flashcards as much or as little as they desired. We recommended that they complete at least one "A" and "B" session each weekday, or 300 repetitions per test in total, but compensation (a small gift) did not depend on this. A post-test of all items introduced and a semi-structured interview completed the study.

Results

Detailed results from study 3 are shown in Table 1. We ran two-tailed paired-sample t-tests between *Progressive* and *Adaptive* methods for the dependent measures of *Items Introduced*, *Repetition Accuracy*, *Items Retained*, *Retention Accuracy*, and *Mean Session Rating*.

User ID	Reps./ method	*Progressive method*					*Adaptive method*				
		II	RA	IR	IR%	MSR	II	RA	IR	IR%	MSR
P1	740	98	23	30	31	1.8	30	71	28	93	3.9
P2	640	95	14	11	12	1.1	19	64	17	89	3.1
P3	540	87	46	29	33	3.1	31	75	27	87	3.8
P4	520	75	53	41	55	3.0	22	78	21	95	3.7
P5	480	76	34	32	42	1.8	22	68	21	95	3.9
P6	400	70	42	20	29	2.3	13	63	9	69	3.3
P7	340	45	7	3	7	1.2	5	24	4	80	2.7
P8	320	53	13	8	15	1.9	9	58	6	67	2.7
P9	300	55	66	35	64	4.0	23	84	19	83	3.9
P10	260	49	29	11	22	2.0	17	68	16	94	3.7
P11	220	45	43	22	49	1.8	18	74	16	89	3.9
P12	160	32	27	13	41	2.6	7	44	7	100	2.4
mean (sd)	**410 (176)**	**65 (22)**	**33 (18)**	**21 (12)**	**32 (17)**	**2.2 (0.8)**	**18 (8)**	**64 (16)**	**16 (8)**	**87 (10)**	**3.4 (0.6)**

Table 1. Detailed Results of Study 3. II = *Items Introduced*; RA% = *Repetition Accuracy*; IR = *Items Retained*; IR% = *Retention Accuracy*; MSR = *Mean Session Rating* (1– 5)

From *Progressive* to *Adaptive*, there were significant differences in *Items Introduced* ($t_{11} = 10.0$, $p < 0.001$) from means of 65.0 (21.6) and 18.0 (8.4); *Repetition Accuracy* ($t_{11} = 8.9$, $p < 0.001$) from means of 33.1% (17.7) and 64.3% (16.3); *Retention Accuracy* ($t_{11} = 11.5$, $p < 0.001$) from means of 32.4% (17.1) and 86.9% (10.5); and *Mean Session Rating* ($t_{11} = 4.9$, $p < 0.001$) from means of 2.22 (0.84) and 3.42 (0.56). For *Items Retained*, there was almost a significant difference ($t_{11} = 2.2$, $p = 0.054$), with means of 20.9 (12.1) for *Progressive* and 15.9 (8.0) for *Adaptive*.

To summarize, the *Adaptive* method doubled learners' repetition accuracy over one quarter as many introduced items, improving the learner experience of each session. In addition, whereas *Repetition Accuracy* predicts *Retention Accuracy* for *Progressive* (means of 33% and 32%), for *Adaptive* this number increases from 64% to 87%. This again indicates stronger, more selective learning with *Adaptive*. All participants also preferred *Adaptive* and all but one (who would rather manage their own rote approach) would continue to use it for their second language learning.

To gain an insight into the possible long-term experience of using both methods, we plotted learners' session accuracies over time. Representative results are shown in Figure 5 (only the four heaviest users are shown for clarity).

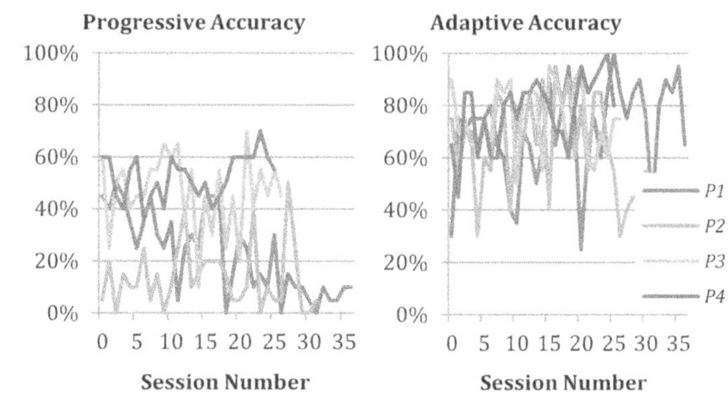

Figure 5. Accuracy over multiple sessions of 20 repetitions

Overall, *Adaptive* succeeds in raising session accuracy levels and holding them high over time. As we shall see in the next section, adapting to abilities, memories, and study schedules is critical in facilitating successful flashcard sessions and for maintaining language learning motivation.

Discussion

In the post-study interview, participants were asked to compare the *Progressive* and *Adaptive* methods in terms of learning experience in the moment and how this relates to their motivation. Participants were also asked to provide feedback on the "mobile microlearning" strategy. We frame our discussion around the themes that arose from these interviews and which provide implications for the future design of such flashcard-based learning systems.

Accuracy motivates by creating a sense of success

Participants widely associated session accuracies with feelings of success. The high accuracies of *Adaptive* sessions were described as creating "the feeling of doing something right" [*P6*], while positive feedback from session percentages amplified the "rewarding" feel of the experience itself, encouraging learners to "invest more time" [*P1*]. The additional statistics of *Adaptive* were also appreciated, with the probability of a correct answer "pushing" learners to try harder [*P5*] and the display of "how things will stay with you in the long term" motivating learners in the moment [*P1*]. However, lower accuracies with *Progressive*, especially from many successive failures, led leaners to feel like they "don't know anything" [*P3*].

Repeating difficult items creates a feeling of control

The predictable approach to item relearning in the *Adaptive* approach gave learners a "reason" to try and remember because they understood items would "come back again soon" [*P3*]. The expectation of coming success encouraged learners to keep items "in the background" of their mind and consequently feel "in control" [*P5*]. This helped learners "remember more difficult words more easily" [*P4*]. In contrast, *Progressive* was like "seeing items and then discarding them" [*P5*], or even feeling "flooded" [*P6*].

New items should feel deserved, not forced

One common complaint with *Progressive* was that new items would be added before existing items had been learned, leading to feelings of reaching a "tipping point" and ultimately ending up "in a hole" with too many items [*P8*]. In contrast, the *Adaptive* method gave learners the ability to "hold on" to items until they could remember them [*P7*], giving learners "the right to move on" [*P9*]. The expectation of "absolutely going to remember" all *Adaptive* items was so powerful it made them feel "precious" [*P1*].

Encourage learning well, not learning more

Most participants (8/11) retained more items with *Progressive* than *Adaptive*, yet all preferred *Adaptive*. Learners thought that choosing "just a few words" that they "really want to learn" helped them to learn better [*P7*], and that "knowing everything really well is so much more important" than the total items learned [*P5*]. *Adaptive* helped learners to feel "secure and confident" in the items they knew since they had been "ingrained" [*P1*]. In contrast, one learner suggested it was just the "volume of words" that meant they learnt more with the "unpleasant" *Progressive* method [*P6*], while another described how the possibility of learning less than half of the taught words made it feel "random" and "not very goal-oriented" [*P4*].

Facilitate self-paced training of fast, automatic recall

In comparison with *Adaptive*, the *Progressive* method often felt slower, "like it went on forever" [*P1*]. It also felt more difficult and "forced" [P9] compared to the "easier way" [*P4*]. In contrast, *Adaptive* was "a lot more satisfying" because it supported learning at "the right speed" [*P3*] and resulted in "instant" recall [*P5*]. For one learner whose prior experience of language learning was to take "one or two minutes" trying to remember each word from a list, the *Adaptive* method helped him to "answer quickly" even though he "thought nothing", indicating automaticity of recall that is "especially helpful for daily life" [*P10*].

Support flexible learning that can fill any time available

Participants appreciated the "flexible" and "modular" nature of mobile microlearning that could fit into their life, preferring it to the "30 minute lessons" of Pimsleur and Rosetta Stone [*P3*]. Mobile microlearning helped learners to make "good use of time" in situations like walking, shopping, or taking a bus [*P4*], as well as in "coffee breaks" with "5 minutes to spare" [*P2*]. One learner remarked that by adding new cards every day, *Progressive* felt like "what other applications already do", which was why he stopped using those applications [*P9*]. Another learner gave the example of Anki as being "so painful" for the same reason: "if you don't study every day, you will never recover" [*P3*].

Summary

The main finding of study three is that by adapting to the learner's patterns of responses over time, we can significantly raise recall accuracies compared with graduated interval recall based on the Pimsleur intervals. These higher accuracies were found to enhance learner control, confidence, and perception of success.

OVERALL DISCUSSION

The overarching message is that microlearning can work across interaction modalities, when mobile and on the move, in ways that enhance learner motivation. The caveat is that small differences in the design of microlearning systems can preclude flexible switching between modalities (e.g., by requiring extended periods of visual attention) as well as negatively impact the learner experience when the focus is on the quantity, not the quality, of learning.

Designing for "Micro Activities"

The implications of this work can be expressed as a set of six design considerations for when transforming a user activity, such as learning, to be more "micro" in nature:

1. *Fixed* → *Mobile*. Support modality switching because user-context changes more frequently and unexpectedly.
2. *Structured* → *Streamed*. Blend sub-activities (e.g., studying, testing) because sessions can end at any time.
3. *Units* → *Bursts*. Deliver success quickly because early experiences motivate further and future use.
4. *Scripted* → *Adaptive*. Let user data drive content delivery, because users and usage develop over time.
5. *Quantity* → *Quality*. Give users control over the pace of progression, because needs vary over time and users.
6. *Scoring* → *Modeling*. Offer time-based ability estimates, because scores do not convey the effects of inaction.

Limitations and Future Directions

Neither flashcards nor microlearning are tools to be used in isolation. Future work is required to connect this fundamentally behaviorist approach to more situated, constructivist, and collaborative pedagogical methods.

For short-term learning, a promising direction for language learning is the explicit preparation of learners for upcoming conversations with native speakers. A similar approach to preparation could also support the rehearsal of material to be delivered in any kind of public speaking or presentation.

For longer-term learning, adaptive flashcards could be used to help people remember all of the interesting things they read online or in eBooks, using some kind of "clipping" functionality to capture content worthy of retention.

Expanding beyond the individual learner, we would like to derive large-scale insights from aggregate use of our adaptive learning algorithm, both in terms of parameters and content. We have already taken our first step in this direction, by incorporating our adaptive flashcard algorithm into a desktop application for language lookup and adaptive flashcard microlearning [5]. There are currently over 100,000 English as Second Language (ESL) learners using this application each day, and we will continue to evolve our system as we learn about its use in practice.

CONCLUSION

We began this paper by highlighting the opportunity for *mobile microlearning*, before introducing theories, studies, and systems based on *cued recall*, which we used to motivate the design of our MemReflex *adaptive flashcards*. Our evaluation was then set around five research questions.

The first question addressed the effectiveness of *microlearning* as a strategy. In both study one and study three, the items retained in each method suggests that this strategy is a worthwhile addition to a learner's repertoire.

The second question targeted the relative benefit of *adaptive learning* over learning with a fixed progression, and in this case the higher repetition accuracies for the adaptive approach in both study one and study three suggests that adaptation makes a substantial difference.

The third question investigated the appropriateness of audio and text as *interaction modalities* for flashcards. Study one made an initial contribution by demonstrating the effectiveness of audio flashcard learning, while study two built on this by showing equivalent retention for audio-only and text-only flashcards in mobile learning while walking.

The fourth question built on the third by seeking evidence for new *mobile learning opportunities* opened up by the flexible nature of adaptive flashcards. The quantitative results of study two and the usage pattern descriptions from study three provide compelling evidence in support of this.

The fifth and final question about the longer-term *motivational effects* of mobile microlearning was tackled solely by study three, which conclusively established the relationship between recall accuracy and learner satisfaction. By matching learning challenges to demonstrated learner skills, our adaptive flashcards were strongly preferred to a fixed progression modeled on the popular Pimsleur method.

We have only just begun to explore how technology can mediate and connect all forms of learning – from the micro to the macro, the mobile to the ubiquitous, and the personal to the social – but this paper demonstrates how mobile HCI can successfully transform a challenging activity into something more mobile, micro, and motivational in nature.

ACKNOWLEDGEMENTS

We thank all of our study participants and reviewers.

REFERENCES

1. Anki Spaced Repetition System. http://ankisrs.net/
2. Bateson, G. (1972). Steps to an ecology of mind. New York: Ballantine Books
3. Benyon, D. & Murray, D. (1993). Developing adaptive systems to fit individual aptitudes. IUI'93, 115–121
4. Bergstrom-Lehtovirta, J., Oulasvirta, A. & Brewster, S. (2011). The effects of walking speed on target acquisition on a touchscreen interface. MobileHCI '11, 143–146
5. Bing Dictionary Desktop. http://dict.bing.msn.cn/
6. Carpenter, S.K., Pashler, H. & Vul, E. (2006). What types of learning are enhanced by a cued recall test? Psychonomic Bulletin & Review, 13(5), 826–830
7. Carpenter, S.K., Pashler, H., Wixted, J.T. & Vul, E. (1998). The effects of tests on learning and forgetting. Memory & Cognition, 36(2), 438–448
8. Cepeda, N.J., Pashler, H., Vul, E. & Wixted, J.T. (2006). Distributed Practice in Verbal Recall Tasks: A Review and Quantitative Synthesis. Psychological Bulletin, 132(5)
9. Chomsky, N. (1965). Aspects of the Theory of Syntax. MIT
10. Csíkszentmihályi, M. (1990). Flow: The Psychology of Optimal Experience, New York: Harper and Row
11. Ebbinghaus, H. (1964). Memory: A contribution to experimental psychology. Dover Publications (original 1885)
12. Edge, D., Searle, E., Chiu, K., Zhao, J. & Landay, J. (2011). MicroMandarin: Mobile Language Learning in Context. CHI 2011, 3169–3178
13. Gassler, G., Hug, T. & Glahn, C. (2004). Integrated Micro Learning – An outline of the basic method and first results. Interactive Computer Aided Learning '04
14. Gradint. http://people.pwf.cam.ac.uk/ssb22/gradint/
15. Leitner System. http://en.wikipedia.org/wiki/Leitner_System
16. Nakamura, J, & Csikszentmihayli, M. (2002). The Concept of Flow. The Handbook of Positive Psychology: Oxford University Press, 89–92
17. Pavlik, P.I. Jr. & Anderson, J.R. (2003). An ACT-R Model of the Spacing Effect. ICCM-5, 177–182
18. Pavlik, P.I. Jr., Presson, N., Dozzi, G., Wu, S.-M., MacWhinney, B. & Koedinger, K. (2007). The FaCT (fact and concept) system: A new tool linking cognitive science with educators. 29th Conf. of the Cog. Sci. Soc., Nashville, TN
19. Pimsleur, P. (1967). A memory schedule. The Modern Language Journal, 51(2), 73–75
20. Rohrer, D., Taylor, K., Pashler, H., Wixted, J.T. & Cepeda, N.J. (2005). The Effect of Overlearning on Long-Term Retention. Applied Cognitive Psychology, 19, 361–374
21. Schildbach, B. & Rukzio, E. (2010). Investigating selection and reading performance on a mobile phone while walking. MobileHCI'11, 93–102
22. Sharples, M. (2000). The Design of Personal Mobile Technologies for Lifelong Learning. Computers and Education, 34, 177–193
23. Wilson, G., Brewster, S., Halvey, M., Crossan, A. & Stewart, C. (2011). The effects of walking, feedback and control method on pressure-based interaction. MobileHCI'11 147–156
24. Wozniak, P.A. & Gorzelanczyk, E.J. (1994). Optimization of repetition spacing in the practice of learning. Acta Neurobiologiae Experimentalis, 54

Mobilizing Education: Evaluation of a Mobile Learning Tool in a Low-Income School

Vanessa Frias-Martinez
Telefonica Research
Madrid, Spain
vanessa@tid.es

Jesus Virseda
Telefonica Research
Madrid, Spain
jvjerez@tid.es

Aldo Gomero
Pontificia Universidad Catolica
Lima, Peru
aldo.gos@gmail.com

ABSTRACT
The pervasiveness of feature phones in emerging economies has contributed to the advent of mobile learning applications for low-income populations. However, many of these tools lack the proper evaluation required to understand their educational impact. In this paper, we extend the state of the art by presenting the evaluation of a game-based mobile learning tool in both formal and informal settings at a low-income school in Lima, Peru. We show that *EducaMovil* improves knowledge acquisition in the formal environment of a classroom. In addition, use of the tool in more informal settings such as school breaks enhances the level of knowledge, as long as there is continuous engagement over time. We also demonstrate that *EducaMovil* can be used as a paperless complement to homework. Finally, we provide teachers with a set of guidelines for a successful deployment of *EducaMovil* at their schools.

Author Keywords
mobile games; low-income schools; learning gains

ACM Classification Keywords
K.3.1 Computers and Education: Computer Uses in Education

INTRODUCTION
Mobile devices have become an integral part of people's lives and a pervasive platform that we carry around at almost all times. In emerging economies, cell phone penetration rates are very high, frequently leapfrogging landlines and broadband access (ITU 2010). Such pervasiveness has contributed to the advent of various mobile-based services for low-income populations in areas like mobile education, mobile agriculture or mobile health. At its core, mobile services benefit from the familiarity that cell phone users have with the platform, which typically implies a small learning curve. Research in mobile education has covered a broad range of learning environments, from providing educational content as a complement to the formal setting of a classroom [4]; to enhancing learning experiences in informal environments like museums or distance learning [23, 25]. The motivations for using cell phones as learning tools are varied including the improvement of student access to learning materials, offering flexibility to students, reducing the costs of using more expensive technologies (like PCs), or to explore collaborative and individual learning [20]. In the specific case of emerging economies and low-income schools, learning environments become much more challenging. In general, these schools have limited budgets and scarce educational resources which often times have an impact on students' motivation and their performance. Given the high ownership rates of cell phones across the student population, mobile learning has been proposed as an affordable solution to complement formal schooling while keeping students engaged and motivated in the classroom. Additionally, the learn anywhere-anytime paradign also proposes the access to educational contents in informal settings e.g., while commuting or waiting for the public transport [12]. This is specially important in emerging economies where children might benefit from the access to educational contents in their downtime. However, there exists an important debate on whether mobile learning technologies constitute an adequate solution for students in low-income schools [21, 19]. Our research attempts to throw light onto this issue by providing a thorough evaluation of a mobile learning tool in a low-income school.

A large collection of mobile learning tools propose the use of smartphones or high-end phones to deliver educational content [25, 26]. Nevertheless, the availability of mobile learning tools for feature phones, which are the most common platform in emerging economies, is still very limited [22]. Most of the existing learning tools for feature phones deploy SMS- or Java-based solutions to provide school students with educational contents often presented as games [2, 10]. Kam *et al.* have shown that various mobile learning games (*MILLEE*) help rural kids to learn English in after-school programs in India [8]. Similarly, the *DrMath* project has offered Math tutors and learning content to hundreds of kids in South African schools [3]. Although these mobile games have shown promising results, they are typically criticized by their cost as well as by the lack of involvement of local teachers in the creation of contents. To overcome these issues, recent work like *EducaMovil* or the *English Literacy Tool* have advanced the state of the art introducing mobile learning games where the educational contents are created and automatically compiled into a game by the teachers themselves [11, 1]. These approaches have the advantage of highly re-

MobileHCI'12, September 21–24, 2012, San Francisco, CA, USA.

ducing educational costs while enhancing localized content authoring, both critical for low-income schools in emerging economies. Additionally, by involving teachers in the mobile learning process, it allows for a continuous and sustainable adaptation of the game to the curricular activities of the classroom. For these reasons, our research focuses on the evaluation of the educational impact of *EducaMovil*– a game-based mobile learning tool that is both low-cost and sustainable– at a low-income school in Lima, Peru.

Understanding the educational impact of a mobile learning tool in the long term is critical for its future deployments. Teachers need to evaluate whether such tools are convenient or not for their classrooms before involving themselves and their students in mobile learning programs. However, many of the mobile learning tools lack the proper evaluation required to understand their educational impact. Although there exist some studies on the impact of mobile learning tools in low-income schools, most of them either carry out only qualitative evaluations [15, 24]; or analyze the tool only in formal or informal settings but never both [16, 3]; or involve small numbers of students [4, 8]. Our research extends the state of the art by presenting a thorough quantitative and qualitative evaluation of the educational impact of *EducaMovil* when used in both formal and informal settings.

Our impact evaluation focuses on three important research questions: (i) the impact of *EducaMovil* on the students' knowledge acquisition *i.e., do students using the tool improve their level of knowledge more than students not using it? and, if so, under which formal or informal learning settings?*; (ii) the impact of the student's prior level of knowledge on her learning gains *i.e., do students need a minimum level of prior knowledge in order to benefit from the tool?*; and (iii) the relationship between game performance and knowledge acquisition *i.e., can teachers use EducaMovil as a proxy to measure a student's level of knowledge thus offering a paperless complement to student homework?* By answering these questions, we expect to provide outcomes and insights about the educational impact of deploying a game-based mobile learning tool at a low-income school. Our final objective is to propose a set of guidelines that will help teachers identify the ideal set up for the implementation of a successful *EducaMovil*learning program at their schools. Finally, although our findings are solely based on analyses for one specific school, we believe that teachers from other low-income schools with similar socio-economic and curricular conditions could potentially extend our results to their schools and decide on the usefulness of *EducaMovil* for their students. In the rest of the paper we present the related work; describe the low-income school and the mobile learning tool used in our evaluation; explain our research questions and methodology; describe our main research results and propose a set of guidelines for teachers willing to deploy *EducaMovil* at their schools. We finish with conclusions and future work.

RELATED WORK

Mobile Games

In recent years, the world has experienced an explosion in the amount of mobile learning tools that have been created for children and adult education in both emerging and developed economies. Game-based learning tools are present in different curricular areas such as: language learning [8] [18] or mathematics among others [7, 3, 9]. Kam *et al.* explored the use of mobile learning games to improve English literacy among Indian children [8]. The results of their pilot study with 27 students, showed that mobile phones have the potential to improve English literacy. However, the results were uneven among the participants: the students that had a higher English level at the beginning of the pilot benefited more from the use of the mobile learning application. In order to solve this discrepancy, the authors proposed as a solution the creation of adaptive mobile learning games that offer personalized contents depending on the students' knowledge. Similar research was presented in Tian *et al.* who studied how culturally inspired mobile learning games could help to improve Chinese literacy [18]. The research analyzes different traditional Chinese games, and uses them as a motivation to design cell phone games that follow similar rules. The authors show that culturally inspired games have more potential than western games to attract the interest of young students in China.

In the area of mathematics skills, a couple of interesting projects are *MobileMath* [7] and *DrMath* [3]. Although none of them rely solely on games for delivering educational content, the games are an important part of their educational models. *MobileMath* is an architecture that provides games, lessons, tutorials, examples and quizzes as separate entities for students to practice concepts in algebra. On the other hand, *DrMath* is a system that allows children to consult a tutor, participate in competitions, or to play single or multiple user text adventure games in the area of arithmetics. There exist other game-based mobile learning tools, like *EducaMovil* or *English Literacy Tool*, that provide more general frameworks to create quizzes for any curricular subject [11, 1]. These tools allow teachers to create collections of quizzes for different subjects, which enhances the creation of localized content authoring adaptable to the curricular activities of the classroom. Additionally, these tools do not require large budgets or engineering knowledge because they automatically embed the educational contents into the games while reducing the costs of creating educational games. Given that sustainability and low cost are critical variables for low-income schools, we focus our research on analyzing the educational impact of using *EducaMovil* at a low-resource school in Lima, Peru.

Impact Evaluation

There exists a large variety of methodologies to evaluate the educational impact of a mobile learning tool [15]. Price *et al.* proposed a research framework that grouped all methodologies into three well differentiated epistemological groups: *anticipated*, *ongoing* and *achieved* impact. Anticipated impact mostly refers to the description of the intentions that a specific educational tool has, and its resuls are of relevance for policy makers. On the other hand, ongoing impact refers to the evaluation of practices and is typically shared with staff development. Finally, achieved impact promotes particular kinds of outcomes and is relevant to support staff. Our research focuses on *ongoing impact* as we evaluate how impact

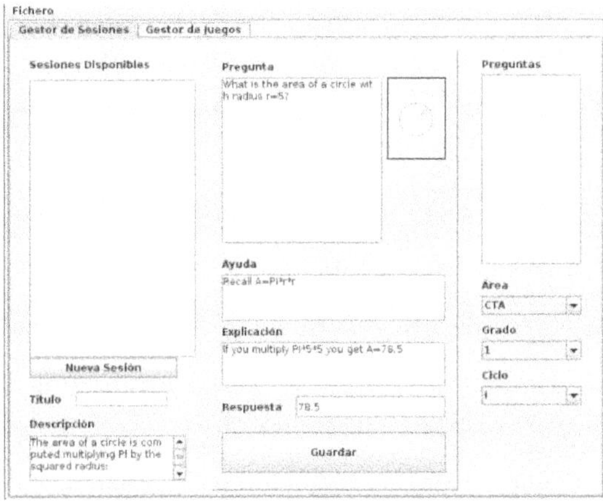

Figure 1. PC tool with a lesson created by a teacher.

took place and the outcomes will be relevant to teachers willing to deploy a mobile learning program at their schools.

In terms of impact measurement, Sharples *et al.* distinguished between impact measured as learning gains of the student (*effectiveness*); impact measured as motivational changes (*satisfaction*, and impact measured as *usability of the tool* [17, 13]. For example, Vavoula *et al.* analyzed the educational impact of *Myartspace* through qualitative analyses based on structured diaries and interviews to measure both effectiveness and satisfaction in informal learning environments [23, 24]. On the other hand, Ramos *et al.* used a mixed-method approach with interviews and logs to evaluate the effectiveness of a mobile learning tool for non-formal, distance education [16]. Given that the usability of *EducaMovil* was already analyzed in [6], our research focuses on the use of quantitative analyses to evaluate educational impact in terms of effectiveness, both in formal and informal environments. Additionally, we also propose a qualitative evaluation through personal interviews with teachers and students so as to draw some hints and insights on the satisfaction of the tool.

LEARNING ENVIRONMENT

In this Section, we present a description of *EducaMovil* and we give an overview of the school and the setup of the pilot for the evaluation.

EducaMovil

EducaMovil is a platform that has two main components: (1) a PC tool for teachers to create educational contents and (2) a mobile game-based educational application for Java-enabled cell phones, which constitute more than half of the cells present in Latin American economies [5]. On the PC, teachers can create the educational contents that will be shown in the games [11]. On the cell phone, the mobile game-based application consists of an open-source cell phone game where points and lives are won after correctly answering a specific educational content. The PC tool allows teachers to bundle together educational content and game in a seamless manner: the teacher simply needs to select the set of lessons that wants to deliver with the game, and click on a button. The package is then automatically downloaded to all student cell phones

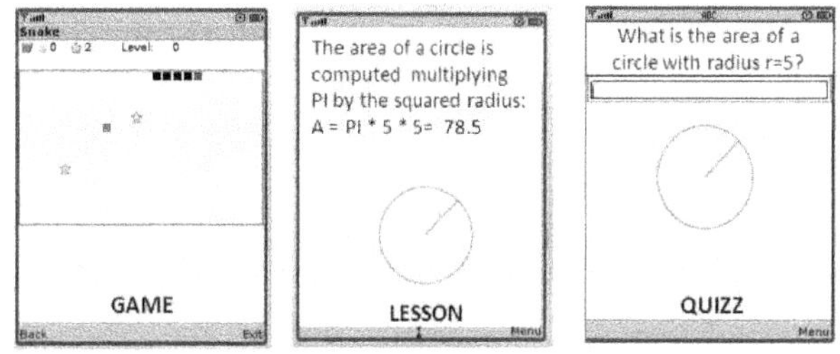

Figure 2. (a) A student eats an item in the Snake game (b) A lesson is shown (c) Quiz asking about content in the lesson

via Bluetooth. Next, we explain the main components of the EducaMovil in detail.

PC Tool

The PC tool allows teachers to create the educational contents that will be shown in the mobile game. Each educational content is composed of a lesson and a quiz, although only quizzes are also possible. The lesson typically contains an image and/or an explanation about a specific concept. A lesson is always followed by a quiz, which can be a simple- or multiple-choice test question. Students' answers are used to evaluate their learning gains. For that purpose, their answers are compared against the correct quiz answers given by the teachers while creating the lessons. Additionally, the PC tool allows teachers to provide a *hint* that is shown whenever students press the *help* button during a quiz. Finally, teachers can also add an *explanation* that is displayed to the student once he runs out of chances to answer the quiz (each quiz is shown a maximum of three times). Figure 1 shows an example of the use of the PC tool by a teacher. As can be observed, the teacher has edited a lesson about how to compute the area of a circle, providing its answer, some hints in case the student asks for help, and an explanation on how to reach the correct answer, given the student fails to do so.

Figure 2 shows how the educational content created by the teacher is shown in the game after the student has eaten an item in the Snake game (2(a)). The lesson contains the explanation about the area of a circle written by the teacher (2(b)). Once the student feels confident with the concept explained, he/she can jump to the quiz (2(c)).

Cell phone Tool

The mobile phone application that students run on their cell phones consists of two elements: the game and the educational contents created by the teachers. EducaMovil offers the possibility of embedding the educational contents into different open-source games for cell phones like Snake, Tetris or Rally. The games are modified to add a module that handles the management of the educational contents. This module consists of three components: Game Model, Adaptation Model and User Model.

The *game model* is responsible for the interaction between the open-source game and the educational contents created by the teachers. The game model is fired every time an event in the game allows players to win points and introduces the educational contents as the units that need to be solved before winning the points. After the student finishes exploring the lesson, s/he will be prompted with a quiz, which is based on the lesson's content. If the learner provides a correct answer to the quiz, she is awarded one point. At any time, students can check their points and compare them against the top 10 highest scores.

The *adaptation model* determines the specific educational content that is going to be shown to the student at each step of the game. The educational contents are randomly selected from the pool of educational contents created by the teachers which are embedded into the game and downloaded to the cell phone. Each lesson and quiz are posed to the student up to three times, but never in a consecutive manner. If the student needs help, she can press the *help* button and the game will show a hint to help her answer the quiz. If the student does not successfully answer the quiz after three attempts, an explanation with the correct answer is shown and the lesson is eliminated from the pool of educational contents.

Finally, the *user model* stores the interactions of the student with the educational contents and the game. The model keeps counters about the lessons explored by the student, whether the quizzes were answered correctly or not, the time invested to answer quizzes, and whether the *help button* or the final *explanation* were instantiated. This model, which can be transfered to the PC tool via bluetooth, is primarily used for the quantitative analysis of the educational impact of *EducaMovil*, as shown in the Evaluation Section.

School and Pilot Setup

We have worked with a public school in a low-income peri-urban area of Lima, Peru (see Figure 3). The school, which offers both primary and secondary education, is part of the *Peru Educa* program run by the Peruvian Ministry of Education which focuses on providing educational tools and contents to teachers and students through an online portal [14]. For that purpose, the school has a very modest lab with second-hand computers where teachers and students can access contents online. The teachers told us that most students are highly motivated when classes are held in the *Innovation Lab*. However, given the large number of students at the school, the computer lab can be used only once a month by each class. Additionally, computers are often times infected by viruses and students have to share the PCs at a ratio of about five students per computer.

These issues pushed us to look for alternatives to the PCs that would be both engaging and attractive to the students while being more affordable and sustainable (in terms of maintenance). Given the high penetration rates of cell phone ownership at the school, we decided to explore the deployment of a mobile learning program. In order to understand the type of mobile learning tool that would better suit the curricular needs of the school, we hold interviews with both teachers and students. The teachers commented that they often test students with multiple-choice exams due to the characteristics of the Peruvian educational system. In Peru, students willing to move from secondary school to a public or private university are required to pass a multiple-choice exam that covers all curricular areas. Thus, teachers put a lot of emphasis on multiple-choice tests, specially in the secondary school, to prepare students for these highly competitive exams. Additionally, interviews with the students revealed that they were also very interested in having access to tests on their cell phones to be able to practice as much as possible; and more than 90% of the students declared that they used their cell phones mostly to call, send SMSs and to play games. These findings made us believe that *EducaMovil* could be the most adequate tool since it provides game-based learning on mobile platforms and the possibility to test students with multiple-choice quizzes.

The academic year at the school is divided into three terms and classes are run throughout the year covering different curricular objectives each term. At the end of each term, students take a final test -heavily based on multiple-choice questions- to evaluate their performance. We deployed our research pilot on the last term, from September'11 to December'11. The teacher for the *Science and Technology* class volunteered to run the pilot with two first grade groups at the secondary level ($ST1$ and $ST2$). During the last two weeks of August'11, we offered a workshop for the teacher to become acquainted with the PC tool and sessions with the students to learn how to use the mobile games. Although *EducaMovil* works on any Java-enabled feature phone, all students were provided with the same feature phone during the sessions to be able to focus our study exclusively on learning gains. Both the teacher and the students had help from a lab technician throughout the term. At the beginning of the pilot, we assigned each first grade group to one usage scenario: students in $ST1$ used *EducaMovil* in the classroom while students in $ST2$ used it during the school breaks. Students that participated in the classroom sessions, did not participate in the break environment and viceversa. The classroom setting constitutes a formal scenario where at the end of the class, and twice a week, each student was given a cell phone and was required to play during 20 minutes. The game always contains 10 lessons that the teacher prepares specifically for the content that has been presented during the class. Students were allowed to ask the teacher for help during the game sessions. On the other hand, the school breaks represent an informal environment that allowed students to go to the Innovation Lab twice a week during the breaks and play with *EducaMovil*. It is important to highlight that in this scenario students were not forced to play and it was up to them to decide when to go and for how long they wanted to play (the duration of the break was 30 minutes). However, the quizzes shown to them in every session were the same that the students in the classroom were shown. We believe that the school break setting can be used as a proxy to other informal scenarios like, for example, playing the game on a bus or while staying at home, which also are noisy environments and have no teacher's supervision. Finally, for control purposes, we also worked with two other first grade groups $C1$ and $C2$ that were taking the same class as $ST1$ and $ST2$. Students in $C1$ used the last 20 minutes of their class to solve paper-based quizzes at their own pace whereas students in $C2$ could voluntarily ask for paper-based quizzes during the breaks. These control groups were selected in such a way that the initial average grade was similar across all classes *i.e.,* the four groups start the pilot with a similar level of knowledge.

Figure 3. Classroom at the Principe de Asturias School, Lima, Peru.

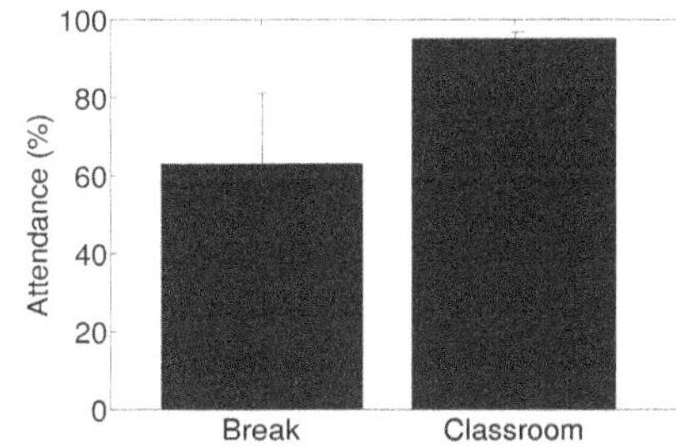

Figure 4. Average percentage of students that attend EducaMovil sessions in the classroom and during the breaks.

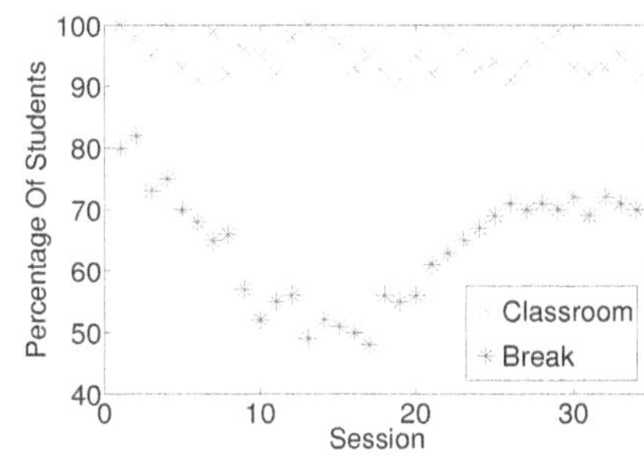

Figure 5. Student participation per session in the classroom (around 90%) and during the breaks (from 50% to 80%).

RESEARCH QUESTIONS AND METHODOLOGY

The focus of our research is to evaluate the educational impact of *EducaMovil* in terms of learning gains (*effectiveness*) when used in the classroom or during the school breaks. For that purpose, we carry out quantitative and qualitative analyses to reveal statistically significant learning outcomes and to gain insights into why these are taking place. Our end objective is to draw a set of guidelines that will help the teachers' community understand the educational impact of *EducaMovil* and decide about the convenience of deploying such tool at their schools. We formalize our study into three research questions.

The first research question (Q1) focuses on *analyzing whether the use of EducaMovil has an impact on knowledge acquisition, and if so, under which learning settings.* The fundamental underlying questions are whether students using *EducaMovil* can improve their level of knowledge more than students using paper-based tests; and whether informal environments like the school breaks promote more or less these gains than the classroom setting. We measure the level of knowledge with the final test grades that students get at the end of the term. In order to evaluate the educational impact, we collect the final test grades of the *Science and Technology* class for all the students using *EducaMovil* (groups $ST1$ and $ST2$) as well as for all the students in the control groups $C1$ and $C2$. Statistically significant differences in test grades between control and EducaMovil groups will determine that the tool probably has an educational impact on knowledge acquisition. Additionally, by measuring the difference between the initial and the final test grades in the classroom and break scenarios, we will be able to evaluate what type of environment favours more knowledge acquisition.

Our second research question (Q2) *evaluates what type of students benefit the most from using EducaMovil.* In fact, it is highly important for teachers to understand whether a minimum initial level of knowledge is necessary to experience significant individual learning gains or, on the contrary, whether even students with very low performance records can benefit from *EducaMovil*. We measure the prior level of knowledge of a student with his initial test grade before using *EducaMovil*, and the individual learning gain is computed as the percentage change between the initial and the final test grades of the *Science and Technology* class. In the end, we seek to understand if there exists an initial performance threshold for students in $ST1$ and $ST2$ to guarantee a significant learning gain in the classroom or the school break setting.

The third research question we pose (Q3) *analyzes the relationship between game performance and classroom performance so as to understand whether* EducaMovil *can be used as a proxy to measure a student's level of knowledge.* The final objective of this research question is to propose the use of EducaMovil as a paperless complement to student homework in order to help teachers with their evaluations. For that purpose, we study the relationship between the final test grades obtained by the students at the end of the term and their average game points across all game sessions. The existence or absence of strong correlations between the two distributions will reveal the potential of EducaMovil to approximate students' test grades. Finally, we use the outcomes from these research questions to build a framework for the semi-structured interviews that we carry out at the end of the pilot. By talking with the teacher and the students that used *EducaMovil*, we expect to gain a better understanding of the reasons behind some of our findings.

EVALUATION OUTCOMES AND INSIGHTS

This section first presents the datasets containing the student information we use for our analyses. Next, we describe general statistics about the usage of the tool and we close presenting our analytical results and insights for each research question.

Data Collection

Four groups participate in the evaluation: classes $ST1$ and $ST2$ use *EducaMovil* in the classroom and during the school breaks, respectively; and groups $C1$ and $C2$ act as control groups. Classes $ST1$ and $ST2$ are composed of 30 and 29 students from the first grade in secondary school; and classes $CT1$ and $C2$ have 28 and 32 students also from the first

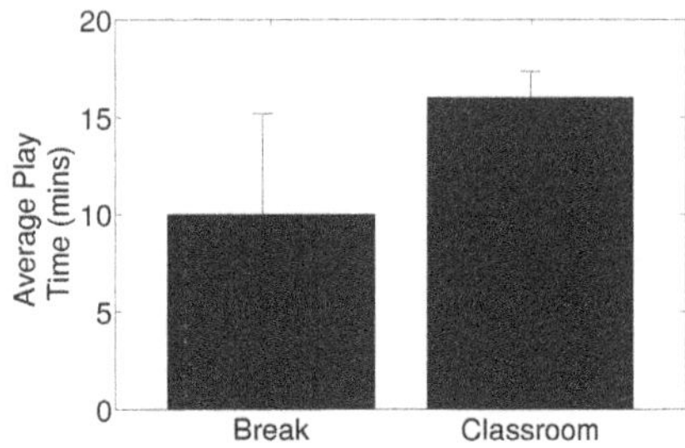

Figure 6. Average playing time with EducaMovil in classroom and break sessions.

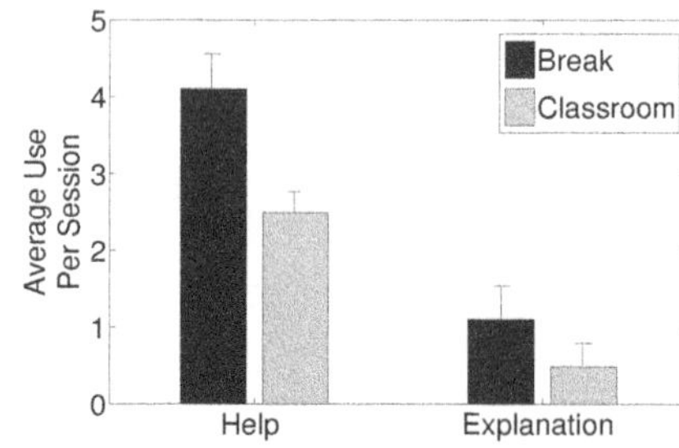

Figure 7. Usage of the *Help* button and instantiation of final Explanations.

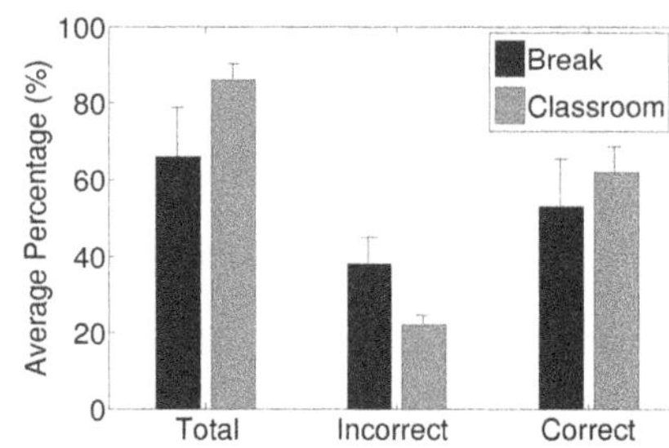

Figure 8. Average percentage of total quizzes answered, incorrect and correct ones both in the classroom sessions and during the breaks.

grade. Recall that all student groups were selected in such a way that the initial average grade was similar across groups, which allows us to compare them in a fair manner. For analytical purposes, we collect the initial and final *Science and Technology* test grades for each individual student in the pilot and control groups. The initial grades for the third term are the final grades obtained by each student at the end of the second term for the same subject.

EducaMovil was used by the students in $ST1$ and $ST2$ during a total of 34 sessions, which happened twice per week. For each session, the teacher prepared a set of 10 lessons that query about the curricular content presented by the teacher during the class. At the end of each session, we collected a user model for each student containing the number of lessons explored, the number of correct answers, time of exploration per lesson, and number of times the *help button* or the final *explanation* were instantiated. It is important to highlight that we did not have access to the results of the paper-based quizzes from $C1$ and $C2$ which they took home together with the results sheet. Although we missed analytical insights, we believe that this replicates best the anonymity that students feel while playing with *EducaMovil*. Additionally, at the end of the term, we also collected the notes from all the semi-structured interviews that we carried out with the teacher, the lab technician and the students.

General Statistics

Figures 4 and 5 reflect the student participation in both formal and informal learning environments. Figure 4 shows the average percentage of students that attend the *EducaMovil* sessions in the classroom and during the breaks. We observe that, on average, 95% ($\sigma = 1.2$) of the students in the classroom attended the game sessions whereas only an average of 63% ($\sigma = 23.2$) of the students played during the breaks. These statistics clearly show the differences in nature of both scenarios: in the classroom environment teachers require students to play during the last 20 minutes of the class which makes it almost impossible to miss the session, unless the student has not attended the class. On the other hand, students that use *EducaMovil* during the breaks, are encouraged but not forced to play. Figure 5 shows the participation of the students per individual session. We observe a high attendance of students during the first break sessions. However, it decreases over time until stabilizing at around an average of 65% of participation. Classroom students show consistently high participation rates throughout the pilot.

Figures 6, 7 and 8 delve into the game and quiz outcomes. Figure 6 shows that the average playing time of students in a classroom session is of $16.2m$ ($\sigma = 1.1m$) compared to the average playing time during the breaks which is shorter ($10.1m$ with $\sigma = 5.5m$). On the other hand, Figure 7 shows the average number of times per session students required help from EducaMovil as well as the average number of times the tool output an explanation. We observe that students in the classroom use less the help button (2.5 times per session on average) and reach less times the final explanation (0.49 times per session), probably due to the fact that they can ask their teacher who is present while the session takes place. On the other hand, students that play during the breaks use more the help button (an average of 4.1 times per session) and reach more times the final explanation (1.1 times on average per session). Since the final explanation is shown only when the student has given an incorrect answer three times for the same quiz, these findings reveal that students during the breaks have more problems reaching final correct answers.

Figure 8 shows that students playing in the classroom give more answers, correct or incorrect, than students playing during the breaks. On average, classroom students answer an 86% ($sigma = 6\%$) of the 10 quizzes that the game session contains as opposed to the 66% ($\sigma = 16\%$) of the quizzes answered by students during the breaks. Additionally, students that play during the breaks make a higher percentage of mistakes in their answers than students playing in the classroom, precisely a 16% more (38% versus 22%). Recall that these are just incorrect answers meaning that the student might answer a quiz wrong the first time but correct the next one. In

Group Final Grade	Significance
ST1 vs. C1,C2	$p = 0.04$ ($t = 2.14, df = 56; t = 2.13, df = 60$)
ST1 vs. ST2	$p = 0.03$ ($t = 2.26, df = 57$)
ST2 vs. C1,C2	-

Table 1. Statistical difference in grades between control groups and students that participated in the pilot.

terms of percentage of correct answers, we see that on average students in the classroom answer correctly a 62% ($\sigma = 12\%$) of the questions whereas during the breaks the percentage of correct answers goes down to 53% ($\sigma = 16\%$). These general statistics show that, on average, students in the classroom seem to use *EducaMovil* more frequently and with better results than students playing during the breaks. Next, we answer the research questions that will allow us to delve more into these observations.

Q1: Educational Impact

To evaluate the impact of *EducaMovil* in terms of *effectiveness*, we run statistical *t-tests* between the final test grades of the control groups and the groups that used *EducaMovil* both in the classroom or during the breaks. The underlying assumption is that improvements in the final test grades are related to the use of *EducaMovil* as opposed to paper-based quizzes. This is a reasonable assumption given that a game-based approach might engage students more through interactivity and practice repetition thus increasing learning gains. Since the student groups are sufficiently large, and since they represent independent sample groups, we use *unpaired t-tests*. Recall that all groups start with a similar level of knowledge *i.e., t-tests* between the initial test grades across all groups did not reveal statistical differences. As shown in Table 1, we observe statistically significant differences between the final test grades of the classroom $ST1$ and the control groups, as well as with the break group $ST2$, at a p-value $p < 1\%$. However, we do not observe any statistical difference between the final test grades of the control groups and the group of students that played with *EducaMovil* during the breaks ($ST2$). This analysis shows that *EducaMovil* might enhance knowledge acquisition when used in the formal environment of a classroom. In order to quantify its impact we applied a *paired t-test* between the students' test grades at the beginning (pre-use) and at the end of the term (post-use). The test showed statistically significant differences with $p < 1\%$. The average pre-use grades were of 10.2 and the post-use grades increased to 11.6 (in a scale of $0 - 20$ with passing grades starting in $7 - 10$).

Next, we delve into the possible reasons behind the lack of impact of the tool when used during the school breaks. There are two elements that differentiate the break environment from the classroom environment: (i) not all students attend all sessions *i.e.,* some students might go very often while others might go from time to time unlike the classroom environment where all students are required to attend the sessions; and (ii) not all students play the same amount of time. In the classroom, all students play for $20 minutes$ which is the time

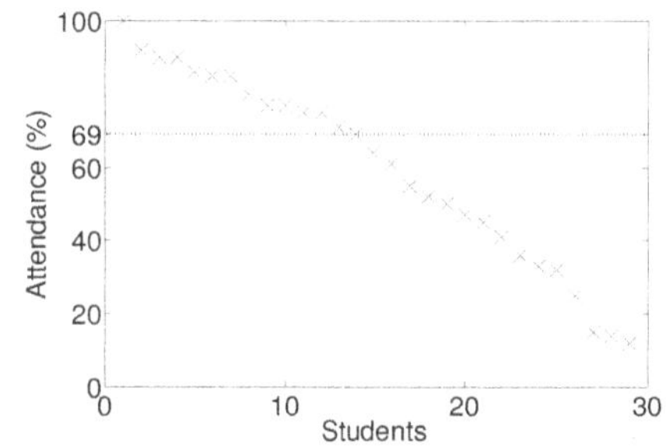

Figure 9. Percentage of sessions that each student attended throughout the duration of the pilot during school breaks. With attendance above 69% knowledge acquisition becomes statistically significant.

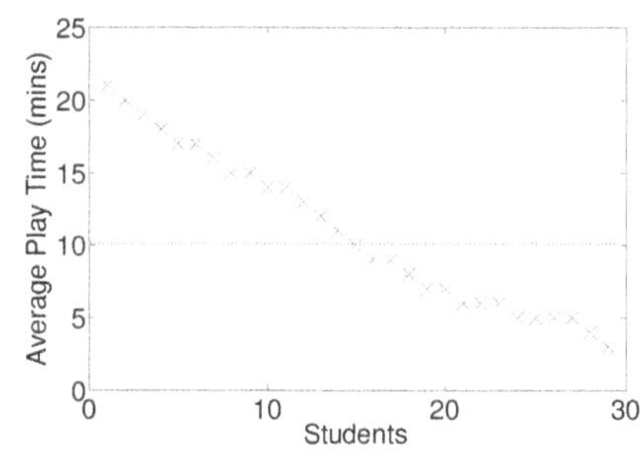

Figure 10. Average playing time per student during school breaks. Students that play for at least 10 minutes per session show statistically significant learning gains when compared to the control groups.

allocated by the teacher, whereas during the $30 - minute$ breaks students are free to play as much time as the want.

Figure 9 shows the percentage of sessions that each student in $ST2$ attended during the breaks (sorted in descending order). We observe that some students attended almost all sessions whereas others attended very few. Thus, it is critical to evaluate whether there exists a minimum number of sessions that students need to attend in order to show significant improvements in knowledge acquisition. For that purpose, we build distributions of students that use *EducaMovil* for at least a minimum percentage of sessions x (with $x \in (0, 100)$) and compare them to the control groups. In this case, given that the sizes of the distributions might be really small and of different sizes, we run the non-parametric version of the *t-test*, the *Man-Whitney test.* The tests highlight that there exist statistically significant differences between the final test grades of the control groups and the students using *EducaMovil* during the breaks when these attend at least 69% of the sessions (with the mean grade of the control groups being smaller). This analysis suggests that *EducaMovil* might also have an educational impact when deployed in informal environments as long as students use it for a minimum number of sessions.

Figure 10 shows the average playing times per session for the students that used *EducaMovil* during the breaks (sorted in descending order). We observe that there are students that use the tool for long intervals whereas others stop playing after a few minutes. In order to understand the role of the average playing time on the educational impact of the tool, we first build distributions of students with average playing times of at least x minutes ($x \in (0, 30)$). Next, we run *Man-Whitney*

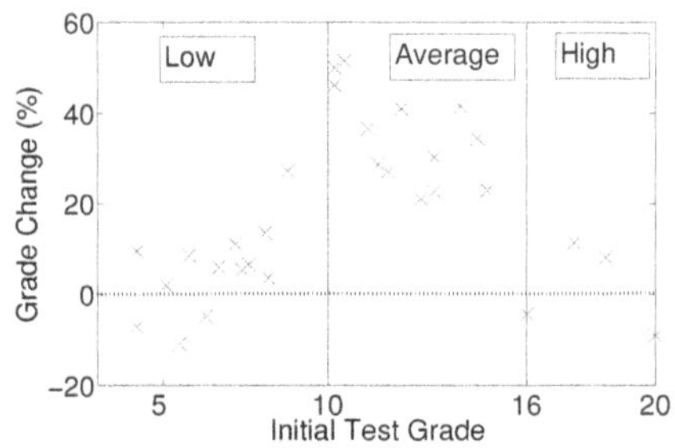

Figure 11. Percentage of change between the initial and the final grades for each group of students that use *EducaMovil* in the classroom.

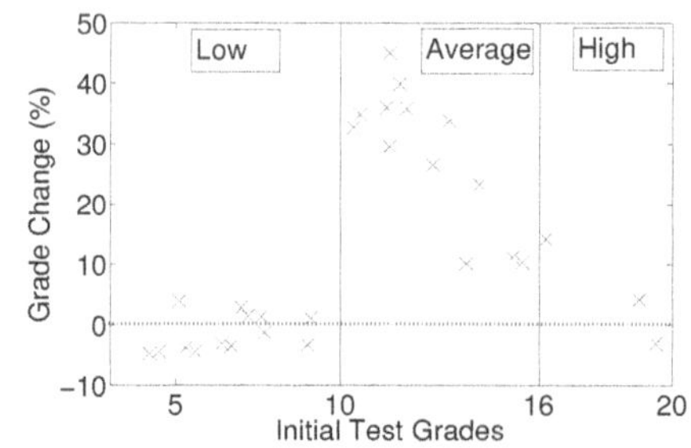

Figure 12. Percentage of change between the initial and the final grades for each group of students that use *EducaMovil* during school breaks.

tests between the final test grades of the students in these distributions and in the control groups and evaluate the differences. The tests showed statistically significant differences (with lower mean grades for the control groups) when the students use *EducaMovil* for at least 10 minutes per session on average (which corresponds to exploring at least 6 quizzes). To conclude, we propose **Guideline #1**: *EducaMovil* can improve knowledge acquisition in both formal and informal environments. However, in informal environments, it is important to make sure that students interact with the tool for a minimum amount of time, otherwise the educational impact will not be statistically significant.

Q2: Who benefits the most?

To analyze what type of students benefit the most from using *EducaMovil*, we divide the students in $ST1$ and $ST2$ into three groups based on their initial test grades before using the tool: high-grade group (from 16 to 20), average-grade group (from 10 to 16) and low-grade group (from 1 to 10). We focus our analysis on evaluating which group of students experiences the largest learning gains. As with $Q1$, the underlying assumption is that improvements in the test grades are related to the use of *EducaMovil* and imply knowledge acquisition. Specifically, we represent individual learning gains as the percentage of change between initial g_0 and final grades g_f *i.e.*, $100*(g_f-g_0)/g_0$ and use this value as a proxy representation of the benefits of the tool.

Figure 11 shows the percentage of change between the initial and the final grades for the students that use *EducaMovil* in the classroom. In general, we observe that the majority of the students show a positive change in their grades *i.e.*, their final test grades are typically higher than their initial test grades. The negative grade changes are of at most -10% which means that the students that obtained worse grades at the end of the term, experienced a decrease of at most two points in their final grades. In terms of groups, we observe that students with initial high grades do not experience large changes in their final grades. This is probably due to the fact that their grades are already high and there is very little room for improvement. At the other extreme, students with initial low grades experience improvements in their final grades of at most a 13% (with the exception of one student that shows an increase of a 22%). Such improvement translates into improvements in the final test grades of approximately two points after using *EducaMovil*. Finally, we observe that the students that show the highest percentages of improvement in their final grades are the students with average initial grades. In fact, this group has students with improvements from 20% all the way up to 50%, which means that the final test grades have incremented at most five points.

On the other hand, Figure 12 shows the percentage of change between initial and final grades for the students that used EducaMovil during the school breaks. We observe that, similarly to the classroom environment, students with high initial grades do not show an important change in their grade evolution over the duration of the pilot. Students with low initial grades, show grade changes of up to 5% which translates into increments of at most one point in the final test grades. Compared to the low-grade group in the classroom environment (see Figure 11), the percentage of change in the school break setting is considerably smaller (5% versus 13%). Digging more into these low-grade students, we observed that they all shared lower average playing times and lower session attendance than their classroom counterpart, confirming the need to require a minimum participation so as to guarantee an educational impact (Guideline #1). Finally, students with average initial grades are again the ones that appear to benefit the most from using *EducaMovil*, showing percentages of grade change of up to 45%. In general, the learning gains for each student group (low, average and high) in the break scenario are smaller than the gains for students using *EducaMovil* in the classroom. Unfortunately, we cannot report on the statistical significance of this observation given the small size of each group. However, differences in percentage of learning gains between the classroom and the breaks are around 5%. To sum up, we propose **Guideline #2** for teachers: students that start using *EducaMovil* with an initial average grade are the ones that benefit the most from using the tool. Thus, before deploying *EducaMovil*, it is important to check that the students have a minimum working knowledge base of the subject to guarantee a significant educational impact. Additionally, teachers should bear in mind that classroom deployments appear to produce higher learning gains –across all groups– than more informal environments.

Q3: EducaMovil and Classroom Performance

To evaluate whether *EducaMovil* can be used as a proxy to measure a student's level of knowledge, we analyze

the relationship between test performance and game performance across all the students using the tool. Test performance

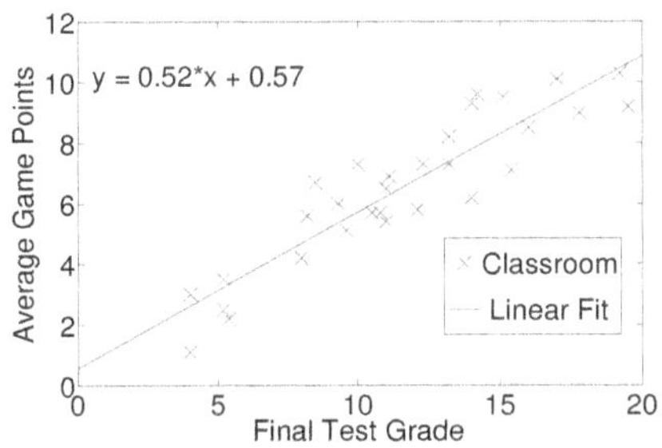

Figure 13. Linear regression of test grades and average game points for students that used *EducaMovil* in the classroom. $R^2_{adj} = 0.86$.

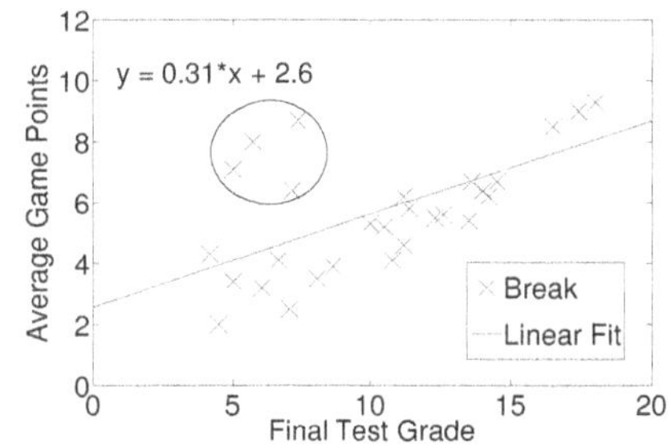

Figure 14. Linear regression of test grades and average game points for students that used *EducaMovil* during school breaks. $R^2_{adj} = 0.64$.

is represented as the final test grade and game performance with the average game points obtained by the student throughout all *EducaMovil* sessions. We study the relationship between the two variables applying linear regression (with the least squares approach) and Pearson's correlation analyses.

Figure 13 represents the final test grade and the average game points for each student using *EducaMovil* in the classroom, and its linear regression. We observe that the trendline appears to fit the data quite well, with a residual sum of squares of $R^2_{adj} = 0.86$. The correlation analysis between the final grades and the game points distributions shows a strong relationship with a coefficient of $r = 0.87$. The linear relationship as well as the strong correlation determines that students with high test grades (17 and above) show high average points per game (around 7 on average); students with low test grades (8 and below) share low average game points (4 and below); and students with average test grades (between 8 and 16) have average game points between 4 and 7.

On the other hand, Figure 14 shows the relationship between final test grades and average game points for the students that used *EducaMovil* during the breaks. We observe that the linear fit is not as good as the classroom trendline in Figure 13, with a residual sum of squares (adjusted R^2) of 0.64. The correlation analysis reveals a medium correlation coefficient of $r = 0.6$. These results are probably due to the fact that there exists a group of students (grouped within a circle in the Figure), that have low test grades but show high average game points. We analyzed each of the students in this group and observed that all four rarely went to any of the sessions (less than 20% of the times). Their high average game points are the result of having played only two or three sessions and having provided a high percentage of correct answers. However, given the small number of sessions they participated in, it is hard to determine whether the high game points are due to randomness or to the students' knowledge. In order to eliminate the impact of these spurious outliers on the fitting, we suggest adding a filter that requires a minimum percentage of session attendance per student. By doing so, the linear fitting in our analysis highly improves with a residual sum of squares $R^2_{adj} = 0.79$ and a correlation coefficient of $r = 0.81$. We suggest **Guideline #3**: *EducaMovil* game points can be used as a proxy for student test grades in the classroom environment; in the break environment, it acts as a proxy only when attendance requirements are put into place. Thus, teachers could potentially use *EducaMovil* as a complementary tool to homework so as to help them with student evaluation.

Qualitative Analysis

To gain insight into some of the previous findings, we designed semi-structured interviews based on the main outcomes from the quantitative analysis. At the end of the pilot, we conducted individual interviews with the teacher, the lab technician and a total of 20 students with different levels of knowledge. Next, we describe the interview questions and highlights from our conversations.

Research questions *Q1* and *Q3* have revealed that the educational impact of *EducaMovil* in terms of learning gains highly depends on a minimum engagement of the student with the tool. In fact, students that used *EducaMovil* frequently and during long periods of time appear to benefit more than students that had a scarce interaction. Although the classroom environment *forces* students to participate in two sessions per week, during the breaks students are free to decide whether to play or not. In an attempt to guarantee a minimum engagement also for students that use *EducaMovil* during the school breaks, we seek to understand what motivated some to engage frequently and what prevented others from doing so. In our interviews, the teacher and the lab technician explained that most of the students participated during the first break sessions of *EducaMovil*. However, they observed that for some students the motivation fell as time passed. They hypothesize that some of the students that failed to participate in the long run, might have felt *left behind* and discouraged because they were not doing as well as their peers *i.e.,* in a competitive game, they were getting less points. The teacher suggested that these students might have felt ashamed and thus might have stopped attending the sessions. They recommended that it would be advisable to personalize the quizzes and adapt them to each student's level of knowledge so as to maintain the engagement throughout the semester. On the other hand, students with low participation records mentioned in their interviews that the questions in the game were too difficult, which might confirm the hypothesis that they felt discouraged because they could not answer many of the quizzes. Although some students in the classroom environment shared the same feeling, these tended to ask their teacher to help them with the quizzes thus maintaining their motivation.

Research question *Q2* identified that students with initial low grades do not benefit as much from *EducaMovil* as students with average initial grades, consistently showing better results in the classroom setting. To understand possible reasons behind this, we interviewed low-grade students who complained about the complexity of the quizzes, which sometimes went beyond class content and required a little bit of research on the students' side. The teacher, in fact, did put some quizzes that required the students to go through the book, find information and reason a little bit before being able to provide an answer. This thinking process might have put back students with lower levels of knowledge for whom researching for an answer could be more difficult. However, low-grade students in the classroom could ask their teacher and engage in conversations whereas students that played *EducaMovil* during the breaks did not have access to teachers or books and played in noisier environments, which might have also affected their concentration. To overcome this problem, we observed that during the breaks low-grade students used much more the help button than the students in the classroom environment. Unfortunately, the help that *EducaMovil* gives, focuses on providing the solution instead of explaining how to do the research to find a specific answer. Thus, the teacher suggested that the help button could be enhanced by engaging the student in an *informal* conversation with an avatar or a character in the game to provide supervision and guidance. These insights will be integrated into future versions of *EducaMovil* which will incorporate personalization techniques to adapt the complexity of the quizzes to each student's knowledge base. Such adaptation will hopefully solve the motivation problem that some students had during the breaks where no teacher supervision was provided. Additionally, we will investigate ways to improve the help offered in *EducaMovil* by stimulating the student towards an inquiry process with a character in the game, instead of simply providing the formula for the answer.

CONCLUSIONS

The pervasiveness of feature phones in emerging economies has contributed to the advent of mobile learning applications for low-income populations. Our research extends the state of the art by presenting a quantitative and qualitative evaluation of a game-based mobile learning tool deployed in both formal and informal learning settings at a low-income school in Lima. We have provided teachers with a set of guidelines for the successful implementation of *EducaMovil*. Among our main findings, we have shown that EducaMovil has an educational impact both in formal and informal environments as long as a minimum interaction with the tool is guaranteed. We have also shown that students with initial average grades benefit the most from using the tool and we have demonstrated that *EducaMovil* could be used as a paperless complement to homework for student evaluation. We finish proposing a set of improvements for *EducaMovil* based on our qualitative assessments.

ACKNOWLEDGEMENTS

We would like to thank Justino Rivero, Sumbi and Telefonica Foundation for all their support.

REFERENCES

1. Alismail, H., and et al. Combining web technology and mobile phones to enhance english literacy in underserved communities. In *First Annual Symposium on Computing For Development* (2010).
2. BBC, Banglalink, Citycell, Grameenphone, TeleTalk, Robi, and Warid. `http://www.bbcjanala.com/`.
3. Butgereit, L. Math on mxit: using mxit as a medium for mathematics education. In *Meraka INNOVATE Conference for Educators* (2007).
4. Corlett, D., Sharples, M., Chan, T., and S., B. Evaluation of a mobile learning organiser for university students. *Journal of Computer Assisted Learning 21* (2005), 162–170.
5. Frias, V., J.Virseda, and Frias, E. The anatomy of mobile handsets: On the development of effective cell phone services. In *Mobile Communication Technology for Development (M4D)* (2010).
6. Frias-Martinez, V., and Virseda, J. Personalization of mobile learning tools for low-income populations. In *Personalization Approaches in Learning Environments Workshop, PALE'11 (UMAP)* (2011).
7. Kalloo, V., and Kinshuk, M. Personalized game based mobile learning to assist high school students with mathematics. In *IEEE International Conference on Advanced Learning Technologies* (2010).
8. Kam, M., and et al. Improving literacy in rural india: Cellphone games in an after-school program. In *ACM Conference on Information and Communication Technology and Development* (2009), 139–149.
9. Ketamo. An adaptive geometry game for handheld devices. *Educational Technology & Society 6(1)* (2003).
10. Malone, T. What makes things fun to learn? In *3rd ACM SIGSMALL* (1980), 162–169.
11. Molnar, A., and Frias-Martinez, V. Educamovil: Mobile educational games made easy. In *Proceedings of the World Conference on Educational Multimedia, Hypermedia and Telecommunications* (2011).
12. Ogawa, M. Augmenting large-enrollment instruction with mobile learning. In *Annual Technology, Colleges and Community* (2010).
13. Oliver, M., and Harvey, J. What does impact mean in the evaluation of learning technology? *Educational Technology and Society 5(3)* (2002).
14. PeruEduca. `http://www.perueduca.edu.pe`.
15. Price, S., and Oliver, M. A framework for conceptualising the impact of technology on teaching and learning. *Educational Technology and Society 10(1)* (2007), 16–27.
16. Ramos, A. J. Project mind: The viability of mobile sms technologies for non-formal distance learning in asia. *Philippines: Molave Development Foundation, Inc.* (2008).
17. Sharples, M. Methods for evaluating mobile learning. *Researching Mobile Learning: Frameworks, Tools and Research Designs. Oxford: Peter Lang Publishing Group* (2009).
18. Tian, F., and et al. Let's play chinese characters: Mobile learning approaches via culturally inspired group games. In *International Conference on Human Factors in Computing Systems* (2010).
19. Toyama, K. Can technology end poverty? *Boston Review 36(5)* (2010).
20. Traxler, J., and Kukulska-Hulme, A. Evaluating mobile learning: Reflections on current practice. In *mLearn 2005. Mobile technology: The future of learning in your hands* (2005).
21. Trucano, M. Worst practice in ict use in education, 2010. EduTech, World Bank Blog.
22. Trucano, M. Mobile learning in developing countries in 2011: What's new, what's next?, 2011. EduTech, World Bank Blog.
23. Vavoula, G., and et al. Myartspace: Design and evaluation of support for learning with multimedia phones between classrooms and museums. *Computers and Education 53*, 2 (2009).
24. Vavoula, G. N. A study of mobile learning practices, report of mobilearn project. `http://www.mobilearn.org/download/`.
25. W., D. Building mathematical knowledge in an authentic mobile phone environment. *Australasian Journal of Educational Technology 26*, 1 (2010), 85–104.
26. Yin, C., Ogata, H., and Yano, Y. Japelas2: Japanese polite expressions learning assisting system in ubiquitous environments. In *Proceedings of Supporting Learning Flow through Integrative Technologies* (2007).

Author Index

www.ingramcontent.com/pod-product-compliance
Ingram Content Group UK Ltd.
Pitfield, Milton Keynes, MK11 3LW, UK
UKHW051413290926
15471UKWH00009B/1578

9 781450 318853